Third Edition

DEVELOPING MULTICULTURAL COUNSELING COMPETENCE

A SYSTEMS APPROACH

Danica G. Hays
University of Nevada, Las Vegas

Bradley T. Erford
Loyola University Maryland

 Pearson

330 Hudson Street, NY, NY 10013

Director, Teacher Education & the Helping Professions: Kevin M. Davis
Content Producer: Janelle Rogers
Content Project Manager: Pamela D. Bennett
Media Project Manager: Lauren Carlson
Portfolio Management Assistant: Anne McAlpine
Executive Field Marketing Manager: Krista Clark
Executive Product Marketing Manager: Christopher Barry
Procurement Specialist: Deidra Smith

Cover Designer: Melissa Welch
Cover Photo: Thapakorn Karnosod/Getty Images
Full-Service Project Management: Sudip Sinha, iEnergizer Aptara LTD
Composition: iEnergizer Aptara LTD
Printer/Binder: LSC/Crawfordsville
Cover Printer: LSC/Crawfordsville
Text Font: 10/12 Times NR MT Pro

Library of Congress Cataloging-in-Publication Data

Names: Hays, Danica G., editor. | Erford, Bradley T., editor.
Title: Developing multicultural counseling competence : a systems approach / [edited by] Danica G. Hays, University of Nevada, Las Vegas, Bradley T. Erford, Loyola University Maryland.
Description: Third edition. | Boston : Pearson, [2018] | Includes bibliographical references and index.
Identifiers: LCCN 2016035831| ISBN 9780134523804 | ISBN 0134523806
Subjects: LCSH: Cross-cultural counseling—United States. | Multiculturalism—United States. | Minorities—Counseling of—United States.
Classification: LCC BF636.7.C76 D48 2018 | DDC 158.308—dc23 LC record available at https://lccn.loc.gov/2016035831

19 2020

ISBN 10:   0-13-452380-6
ISBN 13: 978-0-13-452380-4

To those marginalized in our society, who face and survive unparalleled levels of violence and oppression for no other reason than the color of their skin or whom they love. I am grateful for what you teach us about the importance of cultural identity and understanding and the cycle of injustice. I dedicate this work to you and those we have lost in the struggle for peace.

—dgh

This effort is dedicated to The One: the Giver of energy, passion, and understanding; Who makes life worth living and endeavors worth pursuing and accomplishing; the Teacher of love and forgiveness.

—bte

PREFACE

Becoming culturally competent is a lifelong process. It is both a personal and professional journey of cultural understanding and political changes. It is a personal as well as a professional journey in that we are constantly striving for meaning as cultural beings. We define culture in terms of our race, ethnicity, nationality, geographic origin, gender, sexual orientation, education level, family values, language, immigration history, socioeconomic level, ability status, and spirituality, to name only a few ways. At times culture may be visible: our race or gender might be quite apparent to others. However, culture is not always visible; it may be a shared history of kinship, community practices and norms, discrimination, historical and political power, or resilience. Developing multicultural competence is a professional journey in that it involves promoting optimal counseling relationships, processes, and outcomes among individuals of unique cultural identities. This practice may occur in the counseling session and in the larger community.

Many concepts are related to the process of developing multicultural counseling competence: self-awareness, sensitivity to diversity, knowledge of cultural values, and social advocacy. The core of developing multicultural counseling competence is possessing awareness, knowledge, and skills related to each of these concepts. It is also recognizing resilience in our clients as well as in ourselves. Resilience grows from adversity, which can result from interacting with others in a multicultural world. Oftentimes, the cultural values and identities we possess are partly a product of our resilience from systemic barriers. We build community by identifying with others with similar social, political, and historical experiences.

Developing multicultural counseling competence challenges us to do what we ask of our clients: to aspire to greater personal insight about what makes us members of various cultures and to examine the ways we grow from adversity borne from familial, community, and historical systems. Multicultural counseling competence involves allowing ourselves to be vulnerable and to reflect on our personal wounds, addressing mixed emotions of anger, grief, sadness, guilt, shame, and many others that accompany our privilege and oppression experiences. To this end, developing multicultural counseling competence means acknowledging our resistance to engage in lifelong cultural learning and reveal how our privilege and oppression experiences affect our relationships with others. Only after we engage in self-exploration, experience the consequences, and begin to change because of these consequences can we be free to understand and counsel others. Social advocacy starts when we can connect our personal growth and initiative to change the status quo for those unjustly affected within various social systems by forms of oppression such as structural racism, sexism, heterosexism, classism, ableism, and ageism.

NEW TO THIS EDITION

- Expanded number of case studies and "Voices from the Field" to illustrate clinical application of material
- Additional information on ethics in multicultural counseling and operationalization of the 2015 multicultural and social justice counseling competencies
- Greater attention to international and refugee populations and immigration issues
- Increased discussion of alternative counseling approaches with multicultural competencies

- Greater inclusion of current events that impact multicultural populations
- Updated references and statistics related to theory, research, and practice with multicultural populations

ORGANIZATION OF TEXT

This text is intended to facilitate the journey of developing multicultural counseling competence. Each of the 18 chapters is infused with several self-development opportunities that foster an increase in awareness, knowledge, and skills for understanding cultural makeup, understanding others of diverse identities and experiences, and engaging in facilitative counseling relationships. These opportunities are outlined in boxes inset throughout the text and include case studies, classroom and outside activities, self-reflection activities, tables, figures, and knowledge-building exercises. In addition, "Voices from the Field" are included throughout the text to highlight student, client, practitioner, and scholar perspectives on various cultural topics.

The text is divided into four sections that build on one another. Foundational aspects of multicultural competence are presented in Section One. Some of the major constructs described in multicultural counseling scholarship over the past several decades are described. The authors of Chapter 1 (Hays & McLeod) provide an overview of key multicultural terms and the processes that competent counselors should be aware of as they work toward a systems approach in developing multicultural competence: culture, cultural encapsulation, individualism and collectivism, race and ethnicity, generational status, gender, sexual orientation, socioeconomic status, disability, spirituality, advocacy, privilege, oppression, and worldview. The unique manifestations in counseling of clients' cultural experiences are introduced, including the role of communication and contextual variables such as prejudice and discrimination, acculturation, and violence and trauma. After presenting an approach to multicultural counseling competence that incorporates individual, family, community, and historical systems, key considerations and challenges to developing multicultural competence are presented. Moore-Thomas (Chapter 2) integrates some of these foundational aspects of multicultural competence and presents several cultural identity development models. These models highlight racial, ethnic, gender, sexual, and spiritual identity development among counselors as well as clients. This chapter specifically highlights that cultural identity can develop only in reflection of one's social, political, and historical contexts.

With a fundamental knowledge of key multicultural constructs and interpersonal processes relevant to counseling, the reader is presented in Section Two with scholarship of how differential amounts of power, access, advantage, and social status are available to clients based on cultural makeup. Because shared contemporary and historical experiences of privilege and oppression partly guide our personal development and thus cultural values for the cultural groups to which we belong, it is imperative the origins of and rationale for social injustices and subsequently social advocacy are discussed. Specifically, Section Two opens with a discussion of social justice counseling, the fifth force of counseling (Chapter 3, Gnilka, O'Hara, & Chang) and continues with a focus on racism and White privilege (Chapter 4, Hays & Shillingford-Butler), gender and sexism (Chapter 5, Singh & Mingo), sexual orientation and heterosexism (Chapter 6, Chaney & Brubaker), social class and classism (Chapter 7, Newton & Erford), and disability, ableism, and ageism (Chapter 8, Berens & Erford). Discourse for each newly presented form of privilege and oppression integrates that of previous chapters so the reader can better understand how clients may have unique combinations of privileged and oppressed statuses.

Section Three incorporates various privilege and oppression experiences into the framework of counseling multicultural populations that include individuals and families of those of African, Arab, Asian, Latin, Native American, European, and multiracial backgrounds. Specifically, common cultural values, support systems, mental health concerns, and culturally specific interventions are presented in Chapters 9 through 16. The authors of Chapter 9 (Bounds, Washington, & Henfield) outline African-American culture and values that characterize families, couples, children, Black middle-class individuals, males and females, elderly people, and Black gays and lesbians. Common mental health issues and support systems are presented, and an Afrocentric psychological perspective is described. Nassar-McMillan, Al-Qimlass, and Gonzalez (Chapter 10) provide information about the immigration history, cultural values, role of Islam, discrimination and resilience experiences, and individual differences in acculturation, ethnicity, and gender identity of Arab Americans. In addition, best practices for working with individuals and families of Arab descent are provided.

Luu, Inman, and Alvarez (Chapter 11) outline heterogeneity among Asian Americans, shared cultural values, individual differences based in differential experiences of immigration, enculturation and acculturation, ethnicity and race, gender roles, and sexual identity. Guidelines for working with individuals and families of Asian descent are presented in the context of common mental health concerns and help-seeking and coping behaviors. In articulating multiculturally competent practice with individuals and families of Latin descent, Villalba (Chapter 12) discusses the four major Latin American groups, Latina/o values, and individual differences with respect to immigration, generational, and socioeconomic statuses. After articulating mental health issues related specifically to Latin Americans negotiating their cultural identities, counseling considerations across the life span are discussed. The final commonly presented racial/ethnic minority group, Native Americans, is described in Chapter 13 (Garrett et al.). Garrett et al. present an account of Native American history, common social and political issues, Native American values, and guidelines for counseling Native American clients. McMahon, Paisley, and Skudrzyk (Chapter 14) offer the reader a conceptualization of the evolution and maintenance of the "White American ethnic," describing European-American history and heterogeneity, experiences of European immigrants, and counseling considerations for European-descent individuals and families and recent European immigrants. Kenney and Kenney (Chapter 15) provide information on counseling individuals and families of multiracial descent, a new chapter for the second edition. Definitional, historical, and clinical perspectives for addressing the experiences of this growing population are provided. Section Three closes with a chapter on spiritual diversity (Chapter 16, Cashwell & Giordano). Cashwell and Giordano highlight important cultural dimensions universal to individuals and families of racially and ethnically diverse backgrounds.

The final section of the text is intended to challenge the reader to think about how multicultural client concerns can be conceptualized. With an understanding of current social and political issues as well as racially and ethnically specific cultural values and counseling practices, it is imperative to consider how cultural awareness, knowledge, and skills manifest in counseling practice. Chapter 17 (Orr) connects the concept of worldview and introduces alternative approaches to the development of theory in multicultural counseling. Specifically, applications of counseling theory across cultures are presented. The text concludes in Chapter 18 (Kress, Dixon, & Shannonhouse) as concerns of misdiagnosis and ethnocentric views on normality and psychopathology are raised to challenge the reader to be cautious when applying a diagnostic label for culturally diverse groups that typically experience social injustices, including racial and ethnic minorities and females. The authors provide some solutions for culturally competent case conceptualization and diagnosis.

SUPPLEMENTAL INSTRUCTIONAL FEATURES

Supplemental to this text are pedagogical tools helpful to counselor educators choosing to use this text as a course text. The companion Instructor's Manual contains at least 45 multiple-choice questions and 15 essay questions per chapter. PowerPoint® slides are available to help instructors prepare presentations focusing on chapter content. Numerous case studies and activities included in the text can stimulate lively classroom discussions.

ACKNOWLEDGMENTS

All the contributing authors are to be commended for lending their expertise in the various topical areas. As always, Kevin Davis of Pearson has been wonderfully responsive and supportive. Finally, special thanks go to the reviewers, whose comments helped provide substantive improvement to the original manuscript: David Angeloni, University of Scranton; Britney G. Brinkman, Chatham University; Michael P. Chaney, Oakland University; Cirleen DeBlaere, Georgia State University; and Maria del Carmen Rodriguez, Kean University.

BRIEF CONTENTS

CONTENTS

ABOUT THE EDITORS

Danica G. Hays, PhD, LPC, is a professor and Executive Associate Dean of the College of Education at the University of Nevada, Las Vegas. She earned a doctorate in Counselor Education and Supervision, with an emphasis in multicultural research, from Georgia State University. Her research interests include qualitative methodology, assessment and diagnosis, trauma and gender issues, and multicultural and social justice concerns in counselor preparation and community health. She has published approximately 100 refereed journal articles and book chapters in these areas. In addition to this text, she is co-editor of *Qualitative Inquiry in Clinical and Educational Settings* (1/e, Guilford Press) and *A Counselor's Guide to Career Assessment Instruments* (6/e, National Career Development Association). She is also an associate and content editor of the *American Counseling Association Encyclopedia of Counseling* (1/e, ACA), co-author of *Mastering the NCE and CPCE* (2/e, Pearson), and author of *Assessment in Counseling: A Guide to Psychological Assessment Procedures* (6/e, ACA). She has extensive leadership history in the Association for Assessment and Research in Counseling and the Association for Counselor Education and Supervision. The American Counseling Association has recognized her nationally for her research and advocacy as a counselor educator.

    Bradley T. Erford, PhD, is a professor in the school counseling program in the Education Specialties Department at Loyola University Maryland. He was president of the American Counseling Association during 2012–2013. He is an American Counseling Association (ACA) Fellow and the recipient of several ACA awards, including the Research Award, Extended Research Award, Thomas J. Sweeney Award for Visionary Leadership and Advocacy, Arthur A. Hitchcock Distinguished Professional Service Award, Professional Development Award, and the Carl Perkins Government Relations Award. He has received the Association for Assessment and Research in Counseling (AARC) Exemplary Practices Award; Association for Counselor Education and Supervision (ACES) Robert O. Stripling Award for Excellence in Standards; and the Maryland Association for Counseling and Development (MACD) Maryland Counselor of the Year, Professional Development, Counselor Visibility, and Counselor Advocacy Awards. His research specialization falls primarily in development and technical analysis of psychoeducational tests and has resulted in the publication of more than 30 books, 70 journal articles, 100 book chapters, and a dozen psychoeducational tests. He is a past chair of the ACA, Southern Region; past president of the AARC, the MACD, the Maryland Association for Counselor Education and Supervision (MACES), the Maryland Association for Mental Health Counselors (MAMHC), and the Maryland Association for Measurement and Evaluation (MAME). Dr. Erford is the past chair of the ACA Task Force on High Stakes Testing, Task Force on Standards for Test Users, Public Awareness and Support Committee, Bylaws Committee, and Interprofessional Committee. Dr. Erford is a Licensed Clinical Professional Counselor, Licensed Professional Counselor, Nationally Certified Counselor, Licensed Psychologist, and Licensed School Psychologist. He teaches courses primarily in the areas of assessment, human development, research and evaluation, school counseling, and stress management.

ABOUT THE CONTRIBUTING AUTHORS

Aisha Al-Qimlass, MS, is a doctoral candidate at the counseling and counselor education program in the Leadership, Policy, and Human Development Department at North Carolina State University. Her research interests include the globalization of counseling, Islamic feminism, and chemical dependency. Her dissertation focused on career development factors of Kuwaiti women. She is a Certified Rehabilitation Counselor and provisionally licensed as both a Licensed Professional Counselor and Licensed Clinical Addiction Specialist. She has more than eight years of counseling experience with adults, adolescents, and families in a variety of settings focusing on issues of substance abuse and co-occurring disorders.

Alvin N. Alvarez, PhD, is Dean of the College of Health and Social Sciences and professor of Counseling at San Francisco State University, where he trains master's-level students to be college counselors and student affairs practitioners. He completed his counseling psychology degree from the University of Maryland at College Park and his undergraduate work at the University of California at Irvine. He is a former president of the Asian American Psychological Association. His professional interests focus on Asian Americans, racial identity, and the psychological impact of racism.

Debra E. Berens, PhD, is a Certified Rehabilitation Counselor, Certified Case Manager, and Certified Life Care Planner in private practice in Atlanta, Georgia. She also is a counselor educator in the graduate Rehabilitation Counseling program at Georgia State University. Since entering the counseling field in 1989, Dr. Berens has contributed over 35 publications to the professional literature and over 40 presentations in the areas of rehabilitation counseling, rehabilitation ethics, catastrophic case management, and life care planning. She recently completed a 10-year term as editor of the *Journal of Life Care Planning*.

Patrice S. Bounds is an assistant professor in the Department of Leadership and Counseling at Eastern Michigan University. She is a Nationally Certified Counselor (NCC) and a Licensed Professional Counselor (LPC) in the state of Illinois. Her research focuses on multicultural issues in counseling, academic achievement and self-concept of ethnic minorities grades K–12, and career decision making. To date, she has presented at over 20 national, regional, state, and local professional conferences and has published two book chapters in counseling textbooks and several manuscripts in progress for publication in scholarly professional journals.

Michael D. Brubaker, PhD, is an associate professor and program coordinator of the counseling program in the School of Human Services at the University of Cincinnati. His research, clinical, and advocacy interests center on addressing the barriers to treatment and prevention services among underserved and socially marginalized populations, namely the homeless, individuals identifying as LGBTQQI, and ethnic minorities. His publications have focused on counseling practices with LGBT and homeless populations and stigmatizing attitudes that may impact mental health care. He is a former trustee of the Association for Lesbian, Gay, Bisexual, and Transgender Issues in Counseling as well as a former chair and founding member of Chi Sigma Iota's (CSI) Counselor Community Engagement Committee.

Craig S. Cashwell, PhD, LPC, NCC, ACS, CSAT-S is a professor in the Department of Counseling and Educational Development at The University of North Carolina at Greensboro and an American Counseling Association (ACA) Fellow. He has over 125 publications and has received multiple research, teaching, and service awards. Dr. Cashwell is a past-chair of the

Council for Accreditation of Counseling and Related Educational Programs (CACREP) and has served as the Association for Counselor Education and Supervision (ACES) Governing Council Representative to ACA and President of Chi Sigma Iota, the international honor society for the counseling profession.

Michael P. Chaney, PhD, is an associate professor at Oakland University in Rochester, MI. He received his doctorate in counseling from Georgia State University. A Licensed Professional Counselor and National Certified Counselor, he has provided mental health services to LGBTQI individuals struggling with addictive disorders and to people living with HIV/AIDS in clinical and governmental agencies. Dr. Chaney is the past-president (2010–2011) of the Association of LGBT Issues in Counseling. He serves as an Editor-in-Chief for the *Journal of LGBT Issues in Counseling* and is an editorial board member for the *Journal of Addictions and Offender Counseling*. His research interests include sexual compulsivity, substance use disorders, HIV/AIDS prevention, male body image, and social justice and social advocacy in counseling.

Catherine Y. Chang, PhD, is a professor and program coordinator of the counselor education and practice doctoral program in the Counseling and Psychological Services Department at Georgia State University. Her research interests include multicultural issues in counselor training and supervision and Asian American and Korean American concerns. More specifically, she has published articles related to racial identity development, privilege and oppression issues, and multicultural counseling competence.

Andrea L. Dixon, PhD, is an associate professor of counseling and counselor education at Georgia State University. She has worked as a K–12 school counselor and a professional counselor in private practice. She is an active member of the American Counseling Association, the Association for Multicultural Counseling and Development, Counselors for Social Justice, and Chi Sigma Iota. Dr. Dixon conducts research and publishes in the areas of racial/ethnic and gender identity and wellness across the life span, mattering and meaning in life, adolescence, and school counseling and school counseling supervision.

J. T. Garrett earned an EdD in Public Health. He retired from the U.S. Public Health Service, Indian Health Service, where he worked for over 40 years with American Indian programs. He is a member of the Eastern Band of Cherokee Indians in North Carolina. He was trained by Cherokee Medicine Men and Women in traditional, cultural, and spiritual ways passed down by ancestors with practical uses of natural plants, healing ways, and traditional ceremonies. He coauthored two books with his son, Michael T. Garrett, entitled *Medicine of the Cherokee* and *The Cherokee Full Circle*. He also authored *Herbal* and *Meditations with the Cherokee*. He spent ten years working with the Eastern Band of Cherokee Indians and the Cherokee Historical Association, but spent his life collecting and gathering traditions, stories, history, plant lore, ancestry, and healing ways of the Cherokee Indians through his grandfather and other elders of the tribe.

Michael Tlanusta Garrett, Eastern Band of the Cherokee Nation, is a School Counseling Director and Certified School Counselor with Broward County Public Schools in Fort Lauderdale, Florida. He holds a PhD in Counseling and Counselor Education and a MEd in Counseling and Development from the University of North Carolina at Greensboro, and a BA in Psychology from North Carolina State University. Dr. Garrett's central research focus has emphasized exploring the relationship between cultural values, acculturation, and wellness with implications for developmental, culturally based therapeutic interventions; strength-based work to improve wellness and resilience of children, adolescents, and adults in families, schools, and communities; better understanding bicultural competence and cultural identity development; enhancing school persistence among at-risk youth; counseling indigenous and diverse populations; and spiritual issues in counseling. As author and coauthor of more than 90 professional publications dealing with multiculturalism and social justice, group work, wellness and spirituality, school counseling, working with youth, and counseling Native Americans, Dr. Garrett has authored the books *Walking on the Wind: Cherokee Teachings for Harmony and Balance* (1998), *Native American Faith in America* (2003, 1st ed., and 2012, 2nd ed.), *Counseling and Diversity: Counseling Native Americans* (2011), and edited the book *Youth and Adversity* (2014). In addition, he has coauthored the books *Medicine of the Cherokee: The Way of Right Relationship* (1996), *Cherokee Full Circle: A Practical Guide to Ceremonies and Traditions* (2002), and *Counseling and Diversity* (2012). Dr. Garrett has sought to advance professional understanding of working with diverse populations across therapeutic and educational settings and integrating indigenous healing practices as a way of bridging the cultural gap.

Amanda L. Giordano, PhD, LPC, NCC, is an assistant professor at the University of North Texas. She specializes in addictions counseling and religious/spiritual issues in counseling.

Philip B. Gnilka, PhD, is an assistant professor of Counseling at DePaul University. He has over 30 professional articles and presentations focusing on social justice, stress, coping, and perfectionism. He received his bachelor's degree from the University of North Carolina at Chapel Hill, his master's degree from Wake Forest University, and his doctorate from Georgia State University.

Laura McLaughlin Gonzalez, PhD, is an associate professor of counseling and educational development at the University of North Carolina at Greensboro. She completed her PhD in counselor education at North Carolina State University. Her research interests relate to social justice and multiculturalism with a focus on college access and success for Latino immigrants in emerging communities.

Lisa Grayshield, PhD, an enrolled member of the Washoe Tribe of Nevada and California, is an associate professor in the Department of Counseling & Educational Psychology at New Mexico State University. She holds an MA in Counseling and Educational Psychology, and a PhD in Counseling and Educational Psychology, both from the University of Nevada, Reno. Her research interests focus on Indigenous Ways of Knowing (IWOK) in counseling and psychology, specifically the incorporation of indigenous knowledge forms as viable options for the way counseling and psychology is conceptualized, taught, practiced, and researched. She has written, researched, and served on numerous boards and committees to address issues of cultural appropriate practices with Native and Indigenous people. She is currently teaching course work in a new IWOK Graduate Minor Degree program at New Mexico State University.

Malik S. Henfield, PhD, is program coordinator and associate professor in the Counseling Psychology Department at the University of San Francisco. Dr. Henfield teaches courses in the School Counseling Program, and his research focuses on psychosocial factors that serve to enhance and impede the academic achievement of African American students, particularly males.

Arpana G. Inman received her PhD in counseling psychology from Temple University. She is currently a professor in Counseling Psychology and Chair in the Department of Education and Human Services at Lehigh University in Pennsylvania. Her areas of research include South Asian–Asian American mental health, international counseling, and multicultural competencies in supervision and training.

Kelley R. Kenney, EdD, is a professor and coordinator of the Student Affairs in Higher Education Administration and College Counseling programs in the Department of Counseling and Human Services at Kutztown University, Kutztown, PA. She is also a Licensed Professional Counselor. Her research interests include multicultural and social justice/advocacy issues related to interracial couples, individuals, and families. Dr. Kenney is a coauthor of *Counseling Multiracial Families* (Sage Publications) and *Counseling the Multiracial Population: Couples, Individuals, and Families*, a training video distributed by Micro-training Associates, as well as an author and coauthor of numerous articles, monographs, and book chapters regarding the multiracial population. She's been the recipient of several state and national awards for her service to this population, most notably the American Counseling Association's Don Dinkmeyer Social Interest Award. She is co-chair of the American Counseling Association's Multiracial/Multiethnic Counseling Concerns Interest Network and served on the American Counseling Association's Governing Council, representing the North Atlantic Region.

Mark E. Kenney, MEd, is an adjunct professor at Chestnut Hill College/DeSales University campus in the Department of Clinical and Counseling Psychology in Center Valley, PA, and Albright College Department of Interdisciplinary Studies, Reading, PA. He is also a Licensed Professional Counselor. His research interests include multicultural and social justice/advocacy issues specific to interracial couples, individuals, and families, and the lesbian, gay, bisexual, and transgender population. He is a coauthor of *Counseling Multiracial Families* (Sage Publications) and *Counseling the Multiracial Population: Couples, Individuals, and Families*, a training video distributed by Micro-training Associates, as well as a coauthor of several book chapters addressing the multiracial population. He's been the recipient of several state and national awards for service to underrepresented populations and to the profession of counseling. He is co-chair of the American Counseling Association's Multiracial/ Multiethnic Counseling Concerns Interest Network.

Victoria E. Kress, PhD, is a clinic director, professor, and the coordinator of the clinical mental health, addictions, and college counseling programs at Youngstown State University; she is also a contributing faculty member at Walden University. She has over 20 years of clinical experience in various settings, including community mental health centers, hospitals, residential treatment facilities, private practice, and college counseling centers. She has over 125 publications, and coauthored three books on clinical counseling.

Linh P. Luu, MS is a doctoral candidate in counseling psychology in the Department of Education and Human Services at Lehigh University. Her scholarly interests include issues regarding multicultural competence and social justice advocacy in counselor training and supervision and Asian-American concerns. More specifically, she has published articles and book chapters on factors supporting and hindering trainees' social justice advocacy and multicultural competence, as well as multicultural issues in supervision. Linh has been honored with the Pioneer Award of Section 5 Psychology of Asian Pacific American Women, Society for the Psychology of Women, American Psychological Association, for her contributions to advancing Asian-Pacific-American feminism in psychology.

Amy L. McLeod, PhD, is the Counseling Department Chair and an associate professor at Argosy University Atlanta. Dr. McLeod's research interests include counselor education and supervision, multicultural issues, women's issues, assessment, and crisis intervention.

H. George McMahon is an assistant professor in the Counseling and Human Development Department at The University of Georgia. His professional interests include the ecological model of school counseling, social justice and privilege, and group work, and he has published several journal articles and book chapters in those areas. He has served on the editorial boards for *The Journal for Specialists in Group Work* and *the Journal of School Counseling,* and is currently an Associate Editor for *Professional School Counseling.* Prior to becoming a counselor educator, George earned his PhD in counseling psychology from The University of Georgia and his MEd in school counseling from The University of Virginia. George also worked as a professional school counselor in New Orleans, LA, from 1996–2000.

Taryne M. Mingo, PhD, is an assistant professor at Missouri State University in the Counseling, Leadership, and Special Education Department. She has a professional background in elementary school counseling, bullying and sexual abuse prevention, and advocating for social justice across P–16 settings. Her research interests include supporting students in rural education settings, promoting an intersectional approach to address the needs of diverse students, and incorporating womanist theory into counselor preparation programs.

Cheryl Moore-Thomas received her PhD in counselor education from the University of Maryland. She is an associate professor in the School of Education at Loyola University Maryland and has published and presented extensively in the areas of multicultural counseling competence, critical race theory and leadership, racial identity development of children and adolescents, and accountability in school counseling programs.

Sylvia C. Nassar-McMillan, PhD, is a professor and program coordinator of counselor education at North Carolina State University. She has served in a variety of clinical mental health, school, and college settings over the past 30 years. Her scholarship spans multicultural, gender, and career development issues, with a special focus on Arab-American acculturation and ethnic identity development, and she has published nearly 90 books, refereed articles, and other instructional materials and delivered over 100 conference presentations. She has served as a member of the CACREP Standards Revision Committee, the Census Information Center Advisory Board to the Arab American Institute, and as a board member for the National Board for Certified Counselors and the North Carolina Board of Licensed Professional Counselors. She is past Associate Editor for Multicultural Issues for the *Journal of Counseling & Development*, for which she currently serves as senior associate editor. She was named the Michael G. Morris Endowed Chair by Eastern Michigan University in 2014 for her research and capacity building work on behalf of Arab Americans.

Kathryn S. Newton, PhD, is an assistant professor at Shippensburg University of Pennsylvania. She has been recognized for innovative methods in teaching multicultural counseling, including the use of mindfulness and progressive immersion. Her research focuses on the intersection of race and class oppression, traumatic stress, and resiliency. She provides professional training and consultation in complex trauma, mindfulness, and culturally competent practice.

Caroline O'Hara, PhD, is a scholar and advocate working as a faculty member at the University of Toledo. Her research interests include multicultural counseling competence and advocacy in professional counseling and counselor education. She has numerous publications and presentations in the areas of micro-aggressions, social justice, sexual and gender diversity, multicultural competence, counseling supervision, and advocacy (both client and professional). She has also held multiple leadership positions. She is active with several ACA divisions, including the Association for Assessment and Research in Counseling, where she serves as Treasurer and Diversity Committee Chair, and is also an active member of Chi Sigma Iota and currently serves as the Primary Chapter Faculty Advisor for the Alpha Omega Chapter of Chi Sigma Iota. She has been honored with several awards including the American Counseling Association's Courtland C. Lee Multicultural Excellence Scholarship Award.

Jonathan J. Orr, PhD, is a clinical assistant professor in the Department of Counseling and Psychological Services at Georgia State University. He received a bachelor's degree in English and Classical History from Tulane University, a master's degree in Counseling from the University of New Orleans, and a PhD in Counselor Education from the University of New Orleans. His counseling and research interests include groups, social justice, supervision, multicultural counseling, counseling theory development, and professional counselor identity. He has coauthored or authored several journal articles and conducted workshops and presentations at the local, state, regional, and national levels. He is a Nationally Certified Counselor and a Licensed Professional Counselor in Georgia. He is an active leader within the Association for Specialists in Group Work, the American Counseling Association, and the Association for Counselor Education and Supervision.

Pamela O. Paisley, EdD, is a professor at the University of Georgia and has been at UGA since 1994. Previously, she lived in North Carolina and worked as a teacher and counselor in public schools for 10 years and as a counselor educator at Appalachian State University for seven years. She has won teaching awards at both Appalachian State University and the University of Georgia, has been principal investigator on a national grant to transform school counseling preparation and practice, and has previously served as president of the Association for Counselor Education and Supervision (ACES), a member of the Governing Council of the American Counseling Association (ACA), and an Associate Editor for the *Journal of Counseling & Development*. Dr. Paisley is committed to principles of social justice and is active in related initiatives at the local, state, and national levels. She has received the O'Hana Award and the Reese House Social Justice Advocate Award from the Counselors for Social Justice, has been named an ACA Fellow, and has received the David Brooks Outstanding Mentor Award from the American Counseling Association.

Mark Parrish, PhD, is an associate professor and department chair in the Department of Clinical and Professional Studies at the University of West Georgia. His research interests include multicultural issues in counselor training and supervision related to providing mental health services to diverse populations in schools and in the community and integrating spirituality into the counseling process. His specific research focus has been on serving Native American, Alaskan Native, and First Nations mental health clients. He has published articles related to the use of spirituality in counseling of college students, assessment of spirituality as it relates to holistic wellness, and alternative counseling approaches for adolescents with sexual behavior disorders. Dr. Parrish is active in a number of professional organizations at the national, state, and campus levels.

Tarrell Awe Agahe Portman, PhD, is Dean of the College of Education at Winona State University and emerita professor of the counselor education and supervision doctoral program in the College of Education at the University of Iowa. Her research interests include multicultural counseling issues, particularly those of American Indian populations. She has published multiple articles and book chapters on multicultural issues related to school counselors, multicultural counseling, and social justice. She was the first recipient of the Counselors for Social Justice Mary Smith Arnold Anti-Oppression award and past president for the Association for Multicultural Counseling and Development.

Edil Torres Rivera is a professor at the Counselor Education program and associate director of the School of Human Development and Organizational Studies in Education at University of Florida in Gainesville. He received a PhD in multicultural counseling from the University of Connecticut, Storrs. His research interests are multicultural counseling, group work, chaos theory, liberation psychology, technology, supervision, prisons, and gang-related behavior among Latinos. He has been honored with the following awards: (1) The Samuel H. Johnson Distinguished Service Award; (2) Association for Specialists in Group Work Fellow; and (3) the Ohana Award.

Laura R. Shannonhouse, PhD, is an assistant professor in the counseling and psychological services department at Georgia State University (GSU). She teaches in the school counseling and clinical mental health masters programs, as well as the counselor education and practice doctoral program. Her research interests include multicultural issues in counselor preparation, crisis intervention and suicide prevention in K–12 schools and the role of religion/spirituality and meaning making in the context of disaster. She has been appointed to the *Center for School Safety*, and the *Center for the Study of Stress, Trauma, and Resilience* at GSU, and been honored with the Courtland C. Lee Multicultural Excellence Scholarship Award from the American Counseling Association, the Marian Pope Franklin Fellowship from UNC Greensboro, and the Courtland C. Lee Social Justice Award from the Southern Association for Counselor Educators and Supervisors (SACES).

Ann Shillingford-Butler, PhD, is an associate professor of counselor education at the University of Central Florida in Orlando, FL. She has several years of experience as a professional school counselor prior to completing her doctorate at the University of Central Florida. She has written several articles and book chapters on multicultural issues, particularly those that affect children and youth of color, and one co-edited book, *The Journey Unraveled: College and Career Readiness of African American Students.*

Anneliese A. Singh, PhD, LPC, NCC, is an associate professor at the University of Georgia. Her research interests include qualitative and community-based approaches examining resilience and coping of marginalized populations (e.g., transgender people, LGBQQ people, South Asian immigrants and refugees, people of color), traumatology, and counselor training that is grounded in multicultural, feminist, and social justice frameworks. She is the coauthor of *Qualitative Inquiry in Clinical and Educational Settings* (2012) and the *Affirmative Counseling and Psychological Practice with Transgender and Gender Nonconforming Clients* (2017). Anneliese is also a co-author of the ACA *Multicultural and Social Justice Counseling Competencies, Competencies for Counseling Transgender Clients, Competencies for Counseling LGBQQIAA Clients,* and the *ASGW Multicultural and Social Justice Principles for Group Workers.* She has served as the president of the Association for Lesbian, Gay, Bisexual and Transgender Issues in Counseling (ALGBTIC) and the Southern Association for Counselor Education and Supervision (SACES). Dr. Singh has received several awards for the connection between her research, service, and advocacy, such as the CSJ O'Hana Award, AAMCD Advocacy Award, and ASGW Early Career Group Work Practice Award.

Bogusia Skudrzyk, PhD, NCC, LPC, is a professor and program director of the counselor education program at Palm Beach Atlantic University in West Palm Beach, Florida. She has been working in the field of counseling in residential, outpatient, and educational settings for over 28 years. Her area of specialty includes creative multicultural perspectives on healing and wellness; group work; and coping with losses and trauma across the life span. Her scholarly work includes over 60 presentations and publications in six refereed journals. Recently she co-edited a book called *International Perspectives on Group Work.* She has been a member and chair of various ACA committees and served as a President of ASGW—Association of Specialists In Group Work. She is a native of Poland.

José A. Villalba, PhD, received his doctorate in counselor education from the University of Florida. He is a professor in the Department of Counseling at the Wake Forest University, as well as Associate Dean of Wake Forest College. His teaching interests include multicultural counseling, counseling in school settings, and health and human services. His research interests include addressing Latina/o health disparities in emerging Latino communities. He has published several articles and book chapters, presented at national and international scholarly conferences, and served as keynote speaker for various organizations looking to promote multicultural competence and awareness.

Ahmad R. Washington, PhD, NCC, is an assistant professor in the school counseling program in the Department of Counseling and Human Development at The University of Louisville. His research interest involves how school counselors can use social justice counseling strategies to effectively remove the socioeducational barriers confronting marginalized students. He is particularly interested in how school counselors can use culturally relevant practices to promote the holistic (e.g., personal/social, academic, and occupational development) success of adolescent and young adult African-American males. He has received various awards, including the Association of Counselor Education and Supervision Emerging Leaders Fellowship and the First Annual Association of Multicultural Counseling and Development Asa Hilliard Scholarship Award.

Cyrus Williams, PhD, is an assistant professor in the Counseling Department located in the School of Psychology and Counseling at Regent University. His research interests include multicultural issues and competences, privilege and oppression as it relates to education, supervision, career development, and addictions. He uses this perspective as he teaches, presents, and publishes scholarly works. He has written articles and book chapters that focus on first-generation college students, multicultural issues concerning Native Americans and African Americans, multicultural supervision, as well as advocacy counseling as it relates to education, career development, and addictions.

SECTION 1

The Foundations of Multicultural Counseling

1 The Culturally Competent Counselor

Danica G. Hays and Amy L. Mcleod

PREVIEW

This initial chapter provides essential context for the development of culturally competent counseling. Included in that context are trends in demographic projections for the United States and explanations of the complexities and key concepts of multicultural counseling. The discussion concludes with an introduction to multicultural counseling and social justice competence from a systems approach, and a review of ethical considerations in developing multicultural counseling competency.

THE CULTURALLY COMPETENT COUNSELOR

Since the inception of the helping professions around the time of Freud, counseling and psychotherapy have typically involved one-on-one interventions primarily with White and middle- to upper-class clients who would receive treatment for several years. Approaches and interventions in counseling throughout most of the 20th century assumed that clients were similar in demographics (e.g., White, middle to upper class, heterosexual); thus, techniques could be applied universally. The first three *forces*, as they are called, of counseling (i.e., psychodynamic, behaviorism, and existentialism/humanism) reflected this assumption. But as the U.S. population became increasingly diverse, the counseling profession shifted its focus to attend to the changing demographics of the American client.

These dynamics within counseling theory, practice, and scholarship have sparked two additional forces. Multiculturalism and social advocacy have been described as the fourth and fifth forces of counseling, respectively (Chung & Bemak, 2011; Ratts, 2011). As a profession, counseling is attending more to the complexities of both counselors and clients in their cultural makeup, the systems by which they are surrounded, and the impact these two components have on what earlier counselors and psychotherapists viewed as "universal" expressions of mental health. In addition, as counseling professionals, we are challenging one another to address personal biases and assumptions that prevent us from forming an affirming, therapeutic alliance with clients we counsel. These more recent forces of counseling—multiculturalism and social advocacy—are creating space for counselors to focus on cultural diversity, privilege, oppression, and the resilience strategies that clients have. Before discussing how we can develop our multicultural competence while focusing on systemic influences, current and projected demographics of the U.S. population are presented, particularly across categories such as race, ethnicity, age, and socioeconomic status.

U.S. DEMOGRAPHICS

The portrait of the typical U.S. citizen has changed significantly since the 1970s. Reasons for the increased diversity that now exists include aging trends, higher birthrates for some racial and ethnic minority groups, and immigration trends that have led to an increase in non-English-speaking individuals (U.S. Census Bureau, 2015a). Statistics on population growth provide evidence that counselors will have to make adjustments to serve varying client needs. The counseling relationship thus becomes more complex as client diversity increases. Clients and counselors bring to that relationship unique cultural identities coupled with contemporary and historical experiences of oppression and other forms of discrimination. Counselors are charged with becoming familiar with current and projected demographic trends within the United States and becoming culturally competent to work with a changing clientele.

The United States is the third most populous country in the world, with a population of approximately 321.5 million (U.S. Census Bureau, 2015a) people from various racial and ethnic groups. Of the total U.S. population, 97.43% identified themselves as being of one race only. The predominant racial group in 2015 was White (77.28%), followed by Black/African descent (13.21%), Asian descent (5.46%), and all other races (e.g., Native American, Alaska Native, Native Hawaiian, multiracial) constituting 4.05% of the total U.S. population. Individuals identifying within these groups may also identify themselves as being of Hispanic or Latino descent. More than 54.6 million individuals (17.66% of the U.S. population) identify as such when asked about ethnicity alone; of the remaining 82.34% not identifying as Hispanic or Latino, 61.72% identified as White alone (U.S. Census Bureau Population Division, 2014b).

With individuals of Asian and Hispanic/Latino descent representing the fastest-growing populations, the racial and ethnic group distribution in the United States will change dramatically over the next few decades. According to U.S. Census Bureau projections, individuals who are White non-Hispanic will make up less than half of the U.S. population by 2044. By 2060, the total U.S. population is expected to reach 417 million, with a substantial decrease in the percentages of White, non-Hispanic/non-Latino individuals (43.6%), a stable percentage of those of Black/African descent (14.3%), and increases in the populations of those of Hispanic/Latino descent (29%) and Asian descent (9.3%; Colby & Ortman, 2015).

The overall foreign-born population in 2014 was approximately 13% of the U.S. population (Colby & Ortman, 2015). Foreign-born individuals are those in this country not originating from the United States, including Puerto Rico, Guam, American Samoa, the U.S. Virgin Islands, and the Northern Mariana Islands. Examining the foreign-born population reveals that individuals from Latin America (e.g., the Caribbean, Central America, South America) represent the largest percentage (53%) of foreign-born people presently in the United States, with those originating from Asia (29%), Europe (11%), and other regions (e.g., North America, Africa, Oceania) accounting for the remaining foreign-born individuals. These percentages represent a marked change from 1970 percentages, when a majority of foreign-born individuals were from Europe. More specifically, from 1970 to 2012, the percentage of foreign-born

TABLE 1.1 Projected Age Trends (Percentage of Total U.S. Population)

Age Cohort	2020	2030	2040	2050	2060
0–4 yrs	6.15	5.89	5.56	5.56	5.47
5–17 yrs	16.01	15.33	14.62	14.49	14.28
18–44 yrs	35.89	35.22	33.84	33.23	32.70
45–64 yrs	25.07	22.94	23.94	24.62	24.00
65–84 yrs	14.86	18.08	17.81	17.33	18.82
85+ yrs	2.01	2.54	3.85	4.76	4.73

Source: U.S. Census Bureau Population Division (2014a).

individuals immigrating from Europe decreased from approximately 62% to 11%, whereas, during the same period, the percentage of foreign-born persons coming to the United States from Asia increased from 9% to 29%, and individuals immigrating from Latin America grew from 19% to 53% (U.S. Census Bureau Population Division, 2014b). Overall, the projected foreign-born population by 2060 is expected to be 19% of the estimated U.S. population that year (Colby & Ortman, 2015).

In addition, the U.S. population is living longer. (See Table 1.1.) Age trends vary by racial and ethnic group (see Table 1.2). In the group ages 55 to 64 years, there are approximately 29 million White non-Hispanics, 4.65 million Blacks/African Americans, 4.05 million Latinos/Hispanic Americans, 1.9 million Asian Americans, and 377,000 Native Americans. Among those 65 to 74 years, there are approximately 20.3 million White non-Hispanics, 2.5 million Blacks/African Americans, 2.13 million Latinos/Hispanic Americans, 1.14 million Asian Americans, and 196,000 Native Americans. In the group ages 75 to 84 years, there are approximately 10.81 million White non-Hispanics, 1.17 million Blacks/African Americans, 1.03 million Latinos/Hispanic Americans, 548,000 Asian Americans, and 80,200 Native Americans. Finally, among individuals 85 years and older, there are approximately 5 million White non-Hispanics, 456,000 Blacks/African Americans, 387,000 Latinos/Hispanic Americans, 206,000 Asian Americans, and 26,000 Native Americans (U.S. Census Bureau, 2015a).

TABLE 1.2 Age Trends by Racial/Ethnic Group Membership (Percentage of Total U.S. Population)

	55 to 64 years (n = 40,076,000)	65 to 74 years (n = 26,398,000)	75 years + (n = 19,845,000)
White, non-Hispanic	72	77	81
Black/African American	12	10	9
Hispanic origin	10	8	5
Asian	5	4	4
Native Hawaiian, Alaskan, and Indian; Other Pacific Islander	1	1	1

Note. Population size and percentages are approximate values.

Source: U.S. Census Bureau (2015a).

Of all U.S. residents, 15.8% reported annual incomes below the poverty line in 2013. Rates of poverty in the United States increased between 2007 and 2011, but held stable between 2012 and 2013 (DeNavas-Walt & Proctor, 2014). Females outnumber males and experience disproportionate poverty rates. In 2013, the female-to-male earnings ratio for full-time, year-round workers was 78%. Female heads of households with no husband or partner present represent approximately 32.5% of poor families and have annual median household incomes of $35,154. The majority of these families with female heads of household have children under the age of 18 years. More than half of children under the age of 6 in female-headed households with no partner present live in poverty. Further, median household income varies significantly by racial and ethnic group. The group with the highest median household income in 2013 was Asian Americans ($67,065), followed by White non-Hispanics ($58,270), Hispanics/Latinos ($40,963), and Blacks/African Americans ($34,598). The median household income for all racial and ethnic groups in 2013 was $51,939, which is 8% lower than the inflation-adjusted median household income in 2007, prior to the most recent economic recession in the United States. Disparities in earnings are further indicated by poverty rates; that is, whereas the poverty rate for White non-Hispanics was approximately 9.6%, the poverty rates for Hispanics/Latinos and Blacks/African Americans were 25.3% and 27.2%, respectively. At 10.5%, Asian Americans were the only major racial/ethnic group who experienced a decreased poverty rate over the past decade.

KEY TERMINOLOGY OF MULTICULTURAL COUNSELING

Multicultural counseling may be defined as counseling that integrates cultural identities and takes into account their influence on the counseling relationship, process, and outcome. **Culture** consists of the shared values, practices, social norms, and worldviews associated with a particular cultural group. Cultural groups may be based on race, ethnicity, gender, sexual identity, socioeconomic status, disability, age, and spirituality, to name a few categories. Within each of these cultural categories, we can most likely articulate subgroup memberships. For example, one individual might identify as a Latina, heterosexual, able-bodied, young female from a middle-class background while another individual might select characteristics such as being European American, gay, male, and of lower socioeconomic status in identifying his cultural group memberships. Every individual—counselor and client alike—has a unique combination of cultural group memberships that bring different social, political, biological, and historical experiences to the counseling process. Thus, counselors should view all counseling relationships as cross cultural in some manner. Table 1.3 introduces brief definitions of various cultural categories and terms with which counselors should be familiar; terminology is further discussed and applied to specific populations in the chapters that follow. Further, because counselors have a unique "story" involving these key multicultural concepts that they bring to the counseling relationship, we encourage you to begin creating your own cultural narrative. (See Reflection 1.1.)

The extent to which a group membership is labeled as "cultural" depends on how broadly individuals define culture. For example, a broad definition might include variables such as race, ethnicity, gender, sexual orientation, educational status, language, and geographical origin. A narrower definition might label culture as consisting of race and gender only. For example, consider a multiracial male who presents for counseling. A counselor who uses a broader definition of culture may attend to how characteristics such as the client's race, gender, age, education level, nationality, degree of spirituality, family characteristics,

---

REFLECTION 1.1

Construct a narrative or story of your cultural background. Discuss group memberships that you have with respect to race, ethnicity, gender, sexual orientation, socioeconomic status, spirituality, age, ability status, and any other characteristics that seem significant to you. In your narrative, articulate how you or your family immigrated to the United States (if applicable), your acculturation experiences, and how your family and community shape your cultural identity. In addition, discuss both positive and negative events that have shaped who you are culturally. Outline how values you hold and communication patterns you engage in are influenced by your cultural group memberships.

TABLE 1.3 Key Terms Related to Culture and Multicultural Counseling

Terminology	Description
Acculturation versus Enculturation	**Acculturation** refers to changes in behavior, cognitions, values, language, cultural activities, personal relational styles, and beliefs that a cultural minority group undergoes as it encounters the dominant culture. Alternatively, **enculturation** is the socialization process through which individuals learn and acquire the cultural and psychological qualities of their own group.
Cultural Dimensions	Three overlapping dimensions may be used to broadly define culture. **Universal culture** refers to commonalities shared by all cultures and, in fact, all humankind (e.g., use of language as a method of communication, establishment of social norms, bodily functions, physiological fear responses). **Group culture** involves the characteristics shared by a cultural group or subgroup (e.g., Asian Americans, females, individuals raised in the southern United States, those living in poverty). **Individual culture** consists of those behaviors, attitudes, and cognitions which are unique to specific individuals. Among these may be behaviors that are outside the norms of the groups to which the individuals belong.
Cultural Encapsulation	Also referred to as **ethnocentricism**, **cultural encapsulation** is the narrow and rigid view of the world and other cultural groups that ensues when one uses one's own cultural groups as a reference and standard of normality. This attitude could impair a client's well-being, lead to early termination of counseling services, or both.
Cultural Identity	**Cultural identity** refers to the degree to which individuals identify themselves as belonging to subgroups of various cultural groups or categories. **Cultural identity development** is the intrapersonal and interpersonal process in which individuals engage in order to build a clearer and more complex cultural identity in terms of race, ethnicity, gender, sexual orientation, and other areas.
Disability	As part of the continuum of ability status, a **disability** is a mental or physical impairment that affects at least one of an individual's daily activities. Individuals with disabilities often face discrimination referred to as **ableism**.

Ethnicity	**Ethnicity** refers to the shared characteristics of culture, religion, and language, to name a few, with which a group may identify. Examples of ethnic groups include Latin Americans and Arab Americans. **Nationality**, a common component of ethnicity, refers to one's nation of origin, such as France, Kenya, China, or pre-Columbian America. Several racial groups may share the same ethnicity (e.g., Whites and Africans share South African heritage). Some racial groups, such as Whites, may be unaware of their ethnic group membership.
Etic versus Emic Perspective	An **etic** perspective focuses on the universal qualities common to all cultures and on aspects of counseling that are generalizable across cultures. A limitation of the etic approach is the failure to account for legitimate cultural variations. An **emic** perspective involves viewing each client as an individual and evaluating the client by using norms from within the client's culture. The majority of multicultural counseling literature recommends the emic approach when working with clients from diverse cultural backgrounds; this approach helps reduce stereotyping, prejudice, and the tendency to impose a cultural bias.
Gender	Whereas **sex** refers to the biological distinctions between males and females (e.g., hormonal and anatomical differences), **gender** is the expression of social categories, or **gender roles**, that describe behaviors deemed appropriate by a particular culture for males and females. Three terms are useful in thinking about gender and gender role expression: masculinity, femininity, and androgyny. **Masculinity** and **femininity** are the normative expressions of stereotypical and socially accepted behaviors for males and females, respectively. **Androgyny** is the blending of masculinity and femininity. Further categories, such as **intersex** and **transgender**, demonstrate the complexity of gender and gender norms.
Generational Status	**Generational status** refers to clusters of particular age groups within a particular social and historical context. Generations typically span a range of 15 to 20 years and represent individuals who share common characteristics due to their particular experiences in history based on their cohort. Some of the living generations include the GI generation ("government issue," 1901–1924); the silent generation (mid-1920s to about 1945); the baby-boomer generation (1946–1960); Generation X (1961–1981); Generation Y, or the Millennial Generation (1982–2000); and Generation Z (those born after 2000). Generational status is an important identity for those who become acculturated to the United States, given that younger generations may have an easier time navigating U.S. culture.
Individualism versus Collectivism	**Individualism** is the notion that our behaviors and attitudes are guided by incentives that promote self-determination or independence (e.g., competitiveness, self-disclosure, agency, self-promotion). **Collectivism** refers to the idea that decisions, and thus what is deemed important, are based on the betterment of others, such as community or family members. Collectivistic values might include cooperation, "saving face," and interdependence. Individuals may have a combination of individualistic and collectivistic values.

(Continued)

TABLE 1.3 Key Terms Related to Culture and Multicultural Counseling (Continued)

Privilege versus Oppression	**Privilege** refers to the often unconscious and unearned power, access to resources, advantage, and social position based on cultural group memberships. Privileged cultural groups in U.S. society typically include Whites, males, heterosexuals, those with a higher socioeconomic status, the able bodied, and Christians. Because certain individuals have privilege, others within various cultural groups experience **oppression**: lack of power, inaccessibility of resources, disadvantage, and minority social status. Oppressed cultural groups include racial and ethnic minority groups, females, sexual minorities, the less able bodied, those of lower socioeconomic status, and religious minorities.
Race	**Race**, or **racial group membership**, is the arbitrary, socially constructed classification of individuals and is often based on physical distinctions such as skin color, hair texture, facial form, and shape of the eye. Throughout history, race as a classification system has divided and exploited individuals, and has resulted in both **racism** and lowered social, political, and psychological well-being. Examples of current U.S. racial categories include White, African American, Asian American, and Native American.
Sexual Orientation	**Sexual orientation** refers to sexual or affectional attraction to the same or opposite gender, or both. **Sexual identity** describes the degree of identification with a particular sexual orientation (e.g., heterosexual, gay, lesbian, bisexual, questioning). Sexual identity and sexual orientation overlap in that sexual orientation falls on a continuum, at one end of which an individual of one gender may be attracted solely to another of the opposite gender (i.e., the sexual orientation of the first individual is heterosexual) and at another end of which an individual of one gender may be attracted to another of the same gender (e.g., the sexual orientation of the first individual is gay). Between these points fall various other sexual identities, including bisexual and questioning.
Social Advocacy and Social Justice	**Social advocacy** refers to the promotion of an idea, policy, or cause that betters the lives of those who experience oppression. **Social justice** is the realization of a just and equitable world for all individuals.
Socioeconomic Status	**Socioeconomic status (SES)** is typically indicated by household income, education level, occupational status, use of public assistance, and access to health care. Those who belong to lower SES groups (e.g., working class, underclass) often have negative mental health outcomes as a result of detrimental social, educational, and economic experiences. Racial and ethnic minorities and women heads of household disproportionately represent lower SES groups, making the intersection of SES, race, ethnicity, and gender an important component of multicultural counseling.
Spirituality and Religion	**Spirituality** refers to the connections individuals have with themselves and the universe as a whole. It provides direction, meaning, and purpose, and guides other aspects of cultural identity so that individuals can promote optimal mental functioning. **Religion**, an organizing construct of spirituality, consists of the behaviors and practices of individuals' faith. There are several Western and Eastern religions of the world, including Buddhism, Christianity, Confucianism, Hinduism, Islam, Judaism, and Taoism.

Worldview

A **worldview** is defined as individuals' conceptualization of his or her relationship with the world. Sue (1978) described individuals' worldviews as embedded within two intersecting dimensions—locus of responsibility and locus of control—that individuals and groups use to guide their behaviors. **Locus of responsibility** refers to the system that individuals believe is accountable for things that happen to them. An internal locus of responsibility (IR) refers to the idea that success (or failure) is viewed as the result of individuals' own doings. An external locus of responsibility (ER) refers to the notion that the social environment is responsible for what happens to individuals. The second dimension, **locus of control**, represents the degree of control that individuals perceive they have over their environment. An internal locus of control (IC) refers to the belief that consequences are dependent on individuals' actions. An external locus of control (EC) refers to the notion that consequences result by chance and are outside individuals' control. There are four combinations of IC and EC. (See Build Your Knowledge 1.1.) Kluckhohn and Strodtbeck's (1961) theoretical model creates a different definition of *worldview*, using five dimensions. Specifically, Kluckhohn and Strodtbeck maintain that individuals have perspectives on (1) the nature of humankind, (2) individuals' relationship to nature, (3) individuals' sense of time, (4) the nature of self-expression (e.g., being vs. doing), and (5) how social relationships are organized (e.g., hierarchical vs. collateral–mutual).

BUILD YOUR KNOWLEDGE 1.1

According to Sue (1978), individuals' worldviews may be conceptualized as one of four combinations of locus of responsibility and locus of control (see Table 1.3, definition of *worldview*): (a) IR–IC is a common combination among those who hold White middle-class values according to which individuals control and are responsible for their own actions in the world; (b) IR–EC describes individuals who believe they cannot control actions that occur to them and may blame themselves for any negative consequences; (c) ER–IC addresses those who view individual ability to be possible if people are given an opportunity by those in their environment; and (d) ER–EC involves those who believe they have little control over their actions because of oppression and other systemic pressures and who thus see addressing the consequences of this state of affairs as outside their responsibility.

On the basis of Sue's (1978) four types of worldviews, list at least two situations in which clients may present in counseling with each of the following combinations: IR–IC; IR–EC; ER–IC; and ER–EC.

EXAMPLE: IR–IC *A client visits a career counselor to seek assistance in selecting a college major. The client reports difficulty in the decision-making process. He is interested in a prestigious career that will allow him to be successful, and he wants to select the best college major to obtain this goal. He states that he holds himself accountable for any decision he makes.*

and sexual orientation influence both his presenting symptoms and the counseling relationship. By contrast, a counselor who views this client through a narrower definition of culture may attend only to how his being multiracial and male affects his well-being and the counseling relationship.

In addition to the cultural identities that counselors and clients bring to the counseling relationship, "U.S." or "American" culture is important to attend to, as American values may not always be congruent with values we hold regarding various cultural identities. Activity 1.1 presents some questions to reflect on with respect to U.S. culture and multicultural counseling.

ACTIVITY 1.1

Together with a partner, discuss the following questions about U.S. culture and multicultural counseling:
- What does being an American mean to you?
- What values are associated with being an American?
- What values are associated with not being an American?
- How would you describe U.S. culture to a newcomer to the United States?
- What images come to your mind about U.S. culture as you reflect on media images?
- How might images and descriptions of U.S. culture be beneficial to counseling diverse populations? How might they be a challenge?

USE OF COUNSELING SERVICES AND MULTICULTURAL POPULATIONS

Cultural factors play a role in whether individuals—particularly racial and ethnic minority group members, those of lower socioeconomic status (SES), and nonnative English speakers—seek and remain in mental health treatment (Gonzales, Alegría, Prihoda, Copeland, & Zeber, 2011; Leong & Kalibatseva, 2011; Weissman, Pratt, Miller, & Parker, 2015). Further, individuals with lower levels of acculturation may perceive or experience more barriers to seeking help and may report stigma or mistrust of the counseling profession (Leong & Kalibatseva, 2011). While a perceived or actual lack of access to mental health services is, in general, linked to poorer clinical outcomes, such as suicide, hospitalization, and maladaptive social and occupational functioning (Lee, Xue, Spira, & Lee, 2014), the failure to provide culturally and social justice–oriented care as part of any services delivered can be detrimental to clients from oppressed statuses and lead to premature termination of mental health services.

Thus, understanding the attitudinal and structural factors that deter culturally diverse populations from participating in and completing counseling services is imperative for counselors. *Attitudinal factors* include beliefs about the counselor personally and professionally, as well as those perspectives related to the counseling process and outcome. *Structural factors* involve systemic barriers that make counseling disproportionately available to different clients. We view these two types of factors as interdependent and mediated by culturally based experiences that ultimately serve to influence the type and amount of care individuals seek and obtain. In this section, we first discuss the potential conflict between the "culture" of counseling and common cultural norms of diverse populations. Next, we discuss discrimination experiences that may occur within counseling. We then outline attitudinal factors, such as stigma and cultural mistrust, as well as discrimination experiences those from minority groups encounter. Finally, we examine structural factors, such as barriers associated with geography, SES, language, and the general knowledge base related to culture and mental health.

Counseling versus Cultural Norms of Diverse Populations

The values of counseling may not be congruent with the values of various cultural groups. For example, counseling values mirror the dominant U.S. values of individualism and autonomy; a preference for increased self-awareness, self-disclosure, and emotional expression; and an emphasis on a linear time orientation and goal-directedness (Leong & Kalibatseva, 2011). Many cultural groups have values that are different from these, such as collectivism and interdependence, limited disclosure out of respect for family and community members, and a circular time orientation. In addition, traditional counseling theories tend to minimize a systems approach, often pathologizing close connections among family members through terms such as *enmeshment* and *codependency*, as well as minimizing community and historical factors.

The way normality and abnormality are defined in counseling is culturally based. What constitutes normal behavior and thus optimal mental health? A common assumption in traditional counseling practice is that normality is a universal and consistent construct across social, cultural, historical, and political contexts. The role of culture is often ignored. Culture, however, defines the expression and attribution of mental health symptoms and thus what is considered normal and socially acceptable. Further, culturally diverse groups often view mental health as a function of a mind–body–spirit connection that has implications for how symptoms are diagnosed, understood, and treated (Leong & Kalibatseva, 2011). To present the potential conflict between values associated with mental health and the cultural values of various groups, Reflection 1.2 presents process questions to help you think about your views on help-seeking behaviors.

Stigma and Mistrust

Culturally diverse clients may perceive counseling to be a stigmatizing process because some cultures may view mental illness as something to be discussed only within a specific community. Many cultural groups rely on family members, community leaders, and spiritual healers to provide assistance with mental and physical health problems. Further, a client's informal support network may perceive traditional counseling to be a threat to community practices.

REFLECTION 1.2

Respond to the following questions:
- How does your family of origin view the seeking of formal mental health services?
- What messages have you received about seeking formal mental health services from religious or spiritual organizations?
- Of which cultural groups are you a member?
- How do the media portray "appropriate" help-seeking behaviors?
- When do you think it is necessary for someone to seek formal mental health services?
- How can your beliefs affect your work as a counselor?

Culturally diverse clients are often mistrustful of counselors, who tend to be predominantly White (Cheng, Kwan, & Sevig, 2013), because of historical racist, sexist, classist, and heterosexist undertones in counseling practice. Counselors and counselor trainees have varying levels of awareness of the roles that cultural privilege and oppression play in both the counseling relationship and clients' daily lives (Hays, Chang, & Dean, 2004; Hays et al., 2007). As part of their mistrust, clients from diverse populations may fear being institutionalized should they disclose mental health concerns (Cheng et al., 2013; Lee et al., 2014). Further, cultural stigma and mistrust can create discomfort in talking with someone, especially when the client has higher levels of psychological distress (Cheng et al., 2013; Leong & Kalibatseva, 2011). Research (Lee et al., 2014) examining utilization rates, particularly among those with significant psychological distress (e.g., severe depression), shows that racial and ethnic minorities either lack access to mental health care or select emergency rooms and inpatient facilities instead of more specialized mental health resources because they mistrust the latter. This choice may be associated with stigma, and such mistrust may indicate that these populations, particularly Asian Americans, may attend merely to physical components of mental illness or delay psychological help until conditions are severe.

Discrimination Experiences

Counselors and counselor trainees have varying levels of awareness of the role that cultural privilege and oppression play in both the counseling relationship and clients' daily lives (Hays et al., 2004). Stigma and mistrust of helping professions have been linked to discrimination experiences. Cheng et al. (2013) noted that racial and ethnic minority individuals who perceive culturally based discrimination are more likely to feel ashamed about seeking psychological help and are more concerned with being stigmatized by others for doing so.

There is also evidence that counselors may underdiagnose, overdiagnose, or misdiagnose culturally diverse clients' problems because of prejudice (Eriksen & Kress, 2008). Under-, over-, and misdiagnosis typically happen when the role of culture and sociopolitical issues are inappropriately applied in understanding clients' presenting concerns. A more detailed discussion of diagnosis and culture may be found in Chapter 18.

Inaccessibility of Services

Counseling services tend to be inaccessible to culturally diverse populations for several reasons. First, there are geographic and economic barriers to the use of services, and these barriers are intertwined. Residential areas of people of color and lower SES groups, who often are nonnative English speakers, tend to have few to no mental health resources, given the costs and physical locations of those resources. For individuals from lower SES backgrounds, additional economic barriers arise when they are unable to take time away from work to find or receive services. Further, the traditional practice of counseling lends itself to face-to-face, 50-minute sessions that only a small percentage of individuals can afford. Moreover, with approximately 75% of those with mental health–related disabilities unemployed and about 15% with common psychotic and mood disorders identifying as homeless (World Health Organization, 2010), these services are even more inaccessible to those in greatest need. A second factor associated with inaccessibility relates to the paucity of culturally relevant knowledge concerning the mental health needs and best practices for treating these clients. As Leong and Kalibatseva (2011) noted, the "road to treatment is often blocked by . . . a critical deficiency of studies pertaining to nonwhite populations" (p. 1).

In sum, although the prevalence of mental health disorders is generally similar across cultural groups (APA, 2013; Substance Abuse and Mental Health Services Administration [SAMHSA], 2014), the underuse of services due to the interplay among cultural, attitudinal, and structural factors means that a higher proportion of individuals of minority status may have significant unmet mental health needs (Leong & Kalibatseva, 2011). Given culturally specific stressors (e.g., prejudice, discrimination, immigration and acculturative stress, violence and trauma), it is imperative that counselors engage in multicultural counseling practices that better serve the needs of a diverse population. Counselors must continue to evaluate the current methods by which mental health services are delivered, the disproportionate distribution of mental health services, counselors' own biases about the values of counseling as well as the values of culturally diverse clients, and the ways by which the counseling profession may connect with other social, interpersonal, economic, and political institutions within communities. To illustrate the underuse of counseling services, Voices from the Field 1.1 showcases Dr. Michael Hannon's research (e.g., Hannon, 2013) with Black fathers of children with an autism spectrum disorder.

We conclude this section by offering some cautions regarding reviewing available research on counseling utilization and completion rates for culturally diverse populations. First, underreporting of mental health symptoms and help-seeking behaviors occurs. Underreporting can happen on the part of some individuals because they perceive a stigma associated with admitting mental health concerns and requesting assistance, among other factors. Further, in both their practice and their research, counselors and other health

Voices from the Field 1.1

Black fathers of children with an autism spectrum disorder (ASD, or *autism*) represent a unique population, with a number of intersecting identities. As diagnosis rates of autism continue to rise (Centers for Disease Control and Prevention [CDC], 2016), counselors are increasingly providing services to this population and their families. Parents raising children with disabilities are challenged in finding an identity for their families that is healthy and affirming. However, the process of doing so can be challenging because of a number of factors that include, but are not limited to, disparities in diagnosis, disparities in access to care, missed or delayed diagnoses, and higher rates of dual diagnosis for Black children with autism (CDC, 2016). Counseling support for Black fathers who are making meaning of these realities might assist in the development of a healthy identity. Unfortunately, my research indicates that Black men have been found to underutilize or refrain from seeking counseling services for a number of reasons.

In my research, Black fathers with children with an ASD identified several perspectives regarding the relevance or need for counseling services. Although these men articulated openness to counseling to help them with challenges associated with autism, none sought it for themselves either individually, with their partners or families in couples or family counseling, or with other fathers of children with autism in group counseling. Reasons noted included not being oriented toward the preventative nature of counseling, not being encouraged to seek counseling, relying more on spiritual support than counseling support for hardships, and wanting support solely from someone who had their direct experience (i.e., fathering a child with autism). The three narratives that follow help to underscore fathers' experiences with counseling; pseudonyms have been used to protect the fathers' identities.

(Continued)

Case of Darryl

Darryl is a 49-year-old, Black father and husband. He has been married to his wife, Janine, for over 25 years. He and Janine have one son, Malik, who is 22 years old. Darryl shared that Malik was diagnosed with autism when he was 3. Darryl is a banking executive who works in the greater metropolitan region of a northeastern city. I would describe Malik as a person whose major challenge with autism is his receptive and expressive language. I saw Malik demonstrate his receptive language capacity and saw how he struggles with expressive language. Darryl stated: "In 22 years, I have never sought counseling services for this stuff. Why? BECAUSE WE'RE AFRICAN-AMERICAN!! We don't go to counseling. We go to church and pray about this stuff. If you have a problem, you get you some Jesus and he's going to take care of it all! That has been the mindset. My sister-in-law is a licensed clinical social worker and she has never suggested counseling.

"Now, do I still have that mindset? No. But it's hard to shake something that you have been taught for your entire life. We don't need to see counselors. And then I think—God has blessed these people with training and degrees and talent enough so you can sit down with them and talk about your life problems. But, in African-American households things have to be really bad if you get counseling. Do I think counseling could help with some things? Yeah, I do. There are day-to-day things that we confront and a counselor could help with those things. The stuff related to Malik, though, God has blessed me to have a great relationship with my wife for us to be good parents. He has guided our footsteps through 22 years. Counseling just hasn't been the route we have chosen to take while on this journey. I can't say we won't ever try it. We just haven't tried it up until now. And I have to be honest, because I have had the chance to finally talk about this stuff with someone about MY experience—now it's been 22 years and I have never had anyone ask me about my experience—it has been very, very helpful. I feel like I have been able to exhale a little more."

Case of Cameron

Cameron is a 41-year-old Black father who has been married to his wife, Liz, for 15 years. They have three children: Tyler, Jermaine, and Nicole. Tyler, who is 13, is the oldest child. He was identified with ASD when he was two years old. Cameron is a man of deep Christian faith. Cameron shared that Tyler had been suspended out of school three times that year for issues he argues are symptoms of his son's diagnosis. It has been very contentious between Cameron's family and the school, which was very stressful for Cameron. Cameron is currently seeking legal recourse against his son's school district. Cameron noted: "I never thought about getting counseling throughout this experience with Tyler. Well, let me just say I have no issue with seeing a counselor. I think if someone would have suggested I see one during that early discovery phase, I probably would have jumped on it. Now we've got thirteen years in to this and I don't think the need is as great. That doesn't mean that everything is easy but I have had some people in my life that probably functioned kind of like counselors to help me get to a healthier place. There is no way my wife or I could be at the place we are now without good people who have "counseled" us in hard times.

"Really, the only time I think of counseling is for marriage counseling with the pastor. Many of us think about counseling for couples when something is wrong or for pre-marital counseling but I can see the need to just go see a counselor for the benefit of just talking to someone. Put it this way: I bet I'll have a conversation with my wife about it now! I would not just want to see any counselor, though. I would want to see someone who knew my experience and could relate. I can't just talk to some random person who knows nothing about why I am coming to see him or her. That would be a requirement."

Case of Broderick

Broderick is a 27-year-old married fitness entrepreneur who lives and works in a major northeastern city. His son, BJ, is a six year old with ASD. His family's experience with autism prompted him and his wife to launch a nonprofit educational organization for parents and caregivers of children with disabilities. Broderick asserted, "Um, never really been considered [counseling] for a lot of reasons. I grew up in a house where my mom—she's always been trying to get her social working [degree]—she had a master[']s. She wanted to be a social worker. She always believed in that. She used to take us to a family [counselor] and I was one of those kids that, you know, played with it. I didn't really take it serious. Um, growing up you know you don't really listen to anybody when you don't have anybody to look up to. And, um, that was my issue with counseling. Um, I didn't believe anyone could really tell me or give me a perspective to understand. . . .

"I've been in meetings and one-on-ones and been told about myself, [but] I've never really been able to honestly get—give and get what I feel is counseling . . . So, um, that has never really crossed my mind because, um, I'm more of a trial and error guy. I know how to get up when I fall, and I don't stay down, so it's like I'm—how do I say this, I don't need my hand—I don't really have my hand out for counseling. I understand it now. I understand the idea of it, and I respect it more than I did before because I guess I was just a child . . . But if I did ever get counseling, it would have to be from someone that understands what I'm going through and has a perspective based on helping others with it or being through it themselves."

~Michael D. Hannon, PhD, Counselor Educator, Montclair, New Jersey

professionals may not be asking the right questions, in the right settings, and with the right populations, and this misdirection may lead to a limited or distorted perspective of prevalence rates. As examples, available cross-cultural survey data often have limitations, such as few to no questions regarding the frequency and intensity of symptoms, a lack of within-group information, and a limited understanding of how intersecting identities (e.g., gender, SES, sexual orientation) might affect how data are understood and reported, and scholarship focused on culturally diverse samples is, in general, insufficient (Leong & Kalibatseva, 2011).

A second area of caution is that findings about cultural differences in mental health symptoms and help seeking tend to be mixed. Some reasons for this fluid situation relates to the underreporting factors just discussed; however, there are methodological issues inherent in published research involving racially or ethnically diverse populations as well. A major methodological concern relates to the assessment tools used to evaluate mental health symptoms and help-seeking behaviors: These tools often yield (1) unreliable and invalid scores, because certain groups may possess minimal or insufficient norms or have other test construction issues; (2) bias, because cultural groups experience events differentially on the basis of their cultural makeup and other intersecting variables, such as values, communication patterns, and spirituality; and (3) selection bias, because analyzing data by cultural groups such as race or ethnicity fails to control for either general confounding variables such as SES or language differences, significant within-group variation that may exist, or limitations of the sample itself (Cokley & Awad, 2008). These unreliable or invalid scores and biases lead not only to the misinterpretation of findings, but also to the misapplication of results to a larger population.

THE ROLE OF COMMUNICATION IN MULTICULTURAL COUNSELING

Communication is central to the therapeutic process. Clients communicate their self-concepts, emotions, perspectives, and realities both verbally and nonverbally. Through communication, relationships are built, trust is established, and understanding and empathy are expressed.

In the context of multicultural counseling, differences in language and styles of communication can create a significant barrier to establishing a therapeutic relationship and working toward change. Multicultural counselors, as well as counselors who are competent in social justice issues, are charged with taking action to overcome this barrier by educating themselves about how their own communication styles and the communication styles of clients are influenced by privileged and marginalized statuses. In addition, counselors must develop culturally responsive communication skills to meet the needs of culturally diverse clients (Ratts, Singh, Nassar-McMillan, Butler, & McCullough, 2015).

Verbal Communication

Most of the major counseling theories rely on spoken words as a primary tool for promoting growth and change. Freud referred to psychoanalysis as "the talking cure," and many people still refer to counseling as "talk therapy." For this reason, language differences between the counselor and client create tremendous challenges. In the United States, English is the dominant language; however, as the population becomes increasingly diverse, counselors are likely to encounter clients who are not fluent in English, speak English as a second or third language, or speak a dialect of standard English. In fact, more than 60.6 million people in the United States speak a language other than English at home (Ryan, 2013). Unfortunately, the ethnocentric belief that everyone who lives in the United States should speak only English is still prevalent. Power is embedded in language, and clients who do not speak the dominant language are routinely marginalized and experience discrimination (Moodley, 2009). Individuals who are not fluent in the dominant language may be viewed as unintelligent or childlike and are blocked from accessing resources and opportunities that are available to individuals who are fluent in standard English. Thus, language differences create barriers that may lower self-esteem in clients who speak little to no English.

Feelings of frustration and invalidation are likely to occur when counselors are not able to convey understanding to culturally and linguistically different clients. Research indicates that, within the multicultural counseling setting, clients in the initial stages of counseling are preoccupied with making themselves understood (Ramos-Sánchez, 2007). One way to deepen the level of understanding shared by a counselor and client is to incorporate the use of traditional **metaphors** from the client's culture into the therapy session (Parham, 2002). Metaphors are rich in cultural meaning and may be related to religious teachings or cultural values. Santiago-Rivera, Arredondo, and Gallardo-Cooper (2002) described the use of metaphor with Latina clients. The metaphor "Camina la milla" (p. 138), which translates to "walk the mile," can be meaningful in discussing life's struggles and hardships. The metaphor "El oro brilla hasta en el basurero" (p. 139), which translates to "Gold shines even in the garbage can," may be used to describe perseverance despite discrimination and oppression. As metaphors are passed among generations, they become internalized. Alternative forms of communication, such as music, poetry, art, and dance, can be used to enhance counselor and client understanding as well.

Many clients who speak English as a second language may prefer to express themselves in their native language during the counseling process. Often, culture-specific phrases, or subtle nuances of words in one's native language, are best able to articulate emotions. Counselors should encourage clients to use the language with which they feel most comfortable expressing themselves (Ramos-Sánchez, 2007). At a minimum, counselors need to be aware of resources in the community for clients whose primary language is not standard English. Counselors may employ specially trained interpreters to assist in communicating with clients when a language barrier exists. In addition, English-speaking counselors are encouraged to learn a second language in order to increase the accessibility of counseling services for non-English-speaking clients and to deepen and enhance the counseling relationship with clients who prefer to express themselves in a language other than English (Ivers, Ivers, & Duffey, 2013).

Nonverbal Communication

Understanding a person's nonverbal behavior is essential to the counseling process. Approximately 85% of communication is nonverbal (Ivey, Ivey, & Zalaquett, 2014). Nonverbal communication includes facial expressions; **proxemics**, or the use of personal physical distance; **kinesics**, or body movements, positions, and postures; and **paralanguage**, or verbal cues other than words (Neuliep, 2009). Nonverbal communication may relate to or provide additional information about verbal communication. In addition, nonverbal communication often operates outside conscious awareness and is difficult to falsify, therefore making it key to understanding a client's genuine experience. Herring (1990) noted that nonverbal behavior is often ambiguous and culturally bound. In other words, the same nonverbal expressions can have substantially different meanings in different cultures. For example, interpersonal distance varies according to culture. "Arm's length" is a comfortable distance from which to communicate for most European Americans. However, in some Arabic cultures, for example, communicating at arm's length may be perceived as cold or unfriendly because very close physical proximity is considered comfortable interpersonal distance (Ivey et al., 2014). The meaning of engaging in direct eye contact also varies considerably by culture. In traditional Western cultures, a lack of direct eye contact may indicate shame or depression. In some Eastern cultures, a lack of direct eye contact indicates respect.

It is imperative that counselors interpret a client's presentation on the basis of norms from within the client's culture. Imposing Western norms may lead to misdiagnosis and pathologizing of a client when no pathology exists (Buse, Burker, & Bernacchio, 2013; Hays, Prosek, & McLeod, 2010). Counselors should also be aware of how their own nonverbal behavior may be interpreted by clients and should make an effort to communicate respect through their nonverbal behaviors. To increase your awareness of your nonverbal and verbal communication patterns, complete Activity 1.2.

ACTIVITY 1.2

Increase your awareness of your own verbal and nonverbal communication patterns. Work in triads in which two students role-play, conversing about a topic of their choice, and the third student observes and records notes about the communication patterns of the other two students. Switch roles until each student has had an opportunity to observe a conversation.

Share your observations with the other students. In receiving feedback about your nonverbal and verbal communications, reflect on the following: What patterns do you observe? What messages are you conveying through verbal and nonverbal communication? How might you modify your verbal and nonverbal communication patterns when working with clients from other cultural groups?

Emotional Expression

All human beings experience emotions. Feelings of sadness, anger, gladness, fright, surprise, and disgust are thought to be universal emotional experiences (Ivey et al., 2014). However, the ways in which emotions are expressed and the beliefs about the causes of emotions vary widely among and within cultural groups. The degree to which a cultural group emphasizes a connection between body and mind, the spiritual and religious beliefs of a cultural group, and the individualistic or collectivistic focus of a cultural group may influence emotional expression (Buse et al., 2013). For example, emotions are usually considered either reactions to external events or the result of chemical processes in the brain. In the dominant culture, the expression of emotions is typically viewed as a component of mental health. In non-Western cultures, emotions may be experienced somatically and viewed as a component of physical health, since the verbal expression of strong emotions may be considered culturally unacceptable (Buse et al., 2013). Negative emotions may be attributed to an imbalance of fluids in the body, possession by a spirit, or the violation of a moral or religious principle.

Socialization influences the way emotions are expressed. For example, within European-American culture, females are typically socialized to be more outwardly emotionally expressive than males. In Asian and Latino cultures, individuals may be guarded in the display of emotions because of the social stigma associated with mental health issues (Shea & Yeh, 2008). Reflection 1.3 can assist you with considering the origins of your emotional expressions.

When responding to a client's emotional expressions, counselors should use norms from within the client's culture to determine whether an expression is indicative of pathology. The client's beliefs regarding the origin of emotions should also be considered and incorporated into the counseling process.

REFLECTION 1.3

Think about the following questions to increase your awareness regarding ways in which you experience and express emotions:
- What messages did you receive as a child about emotional expression?
- What messages are present in society about emotional expression for cultural groups you identify with personally?
- Which emotions are you most and least comfortable expressing?
- How do you typically experience and express feeling sad, mad, glad, scared, surprised, or disgusted?
- Which emotions are you most comfortable expressing with others in your presence? Least comfortable?

Communication Patterns of Clients and Counselors

Patterns of communication between a counselor and a client are ideally characterized by openness and honesty. To increase open communication, counselors should consistently check with clients to ensure that they are accurately interpreting and understanding the clients' verbal and nonverbal messages. Clients who are engaged in multicultural counseling report that the feeling that they are accurately being understood by the counselor leads to increased trust and reduced levels of defensiveness (Ramos-Sánchez, 2007).

In addition, counselors should engage in a self-reflective process to evaluate how the counselor inadvertently communicates personal biases, values, and assumptions to a client. For example, the aspects of a client's story a counselor chooses to respond to indicate what the counselor considers important. A counselor's response should be based on the client's frame of reference.

Minority clients are often reluctant to use formal counseling services because they distrust the mental health profession, which has historically pathologized and discriminated against individuals who are not White, middle- or upper-class, heterosexual males (Moodley, 2009; Smith, 2015). Shame and stigma about discussing personal problems with a person outside one's culture or family may also be a barrier to open and honest communication. To build a therapeutic relationship with minority clients, an increased level of self-disclosure on the part of the counselor is often necessary. In addition, research indicates that many minority clients prefer a practical, directive, didactic style of communication from counselors.

CONTEXT AND MULTICULTURAL COUNSELING

As the U.S. population becomes more diverse, counselors are becoming more aware of the role that culturally based contextual factors play in the counseling process. These factors, which include prejudice and discrimination, immigration, acculturation, and violence and trauma, play a significant part in a systems approach to counseling, facilitating multicultural counseling competency when the counselor is not aware of them. In addition, some factors, such as the incongruence between traditional counseling practices and culturally diverse clients' mental health needs, as well as the clients' general attitudes toward counseling, relate specifically to experiences within the counseling process. In sum, contextual factors may influence culturally diverse clients' attitudes and behaviors and increase their risk of mental health problems, given that they may have limited resources and support in U.S. society (Smith, 2015).

Prejudice and Discrimination

Clients with minority status (e.g., non-Whites, females, those of lower SES, and lesbian, gay, and bisexual individuals) often deal with prejudice and discrimination in their daily lives. **Prejudice** is defined as the premature holding of a belief or attitude without appropriate examination or consideration of actual data. A prejudice may be either positive or negative and is based on stereotyped views and accompanying emotions. For example, someone might prejudge Asian Americans to be high achievers or females to be too emotional. Prejudice differs from **discrimination**, which refers to covert and overt *behaviors* based on prejudices held about individuals because of their cultural group memberships. Examples of discrimination include hiring or firing someone on the basis of his or her sexual orientation and supporting laws that may be oppressive to certain racial groups. Forms of prejudice and discrimination are based largely on **stereotypes** we hold about various cultural groups.

Examples of prejudice and discrimination include various forms of oppression, such as racism, sexism, heterosexism, and classism. Depending on their cultural makeup or their perceived cultural makeup, culturally diverse clients will have unique experiences with prejudice and discrimination. Clients have these experiences within several settings, including schools, neighborhoods, churches, temples, and mental health settings. Forms and manifestations of various oppressions will be discussed throughout the remainder of the text.

Prejudice and discrimination may pervade individual, cultural, and institutional practices, and clients may suffer social, economic, political, and mental and physical costs. Prejudice and discrimination affect their amount of social support, occupational status, and

SES; encourage maladaptive coping responses; serve as a catalyst for depression, suicide, substance abuse, violence, anxiety disorders, and chronic and acute stress; and may fuel medical complications such as hypertension, low birth weight, heart disease, and cancer (Nadal, Griffin, Wong, Hamit, & Rasmus, 2014). In addition, experiences of homophobia and heterosexism could foster self-deprecation; lead to anger and frustration; create developmental issues for adolescents; result in lack of family and peer support; and produce the posttraumatic stress disorder symptoms of somatization, denial, guilt, and numbing of emotions (Nadal, Wong, Griffin et al., 2011; Smith, Foley, & Chaney, 2008).

As counselors work with clients who may experience daily prejudice and discrimination, it is important that they examine these clients' environmental stressors associated with stereotyping. Counselors are encouraged to explore with clients any attitudes and behaviors that the clients perceive are in response to their cultural group memberships. In addition, culturally sensitive counselors need to identify various stereotypes that they themselves hold of various cultural groups. Reflection 1.4 offers space to reflect on stereotypes you may possess.

REFLECTION 1.4

Stereotypes are generalizations we hold about individuals based on their cultural group memberships. Describe the following groups honestly and thoroughly with the first thoughts that come to your mind:

Males: _____

Catholics: _____

Native Americans: _____

Gay males: _____

Homeless individuals: _____

Asian Americans: _____

Females: _____

Lesbians: _____

Latin Americans: _____

Jews: _____

Protestants: _____

Whites: _____

Wealthy individuals: _____

African Americans: _____

Middle-class individuals: _____

Muslims: _____

Transgender individuals: _____

Bisexual individuals: _____

Arab Americans: _____

Buddhists: _____

Review the sentences you created. How and from whom did you learn these stereotypical generalizations? Have any of them changed for you throughout your life so far?

Immigration

Immigration is another consideration in multicultural counseling. Immigration is the process by which foreign-born individuals settle in a new country. Most U.S. racial and ethnic groups were immigrants to the country at some point; the only exceptions were groups such as Native Americans, Aleuts, and Native Hawaiians. Immigration can be either voluntary or involuntary. Many individuals choose to enter the United States to flee political or religious persecution or to improve their economic conditions. However, African immigrants arrived in this country involuntarily and were enslaved on arrival. Other immigrants were indentured servants on entry, and many were able to obtain their freedom eventually. In either case—voluntary or involuntary immigration—individuals often are separated from their family and their homeland, creating several mental health considerations. Voices from the Field 1.2 highlights one counselor's considerations when working with immigrants.

Voices from the Field 1.2

At first, I did not know what it meant to be an immigrant. Eighteen years after I unpacked four suitcases containing 30 years of my life I still find myself metaphorically packing, repacking, and pondering. Coping with personal and professional identity shifts, restorations, and amalgamations that this continuous journey has entailed has been my main psychosocial task. I was able to make sense of the very real theoretical stages that manifest in the everyday lives of immigrants because of a core paradox: "I used-to-be" and "I-am" a clinical psychologist in my country of origin. I had the words to name my affects, the support of many hours of psychotherapy, and the privilege of witnessing hundreds of other immigrants' narratives in my work. I am finally able to return to where I already was *and* practice as a soon-to-be clinical counselor. My passion is collaborating with immigrant clients to "edit" the narratives of their journeys, to sort out stories related to cultural and social gaps, and ultimately to integrate who they were, who they are, and who they want to become. Immigration is not a moment in time, but an accumulation of more or less disruptive alterations characterized with peaks of accomplishment and lows of loss and grief. In my experience, I focus on these three elements when counseling immigrant clients:

1. *The counselor's professional worldview.* Built on the advice of one of my supervisors, Dr. Werther, to spend ample time talking about the informed consent, in plain language I further clarify my own tenets to my clients. Periodically, I answer mindfully to questions that operate as detectors of professional biases: what is mental health, what is counseling, my school of thought, other colleagues' schools of thought, what are good therapeutic outcomes. Professional worldviews contain preferences that, if undetected, may hinder the open communication with clients who are transitioning culturally. A counselor and client validate their work together by building trust in each other.

2. *The client as expert in his or her own immigration journey.* Although tempting, I do not use my immigrant clients to learn from their culture as a whole; they are only experts in their particular psychosocial narrative. I may speak the same language as my clients, but our nationalities are different, and we generally do not share a historical context, financial situation, or even religious background. In our encounter, we lend the space for the client to see himself or herself as the expert, to give words to their experience.

(Continued)

> **3.** *The story of the immigration and the dream behind the journey.* Not every concern of every client has to do with the immigration experience, but the transition from the country of origin to the current situation touches affects, cognitions, and social relationships. As my colleague Heidy Guzmán posits, the immigrant dream is at the center of the experience. It is crucial to know the story and the dream: What is the story? Is he or she the creator of that story? Has someone else created a dream for them? Within encounters between counselor and client, there is voice given to the connection between the presenting problem, the story, a eam.
>
> ~*Edurne Chopeitia, M.A., Mental Health Counselor, Atlanta, Georgia*

There are different immigration patterns throughout U.S. history as a result of changing immigration policies. Oftentimes, these policies are shaped by current economic needs. However, some may argue that policy is often guided by a desire to keep the United States largely White, as evidenced by the differential numbers of immigrants on the basis of their countries of origin (Takaki, 2002). For example, between 1820 and 1930, because of policies that existed at the time, about 38 million immigrants came to the United States from Europe, with few arriving from Asia or Africa. This influx was largely in response to the melting-pot concept, whereby Europeans especially were encouraged to immigrate to the "land of opportunity." However, the U.S. government needed cheap labor in the mid-1800s to construct the Central Pacific Railroad, a project that represented a commercial opportunity to conduct business with Asia. Thus, the Chinese were encouraged to immigrate to California to improve their economic conditions. However, borders were closed to the Chinese in 1892 after they were viewed as an economic threat. Since 1950, European immigration has declined from about 60% to only about 20%, while 75% of legal immigrants settling into the United States have come from Latin America or Asia. An estimated 12 million undocumented Latino/a immigrants are working and living in the United States. Politicians have discussed strategies that would criminalize illegal immigration while creating pathways for citizenship for those who are willing to pay fines and wait some time before receiving a green card (American Immigration Council, 2015).

Recent legislation aimed at reforming the immigration system in the United States includes the Deferred Action for Childhood Arrivals (DACA) program and the Deferred Action for Parental Accountability (DAPA) program. These deferral programs provide temporary relief from deportation and offer work authorization for unauthorized individuals who were brought to the United States as children (DACA) and for unauthorized parents of U.S. citizens or legal permanent residents who meet specific criteria (DAPA; American Immigration Council, 2015). Thus, culturally diverse clients will have different immigration histories that affect their sense of belonging. In assessing the role that immigration plays in multicultural counseling, understanding the reasons for a person's entry into the United States, knowing the length of time he or she is in this country, possessing information about the cultural climate of the person's country of origin, and being aware of the degree of prejudice and discrimination faced by a client's family historically and currently become especially important. For example, the historical oppression experienced by southern and eastern Europeans living in urban ghettos is quite different from that experienced by Africans in the South or Asians in the western United States. Further, the experiences of, and thus mental health impact on, Latin Americans seeking political refuge in the United States within the past few years are quite different from those of someone whose family arrived seeking educational and career opportunities several generations ago.

Acculturation

Acculturation is highly related to immigration. As described in Table 1.3, **acculturation** refers to the degree to which immigrants identify with and conform to the new culture of a host society, or the degree to which they integrate new cultural values into their current value system. Acculturation may involve individuals identifying with both the homeland and host cultures, embracing one culture over the other or rejecting both cultures (Phinney, 1993). There are four main models of acculturation with which counselors should be familiar: (a) the *assimilation* model, in which highly acculturated individuals identify solely with the new culture, so one group (typically a racial or ethnic minority group) adopts values and customs of another, more dominant group (i.e., European Americans); (b) the *separation* model, wherein individuals refuse to adapt to cultural values outside their own; (c) the *integration* model, which refers to **biculturalism**—a process in which individuals identify with both their own culture and that of the host culture; and (d) the *marginalization* model, according to which individuals reject the cultural values and customs of both cultures (Paniagua, 2014). There may be unique counseling considerations pertaining to each of these four models of acculturation. Review Case Study 1.1, and apply each of the acculturation models.

CASE STUDY 1.1

You are a middle-school counselor in a small, close-knit community in the Midwest. Lian, a 14-year-old Asian female, was referred to you for social and academic issues. Specifically, her teachers are concerned about Lian's failing grades and isolative behaviors. During your initial session with Lian, you discover that she has been in the United States since age 7 and has lived in your community since age 13.

- How might you conceptualize her acculturation experience on the basis of the four models of acculturation: assimilation, separation, integration, and marginalization?
- To what degree would your interventions differ, according to various acculturation levels?
- How might Lian's cultural group memberships factor into your intervention?

A client's acculturation level is determined largely by the number of years the client has been involved in the acculturation process, the client's country of origin, and the age at which the client began the acculturation process (Paniagua, 2014). It may be assumed that the longer a client is in the United States, particularly if he or she enters the country at a young age, the easier the acculturation process will be. Also, if a client originates from a country that is similar to the United States in some way (e.g., is English speaking, has shared customs and values), the easier the transition will be. Acculturation is also affected largely by immigrants' ethnic identity: The more immigrants identify with and belong to a particular ethnic group, particularly if their ethnic values contrast with general U.S. cultural values, the more difficult the process of acculturation becomes.

Even when the acculturation process seems easier for some culturally diverse clients, there are many stressors associated with it. The process of acculturation can be a significant stressor for racial and ethnic minorities because they must give up, limit, or deny part or all of their cultural values and customs and become more like the dominant group in order to increase their chances of attaining social and economic mobility. Among the responses to these stressors are depression, anxiety, isolation, substance abuse, physical health concerns, and identity confusion (Gonzales et al., 2011; Leong & Kalibatseva, 2011; Weissman et al., 2015). For many groups, acculturation coupled with prejudice and discrimination experiences does little to help them "succeed" in the United States. Many racial and ethnic minorities continue to experience oppression, regardless of how long they have lived in this country and how much they have compromised their cultural identities to increase their sense of belonging in the general U.S. culture. In fact, research indicates that the more acculturated some racial and ethnic minorities are (e.g., Latino Americans, Asian Americans), and thus the longer they have lived in the United States and have been exposed to oppression, the more mental and physical health problems they report (Leong & Kalibatseva, 2011).

Interpersonal Violence and Trauma

Interpersonal violence and trauma are stressors that apply across cultural identities, including race and ethnicity, gender, SES, and sexual orientation. Some immigrants were refugees and fled countries involved in war, killings, starvation, and sexual trauma. Research has linked repeated exposure to these forms of violence and trauma to mental health problems, such as posttraumatic stress disorder and depression. These experiences, coupled with prejudicial attitudes and discriminatory practices in the United States, often make the immigration and acculturation processes more difficult (Liao, 2006; Mahapatra, 2012; Nava, McFarlane, Gilroy, & Maddoux, 2014).

For those who have been in the United States for some time, there can be repeated experiences of violence and trauma. Many lower SES neighborhoods have a disproportionate number of racial or ethnic minorities and women heads of household (DeNavas-Walt & Proctor, 2014) and experience high levels of unemployment, crime, and violence. In addition, sexism (i.e., negative beliefs and behaviors about the ways in which women should be treated that are based on the notion that femininity is to be devalued and is "less healthy") often has negative consequences for women by exposing them to potential sexual victimization and other forms of domestic violence. Individuals who identify as gay, lesbian, or bisexual also experience both violence and trauma as they seek safe, affirmative environments and experience homophobic reactions from many in their schools and communities (Nadal, Wong, Issa et al., 2011; Smith et al., 2008). Thus, culturally competent counselors are encouraged to explore any incidents of violence or trauma in each of their clients' daily experiences in school, at work, and in their communities. Violence and trauma are especially significant for clients who have suffered many oppressive experiences.

DEVELOPING MULTICULTURAL COUNSELING COMPETENCE

The Multicultural and Social Justice Counseling Competencies (MSJCC; Ratts et al., 2015) comprise a set of guidelines that calls attention to the awareness, knowledge, skills, and counseling and advocacy interventions required to counsel in a multiculturally competent manner. According to the MSJCC, the counseling relationship is assumed to occur within a context of counselors and clients with varying degrees of privilege and oppression experiences. These differential levels of power within the counselor–client relationship are important to consider as counselors build their competency for working with culturally diverse populations. The MSJCC Conceptual Framework provides quadrants that illustrate the different combinations of privilege and oppression which may occur between counselors and clients. (See Figure 1.1.)

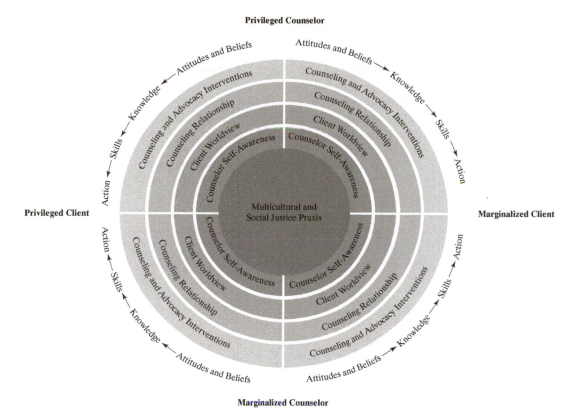

FIGURE 1.1

Source: From "Multicultural and Social Justice Counseling Competencies" by Manivong J Ratts, Anneliese A Singh, Sylvia Nassar McMillan, S Kent Butler and Julian Rafferty McCullough. Copyright © 2005. Published by American Counseling Association.

The counseling profession has increasingly focused on social advocacy as an embedded component of multicultural counseling. Even within the original multicultural counseling competencies (Sue, Arredondo, & McDavis, 1992), it was articulated within some of the guidelines that counselors are to possess awareness and knowledge regarding the role of culturally based power in the counseling relationship, as well as have the skills needed to dismantle differential levels of power in order to enact an effective counseling process and outcome. With this revision, the MSJCC provide a stronger voice about the intersection between multicultural counseling competencies and social advocacy competencies.

Appendix A provides the complete set of MSJCC. The MSJCC include four developmental domains that counselors should attend to as they work with culturally diverse clients: counselor self-awareness, the counseling relationship, the client's worldview, and counseling and advocacy interventions. For the first three domains, the MSJCC include guidelines in the areas of attitudes and beliefs, knowledge, skills, and action. For example, for the counselor self-awareness domain, counselors are to be cognizant of their own worldview and combination of privileged and oppressed statuses (*awareness*); be familiar with how their cultural identity plays out in their personal and professional experiences (*knowledge*); engage in skill development to communicate, apply, and assess their knowledge (*skills*); and make changes on a personal and professional level through cultural immersion and professional development opportunities (*action*). The fourth developmental domain, counseling and advocacy interventions, specifies that social action should be employed in six areas—the intrapersonal, interpersonal, institutional, community, public policy, and international levels—in order to build multicultural counseling competency. As Figure 1.1 shows, the developmental domains are depicted by concentric circles that build upon each other, beginning with counselor self-awareness on the circumference of the innermost circle and culminating in counseling and advocacy interventions just below the circumference of the outermost circle. In addition, Voices from the Field 1.3 highlights how counselors of various specialties define multicultural counseling competence in their own personal and professional lives.

Voices from the Field 1.3

We asked counselors practicing in various specialties how they define multicultural counseling competence. Here are their definitions, with examples from their practice:

> Being multiculturally competent means meeting my clients where they are and removing barriers created by my own cultural biases that may hinder clients from reaching their goals. An example that comes to mind for me was working with an international student from a Middle Eastern country who was in distress related to her engagement to a man who lived in her home country. As a counselor, it was important for me to understand her presenting concerns in the context of her cultural background, and in particular to take into account the influences of her personal and family values. Moreover, it was important for me to consider additional stressors and risk factors this client might face living in a foreign country and being geographically isolated from her family and friends.

~*Brian Shaw, PhD, University Counselor and Clinical Coordinator, Milledgeville, Georgia*

Multicultural competence involves a fine mixture of confidence and humility, knowledge and consideration. Having the confidence to challenge, dissect, clearly define, and embrace my own values and beliefs while being humble enough to give my clients the freedom to do the same makes me relevant as a counselor. To go a step further to understand and consider a client's different experiences as just as valid as one's own and being able to utilize that knowledge and awareness to empower clients to achieve a wellness that is unique and effective for them and their value system makes me relevant as a *multiculturally competent* counselor.

My continued evolution into multicultural competence has been nurtured by a commitment to be proactive in consulting with others for various populations in which I have been unfamiliar. As my clientele at a Christian-based agency increased to include clients of sexual minority statuses, I consulted with a lesbian and gay rights activist to learn more about the plight and values of Christians who are gay and lesbian. I had one client who seemed at an impasse after several weeks. When I shared my observations with her, she acknowledged that she was hesitant to really delve into certain things because she was afraid of my perception of her as a lesbian. Understanding that she needed to know for sure that I accepted her unconditionally, I decided to self-disclose my experience with the gay community and explained the process of clarity and understanding I obtained from the experience. She let out a huge sigh of relief; her body literally and visibly decompressed as if releasing considerable weight and tension. The course of her treatment picked up significant momentum after that session.

~*Carlita L. Coley, MSEd, Counselor, Bakersfield, California*

The fiber that weaves our connectedness is that of human decency, in spite of the harmful effects of prejudice, hatred, and the "isms" that divide rather than bind. Multicultural competence refers to the skillful ability to recognize and regard the lived experiences of diverse populations. I enter therapeutic relationships believing that I am endowed with the capacity to restore clients to higher levels of functioning, while embracing their uniqueness and the uniqueness of others. In order to accomplish this, I must first meet the client where he or she is; value the client as an expert on her/his lived experience; consider the client's experience from the lens which he or she provides; value her or his individuality; and then gradually stretch the client's belief in her or his ability to craft a personal narrative which may differ from that endorsed by the dominant culture.

As a professional school counselor in an urban setting, I am aware of the frequency with which African American males become acquainted with school disciplinary procedures. All too often these students face punitive measures that are deficient of understanding and instruction. For this reason, I agreed to expand my professional role within my elementary school. I accepted the challenge to lead the charge to cultivate an effective school wide discipline philosophy, which emphasizes teaching, modeling, practicing, and reviewing behavior expectations that we maintain for all students. With this new practice, we attempt to level the playing field by taking into account the reality that culture and child-rearing practices within homes differ; yet we can unite around the universal belief that educating students on the ideals of kindness, respect, cooperation, and human decency may result in greater appreciation for the lived experiences of others.

~Caron N. Coles, PhD, NCC, Counselor Educator and Professional School Counselor, Norfolk, Virginia

Being multiculturally competent in counseling has evolved beyond knowledge, skills, and awareness and has moved toward actual implementation. It means taking what has been learned in the classroom into local, national, and international communities and making an impact. Counselors are moving toward participating in social advocacy, giving their time and accepting discomfort at times to give back and participate in change. This was exemplified for me at the 2011 [American Counseling Association] conference when more than 150 counselors used culturally appropriate intervention strategies by working at the HOLT cemetery in New Orleans. The HOLT cemetery was established in 1879 for indigent African-American families and was in very poor condition. The counselors, including myself, all pulled together to respect a local community and give back to a city that means so much to so many people.

~LaShauna Dean, PhD, LPC, ACS, NCC, CSAC Counselor Educator and Substance Abuse Counselor, Wayne, New Jersey

I feel strongly that multicultural counseling is a key component of my work as a counselor. It helps me build rapport, accentuates my empathic responses, and provides me a beacon to search beneath the surface of my clients' presenting issues. My theoretical orientation is humanistic and I find that my work with clients has an element of peeling back the onion layers to highlight their inner core—their true selves, while at the same time providing my clients with empathy, genuineness and unconditional positive regard. I believe multicultural counseling helps me to provide my clients with a deeper empathic understanding.

(Continued)

In counseling I am in a constant search for the patterns in my work that appear ineffective or in need of improvement. I search for patterns in the cultural nuances I may have overlooked, in my cultural misunderstandings, or in my cultural preconceptions as a clue to seek out additional training. I am continuously accessing the literature, seeking consultation and additional training in cultural areas where I have found patterns in my work that may indicate room for improvement.

Because of my background living in Latin America I make myself available as much as I can to Hispanic or Latino clients. I work with many clients who have experienced oppression due to acculturative stress—including language proficiency stress; prejudice and discrimination due to their immigration status and being a member of the marginalized Hispanic/Latino population; and with clients who experience assimilation stress in their efforts to become "normal citizens." I conduct counseling in Spanish, I maintain a working knowledge of immigration visas and the like, and maintain a comprehensive referral source in the community for this particular client base.

~Nial Quinlan, PhD, LPC, NCC, Private Practice, Norfolk, Virginia

A multiculturally competent counselor is a life-long learner committed to understanding the complex interplay between individuals, communities, and systems, while demonstrating willingness to advocate for social justice and participate in social change. This understanding occurs through reflection and dialogue that deepens self-awareness; and by moving beyond comfort zones to experience new cultural and social groups. At a recent orientation for new counselor trainees, my colleagues and I used a fish bowl activity to facilitate a discussion amongst ourselves about our client population. My colleagues and I sat in the inner circle and the counselor trainees sat in the outer circle. In the outer circle, they were charged with observing our interaction, writing parts of the dialogue that stood out to them, reflecting on the meaning of those stand-out parts, and sharing their reflections with the group. In preparing for this, my colleagues and I decided we would be intentional about talking about personal biases that we encountered when working with our client population in hopes that through modeling, we would begin to lay a foundation for holding these dialogues in future clinical supervision sessions. Much to our delight, it worked! By the end of the fish bowl activity, everyone shared about biases related to police brutality, early pregnancy, gang involvement, high school dropouts, various forms of privilege (e.g., white, middle class, education), and more. We also talked about ways in which we will respond to our biases when they come up when working with clients.

~Jayne E. Smith, PhD, LPCC, NCC, Director of School Support Services, John Muir
  Charter Schools, Grass Valley, California

Multicultural counseling competence can be simply defined using one word, BOLD. I have discovered that one must be bold enough to ask questions, bold enough to accept answers, and bold enough to get uncomfortable. This process extends itself beyond therapeutic limitations, but delves into the personal space of the one who seeks competence. It should not be confined to the therapeutic environment, for that is a space with many controlled and defined variables. The best multicultural counseling competence is phenomenological, the lived and experienced, to which its residue is carried into counseling.

For instance, in practice, I find myself indulging in cultural inquiries, seeking answers, and working through uncomfortable variables. Most often, clients delight in cultural dialogue, perhaps because of a warm invitation to be the expert. In my personal life, I am intentional about going, seeking, and doing culturally diverse activities, getting uncomfortable, and enriching my experience of the existence of others. It is boldness that allows individuals to go beyond the known, in search of the unknown and healing of others. That is multicultural counseling competence.

~*Mary Sanderfer, PhD, LPC, NCC, Counselor Educator and Mental Health Counselor, Hampton, Virginia*

A Systems Approach to Multicultural Counseling Competence

Developing multicultural counseling competence involves taking a systems approach to working with culturally diverse clients. We cannot become multiculturally competent without considering the influence of family, community, and other environmental factors (e.g., social injustice) on clients' and our own lives, as well as how these systems intersect to create unique cultural experiences. In fact, the MSJCC clearly highlight the interdependent nature of multicultural counseling competence and social justice competence. Further, the MSJCC's fourth developmental domain—*counseling and advocacy interventions*—intentionally provides guidelines in six arenas for addressing power differentials that affect culturally diverse clients. (See Ratts et al., 2015.) In what follows, we describe how the MSJCC's six levels configure into a systems approach to multicultural counseling competence.

LEVEL 1: INDIVIDUAL   Culturally sensitive, multiculturally competent counselors encourage intrapersonal awareness, knowledge, and skills within themselves and their clients, and engage in actions that facilitate intrapersonal learning. These individual-level competencies include understanding their own cultural group memberships (e.g., race, ethnicity, gender, sexual orientation, SES, spirituality, disability) and identity development statuses (e.g., racial identity development, level of acculturation, spiritual identity development) and associated levels of power that accompany the various memberships.

LEVELS 2, 3, AND 4: FAMILY, FRIENDS, AND PEERS   Family, friends, and peers play a significant role in the cultural identities of many culturally diverse clients and are identified as part of the interpersonal level of the MSJCC (Ratts et al., 2015). Thus, it is imperative that multiculturally competent counselors understand how family, friends, and peers, as a system, affect clients' worldviews and behaviors. For example, families often affect clients' views of gender role socialization, culturally appropriate behavior, career and educational aspirations, and intimate relationships. In addition, violence and trauma within peer groups could affect how clients perceive various cultural group memberships. To develop multicultural counseling competence, counselors acknowledge how families, friends, and peers influence aspects of clients' cultural identities. In addition, they include these groups in a culturally sensitive manner in counseling interventions, as appropriate.

LEVEL 5: COMMUNITY SYSTEMS   Community systems include schools, mental health and other social services, spiritual institutions, public health systems, legal and economic resources, and within-group and between-group cultural diversity; these systems are included as part of the institutional level of the MSJCC (Ratts et al., 2015). In developing multicultural counseling competence, counselors are encouraged to increase their awareness, knowledge, and skills in a manner that connects individuals and families, friends, and peers to community systems. Achieving this aim may involve connecting clients and their immediate supports to available resources, working to change community practices so that clients and their families may have positive mental and physical health outcomes, and increasing community awareness and resources to better serve culturally diverse clientele. Many of these tasks are congruent with the social advocacy movement described later in the text.

In addition to integrating systems, counselors are encouraged to understand how a community as a system, as well as current events that take place in that community, influences clients' worldviews and behaviors. It is important that counselors have an awareness of how a client defines community because community may be defined in various ways. Counselors should explore within-group and between-group cultural diversity within a community along dimensions such as race, ethnicity, sexual orientation, and SES. In addition, counselors should understand how current violence and trauma, and prejudice and discrimination, affect a client's view of community.

LEVEL 6: HISTORICAL   Historical systems are culturally based events in a community that have an impact on a client. As Ratts et al. (2015) described in the community, public policy, and international levels of their MSJCC framework, there are historically embedded norms and regulations that precipitate and sustain inequities on clients with less power. In addition, many historical systems have contemporary implications. Examples of the MSJCC levels include racist acts against a particular racial group, the economy of a community, immigration patterns, discrimination toward international refugees, civil rights events, laws that deter particular groups from treating others inequitably within society, and historic discrimination based on gender or sexual orientation. In particular, historical experiences of oppression can create problems for many culturally diverse clients within a community, affecting their access to resources, sense of belonging, and, thus, mental health. Reflection 1.5 highlights a passage by Marilyn Frye (1983) that likens some historical systems to birdcages.

In sum, counselors are charged with understanding how various systems intersect in their clients' and their own lives to create unique cultural identities. This mutual understanding may allow counselors to have more developed competencies for multicultural counseling practice. We encourage you to complete Activity 1.3 to familiarize yourself with resources that can foster effective multicultural counseling within your community.

Resistance to Multiculturalism

Resistance to the multicultural movement in the field of counseling is still present today. Racism, sexism, ethnocentrism, heterosexism, and ageism are evident within the counseling profession and create barriers to change. In addition, multicultural counseling approaches call for counselors to exercise creativity and try new techniques. Competent multicultural practice requires extra effort on the part of the counselor and may not look like the empirically supported treatments that many counselors are comfortable with. Moreover, while multiculturally competent counselors strive for collaborative relationships with clients and the community, some counselors may be unwilling to relinquish the power associated with the expert role.

REFLECTION 1.5

Marilyn Frye (1983) writes:

> Consider a birdcage. If you look very closely at just one wire in the cage, you cannot see the other wires. If your conception of what is before you is determined by this myopic focus, you could look at that one wire, up and down the length of it, and be unable to see why a bird would not just fly around the wire any time it wanted to go somewhere. Furthermore, even if, one day at a time, you myopically inspected each wire, you still could not see why a bird would have trouble going past the wires to get anywhere. There is no physical property of any one wire, nothing that the closest scrutiny could discover, that will reveal how a bird could be inhibited or harmed by it except in the most accidental way. It is only when you step back, stop looking at the wires one by one, microscopically, and take a macroscopic view of the whole cage, that you can see why the bird does not go anywhere; and then you will see it in a moment. It will require no great subtlety of mental powers. It is perfectly obvious that the bird is surrounded by a network of systematically related barriers, no one of which would be the least hindrance to its flight, but which, by their relations to each other, are as confining as the solid walls of a dungeon.
>
> It is now possible to grasp one of the reasons why oppression can be hard to see and recognize: one can study the elements of an oppressive structure with great care and some good will without seeing the structure as a whole, and hence without seeing or being able to understand that one is looking at a cage and that there are people there who are caged, whose motion and mobility are restricted, whose lives are shaped and reduced. (p. 6)

- What are your reactions to this passage?
- Describe how various forms of prejudice, discrimination, and other contextual factors discussed earlier in this chapter may be conceptualized as a birdcage for clients of minority status.

ACTIVITY 1.3

Investigate resources in your local community that help serve culturally diverse clients (e.g., clients of different races, ethnicities, gender, sexual orientation, SES, spirituality, and ages, and with different disabilities). Compile a referral list with contact information and a brief description of services provided.

ETHICAL CONSIDERATIONS IN MULTICULTURAL COUNSELING

Counselors have an ethical imperative to engage in multiculturally competent counseling, as honoring diversity and promoting social justice are core values of the American Counseling Association (ACA, 2014). But what does this imperative mean as regards effectively incorporating ethical practice into multicultural counseling? The answer is that counselors are to familiarize themselves with specific statements and standards from the *ACA Code of Ethics* (ACA, 2014) that address cultural diversity and social advocacy considerations in terms of client welfare. Although the guidelines as a whole promote ethical competency within a cultural context, there are several areas that more explicitly direct counselors toward multicultural counseling competency. (See Table 1.4.)

TABLE 1.4 *ACA Code of Ethics* **Standards and Multicultural Counseling Considerations**

Section A: The Counseling Relationship

"Counselors actively attempt to understand the diverse cultural backgrounds of the clients they serve. Counselors also explore their own cultural identities and how these affect their values and beliefs about the counseling profession." [Introduction]

"Counselors communicate information in ways that are . . . culturally appropriate" [A.2.c]

"Counselors are aware of—and avoid imposing—their own values, attitudes, beliefs, and behaviors. Counselors respect the diversity of clients . . . especially when the counselor's values are inconsistent with the client's goals or are discriminatory in nature." [A.4.b]

". . . counselors advocate at individual, group, institutional, and societal levels to address potential barriers and obstacles that inhibit access and/or growth and development of clients." [A.7.a]

"Counselors consider the cultural implications of bartering and discuss relevant concerns with clients and document such agreements . . . ." [A.10.e]

Counselors ". . . recognize that in some cultures, small gifts are a token of respect and gratitude." [A.10.f]

"Counselors refrain from referring prospective and current clients based solely on the counselor's personally held values, beliefs, and behaviors. Counselors respect the diversity of the clients and seek training in areas in which they are at risk of imposing their values onto clients. . . ." [A.11.b]

Section B: Confidentiality and Privacy

"Counselors maintain awareness and sensitivity regarding cultural meanings of confidentiality and privacy." [B.1.a]

Section C: Professional Responsibility

"Counselors facilitate access to counseling services, and they practice in a non-discriminatory manner within the boundaries of professional and personal competence. . . . Counselors are expected to advocate to promote changes at the individual, group, institutional, and societal levels that improve the quality of life for individuals and groups and remove potential barriers to the provision or access of appropriate services being offered. . . ." [Introduction]

"Counselors practice within the boundaries of their competence. . . . Whereas multicultural counseling competency is required across all counseling specialties, counselors gain knowledge, personal awareness, sensitivity, dispositions, and skills pertinent to being a culturally competent counselor. . . ." [C.2.a]

Counselors ". . . remain informed regarding best practices for working with diverse populations." [C.2.f]

"Counselors do not condone or engage in discrimination against prospective or current clients . . . based on age, culture, disability, ethnicity, race, religion/spirituality, gender, gender identity, sexual orientation, marital/partnership status, language preference, socioeconomic status, immigration status, or any basis proscribed by law." [C.5]

Section E: Evaluation, Assessment, and Interpretation

"Counselors use assessment . . . taking into account the clients' personal and cultural context." [Introduction]

"Counselors recognize that culture affects the manner in which clients' problems are defined and experienced. Clients' socioeconomic and cultural experiences are considered when diagnosing mental disorders." [E.5.b]

"Counselors recognize historical and social prejudices in the misdiagnosis and pathologizing of certain individuals and groups and strive to become aware [of] and address such biases in themselves and others." [E.5.c]

"Counselors select and use with caution assessment techniques normed on populations other than that of the client. Counselors recognize the effects of age, color, culture, disability, ethnic group, gender, race, language preference, religion, spirituality, sexual orientation, and socioeconomic status on test administration and interpretation, and they place test results in proper perspective with other relevant factors." [E.8]

"When counselors report assessment results, they consider the client's personal and cultural background. . . ." [E.9.a]

Section F: Supervision, Training, and Teaching

"Counseling supervisors are aware of and address the role of multiculturalism/diversity in the supervisory relationship." [F.2.b]

"Supervisors. . . recommend dismissal from training programs . . . when those supervisees are unable to demonstrate that they can provide competent professional services to a range of diverse clients." [F.6.b]

"Counselor educators infuse material related to multiculturalism/diversity into all courses and workshops for the development of professional counselors." [F.7.c]

"Counselor educators actively infuse multicultural/diversity competency in their training and supervision practices." [F.11.c]

Section G: Research and Publication

"Counselors minimize bias and respect diversity in designing and implementing research." [Introduction]

Counselors ". . . describe the extent to which results are applicable to diverse populations." [G.4.a]

Section H: Distance Counseling, Technology, and Social Media

Counselors ". . . are addressed in the informed consent process: . . . cultural and/or language differences that may affect delivery of services. . . ." [H.2.a]

"Counselors provide information to clients regarding reasonable access to pertinent applications when providing technology-assisted services." [H.4.e]

"Counselors who maintain websites provide accessibility to persons with disabilities. They provide translation capabilities for clients who have a different primary language, when feasible." [H.5.d]

Note. "Section D: Relationships with other Professionals" and "Section I: Resolving Ethical Issues" are not included here, given the absence of direct language that addresses multicultural considerations in those sections.

Now that you have reviewed the areas discussed in Table 1.4, examine Case Study 1.2.

CASE STUDY 1.2

Will is a mental health counseling intern in a midsize southern city. He works for a counseling agency that advertises its services as "Christian based." Recently, Will was assigned a case involving an interracial self-identified Christian gay couple. The partners, Marshawn and Brady, are struggling with the decision to adopt a child and are encountering racial and sexual discrimination from their families of origin, as well as from the church in which they seek membership. Will identifies as a devout Christian and admits to his supervisor and colleagues that he has never before worked with a gay couple. He expresses significant discomfort and is wondering whether he has to work with the couple.

- What ethical guidelines are specifically pertinent to this case?
- What concerns do you have regarding client welfare?
- What concerns do you have regarding Will's competency?
- What would you advise Will to do?

The revision of the *ACA Code of Ethics* (ACA, 2014) contains a greater emphasis on multicultural competency and social justice competency than did earlier versions of the Code, owing partly to three key legal cases involving counselor trainees who expressed value conflicts related to working with lesbian, gay, bisexual, transgender, and questioning (LGBTQ) individuals (*Keeton v. Anderson-Wiley*, 2011; *Ward v. Polite*, 2012; *Ward v. Wilbanks*, 2010). Specifically, the *ACA Code of Ethics* promotes greater accountability on the part of the counselor in addressing potential value conflicts through professional development opportunities as opposed to referrals. While we provide a brief description of these cases here, we encourage the reader to review Hutchens, Block, and Young (2013) and Kaplan (2014) for more detailed information.

Jennifer Keeton, a prepracticum school counseling student at Augusta State University in Georgia at the time of the case, had mentioned to instructors and peers within her training program that she viewed homosexuality as an immoral act and subsequently intended to express this view to any future LGBTQ clients and work to convert them to heterosexuality. Citing Keeton's plan to damage client welfare through discriminatory behavior, program faculty ordered her to complete a remediation plan prior to entering practicum. When she did not comply, Keeton was expelled from the program, whereupon she sued the university on the basis that it had violated her First Amendment speech and religious rights. Keeton lost the lawsuit, on the grounds that the program was not denying these rights but was requiring the student to counsel LGBTQ clients effectively, as outlined in the 2005 version of the *ACA Code of Ethics*.

At the same time that the case was being litigated, Julea Ward, a practicum school counseling student at Eastern Michigan University, had been assigned a client who was dealing with depression symptoms and issues related to a same-sex relationship. Because of her religious teachings, Ward was uncomfortable working with a client who was LGBTQ, and she told her supervisor that she wanted to refer the client to another supervisee. Program faculty charged her with not abiding by the ethical standard which asserts that counselors cannot discriminate on the basis of a client's sexual orientation. Ward was provided several options for dealing with her discomfort and chose a formal university hearing to challenge the discrimination issue; the recommendation from the hearing was that Ward be dismissed from the program. Ward then filed a lawsuit, and a federal district court upheld the university's decision to dismiss her. (See *Ward v. Wilbanks*, 2010.) After she appealed the decision (see *Ward v. Polite*, 2012), a higher federal court overturned the previous court decision: The higher court ruled that the *ACA Code of Ethics* does allow values-based referrals and that the program had inconsistently applied particular codes to students on the basis of what types of values were being considered in previous client referrals. According to Kaplan (2014), the case between Ward and the university has been settled out of court.

Summary

Becoming a culturally sensitive counselor is a journey that lasts an entire professional career. As the U.S. population continues to change and diversify, so must our approach to counseling. Multicultural counseling recognizes the need for integrating cultural identities within the counseling process. Culture is the totality of human experience relating to social contexts and can be discussed within three dimensions: universal culture (common to all humankind), group culture (shared by a particular group), and individual culture (unique behaviors, attitudes, and cognitions). Cultural encapsulation (ethnocentrism) occurs when individuals adhere to a narrow and rigid view of the world and other cultures. Cultures are sometimes described as being on the individualism–collectivism continuum. Individualism values self-determination and independence; collectivism focuses on decision making for the betterment of others.

Race, ethnicity, and nationality are frequently discussed as major cultural group classifications. Other cultural classifications include generational status, gender, sexual identity, SES, disability, and spirituality. All clients present with multiple cultural identities, and these identities come with privileges and oppressions. Privilege involves the often unconscious and unearned power and advantages based on social group membership. Oppression is the hardship suffered by certain social groups at the hands of others because those groups lack the power of the others.

A worldview is conceptualized as one's relationship with the world and has been discussed in terms of the dimensions of locus of responsibility and locus of control. Another way of discussing a person's worldview involves five dimensions: the person's view of human nature (e.g., humans are good or bad), relationship to nature (e.g., in harmony with nature or exerting power over nature), sense of time (i.e., past, present, or future orientation), activity (i.e., individual engaged in behaviors), and social relationships (i.e., lineal–hierarchical, collateral–mutual, or individualistic).

Multiculturally sensitive approaches to counseling consider the intricacies of cross-cultural communication, particularly the differential cultural importance of verbal communication (e.g., the use of metaphors), nonverbal communication (e.g., proxemics, kinesics, and paralanguage), and emotional expression. Counselors need to understand the context of culture, both their clients' and their own, to help clients with diverse needs, particularly those clients experiencing prejudice (i.e., beliefs or attitudes without appropriate consideration of actual data) and discrimination (i.e., covert or overt behaviors based on prejudicial generalizations about cultural group members).

Historically, many foreign-born individuals have come to settle in the United States through a process known as immigration. Acculturation is the degree to which immigrants identify with and conform to the new culture of a host society. Four models of acculturation have been proposed: assimilation, separation, integration, and marginalization. Ordinarily, clients who are younger, have been in the host country longer, or are originally from countries with a similar culture acculturate more quickly and easily. Some immigrants have experienced violence and trauma in their country of origin prior to immigrating. Counselors must be sensitive to the diverse, specialized needs of immigrants, remembering that (a) the values of counseling may not be congruent with the values of various cultural groups, (b) culturally diverse clients may perceive counseling to be stigmatizing, (c) culturally diverse clients are often mistrustful of counselors, and (d) mental health services tend to be inaccessible to culturally diverse clients.

The multicultural counseling and social justice competencies operate along four developmental domains, proposing that counselors be cognizant of the role of power within (1) counselors themselves, (2) the counseling relationship,

(3) the client's worldview, and (4) counseling and advocacy interventions. Attitudes and beliefs, knowledge, and skills competencies are embedded in the first three domains. The fourth developmental domain, counseling and advocacy interventions, specifies that social action strategies occur across intrapersonal, interpersonal, institutional, community, public policy, and international levels. Further, the systems approach to multicultural counseling competence promoted throughout this text must provide for the influences of individuals,

family friends and peers, the community, and other environmental factors on clients' and our own lives.

We conclude the chapter with a discussion of the ethical considerations surrounding multicultural counseling. The most recent edition of the *ACA Code of Ethics* (ACA, 2014) strongly highlights multicultural and social justice competency, with particular attention paid to nondiscrimination and handling value conflicts.

Review Questions

1. What population trends do you note by 2060 in terms of race, ethnicity, age, and SES?
2. To what degree is communication style influenced by cultural and social advocacy factors?
3. What are examples of counselor and client worldview conflicts?
4. What are some considerations pertaining to understanding and addressing the underutilization of

counseling services among culturally diverse populations?
5. Using the systems approach model and the MSJCC as guides, give an example of how counselors can be more multiculturally competent with a diverse clientele.
6. What are key ethical considerations in multicultural counseling?

2 Cultural Identity Development

Cheryl Moore-Thomas

PREVIEW

Cultural constructs contribute significantly to identity and personality development (Han, West-Olatunji, & Thomas, 2011; Summers, 2014). Cultural identity (e.g., race, ethnicity, gender) shapes interactions and experiences, as well as worldviews and beliefs (Ukasoanya, 2014). It also can contribute to psychological well-being and resilience, and in some cases it serves as a protective factor against communal challenges, discrimination, and historical loss (Snowshoe, Crooks, Tremblay, Craig, & Hinson, 2015). Cultural identities, therefore, are important to consider in the movement toward multicultural counseling competence (Gonzalez, Eades, & Supple, 2014; Ratts, Singh, Nassar-McMillan, Butler, & McCullough, 2015). Culturally competent counselors must take into account issues of cultural identity not only as they relate to their clients, but also as they relate to themselves. Cultural identity development is undeniably reflected in the counseling relationship and in client–counselor interaction processes; it may be of particular concern for counselors working with clients who do not share the counselors' racial, cultural, or ethnic heritage. Given the importance of cultural self-awareness, identity development theory, and related interventions and strategies to multiculturally competent counseling (Johnson & Jackson Williams, 2015), this chapter begins with an activity (Activity 2.1), a personal story (Voices from the Field 2.1), and case study (Case Study 2.1) that promote reflection and discussion about the ever-present nature and importance of cultural identity. The chapter continues with a discussion of several specific models of cultural identity development and factors that may affect that development. Finally, the chapter includes additional reflection activities and case studies that provide opportunities for readers to consider and apply key concepts and cultural identity theories in relation to themselves and to the continuing development of multicultural counseling competence in work with clients.

ACTIVITY 2.1

Sometimes the most significant markers of our cultural identity are nonverbal. (See Halim et al., 2014.) In small groups, take a few moments to think about your clothing, personal belongings, home, community, and work environments. Then discuss the following questions:

- What symbols of your cultural identity are present?
- Which are most congruent/salient for you?
- What do these symbols say about you?
- How might clients respond to the symbols?
- How might the symbols affect your work as a counselor?
- What surprised you about this reflection?
- Which finding or learning demands additional consideration as you continue your counselor preparation?

Voices from the Field 2.1

Not a day goes by that I do not think about my identity and how people see me. I make very thoughtful, deliberate decisions about what I wear and my hairstyle, in particular. I know people approach me or make the decision not to approach me based on how I look. I think people make assumptions about how competent I am or the manner in which I will approach my work based on my clothes or hair or even my jewelry. I remember one day at work I was told my clothing was very ethnic. I could tell by the tone of my colleague that he did not mean that as a compliment. In the moment, I was shocked. I often wonder if we had the opportunity to unpack that statement what he would have understood that to mean and how I would have responded.

~CM-T

CASE STUDY 2.1

As a White woman in her mid-twenties, Allison had never thought much about culture. She always referred to herself as *American*, with little thought about the meaning of that identity. She did not believe that she had any special values, beliefs, or worldview; everyone around her, she thought, was pretty much the same. Now, however, in her multicultural counseling class, she is beginning to think about her cultural identity and worldview. She wonders whether being *American* means something different to others. She wonders what it has meant to her all these years and the ways both her cultural identity and her worldview may have shaped her interactions, perceptions, and dispositions.

- In general terms, how would you describe Allison's cultural identity development process?
- How may her growth affect her continued study in her counseling program?
- How could her consideration of her identity and worldview affect her work with clients now and in the future?

RACIAL AND ETHNIC IDENTITY DEVELOPMENT

Race and ethnicity are important dimensions of the complex construct of cultural identity. Activity 2.1 and Case Study 2.1 begin to make more visible the implications of race and ethnicity in the particular contexts of counseling and counselor preparation. To sharpen the lens on the constructs and implications of race and ethnic identity development, this section describes race and ethnicity more fully.

Race is a powerful political and socioeconomic construct with both emic and etic dimensions. Race is correlated with artificial categorical differences in physical appearance. However, race becomes more complex and nuanced as it is constructed, shaped, and reshaped by the lives and experiences of those who live it and as it is described by those observing those lived lives and authentic experiences (Coleman, 2011). **Racial identity development** can be conceptualized as a complex process of moving from a state of racial unawareness and nonidentification to one of awareness and self-identification (Chao, 2012). Racial identity theory can help counselors understand how messages are interpreted, how people view themselves, and how meaning is constructed (Middleton, Ergüner-Tekinalp, Williams, Stadler, & Dow, 2011). Mature racial identity development has been associated with healthy psychological functioning (Gushue et al., 2013), an ability to buffer institutional challenges, and an ability to cope with and navigate in-group and out-of-group interactions (Byars-Winston, 2010). Racial identity development, therefore, is important in counseling and defines a key construct for counselors' consideration in the movement toward multicultural counseling competence (Middleton et al., 2011). Related, **ethnic identity development** is a complex process in which individuals negotiate the degree that particular ethnicities belong to them. This negotiation is influenced in part by external evaluation.

With the foregoing understandings in place, we can now review the major principles and specific models of racial and ethnic identity development theory.

Racial Identity Models

In considering the vast literature base on cultural identity development, discussions often begin with the theory and models of racial identity. Cross's (1971, 1995) groundbreaking work on the process through which African Americans came to understand their Black identity gave birth to other significant models of racial identity development, most notably Helms's (1995) people-of-color and White racial identity models and Ponterotto's (1988) model of cultural identity for White counselor trainees. We next examine the Cross, Helms, and Ponterotto models.

CROSS'S NIGRESCENCE MODEL In the early 1970s, Cross began reflecting on the psychology of *nigrescence*, or the psychology of becoming Black. Cross's model (1971, 1995), which he developed and continued to shape over the years, identified stages that Black people go through as they affirm and come to understand their identity. The stages begin with *Preencounter*, which includes a preexisting identity or an identity to be changed. African Americans navigating this stage may hold a low salience for race or may even have anti-Black attitudes. The *Encounter* stage, the second stage of the model, induces identity change. During this stage, individuals experience a personalized encounter that challenges or gives credence to their personal experience of blackness. During the *Immersion–Emersion* stage, individuals immerse themselves in the symbols and signs of Black culture. This oversimplified cultural identification then resolves as individuals emerge with a more sophisticated and nuanced understanding of Black identity. Cross's fourth stage, *Internalization,* is marked by self-accept-ance and a proactive Black pride that infuses everyday life while leaving room for an apprecia-tion of other dimensions of diversity. *Internalization–Commitment,* the fifth and final stage, challenges individuals to integrate their personal sense of Black identity into a way of being and/or a long-lasting commitment to the Black community and issues.

More recently, Cross's model has been expanded to include a focus on attitudes and social identities (Cross & Vandiver, 2001) that are shaped by events and contexts of group identity across the life span. Rather than invoking developmental stages, the expanded model is marked by three thematic categories—preencounter, immersion–emersion, and internalization—that suggest multiple identities rather than one type of Black identity. Thus, the expanded model of nigrescence allows for the negotiation of various levels of multiple attitudes simultaneously. Each of these thematic categories describes frames of reference or ways of understanding the world (Worrell, Cross, & Vandiver, 2001). *Preencounter* attitudes of the expanded model include assimilation to White culture that may reflect low race salience or self-hatred. *Immersion–emersion* attitudes are marked by changing and intense themes of pro-Black and anti-White involvements that move toward more complex understandings of race and identity. *Internalization* themes can be recog-nized by a positive adherence to a Black cultural identity that acknowledges the salience of disparate racial and cultural identities of self and others (Worrell, Vandiver, Schaefer, Cross, & Fhagen-Smith, 2006). Cross's work on racial identity development theory influ-enced the development of many other models, including Helms's people-of-color and White identity models.

HELMS'S PEOPLE-OF-COLOR IDENTITY MODEL Helms's (1995) people-of-color identity model comprises the ego statuses of Conformity (Preencounter), Dissonance, Immersion–Emersion, Internalization, and Integrative Awareness. The *Conformity* status involves the acceptance of racial characteristics and external self-definition. Individuals negotiating this status (but not yet in it) may feel uncomfortable around other people of color or blame them for societal challenges or social ills. During this status, information is processed selectively and with no awareness of racism or socioracial concerns.

Characteristic of the *Dissonance* status is confusion about one's connection to groups of people of color and to Whites. The confusion may result from cross-racial interactions that elucidate one's personal or reference group's experiences with the use of racism. One may also experience guilt and anxiety about personal feelings or beliefs about people of color. As a result, information related to race is often repressed.

During the *Immersion–Emersion* status, people of color idealize their own racial group while devaluing what is perceived to be White and while expressing resistance to oppressive external forces. Individuals in this stage tend to process information in a dichotomous manner that expresses hypervigilance toward racial stimuli.

The *Internalization* status is characterized by the ability to use internal criteria for self-definition as well to respond objectively to Whites. Flexible and analytic information process-ing are aligned with this status.

The final status, *Integrative Awareness,* includes an assessment of one's collective identi-ties and the recognition and appreciation of the similarities among oppressed people. This status culminates in a universal and inclusive resistance to oppression, a commitment to social and political activism, and the ability to process information by using flexible and complex strategies.

HELMS'S WHITE IDENTITY MODEL   Helms's (1995) White identity model is composed of six ego statuses that describe how Whites interpret and respond to racial cues. Each status is a multifaceted expression of an individual's identity and is accompanied by specific information-processing strategies that reflect certain race-related attitudes, behaviors, and feelings. The model's first status is the *Contact* ego status. This status is characterized by satisfaction with the status quo and the acceptance of socially imposed racial characterizations and rules. The associated information-processing strategy is rooted in nonawareness of race and its associated issues.

The *Disintegration* status is marked by confusion regarding one's commitment to one's own group and being beset by racial moral dilemmas. The way of processing information in this stage involves ambivalence, suppression, or movement between feelings of comfort and discomfort about race. Individuals may respond to their ambivalence and confusion in two ways, as described in the next two statuses.

The *Reintegration* status involves the idealization and championing of one's own group and group entitlement. External standards are used to define self and others. During this status, individuals express out-of-group distortions or a lack of empathy for others.

In the fourth ego status, *Pseudoindependence*, individuals rationalize the commitment to their own group and tolerance of others. Tolerance of others, however, is based on the acceptance of White standards. The information-processing strategy for this status involves selective perception or paternalistic attitudes that reshape reality.

The *Immersion–Emersion* status challenges Whites to understand how they have benefited by and contributed to racism. The status requires questioning, self-reflection, and critical analysis, and it may result in an information-processing strategy that yields hypervigilant responses to racism.

The final status of the model is *Autonomy*. Whites operating in this ego status use internally derived definitions of self, demonstrate positive racial group commitment, and possess the capacity to relinquish racial privilege. Flexibility of thoughts and attitudes is the hallmark of the processing strategy for the status (Daniels, 2001; Helms, 1995). Table 2.1 summarizes Helms's models.

TABLE 2.1 Helms's Models of Racial Identity Development

Racial Identity Model for People of Color	Racial Identity Model for Whites
Conformity (Preencounter) Status	Contact Status
Example: "We would be better off if we would stop talking about race. Focusing on race is keeping us from moving forward."	*Example: "I don't know what Black people complain about. I work hard, too. That is what you have to do in life. You have to work hard to get ahead. It is as simple as that."*
Dissonance (Encounter) Status	Disintegration Status
Example: "I am the only person of color in my class. I don't fit in with the White students, but in high school I never really fit in with the students of color either. I thought this college was a good choice for me. Now, I am not so sure."	*Example: "My college is wonderful, but I am concerned that no students of color are in leadership positions. I didn't even notice it until Helen mentioned it to me. I guess it is true. I wonder what is going on."*

(Continued)

TABLE 2.1 Helms's Models of Racial Identity Development (Continued)

Immersion–Emersion Status

Example: "When I moved into the dorm, I made sure I put Black art on the walls and I only played music by Black artists. I know who I am and I am proud of it."

Internalization Status

Example: "I am not defined by what I choose to wear or what kind of music I like. To me, being Black is so much more than that. I haven't figured it all out yet, but I do know my race is bigger than some particular kind of dress or item."

Integrative Awareness Status

Example: "I enjoy the diversity in my class. I am the only person of color in the class, but through interacting with others, I learn more about them and more about me. It is sort of unexpected, but I think I now appreciate who I am and who others are in a more complete way. I like what I bring to the class as a person of color. I also like what others bring to the class."

Reintegration Status

Example: "I work hard just as my parents and grandparents did. If Whites are willing to work hard to get ahead and others are not, whose fault is that?"

Pseudoindependence Status

Example: "I think people of color can learn from what White people and others have done right in this country. If we all work together, we can make this world a better place. I think I am going to volunteer at the after-school program down the street. I have a lot I can offer those children."

Immersion–Emersion Status

Example: "I did not have anything to do with the fact that no people of color were elected to positions in student government. It isn't even my fault that no people of color were selected to head any of the subcommittees. Still, I have to ask myself some hard questions. An even tougher job will be trying to figure out what I am willing to do about all of this. But, I can't do nothing. I have to do something."

Autonomy Status

Example: "I chose this college because I wanted to learn from diverse people and different points of view. I think that is really valuable. I can't continue to grow by seeing the world from only one point of view. I want true change for the world. That can't happen if we, as people, don't get to know each other in real ways."

For both people of color and Whites, racial identity may mediate relationships, including counseling interactions. Helms's (1995) work on **racial interaction theory** discusses the interaction effects of expressed racial identity development strata between client and counselor and the effects of those interactions on therapeutic change. Specifically, Helms described **parallel interactions**, which emphasize congruent race-based communications that deny or avoid tension. In these interactions, harmony is obtainable because the participants share similar or analogous ego statuses that ascribe to similar racial attitudes and assumptions. For example, counselors and clients working at preawareness statuses of racial identity development may be able to establish comfortable counseling environments, but because of the distinct developmental status of each environment, meaningful exploration of issues of race and culture may not occur.

Regressive interactions are marked by differentiated social statuses of the participants, with the participant of higher social power exhibiting a less complex ego status. A client working with a counselor operating at a regressive status of interaction may be frustrated because the counselor may be unable to recognize or acknowledge the issues of race as related to the client's concerns.

Progressive interactions are also marked by differentiated statuses. In these interactions, however, the participant of higher social power also possesses a more cognitively complex ego status and may therefore be able to respond to racial events in a more complete and growth-engendering manner. Counselors operating from progressive interaction statuses may be able to assist clients in recognizing broader issues of race and culture and work toward possibilities and solutions that facilitate client integration and development.

PONTEROTTO'S MODEL OF CULTURAL IDENTITY DEVELOPMENT   Ponterotto (1988) suggested a model to be used specifically with White counselor trainees. In the *Preexposure* stage, White counselor trainees who are unfamiliar with multicultural issues are comfortable with the status quo. During the *Exposure* stage, trainees become aware of racism and other issues pertaining to diversity. This awareness is often initiated by coursework in multicultural counseling and may lead to feelings of anger, guilt, and motivation for change. In the *Zealot–Defensive* stage, White counselor trainees may become pro-minority and anti-White. In the *Integration* stage, a balanced perspective is achieved as White counselors in training are able to process their emotions and make meaning of their learning and growing levels of cultural awareness. Awareness of this model may help White counselor trainees reflect on their cultural identity development and the manner in which associated information-processing strategies affect values, beliefs, worldviews, and interactions with clients.

Counselors are encouraged to use cultural identity theory and models to understand clients better. The importance of using cultural identity theory and models to understand *oneself* better, however, is equally important. Activity 2.2, which highlights and reinforces some of the themes discussed in the preceding review of many of the field's most significant models of cultural identity development, encourages reflection on several questions that may prove helpful in your exploration of your own cultural identity.

Research suggests that individuals' cultural identities take shape in adolescence and are necessary for the development of a healthy self-concept and cultural socialization (Derlan & Umaña-Taylor, 2015; Hernández, Conger, Robins, Bacher, & Widaman, 2014). Early examination of cultural identity is therefore crucial. Phinney (1996) proposed a model of ethnic identity that explores this important issue taking place in early adolescence.

ACTIVITY 2.2

In small groups, reflect on your cultural identity. How would you describe your cultural heritage? How has that heritage affected your worldview, behaviors, attitudes, beliefs, and values? List three specific ways your cultural heritage is shaping your emerging professional identity. What implications do these manifestations of your cultural heritage have for your work with clients who are culturally similar? What implications do these manifestations of your cultural heritage have for your work with clients who are culturally dissimilar?

Phinney's Model of Ethnic Identity

Phinney (1996) described **ethnic identity** as the self-perceived significance of membership in an ethnic group and the attitudes and feelings that are associated with that group. Phinney's model of ethnic identity suggests that young adolescents may experience a status of identity development that is ill defined because they either have no need for such an identity, have no interest in one, or find such an identity irrelevant. This first stage, of *unexamined or diffused ethnic identity*, leads adolescents to either take on ethnic identities of significant family members without exploration or internalize stereotyped identities that pervade the media and popular culture. Phinney's second stage is marked by an *exploration of identity* and a subsequent *differentiation* of the culture of origin from the dominant culture. This stage, which is called *moratorium,* involves emotional experiences and a rapid sense of personal and cultural awareness as adolescents begin to shape a personal understanding of who they are as cultural beings. During the final stage of the model, individuals gain increased *acceptance* of their identity in ways that are healthy and allow for a full appreciation of multiculturalism.

Some research is available that explores the relationship between ethnic identity and academic achievement in adolescents. Phinney's (1992) foundational work in the area found that high school students with more developed levels of ethnic identity were more likely to report grades of A or B than those with less developed levels of ethnic identity. Similarly, Altschul, Oyserman, and Bybee (2006) found that Latino and African-American adolescents with high racial ethnic identity awareness, connectedness, and embedded achievement (i.e., beliefs about achievement as an in-group characteristic) attained better grades. More recently, using data from a large-scale study of adolescents, Harris and Marsh (2010) found that Black students with a raceless identity (i.e., an identity that is not connected to race or that minimizes the relationship to race, to the Black community, or to the sense of "blackness") do not have higher levels of academic achievement or do not attribute more value to education than students with a race-neutral or race-similar identity; this finding adds insight to previously suggested theories about the effects of race identity on the academic achievement of Black students. Luna, Evans, and Davis (2015) found that Latina/Latino students studying a culturally relevant curriculum addressing ethnic belonging, background, and attachment had increased academic motivation and academic aspirations. Although the research in this area is still developing, it appears that these initial findings could have important implications for counselors who work with young adolescent populations. In far-reaching and perhaps unexpected ways, who adolescents are as cultural beings could have connections with who they are as a person and how they see themselves in other aspects of development. Reflection 2.1 will help you think about Phinney's model in a more personally relevant way. Then use Activity 2.3 to think about how the major concepts of Phinney's model apply to your own early cultural identity development.

REFLECTION 2.1

Phinney (1996) conceptualized ethnic identity as having three statuses. In what ways does her model resonate with your personal experiences of ethnic identity development? Recognizing that ethnic identity development is ongoing, what was one of your earliest memories of movement through the following ethnic identity statuses?

1. Unexamined or diffused identity
2. Search/moratorium
3. Identity achievement

ACTIVITY 2.3

Work in small groups to develop a scenario relating how you would counsel a college-aged client in a community-based counseling center. Describe how this client might respond to academic-related stress and grades from each status of Phinney's model. Your group may determine the client's specific age, gender, racial, and/or ethnic identity. Describe a culturally competent counseling response to the scenario your group developed regarding one of the developmental statuses. Be prepared to share this selected scenario and related counseling response in class.

One of the benefits of Phinney's (1996) model is that it can be applied to all racial and ethnic groups (i.e., it is a multigroup model). It does not, however, address multiracial or multiethnic identity development. The next section introduces models that explore multiracial and multiethnic identity development.

Biracial and Multiracial Identity Development

In recent years, the population of multiracial individuals in the United States has increased dramatically. Given the complex history of race, culture, and identity in America, it is important that specific attention be given to the cultural and racial identity development of biracial and multiracial communities.

BIRACIAL IDENTITY DEVELOPMENT Poston (1990) developed one of the first models of biracial identity development after recognizing the inability of race-specific models to adequately describe the developmental trajectory of biracial individuals or individuals whose parents come from two different races. Poston's five-stage model includes Personal Identity, Choice Group Categorization, Enmeshment/Denial, Appreciation, and Integration. *Personal Identity* occurs when a child or young person's sense of self is based primarily on personality constructs that develop within the family context, rather than in a race or culturally specific group context. As a result of this development, individuals in the personal identity stage may not be aware of their biracial heritage. In the second stage of the model, *Choice Group Categorization*, individuals are forced to choose an ethnic or a racial identity because of peer, situational, community, or physical appearance factors. During *Enmeshment/Denial*, individuals may feel guilt, disloyalty, and self-hatred rooted in choices made during the previous stage of development. During the fourth stage, *Appreciation*, multiple heritages are explored as individuals engage in activities and traditions and learn about the histories and worldviews of their previously ignored racial or cultural group. During *Integration*, the final stage of Poston's model, (individuals experience a sense of wholeness as they learn to integrate their multiple cultural identities in personally meaningful ways. Although many gain a biracial identity as they move through this stage, others may maintain a single-race identity that values multiculturalism.

Research on biracial identity is in its infancy. However, Kerwin and Ponterotto (1995) attempted to integrate existing empirical data into an age-based model that acknowledges variance in identity influenced by personal, social, and environmental factors. In the model, children from birth through 5 years of age recognize similarities and differences in skin color and hair texture. This awareness that is characteristic of the *Preschool* stage may be due to parents' heightened sensitivity or, by contrast, parents' denial of the tangible differences in biracial families. In the *Entry to School* stage, biracial children may be forced to classify themselves, often with a monoracial label or a descriptive term that identifies skin color. During Kerwin and Ponterotto's third stage, *Preadolescence*, youths become increasingly aware of group membership and the social meanings ascribed to skin color, race, hair texture, language, and culture. Increased social interactions and other environmental factors may trigger this heightened level of awareness. In the *Adolescence* stage, developmental (e.g., the need to belong, intolerance toward difference) and societal factors pressure biracial youths to choose a specific cultural group identity. Biracial individuals may enter the *College / Young Adulthood* stage continuing to embrace a single-culture identity; however, the expanding sense of self that is experienced during this period of growth often results in the capability and desire to integrate one's multiple heritages. Finally, the *Adulthood* stage is characterized by further exploration of one's race and culture and by increased flexibility in one's interpersonal relations and understanding of self. In contrast to these models positing stages is a model offered by Gonzales-Backen (2013) that proposes an ecological framework to account for the development of biethnic adolescents. The framework is based in an understanding of *proximal process*, or the bidirectional nature of interactions between the individual and the environment that shape development. In the specific context of biethnic development, Gonzales-Backen identified social position (e.g., majority status, minority status, privileged status, marginalized status), discrimination, segregation, promoting or inhibiting environments, child characteristics, and family as factors significant to the cultural ecological development of biethnic adolescents.

MULTIRACIAL IDENTITY DEVELOPMENT   Root (1998) offered an ecological model of multiracial identity development that recognizes gender, politics, socioeconomic status, inherited influences (e.g., language, phenotype, sexual orientation, nativity, name), traits and skills, social interactions, and racial and ethnic groupings as contributors to identity development. As a result of these ecological factors, Root concluded that multiracial identity can be situational, simultaneous, flexible, and variant in private and public domains. Furthermore, Root's study of multiracial siblings found that multiracial identity development is significantly influenced by family dynamics, sociopolitical histories, hazing (a demeaning process of testing a person's racial or ethnic authenticity through the imposition of strenuous and humiliating tasks), and various group affiliations, including those with religious and career or professional groups. Case Study 2.2 highlights some of the issues that are relevant to multiracial identity development.

CASE STUDY 2.2

Terri, Shawn, and their 5-year-old daughter, Amanda, are a multiracial family living in the Southwest. The family attends a large Christian church in the community. Terri and Shawn are very active in their church. Amanda has attended the church's child-care facility since she was an infant. She now attends the kindergarten program at the neighborhood school. Amanda is doing well at school, but Terri is beginning to have concerns about her daughter's biracial identity development. One day after school, Amanda announced that she was brown like her mom now, but next year she will be white like her dad. Although Terri and Shawn had many discussions about race while they were dating, they never talked about race with Amanda. They now wonder whether they should begin to broach the topic of race with their daughter.

   Because of their strong connectedness to their church community, Terri and Shawn seek counseling from a pastoral counselor in the church's counseling center. The counselor begins work by helping Terri and Shawn identify ways in which their own racial identities have influenced their worldviews. Specifically, the counselor helps the couple identify their beliefs, values, expectations, and perceptions and the ways that those factors have shaped their ideas about family life, family traditions, and child rearing. Over the next several weeks, the counselor helps the couple explore their feelings regarding sharing this information in implicit and explicit ways with Amanda. The counselor explains that, from a developmental perspective, many young children gain a sense of biracial identity from their families. Over time, Terri and Shawn start to notice differences. As a child grows, these differences may lead to choice group categorization, or a sense of feeling forced to choose a group. Specifically in Amanda's case, she may be noticing differences and assigning herself to a racial group or to the groups to which she perceives her parents belong. Even at Amanda's young age, she may be making these categorizations even before she has the language or cognitive reasoning skills to fully understand race. Recognizing this phenomenon as a normal part of a child's development, Terri and Shawn determine that their best course of action is to continue to develop their own understanding of race and the ways it manifests itself in their family while they have open, child-led conversations about race within their family. In response to Amanda's statement about being brown now but white next year, Terri and Shawn decide to affirm their daughter's sense of self and to provide her with increased exposure to a variety of skin tones and features through a careful selection of children's books and toys. Both implicitly and explicitly, they transmit the message that all skin colors are beautiful and created by God. Importantly, they determine that, to discuss race constancy, or the concept that race is permanent, would be developmentally inappropriate for their 5-year-old daughter because many children are not cognitively able to grasp this concept until later in childhood. As Amanda grows, her parents will continue to commit to exploring their own racial identity development and the implications their development may have on the emerging biracial identity development of their daughter.

- How would you characterize the family's identity, given the models presented in this chapter?
- What types of questions would be useful to explore the family's identity further?
- What factors would be important to consider in developing counseling goals?
- If you were a counselor working with this family, what elements of your own identity would it be important to consider?
- In what ways could these issues relating to counselor self-awareness prove helpful in your work with the family?

The racial and ethnic identity development models discussed in this chapter are but a few of the many models currently being examined in the research literature. Several groundbreaking race- and ethnicity-specific models cannot be discussed because of space limitations: Ruiz's (1990) Chicano/Latino ethnic identity model; Choney, Berryhill-Paapke, and Robbins's (1995) health model for American Indians; and Sodowsky, Kwan, and Pannu's (1995) nonlinear model of Asian ethnic identity development, among others. Counselors are encouraged to learn more about these models, as well as those reviewed in this chapter and in other chapters of the text. Furthermore, counselors may find it helpful to use theories and models of racial and ethnic identity development to form initial client case conceptualizations. These important first steps may provide insight and clinical direction for counselors' work with diverse clients. Case Study 2.3 applies cultural identity theory to illustrate this point.

CASE STUDY 2.3

Quang, a Vietnamese student, is new to Oakdale High School. Quang is 14 years old. He has attended school in the northern part of Vietnam since he was a little boy. Quang was sent to America to live with his cousin Vinh and to continue his education. Unfortunately, neither Quang nor Vinh knows the other well. They met only one week ago. Quang and Vinh visit the school counselor's office to register for high school. They do not have any school records of Quang; however, he has been cleared to start high school by the school district's international student office.

After meeting with Quang and Vinh, the counselor recognized that Quang's transition to Oakdale High School would likely be uniquely affected by several multicultural counseling issues, including acculturation and cultural identity development processes. He also realized that, although Quang was his student, Vinh likely would play a significant role in Quang's academic achievement. For that reason, the school counselor reflected on the role of family support in mediating possible feelings of marginalization. Furthermore, the counselor realized that, in his efforts to establish a productive counseling relationship with Quang, he would need to examine his own biases, values, and worldview. Given the school counselor's lack of familiarity with Vietnamese culture, he decided to consult with a colleague and school counseling literature on issues of identity development in the Vietnamese culture. He also understood that to blindly apply any acquired knowledge to Quang would be unethical. He decided that, as he continued to meet with Quang on a biweekly basis, he would seek to gain insight into the salience of cultural identity development and other diversity factors that were relevant to Quang's transition to high school.

- What types of questions would be useful to explore cultural identity further with Quang?
- What factors would be important to consider in developing counseling goals?
- If you were Quang's counselor, what specific aspects of your own cultural identity would it be important to consider?
- In what ways could these issues relating to counselor self-awareness regarding cultural identity prove helpful in your work with Quang?

Addressing Racial and Ethnic Identity in Counseling

Understanding and integrating appropriate principles of racial and ethnic identity may help counselors understand within-group differences (Gushue et al., 2013; Karcher & Sass, 2010; Zane & Ku, 2014) and normalize and process clients' cognitive, emotional, and behavioral responses. While allowing clients the opportunity to appreciate the universality of their emotional and behavioral responses and experiences, using the discussed racial and ethnic identity models and other similar models may provide counselors with opportunities to validate clients' unique experiences and feelings. Counselors do not force movement through developmental statuses. However, counselors can and should assist clients in thinking and responding in more productive ways. This broadening of perspective can lead to beneficial, self-realized cultural identity development. Furthermore, understanding these developmental models in client-specific cultural contexts can assist counselors in providing counseling interventions that not only address clients' presenting concerns, but also foster continued identity development. These aims can be achieved by identifying and using systems of support for clients and by providing opportunities for clients to tell their own stories regarding their identity in culturally relevant ways. (See Zane & Ku, 2014.) Moreover, counselors should consider integrating activities such as writing a journal, engaging in creative writing, working on projects, drawing or painting, creating art and music, and constructing genograms to help clients explore their cultural heritage, beliefs, and values (Gonzales et al., 2014). Questions related to the self-definition of culture and cultural identity; the clarification of value systems, religious and cultural expectations, family experiences; experiences with racism, oppression, discrimination, and marginalization; and the exploration of confusion and dissonance regarding cultural identity may also prove helpful.

Practicing counselors and counselor trainees must also seek to increase their self-awareness and historical competence regarding issues of multiculturalism through continued study, training, and clinical supervision. This stance demands a willingness to confront and challenge negative or distorted culturally based perceptions. Furthermore, counselors must engage in advocacy and social justice issues that address discrimination against individuals of diverse cultures. More specific discussion of these implications can be found in later chapters.

GENDER AND SEXUAL IDENTITY DEVELOPMENT

The identity development models discussed thus far in this chapter have provided a framework for understanding how individuals come to see themselves in their identity as racial and ethnic beings. In reality, people navigate multiple intersecting cultural and social identities throughout life. Another important intersecting identity is gender and sexual identity. Gender identity development, or awareness and acceptance of one's maleness or femaleness, and sexual identity development, or awareness and acceptance of one's sexual orientation, are theorized to move through statuses and processes in ways similar to those of race and ethnicity. As individuals navigate these important aspects of self-identity, their movement is never completely linear or straightforward. Development intersects with and responds to biological, psychological, and social influences. Beginning with a discussion of three major gender identity models, the next section reviews gender identity and concludes with a discussion of several sexual identity models in relation to important contextual influences and counseling considerations.

Gender Identity Models

Any gender identity model must address the convergence of race and gender because these dominant and dynamic statuses may have significant implications for individual development. Among the gender-specific models that have been developed are the Key model (Scott & Robinson, 2001), Downing and Roush's (1985) feminist identity development model, and Hoffman's (2006) model of feminist identity.

Although it is important to note that males and females may develop gender identities that do not conform to traditional, culture-bound notions, data do suggest that some notions of gender are strongly linked to socialized cultural norms. For example, many young boys and girls are socialized around dress. Halim et al. (2014) conducted studies of boys' and girls' appearance rigidity and suggested that 3- to 6-year-olds across racially and ethnically diverse groups show an affinity for gender-typed dress (e.g., pink dresses, glitter shoes, dark-blue pants, superhero shirts). Research also suggests that, at an early age, some girls and boys are exposed to stereotyped gender information and norms beyond those of dress, including behavioral characteristics and dispositions. Many girls, for example, are socialized to be dependent and nurturing, and to display emotion. By contrast, socializing practices often encourage boys to be assertive, powerful, strong, independent, and courageous. Furthermore, as they grow older, many males are encouraged to restrict displays of emotions that suggest vulnerability (e.g., sadness, fear). These implicit and explicit messages often converge into a more specific, and perhaps more dangerous, stereotyped notion of manhood that conforms largely to White, middle-class, Christian, heterosexual images (Scott, Havice, Livingston, & Cawthon, 2012; Scott & Robinson, 2001). Driving this classification is the culturally pervasive and competitive desire for power and control of economic and social structures. Given their position in American society as privileged owing to their race and gender, it is understandable that the theory to describe the cultural development of White men would involve those factors. The situation poses an interesting challenge for White men: The Key model of White male development, discussed next, recognizes that the primary developmental task for men is the abandonment of entitlement; once that claim is abandoned, the result is a greater sense of self that is neither defined nor restricted by debilitating socialized notions of male identity.

THE KEY MODEL   The Key model (Scott & Robinson, 2001) describes four types of gender identity attitudes for White males that are flexible and responsive to situations and experiences. The *Noncontact* type describes attitudes that have little awareness of race: Race is simply ignored, denied, or minimized. Traditional gender roles are valued. In general, the status quo is reverenced, with no recognition of the ways in which current conditions may not meet the needs of diverse people. The second type, the *Claustrophobic* type, holds attitudes that blame women and people of color for any personal discomfort related to the failure to achieve, progress, or obtain privilege. Men in this stage of development believe that "others"—namely, women, immigrants, and people of color—prevent them from acquiring what rightfully belongs to them. The *Conscious* type reevaluates his belief system because of a precipitating event that creates internal dissonance. He begins to recognize the role of racism and sexism in sociopolitical events. The *Empirical* type more fully recognizes the implications of sexism and racism and his role in their perpetuation. Furthermore, he becomes aware of his own unearned power and privilege. Finally, the *Optimal* type has an understanding of diversity and the rewards of interacting with others in a holistic way. He is committed to the elimination of oppression in all of its forms and measures himself on the basis of internal measures rather than stereotyped ideas of maleness.

DOWNING AND ROUSH'S MODEL OF FEMINIST IDENTITY   Like the Key model (Scott & Robinson, 2001), the Downing and Roush (1985) model of feminist identity describes a progression from a stage of unawareness of inequity and discrimination to one of commitment to meaningful action aimed at eliminating discrimination and sexism. The *Passive Acceptance* stage involves the acceptance of traditional or stereotyped sex roles together with a denial or lack of awareness of prejudice and discrimination against women. The *Revelation* stage involves a crisis or series of crises that leads to self-examination of roles and ideas, and dualistic thinking that affirms women and denigrates men. *Embeddedness–Emanation* leads to associations with women who are supportive and affirming and, over time, adopt more flexible thinking regarding men. The fourth stage, *Synthesis*, is characterized by a positive identity that integrates personal and feminist identities. The final, *Active Commitment*, stage focuses on action toward meaningful societal change and the identification of personal goals of empowerment.

HOFFMAN'S MODEL OF FEMINIST IDENTITY   Hoffman (2006) proposed a theoretically inclusive model of female identity that identifies four distinct statuses. The model first moves from women's endorsement of a passive acceptance stance to their endorsement of a stance of revelation. These two endorsements are embodied in Hoffman's *Unexamined Female Identity* and *Crisis* statuses, respectively. The model then moves to a *Moratorium/Exploration* status, characterized by women's commitments to an active identity search, and ends in an *Achieved*

TABLE 2.2 Feminist Identity Models

Downing and Roush Model	Hoffman Model
Passive Acceptance	Unexamined Female Identity
Acceptance of traditional women's roles	*Acceptance of traditional women's roles*
Revelation	Crisis
Consciousness-raising experiences that affirm women and denigrate men	*Awareness of societal discrimination of women*
Embeddedness–Emanation	Moratorium/Exploration
Associations in supportive relationships with women and selected men	*Commitment to active identity search*
Synthesis	Achieved Female Identity
Integration of personal and feminist identities	*Synthesis of female identity*
Active Commitment	
Movement toward empowerment, societal change, and activism	

Sources: Summarized from Downing and Roush (1985) and Hoffman (2006).

Female Identity status, involving an identity synthesis. Integral to this model is an understanding of gender self-confidence: the degree of alignment with one's personal standards of femininity or masculinity. In essence, gender self-confidence is the degree to which one accepts and values himself as a male or herself as a female. Furthermore, in Hoffman's model, gender self-confidence encompasses gender self-definition and gender self-acceptance, thereby offering a new understanding of gender identity development theory. Table 2.2 presents a comparison of this model with the Downing and Roush (1985) model.

ADDRESSING GENDER IDENTITY IN COUNSELING   Although gender is an important identity construct, counselors must be mindful of the varying degrees of salience it holds for individual clients. In therapeutic environments, it is important for clients to have the opportunity to share their personal stories and sexual scripts and ideologies (i.e., images, perceptions, messages, thoughts, and behaviors that guide and shape identity development) in safe, nonjudgmental environments so that counselors may acknowledge feelings and discern the ways in which gender identity intersects with the clients' presenting problems. Counselors must also recognize that gender identity statuses are not hierarchical: one status is not higher or better than another; each represents a worldview that describes values, perspectives, and aims. It is the counselor's responsibility to help clients clarify their worldviews and understand the benefits and costs of particular ways of interacting in the world. This task may require the use of didactic, cognitive, affective, or behavioral counseling interventions, including the facilitation of culturally relevant decision-making processes. Furthermore, counselors must be cognizant of personal gender identity statuses and the implications of their own development on their work with clients. Clinical supervision, training, and self-reflection may provide opportunities to carefully monitor these implications.

Sexual Identity Models

Several identity development models describe the cultural identity process for sexual minorities (e.g., gay, lesbian, bisexual, questioning). In general, minorities' sexual identity is conceptualized as a continuous developmental process that begins with awareness of same-sex attraction and exploration, and culminates in self-acceptance, disclosure, and identity integration. These subprocesses are described next, in Cass's (1979, 1990) model of sexual identity, Coleman's (1981) coming-out model, Troiden's (1989) model of sexual identity, McCarn and Fassinger's (1996) model of lesbian/gay identity formation, and Weinberg, Williams, and Pryor's (1994) model of bisexual identity. Table 2.3 provides an overview of these sexual identity models.

TABLE 2.3 Gay and Lesbian Sexual Identity Development Models

	Coleman	Cass	Troiden	McCarn and Fassinger	Weinberg et al.
Stage 1	Pre–Coming Out	Conscious Awareness	Sensitization	Awareness	Initial Confusion
Key Traits	*No or low level of awareness*	*Realization*	*Awareness*	*Awareness at individual and group levels*	*Unsettled feelings*
Stage 2	Coming Out	Identity Comparison	Identity Confusion	Exploration	Finding and Applying Labels
Key Traits	*Awareness, beginning self-acceptance*	*Tentative commitment*	*Incongruence*	*Exploration of feelings at individual level; assessment of feelings at group level*	*Assignment of meaning*
Stage 3	Exploration	Identity Tolerance	Identity Assumption	Deepening Commitment	Settling into Identity
Key Traits	*Confusion and developing sexual competence*	*Informative and supportive relationships*	*Acceptance*	*Commitment to same-sex intimacy at the individual level; commitment to the gay and lesbian community at the group level*	*Emerging sense of self*
Stage 4	First Relationships	Identity Acceptance	Commitment	Internalization and Synthesis	Continued Uncertainty
Key Traits	*Developing trust, exploration*	*Normalcy*	*Positive identity development*	*Internalization of same-sex love at individual level; synthesis of lesbian culture at group level*	*Recognition of social intolerance*
Stage 5	Integration	Identity Pride			
Key Traits	*Commitment, identity integration*	*Strong commitment*			
Stage 6		Identity Synthesis			
Key Traits		*Full self-integration*			

Note: The McCarn and Fassinger (1996) model of lesbian/gay identity formation describes phases, as opposed to stages, of development. This difference acknowledges the flexibility and fluidity inherent in sexual identity development.

Sources: Based on Cass (1979, 1990); Coleman (1981/1982); Troiden (1989); McCarn and Fassinger (1996); and Weinberg et al. (1994).

While several of the models have been applied to both men and women, Cass (1990) noted that there may be significant differences within the stages of sexual identity development, in particular, due to differing socialization patterns and expectations based on gender. These differences may result in different ways of forming identity, expressing identity, or expressing sexual preference. Cass's appreciation of difference was echoed in Lev's (2004) work, which reminds mental health professionals of the ethical responsibility to become well versed in theory, counseling approaches, and sexual identity models. Lev also noted that it is important to respect and allow for the unique and, at times, nonconforming developmental path individuals may take in growing into their authentic selves.

CASS'S HOMOSEXUAL IDENTITY FORMATION MODEL Cass's (1979) article on sexual identity formation is among the earliest and most seminal works on the subject, integrating psychological and sociological perspectives. Beginning in the late 1970s, Cass proposed a six-stage model of development that affirmed homosexual identity. *Conscious Awareness*, the first stage of the model, is marked by a realization that gay, lesbian, or bisexual identity is possible. Individuals in this stage may feel alienated as they wrestle with this inner realization. *Identity Comparison* begins as individuals leave the first stage of development and start to tentatively commit to a homosexual identity. Here, awareness of the difference between self and those with a heterosexual identity is realized. Individuals negotiating this stage may begin to accept their homosexual identity, reject their homosexual identity because they perceive homosexuality as undesirable, or partially accept their homosexual identity with a rationalization of homosexual behavior as a "one-time" or "special-case" experience. During stage three, *Identity Tolerance*, individuals seek out sexual minorities to help alleviate feelings of alienation and enhance self-awareness. In the *Identity Acceptance* stage, individuals begin to establish a sense of normalcy as issues of incongruence between one's view of self and others' views (or perceptions of others' views) are resolved. The fifth stage, *Identity Pride,* is characterized by a strong commitment to homosexual identity and activism that may not yet be fully integrated with the person's total self-identity. In the final, *Identity Synthesis*, stage, one's homosexual identity is fully integrated with other dimensions of self-identity. As a result, meaningful and supportive relationships are sought and maintained with individuals with diverse sexual orientations and identities.

Informed by Cass's work, Coleman (1981/1982) developed a five-stage model describing the coming-out process. The model allows for varied, recursive movement from the first stage, of initial awareness of same-sex feelings, to the last, public acknowledgement and integration of sexual identity. The stages of the model are Pre–Coming Out, Coming Out, Exploration, First Relationships, and Integration. During the *Pre–Coming Out* stage, individuals may not be fully conscious of a same sex attraction, but are likely aware of a sense of feeling different from their heterosexual peers. Adolescents or young adults in the *Coming Out* stage acknowledge their same-sex attractions and disclose their sexual orientation to others. The *Exploration* stage is marked by individuals' initial involvement in same-sex relationships and an emerging sense of position and place within the gay community. During the *First Relationships* stage, individuals deepen interpersonal commitments and place value on meaningful relationships with same-sex partners. In the final stage of the model, *Integration*, individuals merge their public and private selves as they continue to understand their sexual orientation.

TROIDEN'S MODEL OF SEXUAL IDENTITY Troiden (1989) suggested a model consisting of four stages: *Sensitization*, or awareness of same-sex attraction; *Identity Confusion*, defined by a growing awareness of same-sex attraction coupled with incongruence between assumed heterosexual and homosexual orientations; *Identity Assumption*, or acceptance of one's homosexual identity and same-sex sexual experiences; and *Commitment*, which involves a positive homosexual identity and committed same-sex relationships.

INCLUSIVE MODEL OF LESBIAN/GAY IDENTITY FORMATION   McCarn and Fassinger (1996) argued that many existing sexual identity models do not sufficiently account for environmental context and subtly presume a discriminatory stance against one's private, internal acceptance of homosexual identity. To address this limitation, they proposed a four-phase model of sexual minority identity formation. Their model includes an individual sexual identity process and a parallel and reciprocal process of group membership identity. (See Fassinger & Miller, 1996.) These dual processes recognize that an individual's sense of self can be separate from identity, with or without participation in lesbian or gay culture (Fassinger, 1995). The model begins with an *Awareness* phase, which is marked by an awareness of feeling different at the individual level and the awareness of different sexual orientations at the group level. The *Exploration* phase yields strong, often erotic same-sex feelings at the individual level and assessment about feelings and attitudes at the group level. The third phase of the model involves *Deepening Commitment* at the individual and group levels. During this phase, individuals commit to personal choices regarding intimacy and sexuality while committing to the lesbian and gay community at the group level. Finally, the dual processes of the model conclude with an *Internalization and Synthesis* phase. During this phase, the individual process moves toward internalization of same-sex love while the group process moves toward synthesis of membership within the same-sex culture into one's total self-identity. It is important to note that, although the two phases of the model are in fact parallel and reciprocal, they may not necessarily be experienced simultaneously.

BISEXUAL IDENTITY DEVELOPMENT   Although there may be a tendency to view sexual identity as dichotomous, this conceptualization of the term does not account for all the ways in which sexual identity is experienced. About 70 years ago, Kinsey, Pomeroy, and Martin (1948a, 1948b) presented sexual orientation on a continuum ranging from heterosexual to homosexual. They hypothesized that individuals may be exclusively heterosexual, primarily heterosexual with some homosexual behaviors and feelings, primarily homosexual with some heterosexual behaviors and feelings, or exclusively homosexual. In their theory, they proffered an understanding of bisexuality as an identity aligned with both heterosexual and homosexual behaviors and feelings that shape and inform one's identity equally. They proposed that bisexuality sits in the middle of the continuum of sexual identity.

Elaborating on Kinsey, Pomeroy, and Martin's theory, Weinberg et al. (1994) developed a model that describes bisexual identity as a distinct developmental trajectory. The Weinberg et al. model of bisexual identity development begins with initial confusion and proceeds to a stage in which the individual finds and applies labels. These first two stages involve *Unsettled feelings* regarding attraction to both sexes and *Assignment of meaning* to those unsettled feelings. The third stage of the model, *Settling into identity*, is marked by an emerging sense of self-acceptance. This stage is followed by the last stage of the model, *Continued Uncertainty*, which results from the absence of closure that stems from society's intolerance of bisexual identity.

TRANSSEXUAL AND TRANSGENDER IDENTITY DEVELOPMENT

Today, emerging scholarship is offering models of transgender and transsexual identity. **Transgender identity** is an umbrella term that is often used to describe the gender identity of people who are gendered differently from the vast majority of individuals, including heterosexuals, gay and lesbian individuals, and people with a bisexual identity. Transgender individuals are those whose identity expression, behavior, and sense of self do not conform with the sex they were assigned at birth. Transgender identity can move beyond binary concepts of male and female to include people who identify as intersexed, masculine-identified females, feminine-identified males, transmen, transwomen, and other differently gendered people (Lev, 2004). **Transsexual identity**, on the other hand, includes the identity of those whose bodies have transitioned from one sex to the other. Transsexual people may be preoperative, postoperative, or nonoperative. Devor (2004) offered a 14-stage model informed by the work of Cass (1979, 1990; see Table 2.4).

TABLE 2.4 Devor Model of Transsexual and Transgender Identity Formation

Stage	Characteristics and Behaviors
1. Abiding Anxiety	General discomfort and/or anxiety with assigned gender; preference for, and involvement in, activities or behaviors typically ascribed to the opposite gender
2. Identity Confusion about Originally Assigned Gender and Sex	Expressed doubts about assigned gender that are typically met by social and psychological pressure from significant others to conform to assigned gender
3. Identity Comparisons about Originally Assigned Gender and Sex	Attempts to navigate social expectations and needs for identity expression; comparison of inner feelings with various types and degrees of opposite gender expression
4. Discovery of Transsexualism or Transgenderism	Initial awareness of transsexualism or transgender identity, typically through accidental exposure or contact with information or people
5. Identity Confusion about Transsexualism or Transgenderism	Internal and external questioning of transsexual or transgender identity for oneself
6. Identity Comparisons about Transsexualism or Transgenderism	Multifaceted comparisons between oneself and others who share the individual's assigned gender, on the one hand, and those who identify as transsexual and transgender, on the other; disengagement from assigned gender
7. Tolerance of Transsexual or Transgender Identity	Gradual acceptance of transsexual or transgender identity; transgender or transsexual identity becomes the dominant identity expression
8. Delay before Acceptance of Transsexual or Transgender Identity	Reality testing of identity, often through intimate and emotional relationships; seeking of additional information about transsexualism and transgenderism from others who identify as transsexual and transgender

(Continued)

TABLE 2.4 Devor Model of Transsexual and Transgender Identity Formation (Continued)	
9. Acceptance of Transsexual or Transgender Identity	Full acceptance of transsexual or transgender identity; disclosure to members of extended family, business associates, friends, lovers, and casual acquaintances
10. Delay before Transition	Exploration of steps that must be taken for the process of transition, including saving money for sex reassignment surgery, meeting with psychologists and physicians, and undergoing hormone treatment
11. Transition	Often challenging, yet fulfilling, stage of gender and sex reassignment; may experience grief or sadness related to loss of former identity while feeling joy and deep satisfaction over transition
12. Acceptance of Posttransition Gender and Sex Identities	Typically a long period of months or years toward full acceptance of posttransition identity; marked by new lived experiences and a relinquishing of former anxieties and self-doubts
13. Integration	Full integration into society as posttransition gendered individual; may include some level of stigma management; often includes an integration, acceptance, and appreciation of former gender identity
14. Pride	Sense of pride in transgender or transsexual identity; commitment to transgender and transsexual identity advocacy

Source: Adapted from Table 1, Stages of Transsexual or Transgender Identity Formation from "Witnessing and Mirroring: A Fourteen Stage Model of Transsexual Identity Formation" by Aaron H Devor in Transgender Subjectivities: A Clinician's Guide by Jack Drescher and Ubaldo Leli. Copyright © 2004 by Taylor & Francis.

Importantly, Devor's model does not delineate particular choices, outcomes, or time lines, thereby allowing for the rich diversity and authenticity of personal choice regarding transgender identity. Two interactive themes that undergird the theory and facilitate movement through its stages are witnessing and mirroring. *Witnessing* is the human desire to be authentically seen and validated by significant others in one's environment. *Mirroring* is the concept that expands one's sense of belonging by recognizing possibilities for transgender identity that are manifest in others.

Lev (2004) suggested the Transgender Emergence Model, a complex model of developmental and interpersonal transactions. The steps of her model are not to be viewed as labels or to define transgender developmental maturity. Rather, the steps describe what transgender individuals may negotiate as they come to terms with their own identity. Not every person may experience development exactly as it is described in the model. Rather, Lev notes that some may move back and forth among the stages, often revisiting earlier stages in their development. The steps of this model are *Awareness*, a stage in which people often feel distress about their assigned gender identity; *Seeking Information/Reaching Out*, which is marked by a reaching out for information about transgenderism; *Disclosure to Significant Others*, a stage characterized by the disclosure of gender identity beliefs and feelings to partners, close family members, friends, and significant others; *Exploration—Identity and Self-Labeling*, which involves the exploration of various transgender identities and expressions;

Exploration—Transition Issues / Possible Body Modification, a stage marked by the exploration of options for transition, including body modification and various physical presentations; and *Integration—Acceptance and Posttransition Issues*, the final stage of the model, which includes true synthesis and integration of a transgendered identity.

In contrast to these models, de Vries (2015) offers a model of intersectionality from which to view the experiences of transgender people of color. The model, grounded in feminist theory and Black feminist activism and scholarship, identifies 12 categories or social positions to consider in exploring experiences of transgender people of color: race, gender, sexuality, class, nationality, ability, language, religion, culture, ethnicity, body size, and age. These categories or social positions interconnect and move beyond binary concepts (e.g., male/female, Black/White) to make the experiences and development of transgender people of color central. Analysis of each category is rich and grounded in the individual's experiences, which shift and evolve over a lifetime. For example, the first category, race, could be defined by physical characteristics, perceived categorizations, self-categorizations, legal designations (e.g., as recorded on one's birth certificate or driver's license), institutional categorizations (e.g., as reported on school documents), and familial ties or community relationships—simultaneously or with emphasis given to any particular defining factor or factors at any given time. The model highlights the multidimensional aspects of transgender identity while also acknowledging structural inequality, positionality, social stratification, and cultural narratives.

ADDRESSING SEXUAL IDENTITY IN COUNSELING   Unfortunately, gay, lesbian, and transgender identity formation is often stigmatized by issues of discrimination, marginalization, and prejudice. These painful and unjust realities demand individual and systemic interventions from culturally competent counselors. First, counselors must work to create inclusive and supportive therapeutic environments that provide safety, acceptance, and freedom from heterosexist assumptions and restrictive, stereotyped gender roles and norms. The process begins with a thorough self-examination of biases and attitudes regarding sexual orientation and identities, and includes the use of counseling skills that encourage client disclosure and provide opportunities for validation and normalization of feelings. Second, counselors must recognize that, although some clients may follow models of sexual identity development, others may follow a highly individualized, nonlinear path of identity development. Third, counselors should coordinate and facilitate client awareness of community resources that support lesbian, gay, and bisexual (LGB) individuals. Fourth, counselors must continue to enhance their awareness, knowledge, and skills regarding appropriate counseling interventions for LGB clients through coursework, consultation, training, and other professional development opportunities. Finally, counselors should support and engage in research that furthers understanding of sexual identity formation and the intersection of multiple identities. Case Study 2.4 demonstrates how sexual identity development may involve the counseling practices we offer.

CASE STUDY 2.4

Todd, a first-year college student, is meeting with a counselor at the university counseling center to discuss his transition to college. Academically, Todd is doing well. Socially, he is unsure of how he fits in with his peers. In particular, Todd is confused by his relationship with his friend Michael. Todd is concerned because he is sexually attracted to Michael. Todd does not know what his feelings mean and has been too afraid to share them with anyone, even Michael.

During their first session, the counselor asked Todd what brought him to the office. Todd shared his concerns regarding adjustment to college and being away from home. After sensing that there was something more on Todd's mind, the counselor asked him about his social adjustment. Todd shared a little about his feelings for Michael. Through the use of reflection, the counselor learned of Todd's uncertainty about his sexual orientation and fear of others' perceptions.

The counselor recognized that Todd's presenting problem could be adequately approached only by considering the implications of his sexual identity development. Given Todd's seeming position in the beginning stages of sexual identity development, the counselor provided safe and comfortable opportunities over the next several sessions for Todd to explore who he is in terms of his multiple, intersecting identities. Todd began to define himself more clearly as a man, a student, a son, a friend, and a sexual being. Also, as time passed, the counselor gave Todd access to materials and knowledge designed to dispel myths and stereotypes about same-sex sexual orientation. Although the center offers counseling and support groups for LGB students, the counselor recognized that these interventions would not be appropriate for Todd, given his current stage of development. As Todd gains a clearer level of awareness and comfort with his identity, these interventions may become more appropriate.

- What specific cultural identity issues should be explored in more depth?
- How would you approach these issues?
- What other important considerations should the counselor keep in mind while working with Todd?
- What areas of counselor self-awareness are salient in this case?

Counselors should also be cognizant of available research on sexual identity development. Although most research has been conducted with White, middle-class, gay men, some evidence suggests that gender, race, ethnicity, religious affiliation, cultural context, and historical factors can all influence the sexual identity development process. (See Moradi, DeBlaere, & Huang, 2010.) Thus, the intersection of multiple identities must be considered. For example, research suggests that the experiences, perceptions, and developmental processes of gay, lesbian, bisexual, and transgender people of color may be different from the experiences, perceptions, and developmental processes of White gay men (de Vries, 2015). In particular, the level of involvement with same-sex–related social activities or the LGB community and the level of comfort with disclosure and the coming-out process may differ between Black and White gay men. Case Study 2.5 offers an opportunity to consider these counseling implications through discussion and reflection.

CASE STUDY 2.5

Martina, a 52-year-old, recently divorced woman and mother of one grown son, has made an appointment to meet with a career counselor in a neighboring city 25 miles from her hometown. Facing this time of personal transition, Martina is excited about, yet fearful and uncertain of, the life choices ahead of her. Martina has not worked outside the home since she was in her twenties. Everyone in her town knows about her divorce and her recent decision to move in with her lifelong friend Gloria. Martina is aware that some of her friends and family do not approve of her decision to live with Gloria. Martina's sister has refused to call or visit since Martina moved in with Gloria. Martina is very upset about her strained relationship with her sister. She often feels that she spends all her time simply trying to figure out how to repair her relationship with her sister and how to make enough money to make ends meet. Martina is not sure where her life will take her, but she is sure of three things: she must reenter the workforce, she needs to earn enough money to support herself, and she wants Gloria to be a significant part of whatever her future holds.

- What counseling issues may present in this case?
- What specific cultural identity issues should be explored? How would you approach these issues?
- What important considerations should the career counselor keep in mind while working with Martina?

SPIRITUAL AND FAITH IDENTITY DEVELOPMENT

Spirituality is a personally meaningful and often internal and private experience of the transcendent that is grounded in one's beliefs and values and connected to one's worldview and identity (Gladding, 2011; Gold, 2010). Spirituality informs perspectives and judgments, and provides meaning, mission, and purpose to life. It is associated with well-being and may serve as a developmental socializing force (Gladding, 2011; Lambie, Davis, & Miller, 2008). Spirituality need not evolve within the context of an organized religion (see Sink, 2008), and counselors are likely to encounter clients in a variety of settings who present with spiritual concerns. (See Voices from the Field 2.2.) Counselors may, therefore, encounter clients who believe in God or a supreme being, but have no affiliation with any religious institution.

The terms *spiritual development* and *faith development* are sometimes used interchangeably. **Spirituality** involves a search for meaning, transcendence, and purpose. It often requires reflection on important questions of life regarding purpose, meaning, destiny, and existence. **Faith** is also used to describe the process of making meaning (Love, 2001), or the development of a way of knowing or a way of understanding one's world that is grounded in universal structures of logic, moral reasoning, locus of authority, perspective, social awareness, and the role of symbolic functions independently of any particular religious belief (Gold, 2010;

Voices from the Field 2.2

I've had many school counselors and school counseling interns working in public schools tell me about their reluctance to acknowledge their students' spiritual development when issues emerge in group or individual counseling sessions. The counselors and interns often believed that to acknowledge their students' spirituality would somehow break school policy or endorse a specific faith perspective. Counseling ethical standards (American Counseling Association, 2014; American School Counselor Association, 2010), *Multicultural Counseling and Social Justice Competencies* (Ratts et al., 2015), and faith and spirituality development theories (e.g., Fowler 1995; Spero, 1992) provide strong rationales and tools for understanding and effectively addressing faith and spirituality in counseling. Understanding faith and spirituality development in the counseling context is an imperative for all counselors, including those who work in public schools.

~CM-T

REFLECTION 2.2

What are your beliefs about spirituality and faith? How, if at all, have these beliefs and processes changed over time? How have these beliefs and processes for making meaning affected your personal and professional development? How may they facilitate your work with clients?

Parker, 2011). Faith development is complex and multidimensional. It cannot be reduced to any one universal structure, such as moral reasoning (Parker, 2011). Rather, it is a process, an approach—a way of knowing. For some, spiritual development and faith development are parallel processes; that is to say, some people search for meaning through the process of faith development. For others, the search for meaning and purpose is independent of the development of faith. The questions in Reflection 2.2 may be used to further your consideration of your own spirituality and faith development.

Fowler's Model of Faith Development

Fowler's (1995) theory of faith development has six stages: *Intuitive–Projective Faith*, a stage in which young children become aware of cultural faith taboos and prominent faith figures, guided by significant adult figures; *Mythic–Literal Faith*, a stage of late childhood that focuses on religious stories, systems, and symbols; *Synthetic–Conventional Faith*, an adolescent stage of noncritical evaluation of faith and faith traditions; *Individuative–Reflective Faith*, a stage that challenges older adolescents and adults to demythologize spirituality and critically evaluate spiritual paths; *Conjunctive Faith*, a stage reached by adults who are able to appreciate cultural and traditional faith systems without being bound by them; and *Universalizing Faith*, a stage of spirituality characterized by transcendent moral and religious actions, words, and quality of life. The theory is comprehensive in that it examines faith development from early childhood through older adulthood.

Spero's Development of Religious Transformations

Spero's (1992) framework for the development of religious transformations is based on the psychological process of individuation: the process of understanding oneself as a differentiated, yet integrated being. The process has four stages that simultaneously navigate a relationship with God and a relationship with a religious community. The first stage, *Symbiosis*, refers to the time during which a young child relates to God as a protective figure whose sole role is to respond to the child's needs and wants. The child has a perceived oneness with God that is framed solely by an egotistic stance. A similar relationship is formed with the religious community during this stage in which the young child is unable to differentiate her identity from that of the community. In the *Differentiation* stage, an adolescent typically begins to take in other viewpoints through acknowledging other religious traditions and drawing comparisons and contrasts with the adolescent's own personal religious practice. The adolescent seeks ways to fit in, yet develop a unique relationship with God and the religious community. It is also during this developmental stage that the adolescent begins to see herself as an identity separate from that of God. *Practicing*, the third developmental stage, is marked by growing confidence in one's own religious practice as deeper faith-based belief systems and religious traditions and history are explored. God may be understood as a provider of divine guidance during this time of exploration. The final stage, *Rapprochement*, is characterized by the acceptance of oneself in relationship with God on the basis of a sense of individual, human responsibility.

Genia's Development of Growth

Also following a developmental trajectory, Genia's (1995) model of faith development begins with a stage called *Egocentric Faith*. Individuals in this stage of faith development seek relief from anxiety and from fear through the favor of God. They aim to be perfect and see prayer primarily as a means of petitioning God to protect them from harm and pain. During the *Dogmatic* stage, individuals follow religious rules strictly, in order to receive blessings and eternal reward; affiliation with a religious community is typically an important component of this developmental stage. In *Transitional Faith*, the third developmental stage, religious beliefs are examined and introspection is privileged over religious dogma. In the *Reconstructed Internalized Faith* stage, individuals wrestle with questions and doubts about religion, yet offer praise and thanksgiving to God as creator and sustainer of all. The fifth and final stage, *Transcendent Faith*, is marked by a spiritual relationship with God that seeks universal truths, alignment with spiritual values, tolerance of religious differences, and a celebration of all life.

Genia's five-stage model suggests a path beginning in egocentric faith and working toward a faith defined by spiritual commitment. As children develop into adolescents and then adults, very few will progress to the Transcendent Faith stage, according to the theory. Moreover, as individuals face crises or times of challenge, they may regress to a more familiar style of faith practice temporarily or permanently. For example, it would not be unusual for an adult operating in the Transitional Faith stage and facing a serious health condition or devastating job loss to regress to Dogmatic Faith, seeking the comfort and assurance often found in the strict, unquestioned adherence to faith traditions and regulated ways of seeking God's grace and approval.

Parks's Model of Spiritual Identity

Parks (2011) suggested a four-stage model of spiritual development that moves from reliance on external authorities to a position of self-valuing and self-understanding. The stages are *Adolescent/Conventional*, a stage of growing self-awareness and openness to multiple perspectives; *Young Adult*, a stage of probing commitment and the critical choosing of beliefs and values; *Tested Adult*, a stage of further commitment and the "testing" of spiritual choices. This stage is generally reached by those in their early twenties or older; and *Mature Adult*, a stage of demonstrated interdependence and interconnectedness in which the individual is comfortable within the context of strong, personal conviction.

Furthermore, Parks suggests that imagination, an important concept underlying her theory, allows individuals to put together insights, ideas, and images in a way that makes meaning and approximates truth. Unlike fantasy, which moves toward that which is not real, imagination moves toward that which is ultimately real—toward authenticity and wholeness—in the most personally significant ways. Imagination, or the meaning-making process, must be viewed in light of individuals' socially constructed experiences (Tisdell, 2007). Therefore, in broad terms, the ability of clients who are in counseling to use their imagination and see and create meaningful options for themselves and their lives may be related to their spiritual development.

Poll and Smith's Model of Spiritual Identity

Poll and Smith (2003) offered a model of spiritual development that is based on a sense of self in relation to God. It is important to note that movement through this model is not linear, but may in fact involve doubling back or spiraling through various stages again and again from late childhood throughout the life span. During the *Preawareness* stage, individuals do not recognize themselves as spiritual beings or have low salience for spiritual experiences. Then, generally, because of a crisis, challenge, or series of personally meaningful events, individuals enter the *Awakening* stage. This emotionally charged period leads to an awareness of God that is fragmented and specific to the crisis at hand. *Recognition*, the third stage, involves a cognitive and emotional understanding of God that permeates all of life's existence and experiences. During this stage, individuals begin to develop spiritual themes that shape their faith practices, behaviors, and beliefs. The final stage, *Integration*, is marked by internalized notions of God that order perceptions, interactions, relationships, and behaviors. In this stage, individual factors such as personality, faith traditions, and spiritual experiences color the way spirituality may manifest itself. What is constant in the model, however, is that each stage leads to a developing understanding and relationship with God that is personal and internally derived. Case Study 2.6 explores some important elements of the models of spiritual identity development discussed in this section.

CASE STUDY 2.6

John's 2-year-old son was recently diagnosed with autism. John is trying to process what the diagnosis means for his son and his family, but he cannot get over his anger with God. John believes God has taken away the little boy he once had and given him a stranger to rear. John is hurt, angry, and scared. In his despair, John meets with the pastoral counselor at his church. The counselor recognizes that, whereas John once possessed a fairly integrated sense of spiritual development, his relationship with God is now fragmented and confrontational. This type of relationship is to be expected during periods of crisis. The counselor explained that to John and committed to helping him negotiate his current spiritual relationship. The counselor and John spent time exploring John's value system and worldview. They were later able to connect these explorations to John's understanding of God. Given what they learned, over time John and the counselor were able to identify some spiritual practices and faith-based behaviors that John could incorporate into his daily life. Although John still faces challenges in processing his emotions and learning about and providing for his son's needs, he is able to take comfort in his developing spiritual identity.

- How would you characterize John, using the different spiritual identity models presented in this chapter?
- What types of questions would be useful to explore spiritual identity further with John?
- What factors would be important to consider in developing counseling goals?
- What elements of your own spiritual identity, as John's counselor, would it be important to consider?
- In what ways could these issues of counselor self-awareness regarding spiritual identity prove helpful in your work with John?

Addressing Spiritual Identity in Counseling

The preceding discussion represents the beginning of a fundamental knowledge base needed to move toward the provision of culturally competent counseling services to clients who express and/or value spiritual orientations. However, to enhance spiritual and religious cultural competence, additional steps must be taken. As part of the ethically mandated process of continual education in areas of diversity, counselors should increase awareness of their own spiritual and religious development through coursework, articles, books, conversations, reflection, and experiential activities (see ACA, 2014). In addition, counselors can work to understand clients' faith histories, possible stressors (e.g., social isolation, prejudice, discrimination, oppression), and implications for counseling through collaboration, outreach to community religious leaders, attendance at worship services, continuing education courses, and clinical consultation. This kind of work may lead to a much-needed awareness of, and respect for, the indigenous support (e.g., imams, pastors, rabbis, priests) and healing systems of various faith traditions. With heightened awareness and sensitivity, counselors may be well suited to apply spiritual development theory and principles and use multiple helping roles to aid clients' efforts toward meeting counseling goals. Specifically, this approach may include the following:

- Helping clients identify and talk about personal spiritual experiences (Magaldi-Dopman & Park-Taylor, 2010)
- Establishing a safe therapeutic environment that normalizes and provides language for the discussion of spirituality
- Asking nonthreatening, open-ended questions related to meaning, beliefs, and values that allow for an assessment of the client's spiritual identity status and clear, appropriate definitions of self (Magaldi-Dopman & Park-Taylor, 2010)
- Facilitating client alignment between spiritual values and other personal values
- Referring clients for further spiritual guidance and direction
- Incorporating spirituality and the reliance on God in working toward counseling goals
- Assigning homework and encouraging participation in growth experiences that may include attendance at worship services, spiritual reading and reflection, meditation, prayer, and group work

Importantly, counselors are to consider spirituality and religiosity throughout their work with clients. Further, true counseling competence requires counselors to maintain an ongoing commitment to continuous learning and the acquisition of counseling skills relating to religiosity, spirituality, and all other issues pertaining to client diversity.

Summary

Cultural identity constructs extend beyond the typical categories of race and ethnicity to include, among others, considerations of gender, sexual orientation, and spirituality. This chapter has explored some of the dominant theories of cultural identity development as applied specifically to these areas of diversity. Although empirical research in the field is in its infancy, these constructs, models, and theories hold promise for counselors as frameworks for facilitating an understanding of self and client.

This important work begins, of course, with counselor reflection, self-evaluation, and continuing professional development. In all areas of identity development, culturally competent counselors willingly and repeatedly ask themselves the tough questions as they work to better understand who they are as cultural beings and how their cultural identity shapes their counseling. Although this goal may best be accomplished through supervision and consultation, this chapter has illustrated how self-awareness can also be gleaned through becoming familiar with current research on cultural identity, participating in experiential activities, reading broadly about culture and identity, and developing partnerships with culturally relevant community-based resources.

Moreover, the chapter discussed the ways in which counselors can use an understanding of cultural identity theory and models to develop more accurate case conceptualizations and more fully understand and address clients' needs. Although counseling interventions must never be stereotypically applied to clients, the chapter has discussed assessments, interview protocols, and counseling

strategies and interventions that may prove helpful in addressing client issues that significantly involve cultural identity. All of these tools enable counselors to recognize and discuss relevant cultural constructs and within-group differences along multiple cultural dimensions; use cultural identity models to help clients normalize and process cognitive, behavioral, and emotional responses; employ cultural identity models to help clients understand and broaden their worldviews in culturally appropriate ways; use creative arts to help clients explore multiple aspects of cultural identity; and implement systemic interventions as appropriate. Given the importance of cultural identity to healthy human development, culturally competent counselors must stay ever committed to exploring, processing, and successfully navigating the evolving narratives about cultural identity put forth by both the client and themselves.

Review Questions

1. How do ecological identity development models differ from stage or status identity models? What are the advantages of each?

2. How is race both a political and a socioeconomic construct? What implications does this connection have for counseling?

3. What are the counseling implications of parallel interactions as defined by racial interaction theory (Helms, 1995)?

4. Many theorists (Gonzales-Backen, 2013; Poston, 1990; Root, 1998) noted a situational component in multiracial or biethnic identity development. How could this dimension manifest itself in a counseling session, and what implications does it suggest for a culturally competent counselor?

5. In what ways may environmental contexts influence one's sexual identity development? In particular, what significance may these factors have for counselors working with LGBTQ clients?

6. In what ways does intersectionality affect sexual identity development?

7. How is Spero's (1992) theory of the development of religious transformations related to the psychological process of individuation?

8. How could a personal crisis affect cultural identity development? What could be the implications for counseling?

9. How could counselors use creative arts therapeutic strategies to help adolescent or adult clients tell their stories of racial, ethnic, or sexual identity development? How could these strategies benefit the counseling process?

10. How could counselors use creative arts therapeutic strategies to help young clients tell their stories of spiritual identity development? How could these strategies benefit the counseling process?

SECTION 2

Social Advocacy

3

Social Justice Counseling

Philip B. Gnilka, Caroline O'Hara, and Catherine Y. Chang

PREVIEW

Social justice and social advocacy have been, and will for the foreseeable future remain, fundamental to the practice of counseling. Owing to the convergence of certain economic and societal issues, the roles of social justice and social advocacy have gained more prominence in recent years. On the basis of the momentum from this focus, some have argued that social justice in counseling should be considered the "fifth force" following the psychodynamic, behavioral, humanistic, and systemic/multicultural counseling forces that exist in the profession. We begin this chapter discussing some key constructs related to understanding social justice and social advocacy, go on to explore the historical context of social justice and social advocacy in counseling, and then discuss the relationship between social injustice and mental health issues. Strategies and challenges associated with being agents of change are infused throughout these topics, and professional counselors are called upon to be social change agents.

KEY CONSTRUCTS FOR UNDERSTANDING SOCIAL ADVOCACY

Do you believe that every individual in the world has the same worth? Or do you believe that some people are more valuable than others? Should everyone receive equal benefits from society? Do you believe that all people should have equitable rights? Do you believe that all people have the right to a "good life"? The counseling profession has moved more toward addressing social inequities and their impact on clients' psychological and physical health, both within the counseling session and throughout the systems that clients experience—from their families and schools to local communities and historical institutions that continue to marginalize them.

Social justice counseling and advocacy counseling are used interchangeably in the counseling literature. One can argue that the goal of advocacy leads to social justice. For example, supporting the rights of gay men and lesbians to adopt children (advocacy) could assist in giving them equitable opportunities to be parents (social justice). For consistency, we will use *social justice counseling* throughout this chapter to denote both the act aimed at achieving, and the belief in, a just world.

Social justice counseling refers to counseling that recognizes the impact of oppression, privilege, and discrimination on the mental health of individuals (Chang, Crethar, & Ratts, 2010). According to Hays, Chang, and Chaney (2008), the majority of counselors and counselor trainees define social justice as equitable treatment (e.g., equity among groups, nondiscrimination, and equitable distribution of advantages and disadvantages). Some define social justice in terms of its negation, **social injustice**, such as punishment for not following norms and the unequal assignment of privilege. Thus, *social injustice* refers to the unequal distribution of rewards and burdens. Examples of social injustice include discrimination across cultural identities; the provision of limited housing; the existence of educational achievement gaps in schools; poverty; classism; sexism; child exploitation; racial profiling; homophobia; and violence toward racial, ethnic, and sexual minorities. The goal of social justice counseling is to promote access to resources and opportunities and to advocate for equity for all people, focusing particularly on those groups that have been disenfranchised on the basis of their cultural or ethnic background (e.g., race/ethnicity, gender, age, social class, sexual identity). Based on the belief that all people have a right to equitable treatment and fair allocation of societal resources, the goal of social justice counseling is to establish equal distribution of power and resources through advocacy to ensure that all people have the tools and resources for a "good life" (J. Lee, 2014; Lewis, Ratts, Paladino, & Toporek, 2011). Accordingly, one of the goals of social justice counseling is the eradication of oppression. **Oppression** is pervasive and exists across multiple groups (e.g., people of color, people of lower socioeconomic status or social class, gay men, people with disabilities) and at varying levels (e.g., individual, institutional, cultural). Oppression can be said to have two modalities (i.e., oppression by force and oppression by deprivation) and be of three types (i.e., primary, secondary, and tertiary). **Oppression by force** involves the act of imposing, on an individual or a group, an object, a label, a role, an experience, or a living condition that is unwanted and that causes physical or psychological pain. Examples directed at individuals or marginalized groups include sexual assault, negative media images of minority groups, kidnapping (of either an individual or members of a marginalized group), and physical violence toward an individual or a group of individuals. **Oppression by deprivation** includes the act of depriving an individual or a group of an object, a label, a role, an experience, or a living condition that hinders physical and psychological well-being. Examples include neglecting individuals and withholding job promotions from them because of their minority status, denying certain groups a rich educational experience on the basis of their skin color or socioeconomic status, making it difficult to find affordable transportation from home to a place of employment, and making it practically impossible to find safe, affordable housing.

Primary oppression consists of overt acts representing either of the two modalities of oppression (i.e., oppression by force, oppression by deprivation); **secondary oppression** involves individuals benefiting from overt oppressive acts against others. Although individuals involved in secondary oppression do not actively engage in oppressive acts, they do not object to others who do engage in overt oppressive acts and do benefit from the oppression. For example, one might overhear a racial slur by a family member yet not call direct attention to the oppressive nature of the comment. To this end, the person who hears the racial slur perpetuates the idea that it is "okay" if others use racial slurs. Another example is that of a White couple getting into a taxi after observing that the cab passed by a Hispanic couple. **Tertiary oppression**, also referred to as **internalized oppression**, refers to the identification of the dominant message by members of the minority group, often to seek acceptance by the dominant group. Like secondary oppression, tertiary oppression can be passive in nature (Hanna, Talley, & Guindon, 2000; Sue, 2010). For example, a female who internalizes messages of sexism may buy into the message that males are superior and that women should be subjugated. This internalization process is likely to lead to lowered self-esteem, psychological issues such as depression and anxiety, and an increased risk of physical or sexual violence.

Dispenza (2015) provided one of the first empirical studies of tertiary oppression, examining the connection between internalized homophobia and expectations of stigma, on the one hand, and the dyadic adjustment and career satisfaction of 170 men in same-sex dual-income relationships, on the other. Increased levels of internalized homophobia were negatively related to dyadic adjustment of the same-sex couples, while increased levels of expectations of stigma were negatively related to career satisfaction. Dispenza suggested that counselors focus on interventions that help lower levels of internalized homophobia when their clients are in need of dyadic adjustment and on interventions that increase coping resources when their clients are facing elevated stigma in the workplace.

Oppression is complex and multidimensional in that an individual can be a member of both oppressive and oppressed groups and experience oppression at various levels. By virtue of the diverse combinations of race, sex and gender, sexual orientation, gender identity, class, religious or spiritual affiliation, age, and physical and emotional abilities, all individuals are potentially victims and perpetuators of oppression to some degree. For example, a White gay man, who is majority by race and gender but minority by sexual orientation, can be oppressed by individuals (e.g., perpetrators of hate crimes) and institutions (e.g., religious institutions that do not recognize same-sex marriage), as well as experience cultural oppression (e.g., living in a culture that considers his sexual orientation to be abnormal), yet at the same time be an oppressor (e.g., hold sexist or classist attitudes). The result of oppression is an imbalance of **power** (i.e., one individual or group—the privileged—having control, autonomy, and authority or influence over another individual or group—the oppressed). Specific forms of oppression (i.e., racism, sexism, heterosexism, classism, ableism, and ageism) will be discussed more thoroughly in other chapters.

A concept related to social injustice and oppression is that of **structural violence** (sometimes referred to as **institutional oppression**): the marginalization that results from oppressive institutions. Structural violence results when social, political, economic, and other institutional entities and processes intentionally or unintentionally erect barriers to development, wellness, dignity, and human potential. Structural violence can be overt, although it is often covert, making it harder to detect. Examples of structural violence include providing insufficient funding to inner-city and rural schools, limiting access to healthy and affordable food, accepting high unemployment rates for certain minority groups, limiting access to quality health care and preventative care, and making it difficult to find affordable transportation. One particularly insidious example is the exclusion of gender reassignment surgery for transgender individuals from coverage by health insurance companies (an example of overt structural violence) because this oppressed group lacks legal protections and legal recourse (an example of covert structural violence). Structural violence has a very real and lasting impact on the wellness (or lack thereof) of individuals and communities.

Privilege is made up of several components, such as having power, access, or unearned advantage, and holding a majority status. As mentioned earlier, power involves having control, autonomy, and authority or influence over others. Access relates not only to monetary and material possessions, but also to opportunities (e.g., opportunities for higher education, opportunities to attend more affluent schools and libraries). Having connections, receiving favorable treatment, and possessing entitlement all relate to having an unearned advantage, whereas majority status has to do with being not only the majority in number but also the majority in social standing and having the power to define who is who. Therefore, oppression and privilege can be viewed as inversely related (Hays, Chang, & Dean, 2004; O'Hara, 2014).

To understand privilege, it is important to note that those who experience it find it invisible or difficult to detect. Privilege around race serves as an example. Those who identify as White or identify with European ancestry experience White privilege, while people identifying with other racial backgrounds and biracial or multiracial individuals experience oppression and marginalization. White privilege often conflates Whiteness with what is considered to be normal or with a universal human standard. For example, skin bandages, stockings, undergarments, and makeup often come in colors alluding to skin tone (e.g., nude, buff, tan). These adjectives describe colors that match fair-skinned (White) people and not those with darker or deeper skin tones. This practice implies that Whiteness is normal and that other colors or tones are not. The flip side of this example can also be used to detect and understand White privilege. In other words, how common is it to see stockings that are olive, brown, or black and that are called "nude"? This example of White privilege underscores the idea that Whiteness becomes the unspoken standard by which others are compared. Voices from the Field 3.1 presents three cases of becoming aware of privilege and oppression.

Voices from the Field 3.1

We asked each author about their journey during which they became aware of their privilege and oppression.

As a Korean-American, heterosexual, Christian, able-bodied, middle-class woman who grew up in a working-class family, I hold membership in groups that are considered privileged and groups that are considered oppressed. I believe that it is my multiple group memberships in both privileged and oppressed groups that make me keenly cognizant of the impact that privilege and oppression have on each of our lives. Because of this awareness, it is important that I facilitate an awareness and recognition of privilege and oppression issues in my teaching and supervision. I encourage my students to reflect on their various group memberships and to discuss how being a member of each group either has given them some privilege or has oppressed them in some way. Further, I encourage them to think about the impact of privilege and oppression on the lives of their clients.

Catherine Y. Chang, PhD, LPC, NCC, CPCS Professor, Georgia State University

I have had the opportunity to do some significant amount of traveling by car over the past few years. One trip I frequently make is through the Appalachian Mountains to visit family. During these trips, I have become increasingly aware of the huge differences in how people live throughout our society from a socioeconomic perspective. When I first start out on the trip, I am in predominately middle-class and wealthy neighborhoods in northeast Ohio. The houses are big and have green lawns, the streets are clean, and the schools in the area are lively, are new, and look inviting. There are a lot of stores around the area that are full of cars and shoppers.

As I continue down the street toward the outskirts of the city, the environment slowly changes. I begin to see smaller houses and an increasing number in disrepair. I begin to see an increasing number of signs saying "Foreclosure" and "Abandoned Building." The schools in this area seem to be in need of significant repair. There also is an increasing number of boarded-up storefronts.

(Continued)

As I move out of the outskirts of town and continue down the highway into sections of the Appalachian Mountains, another significant change begins to occur. Many of the houses look like they need quite a lot of repair, and many storefronts and several entire shopping centers are completely boarded up. The schools that I pass seem much more outdated. It is harder to find stores and gas stations to stop at, and when I glance at headlines of newspapers in the area, unemployment and economic hardships are a significant front-page issue.

This experience has shown me how wide the socioeconomic gap is in our society, and it is increasing. Although I live in a relatively well-off area of the country, as I continue on my journey, even a few miles away, poverty becomes very evident. As I reflect on this experience, I wonder about other things. How does access to medical and dental care change? What about access to mental health care? Are there enough school counselors (or even any school counselors) in the schools surrounded by poverty? Am I doing enough to help change this situation? What are the issues and implications affecting our country? Having these experiences continues to challenge and press me to see privilege and oppression, particularly poverty, and how an increasingly large number of Americans are suffering.

Philip B. Gnilka, PhD, LPC, NCC, Assistant Professor, DePaul University

One of the experiences that helped shape my awareness about privilege and oppression has been my work with a university SafeZone program. Similar to secondary schools' Gay–Straight Alliances (GSA), SafeZone or Safe Space programs provide education, training, support, advocacy, and networking around issues of sexual and gender diversity at colleges and universities. While representing SafeZone during a campus outreach event for new students and parents/caregivers, I set up our information table with brochures. I thought I heard someone directing a slur at me related to my sexual identity and saw that someone nearby was smirking with a friend and laughing.

As I reflected on the experience, so many things came to mind. Was I imagining the incident? Who were those people? Why was I so on edge? Should I (could I) leave the table? It occurred to me that, as a heterosexual, cisgender female, I was not accustomed to having to consider my sexual identity or gender identity as ways that I could be attacked. I was used to having privilege in those areas and used to feeling safe and comfortable with those parts of myself. However, by working the table as an ally, I was putting myself in the position of making myself more of a target. Because sexual identity and gender identity are "invisible" social identities, it is less clear to outsiders how individuals may self-identify (although assumptions are often still made). It occurred to me that, if that hour of my life was uncomfortable, how must people in the sexual or gender identity minority feel on a regular basis? What issues of safety and security might they have to consider? How do these chronic stressors affect wellness? This is an example of an experience that helped me to consider some of my privileges.

At another campus orientation fair, a new student tentatively approached my table and asked me about our organization. She then revealed to me that one of her best friends in high school had been murdered "because he was gay." My listening to her and connecting her with resources was one example of the types of experiences that continue to stir my passion for social justice and advocacy work. Hearing stories like hers continues to motivate me to intervene in local, institutional, and political ways.

Caroline O'Hara, PhD, LPC, NCC, Assistant Professor, University of Toledo

---

ACTIVITY 3.1

Consider the definitions of oppression and privilege presented in this chapter. In the first column of the table that follows, make a list of privileges that you have personally experienced or witnessed over the past week. In the second column, make a list of oppressive acts that you have experienced or witnessed over the past week. In the third column, indicate whether the acts are examples of power/ lack of power, access/lack of access, advantage/lack of advantage, and majority/minority status.

Privileges	Oppressive Acts	Power/Access/ Advantage/Status

Discuss your listings in a small group. Are there any acts that you did not include in your list that were in others' lists? Are there any acts that others included that you found surprising?

Privilege, like oppression, is complex and multidimensional. Privilege manifests itself differently based on multiple identities, personal experiences, desire for status, and level of self-awareness. One can have privilege based on many social identities, including, but not limited to, race (White privilege), gender (male privilege), gender identity (cis-gender privilege), class (socioeconomic privilege), sexual orientation (heterosexual privilege), and religious affiliation (Christian privilege). As we understand the concepts of oppression and privilege, it is imperative to reflect on our own experiences with power. Activity 3.1 provides a way to explore personal experiences with privilege and oppression.

Take, for example, an Asian-American, heterosexual, Christian female. How did she become aware of the various cultural groups, both privileged and oppressed, in which she holds membership? Her level of awareness of privilege (Christian and heterosexual) and oppression (Asian American and female) is based on external influences that include the government, religion, the media, industry, and education. Her sexual identity is validated through governmental laws that afford her the rights of marriage and through industry practices that provide her spousal insurance coverage. Her sexual identity is further validated through images of her own parents and images of the "traditional" family espoused by the media. However, her image of being an Asian-American female can be both invalidated through negative images of Asians and women in the media and validated through pride in her Asian heritage that is promoted in her family. These messages have been internalized throughout her life and further validated or invalidated through the visibility or invisibility of her cultural group (sexual identity can be considered an invisible characteristic of a cultural group, and being Asian and female are visible characteristics thereof) as well as self- and others' perceptions of that group.

It is important to consider our own awareness of privilege and oppression and how it has changed over time on the basis of our interactions with various societal systems. Reflection 3.1 provides a forum for considering your experiences with power, and Reflection 3.2 gives you an opportunity to consider your cultural identity in the context of your awareness of privilege and oppression.

REFLECTION 3.1

Membership has its privileges! Memberships in various "cultural" groups can be associated with certain "privileges." Name two cultural groups with which you identify, and list some privileges associated with each group. How might these privileges that you experience affect others who do not belong to your group?

REFLECTION 3.2

Consider your cultural identity. Use a broad definition of culture to identify aspects of your identity, such as race, ethnicity, socioeconomic status, and ability status. Construct a narrative using these components to describe the development of your various cultural identities, and reflect upon that narrative.

Empowerment is another important construct in social justice counseling. The goal of social justice counseling involves the equitable distribution of power—in other words, empowering disenfranchised groups. McWhirter (1994) defines empowerment as

> the process by which people, organizations, or groups who are powerless and marginalized (a) become aware of the power dynamics at work in their life context, (b) develop the skills and capacity for gaining reasonable control over their lives, (c) which they exercise, (d) without infringing on the rights of others, and (e) which coincides with actively supporting the empowerment of others in their community. (p. 12)

As is evident in this definition, empowerment is a complex process involving self-reflection and action from the client and the counselor at both the individual and community levels and thus forms the foundation for social justice counseling (J. Lee, 2014). Some examples of empowerment are validating a client's anxiety regarding coming out to his or her parents, normalizing a trauma survivor's symptomology, supporting clients as they search for positive coping strategies to deal with acculturating to the United States, and collaborating with others to address the lack of resources in a local school.

An instance of intimate partner violence (IPV) can also serve as an example of empowerment. Professional counselors who work with survivors of IPV should engage in self-reflection about how to collaborate with these individuals. Empowerment involves developing resources, options, and advocacy skills. It is important for the counselor not to impose expectations on the client. Instead, the counselor and client are to self-reflect and collaborate to identify values, resources, and skills that the client might choose to develop. At the individual level, counselor actions might include recommending bibliotherapy, including specific books; sharing resources; role-playing; assessing strengths; and modeling behaviors that evoke empowerment. Client actions might involve practicing skill development in and out of session, as well as reviewing resources and developing awareness around strengths and empowerment. At the community level, the counselor might offer outreach to schools or community centers that provide education on empowerment and/or IPV prevention. Political lobbying for resources and laws around IPV would also be useful. In turn, the client might engage in similar behaviors or join a group for survivors of IPV, providing leadership and teaching others about empowerment and advocacy.

A key aspect of empowerment involves building on clients' sources of resilience. **Resilience** is defined as the set of behaviors and attitudes that clients identify as beneficial in coping with stressful situations and adversity (Singh, Hays, & Watson, 2011). The stressful situations may involve violence and trauma experienced on the basis of being a member of an oppressed group, or acculturative stress in clients who have migrated to the United States recently and who are living in a substandard neighborhood that lacks sufficient community, school, and medical resources, to name a few shortcomings. Professional counselors working in mental health, school, rehabilitation, and college counseling settings are encouraged to identify these stressful situations and the coping resources that clients use to combat them. To this end, identifying and building on client resources fosters resilience.

HISTORICAL CONTEXT

Although social justice issues have always contributed to the positive evolution of the counseling profession, recent developments have magnified and reinforced their historical and future role as fundamental to modern counseling. Evidence of this expanded role includes, but is not limited to, (a) Loretta Bradley, American Counseling Association (ACA) president, 1999–2000, selecting social justice and advocacy as the thematic focus of her presidential year; (b) the chartering of Counselors for Social Justice as a division of the ACA in 2001 (www.counselorsforsocialjustice.org); (c) endorsement of the advocacy competencies by the ACA Governing Council in 2003; (d) the formation of the Association for Counselor Education and Supervision's (ACES's) Human Rights and Social Justice Committee in 2006; (e) the sponsorship of the ACES Social Justice Summit in 2007 and 2009 (Chang et al., 2010); and (f) revision of the Multicultural Counseling Competencies (Sue, Arredondo, and McDavis, 1992) to become the Multicultural and Social Justice Counseling Competencies (Ratts, Singh, Nassar-McMillan, Butler, & McCullough, 2015).

However, to appreciate this professional shift, we must first refine our perceptions to acknowledge the lineage of social justice's integral impact on the counseling profession. At its inception, the counseling profession began with individuals responding to social injustice and advocating for changes in social policy (e.g., Clifford Beers spearheaded the mental hygiene movement, Carl Rogers believed that the principles of psychology should be used to address social problems, and Clement Vontress advocated for students in urban schools; see Hartung & Blustein, 2002; Kiselica, 2004; McWhirter, 1997). Frank Parsons held the belief that wealth and power were unequally distributed throughout society, and he was committed to empowering immigrant and poor children in their employment and social roles in the United States during the early part of the 19th century. Parsons did that by founding Boston's Vocational Bureau to provide vocational guidance to the people in society who were the least powerful and had the fewest resources. From this genesis flowed a developing dialogue about social injustice—a dialogue that directly molded the counseling profession. The following time line lists some milestones in that dialogue:

1. 1971: "Counseling and the Social Revolution," a special issue of the *Personnel and Guidance Journal* (currently known as the *Journal of Counseling & Development*) is published. The publication encourages counselors to actively engage in the social change process and address issues related to racism, sexism, destruction of the environment, and ending warfare.

2. 1987: The American Association for Counseling and Development (currently the American Counseling Association [ACA]) publishes a position paper on human rights that urges counselors to advocate for social change through personal, professional, and political activities.

3. 1992: Sue et al. (1992) publish the multicultural counseling competencies and standards.

4. 1998: *Social Action: A Mandate for Counselors,* edited by Courtland Lee and Garry Walz, is published.

5. 1999: A special issue of the *Journal of Counseling & Development*, a publication edited by Tracy L. Robinson and Earl J. Ginter, is dedicated to racism.

6. 2003: ACA endorses the Advocacy Competencies developed by Lewis, Arnold, House, and Toporek (2003).

7. 2005: The revised *ACA Code of Ethics* places an increased emphasis on multiculturalism and social justice issues in counseling. In particular, the new standard E.5.c. directs counselors to "recognize historical and social prejudices in the misdiagnosis and pathologizing of certain individuals and groups and the role of mental health professionals in perpetuating these prejudices through diagnosis and treatment."

8. 2007: The Association for Counselor Education and Supervision (ACES) adopts the theme "Vanguards for Change: ACES and Social Justice" and sponsors a Social Justice Summit as part of the conference. The second Social Justice Summit takes place in 2009.

9. 2010–2011: The profession sees an increase in publications related to social justice issues in counseling. For example, the journal *Counselor Education and Supervision* (editors: Chang, Crethar, & Ratts) and the *Journal for Specialists in Group Work* (editors Singh & Salazar) both published special issues on social justice.

10. 2014: A revision of the ACA *Code of Ethics* increases attention on social justice and advocacy by focusing on those issues.

11. 2015: The revised Multicultural and Social Justice Counseling Competencies (MSJCC) is endorsed by the ACA (Ratts et al., 2015).

As an evolving tenet of the counseling profession, the search for social justice will likely continue to serve as a primary force in the maturation of the counseling profession in the decades to come.

SOCIAL INJUSTICE AND MENTAL HEALTH ISSUES

Social justice counseling becomes clear when one considers the relationship between social injustice (i.e., oppression, discrimination, and prejudice) and the mental health of marginalized groups. A historic U.S. Surgeon General's report titled *Mental Health: Culture, Race, and Ethnicity—A Supplement to Mental Health* (USDHHS, 2001) helped illustrate potential consequences of social injustice and predictors of mental illness for various racial/ethnic minority groups and move the field of multicultural counseling forward. This report was seminal in that it expanded counselors' and other mental health professionals' thinking of what culturally competent (and culturally incompetent) practice focuses on. More specifically, the report's findings served as an impetus for conceptualizing multicultural counseling competence as more than just cultural sensitivity and tolerance of difference. The report called for mental health professionals to examine how cultural "difference" and poor conditions for certain groups might be based on negative social conditions and other experiences of oppression. In addition, it demonstrated how various minority statuses for an individual intersect to create additional adverse conditions. Similar research discusses the need for social justice in school counseling (Bemak & Chung, 2008; Bidell, 2011; Dixon, Tucker, & Clark, 2010; Evans, Zambrano, Cook, Moyer, & Duffey, 2011), rehabilitation counseling (Harley, Alston, & Middleton, 2007; Kelsey & Smart, 2012; Middleton, Robinson, & Mu'min, 2010), career counseling (Dik, Duffy, & Steger, 2012; Hartung & Blustein, 2002; Pope & Pangelinan, 2010), and supervision (Chang, Hays, & Milliken, 2009; Glosoff & Durham, 2010; O'Hara, 2014).

Although racial, ethnic, and cultural minorities (e.g., people of color; women; and lesbian, gay, bisexual, and transgender [LGBT] individuals) are exposed to greater levels of discrimination and poverty than the majority culture, they have limited access to mental health care because of socioeconomic and language factors (USDHHS, 2001; Wilson, Okwu, & Mills, 2011). Experiences of oppression can leave people exposed to chronic stressors and challenges that threaten their well-being (Greene, 2005), making them more susceptible to depression, suicide, substance abuse, violence, anxiety, chronic stress, and acute stress, any or all of which in turn may lead to medical complications, including hypertension, low birthrate of newborns, heart disease, and cancer (USDHHS, 2001).

Stress has been identified as the primary cause of emotional disturbances, and the principal sources of stress are poverty, sexism, and being born unwanted (Albee, 2006; Evans & Cassells, 2014). According to Evans and Kim (2013), poor children have decreased cognitive development, poorer physical health, chronic stress, and increased emotional difficulties, compared with more economically advantaged children. The following statements about poverty were presented at the 1993 Bi-Annual Congress of the World Federation for Mental Health (WFMH):

> Poverty dampens the human spirit creating despair and hopelessness. Poverty underlies multiple problems facing families, infants, children, adolescents, adults, and the elderly. Poverty directly affects infant mortality, mental retardation, learning disabilities, and drug and alcohol abuse. Poverty is the major factor in homelessness. Poverty increases the incidence of racial, ethnic, and religious hatred. Poverty increases abuse against women and children. Poverty results in suicide, depression, and severe mental illness. Poverty is directly linked to violence. (as cited in Albee, 2006, pp. 451–452)

Clearly, marginalized groups are at a greater risk for psychological, physical, interpersonal, and financial difficulties. The remaining chapters of this book provide a more in-depth discussion of the costs of White privilege, racism, sexism, heterosexism, classism, ableism, and ageism.

COUNSELORS AS SOCIAL ADVOCATES

J. Lee (2014) calls for a paradigm shift for counselors to engage more in social justice counseling. If counselors are to be agents of social justice, then they need to look beyond the traditional role and scope of the counselor and reject the notion of neutrality. Counselors must reconceptualize the theory and practice of counseling. Social justice counseling calls for counselors to broaden their scope of practice to intervene at not only at the client level, but the societal level as well. Social justice counseling also calls for counselors to reject the notion

---

REFLECTION 3.3

Develop a personal social justice plan based on Lee's (2007) five personal action steps.

Social Justice Plan	Process Questions/Tasks
1. Explore life's meaning and commitment	"What do I do and why do I do it? How do I do it? Who do I do it for? What do I believe about my clients? Am I committed to fostering and supporting a society that is more enlightened, just and humane through my life and work?" (p. 260)
2. Explore personal privilege	Explore the privileged cultural groups that you are a member of, and challenge yourself to use your privilege to promote social justice. (See Reflection 3.1.)
3. Explore the nature of oppression	Consider how you have oppressed others in the past, as well as how you have been oppressed by others by virtue of your group membership.
4. Become multiculturally literate	• Experience various ethnic groups by traveling locally, nationally, and internationally. • Read newspapers and literature from other ethnic groups. • Be open to new cultural experiences.
5. Establish a personal social justice compass	Develop your own personal agenda for social justice on the basis of your personal principles and ideals.

---

of value neutrality in counseling. The assumption of value neutrality supports the status quo of inequity in society. Counselors following traditional counseling theories and interventions are at risk of not addressing underlying societal issues that are likely the cause of the client's issues (Ratts & Wood, 2010). If counselors want to work for social justice, then they must work for a just and equitable social system.

As a first step toward a just and equitable social system, C. C. Lee (2007) called for action at the personal level through self-exploration. He proposed five personal action steps: (a) exploring your personal life's meaning and commitment, (b) exploring personal privilege, (c) exploring the nature of oppression, (d) working to become multiculturally literate, and (e) establishing a "personal social justice compass" (p. 260). Based on these action steps, Reflection 3.3 offers an opportunity for professional counselors to develop their own social justice plan.

Advocacy in Professional Counseling Standards

As the original multicultural counseling competencies (MCC; Sue et al., 1992) developed and were applied, the multicultural counseling movement evolved to become the social justice movement, which places a greater emphasis on the influence of environmental factors (e.g., oppression and social problems) that affect the well-being of clients. The movement's focus on social justice issues is further heightened by the growing awareness of the relationship between oppression and mental illness; thus, social advocacy increasingly is becoming a part of counselors' roles and responsibilities. Three professional documents illustrate the centrality of advocacy to the profession of counseling: the Multicultural and Social Justice Counseling Competencies (MSJCC, Ratts et al., 2015), the 2014 ACA *Code of Ethics* (ACA, 2014), and the ACA Advocacy Competencies (Lewis et al., 2003).

In 2015, the Association for Multicultural Counseling and Development, a division of the ACA, revised the original MCC, developing it into the MSJCC, a document that further demonstrates the evolution of the multicultural counseling movement toward a social justice perspective. In accordance with the MCC, "Culturally skilled counselors possess knowledge and understanding about how oppression, racism, discrimination, and stereotyping affect them personally and in their work" (Sue et al., 1992, p. 482). The principal shifts in the new competencies relate to the inclusion of the *relationship* between client and counselor as a major developmental domain to consider, as well as to the emphasis on *action* as an area of competence (Ratts et al., 2015).

In addition, in response to an increased awareness of the role of advocacy in counseling, the revised ACA *Code of Ethics* (ACA, 2014) included the following statements in reference to advocacy:

> A.7.a. Advocacy: When appropriate, counselors advocate at individual, group, institutional, and societal levels to address potential barriers and obstacles that inhibit access and/or the growth and development of clients.
>
> A.7.b. Confidentiality and Advocacy: Counselors obtain client consent prior to engaging in advocacy efforts on behalf of an identifiable client to improve the provision of services and to work toward removal of systemic barriers or obstacles that inhibit client access, growth, and development. (p. 5)

The **ACA Advocacy Competencies** (Lewis et al., 2003) answer this call for increased engagement and application of social justice in counseling, spanning levels of advocacy from the microlevel of clients and students, to the middle level involving communities, to the macrolevel of interventions in the public arena. The model also identifies two realms (*acting with* and *acting on behalf*) within each level. Thus, the model encompasses six domains in total when delineating advocacy principles: (a) client/student empowerment, (b) client/student advocacy, (c) community collaboration, (d) systems advocacy, (e) public information, and (f) social/political advocacy.

The microlevel (Lewis et al., 2003) consists of client/student empowerment (acting with) and client/student advocacy (acting on behalf). On this level, professional counselors work with clients to identify strengths aiding, and barriers hindering, their optimal development. Professional counselors assist clients in removing barriers and practicing self-advocacy. In addition, clients can develop and implement action plans in their lives to facilitate growth and development.

The middle level (Lewis et al., 2003) consists of community collaboration (acting with) and systems advocacy (acting on behalf). In this realm, professional counselors can act as allies by identifying other supportive agencies and resources available to clients. Data gathering and presentation are essential to collaborate with community stakeholders and analyze efforts. At this level, professional counselors work to identify the systems that affect the wellness of their clients and to help clients navigate those systems to their benefit whenever possible.

The macrolevel (Lewis et al., 2003) consists of public information (acting with) and social/political advocacy (acting on behalf). This arena may include lobbying at the local, state, and national political levels. It also may include the dissemination of information through media campaigns and educative efforts. At this level, professional counselors work with clients and communities to target large-scale efforts at changing institutions, altering laws, and allocating resources.

As mentioned, the MSJCC emphasize the competency domain of action in addition to attitudes, knowledge, and skills (Ratts et al., 2015). This domain dovetails well with the ACA Advocacy Competencies' (Lewis et al., 2003) focus on action (acting with and acting on behalf). Furthermore, the MSJCC model involves four developmental domains: counselor awareness, client worldview, counseling relationship, and counseling and advocacy interventions (Ratts et al., 2015). Within the last of these domains, the MSJCC specify that "privileged and marginalized counselors intervene with, and on behalf of, clients at the intrapersonal, interpersonal, institutional, community, public policy, and international/global levels" (Ratts et al., 2015). Here we see the influence of the ACA Advocacy Competencies in encouraging engagement across ecosystems from the microlevel to the macrolevel. Indeed, the MSJCC model identifies itself as a socioecological model.

These advocacy competencies assert that advocacy requires social action in partnership with the client, as well as on behalf of the client/student. Table 3.1 is a sample listing of the advocacy competencies (Lewis et al., 2003), and Activity 3.2 is aimed at encouraging professional counselors to operationalize some of the ACA Advocacy Competencies in a manner that is relevant to the setting in which they will be working.

TABLE 3.1   ACA Advocacy Competencies Examples

1. Client/student empowerment	a. Identify strengths and resources of clients and students.
	b. At an appropriate development level, help the individual identify the external barriers that affect his or her development.
	c. Help students and clients develop self-advocacy action plans.
2. Client/student advocacy	a. Negotiate relevant services and education systems on behalf of clients and students.
	b. Help clients and students gain access to needed resources.
	c. Identify potential allies for confronting the barriers.
3. Community collaboration	a. Identify environmental factors that impinge upon students' and clients' development.
	b. Alert community or school groups with common concerns related to the issue.
	c. Develop alliances with groups working for change.
4. Systems advocacy	a. Identify environmental factors impinging on students' or clients' development.
	b. Analyze the sources of political power and social influence within the system.
	c. Assess the effect of counselor's advocacy efforts on the system and constituents.

5. Public information	a. Recognize the impact of oppression and other barriers to healthy development.
	b. Identify environmental factors that are protective of healthy development.
	c. Assess the influence of public information efforts undertaken by the counselor.
6. Social/political advocacy	a. Distinguish those problems that can best be resolved through social/political action.
	b. With allies, prepare convincing data and rationales for change.
	c. With allies, lobby legislators and other policy makers.

Source: From "Advocacy Competencies [Electronic version]," by J. Lewis, M. S. Arnold, R. House, & R. L. Toporek, 2003. Retrieved from http://counselorsforsocialjustice.com/advocacycompetencies.html. Copyright 2003 by the American Counseling Association. Reprinted with permission. No further reproduction authorized without written permission from the American Counseling Association.

ACTIVITY 3.2

This activity will help you become familiar with the advocacy competencies. Review the ACA advocacy competencies (Lewis et al., 2003) outlined in Table 3.1, mark the ones that you have already participated in, and then develop a plan of action in dyads for engaging in some of the other competencies.

THREE-TIERED MODEL OF SOCIAL ADVOCACY

Social justice is necessary for optimal psychosocial health (C. C. Lee & Walz, 1998). Counselors can advocate more effectively for their clients if our profession is recognized by other mental health professionals, legislators, and policy makers. (Mellin, Hunt, & Nichols, 2011; Myers, Sweeney, & White, 2002). Chang, Hays et al. (2009) developed a three-tiered model of advocacy to begin to infuse social justice into counseling practice. (See Table 3.2.) The model urges counselors and counselor educators to consider social justice issues relative to two fronts (client advocacy and professional advocacy) and across three tiers (self-awareness, client services, and community collaboration).

Myers et al. (2002) called for a comprehensive national plan for advocacy that includes advocacy for client well-being and for the profession of counseling: "Counselors can be more effective advocates for clients when our profession is recognized by other mental health professions as well as legislators and policy makers" (p. 401). Social change is necessary for optimal psychosocial health of both counselors and clients (C. C. Lee & Walz, 1998). For counselors to promote psychosocial health for themselves and their clients, we believe that they must work toward self-awareness, consider their clients from a social justice perspective, and work toward social justice with others who share their vision. Activity 3.3 allows students to practice advocating for others.

TABLE 3.2 Three-Tiered Model of Social Advocacy

	Client Advocacy	Professional Advocacy
Self-Awareness	Become aware of one's own cultural values, biases, privileges, and experiences of oppression.	Develop a strong professional counselor identity.
Client Services	Understand how various political, social, educational, and individual systems interrelate and influence their clients.	Advocate for changes that assist counselors in providing high-quality services to clients (e.g., ability to diagnose, insurance reimbursement).
Community Collaboration	Identify and advocate for change in the community by noting the relationship between oppression and mental health.	Create and advocate for policies, marketing, and legislation that helps the public to learn the importance of the counseling profession.

ACTIVITY 3.3

Write down a hypothetical personally challenging scenario that involves advocating for a client or an oppressed group to someone in a decision-making capacity (e.g., a clinical director, politician, or school administrator).

Create triads in which students are assigned the roles of counselor, decision maker, and coach. Each member of the group should have the opportunity to play each of the three roles at least once. The coach provides a scenario that calls for social advocacy. The counselor and the decision maker converse for several minutes about a scenario. Once the conversation has ended, the coach provides feedback and offers suggestions. Then, the roles should be rotated, and the new coach will provide a different scenario. As you role-play, be sure to practice what you would say, rather than simply discussing social justice advocacy.

Once you have completed the activity, discuss the following as a class:

- What are some thoughts you have in advocating for your client or oppressed group?
- Was the experience easier or more difficult than you expected?
- Did any approaches work better than others?
- What else could you do to help make it easier for you to advocate in the future?

Self-awareness includes an awareness of one's own cultural values and biases. Relative to social justice counseling, counselors need to be able to identify and discuss the privileges that they personally hold in society by virtue of race, socioeconomic status, religious affiliation, sexual identity, sex, or physical ability. Others echo the importance of self-awareness in conducting social justice counseling (J. Lee, 2014) and developing professional pride and professional advocacy (Mellin et al., 2011; Myers et al., 2002). One method for developing self-awareness is constructing a cultural genogram. (See Reflection 3.4.) Figure 3.1 provides a sample cultural genogram.

Client services in social justice counseling involve the empowerment of disenfranchised clients. According to this model, the counselor must first have a clear understanding of the client's worldview before the counselor and the client can move toward empowerment. Counselors working from a constructivist framework consider the social factors as well as the developmental, emotional, and cognitive processes of the individual client. These factors

---

REFLECTION 3.4

Construct a "cultural genogram: a graphic depiction of your family tree that highlights the various cultural group memberships of your family members. Next to each cultural group membership, mark whether the group is a privileged group (P) or an oppressed group (O) and outline some of the messages that come from being a member of that group. In the margin of the genogram, include information related to resources (e.g., family, friends, religious affiliation, employment, housing assistance) and stressors (e.g., financial strain, legal difficulties, employment difficulties, day care issues). There are many genogram software programs available online, as well as many Web sites that publish common symbols used in genograms. In addition, McGoldrick, Gerson, and Petry (2008) published *Genogram: Assessments and Intervention*, which provides instructions for constructing a standard genogram, conducting a genogram interview, and interpreting the results.

  Consider the following:
- How does your membership in privileged and oppressed groups either support or not support the development of your various cultural identities?
- Which memberships come from earlier generations and have changed over time?
- Are there memberships that do not come from earlier generations?
- Which memberships exert the strongest influence on your cultural identity?
- Which memberships exert the least influence?

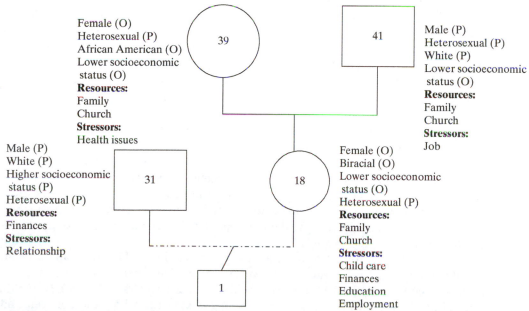

FIGURE 3.1   Sample cultural genogram.

and processes influence and are influenced by various aspects of the client's system. (See Chapter 1.) In addition, counselors recognize the interaction of these systems over time. Working from this model, counselors formulate questions that expose the conditions that promote social, political, and educational advantages and disadvantages. The quality of client services is influenced by the development of a clear professional identity. Accordingly, it is essential that counselors develop their professional identity and professional pride. (See Reflection 3.5.)

REFLECTION 3.5

Questions to Facilitate Professional Identity and Professional Pride

- Describe your role as a professional counselor.
- What qualities make professional counseling unique?
- What role does advocacy play in counseling?
- Suppose you are a counselor working in a shelter for women experiencing intimate partner violence and one of your clients has recently secured a job and housing. What role did you play in assisting your client with her situation?

Community collaboration involves working toward social change at the organizational and institutional levels. Because they work with a diverse group of people, counselors may be the first to become aware of difficulties within agencies, external organizations, and the community. As counselors become aware of external factors influencing their clients, they must look beyond direct clinical work and be willing to intervene at the organizational and institutional levels to promote client and professional advocacy. Several approaches have been suggested by various authors. For example, Dinsmore, Chapman, and McCollum (2000) suggested the following organizational interventions: (a) challenge institutions to provide clients with easier access to critical information that may affect their well-being; (b) serve as a mediator when a client and an institution reach an impasse; (c) negotiate with external agencies and institutions to provide better services for clients; (d) participate in lobbying efforts related to social justice issues; and (e) inform funding agencies of inadequate or damaging practices. In addition, counselors can work toward educating the community about the relationship between oppression and mental health issues through the development of multicultural and social justice programs for different organizations and the community. A more recent example is C. C. Lee and Rogers's "Counselor Advocacy" (2009), which provided additional detail on Kotter's (2012) framework and suggested the following interventions: (a) publicly instilling a sense of urgency regarding one or more identified issues; (b) assisting a group of people in obtaining sufficient power to institute change; (c) designing a vision and strategic plan for change; (d) disseminating the vision publically; (e) nurturing wide support or action, and (f) evaluating actual change.

There are several ways to integrate the three-tiered model of social advocacy in professional counseling. Social justice issues may be addressed in supervision (Case Study 3.1), mental health counseling (Case Study 3.2), school counseling (Case Study 3.3), rehabilitation counseling (Case Study 3.4), college counseling (Case Study 3.5), and counselor education (Case Study 3.6), to name a few venues.

CASE STUDY 3.1

Case of the Three-Tiered Model: Supervision

Consider the following case study and how the three-tiered model can be applied to this case: You are a supervisor who is supervising a certain intern. The intern is at a community agency that includes a shelter and provides crisis counseling for survivors of domestic violence. The majority of the clients in this agency are women who are poor and women of color. The intern is White and from a middle-class background. During the intern's first week of internship, her first client is a woman who is so severely beaten that her face is completely bruised and she has a difficult time speaking because of the swelling. In addition to this case, the intern is asked to see a woman who brought along her 2-year-old daughter because she cannot afford child care. The intern informs you that she did not receive any training on-site prior to seeing her first client.

- What issues related to self-awareness might come up for this intern? Consider cultural identities such as race/ethnicity, socioeconomic status, and education level, to name a few.
- What questions do you have about the quality of client care? Keeping in mind the context of the client, what would you want to consider in working with these women? How would you deal with the presence of a child during the session?
- How can you work with the intern to educate the site about appropriate training (advocacy for the intern and the counseling profession) as well as client care (client advocacy)?

CASE STUDY 3.2

Case of the Three-Tiered Model: Mental Health Counseling

Consider the following case study and how the three-tiered model can be applied to this case: You are a White counselor working at a child advocacy center. You have been assigned a new client, Mia, a 14-year-old Latina who is six months pregnant with her biological father's child. She has been sexually abused by her biological father for the past 4 years. She reports that she loves her father and that they have a "loving" relationship. Her father is currently in prison. Mia's mother is developmentally challenged and considered incompetent to take care of her children; therefore, Mia, along with her three younger siblings, is living with her maternal aunt and uncle and their two children. Her aunt speaks very limited English and requires a translator during the counseling sessions. In addition to your concerns about this client, you have been informed that a major source of funding has been cut from the child advocacy center and may result in some counseling positions being terminated, thus increasing the caseload for the remaining counselors, who already have a heavy caseload.

- What issues related to self-awareness might come up for this professional counselor? Consider cultural identities such as race/ethnicity, socioeconomic status, and education level, to name a few. What potential biases might be an issue for this counselor?
- What questions do you have about the quality of client care? Keeping in mind the context of the client, what would you want to consider when working with the client and her aunt?
- As the professional counselor, how would you balance concern for this client with concern for your job?

CASE STUDY 3.3

Case of the Three-Tiered Model: School Counseling

Consider the following case study and how the three-tiered model can be applied to this case: You are a school counselor currently working at a suburban high school in a conservative part of the country. During the course of the school year, several students individually confide in you about the struggles they have at school because of their sexual orientation. All of them described being called names such as "faggot" by other students and a number of teachers. Several of the students asserted that they had been physically assaulted by other students and nothing was done by the school. When you review the grades and attendance records of the students, you find that all of them are performing below their abilities and show an increasing number of absences.

- What issues related to self-awareness might come up for this school counselor? Consider sexual orientation identities, cultural identities such as race/ethnicity, and socioeconomic status. What potential biases might be an issue for this counselor?
- What concerns do you have about the quality of education being provided for these students?
- What are some community resources and schoolwide resources or programs you could assist in forming?
- What are some of the benefits and risks you might encounter in advocating on a systems or community level?

CASE STUDY 3.4

Case of the Three-Tiered Model: Rehabilitation Counseling

Consider the following case study and how the three-tiered model can be applied to this case: You are a rehabilitation counselor working in an outpatient clinic. One of your new clients has come to the clinic with feelings of hopelessness and despair. Your client is a married, middle-aged Latina who has two children and has never been in trouble before. When you usher her into your office, she is accompanied by her service dog. After brief introductions, you inquire what brought her to your office. She stated that she was in the public library attending a public forum with her service dog when a librarian told her that her dog would have to leave the building. After the client explained that she was blind and it was perfectly legal to have a service dog with her, the librarian contacted the police. When the police responded, they would not listen to the client's side of the story, so she refused to leave the building, forcing the police to place her under arrest. She states that no one will listen to her, and she is unsure as to what to do.

- What issues related to self-awareness might come up for this rehabilitation counselor? Consider cultural identities such as race/ethnicity, socioeconomic status, disability status, and gender, among others. What potential biases might be an issue for this counselor?

- Keeping in mind the context of the client, what would you want to consider in working with this client?
- What are some community resources and communitywide programs that you could assist the client in either finding or establishing? What other interventions would you consider when working with this client?

CASE STUDY 3.5

Case of the Three-Tiered Model: College Campus Hate Crime

Consider the following case study and how the three-tiered model can be applied to this case: You are a counselor working in a college counseling center. One of your new clients has come to the center with feelings of hopelessness and despair. Your client is an African-American male who just started his first year at college. After several sessions, your client reveals that he is gay and was recently assaulted on campus while sleeping in his dorm room. His roommate had seen a pamphlet titled "Coming Out" on his desk the previous night and became enraged. The roommate and several of his friends burst into the room late at night, tied the client up, and began burning him with cigarettes and hitting him repeatedly, giving him a severe concussion and breaking several ribs. They also repeatedly made homophobic and racist remarks. The police were called and eventually arrested the roommate and the other perpetrators; however, hate crime charges were not being considered. Your client was clearly angry as he discussed this and was unsure why his attackers were getting off so easily. He feels that he is falling into a deeper depression and that no one will listen to him.

- Do you consider what the roommate and his friends did a hate crime? Why or why not? Are there differences between hate crimes and other crimes? How do you determine whether these differences exist?
- What issues related to self-awareness might come up for this college counselor? Consider cultural identities such as race/ethnicity, socioeconomic status, disability status, and gender, among others. What potential biases might be an issue for this counselor?
- Keeping in mind the context of the client, what would you want to consider in working with this client?
- What are some community resources and communitywide programs that you could assist the client in either finding or establishing? What other interventions would you consider when working with this client?

CASE STUDY 3.6

Case of the Three-Tiered Model: Counselor Educator

Consider the following case study and how the three-tiered model can be applied to this case: You are a counselor educator who is supervising an intern at a community agency that provides counseling for the general community. The majority of the clients in this agency are poor, although there are many other individuals that the center sees on a regular basis. The intern,

Anita, is an African-American female who also identifies as a conservative Christian from a middle-class background. To date, Anita has had excellent reports from her site supervisor and has been described as an "outstanding intern with superior counseling skills." Close to the end of the semester, the supervisor calls you about a concern she has about Anita. An African-American male who identified as gay came to the clinic seeking counseling for relationship difficulties he was experiencing with his partner. According to the site supervisor, the client was in a serious state of distress. Anita had begun working with the client; however, on learning that the client was openly gay, she excused herself from the consulting room and sought out her site supervisor. She told her supervisor that she believed that her personal religious beliefs would not allow her to continue to counsel the client any further and that she was not a good fit for him. She wanted to be removed from the case and have other clients assigned to her. The site supervisor urged Anita to continue to see this client for the rest of this session and then discuss the matter in supervision. Anita refused and again noted that her religious beliefs were not congruent with her client's "lifestyle." The site supervisor eventually had to finish the session with the client, who found out that Anita no longer wanted to see him. This news caused the client even more distress about his sexual orientation, and he began to feel abandoned and judged by Anita. The site supervisor asks you for help and is unsure what to do going forward.

- What issues related to self-awareness might come up for Anita? Consider cultural identities such as race/ethnicity, socioeconomic status, and education level, to name a few.
- What questions do you have about the quality of client care? Keeping in mind the context of the client, what would you want to consider in working at this site?
- As the counselor educator, how can you work with Anita to educate the site about appropriate training (advocacy for the intern and the counseling profession) as well as client care (client advocacy)?
- Did Anita act in an ethically appropriate manner? Were Anita's actions appropriate from a social justice perspective? Why or why not?

CHALLENGES AND BENEFITS OF SOCIAL JUSTICE COUNSELING

Despite the importance of social justice work, several factors may prevent counselors from engaging in social justice activities. Hays et al. (2008) identified three reasons that may prevent counselor trainees from engaging in social justice counseling: (a) the high intrapersonal and interpersonal costs for counselors (e.g., burnout, job loss, harassment); (b) social justice initiatives that may be incongruent with traditional counseling theories and interventions and traditional ethical standards; and (c) lack of appropriate training in dealing with oppression issues on behalf of the client. Counselor trainees further identified the following areas that challenged the implementation of social justice initiatives: (a) dominant groups (e.g., the closed-mindedness of others, a minimal support system); (b) the counseling process (e.g., communication difficulties, counselors and clients with different levels of awareness of social justice); (c) logistics (e.g., administrative and time constraints); (d) ethics (e.g., the imposition of values); and (e) counselor emotions (e.g., feelings of isolation or helplessness). In addition, reasons that counselor trainees gave for not engaging in social advocacy activities included counselor emotions (e.g., feeling powerless), multicultural incompetence (e.g., lack of advocacy skills), and dominant groups (e.g., fear of conflict and rejection). Reflection 3.6 is designed to assist counselors in identifying resources aimed at offsetting the danger of burnout.

REFLECTION 3.6

Consider the following statement: "Enjoying the pleasures of life can help sustain us in advocating for change." What does that statement mean to you? What are some of the "pleasures of life" that sustain you? How does this statement fit in with the burnout that many counselors face?

Despite the challenges and costs of social justice counseling, it can also be rewarding. Social justice work can lead to personal satisfaction and growth through empowering others and learning from that experience (Kiselica & Robinson, 2000; Klar & Kasser, 2009). Additional perceived benefits of social justice initiatives in counseling include general benefits for society (e.g., promotion of equal rights), general benefits for clients (e.g., culturally appropriate counseling for all), an improved counseling process (e.g., increasing client self-advocacy), general benefits for the counselor (e.g., increased awareness of self), and an imparting of knowledge to clients and communities (Hays et al., 2008). It is important for professional counselors to identify their own personal challenges and benefits that arise from social justice work. (See Reflection 3.7.) In doing so, they are more inclined to locate activities that they can engage in to help end oppressive acts as they attend to the resilience in clients' lives. Table 3.3 offers several activities in which professional counselors may get involved. In addition, Table 3.4 provides several web resources to introduce counselors to national social justice initiatives.

REFLECTION 3.7

Have you engaged in any social justice initiatives? If so, what were some of the challenges and benefits that arose from those experiences? If not, were there any situations in which you would like to have engaged in social justice work but did not? What kept you from intervening?

TABLE 3.3 Additional Social Justice Activities

1. Become a member of a professional counseling organization, such as the American Counseling Association (ACA) or the American Mental Health Counselors Association (AMHCA). Our professional organizations lobby on behalf of our profession and clients. The larger our organizations, the more clout we have in Washington, DC, and in state capitals across the country. You can also find a list of ACA state branches on ACA's Web site under the divisions/regions/branches icon.

2. Join and get involved in an ACA division, such as Counselors for Social Justice (CSJ), the Association for Lesbian, Gay, Bisexual and Transgender Issues in Counseling (ALGBTIC), or the Association for Multicultural Counseling and Development (AMCD), that advocate for social justice causes. By getting involved in divisions of our profession, you can help institute change on social justice issues within the profession.

3. Join the ACA Government Relations Listserv to stay updated on events affecting our profession and how you can make a difference in it and the world. Send an e-mail to Art Terrazas (aterrazas@counseling.org) with the subject line "GR Listserv Sign Up" to subscribe.

(Continued)

TABLE 3.3 Additional Social Justice Activities (Continued)

4. Have your voice heard by sending a fax or an e-mail to your legislators through the ACA Legislative Action Center located at https://www.counseling.org/government-affairs/actioncenter. Through this center, you will be able to send personal e-mails to your U.S. senators and representatives about important legislation that has an impact on our profession. It takes only a few minutes to set up and under a minute for each fax or e-mail.

5. Organize a lobby day at your state capitol with other counselors. When you find a group of counselors who want to join you on the lobby day, find out when your state legislature is in session. Then, figure out who your representatives are and contact them to set up an in-person meeting. Once you have appointments set up with your state legislators, prepare a brief presentation that explains who counselors are, what we do, and why counseling is needed. The ACA Public Policy Web page, at https://www.counseling.org/government-affairs/public-policy, has excellent resources that summarize the effectiveness and benefits of counseling services in both school and community settings.

6. Start a letter-writing campaign at your office or school. First, obtain a list of people who are interested in participating and get their names, phone numbers, and home addresses. Next, find out who their legislators are in Congress and at the state level. You can enter all this information into an Excel spreadsheet. Then, join the ACA Government Relations Listserv to keep abreast of current activities in Washington, DC, that affect the counseling profession or your state counseling association for state issues. When you receive an alert, use a mail merge function in a word processor to prepare a form letter for each individual to send. Some may want to personalize the letter or even compose handwritten letters, so you may need to provide them with talking points. Keep in mind that legislators put much more emphasis on handwritten letters than form letters. Writing letters is an excellent way to get people in an organization to be active in public policy matters.

7. Volunteer for a political campaign. By volunteering for a politician, you will be much more influential in that particular politician's eyes. You can do many things, such as work a phone bank, campaign in your neighborhood and among friends, or simply make a cash contribution. If the politician is elected, you will have more access and influence in having her or him support your issues.

8. Support or volunteer your time with other local service organizations that work for social justice issues you are interested in. For example, you could volunteer for the local domestic violence shelter or HIV/AIDS service organization. Some of these organizations have public policy directors and lobbyists who may need help in finding and summarizing counseling research and literature about their particular issues. Supporting these organizations is an excellent opportunity to use your skills to interpret research for politicians and the general public.

9. Create a giving circle, which is a popular way for individuals to leverage the power of their contributions by pooling those contributions with those of others to achieve a greater impact. Giving circles can be small and informal, with a few people pooling their money and giving it to a chosen charity, or they can be highly organized, requiring multiple contributions and a commitment of many years. Most giving circles are democratically arranged, meaning that donors have an equal voice in deciding where their contributions go. To obtain more information on what a giving circle is and how to start one, check out the Forum of Regional Associations of Grantmakers at www.givingforum.org.

TABLE 3.4 Selected Web Resources

2-1-1 Information and Referral Search (http://www.211.org/): Provides contact information for services regarding multiple issues, such as human trafficking, disaster assistance, health issues, and crises.

American Counseling Association Advocacy Competencies (www.counseling.org/Resources/Competencies/Advocacy_Competencies.pdf): Full text of the advocacy competencies.

American Counseling Association Multicultural Counseling Competencies (www.counseling.org/Resources/Competencies/Multcultural_Competencies.pdf): Full text of the multicultural counseling competencies.

American Counseling Association Government Affairs Web Site (http://www.counseling.org/PublicPolicy): Provides a wealth of information about current issues facing the counseling profession and its clients. Informational resources and advocacy tools are available.

Amnesty International (www.amnesty.org): Nonprofit organization focused on exposing human rights violations across the world.

Association for Lesbian, Gay, Bisexual and Transgender Issues in Counseling (ALGBTIC) (http://www.algbtic.org): Advocates for LGBT clients and counselors, as well as supporting scientific information regarding LGBT issues. A wealth of resources for counselors and clients is provided.

Association for Multicultural Counseling and Development (AMCD) (http://www.multiculturalcounseling.org): Provides a significant amount of resources for clients and counselors in advancing racial and ethnic issues across the globe.

American Counseling Association Action Center (https://www.votervoice.net/COUNSELING/Home): Provides advocacy and survey tools for counselors to contact elected officials about important issues facing the counseling profession.

Corporation for National and Community Service (http://www.nationalservice.gov): A federal agency that provides and coordinates services for communities in the United States.

Counselors for Social Justice (http://www.counseling-csj.org): A division of the American Counseling Association that promotes social justice in the counseling profession and society. Resources are available for counselors.

GLSEN: The Gay, Lesbian, and Straight Education Network (http://www.glsen.org): Advocacy group for LGBT issues in K–12 schools across the country. Tool kits and multiple resources are available for school counselors and anyone working with youths in schools.

GovTrack (http://www.govtrack.us): This Web site provides access to information about governments and the voting records of elected officials.

Human Rights Campaign (www.hrc.org): The largest LGBT civil rights group, with over 1.5 million members. Information and advocacy tools are provided.

Jobs with Justice (www.jwj.org/): A leading organization that provides advocacy and organizing tools for workers' rights.

National Alliance on Mental Illness (http://www.nami.org/): The largest mental health advocacy organization in the United States. This site provides a lot of information regarding current legislation that may affect mental health and discusses multiple ways to get involved.

(Continued)

TABLE 3.4   Selected Web Resources (Continued)

National Coalition for the Homeless (www.nationalhomeless.org): Provides multiple resources and opportunities to advocate for and assist the homeless in the United States.

The National Organization for Women (NOW) (www.now.org): A grassroots advocacy group that focuses on women's rights.

Rape, Abuse, Incest National Network (www.rainn.org): One of the largest anti–sexual violence advocacy groups in the United States. Information for clients that may need help as well as ways to volunteer is listed.

Teaching Tolerance: A Project of the Southern Poverty Law Center (www.tolerance.org): Provides information and tool kits for teachers and schools to help in reducing discrimination and increasing tolerance in schools.

United Nations International Children's Emergency Fund (UNICEF) (www.unicef.org): One of the largest advocacy groups that assists in providing equal rights for children. This Web site has a multitude of information and resources available for counselors.

Universal Declaration of Human Rights (www.un.org/en/documents/udhr): Access to the full copy of the declaration.

World Health Organization (http://www.who.int): One of the largest organizations that fights for the well-being of humans across the world.

Summary

If counselors are going to be agents of change for the prevention of emotional disorders in society, then they must jettison the notion of neutrality in counseling and begin to intervene for change on all levels. Social justice counseling focuses on the fact that both social and economic forces are powerful influences on how people and our society develop. The differences in power that we see in the world are a result of oppression that exists across multiple groups and different levels of society. Oppression, in turn, gives some groups privilege over others, resulting in an inverse relationship between oppression and privilege for a person or group. A person's awareness of privilege and oppression is a complex cyclical process that develops not only in response to external factors but also in response to one's perception and internalization of external factors. The visibility or invisibility of various external factors also influences the processes of internalization and awareness.

One key goal of social justice counseling is the empowerment of clients on all levels (e.g.,

individual, community). Empowerment is the process by which people or organizations that are oppressed become aware of the power differential in their life and then learn and exercise the skills necessary to control their lives without being oppressed and without oppressing other groups.

The relationship between oppression and the mental health of marginalized groups was identified through the U.S. Department of Health and Human Services (2001) report on mental health. The report linked discrimination and oppression experienced by marginalized groups to a greater risk of emotional disturbance and illness. The report helped the counseling profession's viewpoint of multiculturalism evolve from just promoting cultural sensitivity and understanding to exploring how oppression creates poor conditions for certain groups. Counselors must actively promote change in power dynamics, in addition to promoting multicultural awareness, tolerance, and understanding.

Counselors should be aware of the social justice advocacy competencies for counseling professionals that span multiple levels of advocacy across six domains. These advocacy competencies require social action by the counselor on behalf of the client, in addition to personal counselor participation in social action. A three-tiered model of advocacy was created for counselors to view social justice issues on two fronts—client advocacy and professional advocacy—and across three tiers: self-awareness, client services, and community collaboration. Self-aware counselors should be able to identify and discuss the privileged and oppressed groups they belong to, as well as have a sense of professional pride and identity. Client services involve the process of empowering oppressed clients and providing privileged clients an ability to become more self-aware. Community collaboration involves counselors engaging at the institutional and societal levels for change that would affect oppressed clients.

While counselors engaged in social justice counseling face multiple challenges (e.g.,

harassment, burnout, isolation, difficulty integrating traditional theoretical counseling models), many benefits can be gained from social justice advocacy (e.g., personal satisfaction from empowering oppressed clients, personal growth, a more just society).

If the counseling profession wants to create meaningful change in the prevention of mental disorders, the disequilibrium of power that causes oppression and privilege must be confronted. Counselors are the leaders of the fourth wave—the multicultural movement that is sweeping the helping professions—and are once again positioned to bring about a fifth wave in the profession: social advocacy counseling. If social and economic power that breeds oppression is directly challenged and altered, emotional disorders across our society and the world will be significantly reduced. Counselors have the opportunity to make a serious impact on the mental health of people all over the world.

Review Questions

1. Compare and contrast the MSJCC and ACA Advocacy Competencies.
2. Discuss the relationship between oppression and the mental health of individuals from marginalized groups.
3. Give examples of interventions in the following domains in the ACA Advocacy Competencies for counseling professionals: (a) client/student empowerment, (b) client/student advocacy, (c) community collaboration, (d) systems advocacy, (e) public information, and (f) social–political advocacy. Discuss why you selected the particular intervention you did and how you think it will be effective in that specific domain.
4. Compare and contrast the two community collaboration frameworks.
5. Discuss how oppression and privilege can coexist for a client.

4

Racism and White Privilege

Danica G. Hays and Ann Shillingford-Butler

PREVIEW

Racism and associated racial privilege is one of the prominent social justice issues in the counseling profession today. In this chapter, we define racism and White privilege and provide examples of how they have been perpetuated throughout history and continue to pervade society, affecting health in general and mental health specifically. Costs for both people of color and Whites are discussed, and strategies for eradicating racism are provided.

HISTORICAL FOUNDATIONS OF RACE AND RACISM

Being exposed to, reflecting on, and discussing racism and White privilege is a challenging task. For Whites, reading about these concepts and ways in which they manifest themselves in U.S. society can incite confusion, anger, guilt, frustration, and sadness, perhaps all at the same time. Because of these emotions, it may be tempting to forgo learning more about racism and White privilege or take some personal ownership for perpetuating it. For people of color, these topics can reopen old wounds and create new ones, stimulating emotions similar to those of Whites but for different reasons. We encourage you to be open to the material in this chapter; it will challenge you in different ways and, depending on other aspects of your cultural identity, it will resonate with you in different ways. Thus, this material may be difficult to integrate into your worldview. As you read the material in the chapter, we hope that you will consider how the concepts presented arise and appear in your everyday life and whether you find examples of racism and White privilege in yourself, in your family and peers, within the media, or in government policies, educational institutions, the workplace, and so on. We also hope that you will consider how you may be intentionally or unintentionally perpetuating the status quo through your actions and inactions.

Sue (2013) described fears expressed by White students and faculty during conversations of race, racism, and White privilege—conversations referred to as "race talk." Among such fears are the fear of appearing racist, realizing one's racism, confronting White privilege, and taking responsibility to end racism. These are common fears expressed particularly in more in-depth race-related conversations. We hope that White students reflect on such fears and how they may manifest themselves in the counseling relationship. For students of color who are training to become counselors, we hope that understanding these fears can in some way help put into context some of the potential challenges they may face with peers and White clients in the future.

To extend your knowledge, Table 4.3, presented at the end of the chapter, provides several resources to help you achieve a better understanding of White privilege and how to address racism.

Individuals are routinely asked to identify their race on school and employment applications, state and federal documents, and even church and local advocacy group membership forms. The complexity of race is often simplified and masked by everyday social tasks and perceived physical and human differences. Race can appear to be innate and concrete, rather than an ascribed human characteristic used to categorize human beings into subgroups (Byng, 2012; Feagin, 2014; Graves, 2015). Racial "differences" are largely a result of genetic drift, isolation, the effect of temperature on mean body size, and the interaction between geography and biology (e.g., the production of melanin as a biological adaptation of those with lighter skin tones in latitudes that receive less sunlight, the development of sickle cell disease as an adaptive response to living in malaria-prone regions; Feagin, 2014; Graves, 2015). However, such physical distinctions among individuals have served as a method for classifying those individuals and mistakenly assigning complex traits, such as musical ability, intelligence, and athleticism, to name a few biological markers. These racial classifications are so ingrained in our psyche that we believe that physical differences are a natural justification, and evidence for, the existence of racial differences.

When two people who have lived in a society with an institutionalized racial classification system (e.g., the United States) meet for the first time, visual cues such as skin color, apparent hair texture, and eye color initiate an automatic cognitive process that results in their perceived racial identification of each other (Feagin, 2014). Auditory cues, including dialectical and vernacular information, are used similarly to place people into particular racial groups. For example, have you ever called a customer service phone line and almost immediately assumed the race of the customer service representative on the basis of his or her accent or manner of speech? Because race can be defined as the subjective interpretation of individual physical characteristics or human differences, there are almost automatic beliefs we hold about our own race as well as others'. Reflection 4.1 offers some considerations related to our beliefs concerning our own racial membership or memberships.

Although it is confused with ethnicity, **race** implies a "common descent of heredity" (Cameron & Wycoff, 1998, p. 278), whereas **ethnicity** involves cultural characteristics (e.g., rituals, a work ethic, social mores, and values). Race has often been erroneously associated with biological distinctions among groups of individuals. That is, the notion exists that members of a given race would most likely have very minimal genetic differences. Scientific studies, however, support the idea that race refers to a common ancestry. By contrast, ethnicity, as it relates to cultural practices and commonalities (e.g., customs, language), is attributed to individuals from particular regions. For example, an individual who self-identifies as Black is telegraphing that he or she belongs to the Black race. However, this individual's ethnicity may be African American, West Indian, or even African, exhibiting different cultural customs and social norms. Nonetheless, the concepts of race and ethnicity often overlap and are used synonymously in discussions of culture, with the result that individuals group (often erroneously)

REFLECTION 4.1

What are some things you like about being a member of your race or races? What are some things you dislike about it? How do you think your life would be different if you were a member of other races?

various ethnicities into the same racial category even though an ethnicity can contain several "races." In addition, some individuals fail to acknowledge their ethnicity because of the salient, privileged status of their racial category (e.g., White). Reflection 4.2 provides space for thinking about ethnicity, particularly how it relates to race.

REFLECTION 4.2

With which ethnicity or ethnicities do you identify? How does your identified ethnicity relate to your racial group membership or memberships? List the values and traditions that you associate with your combined racial and ethnic heritages:

_____

_____

_____

_____

Review your list of values and traditions associated with being a member of your race and ethnicity. How might your racial and ethnic heritage influence your work with clients?

_____

_____

_____

_____

Traditionally, for the U.S. federal government, racial categories are not biologically based, but rather represent social constructs used for collecting data on race and ethnicity (Office of Management and Budget [OMB], 1997). The OMB, within the Executive Office of the President of the United States, provides the *Standards for the Classification of Federal Data on Race and Ethnicity*:

> Development of the data standards stemmed in large measure from new responsibilities to enforce civil rights laws. Data were needed to monitor equal access in housing, education, employment, and other areas, for populations that historically had experienced discrimination and differential treatment because of their race or ethnicity. . . . The standards have been developed to provide a common language for uniformity and comparability in the collection and use of data on race and ethnicity by Federal agencies. (OMB, 1997, p. 2)

Through these standards, the OMB designates a minimum of five racial categories—(a) American Indian or Alaskan Native, (b) Asian, (c) Black or African American, (d) Native Hawaiian or Other Pacific Islander, and (e) White—and two ethnic categories— (a) Hispanic or Latino and (b) Not Hispanic or Latino—that are to be used to collect federal information. The justification and categories provided by the OMB for the current racial classification system acknowledge historical social injustices related to race, without reference to the essential oppressive nature of the system itself (i.e., racism) enabled by the social construction of race. (Notice, however, that there is no category for Arab Americans, an ethnic group discussed in Section 3 of this text.)

Social Construction of Race

In Spanish, Portuguese, Italian, and French folklore prior to the 16th century, race was usually identified with a breeding line or stock of animals (Feagin, 2014). The primary definition of race began to change in the 16th century, when the term was used by Spanish writers as "one of several ways of referring to new populations discovered in their travels" (Smedley & Smedley, 2005, p. 39). Later the term *race* was adopted by other European settlers in the Americas, particularly the English, for whom "it generally denoted populations of differing origins in the heterogeneous mix of peoples" (p. 37). Smedley and Smedley asserted that "the term 'race' made possible an easy analogy of inheritable and unchangeable features from breeding animals to human beings" (p. 40).

Throughout history, we have seen race classified in various ways. Carl Linnaeus, a Swedish scientist and explorer, began the task, subdividing humans into four geographic regions (the Americas, Europe, Asia, and Africa); he further proposed that individuals exhibited different natures, depending on their predominant "fluid" (i.e., blood, phlegm, choler, and melancholy). In essence, humans from the four regions were described as obstinate, happy, and free (the Americas); white, optimistic, muscular, active, and intelligent (Europe); melancholy, stiff, and severe (Asia); and black, slow, foolish, and negligent (Africa). In the mid- to late 1770s, Johann Blumenbach, a German physician and anthropologist, expanded Linnaeus's classification system and coined the term *Caucasian* to describe White (European) people as possessing ideal beauty, on the basis of his belief that humans originated from the Caucasus Mountains in Russia and were created from "God's vision." He also labeled other racial groups as the "Mongolian variety" (East Asian inhabitants), "Ethiopian variety" (Africans), "American variety" (Native Americans), and "Malay variety" (Melanesians, Polynesians, and Australian Aboriginals; Feagin, 2014). Thus, early racial categorizations were quite Eurocentric and hinted at a rank order of races, with Whites or Europeans at the top, Asians and Native Americans in the middle, and Africans at the bottom. Other "scientific" methods for distinguishing races at the time included measuring skulls to indicate degree of intelligence (to attempt to demonstrate that European Americans had "superior intellect" and African Americans' brains were the most inferior) and examining blood quantum, in which "one drop" of African American or Native American blood was said to be predictive of lower intelligence (Feagin, 2014; Graves, 2015). Early racial classification systems based on physical characteristics paved the way for other forms of racism discussed in later sections of this chapter.

As described earlier, individual physical characteristics (e.g., the shape of one's nose) and human differences (e.g., how one talks) are often used as social criteria for the identification of race. These criteria are seemingly consistent with a genetic or biological foundation for race, in accordance with the origin of the word. Physical characteristics alone, however, are insufficient to make distinctions among people, for several reasons (Feagin, 2014; Graves, 2015). First, with early exploration and colonization, people of different ethnic backgrounds (i.e., different geographic regions, national origins, and cultures) reproduced multiethnic offspring that varied in their physical appearance. Individual ancestry, therefore, is responsible in part for the diversity that exists in the physical characteristics of individuals who identify with the same racial group. Alternatively, these same individuals may be perceived by others as either being or not being within the same racial group in accordance with those others' subjective interpretation of the physical characteristics of the individual. The use of physical characteristics to define race, then, is in large measure arbitrary. Second, genetic information is contrary to biological or physical definitions of race (Graves, 2015). The genetic makeup of all human beings in the world is nearly 100% identical, with more genetic variation occurring *within* so-called racial groups than *between* them. Only 0.1% of all human genes are responsible for individual differences such as physical appearance and the risk of disease. Finally, anthropological and genetic evidence indicate that (a) the earliest modern human fossils were found in Omo Kibish, Ethiopia; (b) the diversity of genetic markers is greatest within the African continent; and (c) the genetic makeup of all human beings is a subset of Africa's gene pool (Shreeve, 2006). On the basis of all these considerations, the physical, biological, or genetic definition of race is, therefore, unfounded. It is important to note that it was the scientific community as well—including anthropologists, psychologists, and others—that played perhaps the most prominent role in the justification of the concept of race and its associated ideologies of White superiority and the inferiority of all other "races," through self-serving theories and research motivated by social and political agendas (Graves, 2015).

Human differences in behavior are also better explained through social learning than inherent genetic or biophysical differences. Although classic research indicated that race plays a part in the identification of others within a society that uses a formal racial classification system, self–racial identification (i.e., racial identity) is essentially learned from the family (or primary caregivers) and the immediate social and cultural environment of the individual (Helms, 1995). The process of learning to identify oneself with a particular racial group and to make distinctions and associations among people on the basis of race is the result of indirect and direct racial socialization enabled and sustained by an institutionalized racial classification system known as racism.

Defining Racism

Physical buildings are designed and constructed for particular functions. A grocery store requires storage space and refrigeration. The concept of race, similarly, was created or constructed to serve a particular social function. Race and the original racial classification system were instituted by English colonists to ensure that the demand for agricultural labor would be met as transatlantic entrepreneurial markets emerged. That aim was accomplished by the establishment of a hierarchical system of oppression that exclusively granted basic human rights, social privileges, and prestige to individuals of European descent (Feagin, 2014). In the late 17th century,

> [c]olonists used the physical differences among various populations interacting in the New World to establish categories that were economically, socially, and politically unequal. The ideology homogenized a diverse assemblage of Europeans into a "White" category; subsumed peoples of varying cultures, religions, and languages from Africa into a "Negro" category; and meshed all indigenous peoples together as "Indians." (Smedley & Smedley, 2005, p. 181)

Native Americans, or American Indians, the original inhabitants and cultivators of the land and society in North America, had their land and resources stolen or destroyed, and their tribespeople killed, in the violent conquests and wars that were waged by the English colonists to dominate and control the people and the land. American Indians, and Africans captured and transported to the first American colony in Jamestown, Virginia, were the most disenfranchised in terms of their access to, and participation in, the emerging English civilization and had the least resources to protect themselves or to appeal for protection of the government.

(Indeed, they needed protection *from* the government.) Without legislative representation or economic power, American Indians and Africans had no voice in the establishment of the oppressive, alien government that created laws making them slaves for life on the basis of the "new" concept of race. Africans were particularly vulnerable, given their absence of political power and easily identifiable brown skin, and suffered the chronic traumatization of being captured, held hostage, and being brutalized, enslaved, and forcibly acculturated into an unfamiliar social system (Feagin, 2014).

Racism is an ongoing, multidimensional, and dynamic process inherent in the development and maintenance of an institutionalized, hierarchical racial classification system (Byng, 2012; Feagin, 2014). It operates simultaneously on individual, group, and system levels and involves intentional and unintentional negative, erroneous, or stereotypical beliefs about race and the consequences of actions (e.g., interpersonal behavior, public policy decisions). The use of racial classifications in all institutions of society (e.g., family, schools, employment, government) results in the socialization of a racial worldview for all its members. A **racial worldview** is a defining cultural characteristic in that individuals and groups perceive and understand each other through this socially constructed prism that will be transmitted to succeeding generations. The process of racism engineers a racial worldview that is securely fastened to the cognitions of all members of a society, initially without their detection or protest. Like other process-defined systems, racism is built to maintain itself (Feagin, 2014). The components of the system are individuals who are actively (e.g., lobbying to eliminate affirmative action policies) and passively (e.g., ignoring racist comments by a colleague) complicit in the reinforcement of racial worldview structures (e.g., prejudices, discrimination, racial inequities) through intentional (e.g., voting, gentrification, employment practices) and unintentional (e.g., obliviousness to the absence of workplace diversity) actions. The preservation and perpetuation of racism enabled by a racial worldview and an institutionalized racial classification system continues to serve its initial purpose: to give unmerited social power to European descendants and to thwart meaningful human connections between diverse peoples—connections based on trust, understanding, and solidarity. Hope lies in the parallel process of racial identity development, driven, ironically, by both racism and a racial worldview. The process matures with a commitment to dismantle the structures, internal and external, of racism and to develop relationships with like-minded allies.

Jones (2000) identified three levels of racism: individual (i.e., personally mediated), institutional, and internalized. These levels intersect and influence one another and may be covert or overt and unintentional or intentional. Reflection 4.3 provides an opportunity to consider how the three levels of racism may affect professional counselors' work with clients. **Individual racism** refers to personal attitudes and beliefs in White superiority and the inferiority of people of color, with physical differences among individuals used as an explanation of social, moral, and intellectual behavior. It involves adverse behavior by one individual or a small group of people. Examples are racial slurs and stereotyping. Jones further defined personally mediated racism as "prejudice and discrimination, where prejudice means differential assumptions about the abilities, motives, and intentions of others according to their race, and discrimination means differential actions toward others according to their race" (p. 1213).

Institutional racism is defined as "differential access to the goods, services, and opportunities of society by race" (Jones, 2000, p. 1212). The term **structural racism**, closely related to, and often used interchangeably with, institutional racism, emphasizes that the oppression of racial and ethnic groups, originating with the social construction of race and racial classification systems, is organized by institutional, cultural, and social structures (i.e., components of

---

REFLECTION 4.3

Identify overt and covert, and intentional and unintentional, forms of racism that may affect your work with clients of color.

Individual: _____

_____

_____

Institutional/Structural: _____

_____

_____

Internalized: _____

_____

_____

Cultural: _____

_____

_____

---

institutions) that create and maintain racial inequities. Gee and Ford (2011) use the metaphor of an iceberg to illustrate structural racism:

> The tip of the iceberg represents acts of racism, such as cross-burnings, that are easily seen and individually mediated. The portion of the iceberg that lies below the water represents structural racism; it is more dangerous and harder to eliminate. Policies and interventions that change the iceberg's tip may do little to change its base, resulting in structural inequalities that remain intact, though less detectable. (p. 117)

Comparative research demonstrates that policies, procedures, laws, and even physical structures that are governed by international, federal, state, and local institutions, both public and private, directly, if not intentionally, contribute to disparate social outcomes for people of color in the United States. Structural racism can be attributed to health inequities among racial minorities (Gee & Ford, 2011; Sondik, Huang, Klein, & Satcher, 2010); disproportionate rates of suspension, expulsion, and corporal punishment for African-American males compared with their White American peers (Feagin, 2014); and disproportionate representation of children of color in the child welfare system (Feagin, 2014; Miller & Ward, 2008).

Internalized racism refers to members of marginalized groups believing and accepting, knowingly or unknowingly, negative social messages about their own racial and ethnic groups. Self-devaluation and the lionization of White American culture as normal and preferable are indicators of internalized racism. **Cultural racism** involves the belief that the cultural values and practices of individuals of White, European descent are superior to those of other racial groups. Self-devaluation and the lionization of White American culture as normal are consequences of cultural racism. The values associated with institutional/structural racism, internalized racism, and cultural racism may also be evident in things such as art, economics, religion, and language. A few examples of institutional and cultural forms of racism throughout U.S. history are listed in Table 4.1. These levels of racism have several detrimental cognitive, affective, interpersonal, and physical costs for people of color.

TABLE 4.1 Examples of Institutional and Cultural Forms of Racism in U.S. History

Naturalization Law (1790)	Excluded Asians and Native Americans from gaining citizenship.
Indian Removal Act (1830)	This congressional act mandated the removal of American Indians from east of the Mississippi River to territory west of the Mississippi.
Manifest Destiny (mid- to late 1800s)	Belief that the United States was destined to expand to the Pacific Ocean. Right of discovery of Western lands outweighed Native Americans' right of occupancy of their lands. This form of racism led to the concept of the "White Man's Burden," perpetuated as the title of Rudyard Kipling's infamous poem in which he saw Whites as exercising their power to "civilize" others. White people in the Western world internalized this viewpoint, to the detriment of people of color everywhere.
People v. Hall (1854)	Supreme Court decision in which George W. Hall was acquitted of the murder of a Chinese man because it was ruled that three of the witnesses who were Chinese could not, by law, testify against Whites.
Dred Scott Decision (1857)	A decision handed down by the U.S. Supreme Court ruling that African slaves could not become free citizens. Dred Scott, a freed slave of a U.S. Army officer, had sued for his freedom. The decision stated that U.S. citizenship could not be granted to any African descendant, freed or enslaved. The decision was a major catalyst for the Civil War, because it also declared unconstitutional the Missouri Compromise, a law stating that slavery could not spread north past a particular boundary of lands gained in the Louisiana Compromise.
Boarding School Movement (1870s)	Program used to assimilate Native American children into the mainstream educational system. The program isolated them from their families, subjected them to emotional and physical abuse when they tried to retain their culture, forced them to work in underfunded schools, and mandated that they change their names and appearance to conform to Western or White culture.
Indian Appropriation Act (1871)	Congress specified that no tribe thereafter would be recognized as an independent nation with which the federal government could make a treaty. All future Indian policies would not be negotiated with Indian tribes through treaties, but rather would be determined by passing congressional statutes or executive orders.
Jim Crow Laws (1876–1965)	Enacted a "separate but equal" status for African Americans in U.S. southern and border states. These laws required separate facilities (e.g., public schools, public transportation) for Whites and African Americans, limiting civil liberties for African Americans.

(*Continued*)

TABLE 4.1 Examples of Institutional and Cultural Forms of Racism in U.S. History (Continued)

Chinese Exclusion Act (1882)	This law limited Chinese immigration after many were fearful that Chinese Americans were hurting the U.S. economy.
Eugenics Movement (1883)	Concept coined by Francis Galton which asserted that scientific progress could be sustained only by racial "purification" and that the "superior" race (i.e., Whites) was endangered, so selective breeding was necessary to keep the race "pure" (Turner & Collinson, 2003).
Dawes Act (1887)	Driven by those who believed that reservations limited integration and progress, Congress allowed the president to allot Native American heads of families 160 acres of a certain reservation, although many tribes were excluded from this act. "Excess" lands were designated for Whites to build schools for "education and civilization" (Takaki, 2002, p. 234). The federal government was to hold title to the land in trust for 25 years. The Dawes Act was one of several that Congress passed to assimilate Native Americans and expand U.S. territory to the west.
Indian Reorganization Act (1934)	This act encouraged Indians to "recover" their culture and sought to promote tribal self-government by encouraging tribes to adopt U.S.-style constitutions and form federally chartered corporations. Many tribes rejected the act, most fearing the consequences of more government control.
War on Drugs (1971)	Campaign initiated to enforce stricter laws on drug use and sales. However, minority populations have been disproportionately targeted with high arrest and incarceration rates, particularly in low-income urban communities.
Zero Tolerance (1994)	This model of discipline resulted in Blacks, Latino youths, and children from low-income minorities becoming at greater risk for the school-to-prison pipeline. Schools enforced punishments through suspensions and expulsions that drastically affected students of color. Black students were three times as likely as Whites to be suspended; Latinos were almost twice as likely.
Glass Ceiling Commission (1995)	Found that Asian Americans were being paid far less than Whites in most occupations.
California Proposition 227 (1998)	Sought to establish English as the only legitimate language in schools and the workplace.
Bank Redlining (2000s)	Discriminatory practice by banks to avoid lending to minority communities. Numerous lawsuits were filed in 2014, with recoveries of up to $33 million.
Arizona Profiling (2010)	The state of Arizona declared that police have the right to check the immigration status of any individual whom they suspect of being in the United States illegally. Many Mexican Americans have experienced discrimination via profiling because of this practice.

Historically, racism has been associated with varied levels of injustice and has been identified as the culprit in the disintegration of identities such as gender and sexual orientation. For example, race and racism have received much scrutiny as factors contributing to organizational inequalities based on gender differences of employees. Women of color have especially been victims of gender-based racism (Shillingford, Trice-Black, & Butler, 2013; Hirshfield & Joseph, 2012). In fact, Shillingford and colleagues indicated that, in academia, women of color experience injustices such as feeling invisible, alienated, and demoralized solely because of their gender and race. Racial differences have also affected the lived experiences of sexual minorities. Though not widely explored in research, race does seem to play a role in incidents of bullying and reports of bullying of sexual minorities. For example, being White and male is associated with selecting sexual minorities as targets for bullying (Paceley & Flynn, 2012).

COSTS OF RACISM FOR PEOPLE OF COLOR

Just as a part of your everyday experience, imagine wondering whether you were overlooked or ignored in a store; whether people were staring at you in a restaurant; whether someone discounted a comment that you made; or whether you did not get a job, appropriate medical or legal advice, a bank loan, an apartment lease, or a reasonable interest rate on a car loan, all because of your race. Experiences like these cause anxiety and guardedness because discriminatory social rules are not explicit, nor are individuals who participate in discrimination against people of color typically able to recognize their prejudicial behavior, because systemic injustices validate and normalize their actions (Byng, 2012; Feagin, 2014).

Racism is an inescapable reality for people of color in the United States. The imprint of racism is historically rooted in the social structure (i.e., laws, traditions, customs) of the United States and lives within its social systems (e.g., occupational, educational, judicial; Gee & Ford, 2011). Racism, therefore, is a complex and dynamic form of social oppression that fundamentally affects the daily lives of people of color. The effects of racism essentially amount to quality-of-life costs imposed on people of color within an oppressive system. Consequently, racism has associated cognitive, affective, interpersonal, and physical costs for people of color. After reviewing each of these costs, complete Activity 4.1 to identify unique expressions or consequences of racism for racial and ethnic minorities. Also, review Case Study 4.1 to examine how these costs may affect Jacob, depicted there.

ACTIVITY 4.1

In dyads, list below as many costs of racism for people of color as you can. Consider costs as they relate to daily lived experiences in families, schools, workplaces, communities, and society in general. After you create the list of costs, consider how these costs may differ for various racial minorities. Why do you think that such differences might exist?

Cognitive Costs:

_____

_____

_____

Affective Costs:

_____

_____

_____

Interpersonal Costs:

_____

_____

_____

Physical Costs:

_____

_____

_____

CASE STUDY 4.1

Consider the potential costs of racism associated with following case study:

Jacob is an 11-year-old African-American male living in an impoverished community characterized by high crime rates relative to those of nearby communities. He has been suspended several times this school year for physical fights, possession of marijuana, and truancy. Because of his missed school days, he is performing poorly academically. Recently, his teacher noticed that Jacob had two knives. Jacob seems to have some friends at school and socializes primarily with older students of color.

When you discuss with Jacob the concerns you have about him, he appears resistant to speaking with you. You also have difficulty contacting his parents.

- As a counselor, how might racism play a factor in Jacob's life, if at all?
- How would you intervene with Jacob, his parents, and other school personnel?

Cognitive Costs

The cognitive costs of racism include the mental energy and psychological processes (e.g., assessing, reflecting, questioning, interpreting) used to evaluate life incidents and experiences in which racism might be involved. An individual's perception and understanding of racism is related to his or her racial identity development. People of color who are at earlier stages of racial identity development assess, interpret, and cope differently with racism-implicated life events (e.g., racial profiling) than those who are in later stages.

During the process of racial identity development, an inevitable question that effectively sums up the cognitive costs of racism emerges in the minds of people of color: Did this happen to me (or others who share my racial classification) because of my (or their) race? This question usually comes to life as a result of an ambiguous cross-racial incident, or a potentially racism-related life experience, which causes people of color to think or feel that they may have been treated differentially, unfairly, or disrespectfully because of their race. The question develops into a cognitive filter that is used to assess subsequent cross-racial situations as well as social experiences in general. A person of color, then, is left to reflect on her or his daily interactions, situations, and behaviors, and those reflections produce a general psychological vigilance in cross-racial interactions that taxes the mind, body, and spirit (Sue, Capodilupo, et al., 2007). Thus, social evaluation is necessary for people of color, yet contains many cognitive costs. Worse, generalized negative thinking as a result of experiences with racism can create additional costs, such as chronic anxiety, lowered self-esteem, a pessimistic outlook, and lack of motivation.

A salient cognitive cost for people of color is internalized racism, as described earlier. Internalized racism supports the belief in White superiority and White values and culture as normative for people of color. In essence, people of color discount the value of their individual, institutional, and cultural contributions to society and engage in self-hatred. This attitude may lead them to deny their racial heritage or isolate themselves from their racial group. Internalized racism can create cognitive dissonance in that, as people of color increasingly introject ideals characteristic of Whites and ignore the values of their own group, they may find that they do not belong in either group.

Affective Costs

By-products (i.e., cognitive costs) of psychological vigilance include frustration, irritation, and hostility, which are antecedents of anger and, possibly, depression. Similarly, emotional responses may be triggered outright by unintentional and intentional racist acts or covert and overt institutionalized forms of racism. Direct links have been noted between racial discrimination and mental health concerns such as depression, somatization, anxiety, and even posttraumatic stress disorder (Pieterse, Todd, Neville, & Carter, 2012). In fact, Pieterse and colleagues suggested that increased experiences with racism may present in the form of trauma-related traits. Prolonged exposure to racism was also determined to be predictive of heightened psychological distress leading to high blood pressure and other physical ailments (Singleton, Robertson, & Robinson, 2008). In light of the psychological effects of racism, emotional awareness of racism can be a beneficial tool for people of color, because affective cues provide information within social situations that can be used for self-preservation, self-protection, and empowerment.

The emotional costs of racism accompany racism-related stress (Feagin, 2014). As described earlier, the psychological exercises that a structural system of racism produces set the stage for hypervigilance or psychological stress. When a person of color perceives that vigilance is necessary, that perception can lead to anger, disappointment, and sadness. Such emotions inevitably develop in people of color in the process of their racial identity development and understanding of racism.

People of color experience historical and generational emotional costs of racism as well. Within specific families and racially classified groups in the United States, the emotional costs of racism can be transmitted through generations, given their particular histories and experiences with racism. Children of parents who have experienced racial discrimination, for example, can sense and take on the emotional resonance of those experiences. This phenomenon can happen either directly or indirectly, even if the parents desire to shield their children from the harmful experiences or deliberately try not to transmit negative messages to their offspring. Other parents, educators, or adults, conversely, may be emphatic in *sharing* their experiences with their children, either to help protect, educate, and empower them or because of their own unresolved racism-related issues or diffuse parent–child boundaries. In either case, the emotional resonance that accompanies historical experiences of racism within families or racially classified groups factors into the individual emotional responses that people of color have to racism.

Finally, emotional costs are associated with overt manifestations of racism, such as racial slurs, direct references to skin color, or culturally ubiquitous racial stereotypes (e.g., media portrayals of people of color). Occurrences such as these, expectedly, rouse an emotional response in many people of color. The principal distinction possessed by racial offenses, however, is that these incidents have historical and cultural implications that demean the individual or his or her family, culture, ancestry, and history, as well as all other people who identify with the person's racial classification.

Interpersonal Costs

The interpersonal costs of racism are perhaps the most visible and concrete of all the costs of racism described. Most people in the United States grow up in parts of cities, communities, neighborhoods, schools, and places of worship that are physically as well as functionally segregated. The segregation of people by racial classification as a result of institutional racism presents a social, even physical, barrier to the establishment of meaningful relationships between people from different racial groups. Social segregation creates an environment for misinformation, misunderstanding, and miscommunication between White people and people of color, as well as between different groups of people of color. It places barriers to, and limitations on, the development of cross-racial relationships, perpetuates racism and discrimination, and maintains social inequities.

Interpersonal costs are, therefore, "fixed" in a social system of racial oppression. Specifically, the social structure that preserves dominant and subordinate groups does not support the development of trust between those groups, between different oppressed groups, and even between members of the same oppressed group (Byng, 2012). As a result, people of color are often ambivalent about developing relationships with members of the "dominant group," including Whites. At the same time, internalized racism contributes to intergroup and intragroup relational discord among people of color. The interpersonal costs of internalized racism, then, are fear, suspicion, and distrust, even between and among people of color, who are similarly oppressed in a racist society.

Physical Costs

Distinctions made among mind, spirit, and body are largely conceptual, in that they are used for identification, explanation, and other functional purposes. It is understood, therefore, that the effects of racism are experienced not only cognitively, affectively, and interpersonally, but physically as well. The physical costs of racism relate specifically to associated physical and physiological symptoms and consequences experienced by people of color: hypertension, chronic fatigue, delivery of low-birth-weight preterm infants, and physical violence, among others (Peters, 2004; U.S. Department of Health and Human Services [USDHHS], 2001). Physical costs of racism also include outcomes related to health care. An Institute of Medicine (IOM, 2002) report concluded that "minority patients [people of color] are less likely than Whites to receive the same quality of healthcare, even when they have similar insurance or the ability to pay for care. To make matters worse, this healthcare gap is linked with higher death rates among minorities" (p. 2). In this chapter, the review of the physical costs of racism cannot be concluded without mentioning recent incidents related to racial discrimination and the deaths of several people of color at the hands of police officers and, by implication, the American justice system.

Over the past few years, Black communities across the United States have railed against what is considered to be profound injustices leading to several documented deaths. In 2012, Trayvon Martin, a 17-year-old Black youth, was gunned down in Sanford, Florida; his killer was found not guilty by reason of self-defense. Eighteen-year-old Michael Brown, an unarmed African American youth, was killed by a police officer in Ferguson, Missouri; the officer was later cleared of any civil rights violations. In 2014, Eric Garner, an African American residing in Staten Island, New York, was killed by a choke hold by police officers. The Nation echoed Mr. Garner's last cries for help, "I can't breathe," as an indication of Black people's frustrations at unfair and unjust implicit profiling of people of color. The list of young Black men and women losing their lives has increased since then, causing mayhem across political arenas, news media, and residential communities all over America.

Efforts to Combat the Costs of Racism

So far in this chapter, we have tried to present the history of racism, as well as the disturbing, often deadly effects it has on people of color. Minority populations, however, are resilient, rising above injustice and advocating for fairness and impartiality. For example, the **Black Lives Matter** movement was developed as a grassroots effort to bring light to the killings and other recognized racial injustices in Black communities across America. In addition, the **Congress of Racial Equality** (2017) has been working to promote the social, political, and economic well-being of minority populations since 1942. The group focuses on creating solutions to difficult problems that underprivileged individuals may face. The **National Council of La Raza** (2014) was established in 1968 and continues to serve as an advocacy sounding board for the betterment of Latinos in the United States. This organization is directly involved with Latino communities and works toward the social, political, and economical progression of their people. Further, the **American Civil Liberties Union** (ACLU, 2017) has been a long-standing figure in the fight for justice for disenfranchised groups; ACLU causes include human rights, immigration rights, and racial rights. The ACLU highlights the U.S. Constitution as its guiding principle in providing equality and liberty for all. This brief list of grassroots advocacy groups is a small sample that represents the efforts being made to protect and empower people of color. Communities, families, and individuals are continuing the struggle daily to create a better future for the next generation.

WHITE PRIVILEGE

Imagine if you never had to think about what it is like to be a member of your race. You go through your day with academic, social, and career opportunities that seem natural to you, surrounded by people who look like you and share similar histories as you. You choose not to notice that racism exists because, in your daily life, you do not feel affected by it. You do not think about racism because you cannot recall significant experiences, like those described thus far in this chapter, in which you were discriminated against because of your race. In fact, you may sometimes have had advantages over others of different races. You are not concerned with being ignored in a store or restaurant, or being feared or thought of as a criminal because of your race. You may feel comforted by your skin color, but still may feel guilt and sadness regarding the access and status your race affords you. And one of the greatest advantages is that you can speak about race without incurring any penalty. This cluster of advantages is common for Whites and is known as **White privilege**.

Although many scholars discuss racism as a White problem (e.g., Knowles & Lowery, 2012; Sue, 2013; Todd & Abrams, 2011), White privilege is the "other side of the coin" that typically receives little attention in the discussion of racism. White privilege encompasses the positive ways that Whites benefit from racism. Oftentimes, these benefits or privileges are unintentional and unconscious. White privilege is related to the idea of **White supremacy**, the belief that the superiority of Whites justifies their disproportionate access to social and economic resources:

> [It] is the belief that only one's standards and opinions are accurate . . . and that these standards and opinions are defined and supported by Whites in a way to continually reinforce social distance between groups, thereby allowing Whites to dominate, control access to, and escape challenges from racial and ethnic minorities. (Hays & Chang, 2003, p. 135)

Peggy McIntosh (1988) wrote the classic and highly cited work on White privilege wherein she described 46 conditions of unearned advantages of having White skin color. These advantages include individual experiences (e.g., favorable situations in stores and job interviews, and not experiencing discrimination in daily living), institutional advantages (e.g., a positive portrayal in the media, adequate housing, and educational opportunities), access to things representative of culture, and the ability to avoid or ignore cultural contributions of other racial/ethnic groups.

Having racial privilege is like having an "invisible weightless knapsack of special provisions, assurances, tools, maps, guides, codebooks, passports, visas, clothes, compass, emergency gear, and blank checks" (McIntosh, 1988, p. 77). Racial privilege embraces unearned advantages based on being constructed as White. Many of these advantages are derived from a history of Whites implementing individual, institutional, and cultural racism, dating back to when Columbus "discovered" America. Because race may be invisible to Whites, it is imperative to reflect on one's early memories of being a member of a particular racial group or racial groups. Consider the questions in Reflection 4.4, and then read "Early Memories of Whiteness and White Privilege," provided in Table 4.2.

REFLECTION 4.4

Describe a specific memory or critical incident when you first realized that you were a member of your race. Who was involved in the experience? What thoughts, feelings, or behaviors did you note from the experience? What thoughts, feelings, or behaviors do you note now as you remember the incident?

Additional characteristics of White privilege include the following:

• *White privilege is often invisible to Whites.* Given the advantages received based on lighter skin tones and other physical features associated with Whiteness, it might seem that White privilege would be more visible to Whites. Whites engage in interracial interactions daily, yet they do not experience prejudice or discrimination from people of color.

TABLE 4.2 Early Memories of Whiteness and White Privilege

The following are quotes from counseling students as they reflected on their earliest memories of being a member of the White race:

"When asked to recall my earliest memory of being a member of my race, I was unable to come up with a specific event. I think that this is because I am White and I have always gone to school in White communities and I always remember being a part of the majority . . . The fact that I don't have a major event that comes to mind when remembering my race demonstrated that, because I am White, I am oblivious to recognizing that I had White privilege." (28-year-old White female)

"My first recollection of identifying with the White race was at age 8. I had a really good friend who was African American, and she invited me to her birthday party one weekend. I was the only White kid there; however, I did not think anything of it. At first, I had not noticed differences of skin color. Everyone was having a great time until one of my friend's cousins said 'who invited the white hoagie?' At that moment, I realized that I had different skin color from everyone at the party. I did not realize that skin color played such an important part in our society until my parents explained it later." (23-year-old White male)

"My first memory of discovering my race was in third grade. . . . I was not in a complete bubble and knew that Black people existed. However, I never had contact with a Black person. . . . I made the transition to the public school system. . . . I noticed things were 'different.' There were kids who had a different skin color than mine. I recall being afraid of them and found many of these kids to be rather rambunctious. . . . One time I dreamed that people from the library were painting me black and it would not come off." (39-year-old White female)

"One specific interaction I had with an African-American classmate in second grade has always stuck with me. After I had asked him to come over for a play date, he responded with something like 'Does your mom let Black people come to your house?' In the midst of my confusion, I remember literally glancing down at my arms, then looking back at his face—a silent pause that brought about some sort of awkward awareness to the differences of our skin color. I unfortunately didn't give much thought to this experience until later in my development, but we enjoyed a game of catch later that day nonetheless." (27-year-old White male)

"Growing up in the South in the 1940s and 1950s, I knew that I was privileged because I was White. My dad took me with him to pick up farm machinery shipped by train. Our little town's depot had 'colored' restrooms and 'colored' drinking fountains . . . Even at 8 or 9 years of age, I knew that something was not quite right about the treatment of 'colored' people. My parents never questioned the situation and became disturbed with me in high school when I professed to believe in the civil rights movement." (65-year-old White female)

"My earliest memory about being White was in first grade. I attended an elementary school located in the southwestern corner of Arizona and, naturally, many of my classmates were Mexican American. One day, to my surprise, a Mexican boy kissed me on the playground! I remember that my father became upset after hearing about the incident and tried to teach me 'self-defense' skills. What I took away from his response was the belief that there were 'others'— that is, people who were racially different from me—that I needed to be protected from. It made me feel *different.*" (29-year-old female)

"I grew up in a bubble. I lived in a White community, I went to a White school, and I did not know any other way. Honestly, I do not remember giving much thought to the idea of personally benefiting from White privilege. I was living in ignorance. It was not until I started college, when I began to learn of other people's experiences and hear their stories, that I realized that I had White privilege. It was only when I became the minority that I first recall being a member of the White race." (24-year-old White female)

(Continued)

TABLE 4.2 Early Memories of Whiteness and White Privilege (Continued)
"In the early to mid-90s, I was a young White male who had grown up in an area with little to no cultural diversity. I remember watching things like the Rodney King riots and the O.J. Simpson trial on television with my family. I distinctly recall an overwhelming majority of rioters being people of color, as well as the same being true of those individuals who believed O.J. Simpson was innocent. I asked my parents why so many Black people were so upset about one of these situations, and I was told, 'Because Black people stick together and support each other even when "one of their own" has done something wrong.' I remember thinking how great it was to have that kind of camaraderie, but also thinking how silly it was to support someone who had done something wrong. Even to this day, I still see my family as a fairly liberal and accepting people, but even with that being said, it was still seen as a 'them' and 'us' mentality." (30-year-old White male)

White privilege also remains invisible to many because addressing racial issues is challenging. For those who become aware of their racial privileges, not only is it difficult to address racism, but also, to address how one has benefited personally from racism seems nearly impossible. For example, many counselor trainees have difficulty identifying examples of personal racial privilege (Todd & Abrams, 2011).

- *White privilege contains psychological and intellectual costs to Whites.* Depending on their level of awareness of White privilege, feelings associated with dealing with that awareness include helplessness, frustration/anger, defensiveness, sadness, anxiety, guilt, and shame. In addition, Whites may experience cognitive dissonance between their beliefs in individualism and equality and their overt and covert racist behaviors. Thus, even though White privilege is a benefit, many costs are associated with being White. The costs of racism for Whites are described more fully shortly.
- *There are several myths Whites hold that can perpetuate White privilege.* Oftentimes, Whites perceive their daily experiences and cultural values inaccurately. These experiences and values include the myths that Whiteness and White culture are desirable and universal, that power affects everyone the same, that guilt is a sufficient response to addressing racial privilege, that feelings of discomfort can be used to resist change or accept privilege, and that those with less power can be truly honest about their feelings regarding racism without consequences (Knowles & Lowery, 2012; MacLeod, 2013; Neville, Awad, Brooks, Flores, & Bluemel, 2013; Pierce, 2013a; Sue, 2013).
- *White privilege differentially benefits Whites.* Whites may possess a combination of privileged and oppressed statuses, making their experiences with White privilege unique at times (MacLeod, 2013). For example, a White lesbian may experience oppression from her statuses as female and a sexual minority. Because of these forms of oppression, she may find it difficult to see that she enjoys specific advantages attributed to her skin color.
- *Individuals who do not identify as White may have some degree of White privilege.* White privilege is the valuation of lighter skin tones, particular hair texture, nose shapes, cultural values, and language. The more "White" an individual appears or the more the individual approximates the White value system, the more privileges he receives. For example, a light-skinned Latino may identify as Latino, yet can be perceived as White if her physical features approximate Whiteness.

COSTS OF RACISM FOR WHITES

Racism has been described as a major mental health problem, a psychological disease beginning as early as 4 years of age. Racism as a disease contributes to a distorted sense of self, reality, and others. The ways in which Whites cope with and respond to racism and racial privilege have cognitive, affective, and interpersonal costs for them, although these costs are minimal compared with those for people of color (Neville et al., 2013).

Cognitive Costs

Among the cognitive costs of racism for Whites is the delusion of White superiority and individuality such that Whites cannot see themselves as White and can deny racism because they are "individuals" (Knowles & Lowery, 2012; Neville et al., 2013; Pierce 2013b). This delusion is created primarily as a result of an inaccurate portrayal of history and can isolate Whites from fully experiencing their culture and ethnicity. Thus, they lack an accurate awareness as a racial being and experience intellectual deficits because they are unable to develop a full range of knowledge of racial issues and culture in general.

White racial identity development (see Helms, 1995) is greatly affected by racism and White privilege (Malott, Paone, Schaefle, Cates, & Haizlip, 2015). White racial identity models assume a component of White guilt and rely on Whites abandoning their entitlement to societal resources and privileges (Hays & Chang, 2003). In these models, lower White racial identity statuses (i.e., *Contact, Disintegration, Reintegration*) serve to enhance opportunities and cultural preferences for Whites and thus maintain the racial status quo, whereas higher White statuses (i.e., *Pseudoindependence, Immersion–Emersion, Autonomy*) view race as a complex construct that is often laden with misconceptions of minorities. A challenge of White racial identity development is that it is difficult to promote a nonracist identity when Whites mostly do not think of themselves as racial beings. Whites at varying levels of White racial identity statuses will experience various psychosocial costs (Neville et al., 2013). As individuals transition among racial identity statuses, they have emotional responses when confronted with the "White as oppressor" role.

Affective Costs

Emotional costs vary with Whites' awareness of racial issues. Fear is one common emotion that Whites possess. Whites may have an irrational sense of danger or of not being safe around people of color. They may fear certain neighborhoods because of stereotypes they hold. They may fear supporting racial affirmative action laws and policies because they are afraid of the impact that those laws and policies may have on White norms. As Whites acknowledge their racial privilege, they may become fearful of losing privileges to which they have become accustomed. Anger is another emotional cost for Whites. Anger may create apathy in Whites, and they may demonstrate a lack of interest in addressing racism. Anger can also result in the use of denial, which is discussed shortly.

Awareness of racism and White privilege could create guilt for Whites. This guilt is often associated with a sense of helplessness and sadness, as Whites may feel incapable of ending racism. Whites may feel anxious because of this guilt and, as a result, may experience lowered self-esteem. Guilt can be felt individually or collectively (Case, Iuzinni, & Hopkins, 2012). For example, White guilt may result from a race-associated action (or inaction) that an individual engages in or from a newfound understanding of how Whites have been oppressive to people of color. Whites may not feel personally guilty, but may feel guilt for being a member of their racial group. In counseling, a counselor's guilt may manifest as **color consciousness**, a term that refers to being intentionally cognizant of racial issues and potentially overemphasizing the role that race and racism play in the client's problems (Ridley, 2005).

Interpersonal Costs

Interpersonal costs can involve the loss of relationships with either people of color or other Whites. The distorted sense of others that accompanies White racism indicates a greater reliance on stereotypes and thus a lack of understanding of people of color. This combination often results in limited interactions with people of color and hence limited social competencies as Whites continue to restrict themselves when learning about other cultures, races, and ethnicities.

The more people connect with people of color, the more they disconnect with racist friends and family and with segregated institutions (Neville et al., 2013). As Whites address racism and racial privilege, they may lose relationships with other Whites, including family members and friends, who are not engaged in social advocacy and personal growth. This dilemma is a particular challenge for Whites that often prevents them from acknowledging racism and White privilege. Now consider specific interpersonal costs, and complete Reflection 4.5.

REFLECTION 4.5

List some potential interpersonal costs that you may experience as you engage in multicultural counseling and social advocacy in your personal and professional roles.

_____

_____

_____

_____

_____

_____

WHITES' PSYCHOLOGICAL RESPONSES TO RACISM AND WHITE PRIVILEGE

Racism contradicts what we have been taught about being an American: "liberty and justice for all"; "equal opportunity for all"; and "All [humans] are created equal." As deKoven (2011) noted, the history that most Whites have been exposed to "is the *only* history that they know, and there is no need to question it because it accurately reflects their own realities and lived experiences" (p. 156). When that history is challenged, how do Whites negotiate thoughts and feelings that come with the conflict between believing in racial justice and wanting to maintain their sociocultural and economic statuses?

Whites' psychological responses to racism and White privilege are linked to how they orient themselves with people of color. Responses can include (a) minimizing the notion that racism and White privilege exist in general or for particular individuals; (b) locating instances in which people of color are to blame for, and Whites are deserving of, the experiences they respectively have; and (c) drawing attention to specific instances of racism and White privilege in general society or their personal experiences. Understanding why and how Whites respond to these constructs is further complicated by the notion that the same White person engages differently with people of color, depending on the setting, time, or circumstance.

As regards the foregoing responses, Whites can engage overtly in racism and acknowledge explicitly that they deserve privileges, or they may understand that racism and White privilege exist but may enact racial microaggressions to some degree. **Racial microaggressions** are "brief and commonplace daily verbal, behavioral, and environmental indignities, whether intentional or unintentional, that communicate hostile, derogatory, negative racial slights and insults to the target person or group" (Sue, Capodilupod, et al., 2007, p. 273).

In essence, these responses are defense mechanisms used to maintain a particular racial identity. It is important to remember that individuals' personal identity, particularly their racial identity, guides how they think about or process new information and how they interact with members of their own and other racial and ethnic groups. Racial identity tends to remain fairly stable, as individuals often distort new race-related information in a way that serves to preserve their identity (Rudman, Dohn, & Fairchild, 2007). Thus, their responses remain quite stable and difficult to change.

A common denominator among the responses discussed subsequently is denial. **Denial** is one of the key defense mechanisms that Whites resort to in order to maintain White privilege and alleviate dissonance and emotional discomfort. Most Whites do not believe that they are racist; thus, any discussion of racism and White privilege soon dissipates. Denial can involve denying either that racism and White privilege exist or that a particular White individual is a racist or personally participates in White privilege. A common comment includes "I have Black friends." The particular denial that one is not personally engaging in racism (and likely not benefiting from White privilege) has been documented in research on White middle- and upper-class individuals. More specifically, members of these groups can sometimes accuse working-class Whites of being racist perhaps because they have heard racial slurs that working-class Whites have made, yet they themselves practice racially exclusionary behavior. (See Pierce, 2013a, 2013b.)

Whiteness and Being American

Whites often assume that being White equates to being American. The common experience acquired through media, politics, business practices, educational opportunities, religious teachings, and family and community conversations is this: White people are everywhere, they are intelligent and educated, their views and actions matter most and should get the most attention, they are to be trusted, and they represent what it means to be American. The term *all-American* has been used in the media to describe a White person who is clean cut, blond haired and light eyed, conventional, Protestant, educated, and middle class. Although this image is slowly changing, it remains the dominant standard that Whites use to judge who gets to be American.

For those who diverge from this all-American image, Sue, Capodilupo, et al. (2007) highlighted several forms of microaggressions that can occur. First is a form referred to as *Pathologizing Cultural Values/Communication Styles*: appearances, practices, and views outside of the all-American standard may be considered abnormal or inappropriate. Scholars (e.g., Nadal, Griffin, Wong, Hamit, & Rasmus, 2014) cite examples of this form, including telling someone of Asian descent that using chopsticks is strange and saying to a woman of African or Black descent that the way she wears her hair is unprofessional.

Second is the *Alien in Own Land* phenomenon: people of color, particularly those who may be of Latin, Asian, Arab, or multiracial descent, are often assumed to be foreign born and hence not "real" Americans. Contemporary examples of this phenomenon are often part of political discussions. For example, the "birther movement," inspired by conspiracy theories about politicians' (e.g., President Barack Obama's, Senator Ted Cruz's) birthplace, asserts that they were not natural-born citizens and thus could not be eligible for the office of President of the United States, on the basis of Article Two of the U.S. Constitution. Other examples are statements such as "Go back to your country" or the offensive reference to "anchor babies," whereby a noncitizen mother (usually of Latin descent) gives birth to her child in the United States as a way to provide advantage for a family to seek legal residency or citizenship there.

A third form of racial microaggression is the *Second-Class Citizen* form, in which Whites are given preferential treatment in stores, the workplace, politics, and the media, to name a few areas (Sue, Capodilupo, et al., 2007). Related to this phenomenon, people of color may feel invalidated and be clustered together as having the same physical characteristics or actions (Nadal et al., 2014). Examples include mistaking one African American for another African American, stating "All Asians look alike," and describing women of color as "exotic."

A final form of microaggression relates to the *Assumption of Criminal Status*, whereby people of color are assumed to be deviant in some way. For people of color, there are, unfortunately, several examples of this theme: being followed in a store because they are assumed to be a shoplifter, being profiled by law enforcement or being more heavily scrutinized as a potential "terrorist," encountering individuals who avoid them because they fear them or think that they are dangerous, having inadequate legal representation, receiving stricter punishment from the legal system, and more.

Color-Blind Racial Attitudes

Color blindness, or **color-blind racial attitudes**, is a form of racial microaggression that involves unawareness of racial privilege, institutional discrimination, or overt racial issues (Neville et al., 2013). For example, using contemporary examples of people of color "overcoming" discrimination (e.g., Barack Obama being elected and then reelected), Whites will claim that racism is a thing of the past and thereby deny the existence of racial inequality and privilege. In addition, they can view the world as offering equal opportunity, thus endorsing the myth of meritocracy. (See next subsection.) The intent for Whites in supporting the concept of color blindness is to treat all humans the same, as if race did not matter or as if the United States were a place in which all racial groups participate equitably in society and racial differences were celebrated. Examples include the following: "I don't see a person's color. I see only a person," "We celebrate our differences," and "There is only one race: the human race." In other words, when Whites assume that there is a level playing field and that race does not matter, they distort or minimize how important race is for an individual. Applied to the counseling profession, when counselors act in a color-blind manner, they may have difficulty establishing a therapeutic alliance, particularly with racial and ethnic minorities (Neville, Spanierman, & Doan, 2006).

Not having to view people or events through a race filter would be ideal. Because of the existence of several forms of racism within society, however, it is not possible (Neville et al., 2013). In fact, several studies show a link between high color-blind racial attitudes (i.e., greater endorsement of the notion of color blindness) and greater racial prejudice and discrimination, particularly on the part of Whites (Oh, Choi, Neville, Anderson, & Landrum-Brown, 2010). Examples of racial prejudice and discrimination perpetrated by these individuals include holding people of color more accountable than they hold Whites for their actions, increased racial fear, limited empathy toward people of color, reverse discrimination, and the development and sustainment of all-White communities. For people of color, endorsing high color-blind racial attitudes has been linked to internalized oppression (Neville et al., 2013).

Myth of Meritocracy

A meritocracy, also referred to as the meritocratic norm, is a system in which individuals are believed to be deserving (or meritorious) of resources and, ultimately, of a societal level that is commensurate with what they contribute to society. What they contribute can include intelligence, ability, skill, effort, and educational attainment, to name a few things. A meritocracy thus is a belief in distributive justice or that rewards should be distributed on the basis of merit. Conrad (1976, pp. 141–143) noted several essential principles of a meritocracy:

1. Merit should be the sole determinant of an unequal share.
2. The test of merit should be individual talent.
3. The most talented should receive a greater share of society's rewards than the less talented receive.
4. Everyone should have an equal chance to display his or her talent or lack thereof (equality of opportunity).
5. Social inequality (deference, income, class standing) is just when it is the outcome of the previous four principles.

If these principles are met, a meritocracy can be viewed as a positive system. Unfortunately, principles 4 and 5 are not present in U.S. society (Knowles & Lowery, 2012), making the notion of meritocracy a myth. Applied to race, the **myth of meritocracy** is the notion that all individuals, regardless of their racial makeup, can succeed if they try.

Literature shows that Whites tend to view themselves as members of a meritocracy, that they are successful, and that they are personally deserving of the rewards afforded to them (Knowles & Lowery, 2012; Liu, 2011). In addition, there seems to be resistance to "attributing inequality to inequity" (Knowles & Lowery, 2012, p. 203): Whites want to believe that equal opportunity exists and that social immobility is possible only because of a lack of individual effort by persons of color. Thus, because Whites value the meritocratic norm on a very personal level, they may feel threatened by the idea of group marginalization and may avoid reflecting on the possibility of a flawed meritocracy. Whites have to be willing to see that there is inequity based on inequality and that they are not necessarily deserving of rewards, because the playing field was not level. This resistance serves only to further limit awareness and the exploration of White privilege.

Focus on Exceptions

Oftentimes, Whites will deflect their role in perpetuating racism by focusing on times when they were discriminated against by people of color, a concept known as **reverse discrimination**. Reverse discrimination may be seen in several responses of White people to laws and policies such as affirmative action in universities and the workplace and increased immigration allowances. Examples include the following: "We are oppressed in that we are required to include everybody" and "I was more qualified, but they had to hire someone who was not White." Further, they may select instances when they experienced oppression due to their cultural makeup. This defense is a natural one because many Whites hold both privileged and oppressed statuses and can easily recall occasions on which they had been treated unfairly because of their gender, socioeconomic status, religion, and so on.

Psychological Dispositions of White Racism

In a 15-year qualitative study involving over 1,200 White individuals across the country, D'Andrea and Daniels (1999) assessed how these individuals thought about and reacted to issues of racism and race relations in the United States at that time. From this research, the authors identified five psychological dispositions of White racism, each characterized by cognitive, behavioral, and affective responses:

- *Affective–Impulsive Disposition.* Whites demonstrating this disposition engage in limited, stereotypical thinking about non-Whites and deny the existence of racism. These thoughts are often related to aggressive and hostile feelings toward people of color and to impulsive actions (e.g., destroying property, racial slurs, physical violence). Whites who identify predominantly with this disposition often exhibit little to no shame or guilt in their interactions with people of color.
- *Rational Disposition.* Whites of this disposition are somewhat aware of how racism exists, yet they tend to engage in either–or thinking about race relations. Further, Whites operate from a superficial tolerance of people of color until they encounter them, when they then exhibit negative (yet often not as hostile and impulsive as those of Whites of the Affective–Impulsive disposition) reactions to any policies or practices that encourage racial integration (e.g., affirmative action, integration of neighborhoods, interracial relationships).
- *Liberal Disposition.* This worldview is characterized by a greater understanding of racism and other forms of social injustice, including insight into others' perspectives and experiences. The disposition was dominant in most of the White counselor educators and students who participated in D'Andrea and Daniels's study, with individuals reporting an interest in multicultural issues in general, yet apathetic or not motivated to explore how White racism influences the mental health and social issues of people of color. Although these Whites demonstrate some sadness, they often fail to act because they perceive that they will experience negative reactions from others or will have to confront their own White privileges (see McIntosh, 1988).
- *Principled Disposition.* Whites operating from the principled disposition are very knowledgeable about how White privilege in their personal and professional lives influences racism, can cite specific examples of systemic racism in the United States, and (for those in counselor training programs) can note gaps or flaws in the ways in which multicultural issues are addressed in counselor preparation. Even with a passion for, and sensitivity to, racial issues, however, these individuals tend to discuss racism with others in a superficial manner and report that they are cynical that current racial dynamics in the United States will change.
- *Principled Activistic Disposition.* Constituting less than 1% of the sample, Whites with this disposition are similar to those with dispositions discussed earlier, because they have an understanding of racism, yet are different in that they are hopeful and active in creating sociopolitical change. Oftentimes, these individuals are not overwhelmed by making systemic changes, and they state that other Whites have the potential to have this perspective and facilitate "spiritual connection and moral empathy" to eradicate racism. Whites of this disposition are considered social advocates who seek to eliminate racism in specific ways within their personal and professional lives.

In sum, racial issues, particularly racism and White privilege, affect the counseling process significantly (Malott & Schaefle, 2015). Clients of color may react to a counselor's racial makeup (i.e., White) or to race-based discussions (or the lack thereof) on the basis of specific racial events that they experience within or outside the counseling session. These reactions will vary with the racial identity status of both the counselor and the client. When racial issues are not discussed in the counseling relationship, the session can be considered a form of racism because it harms the relationship: clients may become frustrated and feel ignored and distrustful. White counselors who avoid racial discussions or disregard how race plays into the client's problems may perceive the client to be defensive or resistant, a perception that could, in turn, lead to labeling the client's behavior as pathological. Further, if White counselors have a high need for power or control over a client of color based on the counselor's racial identity status, the client may be oppressed further, affecting her or his mental well-being. Thus, White counselors who address racism and White privilege are less likely to rely on stereotypes; are more likely to have more therapeutic relationships with clients of color, to contextualize problems and thus consider social and other environmental causes of clients' problems, and to have increased empathy for clients of color; and will definitely be more in tune with racial dynamics within the counseling session (Neville et al., 2013).

ERADICATING RACISM

Eradicating racism involves a systematic approach that focuses on counselor self-awareness, client services, and community collaboration. There are four developmental domains (counselor self-awareness, client worldview, the counseling relationship, counseling and advocacy interventions) within the multicultural and social justice counseling competencies (MSJCC; Ratts, Singh, Nassar-McMillan, Butler, & McCullough, 2015) that counselors are to attend to in seeking to eradicate racism. Applying the three-tiered model of advocacy, we highlight how each of these domains interfaces with the tiers of counselor self-awareness, client services, and community collaboration.

Counselor Self-Awareness

Achieving self-awareness of one's own attitudes and behaviors regarding racism and racial privilege is the first step toward social change. (See Activities 4.2 and 4.3.) Ridley (2005) outlined various factors that contribute to counselor racism. Counselors should reflect on these factors and on how they might play into counseling relationships. Although the following factors were developed as guidelines for White counselors, counselors of color are also encouraged to reflect on them:

- *"Cultural tunnel vision," or ethnocentrism.* Counselors who maintain cultural tunnel vision view client problems from the perspective of their own cultural socialization. Counselors may fail to view presenting problems from the client's worldview and may minimize the role of racism and other forms of oppression in the client's issues.
- *Victim blaming.* Victim blaming consists of labeling clients as the sole cause of their presenting issues or identifying as pathological or a form of resistance client behaviors in counseling that differ from the counselor's expectations. Thus, counselors may exhibit racist attitudes and behaviors and ignore the potential effects of racism on client problems.
- *The limitations of consciousness raising.* Consciousness raising often involves increasing knowledge and awareness of racism; however, the awareness frequently occurs only at a superficial level. For example, counselors may be aware of the definitions and causes of racism and racial privilege, yet fail to identify specific overt and covert behaviors associated with each, as well as have only a limited repertoire of behavioral options to address them. For example, many counselors who are aware of racism and its effects might suggest cultural sensitivity as a sole goal, minimizing the need to end racism.

ACTIVITY 4.2

Bring in items that symbolize what it means to be a member of your race. As an alternative to concrete items, use indirect representations (e.g., photos, magazine pictures, songs, poems, food). Each student may discuss the following in small groups or as a class:

a. Describe your cultural identity via props.
b. What is your definition of mental health? What is your racial/ethnic group's definition of mental health? How is that definition similar to and different from yours?
c. When your family or friends discuss (or discussed) "other" people, how did they describe them?
d. What does *racially different* mean to you? How do you think clients who are racially different from you view you or react to you as their counselor?
e. What does *racially similar* mean to you? How do you think clients who are racially similar to you view you or react to you as their counselor?
f. Articulate one contribution regarding how your race or racial identity influences your counseling style and relationships with clients.

ACTIVITY 4.3

Attend a school or community event that focuses on a racial or ethnic group other than your own. Record your observations of the content and processes that take place within the event. Write a reaction paper that addresses the following questions:

• What were your expectations of the event prior to attending?
• What thoughts and feelings did you have before, during, and after the event?
• How, if at all, did these thoughts and feelings relate to concepts discussed in this chapter?
• To what degree did you participate in the event?
• What factors affected your level of participation?
• What did you learn from the immersion experience?
• How can this learning apply to your work as a counselor?

• *Race-based stereotyping.* Counselors of all races and ethnicities hold various stereotypes of themselves and racially/ethnically different individuals. These stereotypes may be based partly on thinking of race as a biological construct and viewing racial groups as distinctly superior or inferior. Examining one's own stereotypes could provide important insights for counselors.

In addition to contemplating these factors, counselors should attend more closely to personal experiences of privilege (see Chapter 3), along with the degree to which they have encountered or engaged in racism and its impact on their worldview and interactions with others. White counselors are to consider each of the psychological responses presented in the previous section and brainstorm specific incidents when they have responded in a particular manner or held a particular disposition. In addition, they are encouraged to engage in dialogues with peers—those who identify as White and those who identify as a person of color—about their personal or interpersonal experiences with each type of response or disposition. Discussions in a safe environment, particularly one that is cross racial in nature, can be especially facilitative in fostering multicultural counseling competence.

White counselors may also want to self-administer the Color-Blind Racial Attitudes Scale (CoBRAS; Neville, Lilly, Duran, Lee, & Browne, 2000). The CoBRAS contains 21 self-report items rated on a 5-point scale (1 = *not at all appropriate or clear*, 5 = *very appropriate or clear*); there are three subscales (Racial Privilege, Institutional Discrimination, Blatant Racial Issues). Sample items include "It is important that people begin to think of themselves as American and not African American, Mexican American, or Italian American" and "White people in the U.S. are discriminated against because of the color of their skin." In addition to reflecting on the total score for the CoBRAS, White counselors may want to consider, for each item, how endorsing color blindness actually serves to perpetuate racism and thus negative consequences for themselves and people of color.

For counselors of color, it is important to reflect on their encounters with psychological responses of Whites to racism and how these encounters represent racial microaggressions. As they consider these encounters, counselors of color are to contemplate the degree to which racial micro-aggressions have shaped their worldviews, the reasons they entered the counseling profession, and ways in which they work with clients of various racial and ethnic groups. In addition, counselors of color may consider reflecting on some of the suggested interventions presented shortly for counseling clients. Further, counselors of color are to think about instances in which they may have responded in a manner similar to that of Whites regarding race-related events or in which they they have perpetrated microaggressions toward members of their own group or another racial or ethnic minority group. In thinking about these instances, it may behoove them to consider whether and, if so, how particular race-based attitudes shifted and where they faced challenges in doing so. Such consideration may help foster empathy for clients who may be culturally different from them.

With an increased understanding of personal encounters with White privilege and racism, counselors can explore how these phenomena are manifested in the professional realm of counseling and how they might apply new self-learning in professional advocacy efforts. Activity 4.4 offers an opportunity for counselors to consider the link among White privilege, racism, and the profession of counseling as a whole.

ACTIVITY 4.4

In small groups, reflect on these questions and share your responses:

- How might White privilege and racism play a role in common counseling approaches?
- How could White privilege and racism influence a client's presenting concerns, even those that may not seem race based?
- In establishing a counseling relationship and considering in-session counseling processes, what are ways in which White privilege and racism could hinder that relationship?
- In considering the prominence of counseling services in your community, to what degree does race influence the availability of resources and for whom?
- In considering trends in the counseling profession, how has White privilege and racism influenced what conversation shifts are made? What have been the impacts of various conversations in professional counseling organizations?

Client Services

As mentioned in Chapter 3, client services relate to empowering the client at the individual level, with direct change anticipated for the client. When addressing White privilege and racism at the client level, counselors reflect upon both client worldview and the counseling relationship as defined in the MSJCC (Ratts et al., 2015). In this section, three ways are presented in which counselors can engage with clients on an individual level: assessing the client's racial identity, addressing clients who have experienced microaggressions, and addressing client racial prejudice.

ASSESSING THE CLIENT'S RACIAL IDENTITY Racial identity development models outline statuses that describe racial attitudes toward oneself and others, attitudes that vary according to which status(es) is (are) most prominent for individuals. (See Chapter 2 for a complete description of these models.) Assessing a client's racial identity with the use of available tools can illuminate which attitudes the client holds about race, racism, and White privilege. Counselors can present the results, discuss specific items, and process how racial identity development may affect the client's experiences within the counseling relationship and the surrounding community.

As clients present their concerns in counseling, counselors may want to investigate with them how those concerns may be affected by the clients' racial makeup and others' racist attitudes. Knowing which racial identity statuses are most salient for each client may assist in this discussion. Counselors are encouraged to assess any examples of racism clients may be experiencing that created, is maintaining, or will hinder psychological healing. Counselors should remain empathic during this exploration and disclose their own struggles as appropriate.

Recent research (Malott et al., 2015) on White racial identity shows that achieving a positive White racial identity, and thus relinquishing racial privilege, is problematic. As indicated in Chapter 2, Whites move from a lack of awareness of race and racial privilege to a more complex understanding of racism and White privilege at a personal level, presumably with the aim of allowing for the abandonment of entitlement and racial privilege. Malott et al. (2015), conducting a qualitative study of 10 participants who were characterized as predominantly at the autonomy status, found that most participants concluded that a positive White racial identity was not possible, because the notion of Whiteness had been founded upon a racial hierarchy. In addition, most participants asserted that an autonomy status could never be achieved and that relinquishing privilege was an ongoing effort that would likely never be realized. Finally, most participants noted that cross-racial relationships remained difficult owing to a distrust of persons of color and participants' continual failures to avoid individual, institutional, and cultural racism. Sharing these findings are intended, not to discourage White counselors from moving toward a nonracist White racial identity, but to show that this movement toward achieving a positive White racial identity and relinquishing racial privilege, like the development of multicultural counseling competence, is a lifelong, challenging process that has opportunities for deconstructing and redefining cultural constructs.

ADDRESSING CLIENTS WHO HAVE EXPERIENCED MICROAGGRESSIONS The experience of racism can itself be considered a traumatic event, no matter how subtle. Accordingly, Malott and Schaefle (2015) noted that counselors should parallel interventions that have been linked to recovery from trauma—interventions such as establishing client safety, identifying and fostering strengths and positive coping techniques, reducing symptomology, and providing skills training that embody a holistic approach (e.g., career, academic, interpersonal, physical training). Because racism may be pervasive for clients, addressing it at the client level is an ongoing process.

Further, because clients come to counseling with multiple cultural identities and life experiences, they may also present with issues concerning negative events within their families and communities. These issues may result from violence or trauma, or from being a member of a sexual minority or having lower socioeconomic status or some other minority status. Thus, racial microaggressions can intersect with other types of microaggressions. It is important as well to understand that, while research has noted a significant difference in the number of microaggressions experienced between Whites and people of color (see Nadal et al., 2014), there are racial and ethnic differences in forms of microaggressions experienced among people of color. For example, Nadal et al. (2014) noted that individuals of Black and Latin descent reported experiencing feeling invalidated and treated as a criminal while those of Asian descent reported being treated more as exotic, as well as invisible, in the media.

It is important to address directly with clients of color the degree to which they experience racial microaggressions and how these encounters relate to their current functioning. Although the term *microaggression* may be mistakenly interpreted as less harmful than aggression, this is simply not true: microaggressions tend to be more subtle and harder to identify by those who perpetrate them, yet more pervasive for those who experience them. Studies (e.g., Nadal et al., 2014; Nadal, Wong, Griffin, et al., 2011; Rivera, Forquer, & Rangel, 2010; Sue, Capodilupo, & Holder, 2008) indicate that people of color report significant distress from racial microaggressions and cite a long-term impact on their psychological well-being.

By conveying to clients of color an understanding of a link between racial microaggressions and well-being, counselors begin to validate the injustices experienced, an interchange that may begin to foster an affirmative environment and a stronger therapeutic alliance. After outlining with clients some of the research on racial microaggression, the following are some questions that counselors may use with clients to broach the topic of racial microaggressions:

- Have you been told directly or indirectly that racism is no longer an issue or that you are not as affected by it because of other privileged identities you have (e.g., heterosexual, able bodied, male, higher socioeconomic status)?
- What has it been like for you to experience discrimination due to multiple statuses you hold?
- Has someone ever assumed that you were of a particular race but was wrong?
- Has someone ever assumed that you were not born in this country?
- Has someone ever spoken more slowly to you, used a different cadence or vernacular, or stated that you speak "good English" or "White"?
- Have you ever been watched in a store, or avoided, because someone feared you because of your race?
- Has someone asked you to speak on behalf of your race?
- Has someone assumed things about your sexuality on the basis of your race? Your gender? Your socioeconomic status?

As an alternative to these questions, counselors may consider using a quantitative assessment to review more specifically racial microaggressions. The Racial and Ethnic Microaggressions Scale (R28REMS; Forrest-Bank, Jenson, Winn, & Trecartin, 2015), which assesses individuals' experiences with 28 instances of racial microaggressions across various settings, could be useful to administer in order to initiate dialogue about racism. The R28REMS contains five subscales based on Sue, Capodilupo, et al.'s (2007) work: Second-Class Citizen and Assumptions of Criminality, Assumptions of Inferiority, Assumptions of Similarities, Microinvalidations, and Media Microaggressions. Sample items include the following: "I was ignored at school or work because of my race," "Someone assumed that I ate foods associated with my race/culture every day," and "Someone told me that people should not think about race anymore."

However the topic of microaggressions is addressed, counselors have a responsibility to assess how clients responded to a particular event at the time it occurred. Did a particular client address the microaggression with the perpetrator? How? Why or why not? What was the impact of that encounter? In addition, counselors should evaluate the clients' coping style and how active that style has been when the client was faced with microaggressions. What has been the coping style or response each time a microaggression was experienced? What has been the result of employing a particular coping method? Does the client have any regrets? Counselors of color may choose to share instances when they experienced racial microaggressions, how the microaggressions affected them, how they responded, and what supports and actions were useful for them. Nadal et al. (2014) suggested that it might be useful for counselors, no matter their cultural makeup, to process any unresolved feelings with clients regarding past experiences with racial microaggressions, because some people of color have reported that they did not deal effectively with an encounter (Sue, Nadal, et al., 2008). Some clients may have not addressed the experiences as they wanted, or the experiences have pervasive effects that need to be addressed.

Finally, counselors should brainstorm with clients ways in which each of them can advocate for dismantling microaggressions and who should be involved in that advocacy. How would the client like to move forward? In addition, counselors should review with clients strategies for addressing racial microaggressions in the future.

There are a few other considerations pertaining to addressing racial microaggressions in counseling. First, no matter the method for assessing racial microaggressions experienced by clients of color, counselors who identify as White are not to present an image that they have not ever engaged in perpetrating various microaggressions. Because of the various ways in which racial microaggressions can occur, it is not realistic to believe that counselors have not participated in some manner, intentionally or not. Second, because racial microaggressions may occur in the counseling setting itself, it is imperative that counselors prevent this from happening. Nadal et al. (2014) suggested that counselors refrain from behaviors such as communicating verbally or nonverbally that clients complain about racism too much and treating clients of similar backgrounds the same way. Third, clients will have different responses to discussing race, racism, and White privilege, depending on their racial identity status or the counselor's racial identity status. Some clients may not be aware of these constructs, while others may be resistant to discussions based on negative experiences that they have had. Dialogue could be particularly difficult between clients of color and counselors who identify as White, no matter what a particular counselor's racial identity status is. Finally, because intersections of identity exist for people of color, counselors must be ready to assist clients in determining whether a microaggression experience is related to their race, ethnicity, gender, sexual orientation, socioeconomic status, and so on.

ADDRESSING CLIENT RACIAL PREJUDICE   Because professional ethics are often closely tied to personal values, counselors who are developing multicultural competence may experience ethical tensions when working with clients who display racial bias (MacLeod, 2013). The dilemma is that, on one hand, counselors want to respect client worldviews while on the other hand they want to promote social change. When this tension exists, counselors must determine if, how, and when racial prejudice should be addressed. No matter the racial and ethnic makeup of the counselor or client, broaching the topic of racism and White privilege shows an openness to discuss challenging topics and may ultimately foster the therapeutic relationship. MacLeod identified several strategies for counselors considering addressing prejudice in the session:

- Consider the client's goals and how race is related to these goals and [the] presenting issue;
- Assess the client's racial identity status;
- Assess the defense mechanisms being used and how they maintain the problem;
- Consider how the racist comments relate to cultural racism;
- Consider what cultural values and strengths maintain the defenses;
- Find cultural strengths that the client can use to stop relying on defense mechanisms;
- Clarify the counselor's motivations and countertransference in the process of addressing racist comments; and
- Assess the client's motivation for change. (p. 173)

MacLeod (2013) recommended that, if a counselor decides to address client racial prejudice, then the counselor should help the client locate contradictory statements and then validate that these contradictions, or cognitive dissonance, are a normal aspect of moving to a more advanced or authentic racial identity. MacLeod referred to Todd and Abrams's (2011) work on White dialectics for addressing discrepant messages or views about race that serve to perpetuate racism. Specifically, Todd and Abrams noted six dialectics, two each found on three continua. The first continuum, *relationships*, involves the tension between the degree of awareness of clients' awareness of being White and the quality of their multicultural relationships. The second continuum, *importance of race/racism*, refers to the conflict between the extent that clients acknowledge the existence of race and racism with how much they minimize it. The third continuum, *understandings of inequality*, refers to the tension between the degree of awareness that clients have about differential racial privilege with their beliefs about the extent that racism has caused variations in racial privilege.

In addition to adopting these strategies, counselors should help clients create opportunities for meaningful cross-racial interactions; such interactions could help to reduce color-blind racial attitudes or increase awareness of racism and White privilege. As Neville et al. (2013) noted, cross-racial exchanges through emerging friendships put "a human face to racism" (p. 463). The more authentic exchanges are with peers of different races and ethnicities, the more that dissonance is introduced, a necessary precursor to a nonracist identity

Community Collaboration

ADDRESSING RACISM IN THE CLIENT'S SCHOOL AND COMMUNITY   In addition to addressing and dismantling racism within the counseling session, counselors are encouraged to examine the systems in which clients live and experience racism. Further, counselors should work to build stronger coping mechanisms for clients by strengthening and developing community resources. As clients present their stories, counselors are encouraged to search for personal, cultural, and community resources that clients may draw on in counseling. Clients may present their concerns in the form of challenges, and counselors can uncover hidden strengths that the clients have which enable them to deal with these challenges, as well as point out instances when they overcame specific challenges in the past. In addition, counselors should collaborate with clients and identify not only existing support systems and personality attributes, but also resources that clients would like to integrate into their lives.

As social advocates, counselors are responsible for establishing and participating in school and community initiatives that will assist in eradicating racism. To this end, counselors collaborate with others to develop and implement programs that educate teachers, administrators, parents, legal and health services professionals, and community leaders about the impact of racism on people of color. As these programs are developed, counselors are encouraged to ensure that clients and their families have knowledge of, and access to, the programs. For deeper thoughts on this topic, complete Activity 4.5.

ACTIVITY 4.5

Consider the following in small groups, and compile a list for each of the questions:

- What resources are available to clients of color in your local schools and community?
- Where are there opportunities for program development?
- What are the needed economic, legal, and public health services for clients of color?

ADDRESSING RACISM WITHIN OTHER SYSTEMS

Changing existing political, legal, economic, and public health systems is another major component in eradicating racism. Counselors are encouraged to assess each of these systems to better understand how racism and racial privilege are present in them.

Political and Legal Concerns

In addition to attending to race-related issues within the counseling relationship and the client's immediate environment, counselors need to be familiar with historical and current legislation and court decisions that address racial issues or that have implications for racism. In familiarizing yourself with these laws and legal decisions, consider both positive and negative consequences. Also, some of these laws may yield unintended consequences. Have some laws and policies made racism and White privilege issues worse? Examples of historic laws and policies that have attempted to address racial/ethnic issues and oppression include the following:

- *Treaty of Guadalupe Hidalgo (1849):* This treaty granted citizenship to Mexicans living within territories acquired by the United States after the Mexican–American War.
- *Reconstruction (1865–1877):* This era ended slavery and briefly gave African Americans voting rights and "40 acres and a mule."
- *Indian Reorganization Act (1934):* This act abolished the land allotment program originally established by the Dawes Act of 1887 and provided funding for tribes to allow them to redevelop and establish self-governments.
- *Brown v. Board of Education, Topeka, Kansas (1954):* This decision ruled that "separate was inherently unequal" and made racial segregation in schools illegal.
- *McCarran-Walter Act (1952):* This act permitted non-White immigrants to be naturalized, thus abolishing racial restrictions found in U.S. statutes since 1790.
- *Civil Rights Act (1964, 1991):* The 1964 act prohibited employer discrimination in hiring, placement, and promotion of employees on the basis of race, color, religion, or ethnicity. The 1991 act expanded rights by allowing those who had experienced employment discrimination the opportunity to a trial by jury and the possibility of remuneration for emotional distress damages.

- *Immigration Act (1965):* This act abolished the national origins quota system in place at that time and set the stage for future immigration laws whereby individuals of various nationalities had an equal chance for immigration.
- *Voting Rights Act (1965–2013):* This federal act prohibits racial discrimination in voting and is intended to make voting a free and fair process. It has undergone multiple revisions, the most recent in 2013, declaring that jurisdictions that were required to seek preapproval for changes in some voting rules no longer had to get that preapproval. Some of the changes introduced by the act were that documented proof of citizenship was now required in order for a person to register or vote and that same-day registration, early in-person voting, and mail-in absentee voting were made more difficult—provisions that disproportionately affected minorities of color.
- *Affirmative Action (post–civil rights era):* Legal policies implemented to help level the playing field and create occupational, educational, and business opportunities for racial/ethnic minorities.
- *Public Law 93-638 (1975):* Also referred to as the Indian Self-Determination and Education Assistance Act of 1975, this law provided Native Americans more authority in developing community-specific educational and federal services.
- *Indian Health Care Improvement Act (1976):* This act allocated funds for health care services for Native Americans in tribal communities.
- *No Child Left Behind Act (2002):* This act stated that public schools should make adequate yearly progress. One of the main goals of the act was to close the achievement gap between various racial/ethnic minority groups, on the one hand, and Whites and some Asian groups, on the other.

Besides paying attention to these laws and policies, counselors should attend to current legislation in order to ensure that they have no potential negative effects on people of color.

Economic Concerns

Even with affirmative action, people of color receive disproportionate incomes and job opportunities in comparison to their White counterparts. This effect is often based on forms of racism discussed earlier in the chapter. Counselors should remain mindful, particularly in career counseling with people of color, of how racism affects economic opportunities for them. Chapter 7 explains the economic disparities associated with race and how poverty influences people of color.

Public Health Concerns

People of color experience a variety of health-related concerns as a result of racism. The U.S. Surgeon General's supplementary report on race, ethnicity, and mental health (USDHHS, 2001) has numerous examples of how oppression affects mental health—specifically in the areas of misdiagnosis; staff, facility, and program resources; length of treatment; and dissatisfaction with treatment. Since that report, numerous studies have been conducted which show that racism is significantly linked to mental health concerns, problems with pregnancy and childbirth, and behavioral problems (Pieterse et al., 2012; Priest et al., 2013). Counselors need to be aware of health disparities for people of color and how racism contributes to these disparities. Several chapters throughout this text highlight how racism and other forms of discrimination affect various racial and ethnic groups.

Taking Action

In sum, race-related stress in the forms of racism and White privilege has detrimental effects on clients' psychological, physical, and social well-being. In addition, clients often experience oppression and other forms of trauma from other cultural identities they possess. Taking into account the strategies listed for building counselor self-awareness, for advocating for clients within the counseling session and their communities, and for examining and creating institutional changes, counselors are encouraged to develop a vision for ending racism and other intersecting oppressions. Activity 4.6 provides a beginning forum for this vision, and Table 4.3 provides a list of resources to extend your knowledge related to race, racism, and White privilege.

ACTIVITY 4.6

Divide into small groups, and distribute various materials and resources that could be used to develop a model for what a nonracist community would look like. After completion of the project, have each group discuss its proposed community and consider the following:

a. What would nonracist counseling services in schools and communities look like?
b. What school and community services would be available?
c. What existing school and community services would be adapted?
d. How are the various proposals similar and different?
e. What is one thing you could do to achieve a nonracist community?

TABLE 4.3 Resources Having to Do with Race, Racism, and White Privilege

Selected Advocacy Organizations

American Association for Access, Equity, and Diversity (http://www.affirmativeaction.org): Founded in 1974 as Americans for Affirmative Action, this organization is dedicated to promoting affirmative action and equal opportunity for women and people of color.

American–Arab Anti-Discrimination Committee (http://adc.org): Founded in 1980, the ADC is the largest grassroots organization that represents Arab–American culture and highlights hate crimes against Arab–Americans.

National Association for the Advancement of Colored People (http://www.naacp.org): Cited as the oldest and largest civil rights organization in the United States, the NAACP seeks to promote equality for minority groups and provide various legal, career, and advocacy services.

United to End Racism (http://rc.org): This ongoing program of the organization Re-evaluation Counseling is designed to connect individuals around the world in international advocacy efforts to address racism.

YWCA Stand Against Racism (http://standagainstracism.org/): Founded in 2007 in New Jersey, the organization raises awareness of racism and racial justice and engages in legislative efforts.

Selected Books

Alexie, S. (2007). *The absolutely true story of a part-time Indian.* New York, NY: Little, Brown and Company.

Asim, J. (2008). *The N word: Who can say it, who shouldn't, and why.* Boston, MA: Houghton Mifflin Harcourt.

Colby, T. (2012). *Some of my best friends are Black: The strange story of integration in America.* New York, NY: Viking Press.

Davis, A. Y. (1983). *Women, race, & class.* New York, NY: Vintage Books.

Griffin, J. H. (2010). *Black like me.* New York, NY: Penguin.

Jensen, R. (2005). *The heart of Whiteness: Confronting race, racism, and White privilege.* San Francisco, CA: City Lights Publishers.

Kendall, F. (2012). *Understanding White privilege: Creating pathways to authentic relationships across race.* New York, NY: Routledge.

Kenneally, C. (2014). *The invisible history of the human race: How DNA and history shape our identities and our futures.* New York, NY: Viking Press.

Rothenberg, P. S. (2011). *White privilege: Essential readings on the other side of racism.* New York, NY: Worth Publishers.

Tatum, B. D. (2003). *Why are all the Black kids sitting together in the cafeteria: And other conversations about race.* New York, NY: Basic Books.

Thurston, B. (2012). *How to be Black.* New York, NY: HarperCollins Publishers.

Walsh, J. (2012). *What's the matter with White people?: Why we long for a golden age that never was.* Nashville, TN: Turner Publishing.

Wise, T. (2012). *Dear White America: Letter to a new minority.* San Francisco, CA: City Lights Publishers.

X, Malcolm. (1965). *The autobiography of Malcolm X.* New York, NY: One World Books.

Selected Films (Descriptions extracted from www.imdb.com)

American History X (1998): A former neo-Nazi skinhead tries to prevent his younger brother from going down the same wrong path that he did.

The Butler (2013): As Cecil Gaines serves eight presidents during his tenure as a butler at the White House, the civil-rights movement, Vietnam, and other major events affect this man's life, family, and American society.

Black Like Me (1964): Based on the true story of a White reporter who, at the height of the civil-rights movement, temporarily darkened his skin so that he could experience the realities of a Black man's life in the segregated South.

Crash (2004): Los Angeles citizens with vastly separate lives collide in interweaving stories of race, loss, and redemption.

Guess Who's Coming to Dinner (1967): A couple's attitudes are challenged when their daughter introduces them to her African-American fiancé.

The Help (2011): An aspiring author during the civil-rights movement of the 1960s decides to write a book detailing African-American maids' points of view about the White families for which they work and the hardships they go through on a daily basis.

12 Years a Slave (2013): In the antebellum United States, Solomon Northup, a free Black man from upstate New York, is abducted and sold into slavery.

Dear White People (2014): The lives of four Black students at an Ivy League college.

Other Resources

White Like Me: Race, Racism, & White Privilege in America (2013). Antiracist educator and author Tim Wise explores race and racism, with a focus on Whiteness and White privilege.

White Privilege Pop Quiz (http:www/mollysecours/com): Developed by activist Molly Secours two months before the killing of Trayvon Martin, this quiz is intended to gauge awareness of personal experiences of White privilege.

Summary

The way race has been defined throughout history has created significant physical, psychological, social, academic, legal, political, and economic consequences, to name a few. Racial classifications have brought forth an oppressive system for both Whites and people of color (i.e., American Indians or Alaskan Natives, Asian, Blacks or African Americans, Native Hawaiians and Other Pacific Islanders) known as racism. Racism exists at three interlocking levels (i.e., individual, institutional, and cultural) that continue primarily to serve the interests of Whites and justify the exploitation, both covert and overt, of people of color.

The costs of racism for people of color include cognitive (e.g., internalized racism, challenges in racial identity development), affective (e.g., race-related stress, hypervigilance, anger, sadness), interpersonal (e.g., segregation, relational discord), and physical (e.g., hypertension, physical violence) costs. Although people of color have suffered more severe consequences of racism, Whites also experience personal costs from a system in which they benefit. Some of these costs are a false sense of cultural identity, feelings of guilt and fear (depending on Whites' level of awareness of their privileged status), and diminished relationships with people of color and thus limited social competence. These costs are often associated with a lack of awareness of, and motivation to, dismantle White privilege.

White privilege encompasses the benefits that Whites or individuals who approximate a whiter skin tone receive on the basis of their skin color. These benefits include favorable treatment in daily activities such as job interviews and purchases in stores; adequate and positive representation of the White race in the media; and assumptions of intelligence, a good work ethic, and success. White privilege is often invisible to Whites, preventing many of them from understanding their racial and ethnic identities as well as the experiences of people of color, who often do not receive racial privilege. Depending on their level of awareness of racism and racial privilege, Whites possess several psychological responses, including color-blind racial attitudes, a belief in the myth of meritocracy, and a focus on exceptions to White privilege and White racism.

Eradicating racism for clients involves a systematic approach in which counselors engage in awareness of their own experiences with racial privilege and oppression, integrate discussions of race and racism in counseling sessions and the larger community, and work to change political, legal, financial, and health disparities that adversely affect people of color.

Review Questions

1. How has the term *race* been conceptualized throughout history? What have been the consequences for Whites and people of color?
2. How do the examples presented in Table 4.1 relate specifically to institutional and cultural racism? How might these historical shifts affect your work with clients?
3. How do the costs of racism for people of color and Whites compare? How might you use similarities to work more closely with clients?
4. What are the characteristics of White privilege? How might these characteristics relate to psychological responses to racism and White privilege by Whites?
5. What are some specific ways you can promote a nonracist community for your clients?

5

Gender and Sexism

Anneliese A. Singh and Taryne M. Mingo

PREVIEW

In this chapter, the two interrelated constructs of gender and sexism are introduced to continue the discussion of social justice and its impact on individuals' mental health. In assessing the degree to which gender and sexism affect clients, as well as the counseling relationship, it is important for counselors to pay attention to the convergence and intersection of client and counselor multiple identities (e.g., race/ethnicity, sex, gender expression, sexual orientation, ability, age, social class). Multicultural competence with respect to gender and sexism may be addressed through increased counselor awareness of one's own assumptions, values, and biases regarding gender identity and gender expression; counselor awareness of clients' worldviews regarding gender identity and gender expression; and culturally appropriate intervention strategies. Counselors should strive to understand the powerful roles that gender and sexism play in their own lives, as well as the lives of their clients. In this chapter, we define gender and sexism, discuss the concepts of gender identity and gender expression, describe some implications of gender-affirmative counseling, and discuss the intersection of gender and gender identity with race, ethnicity, and other cultural identities.

UNDERSTANDING GENDER AND RELATED CONSTRUCTS

Gender socialization begins from the moment humans are born and includes how people learn what gender they are, what gender others are, and what so-called gender-appropriate behavior entails. For instance, when babies are born, they are typically assigned a sex, male or female, based on a limited, binary view of sex characteristics and anatomy. Society then maps gender identity onto sex assignment, with assigned females designated as having a girl or woman gender identity and assigned males designated as having the gender identity of a boy or man. Gender expression is then mapped onto sex and gender identities, establishing binary gender expectations, notions, and roles of femininity and masculinity. For instance, as early as age 2, children begin to associate certain behaviors with gender. By age 4, children understand that there are certain jobs, toys, and play associated with boys or with girls. At age 6, most children can identify "what boys do" versus "what girls do" as a demonstration of their understanding of personality characteristics and mannerisms assigned to each gender.

One of the challenges, however, of societal gender socialization is that this gender assignment system does not account for the existence of transgender and gender-nonconforming (TGNC) people, who often do not fit into the binary categories of male–female or man–woman. Therefore, when seeking to understand gender socialization, counselors should have knowledge of the terms *cisgender* and *TGNC*. **Cisgender** describes people who feel that the sex they were assigned at birth is in alignment with their identified gender, whereas **transgender and gender nonconforming** (TGNC) describes people whose gender identities and expressions do not fit into societal norms of sex assignment (male, female) and the gender binary (man, woman). This definition of TGNC may include people who identify as cross-dressers, transsexuals, genderqueers, bois, grrls, and other terms that people who are TGNC use to describe themselves. These identities are discussed in more detail later in the chapter.

Gender socialization complicates and disempowers the experiences not just of people who are TGNC: people who are cisgender also experience limitations when socialized under the gender binary, being told how to be, look, and act as a result of their sex, gender identity, and gender expression assignment. Throughout this chapter, the words *man* and *woman* are umbrella terms used to encompass both people who are TGNC and people who are cisgender, unless noted differently. The interactions that people have with one another in society shape their own gender expectations, and how they make meaning of their own gender significantly affects their views of themselves—views that have numerous mental health implications. For example, people are often socialized so as not to express certain emotions, and such socialization is based on whether they are an assigned male (e.g., do not express sadness) or an assigned female (e.g., do not express anger); moreover, these notions vary across cultural worldviews. As with other social identities, personal experiences of gender are fluid and are grounded in personal experiences; yet they also contain multiple realities and narratives about who we are and how we interact with others. These narratives are woven into racial/ethnic, religious, sexual orientation, socioeconomic class, and other identity contexts. Reflection 5.1 provides key considerations relating to thinking about counselors' personal experiences with gender.

REFLECTION 5.1

Self-reflection on sex, gender identity, and gender expression is a foundational part of counseling women and men. Write an answer to the following questions:
- When was the first time you "knew" or were told by someone that you were a boy or a girl?
- What gendered messages did you receive on the basis of your sex assignment?
- What have been the consequences of stepping outside of traditional gender roles for your assigned sex?
- How did your cultural background influence gender roles, norms, and expectations within your family and community?

UNDERSTANDING SEXISM

Across cultures, the gender binary creates unique gender socializations; however, many of these socializations are grounded in sexism. **Sexism** is a system of oppression based on sex, gender identity, and gender expression; many have defined sexism as a system in which men hold privilege and women do not. **Male privilege** refers to unearned rights and societal benefits afforded to men solely on the basis of their sex assignment. Scholars have traditionally defined sexism as the exploitation and dominance of women by men under the system of *patriarchy* (hooks, 2000). However, the oppressive system of sexism is seen to be much more complex when one considers how people who are cisgender or TGNC experience it. For instance, both women who are cisgender and women who are TGNC experience sexism, such as being subjected to rigid and stereotyped notions of femininity. Men who are cisgender hold power within patriarchy, yet men who are TGNC may or may not have access to this privilege, depending on stereotyped notions of masculinity and how much society sees those men within their identified gender as a man. Therefore, the system of cisgender privilege is related to the systemic mechanisms of sexism as well, wherein both women and men who are cisgender hold privilege but women and men who are TGNC do not. Among the advantages that women and men who are cisgender possess are not having to explain their gender identity to others, not having to educate health-care personnel on how to best serve them, and not having to think carefully about using public restrooms.

Sexism is further complicated because it intersects with many other identities, such as race/ethnicity and sexual orientation. Therefore, counselors should understand sexism within the specific sociocultural context in which it operates. Examples of sexism include women being sexualized in popular media solely for entertainment, as well as women earning, on average, less money than their male counterparts with the same experience and position. An additional example pertains to an inequitable distribution of labor within the family system for women who may work outside the home. Women often are expected to take on double (sometimes triple) duties by managing a home, family, and career. Also, women frequently receive negative information about being female, and many women begin to believe these negative messages. This internalization of negative beliefs is called **internalized sexism**, which is a manifestation of male privilege. Activity 5.1 explores male privilege and its effects on both men and women. Examples of male privilege include men generally being socialized not to be afraid to walk alone at night in a public place and men having multiple sex partners without being labeled "promiscuous."

ACTIVITY 5.1

In small groups, identify some forms of male privilege at the individual, interpersonal, community, and institutional levels. What are the negative effects for both men and women? Discuss strategies to minimize the effects of male privilege. How might male privilege manifest itself in a counseling session?

As you reflect on the gender socialization that you experienced as a child, as an adolescent, and now as an adult—in addition to how male privilege may influence the counseling process—consider that the sources of gender socialization occur across all facets of society. For instance, in school settings—from day care and prekindergarten through community college and university settings—students receive clear and specific gender messages. Children are asked typically to line up in school activities according to gender, and adults tend to interact differently with girls and boys. For instance, teachers may call on boys more than girls in classroom activities, use more critical language with girl children, and praise boys more than girls for correct answers—all of which contribute to classroom gender inequities (Blaise, 2009;

Brinkman, Jedinak, Rosen, & Zimmerman, 2011; Thornton & Goldstein, 2006). On the basis of your reflections on gender, you may have noticed that there are also gender stereotypes within families. For example, in what ways were you asked to or expected to engage in various behaviors assigned specifically with a certain gender? In addition to gender inequities found in schools and families, sexism and gender stereotyping continues into workplaces and careers, with covert or "modern" forms of sexism having direct impacts on the perceptions and outcomes of career women and men. Becker (2010) found that women and men were more likely to internalize sexist belief systems when asked about their perceptions of nontraditional stereotypes of women, such as career women or women who are considered to have defied norms. As a result, men were presumed to think more positively of women who conformed to traditional stereotypes (i.e., housewives) because they were not seen as a threat to the men's perceived higher status. Watkins et al. (2006) found that people endorsing the more subtle aspects of sexism shared the fact that they turned to men—not women—for advice concerning their jobs and were able to advance further in their careers through promotions than people who did not ascribe as much to covert sexist beliefs. In Activity 5.2, identify the systemic influences of sexism that are embedded in societal institutions and the covert sexism that exists within these systems.

ACTIVITY 5.2

Make a list of all the different institutions you have interacted with throughout your life (e.g., day care, school, university, family, government). For each of these institutions, list at least one way that covert or overt sexism (e.g., the presence of male privilege or the absence of female privilege) arose in your experiences.

Counselors should carefully consider how sexism is experienced, minimized, or discussed not only in the United States, but also in other countries around the world. There may be a tendency, for instance, for counselors and clients to minimize the influences of sexism on mental health in the United States, especially when sexism has more of a covert influence on women's lives. However, U.S. women experience a range of sexist influences on their mental health, from internalized sexism such as a dislike of their bodies and low self-esteem to experiencing high rates of sexual violence. However, in other countries, sexism may be experienced differently, and counselors should seek to understand the differences when working with clients raised in non-U.S. or non-Western cultures. In addition, the sexism that women who are cisgender and women who are TGNC experience around the world may share significant similarities (e.g., devaluing of women, being forced into sex work for survival), but also may have some distinct differences as well (e.g., relative ease of social and/or medical transition for U.S. women who are TGNC).

GENDER AND COUNSELING CONSIDERATIONS

When working with issues of gender among clients counselors may use the American Counseling Association Multicultural and Social Justice Counseling Competences (MSJCC; Ratts, Singh, Nassar-McMillan, Butler, & McCullough, 2015) to focus attention on, and inform understanding of, gender and sexism in counseling. In these competencies, the most important first step is an awareness of your own assumptions, values, and biases regarding gender; this step also entails learning about your client's worldview regarding issues of gender in order for you to work effectively with clients. Second, acquiring the knowledge that counselors need in order to work with issues of gender and sexism is important, such as having knowledge of South Asian patriarchal and gender norms when working on issues of self-esteem with a women client of South Asian descent. Third, developing the skills to work with gender and sexism in counseling is an outgrowth of self-reflection and knowledge, such as having the skills to counsel a women who is TGNC on issues of societal discrimination. Finally, as discussed earlier, there are multiple mental health impacts on both women and men due to sexism, so counselors should be able to take action in identifying and reducing sexism both inside and outside of their counseling practice. Within these four areas, the MSJCC (Ratts et al., 2015) describe how issues of privilege and oppression may influence both the client and counselor in counseling interactions. Now complete Reflection 5.2 to consider the interplay among sex, gender identity, and gender expression.

REFLECTION 5.2

Think about your sex, gender identity, and gender expression assignment, and how these identities may influence how you will work with the following groups: women who are cisgender; men who are cisgender; women who are TGNC; and men who are TGNC. Identify how gender and sexism, in addition to issues of culture, might influence your counseling work with these groups and how the MSJCC (Ratts et al., 2015) can guide you to work with each group.

In addition to developing the awareness, knowledge, skills, and actions required in order to address gender and sexism in the counseling process, there are certain factors to consider that may lead to more effective counseling processes and outcomes: client–counselor matching, exploration of racial and cultural differences, and communication styles (Kim & Park, 2009). Although one might assume that same-race or same-gender client–counselor dyads would always provide better outcomes, the literature actually shows mixed results (Whitfield, Venable, & Broussard, 2010). Some researchers identified the counseling relationship as having a significant role in facilitating change within clients (Wampold, 2010). This result is further emphasized by Owen, Leach, Wampold, & Rodolfa (2011), whose study found that a counselor with extensive knowledge, skills, and awareness could use her or his abilities within any counseling relationship to meet the specific needs of diverse clients. In addition, a strong alliance between the counselor and client was viewed as a significant factor in therapy outcomes because cultural variability was believed to exist with counselors and clients of similar races/ethnicities or genders.

Gender-related variables within the context of counseling have been examined more closely in recent years because today the majority of counselors identify as women (Cannon, 2008). Not surprisingly, because of gender role socialization, counselors tend to invoke different strategies when interacting with clients according to their gender identities. Men tend to speak more assertively overall with both men and women, whereas women tend to speak more assertively with other women but more tentatively with men. These behaviors are manifestations of sexism and internalized sexism and, as previously discussed, must be carefully considered within the sociocultural context. For example, Cannon's study had large numbers of White counselors in its sample, and the findings may be very different across other racial/ethnic backgrounds. Activity 5.3 challenges you to discuss other examples of sexism in popular culture.

ACTIVITY 5.3

Identify something from popular culture (e.g., a song, an advertisement, a movie) that is sexist in nature. As a group, discuss how popular culture perpetuates sexism. What are the mixed messages portrayed in the thing you found? Discuss how these representations of popular culture affect the mental health of men and women who are cisgender and the mental health of men and women who are TGNC.

Does gender make a difference in counseling dyads? Prior research has shown little evidence of an influence of gender alone; however, certain problems or situations presented by a client that are not considered gender stereotypical (i.e., a wife abusing a husband) could influence gendered perceptions of the client's problem on the part of the counselor (Fäldt & Kullberg, 2012). For example, women exhibiting behaviors that are stereotypically male may be perceived by their counselors as more aberrant than if they were male. Regardless of the makeup of gender dyads, clients generally report perceptions of improvement in counseling, meaning that they feel that they are resolving the problems which brought them to treatment. In terms of race/ethnicity and gender, same-race and same-gender dyads allow for the client and counselor to establish rapport more quickly, yet it is debatable whether this factor makes a difference in treatment outcomes (Goode-Cross, 2011). In addition, the threat of overidentification and failure to recognize how multiple intersections of identity can influence the counselor–client relationship within same-race dyads should be considered. Although the literature on client–counselor matching is in its infancy and provides mixed results, particularly concerning intersecting cultural identities, it is imperative that counselors consider the complex role that gender and sexism play in the counseling process and outcome. The sections that follow will discuss gender-specific counseling considerations and strategies.

Assumptions about gender can be detrimental to clients by influencing the techniques and treatment strategies you choose. Chao and Nath (2011) examined issues related to race and gender roles in training college counselors. Their study indicated that counselors who embodied stereotypical gender roles exhibit lower levels of multicultural competence. As a result, they recommended that counselors examine their own gender roles and awareness of gender. In addition to leading to gender-sensitive counseling, continued professional development in the areas of multicultural competence is believed to reduce stereotypes about male and female clients. There are several issues to consider in providing gender-sensitive counseling to clients. For example, if you believe that women should not show anger, you may help only male clients express this emotion. Similarly, if you have strong beliefs about how men and women should act (e.g., according to culturally endorsed gender roles), you may send negative signals to clients who do not conform, thus impeding the counseling relationship. The next section discusses these and related issues in more depth.

Counseling Girls and Women

In the past several decades, women's rights advocates have made great strides in the quest for gender equality and equity. However, there have also been significant setbacks in the women's liberation movement, and the U.S. Congress has yet to pass the Women's Equality Act addressing issues of pay equity, among others. Even today, to be judged on the basis of intelligence, character, and accomplishments rather than on the basis of gender remains a challenge for women under the system of sexism. Patriarchal norms often, but not always, intersect with race/ethnicity, social class, sexual orientation, and other identities; therefore, the degree of sexism that women experience, and even are able to acknowledge, varies. Despite the great societal changes that have led to increased opportunities for half of the world's population, girls and women continue to face particular challenges. Stressors in women's lives can entail experiencing harassment, violence, negative media messages, economic inequity, and multiple-role overload (American Psychological Association, 2007).

Counselors working with women and girls have a responsibility to evaluate their own awareness, knowledge, and skills related to that population. According to government statistics, women are more than twice as likely as men to experience an anxiety disorder in their lifetime, and, while depression affects many men and women, women are more likely to be diagnosed with depression each year. In addition, women and girls make up 85–90% of those diagnosed with anorexia nervosa. Chapter 18 provides additional information on the prevalence and diagnosis of mental health issues by gender.

One area of particular concern for counselors is women's gender role expectations. Research supports the existence of a sexual double standard regarding women's expression and the limits of sex roles. The media are a source of many of these messages: across advertisements, television shows, websites, and print magazines, women receive the message that there is an ideal they must achieve that is often out of reach. Young women, in particular, are continuously bombarded with mixed messages of sexual subordination and constraint. Women are encouraged to cast themselves as heterosexual objects of male desire while being admonished never to succumb to that desire or to acknowledge it. Thus, young women are told to be sexual objects but not to have overt sexual desires. Counselors can take a sex-positive approach when counseling women, exploring how women relate to and enjoy their bodies, including what sexual pleasure means to them and how to communicate their desires to their sexual partners. Using bibliotherapy and creating a counseling environment in which these issues may be discussed in an affirmative and open way is important.

In addition, young women's primary sexual role is often culturally defined as bearing the burden of rejecting or accepting men's advances. This sexual ideology denies the possibility of sexual negotiation based on a more equitable sexual dialogue. It reminds women that they are defined by their bodies and reinforces the belief that male sexuality is uncontrollable whereas women's sexuality must remain restrained (Brown, 2011). These societal forces, coupled with lower economic statuses generally afforded to women and girls, create a context that can be toxic to both women and men, although it is generally more harmful for women. The sexism embedded within those forces also assumes that all women are straight, neglecting to recognize the existence and value of women who are lesbian, bisexual, queer, and questioning.

Internalized prejudices resulting from oppression and sexual double standards within cultural, societal, and religious beliefs can provide societal barriers to women's development over the life span (Bearman & Amrhein, 2014). These prejudices may also have detrimental effects on a female's self-concept. For example, if a woman adheres to societal role and gender socialization expectations, she may repress her sexual expression or experience unhealthy sexual development according to which she is trained to attend to others' needs rather than be connected with her own sexual needs and desires. Yet, if she responds to her sexual desires and needs and expresses her sexuality, then societal norms that endorse women's sexual passivity may stimulate feelings of guilt or being "deviant." Consider these findings as you review Case Study 5.1.

CASE STUDY 5.1

Deborah is a 42-year-old, cisgender, heterosexual, African-American woman who has made an appointment with you because, she states, "I don't know what to do any more. . . . I think I am depressed and I am hoping you can help me sort it out." During your first session, she reveals that she recently reentered the workforce because her two children will soon be heading to college and the family needs a second income. She also explains that she has seen four other counselors and they were not helpful. As the session begins, Deborah slumps in her chair, exhales loudly, and avoids eye contact. In a muted voice, tearfully, and almost in a whisper, she says, "I don't really think this is going to make any difference. My husband thinks I need to see someone, and I think he just wants me off his back."

- From a gender-affirmative perspective, what would you say to Deborah?
- How would you feel about working with her?
- What might be some gender-specific themes that come up during your sessions?
- How might your beliefs about men and women influence your reaction to Deborah's strong emotions?
- How does Deborah's race/ethnicity affect your reactions to her gender?
- How might things be different if Deborah identified as a woman who is TGNC?
- Sometimes the counselor and the client have conflicting values regarding gender roles and oppression. How does a counselor decide whether to challenge a client's beliefs regarding women's oppression?

Counseling Men

Incorporating a gender-affirmative perspective is as important for the counselor working with men as it is for the counselor working with women. In much of U.S. culture, men often exhibit difficulty seeking help for a wide variety of issues, from everyday stressors to more significant mental health concerns (Reed, 2014). Conformity to masculine norms reflects an important social reality that men and women often do not understand or think about consciously, yet that profoundly shapes our lives. Reflection 5.3 speaks to some messages that counselors might have encountered about males personally.

REFLECTION 5.3

Compile a list of messages you received from your parents, friends, community, and the media about male behavior. How do these messages contribute to your beliefs about what are the right and wrong ways for boys and men to behave? How might messages given to males influence their mental health? How might these messages influence men who are TGNC?

Are men emotionally shut off? Is there something about the way our culture shapes boys into men that makes them emotionally unavailable? Although it is impossible to answer these broad questions adequately, it is important for counselors to be able to identify the ways that men are socialized across cultures. For example, masculine norms in the West are commonly communicated to males in the form of "boys don't cry" or that "it isn't manly to be dependent on others." At the same time, society still expects men today to be able to communicate effectively in their interpersonal relationships and to contribute to raising children. These mixed messages can be confusing, and men often err on the "macho" side by repressing their feelings.

This stifling of emotions can take its toll, and researchers have described the inability men may have to put feelings into words that results from a long socialization process in which boys are taught to suppress and deny their feelings of vulnerability (Levant, Allen, & Lien, 2014). Many behavioral and emotional differences between people assigned as male and people assigned as female can be viewed as rooted in early socialization practices. Research on children from infancy through the school years shows how these differences can happen. Mothers, for instance, expose baby girls to a wider range of emotions than baby boys and work harder to control their sons' emotional volatility. Fathers often step in to socialize their toddlers along gender lines at around 13 months, verbally roughhousing their sons and talking in more emotional terms with daughters. As children get older, both parents can foster this rift by discouraging sons from expressing vulnerable emotions and encouraging such expression in daughters. Finally, peer-group interactions cement boys' unhealthy emotional development by promoting structured group activities that foster toughness, teamwork, stoicism, and competition.

Reed (2014) argued that problems we think of as typically male (e.g., difficulty with intimacy, workaholism, alcoholism, abusive behavior, rage) may be attempts to escape depression. Unfortunately, their attempts to escape this pain may hurt the people they love the most, and they often pass their condition on to their children. In addition, some of the experiences men have—such as experiencing sexual abuse—may be difficult for them to seek counseling for, because of feelings of shame or stigma around seeking help as a man (Singh & Crete, 2014).

European-American values prescribe what behavior is acceptable for men, and anything that strays from this norm is met with disapproval by society. According to Farkas and Leaper (2016), girls become women through relational activities whereas boys become men through oppositional behaviors, learning to be independent, tough, and emotionally reserved. The demands of gender roles for men tend to exclude anything that could be perceived as feminine. In essence, masculinity is defined by how behaviors and attitudes are *not feminine*. Boys learn that becoming men means avoiding feminine attitudes and behaviors and not getting too close emotionally to other boys. In addition, boys and men receive constant messages regarding male privilege that reinforce that privilege, from accepting inequitable work distributions within personal and professional settings to receiving praise that might not be warranted in those settings. These gendered messages for men across racial/ethnic identities can lead men to feel overconfident or to believe that they must present themselves as lacking any weakness (Rogers, Sperry, & Levant, 2015). Such messages can inflict wounds on people across the gender identity spectrum: both men and women who are cisgender or TGNC. Counselors may use role-playing to explore male privilege and its manifestation in individual, family, and group contexts. Reflection 5.4 speaks to this code with respect to the counseling profession.

REFLECTION 5.4

Gender socialization has an influence on all genders. The price for traditional gender socialization for girls is the prioritization of others' needs before their own, whereas the price for boys is disconnection—from themselves and from those around them. Discuss how these concepts have related to your own development and your decision to become a counselor. How many men are there in your counseling classes? What is the connection among the low rate of men who are counseling students, sexism, and gender stereotypes? Answer these same questions about people who are TGNC across their gender identities and expressions.

Many men will use shame-based responses, denial, minimization, and silence as their tools to relate to others emotionally. Some men find asking for help to be shameful. According to Hooker, Wilcox, Burroughs, Rheaume, and Courtenay (2012), traditional masculine ideology reinforces the desire to appear strong and engage in risky behaviors, including behaviors that would jeopardize one's health, in an effort to prove a man's masculinity. One study found a high association between men who adopted a masculine ideology of restrictive emotionality and potential health risks, including an unwillingness to seek help during times of stress (Houle et al., 2015). One study examining the relation between the endorsement of a traditional masculine ideology and restrictive emotionality of men of color suggested that restrictive emotionality might differ for diverse groups of men because cultural norms may reinforce or conflict with masculine ideologies (Levant, Karakis, Wong, & Welsh, 2015; Wong et al., 2012). **Male gender role conflict (male GRC)** is a term used to describe a theory of understanding how traditional gender role socialization can result in negative consequences for men who remain rigid in changing circumstances (O'Neil, 2013). For example, men in traditionally masculine professions, such as law enforcement, may have difficulty switching from being tough, stoic, and independent while on duty to being warm and affectionate while off duty. Wester and Lyubelsky (2005) described four overall patterns of male GRC: (a) success, power, and competition; (b) conflict between work and family relationships; (c) restricted emotionality; and (d) restricted affectionate behavior between men. A discussion of each of these patterns follows.

Success, power, and competition describes the degree to which men are socialized to focus on high achievement personally and professionally, as well as to seek out positions of power and assess their achievements in relation to others' achievements (Wester, Vogel, O'Neil, & Danforth, 2012). For example, many men prefer to excel competitively rather than collaboratively. An authoritarian communication style usually exemplifies this pattern, and men with this trait are used to dealing with problems on their own instead of asking for help. These men get into trouble because interpersonal and spousal relationships require a collaborative approach that can be difficult to accommodate.

The second GRC pattern, *conflict between work and family relationships,* concerns the difficulty many men have balancing work, school, and family relationships. Of course, many (if not most) women across diverse cultural backgrounds may have experienced this difficulty as well, but it is more socially acceptable for women to ask for help than it is for men. Because of increasing competition and the rising costs of living, some men may inadvertently place their careers ahead of their families. Of course, in many cultures, women have been working outside the home—yet their work may be underpaid, overlooked, and undervalued.

The last two GRC patterns, *restricted emotionality* and *restricted affectionate behavior between men,* are closely related and refer to the degree to which men are taught to avoid feelings (Wester et al., 2012), both within themselves and expressed toward other men. Depending on their cultural backgrounds, men have a tendency to avoid showing feelings, out of fear of appearing weak or vulnerable. Consider these GRC patterns as you review Case Study 5.2.

CASE STUDY 5.2

As John and his partner Sandra (both cisgender, Latin American, and from middle-class backgrounds) present for family counseling, they report that they have been constantly fighting about their 10-year-old son, James. John is angry about his son's serious weight problem and reportedly teases James about his weight. Sandra says that she wants John to stop putting down their son. During the course of counseling, John shares with his son for the first time his own experience of being a "fat kid," much heavier than James. He shares the story of the humiliation he felt as a 10-year-old boy, having been teased and beaten regularly by older boys on his way home from school.

- From a gender-sensitive perspective, how might you see John's preoccupation with his son's weight? How may norms of masculinity intersect with John's race/ethnicity and class?
- What does John's childhood experience have to do with his son? How might you assist John in showing concern for his son appropriately?
- How might your answers change if the race/ethnicity or class backgrounds were different in this case?

Counselors working with men should attend to the aforementioned socialization processes, while engaging in specific behaviors that will enhance the likelihood that the men they work with experience successful outcomes. For example, setting specific goals early in the counseling process may be consistent with the way in which many men are socialized across diverse cultures. Also, whereas empathy and support may be important skills in developing healthy relationships, Wester and Lyubelsky (2005) recommend that the gender-sensitive counselor maximize men's socialized preference for overcoming obstacles through overt effort. Again, any work with men should also be culturally informed so that the counselor is aware of how gender norms within a specific culture operate for men.

Men may resist counseling. For instance, men may decide that they themselves want to overcome the obstacles that are impeding them. If so, then the counselor has an important opportunity to collaboratively explore and challenge gender norms and roles that are no longer working for men. One strategy involves *transgenerational focus*, the idea that a greater understanding of individual men can be gained through revisiting their relationships with their fathers, grandfathers, and other men in their family tree. Of course, the purpose is not to condemn all men's behavior, nor is it to change the client's core identity, but it is to assist the client in developing a broader range of cognitive and emotional skills. From this perspective, men can benefit from exploring the values ascribed to their gender role within their families as a way to reevaluate how those values and role behaviors align with current needs and circumstances in their lives and in a changing society.

Counseling People Who Are TGNC

There are currently no ACA competencies related to counseling men and women who are cis-gender; however, there are counseling competencies related to practice with people who are TGNC. Still, many counseling programs do not provide adequate training for work with clients who are TGNC, despite the fact that, according to Reicherzer (2008), counselors will see at least one client who is TGNC during their careers. The Association for Lesbian, Gay, Bisexual, and Transgender Issues in Counseling (ALGBTIC) Transgender Committee's (2010) *American Counseling Association Competencies for Counseling with Transgender Clients* (2010) describes competencies in areas of training (e.g., group work, social and cultural foundations, assessment) conducted by the Council for Accreditation of Counseling and Related Educational Programs. Counselors may use these competencies to guide their work with men and women who are TGNC. A large component of gender-affirmative counseling with people who are TGNC entails knowing the wide range of identities (discussed in the introduction to this chapter) and language relevant to these people. Under the TGNC umbrella, **genderqueer** is an increasingly used term, because it may be more inclusive for some individuals—especially youths—who transgress boundaries of gender identity entirely and may not identify with gender pronouns associated with men, women, and so on. People who are genderqueer may not use pronouns related to the gender binary, such as "she/her" or "he/him," but instead use gender-neutral pronouns, such as "they/them." These third-person pronouns are sometimes inaccurately referred to as "preferred pronouns," a term that should not be used, since people who are genderqueeer do not actually *prefer* those pronouns. Instead, these are the pronouns that are respectful to use to refer to many people who are genderqueer, and microaggressions occur when such pronouns are *not* used by people in the lives of genderqueers. In counseling people who are genderqueer, it is important to explore the effects on people not using the names they believe fit them. Youths who are genderqueer may feel further disempowered regarding this concern, as they may be living with families to whom they do not feel safe disclosing their gender identity and gender expression or families who refuse to use the gender-queers' self-designated names and pronouns.

Sometimes people who are **intersex** are grouped into discussions about people who are TGNC. People who are intersex are those who have variations of reproductive or sexual anatomy that do not fit into the socially constructed definitions of male (XX chromosomes) and female (XY chromosomes). People who are intersex may not identify with the TGNC umbrella at all, yet may have some shared experiences with people who are TGNC, such as being misgendered, experiencing microaggressions, and facing societal discrimination.

Because the rates of hate crimes and other forms of violence are so high toward people who are TGNC in the United States, counselors should be prepared to conduct a thorough trauma assessment at intake and throughout the counseling process. People who are TGNC also experience employment discrimination and no access to health care, as well as high rates of homelessness, poverty, and education discrimination (Grant et al., 2008). Typically, TGNC individuals who seek mental health services are assigned a diagnosis of gender dysphoria, according to the *Diagnostic and Statistical Manual of Mental Disorders*, 5th edition (*DSM* 5; American Psychiatric Association [APA], 2013). The diagnosis is a controversial one, because many people who are TGNC do not believe that their gender identity and expression constitute a mental disorder. It is often the stigma attached to being TGNC that creates much of the distress for members of this vulnerable community, and societal transprejudice is a common reason cited for suicide attempts by individuals who are TGNC (Grant et al., 2008).

The counseling profession is another institution where TGNC people face formalized discrimination, with intake forms lacking attention to TGNC identities, counseling settings lacking safe bathroom access, and clients who are TGNC feeling that they need to educate their counselors about the issues they face in their lives and the important resources they need to access. Counselors should not be surprised, therefore, when clients who are TGNC feel anxious about seeking counseling or working with mental health professionals and do not feel comfortable exploring potential areas of distrust.

Sometimes the counselor microaggressions that clients who are TGNC face entail misplaced assumptions about what being TGNC means for a client. For instance, counselors should be well aware that not all people who are TGNC want to have hormone therapy or surgeries (e.g., "top" surgery, "bottom" surgery, orchiectomy, phalloplasty, facial feminization, facial masculinization). For those TGNC clients who do want to pursue these medical interventions, counselors should understand how to identify TGNC-affirming medical providers. Counselors should also know that, for TGNC clients who do select to seek medical interventions, there is typically a requirement to see a mental health professional. The seventh iteration of the World Professional Association of Transgender Health Standards of Care (WPATH SOC, 2011) provides guidance for mental health professionals working with people who are TGNC across the life span in terms of the focus of counseling work, in addition to guidance in referring to a medical provider. In this most recent version of the SOC, people who are TGNC are able to obtain referral letters from master's-level counselors for the first time. When writing these letters of referral, counselors should inform clients who are TGNC about the purpose and content of the letters. Counselors should seek ongoing professional development, consultation, and supervision if they feel inadequately trained to write the letters. In addition, counselors should inform clients who are TGNC of how long they may be in counseling if the presenting issue is only to obtain a letter. Counselors should also be aware that many people who are TGNC access hormone therapy in off-market ways because they lack access to, and are not covered by, health care. Counselors should thus be prepared to explore the safety of these off-market hormone sources, as well as be able to refer clients to more accessible medical resources and providers. For instance, in many major cities, an informed-consent model is used whereby people who are TGNC are able to access their medical providers directly to receive hormone therapy without having to obtain a referral letter from a counselor. Regardless, because of the inequities that TGNC people experience, even in the health-care arena, counselors should focus on teaching self-advocacy skills related to accessing TGNC-affirmative health-care providers and navigating health-care systems by using altercasting scenarios (e.g., "How will you respond if your medical provider does not attend to your needs as a person who is TGNC?").

Because not all people who are TGNC desire medical treatments, counselors should carefully assess the client's goals, self-definitions, and experiences of discrimination and trauma to understand how these experiences intersect and influence the client's well-being. Counselors should also be prepared to explore how issues of privilege and oppression are related to TGNC self-identified gender shifts when these individuals seek a social or medical transition. For instance, many women who are TGNC experience a loss of male privilege when they transition to their self-identified gender, and there may be grief and shock related to this shift that can be necessary for counselors to explore. Recent research suggests that counselors should focus on the resilience strategies people who are TGNC have that help them navigate transphobia and transprejudice (Singh, Hays, & Watson, 2011; Singh, Meng, & Hansen, 2013). Furthermore, counselors should assume the role of advocate in helping clients who are TGNC access

TGNC-affirmative employment, health care, and housing (Singh & Burnes, 2010). Therefore, expanding resilience and exploring opportunities for advocacy are important foci of counseling. An additional and important source of resilience and self-advocacy for men and women who are TGNC is a TGNC-specific support group; however, counselors may need to refer TGNC clients to online support groups and resources when in-person support groups do not exist.

TGNC-affirmative counselors seek knowledge about the TGNC community so that they can perform ethical practice and begin to reduce stigma. Gender identity is included in the American Counseling Association *Code of Ethics* (ACA, 2014) as a status protected from discrimination, so counselors should seek opportunities to learn about this important community. These opportunities may include educating oneself via online resources (see Table 5.1), attending a professional workshop, watching films, or inviting a person who engages in advocacy for the TGNC community to speak to your colleagues and agency or in a school setting. In 2010, the ACA endorsed specific competencies for counseling people who

---

TABLE 5.1 Gender and Sexism Resources

Cisgender Women

Centers for Disease Control and Prevention (www.cdc.gov/Women/): public health information for cisgender women.

National Institute of Mental Health (www.nimh.nih.gov/health/topics/women-and-mental-health/index.shtml): mental health information for cisgender women.

World Health Organization (www.who.int/mental_health/prevention/genderwomen/en/): cisgender global women's empowerment.

Survivors of Violence

Community United Against Violence (www.cuav.org): violence statistics and prevention efforts with cisgender and transgender women.

Feminist Men (http://www.feminist.com/resources/links/links_men.html): resources for cisgender feminist men.

Men Stopping Violence (http://www.menstoppingviolence.org/): healing and prevention resources for men ending violence against women.

Rape, Abuse, & Incest National Network (www.rainn.org): resources for cisgender and transgender survivors of violence.

Transgender and Intersex Resources

ACA Competencies for Counseling with Transgender Clients (www.counseling.org): counselor training competencies for work with TGNC clients.

Center of Excellence for Transgender Health (www.transhealth.ucsf.edu): interdisciplinary TGNC resources.

Intersex Society of North America (www.isna.org): a Web site exploring intersex identities.

National Center for Transgender Equality (www.transequality.org): TGNC policy advocacy organization.

PFLAG (formerly Parents, Families and Friends of Lesbians and Gays) (www.pflag.org): TGNC-inclusive resources for caregivers and families.

Trans Youth Family Allies (www.iamatyfa.org): TGNC youth and family resources.

World Professional Association for Transgender Health (www.wpath.org): interdisciplinary standards of care for TGNC mental and physical health care.

---

are TGNC (ALGBTIC, 2010; see Table 5.1). Those competencies guide counselors, supervisors, and counselor educators in providing TGNC-affirmative counseling and are important to understand in working with people who are TGNC.

CASE STUDY 5.3

Latianna is a 23-year-old African-American transgender woman who presents for counseling with concerns about making a medical and social transition. Latianna shares the information that her last counselor did not know about transgender concerns, and she felt that she had to educate her counselor about her needs. Latianna says that she is afraid that she will never find the right medical providers who are transgender affirming, and she also wants to connect with other transgender women of color. She has a supportive partner, and her family supports her medical and social transition. She shares the fact that she feels "lost" about the process of transitioning, and she is concerned that she does not have health insurance currently, as she was fired from her last job because of her gender identity.

- What are the personal biases and assumptions about transgender and cisgender people which you have that may influence the counseling process?
- What are the multicultural and social justice concerns you should explore with Latianna?
- What are the opportunities for advocacy on behalf of Latianna in her medical and social transition?
- How might your answers change if the race/ethnicity or class backgrounds (e.g., access to employment and health care) were different in this case?

HISTORICAL CONTEXT OF SEXISM

It is important for counselors to understand the historical context of sexism in order for them to have the knowledge to challenge status quo thinking that enforces narrow definitions of gender in our society. According to Chaudoir and Quinn (2010), structures of patriarchy, in almost every culture, are designed to maintain women's lower status in relation to men. The term *patriarchy* refers to a system that provides men with certain privileges, including access to ways of being, that are considered inaccessible to women (Dickerson, 2013). Patriarchal systems have existed throughout time and across cultures, although scholars such as Lerner (1986) assert that patriarchy has outlasted its initial relevance. According to Lerner, patriarchy originally began as a system that benefited both men and women. Lerner postulates that, in the early development of humankind, because of the high rates of miscarriage, strict gender roles were a biological necessity that enabled humans to reproduce. Aggressive roles for men and domestic roles for women were appropriate for a certain cultural period. Yet, Lerner notes that, over time, patriarchy became an entrenched system that not only allowed men to wield more power, but also restricted women to remaining around domestic matters.

Because patriarchy has overstayed its initial purpose of assisting in human survival, it has also become a system of ownership, in which women have become property of men in institutions such as marriage (Lerner, 2010). Although a thorough review of the history of sexism is outside the scope of this chapter, we will review significant events in mental health over the past 75 years. These events provide counselors with an understanding of how females have either resisted or succumbed to cultural norms of gender roles in the United States.

World War II and Women's Return "Home"

In preparation for the large draft of men in the United States who entered the military during World War II (WWII), women entered the workforce in unprecedented numbers (Hall, Orzada, & Lopez-Gydosh, 2015). Although U.S. women, particularly African-American women, had a long tradition of working both within and outside the home, this gender shift in the workforce provided women with opportunities to become wage earners in ways that had not previously been available to them because of their gender. Working-class women populated factories and were placed in management positions in the absence of a large number of men during WWII. During this time women's roles expanded beyond the traditional ones of wife, mother, and homemaker, and the new roles were endorsed by the U.S. government. One can easily recall the "Rosie the Riveter" advertisement, which was laden with the gender and cultural messages of the time. In this governmental propaganda advertisement, the image of a White, middle-class woman with the words "We can do it!" was used to recruit over 18 million women into the labor force to help drive the war industry.

The story of this period was that women were brought into the workforce and then returned "home" to resume their domestic duties at the end of the war, when men came back to the United States. However, there is another side to the story, documenting the significant numbers of women who worked full time before, during, and even after the war. Hall et al. (2015) also noted the sexual and racial discrimination these women faced, often in the form of direct harassment, as they performed their patriotic duty to the country. Women who did resume a culture of domesticity after men returned from WWII disengaged from dreams of academic and career success to fit back into narrow definitions of women's work. The consumer culture that followed WWII provided U.S. families—especially those with middle-class women—with a boom in prosperity. Massive media campaigns marketed household appliances, and women's magazine headlines focused on preparing women to be optimal caregivers to their husbands and children. Societal standards resumed a strict policing of "appropriate" behaviors and thinking for both genders, with women's focus on the work at home and men's focus on work outside the home (Hall et al., 2015).

However, it is important to note that the governmental enforcement of narrow definitions of gender roles was not received passively and did not affect the lives of women of color or working-class women, who had long traditions of work exploitation. One particularly important, well-publicized book that promoted resistance to women's culture of domesticity and presented a discussion of women's mental health was Betty Friedan's 1963 classic, *The Feminine Mystique*. In this work, Friedan (2001) documented "the problem that has no name," a problem which asserted that middle-class, White women were in fact receiving little pleasure from domestic chores and craved connections with their communities and families that would build their sense of worth and support their longing for freedom and pleasure. Friedan's book was a wake-up call for both women and men, and its publication was one of many historical events documenting women's roles in society.

Historical Resistance to Sexism: The Feminist Movement

The history of feminism as a social justice movement in the United States is often understood as three distinct periods, or "waves." The first wave of feminism focused primarily on suffrage and suffrage-related issues, which involved suffragists such as Hubertine Auclert, who organized against male supremacy in Europe (Allison, 2014). According to Hewitt (2012), first-wave feminists were perceived by second-wave feminists as a homongenous group with a narrow focus on political goals that benefited White, middle-class men. This second wave was successful in obtaining the right to vote for women (the Nineteenth Amendment) and proposed the Equal Rights Amendment, which advocated ending all laws that discriminated against women (e.g., laws dealing with property rights and jury service). However, the movement was a predominately White movement, ignoring important issues of racism in the United States, and LGBTQ issues were not included at all.

The second wave of feminism ushered in a time when gay and lesbian issues in particular began to emerge. The major leaders of the second wave (which came to be called the "women's liberation movement"), such as Betty Friedan, who wrote *The Feminine Mystique* to reveal women's relegation to the domestic sphere at the expense of their mental and physical well-being, resisted the inclusion of gay and lesbian issues. These leaders attempted to focus on equality of the sexes, fearing that including sexual orientation would distract policy makers from acting on behalf of gender parity. In 1966, Friedan founded the National Organization for Women (NOW), which expanded feminism's focus on equal rights to reproductive rights for women (Friedan, 2001; Parry, 2010). Most famous from the second wave was the phrase "the personal is political," which was used to describe the connections between systemic and individual oppressions of women. Critiques of the second wave of feminism again referred to an absence of women of color, in addition to the heteronormative focus of the movement.

The third wave of feminism attempted to correct the absence of these voices: young people in particular highlighted issues important to women of color and queer people. Baumgardner and Richards (2000) described the third wave of feminism as focusing on issues of "sexual harassment, domestic abuse, the wage gap . . . and . . . modern problems of . . . equal access to the Internet and technology, HIV/AIDS, child sexual abuse, self-mutilation, globalization, eating disorders, and body image" (p. 21). Although there has been a focus on lobbying and changing laws, third-wave feminists use direct action, independently produced periodicals, the Internet, and other media technologies to deliver their message. Critiques posed by third-wave feminists have included questions of whether the intersections of gender with other identities, such as race/ethnicity, sexual orientation, class, ability, and socioeconomic status, are being addressed.

Counseling theories have incorporated multicultural approaches, such as feminist theory, to provide support for marginalized groups of people, particularly individuals with intersecting identities. Some researchers believe that feminist theory fails to meet the specific needs of women of color, and they consider it a Eurocentric theory because it privileges the experiences of White women over the experiences of women of color. Addressing inequality from a gender-only framework, they say, neglects the experiences of women whose lives are also affected by race, sexual orientation, or class. Feminist theory, therefore, can be considered a theoretical gateway into understanding the complexity of intersecting identities for women of color and should be paired with a theoretical framework that captures the specific experiences of a group of people such as African-American women, Latina women, Asian-American/Pacific Islander women, and others.

Womanism, a term coined by Alice Walker (1983), can be used as a theoretical framework to address the intersections of identity for women of color. Womanism is also considered a social change perspective that is rooted in African-American women's everyday experiences (Maparyan, 2012). The term has been developed further by other scholars. Layli Phillips (2006), in particular, developed the tenets of Womanism, which can be used as a theoretical framework to guide counselors in supporting women of color.

Multicultural counseling approaches within counselor education programs have tended to analyze cultural variables such as race and gender in isolation from one another, rather than as overlapping identities (Williams & Wiggins, 2010). However, cultural variations exist within similar identity constructs, such as gender, race, and sexual orientation. Thus, the compartmentalization of race and gender into single identity categories limits the understanding of people with multiple stigmatized identities. Therefore, counselors are encouraged to move beyond traditional counseling approaches and adopt an approach that is culturally and contextually appropriate for the needs of each client.

CULTURAL INTERSECTIONS OF GENDER

This section describes how gender interfaces within four racial/ethnic minority groups: African Americans, Asian Americans/Pacific Islanders, Latino(a)/Chicano(a) Americans, and Arab Americans. Because these groups are heterogeneous, gender characteristics are not necessarily similar for all individuals. In addition, gender role identity expression may be different for individuals, depending on their level of acculturation, socioeconomic status, degree of spirituality, and other factors. Often, there are more differences *within* a racial/ethnic group than *across* racial/ethnic groups, so caution should be taken so as not to stereotype the discussion that follows to all women and men of a particular racial/ethnic background.

African Americans

African-American women and men have both experienced racism within the United States, so their gender roles are influenced by these experiences and often defy norms of the dominant groups. For instance, African-American women have long histories of working within and outside of the home, and African-American men have historically experienced restricted power and social status in the United States. Further, African-American families may endorse more matriarchal norms, with women's roles described as those of strength and resourcefulness (C. C. Lee, 2013). Willie and Reddick (2010) noted that one of the greatest gifts of African-American families to U.S. culture has been a more egalitarian family model. Chapter 9 provides additional information on gender role expression among African Americans.

There is still a large amount of literature that underscores how racism and sexism are combined to form a system of oppression uniquely experienced by women of color—a system also known as *gendered racism* (Thomas, Caldwell, Faison, & Jackson, 2009) and *racialized sexism* (hooks & Mesa-Bains, 2006). African-American women, in particular, are affected by racism and gender simultaneously, impinging on their psychological processes, behaviors, and interactions (Perry, Pullen, & Oser, 2012). African-American women are 35% more likely to experience intimate partner violence than are White women (West, 2004). According to Black Women's Health Imperative (2012), 60% of African-American girls have experienced sexual assault by age 18. Racialized sexism has led to the devaluing of African-American women's experiences. According to Alexander-Floyd (2014), African-American activists have often sought to restore the patriarchal role of Black men by blaming female-headed, single-parent homes as the root of the problem within the Black community. In addition, African-American women must also contend with the "superwoman" perception, in which they are believed to be strong and able to withstand any obstacle or handle any situation. In 1978, Michelle Wallace wrote *Black Macho and the Myth of the Superwoman* to detail how the assumption of the strong, Black woman can be detrimental to African-American women's health and mental well-being, especially if the woman is unable to live up to the expectation of being strong and able to overcome all obstacles.

Asian Americans/Pacific Islanders

Asian-American/Pacific Islander cultural norms, particularly the more traditional ones, tend to have quite strict guidelines about acceptable behavior for, and social distance between, men and women (Chung & Singh, 2008). Although there is immense diversity and a wide range of values and worldviews within Asian American/Pacific Islander cultures, there tends to be a shared value of family privacy and norms regarding the types of information that are shared only within the family and other information that may be shared with people outside the immediate family (Frey & Roysircar, 2004; Ta, Holck, & Gee, 2010). Levels of acculturation for Asian Americans/Pacific Islanders are important to explore in order to ascertain the degree to which individuals ascribe to traditional gender roles (Singh & Hays, 2008). For example, a female (male) client may feel particularly anxious about sharing very personal information with a male (female) counselor. Of course, much depends on the context, but in any event, clients who ascribe to more traditional cultural norms may feel more comfortable with a counselor who is perceived as culturally responsive (Dewell & Owen, 2015). At the same time, the bicultural and multicultural experiences of children of immigrant Asian-American/Pacific Islander families typically expose them to multiple gender roles and stereotypes during their life span (Singh, 2008). Therefore, tensions may exist between children and parents regarding the expression and endorsement of traditional gender roles—a matter that counselors should be aware of and explore. For instance, Inman (2006) found that cultural value conflicts for South Asian women varied among both first- and second-generation women in areas of gender role expectations and intimate relations and were influenced by their education, ethnic identity, and religiosity. Further information on Asian-American/Pacific Islander issues in counseling is discussed in Chapter 11.

Latino(a)/Chicano(a) Americans

The U.S. Census Bureau (2014d) defines Latino(a) or Hispanic Americans as "persons of Mexican, Puerto Rican, Cuban, Central or South American, or other Spanish culture or origin, regardless of race" (p. 2). One critical cultural norm that may influence gender roles is the concept of **machismo**, which can be equated with masculine values and behavior that are the epitome of idealized manhood based on level of social status. The man with machismo is the one who supports and protects his family in the face of all odds, who disciplines his children to be hardworking, honest, and upstanding citizens of his community. Machismo is a key factor in the molding and sustaining of the family and personal relationships, and, like any aspect of patriarchy, it can also endorse norms of male privilege and dominance. **Marianismo**, a term derived from Catholicism that translates to "Virgin Mary–ism," describes the gender role expression of Latinas. The word refers to extreme femininity and subordination to males. However, the term has a spiritual connotation in that women who bear children hold a higher spiritual status. Latina women interested in positions of leadership may encounter criticism as a result of this prescribed gender role expression. Hall and Donaghue (2013) acknowledged the burden of female politicians, who must balance being seen as "too feminine," in order to avoid being viewed as incompetent or unable to handle the stress of the position, with being seen as "too ambitious," so that they could still be seen as "real women." Although sexism does manifest itself in these cultural contexts, it is important to note that, simultaneously, women are represented in significant leadership positions (e.g., women presidents currently serve in six countries in South America). As a counselor, you should be comfortable broaching the subjects of machismo and marianismo with your Latino clients, to gauge their thoughts on this aspect of their culture and the role it plays in their lives. But you should also refrain from assuming that these concerns are enacted similarly or at all within clients' lives. Additional information about Latina/o gender role expressions may be found in Chapter 12.

Arab Americans

Approximately 3 million Arab Americans reside in the United States, and their countries of origin range from Algeria, to Lebanon, to Yemen (Arab American Institute, n.d.). In Arab-American culture, much as in Asian-American culture, the family is seen as the central foundational structure in society (Cifti, Jones, & Corrigan, 2013). Arab culture emphasizes the importance of behaving in ways that reflect well on others. Men are predominantly the head of the family, and the culture is based primarily on a patriarchal structure. The role of the father is typically strict and authoritative, whereas the role of the mother is nurturing and compassionate (Okasha, Karam, & Okasha, 2012). The preference for boys still exists in much of Arab-American culture, because of the belief that men will contribute to the family. Accordingly, boys are trained from an early age to eventually become the head of the household.

In Arab-American culture, in general, women are expected to remain virgins until married (Al-Krenawi & Jackson, 2014). In some Arab cultures, a woman may lose her family's honor if she violates this sexual code. Naber (2006) investigated Arab-American attitudes about sexuality and found that participants agreed that virginity and a heterosexual marriage were expected of an ideal Arab woman. The study discussed how a daughter who rejects the ideal notion of an Arab woman could cause cultural loss for the whole family. Arab-American families often endorse collectivistic values, which define family structures, gender roles, and expectations (Cifti et al., 2013). Chapter 10 expands on this discussion of gender among individuals of Arab descent.

MENTAL HEALTH CONSEQUENCES OF SEXISM

The psychological consequences of sexism on the lives of women and girls are numerous and potentially devastating. Although it is beyond the scope of this chapter to address all of the mental health consequences associated with sexism, we explore a few issues that future counselors will likely encounter when working with women or young girls. For TGNC women and girls, the literature is still nascent.

Women and Depression

Distress from sexism on women's lives is immense, with the consequences resting in several dimensions. It is also important to acknowledge that the majority of clients seeking mental health-care services are women. In fact, rates of depression are twice as high for women who are cisgender as for men who are cisgender. This gender disparity exists across race/ethnicity, age, and nationality (APA, 2011). Girls appear as likely as their male counterparts to experience depression during childhood. However, by the time girls become adolescents, their incidence of depression begins to spike, and the gender differences in depression first become apparent. This difference points to the importance of early intervention in girls' lives in terms of supporting their mental health. For TGNC women and girls, depression may increase when there is a lack of access to TGNC-affirming family, health-care, school, employment, and community environments.

Disordered Eating

One of the greatest mental health consequences of sexism is disordered eating and a negative body image. Girls' early exposure to media images and messages about an ideal of beauty that is thin, White, and Western may have indelible effects on their lives and self-image (Hine, 2011). In fact, the rates of eating disorders such as anorexia nervosa and bulimia nervosa have increased exponentially over time (Striegel-Moore & Bulik, 2007), with 3% to 10% of females between 15 and 29 years old (the age of most risk) meeting diagnostic criteria (Bemporad, 1997; Polivy & Herman, 2002). The incidence is different for females and males (10 to 1; McGilley & Pryor, 1998; Striegel-Moore, 1997). Eating disorders first gained attention in the helping professions in the late 1960s in the United States, as clinicians noticed women literally starving themselves or using a binge-and-purge cycle in response to having a negative body image (Polivy & Herman, 2002). Myths continue to exist that eating disorders are a White, upper-class women's issue. Although precise statistics on women of color do not currently exist, several studies have identified eating disorders, body dissatisfaction, and attempts to lose weight across all racial/ethnic groups (Kilpatrick, Ohannessian, & Bartholomew, 1999; Robinson et al., 1996; Story et al., 1997).

These disordered eating patterns are now thought to be coping strategies for many women who struggle with identity issues and with managing a sense of control over their environment. According to Smart, Yuying, Mejia, Hayashino, and Braaten (2011), eating disorders in women of color may be linked to the pressure to conform to Western beauty standards and may be used as a coping strategy to emotionally disconnect from intergenerational cultural stress. In fact, research studies that have focused on the cause of eating disorders may present a misleading view that is not culturally based on the images of beauty for women of color and, as a result, could lead to a misdiagnosis for this population (Talleyrand, 2012). Consequently, treating eating disorders may be challenging because there is a low presence of individuals with eating disorders or weight concerns seeking treatment in general (Eisenberg, Nicklett, Roeder, & Kirz, 2011), as well as a lack of literature that focuses on disordered eating and negative body images for women of color. While there also remains a lack of research into the experiences transgender girls and women have of disordered eating, because of the large numbers of women living with disordered eating and a negative body image, counselors should assess for negative body esteem and eating disorders with every girl and woman client and should be informed of the best practices of treatment for these issues.

Internalized Oppression

Regardless of the specific mental health concerns with which women present, it is likely that internalized oppression will play a role in influencing presenting concerns because sexism is so pervasive across cultural groups. For instance, internalized oppression can prevent women from fully expressing themselves and living their full potential, because they may believe that they need to conform to prescribed gender norms and expressions. Alternatively, the fear of appearing bossy or intimidating may prevent women from fulfilling leadership responsibilities. Conversely, some women may feel compelled to be perceived as completely removed from being seen as a woman at all, because they believe that that is the only way they will be taken seriously. Transgender girls and women may feel that they have to "prove" their femininity because of the anti-TGNC bias that exists in schools and workplaces. Both cisgender and transgender women experience internalized oppression that counselors may explore in order to identify areas of self-acceptance, self-efficacy, and empowerment.

PHYSICAL CONSEQUENCES OF SEXISM

The gender depression disparity hints at more serious physical problems left by sexism. If sexism is the undervaluation of cisgender and transgender women and girls, then it is this undervaluation that allows females in our society to be treated as objects. When women and girls are objectified in this manner, they are more easily made to be targets of violence. Indeed, women and girls do face higher rates of sexual trauma, increased exposure to occupational and environmental hazards, and disordered eating related to a negative body image and poor self-esteem. Counselors should be aware of the physical repercussions of sexism and be prepared to discuss such issues openly.

Women are at increased risk for experiencing interpersonal violence, and this risk is recognized as a serious public health and global concern (Ortabag, Ozdemir, Bebis, & Ceylan, 2014; Smith, Parrott, Swartout, & Tharp, 2015). Dillon, Hussain, Loxton, and Rahman (2013) asserted that women living with violent partners—specifically, women who were repeatedly exposed to violent events—had an increased probability of developing severe physical and psychological conditions, such as depression, suicidal ideation, and posttraumatic stress disorder (PTSD). Feminist researchers have criticized the diagnosis of PTSD because it was defined as a result of a traumatic event outside the typical human experience and, for many women, repeated incidences of physical and sexual violence, terror, and harassment were not outside their typical lived experiences (Wilkin & Hillock, 2014). The need for attention to repeated or chronic trauma experiences is critical to acknowledge, as these events often are related to experiences with sexism and other forms of oppression. Researchers have proposed a diagnosis of complex PTSD (Herman, 1992a), which would acknowledge the insidious trauma (Chu, 2011) involving repeated experiences of oppression that women and people from historically marginalized backgrounds experience.

Child sexual abuse and sexual assault are serious concerns for women and are often reasons that women seek therapy. Rates of child sexual abuse for females are 14.2 per 1,000 (U.S. Department of Justice, 2011). Nouri et al. (2012) suggest that, globally, almost 1 in 5 women have been physically or sexually abused by one or more male partners during their life. The National Intimate Partner and Sexual Violence Survey (NISVS; Black et al., 2011) found that 1 in 5 women had experienced rape perpetrated by men. One of the landmark works on women's trauma experiences and treatment is Judith Herman's (1992b) *Trauma and Recovery*. Herman outlines three stages that are vital for women's recovery from sexual abuse. The first stage entails ensuring that survivors are safe from their abusers and free of stressors (e.g., alcohol abuse, financial stress) that may make it challenging to heal from sexual violence. The second stage makes their trauma meaningful by reviewing the details of their experience and acknowledging associated feelings. The final stage consists of clinicians helping trauma survivors reconnect with their sense of self and with important relationships in their lives. Ultimately, because of the high rates of trauma for women, it is imperative that counselors conduct a thorough trauma assessment with every female client in order to determine what experiences of emotional, physical, and sexual abuse she may have experienced. Counselors also must be aware of best practices with female survivors of trauma.

With regard to women's experiences of intimate-partner violence, Worell and Remer (2003) have proposed a three-part model addressing the abuse of women that includes society at large, the male perpetrator, and the female survivor. The importance of this model is that it provides clinicians with a framework that will help them to understand the pervasive impact of intimate-partner violence on women, as well as how sexism reinforces an undervaluing and abuse of women. Through the model, the authors articulate the pattern of victims returning to their abusers—a pattern that is a dangerous reality of intimate-partner violence, in addition to causing frustration on the part of counselors attempting to advocate for the safety of their female clients. The model posits that the societal system of sexism combines with the male abuser to create a hostile climate for women, which ultimately is disempowering for the female survivor. In this disempowerment, a woman is held "hostage to terror and violence . . . [and] escalates her attempts to placate and please; and in doing so, she increases her powerlessness and becomes psychologically and physically entrapped in a relationship from which she feels unable to extricate herself" (p. 261). One limitation of the model is that it applies only to heterosexual relationships.

As noted earlier, men and women who are TGNC experience high rates of violence across the life span, and these experiences range from repeated microaggressions and street harassment to physical and sexual assault. In a large biannual survey that included students who were TGNC, 55.2% reported being verbally harassed, 11.4% reported physical harassment, and nearly 50% reported cyberharassment. Also concerning is the finding that over 60% of participants who reported an incident of harassment reported that there was no school response to the harassment.

SOCIAL CONSEQUENCES OF SEXISM

In addition to causing the aforementioned mental and physical consequences, sexism creates social health consequences. Especially for women of color, the undervaluation of females and narrow definitions of gender roles for women restrict their career development and opportunities. For instance, 26% of African-American families live below the poverty line, compared with 8.6% of White families (U.S. Census Bureau, 2015c). African-American women are typically funneled into jobs that are defined as traditionally female, such as domestic work and child care. These tracking strategies begin early in women's educational experiences and continue into higher educational experiences. For example, girls are still stigmatized about their supposed lack of ability in science, technology, engineering, and mathematics (STEM) fields and continue to remain unsupported in K–12 mathematics and science courses, especially by a lack of role models in the profession (National Coalition for Women and Girls in Education, 2013). In addition, women and girls who pursue careers in STEM-related fields may find themselves isolated and receiving less pay than men occupying the same positions (National Coalition for Women and Girls in Education, 2013). These discriminatory practices undoubtedly affect the types of careers into which women go and the amount of pay they receive, and all of these findings are consistent with data which show that women earn approximately 78 cents for every dollar earned by men (U.S. Department of Labor, Bureau of Statistics, 2015). The disparity in wage earnings is especially likely to harm single-mother families, which constitute approximately 26% of all U.S. families (about 10 million households). In 2012, 27% of households were managed by single mothers, compared with 18.2% in 1960 (U.S. Census Bureau, 2015c).

Another way that sexism manifests itself in women in the workplace is through internalized doubt in their own abilities. Clance (1985) originally identified this kind of internalized doubt and coined the term **impostor phenomenon** to describe how high-achieving women do not trust in their intelligence and work talents, fearing that others will eventually "find out" that they are not as capable as they actually are. The impostor phenomenon was found to occur more frequently in women than men and was attributed to the recognition that women have more roles than men and are expected to fulfill each role perfectly (Cusack, Hughes, & Nuhu, 2013). The impostor phenomenon may help explain why only 19% of full professors at colleges and universities are women (National Coalition for Women and Girls in Education, 2013). Cusack et al. (2013) maintain that the impostor phenomenon is tied to gender roles, and they describe how the phenomenon could affect women who internalize the belief that men are more capable than women in specific areas. Holding an impostor frame of mind results in a work cycle in which a woman

> [f]ace[s] a . . . project. . . . [She] experiences great doubt. . . . [She] questions whether or not she will succeed *this* time. . . . [She] works hard, overprepares . . . or procrastinates and then prepares in a frenzied manner. . . . [She] succeeds [in the task] and receives positive feedback. The whole cycle is reinforced . . . [and] doubting is reinforced. (p. 52)

Therefore, in addition to understanding the barriers to achievement that confront women in the workplace, it is critical that counselors keep in mind the barriers resulting from sexism when working with women who are managing career stressors. For women of color who are TGNC, counselors should be especially attentive to exploring issues of employment discrimination, lack of access to health care, and other anti-TGNC societal biases, because these effects are multiplicative, based on the intersection of racism and sexism (Singh & McKleroy, 2011).

ADDRESSING SEXISM IN COUNSELING

Counselors must be aware of their attitudes and beliefs about women and men who are cisgender and who are TGNC as a first step to providing nonsexist mental health services. Such awareness includes self-examining general and mental health stereotypes that a counselor might have about women clients, because these stereotypes could interfere with the type and quality of counseling provided. Traditionally, many educators teach students to refer clients to another counselor if there is a large discrepancy between the values of the counselor and client or if a counselor is not competent to work with a particular client. However, this recommendation should not be used as a way to avoid working with clients who are culturally different than the counselor. The ACA (2014) *Code of Ethics* states that counselors have an ethical responsibility to continually educate themselves and to become culturally competent practitioners. This responsibility includes being aware of diverse cultural groups and acquiring knowledge about others' cultures. Counselors also have an ethical responsibility not to partake in discriminatory practices. Discrimination in the guise of referring women clients is unethical.

Counselors must also be aware of how their race/ethnicity, gender, age, class status, ability level, and sexual orientation affect the counseling relationship. Boysen (2010) contends that multiculturally competent counselors recognize that bias exists and are aware of how that bias can harm the counseling relationship, including impairing their ability to support clients from diverse backgrounds. Competent counselors will explore with clients what their gender identities and sexual orientations mean to both of them and in relation to the larger social context. Counselors should also critically examine the counseling process, counseling theories, and the counseling format. Boysen purports that even the most competent counselor should remain cautious of implicit bias, those unintentional forms of bias that may take place outside one's conscious, in order to ensure that automatic responses from learned societal messages do not perpetuate the social *status quo*, particularly for women clients.

An additional way that counselors can minimize sexism in their counseling practice is by *not* assuming that clients' presenting problems are related to their gender identity or expression. Rather, counselors should collaborate with clients to explore how sexism permeates the contextual environments of the clients and how the clients are affected by it. When working with clients of color, counselors should integrate ethnic, gender, and sexual orientation identities to achieve maximum wellness. Wester, McDonough, White, Vogel, and Taylor (2010) suggested that GRC theory could provide counselors a framework for understanding the gendered experiences of clients, particularly those who identify as transgender, and for identifying how counselors can support clients who may still be in conflict about their gender identity. In counseling, GRC focuses on the messages constructed by society that determine one's gender expression and that can be used by counselors to understand the complex experiences of clients. In addition, GRC can zero in on components that prevent clients from moving beyond societal teachings. Once these components are assessed, counselors can implement the ACA's multicultural and social justice competencies (Ratts et al., 2015). Specifically, counselors should integrate the multicultural and social justice competencies in ways that empower cisgender and TGNC girls and women. The following are a few recommended strategies adapted from ACA's multicultural and social justice competencies:

- Identify strengths and resources of women clients who are cisgender and TGNC.
- Explore the social, political, economic, and cultural factors that affect clients who are cisgender and TGNC.
- Help clients who are cisgender and TGNC identify external barriers that affect their development.
- Teach self-empowerment skills to clients who are cisgender and TGNC.
- Explore salient intersectional identities with gender for cisgender and TGNC clients.
- Integrate a socioecological model into counseling assessment and practice (e.g., from microlevel to macrolevel).
- Self-reflect on counselor privilege and oppression experiences related to gender and sexism.

MEN AS FEMINISTS   Some people may think that feminist theory is just for women. Because we live in a male-dominated culture, if more men adopted feminist ideologies, greater social change could occur. Intemann, Lee, McCartney, Roshanravan, and Schriempf (2010) described approaches to feminist theory that, while different from one another, center the acquisition of knowledge as it relates to gender and explicate how race, class, nationality, sexuality, religion, and age intersect with gendered experiences. Numerous organizations and writings exist that explore men's engagement in feminist thinking and action are included in the Web resources listed in Table 5.1.

EXPANDING RESILIENCE AND SOCIAL JUSTICE

Although this chapter has detailed the many negative consequences of sexism for the mental health of men and women who are cisgender and TGNC, counselors should still maintain a strengths-based focus on how their clients may be resilient to the detrimental effects of oppression, as well as on how issues of social justice may provide opportunities for counselors to take action to end sexism. As counselors work with clients whose mental health has been compromised by sexism, focusing on areas in which the clients demonstrate strengths in their lives may help them expand their competencies and build further resilience to sexism in their lives.

For example, scholars have examined the resilience strategies of survivors of child sexual abuse. Boss (2010) proposed that positive family responses, social support, and relationships within one's community are an important aspect of developing resilience. The ability to develop resilience, according to Boss, is guided by finding meaning, reenvisioning attachments, reconstructing identity, normalizing ambivalence, and discovering hope. Authors have defined resilience as one's degree of self-acceptance, engagement in positive relationships, and mastery of contextual environments. Counselors can consider resilience when working with clients with multicultural backgrounds. In a study of South Asian survivors of child sexual abuse, respondents shared the consistent message that self-care, connection with community, and social activism were among their resilience strategies (Singh, Hays, & Watson, 2011). Resilience research with adults, youths, and youths of color who are TGNC suggests that expanding hope, teaching self-advocacy skills, increasing health-care and employment resources, and being connected with TGNC activist communities are important areas that counselors should focus on to support clients navigating anti-TGNC societal discrimination.

In addition to using strengths-based approaches in gender-affirmative counseling, counselors should consider ways in which they may work as social change agents to address the issues surrounding sexism in society. For instance, because the rates of trauma for people—especially women who are cisgender and TGNC—are so high as a result of sexism, counselors may find ways to work with community and government agencies to provide presentations or create support groups for survivors of trauma. Counselors may also work with schools, community colleges, and university centers to identify collaborative opportunities to stage events such as "Women Take Back the Night" (a typically on-campus event whereby survivors of sexual assault hold a rally with speakers on women's empowerment) and "Transgender Day of Remembrance," or "Transgender Day of Resilience" (a nationwide event typically held in November that recognizes TGNC victims of hate crimes and murder). Also important is that counselors be aware of the opportunities for social activism around issues of sexism so that they may educate clients on these events as potential experiences of empowerment and healing. Numerous organizations and writings are available that explore public health and social justice interventions related to sexism.

Summary

In this chapter, gender and sexism were discussed, along with how the various interwoven constructs affect clients, counselors, and the counseling relationship. Because gender is such a fundamental component of identity, we often take for granted that it is a binary concept related to sex assignment—either male or female, man or woman. However, it is imperative to remember that gender identity and expression exist along a continuum, with multiple identities. This variation of gender identities and expressions intersects with other cultural identities, such as race, ethnicity, socioeconomic status, religious affiliation, and so on. Therefore, it is easy to see the complexities that counselors face as they strive to become culturally competent with issues of gender identity and expression. The chapter reviewed the relationship between gender and sexism for women and men who are cisgender and TGNC. From defining these terms to exploring best practices for counselors to follow in working with clients, specific influences that gender and sexism have on the mental health of *all* people were identified. The history of sexism was reviewed, and how gender norms both differ and are similar across diverse cultural groups was discussed. Finally, counselors were urged not only to address the negative impacts of sexism, but also to examine where they may focus on the clients' resilience in the face of sexism and on the opportunities for counselors to advocate on behalf of clients and promote social justice.

Review Questions

1. How does gender affect both clients and counselors, and why is it an important consideration in the counseling relationship?
2. How is internalized sexism related to male privilege, and how does it affect relationships among men, women, and people who are TGNC?
3. Why are women's gender role expectations an area of particular concern for counselors?
4. What is normative male alexithymia, and how might it manifest itself socially as well as clinically?
5. Describe some examples of the mental health consequences of sexism and how these might be addressed in counseling.
6. How can counselors address the negative impact of sexism, and what role does client resilience play?
7. What are the important areas of consideration in counseling clients who are TGNC?
8. How are gender identity, gender expression, sex, and sexual orientation different, but overlapping, constructs?
9. How has the women's liberation movement affected counseling as a field? What are the remaining challenges for women's rights?

6

Sexual Orientation and Heterosexism

Michael P. Chaney and Michael D. Brubaker

PREVIEW

Multicultural counseling has expanded to include various intersections of identity, including sexual orientation. Counseling from this perspective must incorporate an understanding of the complexities inherent in clients, including the fact that many come from multiple minority statuses. Multicultural competence with respect to sexual orientation may be addressed through increased awareness of counselors' assumptions, values, and biases regarding sexual orientation; awareness of clients' worldviews regarding sexual orientation; and clinical and advocacy intervention strategies that are culturally appropriate. This chapter defines and discusses concepts relevant to sexual orientation and presents implications for counseling lesbian, gay, and bisexual (LGB) clients. In addition, we discuss the intersections of sexual orientation with race, gender, ethnicity, and culture, because clients may hold minority statuses. Since the research on sexual orientation and heterosexism is often tied to that related to gender and sexism, some information in this chapter relates to a broader group of lesbian, gay, bisexual, transgender, questioning, and intersex (LGBTQI) individuals.

DEFINING SEXUAL ORIENTATION AND HETEROSEXISM

Sexual orientation is sometimes difficult to define and distinguish because it is often related to gender under the term *sexual identity*. **Sexual identity** includes (a) physical identity, (b) gender identity, (c) social sex role identity, and (d) sexual orientation identity (American Psychological Association, 2011). Whereas **physical identity** is the biological sex of individuals, **gender identity** is the belief a person has about his or her gender (i.e., the psychological sense of being male, female, both, or neither), and **social sex role identity** is the gender roles people adopt or adhere to on the basis of cultural norms for feminine and masculine behavior. For example, a physical male may have a female gender identity, feeling more like a female emotionally and spiritually, and may have a female social sex role identity, adopting societal behaviors and appearances of a female. **Sexual orientation identity** is different from gender identity, involving a person's sexual and emotional attraction to members of the other and/or the same sex.

Sexual orientation is described as consisting of a set of seven variables: (a) sexual behaviors; (b) emotions; (c) sexual fantasies; (d) sexual attractions; (e) social preference; (f) living life as a heterosexual, bisexual, or gay or lesbian; and (g) self-identification (American Institute of Bisexuality, 2012). Heterosexuality, homosexuality, and bisexuality are all possible culminations of the process of sexual orientation identity development. **Heterosexuality**, the most common sexual orientation identity, refers to aesthetic, romantic, or sexual attraction to members of the opposite gender (in a binary male–female system). People may or may not use the term *straight* to describe someone who is heterosexual, because it can be considered a value-laden term. **Homosexuality**, then, is one type of sexual orientation identity; however, *homosexual* is no longer a preferred term used to refer to an individual or a group of people who have same-sex feelings and behaviors and who identify with the gay community. **Gay male** and **lesbian** are acceptable terms because they are associated with positive, nonpathological identities, include individuals' emotional and affectional feelings, and refer to a cultural minority group (i.e., the gay community; American Psychological Association, 2010). In addition, the term *gay* can be used to refer to both men and women and to a broad community and culture that includes both men and women. **Bisexuality**, another sexual orientation identity, refers to aesthetic, romantic, or sexual attraction to members of either the same or the opposite gender. Most bisexual people are not equally attracted to men and women, and many are exclusively attracted to one or the other gender at different points in their lives. In addition, how bisexual people define their relationship may differ from person to person (Beemyn, 2011). **Questioning** is a term that refers to an individual who is questioning her or his sexual orientation and/or gender identity. For many younger people, Q represents **queer**, a broad term that includes anyone who does not identify as heterosexual. As societal attitudes toward nonheterosexuals change, individuals are increasingly using nonbinary categories to describe their sexual orientations, including **pansexual** (an individual whose sexual and/or affectional attractions are not limited to what is based on gender identity or biological sex) and **heteroflexible** (someone who identifies as primarily heterosexual, but may engage in limited situational same-sex sexual behavior yet does not identify as bisexual). Sensitive counselors will ask clients how they refer to themselves and will use language the client uses.

Some researchers have suggested the use of the term **affectional orientation** (Lambert, 2005) to describe sexual minorities (i.e., LGB individuals) because it broadens the discussion beyond simply sexual attraction. Sexual orientation is seen by some as a societal construct that serves to oppress, marginalize, and reduce LGB individuals' identity to the largely taboo realm of sexual behavior. Because LGB relationships are not based solely on sexual attraction, perhaps "affectional orientation" may be a more accurate term. Like heterosexual relationships, LGB relationships involve attraction based on intelligence, emotional stability, communication style, and other interpersonal factors and feelings that exist for many couples. The term *affectional orientation* may also be more appropriate because it allows the LGB or questioning client to use a broader spectrum of emotional language to explore or accurately represent his or her experience of attraction. In sum, LGB identity is one component of sexual orientation identity. A gay or lesbian identity includes having same-sex behaviors, but also includes attractions, emotions, and a sense of connection with a gay community (American Psychological Association, 2011). Reflection 6.1 provides some questions for consideration with respect to the use of terminology.

REFLECTION 6.1

What terminology have you typically used to describe LGB or LGBTQI individuals? Where did you learn these descriptors? How have they changed? What are your thoughts about the term *sexual orientation* versus *affectional orientation*? What are the benefits of using one term over another?

Heterosexism

Heterosexism is defined as the oppression of LGBTQI individuals that involves prejudice and discriminatory behavior (American Psychological Association, 2011). Societal norms valuing heterosexual identity and practices (e.g., marriage, laws) are a major component of heterosexism, which in turn may devalue the lives of LGBTQI people. Heterosexism also includes the enforcement of heterosexual norms that may be consciously or unconsciously endorsed by individuals and institutions. In this manner, prejudicial and discriminatory acts, policies, and behavior are considered to be heterosexist. Heterosexism in these forms is additionally problematic, because it considers heterosexuality to be the "norm" and model of sexual identity for all people. Because heterosexism is a systematic oppression of LGBTQI identity, counselors will likely work with LGBTQI individuals who have internalized this devaluation of their sexual orientation. **Internalized heterosexism**, the internalization of society's negative attitudes toward nonheterosexuals, may emerge in counseling sessions as a comparison to a heterosexual norm and an overriding belief system that heterosexuals are "better than" individuals who are LGBTQI. Internalized heterosexism often manifests itself in LGB clients as unrecognized shame. Heterosexism originates from, and is maintained by, stereotypes that individuals hold about those who are LGBTQI. (See Activity 6.1.)

ACTIVITY 6.1

Generate a list of stereotypes that you have or that you have heard about individuals who are LGBTQI. Review your list in small groups. When did you learn or hear these stereotypes? Where did they come from? Why is it important for you, as a future counselor, to verbalize and name these stereotypes?

A related term that many people often confuse with heterosexism is **homophobia**. Homophobia is defined as fear and hatred of people who are LGBTQI (Bullough, 2018). Homophobic acts may include hate crimes against individuals who are LGBTQI and their communities—crimes that range from verbal to physical assault and are therefore a component of the larger system of heterosexist oppression. Indeed, hate crimes are a real concern for the LGBTQI community, especially because the Federal Bureau of Investigation (FBI) ranks anti-LGBTQI violence as the second-largest group of hate crimes, after racial hate crimes, in the United States (U.S. Department of Justice, 2014b). In fact, 20.8% of all single-bias hate crimes documented by the FBI in 2013 were motivated by sexual orientation (and many anti-LGBTQI hate crimes go unreported), and the number of these hate crimes has consistently increased in the United States. This increase is particularly troublesome because hate crimes involving sexual orientation are some of the most brutal and violent hate crimes that have been documented and include murder (National Coalition of Anti-Violence Programs, 2010). Fortunately, in 2009 the U.S. Congress passed federal hate crimes legislation that included laws against hate crimes motivated by sexual orientation or gender identity (National Gay and Lesbian Task Force, 2014). In thinking about the systemic oppression of people who are LGBTQI, it is important that counselors keep in mind that researchers and social justice advocates have recommended using terms such as *homonegativity* (Slootmaeckers & Lievens, 2014) to acknowledge the devaluation of individuals who are LGBTQI. Regardless of the terminology used, the systemic oppression of heterosexism and homophobia contributes to individuals who are LGBTQI being treated as one of the most denigrated and invisible groups in society, often because they live outside the box of traditional heterosexual norms.

A system of heterosexism confers unearned advantages onto heterosexual people—a phenomenon called **heterosexual privilege**. It is important for heterosexual counselors to recognize this privilege and its related impact on the mental health of people who are LGBTQI. (See Activity 6.2.) Heterosexual privilege includes adoptive and child rights, fewer economic barriers, and family counseling approaches that assume patriarchal family structure as indicative of a functioning family system. Heterosexism also gives heterosexuals the privilege of having their relationships validated by the media and by colleagues in the workplace, in addition to being able to arrange to be in the company of other heterosexual people in most environments.

ACTIVITY 6.2

In small groups, make a list of heterosexual privileges that people who are LGBTQI do not have access to in our society. Then brainstorm a second list of privileges accorded to males simply on the basis of their gender. Identify the commonalities and differences between the two lists. During your discussion, generate ways that one may use heterosexual and male privilege to create LGBTQI-friendly environments in counseling.

HISTORICAL CONTEXT OF HETEROSEXISM

As with other cultural groups, LGBTQI communities have a history. A large part of this history is related to challenging oppressive heterosexist institutions and policies. One of the most noteworthy historical events for members of the LGBTQI communities was the Stonewall Rebellion. This event is credited as starting the gay civil-rights movement.

Resistance to Heterosexism: The Stonewall Rebellion

Duberman (1994) provided an important historical account of the events at Stonewall in 1969 that marked the beginning of the modern LGBTQI rights movement. Police officers in New York City routinely raided the Stonewall Inn, a gay establishment. During a typical raid, police officers harassed and arrested patrons. On June 28, 1969, patrons of the bar (primarily transgender people of color) fought back against the police, thus challenging the systemic oppression. The uprising lasted for several days. The story of Stonewall is especially important for counselors to have knowledge of because clients who are LGBTQI may not be aware of the history of the LGBTQI liberation movement. Sharing knowledge of this movement can help clients normalize the idea that many LGBTQI people were forced into silence and shame. In addition, sharing such knowledge offers the client the hope of visibility, community, and empowerment that Stonewall represents.

INTERSECTIONS OF HETEROSEXISM AND SEXISM Some gay and women studies writers have asserted that heterosexism is a "weapon" of sexism, in that heterosexism functions to systemically and narrowly define gender roles and enforce compulsory heterosexuality. Certainly, the link between heterosexism and sexism is multifaceted and complex and goes beyond the mere fact that "sexism" is included in the word *heterosexism*. In a classic composition, feminist activist and academic bell hooks (1981) asserted that "challenging sexist oppression is a crucial step in the struggle to eliminate all forms of oppression" (pp. 35–36). In terms of complexity, the connection between heterosexism and sexism includes the enforcement of gender roles through socialization practices. For instance, boys are raised with the goal of "becoming a man," which often includes values of emotional restraint, assertiveness, the role of "protector" of the family, competition, and the avoidance of displaying vulnerability. The intersection of sexism and heterosexism becomes clear in the derogatory language (e.g., "faggot," "sissy") that is used when a boy steps outside traditional gender norms for males. Girls, by contrast, are socialized to be caregivers, to be dependent on others, to display emotions, and to avoid being viewed as "too strong." When girls and women cross the boundaries of strict gender roles, they are often the recipients of epithets such as "bitch" or "aggressive" when asserting their needs.

Culturally competent counselors should have a firm understanding of the aforementioned definitions because much of the power of heterosexism is rooted in the meanings society gives to nontraditional behaviors, thoughts, and emotions. In addition, culturally competent counselors should understand how heterosexism intersects with classism.

Intersections of Heterosexism and Classism

Although individuals who are LGBTQI generally have more education than their heterosexual peers, potentially leading to higher paying jobs, home ownership is lower for partnered lesbians and gays than for married heterosexual couples (Goldberg, 2009). Part of the reason may be that many states have laws which prohibit unmarried couples from owning a home together. However, the U.S. Census Bureau (2014a) reported that gay male couples have a higher mean household income than heterosexual couples have, and lesbian couples have lower mean household incomes than heterosexual couples. Although individuals who are LGBTQI live everywhere in the United States, many choose to live in large metropolitan cities, where there tends to be greater tolerance. Gates (2015) reported that the following cities with populations over 100,000 have the highest number of individuals who identify as LGBT: San Francisco (6.2%), Portland (5.4%), Austin (5.3%), New Orleans (5.1%), and Seattle (4.8%). Because many individuals who are LGBTQI choose to live in these more accepting cities, which generally have higher costs of living, members of the LGBTQI community who cannot afford to live in such cities often remain invisible. In fact, according to the Williams Institute (2011), 12% of same-sex couples live in rural areas, and 7% live in exurban areas. Barrett and Pollack (2005) found that working-class gay men may not have the resources to move to higher amenity gay neighborhoods. As a result, many working-class gays and bisexuals remain closeted, living in nonaccepting areas, where there is an increased likelihood of experiencing psychological distress and physical violence. Moreover, 61% of men in Barrett and Pollack's study reported living in poverty or experiencing financial difficulties, such as having to borrow money to meet basic living needs. Because many helping professionals and researchers discuss LGBTQI people only in terms of sexual identity and sexual behavior, issues of race, class, ability, and gender are either forgotten or ignored. Culturally sensitive, nonheterosexist counselors should assess the multiple identities of their clients who are LGBTQI. In addition, culturally competent counselors will examine issues affecting LGB youths.

CURRENT ATTITUDES TOWARD INDIVIDUALS WHO ARE LGBTQI

In 1975, the American Psychological Association adopted a resolution stating that "homosexuality per se implies no impairment in judgment, stability, reliability, or general social or vocational capabilities" (Conger, 1975, p. 633), following a rigorous discussion of the 1973 decision of the American Psychiatric Association to remove homosexuality from its list of mental disorders (American Psychiatric Association, 1973). Although homosexuality is no longer considered a mental illness, societal attitudes and institutional policies toward individuals who are LGBTQI have been slow to improve. For example, many LGB people are not protected from employment discrimination in most states, because sexual orientation is not included in the federal Title VII of the Civil Rights Act of 1964, which prohibits employment discrimination against other minority groups (Ineson, Yap, & Whiting, 2013). Today, 21 states and the District of Columbia prohibit discrimination based on sexual orientation; of those states, 18 also prohibit discrimination based on gender identity (National Gay and Lesbian Task Force, 2014).

Despite the increasing visibility of gays and lesbians in U.S. culture, individuals who are LGB are often unsure when and where it is safe to disclose their sexual orientation. However, Americans' attitudes toward individuals who are LGB and their relationships are shifting, as is evidenced by recent polls, which found that 55% of Americans support same-sex marriage (Pew Research Center, 2015d). The poll also found, however, that 39% of Americans opposed same-sex marriage. These percentages are important information for counselors to have, because some LGBTQI clients will present with relationship issues and will need to work with a counselor who has been exposed to information about current demographics of the LGBTQI community.

LESBIAN, GAY, AND BISEXUAL DEMOGRAPHY

There is much controversy surrounding the actual number of men and women who identify as LGBTQI. Current statistics do not include individuals who may be uncomfortable disclosing an LGBTQI identity, youths and adults who have not yet realized that they are LGBTQI, and heterosexually married individuals who may also identify as LGBTQI. A 2006–2008 survey conducted by the National Center for Health Statistics (2011a) that included 13,495 Americans, aged 15 to 44, found that 6% of men and 12% of women had had same-sex sexual experiences by age 44. Approximately 1% of women between the ages of 18 and 44 identified as lesbian and 3.5% bisexual; approximately 2% of males between the ages of 18 and 44 identified as gay and 1% as bisexual. Note that a same-sex intimate encounter does not necessarily constitute an LGBTQI identity, nor does the absence of a same-sex sexual experience mean that someone is heterosexual. These discrepancies illustrate the difficulty in accurately identifying the precise number of individuals who are LGBTQI. Although the statistics are likely underestimated, it is estimated that there are 9 million LGB individuals in the United States, representing about 3.5% of the population aged 18 and over (Gates, 2011).

LGBTQI Relationship Status and Family Issues

U.S. Census Bureau (2014a) data estimated that over 783,000 same-sex couples (377,903 male–male couples, 405,197 female–female couples) live in the United States. In addition, LGBTQI couples are increasingly choosing to expand their families, with over one-quarter of same-sex couples raising children (Gates, 2013). As will be discussed later in the chapter, the effects of institutional heterosexism on lesbian and gay couples and their children are numerous. One example is in the area of same-sex parent adoption.

The ability to adopt children varies from state to state. In 16 states and the District of Columbia, same-sex couples may petition for joint adoption; in 21 states and the District of Columbia, a same-sex partner may petition for second-parent adoption. In other states, the law is unclear and often depends on the jurisdiction in which adoption petitions are filed. In some states, such as Mississippi and Utah, LGB individuals are banned from adopting children. Some states prohibit them from being foster parents. By contrast, states such as California and New York prohibit discrimination based on sexual orientation in the adoption process (Human Rights Campaign Fund, n.d.). Myths commonly used against LGBTQI individuals seeking to adopt or foster children include the following: "Children need biological parents," "Children raised by same-sex parents are more likely to develop gender and sexual disorders," and "Children need a mother and a father" (Family Research Council, n.d.).

Major national organizations, including the American Psychological Association, the American Medical Association, the American Psychiatric Association, the Child Welfare League of America, and the American Academy of Pediatrics, have rejected these arguments and made statements in support of gay and lesbian parenting. The American Psychological Association (2016) reported that lesbian and gay parents are at least equal to heterosexual parents in terms of mental health, parenting skills, and quality of family relationships. In addition, it reported that research has consistently shown that children of gay and lesbian parents are no different than other children in terms of gender identity development, gender role behavior, sexual orientation, psychological and cognitive development, social relationships, and familial relationships. Although studies have shown same-sex parenting to be no different than opposite-sex parenting, many individuals continue to view same-sex parents as emotionally unstable and to discriminate against same-sex parents and their children (Weiner & Zinner, 2015). Given the increasing attention paid to same-sex parenting, it is important for counselors to consider their own attitudes toward this issue, as well as examine potential counseling considerations. (See Activity 6.3.)

ACTIVITY 6.3

In a dyad, discuss the following questions:

- How do you feel about individuals who are LGBTQI raising children?
- What are some advantages of children being adopted by parents who are LGBTQI?
- What are some of the struggles a child may encounter with parents who are LGBTQI?
- What assumptions do you have about challenges that lesbian parents may experience? How about gay male parents?
- How might these advantages and struggles manifest themselves in counseling families?

Educational Status

In general, individuals who are lesbian and gay have more formal education than their heterosexual counterparts. Approximately 4 in 10 individuals who are LGB have college degrees, compared with 3 in 10 non-LGB people (Gates, 2014a). At first glance, it appears that the myth that LGB individuals have a relatively high disposable income has some truth to it: More education is likely to lead to higher paying jobs. However, viewed critically, these statistics show that an estimated 60% of LGB individuals do *not* have college degrees. This fact is important because higher education and higher income have been found to be related to increased odds of an individual identifying as LGBTQI and to living in a predominantly LGBTQI neighborhood (Barrett & Pollack, 2005). In addition, individuals who are LGB are just as likely as heterosexuals to live in poverty, as is evidenced by a recent report that LGB Americans are less likely than non-LGB individuals to be thriving financially (Gates, 2014b). Possible reasons for these findings are a lack of protection against employment discrimination in most states and a lack of family support (Albelda, Badgett, Gates, & Schneebaum, 2013). Another possible explanation for the discrepancies in educational attainment could be the negative academic experiences that many LGB youths have.

LGB Youths

Counselors who work with adolescents should be aware of the unique pressures faced by LGB youths. Because of the pressure to conform in adolescence, many gay and lesbian youths are harassed for being perceived as gay or lesbian (Centers for Disease Control [CDC], 2014). In fact, the Gay, Lesbian and Straight Education Network (GLSEN, 2014) reported that, among 7,898 middle and high school students surveyed, 74.1% noted experiencing verbal harassment based on their sexual orientation, 36.2% reported physical harassment (e.g., being pushed or shoved), and 16.5% reported physical assault (e.g., being injured with a weapon or punched; Kosciw, Greytak, Palmer, & Boesen, 2014). Some of the bullying was electronic: 49% of students reported being harassed via text or other social media venues, such as Facebook. Many public schools have successfully fought against racism and sexism, but dealing with homophobia has been more challenging. High schools may be reticent to show approval of gay and lesbian youths out of fear of appearing to overstep parental authority or religious doctrine. The general thinking seems to be that the schools are telling students what to think, and they may be teaching them attitudes that are opposite what is being taught at home.

Some adolescents who are LGBT exist in social, emotional, and informational isolation because teachers and other school staff do not take steps to protect them from a hostile environment (Kosciw et al., 2014). GLSEN reported that 71.4% of students identifying as LGBT had heard the word *gay* used in a negative way, and over 64% had heard homonegative words, such as *dyke* and *faggot*, used to describe people who are LGBT. Students who are LGBT risk losing peer status by letting others know about their personal feelings, so they may choose to remain silent and try to "pass."

Although many schools often fail to protect and affirm students who are gay, the federal government, courts, and mass media are taking proactive steps to improve the lives of gay students. The *Equal Access Act* (20 U.S.C. sections 4071–74) states that "it shall be unlawful for any secondary school which receives Federal financial assistance to deny access or a fair opportunity to, or discriminate against, any students who wish to conduct a meeting on the basis of the religious, political, philosophical, or other content of the speech at such meetings." Despite this clear mandate, many local school boards are embroiled in a controversy over the existence of gay–straight alliances. These noncurricular clubs seek to increase understanding, promote respect, and diminish fear around sexual orientation issues. Many school boards are refusing to let such clubs meet, despite protection by the First Amendment and the Equal Access Act. According to Kendra Huard, of People for the American Way (PFAW, a nonprofit civil liberties group),

. . . the school board negatively affects these students because by merely asking for the club they think that they have done something wrong. We just really want the board to understand that if they violate the law, they are opening themselves to litigation. (PFAW, 2003, p. 60)

Another protection for youths who are LGB is **Title IX**, a federal statute that prohibits sex discrimination, including sexual harassment. In 1997, the Office for Civil Rights of the U.S. Department of Education released new Title IX guidelines for schools. For the first time, these guidelines made explicit reference to gay and lesbian students as also being protected. Although Title IX does not provide protection against discrimination related to perceived sexual orientation, it does prohibit discrimination associated with gender identity and gender orientation if it is related to sex-based discrimination (Courson & Farris, 2012). Clearly, more work needs to be done to advocate for and protect LGB youths, but progress is gradually being made. (See Build Your Knowledge 6.1 for important resources.)

Age and Disclosure of Sexual Orientation

Lesbians and gay males in the U.S. population are relatively young, with mean ages in the early forties (Gates, 2014a). Competent counselors are to take into consideration a client's

BUILD YOUR KNOWLEDGE 6.1

The Association for Lesbian, Gay, Bisexual and Transgender Issues in Counseling (ALGBTIC) is a division of the American Counseling Association. Its primary mission is to promote awareness of counseling issues that influence nonheterosexual clients and to improve the delivery of counseling services to clients. The ALGBTIC Web site (www.algbtic.org) contains a comprehensive list of resources for clinicians, students, and the general public. In addition to listing knowledge-based resources, the ALGBTIC website describes ways individuals might advocate on behalf of those who are LGBTQ. Following are other ways to advocate for people who are LGBTQ:

- Have a "safe zone" sticker (available from the Bridges Project of the National Youth Advocacy Coalition or at www.glsen.org) at the entrance to your office or classroom.
- Have literature (e.g., magazines, books) available on LGBTQ concerns.
- Post online resources for students who are LGBTQ, such as resources from the International Gay, Lesbian, Bisexual and Transgender Youth Association (http://orgs.tigweb.org/international-gay-lesbian-bisexual-and-transgender-youth-association); PFLAG (formerly Parents, Family and Friends of Lesbians and Gays; www.pflag.org); Gay, Lesbian, and Straight Education Network (www.glsen.org); Gay and Lesbian Teen Pen Pals (http://penpalslgbt.tumblr.com/); *Oasis* (teen magazine) (www.oasismag.com); Outright (https://www.outright international.org/); OutProud: National Coalition for GLBT Youth (http://msqueer.wordpress.com/2008/07/28/outproud-national-coalition-for-glbt-youth/); The Cool Page for Queer Teens (http://www.bidstrup.com/cool.htm); and National LGBTQ Task Force (www.ngltf.org).
- Use inclusive, stigma-free language, such as "partners" instead of "husbands and wives," in all communication.
- Create a social media page that highlights LGBTQ issues and/or connects individuals who are LGBTQ to form larger advocacy groups.

emotional age, as well as chronological age, when strategizing effective interventions for youths who are LGBTQI. It is common for individuals who come out as LGBTQI in adulthood to experience a late adolescence that they did not have when most heterosexual peers went through adolescence. In relation to the process of disclosing one's sexual orientation to others or the self-realization of an LGBTQI identity (i.e., **coming out**), the average age a person comes out to others is about 25 years old (Rothman, Sullivan, Keyes, & Boehmer, 2012). Further, LGB individuals are more likely to first come out to their mothers than their fathers. This discrepancy is likely due to stereotypical gender roles. For example, it may be easier to come out to mothers, who are socialized to be nurturing and accepting, whereas fathers are expected to be strong and masculine. There may also be a greater fear of being rejected by a father than by a mother. Of those individuals who choose to come out, 10% to 15% are rejected by their parents. Many youths who are LGBTQI and who have been rejected by their parents end up homeless and struggling on the streets, a tragedy that will be discussed later in the chapter. Case Study 6.1 and Reflection 6.2 discuss some coming-out considerations for counselors.

CASE STUDY 6.1

Muna is a 22-year-old, fourth-year student at a large midwestern urban university. She is the oldest of four children. Muna's parents immigrated to the United States from Saudi Arabia when she was 7 years old. In session, she presents herself as an alert, intelligent, and confident young woman. She appears well groomed, wearing blue jeans, a solid-black blouse, and a beige hijab that covers her hair and neck. When asked in the initial counseling session what she would like to work on, Muna nervously revealed that she was having a difficult time deciding whether or not she should tell her traditional Muslim parents that she is a lesbian. Muna went on to say that she realized she was "different" when she was about 12 years old. She shared that, around middle school, when boys and girls were socialized to interact and play with children of their same gender, she wished that she would have been able to socialize with the boys in her school because she was not very interested in the things in which the other girls her age were interested. She remembered a desire to play some of the sporting games with her male peers, rather than engage in some of the activities of her female friends. She also recalled having a crush on one of her female friends at age 16. At the time, she dismissed the crush as just "feeling close to a best friend." Muna went on to share, "Once I left home to attend college, I met other women who felt the way I do. I realized that I was not the only one like this." Muna explained that being a lesbian is not allowed in Islam and that the Quran forbids sexual relationships outside of heterosexual marriage. Muna expressed a great deal of fear about potential negative repercussions from her family and her Islamic community if she were to disclose her sexual orientation, but she also feels like she is being true to herself for the first time in her life.

- What are the presenting problems that you want to focus on as you work with Muna?
- What will be the most challenging aspect working with this client?
- Describe the types of interventions and clinical approaches you believe will be most beneficial for Muna. (Be specific.)
- How will you negotiate Muna's clinical goals and personal values while also taking into consideration the values of her faith, family, and community?

- How will you address her gender, sexual orientation, ethnic, and spiritual identities in your counseling sessions?
- How will your gender, sexual orientation, ethnic, and spiritual identities influence your work with Muna?

REFLECTION 6.2

Write a simulated coming-out letter to someone who is important to you. You do not have to give the letter to the significant person if you do not want to. What was it like to write the letter? How do you imagine the coming-out process is for individuals who are LGBTQI if you do not identify as such? What interventions would you use with a client whose goal is to come out to others?

CULTURAL INTERSECTIONS OF SEXUAL ORIENTATION

Scholars have discussed the phenomenon of double and triple minorities: individuals who have two to three oppressed statuses based on race, culture, gender, or sexual and affectional orientation (Wilson, Okwu, & Mills, 2011). For example, an African-American lesbian may experience oppression in the form of sexism because of her female status, racism because of her African-American heritage, and heterosexism for identifying as a lesbian. A major issue for individuals who are LGB of color is establishing healthy racial and sexual identities simultaneously. It can become quite complex to disentangle how various forms of oppression (e.g., heterosexism, racism) affect an individual's sexual orientation identity. (See Voices from the Field 6.1.)

There are few models that conceptualize the identity development process for LGB individuals of color. One, however, is Morales's (1989) model. Building on earlier gay identity models, Morales's strong model helps explain how some LGB individuals of color establish their identities. The model involves individuals moving through the following states: (a) denying identity conflicts, (b) labeling oneself as bisexual rather than lesbian/gay, (c) being conflicted in allegiance between lesbian/gay and ethnic communities, (d) establishing priorities in allegiance, and (e) integrating multiple identities. According to Morales, people of color who are LGB may experience several of the preceding states simultaneously. This state of affairs is consistent with recent research which found that ethnic and sexual identity development processes occur during similar periods; for most gay and bisexual youths of color, these processes occur at the same time: in early to late adolescence (Jamil, Harper, & Fernandez, 2009). Because clients of color who are LGB tend to experience unique challenges while trying to establish identities in different domains of their lives, it is important for counselors to understand how specific cultural groups view individuals who identify as LGB. What follows is a brief introduction to how certain cultural groups *may* view people who are LGB. We emphasize "may" because it is important that we not generalize the results of the studies that follow to all people who make up the cultural groups represented. There are many heterosexual allies in these groups!

Voices from the Field 6.1

Being a gay Black man, if anything, has taught me to be as kind, compassionate, understanding, accepting, caring and concerned for my fellow humans as I can. I feel that I am a double minority and I haven't the right to show intolerance or prejudicial behavior to others. It would be hypocritical for me to do so.

When I think about how White gay men treat me, it is a tricky and sometimes a sore subject for me. Unfortunately, racism knows no bounds. I have found that some White gay men, as well as Black, can certainly perpetuate prejudice on the basis of the color of my skin. I think it's rather stupid for any gay man or woman to be discriminatory. We are a community (gays) struggling on an hourly basis to be recognized and treated equally, yet some (gays) so readily condemn someone solely on skin color. To me, that's just not logical.

As far as dating is concerned, I find that, because I am a gay Black man, it is hit or miss, feast or famine. In many cases, White gay men are not attracted to me simply because I am Black, and in other cases they are attracted to me *only* because I am Black. Either way, I actually find them both to be equally demeaning. I guess I don't like being ostracized and objectified, whether the intention is good or bad. Ironically, whenever I travel outside of the country, I feel appreciated or rather admired for my "Black-man looks." It's as if I am on equal footing with every other gay man.

When I think about what it's like being gay in the Black community, the first thing that comes to mind is the term "down low." I mean the phrase "DL—down low" is often associated with the gay/bi Black man. It's so ironic to me that, whenever I was in church (and I don't go anymore and haven't for a few decades), I would sit in the pew listening to the preacher denounce homosexuality and then listen to the choir sing while being led by the "gay" choir director. It seems, from my observation, that most of the overtly gay Black men—and by that I mean the "queeny" ones (no offense)—are very visible in the community. I personally have never heard anyone in my family or community (back when I lived in a predominately Black area) really go on about how much they dislike gays. Now that's not to say that it doesn't happen; I've just never experienced it.

~Ty, Rochester, MI

African Americans

Similar to other people of color, African-American LGB individuals have to negotiate two identities that have been historically oppressed. Having to deal with both racist and heterosexist societal messages increases their risk of internalized oppression. Internalized racism and heterosexism are detrimental to one's self-esteem and increase emotional distress (Szymanski & Gupta, 2009; Velez, Moradi, & DeBlaere, 2015). In addition, it seems that, for people who are African American and LGB, internalized heterosexism is a greater predictor of psychological distress than internalized racism. One explanation for this link could be due to the role the Black church has historically played in the lives of many African Americans. Because religion and spirituality have been a foundation within the Black community, persistent negative messages about same-sex behavior are pernicious to Black LGB individuals' identity development and psychological well-being. The problem is that, although individuals may internalize negative messages from the church, many individuals who are Black and LGB look to the church as a source of support. In this regard, Walker and Longmire-Avital (2013) found that Black LGB adults who experienced high levels of internalized heterosexism but had strong religious faith reported a great deal of resiliency to cope with the internalized shame. These findings demonstrate the complex intersection of the multiple identities counselors and clients must navigate.

Asian Americans

Individuals who are Asian American and LGB also contend with the negative consequences associated with multiple oppressed statuses. Stigma management is one strategy used by oppressed groups to deal with the disenfranchisement. Among Asian-American LGB individuals, stigma management is often a collective behavior. Han, Proctor, and Choi (2014) found that one way that Asian-American gay men manage the racial stigma they experience within the larger White gay community is by distancing themselves from all things perceived to be Asian and aligning themselves with things associated with the larger White dominant community. However, this cultural distancing can lead to lower self-esteem and greater marginalizaton from the White gay community. Lack of support and acceptance is not limited to the dominant White gay community. Because some Asian cultures devalue LGB identities, many LGB individuals who are Asian American do not receive needed support from their families and communities after coming out—a situation that can lead to profound distress and rejection. For LGB individuals who are Asian American, heterosexism in Asian-American communities is a predictor of psychological distress (Szymanski & Sung, 2010). Clearly, for many of these LGB individuals who are Asian American, managing their multiple identities becomes a complex balancing act.

Latin Americans

Specific attributes of Latin American culture contribute to the difficulties many LGB individuals who are Latin American experience during the coming-out process. For example, traditionally, many Latin Americans have a strong religious identification (e.g., Catholicism), and, historically, many denominations have judged people who are LGB negatively. For example, Potoczniak, Crosbie-Burnett, and Saltzburg (2009) found that religious and cultural values were viewed as problematic when one comes out and contributed to negative reactions on the part of family members. An additional factor that makes coming out more difficult for some Latin Americans is the role that masculinity plays in some Latin American cultures. Similar to members of the other cultural groups discussed, individuals who are Latino and LGB are just as prone to anti-LGB and racial discrimination because they possess two oppressed statuses: being a person of color and being nonheterosexual (Díaz, Bein, & Ayala, 2006; Ibañez, Van Oss Marin, Flores, Millett, & Díaz, 2009; Velez et al., 2015). Interestingly, Ibañez et al. (2009) noted that Latino gay men reported experiencing more racism within the gay community than in general, although racist experiences were reported in general as well.

Native Americans

The term *two-spirit* has been used frequently in academic literature in multiple ways to describe some Native American individuals, including those who do not identify as heterosexual, those who identify as transgender Native Americans, and those whose gender roles do not conform to the socially expected behaviors of their assigned sex. Adams and Phillips (2009) defined two-spirit people as "contemporary Native American individuals whose sense of self is partially informed by their knowledge of alternate gender roles that functioned within some tribes prior to and briefly following the European invasions" (p. 960). Historically, two-spirit individuals had specific societal roles within their respective communities, such as educating children and possessing specific spiritual responsibilities. In other words, they were valuable members of their communities. Today, LGB individuals who are Native American experience the consequences of heterosexism, just like any other group of individuals who are LGB. This situation is partially due to Western cultural influences, but also due to long-held traditions about strict gender roles for men and women that are passed down by some tribal communities. Gilley (2010) noted exclusionary practices of two-spirit men in their tribal communities if they were openly gay or gender different. Specifically, the men believed that they would not be able to participate in tribal practices if they were open about their sexual orientation. Two-spirit men who were open about their identities were denied the right to engage in ceremonies or were asked to leave a ceremony. What this narrative illustrates is that many LGB individuals who are Native American—especially those who live within tribal communities—often have to negotiate and balance their intersecting identities.

Middle Eastern, Arab, and Muslim Americans

In general, there is very little published information about the counseling needs of Middle Eastern, Arabic, and Chaldean (MEAC) individuals and only a couple of published empirical studies that have focused on LGB members of these cultural groups specifically. One explanation for the lack of attention in the counseling literature is the distinct challenges associated with the multiple oppressed identities of these cultural groups. For many LGB individuals who are MEAC, attempting to integrate their sexual identities and religious or spiritual beliefs can lead to psychological and social conflicts. MEA (Chaldeans are intentionally excluded here because of their Christian affiliation) Muslims may view their nonheterosexual identities as a direct contradiction to Islamic messages that view same-sex attractions or behaviors as an inappropriate social norm. Jaspal and Cinnirella (2014) found that gay Muslim men perceived their Muslim identities as being jeopardized because of their gay identities. This sense of vulnerability led the gay men to hyper-affiliate with the Muslim faith as a way to protect the genuineness of their Muslim identity. Similarly, LGB individuals who are MEAC and Christian may also experience distress as a result of negative messages about the incompatibility of same-sex attractions and behaviors with traditional Christian doctrine.

In one of only two empirical studies that have included MEAC LGB Americans, Ikizler and Szymanski (2014) interviewed 12 LGB individuals who were MEA regarding their identity development and found a number of common themes. Some of the participants had strong connections with their ethnic communities, while other participants had weak connections to their ethnic communities. Strong connections were associated with relationships developed during childhood that continued on into adulthood. The interviewees also reported experiences of racial identity confusion, ethnic oppression, and heterosexism. Although participants experienced disenfranchisement within their Middle Eastern cultures, they also spoke of experiences of strength, resilience, a sense of self, and advocating for others as a result of having to negotiate the complex intersections of their sexual orientations and Middle Eastern ethnic identities.

Spirituality among Individuals Who Are LGBTQ and Ethical Counseling Approaches

Although less so than the general U.S. population, over three-quarters of individuals who are LGB participate in religious organizations, most of which are Christian, identifying as Protestant (29.7%), Catholic (19.7%), or Born Again Christian (17.5%; Herek, Norton, Allen, & Sims, 2010). Other groups represented in the LGB population are Wiccans/Pagans (3.1%), Buddhists (2.6%), and Jews (1.2%), with the remaining quarter (24.2%) identifying as atheist or agnostic, or reporting "none" for their religious affiliation (Herek et al., 2010). National data on transgender, queer, questioning, and intersex populations are lacking. Because of the historical opposition of traditional religious beliefs and same-gender attraction, as well as the rejection of nonconforming gender identity, it is easy to see how many who identify as LGBTQ struggle to integrate religious beliefs and practices into their lives (Kocet, Sanabria, & Smith, 2011; Super & Jacobson, 2012).

Religious Abuse and the Response of Individuals Who Are LGBTQ

Many queer individuals grow up in churches, mosques, or synagogues that abuse them. Super and Jacobson (2012) define this religious abuse as "when a religious group or leader, whether intentionally or unintentionally, uses coercion, threats, rejection, condemnation, or manipulations to force the individual into submission of the religious views about sexuality" (p. 180). Messages about feeling "dirty," becoming a child molester, and engaging in shameful acts are common examples of such abuse (Beagan & Hattie, 2015). Unfortunately, this experience is common among those who identify as LGBTQ, both young and old, and the experience can be quite damaging. Consequences include self-loathing, the loss of close relationships, poor body image, depression, and suicide. Further research has shown that gays and lesbians from nonaffirming Christian traditions have higher rates of internalized heterosexism (Barnes & Meyer, 2012; Bowers, Minichiello, & Plummer, 2010).

The response to oppressive religious institutions varies, with some rejecting their LGBTQ identities, others leaving organized religion altogether, and others integrating their seemingly opposing identities (Beagan & Hattie, 2015). Although negative religious experiences can be damaging, affiliating with affirming religious traditions may benefit psychological well-being among LGBTQ populations (Barnes & Meyer, 2012; Yarhouse & Carrs, 2012). Accordingly, it is less surprising to see how integration is an appealing option for some. Beagan and Hattie (2015) noted that integration strategies may include changing one's beliefs, changing congregations or denominations, changing the degree of participation, or even changing to a new religious practice. With increasing options for affirming congregations, denominations, and religions, it now appears that LGBTQ individuals and families have more alternatives to engage in supportive communities of spiritual practice than ever before. Counselors are often part of this support network, and in order to function in it effectively, they must identify and address any values conflicts that may inhibit their ability to serve their clients who are LGBTQ.

Addressing Values Conflicts

As with other populations, in working with LGBTQ clients, it is important to practice competently, being aware of our own biases and serving our clients with care and respect. The ACA *Code of Ethics* (2014) provides clear guidance on the mandate for counselors not to discriminate on the basis of sexual orientation or gender identity (Standard C. 5.), to practice competently (Standard C.2.a.), and to refrain from imposing one's own values upon clients (Standard A.4.b.). While the Code provides for appropriate termination and referral when a counselor lacks the competence to work with certain populations (Standard A.11.a.), it states that counselors must refrain from making such referrals when they would be made on the basis of the "counselor's personally held values, attitudes, beliefs, and behaviors" (Standard A.11.b). These standards have come into conflict with individuals in the field who claim it their constitutional right to follow their religious beliefs, even when they do not support same-sex relationships (Francis & Dugger, 2014). The case of *Ward v. Wilbanks* (2010) has affirmed the position of the American Counseling Association (ACA), recognizing that counseling services cannot be denied to a client on the basis of the client's sexual orientation; nor can the client be referred to another counselor simply because a counselor's values conflict with the client's (Kaplan, 2014). Other cases against counselors who refuse to provide services to sexual minority clients have been upheld in the courts, suggesting that counselors consider the legal ramifications of not addressing their own biases and not providing competent services (Herlihy, Hermann, & Greden, 2014). To address these biases, Ametrano (2014) found that counseling students appreciated the opportunity to explore differing positions by reading about those positions in ethical dilemma papers and by discussing the positions in small groups. Through these experiences, students were able to expand their tolerance for ambiguity and challenge any black-and-white schemas they held. For those already in the field, obtaining additional training and supervision that will enhance competent and ethical practice is a high priority.

The previous sections briefly touched on the intersections of ethnicity and sexual orientation. The primary purpose was to illustrate that all cultures have specific attitudes, values, and beliefs about individuals who are LGB. As a result, depending on a client's cultural background, unique challenges during the coming-out process may be encountered. In the next section, we look at some of the specific consequences of heterosexism on the lives of people who are LGB, starting with mental health consequences.

MENTAL HEALTH CONSEQUENCES OF HETEROSEXISM

The effects of heterosexism and homonegativism on the lives of clients who are LGBTQI are many. What follows is a brief summary of current research and conceptualizations addressing how individuals who are LGBTQI are harmed by overt and covert heterosexism, homonegativism, and internalized homophobia.

Historically, many mental health providers have attributed mental health problems to individuals who are LGBTQI without considering environmental factors affecting mental well-being. **Attribution bias** is a cognitive bias that influences how we conclude who or what is responsible for an event. Attribution bias is often unconsciously placed on clients who are LGBTQI. Culturally sensitive counselors are starting to realize that mental health problems are not necessarily a product of "broken" individuals; rather, they are a function of social inequities that become toxic for the individuals affected (Chung & Bemak, 2012). One aspect of poisonous social environments that affect the mental health of individuals who are LGBTQI is stereotypes. Often not thought about are the stereotypes associated with the entire LGBTQI community's mental health. Boysen, Fisher, DeJesus, Vogel, and Madon (2011) proposed that the stereotypes that sexual minorities have about their own mental health can foster self-defeating behaviors, self-persecution, and increased psychological distress. Although stereotypes at times may help give meaning to certain situations or groups of people, in general, stereotypes that lead to selective discrimination and prejudice are socially unjust and can cause those to whom they are applied much psychological pain. Some researchers have even proposed that individuals who engage in heterosexist acts have their own psychopathology. (See Reflection 6.3.) Guindon, Green, and Hanna (2003) suggested the following:

> Persons who perpetuate pain and injustice on others through racism, sexism, and homophobia . . . are displaying a type of psychopathology that deserves its own particular category. . . . The common denominator of all the above prejudices seems to be intolerance. . . . This intolerance seems to be descriptive of a personality

disorder, "Intolerant Personality Disorder. . . ." Intolerance becomes psychopathological when rigid beliefs lead a person to suppress the quality of life of another person or group, causing pain and suffering through denial of liberty, equal rights, or freedom of expression. (pp. 167–168)

REFLECTION 6.3

What are some ways in which individuals who are heterosexual are harmed by heterosexism? Brainstorm potential mental health, physical, and social consequences of heterosexism for this population.

In general, individuals who are LGBTQI seek out counseling more than their heterosexual counterparts do (Grella, Cochran, Greenwell, & Mays, 2011). It is not that individuals who are LGBTQI are innately more mentally unstable; rather, persons who are LGBTQI experience the ramifications of heterosexism and homonegativism. Research has consistently demonstrated that heterosexism, sexism, and internalized homophobia are related to psychological distress. Specifically, individuals who are LGBT are more likely than persons who are heterosexual to experience depression, suicide, anxiety, and substance abuse disorders (Burgess, Lee, Tran, & van Ryn, 2008; Cochran, Mays, Alegria, Ortega, & Takeuchi, 2007; McCabe, Bostwick, Hughes, West, & Boyd, 2010). In this regard, let us explore in greater detail the relationship between heterosexism, on the one hand, and suicide and depression, self-esteem and stress, and the mental health of youths who are LGBTQI, on the other.

Suicidality and Depression

One of the most devastating mental health consequences of heterosexism among many individuals who are LGBTQI is depression and suicidality (both ideation and attempts). Individuals who are LGBTQI report disproportionately higher numbers of suicidal thoughts and suicide attempts than their heterosexual peers. This statistic is often attributed to growing up hearing negative messages about being LGBTQI, to shame, and to depressive symptoms related to living in a heterosexist and homophobic society. Specifically, LGBTQI individuals are up to seven times more likely than heterosexuals to attempt suicide (Haas et al., 2011) and are overrepresented in the number of completed suicides (Hatzenbuehler et al., 2014). Meyer, Teylan, and Schwartz (2014) found that LGBTQI suicide attempts are more likely to occur during developmental milestones associated with coming out (e.g., first recognition of same-sex attraction, disclosing sexuality to others). Interestingly, they also found that receiving mental health treatment or medical treatment did not prevent the suicide attempts. In addition, LGBTQI individuals who sought out religious or spiritual assistance were more likely to attempt suicide later than individuals who received no treatment at all. A possible explanation for these results could be the anti-LGBTQI messages conveyed by many, but not all, religious groups.

Bisexual individuals often experience discrimination and intolerance from both the heterosexual and the gay community. This lack of a sense of belonging often leads to feelings of isolation and loneliness, which in turn may result in an increased risk of depression and suicidal behavior. This state of affairs is consistent with research that shows a relationship between internalized heterosexism and depression (Russell, Ryan, Toomey, Díaz, & Sanchez, 2011; Szymanski & Chung, 2003; Szymanski & Gupta, 2009).

For LGBTQI people of color, the risk for depression and suicidal behavior is exacerbated by their additional oppressed identities. For example, Meyer et al. (2014) found that Black and Latino LGB individuals reported a greater proportion of serious suicide attempts than White LGBs. This result is consistent with a recent study which showed that African-American and Latino individuals who are LGB are at an increased risk for suicide attempts (O'Donnell, Meyer, & Schwartz, 2011). Reports such as these are not limited to individuals who are LGBTQI and African American or Latino. For example, Bostwick, Meyer, Aranda, Russell, Hughes, Birkett, and Mustanski (2014) reported that suicidal ideation and attempts tend to be higher for Native Americans, Pacific Islanders, and those who identified as multiracial, but lower for Asians and African Americans. Belonging to multiple stigmatized cultural groups contributes to the disparity in reports of depression and suicide. In addition, greater pressure to conform to cultural values and norms among these populations increases the risk of depressive symptomatology and suicidal behavior.

Among LGBTQI youths, abuse and harassment often lead to low self-esteem, depression, suicidal ideation, and self-harm (Almeida, Johnson, Corliss, Molnar, & Azrael, 2009; Kosciw et al., 2014). Across studies, sexual minority youths report significantly higher rates of depression and suicidality than heterosexual youths, a finding attributed to the stigma, violence, and other forms of oppression those young minorities encounter (Burton, Marshal, Chisolm, Sucato, & Friedman, 2013). Their disproportionately high numbers of suicide attempts and ideation may be attributable to heterosexist and homophobic messages that individuals who are LGBTQI hear in schools, churches, the media, and the larger society that directly attack an individual's self-perception and self-worth. For example, some common negative messages are direct name-calling (e.g., faggot, dyke, queer), homosexuality viewed as an abomination in the eyes of God, and perceiving being gay as unnatural. More covert negative messages are related to the lack of visible mentors and role models who are LGBTQI in schools and universities, on television, and in music and other forms of popular culture, although the number of "out" public figures is increasing. When individuals who are LGBTQI are visible in popular culture (e.g., in movies or on television), they are often stereotyped, pathologized, and used to entertain heterosexual male audiences. (See Activity 6.4.) Visible, positive representations of people who are LGBTQI and of color are nearly nonexistent in popular culture. Thus, these messages increase levels of internalized heterosexism and put members of the LGBTQI community at increased risk for depression and suicide.

ACTIVITY 6.4

Rank the following scenarios from most offensive to least offensive, with "1" being the most offensive and "4" being the least offensive. Compare your responses with those of your peers. Discuss what made you rank the scenarios the way you did.

_____ A televised sexual scene between two women

_____ A televised sexual scene between two men

_____ A televised sexual scene between one man and two women

_____ A televised sexual scene between a man dressed as a woman and a woman

Stress and Self-Esteem

Stress associated with being a member of an oppressed group is called **minority stress**. Meyer (2015) defined minority stress as the extreme stress experienced among individuals from stigmatized social groups due to their minority social position. According to Meyer, people who are LGBTQI have three general sources of minority stress. First, they might experience stress caused by chronic or acute outward events or conditions—for example, anti-LGBTQI slurs, anti–same-sex marriage laws, and bullying of youths who are LGBTQI. A second source of minority stress is the expectation of discriminatory events and the anticipatory energy this expectation requires. It takes a lot of mental and physical energy out of LGBTQI individuals to be constantly "on guard" in anticipation of possible persecution and discrimination. Finally, internalizing society's negative attitudes and feelings toward individuals who are LGBTQI (i.e., internalized homophobia) creates a large amount of stress. Thus, heterosexist acts not only increase the risk of an individual who is LGBTQI experiencing greater levels of stress, but, as studies have shown, also have negative effects on a person's self-esteem (Velez et al., 2015). Because self-esteem is related to self-perception, and because how we perceive ourselves affects how we perceive our environments, it is not surprising that the mental well-being of individuals who are LGBTQI is compromised more than that of their heterosexual peers. At particular risk for diminished self-esteem and psychological distress are youths with LGBTQI.

LGBTQI Youths

The mental health consequences of growing up in a heterosexist and homophobic culture are particularly troubling for youths who are LGBTQI. As with other youths, this period of development can be fraught with many challenges related to identity development, the exploration of intimate relationships, and preparation for an uncertain future in adulthood. But, unlike others at this age, youths who are LGBTQI often lack needed coping strategies, as well as the support of family, teachers, and other potential adult role models to help them navigate the ever-present social and emotional stressors in their lives. A recent National School Climate Survey found that 85.4% of students who are LGBT were verbally harassed in the previous year, and 39.3% reported being physically harassed at school over the same period because of their sexual orientation (Kosciw et al., 2014). These students also reported hostile school climates in which they were treated unequally as regards public affection, gender expression, and the public display of clothing that supports LGBT issues. In such cases, youths are sent a clear message that their nonconforming identities, expressions, and affiliations are not welcomed by peers and adults alike. Beyond the school environment, sexual minority children and youths are more likely than their heterosexual counterparts to be sexually abused or to be abused by a parent (Friedman et al., 2011). In total, youths who are LGBTQI commonly live in unsupportive school or home environments, either of which may contribute to compromised mental health and wellness.

Many youths who are LGBTQI attempt to escape and self-medicate their feelings of worthlessness, depression, and anxiety by abusing substances. In a meta-analysis of 18 studies, Marshal, Friedman, Stall, King, Miles, Gold, Bukstein, and Morse (2008) reported that youths who are LGB use substances at roughly three times the rate of their heterosexual peers. Of particular concern were the higher odds of youths who are LGB using cocaine (3.27:1), injection drugs, (2.87:1), cigarettes (2.76:1), and alcohol (2.55:1). Students who are LGBTQI and who experience direct and indirect heterosexism and homophobia often report experiencing distress well into adulthood. For example, one study indicated that 17% of students who were LGBTQI and who reported being bullied at school because of their actual or perceived sexual orientation experienced posttraumatic stress in adulthood (Rivers, 2004). Furthermore, many people who are LGBTQI and who experienced homophobic acts during their youth reported increased levels of internalized homophobia, depressive symptoms, and anxiety symptoms in adulthood (Russell et al., 2011). As a result of experiencing antigay abuse in their schools, many youths who are LGBTQI drop out of school, and many end up living on the streets. It is also important to note how the increased rates of stressful childhood experiences, such as emotional and physical abuse and neglect, all contribute to higher mental health concerns later in life (Schneeberger, Dietl, Muenzenmeier, Huber, & Lang, 2014). Substance abuse across the life span is further discussed in the next section.

PHYSICAL CONSEQUENCES OF HETEROSEXISM

There also are physical consequences of heterosexism on the lives of individuals who are LGBTQI. Culturally competent counselors are encouraged to pay attention to somatic complaints of clients who are LGBTQI and how physical illness may be related to heterosexism and homophobia.

Substance Abuse

Although substance abuse is classified as a mental health issue, we include it as a physical consequence of heterosexism because of its physical effects, including its relationship to HIV/AIDS. Ward, Dahlhamer, Galinsky, and Joestl (2014) reported that approximately 33% of lesbians and gays are heavy alcohol users, compared with 22% of heterosexuals. Research has demonstrated that heterosexism and internalized homophobia are related to alcohol abuse for the lesbian and gay population (e.g., McCabe et al., 2010; Weber, 2008). Early research indicated that African-American gay and bisexual men have higher rates of heavy substance use, specifically alcohol and cocaine, in comparison to men who are Black and heterosexual (Richardson, Myers, Bing, & Satz, 1997). However, in more recent research, Blacks who identify as lesbian, gay, or bisexual report significantly lower rates of substance use disorders than their White counterparts (Meyer, Dietrich, & Schwartz, 2008). Sexual minority Latinos reported rates of substance use disorders similar to those of Whites (Meyer et al., 2008). Much like the White populations, Black gay and bisexual men are increasingly using methamphetamine (Halkitis & Jerome, 2008).

Because heterosexism can lead to internalized homophobia, shame, and poor self-perception, some members of the LGBTQI community resort to substance abuse as a way to mask these negative feelings. Because places in society where it is safe for people who are LGBTQI to congregate freely are limited, gay bars continue to be the primary gathering place for many who are LGBTQI, a situation that may explain the high rates of alcohol abuse among those in this group. Although many different drugs are used by portions of the LGBTQI community, certain drugs tend to be more prevalent. For example, marijuana, cocaine, psychedelics, methylenedioxymethamphetamine (Ecstasy), nitrate inhalants, and methamphetamine are often abused (Green & Feinstein, 2012; Newcomb, Ryan, Greene, Garofalo, & Mustanski, 2014).

In addition to the aforementioned substances, nicotine (via cigarette smoking) is extremely prevalent in the LGBTQI community. Approximately 25.8% of gay men smoke, compared with 20.3% of men in general (Ward et al., 2014). The smoking rate for lesbians is approximately 25.7%, whereas 15.0% of heterosexual women smoke. One reason the smoking rates are so high among the LGBTQI community could be institutional heterosexism. Washington (2002) explained that cigarette companies intentionally market cigarette advertisements toward the LGBTQI community. The increased rates of smoking put people who are LGBTQI at risk for various types of cancer and other health problems. Smoking partially explains why the life expectancy of gay men is 8 to 20 years lower than that of other men. Interestingly, youths who are LGBTQI have 30% to 87% higher rates of cancer than their heterosexual peers.

HIV/AIDS

Men who have sex with men continue to represent most new HIV infections. Youths who are LGBTQI are increasingly contracting the virus at astounding rates. In fact, according to the CDC (2015), men who have sex with men accounted for approximately 63% of all new HIV infections in the United States in 2010. Men of color were particularly overrepresented in recent HIV infection rates (CDC, 2015). Individuals who are transgender are also affected disproportionately by HIV, with an estimated 27.7% of male-to-female transgender persons found to be HIV positive (Herbst, Jacobs, Finlayson, McKleroy, Neumann, Crepaz, & HIV/AIDS Prevention Research Synthesis Team, 2008).

Heterosexism is partly responsible for the high HIV infection rates among individuals who are LGBTQI. When youths who are LGBTQI come out to their families, many experience homophobic reactions, such as violence and rejection. Some youths who are attracted to the same sex leave home, and others are kicked out of their homes. To survive on the streets, many youths who are LGBTQI engage in sex for money to meet basic needs. They are, however, less likely to practice safe sex. Youths who are LGBTQI and homeless are at increased risk for contracting HIV because some of them engage in survival sex and substance use (Keuroghlian, Shtasel, & Bassuk, 2014). In addition, youths who have been bullied at school for being LGBTQI or because they were perceived to be LGBTQI tend to have more casual sex partners in adulthood than their peers have (Rivers, 2004). This behavior in turn puts them at greater risk for contracting HIV and other sexually transmitted infections. Finally, HIV-positive, LGBTQI individuals who choose to hide their sexual orientation are at greater risk for developing opportunistic infections. Strachan, Bennett, Russo, and Roy-Byrne (2007) found that CD4 cell counts (i.e., counts of cells that fight infections in the human body) increased in men who disclosed their sexual orientation to others. This is likely due to the relief of the distress associated with keeping such an important secret hidden.

SOCIAL CONSEQUENCES OF HETEROSEXISM

The negative stereotypes people have about individuals who are LGBTQI are a social consequence of heterosexism. Historically, gay men have been viewed as displaying feminine characteristics and rejecting masculine gender roles (Madon, 1997), while lesbians were seen as being masculine, aggressive, and sexually deviant (Geiger, Harwood, & Hummert, 2006). Such views have persisted, especially among those with higher levels of homophobia (Brown & Groscup, 2009). Other studies examining mental health trainees' stereotypes of individuals who are LGBTQI have found that trainees believe that most LGBTQI individuals have anxiety, personality, mood, eating, and sexual and gender identity disorders (Boysen, Vogel,

Madon, & Wester, 2006). These stereotypes may contribute to individuals who are LGBTQI reporting dissatisfaction with counseling experiences.

Socioeconomic Status

There is often a distorted view of the socioeconomic status of the LGBTQI population. Many people believe that individuals who are LGBTQI live extravagant lives because of a perception that they have excess financial resources. Thus, people who are LGBTQI are seen as not needing economic, social, or health-related services (Lind, 2004). This stereotype contributes to the invisibility of poverty among individuals who are LGBTQI.

Most people may not think of individuals who are LGBTQI as affected by poverty. However, heterosexism is directly related to financial hardship, for several reasons. One reason is a disparity in LGBTQI personal earnings compared with earnings of coworkers who are heterosexual. Research has consistently shown that men who are openly gay or bisexual earn significantly less than heterosexual men with similar backgrounds (McFadden, 2015). By contrast, women who are openly lesbian or bisexual more often experience a wage premium compared with the wages of heterosexual women, largely because lesbian and bisexual women are less likely to have children and be penalized economically for doing so. However, since earnings contribute to lifestyle, many individuals who are LGBTQI cannot afford to live in the high-amenity metropolitan cities that tend to be more accepting and tolerant of the LGBTQI community. This restriction results in many people who are poor and LGBTQI living in areas that might be more homophobic and less tolerant. (e.g., smaller, more conservative cities).

Research also showed that being of a lower socioeconomic status is related to a decreased likelihood of describing oneself as gay, as well as related to not participating in gay social activities (Barrett & Pollack, 2005). Another factor contributing to poverty among persons who are LGBTQI, particularly youths, is homelessness. Because many youths who are LGBTQI are kicked out of their homes on coming out or run away from abusive homes, many youths who are LGBTQI are homeless. It is estimated that between 30% and 40% of homeless youths identify as LGBTQI (Durson & Gates, 2012). Many of these youths do not attend school and, as a result, have a difficult time finding employment that would financially sustain them.

Institutional Heterosexism

Another social consequence of heterosexism is legalized discrimination in the form of **institutional heterosexism**. Institutional heterosexism is the institutional enforcement of heterosexuality as superior while denigrating homosexuality. Anti–gay marriage laws were an example of institutional heterosexism and have since been overturned by the U.S. Supreme Court. There remain numerous local and state laws, however, that seek to limit the ability of individuals who are LGBT and their families to participate fully in society. In reaction to progressive legislation to advance the rights and protections of sexual minorities, states have passed "religious freedom restoration acts," which allow any individual to refuse secular services (e.g., serving food, renting property) to those who identify as LGBT. There is also proposed and, in some jurisdictions, approved legislation that seeks to restrict transgender individuals from using public accommodations. Such legislation seeks to override local anti-discrimination laws protecting individuals who are LGBT. Conversion therapy has also been debated, with a proposed Oklahoma law that would legally protect any therapist who engages in such practices nearly passing in 2015, even though conversion therapy has been deemed unethical by professional codes of ethics. Activity 6.5 provides an opportunity to consider how you can develop ways to address institutional heterosexism. Voices from the Field 6.2 describes one individual's experience with institutional heterosexism.

ACTIVITY 6.5

As a class, generate a list of examples of institutional heterosexism in addition to those just described. How might various forms of heterosexism affect individuals on the basis of their cultural makeup? What are some small action strategies you can implement to begin to make social change for people who are LGBTQI?

Voices from the Field 6.2

I fell hopelessly in love with a woman who lived halfway around the world. At the time, I was a student in London and she lived and worked in Michigan. Despite all the obstacles and seemingly insurmountable circumstances, we somehow both knew that what we had was special enough that we wanted to find a way to make the relationship work. Terry and I survived nine years long distance, visiting every three months or so, while I finished my studies. I was able to get a postdoctoral position in Detroit and move to Michigan on a work visa. We had a wedding ceremony in front of 180 guests (although it had no legal standing whatsoever) and began building a home and a life together. But then, after three years came disaster: I lost my job. I discovered that I had seven days to get a new employer, find a new visa category, or else leave the country.

Our committed, long-standing relationship gives me no right whatsoever to live with the person I love. Well-meaning friends often ask if we could get married in Canada or in Massachusetts, thinking that would somehow make things better. I have to explain that, because of the *Defense of Marriage Act*, the U.S. government recognized marriage as being only between a man and a woman. In fact, doing either of those things could have actually jeopardized my chance to stay in this country. In order to remain with Terry, I chose to go back to school and switched to a student visa. That let us stay together, but I needed to demonstrate an "intent to leave" the United States after completing my studies, and any evidence of our relationship could have invalidated my student visa and forced me to leave. There was more uncertainty after graduation, as I needed an employer who would be willing to file the immigration paperwork. I was lucky: My current job sponsored me first for a work visa and now for a green card, which will give me the right to remain here indefinitely. However, it has still been eight long years of uncertainty to obtain what heterosexual married couples can get as soon as they arrive in the United States. It's frustrating, to say the least.

With my green card in sight, and with all the recent developments in same-gender marriage rights, we were able to get legally married in Washington, DC, this past autumn, on the 17th anniversary of the day that we met. I was surprised at just how much emotional impact the ceremony and the official wedding certificate had on me. We've always considered ourselves married since our ceremony eight years earlier, so on one level, we talked about the ceremony as "just doing the paperwork" and "no big deal." And yet, in the weeks since the marriage, we've both realized that it *is* a big deal. Standing in front of the judge, hearing her pronounce us legally married—I cried. And then we had to come home to a state where that marriage is not recognized. What we are discovering is that the situation leaves us feeling confused and angry.

The anger was surprising to uncover, as I'd always prided myself on being well adjusted, accepting of my sexuality, and (as a counselor especially!) very self-aware. But it is there, and very real, and, I think, a valid response to the injustice that we face on a daily basis. But it is also only one side of the story. There have been some wonderful benefits from being long distance for so long and from having to work with the immigration system. We have an amazing foundation of communication that came from talking on the phone for at least an hour a day, and countless email exchanges. We joke that we actually talked more when we were apart than we do now, when most conversations are to do with plans for the weekend, whose turn it is to do the laundry, and what's for dinner. Not being able to take our long-term future together for granted has given us a sense of gratitude for every day that we share. Anyone who spends much time around us can tell you how nauseatingly romantic and gooey we are, and a large part of that stems from our sheer joy in finally being together.

Each night for the past eight years, we have gone to bed with a prayer: "Thank you, God, for this day together. May we please have another one tomorrow?" I'm looking forward to the day that prayer is answered for good.

~ *"Kirsti," Detroit, MI*

Diminished Interpersonal Relationships

How heterosexism diminishes interpersonal relationships is another consequence of heterosexism. Internalized homophobia may prevent individuals who are LGBTQI from reaching out to, and participating in, the gay community for fear of being identified as gay. Similarly, heterosexuals who may want to participate in gay-related social events may experience a fear of being perceived as LGBTQI by heterosexual peers. Some individuals who are LGBTQI may isolate themselves from family, particularly if the family is not aware of the LGBTQI identity. Last, heterosexism often prevents meaningful platonic relationships between persons who are LGBTQI and heterosexuals from being realized because of fear, lack of knowledge, and prejudice. Table 6.1 presents several media resources for you to analyze for examples of heterosexism. In addition, consider coming up with your own list of examples of heterosexism in the media.

TABLE 6.1 Media Resources Illustrating Heterosexism

Motion Pictures and Films

A Single Man (2009): A gay male professor who is grief stricken plans his suicide.

Better Than Chocolate (1999): A woman struggles with disclosing her identity to her family as she falls in love with another woman.

Brokeback Mountain (2005): The relationship between two cowboys in the early 1960s is examined.

Hate Crime (2005): A gay man is murdered, and his partner attempts to find the killer, in a conservative town.

Latter Days (2003): A young Mormon missionary struggles with his identity.

(Continued)

TABLE 6.1 Media Resources Illustrating Heterosexism (Continued)

Milk (2008): An exploration of the life of Harvey Milk.

Orange is the New Black (2013–present): Experiences of women in a minimum-security prison.

Out Late (2008): Documentary about LGBT individuals who come out later in life.

Party Monster (2003): True story based on the life of Michael Alig and his experiences in the New York City club scene.

Prayers for Bobby (2009): Based on a true story, this film depicts how a religious mother attempts to "cure" her gay son.

Sordid Lives (2000): What happens when someone "comes out" in a small Texas town?

The Kids are Alright (2010): The story of a lesbian couple with children and the sperm donor.

Books

Burroughs, A. (2003). *Running with scissors: A memoir.* New York, NY: Picador.

Parsell, T. J. (2007). *Fish: A memoir of a boy in a man's prison.* New York, NY: De Capo Press.

Harris, E. L. (1994). *Invisible life.* New York, NY: Anchor.

Holleran, A. (2007). *Grief.* New York, NY: Hachette Books.

Kilmer-Purcell, J. (2006). *I am not myself these days.* New York, NY: Harper Perennial.

Lax, L. (2015). *Uncovered: How I left Hasidic life and finally came home.* Berkeley, CA: She Writes Press.

Lee, M. (2006). *35 cents.* Hong Kong: Suspect Thoughts Press.

Sessums, K. (2008). *Mississippi sissy.* New York, NY: Picador.

Werth, B. (2002). *The scarlet professor: Newton Arvin: A literary life shattered by scandal.* New York, NY: Anchor Books.

Zielinsky, L. (2013). *Turning point.* Falls Church, VA: Supposed Crimes, LLC

Music

Andy, You're A Star (2004, The Killers)

Coming Clean (1994, Green Day)

Doll (2006, Kevin Cahoon & Ghetto)

Hideaway (1987, Erasure)

I Kissed A Girl (2008, Katie Perry)

I'm Still A Guy (2007, Brad Paisley)

Leviticus Faggot (1996, Me'shell Ndegeocello)

Same Love (2012, Macklemore & Ryan Lewis)

She's My Man (2006, The Scissor Sisters)

Ur So Gay (2008, Katie Perry)

Your Gay Friend (2005, Robbie Williams)

SOCIALLY JUST, NONHETEROSEXIST TRAINING AND CLINICAL PRACTICE

Clearly, the negative consequences described in the previous section are just glimpses into how heterosexism affects the lives of many clients who are LGBTQI. Because heterosexism has such a salient presence in the dominant culture, clients are likely to present with their side effects in session. For mental health providers to advocate for their clients who are LGBTQI, counselors need to possess knowledge and skills related to nonheterosexist clinical training and practice.

Counseling Strategies for Addressing Heterosexism

In 1998, both the American Counseling Association (ACA) and the American Psychological Association (APA) passed resolutions opposing prior conceptions that people who are LGB, by their very nature, have mental disorders. In their guidelines for the ethical treatment of lesbians and gay males, Chernin and Johnson (2002) cited the APA resolution "Appropriate Therapeutic Responses to Sexual Orientation," formulated by the Committee on Lesbian and Gay Concerns. This resolution recognizes that homosexuality has been long removed from the *Diagnostic and Statistical manual of Mental Disorders* (*DSM*) and is not a mental disorder; thus, counseling professionals should not pathologize the sexual orientation of clients who are lesbian and gay. In 2009, a revised and updated resolution reiterating that same-sex feelings, attractions, and behaviors are "normal" and that an LGB identity is not a mental illness was created by the American Psychological Association (APA, 2009). The Human Rights Committee of the ACA proposed a similar resolution—"Appropriate Counseling Response to Sexual Orientation"—and the ACA passed it in 1998. This resolution states that the ACA opposes conceptions that people who are LGB have a mental disorder and supports practice and research with LGB people that affirm their sexual orientation. Nonetheless, although the ACA opposes the idea that an LGBTQI identity is a mental disorder, some professionals and paraprofessionals engage in counseling practices that attempt to "treat" LGBTQI identities.

SEXUAL ORIENTATION CHANGE EFFORTS   Efforts to alter same-sex or affectional orientations began in the mid-1800s with studies examining the origins of same-sex attractions. Formerly called **reparative therapy** (psychological approaches that aim to alter, or "repair," sexual orientation from LGB to heterosexual) or **conversion therapy** (attempts to "convert" individuals from LGB to heterosexual), the current umbrella term used to describe any methodological attempts to change sexual orientation is **sexual orientation change efforts (SOCE)**. Historically, biological, behavioral, cognitive, psychodynamic, and religious strategies have been used as part of SOCE. Excessive bicycle riding, testicle transplants, exorcisms, electroshock therapy, forcing men to engage in sexual activity with female prostitutes, aversion therapy, and hypnosis have all been used as "treatments" for nonheterosexual orientations. Even Freud engaged in SOCE with a female client. However, because his therapeutic attempts to change her sexual orientation failed, he came to the conclusion that efforts to change same-sex orientations were futile (APA, 2009). After homosexuality was removed from the *DSM* in 1973, SOCE were not as prominent, but did not dissolve entirely.

Today, there are two primary paradigms of SOCE: secular paradigms and those grounded in religiosity (i.e., ex-gay ministries). Purporting to use secular methods (e.g., chemical aversion therapies, covert desensitization, reinforcement of "appropriate" gender roles and behaviors), the Alliance for Therapeutic Choice and Scientific Integrity and its research and clinical division, the National Association for Research and Therapy of Homosexuality, promotes SOCE to individuals who experience dysphoria associated with same-sex or affectional attractions. Other organizations attempt to change sexual orientation through prayer or a combination of "therapy" and prayer. For example, Homosexuals Anonymous combines prayer and a 14-step model (similar to the traditional 12-step model used by Alcoholics Anonymous). Another organization, Desert Stream Ministries, purports to heal "the sexually and relationally broken" through prayer and repentance. (See www.desertstream.org.)

Because it is common for many individuals who are LGB to experience psychological distress associated with initially negotiating their LGB identities or as a result of living in a heterosexist society, some individuals seek counseling in an attempt to alter their sexual orientation. On the basis of a few empirical SOCE-related studies, it appears that White gay men who identify as Christian are more likely than lesbians and bisexual women to participate in SOCE. LGB adolescents also enter into SOCE therapy, likely brought there by parents. Increasingly, federal courts are banning the use of SOCE on minors. Further, some states—California, New Jersey, Illinois, and Oregon—and the District of Columbia have banned the use of SOCE on minors.

Numerous studies have underscored the detrimental consequences associated with SOCE. Studies have shown that many individuals who have participated in SOCE experienced negative side effects, including depression, anxiety, avoidance of intimacy, sexual dysfunction, internalized heterosexism, and suicidality (APA, 2009). In accordance with these findings, several organizations have resolutions opposing the use of SOCE. The American Psychological Association's Resolution on Appropriate Affirmative Responses to Sexual Orientation Distress and Change Efforts states that there is a lack of evidence to support the use of any type of SOCE (Anton, 2010). The ACA's Governing Council adopted a statement in 1999 that opposed the use of reparative therapy as a cure for LGBT. Further, counselors have an ethical responsibility "not [to] use techniques/procedures/modalities when substantial evidence suggests harm, even if such services are requested" (ACA, 2014, p. 10).

LGB AFFIRMATIVE COUNSELING   LGB affirmative counseling involves counselors being aware of their own strengths and weaknesses in working with LGB clients, being able to use a variety of counseling interventions, countering the negative societal messages often internalized by LGB clients, affirming LGB identities, not pathologizing same-sex behavior and affection, and understanding issues affecting people who are LGB (APA, 2009; Chaney & Brubaker, 2014). Major issues include the impact of negative societal attitudes toward individuals who are LGB; discrimination in the legal, societal, and religious arenas; same-sex relationship dynamics; the effect of HIV/AIDS on the gay community; and identity development issues.

LGB affirmative counseling approaches have been proposed to promote positive identity and psychological adjustment among people who are LGB (e.g., Chaney & Brubaker, 2014; Langdridge, 2007; Matthews, 2007; McGeorge & Carlson, 2007). LGB affirmative counseling extends beyond minimal ethical practice and involves working with LGB clients to minimize feeling stigmatized, validate a client's LGB identity, acknowledge and process the influence of oppression in the client's life, and facilitate clients' sense of self-pride (Johnson, 2012; Langdridge, 2007). In a school setting, LGB affirmative counseling strategies for professional school counselors (American School Counselor Association [ASCA], 2014) include:

- Supporting students who are LGB in an exploration of their feelings about their own sexual orientation as well as the sexual identity of others;
- Advocating for equitable opportunities both in and out of the classroom;
- Promoting a nondiscriminatory, affirming school climate through school policies that confront offensive and hostile language and behaviors, promoting respect and sensitivity, and supporting violence prevention education;

- Addressing the consequences of an unsafe school environment, including diminished psychological well-being, absenteeism, and low academic and career expectations;
- Creating spaces that are safe for students who are LGBTQ and allies to gather in, such as Gay–Straight Alliance clubs;
- Promoting inclusive curriculum, encouraging faculty and staff training on inclusive practices, and modelling inclusive language; and
- Locating LGBTQ resources for families and students.

Remember, youths who are LGB face the same developmental concerns as their heterosexual counterparts, while also dealing with the health and social effects of stigma. By having accurate information, the counselor can provide appropriate interventions, health information, and referrals.

ALGBTIC Competencies

The ALGBTIC has created competencies for working with clients who are lesbian, gay, bisexual, queer, questioning, intersex, and allies (LGBQQIA). These competencies focus on a number of areas promoted by the Council for Accreditation of Counseling and Related Educational Programs (CACREP): human growth and development, social and cultural foundations, helping relationships, group work, career and lifestyle development, appraisal, research, and professional orientation. The competencies can be found in their entirety at http://www.algbtic.org/competencies.html. ALGBTIC has also released competencies for counseling transgender clients. (See Chapter 5.)

Counselor Training

The field of counseling has not been immune to heterosexual bias, and as a result, these biases can be seen in classrooms, textbooks, and research. The lack of consistent and accurate training often leads future helping professionals to feel anxiety and incompetence when sitting across from clients who are victims of heterosexism. An action step that students can take to becoming more competent to work with clients who are LGB is to engage in self-exploration. Because we all are gendered, sexed, raced, classed, and sexually oriented, and because we possess various degrees of ability, we are oppressed and privileged in various ways. Furthermore, we bring these identities into classrooms and counseling sessions. Accordingly, counselor educators and students might begin to examine how these identities function in classrooms, counseling sessions, and society. Once we become aware of how our privileges oppress others, we get closer to the creation of a socially just, nonheterosexist society. (See Reflection 6.4 and Activity 6.6.)

REFLECTION 6.4

Write about a real-life personal experience in which you intentionally or unintentionally oppressed another individual on the basis of your assigned sexual orientation. What privileges come with your assigned sexual orientation? How are these privileges related to the oppressive event you described? Try to identify how the other person may have felt. How did you feel during the event?

ACTIVITY 6.6

In pairs, take turns telling each other of a recent trip you have taken or what you did this past weekend. While one person tells the story without rules, the other person must adhere to the following rules: You cannot mention significant others or friends, you cannot use first names, you cannot use pronouns, and you cannot use gender-specific terms. Now switch roles. What made this conversation difficult? Did you feel empowered to speak freely? Who had more power in the conversation? Do you think that individuals who are LGB have conversations like this often?

The professional literature has additional recommendations for confronting heterosexism in counselor training:

- Raise awareness of heterosexual privilege right from the beginning of one's training. Cannon, Wiggins, Poulsen, and Estrada (2012) suggest a two-day orientation, with activities including understanding each other's contexts, role-playing homoprejudice, exploring privilege in print and video, and understanding one's own privilege.
- Explore queer issues through feminist resources and pedagogies. By developing the concepts of intersectionality by using feminist teaching principles, faculty may create greater opportunities for learning through empowered self-exploration (LaMantia, Wagner, & Bohecker, 2015). The understanding of queer issues may be also developed by incorporating information from other disciplines (e.g., women's studies, human sexuality, anthropology, public policy).
- Use narrative texts and films throughout the curriculum that challenge traditional definitions of sexuality. Rather than viewing sexuality as heterosexist dichotomies (heterosexual or gay), integrate multimedia resources that promote the continuum of sexuality and help provide alternative definitions of these socially constructed terms (Smith, Foley, & Chaney, 2008).
- Emphasize nontraditional approaches to counseling—for example, constructivist and narrative paradigms.
- Choose counseling textbooks and readings that are nonheterosexist. Students need to begin reading texts that are feminist and queer affirmative. In other words, when examining assigned readings and textbooks, students should pay attention to themes of power and control, particularly as they relate to sexual minorities (Carroll, 2001; Jennings, 2014).
- Urge faculty and students to embrace the role of being co-learners. Faculty should not wait to become "experts" in LGB affirming counseling before infusing examples and practices throughout the curriculum (Jennings, 2014). By sharing power in the classroom, all may become resources to identify new research and approaches to best serve LGB clients.
- Create practicum and internship training experiences that include opportunities for counselors in training to work with clients and students who are LGB, and make sure that supervision includes LGB affirmative counseling skill development (Jennings, 2014; Luke & Goodrich, 2012; Smith et al., 2008).
- Familiarize yourself with the constructs of discourse, positioning, and deconstruction (Drewery, 2005). **Discourse** refers to paying attention to the power dynamics in language. For example, in a classroom, who is speaking and who is not speaking? During

discussions, who is being marginalized and who is in control? **Positioning** pertains to the role we take in a particular dialogue. Are we unintentionally (or intentionally) dominating a conversation, causing sexual minorities to be silenced because we believe that our opinions are more important than theirs? Is your voice being silenced because you are fearful of negative repercussions if you expressed a dissenting view? Last, **deconstruction** means removing the hegemonic discourse that is so prevalent in our culture. In other words, it means taking apart and removing dominant ideologies that perpetuate oppression and prevent equal access to resources by persons who are LGB.

Clinical Practice

Research shows that individuals who are LGB seek counseling services more than the general population does. However, they also report greater dissatisfaction with the services received. Therefore, it is important for counselors to be able to provide nonheterosexist clinical services and to create safe nonheterosexist counseling environments. There are several things counselors can do to provide effective counseling to clients who are LGB.

First, counselors must be aware of their attitudes and beliefs about people who are LGB, as an initial step to providing nonheterosexist mental health services. Included in such awareness is a necessary self-examination of the general and mental health stereotypes a counselor might have about clients who are LGB, because these stereotypes could interfere with the type and quality of counseling provided. Traditionally, many educators teach students to refer clients if there is a large discrepancy between the values of the counselor and client or if a counselor is not competent to work with a particular client. However, this recommendation should not be used as a way to avoid working with clients who are culturally different than the counselor. The ACA (2014) *Code of Ethics* states that counselors have an ethical responsibility to continually educate themselves and to become culturally competent practitioners. This includes being aware of diverse cultural groups and acquiring knowledge about others' cultures. Counselors also have an ethical responsibility not to partake in discriminatory practices. Discrimination in the guise of referring clients who are LGB is unethical.

Second, counselors must be aware of how their race, gender, age, class status, ability level, and sexual orientation affect the counseling relationship. In order to become competent when working with any diverse population, one must identify his or her own biases and address them through effective training (Bidell, 2014). Competent counselors will explore with clients what their sexual orientations mean to each other and what the identities mean in relation to the larger social context. Greene (2005) proposed that current models of psychotherapy often perpetuate the social status quo, whereby they become socially unjust tools of oppression, particularly for clients who are LGB.

Examining the power behind the language that counselors choose to use with clients is another way to minimize heterosexism in clinical practice. For example, queer theory views categories such as "straight" and "gay" as contrivances of the dominant culture. These dichotomous labels dismiss individuals who may not identify as heterosexual or gay and who may have adopted identities such as bisexual, queer, pansexual, or asexual (Callis, 2014). Competent counselors will ask clients how they prefer to be addressed and will use language that the client uses. Moreover, the use of the term *homosexual* is not necessarily appropriate, because of its historical significance as a mental disorder. Most persons who are LGB do not describe themselves as "homosexuals," and neither should culturally sensitive mental health professionals. Observe how a client identifies herself or himself (e.g., gay, lesbian, bisexual, queer); that is the appropriate language to use. Last, counselors need to expand the meaning of the word *family*, particularly when working with clients who are LGB. For many clients, *family* does not necessarily refer to biological families of origin. For many persons who are LGB, friends and other community members constitute a family. In addition, because many same-sex couples are increasingly choosing to expand their family through adoption, the term *family* is not limited to a mom, dad, and kids.

An additional way that counselors can minimize heterosexism in counseling practice is by not assuming that clients' presenting problems are related to their sexual orientation. Rather, counselors should collaborate with clients to explore how heterosexism permeates the contextual environments of the clients and how the clients are affected. As the counselor assesses the conversation for evidence of discriminatory acts, including violence, harassment, and other forms of oppression, it is important to explore how clients interpret these acts and the degree to which they are related to heterosexism or other forms of hate (Collier, van Beusekom, Bos, & Sandfort, 2013). Once the form of and source of oppression are assessed, counselors can implement the ACA's advocacy competencies. Specifically, counselors should integrate the advocacy competencies that empower clients who are LGB. (See http://www.algbtic.org/competencies.html.)

Counselors addressing the needs of adolescents may attend to enhancing self-esteem, coping, and general life skills. For youths who are LGBTQI, this focus can mean providing a space for clients or students to discuss their stressors openly and explore strategies to find networks of affirming peers and adults (Chaney & Brubaker, 2014). Counselors should also apply caution when using evidence-based practices that have been unsupported for the population the counselors are serving.

Because "outness" has been correlated with self-esteem and a sense of belonging (Kosciw et al., 2014), counselors may also explore the youth's identity development as well as the level of support in the school and home environment. Youths who are early in the coming-out process often need therapeutic support, as do their parents. Goodrich and Gilbride (2010) found that parental expectations, satisfaction with support, and family flexibility all contributed to higher levels of general family functioning after a youth comes out. In this same study, parental religiosity, fear, and surprise at disclosure all contributed to negative family functioning. Attending to these factors may promote better outcomes for the youths and their families. Case Study 6.2 provides an example of a professional school counselor advocating for LGBTQ students in the high school where she works.

CASE STUDY 6.2

When Julie took her first school counseling job at Tecumseh High School, she had not thought much about the issues of LGBTQ students outside of the chapter she read in her multicultural course. However, when she met her first student for a private counseling session, she quickly learned how gay, lesbian, and bisexual youths can struggle with their sexual orientation, identity, and social support. Angelica was a sophomore in the school who identified as a lesbian and was experiencing a lot of bullying from her peers. Furthermore, when she brought the bullying up to her teachers, they largely ignored her, letting her know that her classmates were just "kidding around" and that "they won't hurt you." Together, Julie and Angelica explored these concerns, assessing her current supports and the resources that might help her. It was during this process that Julie realized that there were other students like Angelica at the school who were

LGB and at various stages of their own identity development and who were often unsupported by the school. Following some investigation, Julie found that some other schools in the district had successfully established gay–straight alliances (GSAs) in their schools, empowering students who were LGBTQ and "straight" allies to come together for support while fighting bullying and other forms of discrimination in the school. She found the GSA Network website (https://www.gsanetwork.org/) and began to explore how to develop an alliance. Finding the support of another counselor at the school, she was able to work with her administration to become the sponsor for a GSA club. Although the club began as a form of social support, it quickly grew into an advocacy group, with students petitioning the administration to increase training for teachers and enact new policies that would be more supportive for students who were LGBTQ. Over time, the students in the group invited their state legislator to come to a meeting so that they could talk about modifying an antibullying law to specifically protect LGBTQ students. Although the legislator did not adopt the recommendation, he did attend the meeting and heard the students' concerns. Similarly, not all of the teachers have changed their support (or lack thereof), but many have—an outcome that has made a difference in the overall school climate.

There can be many obstacles to starting a group whose aim is to challenge the status quo of a school or other type of organization.

- How would you persevere through the resistance that you might encounter from other students, parents, teachers, and administrators?
- What would be the most rewarding aspect of this effort if you were this counselor?
- What other resources might you seek out in order to be most successful?

COUNSELORS' ROLE IN CREATING A SOCIALLY JUST, NONHETEROSEXIST SOCIETY

Historically, one of the goals of counseling has been to make a difference in the community. Over the years, the profession has seemed to lose that focus, but it is once again returning to discussing ways that counselors can become agents of social change. Many leaders in the counseling field believe that counseling and activism should not be separate. Therefore, the following are suggested strategies that counselors and students might use to help create a more socially just, nonheterosexist society.

1. *Lobbying and Supporting Policy Change.* Counselors should actively work together to influence legislators to vote for laws that advocate for people who are LGB. Among such laws are those increasing HIV/AIDS funding, supporting stronger hate crime penalties, banning the practice of conversion therapy, and supporting antibullying laws by protecting youths who are LGBTQ.
2. *Giving Back to the Community.* Counselors need to go into communities where individuals who are LGB reside. Then, they need to advocate for change in those communities. Rather than assuming what needs to be changed, counselors should give voice to community members to hear what *they* think needs to be changed. Counselors can use their counseling skills to build bridges among people who are LGB so that they can work toward common social justice goals that aid their communities. Further, counselors should serve as consultants for community service agencies in order to ensure that clients who are LGB have equal access to services.

3. *Giving Back to the Schools.* On the basis of the work of Stone (2003) and ASCA (2014), school counselors can advocate for LGB youths in the following ways:
   • Collaborate with schools to develop action plans to reduce sexual harassment.
   • Involve heterosexual allies in reforming the social system.
   • Include LGB issues in diversity awareness and multicultural initiatives.
   • Use inclusive language in classroom guidance lessons.
   • Acquire continuing education on young LGB issues.
   • Work to bridge families and schools.
   • Support the Gay, Lesbian, and Straight Education Network (www.glsen.org).
4. *Collaboration with Other Fields.* Counselors and counseling training programs need to expand their areas of competence to include interdisciplinary education (e.g., medicine, human sexuality, public policy, social work, women's studies). Socially conscious counselors will have dialogues with colleagues in these different disciplines to gain knowledge about people who are LGB and to better meet the micro and macro needs of these communities.

The foregoing strategies may be helpful in developing advocacy projects within the counseling community. Brubaker, Harper, and Singh (2011) offer additional suggestions based on actual leadership examples in school and community settings. Activity 6.7 describes a class exercise to develop a project regarding the LGB population.

ACTIVITY 6.7

Find a local organization in your community that provides mental health services to LGB individuals. As a class, create a small advocacy project that will allow you to give back to that organization before the end of your quarter or semester. At the completion of your project, give a written or oral presentation to students and faculty within your department.

Summary

As the field of counseling increasingly stresses the need for competent counselors to work with individuals who identify as lesbian, gay, and bisexual (LGB), it is important to increase counselors' knowledge and awareness regarding sexual orientation. We began this chapter by defining some key terms that counselors should know, because using appropriate language with clients who are LGB is important. For example, although some helping professionals use the terms *sexual orientation* and *gender identity* interchangeably, there are significant differences between the two. Sexual orientation generally involves an individual's

sexual and affectional attractions to others of the opposite or same gender. Gender identity pertains to an individual's sense of being male, female, or some other gender outside the binary of male–female. Individuals typically fall into one of three socially constructed categories of sexual orientation. Lesbians and gay males would fall into the category of same-sex-attracted individuals. Bisexuals may be physically or affectionally attracted to members of either sex. Heterosexuals are typically attracted to members of the opposite sex. The term *Questioning* is used to describe individuals who are in the process of exploring and trying to understand their sexual orientation identity. Although we have terms to delineate the sexual orientations of others, LGB-affirmative counselors should always ask how students and clients prefer to identify their orientation and should never make assumptions about their students' or clients' sexual orientations.

To help better understand their students or clients who are LGB, models of LGB identity development were presented. Cass's model of lesbian and gay identity development not only is historically significant because it was one of the first models, but also has pragmatic application for clinicians. Her model posits that most lesbians and gay men progress through six stages: Identity Confusion, Identity Comparison, Identity Tolerance, Identity Acceptance, Identity Pride, and Identity Synthesis. For many lesbians and gay men, this process may not be linear, and individuals may go back and forth between stages. Assessing at what stage a student or client is within the model could inform affirmative treatment interventions as well as facilitate a stronger therapeutic alliance.

In addition, the construct of heterosexism was delineated. Heterosexism involves the oppression of LGB individuals and entails prejudice and discrimination. Internalized heterosexism occurs when individuals who are LGB internalize the negative beliefs and attitudes that some members of our society have toward people who identify as LGB. To debunk prevalent stereotypes associated with the LGB communities, current demographic information was presented, such as the estimated sizes of the LGB communities, their educational statuses, and their relationships within their communities and to other communities.

To illustrate the harm that heterosexism has perpetrated on individuals who are LGB, we presented examples of the mental health (e.g., depression), physical (e.g., substance abuse), and social consequences (e.g., anti–same-sex legislation) of heterosexism. When working with clients who are LGB, competent counselors should assess the effects of heterosexism in the lives of their clients. Once a culturally sensitive assessment has taken place, competent counselors will implement gay-affirmative counseling interventions. Therefore, we included specific interventions that mental health and school counselors can use on behalf of their clients and students. For example, counselors should be aware of their own beliefs and attitudes about sexual orientation. In addition, competent counselors should be familiar with local resources that could benefit students and clients who are LGB. The Association for LGBT Issues in Counseling has created a set of competencies for working with clients who are LGB. (See www.algbtic.org/competencies.html. LGB-affirming counselors should be familiar with these competencies and integrate them into all aspects of their professional work with students and clients who are LGB. The chapter concluded by recommending specific ways that counselors might advocate for their clients who are LGB at a systemic level, thereby creating a more just nonheterosexist society.

Review Questions

1. What is the relationship between gender identity and sexual identity?
2. Describe the stages of three different identity development models, and explain why it might be necessary to have three different models. In other words, can one, and only one, model be applied to lesbians, gay men, and bisexuals?
3. What is heterosexism, and how is it related to sexism and other forms of oppression?
4. Give an example of a mental health, physical, and social consequence of heterosexism in the lives of individuals who are LGB, and apply at least one ALGBTIC counseling competency to the treatment of the consequences.
5. What are some ways that counselors can foster an LGB-affirmative society? An LGB-affirmative clinical practice?

7 Social Class and Classism

Kathryn S. Newton and Bradley T. Erford

PREVIEW

Socioeconomic status (SES) plays a significant role in personal identity, relationships, and individual and cultural values. It is also a predictive factor for health and well-being. Given the growing resource and income disparities in the United States, and the high likelihood that counselor trainees and counselors will work in communities and schools across the socioeconomic spectrum, the counselor's knowledge of SES and classism is an important area of competence. Although many counseling internship sites serve clients at the lower end of the socioeconomic scale, counselor trainees rarely receive training or supervision that helps them identify, conceptualize, and intervene with issues related to SES and social class identity. This chapter will provide an overview of social class and class-based discrimination in the United States, their effects on mental health, and implications for counselors. Developing the ability to identify and work with the influences of class and classism can contribute to more effective counseling. The activities and resources throughout the chapter are intended to deepen counselor self-awareness, increase knowledge and skills, and provide direction for professional and client advocacy. While reading this chapter, keep in mind that self-awareness is a foundational aspect of cultural competence. Pay attention to topics, issues, or activities which introduce thoughts or feelings that may be uncomfortable and confusing or, by contrast, enlightening and liberating.

CONSIDERING SOCIAL CLASS AND CLASSISM

Social classifications are common, if not universal, to human societies. Classifications may be used to assign social roles such as production, protection, child rearing, and spiritual stewardship. These classifications may be based on family lineage, gender, age, race, ethnicity, ability, or education level. Frequently, they become a way of designating rank and power, or **social class** status. Historically, most social hierarchies have been rigid and institutionalized: individuals were born into a social class that strictly defined their community, vocation, education, language, and behavior toward others, both within and outside their own social classification.

While the general trend is toward more permeable social structures within individual cultures, a rise in global stratification is also being observed as international corporations and political movements compete with national interests. The United States has a multilayered social class history that includes the social organization of the indigenous peoples, the imported values of European settlers, the founding principles of the United States as a nation, and the waves of subsequent immigration. Issues of race, gender, ethnicity, nation of origin, and economic status merge into a complicated system of beliefs and practice. Alongside the prevalent (although not universal) perception of the United States as the "land of opportunity" is the statistical reality that the United States has significantly greater income disparity and lower class mobility than most other developed nations (Chetty, Hendren, Kline, Saez, & Turner, 2014; Torche, 2015). Since social classifications and corresponding markers can vary so widely within and between cultures and across time, it is helpful to make a distinction between class status and the distribution of essential resources. The United Nations Declaration of Human Rights (see Reflection 7.1) provides a useful framework for examining our core beliefs about resource distribution.

REFLECTION 7.1

Article 25 of the United Nations' Universal Declaration of Human Rights, established in 1948, reads as follows:

> Everyone has the right to a standard of living adequate for the health and well-being of himself and of his family, including food, clothing, housing and medical care and necessary social services, and the right to security in the event of unemployment, sickness, disability, widowhood, old age or other lack of livelihood in circumstances beyond his control.

Use the following questions to explore your own beliefs regarding human rights:

a. Do all human beings have a *right* to an adequate standard of living as described in Article 25?
b. Do all human beings have a right to resources adequate for health *and* well-being, and not just for survival?
c. Do you believe that the universal human right to health and well-being is an *attainable* goal?
d. To what degree do you believe that the United States meets these conditions for *all* of its citizens?
e. How do each of these considerations relate to the work of counselors?

A careful examination of social class includes attention to beliefs and values, as in Reflection 7.1, as well as to language and conceptual definitions. One way of defining social class is based on quantifiable socioeconomic factors (e.g., educational attainment, type of employment, income level, savings, investments, housing, and property ownership). Another way of conceptualizing class is subjectively: How do individuals perceive and experience their own SES in relation to others? Yet another perspective examines complex interactions among economics, gender, and race. Class can be defined in terms of access to, and ability to wield, power and influence. Each conceptual lens is both useful and self-limiting. A client or student record will likely indicate educational attainment, but will not indicate the meaning of that status to the individual. Likewise, seemingly objective, descriptive language may be heavy with subjective meaning. Table 7.1 lists some terms commonly used to reference social class status. Although these terms are generally accepted, many of them are also used to covertly reference and perpetuate negative stereotypes. In considering the terms in Table 7.1, notice images that come to mind. Why are certain "profiles" (e.g., race, gender, occupation) associated with specific terms? What is the source of those associations? Complete Activity 7.1 to consider how labels influence individuals' attitudes regarding SES. In Voices from the Field 7.1, a counselor provides her perspective of working with individuals in a low-SES community.

TABLE 7.1 Terms Frequently Used to Reference Social Class

Lower-Class Status	Middle-Class Status	Upper-Class Status
Low income	Middle income	Upper income
Lower class	Middle class	Upper class
Working poor	Working class	Wealthy
Urban poor/rural poor	Professional	New money/old money
Welfare recipient	Home owner	College graduate
High school dropout	High school graduate	Executive
Manual labor	Skilled labor	Elite

ACTIVITY 7.1

In small groups, have a discussion about pejorative words you have heard used to indicate SES. Give special attention to words that indicate the intersection of class, race, and gender. For example, what stereotype is indicated by the term *redneck*? How about the term *welfare mother*? And *trust fund baby*? Where do these terms come from? Who uses them? Do adults and children use different language and markers to indicate class status? What effect might this language have on identity development, peer relationships, and community interactions?

Voices from the Field 7.1

Having grown up in a low-SES rural area, I understand the struggles all too well. As a counselor going back to the same community for work, I can see just how much social class really plays out: "You went to graduate school? How did you afford that?" "Why do we need counseling here?" "So, what, you sit and talk to people as they lay on the couch?" "What do you even do?" I could keep going with the questions, but my point is that there are huge misconceptions about counseling that make advocacy and education extremely important.

The problem that was easiest for me to see was that services are extremely limited and located mostly out of the county, making it difficult for counselors as well as clients. While working with a local high school, I found some services in the next county over, but my clients couldn't get there because of limited transportation. That's where advocacy made a huge difference. I tried calling a few of the services and talking about the possibility of them coming to the school to meet with the student or family. I found that this was possible for a lot of services and that it would overcome a lot of limitations I was originally running into. After talking to possible services, I compiled a list to distribute to the students so that they knew what was available to them. Another set of problems comes with finding services that the client can actually afford. Referring someone to services that they can't afford is not only extremely embarrassing for the client, but can also be a complete turn off to counseling in general. Furthermore, while assistance programs can be helpful, they can also be extremely frustrating and confusing to navigate. Having knowledge of fees, assistance, and system procedures can help so that your client does not get discouraged and give up on you or the service.

Two issues I constantly deal with when providing direct counseling are stigma and confidentiality. In a school setting, being called out of class to see your counselor is "not cool" and can cause others to tease or bully the student. I also have found that the students I worked with did not want to talk to their parents about counseling. They didn't want them to know they were getting help, because it was frowned upon in their family: "Why can't we just help you?" Also, if you are working in an area with a lot of closely connected individuals, it is important to remember to be discrete. One of the ways I did this was to make flyers with different services and put them on the inside of the school bathroom stalls so that students could find out about services and get phone numbers in privacy. Confidentiality is always a big ethical concern and is even more of an issue when you live in a rural area. I worked in the same community where I grew up and went to school, and I found that I knew sisters, brothers, and parents of my clients. This made it difficult at first. I had to constantly be aware of what I was saying and how I was thinking. I did not want my knowledge of another family member to change the way I viewed my client. It was also difficult because I often ran into clients outside of the counseling office. Community events likewise proved to be difficult, because I did not want to make my client or myself uncomfortable. I always explain to my clients when I start working with them that, if I see them in public, I will not make the first move. If they want to say "hello" to me, that's fine, but I do not want to make them feel pressured to explain to individuals who I was. It is a constant battle to break down barriers that these individuals face, but I remind myself daily that these struggles are exactly what made me become a counselor in the first place.

~Kelsi Wiley, M.S., Corrections Counselor, South Central Pennsylvania

What Is Socioeconomic Status?

Socioeconomic status (SES) generally refers to a comparative measure of class standing, or status, based on a combination of educational attainment, income level, and occupational prestige. Other class indicators also may be considered in an assessment of SES, depending on the issue being explored (e.g., a counselor may wish to include peer group status when assessing an adolescent client). In the field of counseling, SES is often used as a descriptor for clients or research sample populations. A "low-SES" client may be assumed to have no more than a high school diploma and to be working in a low-skill position, probably for minimum wage. On the other end of the continuum, a "high-SES" client may be assumed to have a college degree, to be working in a salaried professional career with benefits, and to have acquired assets (property ownership, investments). An example of a "middle-" or "moderate-SES" individual would be a recent graduate of a master's-level counseling program who may be income poor (especially if graduating with student loans), but education rich (just under 10% of the population has attained a graduate-level degree; U.S. Census Bureau, 2012a).

It is important to understand the interaction among social, educational, and economic factors in perceptions of SES. Low, middle, or upper SES does not automatically correlate with income level. An individual's economic **net worth** is based on the sum of the person's *assets* (cash, investments, real estate) minus the sum of her or his *liabilities* (i.e., debt, mortgage, loans). **Poverty** is a condition in which a person's liabilities signiifcantly outweigh his or her assets or the person is unable to meet basic requirements for well-being, such as food, shelter, and clothing. **Wealth**, by contrast, indicates a substantial surplus net worth: the sum of one's assets significantly outweigh the sum of one's liabilities. A person who is wealthy is able to meet his or her basic needs, *and* accumulate resources to satisfy wants, *and* redistribute resources according to personal values (e.g., family inheritance, charitable donations, further accumulation of wealth).

The concrete results of inequitable resource distribution are obvious: hunger, homelessness, educational limitations, inadequate health care, and more. Less apparent are the ways in which class bias and SES influence you and your client. Prejudice (either positive or negative) based on SES influences mental health and the counseling process on multiple levels, including client attitudes toward counseling, counselor perceptions of clients, case conceptualization and intervention choices, and service locations and options. Consider the following profiles of age, education, employment, and income levels:

- Age 38 years, master's degree in business administration, corporate executive, substantial assets, recently unemployed (corporate merger), and no current income
- Age 22 years, vocational degree, employed assistant mechanic, annual income of $100,000 (including lottery payouts)
- Age 45 years, doctoral student, conducting grant-funded research, income falls below federal poverty line
- Age 10 years, attending private school, high-achieving student, on scholarship (from single-parent household living below federal poverty line)
- Age 62 years, general education diploma, senior tollbooth operator, annual salary of $55,000

For each individual, would that individual be considered low, middle, or high SES? As a counselor, how would you feel about approaching each of these individuals? How might each of them perceive and interact with the typical counselor (who holds a master's degree and a professional position, and is of middle-income SES)?

The profiles listed intentionally omitted gender, race, ethnicity, religion, sexual orientation, nation of origin, and ability status. How do your perceptions change if the 38-year-old, unemployed businessperson is also a Muslim, African-American female? What if the 10-year-old student is a White, Christian male? Or a female whose family recently immigrated from Guatemala? What if the tollbooth operator is also a gay male of Asian descent? How might these individuals' SES be perceived by those of the dominant U.S. culture? By their family and cultural community members?

SES ACROSS CULTURES AND NATIONS   The United States will continue to diversify in race, ethnicity, and nation of origin in the coming decades. Social upheaval will increase as our civic, economic, and political systems attempt to adapt to these changes. It is important for counselors to understand differences in defining SES across cultures and nations, especially given that much of our future population growth will be among people of color and among immigrants and their children. Immigrants who have obtained educational and professional status in their country of origin may find their degree or training irrelevant in the United States owing to different professional and legal standards. In countries where status is conferred by family of origin, number of children, religion, or political affiliation, immigrants may gain or lose status when entering the United States. Culturally, a valued elder may experience profound marginalization because of age discrimination. Economically, an individual or a family entering the United States may have lost some or all of their material goods to war, famine, persecution, or the considerable cost of migration. Counselors need to understand that commonly used SES markers (e.g., English language fluency, employment status, type of occupation, income level, attire) may be less and less useful in understanding the social class identity and values of the people they serve.

Looking more closely at language, we may find that literacy, fluency, and manner of speech all play a key role in class status. In a family or community with limited English language skills, anyone who acquires fluency—adult or child—becomes an important community member. This status is especially true for children of immigrants: these children may acculturate rapidly in a U.S. school. In cases where parents came to the United States to provide greater opportunities for their children, lifestyle gains may be tempered by the feeling of "losing" their child to another culture. These disruptions in established class status and social relations can generate profound shifts in identity and in family and community stability (Ainslie, 2011). The following excerpt from Shirley Yee highlights the complexities of class for immigrant families:

> My dad came from China, my Mom from Tokyo. I grew up in an upper-middle-class white suburb and always felt I was supposed to be a way I'm not. Partly it was US/Asian issues. Me and my friends had different lifestyles. I worked 5 days a week throughout the year at my dad's restaurant starting in 7th grade while my friends did summer camp and sports. I'm really interested in immigrants and children of immigrants and why they left. I grew up hearing my mom's story of growing up in Tokyo. She was 5 when the US dropped the bombs, and she saw houses burning and dead people's feet sticking out from under blankets. I wonder what are the privileges I often take for granted having been US born? And what are the costs of immigration? (Leondar-Wright, 2012, p. 1)

Yee's story illustrates a common immigrant experience of contextual and generational fluctuations in class identity and status work. Counselors need to be able to work with clients to understand how these factors contribute to their challenges and strengths. For example, Voices from the Field 7.2 illustrates how a counselor—who is an immigrant herself—experiences providing counseling services in the United States, including services to refugees. Counselors who are native English speakers and who have never experienced immersion in a non-English-speaking culture are likely to underestimate both the value of bilingualism and the stress of acquiring proficiency in a language other than one's own. The next section looks more closely at classism and its implications for counseling.

Voices from the Field 7.2

My story begins with examining how my own social class identity has affected my work as a counselor. I was born and raised in India in an upper-middle-class family (by Indian standards). I am a heterosexual, female, Christian, first-generation immigrant to the United States. In my career path, I believe that my own experiences with adjustment have helped me look for opportunities to advocate around issues influenced by social class identity.

(Continued)

During my eight years working as a drug and alcohol counselor, I found it extremely challenging to help clients access the care they needed, given the limited resources they had. Since addiction is a chronic disease, their recovery often required several episodes of hospitalization and ongoing outpatient treatment. Because the substance use itself had depleted them of finances, and because most of my clients also had a criminal history, they often found themselves trapped in a perpetual cycle of loss. Added to this tragedy was the stigma of being labeled an addict by society. As they fell further into an abyss of hopelessness, I would often hear things like "How am I supposed to get a job if I can't get my driver's license back for several months/years?" "How am I supposed to be a rehabilitated felon if no one will give me a job because of my criminal background?" "How am I supposed to pay my fines, court costs, child support, and bills if I don't have a job?" And now, "How am I supposed to pay for counseling and treatment in order to get better, so that all this does not keep happening in my life, if I don't have a job or even transportation to get to counseling and my family has cut me off?" Clients who were well resourced financially and relationally did not have some of these barriers to accessing services. My approach to counseling the underresourced shifted to helping them see that the birthplace of hope is often where resilience and learning to tolerate discomfort intersect. I connected them with community resources like local drug and alcohol commissions, rehab programs with scholarships, advocacy groups that worked with felons, and free recovery support groups.

A few years ago, I had an opportunity to work with a local refugee community from Somalia in my neighborhood. Many had arrived in the United States through the lottery system and had been living in refugee camps in Kenya after fleeing persecution. This experience really opened my eyes to the unique challenges that are a part of working with refugees who are in the process of resettlement. This population had been severely traumatized, yet they were expected to navigate their way through complex federal and state governmental systems in order to access services for basic needs like health care, food stamps, housing, schooling for their children, and transportation to appointments. Language and literacy barriers provided an additional layer of complexity in gaining timely access to critical services. I remember one incident involving a refugee woman who worked in a factory and kept getting "written up" because of her flowing robe and head covering. Her attire was a central part of her faith as a Muslim but was considered a safety risk at work because it could get caught in the machinery she operated. It took several mediation attempts between an advocacy organization, a translator, and the employer to arrive at the solution of wearing a jacket over her attire for protection without compromising her religious beliefs. This experience challenged me to really examine the work I do as a counselor and ask myself if I could provide services that were not just limited to talk therapy. I began to look for ways to treat trauma that were less confined to verbal processing in a particular language. I found that EMDR [eye movement desensitization and reprocessing] treatment was a helpful alternative. While some translation is still necessary, it is a much more effective approach than using a translator for every session of talk therapy to address trauma.

I currently work in a private Christian college counseling center, and part of my job is to provide support to underrepresented student groups on campus. For the first time in my career, my counseling services are free to all students and unlimited in terms of number of counseling sessions. All students have equal access to high-quality care. That being said, I am keenly aware that getting admitted to a private Christian college and being able to thrive as a student are very much affected by social class identity. Not all students who are able to navigate the complexities of getting financial aid and arrive at college feel comfortable using counseling and support, especially if their social class identity has promoted the belief that counseling is for the sick and troubled. Furthermore, among Christians, there can be guilt and shame in seeking counseling, because some hold the belief that seeking professional help is an indication that you lack trust in God. I see my role as helping students view counseling as a process that can enhance their wellness, not just provide treatment for the sick—a belief that may be linked to their own internalized classism.

~Marcelle Giovannetti MS, NCC, CADC, clinical mental health counselor at the Engle Center for Counseling and Health Services, Messiah College Director of Drug and Alcohol Programs and Multicultural Counseling

What Is Classism?

Classism is having negative biases about, and discriminatory behaviors toward, individuals or groups based on their perceived or actual SES. From childhood, we are exposed to constant messages from family, friends, community members, and the media about relative class status. These familial and social biases shape our sense of self, our relationships, and our worldview. **Internalized classism** refers to unexamined class biases that shape our beliefs about ourselves and our relative merit in our families, peer groups, and community. Depending on our perceived social class position, we may feel ourselves to be diminished, accomplished, or superior compared with others. **Structural classism** refers to social and institutional practices that discriminate on the basis of SES; these practices may be *overt* (e.g., "legacy" admissions in higher education) or *covert* (e.g., lack of public transportation effectively limiting employment options). As counselors, we need to understand how internalized and structural classism may be implicated in mental health issues and barriers to counseling.

Although the counseling profession has made significant progress in addressing issues of gender, race, ethnicity, and sexual identity, class identity and classism are rarely addressed. One factor that may contribute to this relative silence is **psychological distancing**, a term which refers to ways of thinking and behaving that are used by privileged groups to justify and distance themselves from their role in socioeconomic injustice (Lott & Bullock, 2007). One way of distancing is to structure education, work, and spiritual and community activities in a way that maintains the separation between socioeconomic classes. This separation prevents the development of empathy that would naturally follow from open communication and close relationships. Now conduct Activity 7.2 to get a better feel for the economic diversity of your local community.

ACTIVITY 7.2

Part 1: Print out a street map of your local community. Using a color marker, mark all the areas you frequent: your home and the homes of people you often visit, the places you most often go to for food, clothing, gas (if you drive), education, health care and other services, your place of worship, if applicable, and places you go for entertainment or recreation. Using the same color marker, map the routes you travel to and from those places Now take three new color markers:

(Continued)

Use one color to outline the lower-income/impoverished areas of your community, a second color for the working-/middle-class areas, and a third color for the upper-income/wealthy areas. What do you notice about your routes, about where you frequent, and about these three different SES areas?

Part 2: Which socioeconomic class do you have the least exposure to? Can you find out where people from those neighborhoods shop? Access health care? What do they do for entertainment?

Part 3: Spend a few hours or a day in areas you don't usually "see." Find a way to engage people from the economic community in those areas. It would be helpful to do this activity with a partner or in small groups so that you can discuss what you learn about yourself and your community.

Another factor that interferes with actively addressing the consequences of classism is **poverty attribution** (how individuals explain poverty). Studies of both economically privileged and marginalized groups have found that race, gender, education, and political and religious affiliation influence people's beliefs regarding individual wealth or poverty (Bobbio, Canova, & Manganelli, 2010; Flanagan et al., 2014; Robinson, 2009). One belief is that resources are gained or lost through **individual causation** (e.g., people are poor or wealthy because of their personal values, work ethic, or other personal characteristics; people are personally responsible for their economic status). Another belief is that individual wealth or poverty is best explained by socioeconomic and political factors, or **structural causation** (e.g., people are poor because of discriminatory social policy, oppression, or other institutional forms of exclusion; Hunt, 2004). Hunt (2004) conducted a study which found that most participants attributed wealth to individual accomplishment and poverty to external factors, such as a failing economy, politics, or discrimination. The same study found that racial and ethnic minorities were more likely than Whites to attribute both wealth *and* poverty to external factors such as privilege and oppression. Thus, the way we learn to understand and explain relative wealth and poverty is influenced by our life experiences, values, education, and affiliations. Consider, for example, how the values presented in Reflection 7.2 influence interpersonal relationships.

REFLECTION 7.2

Circle five values or expectations from the list that follows that seemed to be the most important in your family of origin. Then, underline five that were discouraged or devalued. In a different color, go through the same process for your current personal values.

- Getting by
- Making a good living
- Gaining social status or prominence
- Communicating openly among family members
- Going to a place of worship
- Keeping up with the neighbors
- Being physically fit or athletic
- Using therapy/counseling
- Helping others

- Getting married and having children
- Respecting law and order
- Defending your country
- Staying out of trouble with the law
- Being polite and well mannered
- Being politically or socially aware
- Gaining personal recognition
- Sticking up for others in your community
- Doing community service
- Being in control
- Being independent
- Saving money
- Making your money work for you
- Enjoying your money
- Getting a high school degree
- Getting a college degree
- Getting an advanced or professional degree
- Learning a trade
- Being smart
- Helping advance your racial, religious, or cultural group
- Maintaining your physical appearance
- Being a professional
- Being an entrepreneur
- Owning a home
- Being patriotic
- Going to a good school
- Not being wasteful
- Being respectful of elders
- Achieving your goals
- Having character
- Other: _____
- Other: _____

Look at the values that you have circled or underlined in both colors. These represent family-of-origin values that have remained the same for you as an adult. Why have you retained such values? How might they support or inhibit your development as a counselor?

Now look over the values that were held by your family of origin but not by you as an adult. Do the same for the values that were not your family's but that you have acquired as an adult. What experiences contributed to these changes in values?

Finally, look at the values that are neither circled nor underlined. What associations do you have with these values? If you had a client for whom these values were primary, would you be able to support, encourage, and empathize with those values?

Source: Adapted from the "Class Background Inventory" created by Class Action: Building Bridges across the Class Divide. Original version available at http://www.classism.org/wp-content/uploads/2010/09/CLASS-BACKGROUND-INVENTORY.pdf

The Evolution of Social Class and Classism in the United States

The cultural mythology of the United States is rooted in the belief that the United States is a "**class-less society**" with equal opportunity for all: the so-called American Dream. James Truslow Adams coined the term "the American Dream" in the book *The Epic of America* (1933), referring to that dream of a land in which life should be better and richer and fuller for every-one, with opportunity for each according to ability or achievement. It is a difficult dream for the European upper classes to interpret adequately, and too many of us ourselves have grown weary and mistrustful of it. It is not a dream of motor cars and high wages merely, but a dream of social order in which each man and each woman shall be able to attain to the fullest stature of which they are innately capable, and be recognized by others for what they are, regardless of the fortuitous circumstances of birth or position. (pp. 214–215)

The concept of social class evolved in 19th-century Europe as societies transitioned from feudal–agricultural societies toward urban–industrial societies, with resulting shifts in eco-nomic and family systems. Social classes helped describe and explain the changing face of economics, politics, and culture, as well as related changes in social stratification. Specifically, the term **upper class** referred to the groups of people who owned the mechanisms and materi-als of production, including inherited wealth and property, and who also had the luxury of leisure time. The *Declaration of Independence* ensured the continuity of this structure, as, during that period in history, the idea that "all men are created equal" and the concept of "inalienable rights" pertained exclusively to White, property-owning men. The **working class** comprised those who provided the labor and were minimally paid. European immigrants to the American continent imported this social structure into what would become the United States. Historically, much of the economic rise of the United States was off the labor of inden-tured servants and the enslavement and oppression of others (e.g., Africans, Native Americans).

Over the past century in the United States, the predominant cultural belief is that, if you work hard enough, you will get ahead (and conversely, if you are not getting ahead, it is because you are not working hard enough). However, actual statistics on income, employ-ment, education, and health indicate otherwise. The more recent transition of developed nations from a manufacturing economy to a service economy has created a new **underclass** of chronically underemployed citizens. For instance, a minimum-wage full-time worker still earns an annual income that is barely above the poverty line for a single wage earner, making class mobility quite difficult for hardworking underclass Americans. The communities we live in, the schools we attend, whether we attend and complete college, our career opportunities, and our social networks are predicted largely by the socioeconomic class of our families of origin.

U.S. CLASS STRUCTURE   In the United States, major class distinctions are based primarily on financial status, source of income, educational attainment, and occupation. (See Table 7.1 for common class designators.) Each economic tier has its own within-group status markers. Among the wealthy, there is inherited versus earned wealth; in the middle class, status may be equated with residence in higher performing public school districts. In lower SES tiers, status may be associated, for example, with one's mode of transportation (private vehicle versus public transportation) or with the degree to which one relies on public assistance. Understanding U.S. class structure requires knowledge of the distribution of wealth in the nation. It is helpful to frame the discussion of wealth distribution by noting that one third of the world's wealth is owned by North Americans, home to the richest 1% of the global popula-tion (Vornovitsky, Gottschalck, & Smith, 2015).

Although the United States is a wealthy nation, the distribution of wealth within the nation is inequitable (Vornovitsky et al., 2015). The wealthiest 1% hold more than one third of total U.S. net worth, and nearly two thirds of the wealth within this country is held by the top 5%. Over the past three decades, the income gap between rich and poor in the United States has increased steadily (Organisation for Economic Co-operation and Development, 2011). Currently, the United States ranks below China, Russia, and even Uganda and Iran in equitable distribution of family income (Central Intelligence Agency, 2018). Simultaneously, tax payment equity has shifted markedly. In 1961, the top income bracket paid 90% of its earnings in taxes, but this top rate was cut to 28% under the Reagan presidency and currently stands at 35%. Simultaneously, investment/capital gains and corporate taxes also declined (Markovich, 2014). Forces of globalization, de-unionization, and technological change have placed lower income and less educated U.S. citizens at substantial employment disadvantages. For example, it is widely believed that the U.S. education system has not kept the U.S. workforce up to speed on integration of technological changes.

The degree to which individuals can "get ahead" (i.e., advance in SES) is referred to as **class mobility**. In the United States, many people continue to believe that there is a high degree of class mobility and that individuals can expect to advance economically within one life span or steadily over generations. Historically, this expectation has held true for the wealthy. For example, between 1998 and 2000, Americans with a net worth of $5 million or more saw their holdings increase by over 40% (Raub & Newcomb, 2012).

Torche (2015) reviewed the sociological and economic literature on intergenerational mobility and suggested that an inverse association exists between inequality and economic mobility at the level of the nation, with the United States featuring higher inequality and lower mobility than other advanced industrial countries. Only the United Kingdom had less class mobility than the United States. However—and surprisingly—mobility has not declined in the United States over the recent decades in which economic inequality has expanded. The inequality–mobility relationship fails to emerge when occupational measures of mobility are used, likely because these measures do not fully capture some mechanisms of economic reproduction.

Chambers, Swan, and Heesacker (2015) confirmed these observations, noting that the general U.S. public's perception is that class mobility has been declining over the past several decades, even though objective measures do not support these subjective perceptions. Indeed, these authors' findings point instead to stable aggregated intergenerational mobility rates. But the most fascinating finding from their study was that class mobility within the United States varies substantially by the geographic area in which a child is raised. The phenomenon was termed a "birth lottery" by Chetty et al. (2014): geographic areas with better residential racial integration, income equality, public schools, and family stability facilitated greater class mobility. These factors are so profound that Chetty and colleagues concluded that a child raised in San Jose, California, whose parents are in the lower fifth of the income distribution has a probability of moving into the upper fifth of the income distribution that is three times greater than that of a child growing up in Charlotte, North Carolina.

At the same time, the standard of living for middle- and lower-income households is stagnating or declining between generations. As purchasing power diminishes, and the cost of food, housing, health care, and a college education increases, we are seeing more downward mobility among the middle class. Approximately 30% of children from middle-class households (households with annual incomes of approximately $34,000 to $64,000 for a family of two adults and two children) fall well below middle-class status as adults (Acs, 2012). Women of all races and Black men are at greatest risk for downward mobility, compared with White men. Economic legislation further compounds the class barriers, with tax policies that favor the wealthy and place the burden of public taxes primarily on middle- and working-class families (Ross, 2009). Voices from the Field 7.3 outlines one counselor's journey working with clients across the socioeconomic spectrum.

Voices from the Field 7.3

My family of origin is Black, post–Great Migration, working poor, and urban. My parents had high expectations, repeating often, "Get an education, stay out of trouble, and make a contribution to make the world around you better." Working with a lot of African-American teenagers, adults, and families was a way of living out these now-internalized expectations. Moving the culture forward meant, in some small way, trying to "give something back."

The early part of my career as a counselor was devoted to working with clients who tended to look like me and who often shared the same demographic and SES characteristics. Whether canoeing through the Everglades with a group of youths ordered to show up by the court, or leading groups for substance-abusing adults and their family members, I believed that I could make connections on a personal level. We had a shared understanding of growing up in a housing project and seeing up close the ways that addiction could wreak havoc.

Working in a low-resource community in which clients had difficulty meeting their basic needs made it difficult to engage clients in conversations that went beyond day-to-day survival. My colleagues would likely write off these conversations as "less than" therapy, a failed facsimile of Rogers or Erickson or Adler. I came to appreciate why clients were reluctant to engage in a "process" while under duress and how challenging it became to sell folks on what that "better alternative" to a life of addictive behaviors could look like.

While my clients and my origin stories often paralleled one another, I was cast in a role of authority and control—a role which negated any rapport that could be established on our shared cultural history. It was a thin wire to traverse: the choices made from moment to moment about how much to self-disclose versus maintaining a "proper" therapeutic distance with clients. Issues as fundamental as speech patterns and word choice could be viewed as an effort to make a client feel more comfortable or as patronizing and hurtful. It was a constant challenge to determine what being authentic looked like for a counselor.

For the last 10 years, I have worked at a highly nationally ranked, predominately White private research university. I was drawn to the position, quite frankly, because budgetary restrictions and onerous regulations had begun to adversely affect the quality of the services my former agency could deliver. I did not wish to witness the demise of a beautiful thing.

In some ways, the clients that I presently work with share commonalities with the lower SES clients from my agency days: They are virtually all mandated to attend counseling, and they have violated alcohol and drug laws and policies. Beyond those factors, however, the life arc of the population I presently work with diverges significantly from the urban, working-poor client I saw in community mental health settings. Many of my present clients come from backgrounds of high SES and financial privilege. They are high-achieving, high-stakes actors who will willingly sacrifice aspects of their health in the pursuit of academic success. Many have had significant interactions with mental health systems, treatment hospitals, and psychiatric medications long before their arrival on campus. Campus Health Services surrounds our students with resources: access to case managers, psychologists, and psychiatrists.

I screen college students for elevated risk of developing substance-use disorders. They are a population that operates with a significantly enhanced risk profile because they have easy access to alcohol and drugs, a high drive to push boundaries, and a desire to explore social relationships as their identity development continues.

On many occasions, the students I interview have committed infractions that would have resulted in their being jailed or put on endless probation and monitoring plans if they were of a lower SES. Student violators rarely encounter the local court system, and when they do, they have the resources to "lawyer up" and avoid the consequences of their acts. Students often express awareness that they live inside of a bubble, shielded from the harsh realities that similar bad choices visit upon those with less stature, less access, and fewer resources.

I often find myself working through a weird sense of survivor's remorse. I sometimes feel like I abandoned people and principles I held close at one time. Having worked both with folks who have always had the brass ring within their grasp and those who have no ring within their reach, I wonder if I have taken the easy way out. Issues of class are always present. I am always taken aback when I let White students into our corridor of offices, only to have them walk right by me. The cognitive dissonance that registers on their faces when they realize that it is me they've come to see is palpable. The attempt to recover from their assumption that I was there solely to open doors for them is unconvincing.

My conversations with students behind that door always reference the reality of life outside the bubble, and the countless ways their status as students becomes less influential as they move away from the campus. It is my small way of challenging their notions of safety arising from their relatively privileged positions.

For many White students, drinking and drug use are referenced as tools used to exercise and celebrate their privilege: Drinking and drug use are, after all, "part of the college experience," right? For Black and Brown student clients, substance use is often discussed as a method for seeking relief from an environment in which privilege is constantly, openly on display and deeply oppressive to the spirit.

~Willie Bannister, M.S., LPC, Associate Director, Substance Abuse Risk Reduction Program

For those at or below the poverty level, stagnating wages, the scarcity of affordable housing, and significant reductions in public assistance are contributing to entrenched economic injustice. Ongoing unemployment, home foreclosures, and the reduced availability of low-income housing units are all contributing to a rising poverty rate within the United States. Culturally competent counselors understand the contradictions between social class mythology and economic reality. Failing to challenge the "classless society" myth serves to maintain the status quo, perpetuating conditions that continue to undermine the well-being of individuals, families, and communities.

Classism, Racism, and Ethnocentrism

Issues of class, class structure, and classism are further complicated by the history of racism and ethnocentrism in the United States. White Europeans who colonized North America brought class structure with them in the form of indentured servants and enslaved peoples, and created a political system that favored the dominant social class of White, property-owning males. Enslaved Africans and their descendants, along with waves of immigrants, supplied the labor that built much of the nation's infrastructure. However, capital accumulation remained primarily in the hands of the propertied class, which controlled policies and the law.

Today, the wealthiest in the nation continue to be predominantly U.S.-born White males; the poorest are disproportionately women, children, and people of color (U.S. Census Bureau, 2014b). One third of all children who are poor and low income are from immigrant families (Migration Policy Institute, 2011). Current projections indicate that, by the year 2050, there will no longer be a White non-Hispanic majority, a demographic shift that is already a reality in some states. Within a few decades, one in five people in the United States will identify as mixed race and close to 20% of the U.S. population will be foreign born (Passel & Cohn, 2008). As a result, intertwined classist, racial, and ethnic tensions are likely to increase within families, communities, and the nation as a whole.

CLASS AND RACE   Over two centuries of racial oppression through legal, political, and social means have contributed to pervasive stereotypes that confound class status and race and serve to perpetuate discrimination. Blackness or Brownness is often associated with poverty, low intelligence, and criminality, and Whiteness with middle- and upper-class status. For example, the term *welfare mother* is a coded derogatory reference to poor, urban Black women who "take advantage" of public assistance. Yet, statistically, if there is a "welfare mother," she is White, maintains at least part-time employment, and lives in a rural area.

Evidence of resiliency, achievement, and community leadership among Black Americans has done little to dispel these deeply held stereotypes of class, race, and identity. People of color who are also poor are more likely to be targeted for surveillance by social services and the criminal justice system. Within communities of color, internalized classism and racism contribute to difficulties in identity formation. Choices about speech patterns, peer groups, clothing, hairstyles, interests, career aspirations, and educational attainment are all loaded with racial and classist connotations. Despite the fact that over a third of Black households in the United States fall within the middle to upper SES range (U.S. Census Bureau, 2014b), being from or aspiring to middle- or upper-class status may still be associated with Whiteness.

CLASS AND IMMIGRATION   Most of us are familiar with the last two sentences of Emma Lazarus's 1883 sonnet, "The New Colossus," inscribed on the Statue of Liberty:

> Give me your tired, your poor,
> Your huddled masses yearning to breathe free,
> The wretched refuse of your teeming shore.
> Send these, the homeless, tempest-tost to me,
> I lift my lamp beside the golden door!

Yet eagerness for plentiful low-cost labor has always been countered by resistance to, and suspicion of, foreign languages and customs. During periods of social upheaval or economic decline, antiforeigner sentiment tends to rise and is often directed at recent immigrants. Targeting an "other" requires some means of "other" identification based on visible (race-based characteristics, clothing style) or audible (speech patterns, accents) differences. Over time, ethnic immigrant groups targeted for exclusionary practices have included those from China (a primary labor force that built the U.S. transcontinental railway system), Ireland, Japan (recall World War II internment camps), and Middle Eastern countries. Most recently, non-White Latinos are the targeted "other," with a growth in legislative changes with the purpose of criminalizing unauthorized immigration.

This exclusion through profiling contributes to both economic disenfranchisement and the perpetuation of classist stereotypes. For many immigrants to the "land of opportunity," exclusion has meant dismal working conditions, limited job prospects, and social ostracism, regardless of skin color. However, although language and observable ethnic behaviors can be acculturated within one to two generations, visible racial characteristics cannot. Thus, the descendants of immigrants of color have faced ongoing challenges to the validity of their "Americanness." By contrast, White immigrants who chose to quickly assimilate to the dominant culture often "blended in" within a generation. The relative ease of being accepted as "American" increased their access to education, employment, and social status; however, the cost was often a loss of lingual, ethnic, and cultural heritage for subsequent generations.

Although overt racial discrimination is no longer included in U.S. immigration law, restrictive caps pertaining to nation of origin, educational attainment, or profession serve as de facto racial and class barriers. Currently, foreign-born residents in the United States tend to fall into one of four categories: educated, skilled professionals; relatives of current legal residents; refugees; or unauthorized immigrants. Now complete Reflection 7.3.

REFLECTION 7.3

Consider the following quotation by Lemieux and Pratto (2003):

> Poverty does not persist because there is a scarcity of resources, nor does poverty exist because some societies have inefficient economic systems, lack natural resources, or because poor people lack ambition. Poverty is a product of human social relationships because social relationships determine how people distribute resources. (p. 147)

- In what ways does this statement support or challenge your own beliefs about the cause(s) of poverty?
- In the context of the given statement, what might an objective observer assume about human relationships in this country on the basis of the distribution of resources?
- In what way might counselors and the counseling profession use social relationships to work toward alleviating poverty and associated mental health issues?

POVERTY AND MENTAL HEALTH

Our particular class status and the corresponding ability to access basic resources interact with mental health on several levels. Poverty has been associated with a higher incidence of mental disorders, more severe symptoms, and greater difficulty accessing services. Worldwide, people living in poverty experience twice the incidence of common mental disorders (e.g., anxiety and depression) as the wealthy (World Health Organization [WHO], 2007). Poverty has been found to be both a causative factor in, and a result of, mental illness. According to the World Health Organization (WHO, 2010), 86% of suicides worldwide occur in economically struggling nations, with the highest rates among men in eastern European countries. Interestingly, social stigma toward people with mental health disorders was found to be highest in urban areas and among people with higher education levels.

Poverty is also associated with a greater incidence of exposure to violence and with related trauma, depression, anxiety, and post-traumatic stress disorder (WHO, 2010). This correlation may hold especially for women and children. Children from impoverished families and communities have higher exposure to pollutants in air, water, and food. The day cares and schools in low-income neighborhoods are usually inferior and often toxic, and children have less access to books, computers, and other tools for learning.

It has been hypothesized that mental illness may precipitate a downward slide into poverty because many of those suffering from the condition have difficulty managing basic life tasks. However, evidence indicates that poverty is just as likely to precede the development of mental illness, owing in part to pervasive and unrelenting life stressors (Hudson, 2005) and less access to quality health-care services. Because of these direct negative correlations between poverty and well-being, it is important to know more about who is poor and to understand the risk factors and mental health consequences associated with poverty. It is also important to understand the relationship among poverty, identity, and well-being.

Who Is Poor?

The incidence of poverty in the United States has been increasing steadily in recent years and, according to the most recent Census statistics, is currently at its highest (15.1%) since 1993 (U.S. Census Bureau, 2014b). Poverty rates vary significantly by race, gender, family status, and age. The 2010 federal poverty threshold was designated as $17,374 for a family of three and $22,314 for a family of four. Looking at absolute numbers reveals that people living below the poverty line in the United States included 16.2 million non-Hispanic Whites, 9.4 million Hispanics, 9.2 million Blacks, and 1.4 million Asians. However, poverty averages indicated significant economic disparities for racial and ethnic minorities. Average poverty rates for racial and ethnic minorities were as follows: Blacks (27.4%); Hispanic origin, any race (26.6%); Native Hawaiian/Pacific Islander (12.2%); and Asian (12.1%). Among Whites, the poverty rate was 13%, with non-Hispanic Whites, registering 9.9%.

Women and children—especially women and children from racial minority groups—are overrepresented among the poor in this country. U.S. Census data (U.S. Census Bureau, 2014b) showed that 24.1% of women and 31.6% of female-headed households were below federal poverty levels, compared with 21.7% of men and 15.8% of male-headed households. The poverty rate among children was reported to be 22%, or 16.4 million children living in poverty. Children made up 25% of the total population, but 49.8% of those in poverty. The poverty rate among Black and Latino children was three times that of White children. Among children nationwide, 17% lived in households with incomes below the poverty line. Forty-two percent of children living in female-headed households experienced poverty, as opposed to 9% of those in married-couple households.

Risk Factors and Mental Health Consequences

Many of the risk factors associated with poverty are related to challenges faced in meeting basic resource needs. Basic resources necessary for security and well-being include sufficient and nutritious food, education, employment at a living wage, safe and stable housing, health care, and child care. Counselors with a basic working knowledge of inequality and stressors in these areas will be better prepared to discuss and assess risk factors with their clients.

SUFFICIENT AND NUTRITIOUS FOOD The U.S. government uses the term **food insecurity** to refer to a reduced quality of diet, disrupted eating patterns, and reduced food intake. In 2010, 14% of all U.S. households experienced some level of food insecurity (Coleman-Jensen, Rabbitt, Gregory, & Singh, 2015). The highest rates of food insecurity were among households below the federal poverty line, single women with children, and Black and Latino households. Households with food-insecure children are likely to include at least one working adult (85% employed at least part time, 70% full-time workers). However, less than half of those adults have an educational level beyond high school. Numerous studies (see Feeding America, 2012; Coleman-Jensen et al., 2015) have linked food insecurity with developmental and social delays in children, lowered immune system functioning, obesity, emotional and behavioral problems, and mental health issues (depression, anxiety, aggression). Case Study 7.1 examines the issue of food insecurity.

CASE STUDY 7.1

An 8-year-old girl, significantly overweight for her age, is referred for counseling for possible behavioral or learning disorders; her intake form indicates that she is both a perpetrator and a target of bullying at her school. During the assessment, she has difficulty focusing and seems listless. Assume that the counselor remembers that these symptoms, as well as obesity, may be indications of food insecurity.

1. What knowledge and skills might be necessary during assessment?
2. How would you intervene in this case?
3. If the assessment uncovers that her family is surviving on fast food and food pantry donations, what impact might this information have on the counselor?
4. What impact might a counselor's intervention choices have on the child and her family?

EDUCATION   A significant factor in public education inequity is the means by which public schools are funded. There are currently no federal standards for funding: states determine allocations, which are generally a combination of local, state, and federal sources. The majority of funding in most states has been generated from local property taxes, and funding is then allocated locally (i.e., a town's property taxes would fund that town's schools). Properties in middle- and upper-income areas generate significantly higher property taxes than those in low-income and poor areas, and the disparity contributes to profound inequities in school facilities, teacher salaries, and teaching materials.

One of the first legal challenges to this system of funding, California's *Serrano v. Priest* in 1971, was filed on behalf of poor students and demanded a more equitable system of taxation and allocation. Since then, more than 40 states have been subject to court cases challenging the constitutionality of their system of public school funding. Increasingly, states are being held accountable for ensuring that all children have access to an adequate education. Recent data from the U.S. Department of Education (USDOE, 2015) indicates that per-student expenditure for students in districts with high poverty has achieved some equity with per-student expenditure for students in districts with low poverty. However, expenditures in middle districts (i.e., districts with moderate poverty) are frequently anywhere from $1,000 to $2,000 less per student than expenditures in low-poverty districts.

Racism, in the form of economic segregation, continues to plague education at all levels of the United States. During the 2014–2015 school year, approximately 1 in 5 public school students were enrolled in high-poverty schools. However, almost *half* of all Black and Hispanic students and 1 in 3 American Indian/Alaskan Native students were in low-poverty schools, compared with only 6% of all White public school students (U.S. Department of Education, 2015). At the postsecondary level, enrollment rates are up among Black and Hispanic students;

however, degree attainment rates are considerably lower than for White students (Complete College America, 2018), because of financial, cultural, and academic preparedness barriers.

Funding disparities in public school are exacerbated by family SES and access to resources. Among students from the wealthiest families, half will attend college, and these families will spend an average of 7% of their income on that child's college education. By contrast, only 1 out of every 17 students from the poorest families will get into college, and their families will spend 25% of their household income on that college education (Complete College America, 2018). Moreover, those who do make it to college face reduced availability of federal grant assistance, higher interest rates on student loans, exorbitant textbook costs, and the challenges of balancing work and academics. Students from poor and low-income backgrounds have significantly lower college graduation rates than those of higher SES. Tomás Aguilar's excerpt highlights the inaccessibility of college for those of low-income backgrounds:

> In Laredo, on the border in Texas, it's all class. The rich landowners are "Hispanics," and everybody else is "Latinos." In high school I knew this kid who always wore a sweatshirt that said "Brown." I thought it meant he had a lot of Chicano pride. He let me think that, then years later told me that all his sisters and brothers went to that college. I had never heard of the Ivy League. (Leondar-Wright, 2012, p. 1)

Oftentimes, a lack of financial resources may affect the pursuit of graduate school or a professional degree. (See Activity 7.3.)

ACTIVITY 7.3

Discuss the following questions in small groups:

- In what ways does the structure of your university and of your counselor training program support or discourage students from poor or low-income backgrounds?
- Is your program structured in a way that would allow students to work while completing their coursework and internship (without compromising their health and well-being)?
- Is work–study available? How about graduate assistantships?

EMPLOYMENT   Educational attainment and employment opportunities are closely linked in perpetuating generational class oppression. The lower the education level, the more likely an individual is to be employed at a minimum-wage hourly job. Although housing, food, utility, clothing, and transportation costs have increased steadily over the past several decades, wages have remained stagnant. Many in this country are experiencing increasing difficulty maintaining their lifestyle; in the world population, few people have "adequate living conditions" as described in the Universal Declaration of Human Rights earlier in the chapter.

In May of 2007, Congress approved a bill to increase the federal minimum wage for the first time since 1997. The minimum wage for adults was gradually increased from $5.15 to $7.25 per hour as of 2009; the current minimum wage for youths under age 20 years is $4.25 per hour (U.S. Department of Labor, n.d.). At the current federal minimum wage, an adult working a 40-hour week, every week of the year, will earn $15,080 annually, or approximately $13,000 after taxes. Compare this net income for a full-time minimum-wage earner with the 2015 federal poverty threshold of $11,770 for a single adult under age 65 years and $24,250 for a family of four with two children (U.S. Department of Health and Human Services, 2015). As of July 2015, 29 states and the District of Columbia have a minimum wage above the federal rate of $7.25, with most in the $8–$9 range. The highest prospective rate is Massachusetts' $11.00 per hour, effective January 2017.

Growing income shortfalls have led to campaigns for a **living wage**, a movement grounded in the belief that no one who is working full time should be living in poverty and that work should be adequately rewarded. Some municipalities have chosen living-wage standards; Seattle has the highest, $15 per hour. (See City of Calgary, 2012, for a list of living-wage ordinance provisions in the United States.) The past decade has seen a rise in grassroots organizations using social media to create successful nationwide civic action movements, such as nationwide protests sponsored by community action groups like Fight for $15 (see http://fightfor15.org/) and the fast-food workers strikes in dozens of U.S. cities.

Employment is, in general, becoming increasingly unstable. Wages have stagnated, health benefits are declining or disappearing, jobs are being outsourced to other countries, and rapidly shifting fields and technologies require constant education and training. The unemployment rate does not count individuals who have already exceeded the benefits period without obtaining work, nor does it count those who became dissatisfied with job programs that funneled them into minimum-wage employment or those who are working part-time or temporary jobs.

It takes only one illness in the family or one job loss to fall from employed, to underemployed, to unemployed, to social welfare. Women and children are especially vulnerable because women are continually subject to gender inequity in wages, limited employment options that are suitable for mothers who are primary caregivers, and the ever-present problem of finding safe and affordable child care. Welfare limitations on lifetime enrollment have been successful in reducing the number of individuals on the welfare rolls; however, results indicate that these "reforms" have succeeded by cutting off access and not by reducing poverty. Over the past decade, **Temporary Aid to Needy Families (TANF)** welfare eligibility and work requirements have been revised in such a way that less than half of very poor families receive public financial assistance, and those who do access benefits may never fully acquire or regain economic stability (Center on Budget and Policy Priorities, 2015). This and other aspects of employment instability contribute to reduced psychological functioning (Booker & Sacker, 2011; WHO, 2016).

SAFE AND AFFORDABLE HOUSING The **Fair Housing Act**, adopted in 1968, prohibits discrimination in housing rentals, sales, and mortgage lending on the basis of race, color, national origin, religion, sex, familial status, and disability. Nonetheless, the act has not eliminated housing discrimination, although it has provided an avenue for complaint and redress. Still, there is no such protection for class discrimination in housing. Steadily increasing housing costs, coupled with stagnating wages, have created a serious shortage in safe and affordable housing for many Americans. Across the country, public housing is being demolished and replaced by "mixed-income" housing units that are in fact unaffordable for lower-income groups. Family homelessness and the use of shelters in both rural and suburban areas has increased steadily, while economic constraints are leading to cuts in related services (U.S. Department of Housing and Urban Development, 2014). A recent federal housing survey found that the national average monthly rent was just over $850, without utilities, representing one third of an average household's monthly income and approximately half the income of a household below the poverty level (U.S. Census Bureau, 2014b). It is becoming difficult, if not impossible, for households to earn sufficient income to cover the cost of housing, food, health care, and other basic necessities, even with two wage earners working full time.

Housing quality and community safety have been found to have positive correlations with mental health. One study randomly moved families out of public housing in high-poverty neighborhoods and into private housing in near-poor or nonpoor neighborhoods. Findings indicate that, among families moved into private housing, parental stress was significantly reduced and male children exhibited fewer anxious and depressive symptoms and fewer dependency problems (Leventhal & Brooks-Gunn, 2003).

HEALTH & HEALTH INSURANCE   The United States is home to the greatest wealth in the world, yet it remains one of the few developed nations without universal health care. In 2014, about 10% of the U.S. population had no health insurance coverage (U.S. Census Bureau, 2015a). Slight racial and ethnic discrepancies are evident in coverage rates: although the percentage of uninsured Whites is just under the national average (7.6%) and uninsured Asians just over (10.3%), the highest uninsured rates are among those of Hispanic origin of any race (19.9%), American Indians/Alaskan Natives (20.0%), and those of African descent (11.8%). Children fare better in insurance coverage because of federal and state plans: more than 90% of U.S. children had health insurance coverage at some point during 2014, of which over a third were insured through government sources (Childstats, 2014). Coverage of White, non-Hispanic children (94%) was slightly higher than the national average; coverage of children of Hispanic and African descent was slightly lower than average (85% and 91%, respectively). Classism has fatal consequences for children and adults from lower income levels, particularly racial and ethnic minorities. The United States has one of the highest levels of per capita health expenditures, but the investment is not benefiting the economically marginalized.

The availability of affordable health care has become a social class issue. The *Affordable Care Act*, the sweeping health care reform law often referred to as "Obamacare" (see https://www.healthcare.gov/), provided numerous consumer protections. The law prohibits plans from denying coverage for children under age 19 who have preexisting conditions, allows some young adults to continue under their parent's health care plans up to age 26 years, bans lifetime limits on most benefits in new plans, and requires insurers to justify unreasonable rate increases publicly. The act also greatly expanded mental health and substance abuse services, requiring most plans to provide preventative mental screenings (e.g., for depression) and child behavioral assessments at no additional cost.

Regarding women's health issues, recent reproductive health legislative actions to defund Planned Parenthood have further exacerbated social class differences in access to preventative health screenings, family planning, and birth control for low-income girls and women. Almost 1 in 5 women were uninsured in 2010, a 15% increase since 2000 (Pais, 2014). The United States is the only developed nation with rising maternal mortality rates, widely attributed to lack of health care and prenatal coverage for low-income women. Furthermore, 43% of women surveyed reported foregoing recommended health care or medication because of the cost (Commonwealth Fund, 2009).

In a comprehensive report on the status of the U.S. health care system—albeit prior to full implementation of the *Affordable Care Act*—Davis, Stremikis, Squires, and Schoen (2014) concluded that the U.S. health care system is the most expensive in the world, while simultaneously ranking near the bottom of industrialized nations in terms of access, efficiency and equity. More than one third of lower-income adults do not go to their doctors for recommended follow-up, treatment, or medication because of cost. The United States also ranks last among the 11 leading industrialized nations in the three categories of infant mortality, deaths due to the lack of medical care, and healthy life expectancy at 60 years of age. Overall, more people per capita in the United States go without health care because of cost than in other leading industrialized nations. Of course, a primary difference between the U.S. health-care system and those in these other nations is the absence of universal health care.

Housing and employment insecurity, coupled with lack of access to health care, can trigger an irreversible decline in economic, physical, and mental health. After interviewing individuals and families across the country and seeing firsthand the fate of the uninsured, Sered and Fernandopulle (2006) referred to this decline as a "death spiral." Without adequate health safeguards, jobs are lost to illness, homes are lost because of job loss, and illness is aggravated by stress, anxiety, depression, and exhaustion suffered in attempting to secure basic needs. Voices from the Field 7.4 describes one counselor's work with migrant workers and their families and reveals how employment insecurity and limited access to health care affect their use of mental health services.

Voices from the Field 7.4

How do you see social class identity and issues affecting your clients and students and the counseling process? The migrant farmworker on the East Coast starts picking citrus in Florida in late winter, moves on to berries in the Carolinas, and ends in Pennsylvania for peaches and apples in the fall. The workers are primarily young men from Mexico and Central America but also include Haitians; many have been doing the same thing for years. Some travel with their families, with wives working in the packinghouses while the men pick in the fields. Others send money home to families that they see only a few months a year.

In our health clinic, they never ask for days off or prescription pain medicine, even when the condition warrants it. Mental health is not a complaint in their lexicon. If they can't take off for tendinitis, why would they miss a day for sadness or anxiety? They report that most problems are fixed with an evening beer and a soccer game. Yet the astute clinician will see frequent somatic complaints for a physical manifestation of mental distress. The skill of the interpreter is also invaluable for understanding the nuances of language and how a direct translation is not always accurate. In our area, there is a single bilingual Spanish–English psychiatrist and a few bilingual counselors; thus, referrals are almost never made.

Once, a young mother presented for headaches. After talking, she revealed that she had lost her baby during childbirth and continued to hear her child's voice calling to her. In the setting of the medicalized United States, we would diagnose postpartum psychosis, possibly committing the woman to an institution involuntarily. But careful conversation showed that she turned to her daughter's spirit as a source of daily strength and guidance—an angel who was now looking out for her. Unfortunately, there was no support group to which she could be referred; no online chat group she could access, because she had no computer; no Internet; no "smart" device; and, at times, no electricity.

It can be extremely challenging facing high levels of distrust of the government, cultural resistance to admitting mental illness, and knowing that, in a few months, the person in front of you will leave to their next destination and may or may not return the next season.

I have found it a perfect opportunity to employ extremely brief interventions, using psychoeducation to normalize emotions and utilizing national and local resources to try to establish care at the next destination ahead of time. In general, a listening ear and validation of their journey in life goes far, as it does in any culture, with any person.

~*Deanna Bridge Najera, MPAS, MS, PA-C, NCC; physician assistant and Nationally Certified Counselor, Keystone Farmworker Program, Pennsylvania*

Poverty: Perceptions and Identity

Although economic status is clearly a powerful factor in overall wellness, it appears that individual perceptions of SES play an equally important role. The degree to which we are satisfied or dissatisfied with our SES, relative to those of others, may influence health outcomes. Classism and the stigma attached to lower SES status may contribute to feeling deprived of power, place, and voice. The psychological consequences of feeling devalued and displaced may include humiliation, lowered efficacy, low self-esteem, and higher rates of suicide (WHO, 2016). The ability to externalize classism, identify structural causes, and take effective action contributes to the ability to cope with stress and to resiliency. It is important to understand evolving perceptions of class and the relationship between social class and mental health counseling over time. Table 7.2 highlights historical events related to social class and economic injustice that have influenced the development of professional counseling. Reflection 7.4 offers an opportunity to reflect on these events.

TABLE 7.2 Noteworthy Events

Late 1700s	The first labor strikes occur in the United States. The rallying cry for the striking carpenters, printers, and cabinetmakers is "in pursuit of happiness," borrowed from the 20-year-old Declaration of Independence.
1850s–1900	As populations in urban centers increase, state mental hospitals are built and used by the state to commit (mostly involuntarily) persons with mental illness, primarily those from the lower class who cannot afford private care.
Late 1800s	The social reform movement takes hold in the United States. Frank Parsons, now referred to as the founder of vocational counseling, is among many people from across class lines who address social inequities in access to education, employment, and housing.
1884	The Federation of Organized Trades and Labor Unions, forerunner of the American Federation of Labor (AFL), passes a resolution stating that a workday should be legally limited to 8 hours. (Adults, youths, and children commonly worked 10- to 12-hour days, 6 days a week.)
1884–1937	Hundreds of American and immigrant workers are injured, deported, or killed by police and state militia in a sustained effort by business owners and politicians to suppress worker demands for basic rights and safety in the workplace.
Early 1900s	In Europe, Alfred Adler advocates for the application of psychological principles to working-class concerns. These principles are soon adopted in the United States.
1908	Frank Parsons founds the Bureau of Vocational Guidance in Boston as a means of advocating for employment opportunities for immigrant youths and families.
1938	The Wages and Hours Act (later called the Fair Labor Standards Act) is passed, banning child labor and setting the 40-hour workweek.

1940s	Carl Rogers advocates for the application of psychological principles to world social issues. (This work continues throughout his life.)
1950s and forward	The civil-rights movement draws people from across race and class lines to address social inequity.
Early 1960s	Funding state mental hospital systems becomes increasingly expensive, and new treatments are allowing patients to return to community life. Federal funding is allocated for the research and construction of community mental health centers (CMHCs).
1963	Congress passes a law mandating equal pay for women.
1980s	There is growing emphasis on a medical model of mental health (including aspects of biology, neurology, the genetics of mental disorders, and the use of medications) and a backlash against social welfare. Funding for CMHCs is scaled down.
1990s	Family systems theory emerges, drawing attention to the influence of larger social structures on individual and family mental health.
1990s and forward	The living-wage movement grows, and numerous cities and businesses implement a living wage for workers.
1999	Counselors for Social Justice (CSJ) is formed, a division of the ACA.
2000–present	The nation sees a rise in managed care and the use of a business model of mental health.
2002	The American Psychological Association publishes the *Resolution on Poverty and Socioeconomic Status.*
2003	The ACA Governing Council endorses the *Advocacy Competencies.*
2009	The Lilly Ledbetter Fair Pay Act, coined the *Equal Pay for Equal Work* bill, restores the right of women to sue for wage discrimination.
2009	The *Affordable Care Act* becomes law.
2011	Two grassroots movements arise: Occupy Wall Street and the 99 Percent Movement.
2014	The ACA revises the *Code of Ethics* to include and encourage client, community, and social advocacy.
2015	The *Multicultural and Social Justice Counseling Competencies* are endorsed by the ACA Governing Council.

REFLECTION 7.4

Classism has a direct effect on individual and family well-being and is also intricately connected with the funding and implementation of mental health services. Select one of the events listed in Table 7.2 to investigate further. Research the influences at the individual, family, community, cultural, and political levels. Consider factors across socioeconomic levels (e.g., how might this event be experienced or viewed by individuals who were poor? Who were working class? Middle class? Upper class?). Also, consider the influence in various settings, including schools, colleges, and community agencies. How did mental health professionals, including counselors, contribute and respond to these events?

ADDRESSING CLASSISM IN COUNSELING

We have known for decades that low-SES clients have some of the highest treatment dropout rates (WHO, 2016), yet research has focused primarily on individual client motivation and practical barriers to services. Individuals from poor and low-income communities have greater difficulty accessing services, and even when they do access them, the services are of a lower quality. Moreover, these individuals are more likely to be involuntarily admitted to a psychiatric hospital. However, there is now a growing awareness that mental health services, as well as the professionals who deliver those services, have played a role in perpetuating class-based discrimination and bias. There are indications that therapist attitudes and values, as well as the quality of the therapeutic alliance, may contribute to dropout among low-SES clients. Class bias has been identified among teachers, therapists, and other helping professionals. Teachers and school administrators have been found to have lower expectations of children and parents who are poor (Center for American Progress, 2014). Classist perceptions are further mediated by the race of both the perceiver and the perceived and by the context in which the perceptions take place.

Borrowing from Maslow's humanistic hierarchy-of-needs model, Smith (2005) outlined ways in which class bias may influence therapeutic interventions. Counselors may assume that people with pressing resource concerns (e.g., shelter, food, clothing, safety) cannot benefit from insight or cannot process therapy until those issues are alleviated. Conversely, counselors may ignore resource stressors and do as they were trained: focus on traditional talk therapy without adequately assessing the most immediate concerns of the client. The pervasiveness of middle-class assumptions and values in counseling affects not only clients, but also counselor trainees and counselors. Current and future counselors who come from poor or lower-class backgrounds may feel pressure to "act" middle class and to adopt values and perspectives that do not match those in their life experience or do not comport with their reason for entering the profession. A study of occupational therapists who identified as being from the lower class found that many felt stigmatized and shamed by their class background and that they expended considerable energy attempting to "pass" as middle class (Beagan, 2007).

Figure 7.1 illustrates a helpful way to conceptualize the many ways that class status, perceptions, beliefs, and biases influence the counseling relationship. Not included is the intersection of classism with other forms of oppression, particularly racial and gender discrimination. As counselor trainees and counselors develop greater awareness of the role of oppression in counseling, they may feel overwhelmed and uncertain about how to be effective in the face of such multifaceted dynamics, many of which involve their own identity and worldview. The next three subsections will introduce strategies for developing awareness, knowledge, and skills regarding classism in counseling.

Awareness

Counselor trainees and counselors come from a range of social class backgrounds, as do the clients they serve. Similarities and differences in class backgrounds influence the development of the counseling relationship, yet this aspect of diversity is often overlooked in training and supervision. Before the first words are spoken, counselor and client have often assessed each other's class standing and made assumptions, often unconscious, that will affect counseling outcomes. Both differences and similarities in class status can evoke a variety of feelings, including discomfort, resentment, guilt, shame, anger, mistrust, pity, avoidance, pride, and jealousy. Counselors must be prepared to identify and address these feelings in themselves and in their clients.

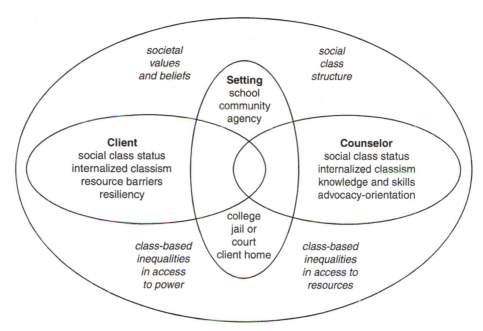

FIGURE 7.1 Classism and the counseling relationship: An illustration of the many external, internal, and contextual social class factors that affect the counseling relationship.

Acquiring awareness is a process that is often accompanied by periods of discomfort. **Cognitive dissonance** describes the state of psychological disequilibrium experienced when we are facing, but have not yet resolved, information that contradicts our worldview. As with any change process, the first step is becoming aware. The move from relative ignorance into a more complex understanding of class issues often fosters a sense of responsibility and interest in social change (Ratts, Singh, Nassar-McMillan, Butler, & McCullough, 2015). The following activities provide several opportunities for increasing one's awareness of class and classism:

- *Write your own class story.* The activity "Exploring Your Class Story" helps you explore your own life story in the context of class and SES. Focus your story on the feelings, values, and beliefs you associate with each area.
- *Volunteer.* Find out about volunteer opportunities at local organizations that work with poor and low-income community members. Allow the staff, clients, and community to educate you.
- *Interact with other social classes.* Which social class seems the most "different" to you? Toward which social class do you have the most negative judgment or biases? Challenge your assumptions, fears, and misperceptions by increasing your interactions with other social classes. Doing so may include reading novels, attending social events or community meetings, and talking to peers about relative class experiences.
- *Educate yourself.* Attend a training session or workshop that explores social class issues. You will find the list of resources given in Table 7.3 helpful in identifying options. If nothing is available in your area, you could create your own workshop by thoroughly exploring the Web sites in the resource list.

- *Interview professionals in your field.* Conduct two informational interviews: one with a counselor who is working with upper-SES clients (e.g., in private schools and colleges, in privately funded mental health agencies or practices) and one with a counselor working with lower-SES clients (e.g., in public schools, in vocational and community colleges, in state-funded agencies). Compare their work experiences and environments, and ask them how SES affects their counseling work.
- *Complete a class privilege inventory.* An interesting version of this kind of resource was created by the Women's Theological Center in Boston. "The Invisibility of Upper Class Privilege" is based on Peggy McIntosh's (1988) work on White privilege. You can find the inventory at www.thewtc.org/Invisibility_of_Class_Privilege.pdf.
- *Explore your social class.* Complete a thorough self-inventory of your socialization experiences regarding SES.

Knowledge

Once counselors become aware of and are able to identify the influence of class and classism, it is important that they have effective tools for addressing these issues in a counseling setting. Professional organizations, including the American Counseling Association (ACA, 2014; Ratts et al., 2015), have begun to outline standards of behavior that address social inequities. In addition, several theories are being revised, and new theories are emerging, that more fully integrate the role of class identity and classism into mental health. The theories that follow are drawn from within and outside the field of psychology. Each theory was in some way shaped by, or has struggled to include, the role of classism in individual and community well-being. Texts, journal articles, and electronic sources are readily available on each of these theories:

- *Feminist Theory.* Originally focused on the social, economic, and political empowerment of women, this theoretical orientation has received criticism for emphasizing the empowerment of middle-class White women. Proponents of feminist theory have strived to improve cultural, economic, racial, and ethnic inclusiveness.
- *Womanist Theory.* This theory emerged as an alternative to feminist theory, which failed to adequately address the needs, concerns, and strengths of African-American and other ethnic minority women. Womanist theory directly attends to the concerns of women, men, and children across class levels and places community and social responsibility in a more central role. It also attends to the intersection of race, gender, and class oppression.
- *Relational-Cultural Theory (RCT).* This theory provides a relational perspective on human development, resiliency, and the practice of therapy (Comstock et al., 2008). The theory has been expanded to address all forms of oppression, including classism.
- *Social Class Worldview Model (SCWM) and Modern Classism Theory (MCT).* The SCWM was developed to provide a more psychologically oriented model for understanding social class. It includes three domains: individual perceptions and attitudes; comparison of self to others; and use of material objects as a reflection of self, lifestyle, and learned social behaviors. MCT calls for the exploration of social class contexts and worldviews, and the impact of external and internalized classism as a means of understanding individual goals and behaviors. Activity 7.4 examines implications of this model for counseling.

Another area of knowledge that is important for effective counseling is familiarity with the needs and concerns of poor and low-income community members of all ages. Any of the following methods can be useful for investigating local issues at the individual, family, community, and political/legislative levels:

ACTIVITY 7.4

Using Liu's (2004) SCWM, create several different client profiles. (Remember to include each of the three domains, along with the client's SES.) If each of these individuals presented for counseling, what would be necessary to build a safe and trusting alliance? What do you imagine would be the strengths of, and challenges for, each client? How might each of the clients present unique challenges and opportunities for you as his or her counselor? What theory and intervention might be most effective with each client?

- *Informational interviews.* Arrange to visit or conduct an informational interview with schools or agencies serving clients from different socioeconomic levels. What are the concerns of those clients? How do the schools or agencies address socioeconomic issues and resource stressors? What resources do they use, and what types of referrals do they commonly make? Do the same with teachers and legislators.
- *Community status reports.* Check local universities, newspapers, and legislators' Web sites for published reports on the status of the community. Know that clients may be directly affected by hospital closings, corporation downsizing, neighborhood and gang violence, changes in property tax rates, and the destruction of public housing.

Finally, it will be very helpful to become more knowledgeable about community resources. This knowledge may be a valuable tool for demonstrating a commitment to clients and for improving counseling effectiveness by providing a holistic response. The following suggestions and activities offer some direction in building a resource knowledge base:

- *Identify local resources.* United Way is a helpful primary resource for becoming familiar with local services and is also an excellent contact to provide to clients. Spend some time using both the phone and the Internet locater services. United Way can be contacted by phone at 211 or through its Web site at www.unitedway.org.
- *Investigate local resources.* Learn about resource assistance and services in the community before providing direct referrals. Before making referrals, research current information on a service: hours, location, phone, address; obstacles clients might face (financial, transportation, hours, wait lists, documentation) in accessing the service; types of services available; and criteria for accessing those services. Visit the services that clients are most likely to need.

Skills

As with race, ethnicity, age, gender and sexual identity, and ability status, there are patterns, but no homogeneity, in social class status and identity. Therefore, one of the most critical skills for identifying and intervening in class-related concerns is assessment.

Consider the fact that clients who appear deprived of resources (e.g., their utilities have been shut off, they wear old and worn clothing, they struggle to get by on welfare and food stamps) may perceive themselves to be rich in spiritual, family, and community resources. Despite an apparent lack of resources, they experience wellness. In contrast, clients who appear to have everything (e.g., a prominent career, a nice home, vacations) may be deprived in relationships and lack a sense of purpose. In general, objective assessments of SES are inadequate to establish whether SES is a factor in the origin, nature, or severity of a client's

Voices from the Field 7.5

As a school-based clinician in an urban school district, I have found my work to be quite challenging. On a daily basis, I am confronted with the effects of long-standing, generations-old socioeconomic inequality on those who live in the community. Many of the families I serve report histories of anxiety, depression, substance abuse, and health issues that can be linked to chronic stress. Both parents and children are often angry and dysregulated. Parents are often cautious or even suspicious when I call, and many are relieved when they realize that it's not yet another negative report or complaint about their child, or a demand that they can't meet. When meeting with me, many parents seem taken aback to be heard or to receive empathy, rather than to be confronted, directed, or dismissed as an irresponsible parent. Coming into this position, I was somewhat prepared to have to help clients locate and access resources. I've found, however, that I have to be prepared not only with a list of potential resources, but with the willingness to assist clients in accessing them. On any given day, I am called upon to play the role of advocate, clinician, or social worker. It's often overwhelming, though not unappreciated, since it inspires growth as a counselor and motivates me to stay up to date on social justice issues. I am better able to empathize and have greater patience with families who may struggle with attendance, timeliness, or following through with treatment recommendations. At times I want to throw in the towel with a child or family, but at other times I want to hang on tight and help, help, help. So I have to continually process my own stuff, seek supervision, and consult with colleagues to maintain my professional equilibrium.

~Monique Talton, MS, LPC, NCC, school-based clinical therapist, South Central Pennsylvania

presenting concern. Furthermore, class stigma and internalized classism may prevent a client from openly sharing the true nature or extent of his or her resource needs until there is trust and safety in the relationship. Voices from the Field 7.5 showcases one counselor's work in building relationships with students and providing them and their families with resources in her lower-SES school.

Assessing class- and resource-related concerns may provide counselors and their clients an opportunity to openly address obvious differences in their respective SES and explore any meaning those differences might have for their work together. It is best not to wait for a client to bring up social class issues. Also, it is safe to assume that, even if a client is not talking about class and power differences, the differences are significant. Clients will not bring up such differences *because* there is a power and class difference and *because* there is social stigma around having or being "less than." As a counselor, it is your job to initiate this discussion in the same way that it is your job to assess other risk and resiliency factors.

There are two significant areas to focus on in assessment: (1) a comprehensive initial assessment of the client, the client's context, and the presenting concern(s); and (2) assessment of counselor values and biases that emerge in response to the client.

• *Comprehensive initial assessment.* Take the time to explore the client's values and beliefs about social class. A competent and socially conscious counselor will routinely assess all clients, regardless of SES, for both stressors and resiliency and will include any concerns or goals, with the client's approval, in the treatment plan. Pay attention to psychological symptoms that may be caused or triggered by aspects of social inequity (either in being subjected to discrimination or in perpetuating inequity). Assess the client's awareness of classism, racism, and gender oppression; internalizing any form of oppression has been found to contribute to mental health issues—in particular, depression, low self-esteem, and substance abuse (Kim & Cardemil, 2012). Now read Case Studies 7.2 and 7.3, which highlight examples of work with clients who are facing economic barriers—among others.

- *Self-assessment.* Assess your own strengths and limitations in addressing the client's concerns. Do you believe that helping a client locate housing resources is "not part of your job"? Where does that belief come from? How are you defining help? When you notice that you're distancing yourself from your clients or their concerns in any way, or, by contrast, becoming overly involved and "doing for" your clients, it is time for a self-assessment. Use individual, group, and peer supervision to reflect on your internal process, the quality of the relationship, and your case conceptualization and intervention choices.

CASE STUDY 7.2

Suppose you are in your first semester of internship and a fellow intern, Chris, is sharing his experience working with outpatient clients in a hospital setting. Chris says that, overall, things have gone well, but he is feeling stuck with his most recent client. All his other clients have been able to talk about their feelings and have responded to his empathetic person-centered interventions—except for his current client, Mia. No matter how much he encourages her to share her feelings, she just won't open up emotionally. He knows that Mia has to be stressed and needing an emotional outlet because of her circumstances: She is due to deliver her fourth child and is living in a shelter after leaving her abusive boyfriend. He also mentions that she is required to come to counseling to continue to receive food stamps and housing assistance.

- What hypotheses do you have about Chris's worldview and how he is conceptualizing the client's issues?
- What do you imagine the client, Mia, is experiencing in her interactions with Chris?
- On the basis of what you've learned so far in this chapter, what suggestions might you have for Chris?
- What would you identify as the client's short- and long-term counseling needs?
- How might Chris become more effective in helping Mia meet these needs?
- How could you advocate for this client?

CASE STUDY 7.3

Part I

James is a 36-year-old White male, referred to your agency by the court after a domestic violence incident. The incident involved his wife of 5 years and occurred in front of their two small children, ages 4 and 6 years. The court is requiring James to attend anger management classes and individual counseling, with the duration to be determined by the agency (in other words, you). If James fails to comply and participate fully, or if he commits further violence, he will go to jail. James is assigned to your caseload, and you read the intake report prior to your first session. The report indicates that James has another child from a previous marriage and is also facing charges for failure to pay child support. The report states that James is currently unemployed and that he tested positive for alcohol when he was picked up by the police.

- What thoughts and feelings do you have as you read the report and prepare to meet with James?

Part II

During your first session with James, he presents as defiant and tight lipped, but gradually he lets down his guard as you discuss the recent local high school football game. You admit your ignorance of game strategy, giving James a chance to reveal his expertise and diffusing the power differential between the two of you somewhat. (Remember, you and your agency are to decide how much counseling he has to do to stay out of jail.) Eventually, James explains that the domestic violence incident happened after he lost his manufacturing job of 15 years because the company was downsizing.

You remember what you learned about the importance of assessing for class-related issues and decide to explore James's values and beliefs about class and gender roles and the meaning he assigns to work. He reveals that, when his wife went out and got a job without telling him, his shame became unbearable and he lashed out at her, resulting in the domestic violence charge. He states that he has never hit her before and that he is afraid of what this event has done to his relationship with his wife and children. James tells you that, unless he secures a regular paycheck soon, his family may become homeless. James handles all the family finances, and he has not shared their precarious position with his wife. He is frustrated that the schedule of the anger management classes prevents him from applying for the one job that is immediately available: the night shift at another plant. When you ask James how he is coping with these stressors, he tells you that he feels trapped and that the only thing that helps relieve the stress has been spending time at the bar with his buddies.

- What is the presenting concern, according to the court? According to James? According to you?
- Is the court-mandated treatment effective for addressing the presenting concern(s)?
- Do you feel prepared and competent to be effective with this client? Why or why not?
- How might a "traditional" counselor intervene? How might an advocacy-oriented counselor intervene?
- What would you want to accomplish with James in your next few sessions?

ADVOCACY

Advocates are made, not born. The personal stories of social advocates often reveal that their commitment to addressing oppression and injustice grew out of personal experiences, relationships, and challenges. Advocacy is a collective response to social injustice. In the individual, advocacy is a developmental process, moving naturally from awareness to action. Empowering a client to speak up at a child custody hearing is as necessary as contacting a state senator or leading community education workshops. Advocacy is a normal and essential element of a counselor's job. The remainder of this section provides ideas for advocacy at several levels of intervention. Advocacy at the professional level includes the following:

- *Self-care.* Engaging in advocacy work can be inspiring as well as exhausting. It is important for counselors and counselor trainees to build up supportive networks, resources, and self-care practices if they wish to engage in effective and sustained advocacy efforts. An excellent source for assessing and building your personal self-care is the Headington Institute's online resources for caregivers worldwide (http://www. headington-institute.org/).
- *Integrated services.* Pilot studies of programs that employ interagency collaboration and training and that include consumers in program design have demonstrated significant improvements in treatment outcomes (Markoff, Finkelstein, Kammerer, Kreiner, & Prost, 2005). These services advocate for increased communication among the work setting, the client, referring agencies, and community service organizations.
- *Counselor training.* Encourage greater inclusiveness of class issues in counselor training and education. Suggestions include developing service-learning programs, engaging in justice-oriented research, and evaluating the training programs' ability to support poor and working-class students.
- *Research.* Participate in or initiate research that moves away from defining poverty (overtly or covertly) as an individual problem by examining social perceptions and sociopolitical structures that perpetuate poverty. Learn more about research methods that include participants in identifying research questions, as well as in designing research and interpreting data.

Interventions at the individual (client) level include the following:

- *Attend to basic needs.* The most effective form of preventing major mental illness is attending to the impact of economic stressors such as unemployment, housing instability, and homelessness. For some individuals in distress, ensuring access to sufficient food may be more effective and cost efficient than a psychopharmacological intervention (Heflin, Siefert, & Williams, 2005); historically, reductions in poverty have been found to provide relief of mental health symptoms (Dearing, Taylor, & McCartney, 2004).

Community-level interventions include the following:

- *Empowerment.* Work with and for economically marginalized communities to promote mental health, assertiveness, and general empowerment as a means of countering the deprivation of power and the pathologizing and medicalization of poverty. It is important that this work be at the invitation of, and in collaboration with, the community and not imposed "from above by experts." Creating social networks and training peer counselors can increase their efficacy, competence, and skills; more cohesive social networks increase the community's relative power and voice.
- *Education and training.* Training areas that may be most relevant to economically marginalized communities include community development, leadership skills, trauma and violence intervention, conflict resolution, and workers' rights.

- *Advocacy in schools.* Suggestions from the World Bank (2005) include increasing teacher incentives and improving basic school infrastructure. Join or start a group that advocates for equitable funding for all public schools. Create a classism or economic injustice awareness program for students in the school.

At the sociopolitical level, advocacy includes the following:

- *Public policy.* Contact local, state, and regional professional organizations for counselors, and ask about past, current, and pending advocacy efforts related to class issues. ACA, the National Board for Certified Counselors (NBCC), the American School Counselor Association (ASCA), and other professional counseling organizations provide current information on legislative issues on their Web sites, along with suggested actions.
- *Universal health insurance.* Join the effort to ensure access to quality health care for everyone. Educate others about the connection between health care and mental health issues.

Information about these and other activities, resources, and volunteer opportunities is described in Table 7.3 and Activity 7.5. In the table, organizations are grouped by focus area, including (a) social justice; (b) women and children; (c) poverty, hunger, and homelessness; and (d) health care.

TABLE 7.3 Resources for Learning and Advocacy

Understanding and Awareness of Classism

Activist Class Cultures (http://www.activistclasscultures.org):

This website includes two key resources: the *Class Culture Traits Quiz* and *The Activist Class Cultures Kit: Glossary*.

Class Action: Building Bridges Across the Class Divide (http://www.classism.org/):

Class Action began in 1995 as a cross-class dialogue group and is now a nonprofit organization offering resources, programs, consultation, professional development, and opportunities for self-awareness and advocacy. Its mission is in its name. The organization provides programs for K–12 and first-generation college students.

Highlander Research and Education Center (http://highlandercenter.org/):

The Highlander Center was started in 1932 to support politically disenfranchised groups in building a progressive labor movement in the South. The center was fully racially integrated by 1942 and became a significant planning, education, and retreat center for civil-rights leaders. Today, the center provides support and training to address all areas of social oppression.

United for a Fair Economy (http://www.faireconomy.org/):

United for a Fair Economy provides information and resources for addressing economic injustice, especially as it pertains to tax fairness.

Women and Children

Children's Defense Fund (CDF) (http://www.childrensdefense.org/):

Founded in 1973 with roots in the civil-rights movement, CDF advocates for poor and minority children and those with disabilities. The Web site contains statistics, research, public policy information, and advocacy opportunities.

Institute for Women's Policy Research (http://www.iwpr.org/):

The institute conducts research and is involved in women's issues relating to public policy, poverty, employment, the family, health, safety, and political participation. The Web site also lists conferences and events, Listservs, public policy action initiatives, and advocacy opportunities.

National Center for Children in Poverty (NCCP) (http://www.nccp.org/):

Housed in the Mailman School of Public Health at Columbia University, the NCCP is a public policy group promoting policies and practices to improve economic solutions for low-income families and children. The Web site includes state profiles, data tools, projects, and publications.

Hunger and Nutrition

Feeding America (http://feedingamerica.org/):

Feeding America (formerly America's Second Harvest) is the largest organization dedicated to addressing and relieving hunger within the United States. The Web site provides access to aggregate, as well as community-specific, hunger statistics and reports. Other resources include food resources, advocacy and policy updates, and volunteer opportunities.

Education and Employment

Living Wage Calculator (http://www.livingwage.geog.psu.edu/):

Enter your location within the United States to calculate a minimum cost of living for low-income families. The calculator will compare the actual cost of living in the selected community with poverty wages and with the federal minimum wage.

Universal Living Wage Campaign (http://universallivingwage.org/):

This Web site provides links to dozens of sites with information on wage rates, employment benefits and laws, and the living-wage movement.

University of California Berkeley Labor Center (http://laborcenter.berkeley.edu/):

The Labor Center conducts research, education, and community outreach pertaining to employment, health care, workforce development, and policy issues. Resources include current projects, trainings, curriculum, and research findings.

Housing and Homelessness

National Law Center on Homelessness and Poverty (NLCHP) (https://www.nlchp.org):

The NLCHP is an organization of lawyers working to prevent and end homelessness through legislative advocacy and public education. Resources include information, tools, training, advocacy opportunities, and legislative alerts pertaining to homelessness and poverty.

Health Care

Access Project (http://www.theaccessproject.com):

The Access Project provides a policy voice for underserved communities and works to improve health for those who are most vulnerable. The site contains information on medical debt, insurance and hospital billing, and language services.

Community Catalyst (http://www.communitycatalyst.org/):

Community Catalyst works in partnership with consumer and community groups nationwide to increase participation in health system decision making. The goal of the organization is quality, affordable health care for all through community action, legal means, and policy advocacy.

Families USA (http://www.familiesusa.org/):

Families USA is a national nonprofit, nonpartisan organization working toward quality, affordable health care. The organization has been in existence for 20 years and functions as a government watchdog and public information clearinghouse. It also provides training and community collaboration.

ACTIVITY 7.5

Here are some activities aimed at increasing knowledge about social injustices outside the classroom:

- Listen to the podcast "Race, Schools and Neighborhoods: Reducing Barriers to Achievement." This online audio recording is of an extended panel of several experts in educational equity discussing the role of poverty and racial segregation. The podcast includes a discussion of the No Child Left Behind Act. You can access the podcast through the Urban Institute Web site at http://webarchive.urban.org/publications/500021.html.
- Read *Savage Inequalities: Children in America's Schools*, by Jonathan Kozol (New York: Broadway Books, 2012). Although the book was set in time years ago, the conditions in many public schools across the country remain the same. What are the social and economic costs we all pay for depriving many of our children of a quality education in a safe environment? What are the social beliefs and values that allow these inequalities to continue? What would you do if you were a school counselor assigned to one of the schools that Kozol describes?
- Watch the movie *The Pursuit of Happyness* (Columbia Pictures, 2006). If the father were your client, would you have supported his career goal? If you were a school counselor and the son was your client, would you have reported the situation to child and family services? In what ways does this film challenge social beliefs about poverty and homelessness? In what ways does the film perpetuate classist stereotypes?

Summary

Multiculturally competent counselors are knowledgeable about the history of social class in the United States, as well as about current sociocultural, political, and economic manifestations of classism. Although many continue to believe in the myth of a "classless society," the fact is that the United States has one of the highest disparities in standard of living among developed nations. Culturally marginalized groups, particularly women, children, persons of color, and immigrants, continue to experience disproportionate rates of poverty. Classism is discriminatory beliefs about, and behaviors toward, others based on class indicators (i.e., educational, employment, or social status; income level; housing; peer groups).

Class-sensitive counselors understand that class privilege and discrimination shape social, political, and cultural practices (structural classism) as well as individual identity (internalized classism). Counselors are aware that classism contributes to barriers to interpersonal communication and to building rapport. Counselors may engage unknowingly in *psychological distancing*, a term that refers to individuals with class privilege distancing themselves physically, emotionally, and psychologically from impoverished individuals, groups, and communities. This distancing may be reinforced by the counselor's unconscious or conscious poverty attribution (attributing the cause of poverty to internal/individual or external/structural factors). Effective counselors also have knowledge of the relationship between poverty and mental health. Individuals, families, and communities that do not have consistent access to basic needs such as food, education, employment, housing, and health insurance suffer significant physical and mental health consequences therefrom. But it is not only the very poor who experience these consequences: Increasingly, the working and middle classes are struggling with a declining standard of living.

Culturally sensitive counselors understand the pervasiveness of classism and its influence on the counseling profession. Counseling is based primarily in middle-class values, which are infused into theories, training, and practice. Classism has played an integral role in the development, implementation, accessibility, and effectiveness of mental health services. Although it has been known for some time that clients from lower-SES groups have higher counseling drop-out rates, it is only recently that counselors have begun to seriously examine the role of professionals in perpetuating class bias. Multiculturally competent counselors are aware that they may be inadequately prepared to work with class-related issues in the counseling process. For this reason, self-awareness is essential for counselors who wish to develop sensitivity to classism in themselves, their practice, and the system(s) within which they are working. Counselors who engage in developing social class awareness should be prepared for some discomfort and disorientation (cognitive dissonance) as they recognize how class has shaped their identity and relationships.

Although self-awareness is a critical foundation, it is also essential that counselors develop knowledge of social class structure and classism within their local community. In addition, counselors develop a working knowledge of local social service organizations and build relationships with service providers. Within their professional practice, counselors understand and are able to apply theories that integrate or emphasize the role of classism. Counselors also understand the importance of addressing class-related issues in client assessment. Comprehensive initial assessments include an inventory of client resources, stressors, strengths, and class-related values. When interpreting assessment data, counselors carefully consider the relationship between social inequity and psychological symptoms.

Culturally competent counselors understand the need to address classism at multiple levels. Best practices are increasingly emphasizing the need for counselors to take an advocacy stance in addressing causative factors of mental distress, especially social inequities. Regarding class-based inequity, counselors are encouraged to advocate for clients in meeting basic needs as well as having a voice within their community. Counselors are also encouraged to take an active role in advocating for attention to class-related issues in counselor education and training, community services, mental health programs, and public policy. By developing awareness, knowledge, and sensitivity to social class issues, counselors may play an important role in improving the overall health and cohesiveness of their clients and communities. To sustain these advocacy efforts, counselors build a supportive network of personal and professional resources and attend to their own well-being. Counselors understand that calling attention to economic and class disparities may initially create disruption and discomfort; however, they remain committed to the longer term benefits for themselves, their clients, and their communities.

Review Questions

1. Review the terms *socioeconomic status* and *classism*. What is the relationship between these two terms, and how does each contribute to personal identity development?
2. What is the relationship between mental health and the ability to access sufficient basic resources?
3. How does class bias influence counseling services? Consider the counseling relationship, interventions, and service locations.
4. Why is assessment referred to in the chapter as "one of the most critical skills for identifying and intervening in class-related concerns?"
5. Review the advocacy ideas at the end of the chapter. Describe the relationship between all four levels of advocacy (professional, individual/client, community, sociopolitical).

8 Disability, Ableism, and Ageism

Debra E. Berens and Bradley T. Erford

PREVIEW

This chapter will explore the concepts of ableism and ageism, with applications to the practice of counseling. For ease of counselor awareness, learning, and understanding, the chapter will be divided into two major sections—"Ableism" and "Ageism"—although, in clinical practice, there may be some overlap or similarities between these concepts within the counseling relationship. Importantly, the two concepts often intersect in older people, but this overlap is certainly not always the case. The chapter will begin with definitions of disability, including models of disability and an overall systematic view of disability together with relevant legislation and advocacy action, then will explore deeper the concepts of ableism and ageism in more depth, as well as implications for the counseling process. Because disability and age-related issues can involve not only medical considerations, but also social, economic, and cultural considerations, the chapter is designed to help counselors and counselors in training become familiar with, and aware of, ableism and ageism issues in order to develop a more culturally competent and meaningful level of service to clients. Specific strategies with regard to awareness, advocacy, and activities for building counselor knowledge and skills are included.

DISABILITY DEFINED

Historically, family members, relatives, and, to some degree, society in general have demonstrated a certain amount of responsibility in caring for one another, especially people who are aged, young (children/adolescents), ill, or disabled. The extent to which family or society has the available economic resources generally defines the amount of support and services that are available to people who belong to these groups (i.e., it has to do with their **economic security**). Although the need for economic security affects people of all ages and in all classes of society, for individuals who have a disability or who are young or old—people who traditionally go unheard and have limited resources to access care and services—this form of security is even more important. What does *disability* refer to? Complete Reflection 8.1 before continuing to read this chapter.

REFLECTION 8.1

What is the first thing that comes to mind when you hear the word *disability* or *disabled*? Write down at least three descriptors and three reasons these descriptors come to mind.

As a prerequisite for understanding this section on ableism, it is helpful to define the term **disability** and offer some global constructs surrounding disability in the United States to provide a foundation. However, the very definition of disability can and does vary, depending on the particular service delivery system; legislative act (law); or individual, entity, or agency that is using the term, and disability can have different meanings to different groups. As an example, *Merriam-Webster's Online Dictionary* (2016) defines disability in two ways: "a disqualification, restriction, or disadvantage" and a "limitation in the ability to pursue an occupation because of a physical or mental impairment." More specific perhaps to the field of disability and to working within systems designed for people with a disability are four commonly recognized definitions of the term from four different government sources:

- *Social Security Administration:* The definition of disability differs even within the Social Security Administration's (SSA's) two national benefits programs for eligible people (children and adults) with a disability: Social Security Disability Insurance (SSDI) and Supplemental Security Income (SSI). Under the SSDI program (for eligible individuals who have a previous work history and have "paid into the system" through taxes assessed under the Federal Insurance Contributions Act and usually withheld from each paycheck, or through self-employment taxes for the self-employed), disability is defined as arising from any medically determined physical or mental impairment specifically diagnosed by a qualified medical provider. The condition must be a "total disability," not a partial disability or temporary or short-term disability. Examples of such impairments are provided by the SSA within various diagnostic categories. (See www.ssa.gov/disability/professionals/bluebook/listing-impairments.htm for specific listings of impairments for adults and children.) Further, under SSDI, disability is defined as the individual's inability to work in a job that he or she previously held or an inability to "adjust to work" in another job within the national labor market, given the person's disability, age, education, and work experience. The disability must have lasted or be expected to last a minimum of 12 months or to result in death. In contrast, although the SSI program uses essentially the same disability criteria as SSDI, it defines disability, not by its effect on one's ability to perform work, but rather by the individual's income, assets, and net worth. Given this definition under SSI, children with a significant disability may be eligible for the SSI program but not for the SSDI program.
- *Americans with Disabilities Act (ADA) and other federal nondiscrimination laws:* The definition of disability under the ADA includes three critical elements: (a) a physical or mental impairment that (b) substantially limits (c) one or more major life activities. As defined by the ADA, a physical or mental impairment includes any physiological disorder or condition, cosmetic disfigurement, or anatomical loss affecting one or more body systems, or any mental or psychological disorder. A major life activity includes those necessary daily activities, such as caring for oneself, performing manual tasks, seeing, hearing, speaking, breathing, learning and working, sitting, standing, walking, lifting, and reaching, which an individual without a significant impairment generally can perform with little or no difficulty.

- *Individuals with Disabilities Education Improvement Act (IDEA):* For school-age children who have a disability, the federal law under IDEA defines disability as a physical or mental impairment that adversely affects a child's educational performance. Specific disability categories are defined in the legislation, and specialized educational services can be provided by the public school system.
- *State Vocational Rehabilitation (VR) Programs:* Disability, as defined under the federal–state vocational rehabilitation program, includes a physical or mental impairment that cannot be acute or of an emergency nature and that must be stable or slowly progressive. The impairment must constitute or result in a substantial impediment to employment such that there is an expectation the individual will benefit from rehabilitation services to achieve successful employment [work] outcomes.

In addition to the previous definitions, the definition of disability often varies with the social system or agency providing services to the individual. Another unique challenge is that the overall concept of "disability" generally is not considered universal, and many cultures and languages do not have a single word or definition for "disability." In actuality, different societies from around the world seemingly tend to group together individuals with specific types of disabilities (e.g., blindness, paralysis) and respond to these groups differently, depending on the cultural and social interpretations associated with the disability in question. It is important for counselors to be aware of various types of disabilities and their meanings across cultures. (See Activity 8.1.)

ACTIVITY 8.1

Awareness of disabilities and the cultural meanings attached to them is one step in developing multicultural counseling competence for counselors working with clients with disabilities. With your classmates, create a list of various disabilities or disabling conditions. Beside each one, list some of the common cultural meanings attached to the particular disability. Give special attention to classmates from cultures other than the dominant culture and to the meanings regarding each disability that may come from those cultures. Are certain disabilities more accepted or less feared than other disabilities? If the answer is yes, think about why that might be. Does it vary with the culture? Why or why not?

Types of Disability

Given the previous definitions of disability, it can be confusing to identify which of these definitions apply to which specific types of disability and whether one of your clients falls into one of the disability categories. Following is a by-no-means complete list of some types of disabilities or disabling conditions that counselors may encounter with clients:

- Blindness or vision impairment
- Deafness or hearing impairment
- Developmental delay in one or more areas of physical development, cognitive development, communication/language development, social/emotional development, and/or adaptive development that constitutes an impairment or impediment

- Medical conditions severe enough to fit a definition of disability, including heart/cardiovascular disease, diabetes, sickle-cell anemia, HIV/AIDS or other immune system disorders, gastrointestinal difficulties, respiratory/pulmonary disease, and other conditions significantly affecting one or more body systems or functions
- Mental retardation
- Neurologic impairment, such as uncontrolled epilepsy (seizures) and severe peripheral neuropathy (damage to nerves usually leading to the upper and lower extremities; the condition includes significant numbness, tingling, burning, or weakness)
- Orthopedic or musculoskeletal (motor) impairment caused by congenital problems, traumatic events (spinal cord injury), disease (bone cancer), or conditions such as cerebral palsy and amputation or the loss of a limb by other causes
- Psychiatric or mental health impairment or mental illness
- Traumatic brain injury that causes cognitive and learning/memory disability

Disability Statistics

Have you ever taken the time to notice how many people whom you pass in your daily life have a disability? If you notice them, it is because these individuals generally have a "visible" disability and are noticeable by something external or observed with the eye, typically the use of a wheelchair, a cane, a walker, a walking stick or guide dog, dark glasses, a hearing aid, a personal attendant, a prosthetic/artificial limb, obvious burn scars, supplemental oxygen, unusual or atypical behaviors—and the list goes on. In addition, some in our community have an "invisible" disability, such as a traumatic brain injury or any number of medical conditions that constitute a disability and are not obvious to the casual observer. The U.S. Census Bureau (2012b) reported that more than 56 million people (18.7% of the total U.S. population) living in the United States have a disability, with more than 38 million (12.6% of the total U.S. population) of them living with a severe disability. In this context, the definition of disability includes a person who has difficulty performing a specific task or activity, such as seeing, hearing, bathing, or doing light housework, or has a specified medically diagnosed condition. The disability is defined as severe if the individual is completely unable to perform one or more of these tasks or activities, needs personal assistance to perform them, or has a severe condition as defined by the U.S. Census Bureau.

Of those people with a disability, almost 30 million are reported to be between the ages of 21 and 64 years, the age range whose members are considered by the U.S. Census Bureau to be "of working age" (U.S. Census Bureau, 2012b) and the age range when people generally are considered to have reached the "prime" of their life in terms of educational achievement, career attainment, social status, partner relationships, and family life. However, it should be no surprise that disability occurs across the life span and touches people of all ages, including the approximately 4 million children aged 6 to 14 years who have a disability. Also, about 50% of people over the age of 65 and 72% of people aged 80 and older have a disability. With regard to gender differences, more people with disabilities, including severe disabilities, who are living in the United States are female (19.9% of females) than male (16.9% of males).

Given these numbers, it is clear to see that counselors will likely see clients, young and old and across the life span, who have some type of disability. It is important to note, however, that these statistics do not include soldiers injured while serving in the military (veterans) or people with a disability who live in institutionalized settings (e.g., nursing homes, mental health facilities, psychiatric hospitals), thus making the number of individuals living with some type of disability in the United States higher than the statistics suggest. This additional number of people living with disabilities can only increase the odds that you will have a client with a disability seek out your professional counseling services. Activity 8.2 provides an opportunity to reflect on current images of people with disabilities that are important to consider, with an increasing number of these individuals seeking counseling.

ACTIVITY 8.2

Cultural stereotypes regarding people with disabilities are created or perpetuated by how individuals are portrayed in the media. As you read this chapter, think about the periodicals you read (e.g., newspapers, journals, magazines) and the television shows you watch (e.g., news reports, sitcoms, documentaries, movies) to become aware of how people with disabilities are portrayed in the media. A common example is the statement "He is *confined* to a wheelchair" or "She suffered a tragic condition that left her with an *intellectual disability*." Cut out articles that include references to people with disabilities or that are written specifically about people with disabilities. Also, write down the name of the television show, movie, or news report (and the date that it aired) that mentions someone with or something about a disability. Present the information to the class to identify how often and in what ways people with disabilities are depicted in the media, even in the 21st century.

MODELS OF DISABILITY

The past several years have seen a gradual paradigm shift in the conceptualization of health and disability, with a focus away from a purely medical model. Historically, disability and rehabilitation models have relied on the medical model that uses the individual's medical diagnosis as the basis for counseling and for determining the needs and functional abilities of the individual with a disability. A more recent development, however, is the inclusion of a social model, which considers the consequences of a diagnosed health condition or disability that is experienced not only by the individual with the diagnosis, but also in the overall social context in which the individual lives. With this model comes a need to understand the full experience of health, which also includes functioning, disability, quality of life, and well-being.

Models of disability have long existed as a way to categorize or understand the concept both in practice and in the professional literature. Smart and Smart (2006) described four broad models of disability: biomedical, functional, environmental, and sociopolitical (also called social). However, for purposes of this chapter, three of the more well-known models of disability—the biomedical model, the functional model, and the sociopolitical model—will be presented, together with a discussion of each and a description of some variations of the social model of disability.

A **biomedical model** of disability can be defined as a model in which disability or illness occurs as the result of a physical or mental condition. Because something is identified as "wrong" with the individual, curing or managing or controlling the disability or illness becomes important. In the United States, one way to cure or manage disability is to invest resources in health care and related services that not only focus on the medical aspects of the disability or illness, but also promote the person's maximum level of functioning and restore the person to as near normal a life as possible. The biomedical model focuses on medical procedures, surgeries, diagnostic tests, therapies (physical and/or psychotherapeutic), and assistive or adaptive devices that can be used to help "normalize" the individual with a disability.

The functional and environmental models interact in a commonsense manner. Their joint thesis is that the environment and how one functions within it can cause or contribute to a disability. Thus, interventions are aimed at adapting the environment and the individual's concomitant functional demands to the needs of people with disabilities. We see this approach being adopted more frequently as technological innovations allow "disabled people" to see, hear, and speak when they previously could not.

Over the past several decades, some disability rights groups and advocates have criticized the medical model for focusing on what is wrong with the person with a disability and the resultant need to "fix" the person. In partial response to this criticism, the sociopolitical model, or **social model**, of disability has gained recognition in recent years. The focus of this model is on societal barriers and biases against people with disabilities, not on the person, the disability, or the medical condition itself. The social model recognizes that, although some people may have a physical, mental, social, psychological, or other condition that is considered different from what is "normal" in a society, the disability is created from society's failure or perceived inability to embrace and accommodate the person and incorporate him or her into society to the fullest extent. Maki and Tarvydas (2011) suggest that, in this model, the limitations and disadvantages experienced by people with disabilities, not the actual condition or difference itself, are what define the disability in our society. In the model, disability is viewed, not as a personal fault based on a medical diagnosis or limitation, but as a public concern. The counseling perspective, therefore, falls nicely in line with this view in that the focus of the helping process is on the strengths, interests, and abilities of each person, not on the person's diagnosis, weaknesses, or deficits.

The origins of the social model of disability in the United States can be traced to the civil-rights movement of the 1960s and the belief in equal rights for all people. The emphasis on equality for people with disabilities applies as well to other socially marginalized groups in our country, in that equal rights for all individuals lead to empowerment and the ability to have choices and make informed decisions. This ability, in turn, leads people with disabilities (and other marginalized groups) to have the ability to participate in society fully and freely.

In comparison with the medical model of disability, which focuses on what is wrong with the *person* that makes her or him different from others (and creates a need to "fix" the person), the social model of disability focuses on what is wrong with *society* that makes us view the person as being "different." The social model suggests that attempts to change, fix, or cure someone with a disability, rather than look at society's contributions that perhaps make the person disabled, can be discriminatory and prejudiced. Examples of society's contributions to the disability process are attitudinal barriers, physical or architectural barriers, and communication or language barriers.

Variations on the Social Model of Disability

The social model of disability attempts to explore the effect that society and the environment have on determining whether someone with a physical, mental, or psychological difference is disabled. The social model implies that disability is more than the individual's difference and includes attributes that are outside the individual (i.e., socially or culturally based). According

Pathology ⟶ Impairments ⟶ Functional limitations ⟶ Disability

FIGURE 8.1   One Model of the Disability Process.

to Stevenson, Cohen, Tell, and Burwell (2010), disability is highly correlated with low education, poverty, the community setting, the environment, and low resources. In support of this correlation, the U.S. Census Bureau (2012b) found that people 25 to 64 years of age with a severe disability have an increased likelihood of living below the poverty level, having "fair to poor" health status, receiving public assistance, having Medicare or Medicaid coverage, and having an annual household income of less than $20,000. By comparison, the poverty rate for other people 25 to 64 years of age was 8% for those with no defined disability, 11% for individuals with a "nonsevere" disability, and 26% for those with a severe disability (U.S. Census Bureau, 2012b). Yet it has not sufficiently been shown whether low education and low socioeconomic status are risk factors for the development of disability or whether disability is a risk factor for poverty.

In considering models of disability, one classic model of the disability process, espoused by Verbrugge and Jette (1994), partially adapted by the World Health Organization in 1980 and the U.S. Academy of Science Institute of Medicine (Pope & Tarlov, 1991), and based on the classic work of the sociologist Saad Nagi (1965, 1991), emphasizes the relationship among four main factors: pathology, impairments, functional limitations, and disability. (See Figure 8.1.)

In this classic model, **pathology** refers to the individual's diagnosis, disease, injury, condition, or illness; **impairments** refers to the individual's dysfunction or structural abnormalities in a specific body system (e.g., neurologic, cardiovascular, or respiratory); **functional limitations** refers to the individual's ability to perform daily or life activities, such as walking, reading, or speaking; and **disability** refers to the individual's difficulty in doing basic activities, such as work, household management, hobbies, leisure/recreation, and social interactions (Verbrugge & Jette, 1994).

This model is helpful in that it enables counselors to gain a greater understanding of the disability process, not only because the model includes an explanation of a main pathway to disability, starting with a specific pathology or diagnosis, but also because it considers risk factors that may influence the onset of pathology, which then leads to the disability. Examples of these risk factors include low socioeconomic status, chronic health conditions, poor health habits, and poor access to health care. Further, the model takes into account **extraindividual intervention** strategies, such as effective medical and rehabilitative care, caregiver support, adaptive/assistive devices, social service programs, and structural or architectural modifications. In addition, it takes into account **intraindividual intervention** strategies, such as lifestyle and behavior changes, psychological attributes, coping strategies, and activity accommodations that help the person maintain independence for as long as possible (Verbrugge & Jette, 1994).

COUNSELING INDIVIDUALS WITH A DISABILITY

In considering the social model of disability, the counselor can begin to understand that different societies view and present people with disabilities with different challenges based on the beliefs and biases of those societies. (See Case Study 8.1.) Within and among societies and cultures, individuals, families, and communities perceive and respond to disabilities differently. One example of this difference is that some Southeast Asian cultures view a person with blindness in a favorable way and believe that a blind person possesses a specific and valued insight while some Western societies view that same individual as someone who has a vision disability and cannot see (Maki & Tarvydas, 2011). In counseling individuals with various disabilities as well as various cultural backgrounds, it is important to be aware of these factors. Following Case Study 8.1 is a discussion, based on Groce (2005), of the various roles that may intersect when one counsels individuals with a disability.

CASE STUDY 8.1

Alex is a 27-year-old first-generation Mexican American who immigrated to the United States when he was 17 years old. He graduated from high school and attended technical school to become a welder. He currently works full time in that capacity. Three years ago, he married Elaine, and they have a 2-year-old child. Elaine is now pregnant with their second child. Together, they had planned to work and raise their family, living the American Dream. But Alex became injured on the job and is no longer able to work. Alex and Elaine wonder what the future holds for them, given that he is permanently disabled and of an ethnicity and a cultural background different from the White majority.

- On the basis of what you have read so far in this chapter, does Alex have a disability? Why or why not?
- What cultural implications should the counselor consider when working with Alex, a Hispanic male with a disability who is living in the United States?
- In providing counseling services to Alex, what strategies should the counselor use to focus on Alex's strengths, interests, abilities, and capacities?
- Under the social model of disability, and on the basis of what you know about American society's view of an individual with a physical injury, what disabilities may be imposed on Alex?

Role of the Individual. The role that a person with a disability is expected to have in the community helps shape the willingness of the community to integrate the person with a disability into the culture, including the willingness to spend financial or other resources on the person. For an adult, the person's contribution to the family income, full integration into society, and ability to contribute to society are all considerations that must be explored both intrinsically (within the person) and extrinsically (within the culture or society). The counselor must take note of the tension that may exist between the views of the person with a disability and the views of the greater society. Conflict can occur in trying to balance the person's needs and expectations, as well as the concerns of the family and community, against the person's plans and aspirations for life, both now and in the future.

Role of the Family. In approximately 94% of the world's societies, the extended family, not the nuclear family, is the norm and influences where a person lives, works, marries, and even seeks health care (Groce, 2005). This relationship is in contrast to the United States and most Western societies, which emphasize individualism and agency. The Western view of rehabilitation and counseling tends to foster independence and individuality and to maintain an already existing view of economic self-sufficiency and productivity that seems to pervade U.S. culture. Clearly, this view may be at odds with individuals from other cultures or societies with regard to the very basics of rights of those with disabilities and their specific cultural beliefs.

Role of the Community.   In the United States, the right and ability of a person with a disability to obtain and maintain employment is a primary goal of rehabilitation and rehabilitation counseling and is a key outcome in the delivery of rehabilitation services. By contrast, in many other cultures, which typically have a more communal society and recognize the influence and importance of extended families, involvement by family, friends, and neighbors can have a significant impact on an individual with a disability. More specifically, in many cultures, having an individual with a disability engage in the workforce can be considered a sign of neglect and abuse by the family and a "shirking" of the family's role and responsibility toward caring for the individual.

One "subgroup" of clients with a disability who are seeking counseling services in greater numbers comprises combat soldiers/veterans with physical or psychological war wounds who have returned from battle. Counselors need to be aware of the increased numbers of servicemen and women who are living in our communities and seeking counseling services. Counselors also must be aware of some of the issues that are unique or specific to this group. One unique issue is that combat veterans from current-day wars have increased rates of polytrauma compared with what has been seen in previous wars or conflicts. **Polytrauma** is defined as two or more permanent injuries to the body that result in physical, cognitive, psychological, or psychosocial impairment and functional disability (e.g., traumatic brain injury, hearing loss and/or visual impairment, major loss of limb, bone fractures, and burns; Griffin & Friedemann-Sánchez, 2012; McFarland, Choppa, Betz, Pruden, & Reiber, 2010). In addition to incurring polytrauma, combat veterans often present with posttraumatic stress disorder as a result of their experiences in combat. Data suggest that advances in body armor technology, coupled with medical and scientific advances in the 21st century, have enabled over 90% of veterans injured in current wars to survive with injuries that would have been fatal in previous wars. Moreover, for every service member killed in war, an estimated 16 wounded veterans will return to the United States with some form of disability (Frain, Bishop, & Bethel, 2010). Given the multiplicity of needs of combat veterans, Pramuka, MacAulay, Sporner, and McCue (2009) identified five areas for consideration for the returning veteran, three of which apply to counseling services with veterans:

- The veteran will need to change his or her outlook from the "we" mentality of being in the military and part of a bigger group, back to an "I" mentality in order to plan for and achieve individual goals.
- The cultural background of the service member is an important consideration. Just because the service member fought for the United States does not mean that he or she is American.
- The service member's individual strengths and limitations are important to identify in order to assist him or her in overcoming barriers.

This information is not intended to be an exhaustive exploration of the unique counseling needs of wounded veterans; however, it may be useful to consider the special needs of this population. Despite the many barriers that face wounded combat veterans returning with multiple needs, the outlook for their treatment, integration back into society, and productivity is still positive overall because of the inherent characteristics of today's military service men and women who are strongly motivated to be as independent as possible (Nichols, 2010).

ABLEISM

With a good foundation of the various definitions of disability and a description of some models of disability, it is important now to turn to the concept of ableism. **Ableism** refers to social attitudes, rehabilitation and counseling practices, and policies that favor individuals who have or are perceived as having full physical and mental health abilities. In contrast, individuals who have or are perceived as having physical and mental health limitations (i.e., disabilities) typically are excluded from having social power and full access to the same services and resources as individuals without health limitations. In defining ableism, there must be a focus on not only the individual's functional abilities but also the role of the larger society. Included in the larger context are cultural attitudes, beliefs, and perceptions regarding a person's abilities (or disabilities). Language is also an important component of ableism. (See Table 8.1.)

It is perhaps no surprise that different cultures may have different expectations surrounding an individual's ability or function and that those expectations are based on the individual's age, gender, socioeconomic status, education level, geographic location, and other factors. It is important to note, however, that in all societies, ableism exists to some extent, in that, not only are individuals with disabilities recognized as different from the general population, but also, many times a specific value and meaning is attached to their particular condition (Groce, 2005). For example, in our own culture, individuals who are blind or visually impaired are shown a degree of acceptance that is greater than that shown individuals with mental health disabilities, who may, in fact, be ignored, shunned, or even ridiculed.

TABLE 8.1 Words That Empower

Language is a powerful tool and can be used in either a positive or a negative way. In the media and elsewhere, people with disabilities are frequently referred to in ways that promote stereotypes. Following is a chart of words and phrases commonly used to describe individuals with disabilities:

Positive Attributes	Negative Attributes
Brave	Weak
Courageous	Unfortunate
Inspirational	Pitied
Superhuman	Burdened
Defeated a terrible fate	Infirmed
Survived against all odds	Suffering
Differently abled	Challenged

What other words or phrases can you add to either list? What words or phrases have you used in the past when referring to someone with a disability?

Remember:

• People with disabilities are people first—who happen to have a disability. They prefer to be called just that: a person with a disability.

• Having a disability is the only "culture" or minority group that any one of us can join at any time.

DISABILITY, ABLEISM, AND THE COUNSELING PROCESS

The preceding sections of this chapter have provided an overview of the concepts of disability and ableism as demonstrated in the current culture of the United States. Understanding the complexity, sensitivity, and variability of how these concepts are portrayed in our diverse culture can give counselors and counselors in training a greater appreciation of the importance of providing multiculturally competent counseling services. Because few counselors have a disability, they may be perceived as not being able to fully understand the client with a disability or as being "superior" to the client. Further, different definitions or interpretations of disability can create conflict or a disconnect between the client and counselor. For this reason, counselors must be attuned not only to the basic tenets and philosophies of the counseling process—most notably, the tenet to do no harm to the client—but also to the individual client's beliefs and value system. To be sensitive to the unique beliefs, needs, and abilities of clients who are physically, mentally, cognitively, or socially different from you, as a counselor, means that you have reached a certain level of awareness and competence to work with clients with different abilities (and, potentially, with their families) in order to facilitate their understanding of the counseling process as a tool to reach their goals.

Awareness

Counselors who become more aware of ableism and its effects on individuals with disabilities are better able to deliver effective counseling services. The need for counselors to become social advocates and get more directly involved in helping clients overcome barriers to full inclusion in society, rather than maintaining a professional objectivity and neutrality, is becoming more important and more impactful on the lives of the clients they serve. In this way, the counselor takes on more of an advocacy role in addition to a counselor role, and counselors are now seen as taking a more proactive and less passive role when working with clients who are confronted by oppression and injustice (Maki & Tarvydas, 2011). Culturally competent counselors who wish to be fully attentive to, and have an understanding of and appreciation for, their clients' needs should have a general awareness of the range of human beliefs with regard to ableism, disability, and functional impairment—a range that crosses cultures, societies, and even individual beliefs. Activity 8.3 and Activity 8.4 provide methods for increasing counselor self-awareness.

Knowledge

Despite the best intentions, the most intensive advocacy efforts, and well-meaning legislation, the rehabilitation service delivery system and laws that govern the system in the United States are not "culture free" (Groce, 2005). The population of individuals with a disability is probably one of our country's largest minority groups with a long history of disability policy and legislation. Although a detailed account of U.S. disability legislation is beyond the scope of this chapter, an overview of key disability policy and legislation will provide historical context. In a very broad context, social policy can be considered to both follow and lead public opinion about relevant social issues. Overall, the view of disability in the United States has evolved from treating it as a military matter and the "unfortunate outcome" of patriotic service to our country, to a conceiving it as an unintended consequence of the Industrial Revolution, to promoting it as a societal cause for charitable treatment, to, finally, considering it as an indication of membership in a minority group with a push for empowerment and equal rights of individuals with disabilities (Maki & Tarvydas, 2011).

Dating back to 1776, the U.S. government established a support program for individuals with disabilities through a system of monetary compensation for soldiers wounded or disabled

ACTIVITY 8.3

Obtain enough loaner wheelchairs for each dyad in the class. Getting wheelchairs can be arranged through local rehabilitation hospitals, local wheelchair equipment vendors, local wheelchair repair shops, or local facilities or programs for people with disabilities, such as Goodwill Industries.

Have one person from each dyad use the wheelchair to navigate through campus to a prese-lected site (e.g., the library, student union, campus dormitory). The other person serves as a re-corder and safety monitor and accompanies the classmate in the wheelchair with a pad and pen. As the classmate in the wheelchair navigates through campus, the other classmate ensures his or her safety (and that of others), as well as writes down campus areas that are inaccessible (or dif-ficult to maneuver with a wheelchair), bumps along the way (both literally and figuratively), and time in transit to get to the desired location. Safety and courtesy are to be kept at the forefront at all times. Once at the preselected location, the classmates switch places, and the recorder now uses the wheelchair, with the other classmate serving as the new recorder and safety monitor. The same information is recorded for the ride back to class.

Once back in class, allow time for each member of the dyad to debrief the other about the experience and the information recorded during their travels. Were the experiences similar or dis-similar? Were there common challenges or difficulties? Were some classmates better able to navi-gate the campus in a wheelchair than others? If so, what may be some reasons? What reactions did the classmates experience from other students on campus? How might this activity be in line with our views of a person with a disability whom we see in public on campus, at the mall, in the grocery store, or at the airport?

ACTIVITY 8.4

Bring enough clean bandanas or scarves to blindfold one student in each dyad in the class. Have one student wear the blindfold and the other student serve as the guide and safety monitor to navigate through campus to a preselected site such as a library, the student union, a campus dorm, and so on. (If you have done Activity 8.3, you should select a different site for the current activity.) As before, safety and courtesy should be kept at the forefront at all times. The guide is responsible for getting the blindfolded classmate to the preselected site safely and without incident. Once at the preselected location, the classmates switch places, and the guide is blindfolded, with the other classmate serving as the new guide and safety monitor. The same task is done for the students to walk back to class. Once back in class, allow time for each member of the dyad to debrief the other about the experience. Consider the questions listed in Activity 8.3 for discussion purposes. Additional questions might be the following: How did it feel to be dependent on another person for getting you where you needed to be—and safely, too? Was it difficult to give up your control to someone else? What amount of control did you feel you kept during this exercise? What would have been helpful from your classmate as you walked through campus wearing a blindfold?

in the Revolutionary War. Current-day programs administered through the U.S. Department of Veterans Affairs continue to serve soldiers and veterans. These programs are perhaps receiving more notice and recognition today because of the large numbers of service men and women returning from Iraq and Afghanistan with injuries and lifelong disabilities.

Although modern-day society is more familiar with current programs administered by the Social Security Administration, Social Security did not really arrive in America with the passage of the Social Security Act in 1935. Indeed, it was not until the Social Security Act was amended in 1960 that the federal government included benefits to individuals who were of working age and were disabled, and to their dependents. In the 1970s, the Social Security Act was again amended to offer benefits to individuals who were not of working age and did not have a history of working (i.e., children).

However, not until 1918, with the passage of the **Soldier Rehabilitation Act**, did the U.S. government establish a formal program of training *and* counseling (i.e., vocational rehabilitation) for U.S. veterans. Almost simultaneous with the desire to support the country's soldiers with disabilities was a growing awareness of the needs of individuals who had received industry- or occupation-related injuries as a result of the nation's ever-increasing industrialization. By the 19th century, improved societal attitudes toward people with disabilities began, in large part, as a result of advances in technology and machines; an improved economic situation in the nation, spurred by the Industrial Revolution; greater societal understanding, compassion, and optimism; and better science and medicine, which influenced individuals and families (Neulicht & Berens, 2004; see Voices from the Field 8.1 and Reflection 8.2).

Voices from the Field 8.1

Two important demographic changes happened in our society beginning in the mid-19th century that altered social programs for individuals with a disability and older individuals: the disappearance of the "extended" family and the increase in life expectancy. Today's society in the United States generally considers "family" to include parents and children, or what is commonly known as the "nuclear family." This viewpoint is in stark contrast to that held by our society for most of our history: an "extended family" that included children, parents, grandparents, and other relatives. The advantage of the extended family was that, when a family member became ill, disabled, or old, other family members were available and commonly assumed responsibility for the care and support of the afflicted member. In the present day, however, our society is more mobile, with children commonly moving away from their family of origin once they become adults. As a result, with the more transient nature of society today, the role of the nuclear family has become more important.

Similar to a change in the role of the nuclear family in present times is an increase in life expectancy of people in our society. It is a common occurrence these days to hear about the aging of the baby-boomer generation. But did you also know that, as life expectancy has been increasing, the birthrate in our country has been decreasing, thus creating more of an emphasis on the older population? With the increase in life expectancy comes a concurrent need for increased services for the older and aging population. This need is seen as well in the mental health and counseling professions, where practitioners are, and will be expected to continue to, provide services to a population of clients who are living to an old age and experiencing life as an older adult. So what is an American society to do?

Consider some of the following questions as you ponder your future as a professional counselor, reflect upon your past as a child to your parents, and ponder your future again, possibly as an aging parent to your children: What are some of the needs and issues of the older and aging population? What are some of the life transitions of an older adult? With women generally living longer than men, what is the impact of gender differences among older adults? What impact does health have on older and aging clients? The ageism section in the second part of this chapter attempts to address some of these questions and other effects of increased life expectancy. We hope that, by the end of the chapter, you will find your voice as a professional counselor advocate—and citizen.

REFLECTION 8.2

Take a moment to define your nuclear family and extended family. Note the individuals you place into each category. Include the geographic location of each family member. As you list family members, think about the frequency with which you communicate with each of them. Think, too, about the health status and age of the family members. Consider a plan of action in the event that one or another of your family may become injured, ill, or disabled, or approach advanced age. Be sure to "customize" the plan to each family member's unique traits and personality in order for the plan to be most effective. Now consider how *you* would wish to be taken care of, and by whom, if you should experience chronic illness, disability, or advanced age.

An important social issue in the nation's consciousness over at least the past half century has been the incidence of occupational injuries and the incidence of disabilities as a result of those injuries. Statistics on occupational injuries contributed not only to the formation of labor unions, but also to state-based workers' compensation systems designed to compensate workers injured on the job. In general, state workers' compensation programs, both then and now, pay health-care costs related to the employee's work injury, as well as provide a percentage of the employee's average weekly wages for the time in which the employee is out of work because of the injury. As early as 1921, 45 states and territories of the United States had some form of workers' compensation law. Today, all U.S. states and territories have workers' compensation laws that offer some form of remuneration for medical care and treatment related to an injury and provide compensation for lost wages as a result of the injury. Some states also provide vocational rehabilitation for injured workers who fall within a certain disability category or level of severity of disability.

To expand disability policy in the United States at the time, the **Civilian Rehabilitation Act** was passed in 1920. The act granted funds to states to implement programs that addressed the needs of ordinary citizens with disabilities. Over about the last 90 years, numerous other laws have been passed that are designed to protect the rights of individuals with disabilities, provide for their care, and prevent discrimination against them as a minority group. The first half of the 20th century saw a proliferation of federal programs, initiatives, and disability legislation with the twin goals of repaying a societal debt to those who had served and become injured or disabled in the military or in the workforce and providing care for those who were not involved in military or work injuries (and therefore were not covered under their respective compensation systems) but were seen by society and public policy as a population of people who deserved help and support.

Disability laws, although presumably well intended, generally reflect the values of society at each point in time and, therefore, appear to favor some social roles over others. For example, the laws appear to have a gender bias favoring men over women, as well as a disability-specific bias favoring individuals who are blind over individuals who are deaf, individuals who are physically impaired over individuals who are mentally impaired, and so on. Further, although it was many years later, disability legislation eventually spilled into the education arena with the passage of the **Elementary and Secondary Education Act of 1965**, which authorized federal monies to states to educate "deprived" children, including children with disabilities. Subsequent amendments have led to the **Education for All Handicapped Children Act of 1975**, with the goal of helping children with disabilities receive a free and appropriate public education in the least restrictive environment, as well as providing early intervention programs for children with disabilities from birth to age 3 years and special-education preschool programs for children with disabilities who are ages 3 to 5 years. In December 2004, the **Individuals with Disabilities Education Improvement Act** was signed into law, amending the 1990 **Individuals with Disabilities Education Act (IDEA)**, which had introduced a number of new provisions related to the education of children with disabilities Both pieces of legislation are commonly referred to as IDEA.

Consistent with the historical path of legislation regarding children with disabilities in a public school setting is legislation regarding people with disabilities in a *general* public setting. The passage of the **Americans with Disabilities Act (ADA)** in 1990 is regarded by some as the culmination of a quarter-century trend toward the establishment of legal protections for people with disabilities and a major victory in the disability rights movement. The ADA protects the rights of people with disabilities and prohibits discrimination in employment, public accommodations, government services, some communication services, and public and private transportation systems. On July 26, 1990, at the signing of the ADA, then-president George Herbert Walker Bush said, "Let the shameful wall of exclusion finally come tumbling down." Sadly, despite President Bush's exhortation, almost three decades after passage of the ADA individuals with disabilities in the United States continue to experience discrimination and exclusion in the very areas that the law was designed to address, particularly employment.

Despite what has been mostly a long history of change and proactive legislation, disability policy in our country has created boundaries that separate people with disabilities from people without disabilities. By allowing "positive discrimination" in the implementation of services, programs, and benefits designed specifically for people with disabilities, we also strive to eliminate "negative discrimination" against people with disabilities (Schriner & Batavia, 1995, p. 269). Martha Minow perhaps sums up this historical situation best by describing it as "the dilemma of difference" (Minow, 1991, p. 20): on the one hand, focusing on differences (e.g., in ability, age, or a combination of the two) between an oppressed group and a privileged group risks creating or perpetuating disadvantages for members of an oppressed group; on the other hand, glossing over the very differences that make each person unique and individual in his or her own right, regardless of the fact that the person is a member of an oppressed group, also risks creating or perpetuating disadvantages for the individual. Reflection 8.3 provides an opportunity to consider this dilemma as it might pertain to your future work with clients with disabilities.

It is important to note that there is no expectation for multiculturally competent counselors to have a thorough knowledge or deep understanding of all cultures; rather, they should understand some of the basic principles and common themes of a number of cultures. Included in that understanding is a better sense of how individuals with a disability perceive disability within their culture and what goals and methods of rehabilitation are commonly accepted. Understanding the

---

REFLECTION 8.3

On the one hand, in discussing counselor awareness, knowledge, and skills used in working with individuals with a disability, relating to clients in a way that emphasizes differences in ability may reinforce the stigma and social isolation they receive in the broader social context (i.e., they are different from what is considered normal). On the other hand, treating all clients the same despite differences in ability may be perceived as being insensitive, ignorant, and privileged. How would you resolve this dilemma if you were working with a client with a significant physical, intellectual, or emotional disability?

challenges associated with different cultures and different disabilities or abilities is crucial in providing counseling services that help eliminate the concept of ableism (or, perhaps more to the point, "disableism"). To assist in this process, a culturally competent counselor will use counseling and advocacy strategies that involve not only the individual client, but also family, peers, and community members, as appropriate, to assist with and inform the individual with a disability (and, potentially, the family) about the possibilities that exist for reaching his or her fullest potential and inclusion in society. Table 8.2 lists some resources for advocacy for ableism that may be helpful as counselors build their level of knowledge and awareness requisite for working with this population.

TABLE 8.2 Resources for Learning and Advocacy Related to Ableism

---

American Rehabilitation Counseling Association (ARCA; www.arcaweb.org/): The mission of ARCA is to enhance the development of people with disabilities throughout their life span and to promote excellence in the rehabilitation counseling profession. Free online access to the organization's quarterly publication *Rehabilitation Counseling Bulletin* and newsletter is available to ARCA members through this Web site.

Careers in Vocational Rehabilitation (www.rehabjobs.org): This Web site provides information on careers in rehabilitation counseling.

Commission on Rehabilitation Counseling (www.crccertification.com): This Web site provides information on the Commission on Rehabilitation Counselor (CRC) certification credential, as well as links to the Code of Professional Ethics for Rehabilitation Counselors and the scope of practice for Rehabilitation Counseling.

Council on Rehabilitation Education (CORE; www.core-rehab.org): CORE is the accrediting body for graduate programs in Rehabilitation Counselor Education (RCE). The organization's purpose is to promote, through accreditation, the effective delivery of rehabilitation services to individuals with disabilities by fostering continuing review and improvement of master's degree–level RCE programs.

International Association of Rehabilitation Professionals (www.rehabpro.org): The International Association of Rehabilitation Professionals is a professional association that serves a diverse membership practicing in the fields of long-term disability management consulting, case management and managed care, forensics and expert testimony, life care planning, and Americans with Disabilities Act (ADA) consulting.

National Council on Rehabilitation Education (https://ncre.org/): The National Council on Rehabilitation Education is a professional organization dedicated to providing quality services for people with disabilities through education and research.

National Rehabilitation Counseling Association (NRCA; http://nrca-net.org): The NRCA is a professional association that is a division of the National Rehabilitation Association and represents professionals in the field of rehabilitation counseling in a wide variety of work settings.

Art and Advocacy

AXIS Dance Company (www.axisdance.org/): This Web site describes AXIS, which "exists to change the face of dance and disability."

DisTHIS! Film Series (https://www.facebook.com/disthis): This resource is an arts/humanistic Web site about disability in film.

Nicu's Spoon Theater Company (www.spoontheater.org/): This New York–based theater group is all inclusive, "offering a home for everyone regardless of color, ability, ethnicity, age, or gender."

Theater Breaking Through Barriers (http://tbtb.org): This theater is dedicated to promoting actors and writers with disabilities.

(Continued)

TABLE 8.2 Resources for Learning and Advocacy Related to Ableism (continued)

Visible Theatre of the National Arts & Disability Center (https://www.semel.ucla.edu/nadc/support-resource/visible-theatre): ". . . dedicated to promoting social justice through the production of new plays."

Legislative/Policy Resources

Americans with Disabilities Act (www.ada.gov/pubs/ada.htm): The Web site provides a direct link to this legislation.

Developmental Disabilities Assistance and Bill of Rights Act of 2000 (http://frwebgate.access.gpo.gov/cgi-bin/getdoc.cgi?dbname=106_cong_public_laws&docid=f:publ402.106): The Web site provides a direct link to this legislation.

Individuals with Disabilities Education Improvement Act (IDEA) of 2004 (http://idea.ed.gov/): The Web site provides a direct link to this legislation.

National Council on Disability (NCD; www.ncd.gov): The NCD is an independent federal agency charged with advising the President, Congress, and other federal agencies regarding policies, programs, practices, and procedures that affect people with disabilities.

Rehabilitation Act of 1973 (www.ed.gov/policy/speced/reg/narrative.html): The Web site provides a direct link to this legislation.

Advocacy and Issue-Specific Resources

Brain Injury Association of America (www.biausa.org): This organization reports that it is "the country's oldest and largest nationwide brain injury advocacy organization."

National Institute on Disability, Independent Living, and Rehabilitation Research (NIDILRR; http://www.acl.gov/programs/nidilrr/): The NIDILRR is focused on generating new knowledge about disability and rehabilitation and promoting the use and adoption of that knowledge.

Online Resource for Americans with Disabilities (www.disability.gov): This Web site connects people with disabilities, their families, and caregivers to helpful resources on topics such as how to apply for disability benefits, find a job, get health care, or pay for accessible housing.

Skills

The strength of the counseling profession is defined by the skills of the practitioners. Counselors are trained and qualified to provide counseling services to a diverse population of clients. The following list, compiled by Smart and Smart (2006), may be helpful for counselors to consider when working with clients with a disability:

1. Fully and continually assess both the client's feelings about her or his experiences with having a disability and the counselor's understanding of those experiences and how they interplay with the counselor's own identity.

2. Recognize that, depending on where they are in their adjustment to disability, most clients with a disability may view their disability as a basic and valued part of their identity, so that, in actuality, they discern positive aspects of the disability rather than negative ones. Counselors must be comfortable asking a client about the client's identity as an individual with a disability and what the client's expectations of the counseling process are. It is important for counselors to understand that offering sympathy and lowered expectations for a client just because of the client's disability may be viewed as stigmatizing and prejudicial and may contribute to increasing negative attitudes toward people with a disability.

3. Believe that the client with a disability is a person first, who also happens to have a disability. As with all human beings, clients with a disability have multiple identities and multiple roles that they serve in their lives, and the competent counselor will acknowledge and facilitate an understanding of the client's multiple identities, functions, and social contexts.

4. Collaborate with the client in identifying and promoting the client's full participation in, and integration into, society on the basis of identities and roles.

5. Avoid imposing the counselor's values onto the client with a disability, and avoid the tendency to put a client into a "disabled role" just because the client has a disability.

6. Allow the full development of a rapport and trust between counselor and client by minimizing the power differential between the counselor, who oftentimes does not have a disability, and the client who has a disability. Not only is this power differential counterproductive to the counseling relationship, but it also may be a continuation of the views of the larger society in which the client lives.

7. Listen and hear what the client's experiences are as a person with a disability to fully understand what the client may share about experiences of discrimination, oppression, and prejudice.

8. Be competent in working with clients with disabilities, and obtain appropriate training to advance your skills.

9. Be knowledgeable about various topics that relate to disability issues in order to be better informed about the ways to serve clients with a disability.

10. Establish professional relationships and partnerships with agencies that typically serve people with disabilities in order to broaden your knowledge about the disability experiences of others with similar challenges.

11. Create effective change within local, regional, state, and national policies and systems that affect individuals with disabilities.

12. Contribute to research efforts by ensuring that the assumptions made about the various models of disability and the values about people with disabilities are clear.

Further, when counseling individuals with a disability, the counselor must serve as an advocate for the client and the client's needs. With regard to social advocacy, the advocate's role is to promote the rights of the client or change the system on behalf of the client's needs. In this way, social advocacy involves the counselor initiating or participating in activities that are aimed at redistributing power and resources away from those individuals or groups that are considered the most "able" and toward those individuals or groups who demonstrate a need for such power and resources. Another component of social advocacy for a counselor is the ability to inform, empower, encourage, and support clients so that they are better able to make informed decisions that will meet their own needs (Maki & Tarvydas, 2011).

Throughout the long history of individuals with a disability, disability legislation, and rehabilitation policy in the United States, numerous social advocates have made their mark on improving social systems and societal attitudes toward individuals with a disability. Table 8.3 lists some individuals who have contributed to our understanding of ableism and social advocacy. The list, of course, is by no means all inclusive.

Disability-Affirmative Counseling and Cultural Intersections

Expanding on the social model, **disability-affirmative counseling** (D-AT; Olkin, 2009) views individuals with disabilities as having value and worth, rather than as being deviant or pathological. As with other diversity characteristics (e.g., race, gender, ethnicity, religion, sexual

---

TABLE 8.3 Social Advocates for People with a Disability and for Rehabilitation

This list features some of the more prominent contemporary advocates for those with a disability and for rehabilitation in the United States.

• **Billy Barner**—First African-American student at the University of California at Berkeley's Cowell Residence Program for Physically Disabled Students, 1969–1973.

• **Henry Betts, MD**—Pioneer in the field of rehabilitation medicine. Strong advocate and leader for people with physical disabilities.

• **Mary Lou Breslin**—Cofounder and director of the Disability Rights Education and Defense Fund.

• **Justin Dart Jr.**—Strong disability rights activist. Cofounder, with Paul Hearne, I. King Jordan, John Kemp, and Dr. Sylvia Walker, of the American Association of People with Disabilities. Sat on stage with President George H. W. Bush at the signing of the ADA in July 1990.

• **Senator Bob Dole**—Republican senator from Kansas who is partially disabled from war injuries and was an original cowriter of the ADA with Senator Tom Harkin.

• **Isabelle Goldenson**—Cofounder of the United Cerebral Palsy organization. Lobbied U.S. Congress to pass legislation to assist individuals with a disability.

• **Judy Huemann**—Cofounder of Disabled in Action. Also, cofounder (with Joan Leon and Ed Roberts) and codirector of the World Institute on Disability. Deputy director of the Center for Independent Living.

• **Mark Johnson**—Grassroots leader and strong advocate for individuals with disabilities. In 1984, helped create the American Disabled for Accessible Public Transportation, which has been an effective force for change in the national disability rights movement. Current director of advocacy at Shepherd Center in Atlanta, GA.

• **Douglas Martin**—National leader in Social Security health benefits reform. Helped pass the ADA. First executive director of the Westside Center for Independent Living.

• **Mary Switzer**—Commissioner of Vocational Rehabilitation. Helped shape the Vocational Rehabilitation Act of 1954.

---

orientation), all individuals have diverse disability statuses. Furthermore, disability intersects with these diverse client characteristics to create advantageous and disadvantageous circumstances and privileges in much the same way that gender and race intersect. Disabilities provide learning opportunities for coping and compensatory mechanisms for people with disabilities, but also for those who work and socialize with individuals with disabilities. These opportunities are integrated into selfhood and can lead to a greater appreciation of all people within the work, family, and community environments and the greater society.

The goals of counseling for clients with disabilities usually are not limited simply to a reduction of symptoms: Ordinarily, clients with disabilities want to feel fully included and functional within their family and community. D-AT helps clients take responsibility for their disability, manage and prevent the internalization of negative reactions, and feel important connections with peers and family members. Olkin (2009) suggested that counselors need to learn to talk openly with clients about disabilities, locate information about specific disabilities, pursue reasonable and accessible accommodations, and refer clients to relevant support groups. Importantly, counselors must manage countertransference and not use derogatory or value-laden language. In sum, D-AT considers the multisystemic (e.g., political, legal, economic, educational) implications of disability and is not limited to just the personal impact on the client with a disability. Counselors practicing D-AT also display the awareness, knowledge, and skills necessary to deal with the complex intersections of disability with gender, race, religion, sexual orientation, and other human characteristics.

AGE DEMOGRAPHICS

Estimates are that, by the year 2030, older adults will account for 20% of the U.S. population (U.S. Census Bureau, 2014b). The U.S. Department of Health and Human Services (USDHHS) Administration on Aging (2016) reports that nearly 45 million Americans are aged 65 years and older and that more than 3 in 5 people in this age group are female. Over the next 40 to 50 years, the number of people aged 65 years and older is expected to double and the number of people aged 85 years and older is expected to triple. Among with America's population in general, minority populations are living longer and getting older; therefore, U.S. senior citizens as a group are becoming more racially diverse.

The growth of the older population is in contrast to historical trends. For example, in the year 2000, there were many more people between their midthirties and midforties than any other age group in this country. By the year 2025, when nearly all of the **baby boomers** (i.e., individuals who were born between the years 1946 and 1964) will have reached the age of 65, the age distribution will increase accordingly such that it is projected that, by 2050, people will continue to live into their eighties, nineties, and even one hundreds. The biggest change by the turn of the 22nd century is expected to be in the number of older men (Cavanaugh & Blanchard-Fields, 2014).

Data from the USDHHS Administration on Aging (2016) show that the number of older adults among ethnic groups in the United States is increasing faster than among European Americans, with larger increases in the numbers of Asian/Pacific Islander and Latin American older adults than in the number of African-American older adults. The advancing age of the baby boomers, combined with the increased life expectancy and increased racial and ethnic diversity of older adults, will put more emphasis on social policies that directly benefit older adults. Given that the United States is composed of immigrants, attitudes in other countries about aging with a disability may be relevant for counselors to understand. According to the World Health Organization (2011), rates of disability vary by country; for example, less than 1% of people in Kenya and Bangladesh, but 20% of people in New Zealand, are reported to have a disability. Data compiled by Rose and Hambleton (2008) indicate that 19% of people in Latin America and the Caribbean reported having a disability. In the United States, studies have further broken down the rate of disability by ethnicity and show that African Americans have the highest rate of disability, followed by American Indians, Whites, Latin Americans, and Asian Pacific Islanders (USDHHS Administration on Aging, 2016).

Gender differences among older adults within different countries reveal that, overall, women in the United Kingdom, the United States, Canada (Chappell & Cooke, 2010), and Spain (Sagardui-Villamor, Guallar-Castillón, García-Ferruelo, Ramón Banegas, & Rodríguez-Artalejo, 2005) experience more disability in old age than do men. In the same vein, Andrade (2009) reported that, although Mexican women live longer than Mexican men, Mexican women experience a higher disability rate than do Mexican men. Moreover, the same is seen in older women from countries outside Mexico, such that, although women generally have a longer life expectancy than do men, women are more likely to have poorer health that leads to some measure of disability or functional impairment in old age (Chappell & Cooke, 2010). Chappell and Cooke (2010) also pointed out other factors to consider when counseling older adults with a disability, including socioeconomic status (coming from a developed or developing country), education level, and marital status, among others. For additional discussion on this topic, Padilla and Griselda (2007) offer a fascinating account of the cultural responses to health among Mexican-American women and their families that explores the complex ways in which individuals from Mexico and other countries integrate their cultural values in their responses to health, aging, and disability. The concern over health disparities among minority groups in the United States is so great that the USDHHS's Agency for Healthcare Research and Quality and the National Ad Council launched a nationwide public service campaign to educate and encourage immigrant groups, especially Latin Americans, to become more knowledgeable about, and more involved in, their own health care. The program, called Conoce las Preguntas, or "Know the Questions," is designed to increase cultural competency among health-care providers and decrease health disparities among minority groups (USDHHS Agency for Healthcare Research and Quality, 2012).

Although a thorough examination of attitudes on aging and disability in other countries is beyond the scope of this discussion, it is important for the counselor to appreciate that old age and disability are not the "doom and gloom" that one might expect. Among older adults, life satisfaction ratings in the areas of happiness and well-being are reported to be high despite a general decline in their health and life with a disability (Chappell & Cooke, 2010). For example, in the United States, 94.4% of older adults report being satisfied or very satisfied with their lives (Strine, Chapman, Balluz, Moriarty, & Mokdad, 2008); in China, 77.8% report being quite or very happy (Appleton & Song, 2008); in Canada, over 90% report being satisfied or very satisfied with life (Statistics Canada, 2010); and in both Italy and Germany, older adults scored 7.5 out of 10 on a life satisfaction scale (Gagliardi, Marcellini, Papa, Giuli, & Mollenkopf, 2008). Having an understanding of the attitudes and cultural experiences of older adults from different countries enables counselors to provide counseling services in a way that is meaningful and that culturally makes sense to their clients.

As medicine, science, and technology improve, the life expectancy of people in the United States has lengthened to the point where people are now living and working longer into old age. For these reasons, it is inevitable that counselors will find themselves working with an older and aging population. According to the USDHHS Administration on Aging (2016), national demographic estimates predict that, by the year 2020, there will be 53.7 million people aged 65 years and older, compared with 34.8 million people aged 65 years and older who were alive in 2000. Whereas in the early 1900s an average person could be expected to live to 47 years of age, data now published by the Centers for Disease Control and Prevention's National Center for Health Statistics (NCHS) show that the life expectancy of the average person born in the United States has reached a record high of 76.4 years for males and 81.2 years for females, for all races combined (USDHHS, CDC, NCHS, 2015). This increased life expectancy means that aging-related issues that previously have not been experienced by society in general and counselors in particular will now begin to surface. To address these issues, counselors must be ready to assess and treat clients in an effective and competent way. (See Case Study 8.2.)

CASE STUDY 8.2

Agnes is a second-generation divorced Greek American who recently was referred to counseling by her adult daughter. Agnes is 60 years old and has been working for over 2 years as the maintenance manager at a large Greek Orthodox church. The pay is not great, but she has full health benefits, and she enjoys the work and the people. With her daughter's help, she recently bought a small house. Last month, she lost her job when the church realized that it needed to reduce its operating budget. Although church members took up a collection that is helping Agnes pay for food and utilities, she has enough in her account for only one more mortgage payment. She also has no savings. She is afraid and ashamed to ask her daughter for help, knowing that her daughter's household is on a tight budget with three young children and a single income. Agnes is afraid that she will not be able to get a job with benefits because of her advanced age. Although her physical health is good, she is afraid that she cannot continue much longer doing physically demanding work. Her anxiety and fear have triggered acute depression, and she is finding it difficult to get out of bed, which exacerbates her anxiety about her ability to find work. If she does not find a job soon, she will lose her home, which she loves. Agnes has been willing to try counseling, yet she doubts that her "twenty-something" counselor can really understand her experiences as an aging adult and what it is like to face these issues as an older adult.

- What feelings and thoughts did you notice in yourself as you read this scenario?
- As a counselor, do you feel adequately prepared to address Agnes's concerns?
- What role (or roles) could a counselor take in working with Agnes?
- What would Agnes's counselor need (knowledge, skills, resources, supervision) in order to be effective?

AGEISM

Ageism is defined as the assumption that chronological age is the main determinant of human characteristics and that one age is better than another. In this context, ageism generally refers to a form of discrimination against those age groups with higher vulnerability and less access to resources and power (i.e., the chronologically youngest and oldest of a population). Children, youths, seniors, and elders are all subject to ageism as a form of discrimination and, as a result, are among the most marginalized populations in our society. Similar to disability and ableism stereotypes, cultural attitudes toward aging are evidenced in the media, social policy, and legislation, and similar to ableism, ageism in the media seems to promote stereotypes that our society places on remaining young, healthy, beautiful, and successful.

Another form of discrimination that is distinct from, yet is related to, ageism because of an awareness of one's age is adultism. **Adultism** refers to discrimination against young people (youths) and children. In a very broad sense, adultism occurs when adults form beliefs about youths and children and behave toward them in ways that generally do not show respect for who they are. Some commonly held beliefs are that youths and young people are ignorant, untrustworthy, and unpredictable, and that they have nothing to contribute to their own well-being or to society as a whole. Along with these negative beliefs about young people comes a power differential in which adults believe that they can and should exert control over young people and orchestrate their lives. This form of discrimination creates a sense of oppression and disempowerment among young people that can be carried on and perpetuated once they become adults. Specific child and youth advocacy organizations, such as the Child Welfare League of America, have been formed to protect children, youths, and their families from adultism (Child Welfare League of America, n.d.).

The remainder of this section will focus on issues prevalent in the population of older and aging adults, given the expected increase of older Americans over the next several years. It is this group of older Americans for whom counselors will likely be providing services over that time span.

Ageism and Older Americans

Older Americans have distinct psychological and physical issues associated with aging that may result in experiences with ageism. (See Build Your Knowledge 8.1.) From a physical standpoint, some of the more obvious changes in older adults that may present themselves during a counseling session are changes in skin (wrinkles and less elasticity), hair (thinner and grayer), and voice (softer and weaker). Other obvious changes are those in height (shorter) and in mobility (slower gait, off balance). Age-related medical or health conditions common among older adults that may affect the therapeutic relationship include cancer, cardiovascular disease, arthritis, and, especially among women, osteoporosis. The CDC reports that, although 88% of people over age 65 years have at least one chronic health condition, the majority of older Americans are able to cope with the physical and cognitive changes associated with aging (USDHHS, CDC, NCHS, 2015). For those unable to cope with changes associated with advanced age, an awareness of these issues is imperative for the competent counselor.

Psychological concerns common among older adults can be related to the physical changes already described and can affect their self-concept, as well as reduce their independence and ability to take care of themselves or perform their normal daily routines. Further, the onset of age-related dementia is one of the worst stereotypes about aging (Cavanaugh & Blanchard-Fields, 2014), a stereotype that affects both how society views older adults and the fear that adults have of living to an old age. Although dementia is not a specific disease, but is more like a family of diseases producing cognitive and behavioral deficits, with Alzheimer's disease the most common form, data show that almost 10% of people older than age 65 years develop dementia, with the risk doubling about every 5 years (USDHHS, CDC, NCHS, 2015). Some characteristics of dementia are significant memory problems (as opposed to the occasional memory lapse), difficulty with abstract thinking, reduced decision making that may affect safety and judgment, lack of insight, and personality changes. Alzheimer's disease has received much media attention in recent years, and it is easy for a counselor to realize that the impact of age-related dementia can be severe and progressive; indeed, at its most significant level, it can alter a person's total daily functioning, as well as the lives of that person's family and caregivers.

Coupled with the loss of memory that is common in dementia, as well as the loss of thinking and functioning that can occur in advanced stages of the condition, are various other

---

BUILD YOUR KNOWLEDGE 8.1

Read the following statements and answer True or False.

1. People naturally know when they are old.
2. Most adults over age 65 years face a steady decline in physical and mental well-being.
3. Older people are similar in their habits, beliefs, and ideas.
4. As people age, they are less able to adjust to changes in the world around them.
5. Older people tend to become more irritable, critical, and demanding as they age.
6. Most older adults (men and women) have little or no interest in sex or sexual activity.
7. Older adults typically are lonely and would like to live with their adult children.
8. Older adults ultimately become a financial burden on their adult children or on society.

Responses to all these statements are false on the basis of what we know about older adults today!

losses that are experienced by older adults, such as the loss of a spouse, family members, and aging friends. Probably each of us has experienced loss in some way and has an appreciation of the grieving process as being complex and individualized to the person grieving. There is no right or wrong way to grieve. In fact, what works for one grieving person may not, and probably will not, work for another person. Further, the length of time needed for the grieving process will vary among persons. Cross-cultural differences in grieving also vary, and the astute counselor must be sensitive to these differences. In older adults, the experience of loss and grief may be prolonged and frequent and may have a greater impact as they realize the finality of their own life.

In addition to psychological and physical issues, socioeconomic issues are relevant for older adults. In the United States and most of Western society, views of older people generally have been based on their role in the economy. The economics of older people living in the United States seems to have the greatest impact on individuals who are single—especially single older women, those from ethnic minorities, those who are seriously ill, and those who are considered "old-old" (generally over 85 years). It is interesting to note that, as a group, 13% of older adults live below the poverty level, compared with 14.8% of younger people (U.S. Census Bureau, 2015c). However, federal figures on older people and poverty can be misleading in that figures used to compute the poverty level are adjusted by age, such that older people aged 65 years and older have a lower poverty level than people in the age range from 15 to 64 years.

Related to socioeconomic concerns, employment is perhaps one area in which ageism or age discrimination may be directed at older individuals. The Social Security Administration's definition of retirement age has been extended from the traditional, or "normal," age of retirement, namely, 65 years to the current age of retirement, 67 years, for all people born after 1959 (Social Security Online, n.d.). Counselors should strive to eliminate age discrimination, as well as increase their own awareness of, and sensitivity to, ageism when working with an older client. Due care must be given to ensure that myths and stereotypes regarding older clients do not bias the counselor's judgment in working with an older client. **Age discrimination** involves denying a job or promotion to an individual solely on the basis of age and is illegal in the United States (Cavanaugh & Blanchard-Fields, 2014). Although passed into legislation more than three decades ago, the **U.S. Age Discrimination in Employment Act of 1986**, which protects workers over age 40 years of age, has done seemingly little to reduce age discrimination at work. Reports of age discrimination in employment continue to exist and have actually risen.

In more recent legislation, the **Older Americans Act Amendments of 2006** protect the rights of older people who, under the act, are entitled to

(1) An adequate retirement income in retirement in accordance with the American standard of living, (2) The best possible physical and mental health which science can make available and without regard to economic status, (3) Obtaining and maintaining suitable housing, independently selected, designed and located with reference to special needs and available at costs which older citizens can afford, (4) Full restorative services for those who require institutional care, and a comprehensive array of community-based, long-term care services adequate to appropriately sustain older people in their communities and in their homes, including support to family members and other persons providing voluntary care to older individuals needing long-term care services, (5) Opportunity for employment with no discriminatory personnel practices because of age, (6) Retirement in health, honor,

dignity—after years of contribution to the economy, (7) Participating in and contributing to meaningful activity within the widest range of civic, cultural, educational and training and recreational opportunities, (8) Efficient community services, including access to low cost transportation, which provide a choice in supported living arrangements and social assistance in a coordinated manner and which are readily available when needed, with emphasis on maintaining a continuum of care for vulnerable older individuals, (9) Immediate benefit from proven research knowledge which can sustain and improve health and happiness, (10) Freedom, independence, and the free exercise of individual initiative in planning and managing their own lives, full participation in the planning and operation of community based services and programs provided for their benefit, and protection against abuse, neglect, and exploitation. (Older Americans Act, 2012)

AGE, AGEISM, AND THE COUNSELING PROCESS

Aging individuals and older individuals are accustomed to being independent and living their life being able to make their own decisions, much as they have throughout their lifetime. The counselor's role, therefore, is to facilitate guiding the older client in making informed decisions and to show respect for the years of life experiences, knowledge, and expectations that inform the client's individual decisions. As with disability issues discussed in the previous section, counselors need to be aware of discrimination against people because of their age. Ageism can affect how the counselor views the client, as well as how society views older adults in general, and people of all ages and abilities need to be viewed in terms of their strengths and abilities. Thus, counselors are encouraged to increase their awareness, knowledge, and skills required for working with an aging and older population.

Counselors who specialize in working with aging and older clients are known within the counseling profession as gerontological counselors. A **gerontological counselor** is a counselor who provides counseling services to elderly clients and their families faced with changing lifestyles as they grow older (United States Bureau of Labor Statistics, 2014). Recognizing counselors' general lack of formal training in gerontological issues, and in an effort to enhance training opportunities for counselors working with older clients, the American Counseling Association (ACA) conducted five national projects on aging between 1977 and 1991 that focused on developing models and resources for preparing counselors to work with older adults. Myers (1992) wrote about efforts taken by the ACA to propose and approve standards for training in gerontological counseling. The standards, which were adopted by the Council for Accreditation of Counseling and Related Educational Programs (CACREP), were designed to infuse gerontological counseling into the common core areas of accredited counselor training programs so that all graduates from accredited programs would have at least some knowledge of issues unique to counseling older adults. Although most citizens aged 65 years and older do not have a disability, they are at increased risk of incurring one. So, in gerontological counseling, it is important to consider a "relational perspective" and to view aging and the disability process as a dynamic interaction between cultural norms and socioeconomic status. Such a view allows the counselor to encompass the client's attitudes, emotions, stigma, availability (or lack thereof) of appropriate health-care and support services, and attitudinal and environmental barriers (e.g., buildings not accessible to wheelchairs) that may impede the older client's independence (Chappell & Cooke, 2010) and empower the client toward effective growth and change.

Awareness

It is important that counselors be aware of their attitudes toward individuals of various age groups, including any common myths they may hold. (See Reflection 8.4.). Myths and stereotypes about aging and older adults can often be found in the media, for example. (See Activity 8.5.) In the counseling process, ageism may be manifested in the following ways:

- Assumptions of limitations on behavior due to youth *or* aging
- Positive or negative stereotypes about younger *or* older persons
- The belief that children and youths are not competent and must be directed (adultism)
- The belief that older people have been socialized to handle their own problems
- The belief that one's mental health needs decrease with age

---

REFLECTION 8.4

Following are some common myths held by mental health professionals about the counseling needs of older people. What myths can you add to the list?
- Mental health issues disappear after midlife.
- Depression, anxiety, and other problems in old age are to be expected (by the mere act of getting old), and they are not worth treating.
- Older people are "developmentally static," and coping mechanisms learned in their youth and young adulthood should work for them into old age.
- Older people lack resources to seek counseling.
- Older adults are "too old" to change.

The sheer numbers of older individuals living in the United States and elsewhere are making society increasingly aware of the mental health needs of older adults. How can you respond to their needs?

ACTIVITY 8.5

In our society, there are many misconceptions about aging and older adults. Look for examples of myths and stereotypes about aging in cartoons, magazines, and newspapers, on television, and in movies and other forms of media. Select three of your examples and discuss the possible origins of these stereotypes. Use the information and resources on aging provided in this chapter to refute each stereotype.

Knowledge

The **ACA gerontological competencies** (American Association for Counseling and Development [AACD], 1990) include competence statements that were prepared to assist counselor educators in developing curricula and other training experiences to ensure adequate preparation of counselors in gerontological issues. The statements provide a listing of minimum essential competencies required of effective generic and specialty counselors in working with older persons. In addition, It lists competencies for generic and specialty training based in the core areas of counselor preparation as defined in CACREP standards. CACREP is the national accrediting body for training in the counseling and human development professions. According to the standards (AACD, 1990), a gerontological counselor

- Exhibits positive, wellness-enhancing attitudes toward older people, including respect for the intellectual, emotional, social, vocational, physical, and spiritual needs of older individuals and the older population as a whole.
- Exhibits sensitivity to the sensory and physical limitations of older people through appropriate environmental modifications that facilitate helping relationships.
- Demonstrates knowledge of the unique considerations in establishing and maintaining helping relationships with older persons. Demonstrates knowledge of human development in older people, including knowledge of the major psychological theories of aging, physiological aspects of "normal" aging, and dysfunctional behaviors of older people.
- Demonstrates knowledge of the social and cultural issues that affect older people, including knowledge of common positive and negative societal attitudes, major causes of stress, needs of family caregivers, and the implications of major demographic characteristics of the older population (e.g., numbers of women, numbers of widows, increasing numbers of older minorities).
- Demonstrates knowledge of special considerations and techniques required for group work with older people.
- Demonstrates knowledge of lifestyle and career development concerns of older people, including knowledge of the effects of age-related physical, psychological, and social changes on vocational development, factors affecting the retirement transition, and alternative careers and lifestyles for those in later life.
- Demonstrates knowledge of the unique aspects of appraisal of older people, including knowledge of the psychological, social, and physical factors that may affect assessment and knowledge of the ethical implications of using assessment techniques.
- Demonstrates knowledge of sources of literature reporting research about older people and knowledge of ethical issues surrounding research with older subjects.
- Demonstrates knowledge of formal and informal referral networks for helping older people and knowledge of ethical behavior required in working with other professionals to assist older people.

In addition to consulting the competencies for gerontological counselors, counselors interested in working with the aging and older populations may want to investigate available professional and community resources presented in Table 8.4.

Skills

Like disability, aging can be viewed as negative or positive, as loss or gain. As counselors, we find it more helpful to facilitate our clients in building resiliency on the positive aspects of aging, such as lessons learned from a lifetime of experiences, knowledge, and skills, than focus on the client's losses or perceived losses due to old age. In this way, clients can understand that aging is inevitable and we can be successful in the outcome. But how is "successful" defined when applied to the aging process, and who determines whether the way a person is aging is

TABLE 8.4 Resources for Learning and Advocacy Related to Ageism

Association for Adult Development and Aging (AADA; www.aadaweb.org): The mission of the AADA is to support the professional development of counselors, advocate on issues related to adult development and aging, and address counseling concerns across the life span. The *ADULTSPAN* journal and newsletter are available with AADA membership or by subscription.

American Geriatrics Society (www.americangeriatrics.org): This society is devoted to improving the health, independence, and quality of life of all older people. The Society provides leadership to health-care professionals, policy makers, and the public.

American Psychological Association, Division 20, Committee on Aging (CONA; http://www.apa. org/pi/aging/cona/efforts-summary.pdf): This URL provides a direct link to a summary statement of CONA on its efforts over a 20-year period.

American Society on Aging (www.asaging.org): The American Society on Aging represents a multidisciplinary group of professionals who seek to improve the quality of life of older adults and their families.

Administration on Aging (www.aoa.gov): The Administration on Aging is the principal agency of the U.S Department of Health and Human Services designated to carry out the provisions of the Older Americans Act of 1965.

Centers for Disease Control and Prevention (CDC; www.cdc.gov/nccdphp/sgr/olderad.htm): This link provides direct access to the CDC *Report on Older Adults*.

National Association of Area Agencies on Aging (www.N4A.org): The mission of N4A members is to help older adults and people with disabilities live with dignity and choices in their homes and communities for as long as possible.

National Council on Aging (NCOA; www.ncoa.org): The NCOA is dedicated to improving the health and economic security of 10 million older adults by 2020.

National Institute on Aging (NIA; www.nia.nih.gov/): As 1 of the 27 Institutes and Centers of the National Institutes of Health, the NIA engages in research activities dedicated to understanding the nature of aging, supporting the health and well-being of older adults, and extending healthy, active years of life for more people.

Resources and Organizations for Clients

AARP, formerly the American Association for Retired Persons (www.aarp.org): This 37+ million member organization helps strengthen communities of those approaching retirement, while advocating for issues such as health care, employment security, and retirement planning.

Alzheimer's Association (www.alz.org): The mission of this organization is to advance dementia research and provide care to those affected.

Children's Defense Fund (www.childrensdefense.org): The Children's Defense fund is a non-profit child advocacy organization working for policies and programs that address poverty, child abuse and neglect, and access to health care and education.

Child Welfare League of America (http://cwla.org): The Child Welfare League of America advocates for children and youth issues such as abuse and neglect, family disruption, or other factors that jeopardize children's and youths' safety, permanence, or well-being.

Eldercare (www.eldercare.com): This website offers a searchable directory whereby the elder population can locate a variety of personal and medical care services.

National Youth Rights Association (www.youthrights.org): The National Youth Rights Association is dedicated to defending the civil and human rights of youths in the United States.

(Continued)

TABLE 8.4 Resources for Learning and Advocacy Related to Ageism (continued)

Youth for Human Rights International (www.youthforhumanrights.org): The purpose of this international organization is to teach youths about human rights—specifically, the United Nations Universal Declaration of Human Rights—and inspire them to become advocates for tolerance and peace.

Issue-Specific Resources

AARP, formerly the American Association for Retired Persons (AARP; www.aarp.org): AARP is a nonprofit membership organization of people aged 50 years and older that is dedicated to addressing their needs and interests.

Americans for a Society Free from Age Restrictions (ASFAR; https://web.archive.org/web/20110314110939/http://asfar.org/): The ASFAR is dedicated to protecting and advancing the legal civil rights of youths.

Center for Successful Aging (CSA; http://hhd.fullerton.edu/csa): "The specific goals of the Center are to: (1) conduct interdisciplinary research on issues related to healthy aging; (2) provide professional training of students and healthcare practitioners working with older adults in a variety of settings; (3) offer a variety of health, psychological, and functional assessments; (4) conduct a range of community-accessible programs based on the principles of whole-person wellness; (5) collaborate and partner with community agencies and organizations to provide innovative programming and services aimed at improving the quality of life in later years; and (6) serve as an advocate for affecting public policy relative to healthy aging and fall risk reduction."

Gray Panthers, Age and Youth in Action (http://www.graypanthersnyc.org/): The Gray Panthers is an intergenerational, multi-issue organization working to create a society that puts the needs of people over profit, responsibility over power, and democracy over institutions.

National Youth Rights Association (NYRA; www.youthrights.org/): This national youth-led organization defends the civil and human rights of young people in the United States through educating people about youth rights, working with public officials, and empowering young people to work on their own behalf. The organization holds the belief that certain basic rights are intrinsic parts of American citizenship and transcend age or status limits.

---

successful? More than five decades ago, Havighurst (1961) defined successful aging as the process of adding life to one's years (rather than years to one's life) and getting satisfaction out of life. Likewise, Rowe and Kahn (1998), in their classic work, *Successful Aging* (1998), defined **successful aging** as the avoidance of disease and disability, the maintenance of cognitive and physical function, and sustained engagement with life. Although this three-part definition of successful aging has become a central theoretical paradigm in the study of gerontology and geriatrics, it appears to assume that people have the resources to live a healthy life, adequate access to health care, a safe living environment, and the ability to make their own decisions. These desiderata may indeed be aspirational for most, if not all, of us as we age, but the reality is that not all older adults experience lives that support this definition of successful aging. Does it, then, mean that older people who have physical, psychological, or emotional health problems have not aged successfully? Just as "beauty is in the eye of the beholder," successful aging is defined by the person living the process. In other words, as counselors, we will find it helpful to understand (and even facilitate) *our client's own definition* of successful aging in his or her own terms. Reflection 8.5 offers you a chance to process your ideas of successful aging; Voices from the Field 8.2 presents one senior's perspective on successful aging.

REFLECTION 8.5

Is there a problem associating successful aging with having good physical and psychological health and the resources to maintain that condition into old age? Why or why not? Given what you have read on aging and ageism, how do you think older adults will define successful aging in the future? What is a counselor's role in helping clients assess their own definition of successful aging and facilitate their personal growth into old age?

Voices from the Field 8.2

I don't feel old at all, and I am busier now than I was when I worked full time. Yes, being a full-time grandmother can be every bit as fulfilling and active as being a full-time employee!! I was a secretary at a major worldwide corporation my entire career. My husband and I were both forced into retirement a few years before our 65th birthdays—they say it was corporate downsizing, but we both feel that they wanted younger, cheaper workers who would work longer hours. It was sad to close that chapter on our work and careers.

But it has been pure screaming, hair-on-fire excitement ever since. We have eight grandchildren that we see every week, because they all live within an hour of our home. Every year we have two-weeks-with-grandma-and-grandpa parties for the boys and two more weeks for the girls. Yes, that is four weeks a year! One of my grandsons is very special: He has autism. I arranged with the school system to be his transportation to and from school every day to help transition him and reduce the intense stress he feels. My husband and I also work part-time jobs now and then to stay active and pick up a little cash to pay for my husband's golf addiction!

All of this keeps me feeling young and focused on helping others, so I don't get bogged down into myself. You see, we also both are quite overweight and have diabetes, cholesterol, and heart problems. And we have a family history of heart problems, cancer, and Alzheimer's. Looking forward scares me sometimes, particularly when I consider life without my husband, or him living on without me. Still, I am thankful for my children, grandchildren, and extended family, and remain hopeful that my best years are still ahead!

Summary

This chapter was designed to give counselors and counselors in training an understanding of the concepts of ableism and ageism, both of which continue to exist in our society today. Given the large and growing minority group of individuals with disabilities in our society, it is likely that counselors, regardless of their specialty area or theoretical orientation, will be providing services to clients with disabilities or chronic medical or physical challenges at some time in their careers.

In working with clients who are "differently able," it is crucial for counselors to view the client with a disability as an individual first, to use disability-affirmative approaches, and to acknowledge that the client has multiple roles and functions within the family, community, culture, and society, all of which may affect the counseling process.

Similarly, the growing population of individuals in our society who are older (typically, aged 55 years and older) forms the basis for the section on ageism and older adults. Although ageism as a concept refers to any form of discrimination based on age (young or old), most of the chapter focused on older adults because they are projected to be the largest-growing segment of our population over the coming years. Clearly, on the basis of the projected numbers alone, there is a growing need for counselors and counselors in training to specialize in addressing the needs and concerns of older adults and to advocate for effective services for that population. In this way, counselors who are competent and interested in working with older adults may be considered to be on the cutting edge of the counseling profession and are poised to fill a great need both now and in the future. By recognizing that ability and age are diversity issues within our society, the multiculturally competent counselor can facilitate the counseling process and help clients of all ages and abilities achieve their goals.

Review Questions

1. How has disability been defined by various federal programs and legislation?
2. How do the two major models of disability compare and contrast?
3. What are some counseling considerations that are relevant to working with clients with a disability? How do various systems and cultural considerations play a role in the counseling process?
4. What is ageism, and how might it affect older adult clients?
5. What are some counseling considerations that are relevant to working with older adult clients? How can counselors increase their awareness, knowledge, and skills required for working with this population?

SECTION 3

Counseling Multicultural Populations

9 Individuals and Families of African Descent

Patrice S. Bounds, Ahmad R. Washington,
and Malik S. Henfield*

PREVIEW

This chapter will explore the experiences, cultural values, and common presenting issues for individuals, families, and couples, as well as various subpopulations, of African descent in the United States. The chapter will review common past and present experiences of African Americans, racial identity development, acculturation and racial identity as mental health indicators, African-American culture and values, common support systems for African Americans, the efficacy of traditional psychotherapies and assessments with this population, and the efficacy of multiculturally sensitive interventions.

INDIVIDUALS AND FAMILIES OF AFRICAN DESCENT

Individuals of African descent have a rich and varied history of survival in the United States despite unfavorable odds. Although the United States was a country founded on principles of religious and ethnic freedom, discriminatory laws and historically poor treatment of individuals of African descent contradicted these principles. One must understand the history of this group in the United States to truly comprehend and provide a context for how African-American culture developed and is maintained; how the psyche, racial identity, and worldview of individuals of African descent formed over time; what presenting treatment issues African Americans commonly bring to therapy; and what forms of deeply ingrained racism and discrimination many individuals of African descent face on a daily basis. Included in this history is a discussion of enslavement. The impact that one group of people being the legal property of another group of people had, and still has, on the collective psyche and mental health of individuals of African descent cannot be underestimated. This impact also underlies many of the common treatment issues that African Americans present when seeking counseling. Despite the fact that, as a group, African Americans share a deeply ingrained cultural experience, counselors must be mindful that African Americans exhibit tremendous within-group diversity (Richardson, Bethea, Hayling, & Williamson-Taylor, 2010; Sue & Sue, 2013). In other words,

*The editors want to thank Katherine M. Helm and Lawrence James, Jr., for their contributions to this chapter in the first edition.

counselors must strike a delicate balance between having an awareness of the historical and contemporary barriers that have affected people of African descent and recognizing the subtle and explicit idiosyncrasies each of these individuals possesses and presents during any given therapeutic encounter. In achieving this balance, clinicians will recognize the rich sociocultural history of people of African descent without making sweeping generalizations about them.

You may ask yourself, "How is counseling a person of African descent different than counseling individuals of other backgrounds?" The answer is that it is very different in some ways and not so different in other ways. Individuals are treated and judged differently on the basis of perceived race, ethnicity, gender, sexual orientation, religious background, height, weight, disability, and level of attractiveness, as well as other characteristics that are given a status in our society. Because skin color is readily seen, it is often the characteristic by which we are judged most quickly. In working with clients of African descent, multiculturally competent counselors develop a self-awareness of their social identities, social group statuses, power, privilege, oppression, strengths, attitudes, beliefs, and bias, and combine their academic knowledge, practical and personal experiences, and common sense to understand and be sensitive to clients' varied experiences in their individual worlds (Ratts, Singh, Nassar-McMillan, Butler, & McCullough, 2015). Reflection 9.1 offers counselors an opportunity to explore their own assumptions and biases about the African-American population.

REFLECTION 9.1

Compile a list of initial thoughts that come to mind about individuals of African descent. Examine your assumptions and beliefs about this population. Explore how these views could affect your work, both positively and negatively, with these clients.

Terminology

This chapter is titled "Individuals and Families of African Descent" because that is the most inclusive title of that population at this time. The chapter does not include individuals of North African descent (e.g., Egyptians, Libyans, Moroccans); however, information on this population is discussed in the next chapter, on individuals and families of Arab descent.

Throughout time, Black Americans have been referred to as Negroes, Colored, Blacks, Afro-Americans, and African Americans. Historically, Black Americans began labeling themselves publicly as a group most noticeably in the 1960s, with the expression "Black is beautiful" (Camp, 2015). This choice of words represented the idea that, as a people, Blacks could celebrate their own diversity of skin tones and that Black people had a proud heritage to celebrate. Prior to the "Black is beautiful" movement, African Americans in the United States were named by those in power. The term *African American* came about in the 1980s. Coined by Reverend Jesse Jackson, it emphasized Black Americans' ties to Africa as well as to the country of their citizenship, the United States. Not all African Americans wish to be called "African American" or "Black." Therefore, multiculturally competent counselors should ask their clients of African descent what they prefer to be called. This chapter will use the terms *Black, African American*, and *individuals of African descent* interchangeably to reflect the ways in which many Blacks in the United States refer to themselves; however, each term is different and can represent an individual's sense of his or her own identity and pride.

Demographics

According to 2010 U.S. Census data, African Americans make up approximately 12.6% (38.9 million) of the U.S. population. Since 2000, the Black population has grown by 12% (34.7 million; U.S. Census Bureau, 2011a). The Black population has slightly more females (52.3%) than males (47.7%), with nearly 26% of the population under 18 years and only 9.7% over 65 years (U.S. Census Bureau, 2014b). The U.S. Census Bureau projects that, by the year 2060, the African American population will increase to 74.5 million, accounting for 17.9% of the total U.S. population. An analysis of immigration patterns finds that individuals of African descent come from diverse places, including Africa, the Caribbean, the West Indies, Latin America, central Europe, and South America, among others (Pew Research Center, 2015a). During fiscal year 2013, 98,304 immigrants from the continent of Africa lawfully applied and subsequently received permanent residence in the United States (Office of Homeland Security, 2013).

But it would be shortsighted to ignore just how ethnically diverse that group of immigrants actually was. Indeed, the following statistics vividly illustrate that the people immigrating to the United States from the continent of Africa were not monolithic: Of those 98,304 African immigrants (Office of Homeland Security, 2013), 13,097 were from Ethiopia; 10,265 came from Ghana; 6,123 identified Kenya as their country of origin; 13,840 were Nigerian; and 59 were from South Sudan. If we examine these data in greater detail, we can see that, since 2004, there has been a sharp escalation in the number of immigrants from all of the aforementioned African countries (Ethiopia, 8,286; Ghana, 5,337; Kenya, 5,335; Nigeria, 9,374; South Sudan was not an independent country in 2004). There has also been a steady and consistent uptick in the number of Black Caribbean immigrants seeking permanent residence in the United States. Again citing data accumulated by the Office of Homeland Security (2013), we see that large numbers of Black Caribbean immigrants came to the United States primarily from three countries: Haiti (20,351), Jamaica (19,400), and Trinidad and Tobago (4,724). To this list of countries we must add and consider the unique case of Haitians coming from the Dominican Republic (41,311). Recently, the Dominican Republic expelled thousands of Haitians who had been residing in that country, leaving them to shelter in tent campuses along the border between the two countries. Because of the physical violence and social persecution these Haitians have had to endure, it is not inconceivable that many of them may be seeking refuge in the United States. Although Black immigrants to the United States are outnumbered by non-Black Latino/a and Asian immigrants, the Black immigrant population has more than quadrupled, from 816,000 in 1980 to 3,793,000 in 2013.

People of African descent disproportionally face many issues, including struggles with poverty and unemployment. According to data from the Cable News Network (CNN, 2014), approximately 15% of Americans now live in poverty; however, the poverty rate for African Americans remains nearly 3 times higher than that of White Americans (27.2% vs. 9.6%; U.S. Census Bureau, 2014b). Also, the unemployment rate for African Americans remains twice as high as that of White Americans (13.1% vs. 6.5%; U.S. Bureau of Labor Statistics, 2014). This gap could both stem from and contribute to physical and mental health disparities (e.g., less access to affordable health insurance, a lower average life expectancy than Whites by almost 7 years), low educational attainment, and systematic and discriminatory practices based on race (Byars-Winston, 2010; Parris, Owens, Johnson, Grbevski, & Holbert-Quince, 2010). In addition, Blacks are incarcerated at a rate 5 times higher than Whites. According to the U.S. Department of Justice (2013, 2014a), there are 1.5 million inmates in federal and state prisons in 2013, an increase of 0.3% (4,300 inmates) over 2012. Of the total prison population, non-Hispanic Blacks made up 40% (2,306 per 100,000 people) of the incarcerations even though Blacks were only

12.6% of the U.S. population; by way of comparison, non-Hispanic Whites made up 39% (450 per 100,000) of incarcerations and accounted for 64% of the U.S. population and Hispanics were 19% (831 per 100,000) of incarcerations and constituted 19% of the U.S. population.

With regard to educational attainment, 20.8% of Blacks are college graduates from 4-year universities, as opposed to 43.3% of Whites (U.S. Department of Education, 2014). Among high school students enrolled in public schools, African Americans have the lowest graduation rate (66.1%, vs. 83% of Whites; Stillwell & Sable, 2013). Urban school districts (in which many school attendees are Black) receive about 12% less funding for each child, compared with predominantly White school districts. Poor urban schools often lack important resources, such as computers, current textbooks, after-school activities, and Advanced Placement (AP) courses. So many of these struggles are reflective of the oppression Blacks face in American society because of historic and current racial discrimination. Despite these serious issues facing individuals of African descent, African Americans' history of resilience and survival in an often hostile and highly racialized climate cannot be denied.

AFRICAN-AMERICAN HISTORY

People of African descent living in the United States have been labeled in many different ways. Historically, as discussed in Chapter 4, race was considered a biological construct. However, there is a general consensus among contemporary scholars and researchers that race, as a construct and organizational framework, was devised and used deliberately by Europeans in the 18th century to facilitate the colonization of indigenous and native peoples around the globe, but especially from Africa (Feagin, 2014; Feagin & Elias, 2013). Because race was deployed to achieve the material, sociopolitical, and economic motives of the European elite and professional classes, some of the most influential writings used to legitimize race as a biological construct came from the most influential European institutions. Consequently, a litany of European scientists (e.g., psychologists, anthropologists, psychometricians) undertook the task of codifying and buttressing this fundamental premise through the practice of **scientific racism**. Scientific racism was an unethical practice initiated during the middle of the 18th century through the beginning of the 20th century whereby pseudoscientists played an integral role in promulgating myths that indigenous non-Whites were racially inferior (Roberts, 2014). Without knowing this bit of Black history, it is impossible for counseling professionals to truly appreciate how pseudoscience helped to deeply entwine biological notions of race with almost every American social institution (Muhammad, 2010).

Because Europeans were responsible for the categorical system based on race, the darker one's skin and the further an individual's features were from the European standard, the lower was the status of the individual in society. Racial categories were always hierarchical, with the darkest individuals compared to animals and the lightest individuals considered to be made in "God's image." This hierarchical system is evident in the **one-drop rule**, which states that having one drop of Black blood makes one Black (Bernasconi, 2012; Davis, 2010; Khanna, 2010). Slave owners and subsequent laws obsessively classified individuals of African descent according to how much White blood one had. For example, mulattoes were half Black and half White, quadroons were one fourth Black, and octoroons were one eighth Black (Gullickson, 2010). Often, the more White blood slaves had, the more privileges they had over their darker counterparts. Lighter skinned slaves were able to work in the slave owner's house, and darker skinned slaves had to work outdoors all day. Slaves with lighter skin were also considered more attractive by White slave owners because they were closer to the White beauty ideal.

Lighter skinned slaves were often the result of the slave owners sexually assaulting darker slaves. These sexual acts are why many slaves were actually related to their slave owners for generations.

Colorism still exists in the Black community, where African Americans with lighter skin are often perceived as having an easier time than African Americans with darker skin (Burton, Bonilla-Silva, Ray, Buckelew, & Hordge Freeman, 2010; Hannon & DeFina, 2014; Wilder, 2010; Wilder & Cain, 2011). There is some basis to this perception, both currently and historically. It is a form of internalized racism, wherein lighter skin is sometimes more valued than darker skin in the African-American community. Occasionally in Black families, parents or grandparents may knowingly or unknowingly prefer children on the basis of their skin tone. This issue can often be a very painful one that may not be openly discussed or acknowledged (Burton et al., 2010). In working with African-American women especially, colorism may be a hidden treatment issue, because skin color can be related to self-esteem, body image issues, and feelings of attractiveness. A multiculturally competent counselor might therefore explore the salience of clients' self-perceptions related to skin tone because such perceptions might be relevant to their self-concept or presenting issue.

In sum, race today is a social, economic, psychological, and ideological construct. In other words, what race someone is has economic and social consequences for living in the United States. Race also shapes one's worldview and oftentimes how the person is perceived and treated by others in society. In the United States, race and social class are frequently confounded. For example, it is often assumed that most Blacks are poor. The media tends to enhance this perception by depicting news stories, movies, and television programs that support it. The perception does not allow for the economic heterogeneity among African Americans. It is true that a disproportionate number of African Americans are poor relative to their numbers in the population; however, it is also true that most African Americans are *not* poor (Macartney, Bishaw, & Fontenot, 2013).

Individuals of African descent have a distinct culture that is influenced by geographic region, origins (e.g., Haitian American vs. Dominican American), ideology, social class, and many other variables. Without understanding the diversity within African-American culture, a counselor cannot work effectively with clients of these backgrounds. Those with "black skin" do not all have the same culture. Afro-Cubans, Black Americans, individuals from Ghana, and people from the Caribbean may all have similar skin tones, but their cultures, values, experiences, and worldviews may be vastly different. Accordingly, multiculturally sensitive counselors educate themselves about their client's personal (individual) and collective (group) culture, assessing the clients' levels of acculturation with an eye toward understanding some of their cultural values. (Assessment of acculturation level will be discussed later in the chapter.)

DISCRIMINATION EXPERIENCES

The first Africans arrived in the United States in 1619 as indentured servants, the way many White settlers came. Within 20 years, there were laws against racial mixing and interracial marriage (Djamba & Kimuna, 2014; Field, Kimuna, & Straus, 2013; McClain, 2011). Very soon after that, Africans began arriving on the shores of the United States as slaves. From the mid-1600s through 1965, laws were used to justify the physical, mental, and spiritual abuse of African Americans. Early models of mental health pathologized Africans (Jarvis, 2012). For example, **drapetomania** was said to be a noted mental illness of slaves who tried to escape from their owners (Jarvis, 2012; Matus, 2010). White Americans at the time justified slavery by assuming that Blacks were not human beings and that they could not feel pain to the same extent as Whites. Laws considered slaves to be one tenth of a human being.

During the years of the slave trade, Africans from different tribes were ripped from their families and culture and forced onto severely overcrowded ships, where over half of them died before coming to the shores of the United States. Upon arrival, they were sold away from other family members to White slave owners. They were beaten, starved, and forced to work 18 hours a day. Africans were forced to give up their African names and culture and were given European names. Even their reproductive lives were not their own, as men were frequently used as "studs" to make more slaves and women were seen as breeders. All children born were considered the property of slave owners, and many children were promptly sold away from their families. Thus, the nuclear family unit was seldom allowed to form among slaves. Often, slave children were raised by whichever adults and older children were left on the plantation. Rarely were these the children's actual relatives. Thus, slaves made family where they found it. Although more traditional mental health models and models of family therapy have pathologized Black families because many of them are not "nuclear," this situation clearly has a historical basis and is not pathological (Gans, 2011; Williams, Gooden, & Davis, 2012). It is still true that Black families are not strictly nuclear, and Black children are often raised by their close biological relatives and extended family. Although the dehumanization and denigration of Blacks and Black culture began in times of slavery, current society often continues to reflect this pattern. These practices can be seen in racial profiling, the criminalization of Blacks, and the view that Blacks are undesirable people and a group to be feared.

Post–Civil War Reconstruction is the brief historical period between the end of enslavement in 1865 and the beginning of the **Jim Crow** era in 1877. Despite suffering unrelenting violence at the hands of angry and envious White southerners, emancipated Blacks made several noteworthy tangible strides, perhaps most notably being elected to prominent political offices at the state and federal levels (e.g., governors, congressional representatives). Briefly, Jim Crow laws maintained and supported segregationist policies that governed the lives of Blacks in America. These racist policies were enforced by legal institutions such as the police and courthouses through the 1960s. Thus, throughout their history in the United States, Blacks have been made to feel unwelcome, undesirable, and pathologized. Blacks have been seen as a "problem people," a people to be hated and feared, and a threat. It is on this backdrop that African values with American influences were maintained in the traumatic war zone of slavery, the Jim Crow era, and continued racism and discrimination. Although racism and discrimination are rarely openly tolerated in today's times, they still exist.

As discussed in Chapter 4, racial microaggressions are subtle statements or behaviors, whether intentional or unintentional, that convey insulting or demeaning messages to people of color (Nadal, 2011; Pittman, 2012; Sue, 2010; Sue & Sue, 2013). Although today's racism is often passive, hidden, unconscious, and systemic, it is still extremely damaging and hurtful. For example, research on health-care disparities and medical treatment document well that African Americans often receive poorer health care and are frequently diagnosed with life-threatening illnesses and mental illnesses later than their White counterparts (Smith, 2015). In assessing the symptomology of psychiatric disorders, experiences with discriminatory practices have been linked to generalized anxiety disorder, depression, and increased psychological distress (Hammond, 2012; Krieger, Kosheleva, Waterman, Chen, & Koenen, 2011; Smith, Hung, & Franklin, 2011). According to the National Alliance on Mental Illness (NAMI, 2012), African Americans are less likely to use mental health counseling services and are more likely to be misdiagnosed. This difference in care could be attributed to bias, prejudice, and stereotyping on the part of the health-care provider (Hatcher, 2012; Smith, 2015).

Thus, passive and unconscious racism can have devastating life-threatening consequences for the lives of individuals of African descent. As a result, many African Americans are distrustful of medical and mental health professionals because, in the not-so-distant past, Blacks were victims of medical experiments done without their permission (e.g., the Tuskegee syphilis experiment) and involuntary sterilization in which they were harmed and even died as a result. The *New York Press* (Bergman, 2005) reported that the New York City foster care system (most of the children in foster care across the country are Black) gave HIV-positive children toxic experimental drugs for treatment without the children's or guardians' permission. Children of parents who were aware of experimental treatments and whose parents refused to allow them to participate were removed from their parents' custody. It is also true that often the only contact some members of the Black community have with mental health professionals is when social workers come in to remove children from their homes or through the welfare system (Harris, 2014).

Amid the ongoing struggle for racial equality, the historic election of this country's first African-American president, Barack H. Obama, warrants considerable examination. President Obama's election represented a unique, yet challenging, opportunity to consider the relative progress of African Americans collectively, as well as to examine this country's latent and covert thoughts and feelings regarding race. Although Obama's presidency was certainly laudable, given the nation's racial past and present, many Americans erroneously equated Obama's election with validation for the position that cries of racism were obsolete (Baldridge, Hill, & Davis, 2011; Hehman, Gaertner, & Dovidio, 2011; Howard & Flennaugh, 2011). Correspondingly, this faction would contend that the election of President Obama demonstrated unequivocally the existence of a postracial society. As those who support this position believe, the fact that an African American occupied the highest office in the land rendered claims of systemic and institutional racism pointless. In other words, the ascent of President Obama purportedly signified the triumphant arrival of a postracial society in which race no longer dictated one's station in life, as it once did in the United States.

Interestingly, as the postracial sentiment continues to resonate among segments of Americans, it rings hollow in the face of research which suggests that White Americans' condemnation of the Obama presidency is motivated by racial prejudice (Hehman et al., 2011). In addition, this cynicism increases when it is revealed that, despite President Obama's presence in the White House, the status of African Americans in relation to health and education, for example, continues to lag behind Whites (Baldridge et al., 2011). Moreover, the Obama Presidency has done nothing to interrupt the disproportionate representation among African Americans in the American penal system (Alexander, 2012).

No contemporary conversation about the overwhelming number of incarcerated Black Americans would be complete without a critical examination of the historical sociopolitical variables that first relegated and then confined poor and working-class Blacks to the most undesirable parts of large urban cities (e.g., housing discrimination, Housing and Urban Development public housing policies, redlining; Wacquant, 2010; Wilson, 2012). These cities, which had become largely dilapidated, did not possess the requisite educational and employment opportunities and social services to support Black residents who were struggling literally to survive. Rather than incentivizing corporations to invest in those cities in order to promote economic stimulation and revitalization, local and federal agencies, under the auspices of the Nixon and Reagan administrations, initiated a War on Drugs that has had a debilitating impact on Black communities throughout this country and that continues to this day (Alexander, 2012). Rooted in the presumption that these neighborhoods are inherently more criminal than others, local and federal police forces can justify their surveillance of Black communities. The ostensible ubiquitous presence of law enforcement in Black neighborhoods virtually guarantees police contact with Black residents (e.g., through stop and frisk) and, with increasing regularity, these encounters are proving deadly for Black American children (e.g., Aiyana Stanley-Jones, Tamir Rice), women (e.g., Rekia Boyd, Tanisha Anderson), and men (e.g., John Crawford, Eric Garner).

In the U.S. school system of the mid-to-late 20th century, mental health professionals were also involved with the disproportionate labeling of Black children as having an intellectual disability. Intelligence tests, which had not at the time been normed on Black children or children of lower socioeconomic status (SES), were used as the sole measure for placing children into special-education programs. Historically, these children were often placed in a special-education curriculum without their parents' knowledge or consent. This past negative history has contributed to the general cultural mistrust that some African Americans have of the government, as well as of medical and mental health professionals and institutions (Scott, McCoy, Munson, Snowden, & McMillen, 2011).

BLACK RACIAL IDENTITY

Understanding racial identity among African Americans is essential to counseling members of this group effectively. Counselors must also understand Black cultural variables and their clients' level of acculturation. The Cross (1971) model of Black racial identity development (see Chapter 2) is a prominent framework for understanding Black racial identity. It has been modified, researched extensively, and applied to counseling settings with cross-racial dyads of clients and counselors (Parham, 1989; Parham & Helms, 1981), to client racial preferences for counselors (Boyd-Franklin, 2013), and to supervisor–supervisee cross-racial pairings and used to explore how racial identity can change over the life span (Parham, 2002). The Cross model has been updated (Cross & Vandiver, 2001); however, the basic core of the model has remained the same. The model describes a process by which most African Americans come to embrace and internalize a positive Black identity despite instances of racial discrimination and negative societal messages about being Black. Some individuals of Black descent do not embrace a positive Black identity and do not consider their Black heritage to be an important aspect of their identities, whereas others see being Black as a central part of their identities (Barnes, Williams, & Barnes, 2014; Byrd & Chavous, 2011). Sellers, Smith, Shelton, Rowley, and Chavous (1998) developed a multidimensional model of racial identity that provides a framework for understanding both the significance of race in the self-concept of African Americans and the qualitative meaning that is attributed to being a member of that racial category. It is therefore essential in working with clients of African descent that counselors assess how central clients' racial awareness and identity is to who they say they are as individuals.

Other literature finds that a client's Black identity (especially if seen as excessively negative) can have negative implications for mental health issues and self-esteem (Baillargeon, 2014; Banks, Murry, Brown, & Hammond, 2014; Thompson & Gregory, 2011). This identity can present as the internalization of the White beauty ideal, the rejection of a Black identity and high negative feelings about being Black, the disparagement of other Blacks, and other forms of internalized racism. It is important that counselors recognize how stifling these messages can be on the psyche of African Americans and examine the ways more affirming messages can promote healthier psychosocial outcomes for African Americans.

Research demonstrates that a positive racial identity serves a protective function for individuals of African descent (Banks et al., 2014; Wang & Huguley, 2012), shielding them from negative societal messages about being Black. Wang and Huguley (2012) found that African-American adolescents who received affirming cultural socialization messages within schools were less likely to experience adverse consequences (e.g., a lower grade point average and diminished educational aspirations) even under teacher discrimination. These studies lend credence to the belief that the assessment of racial identity is useful in the counseling process because it allows a counselor to hypothesize the types of conflict a client deals with and how the client views the world.

ACCULTURATION

In addition to assessing and understanding clients' racial identities, their level of acculturation must be explored. In this respect, it is important to consider acculturation to racial identity especially when working with individuals of African descent. Briefly, the difference between racial identity and acculturation is that racial identity has to do with how one identifies oneself and whether race is a key component of one's identity, whereas **acculturation** refers to specific influences on socialization and how one's racial identity is practiced. Thus, acculturation speaks more to culture than to race. Loosely speaking, acculturation is the extent to which ethnic minorities and immigrants participate in the cultural values, beliefs, and practices of their own culture versus those of the mainstream culture (Yoon et al., 2013). Given the importance of acculturation, a multiculturally competent counselor should assess how invested a Black client is in traditional African-American religious beliefs and practices, traditional African-American socialization experiences and values, and preferences for African-American things. Such an assessment will give the counselor an indication of the client's level of acculturation. The issues discussed here are illuminated in Voices from the Field 9.1.

Understanding a client's racial identity and level of acculturation will guide the counselor in recommending or acknowledging appropriate support systems for clients. Highly acculturated clients may wish to use Black organizations (e.g., churches, fraternities and sororities, Black-run charities, Black-owned businesses) as a source of emotional, financial, and social support. Referring a Black client who does not consider being Black an important part of her or his identity to traditional Black support systems in the community would be contraindicated, and the client could be offended.

Acculturation is also a phenomenon germane to the experiences of people of African descent born outside this country. According to McCabe (2011), Black immigrants, unlike African Americans, are people of African ancestry who arrive to this country after having departed from the continent of Africa or other places throughout the African diaspora. Although it is important to be respectful of the dissimilarities between African Americans and Black immigrants, counselors should also recognize the within-group differences exhibited by those categorized as Black immigrants. Just as the racial category of individuals of Asian descent encompasses tremendous diversity, so do Black immigrants (Rong & Fitchett, 2008).

Although Black immigrants and African Americans often possess phenotypic traits supposedly indicative of membership in the Black racial categories, Black immigrants encounter

Voices from the Field 9.1

School culture is the foundation for a learning environment. The level of acceptance and respect in the classroom sets the stage for students to excel in their academics. Currently, our ninth-grade students are reading *Kaffir Boy* by Mark Mathabane during their English class. Sierra, an African-American student, is struggling with her level of comfort in the classroom, since she is the only African-American student in the room. She told me of her feelings of being singled out, judged, and stared at while the book is being discussed. She does not feel that public opinion or oppression has changed since the 1970s, the period discussed in the book. From her perspective, she is a lone martyr for the race within the classroom. She does not want to be in the class and struggles to attend on a daily basis.

The first step in working with Sierra was to validate her feelings and try to understand her perspective better. I let her know that I have not had the experience of being the only White person in an all–African-American group. I can only envision how uncomfortable it makes her feel. She reassured me that she was comfortable with her classmates; however, with the topic at hand, she could not remain in the room. As she continued to process her emotions with me, I asked probing questions to help her think about the situation from different perspectives. She struggled to see the perspective of her peers or the teacher. I abandoned the view of the situation and focused on Sierra. We then discussed leadership and self-advocacy. She sees herself as a strong African-American female. She wants to be able to be a part of the discussion but does not want to be the lone African American in the room. We moved to focusing on the positive and the future. I felt that it was imperative that she see the situation as an opportunity for her to learn more about herself and how she can grow in the situation. Empowering her with self-advocacy skills through a brainstorming process enabled her to make the situation not only bearable, but also a learning opportunity for her peers and herself.

~Natalie Hess, Certified School Counselor

a unique set of barriers that can interfere with their assimilation into American culture and society (Venters et al., 2011). Black immigrants, much like African Americans, must contend with episodes of racism, whether blatant or subtle in nature, as they attempt to transition successfully to this country (Thomas, 2011). Moreover, those Black immigrants possessing markers of immigrant status (e.g., a distinct accent) are more susceptible to this type of discrimination. Black immigrants' class status can also have a tangible impact on their level of assimilation. As Thomas (2011) pointed out, working-class Black immigrants are often less able to reside in adequate or desirable housing. Thus, in working with Black immigrants, it is imperative for counseling practitioners to be sensitive to the multitude of variables affecting this minority group.

AFRICAN-AMERICAN CULTURE AND VALUES

According to Sue and Sue (2013), some of the quintessential components of the traditional American cultural ethos are rugged individualism, dogged competition, a belief in the existence of a meritocratic society, and the centrality of nuclear families. This ethos differs starkly from African-centered values in (1) the significance of the collective over the individual; (2) the importance of kinship and affiliation; (3) the prominence of the extended family; (4) the notions of spirituality, connectedness, and harmony with nature; and (5) an overall holistic outlook (Hartung, Fouad, Leong, & Hardin, 2010; Mattis & Mattis, 2011; Sue & Sue, 2013).

Many individuals of African descent in America perceive kinship or a connection to other African Americans because of a shared history of oppression and discrimination. However, counselors should not assume that all African Americans feel connected to one another. In addition to natural feelings of being linked because of this shared history, there is also a forced collectivism that exists for individuals of African descent in America that comes from the way society as a whole views African Americans. For example, most African Americans understand that, if one African American does something negative (e.g., a criminal act), the collective (i.e., African Americans as a group) are judged by this act, especially if the negative act of the Black individual reinforces a stereotype about Black people. Most individuals of African descent understand, even though it is unfair and oppressive, that, for racial ethnic minorities in America, the whole group is often judged poorly by the negative acts of a few. This forced collectivistic view affects the way African Americans are seen as a group in society and does not acknowledge the heterogeneity among them. A summary of general values for individuals of African descent is given in Table 9.1. These values will be discussed more thoroughly in the material that follows.

Families of African Descent

In Boyd-Franklin's extensive work with Black families (Boyd-Franklin, 2013; Boyd-Franklin & Hafer-Bry, 2001), she stated that there is no such thing as the typical Black family. As

---

TABLE 9.1 General Values Associated with Individuals of African Descent

- Collectivism and group consciousness (a group identity)
- Communalism—person centered (as opposed to object centered)
- Care for elderly at home
- Flexible time orientation
- Racial socialization of children (helping children deal with the realities of racism)
- Kinship bonds (relationship bonds with family, extended family, and nonrelatives)
- Spiritual or religious orientation
- Harmony and interrelatedness with nature
- Extended family relationships
- Collective child-raising practices (multiple adult and adolescent caregivers may be involved in raising young children)
- Nonrelative familial relationships
- Educational attainment
- Gender-egalitarian romantic relationships
- Respect for adult figures by children
- Assertiveness
- Expressiveness in communication style
- The "family business" stays in the family

---

mentioned previously, since slave times Black families have not been strictly nuclear. In Africa, of course, children were raised in tribal cultures that did not emphasize the nuclear family as the primary unit. In the United States, early models of mental health and family therapy pathologized Black families, characterizing them as "disorganized, deprived, disadvantaged kids coming from broken homes" (Boyd-Franklin, 2013, p. 14) and "fatherless homes promoting a matriarchal culture which is abnormal" (Peters, 2007, p. 207). Deficient views of Black families were perpetuated by applying Eurocentric models of family therapy to them (Moore & McDowell, 2014).

Many Black families are led by females. However, this does not automatically mean that there is no male involved in raising the children (Boyd-Franklin, 2013). Thus, counselors need to be sensitive to the role of large numbers of Black women as single parents, as well as to Black men who may be involved with their children but not living in the same household. Both roles involve multiple stressors.

Many researchers have suggested a strengths-based approach when working with Black families (Bell-Tolliver, Burgess, & Brock, 2009; Moore & McDowell, 2014; Pollock, Kazman, & Deuster, 2015). This approach involves assessing a family's strengths (skills, abilities, and knowledge) and using these strengths in counseling in order to empower clients (Jokes, 2009; Sheely-Moore & Bratton, 2010). Hill (2003) cited that, historically, some of the strengths of Black families have been strong kinship bonds, a strong work orientation, adaptability, a high achievement orientation, and versatility. These strengths represent African-centered values (Boyd-Franklin, 2013) and are coping strategies that people of African descent have used to survive societal oppression. For example, the versatility of family roles grew out of necessity: often, in Black families, older siblings are responsible for helping to raise other siblings. In addition, Peters (2007) stated that these roles are not restricted to gender (e.g., an older brother would be as responsible for helping raise younger siblings as an older sister would). In Black families, many such roles are determined by age and not gender.

Black families often keep generational secrets that are never talked about inside or outside the family. Boyd-Franklin (2013) reported that common family secrets include informal adoptions of children, true parentage of children, unwed pregnancies, a parent who had "trouble" early in life, substance abuse, HIV status, an ancestor who was mentally ill, domestic violence, White relatives, and skin-color issues.

Black parents and other adult caregivers often racially socialize Black children, whereby they foster a sense of racial pride, teach children about their African-American heritage, help the children develop a positive racial identity, and discuss ways in which to deal with racism (Banks et al., 2014; Barnes et al., 2014; Bell-Tolliver et al., 2009; Boyd-Franklin, 2013). This socialization often serves as a protective function against lowered self-esteem when children face racism. For example, when an African-American child comes home and tells his mother about a racist incident at school, the child is less likely to believe that something is wrong with him or her personally because of this racial socialization.

Black families come in all different skin tones within the same family. As mentioned previously, given that light skin was historically, and continues to be, valued over dark skin in our society, some Black families may have internalized this form of racism. Therefore, caregivers may deliberately or inadvertently choose favorites or scapegoat children on the basis of the darkness or lightness of skin color (Hannon & DeFina, 2014; Wilder, 2010). This may present as a treatment issue in counseling or may be simply related to other treatment issues such as self-esteem or family conflict.

African American parents, especially working-class parents, are more likely than Whites to use physical punishment to discipline their children (Westbrook, Harden, Holmes, Meisch, & Whittaker, 2013). Unlike the situation with White children, physical punishment was not associated with more acting out among Black children (Lansford et al., 2009; Westbrook et al., 2013). In some Black families, obedience is valued and is seen by parent and child as a sign of respect and an eventual survival skill for success in school and future employment (Peters, 2007). Obviously, as with other racial/ethnic groups, level of education and SES influence how families discipline their children. African-American families are not an exception. In the clinical realm, physical punishment should be separated from physical abuse, and one should not be confused with the other.

In working with Black families, Boyd-Franklin (2013) and Sanders (2007) recommend that counselors be flexible. Because religion and spirituality often play a part in African-American family life, including child rearing, counselors are encouraged to be aware of and involve community resources in treatment—especially the Black church if the family is religious or spiritual (McAdoo, 2007; McAdoo & Younge, 2009). In addition, counselors should be flexible in their conceptualization of Black families. An assessment of involved extended family and fictive kin (i.e., nonrelatives who are as close to, and involved in, the family as blood relatives are) is common (McAdoo, 2007) and should be included in the picture of what a family is. Counselors need to ask who lives in the home and who helps take care of the children, and they need to understand how the multigenerational role of racism, oppression, poverty, and victimization, both past and present, has an impact on Black families (Boyd-Franklin, 2013; McAdoo, 2007; McAdoo & Younge, 2009).

In using a strengths-based approach with a Black family, a counselor should emphasize the positive values, support systems, and strengths of that family (Awosan, Sandberg, & Hall, 2011; Boyd-Franklin, 2013; Pollock et al., 2015). Counselors should focus on empowering the family to function effectively. Empowerment can include restructuring the family so that power is appropriately used to mobilize the family's ability to interact successfully with external systems (Awosan et al., 2011; Boyd-Franklin, 2013).

Common presenting issues of Black families include finances, blended families, missing father figures, siblings in the same family who have different fathers and different levels of involvement with those fathers, violence, multigenerational role conflict, the negative impact of colorism, and unemployment. Obviously, understanding the social and cultural context of each family is essential to working effectively with individual Black families. Once again, SES affects presenting issues of Black families and their access to community and other resources. The multiculturally competent counselor readily understands issues common to most Black families, is connected to important community resources, uses a strengths-based approach, and views the family through the family's cultural lens. Case Study 9.1 offers an example of how family dynamics may be considered in counseling.

CASE STUDY 9.1

Bernadine is a 42-year-old woman of African descent. She has been heavily encouraged to go to counseling by her supervisor at work, who maintains that she has an anger problem. Bernadine has been short tempered and highly irritable at work. She has repeatedly gotten into tense disagreements with colleagues when she feels that they are not showing her respect. Bernadine is one of two African Americans in her office. She works for a Fortune 500 company as a middle-level manager. She has threatened to sue the company for discrimination because several younger White employees whom she has trained have superseded her into top-level management positions, whereas her ascent to the top has been stalled for several years now. When she brought this situation up at work, she was accused of playing the "race card." Bernadine has an MBA from a prestigious university and was recruited 12 years ago directly out of graduate school.

Bernadine's husband of 17 years filed for divorce 6 months ago. The couple has two children, aged 10 and 12 years. Her husband left her for a woman who is not African American. In your first intake session with Bernadine, you find her to be angry at being forced into treatment and hostile toward you, the counselor.

Reflect on the following questions:

- How might the history of discrimination against individuals of African descent in the United States affect the way this client views her situation? How might that history affect the way others see this client?
- How would you cultivate therapeutic rapport with this client, given that she may not be receptive to receiving treatment?
- Pretend that you are ethnically different from this client. When and how would you address this difference in counseling?
- What would you hypothesize this client's underlying treatment issue(s) to be?
- What are some possible diagnoses for this client?
- How would you assess this client's racial identity? Level of acculturation?
- What other things do you need to know before beginning treatment with this client?
- How would you assess whether this client's claims of discrimination on her job are accurate?
- How would you go about validating this client's perception of her experiences at work?
- What kind of evidence of resilience might there be for this client?

Couples of African Descent

Couples of African descent often have unique challenges to face in addition to the common issues that couples of all ethnic backgrounds face (Bethea & Allen, 2013; Dixon, 2009). According to Chapman (2007), in 1970, couples headed more than 68% of African-American families. Currently, the proportion of African American families headed by couples is 41%. The national first-divorce rate for U.S. residents (excluding residents of California, Georgia, Hawaii, Indiana, Louisiana, and Minnesota) in 2010 was 17.5 per 1,000 women 18 years old or older (U.S. Census Bureau, 2011a). Breaking down the divorce rate by race and ethnicity reveals, however, that the divorce rate for Black couples is higher than it is for White couples. For example, in a research study conducted by the National Center for Family and Marriage Research (NCFMR), Black women were found to experience a first divorce at a rate of 30.4 divorces per 1,000 women, compared with 16.3 and 18.1 divorces per 1,000 White and Latino women, respectively, in 2010 (Bowling Green State University, 2011).

Many predictors of marital dissatisfaction among Black couples (e.g., conflicts, affairs, feelings of marital unhappiness) are similar to those of other groups. The number of unmarried women has increased across all groups, but especially among African-American women. According to Wicker and Brodie (2004), the increase among African-American women is due in part to the disproportionate number of incarcerated African-American men, the growing disparities in educational attainment between African-American men and women, a high mortality rate of African-American men due to homicide, the number of African-American men who marry non–African-American women, and the number of African-American men who are gay. Marriage trends demonstrate that African-American women are less likely to marry than their counterparts in other ethnic groups (Dixon, 2009). Dixon found that African Americans report significantly less happiness in their marriages than Whites do and are less likely to remarry after divorce.

On the one hand, among the issues affecting Black couples—some of which are unique to them—are economic problems; unemployment due to the decreasing number of blue-collar jobs available; women making more money than their male partners, a situation that may cause conflict between spouses; substance abuse; blended families involving multiple children in the same household with different biological parents; a sex ratio that favors men over women, so fewer marriageable men are available (often contributing to a power imbalance in the marital relationship or an increased incidence of affairs on the part of the male); internalized racism of one or both partners; and the realities and pressures of daily racism faced by Black couples (Bethea & Allen, 2013; Green, Doherty, Fothergill, & Ensminger, 2012). These issues can significantly contribute to marital dissatisfaction. On the other hand, strengths of Black couples include the support system often provided by the couples' extended families and by the Black church and other Black organizations, the gender-egalitarian nature of Black couples' relationships, a cultural connectedness often shared by Black couples, and a flexible role orientation within the relationship. Black couples (and individuals) are more likely to seek support from religious leaders than counselors when they begin to experience relationship problems. Therefore, multiculturally sensitive counselors need to consider collaborating with clients' community resources (e.g., church leaders) when working with couples. In addition, in a strengths-based approach, sensitive counselors integrate couples' spiritual belief systems into psychotherapy. Review Case Study 9.1 for some insights into the complex issues that sometimes arise in counseling individuals of African descent.

Interracial Couples

Since the last of the miscegenation laws were repealed in 1967, there has been an increase in the number of interracial and intercultural couples in the United States. Like Black couples, interracial and intercultural couples face unique challenges, including lack of support by one or both members' families, the social stigma that continues to exist for those dating or marrying a partner of a different ethnic background, criticism within their own same-race communities, fears about their children's adjustment to a biracial identity, and social pressure from being stared at in public or being socially rejected solely on the basis of their being an interracial couple. Multiculturally competent counselors understand the common issues most couples deal with, as well as the unique issues faced by Black couples and interracial couples. (See Chapter 15 for additional information.) These unique issues can have a significant impact on the quality of the couple's relationship.

Children of African Descent

Children of African descent will often face different issues, depending on whether they come from middle- or working-class backgrounds and where they reside (e.g., urban, suburban, or rural areas). Inner-city children often face issues of poverty, disparity in educational resources, poorer mental and physical health care, the temptations of drugs and violence, teen pregnancy, growing up in predominately female-supported households, and fewer community support resources. Middle-class children of African descent, particularly those living in suburban areas, may face difficulty with issues regarding fitting into predominately White environments, feeling isolated from other children of color, being the only person of color in a classroom, having to develop bicultural skills that enable them to fit into all-Black and all-White environments, suffering parental divorce, growing up in predominately female-supported households, and having feelings of not being "Black enough" or "White enough," depending on their social environments (Day-Vines, Patton, & Baytops, 2003). When working with children of African descent, multiculturally competent counselors are aware of several issues, including racial identity; problems children might face given their school, home, and social environments; and how racism affects normal developmental challenges that children face. Effective counselors are aware of available culturally appropriate community resources for children and their families. Counselors also are open to including significant community members (e.g., one's minister) in a child's treatment if therapeutically indicated and if parental permission is given.

In addition to recognizing the aforementioned concerns, clinicians should be aware of the ongoing conversation about African-American children and their academic performance. In discussing the matter, it is highly probably that the concept of the "achievement gap" will be introduced. Simply put, the achievement gap is the chronic disparity in academic performance between White students and some ethnic minority students, including African-American students (Thomas, Caldwell, Faison, & Jackson, 2009; Lewis-McCoy, 2014). By no means is this a new dialogue; in fact, interest in the observed academic disparities between African-American and White students has existed for quite some time. However, although these examinations of the achievement gap have been undertaken by professionals from disparate professions (e.g., psychology, education), often they have been firmly entrenched in scientific racism and pseudoscience, which unfairly disparaged African Americans. As a consequence, the conversation about African-American students, education, and the achievement gap operated from the deficit perspective. According to the **deficit perspective**, students who underachieve academically, especially African-American students, are responsible for their own failure because they either lack the innate intellectual ability to perform better or they behave in a manner that is incongruent with the cultural values espoused by members of the educational setting. In either case, failure is held to be a function of the student alone.

Although the deficit perspective has had its share of ardent supporters, a number of scholars have criticized it because it does not account for the contextual/environmental variables that also contribute to African-American students' academic performance (Lucier-Greer, O'Neal, Arnold, Mancini, & Wickrama, 2014). By contrast, the **ecological perspective** asserted that academic performance cannot be adequately understood without taking into account the confluence of environmental variables (e.g., poverty, crime) and educational resources (e.g., qualified and supportive teachers; pedagogical strategies) and how they affect learning. For instance, wealth and income disparities, as well as an opportunity gap between Whites and African Americans borne of years of racial subjugation, leave urban and inner-city schools more vulnerable than schools in suburban and affluent neighborhoods (Carter & Weiner, 2013). For counseling professionals working in K–12 educational settings, an ability to advocate on behalf of students with the aim of alleviating the aforementioned barriers to the performance of students is essential (Woo, Henfield, & Choi, 2014). Activity 9.1 provides an opportunity to consider how an ecological perspective can be used to advocate for policies that address disparities that African Americans face.

ACTIVITY 9.1

In small groups, develop a list of policies that have disparate impacts on African Americans within the school and community contexts. Using an ecological perspective, discuss some policy revisions that could help level the playing field for African Americans and lead to more positive outcomes.

Black Middle-Class People and Mental Health

More than one third (38.4%) of the African-American population is middle class (U.S. Census Bureau, 2011a). Middle-class African Americans often face issues different from those encountered by working-class African Americans (Lewis-McCoy, 2014). For example, middle-class African Americans are more likely to have to operate biculturally—that is, in both all-Black and all-White environments. Trying to meet this challenge can be very stressful, especially for children and adolescents who are just learning the implications of being Black in predominately White environments. Middle-class Blacks who are isolated from the Black community may experience symptoms of depression and guilt for "making it" (i.e., "survivor guilt") when others in the Black community have not (Boyd-Franklin, 1989, 2013). Thus, social class can have a distinct impact on the presenting treatment issues of clients of African descent. Counselors need to assess and understand how social class interacts with, and affects, Black clients' treatment issues and experiences with discrimination.

Across all socioeconomic levels, institutional racism increases psychological distress for African Americans (Bryant, 2011; Paniagua, 2014; Pittman, 2011). Sawyer, Major, Casad, Townsend, and Mendes (2012) reported that racial discrimination is a strong predictor of psychological symptoms in general and somatization and anxiety in particular (Williams, Neighbors, & Jackson, 2008). A meta-analysis conducted by Paradies et al. (2015) found a relationship between internalized racism, on the one hand, and alcohol consumption, psychological distress, depression, and lower self-esteem, on the other. In sum, Blacks experience mental illness proportional to that of Whites, but the contributing factors may be different (Paniagua, 2014). Clearly, regardless of SES, the psychological and physical effects of racial discrimination are damaging. Counselors should assess the impact of discrimination on the lives of their clients of African descent.

Gender

African-American men and women often bring different treatment issues into the therapeutic realm. Obviously, environmental influences affect these issues. In the authors' individual counseling practice settings, some presenting issues of Black women were found to be single parenthood, weight, skin color, self-esteem, depression, anxiety, parenting issues, economic struggles, a perceived lack of available same-race romantic male partners, childhood sexual abuse, domestic violence, inappropriate use of anger as a defense, relational mistrust, and emotional intimacy. Presenting issues for men of African descent may include the formation of a Black male identity in a society that fears and rejects Black men as "problem people," absent or distant relationships with father figures, self-esteem, economic struggles, domestic and other violence, relational mistrust, emotional intimacy, depression, anxiety, and substance abuse.

All these issues are profoundly influenced by Black men being perceived as threatening or dangerous in our society and Black women being perceived as angry and unapproachable. These stereotypes can be internalized by Black men and women themselves, impeding the formation of healthy relationships. In addition, counselors who hold such stereotypic views are ineffective and often harm their clients of African descent.

Black Elderly Individuals

Black elderly people in the United States often face issues associated with poverty, poor mental and physical health care, illiteracy, gender discrepancies (e.g., Black elderly women far outnumber Black elderly men), employment discrimination, social and physical isolation, disability, and grief and bereavement (Schmitt, Branscombe, Postmes, & Garcia, 2014; Waite et al., 2013). Some of these issues are identical to those faced by elderly individuals as a whole in the United States. However, a higher percentage of Black elderly people than White elderly individuals is poor. Normal developmental aging issues are complicated by the interplay of poverty and racial discrimination. Issues faced by Black elderly Americans will vary with the individual's SES, health, and familial and community support. As with all subgroups within the Black community, multiculturally competent counselors are aware of economic, social, emotional, and spiritual resources in the community that can be helpful to this population. Counselors also attend to any negative stereotypes or assumptions they have about this client population.

Black Gays and Lesbians

Gay and lesbian African Americans often deal with multiple sources of oppression and discrimination (Choi, Paul, Ayala, Boylan, & Gregorich, 2013; Graham, Aronson, Nichols, Stephens, & Rhodes, 2011). They may feel conflicts in allegiances (i.e., allegiance to the Black community or allegiance to the gay community), struggle to integrate different aspects of their identities (e.g., being an individual of African descent, being a woman, and being a lesbian), and feel the pressure to hide their gay identity from friends and family. In addition, many African Americans hold a religious orientation, and many conservative Black churches do not support gays and lesbians. This stance on the part of those churches is often a painful experience for gays and lesbians who look to the Black church for social support and spiritual guidance, and it may increase the likelihood that they face discrimination in their own communities and families. Dealing with multiple sources of oppression can be extremely stressful. When working with gay and lesbian clients of African descent, it is important to assess whether identity conflict (e.g., issues as a Black person, a gay person, or both) are relevant to the presenting treatment issue in therapy. Finally, as with all other client populations, multiculturally competent counselors are aware of relevant community resources and are cognizant of their own negative assumptions about the client population with which they are working.

GENERAL MENTAL HEALTH ISSUES OF INDIVIDUALS OF AFRICAN DESCENT

The Centers for Disease Control and Prevention (2013) provides an excellent overview of many of the common physical and mental health issues that individuals of African descent face in America. In brief, some of those common health issues are diabetes, heart disease, HIV/AIDS, prostate cancer, higher infant mortality rates, substance abuse, sickle-cell anemia, lead poisoning, and teen pregnancy. As mentioned previously, lower-SES African Americans are more likely to receive poorer health care and not have health insurance. Many of these physical illnesses have an impact on the development of psychological disorders as well.

Wicker and Brodie (2004) found that African Americans are disproportionately represented in the lower-SES group, and research indicates that there is a correlation between SES and diagnosed mental health disorders. Ostrove, Feldman, and Adler (1999) found that both African Americans and Whites exhibited more depressive symptoms in lower-SES individuals in their respective populations than among those with higher levels of education, wealth, and income. Higher rates of mental illness often go hand in hand with poverty, higher rates of violence, and little attention to mental health treatment. In addition, there remains a negative social stigma within the African-American community around mental illness and treatment for mental illnesses (Wicker & Brodie, 2004). As a result, African Americans may underutilize mental health services, may seek them out only in times of crisis, and may have more severe symptoms once obtaining treatment. African Americans also are more likely to be misdiagnosed and to drop out of treatment earlier than their White counterparts (National Alliance on Mental Illness, 2012). Research has shown that African-American adolescents drop out of counseling between the first and third appointments, usually failing to complete a course of treatment (Copeland, 2006). Finally, African Americans are more likely to express their psychological symptoms in a physical form. Thus, they may seek medical treatment for physical complaints when they are actually suffering from psychological issues, thus leaving the psychological issues untreated (Eap, Gobin, Ng, & Nagayama Hall, 2010).

Disorders such as depression, anxiety, posttraumatic stress, and schizophrenia are seen in the African-American community at rates similar to those of Whites, even though misdiagnosis may be common. (See Chapter 18 for a detailed discussion.) However, it is important to recognize cultural influences on the presentation of symptoms, as well as to understand that racism, either blatant or institutional, can be a significant contributing factor to feelings of depression and anxiety, even if the client does not recognize that to be so. For example, Black women with depression may present with feelings of irritability or physical complaints, opening the door to misdiagnosis.

As discussed earlier, the Black community faces some uniquely negative environmental influences that affect African Americans' mental health. Among those influences might be higher unemployment rates, educational and occupational deficits, more grief and bereavement issues, higher rates of incarceration for Black men, higher rates of violence in urban communities, single-parent status and its concomitant economic hardships, the unavailability of same-race male partners for Black women, poverty, and lower educational attainment (Lawson & Lawson, 2013). These environmental issues most certainly influence the presentation of psychological issues in Black clients and are heavily influenced in turn by SES. For example, middle-class African Americans may not experience poverty, but they may be more likely to encounter institutionalized racism in the form of "glass ceilings" at work. In light of the relationship between psychological issues and environmental stressors due to race and cultural differences, complete Reflection 9.2 to begin considering how to address these differences in counseling.

REFLECTION 9.2

How might counselors of non-African descent address issues of racial and cultural differences with clients of African descent?

COMMON SUPPORT SYSTEMS FOR INDIVIDUALS OF AFRICAN DESCENT

Religion and spirituality are both vital components of traditional and contemporary African-American cultural values and practices (Pedersen, Lonner, Draguns, Trimble, & Scharron-del Rio, 2016). Therefore, a common support system for many clients of African descent will include "spiritually directed activities" (e.g., involvement in Black churches or mosques). Spirituality and religion "help combat societal oppression and increase economic support" (p. 299). In fact, African Americans are more likely to seek religious or spiritual experiences than admit to mental health concerns (Bryant-Davis et al., 2015; Debnam, Holt, Clark, Roth, & Southward, 2012; Ojelade, McCray, Ashby, & Meyers, 2011). Participation in religious activities allows for opportunities for self-expression, leadership, and community involvement. Counselors should elicit and encourage the use of spiritual resources if that approach is amenable to the student or client (Pedersen et al., 2016).

Other support systems include Black organizations, such as fraternities and sororities, and the National Association for the Advancement of Colored People (NAACP); the client's extended family; Sister Circles, which are social groups for Black women whose sole purpose is to provide one another with emotional and spiritual support; Brotherhood opportunities, which are social experiences for Black men that provide a connection with, and support for, Black men; and activities for children (e.g., sports, music). Activity 9.2 provides a method for accessing these support systems in counseling.

ACTIVITY 9.2

In small groups, develop a list of questions or areas for exploration that could be used in counseling individuals and families of African descent to identify and strengthen support systems.

AN AFROCENTRIC PSYCHOLOGICAL PERSPECTIVE

Earlier, we discussed and shaped an argument for and about the uniqueness of the life experience of people of African descent in America. Even with all the differences elaborated, however, it is not clear, nor has it been definitively established, that there exists a need to have counseling techniques that are designed specifically for this group of people and its subgroups. Still, Afrocentric psychotherapies are supportive of, and sensitive to, the cultural values of people of African descent. Thus, these psychotherapies can be used as a primary treatment modality or as an adjunct to other modes of treatment. In pursuit of that aim, this section will briefly explore Afrocentric therapeutic approaches and theory, as well as some traditional (Eurocentric) models of counseling with clients of African descent.

Much of the critical thinking in this area has centered on the inadequacies of Western psychological principles and techniques for understanding and treating individuals of African descent (Pedersen et al., 2016). Equally, many scholars of African descent have focused their attention on or around the concepts underlying the empowerment of African Americans to incorporate positive thoughts of themselves and their communities into their self-concepts—for example, "Black is beautiful" and "I'm Black and I'm proud" (Camp, 2015). The goal of these concepts as interventions is to endeavor to bring about individual and collective empowerment and to support a client's positive self-image, sense of self-respect, growth, and healthier emotional functioning.

NTU Psychotherapy

An Afrocentric approach to psychotherapy developed by Phillips (1990) is described as "spiritually based and aims to assist people and systems to become authentic and balanced within a shared energy and essence that is in alignment with natural order" (p. 55). NTU (pronounced "in-too") is a Bantu (central African) concept that describes a universal, unifying force that touches on all aspects of existence. The concept includes a spiritual force inside an individual and a spiritual force outside the individual and focuses on the essence of one's life. The basic principles of NTU psychotherapy include harmony, balance, interconnectedness, cultural awareness, and authenticity, all of which are Afrocentric values (Phillips, 1990; Jackson, Gregory, & Davis, 2004; Woods-Giscombe & Black, 2010; Wynn & West-Olatunji, 2008).

Counseling is considered to be a healing process based on a spiritual relationship between the client and the counselor (healer). The counselor assists the client in rediscovering his or her own natural alignment. There are five phases of NTU psychotherapy: Harmony, Awareness, Alignment, Actualize, and Synthesis. These phases of treatment are considered in a circular rather than linear time frame, so they may occur simultaneously or even "out of sequence" (Phillips, 1990; Jackson et al., 2004). The goal of treatment is to assist people and systems to become harmonious, balanced, and authentic within a shared energy and shared essence that are in alignment with the natural order. An additional goal is to help the client function within the guidelines of the Nguzo Saba (the seven principles of Kwanzaa). Natural order is described as a unity of mind, body, and spirit throughout life. Relationships within one's life are purposeful and orderly and, at their base, spiritual. Further, Phillips (1990) asserted that "natural order" implies that our lives and our relationships have a purpose and a direction. Consequently, it is our ongoing task in life to be in tune with the natural order.

In NTU counseling, the counselor's role is to assist the client in reestablishing harmony. This role implies a shared responsibility between the client and the counselor—a role that is generally contrary to the more traditional approaches of doing therapy whereby the client assumes most of the responsibility for his or her own treatment. Although NTU emphasizes the special nature of the relationship between the counselor and the client, it also encourages counselors to explore their own connections with clients more clearly. Counselors (healers) are encouraged to use their intuition and inspiration as a part of the therapeutic experience. This kind of exploration is not pathologized, as in the concept of Freudian countertransference, nor is it diminished, as in client-centered therapy.

Pros and Cons of Traditional (Eurocentric) Counseling Approaches with Clients of African Descent

Three traditional counseling approaches are the client-centered, psychodynamic, and Adlerian psychotherapy approaches. We discuss each of these in turn, with particular attention to their utility with African-American clients. Reflection 9.3 challenges the reader to consider how the three approaches may be applied in counseling.

REFLECTION 9.3

In reviewing the key characteristics of the three traditional counseling approaches presented here, consider how you could apply concrete techniques and assumptions from these approaches when counseling individuals and families of African descent.

Client-Centered Counseling

The primary characteristic of this treatment modality is its focus on the therapeutic relationship between the counselor and the client and on how client change is facilitated through the development of that relationship. Conditions sought in the therapeutic relationship include genuineness, congruence, positive regard, acceptance of the client, and empathic understanding (Johnson, Kim, & Church, 2010; Witty & Adomaitis, 2014). The therapeutic process moves a client from a place of rigidity, remoteness from feelings and experience, and distance from other people toward fluidity, acceptance of feelings and experiences, and unity and integration of one's self. This approach's ultimate goal of client self-acceptance is consistent with the African worldview (i.e., unity and integration).

With the client of African descent, client-centered counseling has utility especially when helping to set or create conditions in which the client may feel comfortable and supported within the counseling relationship. Creating those conditions is accomplished by developing rapport and being empathic, understanding, and nonjudgmental with clients. That accomplished, it is then possible for clients to begin the process of exploring their own problems (Witty & Adomaitis, 2014).

A limitation of this approach is its idea that the counselor's intent to promote growth in the client seems to suggest a hierarchical relationship that is more consistent with a European rather than an African worldview. Further, the approach appears to suggest that the client lacks, in some basic way, an understanding of self or the concept of harmony and unity that is inherent in the African worldview. Finally, the focus remains solely on the individual, primarily without any focus on the connection to others as a part of the concept of self, which is rooted in a connection or existence within a community. In an African worldview, the concept of the individual exists within the context of community (unity), as well as harmony or balance within the larger universe structure. This concept brings to mind the Akan proverb, "I am because we are. We are because I am."

Psychodynamic Counseling

Psychodynamic theory focuses on the individual and not the community. The idea of individualism is expressed in the notion that the change process is dependent on the work or effort of the individual undergoing treatment. Mental processes are considered to be largely unconscious. Psychoanalysis, which is based in psychodynamic theory, believes that impulses, which are described as sexual, cause nervous and mental disorders (Freud, 1924). These general principles are inconsistent with an Afrocentric framework.

In Hall's (2004) review of the book *Psychotherapy with African American Women* by Jackson and Greene (2000), she acknowledged some of the benefits (e.g., the capacity to deal with the individual and multiple complexities of their lives, a focus on early childhood experiences and their impact on client functioning in later life) and limitations associated with psychodynamic psychotherapy with a population of African descent. The primary limitation discussed is the lack of attention to cultural factors. In particular, the authors asserted that theories and treatment approaches need to be reformulated to acknowledge the effects that racial and class stereotypes—legacies of slavery, present-day racism, African or Caribbean cultural influences, and gender-based maltreatment—have on the psychological lives of women and the interplay between these factors and the individual Black woman's intrapsychic world. Exploration of these factors needs to be encouraged and understood in the context of the therapeutic dyad. Other shortcomings of traditional psychodynamic theories include a tendency to pathologize cultural differences, the limited experience that many analysts have with women patients of African descent, the authoritarian style of the analyst with respect to the client, heterosexism, and the likelihood that White therapists will hold racial attitudes that have not been addressed in their own therapy (Pedersen et al., 2016).

Adlerian Counseling

The Adlerian approach focuses on social interest as an organizing principle (Guardia & Banner, 2012; Perkins-Dock, 2005). The approach explores an individual's social nature during interactions and the influences of the social environment on the individual's development. Thus, the Adlerian approach is thought to be respectful of both the individual and her or his cultural heritage. Inherent in the approach is attention to the influence of cultural factors on development and on the client's presenting treatment issues. The theoretical principles of the Adlerian approach appear conducive to therapeutic work with clients of African descent. These principles include the concept of collective unity and social interest, the importance of the family atmosphere, an emphasis on collaborative goal setting, the influence of a multigenerational legacy, and the flexibility of intervention strategies (Moore & McDowell, 2014). Collective unity and social interest consists of working toward fitting in within the community, contributing to the community, and supporting the cultural value system of many Blacks.

The family atmosphere concept emphasizes harmony in interpersonal relationships, interdependence, and mutual obligation for creating harmony and peace. The concept focuses on cooperation, and the goals of counseling are chosen collaboratively. Finally, Perkins-Dock (2005) asserted that Adlerian counseling is congruent with many traditional beliefs of people of African descent and provides flexibility within the range of interventions that it is able to offer.

Clearly, there is some utility in the use of traditional counseling approaches with clients of African descent. However, the treatment outcome research has been equivocal. For example, cognitive behavioral therapy has been found to be effective with African Americans and Whites in the treatment of anxiety disorders (Carter, Mitchell, & Sbrocco, 2012; Kendall, Hudson, Gosch, Flannery-Schroeder, & Suveg, 2008; Stewart & Chambles, 2009). Yon and Scogin (2008) found behavioral treatment generally effective in a sample of older Black medical patients. Multiculturally competent counselors are aware of the current literature on the effectiveness of treatment approaches for the population for which they are providing services; hence, they do not assume that "one approach fits all" when working with clients of African descent.

GUIDELINES FOR WORK WITH CLIENTS OF AFRICAN DESCENT

The ideal or "gold standard" for counselors is to be trained in an African-centered worldview counseling system and to employ the theory and techniques of that system when working with clients of African descent. The belief in the values espoused by this worldview system could be employed by counselors of African descent and non-African descent alike. Voices from the Field 9.2 illustrates one view from an African-American licensed clinical professional counselor.

Voices from the Field 9.2

Providing services to African Americans requires an understanding of the historical, cultural, and socioeconomic factors that may affect physical and mental health care. For instance, it is highly probable, within the context of U.S. culture, that minority groups live in impoverished conditions that are compounded by a lack of community, medical, and behavioral resources. Socioeconomic factors often affect one's ability to maintain health and wellness, because of the rising cost of medications, insurance premiums, co-payments, and clinical procedures. Even with the implementation of the Patient Protection and Affordable Care Act in 2010, many African Americans are reluctant to seek care for mental health problems. Some are underemployed and underinsured, and even when they have insurance coverage, they encounter many challenges regarding access to care and poorer quality care. Counseling professionals should be cognizant of these topics when working with clients of African descent.

I worked with an African-American client by the name of Lisa. She resides in a segregated, crime-ridden neighborhood with low property values and limited job opportunities. Living with multiple complex physical ailments made it difficult for her to address her feelings of anxiety and depression. Lisa didn't graduate from high school but was able to maintain her family duties despite the stressors associated with being a single, unmarried woman with four children. As her counselor, I used mindfulness to help Lisa relax, monitor her thoughts, and change her perceptions of her current situation, all of which together improved her ability to cope. As a clinician, I understood that it was important for me to help her realize that depression can be expressed differently in Black women because of the cultural tradition that they are perceived as "strong," in addition to historical and family experiences. Although direct assistance may not be available to address difficulties experienced by clients of African descent, it is essential that counselors acknowledge barriers and help their clients find the best outcome to enhance their daily living. Behavioral health providers with advanced clinical judgment and excellent communication skills can increase the confidence levels of this population. Mental health professionals who master the skills of remaining silent, listening, reading, and observing will demonstrate consistency and trustworthiness, which are vital to the client's adherence to treatment. Motivational interviewing, empathy, respect, assessments, and a person-centered approach are just some of the tools that can be used during therapeutic interactions. For example, when addressing sensitive subjects, implore the client to "Help me understand...." and ask questions such as "What's a typical day...?" and "If it's ok with you, I would like to share some information about...." By questioning and being clearer about using the "right words," counselors can have candid conversations with African-American clients, regardless of their differences, to promote an environment of openness and trust.

~ *Nicole Ford, Licensed Clinical Professional Counselor, Chicago, IL*

Practitioners who continue to use European worldview counseling systems and techniques with clients of African descent must become aware of the limitations of these systems when it comes to treatment efficacy. Case Study 9.2 provides a clinical example of culturally centered practice with a family of African descent. Finally, Table 9.2 provides examples in the popular media that counselors and counselor trainees may want to explore to better understand the experiences of clients of African descent.

CASE STUDY 9.2

Mr. M. called to set up an appointment for his son. Mr. M. admits that no one in his family has ever sought the help of a mental health professional. He seems at a loss as to what to do. His son had recently seen a psychiatrist who had prescribed an antidepressant medication the previous week. The counselor noted that Mr. M. spoke English with an accent.

At the first session, the counselor met with the 15-year-old client and his parents, Mr. and Mrs. M. The three older female children in the family did not attend the session. While the son waited outside, the counselor spoke with the parents about their concerns. Mrs. M. was an energetic African-American female who expressed her concern that her son is depressed and had seemingly been going downhill for several months since entering high school. She noted that he had always been somewhat reserved and had few friends, but things had gotten worse just after he began high school, even though he had a girlfriend. His grades were dropping at school, he seemed sad, and now he was talking about suicide.

Mrs. M. stated that she had a close relationship with her son and tried to talk with him all the time about how he was doing, but she did not really know what was bothering him. Mr. M. stated that he was concerned about his son as well, especially about his son's grades at school and how poor grades would limit his options in life. Mr. M. stated that he was helping his son with his homework and with studying, but that his efforts were not helping at the high school level even though they had made a positive difference in grade school.

Mr. M. noted that he had grown up poor in West Africa and that education had been a way out of that situation for him in the United States. He did not have any idea why his son might be depressed, because he had so much more than what Mr. M. had as a child. However, he did speculate that his son's relationship with his girlfriend, who was Asian, might be a part of the problem, as her father did not like her dating someone Black. Mr. M. did not understand why his son would put himself in such a position knowing that it was against the wishes of the girlfriend's father. He also felt that his wife supported the son remaining in the relationship even though he hoped his son would leave it.

Throughout the conversation, the son, Reginald, sat passively, listening to his parents and completing paperwork. He did not interject or overtly disagree with anything that either of his parents stated about him or his situation when they were speaking about him. When asked about these things in their presence, he acknowledged that he had been depressed, but he did not know why, and that he was having trouble at school.

At this point, the counselor discussed with Reginald and his parents the limits on confidentiality. Included in the discussion were limits related to suicidal/homicidal ideation. Reginald and the counselor both agreed on issues that his parents wanted to be directly informed of, such as drugs, suicide, or violence. But outside of these stated issues, Reginald was allowed to discuss his concerns without having to report everything back to his parents. Both Reginald and his parents acknowledged their understanding of these limitations on confidentiality.

Mr. and Mrs. M. were asked to wait outside while the counselor and Reginald spoke. Reginald was a very quiet, soft-spoken, and reserved young man who was passive in his presentation. His posture, facial expression, and body language suggested a person who was sad, but his verbal responses seemed incongruent with his presentation. Although he said, "I don't know" often, intuitively the counselor felt that such statements were inaccurate. Instead, it felt like he was being somewhat evasive. When talking about his girlfriend, he did not appear to have any joy, but he stated that she was the only thing good in his life. When asked how he felt about his girlfriend's father disliking him because he is Black without ever having met him, he acknowledged that it was dumb, but did not indicate any strong emotional reaction to the situation. Exploring the issue further with him, the counselor introduced emotion-laden words such as *hurt* and *angry*. Reginald stated that he "guessed" he felt a little angry about it, since the father did not know him personally and just assumed that he was dumb and was a "thug with baggy pants." He also stated that it bothered him that he could not see or talk to his girlfriend when her father was in town because of the father's reaction to the relationship. He denied being close to his family and stated that he did not care for his eldest sister because she was mean to him. He stated further that he and his best male friend were no longer close because the friend would not come over to his house anymore. Reginald also stated that his best friend seemed to have made other friends outside their relationship. He denied any plans for suicide, but said that he'd rather be dead if he couldn't be with his girlfriend. He indicated that his goal for counseling was to feel better, but he did not know what that meant to him.

Within this initial session, some of the culture-centered counseling techniques were implemented. However, it should be clear from the case description that the use of these ideas, concepts, and techniques indicated some subtle rather than overt differences in treatment at this initial stage. Examples of culture-centered practices and their use in the session include the following:

1. Establish that counseling is a collaborative process involving, in this case, the client, the counselor, and the family. If necessary, others, including friends, siblings, school personnel, and other members of the community (e.g., a minister), could be brought into the process.
2. Explore the problem or issue as existing with the family system (e.g., the client and his parents) and not just as a problem of the individual. Probing the parents led to an understanding of the family structure and the fact that the family has had a complex primary cultural history (African father, African-American mother) which has influenced their child-rearing practices. For example, Mr. M. is focused primarily on his son's educational development and seems to perceive other issues as secondary. It will be important in future sessions for the counselor to get Mr. M. to understand that he can help his son develop a greater cognitive and emotional balance in his life—a balance that involves an emotional focus. In addition, future sessions might explore whether there are any differences between the parents in child-rearing practices and, if so, what they are. If there are differences, they might account, in part, for Reginald's imbalanced relationships with his parents. The issue can be explored in a meeting with the parents, either together with Reginald or separately. Parental involvement will be maintained in treatment both formally and informally. Often, informal involvement occurs before or after sessions via simple acknowledgments of client progress, parental concerns, and so on.
3. Communicate openly and honestly. The discussion of confidentiality, especially as it relates to the relationship between the counselor and Reginald, as well as the counselor's relationship with Reginald's parents, is respectful and sets the tone for their work together. Speaking with the parents about concerns that Reginald might communicate in counseling exhibits the concept of openness and honesty. Reginald can then feel free to discuss what he believes he needs to talk about in therapy, or he can limit his discussion. Either way, the end result is that he actively makes choices for himself and his own treatment.
4. Set goals collaboratively. Although the responsibility for establishing goals resides with Reginald and with whatever he decides might help him feel better, the role of the counselor is to assist him in achieving his goals.

5. Assess "the problem." Assessment is ongoing and is informed by what is said within the session, by the counselor's intuition or felt sense, and by the counselor's observations and emotional reactions to the client. In this session, the counselor's intuition or felt sense overtly informed his belief about Reginald's level of depression as well as about the depth of the problem, even though it appeared that Reginald was minimizing it.

6. Allow the ebb and flow of the session to be organic. There was no overt limit imposed on the time the counselor spent with the parents or the client, or on the time the counselor spent discussing a particular topic. The exploration occurred in such a fashion as to be thorough enough that any change in topic felt like a natural progression. Topics were explored enough to be satisfactory and were not belabored. The focus of the session was not technique driven. Instead, the approach used the skills necessary and appropriate for Reginald's situation and presenting issues.

7. Focus ongoing treatment on the continued development of the relationship between the client and his or her family. The process of assessing and exploring Reginald in his cultural context will continue, and he will be assisted in becoming more aware of his own wants, needs, and desires, as well as in learning how they may interact and affect his emotional well-being. The organic flow of this exploration will lead to more concrete examples of when Reginald's emotional needs are met, when they are not met, and how the choices that he makes in a variety of situations determine whether his needs are met. Future sessions will help him explore and process "instances of success" (i.e., when he had his emotional needs met and the process which occurred to accomplish that goal). Subsequently, this process will be explored for its utility in how he can make empowering choices for himself. A goal of counseling might be to help Reginald evaluate the efficacy of his own therapeutic process throughout treatment. Ultimately, a hope for this client is that he can accomplish better emotional balance (well-being).

TABLE 9.2 Media Resources of the Individual and Family of African Descent

Movies

12 Years a Slave (2013). Memoir about a free Black man from New York who was abducted and sold into slavery.

American History X (1998). An American crime drama of a former neo-Nazi skinhead who tries to prevent his younger brother from going down the same path as he did.

A Time to Kill (1996). A film depicting the struggles of a young lawyer who is defending a Black male accused of murdering the two men who raped his 10-year-old daughter. The jury's verdict sparks the rebirth of the Ku Klux Klan.

CNN Presents: Black in America (2008). A multipart series of documentaries hosted by Soledad O'Brien on various issues regarding Black people in America.

For Colored Girls (2010). A drama depicting the intertwined lives of nine women revealing different issues that affect women of color.

Ghosts of Mississippi (1996). An American drama film based on the 1994 trial of Byron De La Beckwith, the White supremacist accused of assassinating civil rights leader Medgar Evers in 1963.

Glory (1989). An American dramatic war film about the first formal unit of the Union Army during the American Civil War to be made up entirely of African-American men.

Higher Learning (1995). An American dramatic film that follows the lives of three incoming freshmen at a fictional university and their encounter with racial tension, rape, and the meaning of an education on a university campus.

The Butler (2013). A historical dramatic film produced and directed by Lee Daniels that is loosely based on the real life of Eugene Allen, an African-American butler at the White House who served eight different presidents during his tenure, and the notable political and social events of the 20th century that he witnessed.

Malcolm X (1992). A biographical drama depicting the controversial and influential life of activist Malcolm X.

Precious (2009). A dramatic film depicting the life of Precious, an overweight, abused, illiterate teen who is pregnant with her second child and is invited to attend an alternative school in the hopes that she can change her life's direction.

Remember the Titans (2000). A sports drama based on the true story of Herman Boone, an African-American football coach who tries to introduce a racially diverse team at T. C. Williams High School in Alexandria, Virginia.

Roots (1977). A television miniseries based on author Alex Haley's family line progressing from ancestor Kunta Kinte's enslavement to his descendants' liberation.

Rosewood (1997). A dramatization of the 1923 Rosewood massacre in Florida, when a White lynch mob attacked an African-American community.

Selma (2014). A drama based on the chronicle of events taking place during the 1965 Selma-to-Montgomery voting rights marches led by Martin Luther King, Jr., and other civil rights leaders.

Skin (2008). A British–South African biographical film of a Black girl who was born to two White parents in South Africa during the apartheid era.

The Black Power Mixtape 1967–1975 (2011). A documentary that examines the evolution of the Black Power movement.

The Color of Fear (1994). A film that examines the state of race relations in America from the perspective of eight men from various ethnic and racial backgrounds.

The Color Purple (1985). A dramatic film about a Black southern woman who is faced with racism, poverty, and sexism during the early 1900s.

The Great Debaters (2007). A dramatic film based on the true story of Tony Scherman, who inspired a group of African-American students to form Harvard's f first-ever debate team.

Books

Alexander, M. (2012). *The new Jim Crow: Mass incarceration in the age of colorblindness.* New York, NY: The New Press.

Angelou, M. (1997). *I know why the caged bird sings.* New York, NY: Bantam Dell Publishing.

Bloom, H. (2008). *Zora Neale Hurston's Their eyes were watching God.* New York, NY: Infobase Publishing.

Du Bois, W. E. B. (1903). *The souls of black folk.* New York, NY: Oxford University Press.

Ellison, R. (2010). *Invisible man.* New York, NY: Vintage.

Harris, A. L. (2011). *Kids don't want to fail.* Cambridge, MA: Harvard University Press.

Hayley, A. (2007). *Roots: The saga of an American family.* New York, NY: Vanguard Press.

Malcolm, X., Haley, A., & Handler, M. S. (1992). *The autobiography of Malcolm X.* New York, NY: Ballantine Books.

Morrison, T. (1999). *The bluest eye.* New York, NY: Random House.

Neal, M. A. (2015). *New black man.* New York, NY: Routledge.

(Continued)

TABLE 9.2 Media Resources of the Individual and Family of African Descent (continued)

Obama, B. (2007). *Dreams from my father: A story of race and inheritance.* Edinburgh, UK: Canongate Books.

Shange, N. (2010). *For colored girls who have considered suicide/when the rainbow is enuf.* New York, NY: Simon and Schuster.

Washington, B. T. (1986). *Up from slavery.* New York, NY: Penguin.

Wilkerson, I. (2010). *The warmth of other sons: The epic story of America's great migration.* New York, NY: Vintage.

Woodson, C. G. (2006). *The mis-education of the negro.* San Diego, CA: Book Tree.

Wright, R. (2000). *Native son.* New York, NY: Random House.

Websites

Africans in America (http://www.pbs.org/wgbh/aia/home.html): A companion Web site to Africans in American, a 6-hour public television series.

Black Press USA (http://www.blackpressusa.com/): News outlet reporting stories as the voice of the Black community.

Center for Racial Justice Innovation (https://www.raceforward.org/about): Focuses on complex race issues to help people take effective action toward racial equity.

Celebrating the Fullness of Black Womanhood (http://www.forharriet.com): This Black-owned website features articles based on issues faced by African-American women.

Coalition of Schools Educating Boys of Color (http://www.coseboc.org/): This is the only national educational organization of practitioners focused solely on promoting the educational success of boys and young men of color.

Journal of African American History (http://www.jaah.org): This journal publishes articles based on all aspects of the African-American experience.

Journal of Blacks in Higher Education (http://www.jbhe.com): This journal publishes articles on the status and prospects for African Americans in higher education.

Journal of Black Studies (http://jbs.sagepub.com/): This journal publishes articles on the dynamic, innovative, and creative research into the Black experience.

National Association for the Advancement of Colored People (http://www.naacp.org): This organization focuses on the political, educational, social, and economic equality of rights for all people and on eliminating race-based discrimination.

State Sanctioned Black Lives Matter Movement (http://statesanctioned.com/black-lives-matter-movement/): Web site that reports current news and resources dedicated to documenting and analyzing state-sanctioned violence in the United States.

Schott Foundation for Public Education (http://www.schottfoundation.org): This Web site features articles, resources, blogs, and voluntary information to provide not only a route out of poverty, but also the possibility to transform young lives.

Understanding the Plight of African Americans During the Period of Post-Civil War Reconstruction (http://www.history.com/topics/american-civil-war/reconstruction): This Web site, a division of the History channel, provides articles, speeches, and videos on the plight of African Americans in history.

Summary

This chapter has explored historical and current influences on the experiences of people of African descent in America, the cultural values of this diverse group, racial identity and acculturation, and common issues faced by Black children, men, women, and other subpopulations within the Black community. The narrative presented has some important implications for counseling practice.

The role of the counselor for African-American clients may need to be broader than that for White clients. For example, African-American clients may need help in dealing with agencies and making connections to the community. Multiculturally competent counselors are to bring up differences in background; explore clients' feelings about coming to counseling and how it will be beneficial to them as clients; explore clients' worldviews; establish egalitarian therapeutic relationships that can be aided by self-disclosure; assess assets of clients, such as support systems, family, community resources, and church; explore external factors that might be related to the presenting problem; not dismiss racism as "just an excuse;" and help clients define goals and find solutions to their problems.

Neville and Walters (2004) discussed the harmful effects of counselors employing a color-blind racial ideology, which is a "set of beliefs that serves to minimize, ignore, or distort the existence of race and racism" (p. 95). At its core is the belief that racism is a thing of the past and that race and racism no longer play a significant role in current social and economic realities. This belief is obviously a harmful one in working with the African-American population because it is invalidating and dismissive of clients' experiences. Therefore, in counseling clients of African descent, recognizing, acknowledging, and honoring the client's ethnic and cultural background is an important rapport-building tool for an effective therapeutic relationship.

Multiculturally competent counselors also understand that clients of African descent may display cultural mistrust toward counselors. Effective counselors do not pathologize or personalize this mistrust. Instead, they understand where it comes from and how it develops. They acknowledge it and discuss it openly in counseling.

It is important to explain to clients of African descent what counseling is and what the boundaries of the counselor–client relationship are. It is also important to engage in thoughtful informed-consent procedures with the clients. Black clients may see counseling as intrusive, so counselors should not use first names with older clients, as doing so might be seen as disrespectful. The multiculturally competent counselor asks clients what they would like to be called. Finally, African-American clients may prefer African-American counselors. Thus, if a client has a racial preference for a counselor and it is possible to meet that client's need, every attempt should be made to do so. Not all clients of African descent will have a same-race counselor preference, but some will.

Review Questions

1. What are microaggressions? Describe the different types of microaggressions and provide examples of each.
2. Why is acculturation important to assess when working with individuals and families of African descent? How might you assess an individual's level of acculturation?
3. Identify and describe general values associated with individuals of African descent. How might these values affect the counseling process?
4. Describe some of the common physical and mental health issues that individuals of African descent face in America. What factors might contribute to the underutilization of mental health services among African Americans?
5. What counseling approaches were discussed in this chapter? What are the benefits and challenges of each?

10 Individuals and Families of Arab Descent

Sylvia C. Nassar-McMillan, Aisha Al-Qimlass, and Laura McLaughlin Gonzalez

PREVIEW

Who are Arab Americans? There are many more answers to this question since the New York City Twin Towers tragedy of September 11, 2001, an event that unwittingly seemed to catapult this population into the public eye. This chapter will help you determine the accuracy of your perceptions about Arab Americans. Despite their educational, professional, and economic successes over the past 100-plus years, Arab Americans have had a somewhat turbulent immigration history in the United States. Although leading advocacy groups estimate their number in the U.S. population at over 3.5 million, research on mental health and counseling, particularly within the post-9/11 context, has only begun to emerge. In this chapter, key issues about historic and geographic descriptions of the Arab Middle East, as well as the immigration history from that region, will be addressed. Sociopolitical aspects of the Arab-American experience will be explored next, along with the diversity of the population. Cultural characteristics, such as collectivism, religion and faith, socioeconomic demographics, and communication styles, will be explored, followed by acculturation and identity development from a current-day perspective. The final sections of this chapter will address mental health issues and guidelines for counseling Arab Americans and include illustrative case studies.

ARAB-AMERICAN HETEROGENEITY

For many people in the United States, terms like *Arab* or *Middle Eastern* are associated with a complex mix of images and impressions, but few facts. Efforts to clarify the boundaries and contents of these terms are necessary for counseling students who seek to increase their multicultural competence. Although there is not one comprehensive definition of the Middle East or its Arab citizens, the perspectives discussed next should alleviate some of the confusion.

The region centered around the Persian Gulf became known to English speakers as "the **Middle East**" or the "Near Orient" in the early 1900s. Centuries of important historical events have occurred in the Middle East, one of the earliest cradles of civilization. The area is also rich in religious history, with cities such as Jerusalem and Mecca within its boundaries. Among the religious groups coexisting in the Middle East are Muslims, Christians, Jews, Bah'ai, and Druze.

Such a confluence of political and spiritual activity has meant that the Middle East holds great diversity in a relatively small area. It encompasses both Arab-speaking and non-Arab-speaking countries; examples of the latter include Iran (where Farsi is spoken), Turkey, and Israel (Nassar-McMillan, Ajrouch, & Hakim-Larson, 2014).

Owing in large part to the rich diversity concentrated within the area referred to as the Middle East, not all citizens residing there are Arabs. Even some populations in America can trace their heritage to parts of the Middle East; however, their specific ancestral communities have a cultural and linguistic tradition that distinguishes them from the Arab-speaking majority within the region (Samhan, 2014). For example, those who trace their ancestry to the Kurds, Berbers, or Chaldeans are not considered Arabs, although they are linked to regions in present-day Iraq, Syria, Iran, and Turkey (Nassar-McMillan, 2010; Samhan, 2014). Geographically, **Arabs** are people who have ancestral ties to the Saudi Arabian peninsula and historically have practiced Islam (Salameh, 2011).

Another way of indicating Arab people has been through the common use of the Arabic language; however, this strategy is not without its conceptual limitations, too. Alternatively, Arabs can be described in varying ways in terms of race or skin color, so it is more appropriate to consider the term *Arab* as an ethnic or cultural category (Nassar-McMillan, Ajrouch, et al., 2014). For the purposes of this chapter, **Arab American** is used to mean any individual who defines himself or herself as part of that ethnic group and has a heritage linked to the League of Arab States as described next. Because not all countries in the *geographic* Middle East self-define as "Arab" (e.g., Turkey, Afghanistan), many contemporary scholars define those originating from the **Arab Middle East** (self-defined as a country of origin belonging to the League of Arab States) as being of Arab descent.

The **League of Arab States** was founded in 1945. The 22 member states are Algeria, Bahrain, the Comoros, Djibouti, Egypt, Iraq, Jordan, Kuwait, Lebanon, Libya, Mauritania, Morocco, Oman, Palestine, Qatar, Saudi Arabia, Somalia, Sudan, Syria, Tunisia, the United Arab Emirates, and Yemen (Nassar-McMillan, Ajrouch, et al., 2014). These are sometimes grouped into the Gulf states (i.e., Kuwait, Saudi Arabia, Oman), Greater Syria (including Iraq and Lebanon), and the area of North Africa referred to as the Maghreb (i.e., Egypt, Libya, Morocco). Some Arab-speaking countries are not part of the Arab League, however. This intercontinental alliance again points to the diversity of the Arab world, with some countries having a significant Western influence (e.g., Lebanon) and other countries being fairly isolated from such influence (e.g., Sudan, Yemen). The dialect of spoken Arabic, cultural and religious traditions, political history, and geography are all dimensions along which the Arab League countries may differ.

Of note, recently the term *Middle Eastern/North African* (*MENA*) has emerged to reference individuals of Arab descent. Developed by the World Bank for fiscal use, it does not maintain the same parameters as the term *Arab American* (Nassar-McMillan, Ajrouch, et al., 2014) and should not be used synonymously with the population of interest for this chapter.

Arab Muslims make up about one fifth of the world's **Muslim** population, or adherents of the religion of Islam, indicating that the terms *Muslim* and *Arab* are not completely overlapping or synonymous (Samhan, 2014). In addition, the Arab-American demographic majority is made up of Christian Arabs who immigrated to the United States over a longer period than their Muslim Arab counterparts.

Subject to colonialism over the past several centuries by multiple Western entities, the Arab Middle East has faced a variety of pressures. Although the United States is currently the most powerful Western country attempting to wield influence in the Arab Middle East, both Britain and France have historically held colonies and swayed policy in the region. Some of the borders that are disputed today were dictated at the end of World War I when the Ottoman Empire was carved up by the victorious allies. Although this political history can be complex, it takes on increased importance in light of the current struggles among Western powers and the various religious, ethnic, and cultural groups that populate the Arab Middle East. Misunderstandings, conflicts, and wars have contributed to the flow of Arab refugees and immigrants that now populate the United States and may seek out counseling services.

Arabs have arrived in the United States in four distinct waves of immigration. Each group had different reasons for immigrating, different characteristics, and different experiences in their host or adopted country. The first group of immigrants came primarily from Lebanon, Syria, Palestine, and Jordan at the end of the 19th century and beginning of the 20th century (Abdelhady, 2014; Bale, 2010). Most of them were Christians who wanted to escape the Islamic Ottoman Empire. They tended to be uneducated laborers with little in the way of material resources. Upon arrival, they maintained their communities by settling in ethnic enclaves in various cities in the United States. Their religion allowed them to settle into Christian-influenced areas with fewer challenges than later Muslim immigrants would face (Abdelhady, 2014; Samhan, 2014).

The second group of Arab immigrants arrived after World War II (Abdelhady, 2014; Bale, 2010). These individuals were fleeing their homelands that were wracked with political tensions. Among them were Palestinians who were escaping civil war in 1948 as the British mandate in the area expired and territories were seized by Israel, but the wave also included Syrians, Jordanians, Egyptians, Iraqis, and, to a lesser extent, Yemenis and Lebanese. Some have called this exodus the **brain drain** (Nassar-McMillan, Ajrouch, et al., 2014), because those who left were formally educated Muslims with the means to escape undesirable situations.

The third wave of immigrants was also composed predominantly of formally educated Muslims, but this group's motivation was a search for better lives as part of the American Dream. Restrictions on immigration had been eased in the 1960s, making it easier to take advantage of the opportunity. Many of the people arriving at this time were Palestinians who wanted to escape the Israeli occupation (Samhan, 2014).

Finally, the Gulf War created a situation in which refugees had very few options left and were compelled to flee. This group included, for example, Iraqis who worked with the United States in its war efforts in the region and who faced harsh consequences for that choice (Abdelhady, 2014; Samhan, 2014). Renewed conflict in the region has led more Iraqi refugees to the United States, both directly and indirectly after stopovers in refugee camps.

In sum, Arab Americans have come from a variety of backgrounds (e.g., religious, geographic, ethnic) and have made their homes in the United States at various times and for various reasons. The history, culture, and religion of their country of origin may continue to influence Arabs in their new communities, but it is also possible to meet a fourth-generation Arab American for whom this country is his or her only frame of reference. In terms of U.S. Census categories, most individuals of Arab descent are from Lebanon, Syria, Palestine, Egypt, and Iraq. Estimates are that there are approximately 3.5 million Arab Americans, although census data have not always reflected a category to distinguish this group (Arab American Institute, n.d.). Readers who have spent less time learning about the community of Arab descent in the United States may feel surprise (as described in Reflection 10.1) as they uncover individuals and groups that they did not know were Arab American.

REFLECTION 10.1

Reactions to National Public Radio (NPR) Story (January 31, 2008, Morning Edition)
Kibbe at the Crossroads: A Lebanese Kitchen Story

> I am tuned in to NPR and hear the sweet undulations of a southern drawl. I believe the man's name is Pat Davis, and he is the current owner of Abe's BAR-B-Q in Clarksdale, Mississippi. To my surprise, he is talking about his father, the original owner of the restaurant since 1924 and an immigrant from Lebanon. Another Lebanese immigrant to the Delta area, Chafik Chamoun, tells about how he started his business by going door to door peddling goods to his neighbors. No one had very much then (1950s), and sometimes his neighbors would buy from him just to help sustain him for one more week, not because they needed anything or had much to spare themselves. Indeed, when he opened his restaurant in 1960, he had the chance to return the favor. The civil rights era had created enormous tensions between African Americans and European Americans, so the Lebanese immigrants in the southeast were among the few who would serve food to their Black patrons. I was surprised by this history, generations of Arab Americans building the culture of the United States in ways I had not suspected. I also was touched by the willingness of people on the margin to help each other, looking past their differences and seeing the commonness of humanity.

Reflect on the following:

- What are your thoughts and feelings about this reaction by the Lebanese Americans to the plight of African Americans in the 1960s?
- How might this reflection influence the way you work with clients of Arab descent?
- Do you know anyone who self-identifies as Arab American?
- What do you know about this person's culture, family, values, or lifestyle?
- What have your interactions been with this person?
- How, if at all, has this individual or your interactions informed or affected your view of Arab Americans in general?
- To what degree has your experience with this person "fit in" with stereotypes you may be aware of about Arab Americans?

CONTEMPORARY SOCIAL PERCEPTIONS AND DISCRIMINATION EXPERIENCES

Various scholars have noted the complexity of existence for early-21st-century Arab Americans (Bale, 2010; Salameh, 2011). The post-9/11 United States has become intent on securing its borders against real or perceived threats and has engaged in preemptive actions in the name of the war on terror. The tragedy of the attacks on the World Trade Center towers is certainly real, as is the backlash suffered by the Arab-American community. Changes in national policy over the past decade (e.g., the PATRIOT Act as a precursor to the later National Security Strategy and most recent National Defense Authorization Act, or "Homeland Battlefield Bill") have altered the civil liberties often taken for granted in the United States, including expectations not to be under surveillance or be detained without cause, and have led to worldwide criticism (American Civil Liberties Union, 2010; Gray, 2011). Arab Americans, as well as other leading civil-rights advocates, have challenged these policies, claiming that they are used to target those perceived as "Middle Eastern" or "Arab," rather than being implemented fairly. Such acts of profiling perpetuate the stereotypes of Arab Americans as Muslims and extremists (Nassar-McMillan, 2010).

Hate crimes and profiling against U.S. citizens and immigrants, regardless of how closely they do or do not fit the stereotypical "Middle Eastern" images, have gone up dramatically in recent years. For example, Sikhs, who are often of Indian descent and are not Muslim, have been attacked for their custom of wearing a turban. The American-Arab Anti-Discrimination Committee listed over 600 attacks against people whom the perpetrators assumed to be Muslim Arabs in the months following September 11, 2001 (Nassar-McMillan, 2010). Although the number of hate crimes peaked in 2001, evidence suggests that it has increased in recent years. FBI data document a 50% increase in anti-Muslim hate crimes from 2009 to 2010 (Southern Poverty Law Center, 2012). Only recently (2015) has the FBI created a category for including anti-Arab bias under the religious hate crimes category, so accuracy in reporting should improve (Federal Bureau of Investigation, 2010). Certainly, most non–Arab Americans have not participated in anti-Arab hate crimes; these atrocities can be attributed to an extreme element (Elaasar, 2004). In fact, alongside the many Arab-American organizations publicly condemning the 9/11 attacks, many non–Arab-American counterparts expressed the view, via public opinion polls, that the United States, on the grounds and spirit of tolerance, should extend the benefit of the doubt to citizens of this country who also happen to be Arab. Researchers have explored the impact of discrimination (e.g., Ahmed, Kia-Keating, & Tsai, 2011; Sullivan, Scott, & Nicks, 2011; Widner & Chicoine, 2011) such as psychological distress and other indicators of mental health (e.g., Padela & Heisler, 2010). Some scholars, for example, have recently examined vicarious trauma in American Muslims as a result of their discrimination experiences (e.g., Ashraf, 2015).

Stereotypes of Arabs as callous oil barons, desert nomads, religious zealots, and repressive dictators do not help promote intercultural understanding (Beitin & Aprahamian, 2014; Cainkar & Ghazal Read, 2014; Haboush & Barakat, 2014). Some political media continue to represent "secular dictatorships . . . religious states . . . political Islam . . . and Islamic extremism" as a collective image of Arab culture, an image based on erroneous assumptions that produce detrimental effects on Americans' perceptions of their Arab-American and Arab counterparts (McLarney, 2011, p. 21). For example, the recent media portrayals of ISIS (Islamic State of Iraq and Syria, also referred to as ISIL, or Islamic State of Iraq and the Levant) and its terrorist activities centered geographically in the Middle Eastern region have served to perpetuate this conflated perception of Arab culture through global media. Such images come to the United States in movies, fictional novels, and even the news media and educational textbooks (American Arab Anti-Discrimination Committee Education, 2012). There are very few normalized images to counter those exaggerated and falsified ones that permeate U.S. culture and consciousness, and contemporary attempts at creating normalized images, such as the television show *All-American Muslim*, are fraught with political controversy. Most U.S. citizens would have a difficult time envisioning an average Arab or Arab-American family sitting down to dinner in the evening, celebrating a wedding or grieving at a funeral, getting ready for work or school in the morning, or making purchases at a store. It is ironic and sad that the current historical moments of the Arab Middle East undergoing massive political upheaval and yearning for democracy, a movement commonly referred to as the Arab Spring, yield images of terrorism and pillaging rather than the humanistic struggles of those who strive for a better community, country, and world. Still elusive are these human images to help guide us in better understanding and embracing Arab Americans in their daily lives.

Against this backdrop of stereotypes and misunderstanding, the personal and political choice of Arab Americans to identify strongly with their ethnicity can be a difficult one (Nassar-McMillan, Lambert, & Hakim-Larson, 2011). Some have responded with fear and embarrassment, perhaps internalizing the negative stereotypes of Arabs and denying their heritage. Others have experienced discrimination or threats and have had to decide whether to respond or be silenced by their mistreatment. In addition to documenting hate crimes, the American Arab Anti-Discrimination Committee (2015) recorded countless cases of workplace discrimination, spanning loss of employment to religious or personal harassment. To boot, the federal government became increasingly strict in screening Arab Americans for jobs and other benefits (Nassar-McMillan & Tovar, 2012). In the face of such real discrimination, survival instincts may outweigh the desire to express one's ethnic pride.

Others have responded to the post-9/11 environment by realizing the need for solidarity among members of the Arab-American community (Nassar-McMillan, 2010; Nassar-McMillan et al., 2011). Muslims in particular were involved in community education efforts, opening local mosques to those who wanted to understand Islam and praying for those who had lost their lives (Elaasar, 2004). Some Arab Americans also started to describe the things that they were proud of in their culture, as a way to counter the negative images generated after 9/11.

ARAB-AMERICAN CULTURE AND VALUES

As is true with any large and varied ethnic group, it is an overgeneralization to say that every Arab American adheres to an equal extent to the cultural values mentioned here. The rest of this section brings to light the traditional values that may be moderated over time by exposure to the U.S. culture, but may also be maintained by strong family systems and ethnic enclaves, or communities: collectivism; religion and faith; education, work, and economic status; and communication styles.

Collectivism

Above almost all else, Arab Americans should be understood as holding a collective worldview (Amri, Nassar-McMillan, Amen-Bryan, & Misenhimer, 2013; Hakim-Larson, Nassar-McMillan, & Patterson, 2012). Thus, as opposed to the U.S. system, in which individuals are expected to become more independent as they mature, Arab Americans are likely to continue seeing themselves as part of an extended family and community structure. Decisions are made within this context, help is sought from other members of the collective group, appropriate behavior is defined by the shared beliefs of the community, and interdependence is valued as a sign of dedication and loyalty to the group. As an additional outcome of a collectivistic culture, Arab Americans tend to be highly aware of both major and minor circumstances that could bring either honor or shame to their family and the larger community (Nassar-McMillan, Nour, & Al-Qimlass, in press). The idea of honor and shame tends to play a large role in the decisions, goals, and behaviors made by many Arab Americans (Graham, Bradshaw, & Trew, 2010; Scull, Khullar, Al-Awadhi, & Erheim, 2014). Career counseling, for example, would have a very different feel in this collective context as opposed to the context of helping clarify the work-related interests of an individual (Nassar-McMillan & Tovar, 2012). A person would be expected to sacrifice individual goals or needs for the sake of the extended family. As one common Arab proverb emphasizes, "We rise together, we fall together" (Sayed, Collins, & Takahashi, 1998, p. 444).

The strength of the collective bonds within the group may promote the tendency toward clannish behavior and cause separation between one Arab culture and other cultures that have different countries of origin, religious preferences, races, and the like. Another common proverb states, "It is my brother and I against our cousin; but it is my cousin and I against a stranger" (Nassar-McMillan, 2010). Collective societies value trust, so outsiders must work to gain favor through sustained demonstrations of knowledge, awareness, and skillful assistance. However, before trust is earned, individualistic U.S. influences may be viewed with some suspicion.

Along with a collectivist worldview, the Arab social structure is patrilineal, with males being at the top of the hierarchy (Beitin & Aprahamian, 2014). This patrilineal structure does not immediately mean male dominance and female subjugation, however. Instead, it focuses on how responsibility, security, and personal arrangement within the family and overall society are directly connected to male family members. Examples of some patriarchal, and patrilineal, behaviors that are more typically viewed in the Arab-American women's population, as opposed to other ethnic or racial populations, include abstaining from premarital sex, taking care of the husband and other male elders, and raising the children to align with cultural norms and traditions. There is wide variation, however, within the Arab and Arab-American communities as to how gender roles and power are expressed, including how patriarchal beliefs and behaviors are supported. This type of variation is not usually seen in the relevant literature and therefore continues to contribute to the stereotype of a patriarchal society.

Also within Arab-American families, parenting styles may be even more authoritarian than those of Arabs in their home countries, because U.S. cultural values may be viewed as a threat to the structure of the Arab-American family and its value system, particularly in the case of Muslims (Nassar-McMillan, 2010). Parents may impose social constraints on young girls to prevent them from falling prey to sexual permissiveness or other problematic U.S. influences (Beitin & Aprahamian, 2014). These constraints may fall more so on the daughters of an Arab-American family, rather than the sons, because, traditionally and culturally, the behaviors of women are more closely tied to overall family honor than to men (Cainkar & Ghazal Read, 2014). Counselors in schools may not understand a family's request that their daughter not wear a swimsuit or enter a pool, for example, but pushing the family to reconsider may only heighten their sense of a values conflict and cause them to become even more resolved to protect their children.

Extended family systems, through blood and marriage, are common within Arab households (Nassar-McMillan et al., in press). That tradition may be carried on in the United States, but if immigration patterns have disrupted the connection among generations, the roles of elders may be picked up by other members of an ethnic enclave. These communities tend to be close knit and share common places of origin (the same city or area in the old country), if not blood. The individual's relationship with grandmother or "auntie" is an important source of stability and very important to assess within the context of counseling (Nydell, 2012). Specifically, the extended family provides mental, emotional, spiritual, physical, and economic support to its members (Aboul-Enein & Aboul-Enein, 2010).

Stemming from the collectivistic nature in Arab communities, family becomes the hallmark of Arab culture and the mode with which to pass on cultural traditions and beliefs (Cainkar & Ghazal Read, 2014). This high level of importance placed on the family unit invariably incorporates the idea of marriage and divorce. While divorce does occur in both the Arab and Arab-American communities, it can be "highly frowned upon" (p. 90) by members of the families and society at large. With regard to marriage norms, pairings are typically viewed through the lens of compatibility versus love. When viewing a marriage proposal through the lens of compatibility between the pair, it is assumed that love will occur over time between them. In addition, it is believed that "arranged" marriages can be as successful as "love matches," or marriages that are founded on the love and relationship of the two partners, independently of any social or financial arrangements or accommodations made by the parents; both views of marriage are observed in Arab-American communities.

Counselors in any setting should be careful to ask about family or other important relationships in a very broad and inclusive way. Another way to view the Arab-American family is through the term **kinship**. This term includes "extended family that provide connection, security, and identity for Arab men and women" (Beitin & Aprahamian, 2014, p. 69). Counseling related to family issues should be undertaken with the understanding that relationships will be close and interdependent in a way that might be described as "enmeshed" if one were working with an individualistic family. Care should be taken not to label relationships as unhealthy or inappropriate if they are simply adhering to different cultural standards. Furthermore, the identification of family values adhered to in Arab culture will provide greater context for Arab-American family patterns and issues brought to the counseling session.

Religion and Faith

The religious diversity of the Arab-American community is an aspect that may come as a surprise to those unfamiliar with its traditions. The Islamic heritage of some Arab Americans has received more attention because of its distinctiveness from the dominant religious traditions of the United States. In addition, it is true that the majority of Arabs in the Middle East are Muslim. However, the largest religious group within Arab Americans is Catholic (i.e., 35%; Arab American Institute, n.d.). An additional 20% are Christian Orthodox, followed by 11% who practice a Christian Protestant religion; only 24% of Arab Americans practice Islam, whereas the remaining 13% of Arab Americans describe themselves as not having a religious affiliation (Nydell, 2012; Samhan, 2014). Given that the Arab Middle East is the birthplace of several of these traditions, it makes sense that there would be a range of practices among Arab descendants of the region. In addition, the immigration process may selectively bring more members of one group than another to a host country, so it is also logical that the percentage of Arab Muslims residing in the United States is different from the percentage of Arab Muslims in their region of origin (Abdelhady, 2014; Samhan, 2014).

Because less may be known about Islam than some of the other, more dominant U.S. faiths mentioned, a fuller description of its tenets is provided in Build Your Knowledge 10.1., as well as in Chapter 16 of this text. **Islam** began in the 7th century when the Prophet Muhammad began to deliver God's messages in the area of the Arabian Peninsula. Muhammad did not claim to be divine, but said that he received divine revelations from the Archangel Gabriel. These messages from Allah (the Arabic word for God) were written and became

---

BUILD YOUR KNOWLEDGE 10.1

TENETS OF ISLAM

Some of the basic beliefs of Islam are the beliefs that people are responsible for their own deeds and must always remain accountable to God and aware of his presence. Muslims also share the Christian belief in Heaven and Hell. Islam emphasizes unity among peoples, even across racial or religious lines. Five important spiritual practices, known as the Pillars of Islam, are (a) *Shahada,* the declaration of faith in one God, Allah, and in Muhammad as God's prophet; (b) *Salat,* or the formal practice of worshiping by bowing toward Mecca five times daily and praying; (c) *Sawm,* the monthlong fast observed during Ramadan—a practice that serves to build patience and obedience to God, as well as to teach compassion for those who go hungry; (d) *Zakah,* or the donation of 2.5% of one's income to the mosques as a form of giving alms; and (e) *Hajj,* or the pilgrimage to Mecca. Those who are not able to make the journey to Mecca are encouraged to sponsor someone else's pilgrimage.

known as the Qur'an. In this way, the Qur'an is not drastically different from the Old or New Testament of the Bible, both of which were God's revelations delivered through faithful messengers (Nassar-McMillan, 2010). Muhammad himself was actually an orphan at a young age and was raised in Mecca by a family and community that tended to practice polytheistic traditions. Muhammad made the firm decision to worship only one God, the God of his ancestor, Abraham. Of interest, it is written that the progeny of Abraham's son Isaac became Jews and the progeny of Abraham's son Ishmael became Muslims.

Many Muslims view Islam as not merely their religion, but their guide for everyday life. Indeed, Islamic law is written to help believers lead ethical lives that respect others and promote peace. The very word *Islam* means peace through submission, a concept that does not condone actions taken with the express purpose of hurting or terrorizing another person or group. The goal of global unity is supported by Islamic ethics, including religious unity and racial and ethnic unity (Nassar-McMillan, 2010). For counselors who may not typically include religion as a topic of assessment, the presence of Islamic ethics in all parts of daily life means that an important influence could otherwise be missed.

The role of Islam in everyday life can also be seen in the everyday words and phrases used by Muslim Arab Americans—for example, *insha'Allah* (God willing). The use of these religious phrases does not equate to the level of religiosity that the individual using them has, as most are common colloquial sayings (Nassar-McMillan et al., in press).

Another misconception of Islam is that it asks women to be subservient to men (Douglas, 2002). In actuality, males and females are considered by Islam to be equals before God. Muslim women are able to obtain an education, own property, make their own decisions about marriage and divorce, and vote. Muslim women also pray in the same way that the men do, but as with many other activities in traditional Arab Muslim households, the genders are separated (Cainkar & Ghazal Read, 2014). It should also be noted that local customs and leaders may interact with Islam in such a way as to limit women's rights, but this type of interaction is typically due to sociopolitical influences of the particular country or region, rather than to a tenet of Islam (Nassar-McMillan, 2010).

Although some of the customs may appear different at first, there is much common ground among Islam, Christianity, and Judaism (Nassar-McMillan, 2010). The Catholic tradition that exists in Arab-American communities has its roots in the crusades of the 12th century and the Maronites (mostly from Lebanon) and Melkites (Greek Catholic). In addition, early Christian traditions have led to the emergence, over time, of present-day Orthodox groups such as the Egyptian Copts, the Syrians, the Antiochians, and those of the Greek Orthodox faith. For these Arab Americans, as well as for their Protestant counterparts, traditions in the United States do not represent a dramatic departure from their customary worship.

Just as with other U.S. groups that associate with a religion, some Arab Americans adhere strongly to their faith traditions and maintain a daily or weekly practice whereas others spend relatively less time attending religious services or engaged in other spiritual matters. Degree of religiosity is an important aspect to learn about in a counseling relationship, especially with stereotypes about extremist Muslims influencing U.S. opinions about the more typical members of the group (Nassar-McMillan, 2010). For Arab Americans of any faith tradition, religion is often a source of comfort and strength, a valued connection to cultural roots, and a resource in times of difficulty. For Muslims in particular (as a religious minority in the United States), the strain of being misunderstood and perhaps mistreated in everyday life can be counterbalanced by time spent with other Muslims at the mosque. Moreover, the sense of community that is often generated in the mosque extends beyond religion to the social, psychological, and physical well-being of its members.

The Imam (i.e., religious leader) may be sought for counsel in handling daily stressors, and the worshipers may assist each other with issues related to family life, work, and education. Of course, daily transactions with non-Muslims have meant that members of the Islamic faith must integrate themselves into the wider community to a certain extent. However, in personal matters of values, religion, and family, Muslims may choose to maintain their cultural traits and traditions. For a counselor working with a traditional Arab American of Islamic faith, the option to include an Imam or other important religious figure in the process may be greatly appreciated by the client.

Education, Work, and Economic Status

Contrary to some stereotypes, education is strongly encouraged for boys and girls alike in the Arab-American community (Haboush & Barakat, 2014). Although some schoolchildren in the Arab Middle East may be segregated by gender, Arab-American children follow the norms of schooling in the United States. Some children attend private Islamic schools, where they also learn Arabic culture and language, but many are students in the public schools of their communities (Haboush & Barakat, 2014; Nassar-McMillan et al., in press). Education and professional preparation are both emphasized across the Arab Middle East and therefore are carried over into the United States. An example of this emphasis can be found in Christian and Muslim Arab-American women. For this population, obtaining a high-quality education is often viewed as a positive resource for parenting, and such an education increases overall family value (Cainkar & Ghazal Read, 2014). Whether an Arab-American woman chooses to enter the labor market, however, is another consideration altogether: Even with a high level of education, an Arab-American woman may choose to remain in the home because of a value system that prioritizes family, with the woman holding an important and integral role.

The Arab-American community has a laudable record of educational accomplishment, with 85% of Arab Americans having a high school diploma and over 40% having bachelor's degrees (Nassar-McMillan, 2010). Arab Americans tend to have career paths similar to those of other groups in this country, although there are more participating in business and other entrepreneurial activities and fewer participating in government, perhaps for reasons mentioned earlier in the chapter (Nassar-McMillan & Tovar, 2012). Some of the most recent immigrants have professions and educational certifications from their home countries, but may not be able to practice those professions in the United States. The overall rate of employment among Arab Americans is high, as is the mean household income. This fact, however, does not mean that Arab Americans would not present for career-related counseling. In addition to some of the typical career-related concerns seen with any client (e.g., occupational exploration, workforce transition issues, balancing career and family) Arab Americans may discuss issues related to workplace discrimination, expectations from a collectivistic cultural viewpoint, or the impact of immigration or cultural adjustment on work.

Communication Styles

Because counseling is an activity that is highly dependent on the quality of communication between counselor and client, it is important to understand some manners of expression that Arab Americans may use. Some of the characteristics that are different from the average U.S. conversational style are the use of nonverbal gestures to express emotion and respect, comfort with touching and standing in close proximity while communicating with those they are familiar with, and the use of volume, loud voice, or repetition to emphasize a critical point (Graham et al., 2010; Nassar-McMillan et al., in press; Nydell, 2012). At the same time, such expressiveness may not extend to the sharing of emotional feelings or issues. On the contrary, Arab Americans may be reluctant to share in that way, particularly with those outside their culture, and they may resort to somaticizing their emotions, a phenomenon in which deep emotions are inadvertently expressed through physical symptoms (Graham et al., 2010; Nassar-McMillan et al., in press; Nassar-McMillan, Hakim-Larson, & Patterson, 2014). Moreover, they may be reluctant to say anything negative about another person, particularly within their family or community. Kissing cheeks as a greeting and holding hands (even among adult males, though not usually between male and female) is common in the Middle East, and these customs may or may not be observed in the United States.

There may be a hierarchy in terms of communication among family members, with an emphasis on children speaking respectfully to their elders and women being respectful to men while in public settings. This behavior may be seen as women being less direct and less intense than men when communicating in public and around strangers (Nassar-McMillan et al., in press). The tenet of respect, especially as it relates to elders and others in positions of perceived authority, is a foundational building block of Arab culture and is derived from the patriarchal/patrilineal family system (Beitin & Aprahamian, 2014; Nassar-McMillan, 2010; Nassar-McMillan et al., in press). If counseling is being sought for marriage- or family-related issues, the counselor may consider one separate meeting before working jointly with the couple, to have the opportunity to hear the woman's concerns when she is not guided by custom to defer to her husband. If the counselor is seen as an authority figure, the client (in any setting) may expect him or her to provide concrete solutions to problems rather than to ask questions designed to promote insight into the situation (Nassar-McMillan, 2010). Arab Americans may initially be reserved with members of other ethnic groups, until an initial sense of trust is established, especially in matters of emotional importance. Some clients could feel that they are betraying their families by sharing personal matters with an outsider, such as the counselor. Another tendency that may affect counseling is the traditional Middle Eastern custom of gender separation during certain activities. Same-gender pairs, where available, may be more comfortable for Arab-American clients. Therefore, both the communication style and the content of counseling sessions may be affected by these customs, a situation that would be most relevant with the client who holds fast to cultural traditions. As a counselor, particularly a non–Arab-American one, you may find that learning a few key Arabic greetings and other phrases, along with cultural traditions, from one's clients could go a long way toward building rapport.

INDIVIDUAL DIFFERENCES AND IDENTITIES

Identity is a multilayered construct, one that may operate at a subconscious level for some areas and may be foremost in our minds for other areas. Our identities include our sense of who we are as gendered, ethnic/racial, and religious beings. For individuals of Arab descent in particular, they are likely to be influenced by demographic characteristics such as religion, gender, refugee status, acculturation, and discrimination experiences (Amer, 2014; Kira, Amer & Wrobel, 2014; Nassar-McMillan et al., 2011; Nassar-McMillan, Rezcallah & Nour, 2014), among a host of other factors. Our identities are shaped by where we work and live, with whom we partner, and what we believe to be good and just. All of these interacting streams of identity develop at different rates, continue to change over time, and respond to different influences. Identity development for an Arab American may be complicated for additional reasons. For example, there may be differences between the self that can be presented while at school or working in the community and the self that is nurtured and accepted in the family home or among friends

(Hakim-Larson & Nassar-McMillan, 2006). For counselors, it is useful to consider some of the external and internal influences that may be important to the identities of Arab-American clients.

Acculturation

Immigration and the resultant process of acculturation (the multidimensional changes that occur when two or more cultural groups come into contact with each other) are never easy. Acculturation is not a simple linear progression to one final solution, but rather a process that occurs at different rates within individuals, families, and communities. For the newest members of the community, the process of encountering an unfamiliar culture can result in a variety of outcomes. Some individuals invest years learning about their new home and become so assimilated to those customs that they leave behind their former cultural values. Others may add the new cultural competencies to the old and become bicultural or integrated in their acculturation status. Other individuals may keep themselves separated from the new culture and cling tightly to their original traditions. Still others may come to feel marginalized in both cultures, not belonging to either one, not feeling comfortable anywhere (Amer, 2014; Nassar-McMillan, Rezcallah, et al., 2014). It is certainly possible to sustain one's original Arab identity and take on a U.S. citizen identity over time (Nassar-McMillan, 2010), but this biculturalism is challenging when one identity is being actively disparaged by the dominant culture (Nassar-McMillan et al, 2011). Indeed, research is just beginning to identify the long-term impact of trying to build a secure Arab-American identity in the context of ongoing U.S. war efforts in the Arab Middle East and the so-called war on terror that has targeted Islamic extremists as the enemy (Cainkar & Ghazal Read, 2014; Hakim-Larson & Nassar-McMillan, 2006). The adherence to Arab cultural values and traditions can provide the Arab American or recent Arab immigrant with a bridge to his or her heritage—a bridge that can increase feelings of security and camaraderie with others (Beitin & Aprahamian, 2014).

For some of the Arab immigrants to this country, similarities to the predominant U.S. culture provided initial pathways to connect with their new homeland and perhaps eased part of the acculturation process. For example, Arabs with lighter skin tones and a Christian religious heritage would not draw as much attention in the United States as would darker-skinned Arabs who maintained Islamic religious practices (e.g., wearing a veil, praying five times a day, fasting; Nassar-McMillan, 2010). Some of the factors influencing the ease or difficulty of the adjustment process are the specific country of origin, the reason for coming to the United States, the language used in the home, and proximity to an Arab-American enclave. For example, Muslim immigrants often were mistreated because of their noticeable differences. The negative images of Muslims in the media and in common conversation could influence how new immigrants come to see themselves as they consolidate their identity in a new place (Nassar-McMillan, Tovar, & Conley, 2014). Counselors who have worked with new immigrants from other parts of the world already have some basic knowledge about common adjustment issues and how they pervade all aspects of life. This perspective will be helpful when working with new immigrants from the Arab Middle East, although each group still has specific issues that need to be explored as well.

Involuntary immigration, or situations in which newcomers seek refuge because conditions in their original country are intolerable, carries unique difficulties and stressors. Refugees from war, violence, occupation, and instability may experience posttraumatic stress disorder (PTSD) and are less capable of attending to the process of establishing themselves in their new communities (Kira et al., 2014). These individuals often have been forced to leave and may continue to grieve the losses of home, family, and a familiar way of life for some time. Frequently, they have arrived with few, if any, supportive resources, either economic or social. Families may be separated, communities torn apart, and familiar sources of comfort (e.g., mosques, religious leaders, customs, traditions) no longer present. To compound these difficulties, refugees might also face a lack of understanding, ranging from neglect to hostile discrimination, in their new host country (Jamil, Nassar-McMillan, Lambert, Wang, Ager, & Arnetz, 2010; Kira et al., 2014; Nassar-McMillan, Rezcallah, et al., 2014). Iraqis, making up some of the current wave of Arab immigration, provide an example of the problems associated with refugee status (Jamil et al., 2010; Samhan, 2014). Many of these individuals were allies to the U.S. military forces in their country, only to find themselves in danger in their homelands and facing discrimination and misunderstanding in the United States, their host country. Refugees who left war, famine, ethnic cleansing, or political turbulence behind them have a distinct set of issues. For example, nearly half the total population of Syria have fled their homes from 2010 to 2014 in response to the war that continues to destabilize the country. The Church World Services estimate "3.9 million Syrians escaping to surrounding countries and another 7.8 million displaced within Syria" in a recent posting (Weaver, 2015). Currently, only 1,600 Syrian refugees have been admitted for asylum in the United States, but government officials have promised to accept 10,000 more over the next year (Robbins, 2015). European countries are also responding with varied levels of flexibility to accommodate the millions of Syrians seeking shelter. The refugees may not be likely to seek counseling as a primary resource, although they may be referred when they contact agencies for basic needs such as food, medicine, or shelter. Counselors living in areas that are receiving groups of refugees have an ethical obligation to educate themselves about posttraumatic stress and to be prepared to work with these individuals.

Ethnicity

Beyond the Hollywood images of sheiks or the evening news images of women wearing veils, what does a contemporary Arab American look like? Interestingly, even the U.S. government has categorized Middle Easterners with terms as various as *Asiatic, Colored,* and *White* since the late 1800s (Samhan, 2012). Given the many skin tones and hair and eye colors that are possible, there is no phenotypical look that is common to all Arabs. Also, in the United States intermarriage causes new variations in the physical attributes of Arab Americans, making cultural identity a more complex issue for their children (Haboush & Barakat, 2014). Therefore, some members of the community may go unnoticed or unidentified by their neighbors or associates, especially if their names have changed from the original Arabic surname. One clear exception would be practicing Muslims whose attire or customs may trigger some of the common Middle Eastern stereotypes and thus receive unwanted attention from non–Arab Americans. Other external influences on Arab-American ethnic identity include the political discourse of the times, the predominant religions in the local communities, the absence or presence of other Arab Americans, and any other acculturation-related factor, such as length of time in the United States or language spoken at home. Voices from the Field 10.1 highlights a counselor's conceptualization of his ethnicity.

Nassar-McMillan (2010) noted that ethnicity and religion must be understood together in any attempt to investigate the ethnic identity of Arab Americans. This intersection is demonstrated in a more personal way in Reflection 10.1. White Christian Arab Americans would be likely to integrate with ease, whereas Black Christian Arab Americans and White Muslim Arab Americans would each have some unique challenges to navigate. Black Muslim Arab

Voices from the Field 10.1

"What box do I check?" My earliest recollection of trying to understand what being an Arab American meant was when I asked this question to my teacher in elementary school. Our class was preparing to take a standardized test, and I was perplexed by the demographics question. When I explained that my family was from Syria, she told me to select Caucasian. Many other times in my life, I have defined myself and been viewed by others as simply Caucasian. The reasons are related to my family history and how I was raised.

My maternal grandfather arrived in New York Harbor by way of Damascus, Syria, as an infant at the turn of the 20th century. My grandfather never learned to speak Arabic and made all efforts to blend in and raise his children, all born in the United States, as Americans. My father, on the other hand, arrived in New York City during the early 1970s, leaving Damascus to escape the instability of the region and to find success in America. I was the second of three children, two boys and a younger sister, all born in the United States.

Our home life and upbringing were influenced by both Arab and American cultures. Both my parents are Melkite Catholic, a branch of Catholicism more common in the Middle East, but because there were almost no other Melkite Catholics in our neighborhood and the nearest parish was Roman rite, I was raised Roman Catholic. Although my family regularly attended Roman Catholic services, on certain holy days we traveled downtown to the Melkite Church for mass. Being Arabic on "special occasions" was also true when it came to meals. Most nights, my mother would prepare American food staples such as pasta, burgers, and hot dogs. On holidays, however, my mom would unearth dusty old recipes written on yellowing paper and, with help from my father, prepared traditional Arabic dishes.

Although many of the values and traditions emblematic of Arabic culture were present at home, because my mother had been born in America, I was raised differently compared with the other Arab American children I would meet during our occasional visits to the Melkite Church. Because I had fair skin and never learned to speak the language, I often felt like I did not fit in among them and that I had more in common with my friends who lived in my neighborhood. I felt the same way about my relatives in Syria. We rarely visited, and when we did, the language barrier prevented us from developing close relationships.

I rarely discussed or even thought of my Arabic background with my peers or at school, which is likely why I was so confused by the demographics question. When this part of my identity was broached, however, it usually was under inauspicious circumstances, such as during Desert Storm or after the first World Trade Center bombing. During these times, I felt isolated by my classmates, who viewed me as someone different from them, somehow affiliated with the "bad guys." I remember at times wishing that I had simply just been generically "Caucasian" and was not associated with people who would threaten or harm my home country.

As I have grown older, I have been able to integrate aspects of Arabic culture into my life. I also have a much better understanding of the friction between the collectivist culture of my father (and somewhat of my mother) and the values of individualism passed on to me through my education. It took many years for my father to accept my vocation as a counselor and the likelihood that I would not take over the family business. This acceptance no doubt was aided by my success as a counselor and my utter failure to learn the family business when I worked with him during the summer months when I was in high school.

Meeting Arab Americans who come from similar circumstances and connecting through social networking with my cousins in Damascus have helped me incorporate my cultural roots as part of my identity and have provided me with a more nuanced understanding of the culture. These relationships helped me feel less isolated at times when the Arab American community in

(Continued)

the United States has been scrutinized, such as during the time after 9/11/2001. Nowadays when asked, I self-identify as an Arab American; not having a specific box to select when answering demographics questions no longer distresses me. In fact, I am quite proud that my family history and cultural heritage are so complex and rich.

~Ed Wahesh

In dyads, consider the following:

- What are some of the complexities in Ed's identity development process?
- In what ways did Ed's family's faith serve as a value, and in what other ways did it serve as a tradition?
- In what ways did Ed experience "profiling" or other negative aspects of his ethnicity?

Americans may be faced with the most difficult road in terms of finding acceptance in mainstream U.S. society. Religion is clearly one of the key determinants of how acculturation proceeds (or is impeded) in this community.

If those with the ability to blend in and integrate cause confusion for non–Arab Americans, then Arab Americans themselves may have difficulty in defining their ethnic identity. There are already differences among members of the community with respect to country of origin, education, generation of immigration, religion, and social status. Some individuals may identify themselves mostly by their religion or their country of origin (e.g., "I'm Lebanese, you are Yemeni.") and not with the panethnic term *Arab American* (Samhan, 2014). Some Arab Americans may adhere more strongly to traditional value systems, whereas others may be comfortable assimilating to U.S. value norms. Indeed, there can be occasional infighting, with more traditional Arab Americans referring to the more assimilated as "White" whereas the more assimilated may think of the others as "boaters": newly immigrated and thus too old fashioned (Hakim-Larson & Nassar-McMillan, 2006). It should not be assumed that all Arab Americans consider themselves ethnic minorities: Some—particularly those who have successfully integrated into U.S. society—may identify more with the dominant White culture within the American mainstream. It may be more challenging for some adolescent Arab Americans to identify with their Arab culture of origin, especially if a family does not live near an ethnic enclave and does not have ties to a cultural community (Ajrouch & Jamal, 2007).

An in-depth focus on some of the identity development tasks of young Arab Americans may be useful for those preparing to become professional counselors. School counselors in particular will want to complete Activity 10.1, which provides a multidimensional way to conceptualize Arab-American adolescents in the context of a non-Arab-majority school. There are three levels that should be considered in thinking about how an Arab-American identity could be constructed (Hakim-Larson & Nassar-McMillan, 2006). On the individual level, all adolescents must navigate gender identity as they approach adulthood, but the process is likely to intersect with religion, social values from the country of origin, and acculturation status for young Arab Americans. Also on the individual level, these adolescents must come to understand their ethnicities, build a sense of self-esteem, and confront the roles that take up most of their time (e.g., student, family member, friend). On the level of family and peers, there may be differences among Arab-American youths regarding how much they feel that their values are similar to or conflicting with those of the parental generation. It is likely that they will have absorbed some emphasis on collectivism from their family life, but this conception will bump up against the predominant U.S. value of individualism in school and other settings. Finally, at the sociocultural level, Arab-American children may come to learn that discrimination exists in the United States and is occasionally directed at members of their community. They may learn more about the politics of the Arab Middle East or what types of pressures led their family to immigrate in the first place. If a level of fear accompanies these growing realizations about the difficult place of individuals of Arab heritage in the United States, it could also cause insecurity in their nascent identities. This process is parallel in some ways to the role of internalized oppression in the identity development of other racial minorities in the United States. (See Chapter 2.)

In some of their typical developmental tasks, children from collectivistic families are less likely to struggle for independence or have noticeably turbulent relationships with their parents (Beitin & Aprahamian, 2014). Adolescents of any culture are likely to focus on building competence in schoolwork, finding a group of friends, and preparing themselves for an acceptable future. For children of individualistic families, part of preparing for the future is learning how to be independent of their parents by making their own choices and defining their own roles. In contrast, among children of collectivistic families, preparing for the future is not something that requires moving outside the family influence. Indeed, if the Arab-American parents have chosen the culturally preferred authoritative parenting style, then the children may come to understand and expect that someone in the family hierarchy is looking out for their interests and will help them with important decisions. There are benefits and liabilities to each system, but the critical point for Arab-American youths who are raised in this way is that they observe the individualistic system by day as they interact with classmates and teachers, and they live the collectivistic system by night at home with their families. The contrast between the two could be confusing for a young person trying to build an identity. Of course, the less difference there is between the school environment and the family environment (e.g., in an Islamic school) or the less overlap between the two systems (e.g., the student goes to school only to learn, does not try to make friends, and fulfills all social needs through a mosque, church, or community center), the less friction will result. Other characteristics that may be present among some students of Arab descent, particularly the less acculturated, are a prevailing respect for authority, and a corresponding participatory role that might appear to be less active than that of students who are not of Arab descent (Haboush & Barakat, 2014). Moreover, refugee children may suffer from PTSD and other symptoms that would likely affect their academic performance. Parental support has been found, in some cases, to mediate such challenges. Now complete Activity 10.1.

Gender Identity

Non-Arab U.S. citizens may hold multiple stereotypes about Arab or Arab-American women, particularly those who are Muslim. There are movie images of harem girls doing belly dances, contrasted with news images of oppressed women cloaked in dark fabrics who could not leave the house, drive a car, or have an opinion (Shaheen, 2014). As is most often true with stereotypes, these images are not a good portrait of the majority of Arab women and even less so of Arab-American women. In addition to media stereotypes, there are gaps in Arab-American research regarding the topic of gender (Cainkar & Ghazal Read, 2014). The first gap occurs because of research that focuses on an ethnically homogenous group of Arab Americans as the sample population. As reported by Cainkar and Ghazal Read in a large sample of Arab Americans, women living in ethnically homogenous communities tended to follow more traditional gender roles as opposed to Arab-American women living in more ethnically diverse communities. A second gap in gender research stems from the

ACTIVITY 10.1 SCHOOL COUNSELING CONSIDERATIONS

Consider Sahara, a child of a Lebanese family. As she enters high school, her mother insists that she adopt the hijab as a part of her wardrobe. Although she is very stylish in her attire, including the hijab, Sahara is quite upset about this new familial expectation. In the past, she has been a popular girl at school, well adjusted academically and socially. Since she began wearing the hijab, her grades have quickly fallen in all of her classes and she has become depressed. Suddenly, she feels as though she is being treated differently, and she has lost some of her close friends. A school counselor working with Arab-American students may wish to maintain awareness of some important influences (Hakim-Larson & Nassar-McMillan, 2006):

- Is the student different in a way that is obvious to non-Arab peers, perhaps prompting them to express discriminatory attitudes and reject the Arab-American child?
- How can this uniqueness be addressed constructively, given the possibility that the non-Arab students are repeating comments they hear at home?
- How long has the Arab-American family lived in this country, or when did they arrive?
- If they are recent immigrants or refugees, how old was the child on leaving the country of origin?
- Was the social and political situation in the home country dangerous and destabilized?
- Is the family highly traditional? Do they seem to keep their social contacts within their ethnic community?
- Does the student appreciate or resist the type of support offered by his or her family—especially Muslim families, which may try to counter the influence of U.S. values?
- If the student seems to have any conflict about his or her ethnic group membership, school counselors need to be aware that the student is not likely to criticize his or her parents to an outsider and that questions must be asked in a context of respect for collective values.

dearth of information regarding Arab-American men. This deficiency also perpetuates the stereotypes of Arab women, because it disproportionately focuses on women's experiences while ignoring those of men. The impact of traditional Arab values on Arab-American women's attitudes and behaviors is difficult to determine because of both the diversity within the population itself and the varying opinions held by society about Arab-American women.

Arab-American men and women may support and adhere to traditional gender roles of their culture for various reasons, the most prominent being that they agree with those roles, but also because not doing so could mean that they are inadvertently complying with the prejudices and stereotypes that others have put on them, whereby they may lose a sense of personal dignity (Cainkar & Ghazal Read, 2014). Viewing cultural gender norms in this way, a Muslim Arab-American woman who chooses to wear the head scarf may be understood as choosing to express both her religious faith and her commitment to her culture's traditional gender role, as well as the "dignity of Muslims in the context of social derision" (p. 100).

The personal perspective provided in Voices from the Field 10.2 helps situate gender as an important aspect of identity, but not the only relevant one. Many Arab-American women are quite modern compared with the stereotypes: they dress as most other Americans do, divide time between work or school and family, hold political opinions, and are active in a variety of communities (Beitin & Aprahamia, 2014; Cainkar & Ghazal Read, 2014). Even

Voices from the Field 10.2

As an Arab-American woman, I have struggled throughout my life to develop and rightly claim my ethnic identity. During that process, I never considered that I would arrive at the intersection of having to decide if I would adopt the traditional Islamic head covering.

After all, my mother didn't cover, nor did my grandmother. My great-grandmother wore a white scarf, tied casually under her chin, in the style of all the other women from her Lebanese village. Absolutely no one expected me, a college-educated, independent, articulate daughter of a progressive-minded mother to begin covering her hair, more than 10 years after her marriage to a non-Arab. Yet, after all the protests I had personally waged against this "requirement" at religious and social gatherings, I found myself looking at the young, veiled women around me with fresh eyes. I began to feel less constricted as I pinned a scarf on to attend religious services. I began to wait just a little longer each time I departed before taking it off.

This newest phase of my interest in Islam became a trajectory of yet another dimension of my identity. This path toward a broader Islamic identity was certainly fuelled by the post-9/11 environment. Profiling had become the accepted, even preferred, method of policing and security interventions. Conspiracy theories of camps being set up just for Muslims took on new validity. I had a dual platform to achieve: help to repair the trust that had been damaged while projecting a positive image of Islam, and have the courage to publicly display myself as a Muslim in an ever increasingly hostile atmosphere. The scarf satisfied both of these goals for me.

My ethnic values that were simultaneously comforting and familiar, yet often difficult for me to manage due to a lack of Arabic language skills, were starting to recede in the background. In their place emerged a global Muslim identity that not only cut across every barrier, but acknowledged the differences as a plan from God. This was the vessel of global human values of which I could be the respected flag bearer—with just some modifications in my attire! And of course, nothing is that simple.

How was I going to convince my husband this was the right thing for me and us collectively? Did I trust myself to maintain this commitment for the rest of my life? How will I cope in hot weather? How will other family members, friends, colleagues, and clients react?

As might be expected, all the reactions were a mixed bag of questions such as "Why?", surprise (no one more so than myself, actually), and a lot of admiration, for which I was unprepared—and those responses had the most humbling effect. In the past, whenever I had noticed a woman of any age begin to wear the hijab, I likely never acknowledged it, and certainly did not offer positive encouragement. Now I had men and women telling me how much they respected my decision. I never would have imagined it meant so much to them. My feelings of hypocrisy intensified as I recalled how much I had railed against the tradition of veiling, or wearing the hijab.

From the inner perspective, my head covering is my integrity check. I confront myself with questions that determine if my worship, behavior, and manners are honoring the public symbol I choose to display. And, with those same eyes, I still struggle with wanting to adorn myself with what the fashion industry defines as beautiful, attractive, and stylish.

The scarf is far beyond just being a piece of cloth. It becomes a part of one's identity, blurs the ethnic edges, and defines religious parameters. It keeps one's head warm on cold, windy days, and hides the gray hairs that grow in much too fast! ~Sandra Amen-Bryan

In dyads, consider the following:

- What are your reactions to Sandra's identity development?
- What have some of Sandra's challenges been?
- With which aspects of Sandra's identity development can you personally identify—how and why?

historic images of Arab women that are held by Westerners are often one sided. The late Arab-American sociologist Evelyn Shakir (1997) shared an interesting story of an 18th-century British woman who was living with her diplomat husband in Turkey. The woman's view of the "oppressed" Arab woman changed after some Turkish women were helping her change clothes and remarked on the cruel and unusual punishment that she was enduring: the bone corset. In her later work, *Remember Me to Lebanon*, Shakir (2007) shared many other such stories told through the eyes of multiple generations of Arab-American women. This chapter offers a special focus on understanding "**bint Arabs**," or Arab daughters.

Some of the traditional social customs from the Middle East that encourage separation of the sexes for various activities are particularly hard for non–Arab Americans to understand (Cainkar & Ghazal Read, 2014). From the U.S. perspective, it is unfair to put girls in separate classrooms, whereas from some Arab perspectives, this segregation protects them from harassment or inappropriate male behavior. From a traditional Arab perspective, allowing an unmarried and sexually protected young woman to go on a date with a young man would be putting herself and her reputation in danger; from the U.S. perspective, it is a necessary ritual for finding a partner. The absence of such restrictions for young men does indicate a double standard, but Arab culture would not be the only one to provide different social instructions to women and men (Nassar-McMillan, 2010). Arab-American women may decide to adhere to their Arab culture's gender roles to different extents. Some may pray or worship in a setting apart from men to improve their focus on God and yet may work and share living space comfortably with men (Cainkar & Ghazal Read, 2014). Indeed, some may be third- or fourth-generation American women who feel less of a connection to a distant country in the Arab Middle East. The important point for counselors is to explore a client's perspectives on gender without preconception or judgment based on stereotypes.

A person's generation of immigration and time spent in the United States can influence her or his acculturation status and, hence, choices about cultural norms and gender roles. Haddad (2004) described an interesting change that occurred in the Arab-American enclave in Dearborn, Michigan. The earlier immigrants had adopted some American customs, such as allowing women to take charge of activities outside the home (e.g., raising money for establishing a new mosque, planning weddings and other social events at the mosque, helping with family business ventures), but later male immigrants from a more traditional culture in the Arab Middle East found this level of involvement to be unacceptable. They took control of the mosque via court action and told the women that they would be allowed to enter only through a back door that led to the basement. They brought in a more traditional Imam who supported their perspectives and eliminated all social activity in the mosque, returning it solely to a place of prayer. Thus, the way women's roles are defined in the Arab-American community may shift with time and religious traditionalism. Trying to bridge the two cultures at their points of greatest differences could cause frustration and a sense of incongruence in women.

Another example of the variations in Muslim Arab-American gender identity is the practice of veiling (Cainkar & Ghazal Read, 2014). The use of the veil may be viewed by non-Muslims as oppressive, whereas Muslim women and girls who agree to wear veils may feel that it is a sign of their religious devotion and cultural pride. Some women who veil their faces or dress in modest attire also indicate that they are free to develop their minds and opinions when attention is taken away from their physical selves. Other Muslim women may have an ambivalent relationship with the practice of veiling, accepting it at certain times and places in their lives and rejecting it at others. As is the case with many things, it is easier to reject and criticize that which we do not understand as outsiders to a community. Women who wear veils have not forfeited their rights:

they can study, they can choose professions, and they can exercise authority in the family and the community (Beitin & Aprahamian, 2014; Cainkar & Ghazal Read, 2014). At times, they face discrimination for adhering to their choice in non-Muslim settings, such as work and school (Haboush & Barakat, 2014). Recently, some European countries have debated laws aimed at not allowing students to veil (seen as a symbol of religion) in, for example, public schools.

Consequently, regardless of whether a Muslim woman does or does not wear a veil, her religious identity and her gender identity can still take a variety of forms. In many cases, the person's degree of religiosity and other factors have more influence on the content of gender roles for Arab-American women than being Christian or Muslim does (Cainkar & Ghazal Read, 2014; Nassar-McMillan et al., in press). That is, more fundamental belief systems tend to have more restrictions on how men and women should act, irrespective of the actual religion. For example, a Christian Arab-American (or Christian non–Arab-American) woman may be strongly opposed to the practice of premarital sex. Counselors who meet a client for the first time and observe her wearing a veil would be wise not to make interpretations about that choice until other aspects of the client's personality and values become clear.

It can be complicated to construct a gender identity if one is also influenced by two fairly distinctive cultural or religious traditions. A wonderful interview from Shakir (1997) sheds light on this issue as the subject discusses wearing traditional Muslim attire:

> The more in touch with reality I became through the teachings of Islam, the more of a feminist I became, meaning that yes I wanted to be free, free from all these lies they're telling me, free from cultural influences that tyrannize young people. I wanted to be emancipated from having to wear my skirts up to here or heels this high or being a slave to fashion. (p. 121)

Throughout one's lifetime, the process of constructing and adapting one's gender identity can be viewed as a dialogue between the values of the self and the values of the outer world (Adams & Markus, 2001).

RISKS AND RESILIENCIES: MENTAL HEALTH ISSUES AMONG ARAB AMERICANS

In this section, we detail key potential mental health consequences related to some of the issues presented earlier in the chapter, such as oppression, immigration and acculturation, ethnic identity development, and other psychosocial issues. Mental health–based research within Arab-American communities indicates that these presenting issues are most relevant to the clients they serve (e.g., Hakim-Larson et al., 2012; Nassar-McMillan, 2010). Later, Case Studies 10.1 and 10.2 illustrate the issues presented. We will frame each in terms of both risks and resiliencies on the part of the client that may be present within the overall counseling context or that may be positively facilitated by the counselor. In the next section, on counseling considerations, we will revisit these scenarios, along with empirically based information about clinical interventions and accompanying probes to facilitate thought and discussion about possible ways to handle each case.

Oppression and Discrimination

As popular media sources portray Arabs and Arab Americans in a manner that reflects the politically tense relations between the United States and various Arab Middle East countries, such portrayals are internalized by both non–Arab Americans, as they "learn" more about individuals of Arab descent, as well as Arab Americans themselves—particularly those in earlier stages of developing their cultural identities—as they learn more about themselves. Both overt and covert discrimination are detrimental to the mental health of individuals toward whom those acts are directed. Ethnic pride can be either promoted or discouraged by such oppression; appropriately developed or supported, it can serve as a strong source of resilience among Arab Americans.

Acculturative Stress

Increasingly, attention is being given to researching the various types of stressors encompassed by the acculturation process. Along with learning a new language and cultural customs, immigrants must learn to navigate within new societal structures, such as education, employment, and government. These transitions are often quite challenging; consider, for example, "transferring" from former levels of education or employment credentials to new host systems that might not recognize them. In this context, it may be difficult to determine student grade levels within a new structure, particularly in postsecondary institutions. It also might be challenging, and at times impossible, for professionals to have their former credentials recognized in a reciprocal way. For instance, a person who was a pharmacist in the country of origin might have to either undergo an entire training program in the United States in order to achieve recognized credentials or forgo that career path altogether. Understandably, these difficulties can sometimes lead to anxiety or depression in recent immigrants. Resilience within this arena can be fostered if immigrants are able to transfer their former training, if not credentials, to comparable or similar careers in the new host country.

Intergenerational stress, among both recent and later generations of immigrants, may pose additional family stressors. In some cases in which English language acquisition has not been fully achieved, particularly by the parents or older generation, children may be inadvertently placed in a situation of having to translate notes or other directives from school to their parents, thus creating a role reversal in terms of a traditional hierarchy. In addition, rules or expectations from the culture of origin may be stricter than, or otherwise different from, those recognized by the children's school and community peers, in this way causing conflicts in the parenting arena. For example, rules about curfews, dating, or other aspects of supervised activities may be imposed that may result in children feeling "different" from the peers with whom they are trying to fit in. Such situations can pose additional stressors for all generations and family members involved. Dialogue between Arab-American youths and their families around these acculturation issues can yield self-exploration opportunities to identify psycho-emotional stressors, as well as cultural strengths and positive values.

Ethnic and Gender Identity Development

Historically, "Arabism" and ethnic identity development among Arab Americans have paralleled their immigration history in the United States. As discussed earlier in the chapter, demographic definitions of Arab Americans, especially for census purposes, have evolved significantly over the years. Paralleling such U.S. trends, along with overall global relations and other politics, pride in ethnic heritage, particularly for Arab Americans, did not emerge fully until the 1960s. Over the course of the last 50 or so years, political and other conflicts between the United States and the nations in the Arab Middle East, as well as domestic acts of violence either legitimately or falsely attributed to Arabs or Arab Americans, have often served as the catalyst for the ebb and flow of ethnic pride within the Arab-American community nationally. Even within Arab-American enclaves, where young people, who are in the midst of their identity development, may have access to role models and peers who share their heritage, negotiating such an identity development process in the face of sociopolitical challenges has not been easy. Intentional mentoring can support resilience among Arab-American youths and young adults as they mature through the stages of process.

Relationships between Arab-American parents and their children may be affected by the cultural differences between their country of origin and their current country of residence (Beitin & Aprahamian, 2014). For example, although Arab-American parents want their children to fit in and be successful in their new home (i.e., the United States), they would also like them to maintain a connection with their heritage. Certain Arab-American adolescents, in their ethnic identity development, may worry that integrating United States culture and society into their lives will further distance themselves from their cultural heritage or even make them lose that heritage altogether.

Along with overall identity development, mixed messages about "appropriate" gender development may cause additional challenges. These messages can emerge from families of origin, communities—either ethnic enclave communities or the community at large—and, of course, the media and other sources to which young people are constantly exposed. Questions such as "Should I seek postsecondary and graduate education?", "Which careers are appropriate for me?", or "Should I get married?" are thought about by young women of most ethnic groups, and Arab Americans are no different.

In more traditional Arab-American families, the issue of gender may more significantly affect the "experience of individuation—which refers to the process of becoming an individual and having distinct characteristics from others" (Beitin & Aprahamian, 2014, p. 70) because of some of the cultural values and beliefs, such as collectivism, discussed earlier. For example, a son or daughter raised in a more traditional Arab-American family and community may find that his or her formation of gender identity will differ notably from an average non–Arab American's gender identity formation (Cainkar & Ghazal Read, 2014). For Arab-American girls, as opposed to boys, the difference can lead to a more complex negotiation of values, beliefs, and ideals between their traditional cultural upbringing and the modern, liberal surroundings found in the United States. This issue often is at the crux of related, sometimes concurrent issues, such as sexual or career identity development. Here, too, role modeling and mentoring can promote resilience among Arab-American youths, particularly those who may perceive themselves or be perceived by others as in the "minority" with regard to sexual orientation, career choice, or other issues.

Other Psychosocial Issues

Arab Americans, like their non–Arab-American counterparts, experience any number of developmental and crisis issues, along with psychological disorders. Particularly because Arab Americans are not identified as a special population by most governmental or mental health agencies, there are no specific data on the prevalence of issues within this population compared with that in the overall population of communities.

For one group, however, there are at least certain data: recent immigrants who are refugees exhibit a high prevalence of PTSD, often accompanied by elevated rates of anxiety and depression, as well as other psychoemotional and medical complaints. These refugees came from Lebanon in the 1970s and 1980s and, most recently, from Iraq, as veterans who fought in, and civilians who fled from, the 1991 Gulf War, often via refugee camps elsewhere in the world. Accurate diagnosis and treatment of their medical illnesses is a prerequisite to tackling any other issues with any kind of success and to developing overall resilience within this population. To date, few Syrian refugees have been resettled in the United States in response to the civil war and chaos occurring in Syria, but in September of 2015 President Obama pledged asylum to at least 10,000 Syrian refugees in the upcoming year (Robbins, 2015). This newly emergent population will most certainly bring with it a similar base of risk factors, along with a potentially unique set of circumstances.

Psychosocial issues for Arab Americans often present as somatic or physical issues (Nassar-McMillan et al., in press). Depression or anxiety, for example, may become manifest in digestive, sleep, or any number of other physical disorders. It is important for all health and mental health care providers to be attuned to this pattern when working with Arab-American clients or patients. Again, effective identification and treatment better ensure resilience in working through other, related psychosocial issues. Now read Case Studies 10.1 and 10.2 which will continue later in the chapter.

CASE STUDY 10.1

Meet Ahmed: A Saudi Arabian Middle Schooler

Ahmed was born in Saudi Arabia. When he was 10 years old, his father, a university administrator, took a position at a midwestern U.S. university to direct the new Middle East studies program there, about an hour outside of a large Arab-American community, or enclave. Ahmed's family (his mother, father, three brothers, and one sister) relocated to the United States for an indefinite time. His mother was a nurse in Saudi Arabia but was not able to transfer her credentials to the United States and so is not able to work professionally, a situation that has caused some depression on her part and financial stress in the home. She has been unable to secure even lower level positions as a nursing assistant. Nor has she been sufficiently attentive to Ahmed's emotional needs, because of her own acculturative stress and resulting depression. Ahmed is now in middle school in their urban community school system. There are a number of other Arab-American students in the school community. Some of them are second- and third-generation Arab Americans from Lebanon, although they still maintain strong ties to their ethnic heritage. Another group is first-generation students from Yemen, a relatively rural country with a lower socioeconomic and educational base. Along with these groups, there is a military base within a few hours of the city, and a large number of students in the school have at least one parent affiliated with the U.S. military, with some currently deployed in Iraq.

Ahmed often feels lonely and sad. He doesn't seem to fit in with either group of Arab-American students, even though most of them, except for some of the Lebanese students, are Muslim. The Lebanese group calls him a "boater," as they do the Yemeni students, because he is less acculturated to U.S. cultural norms and speaks English with an Arabic accent. The Yemeni students also do not accept Ahmed, because he comes from a more affluent and educated background than they do. Moreover, when there are military or political flare-ups related to the situation in Iraq, some students in the school make anti-Arab remarks to him, along with others, about "going back where they came from," calling them "camel jockeys" and the like. Despite the sizeable Arab and Muslim population in the school, there is considerable misunderstanding between those groups, on the one hand, and non–Arab Americans, on the other. Some of the sentiments expressed within the school by these non–Arab-American students have reflected those presented in the media by public figures as expressing Islamophobia (equating Islam and Muslims with hatred of Western culture, terrorism, etc.).

CASE STUDY 10.2

Meet Laila: A Lebanese Graduate Student

Laila is a graduate student in engineering at a university in a large Arab-American enclave. Her family is of Lebanese descent, with several of her grandparents being the first immigrants from the family. Originally merchants, these individuals expanded the family business enough to provide more than adequate financial support for later generations to better themselves economically. Laila is not the first of her siblings and cousins to pursue graduate education. She is, however, the first female to pursue a graduate degree in a male-dominated field. Living in the large Arab-American community, she knows numerous other young women in her program and understands the struggle that some of them have had in terms of negotiating their gender identities within their families, communities, and the university program, which is male dominated among both students and the faculty. She also has begun to question her sexuality. She thinks that some of this questioning may be related to her school environment and the absence of role models, but she does not feel comfortable talking to any of her peers about it.

On the one hand, Laila loves the academic challenges of her program and has considered going on to pursue her doctorate in engineering. On the other hand, she has experienced some strain from not having adequate role models or mentoring in her program and sometimes feels as though she is floundering in her career direction. She has not seen many females go on to the doctoral program, even though they may have initially planned to.

Lately, the strain of Laila's identity negotiation processes, coupled with her career decision challenges, has resulted in heightened anxiety. In turn, this anxiety has led to insomnia and digestive issues, both of which affect her ability to concentrate, as well as her ability to attend classes.

CONSIDERATIONS IN COUNSELING ARAB AMERICANS

Within the most recent decade, both scholars and practitioners have focused on "best practices" counseling interventions with clients of Arab descent (e.g., Amri et al., 2013; Hakim-Larson et al., 2012; Nassar-McMillan, 2010). In implementing best practices, counselors should avoid the tendency to impose Western biases and approaches, engage community and family members as much as possible, understand and identify the nature of stigmas and help-seeking behaviors, and be mindful of standards for cultural competence.

Approach

Many Western approaches to counseling apply insight-based strategies. For Arab-American clients who are more acculturated, this approach may be beneficial. However, think for a moment about what you have learned about Arab culture and societal structure. Family and community units are tight knit, and each person has a role that is critical within those structures. Thus, any goals aimed at building additional client insights run the risk of concurrently creating more internal conflicts. Instead, Arab Americans as a group tend to prefer solution-focused, cognitive–behavioral, or other pragmatic or practical interventions. It is important to add, though, that constructivist approaches may be useful, particularly in a situation in which the counselor is non–Arab American, in that they allow clients to tell their own story and be heard, understood, and validated.

Other issues mentioned earlier in the chapter, having to do with, for example, emotional expressions or concepts of time, may emerge in counseling as well. Thus, clients may be reluctant to express a negative emotion or thought toward a parent or another respected person in the community. Or, by contrast, if they are engaging in an emotive process with a counselor with whom they feel comfortable and have established a rapport, they may be highly expressive in aspects such as tone, volume, gesticulation, and so on, perhaps more so than a non–Arab-American client. Building a positive working alliance with an Arab-American client will involve both intellectual skills (e.g., understanding preferred approaches, learning about the individual and the group) and personal skills (e.g., monitoring internal prejudices, becoming empathetic, finding ways to relate). Reflection 10.2 provides a metaphor for considering and combining these skill sets. Then, going one step further, Activity 10.2 addresses specific knowledge, self-awareness, and skills related to working with Arab-American clients.

Family and Community Involvement

Remember, Arab Americans tend to be collectivistic peoples. Therefore, to promote resilience, individual counseling not only should be focused on the collective unit rather than the individual, but also should involve individuals within that unit. Whenever possible and appropriate, it can be beneficial to bring in other family members. Engaging the support of community leaders, such as Imams or other trusted individuals can also serve as a powerful intervention or strategy.

Along those lines, whenever attendance at a local community event can be incorporated into the treatment plan, it could be important to do so. For example, inviting a person who is self-conscious about her or his appearance or social skills to a community event, together with homework involving the counselor or others, can be beneficial. This approach may appear to run counter to the traditional Western view, but, for the Arab and Arab-American populations, it may be far more effective.

REFLECTION 10.2

As a counselor trainee, you are perhaps like a carpenter learning to use all of the tools assembled in your tool belt. The first few times you hold them, they may seem awkward, but with repeated practice, they become more familiar to you. You are unlike a carpenter, however, in that the most important tool is yourself. We could make the analogy that the tool belt represents your personality, your skills, your life history, and your view of the world. Thus, in order to help clients of any culture or background, you should be familiar with the tools of our trade (e.g., theoretical approaches and techniques, methods for assessing and evaluating problems, exercises to improve health or to work through those problems, resources for assistance) and the condition of your tool belt.

What is the state of your knowledge, awareness, and skills with respect to Arab-American clients? Have you taken an opportunity to broaden your horizons by talking to people from a variety of backgrounds? Do you recognize any stereotypes or limited ideas present in your thinking about Arab Americans? Do you have an emotional response to the information presented in this chapter?

To reach out to clients, counselors can use some of what they know as part of the human experience, some of what they have learned about the specific journeys of others, and some tools that may clarify or resolve the physical, mental, emotional, or spiritual stress of the client. Spend some time thinking about how the tools you have acquired so far in your training would be useful with Arab-American clients and how you can polish up your tool belt (yourself) so that you are ready to respond.

ACTIVITY 10.2

According to the Multicultural and Social Justice Counseling Competencies (Ratts, Singh, Nassar-McMillan, Butler, & McCulloch, 2015), attitudes and beliefs, knowledge, skills, and action are the key components in developing basic multicultural competence. These competencies are embedded within the four developmental domains of counselor self-awareness, client worldview, counseling relationship, and counseling and advocacy interventions. Moreover, the privileged and oppressed statuses of both client and counselor should be considered at specific points in time, because they are particularly relevant to the counseling relationship. In counseling Arab Americans, these competencies can be addressed in the following ways (feel free to add your own ideas to the list):

I. **Attitudes and beliefs:** Learning about our own personal and cultural biases toward Arab Americans and determining ways to overcome them. In so doing, counselors can gain increased respect for their Arab-American clients' culturally different backgrounds, experiences, and values. Identifying these attitudes and beliefs should include an exploration into (1) counselor and client experiences with privilege and oppression, (2) the ways in which counselor and client attitudes and beliefs play out through the counseling relationship, and (3) the ways in which counselors can act on the basis of these experiences and resulting worldviews on various sociological levels (e.g., intrapersonal; interpersonal; institutional; community; public policy; international and global affairs).

II. **Knowledge:** Learning about how our own culture personally and professionally affects our attitudes toward Arab Americans and how oppression, racism, discrimination, and stereotyping against Arab Americans may affect our counseling relationships with Arab-American clients (e.g., in the way, and even whether, we assess internalized oppression; in how traditional counseling settings may be incongruent with the cultural values of some Arab-American clients; in how Arab Americans' help-seeking behaviors may affect the counseling process; and in how testing and assessment may be culturally biased). Counselors should apply this knowledge to multiple sociological levels relevant to their work with Arab-American clients (e.g., intrapersonal; interpersonal; institutional; community; public policy; international and global affairs).

III. **Skills:** Learning ways to seek out education, training, and consultation to improve our effectiveness in working with Arab-American clients; in employing a wider range of verbal and nonverbal communication styles and responses in our client–counselor relationships; in seeking consultation with supporting personnel; and in working to eliminate biases, prejudices, and discriminatory practices across sociological levels (e.g., intrapersonal; interpersonal; institutional; community; public policy; international and global affairs).

IV. **Action:** Extending our professional counseling work beyond the traditional counseling setting and into broader systems that are relevant to our clients, such as their schools, institutions, communities, and public policy (more broadly, into intrapersonal; interpersonal; institutional; community; public policy; and international and global affairs levels). For Arab-American clients in particular, this task involves understanding and taking action in cases where legislative policies and practices, both formal and informal, may have a direct effect on our clients' well-being and mental health.

In small groups, discuss other ways by which you can examine and enhance your attitudes and beliefs, knowledge, skills, and action for working effectively with individuals and families of Arab descent.

It is important to gauge with each client or family whether the level to which the counselor is perceived as being a member of the greater community is a positive or negative attribute to the counseling relationship. On the one hand, it may be viewed as positive, in the sense that the counselor may have a better understanding and appreciation of cultural issues. On the other hand, issues of confidentiality and other boundaries may be less clear and may need to be reiterated more as a part of the counseling process.

Stigmas and Help-Seeking Behaviors

In the previous section on mental health issues, the high prevalence of somatization, or the physical manifestation of psychological distress, was mentioned. This presentation is rooted historically within Arab culture, although there have been, and still are, numerous tribal and other indigenous individuals whose holistic treatment of the person includes psychological as well as physical symptoms and etiology. For counselors, being aware of this tendency toward somatization can help develop an authoritative stance, perhaps more consistent with that of a medical professional, that may be most effective.

In addition, counseling is viewed as a Western concept and therefore is more likely to be sought out by later generations of Arab Americans. More recent immigrants, if seeking help at all, might do so from medical professionals or members of the clergy. Thus, particularly for counselors living near an Arab-American enclave or an urban community with a large population of Arab Americans, it is important to collaborate with helping professionals across a variety of arenas to develop client education interventions about counseling services, as well as referral networks to promote resilience among individuals and communities. For counselors of Arab descent, ethnicity may serve either as an advantage, in the sense that prospective clients might feel more culturally understood, or as a disadvantage, in the sense that issues of confidentiality may arise if the client and counselor live in the same community.

Case Studies Revisited

Now that we have explored some of the issues that might be likely to emerge in working within an Arab-American community or with Arab-American clients, as well as counseling and other treatment considerations, we will review each case study in further detail.

CASE STUDY 10.1 CONTINUED: AHMED: A SCHOOL COUNSELING CASE   Recall the case of Ahmed, the middle schooler who recently relocated to the United States. Lonely and sad, not fitting in with either the other Arab-American kids or the non–Arab-American ones, Ahmed got involved in several fights at school. The principal has asked the parents to come in and meet with him and one of the school counselors for consultation. Both parents came to discuss the situation. The principal is recommending that Ahmed work with the school counselor and, possibly, a counselor from the outside community. During the meeting, the parents express their concerns. They have some questions about the counseling process and share some hesitation about having their son involved in it, but they are assured that it is viewed as academic support. They are less willing to participate in community counseling at this point.

Imagine that you are the school counselor to whom Ahmed is assigned. You decide to conduct some research into issues that Ahmed or others like him might be facing. Here are some of your findings:

- Arab-American adolescents who perceive greater levels of racism and discrimination have been found to be at higher risk for acculturative stress, depression, anxiety, and both internalizing and externalizing symptoms (Ahmed et al., 2011).

- Parental support for younger children (Ahmed et al., 2011; Lewandowski, Chiodo, Peterson, & Kira, 2007) and peer support for older adolescents (Sheikh, 2009; Tabbah, Miranda, & Wheaton, 2012) have been identified as providing protective factors and bolstering resilience.
- Ethnic identity development processes that effectively navigate the culture of origin and the mainstream culture, along with higher levels of religious coping, have been associated with decreased levels of psychological distress among Arab-American adolescents (Ahmed et al., 2011).
- Arab Americans with distinctively Arab names have been found to experience employment discrimination, with such applicants applying to twice as many jobs for the same result (Widner & Chicoine, 2011).
- Language and other communication barriers may have detrimental effects on the counseling process (Aboul-Enein & Aboul-Enein, 2010).

These findings collectively suggest that you will need to be holistic in your initial meetings and assessments with Ahmed, and perhaps his parents as well. Because of the key role his parents can and should ideally play in supporting Ahmed's successful acculturation and development, the mother's employment discrimination and depression should be addressed and she should be referred for outside counseling services. If there are language barriers in working with Ahmed's parents (in particular, his mother), it will be essential to bring in a translator to ensure that the communication is as effective as possible. Think about the following list of questions as you prepare for your work with Ahmed:

In terms of your approach,

- What are some of the approaches that might be less helpful? More helpful?
- What are some of the strategies/techniques that might be least helpful? Most helpful?

In terms of engaging the family and community,

- How, if at all, should or could the family be involved?
- Which family members should or could be involved, and in what ways?
- To what extent is the family involved with the local community?
- To what extent is the family involved with the nearby Arab-American community?
- To what extent is Ahmed interested in connecting with the various communities?
- Are there key individuals or community leaders who could be helpful in providing support to Ahmed or his family? If so, who are they?
- How can these or other approaches foster resilience among Ahmed and his family?

In terms of stigmas,

- How do you think Ahmed might feel about seeing the school counselor?
- How do you think Ahmed might feel about having his family involved?
- How do you think Ahmed's family feels about him (and them) needing this extra support?
- Are there other ways in which this psychological distress and other stressors may be manifesting for Ahmed? For other family members?

CASE STUDY 10.2 CONTINUED: LAILA: A COLLEGE COUNSELING CASE Laila's master's program is coming to an end, and she is feeling pressured by her family to make a decision. Although her family members have been supportive of her educational pursuits, they feel that it is time for her to focus on finding a marital partner alongside her upcoming career goals.

Her brothers tease her about being in a "men's" program and profession, adding to her self-questioning of gender, sexual, and career identity issues. With her anxiety-based digestive issues spiraling out of control, Laila ends up making an appointment with the student health center on campus to get help with her digestive problems. The physician treats Laila's physical symptoms but discerns that the underlying cause might be psycho-socio-emotional. He strongly urges her to make an appointment next door at the counseling center. At first, Laila is reluctant, but after a few weeks of continued physical issues despite the medication she is taking, she decides to go to the counseling center to talk to someone about her concerns. You are her assigned counselor.

You have counseled women college students on gender and career issues, but have not worked with many Arab-American students thus far. In your preparations, you identify a number of issues in the literature that may be particularly relevant in working with Laila:

- Peer support for older adolescents and young adults (Sheikh, 2009; Tabbah et al., 2012) have been identified as providing protective factors and bolstering resilience among Arab Americans.
- High percentages of today's college students have reported experiencing anti-Arab discrimination, which can have an adverse effect on mental health (Haboush & Barakat, 2014).
- Intergenerational and acculturation differences between college-aged Arab-American youths and older family members, particularly with regard to individualistic versus collectivistic decision making and expectations, can create challenges to navigating identity issues successfully (Nassar-McMillan et al., in press; Rasmi, Chuang, & Hennig, 2014).

The information you found prompts you to consider the possibility that Laila may need to extend her peer support group both within and outside of her academic department and even the university. Ideally, this reaching out should include peers from her Arab-American community who may be successful women professionals or currently seeking an advanced college degree. She might find some candidates who are pursuing or are currently in "nontraditional" careers. It is also important to discern whether Laila has experienced discrimination or "hostile environment" issues in her classes or department that are related to her ethnicity. If so, these experiences need to be incorporated into her initial overall assessment process. Finally, it may be important to explore with Laila, perhaps through narrative or other constructivist approaches, the relationships within her family structure, the influence of ethnicity within them, and the culturally based values that various key individuals hold. In terms of your approach,

- What are some of the approaches that might be less helpful? More helpful?
- What are some of the strategies/techniques that might be least helpful? Most helpful? Most likely to foster resilience?

In terms of engaging the family and community,

- How, if at all, should or could the family be involved?
- Which family members should or could be involved, and in what ways?
- To what extent is Laila involved with the local Arab-American community?
- To what extent is Laila involved with the local community at large?
- Are there key individuals or community leaders (in the Arab-American community or the larger community) who could be helpful in providing support to Laila?

In terms of stigmas,

- How do you think Laila might feel about counseling?
- Can you identify any cultural stigmas (e.g., gender, sexual, career) that might be involved in Laila's identity development processes?

COUNSELING CONSIDERATIONS ENDNOTE

More than ever before, today's counselors are charged with the task of serving as advocates for their clients individually, locally, and nationally. Most helping professions have identified this new role as a critical one in today's world, with its vast diversity across cultures, religions, sexual orientations, and the like. Working with Arab Americans, given the sociopolitical climate over the recent decade or more, requires a certain level of knowledge of a number of topics: U.S. foreign policy toward the Arab Middle East and neighboring regions, civil liberties issues around profiling and harassment, and laws surrounding immigration and seizure of people and their property (Nassar-McMillan, 2003, 2010). All these, in addition to the basic multicultural competencies applied to Arab-American clients, are requisite for building resilience effectively. (For more information about multicultural competencies applied to Arab Americans, see Nassar-McMillan, 2007a, 2007b.)

Living within an ethnic enclave can provide the support necessary for Arab Americans to move beyond the initial stages of identity development and arrive at a mature and consolidated sense of ethnic identity. Individuals moving into those advanced identity stages could focus on projecting the positive aspects of their culture with pride. In various communities, support organizations have formed to promote employment, expand religious tolerance and understanding, provide accurate information about the history and politics of the Middle East, and support members of the community. These resources also are available to counselors who are interested in working with this population. Even outside ethnic enclaves, these organizations have a national scope that seeks to provide information and resources necessary to help counselors develop their competencies further. Table 10.1 provides a preliminary list of resources.

TABLE 10.1 Resources for Counseling Individuals and Families of Arab Descent

General Web Resources

America–Mideast Educational and Training Services, Inc. [AMIDEAST] (www.amideast.org): This American nonprofit organization is engaged in international education, training, and development activities in the Middle East and North Africa.

American Arab Chamber of Commerce (http://americanarab.com/): The American Arab Chamber of Commerce builds economic bridges by promoting and empowering the business community it serves on a local, national, and international level.

American-Arab Anti-Discrimination Committee (www.adc.org): The American-Arab Anti-Discrimination Committee is a civil rights organization committed to defending the rights of people of Arab descent and promoting their rich cultural heritage.

Arab American Institute Links and Resources (http://www.aaiusa.org/links-resources): This Web source includes documents and links promoting education on Arab Americans, their religions, and the Middle East.

(Continued)

TABLE 10.1 Resources for Counseling Individuals and Families of Arab Descent (Continued)

Arab American Institute (www.aaiusa.org/): The Arab American Institute represents the policy and community interests of Arab Americans throughout the United States and strives to promote Arab-American participation in the U.S. electoral system.

Arab American National Museum (http://www.arabamericanmuseum.org/): The Arab American National Museum documents, preserves, and presents the history, culture, and contributions of Arab Americans in an effort to dispel misconceptions about Arab Americans and other minorities.

Arab Community Center for Economic and Social Services [ACCESS] (www.accesscommunity. org): ACCESS strives to enable and empower individuals, families, and communities to lead informed, productive, and culturally sensitive lives; ACCESS also seeks to honor our Arab-American heritage through community building and to provide services to those of every heritage who are in need.

Arab-American Women's Business Council (http://www.aawbc.org/): The mission of the council is to empower Arab-American women of diverse professions and industries through networking, leadership, and educational/professional development opportunities.

Center for Muslim–Christian Understanding (https://acmcu.georgetown.edu/): The Center's mission is to improve relations between the Muslim world and the West and to enhance understanding of Muslims in the West.

Middle East Institute (http://www.mei.edu/): This is the oldest Washington-based institution dedicated solely to the study of the Middle East, to increasing knowledge of the Middle East among the citizens of the United States, and to promoting a better understanding between the people of these two areas.

Middle East & Middle Eastern American Center [MEMEAC] (http://memeac.gc.cuny.edu): Since 2001, MEMEAC has worked to promote the study of the Middle East and Middle Eastern Americans.

Middle East Policy Council (www.mepc.org): The Middle East Policy Council is a nonprofit organization whose mission is to contribute to American understanding of the political, economic, and cultural issues that affect U.S. interests in the Middle East.

National Network for Arab American Communities (http://www.nnaac.org/): This organization's mission is the development of Arab-American community-based nonprofit organizations that understand, meet the needs, and represent the concerns of Arab Americans at a local level while also collectively addressing those issues at a national level.

Network of Arab-American Professionals (http://www.naaponline.org/): The organization's mission is to promote professional networking and social interaction among Arab-American and Arab professionals in the United States and abroad; educate both the Arab-American and non-Arab communities about Arab culture, identity, and concerns; advance the Arab-American community by empowering, protecting, and promoting its political causes and interests in the United States and abroad within all levels of society; support the Arab student movement in the United States; and serve society through volunteerism and community service efforts.

One Nation For All (http://www.onenationforall.org/): One Nation For All can help find the best possible outcome of a case or settlement when it matters most. The public deserves the right to understand legal proceedings, and this organization is here to help.

The Arab-American Business and Professional Association (http://www.a-abpa.org/web/): This organization aims to provide networking opportunities for the growing Arab-American business and professional community and to promote trade and investment between Illinois businesses and the Arab World.

Books

Al-Faruqi, L. (1991). *Women, Muslim society, and Islam.* Plainfield, IN: American Trust Publications.

Amer, M., & Awwad, G. (Eds.). (in press). *Handbook of Arab American psychology*. New York, NY: Brunner-Routledge.

Haneef, S. (1985). *What everyone should know about Islam and Muslims*. Chicago, IL: Kazi Publications.

Kahf, M. (1999). *Western representations of the Muslim woman*. Austin: University of Texas Press.

Maqsood, R. (1994). *Teach yourself Islam*. Chicago, IL: NTC Publishing Group.

Nassar-McMillan, S. C., Ajrouch, K., & Hakim-Larson, J. (Eds.). (2014). *Biopsychosocial perspectives on Arab Americans: Culture, development, and health*. New York, NY: Springer.

Peters, F. E. (1990). *Judaism, Christianity, and Islam*. Princeton, NJ: Princeton Paperbacks.

Shaikh, M. A. (Ed.). (1995). *Teaching about Islam & Muslims in the public school classroom: A handbook for educators* (3rd ed.). Fountain Valley, CA: Council on Islamic Education.

Legal Resources

• For resources on civil rights and civil liberties:

Arab American Institute. (2015). *Domestic policy*. Retrieved from: http://www.aaiusa.org/domestic-policy.

• The U.S. Commission on Civil Rights Hotline, 1-800-552-6843

U.S. Commission on Civil Rights. (2015). *Contact information*. Retrieved from: http://www.usccr.gov/contact/

• U.S. Department of Justice Civil Rights Division. (2015). *Combatting post-9/11 discriminatory backlash*. Retrieved from: http://www.justice.gov/crt/nordwg.php

• To file a complaint about an alleged civil-rights violation by a U.S. Department of Justice employee, including employees of the FBI, the Drug Enforcement Administration, the INS, the Federal Bureau of Prisons, and the U.S. Marshals Service:

U.S. Department of Justice Office of the Inspector General. (2015). *Hotline*. Retrieved from: https://oig.justice.gov/hotline/index.htm

• For a brochure, in English and Arabic, on federal protections against discrimination because of national origin:

United States Department of Justice Civil Rights Division. (2015). *Federal protections against national origin discrimination*. Retrieved from: http://www.justice.gov/crt/legalinfo/natlorg-eng.php and http://www.justice.gov/crt/legalinfo/natlorg-ar.pdf

• *Summary: Civil Liberties Restoration Act of 2004*. Retrieved from: https://www.americanprogress.org/wp-content/uploads/kf/CLRASUMMARY.pdf

• *I am in immigration detention . . . what are my rights?* Retrieved from: http://www.nationalimmigrationproject.org/community/Detention%20-%20Know%20Your%20Rights%20-%20English.pdf

• American Civil Liberties Union. (2015). *Immigrants' rights*. Retrieved from: https://www.aclu.org/issues/immigrants-rights

• U.S. Equal Employment Opportunity Commission. (n.d.). *Questions and answers about the workplace: Rights of Muslims, Arabs, South Asians, and Sikhs under the Equal Employment Opportunity laws*. Retrieved from: http://www.eeoc.gov/eeoc/publications/backlash-employee.cfm

• U.S. Equal Employment Opportunity Commission. (n.d.). *Questions and answers about employer responsibilities concerning the employment of Muslims, Arabs, South Asians, and Sikhs*. Retrieved from: http://www.eeoc.gov/eeoc/publications/backlash-employer.cfm

• U.S. Department of Justice Civil Rights Division. (2015). *Combating religious discrimination and protecting religious freedom*. Retrieved from: http://www.justice.gov/crt/spec_topics/religiousdiscrimination/religionpamp.php

Summary

Arab Americans are a diverse ethnic group, yet homogenous in certain ways, in the United States today. Their communities and cultures are vibrant with this diversity, intertwined with American cultures and traditions. Learning about some of these Arab-American cultures, whether first, second, or third generation; whether immigration occurred as a voluntary, exciting venture or as a terrifying postwar exile experience; whether hailing from southwestern Asia or northern Africa; whether Muslim or Christian, is likely to become a rich and valuable learning experience for counseling practitioners. You have learned about the complex immigration history of individuals and families of Arab descent, as well as their primary enclaves, or ethnic communities, in the United States. Perhaps some of these are located in your own state or city.

You have also learned about some important overlaps, as well as distinctions, among *Arabs*, *Muslims*, and *Middle Easterners*. Understanding the heterogeneity of Arab-American culture will help you, as a counseling practitioner, become a more savvy consumer of today's media. Once you begin to understand individuals, families, and communities from a human and empathic perspective, you can begin to unravel the contemporary social perceptions that are carefully engineered by political players and their media campaigns. You will be able to discern how the media can perpetuate negative stereotypes and reinforce discrimination on subtle levels. You will realize how your clients may have been or are personally affected by events such as the tragedy of 9/11 or the recent Arab Spring movement. You may begin to better recognize or empathize with individuals or families of Arab descent who might already be in your professional, personal, social, or client circles You will learn of famous people who may have Arab origins. Most important, you will be able to validate your clients' experiences of both overt and subtle discriminations, based on their ethnicity, in the context of a contemporary sociopolitical climate.

You will find yourself pondering more often the what-ifs of cultural values—both similar and different. What if your own cultural background is also collectivistic? What if it is more individualistic? What are the strengths and values of each of these possibilities? What if you begin to recognize the similarities among multiple cultures or between Arab-American cultural backgrounds and your own? How will you begin to recognize these values in your clients or in your own family or community? What if you realize that there are many similarities between your own religious traditions and those of Arabs, whether Christian or Muslim? Will you begin to recognize them when you are out in public places? Dining with your own family? Or as you critique the next novel you read or movie you watch?

You have learned some basics about the religious tradition of Islam. Belief in one God, daily prayer, fasting, charitable giving, and the hajj, or pilgrimage, to Mecca—key tenets of Islam—are not so different from those of other world religions. Moreover, they do not define all Arabs, but are intertwined within the fabric of life for most Arabs and, thus, those of Arab descent who still remain connected to their culture of origin.

You have learned that, despite the overarching Arab cultural traditions and values, heterogeneity cannot be overemphasized. In other words, each individual, family, and community will be self-defined, influenced by many complex variables, such as ethnicity or country of origin, length of time in the United States, gender, educational level, level of acculturation, and, perhaps most important, the ethnic identity of the particular person or people. As counselors, we need to recognize that each complex constellation of these unique variables will determine what kinds of risks and resiliencies need to be considered. Whether you are working with Ahmad or Laila, we hope that the knowledge and insights you have gained from this chapter will stand you in good stead in your development as a professional counselor.

Review Questions

1. Given the complexity of the immigration pattern from the Arab Middle East, how might a client's region or country of origin and year or timeframe of immigration influence his or her acculturation process, ethnic identity, and gender identity?

2. What are some hallmarks of the collectivistic values within Arab-American societies, and how might those hallmarks play out in counseling within your setting of interest?

3. Explain the overlaps and distinctions among the terms *Arab*, *Muslim*, and *Middle Easterner*.

4. What are some of the particular challenges faced by recent immigrants, especially refugees, from regions of the Arab Middle East?

5. In what ways do you believe that your views about Arab Americans, prior to reading this chapter, may have been influenced by the media? In what ways, if any, have your views changed after reading this chapter?

11 Individuals and Families of Asian Descent

Linh P. Luu, Arpana G. Inman,
and Alvin N. Alvarez

PREVIEW

At 5.2% of the population, the 16.1 million individuals who describe themselves as Asian American (U.S. Census Bureau, 2012c) have rapidly emerged onto the racial landscape of the United States (Humes, Jones, & Ramírez, 2011). In addition, 1.7 million people, or another 0.6% of the U.S. population, reported that they were Asian in combination with one or more other races (U.S. Census Bureau, 2012c). With a growth rate of 43.3% between 2000 and 2010, the Asian-American community has been characterized as one of the fastest growing racial and ethnic communities (Humes et al., 2011). In particular, Asian Americans represent three broad, yet distinct, groups: East Asians from China, Taiwan, Japan, the Philippines, and Korea; South Asians from India, Pakistan, Bangladesh, Sri Lanka, Nepal, Bhutan, and the Maldives; and Southeast Asians (including the Hmong) from Vietnam, Laos, Cambodia, Thailand, and Myanmar (formerly Burma; Tewari, Inman, & Sandhu, 2003). Interestingly, the U.S. Census Bureau has been using six detailed Asian response categories (Asian Indian, Chinese, Filipino, Japanese, Korean, and Vietnamese) in the decennial census question on race since 1980 (Hoeffel, Rastogi, Kim, & Shahid, 2012). Despite being categorized under the umbrella of "Asian Americans," these communities exhibit much ethnic, linguistic, and historical diversity (Trinh-Shevrin, Islam, & Rey, 2009). Indeed, the U.S. Census Bureau (2012d) estimates that, by 2060, the diverse Asian-American community will increase by over 200% and constitute about 8% of the U.S. population. Note that numerous scholars have argued that any treatment of this community in strictly aggregate terms obscures the complexities and heterogeneity of the lived experiences of Asian Americans, both currently and historically (Ali, 2014). Consequently, to shift away from broad statistics, the first section of this chapter begins with a historical overview of Asian Americans and the role of discrimination in their lives. Then, the second section examines the ethnic, socioeconomic, linguistic, and educational complexities that characterize the group's heterogeneity. After that, the next three sections provide counselors with a baseline understanding of the culture and values, individual differences, and prevailing psychological distress among Asian Americans. Finally, the remainder of the chapter explores issues related to Asian Americans seeking help and coping with their problems, and outlines counseling guidelines. Before beginning this chapter, complete Reflection 11.1.

REFLECTION 11.1

Assume that you are Asian American. Using the following three lenses, write your thoughts:

1. How do you perceive yourself as a member of this group?
2. How might others perceive you?
3. How would you like to be perceived?

ASIAN-AMERICAN HISTORY

Since the large-scale arrival of Chinese laborers on the sugar plantations of Hawaii and the gold mines of California in the mid-1800s, immigration has been a common thread shared by numerous Asian ethnic groups. Whether they were "pushed" from their countries of origin by political strife, economic instability, social persecution, famine, or war, Asian immigrants have been "pulled" to the United States (what the Cantonese called *gam saan,* or "Gold Mountain") by the lure of several factors: the prospect of earning economic fortunes, the availability of high-paying jobs, and the potential to provide for one's family. Indeed, the same hopes that currently lure Asian immigrants from Taiwan, China, and India to Silicon Valley are reminiscent of what drew Cantonese and Punjabi laborers to the hills and fields of California in the 1850s.

Along with the lure of these factors, Asian immigrants have also faced similar forms of hostility and discrimination (Cheryan & Monin, 2005; Li, 2014). For instance, Chinatowns began to develop because Chinese Americans were restricted from living among Whites and were not allowed to own land, buy property, intermarry with Whites, or obtain an education (Zia, 2001). Because early Asian-American immigrants were perceived as economic and social threats, anti-Asian violence was also a shared experience of theirs, as evidenced by events such as the anti-Chinese riots at Rock Springs, Wyoming in 1885 that resulted in 43 casualties; the armed expulsion of 100 Asian Indian laborers from Live Oak, California in 1908; the armed expulsion of over 100 Japanese farmworkers from Turlock, California in 1921; and the anti-Filipino riots of 1930 in Watsonville, California (Hall & Hwang, 2001; Nadal, 2012).

Parallel to the individual treatment of Asian immigrants, institutional and legislative forms of discrimination were also enacted against Asian-American communities. From anti-miscegenation codes, housing restrictions, and educational limitations to ethnicity-specific business taxes, antinaturalization and anti-immigration laws, Asian Americans faced numerous obstacles in their search for Gold Mountain. Examples of exclusionary immigration laws include the Chinese Exclusion Act of 1882, the first ethnicity-specific ban of its kind; the Gentleman's Agreement of 1907, which restricted Japanese immigration; the Immigration Act of 1917, which restricted Asian Indian immigration; and the passage of the Tydings–McDuffie Act of 1934, which effectively restricted Filipino immigration, despite the fact that Filipinos were considered U.S. nationals at the time (Dinh, Weinstein, Nemon, & Rondeau, 2008; Hall & Hwang, 2001). In effect, no matter the Asian ethnic group that immigrated to the United States, each group faced strikingly similar instances of institutional discrimination. Indeed, the height of institutional discrimination was exemplified by the 1942 incarceration of 120,000 Japanese Americans (62% of whom were U.S. citizens), who were forced to evacuate their homes and sell their businesses as they were being imprisoned in remote internment camps without trial, due process, or the right to appeal (Parker, 2004).

Contemporary Asian America emerged with the passage of the Immigration and Nationality Act of 1965. Prior to 1965, existing immigration laws severely restricted Asian immigration, as previously noted, while also favoring European immigration. After 1965, immigration was based on family reunification rather than on quotas by national origin. As a result, the number of Asian immigrants grew dramatically, from 800,000 in 1970 to an estimated 7.3 million in 2000, an 800% increase (Reeves & Bennett, 2004). The Asian population grew faster than any other major race group between 2000 and 2010, increasing by 43%. Also, showcasing the second-largest numerical change (5.9 million) of all the major race groups, the Asian population grew from 10.2 million in 2000 to 16.1 million in 2012 (U.S. Census Bureau, 2012c). In contrast to the influx of voluntary immigrants after 1965, the experience of Southeast Asian refugees after the 1975 fall of South Vietnam is quite distinct. As a result of U.S. military involvement and brutal communist reprisals, as well as class-based cleansing and genocide, over 1 million Southeast Asians have fled Vietnam, Cambodia, and Laos since the mid-1970s. Enduring starvation, overcrowded conditions, disease, and death in both reeducation camps and refugee camps, as well as the loss of their homes and forced resettlement, these involuntary immigrants suffer from a host of psychological and traumatic experiences not seen in voluntary immigrants.

Given the relatively recent influx of both Asian immigrants and Asian refugees, the notion of an "Asian-American" community is an equally recent phenomenon. Despite the arrival of Filipinos in the bayous south of New Orleans in the 1760s (Nadal, 2012), Asian Americans as a demographic, psychological, and sociocultural community did not emerge until 200 years later. Not until the 1960s did Japanese, Chinese, and Filipino student activists begin to informally use the term *Asian American* in recognition of their commonalities and shared history of oppression. Inspired by the civil-rights movement, the nationalism of the Black Panther Party, and the anti–Vietnam War movement, these activists promoted the notion of a panethnic or racial community in a spirit of political unification that was in stark contrast to a 200-year history characterized more by ethnic separation (Zia, 2001).

Yet, beyond a simple narration of history and migration, the threads of immigration and discrimination that are woven throughout various Asian ethnic communities also reflect their shared psychological experiences. To leave one's country, family, friends, and all that is familiar for a country in which you may not know anyone, may not have a job, may not know the language or customs—and to do so with only the hope of a better life—is a psychological experience that is embedded within Asian-American communities both past and present. Similarly, to be faced with laws, regulations, and attitudes rooted in racism and discrimination, and to receive the message both covertly and overtly that one does not belong, has been, and continues to be, a shared experience of Asian Americans. Consequently, although counselors often place an emphasis on understanding their clients as individuals, it is equally important to recognize that individuals live within a larger community that is shaped by both historical and sociopolitical influences.

CONTEMPORARY FORMS OF DISCRIMINATION AND STEREOTYPES

To better understand the sociopolitical context in which Asian Americans live, it may be helpful to examine how they have been perceived and treated within the United States. Gee, Ro, Shariff-Macro, and Chae (2009) discussed the idea that discrimination can be overt (e.g., hate crimes, poor treatment), covert/symbolic (e.g., an implicit attitude), or structural (e.g., segration, a racial ideology, institutional policies). Consistent with the historical examples of institutional racism that were previously discussed, Asian Americans continue to encounter contemporary forms of the phenomenon. Modern-day examples of institutional racism against Asian Americans include "English-only" language initiatives; income-to-education disparities, in which Asian Americans earn incomes that are disproportionately lower than those of Whites with the same level of education; and glass-ceiling effects in career advancement, in which Asian Americans, despite their experience and training, are underrepresented in administrative and managerial positions (Gee et al., 2009). Asian Americans also continue to experience individual racism. Examples of contemporary individual racism range from differential treatment, verbal insults, and racial slurs to physical harassment, vandalism, and, in some cases, homicide. Indeed, the murder of Vincent Chin in 1982 by ex-autoworkers who regarded him as the reason they lost their jobs and the 1987 murder of Navroze Mody by a Jersey City gang called the Dotbusters (referring to South Asian women's bindis, the red decorative marks worn on the forehead by Hindu and Jain women), have become galvanizing rallying points for the Asian-American community (Asian Americans Advancing Justice, 2012).

The discrimination that Asian Americans face is directly related to stereotypic perceptions and attitudes that people have of them. Beginning with the large-scale arrival of Chinese immigrants in the 19th century and the xenophobic portrayal of this immigration wave as the "yellow peril," Asian American stereotypes have cast this community as "other." Images of Asian Americans as "heathens," "dog eaters," "martial artists," "exotic," and "dragon ladies" have objectified this community by reducing them to one-dimensional caricatures set apart from, and unassimilable into, the dominant White society. Such stereotypes add fuel to the treatment of this community as economic, labor, cultural, and, most recently, national security threats to what is deemed "mainstream America." Of particular relevance to contemporary Asian Americans are the stereotypes of the "perpetual foreigner" and the "model minority."

From the seemingly innocuous question "Where are you from?" to a national headline that proclaimed "American Beats Kwan" in reference to native Californian figure skater Michelle Kwan, the perception of Asian Americans as being "perpetual foreigners" has been a persistent theme in their daily experiences. Despite the repeal of antinaturalization laws that explicitly prohibited them from becoming citizens, Asian Americans continue to be implicitly regarded as being what Tuan (1999) called "illegitimate Americans," regardless of their nativity or citizenship. Events such as the racial profiling of Wen Ho Lee at Los Alamos National Laboratory and the presumptive treatment of South Asians as terrorists since September 11 have further perpetuated the perception that Asian Americans are not only foreigners, but also foreigners who cannot be trusted and are potential threats to national security (U.S. Commission on Civil Rights, 2015).

The implicit second-class status of the perpetual-foreigner stereotype stands in distinct contrast to the **model-minority myth**. Since the 1966 *New York Times Magazine* article titled "Success Story: Japanese-American Style," the model-minority stereotype has been used to describe and elevate the status of Asian Americans. According to this stereotype, Asian Americans as a group have become a model community that has "overcome" its minority status, despite the barriers presented by racism. Presumably, high academic achievement, high family incomes, low mental health utilization rates, and low delinquency rates of Asian Americans are all indicators of this community's success. However, numerous scholars (Museus & Kiang, 2009) have noted that the emergence of this stereotype coincided with the racial unrest of the civil-rights movement and that the "presumed success" of Asian Americans was used to pit racial groups against one another while simultaneously minimizing the racial and socioeconomic inequities perpetrated on communities of color. Voices from the Field 11.1 provides reflections from five professionals about what "model minority" means to them personally and professionally.

Voices from the Field 11.1

"Personally, the model minority is a stereotype that many of us who identify as Asian Americans have lived with, experienced, and even internalized throughout our lives. For me, it means that others do not initially see me as an individual, but only my assumed ethnicity and race. It says that all Asians are successful, smart, educated, economically stable, emotionally healthy, etc. The model minority does not acknowledge the diversity within our group as well as the various paths/experiences that we have had, instead, we are all placed into this melting pot. Growing up, many of my teachers responded and expected certain behaviors/study habits from me: to "behave" and "do what I am being asked" and "not ask questions, work hard." This stereotype has also been used to divide people of color as well, leading to interracial and even interethnic conflict/tension."

~ 49-year-old Japanese American female

"The label 'model minority' makes me feel like I am a trophy. The trophy recipient would show me to all their friends, family, and those he wants to impress. 'Look what I did!' And the people would say, 'Yes, look how it shines in the light' or any other supposedly redeeming aspects of being a trophy. 'It shows your strength, your ability to succeed.' To those who do not have a trophy, the trophy recipient would say, 'This is what you can get if you tried hard. You can be like me and get this trophy!' At first, you might think it is a nice to be a trophy and be seen to have these redeeming qualities. It is good to be thought of in a positive way. But then you realize these are not your own qualities, but that of someone else."

~ 25-year-old Vietnamese-American male

"The model-minority notion to me refers to the idea that Asian Americans are uniformly perceived to excel in academics and be financially successful. While this is a common public conscious and unconscious perception of Asian Americans, the reality is often far more complex. The model-minority concept veils the real experiences of racism, challenges in navigating across multiple cultures, and separating from one's heritage country, language, and religion. It hides the fact that Asian Americans experience loss, sadness, and anxiety, and [implies] that we don't have 'real' problems. 'Model minority' also conveys the idea that, as an Asian-American person, I carry privilege over other minority groups, and therefore, my struggles are less important or less valid."

~ 46-year-old Indian-American female

"['Model minority' is] a set of expectations about achievement and demeanor that I recognize as constraining and humiliating, used to divide Asian Americans from their allies and within themselves. It feeds into our already existing set of cultural norms to make families proud and succeed at any cost. Yet, they have peculiar power where I find myself playing into them when I am recognized with that label (whether said outright or not, because these days, most folks are too sophisticated to use that exact term) on how much I get along as a person of color unlike those 'other' people of color. Feeling shamed when I see other Asian Americans not being dignified or being less than competent. Catch 22—I catch myself in a cringe when my students of color behave to the stereotype, and I cringe when they don't."

~ 47-year-old Indian-American female

"Personally, 'model minority' doesn't mean anything to me, but it is a term that society uses to stereotype Asian Americans and to suppress the legitimate concerns/protest of other minority groups, particularly Blacks/African Americans, about the racist hierarchy or discriminatory system that exists in U.S. society. Societal perception of Asian American as 'model minority' has deep negative consequences for us all (as well as for other minority groups). The effects are complex, but to put it simply, people and society perceive Asian Americans as 'smart' and 'hardworking' but definitely not as 'innovative,' 'creative,' or 'leadership-type.' These are just some examples. People want us to be 'productive' members of society (i.e., soldiers), but they definitely do not want us to be leaders, and in fact, they do not believe we have the capacity (nature or nurture) to be leaders."

~ 47-year-old Vietnamese-American female

Importantly, in contrast to the general public's beliefs that only negative stereotypes could result in hostility or negative outcomes, the model-minority myth, and other seemingly positive stereotypes, can also have deleterious effects on Asian Americans' physical and psychological well-being (Gupta, Szymanski, & Leong, 2011; Ibaraki, Hall, & Sabin, 2014). For instance, one study (Siy & Cheryan, 2013) found that hearing positive stereotypes about their group, such as the stereotype that Asians are good at math, was associated with negative emotions on the part of Asian-American participants. The model-minority myth is damaging because it implies, and attributes positive quality solely to group membership. It minimizes an individual's effort and achievement, as well as generalizes characteristics of a group to individuals to whom they may not apply (Czopp, 2008; Ibaraki et al., 2014). Asian individuals who do not uphold these stereotypical traits may believe that they are not meeting the expectations associated with the model minority and thus may experience psychological distress and be less willing to seek help as a result of feeling inadequate (Gupta et al., 2011). Furthermore, Ibaraki and colleagues (2014) discussed the potential danger of extending the model-minority myth to Asian American's physical health. Because the myth is so widely held, the general public may perceive Asian Americans to be healthier than other ethnic groups and least likely to suffer from various health conditions, such as stroke, diabetes, alcoholism, obesity, heart disease, and cancer. The researchers argued that it could be very dangerous if physicians endorse these common beliefs and become less likely to recommend testing, such as cancer screening, for their Asian patients. In fact, according to the National Center for Health Statistics (2011b), Asian Americans have lower rates of recommendations for cancer screening compared with other racial groups, and the failure to screen is associated with disproportionately high rates of cancer-related deaths among Asian Americans.

Equally important, the adverse impact of the model-minority myth can also be evidenced in institutional neglect and cross-racial tensions resulting from both competition and resentment. To the extent that Asian Americans are uniformly regarded as academically and economically successful, individuals and institutions may be less likely to recognize that educational, health, and other disparities still exist, and therefore, they may be less likely to allocate resources such as funding, staff, and programmatic support to Asian-American communities. As a case in point, the National Commission on Asian American and Pacific Islander Research in Education (2008) found that, in light of model-minority assumptions of success, there has been less urgency in proactively addressing or developing programs to increase Asian-American representation among faculty, staff, and administrators of colleges and universities; presumably, there is less need for equitable representation, role models, or cultural competencies in working with a community that is perceived as being already successful. Likewise, consistent with early critiques of the model minority, the perception of success may be a contributing factor to racial tensions. For example, a number of scholars (Greene, Way, & Pahl, 2006; Rosenbloom & Way 2004) have found that, whereas Latino and African-American students tend to identify authority figures as the perpetrators of discrimination, Asian-American youths faced a higher level of racial discrimination from their peers. Consequently, despite a seemingly beneficial stereotype, the model-minority myth has a clear and negative impact on Asian-American communities. Voices from the Field 11.2 describes some impacts that the label "model minority" has on four Asian-American professionals from the field.

Voices from the Field 11.2

"The model-minority stereotype has contributed to increased levels of stress and tension, and decreased levels of self-esteem, among Asian Americans. I think a big issue is not just that others view Asians as a model minority, but what happens when we internalize this stereotype. So, if we begin to believe that we 'should' be smart, educated, obedient, etc., what happens and do we ask for support when needed?"

~ 49-year-old Japanese-American female

"People do not see you as for what you are—the curves, the shine, the glow—but as a representation of the recipient. You are successful because your recipient was successful. You are strength because your recipient is strength. They do not see the cracks at the base of the frame, the dust collecting in the cup. And the people you were shown off to by the recipient as something they can strive for, they may start to despise you because they despise the recipient for making it hard for them to obtain you. They ridicule you, deface you, trying to crack you in any way as possible because you are seen to be like the recipient, but one that just sits in the trophy cabinet, not capable of fighting back. Why would you need to fight back? You are just a trophy. But because you are a trophy, you are the easiest for others to put their anger on instead of the recipient."

~ 25-year-old Vietnamese-American male

"The model-minority concept impacts me in several ways. First, it means that I may have to work much harder at work in order for my achievements to be recognized as earned, and not as a reflection of some innate capacity. This latter notion is, of course, a fallacy. Second, I experience more internal pressure to achieve as a function of external demands that I excel academically and professionally. Third, it means that my experiences of racism are perceived by others as less harmful to me than racism experienced by members of other racial minority groups."

~ 46-year-old Indian-American female

"What impact does this label have on me? A lot of stress in dealing with colleagues and White society: While they know or think that I am 'smart' and 'hardworking,' they do not like it when I take leadership roles and do the job better than they can, and they definitely do not like it when I question their competence and authority. They want me to stay within the stereotypes they have of me, and even though they will comment in negative ways about Asian Americans being too quiet, they actually do not like it when I speak, especially when I disagree with them. So, they do various things, both in blatant and subtle ways, to undermine or devalue my work and my position."

~ 47-year-old Vietnamese-American female

REFLECTION 11.2

Explore various Asian-American communities via the Web. For a start, you may want to read the discussion forums on Angry Asian Man (www.angryasianman.com) and Mixed Asians (www.mixedasians.com), or the Asian Pacific Islander Blog Network (www.apiablogs.net). What are your reactions to the postings? What resonates with you? Is there anything that is unfamiliar to you? How are these views similar to or different from the perspectives to which you have been exposed?

REFLECTION 11.3

Given that culture is defined as "a shared learned behavior that is transmitted from one generation to another for purposes of human adjustment, adaptation, and growth" (Marsella & Kameoka, 1989, p. 233), it is important to explore values that you and your family share. In the space provided, write about cultural biases, stereotypes, attitudes, and behaviors regarding Asian-American individuals and communities you have observed in your immediate and extended family (adapted from Fawcett & Evans, 2013):

- Cultural biases include
- Stereotypes include
- Attitudes I have inherited from my family include
- Some of my behaviors that are based on cultural bias include
- Some of my unbiased behaviors include
- Feelings I am aware of include
- Thoughts that I have about myself as a person are
- Thoughts the I have about myself as a developing counselor are
- Questions that I have include

To counter such idyllic portrayals of Asian Americans, scholars further argue that the aggregation of Asian Americans into a seemingly homogeneous and monolithic racial group fails to account for the heterogeneity and diversity of this community and thereby overemphasizes Asian-American success while obscuring legitimate racial disparities. Reflections 11.2 and 11.3 provide an opportunity to investigate some Asian-American communities and cultural dynamics. Then, the next section examines both the complexity and heterogeneity within the Asian-American community.

ASIAN-AMERICAN HETEROGENEITY

Given the unidimensional portrayals that characterize the aforementioned stereotypes, multicultural competence with Asian Americans is directly related to understanding this community's demographic heterogeneity. Without such an understanding, counselors may inadvertently generalize their knowledge of the Asian-American community and assume that what applies to one segment of this community will also apply to other segments. Factors such as language proficiency, immigration history, and educational level may influence, in individualized ways, the manner in which Asian-American clients understand their presenting issues, their attitudes toward counseling, their expectations of the counselor, and their access to resources, as well as the effectiveness of counseling itself.

The aggregation of Asian Americans as a racial group obscures the ethnic heterogeneity of this community and the approximately 43 distinct Asian ethnic groups from 20 different countries of origin (U.S. Census Bureau, 2012c). Although historical dominance has led to an assumption that equates Asian with being East Asian (i.e., Chinese, Japanese, Korean), the 10 largest Asian ethnic groups in the United States, according to the U.S. Census (i.e., Chinese, Filipino, Asian Indian, Vietnamese, Korean, Japanese, Cambodian, Hmong, Laotian, and Pakistani), clearly underscore the inaccuracy of this assumption. Moreover, given that the five fastest-growing Asian ethnicities in the United States (i.e., Bangladeshi, Asian Indian, Pakistani, Hmong, and Sri Lankan) are quite distinct from the five largest groups, it stands to reason that the ethnic composition of this community will continue to evolve.

Asian Americans are also diverse in terms of their immigration histories. Although large-scale Asian-American immigration began in the mid-1800s, even today nearly three quarters (74%) of Asian-American adults were born abroad (Pew Research Center, 2013), but with notable ethnic group variability. For instance, whereas majority of those in most Asian ethnic subgroups (e.g., Asian Indian, Vietnamese, Korean) are foreign born, only 27% of Japanese Americans are foreign born. Relatedly, the paths to the United States have been varied across ethnic groups. For example, three-quarters of the foreign-born Vietnamese are naturalized U.S. citizens, compared with two-thirds of Filipinos, about 6 in 10 Chinese and Koreans, half of Indians, and only a third of Japanese. Hence, for counselors working with Asian Americans, it is important to recognize that they may encounter a continuum of immigration and refugee histories, ranging from a fourth-generation Chinese American, to a newly arrived international student from South Asia, to a college-educated immigrant from South Korea, to a Cambodian refugee with little formal education. Even more important, these immigration patterns have significant implications for their clients' understanding of, and adaptation to, U.S. cultural norms.

Particularly in light of the model-minority assumptions about Asian Americans, beliefs about the universal economic and academic success of Asian Americans have rendered issues of poverty and educational inequities in certain Asian ethnic groups nearly invisible. Although a high median income of Asian-American families has often been interpreted as evidence of their economic well-being, the use of such a statistic fails to account for the larger number of wage earners in Asian-American households, the concentration of Asian Americans in high-cost urban areas, and disparities in the ratio of income to education level (Lee, Wong, & Alvarez, 2009). Data over the past couple of decades reveal similar trends and disparities. For instance, in 2004, statistics showed that, in California, Korean men make 82%, Chinese men 68%, and Filipino men 62% of the income that White men make (Uy, 2004). Moreover, Asian-American women made 40% less than White women (Uy, 2004). A recent study examining racial ethnic inequality in earnings (Kim, 2015) found that first-generation Asian-American men earned approximately 30% less than White men with the same college degree. The U.S. Census Bureau (2011c) showed that about 53% of Asian Americans owned homes, compared with approximately 71% of Whites. Further, although Asian Americans on the whole have higher median family incomes than White Americans, their poverty rate is actually higher than that of White Americans. Recent statistics from the U.S Department of Labor (2014) reveal that more than 12% of Asian-American men live below the poverty level whereas only 8% of White men fall into this category. In a study on income gaps among college-educated men, Kim (2015) indicated that Asian-American men earn approximately 9% less than their

White counterparts. In addition, more than 21% of Asian-American men and women ages 18 to 64 do not have health insurance, while only 15% of White Americans are uninsured. Furthermore, although Asian Indian and Japanese-American families have median incomes that are $11,000 higher than the national median, it is also important to recognize that Cambodian and Hmong families have median incomes that are approximately $15,000 *lower* than the national median (U.S. Census Bureau, 2012c).

Similar trends are mirrored in occupational status and educational attainment that obscure achievement gaps within the Asian-American community. For instance, whereas 50% or more of Asian Indian, Chinese, and Japanese Americans are in professional or management positions, only 17% or less of Laotian, Hmong, and Cambodian Americans are in similar positions (Reeves & Bennett, 2004). In regard to educational status, Asian Americans as an aggregate have a higher percentage of individuals with a bachelor's degree compared with the national average (i.e., 52% vs. 29%; U.S. Department of Education, 2010). However, this aggregation masks educational disparities in the community. For example, over 50% of Asian Indians and Pakistanis have a bachelor's degree, whereas less than 9% of Laotian, Hmong, and Cambodian Americans do. Moreover, it is critical to recognize that, for many recent Asian immigrants, this educational capital is reflective of the education they received in their countries of origin, rather than in the United States. Indeed, many of the college-educated, professional immigrants who immigrate to the United States can be rightfully described as the "elites of their countries of origin" (National Commission on Asian American and Pacific Islander Research in Education, 2008, p. 26).

Linguistic diversity may also have implications for counselors working with Asian-American communities. As a group, 41.8% of foreign-born Asians ages 5 and above speak English "very well" and 11.2% speak only English. (American Immigration Council, 2012). However, as with other demographic characteristics within this community, closer scrutiny of the data yields notable within-group differences. For example, limited English proficiency (i.e., speaking English "not well" or "not at all") is prevalent at about 30% each for those speaking the following native languages: Korean, Cambodian, Laotian, and Vietnamese. By contrast, over 57% of individuals with the following native languages said that they spoke English "very well": Japanese, Hmong, and Tagalog (U.S. Census Bureau, 2013). Consequently, in a profession that is highly dependent on verbal expression, counselors need to recognize that their Asian-American clients may enter counseling with a range of linguistic abilities (Reeves & Bennett, 2004).

In sum, the notion of what constitutes "Asian American" is both complex and continually evolving. As the preceding demographic statistics demonstrate, counselors may encounter a wide range of Asian-American clients, many of whom will have immigration experiences and academic and socioeconomic resources that are entirely different from one another. Therefore, multicultural competence will be demonstrated by a continuing and fluid openness to learning the different segments of this community.

ASIAN-AMERICAN CULTURE AND VALUES

Cultural values influence our socialization by influencing our psychological and social functioning (Inman, Howard, Beaumont, & Walker, 2007). Although there is much diversity, Asian Americans are influenced by some common values, ideologies, and philosophies that guide their lives and perspectives (Inman & Yeh, 2007). This section highlights specific values that provide a baseline foundation for understanding their experience. However, it is important to note that the extent to which Asian Americans adhere to these values is influenced by their generational status, immigration histories, and acculturation levels. Thus, it is the counselor's responsibility to assess the extent to which particular Asian-American clients identify with these values and beliefs. To prevent making generalizations, counselors are encouraged to increase their knowledge of the complexities of, and distinctions within, the Asian American culture. To help in this process, various forms of media provide numerous examples of Asian-American culture. (See Table 11.1 at the end of the chapter.)

Family

Within the Asian community, the term *family* or *kinship* refers to an extended network of relationships that encompasses several households (Jones, 2011). In many instances, multiple generations and caretakers may reside in the family (Yee, DeBaryshe, Yuen, Kim, & McCubbin, 2007) and influence decisions. The family is considered to be of primary importance, and family needs often override individual needs. Relatedly, the notions of a private space and an individualistic identity go against the Asian collectivistic value orientation (Lee, Beckert, & Goodrich, 2010), because one's actions are considered to influence the welfare and integrity of the family. This emphasis on a family identity and interdependence makes **filial piety** a strongly espoused value in the Asian-American family. Filial piety is an abstract concept that prescribes the way children need to show respect and obedience toward their parents, elders, and ancestors (Leung, Wong, Wong, & McBride-Chang, 2010). Within this context, obligation, respect, and a strong sense of duty to the parents and elders is not uncommon. In fact, a strong allegiance to parents can continue after adult offspring (especially the male child) are married. For instance, it is common for adult children to reside with their parents until, and even after, marriage and for married sons to take care of their parents in their old age (Periyakoil, 2006). This emphasis on family ties plays an important role in "saving face" and protecting the honor of the family.

Filial piety is influenced by parenting that tends to be authoritarian and directive. Actions that benefit the family are praised, whereas guilt-inducing techniques, such as withdrawing familial support, are often used as a means of enforcing discipline and maintaining family cohesion (Kwon, 2010). Children are taught to be responsible for their actions and to control their emotions, as well as to respect elders (Chang & Smith, 2015). The family structure is typically patriarchal, with children being expected to obey their parents and fulfill their obligations within the family. However, some recent studies (Cheah, Leung, Tahseen, & Schultz, 2009; Nguyen & Cheung, 2009) reveal a shift to an authoritative style of parenting (i.e., greater bidirectional communication and a reciprocal parent–child relationship), suggesting that acculturative processes are at play. Conversely, structural barriers related to their immigration status may push poor Chinese immigrant women to send their newborn children back to China to be cared for by their extended families (Kwong, Chung, Sun, Chou, & Taylor-Shih, 2009).

Given the important role that family plays in Asian-American culture, when working with Asian Americans, counselors should consider family dynamics and other related factors, such as individual and family immigration history, adaptation experiences, cultural values, and generational differences due to differences in acculturation experience (Lui, 2015; Miller, Yang, Hui, Choi, & Lim, 2011). The contrast between collectivism in traditional heritage and individualism in the mainstream American culture presents unique challenges for Asian-American family relationships. Although transitory parent–offspring conflicts over everyday tasks seem to be a normal part of development in American mainstream nonimmigrant families, a sizeable body of research has shown that conflicts in Asian-American families tend to be complicated by the acculturation process and cultural differences (Lui, 2015). In a recent meta-analytic review of intergenerational conflict among Asian-American families, Lui (2015) indicated that intergenerational cultural conflict was found to be negatively associated with youths' mental health and educational outcomes in a sample of 41 Asian Americans. In particular, qualitative analyses found that, among academically high-achieving adolescents (defined by high school grade point average), immigrant Chinese parents with psychologically distressed offspring were reported to apply rigid parenting behaviors that reflected traditional Asian values of high parental authority and hierarchy, emphasize academic achievement, and use non-open communication, resulting in poor parent–offspring cohesion and high levels of intergenerational conflict (Qin, 2008).

Gender Roles

Socialized primarily within a patriarchal society, a well-functioning family is a family that subscribes to the specific gender roles and communication rules set by the family (Schmitt & Wirth, 2009). These authors also note that gender roles and responsibilities are clearly prescribed and based in one's authority and status in the family and social hierarchy. For instance, age is valued, and elders are accorded great respect and importance. Respect is implicit in obedience, formality, and social restraint in relationships with elders. It is important to note, however, that within-group differences exist. For example, Japanese Americans tend to be more acculturated, and hence more egalitarian, in their roles because several generations have lived in this country. Filipino Americans also tend to be more egalitarian, whereas Chinese Americans, Koreans, and Southeast Asians tend to be more patriarchal and traditional in orientation (Dion & Dion, 2001). Interestingly, South Asians have been noted to be traditional in their homes but contemporary in relation to education- and achievement-related issues (Dion & Dion, 2001). Further, Qin (2009) revealed important gender differences. For instance, immigrant adolescent girls were more connected to their heritage, language, and ethnic identity and resisted gender stereotypes, compared with their male counterparts.

Interpersonal Relationships

Among Asian Americans, maintaining harmony governs interpersonal relationships (Andrews & Boyle, 2011). Thus, being nondirective, nonconfrontational, and silent are considered virtues. Moderation in behaviors is valued through self-restraint and self-control. Asians tend not to be too emotionally demonstrative in their relationships, and displaying strong emotions is often seen as a sign of immaturity. Relatedly, humility in deeds and actions is seen as maintaining respect and dignity in relationships.

Intimacy and Marriage

An important aspect of interpersonal relationships involves issues related to intimacy and marriage. Asian-American youths are traditionally not encouraged to date. Dating and sexuality are intimately linked, and parents often fear negative repercussions related to dating (Inman, Howard, et al., 2007). Often, parents and the extended family play an important role in choosing a mate for children through social networks. For example, arranged or semiarranged marriages are a common practice among South Asian communities, with children typically encouraged to marry within their ethnic community. Because marriage is considered a union of two families, the choice of mate involves introducing potential candidates from families with good educational and financial backgrounds. However, marriage based on love and mutual compatibility has increasingly become a norm for Asian-American youths (Yee et al., 2007). Furthermore, although Asian Americans traditionally tend to be modest regarding their sexuality and nondemonstrative in their sexual and physical affection, there are generational variations based on levels of acculturation. For instance, the more acculturated the individual, the greater is the likelihood of being demonstrative and having open discussions regarding sexuality and dating (Inman, Constantine, & Ladany, 1999).

Divorce and interracial marriages have traditionally not been a common practice among Asian Americans. The U.S. Census Bureau indicates that less than 10% (compared with 19% of the total population) of Asians are likely to be separated, widowed, or divorced (Reeves & Bennett, 2004), with Japanese Americans having the highest rates of divorce. However, recent trends suggest a significant increase (31%) in interracial marriages for Asian Americans (Passel, Wang, & Taylor, 2010). Further, there are specific gender and generational differences among Asians who marry interracially. For instance, 25% of Asian women born and raised in the United States married White men in 1990. In 2006, 41% of these Asian women married White men. By contrast, only 30% of Asian men born and raised in the United States married White women (Le, 2010). In terms of ethnic and gender differences, Japanese Americans (20% of men and 41% of women) have a higher percentage of interracial marriages compared with Filipinos (13% of men and 33% of women) and Koreans (4% of men and 27% of women). These trends suggest greater intermarriage among U.S.-born Asians compared with immigrant Asian Americans (Xie & Goyette, 2004). However, it is interesting to note that foreign-born Asian Indians seem to engage in higher interracial marriages than U.S.-born Asian Indians (Le, 2010).

Education

In general, Asian Americans have a high regard for learning. Mello (2009) showed that Asian-American adolescents had higher educational and professional career expectations in comparison to other groups. In most Asian-American families, academic achievement and a successful career are highly valued and indicative of a good family upbringing. The emphasis on education is seen as going beyond the individual to enhance the whole family (Park, Endo, Lee, & Rong, 2007). Relatedly, there is pressure to spend time studying at the expense of other curricular activities. Although the pressure to obtain certain jobs (e.g., science related or technical) over others (e.g., psychologist) has been noted as a cultural expectation, Inman, Howard, et al. (2007) noted that Asian Indian parents believed that these choices went beyond culture, to ensure that their children gained occupational and financial security as minority members within the United States. Indeed, Sue and Okazaki (2009) have convincingly argued that, in response to perceived restrictions and limitations due to discrimination, Asian Americans place a higher value on education as the most viable means of upward mobility, a concept they refer to as **relative functionalism**. One study reflects the important roles of education and schooling among Asian-American youths: Dinh, Weinstein, Tein, and Roosa (2013) found that both acculturation and enculturation were positively associated with school attachment among Cambodian-American youths. The researchers argued that school has a vital role in the lives of Cambodian-American adolescents, as the school context is one of the primary social networks for youths.

Religion

Depending on the geographic region, different religious teachings serve as important spiritual philosophies guiding Asian-American lives. For instance, East Asian Americans, such as Chinese Americans, tend to follow Confucianism, Buddhism, and Christianity. Because of the Spanish influence in the Philippines, Filipino Americans oftentimes tend to be Catholic, whereas Buddhism, Christianity, and Shinotoism are primary religions practiced among Japanese Americans (Carnes & Yang, 2004). Although Hinduism is the major religion in South Asia, Islam, Sikhism, Jainism, Zoroastrianism (Parsi), the Baha'i faith, and Judaism are also practiced in India and other regions of South Asia (Mittal & Thursby, 2006). Southeast Asians such as the Cambodians and Laotians have been strongly influenced by Hinduism and Buddhism, whereas the Vietnamese practice Buddhism and Catholicism. By contrast, the Mien and Hmong tend to believe in supernatural powers and are animistic (Carnes & Yang, 2004). Also, a majority of Asian communities believe in fate, rebirth, and an afterlife, based in either a polytheistic or a monotheistic notion of God. Pain and pleasure are seen as a natural part of one's existence. These religious philosophies influence perspectives on life, health, and illness (Inman & Yeh, 2007). In many of these communities, places of worship (e.g., churches, mosques, temples, monasteries) and religious figures, such as the priest or minister (Christianity), the mullah/Imam (Islam), pundit (Hinduism), or monk (Buddhism), may be key sources of support during times of difficulties. Alternatively, some Asian Americans may be atheists or agnostics.

Death and Dying

Death is a universal phenomenon, but expressions of grief and death rituals vary by ethnicity and religion. However, the basic premise underlying death rituals seems to have a common thread among the different Asian communities. For instance, death is a communal affair among several Asian groups. Burials and cremation ceremonies are traditionally performed by the males in the family, and elders are often consulted in performing rites (Inman, Yeh, Madan-Bahel, & Nath, 2007). Another common theme is the effect of the rituals on the family and the deceased. The Hmong believe that proper burial and ancestral worship influence the health, safety, and prosperity of the family (Lee, 2009), whereas Buddhists believe that proper burial rituals and the state of mind of the dying person influence the rebirth process (Lee, 2009). Similarly, for Hindus, cremations and other death rituals are designed to assist with rebirth and release the soul from its earthly existence; for Muslims, burials are crucial to the Islamic belief in the physical resurrection of the dead (Rees, 2001).

INDIVIDUAL DIFFERENCES AND IDENTITIES

Because of their diversity, to speak of Asian Americans as a single homogeneous entity is misleading. There are multiple ways in which aspects of diversity (e.g., immigration, ethnicity, race, and gender) shape the socialization processes, identity development, and interactions for Asian Americans. Understanding the complexity of Asian Americans involves examining the meaning behind their experiences, situations, and behaviors (Samovar, Porter, & McDaniel, 2014; Tewari, & Alvarez, 2009). In this section, we highlight that complexity by addressing issues related to immigration and the multiple identities that frame Asian-American lives. Although we deconstruct these issues and examine them separately, it is important to note that the multidimensionality of Asian-American identities must be examined through the interrelated axes of the different contexts (e.g., race, gender, sexual orientation).

Immigration, Enculturation, and Acculturation

The nature of immigration, the reason for immigration, the age at immigration, language abilities, past and present exposure to Western cultures, immigration status, socioeconomic status, professional status, ethnic pride, and the length of stay in the United States are factors that mediate Asian-American adaptation to U.S. society (Nandan, 2005). In effect, the emigrational status of an individual is an important determinant of the nature of the transition and adjustment that individuals make in moving to a new environment. Therefore, in discussing Asian-American experiences, it is important to distinguish immigrants from refugees. Immigrants are foreign-born individuals who leave their countries on a voluntary basis. Moving to a new country for economic opportunities and upward mobility, these individuals are free to return to or visit their countries without legal restrictions. It is also important to recognize that there are different types of immigrants: those who come to the United States for short periods (e.g., international students coming for education, consultants coming for employment) and those who choose to stay on a permanent basis (i.e., seek permanent residency or citizenship). By contrast, refugees, although foreign born, are involuntarily displaced from their countries. Often forced to leave their countries of origin due to political unrest, human rights violations, or other chaotic situations, they are in exile from their own lands. Because of their inability to return "home," they seek asylum elsewhere (Kim & Kim, 2014). People from Tibet, Vietnam, Laos, and Cambodia have arrived in the United States as refugees.

To facilitate their success, Asian Americans have been noted to selectively adapt to certain U.S. cultural norms (e.g., English proficiency, career goals, dress) while holding onto fundamental ethnic cultural values related to family relations, religion, and intimate relations. In this context, although Asian Americans might engage in U.S.-based activities, they may not fully identify with the American culture. Still, it is important to note that Asian Americans who are born in the United States may have a stronger identification with the American culture first and Asian culture second. Alternatively, there may be those who are strongly acculturated to the American culture and yet strongly identify with the Asian culture (Kim, Wang, Chen, Shen, & Hou, 2015).

Ethnicity and Race

As described in Chapter 4, **ethnicity** refers to shared, but unique, cultural values, traditions, norms, and customs within an ethnic community whereas **race** refers to an arbitrary classification system based in positions of power and privilege. Although the process of ethnic identification begins at a very young age, with the family playing a significant role, the social construction of ethnic identity within the context of a U.S. society takes on a unique and different meaning for Asian Americans. Growing up in a bicultural setting, a fundamental dilemma that evolves for Asian Americans is the degree to which one's ethnic identity is valued and must be retained (Inman, 2006).

Although ethnic identity research has revealed that a strong attachment and sense of belonging to one's cultural roots and traditions has positive psychological outcomes for Asian

---

REFLECTION 11.4

Acculturation is a significant clinical consideration. In working with a client, how do you determine a client's level of acculturation? What are some indicators of this attribute? What sorts of questions might you ask to determine it? How might these indicators change on the basis of the immigrational status of the individual (e.g., an international student, a permanent resident, U.S. born, or a refugee)? Write your thoughts and discuss them in small groups.

Americans (Museus & Maramba, 2011), Cheryan and Tsai (2007) believed that the tendency to focus on attachment to one's Asian ancestral country of origin alone tends to confuse other identifications that Asian Americans may have. Because ethnic identity may function differently for foreign-born Asians versus U.S.-born Asian Americans, there is a need to understand ethnic identification more broadly as including the attachment one feels to all "cultural heritages, including those not based specifically on one's country of origin" (Cheryan & Tsai, 2007, p. 125). For instance, Inman (2006) found that ethnic identification was a greater buffer against stress for foreign-born first-generation South Asians than U.S.-born second-generation South Asians.

In essence, because of a bicultural influence, Asian Americans internalize two cultures that inform and influence their lives: the Asian identity and the American identity. Although being "American" is not consistent with an ethnic identity (Cheryan & Tsai, 2007), identifying with an American identity and being seen as American provides Asian Americans with a sense of belonging, a sense of legitimacy, and cultural competence that increases their ability to navigate interactions effectively and to access resources (Kim, Shen, Huang, Wang, & Orozco-Lapray, 2014; Phinney, Horenczyk, Liebkind, & Vedder, 2001).

Interestingly, how particular aspects of identity operate in particular situations is influenced by social cues that Asian Americans experience (Cornish, Schreier, Nadakarni, Metzger, & Rodolfa, 2010), as well as by exposure and connection to a cultural context (e.g., visiting Asia or lack of contact with Asia; Cheryan & Tsai, 2007), with some aspects being seen as more salient than others. Thus, different aspects of identity may be activated based on different contexts, a notion termed **cultural frame switching** (Cheng, Lee, & Benet-Martínez, 2006). Related to these varying aspects of identity is the role of race and racial identity in Asian-American lives.

The concept of race and racism has been an elusive one for Asian Americans. Despite a long history of racism and discrimination (e.g., denial of land ownership and citizenship, anti-miscegenation laws, racial profiling, being targets of racial slurs and violence, internment camps; Alvarez & Helms, 2001; Gee et al., 2009), there are varying views of acceptance from within and outside this community. The difficulty in recognizing that Asian Americans experience discrimination is a function of several factors: the model-minority myth (S. J. Lee et al., 2009), the tendency to dichotomize racism as a Black–White issue (Yoo, Steger, & Lee, 2010), the absence of racial socialization and a language to speak to these issues among new immigrants (Kim & Chao, 2009), and related racial politics of success and economics. These factors tend to mask the negative effects of discrimination on the well-being of Asian Americans. In opposition to these factors, Alvarez, Juang, and Liang (2006) found that discussions around race and racism with significant individuals in one's life are critical to enhancing Asian Americans' awareness of racism.

However, the Asian-American community has been paying greater attention to, and becoming more aware of, racism because of discrimination (Inman, Tummala-Narra, Kaduvettoor-Davidson, Alvarez, & Yeh, 2015; Sue, Bucceri, Lin, Nadal, & Torino, 2007) and reports of increased anti-Asian sentiment since the terrorist attacks on September 11, 2001 (Inman, Yeh et al., 2007; National Asian Pacific American Legal Consortium, 2003; Yeh, Inman, Kim, & Okubo, 2006). In fact, some authors (e.g., Sue, Bucceri, et al., 2007; Tummala-Narra, Inman, & Ettigi, 2011) highlight racial microaggressions that can come in the form of microassaults (e.g., racial slurs such as "chinks," "Fresh off the Boats" [FOBs], "American-Born Confused Desis" [ABCDs]), microinsults (e.g., assumption that Asian Americans may not be good managers), and microinvalidations (e.g., Asian American complimented for speaking good English or speaking without an accent, or being asked, "Where are you from?"). These forms of discriminatory acts relegate Asian Americans to a perpetual-foreigner status, despite several generations having grown up in this country. Yet, the experiences of racial discrimination are indeed internalized by Asian Americans in the United States. Through this internalization, Asian Americans can go through multiple stages wherein they may wish to own or disown their ethnic heritage (Millan & Alvarez, 2014). Thus, the intersections of ethnic and racial identities must be considered in working with Asian Americans.

Gender Roles

Traditional Asian cultures suggest clear and stringent gender roles for Asian men and women, with several religious teachings (e.g., Confucianism, Hinduism) seeing masculine and feminine characteristics as intrinsic and complementary to each other. In keeping with this outlook, there is a greater variability in notions of masculinity among Asian men compared with White men (Shek, 2006). Based in Asian cultural values, men are brought up to be group and family focused (Liu & Iwamoto, 2006), fulfilling parental and familial expectations (Chang & Subramaniam, 2008) and expected to be the main breadwinner in the family. Furthermore, the patriarchal emphasis of Asian cultures allows men to experience less stringent rules and expectations in relation to sexual behaviors and intimacy. Asian women, by contrast, experience greater community censures related to gender roles and intimacy issues and bear the disproportionate burden of passing on the cultural traditions (Dasgupta & Basu, 2011).

Asian men and women alike have had to deal with long-standing stereotypes and tensions between multiple cultures and gender role expectations. Although there are some similarities between Asian and White values, the emphasis has often been on the differences. For instance, there are images of Asian women as subservient, passive, childlike, innocent, and exotic;, and then there are other, contrasting images of them as mail-order brides, dragon ladies, and conscientious hard workers. Asian men are often stereotyped as being nerdy or geeky, feminine, industrious, passive, and asexual (Liu & Chang, 2007; Wilkins, Chan, & Kaiser, 2011). The stereotypes attributed to Asian women have led to sexual exploitation and a continued objectification of these women. In contrast, the dominant myth of Asian males as asexual and feminine renders Asian men as less desirable. Within the context of a bicultural socialization, Asian men and women have needed to negotiate competing cultural representations of masculinity or femininity. This challenge has important implications as they manage their gender identity.

Another aspect that has complicated the picture is the shifts in roles and responsibilities. Immigration has created role reversals for some Asian immigrants, significantly influencing their family roles and expectations. The shifts have resulted in a greater need for dual-income families and greater struggles on the part of women to achieve equal access to resources. Because some foreign-born Asian men experience diminished occupational mobility (Sharif, 2010), more women are finding themselves having to work outside the family.

Sexuality and Sexual Identity

Although one's sexuality and being attracted to another individual are an integral part of human life and relationships, the meanings attached to sexuality and sexual behaviors are experienced and informed differently, through cultural, religious, familial, and acculturative influences (Lange, Houran, & Li, 2015). Historically, Asian cultures have depicted their attitudes and openness to sexual issues through the arts, literature, religion, history, and philosophy, with sexual themes covering a range of orientations. For instance, the existence of homosexuality, bisexuality, and other forms of sexuality have been noted in erotic art, paintings, and wall carvings as normal subjects in Japanese and Indian artistic ventures (Adamczyk & Cheng, 2015). Yet, over the years, because of political, social, and religious influences, Asian cultural norms have become more restrictive and now place a strong emphasis on silence surrounding issues of sexuality (Kim & Ward, 2007). This attitude not only is seen within the context of heterosexual intimacy issues, but also takes on great significance within the context of homosexuality (Trinh, Ward, Day, Thomas, & Levin, 2014). Specifically, Asian Americans perceive homosexuality as a Western concept (Cornish et al., 2010). Based in the notion that one becomes gay from contact with "foreigners," homosexuality is often viewed as a "White disease" and therefore not a natural part of the Asian societies (Cheng, 2011).

Although acculturation and exposure to U.S. values may play an important role in achieving more positive attitudes toward sexuality and sexual identity issues (Trinh et al., 2014), familial and cultural influences still may predominate. For instance, in traditional Asian-American families, there is an expectation that children will marry and have their own children. Consequently, as Asian-American sexual minorities develop their identity, pressures related to marriage and the fear of familial rejection may be major hindrances in the ownership of their identity and the coming-out process (Kwon, 2010; Nadal & Corpus, 2013).

Culturally, religion may also play a significant role. For instance, the majority of religions (e.g., Christianity, Islam, Hinduism, Taoism) seem to have negative and stringent attitudes toward sex and homosexuality (van den Akker, van der Pioeg, & Scheepers, 2013). Although some religious teachings (e.g., Confucianism, Hinduism) subscribe to a balance between female (i.e., yin in Confucianism, shakti in Hinduism) and male (i.e., yang in Confucianism, shiva in Hinduism) attributes, the focus is primarily on heterosexual relations. Any leanings toward homosexuality are seen as a sin and thus unacceptable (Adamczyk & Cheng, 2015).

According to Chung and Katayama (1998), it is important to recognize that Asian Americans undergo a dual, but parallel, developmental process in relation to their ethnic and sexual identities. These two processes of identity development may occur simultaneously, or one may follow the other; in either case, they may be complicated by racial socialization issues. How Asian Americans negotiate these minority identities, what the relative salience of each identity might be for the person, and how the identities intersect or interact at different points in a person's life become important. Reflections 11.5 and 11.6 further consider the role of different social identities.

REFLECTION 11.5

Social identities such as race, ethnicity, gender, and sexual orientation are important lenses that shape a person's interactions in society. In considering your own social identities, reflect on the extent to which you think about each of them while interacting with others. What are the circumstances and reasons for this awareness? How do your identities and your awareness of them shift across different situations and groups, if at all? In working with a client, how would you determine when a particular aspect of identity is important or salient to him or her? What are some indicators of that importance? What sorts of questions might you ask to determine it? Write your thoughts.

REFLECTION 11.6

Reflect on your racial identity by completing these statements:
- I believe that [insert your racial group] are . . .
- I am proud that [insert your racial group] . . .
- I am sad that [insert your racial group] . . .
- I wish that [insert your racial group] . . .

In a small group, share your feelings and thoughts about your development as a person and as an emerging counselor after you finish this reflection exercise.

GENERAL MENTAL HEALTH ISSUES OF INDIVIDUALS OF ASIAN DESCENT

Counselors need to understand Asian-American culture and how its manifestations in individuals create unique mental health issues for this population. In this section, the prevalence and expression of common mental health problems and help-seeking behaviors are discussed. Case Study 11.1 and Case Study 11.2 illustrate general mental health issues for the Asian-American population.

CASE STUDY 11.1

Marge is a 20-year-old second-year university student majoring in English. She was raised in a predominantly White neighborhood in the Midwest after being adopted by a White family when she was an infant. Although she is Korean by birth, she identifies herself as being "American" and has never thought of herself as "Korean American." So, she prides herself on her ability to look beyond "race."

Marge had been planning on going to graduate school to study English further, but lately she has had doubts about her abilities. She has been an *A* student in general, but one class has made her think about whether or not she can make it in graduate school. The professor has a reputation as an excellent teacher with high expectations for her students. But no matter what she has tried to do, Marge keeps getting *B*'s and *C*'s on her papers. Her classmates keep pointing out that the professor always ignores her in class, and when she does call on her, she keeps pushing Marge to speak more clearly. On her last paper, the professor commented that Marge needed a better command of English and needed to be more sophisticated in her analysis—which was the first time any instructor had ever said anything close to that kind of comment. Her classmates keep telling Marge that the professor is prejudiced against her by treating her as if she were a foreigner and that it's noticeable because Marge is only one of two students of color in the class. But Marge insists that she's never been treated differently because of her race and that she just needs to work harder and win the professor over. There's nothing racial about any of this treatment as far as she can see, and this professor is well regarded in the field.

Marge has come to counseling because she has had trouble concentrating and studying. She mentions all of this and says, with frustration and ambivalence, "I just don't understand why this is happening to me . . . I don't know why I keep thinking about this. I don't think it's about race . . . or is it?" She says that she doesn't want to dwell on the matter and that what she really needs is to focus on how to cope better with her stress. This is a critical year for Marge, and with her plans to go to graduate school, she knows that she can push herself too hard. So, she just wants to continue discussing how she can "chill and keep from freaking herself out." Imagine that you are a counselor working with Marge, and take a moment to reflect on these questions:

- How does your understanding of Asian-American stereotypes and racial discrimination inform your work with Marge?
- What is your own experience with race and racism? How might that experience facilitate or inhibit your ability to discuss Marge's situation?
- How do you see yourself in terms of your own racial identity, and how might your view of yourself shape counseling?
- Should you address the issue of race and racism with Marge? If so, what is your rationale, and how might you begin the discussion? If not, what is your rationale for not doing so?
- If you are racially similar to Marge, how does that similarity facilitate or inhibit your work with her? If you are racially different from Marge, how does that difference facilitate or inhibit your work with her?
- How might Marge's perceptions or assumptions about you influence what she says and does in counseling?
- What parts of Marge's experience can you empathize and resonate with? What parts are more challenging for you to understand?
- What about Marge's life, family, and social and cultural experiences might help you gain an understanding of how she regards race and racism?
- What can you validate about Marge's experience?

CASE STUDY 11.2

Maya is a 23-year-old South Asian woman who was raised in the United States and lives in the nation's South. She has been married for 2 years and is seeking a graduate degree at your university. She comes to counseling because she is struggling with some of her classes. She reports that she is depressed and is having difficulty concentrating. In further explorations, you find out that she has a perforated ear from repeated beatings by her partner. She indicates that she may be losing the hearing in one of her ears. Maya reveals that her in-laws support her partner and believe that Maya is not a good enough daughter-in-law and wife. Maya's support system—her parents—live in the northwestern part of the United States. Although she is able to speak with them on a regular basis, she is not able to visit them regularly. To complicate the issues, her father has a heart condition, and Maya is afraid to tell her parents about her situation for fear of upsetting her father and his health. Her partner is unaware that she is seeking counseling and would likely prevent her from coming to school if he were to become aware that she is sharing "private issues" with an outsider. Maya shares with you that school is the one place where she experiences a sense of freedom and an opportunity to be herself. Imagine that you are a counselor working with Maya. Take a moment to reflect on the following questions:

- How does your understanding of Asian-American values inform your work with Maya?
- What are your thoughts about women and violence? How might those thoughts facilitate or inhibit your ability to discuss the issue with Maya?

- How do you see yourself in terms of your own gender identity, and how might your view of yourself shape your counseling approach?
- If you share a similar cultural background with Maya, how might Maya's perceptions or assumptions about you influence what she shares with you in counseling? If you do not share a similar cultural background with Maya, how might Maya's perceptions or assumptions about you influence what she shares with you in counseling?
- What parts of Maya's experience can you empathize and resonate with? What parts are more challenging for you to understand?
- What about Maya's life, family, and social and cultural experiences might help you gain an understanding of how she deals with her situation?
- What can you validate about Maya's experience?

Psychopathology

Questions about the prevalence of psychological disorders among Asian Americans are questions of both clinical and empirical concern. For instance, answers to questions such as how prevalent depression is among people of Chinese descent or how common it is for Filipinos to encounter racism are critical in providing researchers and clinicians with a baseline understanding of the psychological status of Asian-American communities. However, despite the value of such questions, counselors should be cautious in reviewing the literature for "answers." As a relatively new field, research on counseling Asian Americans is far from definitive and is more likely to provide conflicting answers as a function of different samples, surveys, and analytical strategies (Sue, Cheng, Saad, & Chu, 2012).

To gain insights into, rather than answers to, these questions, researchers have generally used two approaches: (a) epidemiological studies that attempt to be representative of a particular population at large, and (b) small-scale studies that often use smaller, convenience samples. Although epidemiological studies are clearly valuable, drawing conclusions from national epidemiological studies has been hampered by relatively small samples of Asian Americans and the aggregation of Asian Americans across ethnic groups (Yang & WonPat-Borja, 2007). Nevertheless, a few epidemiological studies, such as the Chinese American Psychiatric Epidemiological Study (CAPES) and the Filipino American Community Epidemiological Study (FACES) have provided valuable insights. To address the limited number of epidemiological studies, Takeuchi, Hong, Gile, and Alegría (2007) conducted the National Latino and Asian American Study (NLAAS), the most comprehensive study of Latino and Asian American mental health thus far. With a probability sample of 2,095 Asian Americans consisting of 600 Chinese, 508 Filipinos, 520 Vietnamese, 141 Asian Indians, 107 Japanese, 81 Koreans, and 138 individuals categorized as "Other," the study has already become a rich source of information. Consequently, in this section we review the existing literature—including findings from the NLAAS—on racism and its relationship to psychological distress and, more specifically, the prevalence of depression, posttraumatic stress disorder (PTSD), domestic violence, anxiety, and schizophrenia.

RACISM   Research on the prevalence of racism is both emerging and far from definitive. Part of the challenge in such studies is in the manner in which a construct such as racism is defined and measured. For instance, a number of researchers indicated that many Asian Americans experience overt racial discrimination, such as hate crimes, racial profiling by police, and employment discrimination (Lai & Arguelles, 2003; Lien, 2002; Umemoto, 2000). In addition, Alvarez et al. (2006) reported that 98% of Asian Americans have experienced at least one instance of racial microagression. Other studies have also pointed out negative attitudes toward Asian Americans. In particular, the Committee of 100 (2001) reported that 1 in 4 Americans agreed that Chinese Americans are "taking away too many jobs from Americans" and 1 in 5 Americans endorsed the view that Chinese Americans "don't care what happens to anyone but their own kind." Hence, counselors may benefit from attending to methodological issues in evaluating such studies.

There has been consistent empirical evidence to indicate that racism has an adverse impact on mental health, health, and health-related behaviors (Alvarez, Liang, & Neville, 2016; Alvarez & Shin, 2013; Carlisle, 2015; Cheng, Lin, & Cham, 2015; Gee et al., 2009; Tummala-Narra et al., 2011). Racism has been shown to have an adverse impact on self-esteem (Greene et al., 2006), depression (Beiser & Hou, 2006; Han & Lee, 2011), race-related stress (Liang, Alvarez, Juang, & Liang, 2007), drug use (Gee, Delva, & Takeuchi, 2006), body image (Iyer & Haslam, 2003), HIV risk behaviors (Yoshikawa, Wilson, Chae, & Cheng, 2004), PTSD (Loo et al., 2001), and chronic health concerns (Carlisle, 2015). Researchers have found that foreign-born Asian Americans tend to experience more racial discrimination than U.S.-born individuals (Yoo et al., 2010). In a large-scale epidemiological study, Gee, Spencer, Chen, Yip, and Takeuchi (2007) found that perceived discrimination was associated with depression and other mental disorders among Asian-American adults, regardless of degree of acculturative stress or generation status.

Most disturbing, using data from the NLAAS, scholars have found that perceived discrimination is associated with an increase in suicidal attempts and ideation (Cheng et al., 2010), an increased likelihood of a mental disorder (Gee, Spencer, Chen, & Takeuchi, 2007), and chronic health conditions (Gee, Spencer, Chen, & Takeuchi, 2007; Carlisle, 2015), such as chronic pain, cardiovascular disease, and respiratory disease. In a further illustration of the insidious impact of discrimination on health, Gee and Ponce (2010) found that Asian Americans who experienced discrimination reported between 19 (for Chinese Americans) and 51 (for South Asians) more unhealthy days (i.e., days in which their mental or physical health was not good) than Asian Americans who did not experience discrimination. Yet further, in a review of research and literature on Asian-American veterans' mental health, Tsai and Kong (2012) mentioned that Asian-American Pacific Islander veterans who served during the Vietnam War encountered racism from fellow soldiers, and race-related stressors were associated with more severe PTSD symptoms. As a group, Asian-American Pacific Islander veterans were found to be physically healthier than other veterans, but reported poorer mental health and were less likely to use mental health services.

Last, perceived discrimination has been associated with the underutilization of both health and mental health care among Asian Americans (Burgess, Ding, Hargreaves, Ryn, & Phelan, 2008; Gupta et al., 2011). Worse, Lee, Ayers, and Kronenfeld (2009) found that, when people of color—including Asian Americans—do seek health care, they are more likely to report discrimination from their health-care providers and less satisfying treatment (e.g., less likely to be treated with respect, less likely to be involved in decision making). In turn, these experiences of discrimination within the health-care system lead to further underutilization of services and ultimately exacerbate individuals' health and mental health disorders. In short, when Asian Americans encounter racial discrimination, it can be part of a cyclical process that creates psychological and physical distress that may be further exacerbated by both the underutilization of treatment and discrimination from the same professionals providing that treatment. Racism, then, appears to be an experience with considerable and adverse psychological consequences.

DEPRESSION Studies of depression among Asian Americans have generally suggested that Asian Americans experience major depressive disorders at a rate that is equal to or lower than that of the general population (Yang & WonPat-Borja, 2007). However, a meta-analysis by Gupta, Leong, Valentine, and Canada (2013) of 38 studies indicates that depression rates may be *higher* than that of the general population. In the CAPES study, with a sample of 1,747 Chinese American adults in the Los Angeles area, Takeuchi et al. (2007) found a 3.4% rate of depression over the 12 months prior to the study—lower than the 6.6% rate found in the general population by a replication of the National Comorbidity Study (Kessler et al., 2003). However, self-reports of depression rates among Asian-American adults have ranged from 12% to 41% (Leung, Cheung, & Tsui, 2012; Yang & WonPat-Borja, 2007). Among studies of youths, Yang and WonPat-Borja's (2007) meta-analysis found that, in 7 out of 9 major studies, there were no significant differences in depression rates between Asian Americans and other racial groups, with rates ranging from 2.6% to 12.8%, using diagnostic interviews. Of the demographic groups that have been examined, elderly Asian Americans appear to be at greatest risk for depression, with rates as high as 40% (Mui & Kang, 2006). However, in their review of seven studies of elderly Asian Americans, Yang and WonPat-Borja (2007) found three studies showing rates lower than that of White Americans, three studies showing comparable rates, and one study showing higher rates.

To add further complexity to understanding the mental health of Asian Americans, immigration appears to be an important factor in mental health. For instance, examining the NLAAS, Takeuchi et al. (2007) found that lifetime rates of mental health disorders were significantly higher (24.6%) for U.S.-born participants than for foreign-born Asian Americans (15.2%). Similarly, Zhang, Fang, Wu, and Wieczorek (2013) found that lifetime prevalence rates of depressive disorder and suicidal ideation were much higher among U.S.-born Chinese Americans than among U.S. immigrants born in China. Specifically, the rates were 23.20% versus 8.25% for depression and 18.40% versus 8.88% for suicidal ideation. Likewise, Takeuchi et al. (2007) found that age of immigration was significantly related to prevalence of psychiatric disorders: Individuals who immigrated as children were more likely to have psychiatric disorders than individuals who immigrated later in life. Acculturation has also been found to be associated with depressive symptoms among Asian Americans (Castellanos, Gloria, Kim, & Park, 2014). Consequently, as counselors explore the empirical literature in this area, it may be helpful for them to recognize the within-group differences found in studies on Asian-American mental health.

POSTTRAUMATIC STRESS DISORDER (PTSD) Premigration traumas, particularly among Southeast Asian refugees, have been consistently associated with the incidence of PTSD, suicide, and depression (Chung & Bemak, 2007). In the most comprehensive study to date on Cambodian refugees, Marshall, Schell, Elliott, Berthold, and Chun (2005) found that 62% suffered from PTSD and 51% had major depression in the previous year. To contextualize these rates, the authors related that 99% of the participants reported near-death starvation, 90% had family or friends murdered, and 54% were tortured prior to coming to the United States. The effects of such trauma can be multigenerational. For instance, in a study of Cambodian-American refugees, Hinton, Field, Nickerson, Bryant, and Simon (2013) found that 52% of those surveyed demonstrated symptoms of PTSD. In addition, it seems that women exhibit higher levels of psychological distress (Chung & Bemak, 2007). More disturbingly, there has been evidence to indicate that the effects of migration trauma can persist over time. In one study, Marshall et al. (2005) found that 62% of the Cambodian refugee participants continued to exhibit PTSD symptoms, and 51% exhibited symptoms of depression, two decades after resettlement in the United States. Hence, the experiences of Southeast Asian–American refugees are significantly different from their immigrant peers. Interestingly, in a recent study on Asian-American and Pacific Islander veterans, Whealin and colleagues (2013) found that the Asian-American veteran participants were significantly less likely to screen positive for PTSD than Native Hawaiian/Pacific Islanders and European Americans (16.4% vs. 44.4% and 39.2%, respectively). Resiliency and social support seemed to be important protective factors for the Asian-American veterans.

DOMESTIC VIOLENCE   Efforts at determining the prevalence of domestic violence among Asian Americans have been hampered by limited research, particularly because of the paucity of representative epidemiological samples (Kim, Lau, & Chang, 2007). Nevertheless, using the NLAAS, Chang, Shen, and Takeuchi (2009) found relatively lower rates of intimate partner violence, with 10.1% of Asian-American women and 11.9% of men reporting that they were targets of such violence (compared with national rates of 17.4% for women and 18.4% for men). The Asian and Pacific Islander Institute on Domestic Violence (2011) indicated that 41% to 61% of Asian women report experiencing physical or sexual violence by an intimate partner during their lifetime. This range of rates is higher than the rates reported by Whites (21.3%), African Americans (26.3%), Hispanics of any race (21.2%), people of mixed race (27.0%), and American Indians and Alaskan Natives (30.7%) in a national study (Tjaden & Thoennes, 2000). In addition, Tjaden and Thoennes cautioned that rates may be underreported because of cultural values surrounding self-disclosure. Indeed, Kawahara and Fu (2007) observed that silence around domestic violence may be perpetuated by cultural values such as the need to maintain group harmony and save face, as well as by tactics such as social isolation and threats to women's "reputation" and their immigration status.

Given the limited research in this area, studies using nonrepresentative convenience samples may be the best alternative to date. For instance, in a relatively large survey of 336 Asian Americans by the National Asian Women's Health Organization (NAWHO, 2002), 8% of the women reported that they had been raped, 19% were pressured to have sex, and 26% said that they were the target of physical or emotional abuse by their partners. In addition, Kim et al. (2007) reported that community-based studies of domestic violence among Asian-American women have found rates of victimization ranging from 24% to 60%. Although the evidence in this area is far from definitive, perhaps the most salient finding for counselors to consider is that the overwhelming majority of Asian-American women (95% to 97%) have never used preventive or treatment services despite the high incidence of violence in their lives (NAWHO, 2002).

ANXIETY AND SCHIZOPHRENIA   Few studies have been conducted on the prevalence of anxiety disorders and schizophrenia in individuals of Asian descent. Moreover, whatever research there is offers a mixed picture about the prevalence of anxiety disorders among Asian Americans. On the one hand, earlier research has been relatively consistent in suggesting that these disorders occur in individuals of Asian descent at rates lower than or similar to those occurring in Whites (Sue, Sue, Sue, & Takeuchi, 1995; Zhang & Snowden, 1999). For instance, in Zhang and Snowden's analysis of the Epidemiological Catchment Area data set consisting of over 18,000 participants across the country, the authors found that Asian Americans reported the lowest lifetime rates of schizophrenia, phobias, and obsessive–compulsive disorders among all racial groups. Similarly, Sue et al. (1995) found that Chinese Americans reported lower rates of generalized anxiety disorder, agoraphobia, simple phobia, and panic disorder.

On the other hand, more recent empirical studies report higher social anxiety among people of Asian heritage compared with people of Western heritage (Hsu et al., 2012; Lau et al., 2009). In fact, a meta-analytic review by Krieg and Xu (2015) indicated that 28 of 32 studies found that individuals of Asian heritage in America, Australia, and Canada reported higher social anxiety than individuals of European heritage. Given the mixed findings, the limited amount of research, and the failure of existing studies to tap the heterogeneity of the Asian-American communities, it is important that counselors and scholars be cautious to not make premature definitive conclusions about the status of psychopathology among Asian Americans.

Help Seeking and Coping

Help seeking is a complicated process. Although a need for mental health services exists, only a portion of those who need professional help seek out such services. Although several variables influence help seeking, researchers have emphasized that coping strategies and their perceived effectiveness must be understood and evaluated against the backdrop of a cultural group's values, norms, and worldviews (Inman & Yeh, 2007; Inman, Yeh, et al., 2007; Miller et al., 2011; Yeh et al., 2006). For us to understand Asian-American help seeking, we need to understand how help seeking may be influenced by Asian values and worldviews. The remainder of this section highlights specific issues related to mental health use among Asian Americans.

UTILIZATION RATES   Literature has consistently revealed that Asian Americans underutilize mental health services (Abe-Kim et al., 2007; Leong, Chang, & Lee, 2007). The National Alliance on Mental Illness (2012) reported that, among Asian Americans with a depressive disorder, 69% did not receive mental health treatment during the previous year. Furthermore, while 33% of non-Latino Whites with depression received quality depression treatment, only 14% of Asian Americans received such treatment In addition, congruent with earlier data from the National Institute of Mental Health (Matsuoka, Breaux, & Ryujin, 1997) on utilization rates, Leong and colleagues (2007) found that Asian-American Pacific Islanders were 3 times less likely than their White counterparts to use mental health services, even in 16 of the states with the highest populations of Asian-American Pacific Islanders.

The NLAAS (Abe-Kim et al., 2007) reports that only 8.6% of Asian Americans with a psychological problem sought any form of professional help, compared with 17.9% of the general population. Of those who received help, only 3.1% of Asian Americans had sought help from a mental health provider, and U.S.-born Asian Americans were more likely than foreign-born Asian Americans to see a mental health provider. In fact, a number of researchers (e.g., Han & Pong, 2015; Leung et al., 2012) indicated that Asian Americans in general were less likely than the general population to seek professional mental health providers as their primary source of help. Moreover, when Asian Americans did seek help, they were noted to terminate psychotherapy prematurely (Kim, Ng, & Ahn, 2005). Comparisons of help-seeking attitudes between Asian international students and European-American students have yielded similar results. Studies have shown that Asian international students have less favorable attitudes than the general population has toward psychotherapy (e.g., J. Lee, 2014; Tedeschi & Willis, 1993). Similar trends have been found in large-scale studies analyzing usage of the public mental health system. Ihara, Chae, Cummings, and Lee (2014) indicated that, irrespective of socioeconomic status, all four groups of Asian-American individuals with mental health needs in their study (i.e., Vietnamese, Filipino, Chinese, and "Other") underutilized both health and mental health services; only 5.8% reported using any mental health specialist provider.

By contrast, some researchers (Maynard, Ehreth, Cox, Peterson, & McGann, 1997) have found that a small percentage of Asian Americans overutilize mental health services. This trend has increased since the 1970s. For instance, Sue, Fujino, Hu, Takeuchi, and Zane (1991) examined data on clients entering the Los Angeles County Department of Mental Health system between 1983 and 1988. Although Asian Americans constituted only 3.1% of outpatients and 8.7% of the county population, they exhibited more severe disorders, engaged in a greater number of treatment sessions, and received medication-based treatments more frequently, than their White counterparts did (Flaskerud & Hu, 1992). Similar trends were found in Chen, Sullivan, Lu, and Shibusawa's (2003) analysis of public mental health service use in San Diego County between 1991 and 1994: In addition to exhibiting more severe symptoms and having longer lengths of stay, Asian Americans were more likely than other ethnic groups to use outpatient and day treatment programs. Furthermore, several Southeast Asian and East Asian groups have been found to overutilize mental health services (Zane, Hatanaka, Park, & Akutsu, 1994).

Research has also revealed other instances when Asian Americans seem to utilize services differently. For example, Ruzek, Nguyen, and Herzog (2011) found that Asian Americans preferred using health centers over counseling and using mental health classes and Web sites over actual therapy. Similarly, acculturation seemed to affect the choice of providers (professional versus community based; Takayama, 2010). Specifically, the more acculturated the person and the greater the English language proficiency, the greater was the likelihood of seeking mental health services. Asians with lesser language proficiency tendeded to seek alternative services (Meyer, Zane, & Cho, 2009).

ATTITUDES TOWARD, AND BARRIERS TO, HELP SEEKING   Although Asian Americans experience difficulties with a range of issues, including academic, interpersonal, familial, and intergenerational issues, as well as issues with substance abuse, health, identity, and racism (Inman & Yeh, 2007), they may display less favorable attitudes toward seeking help from a professional mental health provider (Kim & Lee, 2014; Leong, Kim, & Gupta, 2011). Leong and Lau (2001) identified several barriers that would explain the low utilization rates of Asian Americans: cognitive (e.g., stigmas), affective (e.g., shame), value orientation (e.g., a collectivist nature), and physical (e.g., access to resources) barriers. Although the interaction between client and counselor can influence help seeking, several individual, sociocultural, and structural/institutional barriers have been noted as influencing Asian-American help-seeking attitudes and behaviors.

At the individual level, lack of knowledge or lack of exposure to Western mental health treatment and misconceptions about professional counseling may be barriers to seeking professional help (Kawanga-Singer & Chung, 2002). These conditions may be closely related to the person's immigration history (Takayama, 2010), length of stay in the United States, and level of acculturation. Further, some authors (Akutsu & Chu, 2006; Ting & Hwang, 2009) have observed a significant positive relationship between highly acculturated college students and attitudes toward seeking professional help. Other demographic variables that have been noted to influence help seeking include gender (Nolen-Hoeksema, 2002; Sheu & Sedlacek, 2004), age (Luu, Leung, & Nash, 2009), and history of previous treatment (Ruzek et al., 2011). For example, some authors have found that women and those who have sought previous clinical help tended to be more open to mental health treatment; others (Ting & Hwang, 2009), however, have found no gender differences in help-seeking attitudes. Further, older, more traditional, and less acculturated Asians tend to hold on to traditional cultural beliefs and are likely to have less favorable attitudes toward the use of mental health services (Nguyen, 2011).

In addition, limited language proficiency (Kawanga-Singer & Chung, 2002) and client–counselor ethnic matching are other individual-level factors that influence help seeking among Asian Americans (Meyer et al., 2009). For instance, Gamst, Dana, Der-Karabetian, and Kramer (2001) found that client–counselor ethnic matching not only is associated with higher global assessment, but also is linked to a lower probability of premature termination of counseling services, particularly for clients who do not have English as their primary language. However, given the dearth of research in this area, it is recommended that counselors interprete and apply findings with caution.

At the sociocultural level, cultural values and views of mental health, expressions of distress, stigmatization of persons who have a mental illness and who use mental health services, and the availability of alternative healing practices have been noted to contribute to underutilization of mental health services (Inman, Yeh, et al., 2007), especially for Asian Americans residing in immigrant communities. For example, the notion of shame or loss of face has been identified as a significant barrier to the utilization of mental health services. According to Sue (1994), terms like *Haji* among the Japanese, *Hiya* among Filipinos, *Mentz* among the Chinese, and *Chaemyun* among Koreans are often used to highlight the shame that may be incurred in these communities (p. 203). Utilization of mental health services may be seen as a public admission that something is wrong and thus is likely to compromise the family and its social status (Tuliao, 2014); to Asians and many Asian Americans, not only are personal problems and weaknesses to be shared only by family members, but also, the family is seen as the only party responsible for taking care of the problem (Gomes, 2000; Yeh & Wang, 2000). Seeking professional counseling may be seen as breaking away from, and going against the privacy of, the family (Yeh et al., 2006).

Cultural factors also influence how Asian Americans may perceive the symptoms or causes of a disorder and, in turn, the specific intervention that might be effective (Versola-Russo, 2006). Within Asian cultures, the mind and body are considered inseparable (Sue & Sue, 2013). Health and well-being are seen holistically and include mental, physical, and spiritual components (Hilton et al., 2001). Because the mind and the body are seen to be interconnected, psychopathology is often conceptualized within physical and spiritual frameworks. For instance, it is not uncommon to see Asian Americans present with physical symptoms (e.g., headaches, dizziness) when emotionally distressed. Furthermore, symptoms may also be seen as embedded within a religious context. Studies (Inman, Yeh, et al., 2007; Yeh et al., 2006) of South Asians, Southeast Asians, and East Asians have revealed that these immigrant communities believe that problems are preordained, a result of past lives, and karmic, caused by supernatural forces or an imbalance between the yin and the yang. Consistent with these beliefs, these communities have been known to seek indigenous forms of healing. Activity 11.1 provides an opportunity to obtain more information on indigenous healers.

ACTIVITY 11.1

Interview an Asian-American nontraditional or indigenous healer. How does the method the healer uses compare against Western perspectives of counseling and treatment? What preconceptions, biases, or beliefs based in your own socialization did you have about this type of healing? What did you learn from this experience?

At the structural level or institutional level, conflict between the values endorsed by Western mental health systems and Asian values may be a major deterrent to seeking professional help (Yakunina & Weigold, 2011). For instance, Western approaches to counseling often focus on self-disclosure of personal, highly intense issues and feelings, insight-oriented intrapsychic approaches, and individual goals (Hall, Hong, Zane, & Meyer, 2011; Leong & Lau, 2001; Sue, 1999). Given the focus on self-reliance, emotional management, willpower (Hall et al., 2011), keeping personal issues in the family (Zane & Ku, 2014), and a collectivistic orientation to problems (Kim & Kendall, 2015; Yeh et al., 2006), Western approaches tend to be antithetical to Asian values and thus may deter these communities from seeking help (Hall et al., 2011; Leong & Lau, 2001).

In a meta-analytic review, Cabral and Smith (2011) indicated that perceived counselor credibility was strongly related to utilization of services. In a related fashion, Inman, Yeh, et al. (2007) found that the lack of culturally sensitive and competent counselors has been another reason for high dropout rates or reticence in seeking professional help. Inaccurate evaluations or misdiagnoses due to cultural biases, different social norms, or culturally incongruent scales may create significant difficulties in perceived credibility among Asian Americans (Cabral & Smith, 2011). In addition, a counselor's lack of culture-specific knowledge may result in Asian American clients not receiving necessary care. As mentioned earlier, Asian-American clients sometimes tend to focus on physical discomforts than emotional symptoms. For instance, Chung et al. (2003) found that, while 41.6% of the Asian patients exhibited depressive symptoms and psychological distress, physicians identified only 23.6% of the patients as actually being distressed. Finally, other systemic issues, such as poor access to services (because of transportation or location problems), familial obligations (e.g., child care), and financial costs, are factors that can influence the use of mental health services.

SITES OF RESILIENCY   Sites of resiliency represent those psychological or physical spaces that help Asian Americans cope. In keeping with this idea, several sites of resiliency have been identified for the Asian-American community. For instance, the use of alternative forms of healing has been noted as an important source of resiliency, particularly for Asian immigrants whose cultural values and beliefs greatly influence their daily lives and attitudes toward health and well-being (Inman, Yeh, et al., 2007; Yeh et al., 2006). Alternative forms of healing not only are consistent with Asian cultural values, but also seem integral to maintaining a sense of self within the communities (Constantine, Myers, Kindaichi, & Moore, 2004). For example, alternative healers tend to treat illness within a cultural, familial, and communal context (Hsiao et al., 2006).

Because of a holistic emphasis on health and a spiritually guided life (C. C. Lee, 2007; Lee & Ctian, 2009), themes of fatalism, karma, and religion play a significant role in coping with daily stressors (Yeh et al., 2006). In light of these themes, Asian Americans have been known to seek religious/faith healers and religious organizations (e.g., churches, temples) and to engage in chants, prayers, religious ceremonies, and lighting of lamps. Other, related sources are palm reading and astrology. Also, because of their belief in creating mind–body harmony, Asians may engage in activities such as Tai Chi, yoga, Qigong, acupuncture, and therapeutic massage. Furthermore, because of the belief in bodily imbalance across several Asian cultures (e.g., Chinese, Indian), nutrition is another popular means of restoring health. This concept is exemplified in the use of herbal medicine or specific foods.

A central source of alternative support or resiliency is the family and social community. The family as a major source of support has been discussed across several Asian groups.

For instance, authors have found that first-generation adults (Inman, Yeh, et al., 2007; Yeh et al., 2006) and second-generation Asian-American college students (Kim & Park, 2009) tend to seek support from family members when faced with personal difficulties. Furthermore, social supports beyond the family can provide important psychological and social support. Because of the emphasis on a collectivistic culture and the potential for familial conflicts, social networks with individuals who are ethnically and racially similar may be important in buffering individuals from stressful situations (Frey & Roysircar, 2006).

GUIDELINES FOR COUNSELING CLIENTS OF ASIAN DESCENT

Different cultural values, a lack of familiarity with the counseling process, potential language difficulties, discrimination, and other cultural experiences can challenge the therapeutic relationship, resulting in miscommunication and premature termination of services. Given that counseling may be a foreign concept to many Asian Americans, education about counseling and the utility of mental health services is very much needed among Asian Americans who may not be acculturated to Western conceptualizations of health care (Yakunina & Weigold, 2011). In this regard, counselors should be prepared to answer, in lay terms, seemingly basic, yet critical, questions such as "How does talking help me?" or "Why do I do all the talking?" or "What do you do?" Whether the client explicitly asks or not, she or he may be wondering about the answers to these questions—answers that may be critical to enhancing the client's intrinsic motivation to remain in counseling (Alvarez & Chen, 2012). Hence, counselors must play an integral role in educating clients about the counseling process. In this section, we highlight some critical areas that counselors should focus on as they work with Asian-American clients. Reflection 11.7 may help you conceptualize cross-cultural help-seeking behaviors.

Counselor Self-Assessment

Multicultural competence begins when counselors do a frank assessment of themselves before they enter the session. Counselors are encouraged to obtain training, attend workshops and presentations, and familiarize themselves with the literature on the Asian-American community prior to beginning their work with clients from that community. In essence, counselors should assess the extent to which they are familiar with the information presented in this chapter.

On a personal level, counselors would do well to reflect on their socialization experiences with Asian Americans, their assumptions and biases about that community, and the extent to which all those factors may influence their work as counselors. Indeed, Alvarez and Chen (2012) have argued that this self-reflection is mandatory, regardless of whether the client and the counselor are similar or different in terms of race, ethnicity, gender, or any other cultural dimension. The issue is that, despite phenotypic similarities between a counselor and a client,

---

REFLECTION 11.7

Reflect on what you have been taught in terms of "appropriate" help seeking and support. Whom can you turn to? What can you discuss? How will others react? How does what you have been taught compare with what you know about Asian-American attitudes regarding help seeking? How might what you know shape your expectations about seeking help, and, more important, how might what you know facilitate or inhibit your work with Asian Americans?

the psychological meaning that each attributes to these identities may be entirely different and far more critical. Last, given the significance of issues such as race, gender, and experiences of oppression, counselors may further benefit from an awareness of the extent to which they are comfortable and able to raise those issues in counseling. The problem is that clients are unlikely to raise such relatively "taboo" issues on their own initiative, despite the potential significance of these issues in the counseling relationship. For instance, how often do you think a client will simply say, "I'd like to talk about the fact that you're a White counselor and I'm Asian American." As a result, both the responsibility and the power to do so lie with the counselor.

Imagine yourself working with Maya (the client depicted in Case Study 11.2). Consider the following questions as you reflect on the case: (1) What might be some personal assumptions and values that will influence your work with her? (2) How is your identity similar or dissimilar from Maya's identity? (3) What values do you share with Maya, and what values do you differ on with Maya? (4) How might your beliefs in women's rights and autonomy and in family cohesion, as well as your knowledge about South Asian culture, play a role in your response or reaction to Maya's decision of not wanting to share her experience of abuse with her parents? These are some crucial questions for the counselor to ask herself or himself when working with individuals similar to Maya.

Counseling Process

In treating Asian-American clients, understanding how counseling and the counseling process may be conceptualized within a cultural context plays a significant role in providing culturally sensitive therapy. For example, the emphasis on equality in counselor–client relationships is an important aspect of some Western psychotherapeutic approaches (e.g., feminist therapy). However, depending on their acculturation level, Asian Americans tend to be deferential to people in authority (e.g., the counselor); thus, equality may not be the most effective way of creating a therapeutic alliance (Wong, Beutler, & Zane, 2007). In a related fashion, because of their authoritative roles, counselors are seen as experts. For instance, Asian-American clients who work with a college counselor may expect the counselor to tell them what to do with regard to choosing majors or classes. Furthermore, Asian Americans may not understand the need for intrusive questions and the length of time a psychological evaluation might take. In addition, because of the use of brief interventions with physicians, shamans, or other elders, in which they are evaluated, diagnosed, and given a prescription in one session, there may be a tendency on the part of some Asian Americans to expect a quick fix to their problem. As a result, the client who comes in to see a career counselor may be puzzled by a process that involves a lengthy assessment of his or her values, interests, and career socialization, as well as the administration of a battery of surveys. Because they do not understand or are unfamiliar with the conceptual underpinnings of Western approaches to counseling, Asian-American immigrants may feel frustrated with therapy.

The primary focus in counseling in the United States is on verbal communication. This expectation that clients talk about their issues goes against some Asian cultural values, such as the stigma attached to sharing personal information with strangers. Conducting therapy by first developing a relationship with your Asian-American client is important in creating a trusting environment that will allow conversations to occur. In particular, the use of specific types of counselor self-disclosures (e.g., strategies, intimate disclosures) has been found helpful in the client–counselor relationship. For instance, disclosing tangible ideas used in personal challenges that might share some similarity with those of the client has been noted to increase trust levels in client–counselor relationships (Inman & Tewari, 2003). In a related fashion, initiating a discussion on potential counselor–client differences can also assist with building a relationship with your Asian client. Discussing differences related to aspects such as immigrant/international status, race, ethnicity, and gender allows for contextualizing the client's experience and addressing any potential for miscommunication that may evolve in this emotional and personal relationship. Now think back to Marge in Case Study 11.1. Marge came in specifically wanting to work on her anxiety relating to her class. How do you anticipate Marge might react when you want to explore her cultural identity, adoption history, and experience with racism? What might the counseling process with Marge look like then? In addition, consider how you would work with the client discussed in Activity 11.2, next.

ACTIVITY 11.2

Discuss the following in dyads: Imagine that your client of Pakistani-American descent has just decided that she will follow the career path that her family thinks is best for her. She has considered pursuing her own career interests but feels that doing so would be too disruptive to her family. What is your personal reaction to this decision? How does your reaction compare with your own values and assumptions? How will you manage and address your reaction? How will the way you address it affect the counseling process?

Conceptualization of the Problem

When clients present with specific issues in counseling, it becomes important to align the conceptualization of the problem with the multiple contexts in which individuals exist. In capturing the complexity of an individual's life, assessing the relative significance of various relationships (families, friends), systems (school, work), and environments (immigration, discrimination, racism), and examining the intersection of the three within the lives of Asian Americans, becomes very important (Inman, Rawls, Meza, & Brown, 2002). For instance, owing to the emphasis on family and community within the Asian culture, exploring the makeup of the actual household, the influence of the extended family (whether in the United States or in the country of origin), and the different alliances in the community becomes necessary. However, the ethnic social support that goes beyond the family can, on the one hand, provide Asian Americans with important psychological, moral, emotional, and physical support but, on the other hand, also create great stress for the individual (Yee et al., 2007). Thus, some caution should be taken in this regard.

A second major force shaping Asian-American identities is their immigration experience. Many families migrate to the United States to obtain better opportunities for their families. Within this context, preimmigration experiences (e.g., age at immigration, reasons for immigration, immigration status on arrival [voluntary immigrant or involuntary refugee], exposure to Western values, educational and skill levels, sacrifices made in leaving their country of origin) and the postimmigrant adjustment (e.g., sacrifices made in taking care of families, level of intergenerational conflict, changes in economic and social status, potential gender role and parent–child role reversals, level of community support, religiosity, and experiences of discrimination and racism) are significant factors that need to be considered in understanding the socialization and adjustment of Asian Americans in the United States. Moreover, it is important to recognize that the psychological significance of immigration is not limited to the first generation alone, given that the sense of sacrifice and hardship associated with the immigration period may reverberate across generations. For instance, a school counselor who is working with a young Cambodian-American student may need to consider the idea that the importance of school to this student and her family takes on a unique significance in light of the possibility that they may be refugees who have lost a great deal in coming to the United States. These factors all become important and influential not only in the extent to which families acculturate to the host culture, but also in the responsibilities that Asian Americans experience in their families (Inman, Yeh, et al., 2007).

Further, because of the diversity within the Asian-American groups with regard to educational levels, occupations, socioeconomic status, and experiences of racism, oppression, and privilege, exploring the negotiation among education and class, ethnic and racial identities, and gender and sexual identities is paramount so that counselors can understand the pressures that Asian Americans might be experiencing. For instance, educational and career choices do not occur in a vacuum but are influenced by social systems (e.g., language barriers) and institutional barriers (e.g., access to managerial jobs). Acknowledging and utilizing the different cultural contexts that frame the lives of Asian Americans is an important consideration in delivering comprehensive culturally sensitive psychological services to these individuals.

Now reflect on Marge (the client depicted in Case Study 11.1). A multiculturally sensitive counselor would take into consideration major factors and social systems that influence or cause Marge's nervousness and anxiety-like symptoms, instead of pathologizing her with a disorder. Consider how you would conceptualize Marge's anxiety in the context of her multiple social contexts (e.g., race, social class, gender). How might you explore with Marge her experience growing up as a transracially adopted child living in a predominantly White neighborhood? How do you think Marge's level of cultural identity development plays a role in how she views herself and others. Consider: If Marge views herself as White, how might her experience of discrimination shake her sense of self and thus create anxiety. Do you think its important to explore whether Marge and her adoptive parents have ever discussed the racial differences between her and them? If so, how might you engage in this process? How might your engagement with Marge and her adoptive parents help you develop a good conceptualization of Marge and her clinical issues that she is presenting in counseling?

Intervention

The literature has identified some general counseling principles that the multiculturally competent counselor might use in working with Asian Americans. These principles are based in Asian cultural values. For instance, research suggests that, because of the emphasis on privacy within Asian-American families, Asian Americans might not openly express strong emotions. Neither might they publicly disclose personal and family issues that may bring shame on their families. Others (Sue & Zane, 2009) have noted that Asian Americans typically prefer an authoritarian, directive, and structured approach to treatment. Yet other researchers have observed that Asian Americans do better when there is both ethnic and gender matching in the therapeutic relationship (Meyer et al., 2011; Zyguras, Klimidis, Lewis, & Stuart, 2003). Finally, because of the significant role that families play, family therapy might be an appropriate therapeutic intervention. Nevertheless, rather than automatically "comply" with these findings, counselors would do well in exercising some caution in implementing them.

Although the literature dictates some general guidelines surrounding therapeutic interventions, when working with Asian Americans, it is important to keep in mind that, as a group, they are extremely heterogeneous. Thus, interventions should be responsive to the specifics of your client, rather than following without question what has been found in the literature. To prevent stereotyping or overgeneralization, it is essential to assess individual differences that exist within and across generations and ethnic groups. For example, length of stay in the United States can significantly influence the extent to which Asian Americans hold onto their traditional cultural values or take on the dominant cultural values. The literature suggests that American-born Asians tend to acculturate at a faster pace than first-generation foreign-born Asians. Owing to these different rates of acculturation, the specific needs and adjustment issues of American-born Asians can be quite different from those of foreign-born Asians. For instance, because of unfamiliar systems or limited language proficiency, immigrant parents may not only experience challenges in guiding their American-born children in schoolwork (Shea, Ma, & Yeh, 2007), but also rely on their children to interpret social mores and manage daily chores (Inman & Tummala-Narra, 2010). This reversal in roles can create significant cultural conflicts for these children and their parents as the children become cultural brokers for their parents. Relatedly, the relevance of a racial versus an ethnic identity has been noted to be different for these two groups: Inman (2006) observed that race seemed more salient for American-born Asians, whereas ethnicity appeared more salient for foreign-born Asians. Even within the foreign-born Asians group, those who have lived in the United States for a considerable amount of time can experience issues quite differently from international students, who might live in the United States for short periods. For example, international students are likely to experience greater cultural shock than foreign-born Asians who have lived in the United States for longer periods (Zhou, Jindal-Snape, Topping, & Todman, 2008). Similarly, voluntary Asian immigrants' needs and adjustments can differ from those of nonvoluntary immigrants, or refugees, from Asia. For instance, Southeast Asian refugees (e.g., from Cambodia or Vietnam) have higher rates of PTSD and depression than voluntary immigrants from the region (National Institute of Health, 2005).

Thus, developing a range of treatment modalities is important in working with the diverse Asian community. Assessing whether the problem is individual, systemic (e.g., relational), environmental, or a combination of these is important as well. Moreover, assessing the client's and her or his family's worldview with regard to individualism versus collectivism is vital. Also, counselors need to be sensitive to the cultural norm of placing a family's needs before an individual's needs. Similarly, considerations need to be observed in terms of the application of traditional Western modalities to Asian Americans. The preference this group has for the use of alternative healing approaches (e.g., indigenous healers, family, friends, and other social supports) must be factored into treatment. Moreover, while some authors (e.g., Pinyuchon, Gray, & House, 2003; Tien & Olson, 2003) have highlighted models in working with specific Asian ethnic groups, Bae and Kung (2000) proposed a five-stage model (reparation, engagement, psycho-education, family sessions, and ending) for working with Asian-American clients with severe psychiatric conditions (e.g., schizophrenia). The factor common to these models is their focus on understanding the client's cultural values and stressors, and tailoring treatment to the client's needs, as well as including the family in counseling sessions when appropriate. Leong, Lee, and Chang (2008) suggest several key factors to consider in working with Asian-American clients, such as: adherence to Asian cultural values, acculturation level, immigration experience, communication style, family dynamics and interdependence, proneness to shame, and use of traditional healing methods.

Imagine that you were the counselor working with both Marge and Maya. Although each of them could be identified as an Asian-American woman, their cultural values and stressors, as well as their family and personal histories, are quite different from each other. As a woman of South Asian descent, Maya seems to subscribe to many of the South Asian cultural values, whereas Marge seems to perhaps have had less exposure to Asian values, regardless of her birth origin, and may be identifying more with the American culture. Thus, it is important for counselors to examine with each client their individual values and stories in order to tailor treatment accordingly and to avoid making assumptions and overgeneralizations. For instance, with Maya, the counselor may want to explore how she and her family view domestic violence. It is also important for the counselor to acknowledge the fact that, by seeking counseling and sharing details about her family and marriage, she has gone against her husband's family's beliefs of family privacy. In addition, while Maya's safety is a priority, the counselor needs to be cognizant of her or his own beliefs so as not to push Maya into taking immediate actions that may not be congruent with her values. By contrast, with Marge, it may be important to examine the role that Asian values play in her life. The issue of individualist versus collectivist values may be another area to examine with Marge. Yet another issue to explore with Marge is how she understands what it means to be "Korean American" and how the negotiation of this dual identity may influence her experiences. Complete Activity 11.3, and reflect on the common values and assumptions, as well as the heterogeneous nature, of those of Asian descent.

ACTIVITY 11.3

Discuss the following in dyads: Imagine that you have been assigned a client of Vietnamese descent. You may be similar to the client in terms of race and ethnicity, or you may be different. As you begin working with this client, how do you raise these racial and ethnic differences and similarities? Or do you? What is your rationale for either course of action? Be specific, and develop concrete examples of what you might say.

Outreach and Nonclinical Visibility

For some Asian Americans, the use of mental health or counseling services has been related to whether they know someone who works or who is connected to someone in such a setting (Inman, Yeh, et al., 2007). In essence, "word-of-mouth" referrals play a significant role for Asian Americans who seek counseling. This attitude is strongly related to the issue of credibility.

As noted previously, counselor credibility is an important factor in mental health utilization among Asian Americans. Subsumed within the definition of credibility are notions of expertness and trustworthiness on the part of the counselor. Perceived expertness in a counselor "is typically a function of a) reputation, b) evidence of specialized training, and c) behavioral evidence of proficiency and competency" (Inman, Yeh, et al., 2007, p. 85). For example, a rehabilitation counselor's credibility may be reflected in her familiarity with state and federal legislation on disability issues and how that affects her client's rights. Similarly, a counselor working with refugees will need to have sufficient knowledge of the legal and social issues related to a client's refugee status and how that status may affect the client's access to services. Such a testimony of expertness becomes all the more important when it comes from someone within the community.

Perceived trustworthiness, by contrast, "encompasses such factors as sincerity, openness, honesty, or perceived lack of motivation for personal gain" (p. 87). Intrinsic to developing trust is the extent to which a counselor self-discloses personal information. Knowing counselors at a personal level allows Asian-American clients to develop a sense of safety and kinship that may be needed in building the therapeutic relationship. This sort of personal knowledge may apply especially to immigrants or refugees who have had a negative experiences in relation to their legal documentation and residency. Their experiences may make them distrustful of the system and all people associated with it. In a related fashion, the fact that "actions speak louder than words" is a notion that has been well established in the South Asian community. For instance, Inman, Yeh et al. (2007) noted that, when caseworkers and other professionals went beyond the client to address client systems such as engaging in advocacy and facilitating connections between services, the South Asian participants in the study seemed to accord those individuals more credibility. Thus, the extent to which a counselor is considered credible can manifest itself in the way client issues are conceptualized and the specific interventions that are used in solving problems. Given that Asian Americans are apprehensive toward counseling, engaging in outreach and maintaining visibility (clinical or nonclinical) in the community is extremely important in developing credibility. Activity 11.4 provides an opportunity for you to learn about available resources for individuals of Asian descent.

ACTIVITY 11.4

Outreach is an important clinical activity. Apart from offering clinical services, an important role of an outreach counselor is to provide resources that best meet the client's needs. Accordingly, it becomes important to understand the needs of your community before offering your services. In preparing to work with Asian international students, contact the office of international students at your or a neighboring university and interview a staff member about the legal and social issues pertinent to international students. Similarly, to understand the experience of a refugee, contact an agency that works with refugees and interview a staff member about the resources (e.g., legal, social) that a refugee may need in adjusting to his or her new environment.

Social Advocacy and Social Justice

Issues closely related to outreach are social advocacy and social justice. In examining the ethics codes and guidelines of several mental health organizations (i.e., the American Counseling Association, the American Psychological Association, the National Association of Social Workers, and the American Association for Marriage and Family Therapy), a few recurring themes arise that surround the ethical behavior of counselors and that correspond to social justice. The first recurring theme is *respect for the integrity and strength of clients or communities.* Respecting communities involves acquiring adequate knowledge about those communities and being respectful of the differences among them. Respect is the foundation for engaging in social justice work because it ensures that "counselors understand and abide by a community's strengths, goals, and determination" (Toporek & Williams, 2006, p. 18). Thus, as you work with Asian-American communities, be mindful of the constant shifts and changes in cultural boundaries within different contexts. Although it is possible to be *informed* about the Asian community, it is not possible to know *everything* about it. It is important to engage in a constant process of raising your awareness about Asian Americans in different contexts (e.g., media, work), to understand how meanings of identity shift through different cultural factors (e.g., race, gender), and to sort through your assumptions and stereotypes (e.g., model minority) about this hetero- geneous group. Be aware that theories cannot be universally applied and that imposing Western modalities without modifications and adaptations is culturally insensitive. Thus, theories that are individually focused (e.g., client-centered therapy, psychodynamic theory) need to be critiqued. For instance, the "size of self" may be smaller among Asian communi- ties. How these theories may need to take on a more collective focus would need to be explored.

A second theme in the ethics guidelines is *responsibility*. Responsibility entails an assertion that counselors will help clients have access to resources, will minimize bias and dis- crimination, and will thus be part of the solution. This approach involves challenging the model-minority myth about Asian Americans. When using interventions, assess their impact not only on the individual but also on the Asian-American community. Concretely, when engaged in career counseling with an Asian student, consider the implications of encouraging the student to assert his or her independence in vocational choices that may go against familial desires and circumstances. Be aware of the academic pressures that Asian-American youths face. Engage teachers and other school personnel in dialogues about the need to be mindful of imposing or acting on these pressures to the detriment of the child. Examine the role of exter- nal forces in Asian-American lives. Challenge the oppression and discriminatory behaviors that occur at the individual (e.g., racist jokes, racial profiling), cultural (e.g., the representa- tion of Asians as a model minority in the media), and systemic (e.g., the glass ceiling) levels. Develop multiple hypotheses about issues, and be cognizant of the social and personal costs that Asian Americans may incur as a function of their acculturation and their alliances to their different identities (e.g., race, ethnicity). For instance, when working with Marge, the counselor can help her explore her racial and cultural identity and understand the impact of racism on herself and others. Besides helping her to gain more understanding and awareness of herself and of the challenges she is facing, it is important for the counselor to empower Marge to advo- cate for herself and to navigate the system and cope with discriminatory events. In addition, given that there might be a certain newness for Marge in owning her identification as an Asian- American woman, it might be helpful for Marge to be introduced to one or more support groups of individuals who share similar experiences (e.g., transracially adopted individuals).

Finally, the third theme in the ethics guidelines is *action*. This theme represents an explicit and intentional call to take steps, to contribute professional time to service without compensa- tion or personal advantage. Action can occur through education, advocacy, and lobbying for the betterment of a community (Fouad, Gerstein, & Toporek, 2006). Rather than relegate highlighting Asian-American history and experiences to Asian-Pacific American Heritage Month alone, explore how issues that are salient to Asian Americans are being addressed and integrated in day-to-day curricula, instruction, and activities. Social justice involves becoming actively involved with the "other" outside the counseling setting—for instance, through com- munity events, social and political functions, celebrations, friendships, and neighborhood groups—to develop a perspective that is beyond academics. For instance, Marge's counselor could work with other professionals at the counseling center to develop and implement a psycho-education program for students, staff, and faculty on campus about Asian Americans, discrimination, and how to advocate for Asian-American individuals and their community on campus.

Yet, for counselors accustomed to thinking of their work as strictly involving individual counseling, the question remains: "How do we take action on behalf of Asian-American individuals and communities?" To facilitate the process, it may be helpful to review the revised model of advocacy competencies set forth by Ratts et al. (2015). According to those authors, counselors can move beyond their individual work with clients by forming collaborations with like-minded individuals or organizations, as well as mobilizing these coalitions to address systemic barriers that adversely affect Asian Americans. At the local level, collaboration may mean building alliances with an Asian-American professional association, an Asian-American church or temple, or perhaps a local community service agency devoted to Asian-American communities. At a national level and outside the field of counseling and psychology, counselors may join with national Asian-American civil-rights groups, such as the Organization of Chinese Americans, the Japanese American Citizens League, and the Sikh American Legal Defense and Education Fund, to address systemic and sociopolitical injustices. Counselors can also use their professional affiliations as a path toward advocacy. For instance, counselors can lend their time and energy by becoming members of the Asian American Psychological Association—the nation's oldest professional association dedicated to Asian-American mental health—as well as becoming involved in groups such as the American Counseling Association's Association for Multicultural Counseling and Development and the American Psychological Association's Division 45: Society for the Psychological Study of Culture, Ethnicity and Race. In short, counselors have a range of potential coalitions through which they can channel their interests in advocating for Asian-American communities.

Through their community and professional collaborations, counselors can be advocates for Asian Americans by identifying barriers as well as by developing and implementing action plans that improve the communities and systems in which their clients live (Ratts et al., 2015). A major issue that affects Asian-American communities is the cultural competence and diversity of the service providers in their communities. For example, rehabilitation counselors may serve as advocates by developing training programs, workshops, or curricula that underscore the unique cultural dimensions of working with Asian Americans with disabilities and their families. Relatedly, school counselors can advocate for increased representation of Asian Americans in hiring new counselors, teachers, coaches, and principals in their schools and school districts. In addition, language access and linguistic competence have been significant barriers to Asian Americans in need of counseling. Thus, counselors can be advocates for Asian Americans by making linguistic fluency in an Asian language a criterion for hiring a new counselor, or they can urge their respective agencies to translate pamphlets, intake forms, publicity flyers, Web sites, and so forth into the languages of the major Asian-American ethnic groups in their area. Indeed, although such steps are specific to enhancing access to counseling services, the issue of access to resources in general is of vital importance to Asian-American communities. Given the myth of the model minority (Gupta et al., 2011) and the tacit assumption that Asian Americans are successful and have no need for services, Asian-American communities may be deprived of, and lack access to, numerous services. For instance, college counselors may find opportunities for advocacy in a university that provides minimal recruitment, outreach, financial aid, tutoring, mentoring, and advising to Asian Americans under the erroneous presumption that all Asian Americans are academically successful. In sum, counselors can advocate for Asian Americans by identifying systemic policies, procedures, and regulations that serve as barriers to the welfare of Asian Americans.

Yet, beyond community, agency, or school, Ratts et al. (2015) argued that counselors also have an advocacy role in the larger public and political arena. As educators and researchers, counselors can advocate for Asian Americans simply by helping disseminate accurate information and research that challenge the myths and stereotypes that the larger community may have about Asian Americans. Thus, counselors can help ensure that accurate, culturally competent information is distributed through staff trainings, workshops, community outreach, presentations at conferences, and publications, including books, book chapters, and articles in journals. Moreover, counselors can be advocates by developing research programs that shed light on the needs and concerns of Asian Americans, as well as on practices that are effective in serving that population. Last, counselors can be advocates for effecting change in municipal, state, and federal regulations and policies that influence Asian Americans. For instance, by partnering with civil-rights groups such as the Asian American Justice Center, counselors can draw attention to legislative issues that directly influence Asian-American communities—for example, legislation on immigration policies, funding for research, language access, and monitoring hate crimes. Given that the opportunities for Asian-American advocacy are clearly vast, counselors may find the task daunting. Thus, it is critical that counselors recognize that the power and expertise to effect change beyond individual counseling is within their grasp and that the first step in doing so may simply begin with an openness to learning and self-examination. One mode of learning is to gain knowledge about the Asian-American community. (See Activity 11.5.)

ACTIVITY 11.5

There are different ways that one can learn about a community—through an indirect/observational approach and through an interactive/direct participatory approach. As part of the indirect/observational approach, watch a movie or film, or read a book, related to Asian-American experiences (see Table 11.1 for examples of films and books). As part of the interactive/direct participatory approach, interview Asian Americans about their experiences. Compare the two types of learning. Identify the value or effectiveness of each method of learning. For each, describe and explain whether the learning is cognitive, affective, or behavioral.

TABLE 11.1 Media Resources about Asian-American Culture

Films about Family Relationships and Identity

- *The Joy Luck Club.* (1993). Based on the book by Amy Tan (1989), this film focuses on mother–daughter relationships.
- *Knowing Her Place.* (1990). A film by Indu Krishnan in which an Indian woman looks at her life, her marriage, and her role in contemporary society in both India and the United States.
- *My America (. . .Or Honk If You Love Buddha).* (1997). A film by Renee Tajima-Peña as she travels the United States to search for what it means to be Asian American.
- *Letters to Thien.* (1997). A documentary detailing the life and murder of a gifted young Vietnamese American, Ly Minh Thien, and how the hate crime affected Thien's community.
- *Desi: South Asians in New York.* (2000). This film presents dozens of first- and second-generation New Yorkers who share their insights, reflections, and experiences to illustrate the wide spectrum of Pakistanis, Indians, Bangladeshis, Sri Lankans, Nepalese, and other South Asians who have become an integral part of the city.

(Continued)

TABLE 11.1 Media Resources about Asian-American Culture (Continued)

- *Silent Sacrifices: Voices of the Filipino American Family.* (2001). A film by Patricia Heras about the cultural conflicts that Filipino immigrants and their American-born children encounter on a daily basis.
- *Bend It Like Beckham.* (2002). A film about an Asian Indian family that deals with coming-of-age, interracial relations, and gender issues.
- *The Namesake.* (2007). Based on a book by Jhumpa Lahiri (2003), this film is about names, identity, and Asian Indian family relations.
- *American Adobo.* (2002). A comedy about five Filipino-American friends and their lives in New York.
- *The Search for General Tso.* (2014) (available on Netflix). This feature documentary explores the origins and ubiquity of Chinese-American food through the story of an iconic sweet-and-spicy chicken dish.

Films about Asian Sexuality

- *Chutney Popcorn.* (1999). A film about an Asian Indian lesbian, estranged from her parents, who agrees to carry a child for her infertile sister, much to chagrin of her partner and parents.
- *The Wedding Banquet.* (1993). A film that explores what happens when the parents of a Taiwanese gay male visit him in America.
- *Dim Sum Take Out.* (1988). Focuses on one woman's difficulties and her personal issues of independence and sexuality.
- *Fated to Be Queer.* (1992). Four charming, articulate Filipino men illuminate some of their issues and concerns as gay people of color in the San Francisco Bay Area.
- *Khush.* (1991). Interviews with South Asian lesbians and gay men in Britain, North America, and India concerning the intricacies of being gay and of color.
- *Saving Face.* (2012). A young Chinese-American lesbian and her traditionalist mother are reluctant to go public with secret loves that clash against cultural expectations.

Films about Race Relations

- *Vincent Who?* (2009). An update on the impact of the 1982 murder of Vincent Chin and its effect on the political and social consciousness of Asian Americans.
- *Mistaken Identity: Sikhs in America.* (2004). An investigation of attitudes toward Sikhs in the United States following the terrorist events of September 11, 2001. The film also explores the religion, culture, and history of Sikhs in America, highlighting contributions that Sikh Americans have made to the American society and economy for over 100 years.
- *Raising Our Voices: South Asian Americans Address Hate.* (2008). A film developed to raise awareness about hate crimes and incidents of bias affecting South Asians living in America, with particular reference to the increase in such events since the terrorist attacks of September 11, 2001.
- *Hapa: One Step at A Time.* (2012). Marathon runner Midori Sperandeo talks personally about her biracial heritage and reflects on the phenomenon of being biracial, with interviews from a number of ethnically mixed-raced people with additional viewpoints. Midori, her mother (who is also interviewed), and others offer an overview of the struggle of racially mixed people to be accepted and understood and how that role has changed as the United States becomes a more multicultural society. In describing her own personal struggles, Midori likens them to the challenges encountered in learning to be a long-distance runner.
- *Rabbit in the Moon.* (1999). A very poignant Public Broadcasting System documentary about Japanese and Japanese-American internment during World War II in the United States. The film does a great job exploring the issues these individuals faced via testimonials from survivors.

- *Who's Going to Pay for These Donuts Anyway?* (1992). Addresses the profound effect of the Japanese-American internment on generations of individuals. Chronicles director Janice Tanaka's search for her father.
- *Children of the Camps.* (1999). In this documentary, six Japanese Americans who were incarcerated as children in internment camps during World War II reveal their experiences, cultural and familial issues during incarceration, and the long-internalized grief and shame they felt and how this early trauma manifested itself in their adult lives.
- *The Way Home.* (2002). A documentary about women (of different racial groups) and race relations.
- *Who Killed Vincent Chin?* (1987). A classic about the murder of Vincent Chin in 1982 and its effects on the Asian-American community in Detroit and across the nation.
- *American Sons.* (1995). A provocative examination of the role of racism and stereotypical gender expectations in the lives of four Asian-American men.
- *A.K.A. Don Bonus.* (1995). A moving video diary of a young 18-year-old Cambodian man as he struggles against racism and poverty and adjusts to life in San Francisco.
- *Sa-I-Gu.* (1993). The post–Rodney King 1992 Los Angeles uprising as seen through the eyes of the Korean-American women shopkeepers who were in the midst of the rioting.
- *Carved in Silence.* (1987). A documentary about the detainment of Chinese immigrants at Angel Island during the period of the Chinese Exclusion Act.
- *Conscience and Constitution.* (2000). Documentary about Japanese-American internees who refused to be drafted during World War II as a sign of protest.
- *Yuri Kochiyama: Passion for Justice.* (1999). The story of the legendary activist, from her work with Malcolm X to her advocavy for Japanese-American reparations and prisoners' rights.
- *Combination Platter.* (1993). The story of a Chinese illegal immigrant, his life in New York, and his work at a Chinese restaurant.

Films about Religion

- *In the Name of God.* (2013). This documentary by a South Asian filmmaker shows the political/ religious movement prior to the destruction of the Babri Mosque in Uttar Pradesh, India.
- *On Common Ground: World Religions in America.* (2008). Diana L. Eck and the Pluralism Project at Harvard University capture the fundamental beliefs and practices of different faiths and the transformation of old traditions into new settings.

Web Resources

Asian American Justice Center [AAJC] (www.advancingequality.org): Asian Americans Advancing Justice is a national nonprofit founded in 1991 to protect civil and human rights. The AAJC is a national advocate for Asian Americans.

Asian-Nation (www.asian-nation.org): This resource provides information about different Asian ethnic groups and information about issues that affect the Asian-American community).

Asian American Psychological Association (www.aapaonline.org): This is the home Web page of the Asian American Psychological Association, an organization that aims to advance the mental health and well-being of Asian-American communities through research, practice, education, and policy.

Asian Culture and Media Alliance [ACMA] (www.carmamedia.com/acma.htm): The ACMA is a nonprofit organization whose mission is to unite, empower, and promote Asian-American Pacific Islander communities through the power of media.

Asia Society (asiasociety.org): The Asia Society is an educational organization dedicated to promoting mutual understanding and strengthening partnerships among people, leaders, and institutions of Asia and the United States.

(Continued)

TABLE 11.1 Media Resources about Asian-American Culture (Continued)

Asian and Pacific Islander American Health Forum [APIAHF] (www.apiahf.org): The APIAHF is an advocacy organization that works with communities in order to influence policy and strengthen community-based organizations to achieve health quality for Asian-American Pacific Islanders.

Association for Asian American Studies [AAAS] (saaastudies.org/): AAAS's mission is to advance standards of excellence in teaching and research in the field of Asian American studies.

National Asian American Pacific Islander Mental Health Association [NAAPIMHA] (www.naapimha.org/): The NAAPIMHA is a nonprofit organization whose mission is to promote the mental health and well-being ofAsian-American Pacific Islanders.

Books

Asian Women United of California. (Eds.). (1989). *Making waves: An anthology of writings by and about Asian American women.* Boston, MA: Beacon Press.

Chin, J. L. (1993). *Transference and empathy in Asian American psychotherapy: Cultural values and treatment needs.* Portsmouth, NH: Greenwood Publishing Group.

Dasgupta, S. D. (1998). *A patchwork shawl: Chronicles of South Asian women in America.* New Brunswick, NJ: Rutgers University Press.

Eng, D. L. (1998). *Q & A: Queer and Asian American.* Philadelphia, PA: Temple University Press.

Gupta, S. R. (1999). *Emerging voices: South Asian American women redefine self, family and community.* Walnut Creek, CA: AltaMira Press.

Han, A. (2004). *Asian American X: An intersection of twenty-first century Asian American voices.* Ann Arbor: University of Michigan Press.

Kodama, C. M., McEwen, M. K., Alvarez, A. N., Liang, C., & Lee, S. (2002). *Working with Asian American college students: New directions for student services.* San Francisco, CA: Jossey-Bass.

LEAP Asian Pacific American Public Policy Institute and UCLA Asian American Studies Center. (1993). *The state of Asian Pacific America: Policy issues to the year 2020.* Los Angeles, CA: Authors

Lee, J., & Zhou, M. (2015). *The Asian American achievement paradox.* New York, NY: The Russell Sage Foundation.

Lee, S. J. (1996). *Unraveling the "model minority" stereotype: Listening to Asian American youth.* New York, NY: Teachers College Press.

Okihiro, G. Y. (1994). *Margins and mainstreams: Asians in American history and culture.* Seattle, WA: University of Washington Press.

Pang, V. O. (2004). *Struggling to be heard.* Albany, NY: SUNY Press.

Prashad, V. (2000). *The karma of brown folks.* Minneapolis: University of Minnesota Press.

Shankar, L. D., & Srikanth, R. (1998). *A part, yet apart: South Asians in Asian America.* Philadelphia, PA: Temple University Press.

Takaki, R. (1998). *Strangers from a different shore: A history of Asian Americans.* New York, NY: Penguin Books.

Tewari, N., & Alvarez, A. N. (2009). *Asian American psychology: Current perspectives.* New York, NY: Psychology Press.

Wu, F. H. (2001). *Yellow: Race in America beyond Black and White.* New York, NY: Basic Books.

Wu, J. Y., & Song, M. (2000). *Asian American studies: A reader.* New Brunswick, NJ: Rutgers University Press.

Zia, H. (2000). *Asian American dreams: The emergence of an Asian American people.* New York, NY: Farrar, Strauss, & Giroux.

Summary

Asian Americans are one of the fastest-growing racial and ethnic minorities, contributing significantly to overall population growth in the United States. Although the term *Asian American* denotes a common identity with shared cultural values and beliefs, Asian Americans are composed of distinct and heterogeneous ethnic groups with diverse immigration histories, acculturation levels, discrimination experiences, languages, intergenerational issues, socioeconomic statuses, educational backgrounds, and religious practices. This heterogeneity underscores the need for counselors to conceptualize Asian-American client issues against the backdrop of these multiple influences. In particular, the stereotypes related to the model-minority myth, the assumptions that Asian Americans' incomes might be greater than those of White Americans, and perceptions as a perpetual foreigner obfuscate the discrimination and the educational disparities, as well as the invisibility, experienced by this community within the United States.

What constitutes the Asian-American experience and its relation to mental health is complex. It is influenced by different acculturation levels, generational statuses, immigration histories, and relationships to the dominant communities, as well as the intersectionality and oppressions based in multiple identities (e.g., gender, sexuality, race, ethnicity, religion). Further values, related to family and interpersonal relationships, highlight their assumptions surrounding Asian Americans' mental health and coping mechanisms. In this chapter, we have presented literature that highlights help-seeking attitudes, willingness to seek mental health services, and data on particular aspects of psychopathology pertinent to Asian Americans. The dearth of literature on Asian-American mental health suggests a prevalence of psychological distress (e.g., depression, anxiety, PTSD, suicidality) and chronic health conditions in relation to the group's experiences of racism, domestic violence, and other types of trauma. Yet, the research also highlights Asian-American tendencies to shy away from seeking mental health services, owing to several individual, cultural, and systemic barriers. Thus, although the research provides some glimpses into the underutilization of mental health services, the mixed findings raise several questions about the applicability of both theories and empirical research in understanding the experience of Asian Americans. Obtaining a good history of their pre- and postmigration experiences, their attitudes toward mental health and help seeking, and their experiences with the U.S. health-care systems, as well as the discrimination they have experienced, are important precursors of good mental health assessments. The counselor's understanding of the different systemic levels (e.g., micro, meso, macro) that influence Asian Americans and his or her own knowledge and ability to advocate for his or her clients become important elements in culturally sensitive therapy with this diverse community.

In particular, our intention in this chapter has been to encourage you to critique and challenge the assumptions and practices that tend to reify and deify traditional and stereotypical notions of Asian Americans and the role of the "model minority"—to reconstruct, redefine, and recognize how global shifts, immigration histories, demographic trends, and external experiences and internal processes related to cultural and personal identification are inextricably tied to Asian-American lives. Relatedly, gaining a systemic approach and developing a sense of advocacy and outreach are important elements in working with Asian Americans. In particular, the intent of this chapter has been to provide a cultural framework for working with Asian Americans while highlighting the multiple contexts and intersections within which Asian Americans' identities are embedded.

Review Questions

1. Given the cultural values embedded within the Asian community (e.g., collectivism, hesitance to share personal information with outsiders, the focus on saving face), how might you introduce the idea of talk therapy to individuals in the Asian-American community who may question the validity of this approach?

2. What are some traditional and nontraditional approaches to interventions that you would use with Asian-American clients?

3. The chapter highlights the need for counselors to engage in self-assessment. How might you explore your own cultural identities? How might your identities shape your work with your client? How might you address any cultural differences between you and your client?

4. Do you believe that Asian-American communities need social advocacy? If so, what areas do you believe are in need of this advocacy?

5. What are some examples of social actions that can be taken at the local, national, professional, and political levels for Asian Americans?

12 Individuals and Families of Latin-American and Latin Descent

José A. Villalba

PREVIEW

Generational differences, language preferences, family, legal status, acculturation to U.S. customs, holding onto native traditions, religion, and geographical location are but a few of the factors that influence how U.S. Latinas/os perceive their environment. In turn, these factors contribute to how members of the at-large U.S. society view Latinas/os, the nation's largest minority group. As this group continues to grow, the likelihood of encountering Latina/o clients in clinical settings (e.g., public schools, community counseling centers, college campuses, private practice, inpatient hospital facilities) increases. Therefore, it is in the best interest of counseling professionals to increase their knowledge of this population in an effort to attain heightened multicultural competence. The information provided in this chapter is not intended to be a be-all and end-all regarding the experiences of Latinas/os living in the United States, because these experiences can be quite nuanced. As an example, the title of the chapter references Latinas/os living in the United States who may have been born in Latin America and may identify with their (or their family's) Latin American roots, as well as those who were born in the United States and yet identify with their Latino/a ancestry. The chapter should serve to stimulate further actions on the part of helping professionals, and those training to become helping professionals, in their attempt to assist Latina/o clients. Table 12.1 at the end of the chapter lists some media resources that will deepen your understanding of this population.

A LATIN AMERICAN HISTORY PRIMER

Terms like *Latina/o* and *Hispanic* are grounded in the history of Latin America. For example, *Hispanic* is related to the Spanish word "Hispano," which itself is related to "Hispañola," Spanish for Hispaniola, the island comprising present-day Haiti and the Dominican Republic upon which Christopher Columbus first made landfall in the Western Hemisphere. Consequently, U.S. Census Bureau terminology such as *Hispanic* has an inherent offensive connotation for some, as it references Latin America's colonial period and European heritage (from 1492 through the early 1900s), a period and heritage marred with bloodshed and forced land acquisition from native-born Latin Americans and dismissive of the unique traditions and history of each Latin American country and each indigenous civilization (e.g., Aztecs, Ciboneys, Guaanajatabeys, Incas, Mayans, Taino) on which colonialism was founded

(Shorris, 2012). Unfortunately, Latin America's history also includes political and economic struggles with influential protagonists ranging from "liberators" such as Simón Bolívar (recognized in several South American countries) to "dictators" such as Hugo Chávez (Venezuela) and persecuted philosophers such as Paolo Freire (Brazil) and José Martí (Cuba). In essence, Latinas/os from all countries share a set of common bonds and pride grounded in perseverance, respect for one's ancestors, and the acknowledgement of history's influence. There are 20 Latin American countries from which individuals and families descend. (See Build Your Knowledge 12.1.)

BUILD YOUR KNOWLEDGE 12.1

Write down as many Latin American countries as possible in the next 60 seconds. (Spain and the United States do not count.) Next, have each person share her or his list with the class. Then, explore the customs, foods, traditions, dances, religious practices, and so on that may be representative of immigrants from these different countries (and do not be afraid to "be wrong"; it is okay to become aware of our own perceptions and stereotypes). Finally, discuss how differences among Latinas/os might affect the counseling profession and counseling professionals.

For the foregoing reasons, I consider the term *Latina/o* most appropriate, instead of *Hispanic, Hispanic American,* or *Hispano*; it is a term that honors the indigenous heritage of Spanish-speaking individuals with Latin American ancestry. Furthermore, to differentiate Latinas/os living in the United States from Latinas/os living outside the United States, who may have different experiences and concerns than those living in the United States, the term *U.S. Latinas/os* will be used throughout this chapter. Nevertheless, counselors are encouraged to ask their Latina/o clients how they identify themselves, instead of assuming that one term is better than another.

It also should be noted that individuals from Brazil, Guyana, Surinam, and French Guiana are considered to be *Latino*—but not *Hispanic*—because these parts of Latin America were colonized by French and Portuguese conquistadors. *Hispanic* implies a connection to Spain and the Spanish language, whereas *Latino* alludes to a connection with other popular romance languages—French, Portuguese, and Italian, for example—that are based on the ancient European language of Latin.

LATIN AMERICAN AND LATINO HETEROGENEITY

U.S. Latinas/os currently account for over 17.4% of the U.S. population, or roughly 55.4 million residents (Pew Hispanic Center, 2016a). However, there are as many, if not more, differences within the demographic grouping as there are similarities (Pew Hispanic Center, 2016b). These differences stem from the fact that Latinas/os living in the United States come from 20 countries in addition to the United States. Several Latinas/os living in the southwestern United States are quite proud that their ancestors lived in territories that would later become states or parts of states (i.e., Arizona, California, Colorado, Nevada, New Mexico, Texas, Utah, and Wyoming) *before* these states became part of the United States after the Treaty of Guadalupe Hidalgo ended the Mexican–American War in 1848 and ceded Mexican territory to the United States. Aside from nation-specific foods, Spanish dialects, indigenous tongues, folktales, burial rituals, dances, and religious nuances, U.S. Latinas/os report a wide variety of educational experiences, immigration statuses, career opportunities, and economic realities. In short, besides the traditional use of the Spanish language, a general affiliation and tradition with the Catholic Church, and basic family traits with adherence to collectivistic values, U.S. Latinas/os represent many experiences and worldviews (Organista, 2007; Santiago-Rivera, Arredondo, & Gallardo-Cooper, 2002).

Apart from cultural factors, U.S. Latinas/os generally share certain demographic realities that may stand as obstacles to political, social, educational, and, consequently, emotional stability. For example, 64.6% of U.S. Latinas/os have at least a high school diploma, compared with 91.6% of non-Latina/o Whites (Pew Hispanic Center, 2016b). Furthermore, of those attaining at least a high school diploma or its equivalent, passing the General Educational Development (GED) test, 14% of Latinas/os have earned a 4-year degree compared with 33% of Whites. The Pew Hispanic Center (2016b) also reported that 12% of U.S. Latinas/os are employed in office and administrative support, 9.1% are employed in building and grounds cleaning and maintenance, 9% are in the construction trades, 7.5% are employed in management and business, 4.8% are employed in education, and 4.8% work in health-care trades; comparable figures for non-Latina/o Whites are 13.7%, 3.1%, 15.4%, 9%, and 7.5%, respectively. With regard to personal earnings, 15.9% of U.S. Latinas/os earn more than $50,000 per year, as opposed to 33.7.7% of Whites, 20.0% of African Americans, and 39.8% of Asians and Asian Americans (Pew Hispanic Center, 2016b). One final generalization pertaining to U.S. Latinas/os is their relative youth: The median age for Latinas/os in this country is 28 years, compared with 42 years for Whites, 33 years for African Americans, and 36 years for Asians and Asian Americans. Although these statistics may incline one to lump together all U.S. Latinas/os, many aspects set Latinas/os apart from one another. Therefore, it becomes necessary to address some of the differences among Latina/o groups in the United States. The rest of this section discusses some basic characteristics of the larger groups of U.S. Latinas/os.

Mexicans

Mexicans are the largest group of U.S. Latinas/os. The Pew Hispanic Center (2016b) reported that Latinas/os with Mexican heritage (i.e., those born in Mexico or who were born to Mexican parents) account for 64.1% (34.6 million) of all U.S. Latinas/os. The size of the U.S. Mexican population can be attributed to the shared U.S.–Mexican border, the annexation and cession of Mexican territories (including Texas, California, and New Mexico) at the conclusion of the Mexican War in 1848, and the sustained and increased immigration of Mexicans, particularly during the mid-1970s.

More recently, the U.S. immigration debate has focused on Mexicans because of their large concentration along border states (i.e., Arizona, California, New Mexico, Texas) and the fact that 40% of Mexicans (roughly 15,000,000) living in the United States are not native born. Unfortunately, some individuals assume that these nonnative U.S. residents are in this country illegally, leading to racism and stereotypes. For many Mexicans, issues of discrimination and limited socioeconomic advancement also are compounded by large high school dropout rates (61% for first-generation Mexican immigrants and 40% for second-generation Mexican immigrants) and low 4-year college completion rates (9% of Mexicans and Mexican Americans living in the United States have a 4-year college degree; President's Advisory Commission on Educational Excellence for Hispanic Americans, 2003; Pew Hispanic Center, 2016b). Still, despite educational barriers, immigration-related stressors, and limited employment opportunities, many Mexicans and those of Mexican heritage have managed to influence society (e.g., César Chávez), ascend to governorships (e.g., Bill Richardson), and influence the performing and visual arts (e.g., Diego Rivera, Edward James Olmos). As you consider the experiences of Mexicans and Mexican Americans, it is important to consider your values and assumptions related to these experiences, as well as characteristics of this population. Reflection 12.1 offers an opportunity to reflect on beliefs you hold about this group collectively.

REFLECTION 12.1

Think of common stereotypes regarding Mexicans and Mexican Americans that you may have heard or may believe. List the specific media outlets, instances, and experiences that have contributed to these stereotypes. Now, think about how the stereotypes would affect your work with Latina/o clients of Mexican descent. More important, how could you counter the stereotypes? Where would you acquire the knowledge and experiences to minimize the impact of such stereotypes on Latina/o clients of Mexican descent?

Puerto Ricans

The second-largest group of Latinas/os in the United States is of Puerto Rican heritage and makes up 9.5% (5.12 million) of the U.S. Latina/o population (Pew Hispanic Center, 2016b). Unlike Mexicans, who tend to cluster in the southern and southwestern parts of the United States, Puerto Ricans tend to live in and around metropolitan centers in the northeastern states. Because Puerto Rico is a U.S. territory, all Puerto Ricans born in Puerto Rico are U.S. citizens. For this reason, only 1% of Puerto Ricans living in the United States are considered to be "foreign born" (e.g., a child born to Puerto Rican parents while they were stationed as military personnel in Germany).

As a whole, Puerto Ricans living in the United States have experienced drops in median household income since 2000 and now trail Mexicans and Cubans, but have increased the rate at which they finish high school compared with Mexicans or Cubans living in the United States (Pew Hispanic Center, 2016b). In addition, Puerto Ricans are more likely than Cubans and Mexicans living in the United States to have health insurance, yet they are less likely than these other two groups to own their own homes. These realities confound many theorists and public policy makers, considering the automatic U.S. citizenship status of Puerto Ricans. Regardless, Puerto Ricans have influenced the arts (e.g., Tito Puente, Tony Orlando, Tomás Batista) and politics (e.g., José Serrano). Reflection 12.2 offers an opportunity to reflect on stereotypes regarding the Puerto Rican population.

REFLECTION 12.2

Think of common stereotypes regarding Puerto Ricans and Puerto Rican Americans (Puerto Ricans living outside Puerto Rico but in the United States) that you may have heard or may believe. List the specific media outlets, instances, and experiences that have contributed to these stereotypes. Now, think about how the stereotypes would affect your work with Latina/o clients of Puerto Rican descent. More important, how could you counter the stereotypes? Where would you acquire the knowledge and experiences to minimize the impact of such stereotypes on Latina/o clients of Puerto Rican descent?

Cubans

The third-largest U.S. Latina/o population is Cuban immigrants and those of Cuban heritage, accounting for 3.7% (1.98 million) of all U.S. Latinas/os (Pew Hispanic Center, 2016b). What are your attitudes toward this group? (See Reflection 12.3.) Unlike other groups of U.S. Latinas/os, which tend to be more dispersed throughout the nation, Cubans are concentrated in South Florida and New York City (including neighboring communities in New Jersey). The immigration pattern for Cubans is different from Mexicans and Puerto Ricans for two reasons: (a) most came to the United States for political reasons, and (b) most Cuban immigration is fairly recent (within the last 50 years). With regard to the political nature of Cuban immigration, the rise of Fidel Castro's communist regime in 1959 accounted for the first sustained wave of Cuban immigration, from the early 1960s through the early 1990s (de las Fuentes, 2003). The earliest Cuban immigrants from that postcommunist wave of immigration were well educated, were economically stable, and lost many of their possessions to the Castro government. In 1980 a spike in Cuban immigration to the United States (specifically Miami, Florida) occurred as a result of the Mariel Boatlift, named for the Cuban port of departure for most of these individuals. This wave of 100,000 to 125,000 Cuban immigrants was not as well educated or as economically stable as previous Cuban immigrants. Consequently, some of these individuals, known as Marielitos, were the victims of discrimination by fellow Cubans.

REFLECTION 12.3

Think of common stereotypes regarding Cubans and Cuban Americans that you may have heard or may believe. List specific media outlets, instances, and experiences that contributed to these stereotypes. Now, think about how the stereotypes would affect your work with Latina/o clients of Cuban descent. More important, how could you counter the stereotypes? Where would you acquire the knowledge and experiences to minimize the influence of such stereotypes on Latina/o clients of Cuban descent?

For the most part, Cubans and those of Cuban heritage living in the United States have made large strides in political circles, educational attainment, and economic success. For example, this group of Latinas/os has the highest rate of high school and college graduation (Pew Hispanic Center, 2016a). Furthermore, Cubans generally have higher mean earnings than all other U.S. Latinas/os. Also, considering the relatively small number of Cubans and Cuban Americans in the United States and their limited presence in this country, they held five congressional seats and three senate seats in the 114th U.S. Congress. However, it should not be assumed that all U.S. Cubans are free of economic hardships, acculturative stress, or educational barriers.

Finally, recent changes in United States–Cuba policy and diplomacy have led to an increase in support for, knowledge and awareness of, and interest in the Cuban and Cuban-American experience among Latina/o and non-Latina/o Americans, including overall support for ending the U.S. trade embargo with Cuba and re-establishing diplomatic relations between both countries (Pew Hispanic Center, 2016c). Note, however, that Cubans and Cuban Americans living in the United States are more split about the idea of normalizing diplomatic ties between the United States and Cuba: some support normalization of relations and others oppose it. Mental health practitioners should refrain from drawing too many conclusions from media reports and recent survey data, particularly since the normalization of diplomatic ties is very new and much is left to be determined.

Caribbean Hispanics/Latinas/os, and Central and South Americans

The remaining U.S. Latina/o population comes from the Dominican Republic, Central American countries (not including Mexico), and South America. Dominicans, Colombians, and Guatemalans make up a large percentage of the "other" U.S. Latinas/os, with at least 500,000 individuals from each group residing in the United States (Pew Hispanic Center, 2016b). Recently, Salvadorans have entered into a statistical "dead heat" with Cuban Americans, and there are now over 1.97 million Salvadorans living in the United States. However, Salvadorans have lived in the United States in large numbers for far fewer years than Cubans, thereby mitigating their influence on U.S. politics and society compared with Cubans.

Immigration patterns for Latinas/os of non-Cuban, non-Mexican, or non–Puerto Rican descent are much more difficult to characterize. For example, whereas 45% of all U.S. Latina/o immigrants arrived in the United States prior to 1990, 50% of Dominican and 51% of Salvadoran immigrants were here prior to 1990, compared with 41% of Guatemalan and 44% of Colombian immigrants (U.S. Census Bureau, 2007). In contrast, 20% of U.S. Latina/o immigrants came to the United States after 2000; however, the percentage of Dominicans and Salvadorans who immigrated to the United States after 2000 was lower than the average for all U.S. Latinas/os (13% and 17%, respectively), but the percentage of Colombians and Guatemalans immigrating to the United States after 2000 was higher, by 3% for both groups, than that of the average U.S. Latina/o. It is equally difficult to establish patterns with other U.S. Latinas/os of Central and South American heritage. In addition, Caribbean, Central, and South American U.S. Latina/o immigrants have a plethora of reasons for leaving their native lands, including political persecution, economic hardship, and educational barriers. This heterogeneity is mirrored by the experiences of these immigrants once they are in the United States.

It is difficult to make generalizations about "other" U.S. Latinas/os because of the inherent nature of their heterogeneity as it relates to education level, unemployment, public assistance, and mean earnings. Therefore, counselors are encouraged to find out more about their U.S. Latina/o client's experiences before drawing quick and potentially incorrect conclusions. Part of this knowledge acquisition has to involve reflecting on perspectives on the Latina/o population as a whole. (See Activity 12.1.)

ACTIVITY 12.1

Take a few moments individually to write down how you feel about the U.S. Latina/o population expansion, particularly how it has or has not affected your community. How has the media's representation of Latinas/os, including the coverage on the immigration debate, played a role in your perceptions of U.S. Latinas/os? In small groups, develop steps you can take to reframe any negative stereotypes you may have about U.S. Latinas/os and their increasing numbers, especially because it is quite likely that you will have Latina/o clients in the near future. Discuss your ideas with the rest of the class.

LATIN-AMERICAN AND LATINO CULTURE AND VALUES

Because of the aforementioned colonial and indigenous lineage, the shared experiences of being immigrants in the United States, Spanish-language similarities, and the role of religion and spirituality, it is possible to deduce a shared worldview for the majority of the U.S. Latina/o population. This section presents characteristics and experiences that contribute to a general U.S. Latina/o worldview. After reviewing these cultural values, reflect on the experience of Juan presented in Case Study 12.1.

CASE STUDY 12.1

Juan is a 22-year-old, second-generation "Hispanic." His mother is a 60-year-old Cuban-born U.S. citizen, and his father is a 70-year-old Colombian-born U.S. citizen. Both immigrated separately to the southeastern United States in 1970 and would be considered first-generation immigrants. They still live in the same city they moved to over 40 years ago, an urban center known for its strong Latina/o presence and celebration of Latin American cultures. Unlike their son, they identify themselves as "Cubana" and "Colombiano," respectively, instead of "Hispanic," "Hispanic American," "Hispano," or "Latina/Latino." Juan has an older brother (in his late thirties) who lives outside the home. His brother also is a second-generation American; however, Juan's older brother identifies himself as "Latino" to those who ask, typically coworkers and new acquaintances.

Lately, Juan has been having a few misunderstandings with his parents over his adopting American values, or, as his parents put it, "valores Americanos." His parents define these values as "too much freedom," "too much independence," "acting older than you are," "not being responsible for your actions," and "too much focus on friends and being 'cool,' instead of focusing on the family." These misunderstandings have caused strain in Juan's immediate household: On the one hand, Juan would like his parents to understand that some of their customs, traditions, and values just "don't apply to this country, this era"; on the other hand, his parents cannot understand why Juan fails to see that adhering to traditional customs and values (e.g., wanting to spend time with family first, seeking the advice and input of family members when making decisions, and having an intrinsic desire to practice and use the Spanish language) have benefited them and their older son and, therefore, should work just fine for Juan.

In an attempt to reconcile issues in the home, Juan's parents have sought advice and input from his older brother, his Cuban grandmother, their friends from church, and extended family members. In contrast, Juan has sought support from his old high school friends, his girlfriend, and, on occasion, his older brother. In the end, Juan simply wants his parents to understand him better and "get off my back a bit." His parents, to the contrary, want Juan to start "acting more responsibly" and focus more on his family and studies, and less on his friends and their "bad influences."

- How do you conceptualize the cultural values of both Juan and his parents?
- What individual differences play into conflicting values for Juan and his parents?
- How would you work with this family in counseling?
- What sources of resiliency do you note for Juan?
- How might your cultural values and cultural statuses affect your work with this family?

"Somos Inmigrantes" ("We Are Immigrants")

One of the first attributes binding most U.S. Latinas/os is their identification as nonnative U.S.-born residents or being descendants of immigrants. This factor allows most U.S. Latinas/os to empathize with each other, even if they trace their roots back to different countries. This is not to say that, for example, Mexicans will have many similarities with Cubans. On the contrary, their reasons for immigrating to the United States and their experiences once they are here can be starkly different. However, when confronted, for example, with U.S. immigration policies that limit access to public education for their children, Cubans and Mexicans have bonded together to promote public-policy initiatives.

In addition, the hardships suffered in coming to this country—whether by land for most Mexicans, Central Americans, and South Americans, or by sea for some Cubans—bring various U.S. Latinas/os together (Organista, 2007). It is common to hear older generations of U.S. Latinas/os share immigration experiences and related sacrifices with their children and grandchildren. These stories are partially responsible for a shared resiliency displayed by many Latina/o youths living in the United States, regardless of their national heritage or place of birth.

In recent years, Latino immigration has actually started to decline, reversing a 20-year trend. Specifically, the Pew Hispanic Center (2016d) noted that Latino immigration of undocumented individuals has decreased since 2007—a trend that is especially evident in the decrease in number of those employed in manufacturing and construction jobs. Factors attributed to this decline include anti-immigration policies being enforced more frequently, as well as the economic recession that took place from December 2007 to June 2009 in the United States. For these reasons, documented and undocumented Latino workers actually are a smaller percentage of the current U.S. workforce than they were prior to 2008. Note, however, that an overall and general shift in the attitudes toward undocumented immigrants has changed drastically since 1996. The most significant example of this shift is around the notion of a path to legal residency for currently undocumented immigrants: roughly 72% of Americans believe that undocumented residents should be allowed to apply for citizenship or permanent residency in the United States, as long as they are law-abiding individuals (Pew Hispanic Center, 2016e).

Language

Most U.S. Latinas/os have at least a familiarity with Spanish. However, the dominance of Spanish, for both written and oral communication, is dependent on the generational status of the individual. According to the Pew Hispanic Center (2016f), 34% of first-generation U.S. Latinas/os (those born outside the United States) age 18 years and older indicated that they spoke English "very well," compared with 89% of second-generation Latinas/os (children born in the United States, but whose parents were born in a different country and immigrated to the United States). Furthermore, 60% of second-generation U.S. Latinas/os 5 years and older reported they "speak Spanish at home"; in comparison, 95% of first-generation U.S. Latinas/os reported that they "speak Spanish at home." See Voices from the Field 12.1 for one father's experience learning English.

As with the shared immigrant identity, the use of, and familiarity with, Spanish has helped promote a sense of understanding and community between U.S. Latinas/os from different countries of origin. There is a sense of comfort, for example, when a recently arrived immigrant family can turn on their television in the United States and watch a program, in Spanish, on one of two Spanish-language national networks (i.e., Telemundo, Univision). Most major radio markets now have at least one FM (and several AM) Spanish-language stations, meaning more media choices. In addition, local libraries and national bookseller chains

> ### Voices from the Field 12.1
>
> What I don't understand is why the Americans in my neighborhood assume I don't want to learn English, just because I don't speak it well. Don't they realize how hard it is to learn a new language at age 48? And it's not like the English language is the easiest language to learn. There are three ways to spell the word "to," but only one way to pronounce it. And why is it that "i" comes before "e" sometimes, but not others? And I'm old! It's not easy to "hide" my accent, but it doesn't mean I'm stupid. And when exactly am I supposed to learn how to speak English if I have a job and I like spending time with my kids after school? I just wish my neighbors understood it is harder to learn a language they take for granted.
>
> ~ Anonymous, a 48-year-old father of two children, on learning English

carry Spanish-language books. These types of resources also provide a benefit to counselors and other helping professionals in that they give them access to some aspects of life for U.S. Latinas/os, even if they are not fluent in Spanish.

Religion and Spirituality

The vast majority of U.S. Latinas/os are Christian (89.9%), with most identifying as Roman Catholic (67.6%), although there are Latina/o Jews and Latina/o Muslims (Pew Hispanic Center, 2007). The affiliation with Christianity, particularly Roman Catholicism, is related to the colonization of Latin American countries by Spanish and Portuguese conquistadors, who often drew support for their travels from the Catholic Church and regularly included clergy in their crews. Over the centuries, however, Latinas/os from various nations have combined traditional customs with Catholic practices—a blending that has resulted in a rich and dynamic practicing of faith. For example, in Mexico, *El Día de Los Muertos* (the Day of the Dead) is celebrated annually around November 1 and combines aspects of Catholicism and All Saints' Day with Aztec rituals for honoring and celebrating deceased loved ones. Also, *El Día de Reyes* (known in English as "Three Kings Day," although its literal translation is "The Day of Kings") recognizes the epiphany of the Three Wise Men and the gifts they gave baby Jesus. It is celebrated with particular vigor in Cuba and Puerto Rico on January 6. In fact, it is *Los Reyes* who bring boys and girls gifts around the winter holidays in these countries, along with Santa Claus. With regard to spirituality, U.S. Latinas/os often use terms such as *gracias a Dios* (thanks be to God), *si Dios quiere* (if God wants), *Ay, Bendito* (Oh Holiness), or *hay que tener fe* (you have to have faith) in reaction to stress, happiness, sorrow, or hope—so much so that these expressions are part of the everyday vernacular for many Latinas/os.

Latinas/os who have immigrated to the United States and their U.S.-born offspring have continued their religious traditions. Rites of passage for children are intricately tied to First Communion or Holy Confirmation, the way a Bat Mitzvah might be for a Jewish girl. Religious affiliation is so important to most U.S. Latinas/os that many of their first encounters in the United States occur in churches and places of worship. U.S. Latinas/os also are more likely to turn to a priest, minister, or *curandero* (healing man) in a time of emotional difficulty than a counselor or other mental health expert (Falicov, 2010). Note, however, that the importance of religion, particularly Christianity (and mainly Catholicism), need not always manifest itself in increased church attendance, or even in the attainment of expected religious milestones (e.g., being baptized, confirmed, married in a church); rather, the importance of religion and spirituality is embodied in a heritage that has strong ties to organized religion and the belief in a higher power (Falicov, 2014). As a result, it becomes important for counselors to assess the role that religion and spirituality play in the lives of their U.S. Latina/o clients, in addition to doing their own research on certain practices with which they may be unfamiliar.

Resiliency

Although resiliency is a personality trait attributed not solely to Latinas/os, it is an additional characteristic that adds to the cultural strengths of Latina/o children and adults. Toro-Morn (1998), Fennelly, Mulkeen, and Giusti (1998), and Gallo, Penedo, Espinosa de los Monteros, and Arguelles (2009) are just some who point to resiliency as one of the ways in which Latinas/os manage to cope with both common and extraordinary stressors. With newly arrived Puerto Rican women, for example, resiliency helps them come to terms with the expectations of a new city while they long for family, friends, and customs from their native Puerto Rico (Toro-Morn, 1998). In the case of Latina/o teens faced with the trauma of racism and discrimination, Fennelly et al. credit these youngsters' fortitude and inner strengths as examples of their resiliency in dealing with experiences with which most of their White peers do not have to struggle. The concept of resiliency is so powerful in the Latino culture that Gallo and colleagues (2009) indicate that it can mitigate the stressors of acculturative stress and immigration policies, as manifested in lower anxiety and even improved cardiovascular health, at least for first-generation Latino immigrants. Counselors working with Latina/o clients should, of course, be cautious about always pointing to the resiliency of Latinas/os, as there may be occasions or circumstances that may not be corrected by resiliency alone. Nevertheless, just as family, faith, and traditional customs can serve to alleviate some of the tension experienced by Latina/o clients, resiliency is a concept whose role counselors should consider in their work with Latinas/os.

Gender Roles

Gender roles for individuals of Latin descent are steeped in tradition and religion. To understand the power of gender roles, it is important to become familiar with the concepts of machismo and marianismo (Falicov, 2014; Organista, 2007). **Machismo** represents a strong, virile, omnipotent man who takes care of his family by providing food and shelter. Because of these responsibilities, macho men tend to leave the notions of child rearing and housework to their wives and female daughters. **Marianismo**, in contrast to machismo, is distinctive in that it requires a woman to be pure, make sacrifices for the husband's and children's benefit, not engage in premarital sex, and be a nurturing female role model for her daughters. The ultimate role model for most Latina women is *La Virgen María* (the Virgin Mary), from which the term *marianismo* is derived.

It may be difficult for non-Latinas/os living in the United States not to characterize machismo as chauvinistic, rude, and hypersexualized, and marianismo as a "step back" in the women's movement, both insulting and demoralizing. Although many first-generation U.S. Latinas/os accept these traditional roles, immigration and generational status may influence their degree of acceptance.

Second-generation (and beyond) U.S. Latinas/os (and even some first-generation U.S. Latinas/os) begin to question the merit and practice of traditional roles as they acculturate to the United States. This questioning contributes to attempts by older Latina/o generations to emphasize and facilitate adherence to traditional gender roles in younger generations. The devotion to these gender roles and the subsequent rejection by second-generation (and beyond) U.S. Latinas/os can create dissonance among children, parents, and the rest of the family. See Voices from the Field 12.2 for the perspective of one mother from a younger generation on raising children. As a counselor working with U.S. Latina/o clients and families, you should assess the importance and observance of traditional gender roles. Moreover, counselors must assess and monitor their own attitudes toward marianismo and machismo.

Voices from the Field 12.2

I know it wasn't the smartest thing for me to have a baby this young, but my mom had me when she was 18 and my grandmother had her first child when she was 17. And I love being a mom. No, it's not easy, but I have a great support system, and positive male and female role models for my daughter. Believe it or not, this was an intentional choice of mine; not something I jumped into or a "mistake." Is it the preferred way for most girls my age in this country? No. But I am not from this country, and I'm not exactly crazy about going to the clubs, having a ton of boyfriends, or going away to college. This is what I always wanted to do, and now I am doing it. I want to sacrifice for my family and my child, and it doesn't mean that I am a weak woman. In fact, I think it makes me a strong woman.

~ Anonymous, 19-year-old mother of a 1-year-old female

Families of Latin-American and Latino Descent

The collectivistic nature of Latinas/os in the United States and native lands is directly related to the importance of the family, both immediate and extended. Falicov (2014) and Organista (2007) noted that Latinas/os are more likely to make individual sacrifices for the benefit of their families. This orientation toward the family is known as *familismo*. By definition, **familismo** signifies an individual's consideration of one's parents, siblings, grandparents, aunts, uncles, and even close friends of the family, as well as religious godparents, when making decisions (Falicov, 2014). Familismo also entails a certain level of automatic respect for older generations, including those older adults who remained in their country of origin while younger generations immigrated to the United States. According to Santiago-Rivera et al. (2002) familismo can be traced back to the colonization of the Americas by Spain and is a common cultural principle in Latin-American countries and U.S. Latina/o communities.

As with gender role orientation, second-generation (and beyond) U.S. Latinas/os may not be as willing to practice or honor familismo as their parents and grandparents do. Younger U.S. Latinas/os may actually resent the notion of sacrificing their own interests for their family. As a result, counselors working with U.S. Latinas/os should consider the interplay between a client's age, length of time in the United States, and family size, as well as the presence of older family members, and relevant family members who reside in their native country. Indeed, it may become necessary to gauge how each family member views and defines the immediate and extended family unit. Only by exploring the importance of familismo, and possible resulting conflicts due to generational differences, can counselors demonstrate an understanding of how family systems can influence the individual wellness of U.S. Latina/o clients.

Interpersonal Relationships

Most U.S. Latinas/os hold interpersonal relationships with family and friends in high regard. The warmth, affection, concern about others, and positive regard for those close to an individual is known as **personalismo** (Organista, 2007; Santiago-Rivera et al., 2002). Furthermore, Latinas/os expect these feelings to be reciprocated by their loved ones. So engrained is personalismo in the Latina/o psyche that even strangers and acquaintances are at least afforded the benefit of the doubt and are often greeted with smiles, hugs, and perhaps an offering of help or even food. In other words, what may be misconstrued by some as intrusive and "lacking personal space" is simply seen as demonstrating affection and care.

Confianza is another important facet of interpersonal relationships. The word translates into trust and confidence and is the closest counterpart to rapport in the counseling relationship (Arredondo, Gallardo-Cooper, Delgado-Romero, & Zapata, 2014). Confianza, like trust, must be earned and, once earned, must be maintained. However, once confianza is established between two individuals, regardless of nationality, it is a powerful bond. Without personalismo, confianza is difficult to reach, in that personalismo helps tear down some of the barriers or obstacles to the genuineness and egalitarianism that are crucial to establishing rapport. For this reason, counselors and helping professionals are encouraged to explore the "colder," "more sterile," and "uninviting" nature of clinical relationships and environments in hopes of reaching some semblance of confianza with U.S. Latina/o clients.

INDIVIDUAL DIFFERENCES AND IDENTITIES

The core cultural values that shape the U.S. Latinas'/os' experiences are mediated by immigration status, generational status, and socioeconomic status. Thus, the degree to which U.S. Latinas/os adhere to a Latina/o worldview depends on their current immigration status, length of stay in the United States, and degree of social, educational, and economic barriers and opportunities available to them. Because of the complexities of these three statuses, great variability may exist between Latina/o groups and within Latina/o families and local communities.

Immigration Status

The immigration status of U.S. Latinas/os is crucial to understanding the options, barriers, and opportunities they face living in the United States. Legal residency or U.S. citizenship depends on filing the proper documentation and on the person's nation of birth. For those clients who were born in the United States (including Puerto Rico) or who have taken the appropriate steps to legalized residency or citizenship, qualifying for student financial aid, medical assistance, Social Security, and in-state tuition rates at state colleges and universities, among other resources, is typically not an issue. However, for undocumented U.S. Latinas/os, the doors to economic, educational, and physical wellness tend to be shut, not to mention the stigma that comes with being termed "an illegal," as well as the constant stress from fear of deportation (Arbona et al., 2010; Bemak & Chung, 2003; Organista, 2007). In sum, the immigration experience is an important consideration in counseling. (See Reflection 12.4.)

The concepts of forced migration and voluntary migration also play a role in the heterogeneous nature of the American experience for U.S. Latinas/os. Historically, according to Murphy

---

REFLECTION 12.4

The current contentious immigration debate in the United States makes it is quite possible that some Latina/o clients will come into your office to discuss (either directly or vicariously through a family member, friend, or other source) their experiences with racism and discrimination. How do you suppose your stance toward the immigration debate might facilitate or hinder your work with clients wanting to talk about immigration-related issues?

(1977), those individuals who were forced to leave their native lands because of political persecution, ethnic violence, war, or religious discrimination may experience more acculturative stress, grief and loss, and feelings of hopelessness than voluntary immigrants, who came to the United States for economic opportunities or to improve their lives. As a result, a counselor working with, for example, a Cuban client may have to address experiences involving abruptly leaving family behind, being jailed as a political prisoner for engaging in anticommunist activities, and constant worry about relatives who may suffer repercussions because of your client's decision to leave the country. By contrast, a client from El Salvador who came to the United States with his or her entire nuclear family may want to share issues of frustration with finding resources, adjusting to a new community, or being discriminated against at work because colleagues assume that he or she is here illegally. These two examples are but glimpses of how immigration status and reasons for coming to the United States can influence the client–counselor relationship.

Regardless of why or how Latina/o immigrants arrived in the United States, or their reasons for being here, counselors working with undocumented clients of Latin heritage should pay particular attention to how their clients' undocumented status may be influencing their day-to-day life. The immigration status of undocumented Latinas/os can have a detrimental effect on their emotional stability as well as their general health (Cavazos-Rehg, Zayas, & Spitznagel, 2007; Martinez et al., 2015). Therefore, counselors working with undocumented Latina/o clients are to discuss the anxiety, doubt, and frustration associated with their status, or to check for psychosomatic physical health concerns. Moreover, counselors should provide an environment in which the undocumented clients can feel comfortable talking about being separated from loved ones or returning to a country they may not remember or want to go back to if they were to be deported. Finally, counselors who find themselves employed in communities with a significant number of undocumented individuals should consider networking with local immigration attorneys, immigration advocacy groups, and community centers providing "wraparound" services, and even studying the local and state laws that apply to undocumented individuals. These actions are to be taken not only to improve rapport with Latina/o clients who are undocumented, but also to increase one's multicultural competence. Voices from the Field 12.3 highlights one example of an undocumented college student who is experiencing anxiety and frustration with the threat of deportation.

Generational Status

Although generational status has been discussed previously in this chapter, the confusing nature of the term, as well as the differences between U.S. Latina/o generations, justifies additional information. The Pew Research Center (2015e) defines first-generation U.S. immigrants as those who were born in a different country and immigrated to the United States, thereby signifying that their children would be considered second-generation immigrants and

---

Voices from the Field 12.3

I came here when I was 2 years old. My mom and dad crossed the border with my grand-mother, my 2 brothers, and me. And no one looked back. So all I've ever known is this country. I don't even speak with an accent. But I got a deportation order 2 months ago, and what the hell do I do now. I've been told that I am in this country illegally and I need to go back to my country of birth. But I have never lived there. I've never even visited there; no one in my family has, for that matter, because we never wanted to not be let back into the United States. I was a good high school student, I got a scholarship and went to college, I graduated, and I started my own business. I have never been arrested, and I have never gotten in trouble, and they want me to leave? Why?! I didn't have a choice in coming here or not. No one asked me when I was 2 if it was okay with me to move to the United States. I just don't get it. Someone in the government needs to get his or her priorities in check. I just don't know what the hell I'm going to do now.

~ Anonymous, 23-year-old college student who is undocumented

---

their children's children would be third-generation immigrants. However, other authors (e.g., Delgado-Romero, 2001) consider first-generation immigrants to be U.S.-born children of immigrants. Therefore, it becomes essential that counselors find out from their clients what they consider themselves to be in relation to their generational status. This chapter adheres to the Pew Hispanic Center's definition.

The importance of a U.S. Latina/o client's generational status is due to the influence a generation can have on the client's experiences and perspectives. For example, the median age for first-generation/foreign-born U.S. Latinas/os is 40 years, compared with 19 years for native U.S.-born Latinas/os (Pew Hispanic Center, 2015e). In addition, the rate of second-generation U.S. Latinas/os entering the workforce is growing at 2 and 3 times the rate for third-generation and first-generation U.S. Latinas/os, respectively. In addition, the fact that second-generation (and beyond) U.S. Latinas/os have grown up in a hybrid culture composed of U.S. and Latina/o customs may cause tensions with first-generation U.S. Latinas/os. These are but a few examples of how generational status can affect the relationship between intergenerational U.S. Latinas/os, as well as counselors with whom they are working. As an illustration, a school counselor could be "caught in the middle" between a U.S.-born Latina/o high school student who is get-ting ready to attend an out-of-state university and her U.S. resident parents and grandparents, who wish she would attend a local community college so she can stay close to home.

Socioeconomic Status

An individual's socioeconomic status (SES), or social class, is an amalgamation of income, employment status, educational attainment, experiences with poverty, accumulated wealth, life expectancy, and even the number of individuals living within a household. This merging of factors can essentially lead to individuals identifying with peers, not on the basis of race, ethnicity, religion, or even gender, but rather on the basis of being lower class, middle class, or upper class (Liu & Pope-Davis, 2004; Thomas & Schwarzbaum, 2011). Therefore, although some of the economic data suggest that, in general, U.S. Latinas/os earn less, have less desirable jobs, have lower levels of formal education, and are more likely to live below the poverty line than their non-Latina/o peers (Pew Hispanic Center, 2016b), counselors should not assume that all their U.S. Latina/o clients will share this description. Two telling examples of lower SES for Latinas/os in the United States are that 24.6% live at or below the poverty line, compared with 11% of Whites, and 28.6% lack health insurance, compared with 10.3% of Whites.

The SES of undocumented workers is of particular concern to counselors because of the compounding stressors of possible deportation coupled with losing one's job. Kandula, Kersey, and Lurie (2004) noted additional workplace stressors, such as the vulnerability associated with experiencing more discrimination; perceived disempowerment, resulting in failure to report precarious working conditions; fewer opportunities for upward mobility; and insufficient medical and financial benefits. In other words, if the statistics point to low SES for Latinas/os in general, then the SES of undocumented Latinas/os has the potential to be even lower because of their increased likelihood of losing their jobs and because they work in the kinds of jobs that offer fewer chances to accumulate wealth. Further complicating matters for undocumented workers is that they are paid less than documented workers for doing the same types of jobs, have less access to collective-bargaining opportunities, and have less overall job security (Organista, 2007). Clearly, counselors working with undocumented Latina/o workers have several SES-related issues to discuss with their clients.

MENTAL HEALTH ISSUES OF INDIVIDUALS OF LATIN-AMERICAN AND LATINO DESCENT

Systems (e.g., political, economic, religious, educational) play roles in the experiences of U.S. Latinas/os on personal, family, and community levels. Failing to consider the overlapping and influential nature of these systems in working with U.S. Latina/o clients would therefore greatly limit the effectiveness of counseling theories and interventions. Counselors should keep in mind the richness and expansiveness of the U.S. Latina/o experience as they prepare to assess the counseling needs, strengths, and goals of their clients while they strive to provide the most culturally appropriate and competent mental health assistance possible.

Before detailing some of the principal mental health concerns of U.S. Latinas/os, we must explore the types of cultural and societal factors that infringe on the overall well-being of this population. First and foremost is the use of, and familiarity with, the Spanish language, and consequent limited English fluency, for many U.S. Latinas/os. Roughly 32% of U.S. Latinas/os say that they speak English less than "very well" (Pew Hispanic Center, 2016f), so communication barriers may contribute to or complicate mental health concerns for that group. Whether they are unable to communicate with coworkers, school peers, members of the justice system, or children's teachers, or whether they even understand traffic signs and laws, many U.S. Latinas/os are bombarded with language-related stressors on a regular basis.

U.S. Latinas/os also are faced with overcoming barriers in various social systems, including the workforce and school settings. Such barriers adversely affect mental health and compound mental health problems. For example, over 80% of U.S. Latinas/os believe that job-related discrimination is at least a "minor problem" and interferes with their career advancement (Pew Hispanic Center, 2005). Fox and Stallworth (2005) further explained that racism and on-the-job "bullying" of Latinas/os increases their stress and feelings of being oppressed, while Madera, King, and Hebl (2012) reported that employers sometimes behave in a manner that supresses Latinas'/os' ethnic identity, further resulting in negative feelings and even increased job turnover.

Although many first-generation U.S. Latinas/os report coming to this country for the educational opportunities that are available to their children, the U.S. educational system is not as equally available or helpful to U.S. Latinas/os as it is to non-Latinas/os. For example, non-Latina/o children are at least 50% more likely to be enrolled in preschool programs, are more likely to graduate from high school by the time they turn 19, and can expect to enter and complete college in greater numbers than Latinas/os (Cabrera & Padilla, 2004; Pew Hispanic Center, 2016b). In addition, many first-generation U.S. Latina/o parents are unfamiliar with navigating the U.S. educational system—a problem that leads to their children participating less in extracurricular activities, requiring tutoring programs, and being subsidized by free and reduced-fee lunch programs. Parent participation in school-related activities also is reduced because they have an increased likelihood of working multiple jobs or simply feeling "out-of-place" in their children's schools (Casas, Furlong, & Ruiz de Esparza, 2003; Organista, 2007).

Lower levels of education, apart from offering fewer opportunities for U.S. Latinas/os and potentially affecting self-efficacy levels, also contribute to higher poverty and limited earnings. In addition, the increased U.S. Latina/o presence in the working-poor and lower-SES class is partially to blame for chronic and infectious illnesses, health disparities, increased reliance on the public health-care system, and limited health insurance (Zsembik & Fennell, 2005). A further outcome of lower educational attainment and of social class membership is increased homicide rates for U.S. Latinas/os, particularly males living in urban settings (Organista, 2007).

Struggling to acculturate and get ahead in the United States while managing the obstacles presented by so many social systems is a daunting task for many U.S. Latinas/os. It is easy to understand how mental health issues arise or are exacerbated in the U.S. Latina/o population, given a dearth of Spanish-speaking and Latina/o mental health workers. The remainder of this section examines some common problems affecting the mental health of many U.S. Latinas/os.

Acculturative Stress

The immigration process for many first-generation U.S. Latinas/os, and the resulting negotiation between native and adopted cultures, can lead to acculturative stress. Organista (2007) and Falicov (2014) described **acculturative stress** as the internal psychological reaction to balancing the strains of learning about a new culture while longing for the familiarity of one's previous surroundings. Acculturative stress affects not only first-generation U.S. Latinas/os as they learn English or figure out hidden rules and agendas at work and in schools, but also future generations of U.S. Latinas/os (Falicov, 2014; Organista, 2007). The impact is a direct by-product of observing the negative effects that acculturative stress may have on their parents and grandparents, such as depression, domestic violence, identity loss, and substance abuse. Most alarming of all, it appears that some U.S. Latinas/os may suffer prolonged mental health concerns as they continue to acculturate (Turner & Gil, 2002). Caplan (2007) indicated that a sense of being new to a community and being away from family further heightened the effects of acculturative stress for recently arrived Latina/o immigrants and that continued distance from family and residing in a community with few Latinas/os decreased the mental health of Latina/o immigrants exponentially. Because acculturative stress can be a lifelong occurrence and can range from an unpleasant level of pressure to post-traumatic stress disorder (PTSD; particularly for Latina/o refugees fleeing war-torn lands or political oppression), mental health specialists should regularly assess and monitor their U.S. Latina/o clients' acculturation levels.

Grief and Loss

The grieving and loss associated with leaving loved ones behind, sacrificing cultural traits and mores for those of the host culture, or having one or more minority statuses can contribute to feelings of depression and despair. These feelings, which also are connected to a sense of isolation, can lead U.S. Latinas/os to substance abuse, suicidal ideation, acts of domestic violence, and even heart disease (National Council of La Raza, 2005). First-generation U.S. Latinas/os also feel as if they are losing their children and grandchildren to U.S. society, whether they were born in their native country or in the United States. These emotions and worries often lead parents and grandparents to generational conflicts and disagreements with younger U.S. Latinas/os, increased levels of strictness and protectiveness for the younger generation, and resentment toward the United States and its perceived more "liberal" child-rearing practices (Arredondo et al., 2014). As they attend to these emotional responses, counselors working with U.S. Latinas/os are therefore encouraged to ask their clients about family members, friends, and social networks they left behind, as well as their and their families' current experiences and reactions experienced while establishing new roots in the United States.

Experiences with Discrimination

Unfortunately, the mental health literature contains several examples of Latina's/o's negative experiences with discrimination and prejudice. Experiences with discrimination often are correlated with high levels of stress and depression, low self-confidence and self-efficacy, and an overall limited quality of life for Latinas/os. For example, Negi (2013) provided a glimpse into the hardships that male Latino day laborers experience. Individuals in her study reported difficult working conditions, low wages, high levels of stress, and poor mental health, all of which was compounded by working in isolated working environments. In another study, Arbona and Jimenez (2014) interviewed Latina and Latino college students to determine the impact on them of a variety of issues related to ethnic group membership. Unfortunately, both men and women in their study reported incidents of discrimination on their college campuses, contributing to high levels of stress, increased concerns about their academic performance and capabilities, and depressive symptoms. Further, LeBron et al. (2014) looked at the multifaceted impact of discrimination on mental health and physical health by exploring the links between discrimination experiences and diabetes-related distress and depressive symptoms in African Americans and Latinas/os with Type 2 diabetes. In their study, discrimination was associated with significantly higher levels of diabetes-related stress and depressive symptoms for the Latinas/os.

Focusing specifically on Latino adolescents, Sirin et al. (2015) found that discrimination-related stress was affected by the immigration status of their parents. In this study, the overall depression and anxiety that was related to experiences with discrimination decreased over time for a significant portion of the sample, but the decrease was linked to whether their parents were born in the United States and to adolescents' own experiences with anti-immigration sentiments. Finally, a meta-analysis conducted by Pérez-Escamilla (2011) further identified the strong relationship between acculturative stress (which includes attempting to cope with discrimination) and health disparities in Latinos with Type-2 diabetes. This article points to the preponderance in the health-related quality-of-life literature asserting that the impact of discrimination on Latinas/os can have immediate and long-term effects, both physically and mentally.

Additional Concerns

U.S. Latinas/os, like most of the U.S. population, can experience a variety of mental, physical, and social problems. Some of these (e.g., domestic violence, substance abuse, depression) already have been alluded to and may be directly related to cultural manifestations of grief and acculturative stress. However, divorce, unemployment, teenage pregnancy, physical and sexual abuse victimization, academic struggles, and homelessness are but a few of the factors that may contribute to fear, anxiety, helplessness, hopelessness, or anger in U.S. Latinas/os. For Latino youths in particular, personal positive and negative experiences in their communities can have long-term effects on their aspirational goals, from graduating high school, to going to college, to career trajectories (Gonzales, Stein, Shannonhouse, & Prinstein, 2012). The onus is on counselors working with U.S. Latina/o clients who present with these issues to augment their services by considering Latina/o cultural customs and preferences, history, and immigration experiences. By practicing the basic tenets of multicultural competence, counselors working with U.S. Latina/o clients increase their likelihood of providing effective interventions to this clientele. (See Activity 12.2 and Activity 12.3 for strategies for increasing, respectively, skill development and knowledge in Latin Americans.)

ACTIVITY 12.2

Compile a list of questions or probes that you as a counselor may use with U.S. Latina/o individuals and families to assess the relationship between the clients' cultural stressors and their counseling concerns. Furthermore, take into account the setting in which you are working (e.g., school, community counseling, college counseling center, vocational rehabilitation services) and how that setting may influence your line of questioning or desired outcomes. Discuss your list with the class. How could schools and mental health and community agencies lessen cultural stressors for Latina/o clients?

ACTIVITY 12.3

Immerse yourself in a Latina/o cultural experience in your community, one with which you are unfamiliar. For example, find a Spanish religious service, eat at a new (perhaps non-Mexican) Latin restaurant, or visit a community center serving Latina/o residents. Before you do any of these, write down a list of 10 expectations or assumptions about your forthcoming cultural immersion. After you have engaged in the activity, revisit your list and (a) see which of your expectations or assumptions were met and which ones were not and (b) compare your level of comfort or anxiety prior to and after the cultural immersion exercise.

GUIDELINES FOR COUNSELING CLIENTS OF LATIN-AMERICAN AND LATINO DESCENT

The counseling needs, strengths, goals, and objectives of U.S. Latinas/os vary according to age, immigration status, country of origin, where they live in the United States, economic and socioeconomic status, language preference, and assimilation, to name but a few factors. This section looks at potential considerations and counseling interventions for U.S. Latina/o clients based primarily on their age. What is purposefully absent from the discussion is the type of theoretical orientation to use with U.S. Latina/o clients. Counseling theories and techniques that are effective with Latina/o clients include cognitive–behavioral (Chavira, Bustos, Garcia, Ng, & Camacho, 2015; Pina, Silverman, Fuentes, Kurtines, & Weems, 2003), person-centered (Coatsworth, Maldonado-Molina, Pantin, & Szapocznik, 2005), psychodynamic (Gelman, 2003), and solution-focused counseling approaches (Springer, Lynch, & Allen, 2000). However, although the literature seems to lend more support for using cognitive–behavioral therapy and directive theories with Latina/o clients, counselors working with these clients should not assume a "one-size-fits-all" mentality when deciding on which theories and techniques to use with these individuals. Instead, counselors should explore how the ideas presented next fit in with their theoretical preferences.

Counseling Considerations for Children of Latin-American and Latino Descent

Two key factors must be taken into account in working with U.S. Latina/o children: age and birthplace. Age is rather basic, in that counselors must ensure that their interventions are developmentally appropriate, including chronologically, cognitively, and socially appropriate. Birthplace, however, is not as commonly deliberated when it comes to working with children.

Latina/o children who were born in the United States are less likely to be Spanish dominant or bilingual, or to have academic difficulty and are more likely to identify themselves as "Americans" (Pew Hispanic Center, 2016b). U.S. Latina/o children who were born in their native country and immigrated to the United States (first-generation U.S. Latinas/os) at a young age are more likely to experience academic difficulty, are less likely to attain cognitive fluency in Spanish or English, and face greater risk for acculturative stress (Organista, 2007). Counselors must therefore become knowledgeable about how long the child and the family have been in the United States if they were born abroad. This information should lead to further inquiry related to experiences in their homeland and to possible trauma connected with the immigration process (and perhaps to current stress due to immigration status). Such information may provide the counselor with context for developing counseling interventions, securing interpretative services when necessary, and locating community-based services, as is relevant. Counselors working with U.S. Latina/o children also should be aware of the child's

- knowledge of, and identification with, his or her Latina/o heritage
- family members, both immediate and extended, and where important family members live
- fluency in English and Spanish, and preferred language for communicating in clinical settings
- upbringing regarding the role of gender socialization (e.g., identification with machismo or marianismo traits)
- reactions to experiences with racism and discrimination
- self-concept and self-efficacy as they relate to academic performance

COUNSELING CHILDREN Counselors working with U.S. Latina/o children can use individual, group, and family counseling interventions, just as they would with children of non-Latina/o heritage. However, when working with U.S. Latina/o children, counselors should keep in mind the influence of the family and school systems. For example, a counselor working with a 7-year-old, first-generation Latina/o child in a school setting must determine the child's English fluency if working with the child in English, the school's policy for teaching

English language learners, and even the parents' English fluency (Clemente & Collison, 2000). All these systems will influence how much the child communicates, the level of emotions described, and the details behind the issue presented.

Group work with young U.S. Latina/o children provides a unique opportunity for them to share similar experiences with peers, in addition to enhancing their feelings of universality and cohesion (Torres-Rivera, 2004; Villalba, 2003; Villalba, Ivers, & Bartley Ohlms, 2010). Group interventions can focus on adjusting to a new school, learning a second language, acquiring study skills, or practicing skills for coping with grief and loss. More important, group facilitators can help children link the similarities in their experiences while encouraging them to build relationships with each other. In essence, counseling groups and psychoeducational groups can take on some of the characteristics of a "family," particularly for those children who have recently arrived in the United States.

Family counseling and therapy with U.S. Latina/o children also can be an effective counseling intervention. (See Build Your Knowledge 12.2 for an example.) The strength and influence of the Latina/o family already has been discussed. Specifically, Latino parents can be invited to consider their unique roles in motivating their children and influencing their post–high school choices, while mental health practitioners can be persuaded to consider how their professional expectations and clinical goals can be framed or reframed from the perspective of the Latino culture and family structure (Gonzalez, Borders, Hines, Villalba, & Henderson, 2013). It is therefore easy to justify the inclusion of family members, either as full participants or as sources of information, in providing mental health services to young U.S. Latina/o clients. Moreover, because of the impact of the extended family and friends of the family, children should be afforded the opportunity to share information on as many "relevant" family members and adults as possible.

BUILD YOUR KNOWLEDGE 12.2

COUNSELING ACTIVITY FOR USE WITH U.S. LATINA/O CHILDREN: CUENTO THERAPY

Cuento therapy was first introduced into the counseling literature by Costantino, Malgady, and Rogler (1986). *Cuento* translates into "fairy tale" in Spanish, and Costantino et al. employed this counseling modality to model desirable social behaviors for Puerto Rican children. The stories they used were based on Puerto Rican lore and included Puerto Rican heroes, cultural concepts, and locales. In essence, cuento therapy is similar to bibliotherapy, but instead of reading a book on bullying (like *The Three Little Pigs*) and leading a group or individual discussion with a child, the counselor shares a native folk story with the child(ren) and then processes the events and characters in the story. The stories were unique in that the Puerto Rican children in Costantino et al.'s study felt that they could identify with the cuento's characters, situations, and language. In turn, Costantino et al. used the children's identification with characters and themes to facilitate their discussion and use of positive social behaviors inside and outside counseling sessions. Last, Villalba et al. (2010) applied cuento therapy to groups of Latino middle school students in an emerging Latino community and got positive, though not robust, results. Specifically, children participating in a cuento therapy intervention led by school counselors displayed marginal, but positive, changes in their self-concept.

Of course, the biggest hurdle for most counselors who want to use cuento therapy is where to find the cuentos. (See Villalba et al., 2010.) The best place to start would be to ask parents or guardians for some cuentos, particularly with strong hero figures and clear notions of right versus wrong or with a problem and its resolution. It may be necessary to consult with a translator if a parent is not fluent or comfortable communicating in English. Children themselves also could teach the counselor about cuentos with which they are familiar. Parents and children are great folks to ask because they will often relay a story unique to their culture and country of origin, thereby decreasing the likelihood of using a cuento that may not be familiar to a child (e.g., a cuento related to Cinco De Mayo [May 5], which is a Mexican holiday, would have little relevance to a child from Argentina).

As counselors accumulate cuentos, they can incorporate these stories into their counseling sessions with U.S. Latina/o children. Before doing so, however, the counselor should become familiar with the characters, themes, and outcomes of the story and be able to link them to the expected counseling goals and objectives. It is not necessary for the counselor to tell the cuento in Spanish—just that he or she be able to translate the general concepts and characters to meet the child's needs.

Cuento therapy, therefore, is a great way to demonstrate the counselor's willingness to bring culture into the counseling session while increasing the connection between therapeutic goals and culture. For example, a counselor's eagerness to learn a Latin cuento and adapt it to a counseling session with a young girl who is experiencing acculturative stress shows the child just how important that child's culture and, by association, the child herself is to the counselor. This genuine attempt to bridge cultural traditions and folklore with the counseling process may assuage the child's acculturative stress in that a familiar story is being shared in counseling (which is perhaps an unfamiliar activity). In the long run, the counselor's efforts to use cuento therapy may help the child understand the counseling process even more and will contribute to the counseling relationship.

Counseling Considerations for Adolescents of Latin-American and Latino Descent

Given the important role that school plays in the development and socialization of teenagers, counselors should pay close attention to the academic experiences of their adolescent U.S. Latina/o clients. Peer pressure, puberty, adjustments to more rigorous academic material, and the need to "fit in" can be difficult for most middle and high school students. For U.S. Latina/o youths, however, these problems may be aggravated by English proficiency, a need to achieve a balance between their home (Latina/o) and school (American) cultures, and limited parental involvement in school and social interests (Casas et al., 2003; Organista, 2007).

Because of the increased probability that these adolescents' parents attended school outside the United States, were socialized in their native countries, and typically have traditional expectations for their youngsters, conflict tends to arise between first-generation U.S. Latina/o parents and their U.S. Latina/o teenagers, regardless of where their children were born. Consequently, counselors also must assess the type and quality of the relationships that adolescents have with their parents and other family members. In addition, it would help the counselor to find out what the parents' perspectives are of the relationship, as well as factors that positively or negatively influence it. Counselors working with U.S. Latina/o adolescents also should be aware of the adolescent's

- difficulty reconciling his or her bicultural status
- feelings toward adhering to gender-related expectations in the face of American values

- sexual orientation development, particularly as it relates to males and the culture's intolerance for homosexuality (Agronick et al., 2004)
- limited exposure to culturally related extracurricular school activities and sports
- potential substance use as a mechanism for coping with stress (National Council of La Raza, 2005)
- level of experience and exposure to various career opportunities and should seek to identify the client's career models

COUNSELING ADOLESCENTS Individual counseling interventions are an effective way to help U.S. Latina/o teens deal with, for example, the pressures associated with being bicultural. Counselors can organize one-on-one sessions so that their adolescent clients can talk about the struggles to fit in at school with peers (Latina/o and non-Latina/o) while adhering to parents' wishes and cultural mores. Individual counseling also can be used to help these teenagers gain insight from their experiences while also helping them to frame some of their bicultural skills as assets (Villalba, 2007).

Group counseling, particularly in the form of psychoeducational groups, may be an effective method for helping teenage U.S. Latina/o boys and girls deal with gender socialization struggles. Recall that Latina/o gender socialization (i.e., machismo and marianismo) is often at odds with certain U.S. notions of gender socializations. Counselor-led groups organized for high school–aged youths would provide males and females a medium to discuss issues around "being macho," "being matronly and pure," "having to support the family," or "sacrificing college to be a good wife and mother." Recently, the concept of **caballerismo** (being a gentleman) has been researched in the literature, yielding positive relationships between promoting a more pro-social type of masculinity for adolescent Latinos and improved well-being (Estrada & Arciniega, 2015). Although not all U.S. Latina/o adolescents, particularly third-generation immigrants and beyond, will experience a conflict with gender roles, it would behoove counselors to at least ask these clients if such issues are of concern to them.

Including immediate and extended family members when counseling adolescents can be a tricky task. Some teens are resistant to their parents' suggestions, ideas, and even presence because of normal conflicts that arise between parents and children during adolescence. However, this situation should not lead counselors to omit the participation of family members when counseling U.S. Latina/o adolescents. For example, brief strategic family therapy (BSFT) has been shown to be an effective clinical intervention for helping Latina/o adolescents with substance abuse and behavioral problems (Robbins et al., 2008; Santisteban et al., 2003). In another example from the literature, Burrow-Sánchez, Meyers, Corrales, and Ortiz-Jensen (2015) found that cultural values and norms that are of relevance to Latino adolescents, such as ethnic identity and familismo, were significantly linked with coping with substance abuse issues. In particular, the stronger the sense of familismo and ethnic identity, the more follow-through Latino adolescents with substance disorders displayed while in treatment. Although the success of BSFT with U.S. Latina/o youths can be attributed partially to the overall effectiveness of the technique, BSFT also supports the power of familismo and the family system in Latina/o families. The activity described in Build Your Knowledge 12.3 presents the basic tenets of using BSFT with Latina/o families, with the stipulation that further reading and research would be required to fully implement this technique with U.S. Latina/o adolescents.

BUILD YOUR KNOWLEDGE 12.3

COUNSELING ACTIVITY FOR USE WITH U.S. LATINA/O ADOLESCENTS: BRIEF STRATEGIC FAMILY THERAPY

According to Robbins et al. (2008) and Santisteban et al. (2003), brief strategic family therapy (BSFT) is a three-phase counseling technique whereby the professional counselor "joins with," diagnoses, and restructures the family's communication patterns in hopes of making the parents the "primary source of authority and [where] all individuals have equal opportunities to contribute to the family and to voice their issues and concerns" (p. 123). In the joining phase, the counselor helps the family members analyze and process their communication and interaction by summarizing and paraphrasing the family's emotions and behaviors, as well as emphasizing that they interact in their "typical" manner. This process leads to the diagnosing phase, wherein the counselor looks for power distribution patterns exercised between family members, targeted family members, boundary irregularities, and avenues for conflict resolution. Finally, all the information that is collected directs the counselor in developing a restructuring plan to present the family with more effective, realistic, and appropriate communication methods and interactions.

With U.S. Latina/o adolescents involved in generational conflicts—particularly those who are, in the eyes of parents/guardians and older family members, "rebelling against the old ways"— BSFT can help them and their families take a "time-out" from their culture-centered and generational-centered infighting to gauge why their communication patterns are not leading to family cohesion and solutions to discord. (See Case Study 12.2.) Counselors who join U.S. Latina/o families can help them observe the adaptive and maladaptive communication styles and topics of disagreement in order to identify where the actual problems are centered. Next, by providing support for the adult's role as authority figure (in line with Latina/o cultural norms) while acknowledging that every family member's voice is valid (though not a commonly held belief in Latina/o culture as it pertains to children, this concept is a collectivistic one), the counselor can help each family member develop methods for attaining stronger and healthier relationships. As with most techniques, mental health experts are ethically required to explore and research the merits of BSFT. Once counselors have become more comfortable with the basic tenets of the idea, they will most likely find it to be a counseling technique that takes into account many of the cultural norms and customs of U.S. Latina/o adolescents and their families, thereby increasing the likelihood it will be an effective clinical tool.

CASE STUDY 12.2

Sandra is a 14-year-old Mexican-American high school student. She was born in the United States; her parents were born in Mexico. She has been referred to the community counseling center in which you work by her high school counselor. The school counselor informs you that Sandra is experiencing family issues at home and that these issues are manifesting themselves in the classroom. Among the issues that Sandra is experiencing are an apathetic attitude toward her schoolwork, aggression toward her classmates, and disrespectful behavior toward school personnel. The school counselor elaborates on the issues in the home by saying that Sandra is at odds with her parents' child-rearing practices; in particular, Sandra says that her parents are "much more strict" than her peers' parents. Moreover, Sandra's parents are going back to Mexico this summer for the entire 3 months of summer vacation, and Sandra does not want to go with them. She'd rather be left with an aunt who lives in a nearby town. Finally, your colleague informs you that Sandra has reported "being fed up with all this speaking Spanish stuff in the house, Spanish TV and radio, and tortillas for breakfast, lunch, and dinner. I just wish I was more American like my friends, and not Mexican." The parents have agreed with the school counselor that a community counseling referral would be most beneficial for Sandra. You agree to see Sandra, fully aware of the multiple factors involved in Sandra's presenting school issues, as well as the deeper layers of cultural resentment and parental conflict. Explore the following questions:

- Considering that you will have an intake session with Sandra in the next week, what kind of information would you want to know from that session? Think about what *might not* be on the intake form, that you might also want to know.
- Assuming that you are doing a mental status exam (MSE) as part of the intake, what kinds of formal and informal assessments would you like to include? What cultural considerations would you need to account for as you complete the MSE? What are some of the cultural limitations of the MSE process?
- To what extent would you involve Sandra's parents in the intake session? To what extent would you involve her parents in subsequent sessions? How would you deal with generational conflicts in sessions? How would you address generational conflicts outside of the session, when they are more likely to occur?
- There are two tiers of circumstances here: (1) the school concerns and (2) the family/ home/ cultural identity concerns. How do you prioritize these concerns, and why? What kind of theoretical orientation and techniques would you use to address the concerns?
- What kinds of goals for Sandra and/or her family would you assist in formulating? How would you achieve this goal formation? How would you know when the goals have been attained?
- What countertransference issues, if any, are you experiencing as a result of reading this case study? How do you grapple with these issues and your own self-awareness, and how do you address them?

Counseling Considerations for Adults of Latin-American and Latino Descent

In working with U.S. Latina/o adults, it becomes important to consider the impact of their immigration status and their practice of cultural and religious customs. Particularly for first-generation adult U.S. Latinas/os, their immigration status can be a constant stressor if they do not have the proper documentation to reside in this country. It can also be a source of pride if they have successfully become a U.S. resident or citizen, or a source of guilt if they experience feelings of having to "sacrifice" their affiliation with their country of origin for U.S. citizenship. Even for second-generation U.S. Latinas/os, immigration issues can have an influence on their daily lives. For example, 54% of legal U.S. Latina/o residents and citizens have reported increased discrimination as a direct result of the contentious immigration debate in the United States (Pew Hispanic Center, 2005). U.S. Latinas/os also worry about the immigration status of loved ones living in the United States and about visa procedures for those trying to move to the United States. In short, counselors should not assume that immigration is a nonissue for U.S. Latinas/os, regardless of their status.

The amount of time a U.S. Latina/o adult has lived in the United States also can influence the vigor with which he or she adheres to Latina/o norms, customs, traditions, and even religious practice. The sacrificing or mere fading of one's Latina/o heritage in the name of becoming more "American" can result in feelings of guilt in many adults—almost a feeling of "selling out" the homeland. These circumstances can be moderated by where the client lives. For example, does the client reside in a community with a historically large and active Latina/o presence (e.g., Los Angeles, Miami, New York), or has the client settled down in a more rural community with a burgeoning, yet small, Latina/o populace (e.g., Siler City, North Carolina; Washington County, Arkansas)? In the former case, perhaps the client is more capable of practicing and coming in contact with reminders from home (e.g., ingredients for Latin cooking, Latin restaurants, Catholic services in Spanish); in the latter, there is little likelihood of finding the comforts of his or her native home. As with other considerations previously outlined, it is the counselor's job to assess whether and, if so, how the adult client's presenting problems are associated with immigration and a longing for cultural connections.

Finally, special consideration should be paid to counseling Latino families. As detailed by Falicov (2014), therapy for Latino families and couples requires the counselor to be cognizant of societal norms and expectations and how they may differ from expected behaviors, values, and experiences of Latino families. For example, a counseling goal for an adolescent in a Latino family may be that she or he receives a scholarship and leaves the home to attend a certain school. This goal, however, may be at odds with the parents' wishes to have their child live closer to home. Another counseling goal may be for a counselor to have a family share more with each other how they feel, only to have those goals brush up against the concept of marianismo or machismo. Finally, a family caring for elderly family members may be struggling financially and emotionally to care for a convalescent parent, leading the counselor to incorrectly suggest that they explore the option of moving the elderly family member to an assisted-care facility. Such a suggestion could upset the generational nature of the nuclear and extended Latino family (Falicov, 2014). These three examples are not limited to Latino families: the truth is that most (if not all) families must deal with similar stress-inducing events. And yet, with Latino families and couples in particular, how adults and children in the family react to these experiences is sometimes influenced by the salience of the Latino experience and the cultural heritage of the individual. Counselors working with U.S. Latina/o adults also should be aware of adults who

- struggle with caring for their elderly parents in a society they consider to be not as respectful of the elderly as Latina/o cultures
- experience discrimination in the workplace or who are underemployed as a result of their educational attainment or immigration status
- find it difficult to connect with their children because of differences between the school culture and the home culture
- feel powerless because they must depend on their children to serve as translators if the child's English fluency is greater than their own (Organista, 2007; Santiago-Rivera et al., 2002)
- feel the need to send remittances to family members, friends, or creditors in their native countries while struggling to reach economic stability in the United States

COUNSELING ADULTS   Selecting between individual, group, and family counseling for adult U.S. Latinas/os can be more difficult than it is for children and adolescents. To begin with, U.S. Latina/o adults tend to have stronger Latina/o identities tied to their country of origin, and the ties can often play a role in the type of counseling modality selected. In addition, with the exception of college-aged individuals attending classes or living on a college campus, most U.S. Latinas/os do not have regular access to mental health specialists. Therefore, planning and offering counseling services is more dependent on clients making time for mental health services, despite family, work, and life obligations. And it is precisely because of these types of responsibilities that a systems approach to counseling—that is, an approach that considers all the aspects of a U.S. Latina/o client's environment(s)—is almost as important as selecting between one-on-one counseling, a support group, or family therapy. Now reflect on what modalities would be best for Alejandro in Case Study 12.3.

CASE STUDY 12.3

Alejandro is a 54-year-old Honduran man. He came to the United States 24 years ago and has been a U.S. citizen for 7 years. He recently was laid off from his job as supervisor for a textile company (with 26 garment workers under his management) because of a downturn in the market. For this reason, he has come to you, a vocational counselor, in an effort to find employment in a related field. Typically, you would start off the first session with a new client by asking for some background on his or her past jobs and assessing the client's interests and skills. However, you realize that Alejandro has a lot more that he would like to discuss than finding a new job. In this first session, he also shares how "lost" he feels now that he can't provide for his family and that he knows his age is not going to help him get a new job because "any employer would just as soon hire a younger person with less experience and not have to pay him a living wage." You realize, then, that there are more pressing concerns for this gentleman than finding a new job, and you know that many cultural aspects will need to be considered as you proceed to offer him vocational guidance. Therefore, consider the following questions:

- How do you prioritize his presenting goals of "obtaining a new job" with his anxiety and stigma over not being able to "provide for his family"?
- To what extent does machismo factor into this client's perceptions, if at all? Furthermore, how would you raise these issues (if at all), considering your own gender?
- What about his notion of confianza? What role does it play in setting goals, challenging statements, and even reflecting with this client, considering that this is the first session?
- What about the cultural appropriateness of commonly used career assessments? Would they be appropriate for this client, given his age and ethnicity?
- Finally, how comfortable would you feel providing services that went beyond "vocational guidance" to this client? Think about your setting (i.e., the specific role of your agency) and how that may facilitate or hinder your desire to go beyond "vocational guidance" to address Alejandro's many concerns.

If individual counseling is used with adult clients, attention should be paid to the different culturally related factors that may be affecting the issue presented. For example, if a client is seeking anger management skills, the counselor should help the client explore how her or his experiences as a U.S. Latina/o are connected to antecedents and behaviors associated with anger. In one case, for example, a client from the Dominican Republic may need to consider how the discrimination she experiences at work, the delays she suffers in getting a U.S. work visa renewed, and the feelings she has about her daughter "becoming less Dominican and more American by the minute" are contributing to her anger at home and on the job. With this client, a counselor would be remiss if he or she focused only on helping her learn anger management skills without at least helping her consider the influence of social, political, and family systems on her feelings and reactions. Processing these circumstances becomes crucial to the overall counseling relationship and related goals, particularly because clients are not solely in control of these systems.

The benefits of cohesion and universality attributable to group work make it a "modality of choice" in working with members of any race, age, or ethnicity. However, because of the strong identification that most U.S. Latinas/os have with their country of origin, counselors should proceed with caution before "lumping" U.S. Latina/o clients into any type of counseling group, psychoeducational group, or self-help/support group. Furthermore, counselors should not assume that they can place South Americans (e.g., Peruvians, Colombians, and Brazilians) or Caribbeans (e.g., Cubans and Puerto Ricans) together, expecting mutual empathy from the group members on the basis of geographic proximity. In essence, counselors working with group modalities to assist U.S. Latina/o clients in processing and coping with a variety of issues (e.g., grief and loss, substance use, domestic violence, adjusting to life in the United States) must at least be cognizant of the influence that cultural systems attributed to their country of origin can have, even if the client is a second- or third-generation U.S. Latina/o, because customs, dialects, worshiping nuances, and role models can be very different.

Family counseling would seem to be an effective modality for U.S. Latina/o adults, considering the importance placed on the family system. And, indeed, although family counseling is most likely a viable option, counselors must keep in mind the resistance by some U.S. Latina/o adults to seek mental health help from someone other than a fellow family member or a member of the clergy (Organista, 2007). For this reason, counselors working with U.S. Latinas/os should ask how their clients would feel about involving members of their immediate or extended family. It may be that a particular adult client has not told any family members that he or she is seeking counseling. Clients may feel that family members would be critical of them going outside the family and church, and telling a stranger about their problems. The family system is oftentimes partially responsible for or influenced by an individual's reasons for seeking mental health assistance. The culture-centered genogram, developed by Maritza Gallardo-Cooper, is one method to establish family background, determine relevant family members, and discuss family bonds and relationships for individual and family clients. This information could then be used to enhance family therapy objectives, exercises, and goals. Build Your Knowledge 12.4 presents another technique for counseling adults, and Voices from the Field 12.4 demonstrates a Latina's experiences in counseling. Finally, Activity 12.3 (see earlier) encourages the reader to conduct an immersion experience, and Table 12.1 provides media resources that are helpful for counseling individuals and families of Latino descent.

BUILD YOUR KNOWLEDGE 12.4

COUNSELING ACTIVITY FOR USE WITH U.S. LATINA/O ADULTS: CULTURALLY SENSITIVE ECOMAP

The **ecomap**, formally known as an ecological genogram, was developed by Hartman (1995). Ecomaps are visual depictions of the systems that influence an individual's world. Unlike genograms that focus on someone's family history, the ecomap takes into account microsystems (e.g., the individual and his or her family), mesosystems (i.e., the relationship between systems), exosystems (i.e., systems indirectly connected to the individual or his or her family, such as one's place of work, school, or church), and macrosystems (e.g., religion/spirituality or political systems). Basically, a counselor using an ecomap with a client would ask the client to draw a circle in the middle of a page. The circle represents the client (i.e., "self"). Then, the client can draw, in separate circles, family members, the client's place of work and worship, and greater themes, such as spirituality and the power of government over his or her life. The client is then instructed to consider carefully where he or she places each circle in relation

(Continued)

to the "self" circle because distance from himself or herself to other individuals and systems indicates importance (closeness) or inconsequentiality (remoteness). Finally, the counselor instructs the client to "say a bit more" about the relationship between the "self" and the system, using different types of lines to indicate the type of relationship involved (e.g., a straight line might indicate a positive relationship, a dotted line may signify an indifferent relationship, and a jagged line could indicate a strained or negative relationship—what the lines represent is up to the counselor). The final part of this activity would be to discuss the client's reactions to the ecomap and perhaps develop future clinical goals or foci.

What makes an ecomap particularly useful with U.S. Latina/o adult clients is how it can open up discussions of, for example, extended family members, the influence of the church, or even the strain of an uncertain U.S. residency. In fact, counselors who use ecomaps with U.S. Latina/o clients should stress the importance of placing as many relevant "systems" as possible, while having the client focus on what makes the mesosystems take on the characteristics that they do. If the client is intent on altering mesosystems (e.g., bringing a family member closer or redefining the importance of school or church), then the ecomap provides a visual cue as to how things look now and how the client would like them to look in the future. By definition, ecomaps do not have to be culturally sensitive, but when used by a culturally competent counselor, they can be very useful in helping U.S. Latina/o clients realize the importance of all the systems that influence their daily lives.

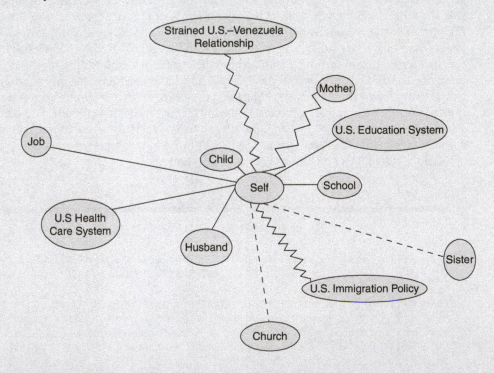

Microsystems: Self, Child, Husband, Sister, Mother

Mesosystems: Straight Line = A Positive Relationship; Broken Line = A Distant, Indifferent Relationship; Jagged Line = A Negative, Strained Relationship

Exosystems: School, Church, Job

Macrosystems: Strained U.S.–Venezuela Relationship; U.S. Education System; U.S. Health Care System; U.S. Immigration Policy

The foregoing hypothetical ecomap was completed by your client ("Self"), a 27-year-old legal U.S. resident who came to the United States from Venezuela when she was 10 years old. She indicates that her child (a 6-year-old son) and her husband represent her most positive and strongest relationships. However, she does not have much contact with her sister back in Venezuela and is estranged from her mother, who lives in the same city as your client. Relevant exosystems include the community college where your client is pursuing studies to become a licensed practicing nurse (as indicated by "School") and her job. Although she indicates an indifferent relationship between the local Catholic church (as indicated by "Church"), she mentions that she would like to increase her family's participation in church activities. Finally, she mentions that her husband's pending immigration status (his worker visa has expired, and he is waiting for an update on if and when it will be renewed) and the current state of U.S. immigration policy, coupled with the strained relationship between the United States and Venezuela, has her worried that he will be deported back to Venezuela before the paperwork is completed. However, she does not want to sound "anti-American," for she is grateful for the U.S. education and health-care systems from which she benefits.

Voices from the Field 12.4

I don't know what I am doing here. Honestly, I don't even know what your job as the counselor is. Did you know that in Spanish there is no direct translation for "counselor"? *Consejero* is more or less a made-up word, a word that has been translated into Spanish from English. I mean, we have psychologists and psychiatrists in my home country who work with crazy people. But we don't have "counselors." We don't even have the word "counseling." It wasn't until my friend from work told me she saw you when she was having problems with her husband that I came to see you. I was even trying to tell my mom that I wanted to get some counseling to talk about getting a divorce, and she didn't even know what "counseling" was. It's not your fault or anything, but I just wanted you to know that I really have no example of what a counselor is or what a counselor does. I hope you can help me, though, because I really don't know what to do about my marriage and my family.

~ Anonymous, 31-year-old Latina coming to a marriage counselor for the first time

TABLE 12.1 Media Resources for Counseling Individuals and Families of Latin-American and Latino Descent

General Web Resources

Hispanic Association of Colleges and Universities (www.hacu.net): An association of more than 400 colleges and universities committed to the success of Hispanic students all over the world.

National Alliance for Hispanic Health (http://www.hispanichealth.org/): An advocacy and educational organization helping Latinos gain access to physical and mental health services and information.

Pew Research Center for Hispanic Trends (http://www.pewhispanic.org): A hub for statistics, data, and policy briefs and reports on Latinas/os living in the United States; from the Pew Charitable Trust.

(Continued)

National Council of La Raza [NCLR] (http://www.nclr.org/): The NCLR is the largest national Latina/o civil rights organization and one of the longest in existence.

Hispanic Scholarship Fund (http://www.hsf.net/): This is a clearinghouse for scholarships and nonfederal financial aid options, as well as a recourse for Latino families and an informational guide on how to apply for and receive scholarships and other financial aid.

National Resource Center for Hispanic Mental Health (http://www.nrchmh.org/): A national nonprofit organization that promotes and advocates for effective mental health options for Latinas/os, as well as influencing mental health public policy.

National Latino Behavioral Health Association (http://nlbha.org/): This organization focuses on mental health disparities afflicting Latino individuals and families, while promoting increases in access to, and funding for, greater numbers of mental health service providers working with Latinas/os in the United States.

Mexican American Legal Defense and Educational Fund (http://www.maldef.org/): A Latino legal civil rights organization established to promote social change for the Latino community through education and, when necessary, litigation.

Films

Please visit www.imdb.com for additional information on these films.

Puerto Rico

- *Lo que le Paso a Santiago* (1989)
- *Linda Sara* (1994)
- *Héroes de Otra Patria* (1996)
- *12 Horas* (2001)
- *Ladrones y Mentirosos* (2006)
- *Talento de Barrio* (2008)
- *Ángel* (2007)
- *Maldeamores* (2007)

Cuba

- *Buena Vista Social Club* (1999)
- *Soy Cuba* (1964)
- *Fresa y chocolate* (1994)
- *Memorias del subdesarrollo* (1968)
- *Guantanamera* (1995)
- *Lista de espera* (2000)
- *La vida es silbar* (1998)
- *Azúcar amarga* (1996)

Mexican

- *El laberinto del fauno* (2006)
- *Amores perros* (2000)
- *Y tu mamá también* (2001)
- *Bandidas* (2006)
- *El ángel exterminador* (1962)
- *Sin Nombre* (2009)
- *Como agua para chocolate* (1992)
- *El crimen del padre Amaro* (2002)

Summary

U.S. Latina/o clients span all races and religions, reside in all parts of the United States, and possess a multitude of strengths. These clients, however, also are exposed to a variety of stressors, compounded by the very systems set up to support them: family, culture, government, their work setting, and local communities. U.S. Latina/o clients seeking assistance from counselors should, at the very least, be able to expect to work with a professional who has knowledge about the unique and expansive U.S. Latina/o experience.

Several key terms were discussed in this chapter. Key values include *marianismo*, the requirement that a woman be pure, make sacrifices for her family's benefit, and not engage in premarital sex; *familismo*, an individual's consideration of one's immediate and extended family, and even close friends of the family as well as religious godparents, when making decisions; *confianza*, trust and confidence; and *personalismo*, the warmth, affection, concern about others, and positive regard for those close to an individual. In addition, *first-generation immigrants* was defined as those who were born in a different country and immigrated to the United States, thereby signifying that their children would be considered second-generation immigrants and their children's children would be third-generation immigrants. Finally, forced migration and voluntary migration were compared. Forced migrants, or individuals who were forced to leave their native lands because of political persecution, ethnic violence, war, or religious discrimination, may experience more acculturative stress, grief and loss, and feelings of hopelessness than voluntary immigrants, who came to the United States for economic opportunities or to improve their lives.

The intent of the chapter was to provide initial information as it relates to potential U.S. Latina/o clients. How a counselor decides to incorporate this information into his or her professional skills and repertoire, however, is up to the individual. Counseling U.S. Latinas/os is a complex, yet necessary, endeavor. Unless counselors are comfortable enough with their own shortcomings to ask their U.S. Latina/o clients for information on their family, country of origin, immigration, and cultural experience, the counseling relationship will suffer from too many cultural assumptions and misconceptions. Therefore, take the information provided here on the richness that is the U.S. Latina/o experience as a mere *sabor* (taste), and use these ideas, concepts, and activities as a foundation for future exploration into the lives of U.S. Latina/o children, adolescents, and adults.

Review Questions

1. How would you, as a counselor, deal with the concepts of *marianismo* and *machismo* if you don't value "women sacrificing their own betterment for that of their families" and/or have strong reservations toward "men who play a dominant role in their families"?
2. How does a Hispanic or Latina/o client's immigration status affect the counseling process?
3. Explain how acculturative stress can affect the personal lives of Hispanic and Latina/o clients. What "clues" does acculturative stress provide about possible concerns of Hispanic and Latina/o clients?
4. How do economic barriers manifest themselves in the counseling concerns of Hispanic and Latina/o clients, and how might you, as a counselor, help the client deal with related issues?
5. According to the literature, what are some common counseling concerns to look for when working with Hispanic or Latina/o adolescents?

13 Counseling Individuals and Families of Native American Descent

Michael Tlanusta Garrett, J. T. Garrett, Tarrell Awe Agahe Portman, Lisa Grayshield, Edil Torres Rivera, Cyrus Williams, and Mark Parrish

PREVIEW

Native peoples existed on this continent long before the arrival of any other group of people and have struggled to survive and continued to thrive. The history and stories of the lives of this ancient people is often portrayed in the media, playing on age-old stereotypes held about this population. But the often untold stories of pain and persistence have carried over from generation to generation beyond what is portrayed in books and movies. The real lives of real people are what counselors must understand to best assist Native clients who may come to them with words, reflections, dreams, and visions of their own. The purpose of this chapter is to facilitate culturally responsive and competent counseling practice with Native people by offering a comprehensive overview and understanding of this population. First, let us begin by understanding what it means to see through indigenous eyes with a reflection by the riverside, then consider a few case studies to help guide our thinking toward application of the concepts that will be discussed throughout this chapter.

UNDERSTANDING NATIVE AMERICANS: REFLECTIONS DOWN BY THE RIVERSIDE

Some of my fondest memories of when I was still a little one go back to times spent with my grandfather, Oscar Rogers, who was Eastern Cherokee. We would spend time sitting on the rocks by the Oconaluftee River in Cherokee, North Carolina. "What do you see when you look into the water?" he would inquire, as he sat on a rock enjoying the afternoon sun. I would look closely to see the water rushing quickly downstream. My eyes would catch the glimpse of a fish, water beetles, flies touching the water, soaked wood floating along at the will of the water, rocks, and green plants.

"I see the water," I said. "What else do you see?" he asked. "Well, I see the fish," I answered, because there were little minnows swimming around in the water. "What else do you see?" he asked. "I see the rocks," I said. "What else do you see?" he asked again. My eyes began to water themselves as I stared intently, wanting so much to please my grandfather by seeing everything he saw.

"Ah, I see my reflection," I responded proudly. "That's good," he replied confidently. "What you see is your whole life ahead of you. Know that the Great One has a plan for you to be the keeper of everything you see with your eyes, 'cause every living thing is your brother and sister." "Even the rocks?" I questioned. "Yes, even the rocks," he answered, "because they have elements of Mother Earth and Father Sky, just as we do."

"Remember to give thanks every day for all things that make up the Universe," said my grandfather. "Always remember to walk the path of Good Medicine and see the good reflected in everything that occurs in life. Life is a lesson, and you must learn the lesson well to see your true reflection in the water." (J. T Garrett, Eastern Band of Cherokee, in Garrett [1996], p. 12)

As we take the journey into gaining awareness, knowledge, and skills about Native people, test your knowledge about Native Americans by completing Activity 13.1.

ACTIVITY 13.1   TRUE OR FALSE

Indicate the correct response by circling True (T) or False (F)

T F **1.** There is a difference socially and legally between people who self-identify as Native versus those who are enrolled tribal members.

T F **2.** Columbus was not the first to explore "the new world" or to have contact with the Native peoples of this continent.

T F **3.** From 1778 to 1871, there were 370 documented treaties negotiated between the U.S. government and Indian tribes.

T F **4.** Indian people were granted U.S. citizenship as soon as they were put on reservations.

T F **5.** All of the major tribes in the United States are located west of the Mississippi River.

T F **6.** Suicide rates are higher for Native Americans than any other group in the United States.

T F **7.** Approximately 50% of the Native American population resides in urban areas.

T F **8.** Native traditionalists worship multiple deities in their tribal spiritual traditions.

T F **9.** In many Native traditions, the eagle feather serves as a sacred reminder that many things in this world are separate and opposite and need to be kept that way.

T F **10.** Indian people are stoic and seldom laugh.

T F **11.** In the traditional style of Native communication, silence means that you lack confidence or that you are hiding something.

T F **12.** In many Native traditions, speaking loudly and drawing a lot of attention to yourself is considered arrogant and boastful.

T F **13.** The one word that encompasses the essence of a traditional Native worldview is *relation*.

Answer key: 1. T, 2. T, 3. T, 4. F, 5. F, 6. T, 7. T, 8. F, 9. F, 10. F, 11. F, 12. T, 13. T.

Native Americans Today

Native Americans represent a group of peoples with a steadily growing population of more than 5.2 million (U.S. Census Bureau, 2011b), or just more than 1% of the total U.S. population. Across the United States there are more than 566 federally recognized tribes (228 of which exist in Alaska), more than 50 state-recognized tribes, and several hundred more tribes in various stages of petitioning the federal government for recognition; in addition, there are 324 federally recognized Native American reservations (Garrett, Garrett, & Melton, 2009; U.S. Census Bureau, 2011b). According to recent U.S. Census Bureau (2011b) data, the 10 states with the greatest number of Native people were California (723,225), Oklahoma (482,760), Arizona (353,386), Texas (315,264), New York (221,058), New Mexico (219,512), Washington (198,998), North Carolina (184,082), Florida (162,562), and Michigan (139,095). Contrary to the stereotypical image that Native Americans live only on reservations or in other rural areas and rarely exist in contemporary mainstream society, approximately 78% of the Native American population resides in urban areas (Garrett, Garrett, & Melton, 2009).

As of the most recent U.S. census numbers (2011b), the largest tribes in the United States by population were Navajo, Cherokee, Choctaw, Sioux, Chippewa, Apache, Blackfeet, Iroquois, and Pueblo. In terms of age, 33.9% of the total population of Native Americans is under the age of 18; the next largest age group is 30.9% with individuals between 25 and 44 years of age, while only 5.6% of Native Americans are over age 65. In 2011, the median age of Native Americans was 31 years, compared to the median age of 37 years for the overall U.S. population. More than half of Native American grandparents are responsible for caring for grandchildren for longer than a five-year period, and over 8% of American Indian and Alaska Native grandparents live with their grandchildren. Furthermore, as of 2011, 27% of Native American youth ages 5 years and older spoke a language other than English at home, compared to 21% for the entire nation (U.S. Census Bureau, 2011a).

Native scholars have written extensively about the ongoing effects of generational and intergenerational trauma on indigenous people, their families, and their tribal communities (e.g., Duran, 2006; Garrett, Portman, Choudhuri, & Santiago-Rivera, 2011; Gone, 2009). These scholars have consistently described the challenges that Native Americans encounter as they navigate a world that is drastically different than that of their own tribal cultures. Numerous authors have highlighted the fact that Native people are at greater risk than other ethnicities for a variety of adverse outcomes that include maltreatment, substance abuse, suicide, accidental death, violence, and mental health problems (Chandler, Lalonde, Sokol, & Hallett, 2003; Fitzgerald, & Farrell, 2012). Many Native Americans grow up in communities characterized by high rates of unemployment, poverty, physical and mental health disparities, violence, and lower levels of educational achievement in comparison to the total U.S. population. Researchers continue to identify links between historical trauma and feelings of anxiety, depression, anger, and avoidance among Native Americans (Sarche & Whitsell, 2012).

Despite these challenges, Native communities across the United States and Canada seek to transcend experiences of trauma and loss by embracing cultural practices that have sustained Native peoples for centuries and to focus efforts toward renewal through cultural and community-based intervention models (Spicer et al., 2012). Examples of such efforts include wellness centers based on indigenous cultural concepts of healing, as well as culture- and language-immersion schools and tradition-based programs that promote Native youth development and community resilience. Research indicates these efforts help reduce many of the health disparities that plague Native communities (Chandler et al., 2003). At the heart of these efforts is the ongoing cultural belief in the sacredness of children as a focal point for the health and well-being of the entire community. In many Native communities, an increasing emphasis has been placed on strong extended kin networks, participation in traditional ceremonies that contribute to a sense of belonging and identity, and the learning and preservation of tribal languages and stories (Kirmayer, Dandeneau, Marshall, Phillips, & Williamson, 2011; Sarche & Whitsell, 2012). Nonetheless, the tensions that exist between the tribal world and that of mainstream society remain a constant challenge for Native Americans.

There are some common elements in Native American worldview. Cultural conflict and acculturation to the dominant American culture play a major role. Common core values exist for traditional Native Americans across tribal groups, including a high degree of psychological homogeneity and some shared cultural standards and meanings (Garrett, Portman, et al., 2011; McLeigh, 2010). For example, Cherokees and Navajos share similarities in basic cultural values and worldview, although their regional cultures, climatic adaptations, and languages differ greatly. However, the worldview and degree of commitment to traditional culture vary within groups of Native people. At the same time, a prevailing sense of indigeneity or "Indianness" based on common worldview and common history in what Grayshield and Mihecoby (2010) refer to as "Indigenous Ways of Knowing" seems to bind Native Americans together as a people of many peoples (Garrett, Portman, et al., 2011).

Grayshield and Mihecoby (2010) defined **indigenous ways of knowing** as "a multidimensional body of lived experiences that informs and sustains people who make their homes in a local area and always takes into account the current sociopolitical colonial power dimensions of the Western world" (p. 6). There are "three central features within Indigenous knowledge forms that have both political and curricular implications: many Indigenous/tribal cultures related harmoniously to their environment; experienced colonization, and provided an alternative perspective on human experience that differed from Western empirical science" (p. 6). Clearly, maintaining a sense of history and continuing to feel a part of both one's tribe and of the entire Native American population through the integration of indigenous ways of knowing will continue to be a key issue among Native Americans (Kirmayer et al., 2011).

Group Membership

It is not uncommon for a Native person to be asked by non-Natives "How much *Indian* are you?" This question refers to **blood quantum**, also known as degree of Indian blood or certificate of Indian blood (CIB card); however, many Native Americans are not enrolled members of federally recognized tribes or are unable to trace their degree of blood in a specific tribe to satisfy the blood quantum requirement. Blood quantum requirements are hot topics on reservations due to intermarriage with nontribal members or those who are not considered enrolled members. Although populations on reservations are growing, especially among the younger generations, tribal membership is vastly declining on many reservations. Issues of blood quantum pose numerous challenges in forming healthy identities for Native American people, but nonetheless remain the primary identifying modality in determining who is an Indian. As such, it is critical that we begin our discussion of what it means to be Native American by clarifying some definitions and concepts around group membership.

The term **Native American** is often used to describe indigenous peoples of the Western Hemisphere whose life and life ways are intricately interwoven with the natural environment. The U.S. Bureau of Indian Affairs (BIA; 2015) legally defines Native American (or American Indian/Alaska Native [AI/AN]) as:

. . . someone who has blood degree from and is recognized as such by a federally recognized tribe or village (as an enrolled tribal member) and/or the United States. Of course, blood quantum (the degree of American Indian or Alaska Native blood from a federally recognized tribe or village that a person possesses) is not the only means by which a person is considered to be an American Indian or Alaska Native. Other factors, such as a person's knowledge of his or her tribe's culture, history, language, religion, familial kinships, and how strongly a person identifies himself or herself as American Indian or Alaska Native, are also important. In fact, there is no single federal or tribal criterion or standard that establishes a person's identity as American Indian or Alaska Native.

Blood quantum is not literally a measure of "degree of blood" as it implies; instead, it refers to the percentage of ancestry that can be traced to people from a specific tribe or nation. Most tribes require one-quarter blood quantum for membership (Russell, 2004), whereas others set alternative criteria to address differing sociopolitical issues. For example, the Cherokee Nation of Oklahoma enrolls members with blood quantum as little as 1/512, whereas the Ute Nation of Utah requires a minimum blood quantum of five-eighths for tribal membership. However, the U.S. Census Bureau (2011b) relies on self-identification to determine who is a Native person. This allows numerous individuals who may not necessarily be members of any tribe to self-identify their Native American heritage. Oswalt (2009) pointed out, however, that

if a person is considered an Indian by other individuals in the community, he or she is legally an Indian . . . [in other words], if an individual is on the roll of a federally recognized Indian group, then he or she is an Indian; the degree of Indian blood is of no real consequence, although usually he or she has at least some Indian blood. (p. 5)

Some of the terms used historically or currently to refer to Native people are American Indian, Alaskan Native, Native people, Indian, First American, Amerindian, Amerind, First Nations people, Aboriginal people, and indigenous people. The terms *Native American* or *Native people* (and sometimes, *Indian*) will be used in this chapter to refer generally to those people who are indigenous to the United States, who self-identify as Native American, and who maintain cultural identification as so-called Native persons through membership in a specific Native American tribe that may or may not be recognized by the state or federal government or through other tribal affiliation and community recognition.

Now that there is a better understanding of some of the definitions and terms involved with group membership among Native Americans, it is necessary to discuss in more depth what it means to be Native American in contemporary society. Consider Case Studies 13.1 through 13.4. Later in the chapter we will analyze each of these cases and address important cultural and counseling issues.

CASE STUDY 13.1

Jose Daugheetee is a teen of Kiowa descent. He struggles with his personal identity as a Native American young man. He is often mistaken for being Latino due to his birth name. He constantly finds himself explaining he is not Mexican, that his mother just liked the name because it sounded like Jesus. Jose feels proud of his Kiowa traditions but feels like an outsider based on his birth name. He is considering going through a naming ceremony with elders so he can be "fully" Kiowa. Jose is in middle school and has visited the school counselor to discuss this major issue in his life. The school counselor tries to be empathetic but admits he has no idea of the cultural issues surrounding Jose's circumstances.

What would be the first steps the counselor could take to help Jose?

CASE STUDY 13.2

Kathy Dawes is a 32-year-old woman of Quapaw descent. She has never been married and recently began to date an African-American male, George, age 36 years. Kathy is excited and feels George could be her soul mate. They have discussed partnering and living together. Kathy seeks out guidance from the counselor who comes to the tribal administration center once per month. Kathy presents a concern that she needs to carry on the Quapaw bloodline due to the diminishing numbers in the tribe. If she has children with George, her children would not be eligible for tribal membership due to falling below the one-half blood quantum line. Kathy has been thinking she should get pregnant by a Quapaw male to allow her children to be in the tribe. She feels strongly that George would understand.

What would a counselor do in this situation? Where would a counselor turn for help?

CASE STUDY 13.3

Jana is an 18-year-old woman of Comanche descent. Jana was removed from her birth parents at the age of 3 years and sent to foster parents living in New York. Jana barely remembers her Comanche relatives but has carried pictures and birthday cards with her to various foster homes. Jana has aged-out of the foster-care system and is on her own now with no employment. Jana comes to the workforce counselor seeking ways to reconnect with her birth family in Oklahoma. Jana feels confident they would take her in, even though it has been 15 years since contact. Jana does not know where to begin but asks for the counselor's help.

How might the counselor respond?

CASE STUDY 13.4

Zed is an 87-year-old Zuni two spirit. Zed has recently had some health issues that caused him to relocate from Arizona to Minnesota to live with his youngest daughter, Suzie. Suzie is a professor at the local university. Zed has lived a traditional lifestyle on the Zuni tribal lands in Arizona all his life. Suzie schedules an appointment for Zed to see a gerontological counselor to deal with his lack of adjustment to Minneapolis. Zed willingly agrees to see the counselor but is reluctant to engage in conversation.

How can a counselor help Zed and Suzie in this situation?

Native American History

By understanding the historical context from which Native American individuals and families come, one can better understand what it means to be Native today. As such, it is important to consider the powerful influence of what many Native people refer to as "generational grief and trauma," or what Brave Heart has simply termed "historical trauma," and the effect this aspect of the Native experience has had on Native worldview and life. Characterized by institutional racism and discrimination, the dominant culture has a long history of opposition to Native cultures. Attempts to assimilate Native people have had a long-lasting effect on Native cultures ways of life (Brave Heart, 2005; Deloria, 2006; Duran, 2006; Duran, Firehammer, & Gonzalez, 2008; Gone, 2009; Turner & Pope, 2009).

It is generally understood that there are five stages of U.S. government policy leading to the state of tribal sovereignty currently experienced by Native tribes (Deloria, 2006; Duran, 2006; Oswalt, 2009). These stages are (a) the removal period (1600s to 1840s), characterized by the saying, "The only good Indian is a dead Indian"; (b) the reservation period (1860 to 1920s), characterized by the saying, "Kill the Indian, but save the man"; (c) the reorganization period (1930s to 1950s) with schools allowed on reservations; (d) the termination period (1950s to 1960s) with Relocation Programs intended to achieve sociocultural integration to end dependence on the federal government (resulting in the sale of huge parcels of Native lands and increased poverty); and (e) the self-determination period (1975 to the present) with increased tribal sovereignty following a period of Native activism, referred to as "Red Power."

Examples of efforts by the United States to destroy or assimilate Native peoples in this country are abundant. By the end of the 18th century, the once abundant population of Native peoples had been reduced to 10% of its original size (Oswalt, 2009). Policies of extermination and seizure of lands were common in the history of the United States' interaction with Native American tribes. Even today, the depiction of President Andrew Jackson on the U.S. $20 bill reminds many Native Americans in the southeastern and western United States of the betrayal by the government in 1838, when Jackson defied the Supreme Court by signing an act that forced the removal of over 16,000 Cherokees and members of other tribes from parts of North Carolina, South Carolina, Tennessee, and Georgia to the Oklahoma territory. This forced movement of people is known as the Trail of Tears. Even after being forced onto reservation lands, many Indian families experienced disruption of their cultural traditions. Many Native American children were deliberately taken from their homes and forced to attend boarding schools, where they were not allowed to speak their Native language or practice their traditions. The children usually spent a minimum of eight continuous years away from their families and communities (Brave Heart, 2005; Deloria, 2006; Duran, 2006; Garrett, Portman, et al., 2011). It was not until 1924 that the U.S. government recognized the citizenship of Native Americans—when they were no longer a threat to national expansion—through passage of the Citizenship Act (Garrett et al., 2009). Native Americans were not granted religious freedom until 1978, when the American Indian Religious Freedom Act was passed. This act overturned the Indian Religious Crimes Code of 1889 and guaranteed Native people, for the first time in a century, the constitutional right to exercise their traditional religious practices (Oswalt, 2009). In more recent times, massive efforts to "civilize" Native people through the aforementioned government-supported, religiously run boarding schools and the Relocation Programs of the 1950s added to the generational trauma and cultural discontinuity (Garrett & Portman, 2011; Gone, 2009; Oswalt, 2009). These events have affected Native Americans psychologically, economically, and socially for generations. From both a historical and contemporary perspective, oppression is and continues to be a very real experience for Native people.

Contemporary Native scholars such as Brave Heart and others have coined the term **historical trauma** as a way of naming the cumulative emotional and psychological wounding, over the life span and across generations, emanating from massive group trauma experiences (Brave Heart, 2005; Crazy Thunder & Brave Heart, 2005; Grayshield & Mihecoby, 2010). The **historical trauma response** is the constellation of features in reaction to this trauma that may include substance abuse as a vehicle for attempting to numb the pain associated with trauma, and often includes other types of self-destructive behavior, suicidal thoughts and gestures, depression, anxiety, low self-esteem, anger, and difficulty recognizing and expressing emotions (Brave Heart, 2003).

To help illustrate, a Navajo elder relates, in the following excerpt, her first experience at age 7 in boarding school over 40 years ago. She was unable to speak any English and had always lived on the reservation until being taken away:

It was the first time I've seen a brick building that was not a trading post. The ceilings were so high, and the rooms so big and empty. It was so cold. There was no warmth. Not as far as "Brrr, I'm cold," but in a sense of emotional cold. Kind of an emptiness, when you're hanging onto your mom's skirt and trying hard not to cry. Then when you get up to your turn, she [the teacher] thumbprints the paper and she leaves and you watch her go out the big metal doors. The whole thing was cold. The doors were metal and they even had this big window with wires running through it. You watch your mama go down the sidewalk, actually it's the first time I seen a sidewalk, and you see her get into the truck and the truck starts moving and all the home smell goes with it. You see it all leaving.

Then the woman takes you by the hand and takes you inside and the first thing they do is take down your bun. The first thing they do is cut off your hair, and you been told your whole life that you never cut your hair recklessly because that is your life. And that's the first thing them women does is cut off your hair. And you see that long, black hair drop, and it's like they take out your heart and they give you this cold thing that beats inside. And now you're gonna be just like them. You're gonna be cold. You're never gonna be happy or have that warm feeling and attitude towards life anymore. That's what it feels like, like taking your heart out and putting in a cold river pebble.

When you go into the shower, you leave your squaw skirt and blouse right there at the shower door. When you come out, it's gone. You don't see it again. They cut your hair, now they take your squaw skirt. They take from the beginning. When you first walk in there, they take everything that you're about. They jerk it away from you. They don't ask how you feel about it. They never tell you anything. They never say what they're gonna do, why they're doing it. They barely speak to you. They take everything away from you. Then you think, mama must be whackers. She wants me to be like them? Every time you don't know what they're doing, they laugh at you. They yell at you. They jerk you around. It was never what I wanted to be. I never wanted to be like them. But my mom wanted me to be like them. As I got older, I found out that you don't have to be like them. You can have a nice world and have everything that mama wanted, but you don't have to be cold. . . . (McLaughlin, 1994, pp. 47–48)

For this elder, the boarding school experience she underwent in childhood is still very real and very vivid in her memory, carrying forward in ways that might be hard to understand.

Yet, her narrative represents a vivid illustration of cultural genocide and a reminder of the soul wound that many Native clients might carry (Duran, 2006; Duran et al., 2008). Across Native populations in the United States and throughout the world, boarding schools were consistently an element of the policy of forced assimilation through removal from, and denigration of, traditional culture. McLeigh (2010) noted the transgenerational effects of the residential schools: disruption of families and communities; confusion of parenting with punitive institutional practices; impaired emotional response (a reflection of the lack of warmth and intimacy in childhood); repetition of physical and sexual abuse; loss of knowledge, language, and tradition; and systematic devaluing of Native identity. Historical trauma, such as the impact of the boarding school experience, captures the "collective emotional and psychological injury (both over the life span and across generations) that is the product of a cataclysmic history of genocide" (McLeigh, 2010, p. 178). Accordingly, recognizing and addressing historical trauma also provides a starting point for the design of ethnically specific preventive and therapeutic interventions that take into account the historical experience of colonization and current social and political issues facing any given tribal community.

CURRENT SOCIAL, ECONOMIC, AND POLITICAL ISSUES

Native American Sociocultural Characteristics in the United States Today

American policies of assimilation have had a pervasive impact on Native peoples and their way of life. The following information based on U.S. Census Bureau (2011b) data help provide a better understanding of the current socioeconomic status of Native people.

FAMILIES Native American families are unique—intergenerational, nonblood (fictive) kinship ties, and pervasive with a history of cultural adoptions. More than half of Native American grandparents are responsible for grandchildren for longer than a five-year period of time. More than 8% of American Indian and Alaska Native grandparents live with their grandchildren.

EDUCATIONAL ATTAINMENT Native Americans have a 70.9% high school graduation rate, and reportedly earn bachelor's degrees at a rate of 11.3%, which is below the national average (U.S. Census Bureau, 2011b). Advanced degrees earned are far below the general population with American Indian/Alaska Native reporting only 3.9%. Native youth have the highest dropout rate in the nation with 29.1% compared to 9.8% for the total U.S. population. The states with the highest Native American graduation rates are Tennessee (89%), New Jersey (87%), Texas (87%), Arkansas (85%), Maine (82%), and Alabama (80%). The states with the lowest Native American graduation rates are Colorado (52%), Nevada (52%), Oregon (52%), Alaska (51%), Wyoming (51%), South Dakota (49%), and Minnesota (42%).

INCOME AND POVERTY The recent average median income for Native Americans has been reported at $35,192, compared to $50,502 for the entire nation (U.S. Census Bureau, 2011b). Native Americans have a reported poverty level of 30%, compared to the 16% total of the U.S. population living in poverty. Native Americans have the lowest monthly expenses for their households with a median of $879. In 2011, 33% of AI/AN (alone) students were living below the poverty threshold, compared to 12% of Whites (alone). Seventy-five percent of the Native workforce earns less than $7,000 per year.

EMPLOYMENT   The average unemployment rate for Native people is 45%; however, on some reservations, the unemployment rate is as high as 90% (U.S. Census Bureau, 2011b). Most American Indians and Alaska Natives who are employed reported occupations in the Management, Professional, and Related Occupations (24.3%) and Sales and Office (24%). The Service category held the next highest percentage of individuals with 20.6%.

OTHER RISK FACTORS   Native Americans are often viewed as a population facing enormous problems illustrated by arrest rates three times those for African Americans, and a rate of alcoholism double that of the general population. In terms of health concerns, fetal alcohol syndrome rates for Native people are 33 times higher than that of non-Native people. One in six Native adolescents has attempted suicide, a rate 4 times that of all other groups. Alcohol mortality is 6 times the rate for all other ethnic groups. Tuberculosis is 7.4 times greater than for non-Indians. Diabetes is 6.8 times greater than for non-Native people (Russell, 2004). As for living conditions, the reality in Native communities is that 46% have no electricity; 54% have no indoor plumbing; and 82% live without a telephone.

Help-seeking behaviors of Native people include mental health, rehabilitation, substance abuse, and school counseling services. Native American health-care access and outcomes still fall well below all other U.S. racial groups. Mortality rates due to behavioral health concerns such as alcoholism, accidents, suicide, and homicide are greater than the current age-adjusted U.S. population statistics for all ethnicities (Indian Health Service, 2014). Mental health issues are the fourth leading cause of hospitalization among Native Americans 15 to 44 years of age and the fifth leading cause for ambulatory visits for indigenous peoples 25 to 44 years of age. In addition to the data presented here, there are social, economic, and political issues that create both challenges and opportunities for Native people: self-determination and sovereignty; federal and state recognition; cultural preservation; achievement gap; gaming; tribal resources; sacred sites, repatriation, and reburial; and mascot issues. Discussions of each follow.

Self-Determination and Sovereignty

Federally recognized tribal governments possess the right to form their own government, enforce laws (both civil and criminal), tax members, establish requirements for membership, license and regulate activities, zone areas, and exclude persons from tribal territories. Existing limitations on tribal powers of self-government include the same limitations applicable to states; for example, neither tribes nor states have the power to make war, engage in foreign relations, or coin money (including paper currency). This sovereignty that exists for Native American nations is the result of the Indian Self-Determination and Education Assistance Act passed in 1975.

Despite this, many Native Americans and advocates of Native American rights point out that the federal government's claim to recognize the "sovereignty" of Native American peoples falls short, given that the United States still wishes to govern Native American peoples and treat them as subject to U.S. law. True respect for Native American sovereignty, according to such advocates, would require that the U.S. federal government deal with Native American peoples in the same manner as any other sovereign nation, handling matters related to relations with Native Americans through the Secretary of State, rather than the BIA. The stated responsibility of the U.S. Bureau of Indian Affairs (2015), according to its Web site, is "the administration and management of 55,700,000 acres of land held in trust by the United States for American Indians, Indian tribes, and Alaska Natives." Native Americans continue to be wary of attempts by others to gain control of their reservation lands for exploitation of natural resources such as coal and uranium. Such attempts have been made throughout U.S. history.

Internationally, regarding the issues of indigenous rights, the UN General Assembly adopted the United Nations Declaration on the Rights of Indigenous Peoples on September 13, 2007, following nearly 25 years of discussion. According to a UN press release, "while the Declaration is not a legally binding instrument under international law, it does set an important standard for the treatment of Indigenous peoples that will undoubtedly be a significant tool towards eliminating human rights violations against the planet's 370 million Indigenous people and assisting them in combating discrimination and marginalization" (United Nations, as cited in Garrett et al., 2009). Thus, the purpose of the Declaration is to set the individual and collective rights of indigenous peoples, as well as their rights to culture, identity, language, employment, health, education, and other issues. Furthermore, it "prohibits discrimination against Indigenous peoples" and "promotes their full and effective participation in all matters that concern them and their right to remain distinct and to pursue their own visions of economic and social development."

Federal and State Recognition

Federal recognition of American Indians and Alaska Natives is based on historical and governmental relationships involving treaties and contracts made in the past with certain tribes. The key word is *tribes*; individual Native Americans are recognized as tribal members. Under federal laws (such as the Indian Civil Rights Act of 1968 and related federal acts and amendments), the tribes are considered sovereign, with the federal government having a trust responsibility over them.

Historically, the Indian Appropriations Act of 1871 instructed the Senate and the president not to make any further treaties with tribes, and reservations were established under executive orders directly from the president. Beginning in 1919, Congress looked to the Secretary of the Interior and later to the BIA to deal with the question of which people comprised a tribe. Authorization under the Indian Reorganization Act of 1934 and subsequent rulings by the U.S. Supreme Court made it clear that the federal government has a trust responsibility for tribes. The tribes, in turn, continue to have responsibility and authority related to civil actions and the education, health, social, and welfare issues of their members. Individual members of a tribe are also citizens of the United States and enjoy those rights granted to all U.S. citizens.

Some tribal nations have been unable to establish their heritage and obtain federal recognition, such as many of the smaller eastern tribes who have been applying to gain official recognition of their tribal status. This recognition brings with it some benefits, including the right to label arts and crafts as Native American and permission to apply for grants that are specifically reserved for Native Americans. However, gaining recognition as a tribe is extremely difficult and includes the requirement to submit extensive genealogical proof of tribal descent as well as continuous existence as a tribe since 1900.

In addition to the 566 federally recognized nations, a number of tribes are recognized by individual states, but not by the federal government. The rights and benefits associated with state recognition vary from state to state. State recognition is based on tribal organizations located within specific state boundaries, which is based on historical and mutual relationships established by state legislatures or executive actions by state governors. As an example, North

Carolina has established the North Carolina Indian Commission, with representation from the state and federally recognized tribes within its jurisdiction. Other states, such as Maine, South Carolina, and Georgia, have recognized tribes within their jurisdiction with commissions or staff in the governor's office or another administrative office to deal with Native concerns.

Cultural Preservation

Increased sovereignty for many Native nations also means increased control over the way that cultural resources are maintained and preserved. In many Native nations and communities across the country, huge efforts are being made to preserve culture by developing programs both inside and outside of the schools to teach Native youth such things as traditional arts and crafts, the language, ceremonies and prayers, songs and chants, as well as dance. Many of these programs began as remedial efforts in programs such as residential youth treatment centers and sobriety programs for all ages. As the efficacy of such programs has become evident, the popularity of these efforts has grown. This cultural appreciation impulse lies in distinct contrast to the previously accepted mainstream notion of only one or two generations ago that "civilizing" Indians was essential. That "civilizing" was done through mandated, largely Christian, government-supported Indian boarding schools, whose primary objective was to strip Native youth of any cultural Indian foundation.

There have been very positive advances in cultural preservation since the passage of the Indian Civil Rights Act of 1968 (which settled some sovereignty and jurisdiction issues), the Indian Education Act of 1972 (which provides funding to help educators learn how to better serve Native American and Alaska Native students), the Indian Religious Freedom Act of 1978 (which protects the practice of Native American religions), and similar legislation in many states. Overall, Native communities across the United States and Canada are seeking to transcend experiences of trauma and loss by embracing cultural practices informed by evidence (Spicer et al., 2012). In fact, Crazy Bull proposed a Native American community research agenda as one that "preserves, maintains, and restores our traditions and cultural practices. . . . We are intensely interested in understanding our circumstances and how our families and communities came to be where they are today" (Galliher, Tsethlikai, & Stolle, 2012, p. 67).

Local programs in tribal communities often operate under a mandate to promote the wellness of Native American tribal members by restoring cultural integrity, eliminating existing disparities in health and development, maintaining sensitivity to and respecting the historical context, respecting tribal sovereignty, building community trust, and fostering ongoing responsibility to tribal members and to the betterment of the tribal community overall (Spicer et al., 2012). Local efforts by tribal communities to preserve and promote their culture have shown positive outcomes by reducing existing health disparities. Given the popularity and effectiveness of community-based participatory research, there are three general efforts happening in Native communities around intervention and inquiry that focus on community engagement and cultural preservation: the American Indian and Alaska Native Head Start Research Center (AIANHSRC); the Circles of Care Initiative; and the American Indian Life Skills Development Curriculum (AILSDC).

First, in the area of education, the American Indian and Alaska Native Head Start Research Center (AIANHSRC) developed out of the unique need and cultural demands of research on Head Start in Native communities, many of which exist in more isolated areas and serve young children who may encounter violence and substance abuse in the home at very early ages, and whose family may be struggling with having or keeping a home, education, and jobs (Spicer et al., 2012). With this in mind, the Office of Planning, Research, and Evaluation at the Administration for Children and Families (ACF) funded AIANHSRC in an effort to coordinate community-based participatory research activities (Allen, Mohatt, Markstrom, Byers, & Novins, 2012). These efforts have focused on producing Native researchers, developing tools for the appropriate assessment of Native children and families, and creating programs designed to assess the true strengths and weaknesses of Native students and teachers while being sensitive to unique cultural factors.

Second, in the area of mental health, the Substance Abuse and Mental Health Services Administration funded the Circles of Care Initiative with the overall goal of providing rural and urban Native communities with tools and resources to plan, implement, and evaluate holistic, community-based systems of care to support mental health and wellness for Native children, youth, and families from a culturally responsive perspective (Spicer et al., 2012). More specifically, this initiative is intended to (a) support the development of mental health service delivery models designed by Native communities to achieve outcomes for their children that they choose for themselves; (b) position tribes, tribal groups, or villages advantageously for future service system implementation and development; (c) strengthen the capacity of tribes, tribal groups, or villages for evaluating their own service system's effectiveness; and (d) develop a body of knowledge to assist tribal and other policy-makers and program planners for all child-serving systems with improving systems of care for the Native population overall (Jumper-Thurman, Allen, & Deters, 2004). The focus has been on developing partnerships of community leaders and members with agency leaders and staff to reduce mental health stigma, improve relationships between provider groups, address service capacity issues, and increase cultural competence in the overall system at the tribal, county, state, and federal levels (Jumper-Thurman et al., 2004; Novins, LeMaster, Jumper-Thurman, & Plested, 2004).

Third, the American Indian Life Skills Development Curriculum (AILSDC) has been widely used with an overall purpose of assisting Native adolescents in developing the tools they need to effectively deal with life's challenges. The basic function of the AILSDC is to reduce adolescent suicide by addressing essential risk factors and empowering Native youth. This process of empowerment occurs by teaching prosocial and problem-solving behaviors while replacing avoidant coping strategies such as social isolation and substance abuse (Spicer et al., 2012). Again, the overall goal of this approach according to LaFromboise and Lewis (2008) is to provide intervention strategies compatible with cultural and community values, strengths, and needs for any specific tribal groups in a way that emphasizes the specific cultural teachings, language, and overall worldview. Again, the focus has been developing partnerships of community leaders and members with practitioners and researchers. Taken together, these three efforts clearly emphasize the need for and effectiveness of community collaboration and interventions that emphasize cultural strengths in order to compensate for the ongoing wounds inflicted by historical trauma on the individual, family, community, and tribe (Fitzgerald & Farrell, 2012).

Achievement Gap

The American education system has had a devastating impact on Native American people, their families, and their tribal communities. The original goal of Indian education was summed up best by Henry Pratt, who established the most famous government boarding school, called

Carlisle Indian School, in 1879. Pratt's motto was "Kill the Indian, save the man" (see Pratt, 1978). However, Lewis Meriam (1928) set the stage for a major shift in attitude toward Indian issues in a report published by the Institute for Government Research Studies in Administration. Meriam pointed out that assimilation policies proved to be destructive to Indian children. For Native American students, the discontinuity among cultural values seems to have its greatest impact around the fourth grade, at which point academic performance has a tendency to begin to steadily decline, eventually leading to academic failure and the dropout of numerous students during the high school years (Garrett et al., 2014). The goals, purpose, value and behavioral expectations, and sequence of learning processes in a traditional Native American approach to education and socialization differ vastly from, and are in direct conflict with, the mainstream U.S. educational approach (Kirmayer et al., 2011). The additional stress associated with achieving a meaningful sense of personal-cultural identity during the adolescent years presents many Native American students with the constant challenge of reconciling cultural differences in personal values and educational expectations (Grayshield & Mihecoby, 2010). Therefore, the period leading up to and during grades 9 to 11 is critical because the majority of Native American students drop out of school around the 10th grade (Garrett, Torres-Rivera, Dixon, & Myers, 2009) when Native adolescents' traditional choices and values are challenged.

Research shows that the achievement gap, defined as a difference between test scores of low-income or ethnic minority students and their majority counterparts, begins early in a Native American student's academic career and broadens with time. When looking at scores of large-scale standardized tests from students with different ethnic backgrounds, such as Native American students, the evidence of an achievement gap becomes clear. Within this gap, Native students perform at least two grade levels below their White peers in reading and math. According to BigFoot and Funderburk (2011) and Garrett, Portman, et al. (2011), Native American students often enter school unprepared to learn. As they proceed throughout the grades with the gap widening, dropout rates increase as well (Freeman & Fox, 2005). According to a 2008 report of the National Caucus of Native American State legislators, Native American students are "237 percent more likely to drop out of school and 207 percent more likely to be expelled than White students" (p. 5). Testing has become the primary focus for determining academic success with the passage of the No Child Left Behind Act (NCLB) in 2001 and continues with its successor, Every Student Succeeds Act, in 2015. As a result, public schools across the nation appear to have abandoned any efforts to include the culture, language, and traditions of the AI/AN students they serve. With little to no consultation with tribes, Native communities, and parents of Native children, resources have focused solely on increasing test scores in the core curriculum areas. Many states have increased the use of testing under this federal mandate. Nichols, Glass, and Berliner (2006) found no convincing evidence that students' academic achievement benefited from the intense focus of meeting standardized test requirements but rather produced great amounts of pressure leading to more problems. They further indicated that "problems associated with high-stakes testing will disproportionately affect America's minority students" (p. ii). Moreover, there is evidence that innovative classroom teaching has been seriously compromised by the pressure of testing students to meet adequate yearly progress (AYP).

Research regarding the formal education of Native American students suggests that the traditional value orientation of these students remains in constant conflict with the value orientation on which U.S. school systems function (Capriccioso, 2005; Garrett, Portman, et al., 2011). Thus, these students often experience poor academic achievement, poor self-concept, low self-esteem, and higher rates of educational attrition (Garrett, Portman, et al., 2011; Garrett et al., 2009). Native American students have dropout rates twice the national average—the highest rate of any U.S. ethnic or racial group (Capriccioso, 2005; Garrett, Portman, et al., 2011). Also, boredom in school and difficulty with teacher and peer relationships are among a few of the reasons for Native American high school students dropping out before graduation (Capriccioso, 2005; Garrett et al., 2009). These statistics suggest that both the quality of relational interactions in schools and the content and presentation of curricula play important roles in the degree of cultural conflict experienced by Native American students.

Literature does not support one clear cause of the achievement gap but indicates there may be several common themes outside the classroom that lead to achievement gaps for students of Native American descent, such as culture and identity, discrimination and institutional oppression, and negotiations of duality (Grande, 2015). The boarding school experience and government oversight created generations of historical trauma. Through the tribal school experience, many tribes are making specific efforts to incorporate culturally based learning such as language immersion, tribal cultural arts and crafts, storytelling traditions, and mentoring by elders in regular classrooms and the general curriculum with successful results. Overall, it has become increasingly clear that if specific attention is not given to cultural and traditional ways of teaching Native American students by policy makers, the achievement gap will continue to widen, with serious implications for the well-being of Native communities throughout the United States. Cultural degradation has served as the greatest barrier to academic achievement for Native American students. Continuing implementation of current Indian education policies and research in culturally based programs is critical in meeting the culturally related academic needs of Native students.

Gaming

When it comes to cultural perceptions of Native people in modern times, one of the biggest issues that comes to mind for many non-Native people is gaming. Native American gaming operations create a stream of revenue that those communities have been using as leverage to build diversified economies. Although many Native American tribes have casinos and/or bingo halls, the cultural impact of the Native American gaming industry is still controversial. Some tribes, such as the Winnemem Wintu of California, have refused to participate in gaming on the grounds that casinos and their proceeds are destructive to traditional cultures that have existed throughout time without the need for dependence on such things.

Although the gaming industry has become a major source of income and economic development for many Native American nations as well as controversy and scandal for some, the challenge for many tribes at this point is how to maintain positive revenue streams and plan for the future so that the growth continues in a positive way, to benefit the people beyond a limited number of extremely successful tribes who have chosen to participate in gaming. Currently in the United States, there are around 400 Native American gaming establishments operated by approximately 220 federally recognized tribes and generating revenues of around $18.5 billion (Garrett et al., 2009). Most of the revenues generated in the Native American gaming industry are from casinos located in, or near, large metropolitan areas such as those in California and other more heavily populated areas of the west coast, which is one of the fastest-growing segments for this industry. Moreover, 12% of Indian gaming establishments generate 65% of Indian gaming revenues. The vast majority of tribal casinos are much less financially successful, particularly those in the Midwest and Great Plains.

Tribal Resources

When considering tribal resources, it is first important to understand what is the most important environmental and spiritual resource from a Native perspective—the land. Although most of the Native population resides in urban areas, reservations, which are lands set aside by the federal government at various points in history for tribes based on treaty agreements, continue to be the primary center of Native traditionalism and cultural preservation. Federally recognized reservations total approximately 55 million acres; however, 11 million acres (20%) within reservation boundaries are owned by non-Indians. This land base provides many Native nations with an array of resources from which to benefit the people and also with a number of challenges about how to maintain, protect, or expand that land base. According to Russell (2004), there are 44 million acres in range and grazing; 5.3 million acres of commercial forest; 2.5 million acres of crop area; 4% of U.S. oil and gas reserves; 40% of U.S. uranium deposits; 30% of western coal reserves; and $2 billion in trust royalty payments.

Native American communities have prevailed in some legal battles ensuring recognition of rights to self-determination and to use of natural resources. In 2009, the federal government agreed to pay $1.4 billion to Native Americans as a result of the mismanagement of Native American land going back to the Dawes Act of 1877. The agreement is subject to Congressional and Federal Court approval. Then, in 2010, the Obama administration announced a $760 million settlement to resolve charges by thousands of Native American farmers and ranchers who say that for decades the Agriculture Department discriminated against them in loan programs. On November 19, 2010, Congress approved a payment of $4.5 billion to both Native Americans (who will get $3.4 billion) and African Americans (who will get $1.14 billion) to settle the Agriculture Department land dispute discrimination case. President Obama signed the law shortly thereafter. Despite some gains, many tribes are locked in heated legal battles with the government and private interests to maintain and protect treaty-based rights to their homelands and sacred sites that are continually being encroached on by outside interests.

Sacred Sites, Repatriation, and Reburial

One of the unique features of traditional Native American religions is the emphasis placed on space rather than time. What this denotes is the importance of the land and existing environment as a source of spiritual power and truths. Native people have sacred places and go to these sacred places to pray, fast, seek visions, conduct ceremonies, receive guidance from spirit guides, and teach youth the traditional ways. Many physical conditions such as dams, fencing, roads, mining, hydroelectric plants, urban housing, tourism, vandalism, and the spraying and logging of trees inextricably affect sacred sites. Unfortunately, many of the sacred sites revered by Native people do not exist under their control, but instead are under the control of federal agencies intent on using the land for the purpose of tourism development, clear-cutting, and uranium mining. Examples of sacred sites include the following:

- Blue Lake, NM (preserved), sacred to the Taos Pueblo
- Kootenai Falls, MT (preserved), sacred to the Kootanai Indians of Montana, Idaho, and British Columbia
- Mount Adams, WA (preserved), sacred to the Yakima
- Badger-Two Medicine, MT (endangered), sacred to the Blackfeet, threatened by companies wanting to drill for oil and gas
- Canyon Mine, AZ (endangered), sacred to the Havasupai, threatened by uranium mining that is permitted by the U.S. Forest Service

- Medicine Wheel, WY (endangered), sacred to the Arapaho, Blackfeet, Crow, Cheyenne, Lakota, and Shoshone, threatened by proposed measures by the U.S. Forest Service to develop the area as a tourist attraction and promote logging activities in the vicinity
- Mount Graham, AZ (endangered), sacred to the San Carlos Apache, threatened by construction of a seven-telescope observatory
- Celilo Falls, OR (desecrated), sacred to the Umatilla, Nez Perce, Yakima, and Warm Springs Indians, flooded by the Dalles Dam, which was completed in 1957
- Rainbow Natural Bridge, UT (desecrated), sacred to the Navajo, Paiute, and Pueblos, destroyed by completion of the Glen Canyon Dam on the Colorado River in 1963 and the rising of Lake Powell
- San Francisco Peaks, AZ (desecrated), sacred to the Apaches, Hopis, Navajos, and Zunis, destroyed by the development of the Snow Bowl, a portion of the peaks used for downhill skiing

Many of these sites form the cornerstone of Native religious traditions and cannot be replaced. Therefore, many legal efforts are being undertaken by tribes across the country to protect and preserve not only the sacred sites on which their culture is based, but also to protect and preserve their very way of life from generations past.

Among the many sacred sites disturbed or destroyed by such things as erosion and flooding, plowing, urban development, road building, land-clearing, logging, and vandalism have been the ancient graves of Native people. Perhaps worst of all has been the desecration of Native graves by pothunters and vandals seeking to loot those graves for objects that are valued in national and international markets. It has been estimated that grave desecration and looting of Native graves reached its peak in the 1980s. Outraged by such disregard and violations of sacred areas, Native American nations demanded the immediate return of all that was rightfully theirs, including skeletal remains, burial goods, and sacred objects. In the end, Native people have persevered through the passage of critical legislation that now protects Native gravesites from looting and provides Native people with legal means for reclaiming both remains and sacred objects. Many of these remains and objects have been ceremonially returned to their original sites when possible under the careful guidance and blessing of tribal elders and Medicine people.

Mascot Issues

As many tribes continue to move toward increased sovereignty and consequent pride in their ethnicity, land and natural resources are only part of the concern. A constant source of controversy between Native peoples and non-Natives in both the United States and Canada has been sports mascots depicting Native Americans in a derogatory manner. Americans have a long history of "playing Indian" that dates back to at least the 18th century and has tended to be based on a stereotypical, romanticized image of the heroic Native American warrior. For the most part, Native mascot images fall into one of two categories: the hostile, warlike Indian; or the dopey, clown-like figure with headdress, big nose, red skin, and big lips, among other stereotypical features. As such, many Native Americans and human rights groups think that the use of Indian mascots is both offensive and demeaning. The question remains, in a day and age where social mores and laws exist to protect the dignity and basic human rights of all groups of peoples, why it is still acceptable to exploit images of Native people this way. Professional, college, and high school sports teams across the country have been challenged to do away with stereotypical, racist images of Native people as mascots, including baseball's Atlanta Braves and Cleveland Indians; football's Washington Redskins; and college sports'

Florida State University Seminoles. Many universities (e.g., North Dakota Fighting Sioux of the University of North Dakota) and professional sports teams (e.g., usage of Chief Wahoo by the Cleveland Indians has diminished but not ended altogether) no longer use such images without consultation with Native American nations. Some tribal team names have been approved by the tribe in question, such as the Seminole Tribe of Florida who approved the use of their name for Florida State University athletic teams. Others ended use of offensive mascots altogether including Stanford University, which changed from Indians to Cardinal in 1972; Miami University, which switched from Redskins to RedHawks in 1997; and the NBA's Golden State Warriors, who originally used Native American-themed logos but have not since 1971. In spite of changes by high-profile sports organizations, some lower-level schools' sports teams continue to use such images and remain under scrutiny by those who maintain that such practices are offensive and perpetuate negative racial stereotypes.

NATIVE AMERICAN CULTURE AND VALUES

Native Americans represent a diversity illustrated, for example, by over 150 different languages. At the same time, a prevailing sense of "Indianness" based on common worldview and many similar experiences in history seems to bind Native Americans together as a people of many peoples (Garrett et al., 2009). Like other groups, Native people's relationship with their cultural heritage and ethnicity can vary with regard to acceptance and commitment to specific tribal values, beliefs, and traditional practices (Garrett, Portman, et al., 2011; Garrett et al., 2009). Those differences are related to variations in (a) level of acculturation, (b) geographic setting (urban, rural, or reservation), and (c) socioeconomic status (Garrett et al., 2009). Although acculturation plays a major factor in Native American worldview, there tends to be a high degree of psychological homogeneity, a certain degree of shared cultural standards and meanings, based on common core values that exist for traditional Native Americans across tribal groups.

Several authors have described common core values that characterize Native traditionalism across tribal nations. Some of these Native traditional values (see Table 13.1) are the importance of community contribution, sharing, acceptance, cooperation, harmony and balance, noninterference, extended family, attention to nature, immediacy of time, awareness of the relationship, and a deep respect for elders (Garrett, Garrett, & Melton, 2009; Hunter & Sawyer, 2006; Rybak, Eastin, & Robbins, 2004). All in all, these traditional values show the importance of honoring, through harmony and balance, what Native people believe to be a very sacred connection with the energy of life and the whole of biodiversity; this is the basis for a traditional Native worldview and spirituality across tribal nations.

Harmony and Balance

Different tribal languages have different words or ways of referring to the idea of honoring one's sense of connection. However, the meaning of honoring connection is similar across nations in referring to the belief that human beings exist on Mother Earth to be helpers and protectors of life. In Native communities, it is not uncommon, for example, to hear people use the term *caretaking* to refer to a desired way of life. Therefore, from the perspective of a traditionalist, to see one's purpose as being that of caretaker is to accept responsibility for the gift of life by taking good care of that gift, the gift of life that others have received, and the surrounding beauty of the world in which one lives (Garrett, Portman, et al., 2011).

TABLE 13.1 Comparison of Cultural Values and Expectations

Traditional Native American	Contemporary Mainstream American
Harmony with nature	Power over nature
Cooperation	Competition
Group needs more important	Personal goals more important
Privacy and noninterference; try to control self, not others	Need to control and affect others
Self-discipline both in body and mind	Self-expression and self-disclosure
Participation after observation (only when certain of ability)	Trial-and-error learning, new skills practiced until mastery
Explanation according to nature	Scientific explanation for everything
Reliance on extended family	Reliance on experts
Emotional relationships valued	Concerned mostly with facts
Patience encouraged (allow others to go first)	Aggressiveness and competitiveness encouraged
Humility	Fame and recognition; winning
Win once, let others win also	Win first prize all the time
Follow the old ways	Climb the ladder of success; importance of progress
Discipline distributed among many; no one person takes blame	Blame one person at cost to others
Physical punishment rare	Physical punishment accepted
Present-time focus	Future-time focus
Time is always with us	Clock-watching
Present goals considered important; future accepted as it comes	Plan for future and how to get ahead
Encourage sharing freely and keeping only enough to satisfy present needs	Private property; encourage acquisition of material comfort and saving for the future
Speak softly, at a slower rate	Speak louder and faster
Avoid singling out the listener	Address listener directly (by name)
Interject less	Interrupt frequently
Use less "encouraging signs" (uh-huh, head nodding)	Use verbal encouragement
Delay response to auditory messages	Use immediate response
Nonverbal communication	Verbal skills highly prized

Source: Adapted from Garrett and Pichette (2000).

Like anyone, the spiritual beliefs of any individual Native American depend on a number of factors, including her or his level of acculturation, geographic region, family structure, religious influences, and tribally specific traditions (Garrett, Portman, et al., 2011; Garrett et al., 2009). However, it is possible to generalize, to some extent, about a number of basic beliefs characterizing Native American traditionalism and spirituality across tribal nations. The following, adapted from a classic book by Locust (1988, pp. 317–318), elaborates on a number of basic Native American spiritual and traditional beliefs:

- There is a single higher power known as Creator, Great Creator, Great Spirit, or Great One, among other names (this being is sometimes referred to in gender form, but does not necessarily exist as one particular gender or another). There are also lesser beings known as *spirit beings* or *spirit helpers*.
- Plants and animals, like humans, are part of the spirit world. The spirit world exists side by side with, and intermingles with, the physical world. Moreover, the spirit existed in the spirit world before it came into a physical body and will exist after the body dies.
- Human beings are made up of a spirit, mind, and body. The mind, body, and spirit are all interconnected; therefore, illness affects the mind and spirit, as well as the body.
- Wellness is harmony in body, mind, and spirit; unwellness is disharmony in mind, body, and spirit.
- Natural unwellness is caused by the violation of a sacred social or natural law of Creation (e.g., participating in a sacred ceremony while under the influence of alcohol, drugs, or having had sex within four days of the ceremony).
- Unnatural unwellness is caused by conjuring (witchcraft) from those with destructive intentions.
- Each of us is responsible for our own wellness by keeping ourselves attuned to self, relations, environment, and universe.

To better understand more generally what it means to "walk in step" according to Native American spirituality, it is important to discuss four basic cultural elements: medicine, harmony, relation, and vision.

MEDICINE *Everything is alive.* In many Native American tribal languages there is no word for religion because spiritual practices are an integral part of every aspect of daily life, which is necessary for the harmony and balance, or wellness, of individual, family, clan, and community (Garrett, Portman, et al., 2011). Healing and worship are considered one and the same. For Native American people, the concept of health and wellness is not only a physical state, but a spiritual one as well. **Medicine**, as a Native concept, implies the very essence of our being, or the life force that exists in all creatures on Mother Earth (Deloria, 2006; Garrett et al., 2009; Garrett, Portman, et al., 2011; Hunter & Sawyer, 2006). In the traditional way, Medicine can consist of physical remedies such as herbs, teas, and poultices for physical ailments, but Medicine is simultaneously something much more than a pill taken to cure illness, get rid of pain, or correct a physiological malfunction. Medicine is everywhere. It is that which gives inner power.

HARMONY *Everything has purpose.* Every living organism has a reason for being. Traditional Native Americans look on life as a gift from the Creator. As such, it is to be treated with the utmost care out of respect for the giver. This means living in a humble way and giving thanks for all the gifts that one receives every day, no matter how big or small. **Harmony** is also represented by numbers. Native American spirituality often places great emphasis on the numbers four and seven. The number four represents the spirit of each of the directions—east, south, west, and north—usually depicted in a circle. The number seven represents the same four directions as well as the upper world (Sky), lower world (Earth), and center (often referring to the heart, or sacred fire) to symbolize universal harmony and balance (visualized as a sphere). In the traditional way, Native people seek to understand what lessons are offered to them by giving thanks to each of the four directions for the wisdom, guidance, strength, and clarity that they receive. Not every tribe practices the directions in this way, but almost all tribes have some representation of the four directions as a circular symbol of the harmony and balance of mind, body, and spirit with the natural environment (and spirit world).

RELATION *All things are connected.* Central to Native American spiritual traditions is the importance of "relation" as a total way of existing in the world. The concept of family extends to brothers and sisters in the animal world, the plant world, the mineral world, Mother Earth, and Father Sky, to name some examples. Respect for **relation** also means practicing respect for the interconnection that humans share. Across tribal nations, certain natural or social laws must be observed out of respect for relation. These often point to restrictions on personal conduct in relation to such things as death, incest, the female menstrual cycle, witchcraft, certain animals, certain natural phenomena, certain foods, marrying into one's own clan, and strict observance of ceremonial protocol (Deloria, 2006; Garrett, Portman, et al., 2011). A general guideline in Native tradition is that you (a) never take more than you need, (b) give thanks for what you have or what you receive, (c) take great care to use all of what you do have, and (d) give away what you do not need (or what someone else may need more than you).

VISION *Embrace the medicine of every living being.* Across tribal nations, many different ceremonies are used for healing, giving thanks, celebrating, clearing the way, and blessing (Garrett et al., 2009). Among the various ceremonies are the sweat lodge, vision quest, clearing-way ceremony, blessing-way ceremony, pipe ceremony, sunrise ceremony, and sundance (Deloria, 2006; Garrett, Portman, et al., 2011). One of the functions of ceremonial practice is to reaffirm one's sense of connection with that which is sacred. By contrast, a major tenet of American mainstream ideology is that the purpose of life consists of "life, liberty, and the pursuit of happiness." From a traditional Native perspective, a corollary would be "life, love, and the pursuit of harmony." Understanding one's **vision** is understanding the direction of one's path as a caretaker moving to the rhythm of the sacred heartbeat.

Cultural Identity and the Tribal Nation

In a very real sense, Native American individuals are extensions of their tribal nation—socially, emotionally, historically, and politically. For many Indian people, cultural identity is rooted in tribal membership, community, and heritage rather than in personal achievements, social or financial status, or acquired possessions. Many children of Native tribes, such as the Cherokee, trace their heritage through the mother or grandmother, and the social structure of the tribe may place more emphasis on power held by women. However, there are those who follow patriarchal/patrilineal ways too (or other variations of gender dominance and tracing of family heritage). This pattern of heritage and social/political power, in turn, affects not only social structure and functioning of the community, but also that of the family/clan. The extended family (at least three generations) and tribal group take precedence over all other affiliations.

The tribe is an interdependent system of people who perceive themselves to be part of the greater whole (i.e., the tribe) rather than to be a whole consisting of individual parts. This principle is expressed in traditional Native people judging themselves and their actions according to whether or not they are benefiting the tribal community and its continued harmonious functioning. In mainstream American society, worth and status are based on "what you do" or "what you have achieved." For Native Americans, "who you are is where you come from." Native Americans essentially believe that, "If you know my family, clan, or tribe, then you know me." As a result, traditional Native people might be likely to describe some aspect of their family or tribal heritage when asked to talk about themselves.

Family

In contrast to the popular conversational question in majority culture when two people meet for the first time, "What do you do?" many Native people may ask, "Where do you come from? Who's your family? To whom do you belong? Who are your people?" The speaker's intent is to find out where she or he stands in relation to this new person, and what commonality exists. In fact, this is a simple way of building bridges—or recognizing bridges that already exist, but that are as yet unknown. Family may or may not consist of blood relatives. It is common practice in the Indian way, for instance, to claim a non-blood-related person as a relative, thereby welcoming him or her as a real family member. From that point on, that person is a relative, and that is that. After all, family can be a matter of both blood and spirit.

In the traditional way, the prevalence of cooperation and sharing in the spirit of community is essential for harmony and balance. It is not unusual for a Native child to be raised in several different households over time. This is generally not due to a lack of caring or responsibility, but because it is both an obligation and a pleasure to share in raising and caring for the children in one's family (Harper, 2011; Hunter & Sawyer, 2006). Grandparents, aunts, uncles, and other members of the community are all responsible for the raising of children, and they take this responsibility very seriously (BigFoot & Funderburk, 2011).

Wisdom Keepers

Native elders are the keepers of the sacred ways. They are protectors, mentors, teachers, and support-givers. Native communities honor their elders as the "Keepers of the Wisdom" for their lifetime's worth of knowledge and experience. Elders have always played an important part in the continuance of the tribal community by functioning in the role of parent, teacher, community leader, and spiritual guide (Harper, 2011). To refer to an elder as Grandmother, Grandfather, Uncle, Aunt, "Old Woman," or "Old Man" is to refer to a very special relationship that exists with that elder, characterized by deep respect and admiration.

There is a very special kind of relationship based on mutual respect and caring between Indian elders and Indian children as one moves through the Life Circle from birth to old age. With increased age comes an increase in the sacred obligation to family, clan, and tribe. Native American elders pass on to the children the notion that their own life force carries the spirits of their ancestors (Hunter & Sawyer, 2006). With such an emphasis on connectedness, Native traditions revere children, not only as ones who will carry on the wisdom and traditions, but also as "little people" who are still very close to the spirit world and from whom we have much to learn. The following anecdote from Brendtro, Brokenleg, and Van Bockern (1990) illustrates the importance of being a caretaker within Native culture as a manifestation of family: "In a conversation with his aging grandfather, a young Indian man asked, 'Grandfather, what is the purpose of life?' After a long time in thought, the old man looked up and said, 'Grandson, children are the purpose of life. We were once children and someone cared for us, and now it is our time to care'" (p. 45).

Humility

Boasting of one's accomplishments and loud behavior that attracts attention to oneself are discouraged in the traditional way. In the traditional value system, self-absorption and self-importance are seen as bringing disharmony on oneself and one's family. In the life circle, the group must take precedence over the individual. And, as discussed earlier, the wisdom of age takes precedence over youth, although age does not make anyone better or more worthy than anyone else. Many times, a traditional Native person may drop his or her head and eyes or at least be careful not to look into the eyes of another as a sign of respect for any elder or other honored person. No one is worthy of staring into the eyes of an elder or looking into the spirit of that honored person. This deferential behavior is also an act that signifies that a person does not view him- or herself as better than anyone else.

Generosity

Traditional Native views concerning property accentuate the underlying belief that "whatever belongs to the individual also belongs to the group," and vice versa. It should come as no surprise to see Native people sharing and/or giving "their possessions" away to others in certain circumstances such as Giveaway ceremonies practiced by many nations. Generosity is considered a sign of wisdom and humility.

Patience

In the Native worldview, everything has its place. Very often, it is simply a matter of time before one recognizes where and how things fit together. In Native traditions, there is a sacred design to the world in which humans live, a design to the process of life itself. And, very often, it is not a matter of whether "things" fall into place, but whether humans' capacity for *awareness and understanding of "things"* falls into place. It is therefore important to be able to learn through careful observation, listening, and patience, as well as asking questions or thinking things through. Everything offers us a valuable lesson, from all our surroundings to each of our experiences. It takes time and a special kind of willingness or openness to receive all the lessons that are offered to us throughout life. Many Native elders will share with younger people how important it is to talk less so you can hear more, for example.

Time

In the traditional Indian view, humans do not always have to live by the clock. Mother Earth has her own unique rhythms, which signal the beginnings and endings of things. One need only observe and listen quietly to know when it is time. So-called Indian time says that things begin when they are ready, and things end when they are finished. For example, a ceremony or gathering might be set to begin at sunrise, per se, rather than a specific "clock time," and end whenever sufficient time has been spent to complete what needed to be done. In that sense, the American Indian view of time is similar to that of all rural people over the world, where tasks and natural rhythms dictate time.

Communication Style

Native interaction style emphasizes nonverbal communication over verbal communication. Moderation in speech and avoidance of direct eye contact are nonverbal communicators of respect for the listener, especially if it is a respected elder or anyone in a position of authority

(Garrett, Portman, et al., 2011). Careful listening and observation are exercised to understand more of what is meant and less of what is actually said. Storytelling is commonly used to express feelings, beliefs, and the importance of experience (Deloria, 2006). Oral recitation is common. It is a time when listeners are expected to be silent, patient, and reflective.

In an attempt to be respectful of harmony, traditional Native people practice self-discipline through silence, modesty, and patience. Direct confrontation is avoided, as it disrupts the harmony and balance that are essential in keeping good relations. There are believed to be more effective ways to deal with discrepancies and dissatisfaction. Cooperation and sharing, as a reflection of harmony, are an important part of interacting with others. By contrast, individuals in the dominant American culture are rewarded for being outgoing and "assertive." Such behaviors as asking questions, interrupting, speaking for others, telling others what to do, or arguing are fairly common in mainstream society. These behaviors severely contradict what traditional Native people have been taught are respectful and appropriate ways of interacting with others (BigFoot & Funderburk, 2011).

Being

Native tradition ("the Medicine Way") emphasizes a unique sense of "being" that allows one to live in accord with the natural flow of life-energy. *Being* says, "It's enough just to be; our purpose in life is to develop the inner self in relation to everything around us." Being receives much of its power from connectedness. Belonging and connectedness lie at the very heart of where Indian people came from, who they are, and to whom they belong. True "being" requires that individuals know and experience their connections, and that they honor their relations with all their heart. So, for many traditional Native people, the relationship with someone is much more important than any personal accomplishment, and as a result, the strength of a person's inner peace and presence in the here-and-now would say more to a traditional Native person than anything else. Voices from the Field 13.1 provides an example of the Native tradition of being, which highlights the role of nature as Medicine.

Voices from the Field 13.1

It's Not the Medicine That Does the Work

Well, my grandfather passed on, matter of fact, he died of cancer. And that's something that really bothered me because I couldn't understand, if he was such a powerful Medicine Man, such a powerful spiritual man, why'd he have to die? Why didn't he have Medicine to cure him? 'Cause he told me, and I do remember this, he said, "There's a plant, there's Medicine for everything. Anything that ever happens to you in your life, there's always a special plant out there for it, all you have to do is go out and seek it, go out and find it."

So I kept thinking, you know, I was so angry when my grandfather died, why didn't he seek it? You know, he always told me there was. And I guess that's one of the first times that I suddenly realized that people die anyway. That was a concept that I couldn't understand. If we've got Medicine, why were people dying? If we've got cures, why would people die? Why would so many people die of influenza, 'cause see, keep in mind, that was a period of time when a lot of people would die every year because of influenza—flu. Also, for me, that was a period of time when there

(Continued)

was diseases like polio, and I had a good friend of mine, matter of fact, who got polio. And I couldn't understand, if we've got all this Medicine. . . .

So I remember, one of the first things I was thinking was why wouldn't people share more? And I remember, I asked one of my uncles, "Why didn't he find his own Medicine?," 'cause I know they had cancer cures' 'cause I remember something about curing everything, and I didn't know what "cancer" was. Matter of fact, back then, they used to call it "consumption," and people died of "consumption" or some other name for a disease. My uncle, oh and by the way this was Tingaling Rogers, and Tingaling went through the Baton Death March during WWII, a decorated soldier like many of my uncles who were in the war at that time. But Tingaling had pretty much survived on what he could find, and he knew plants, he knew how to prepare plants, knew how fix them, knew how to cook them, he knew how to use them for Medicine. And he told me a number of times that's what helped him to survive. He'd always volunteer for details to go out and work in the hardest, hottest, worst work you'd do, working with digging up plants and cutting up logs, 'cause what he'd do is he'd scrape part of the bark off the tree for Medicine. And he'd know what kind of plant it was by something that he called "similars."

Even to this day, Cherokees feel that there's a similar plant for everything that ails you. If it's your heart, it'll be shaped like a heart leaf, if it's your liver, it'll be shaped like a spade, things like that. He told me, he said, "you know, one thing you have to learn is that when it's somebody's time, and everybody has their own time, it's not the Medicine that does the work, it's the person who has to do the work . . . and even with the Medicine, you have to seek your own Medicine. ~J. T. Garrett, Eastern Band of Cherokee

(Note: J. T. is a 72-year-old enrolled member of the Eastern Band of the Cherokee Nation who currently works as Director of Public Health and Human Services for his tribal nation. He is the oldest of three siblings, and resides on the reservation where he grew up. J. T. was the first member of his nation to receive a doctorate. His first dream was to pursue a career as a high school biology teacher, but he has made a stellar career in industry and public health through both the private and public sectors. At age 51, he had a heart attack [which he still refers to as a "heart opportunity"] that forced his retirement from many years of service in the Indian Health Service. As a Vietnam veteran who struggled for years with recurring, restless, and sometimes violent dreams, these days he spends time reflecting more on his life and on the people he loves and has loved the most, as well as working and advocating for his tribe. One person whom he describes as having the strongest influence on his life was his grandfather, Oscar. His grandfather's death, however, came at an early age, something J. T. still wrestles with, especially now that he has recently become a grandfather as well, and worries about leaving this world too soon as so many of the men in his family have done, including his father.)

LESSONS OF THE EAGLE FEATHER

Eagle feathers are considered to be infinitely sacred among Native Americans. These feathers are used for a variety of purposes, including ceremonial healing and purification. Native traditionalists refer to "Eagle Medicine," which represents a state of being achieved through diligence, understanding, awareness, and completion of "tests of initiation" such as the Vision Quest or other demanding life experiences (Deloria, 2006; Garrett et al., 2009; Garrett, Portman, et al., 2011). Highly respected elder status is associated with Eagle Medicine and the power of connectedness and truth. It is through experience and patience that this Medicine is earned over a lifetime, and through understanding and choice that it is honored. There is an old anecdote that probably best illustrates the lessons of the eagle feather by reminding us about the power of perspective: "Once while acting as a guide for a hunting expedition, an Indian had lost the way home. One of the men with him said, 'You're lost, chief.' The Indian guide replied, 'I'm not lost, my tipi is lost.'"

The Eagle feather represents duality in existence. It tells the story of life by symbolizing harmony and balance through which life has been able to persist. It tells of the many dualities or opposites that exist in the Circle of Life, such as light and dark, male and female, substance and shadow, summer and winter, life and death, peace and war (Garrett, Portman, et al., 2011). The Eagle feather has both light and dark colors, dualities and opposites. Though one can make a choice to argue which of the colors is most beautiful or most valuable, the truth is that both colors come from the same feather, both are true, both are connected, and it takes both to fly. The colors are opposite, but they are part of the same truth. The importance of the feather lies not in which color is most beautiful, but in finding out and accepting what the purpose of the feather as a whole may be. In other words, there is no such thing as keeping the mountains and getting rid of the valleys; they are one and the same, and they exist because of one another.

GUIDELINES FOR COUNSELING NATIVE AMERICAN CLIENTS

In working with most Native American clients, counselors should attend to two early assessment factors: (a) assessing the extent to which the process of acculturation has affected the client's cultural identity, and (b) understanding the influence of oppression on her or his experience and current presenting issues (Robinson-Wood, 2013). Therefore, this section begins with a discussion of issues around identity and oppression. Then it continues with a discussion of the counseling implications of traditions, spirituality, values about opposites and balance, and communication style.

Identity, Family, and Acculturation

A first step in the counseling relationship, and a sign of respect, lies in the counselor finding out from which tribe the client comes, and possibly whether that person is directly affiliated with that tribe (federal, state, and/or community recognition). It is not the job of counselors to pass judgment on who is Indian and who is not. Thus, a counselor should not ask a Native client how much Indian the client is or relate personal stories of Indian heritage in his or her own family as a way of connecting with that client. That is often a quick way to lose a Native person's receptivity and trust. If a client says that he or she is Native, then a counselor must assume that it is so. This acceptance of client self-report is a way to understanding that client without having to get into the painful (and sometimes irrelevant) politics of categorization. More important, it gives the counselor insight into that person's perception of her experience and place in the world.

When working with a Native client, it is important to get a sense of that person's level of acculturation. This sense can be gotten by the counselor informally assessing the client's (a) values (traditional, marginal, bicultural, assimilated, pantraditional); (b) geographic origin/residence (reservation, rural, urban); and (c) tribal affiliation (tribal structure, customs, beliefs).

Both verbal and nonverbal cues will give counselors a good sense of a Native American client's level of acculturation (Scholl, 2006). If questions remain, it is important to pose them in a respectful, unobtrusive way. Following are some examples of general leads intended to respectfully elicit important culturally relevant information:

- Where do you come from?
- Tell me about your family.

- What tribe are you? Tell me a little bit about that.
- Tell me about you as a person, culturally and spiritually.
- Tell me how you identify yourself culturally.
- Tell me how your culture/spirituality plays into how you live your life.
- Tell me about your life as you see it, past, present, or future.

To further determine acculturation and subsequent worldview, the counselor should gather information on the family history and structure, as well as on community of origin versus community of choice. Counselors must avoid making assumptions about the cultural identity of Native American clients without gathering further information about both the internal and external experience of that person. As mentioned earlier, one cannot assume because a person "looks Indian" that he or she is traditional in his or her cultural and spiritual ways, or that, because a person "does not look Indian," he or she is not traditional. Instead, it is important to explore the meaning of the core values and beliefs that characterize what it means to be Native for any given client.

Healing from Historical Trauma and the Impact of Oppression

Given the historical and current context of social and political issues facing Native people, a major underlying and ongoing issue in counseling most Native clients is trust versus mistrust, as it is with many oppressed peoples (Grayshield & Mihecoby, 2010). The question that the counselor must ask herself or himself is, "What can I do to create and maintain trust with a Native client?" It may be time well spent to bring up the topic of oppression with the client, asking him or her to relate experiences that have had an impact on his or her life for better or for worse. Counselors can ask where the client is from and, likewise, where his or her family is from. Counselors might further ask what some of the experiences are across generations that have affected the client and helped to shape how he or she sees the world. Specifically, counselors should inquire about what ways family and intergenerational history might be playing into what has brought the client in for services.

According to Brave Heart (2005), both prevention and treatment need to focus on ameliorating the historical trauma response and fostering a reattachment to traditional Native values, which may serve as protective factors to limit or prevent substance abuse as well as further transmission of trauma across generations. Rekindling or imparting traditional cultural values through intervention and prevention activities promise to promote improved parenting skills and parent–child relationships. Improved relationships across generations may serve as protection against both substance abuse and the transfer of the historical trauma response (Gone, 2009). The focus on helping parents heal from historical trauma and improving parenting skills is one type of intervention. An emphasis on traditional culture may also mitigate substance abuse (Brave Heart, 2005). Native culture traditionally fostering extensive familial and social support networks also offers protection against substance abuse. Native ceremonies often require discipline and commitment, delaying gratification, and provide Native children with healthy role models of skills needed in refusal behavior and healthy defenses against substance use and other risk factors.

One model useful in both prevention and intervention programs is the Historical Trauma and Unresolved Grief intervention (HTUG), which addresses risk and protective factors for substance abuse through group trauma and psychoeducational interventions that seek to restore attachment to traditional values (Brave Heart, 2005; Crazy Thunder & Brave Heart, 2005). Intervention goals are congruent with posttraumatic stress disorder (PTSD) treatment, where a sense of mastery and control are transmitted within a traditional retreat-like setting, providing a safe, affectively containing milieu. Participants in the HTUG model are exposed to content, through audiovisual materials, that stimulate historically traumatic memories; this is done to provide opportunities for cognitive integration of the trauma as well as affective cathartic working through, necessary for healing (Brave Heart, 2005). Small- and large-group processing provide occasions for increasing capacity to tolerate and regulate emotions, trauma mastery, and at least short-term amelioration of historical trauma. Traditional prayer and ceremonies, incorporated throughout the intervention as feasible, afford emotional containment and increased connection to indigenous values and a pretraumatic tribal past. Purification ceremonies have been observed as having a curative effect in PTSD treatment.

Preliminary research on the HTUG model and on its integration into parenting sessions indicated that there was (a) a beginning trauma and grief resolution, including a decrease in hopelessness as well as an increase in joy; (b) an increase in positive tribal identity; (c) an increase in protective factors and a decrease in risk factors for substance abuse; (d) perceived improved parental relationships with children and family relationships across generations; and (e) perceived improvement in parenting skills, family connections, and sensitivity to one's children (Brave Heart, 2000). By educating themselves about the history of tribes from which Native clients come and cutting-edge treatment modalities such as HTUG, counselors can better understand the impact of institutional racism and acculturation, as well as the meaning of the Native American experience for any given client, and begin the process of healing in a way that incorporates culture as a central focus.

Drawing on Traditions

In contrast to many of the traditional Native values and beliefs discussed herein, mainstream American values tend to emphasize self-promotion, saving for the future, domination of others, accomplishment, competition and aggression, individualism and the nuclear family, mastery over nature, a time orientation toward living for the future, a preference for scientific explanations, time-consciousness, winning, and reverence for youth (Garrett et al., 2009; Hunter & Sawyer, 2006). Each of these values contrasts to Native ones. For Native people, there is great potential for cultural conflicts due to a clash of values with those of the larger society. Therefore, exploration of cultural conflicts itself may be an important goal for counseling.

Native clients can be encouraged to talk about the meaning of family, clan, or tribe to them as a way of exploring worldview, especially in light of intergenerational differences or the effects of oppression or presenting issues. Once again, counselors must ask themselves, "What can I do to create and maintain trust with a Native client and create a deeper understanding of his or her individual needs?" Counselors should think about some of the traditional Native values, beliefs, experiences, and traditions related so far in this chapter. They should ask themselves which of these their client holds and in what ways they are played out in his or her life. Further, counselors should consider how to build on their knowledge of these values, beliefs, experiences, and traditions to show understanding, develop rapport, and match interventions.

Integrating Spirituality

A counselor must recognize the vast diversity of spiritual traditions and customs that can be tribally specific, ones that may also have been influenced by or replaced by forms of Christianity or other belief systems. It may be important to let the client express what he or she needs in terms of spiritual support or ceremony and how that might be best achieved within the context of counseling. As stated, Native spirituality manifests itself in many different forms, such as traditional tribal ways, Christian traditions, or Native American Church. With a client who seems to have more traditional values and beliefs, it may be particularly helpful to suggest that family or a Medicine person participate in the process to support the client as he or she moves through important personal transitions and subsequent personal cleansing. It should be noted that a general understanding of Native American spirituality does not prepare a counselor to participate in or conduct Native ceremonies as part of the counseling process (Garrett et al., 2009). That is the responsibility of those who are trained as Native Medicine persons and who also can serve as an important resource to counselors working with Native clients.

Values: Using the Rule of Opposites and Seeking Balance

An understanding of the **Rule of Opposites** is essential for working with Native American clients who may be experiencing dissonance in their lives, but who perceive this in a much different way than might be expected within the majority culture. Asking the right questions and being open to what counselors do not readily perceive bridges the gap between what counselors see and what exists underneath perceived facades. Given the understanding that, from the Native worldview, everything has meaning and purpose, one goal of counseling becomes helping Native clients discover their purpose, examine their assumptions, seek an awareness of universal and personal truths, and make choices that allow them to exist in a state of harmony and balance within the Circle of Life. Talking with the client about his or her powerful cultural symbols, such as the eagle feather, and what these symbols represent to that particular client may help open a dialogue that will give much insight into current issues, internal and external resources, and needed approaches. These discussions may provide insight into potential therapeutic goals for achieving harmony and balance among the four directions: mind, body, spirit, and natural environment.

Communication

Once the counselor has some general information concerning the client's cultural identity, background and experiences, spiritual ways, and specific needs, he or she has a better understanding of what may or may not be considered appropriate with and for the client. The following recommendations (Garrett, Portman, et al., 2011) are intended as culturally alert ways for working with a traditional Native client:

1. *Greeting.* For traditional Native Americans, a gentle handshake is the proper way of greeting. Sometimes, just a word of greeting or head nod is sufficient. To use a firm handshake can be interpreted as an aggressive show of power and a personal insult. It may be important to follow, rather than lead, the client in manner of greeting.
2. *Hospitality.* Given the traditional emphasis on generosity, kindness, and "gifting" as a way of honoring the relationship, hospitality is an important part of Native American life. Therefore, it is helpful to be able to offer the Native client a beverage or snack as a sign of good relation. In the traditional way, to not offer hospitality to a visitor or guest is to bring shame on oneself and one's family.
3. *Silence.* In the traditional way, when two people meet, very little may be said between them during the initial moments of the encounter. Quiet time at the beginning of a

session is an appropriate way of transitioning into the therapeutic process by giving both counselor and client a chance to orient themselves to the situation, get in touch with themselves, and experience the presence of the other person. This brief time (perhaps a couple of minutes or so) can be nonverbal, noninteractive time that allows the client to be at ease. This is an important show of respect, understanding, and patience.

4. *Space.* Taking care to respect physical space is an extension of the principle that one need not always fill relational space with words. In Native tradition, both the physical form and the space between the physical is sacred. In counseling, it is important to respect the physical space of the client by not sitting too close and not sitting directly across from the client, which allows scrutiny of the other. A more comfortable arrangement, traditionally, is sitting together either side by side or in two different chairs at an off angle. The burning of sage, cedar, or sweetgrass (a method of spatial cleansing known as "smudging") is customary, but should only be done at the request or with permission of the Native client.

5. *Eye Contact.* Native American clients with traditional values (and possibly those who are marginal or bicultural) may tend to avert their eyes as a sign of respect. To subtly match this level of eye contact is respectful and shows an understanding of the client's way of being. The eyes are considered to be the pathway to the spirit; therefore to consistently look someone in the eye is to show a level of entitlement or aggression. It is good to glance at someone every once in a while, but listening, in the traditional way, is something that happens with the ears and the heart.

6. *Intention.* One of the biggest issues with many Indian clients in the counseling relationship is trust. This should come as no surprise, given the history of broken promises and exploitation experienced by all tribal nations. Typically, an Indian client will "read" the counselor's nonverbals fairly quickly to determine whether the counselor is someone to be trusted or not. Therefore, counselors can focus on honoring the mental space between counselor and client by seeking to offer respect and humility in the counseling process. Acceptance by the counselor means not trying to control or influence the client. This is considered "bad Medicine."

7. *Collaboration.* In counseling, more traditional Native clients may welcome (or even expect) the counselor to offer helpful suggestions or alternatives. From a traditional perspective, respect for choice is important, but healing is a collaborative process. Therefore, offer suggestions without offering directions. There is a difference between encouraging and pushing. With traditional Native American clients, actions will always speak louder than words.

Humor

Although humor is one of the important Native coping mechanisms, it should only be used if the client invites it, meaning that the client trusts the counselor enough to connect on that level. What, in one situation, can be humor between two people, in another can be interpreted as ridicule or wearing a mask. Counselors therefore have to be sensitive to using humor in a way that does not reinforce various means of oppression that the client has endured probably for all of his or her life.

However, on the opposite side of this issue lies the opportunity to connect with the client on his or her ground and share a powerful trust through humor that seems appropriate following the client's verbal and nonverbal cues. In sum, although counselors working with Native clients should exercise caution when using humor, they definitely should not overlook it as a powerful therapeutic technique. Indian humor serves the purpose of reaffirming and enhancing the sense of connectedness as part of family, clan, and tribe. To the extent that it can serve that purpose in the counseling relationship, it is all the better.

Practical Tribally Specific Interventions

One valuable foundation for a counselor's understanding of the experience and worldview of traditional Native clients is for the counselor to imagine what it means to be a member of a tribe and how powerful an influence that is. A helpful way to remember this might be for counselors to think about the people they know who do not have a "tribe," meaning that they do not seem to have a particular place or community to which they belong.

Having now discussed some important overall counseling interventions and treatment modalities, the following section explores ways for incorporating tribally specific interventions to meet the cultural, spiritual, personal, and/or career needs of specific Native clients. The following (Garrett, Portman, et al., 2011) are offered as practical recommendations:

- *Foster cultural connections.* Native clients can reconnect with a sense of purpose by participating in community programs and cultural activities intended to combat the high rates of unemployment, inadequate housing, low educational levels, poverty-level incomes, and isolated living conditions. Participation in communitywide volunteer programs to help those in need has proved to be a successful part of healing for many Indian people. Also, in the past 10 years or so, powwows and other pantraditional events have become more and more popular around Native communities for whom that event is not indigenous as well as those for whom it is.

- *Encourage physical health.* Native people should be encouraged to get regular physical checkups and blood tests (e.g., blood sugar) as a preventive measure in dealing with high incidence of diabetes and other conditions prevalent among Native populations.

- *Examine/teach the historical context.* A critical component of counseling could include facilitating a psychoeducational experience or dialogue about Native experience in the United States. The counselor can discuss or lead the Native client to resources about the exploitation of Native people through discrimination, assimilation through boarding schools and relocation programs, as well as disruption of traditional cultural and familial patterns. Discussions of this nature might be helpful to Native clients in exploring their own level of cultural identity development.

- *Promote positive cultural identity.* Native clients can be assisted with exploration of personal cultural identity and career issues by focusing in on the positive cultural themes of belonging, mastery, independence, and generosity identified as culturally appropriate ways of developing positive cultural identity for Native people (Garrett, Portman, et al., 2011). Counselors can use the following general questions to generate strengths and positive dimensions of clients' lives: (a) (Belonging) Where do you belong? (b) (Mastery) What are you good at, what do you enjoy doing? (c) (Independence) What are your sources of strength, what limits you? (d) (Generosity) What do you have to offer/ contribute? These questions provide an entry into useful dialogue and any number of therapeutic interventions that could be useful for clients based on a variety of issues. In addition, counselors can help the client learn about the expectations and ways of the dominant culture, so that the client is prepared to engage in mainstream activities if she or he wishes.

- *Reduce isolation/enhance social connections.* Participation in social events allows Native clients to experience social cohesion and social interaction in their communities. Some Native clients can benefit, thereby, from a sense of reconnection with community and traditional roles. This has been accomplished through the revival of tribal ceremonies and practices (e.g., talking circles, sweat lodges, powwows, peyote meetings). These revivals can reestablish a sense of belonging and communal meaningfulness for Native people "returning to the old ways" as an integral part of modern life.
- *Reduce generational splits.* Native clients of all ages can benefit from acting as or learning from elders serving as role models and teachers for young people. This, too, has become more commonly practiced by tribal nations across the country in therapeutic programs and schools.
- *Enhance coping mechanisms.* Native clients can learn better methods of dealing with stress, boredom, powerlessness, and the sense of emptiness associated with acculturation and identity confusion. Consultation with or participation of a Medicine person (i.e., traditional Native healer) may prove very helpful.
- *Work with the noninterference principle.* The principle of noninterference has been identified as a value of traditional Native culture and is based on a common cultural practice of showing respect among one's relations (Garrett et al., 2009). Noninterference means that a person is not to interfere with the choices of another, as it would be considered disrespectful and insulting. However, in certain situations, noninterference can also be seen as avoidance behavior of family and community members with regard to persons who may be in need of help. This potential avoidance behavior can be challenged with Native clients, as well as with family and community members, to the extent that it may be destructive. Carol Attneave's (1987) Network Therapy has been very effective with Native clients as a way of working with an individual in family and community context where family and community members are incorporated into the counseling process, often through the use of group interventions that complement the cultural context.

Working from a Social Justice and Advocacy Counseling Perspective

Native Americans have many resources on which to draw, as well as serious individual and community concerns to address. As a result, oftentimes they are focused on the micro or day-by-day issues, such as moving their culture forward, by maintaining their traditions, language, and customs. Additional issues include addressing problems like health care, education, addictions, and trauma associated with current and historic oppression.

Choudhuri, Santiago-Rivera, and Garrett (2012) discussed the need for counselors to focus on three main levels of practice from an advocacy and social justice counseling perspective: (a) client and student advocacy, (b) school and community advocacy, and (c) public arena advocacy. In client and student advocacy, the helping professional implements direct counseling strategies based on understanding the social, political, economic, and cultural contexts in which clients live and facilitating self-advocacy on the part of the client. For instance, a helping professional might join an organization offering counseling services to returning Native American veterans and their families. Furthermore, the counselor may directly address external barriers that impede the client's development that the client is unable to address due to lack of resources, access, or power. For example, a school counselor might intervene directly with a health education teacher who has failed a student for turning in a paper on indigenous healing methods. In school and community advocacy, the helping professional might get involved in assisting community organizations that are working for change, such as developing a cultural sensitivity training program for volunteers at a food bank. Furthermore, counselors might get involved by going to a larger stage to maintain a direction for change that will affect macrolevels of access and resources. An example of this may be to join in ongoing lobbying efforts to maintain funding and services for Native American–based ex-offender employment and rehabilitation programs. Finally, in public arena advocacy, counselors might get involved in disseminating information widely to raise social consciousness that assists in deepening understanding. So, helping professionals might write an article for the local newspaper on Native American mental health concerns, sensitizing public awareness of ongoing discrimination. Furthermore, counselors might get involved with working on large social issues that will then indirectly trickle into an impact on the experience of Native Americans.

Furthermore, counselors must convince Native Americans of the importance of becoming engaged in the macro level of addressing oppression. Counselors need to develop the skills needed to encourage and galvanize individuals and communities to participate in social justice activities. One of the challenges that counselors may encounter when attempting to encourage participation in macro-level change strategies is the history of distrust when dealing with the government. Thus, training, explaining, and empowering may be the most prudent strategy to gain trust and buy in from this population.

Another strategy that may assist counselors to promote Native communities to participate in advocacy initiatives is to identify the strengths of these individuals and use those assets in their strategies. For example, one of the strengths of Native Americans is their comfort, proficiency, and tradition in storytelling. Counselors can impress on the individuals in the communities that storytelling is the foundation of enacting change. If these stories are communicated, they can influence local, state, and federal politicians, which may result in more resources and bring attention to the needs of their community. Grayshield and Mihecoby (2010) highlighted the importance of understanding "how dysfunction became so prevalent in my community, but the fact still remains, if the approach towards social justice is not about land, language and culture, then the approach is not multiculturally competent" (p. 13). Activity 13.2 provides an opportunity for you to explore social justice and advocacy counseling efforts by Native American organizations. Finally, Table 13.2 provides media resources that may help broaden your perspectives on Native cultures.

ACTIVITY 13.2

Investigate Native social, economic, educational, and political organizations such as the American Indian Movement, First Nations Development Institute, Morningstar Institute, American Indian College Fund, American Indian Science and Engineering Society, Native American Public Broadcasting Consortium, or Native American Rights Fund.
  • What are their primary characteristics?
  • How do they compare with one another?
  • How might they be useful when working with clients in schools? Communities?

TABLE 13.2 Media Resources about Native American Culture

Agency Resource Pages

- Bureau of Indian Affairs (http://www.bia.gov/): Web site of the U.S. Department of the Interior's Bureau of Indian Affairs.
- Indian Health Service (http://www.ihs.gov/): Web site provides information about the federal health program for American Indians and Alaska Natives.
- National Indian Council on Aging (http://www.nicoa.org/): national organization focused on advocating for Native American elders and their caregivers and families.

Native American Journals

- *American Indian Culture & Resource Journal* (http://aisc.metapress.com/content/120819): journal published by the UCLA American Indian Studies Center Publications Unit.
- *American Indian Law Review* (http://www.law.ou.edu/content/american-indian-law-review-1): journal published by the University of Oklahoma.
- *American Indian Quarterly* (http://www.nebraskapress.unl.edu/product/American-Indian-Quarterly,673174.aspx): journal published by the University of Nebraska Press.
- *Canadian Journal of Native Education* (http://www.lights.ca/sifc/cjne.htm): journal published by the First Nations House of Learning at the University of British Columbia and the First Nations Graduate Education Program at the University of Alberta.
- *The Canadian Journal of Native Studies* (http://www.brandonu.ca/Library/CJNS/): official journal of the Canadian Indian/Native Studies Association.
- *Indigenous Policy Journal* (http://www.indigenouspolicy.org/): journal published by the American Indian Studies Program at Michigan State University.
- *International Journal of Cultural Property* (http://journals.cambridge.org/action/displayJournal?jid=JCP): journal published by Cambridge University Press.
- *Journal of American Indian Education* (http://jaie.asu.edu/): journal published by Arizona State University.
- *Native Studies Review* (http://publications.usask.ca/nativestudiesreview/): journal published by University of Saskatchewan.

Native American Movies and Documentaries

- *A Good Day to Die* (2010): AIM leader Dennis Banks looks back at his early life and the rise of the American Indian Movement.
- *Bury My Heart at Wounded Knee* (2007): A chronicle of how Native Americans were displaced as the U.S. expanded West; based on the book by Dee Brown.
- *The Business of Fancydancing* (2002): Seymour Polatkin is a successful, gay Indian poet from Spokane who confronts his past when he returns to his childhood home on the reservation to attend the funeral of a dear friend.
- *Dance Me Outside* (1994): Silas and Frank are trying to get into college to train to be mechanics but they find themselves having to deal with girls, family, and murder.
- *Dreamkeeper* (2003): An old storyteller Indian asks his grandson Shane to take his old pony and him to Albuquerque to the great powwow, an Indian meeting.
- *Four Sheets to the Wind* (2007): After his father's untimely suicide, Cufe leaves his home in a Native American reservation in search of a more fulfilling life.
- *Grand Avenue* (1996): When Mollie's boyfriend Jack dies on the reservation, she is forced to pack up her belongings and her children and move to northern California.

(*Continued*)

TABLE 13.2 Media Resources about Native American Culture (Continued)

- *How the West Was Lost I & II* (1993): The story of how Native Americans lost their battle for the West.
- *Imprint* (2001): Shayla Stonefeather, a Native American attorney prosecuting a Lakota teen in a controversial murder trial, returns to the reservation to say goodbye to her dying father.
- *Incident at Oglala: The Leonard Peltier Story* (1992): Robert Redford documentary about AIM activist and political prisoner Leonard Peltier.
- *Lakota Woman* (1994): The story of the American Indian Movement, based on Mary Crow Dog's autobiography.
- *Medicine River* (1993): Two women pressure a Toronto photojournalist on a trip to his Native community.
- *Miss Navajo* (2007): The role of women and tradition in Dine (Navajo) culture is explored through a young girl's quest for the Miss Navajo Nation crown.
- *Older than America* (2008): A woman's haunting visions reveal a Catholic priest's sinister plot to silence her mother from speaking the truth about the atrocities that took place at her Native American boarding school.
- *On the Ice* (2011): In Barrow, Alaska, teenagers Qalli and Aivaaq find their bond tested when a seal-hunting trip goes wrong, resulting in the death of their friend.
- *Pow Wow Highway* (1989): Depicts the struggles of reservation-dwelling Native Americans with a main character who is an introspective and lovable person in a process of seeking pride and identity through traditional and mystical means of gathering power.
- *Reel Injun* (2009): The history of the depiction of Native Americans in Hollywood films.
- *Run, Broken, Yet Brave* (2009): Ashley is sent by her mom to spend a month of her summer holidays with her grandparents on the family farm.
- *Running Brave* (1983): The story of Billy Mills, the American Indian who came from obscurity, to win the 10,000-meter long-distance foot race in the Tokyo Olympics.
- *Skins* (2002): An inspirational tale about the relationship between two Sioux Indian brothers living on the Pine Ridge Indian reservation.
- *Skinwalkers* (2002): The story revolves around skin walkers, a folk legend from Utah about the spirits of murdered Indians returning to seek revenge upon those who disrespect the land.
- *Smoke Signals* (1998): When Victor hears his father has died, his friend Thomas offers him funding for the trip to get Arnold's remains, but only if Thomas will also go with him. Thomas and Victor hit the road.
- *Thunderheart* (1998): A young mixed-blood FBI agent is assigned to work with a cynical veteran investigator on a murder on a poverty-stricken Sioux reservation.
- *Trudell* (2005): A chronicle of legendary Native American poet/activist John Trudell's travels, spoken-word performances, and politics.
- *We're Still Here: Native Americans in America* (2012): A contemporary look at two communities often overlooked in the race dialogue: American Indians and Native Hawaiians.
- *Windtalkers* (2002). Two U.S. Marines in WWII are assigned to protect Navajo Marines who use their Native language as an unbreakable radio cypher.

Summary

Native scholars have written extensively about the ongoing effects of generational and intergenerational trauma on indigenous people, their families, and their tribal communities for decades (Brave Heart, 2005; Deloria, 2006; Duran, 2006; Duran et al., 2008; Garrett et al., 2009; Garrett, Portman, et al., 2011; Gone, 2009). These scholars have consistently described the challenges that Native Americans encounter as they navigate a world that is drastically different than that of their own tribal cultures. If professionals hope to have an impact on this population of people, they must understand that it is simply not enough to know about Indians, be part Indian, go to a sweat lodge meeting, take a class on Native Americans, or have an insatiable curiosity about them. Before anyone can begin to apply conventional psychological principles and theories to an ethno-cultural group, they must first understand its unique life ways and thought ways.

There are, however, some generalizations that can be drawn from the collective experiences of Native Americans as sociopolitical groups, as well as individuals from unique tribal backgrounds. It is a salient thought to know that Native American people as unique tribal groups and individuals do still exist, many within the boundaries of their own homelands. It is also important to note that many tribal people vehemently continue to protect their cultural ways through efforts to promote and revitalize their traditions, spiritual practices, and unique tribal languages despite numerous attempts to assimilate them into the dominant value system. The literature on culturally relevant processes in counseling is growing for Natives and non-Natives alike.

As such, the purpose of this chapter was to facilitate culturally responsive and competent counseling practice with Native people by offering a comprehensive overview and understanding of this population. Specific sections of this chapter addressed the following topics:

- An overview of the people, with particular discussion of demographics grounded in the concept of indigenous ways of knowing
- Terms and definitions of what group membership means for Native Americans
- Historical context of cultural genocide, assimilation efforts, and historical trauma
- Current and ongoing social, economic, and political issues that include self-determination and sovereignty; federal and state recognition; cultural preservation; achievement gap; gaming; tribal resources; sacred sites, repatriation, and reburial; and mascot issues
- Acculturation as seen through the process and impact of cultural change
- Native American cultural values and worldview
- Traditional spirituality defined broadly through the cultural themes of Medicine, harmony, relation, and vision
- Tribal and cultural identity, and the meaning of family; wisdomkeepers, humility, generosity, patience, time, communication style, and being
- Cultural worldview reflected in the teachings of the eagle feather
- Implications for practice with Native American clients using contemporary counseling interventions and treatment modalities
- Practical, tribally specific interventions
- A social justice and advocacy counseling perspective
- A call for culturally relevant research for and by Native peoples

Overall, the real lives of real people are what counselors must understand to best assist Native clients who may come to them with many stories, lived and shared in words, experiences, dreams, reflections, and visions of their own. Maybe the reflection we see down by the riverside offers something valuable for us all to behold in the work we do for and with Native people, as well as the work we do within ourselves.

Review Questions

1. What do the overall demographics and statistics offered in the chapter tell you about the current status of this population in different areas?
2. What is historical trauma as it relates to Native people, and what are the identified outcomes of historical trauma?
3. What are the current social, economic, and political issues that were identified in the chapter as presenting Native people and communities with both challenges and opportunities for change?
4. What are the four general components of traditional Native American spirituality discussed in the chapter?

5. What role do the tribe, family, and elders play in the lives of traditional Native culture and worldview?
6. How are the traditional cultural values of humility, generosity, patience, a present-time focus, and sense of being understood from a Native perspective?
7. What strengths and challenges does the chapter discuss regarding resilience, risk behaviors, and help-seeking for Native people?

14 Individuals and Families of European Descent

H. George McMahon, Pamela O. Paisley,
and Bogusia Skudrzyk

PREVIEW

Multicultural counseling has traditionally been taught as an approach a White counselor might take with clients of color, yet it is also important to understand the cultural factors that lead to identity construction of Americans of European descent. Perhaps, when clients of European descent clarify their identity, they will be able to clearly understand the source of their distress and challenges. It is equally important for counselors of European descent to understand their own cultural perspective to better understand their clients. In this chapter, cultural values and traditions from several European ethnicities, including White American ethnicity, are discussed. In addition, implications for multicultural counseling with recent European immigrants as well as individuals and families who identify as "White American ethnics" are addressed.

EUROPEAN AMERICAN HISTORY

> Martin was, like most inhabitants of Elk Mills before the Slavo-Italian immigration, a typical purebred Anglo-Saxon American, which means that he was a union of German, French, Scots, Irish, perhaps a little Spanish, conceivably a little of the strains lumped together as "Jewish," and a great deal of English, which is itself a combination of primitive Briton, Celt, Phoenician, Roman, German, Dane, and Swede. (Lewis, 1925, p. 6)

To better understand the cultural worldview of European Americans, it is worthwhile to gain an understanding of Europe and the people who settled there. One of the most significant developments of European history is the creation of the idea that "Europe" exists as a distinct region (Baum, 2008). Throughout the first millennium CE, various nomadic tribes traveled across the Eurasian landmass. The Roman Empire helped create an infrastructure for stable living environments throughout the areas now defined as Europe, and after the fall of the Empire, the region slowly gelled, populated by many of the nomadic tribes that had wandered throughout the region for generations, including the Anglos, the Celts, the Gauls, the Saxons, and the Slavs.

The tribes that formed the region of Europe were very different from one another and had experienced conflicts with one another for centuries. The Roman Empire and extensive trading routes, however, had exposed these tribes to cultures from far away. As Bartlett (1994) reported, "When compared to other cultural areas of the globe, such as the Middle East, the Indian Subcontinent, or China, western or central Europe exhibited distinct characteristics" (p. 1). Thus, perhaps in large part due to the rather vague boundaries of the region, these early tribes that collectively formed Europe separated themselves from others along physical and cultural characteristics as much as physical geography (Baum, 2008).

Although the physical features shared by the early European tribes were certainly important in their self-determination of who was and was not European, cultural practices were also very important. Perhaps no sociocultural factor was more important, however, than the adoption of the Christian religion (Baum, 2008). The rise of Islam in the 7th and 8th centuries helped define "boundaries" between Christian Europe and "infidel" (as Muslims were described by European Christians at the time) areas (Glick, 2005). This Christian–Islamic border was not merely one of physical territory, but was an important social distinction as well. Laws were passed in Europe to maintain strict Christian bloodlines within the community, and active participation in the Latin Christian Church and obedience to the pope were seen as essential criteria (although not sufficient by themselves) to be considered part of the proper European societies of the Middle Ages (Baum, 2008). This pattern of European peoples categorizing themselves (and others) based on physical features and sociocultural practices was repeated throughout their history and continues today as "Western" people, culture, and ideas.

The Early Colonial Period

The colonization of North America beginning in the late 15th century brought an influx of European settlers to the North American continent (see Table 14.1). American history texts describe the "discovery of the new world" while minimizing the reality that tribes of Native Americans had lived, farmed, and worked in this part of the world for centuries. The narrative constructed by European conquerors of the "new world" as a wilderness sparsely populated by savages without religion may have helped to justify European immigrants' settlement of land at the expense of current inhabitants, but recent ongoing archaeological and anthropological research is uncovering a very different picture of pre-Columbus America. America's vast population with very diverse cultures created what Mann (2007) called a "thriving, stunningly diverse place" (p. 26), where active trading across cultures took place and advancements in mathematics, astronomy, and agriculture rivaled those of other cultures on Earth. Nonetheless, the Eurocentric view of pre-Columbus America is still taught in public schools and continues to have a powerful influence on the cultural conditioning of U.S. citizens and policy.

American history texts often present a narrative of colonization of North America by freedom-loving individuals who sought an open and free society for all. Most early European immigrants, however, came for purely economic reasons., For those who did come seeking religious freedom, they typically did not seek religious freedom for others but only the freedom to practice their particular set of beliefs without interference (Banks, 2008). In fact, the early colonial period was a time of extreme religious intolerance, characterized by infighting within smaller Protestant sects (e.g., Presbyterians, Baptists, Quakers, and Lutherans), all of whom disliked the Anglicans; about the only thing the different

TABLE 14.1 Early European Settlements in What Is Now the United States

Year	Ethnic Group	Area of Settlement	Primary Reason
1607	Anglos, Germans, and Poles	Jamestown, VA	Financial opportunities
1609	Dutch	New Netherland (Manhattan Island)	Financial (East India Trading Co.)
1638	Swedes	Delaware Bay	Fur and tobacco trading
1664	Quakers (Anglos and German)	Philadelphia, PA, and Germantown, PA	"Holy Experiment" (for people to live in peace)
1718	French	Mississippi River (New Orleans to St. Louis to Detroit)	Farming and plantations

Source: www.spartacus.schoolnet.co.uk.

Protestant groups could agree on was a dislike and distrust of the "Papists" (Catholics) (Parillo, 2015). Despite the reasons for their departure, the very power dynamics (e.g., oppression, class structure) that many were escaping quickly began to appear within the colonies themselves.

The early settlements were very diverse, including colonists from England, Scotland, Germany, France, and Africa, as well as Jews and Christians (see Table 14.1). These diverse communities were not without conflict. The English, who accounted for approximately 60% of the European immigrants, were clearly dominant during this period and had the greatest influence over the creation of the political and social systems developing in the colonies. This social and political dominance led to the colonies using English as the primary language as well as a notion of supremacy of English cultural values. Banks (2008) noted that, for ethnic groups, becoming acculturated meant becoming associated with Anglo-Saxon culture. There were a variety of similarities and differences among the cultural values of the different European ethnicities, but the major differences setting the English value system apart were the focus on individuality, the strong work ethic, and the value of external signs of success. Many scholars relate the English work ethic and external signs of success to the Protestant/Calvinist belief that success on earth (which was achieved through hard work and individual responsibility) was evidence of predestination for salvation (McGill & Pearce, 2005). Thus, the external rewards of success were proof that one had lived a proper and worthy life in the eyes of God. Consider other values of "American" culture by completing Activity 14.1.

During this early colonial period, many of the European ethnic groups intermarried. The English culture and values remained dominant while individuals of other ethnic backgrounds assimilated to the English American culture (McGill & Pearce, 2005). By the time of the American Revolution, the population of the colonies was largely seen as English Protestant, although a great deal of German and Scots/Irish heritage, along with smaller numbers of French, Dutch, Swede, Polish, and Swiss heritage, had been absorbed into the dominant culture. This cultural mix, in addition to the norm of assimilating into the dominant culture, set the foundation for what would become the dominant social system and

---

ACTIVITY 14.1   WHERE IS IT FROM?

Nothing is more American than a hamburger . . . except that it is German. The popular American sandwich is named for the German city of Hamburg, where it is believed to have originated. Even hotdogs are European, based on popular sausages such as the German frankfurter and the Polish kielbasa. Identify some other staples of "American culture" and see if you can identify the cultures from which they originate. Brainstorm in small groups about different foods, games, traditions, holidays, art, education, and so forth associated with American culture. Identify rituals that were created to honor relationships and connections with each other and nature.

---

worldview, as well as the process immigrants were expected to go through on arrival in the United States for years to come.

European Immigration

Although many people associate European settlers with the 1600s, immigration from Europe was by no means limited to the colonial period, and in fact it continues today. Between 1820 and 1998, approximately 61% of the over 64,000,000 legal immigrants to the United States came from Europe (Banks, 2008). European immigration in the 19th century was particularly strong, due in large part to the political and economic turmoil in Europe throughout the mid-1800s.

Immigrant children and families represent a broad range of diverse and intercultural groups, and the experience of immigrants varies greatly by the time period in which they immigrated, their reasons for leaving, the regions to which they came, the political climate of the time, and their own personal circumstances. Table 14.2 identifies European ethnic immigration periods and reasons for immigrating.

TABLE 14.2   Major European Immigration Periods

Approximate Date	Country of Origin	Reason for Immigration	Areas Settled
1845–1854	Ireland	Potato famine and typhus outbreak	Cities along the east coast, Chicago, Ohio
1848–1858	Germany	Political turmoil (failed revolution)	New York and midwestern cities (e.g., Chicago, Milwaukee, Detroit)
1851	France	Political turmoil	New York, Chicago, New Orleans
1890–1900	Italy	Financial concerns (low wages and high taxes)	Industrial cities (e.g., New York, Philadelphia, Chicago, Detroit)

Source: www.spartacus.schoolnet.co.uk.

Although contemporary American media and political debates about immigration rarely refer to European immigrants, this was not always the case. Arbitrary hierarchies that distinguished old immigrants from new ones, or more specifically, that distinguished ethnic groups of northern and western Europe from those of southern and eastern European countries, were in place throughout much of U.S. history (Banks, 2008). Discrimination against ethnic groups was particularly prevalent during periodic mass migrations, particularly migrations from southern and eastern European countries.

Counselors need to take time and help clients of European descent reflect on their cultural identity construction. What does being a White European mean to them? What are their underlying perceptions regarding self and others? Although, historically, European immigrants attempted to run from financial hardship, religious persecution, and lack of freedom, sometimes the oppressed may become the oppressors when their identity construction is based on viewing differences as deficiencies (Banks, 2008). First, counselors may want to visit Reflection 14.1 to consider their own thoughts of what it means to be "American."

Two concepts of particular significance in the waves of colonization and immigration that make up American history are enculturation and acculturation. Though sometimes used interchangeably, the terms represent two distinct processes that have relevance for the experiences of Americans of European descent. **Enculturation** is most clearly used to describe an individual learning the values, attitudes, beliefs, behaviors, and rituals associated with one's primary culture, typically the culture into which one was born. In contrast, **acculturation** refers to encounters between primary cultures resulting in the acquisition of a secondary set of cultural expectations, expressions, and norms (McAuliffe, Kim, & Park, 2008). Acculturation can also be considered bidirectional in that individuals from both or multiple encountering groups may experience changes in their primary set of cultural variables based on their interactions with the "other."

For immigrants or refugees coming into a new dominant culture, the process of acculturation is often a complex and challenging transition to something new (Monk, Winslade, & Sinclair, 2008). Throughout American history, immigrants and refugees coming to the United States were expected to adjust to a new set of cultural values, beliefs, and behaviors that were often grounded in Western European, particularly Anglo-Saxon, expectations. Initially, the pressure to change was placed on those coming into the United States. Immigrants were

---

REFLECTION 14.1

The vast majority of Americans can trace their ancestry to another country, and thus other ethnic backgrounds and culture. Consider these questions:

- What do you think it means to be "American"?
- What are "American values"? Name some specifically. How have these values helped shape American culture? How might these values create conflict among some immigrant groups?
- Think about your family specifically. When did individuals in your family become American? What was the process of becoming American like for them?
- Do you know what your ancestors' names were prior to coming to the United States? How were the names given to them? Did their names change over time?
- To what extent did your ancestors and family members maintain awareness of their previous cultural and spiritual practices that fostered a sense of cultural belonging and well-being?

expected to "fit in," to assimilate, and to abandon or at least minimize their commitment to their primary culture. More recently, certainly within counseling and psychology, an appropriate balance of understanding the new cultural context and expectations while also maintaining primary cultural values, beliefs, rituals, behaviors, and attitudes has come to be a more healthy and respectful goal and position. The degree to which this more healthy balance or bicultural perspective has been achieved has varied greatly across time, circumstances, groups, and individuals.

It is important to realize that European immigrants were not always seen as "White"; that is, for long periods of time, particularly at times of large influx of immigrants from a particular geographic region, the dominant groups in America marginalized immigrants from various European countries, including those from Ireland, Italy, and much of Eastern Europe (Treitler, 2013; see Reflection 14.2). These periods were pockmarked by warnings from policy makers, the media, and even scientists that true American stock (i.e., primarily Anglo-Saxon Americans) were being polluted by "inferior" European (and non-European) people (Brodkin, 2007). These statements not only led to discrimination and oppression of the immigrants themselves, but also created a system that pitted different "ethnic groups" against each other, so that in order to achieve a status uplift, a group would have to differentiate itself from other marginalized groups (often at other groups' expense; Treitler, 2013). This system provided both convenient scapegoats for urban, economic, and political problems in the persons of recent European immigrants who were labeled as vulnerable targets deemed culturally and intellectually inferior (Banks, 2008) and a system that encouraged discrimination amongst marginalized groups, thereby preventing them from uniting for more fair treatment collectively (Treitler, 2013).

REFLECTION 14.2

In the 19th century, many immigrants who are now considered White were not viewed that way and were systematically and sometimes violently discriminated against. For instance, records reveal instances of Italians being lynched in the South and media publications referring to Irish immigrants as "low-browed and savage, groveling and bestial, lazy and wild, simian and sensual" (Roediger, 2007, p. 133). Although the target groups may have changed, what similarities do you see in the way non-White immigrants are characterized in the United States today? What role might portraying immigrants in these ways play in the cultural power dynamics within the United States? What emotions, dispositions, or cultural worldviews do you think underlie the strategies White American ethnics have used in portraying recent immigrants?

TERMINOLOGY

Many different terms have been used at different times and in different settings to describe Americans of European descent. Even within the professional multicultural literature, scholars have used terms including *White, White American, Euro-American, Anglo-American, Anglo,* and *European American* to describe the dominant cultural–racial group in the United States. Members of this group are also identified as being part of the Caucasian or White racial group. For many Americans, these terms are used interchangeably, or the preferred term may vary depending on generation or geographic region.

Although it may seem as though the terms are somewhat arbitrary, there are important differences in the terms and in the ways in which they have been used. Some terms refer specifically to a racial category. Others may refer to ethnicity comprised mostly of the dominant American culture or may involve more specific cultural views of the European ethnicity of origin. It is important to remember that these terms have been used not only to describe the majority culture, but also to maintain political power by separating the majority culture from non-White ethnic groups (Treitler, 2013).

In this chapter, the term **White** will be used to describe the larger racial group. Moreover, the authors acknowledge the ongoing debate about the significance of race, and that the concept of race in biological or genetic terms is illegitimate and that race exists *only* as a social constuct (Kaplan & Winther, 2013; Olson & Beal, 2011). Nevertheless, as a social construct, race is very significant in that those persons and/or groups that have been "racialized" as White have gained advantages over non-White racialized categories in terms of material goods, social status, psychological benefits, and access to resources, among other advantages. Moreover, the term **Caucasian**, although commonly used to describe the privileged racialized group, will not be used because Caucasian is, in fact, an ethnic group of people traditionally from the isthmus between the Black and Caspian Seas and because these groups, ironically, have not been considered European by their neighbors. (In fact, many Russian ethnics have referred to the Caucasian ethnic groups as "Black.") It is important to reflect on how you conceptualize race (see Reflection 14.3).

The term **European American** will be used generally to refer to individuals living in the United States who are recent immigrants from or identify closely with their European heritage in terms of values, traditions, and worldview. When talking about specific examples, the specific ethnic label will be used when it is known (e.g., German American). Finally, the term **White American ethnic** will be used to describe individuals of European descent who identify themselves as American ethnically and who have adopted the culture, traditions, and values of the dominant culture in the United States. In essence, White American ethnics are those who include European Americans who have become socialized and infused as White. The next section will discuss key concepts that contribute to the development of White American ethnics or ethnicity.

REFLECTION 14.3

Race as a biological construct has been largely discredited within the science community, yet the term is still used widely, and the *concept* of race is something that many Americans understand (at least in their own way). Currently, there is debate over use of the term *race*. Although some argue that using terms like *race* and *racial differences* perpetuate the myth that racial differences exist on a biological level, others argue that the social construction of the concept of race is, from a postmodernist view, very real, and must be dealt with as a "real" concept. What are your thoughts on the concept of "race," and how should we address the issue, if at all, to promote a more accurate understanding of race?

DEVELOPMENT OF A WHITE AMERICAN ETHNIC IDENTITY

The multicultural literature in America has long talked about individuals of color being acculturated to the mainstream culture, but little explicit attention is given to the meaning of "mainstream culture." Historically, this is reasonable—multiculturalism developed as a reaction against or an alternative to mainstream culture, so it follows that pioneers in multiculturalism would not focus on mainstream culture in their initial writing. Furthermore, it may have been that assumption that mainstream culture was so apparent to the readers that there was no need to spend time describing it. Although this may have been the consensus among Americans of color, White students have demonstrated little identification with or understanding of their own racial identity compared to other ethnic and racial groups (Kaplan & Winther, 2013). It is important to explicitly describe, therefore, the basic tenets of White American culture, which many people may be aware of only implicitly, to promote a deeper and more accurate understanding of the context in which the White American culture was constructed.

Many diverse factors merged and interacted as the worldview, belief systems, behavioral norms, and traditions of the White American ethnics began to emerge. Certainly, the philosophical base of the White American ethnicity was the English system that dominated the social and political systems of the early colonies, although other (primarily European, initially) ethnicities added characteristics as well. In addition, the wide expanse of the North American continent, which was seen as unsettled by the new White American ethnics, combined with the Calvinist understanding of predestination to lead to a "pioneer spirit" that valued exploration and "conquering" the land as a way to demonstrate evidence of one's worth. This adventurous spirit and the belief that it was White American ethnics' "manifest destiny" to dominate the land is a clear example of how cultural and religious beliefs interacted. Although countless factors contributed to the development of the White American ethnicity, three specific contributions will be discussed briefly: the emergence of the American "melting pot," the development of the American Dream, and the creation of a national heritage.

The Melting Pot

As the newly founded nation of the United States matured and individuals of different European ethnicities intermarried, a new and distinct culturally homogeneous society began to emerge. Although grounded in the cultural values and worldview of the English settlers, other European ethnicities contributed a great deal to the development of this new and unique sociocultural perspective, with its own traditions and beliefs. The term **melting pot** was commonly used as a metaphor to describe the process of combining a variety of cultural backgrounds and beliefs to create a new, virtuous (i.e., White American) culture, with the idea being it's okay to be different, as long as one accepts mainstream (e.g., White Protestant) values (Guy, 2010). Although the vision of the melting pot was an idealized notion used to demonstrate the United States as a utopia, non-Europeans, and in some cases non-English-speaking Europeans, were largely excluded from adding their contribution or flavor to the cultural pot. This led to both marginalization of and discrimination against non-White and non-English-speaking Americans.

The popular notion of the United States as a melting pot began to dissolve during the civil rights movement of the 1960s, when people of color demanded that their identity be recognized and respected separate from the White mainstream culture (Guy, 2010). The melting pot idea was replaced with a new sense of multiculturalism focusing on inclusion and ethnic pride. Several metaphors have been suggested to replace the melting pot, such as viewing the United States as a **salad bowl** where several different ethnic flavors coexist and add to the overall culinary gestalt while maintaining their own distinct characteristics (C. C. Lee, 2013). In some arenas, this view has since been replaced by the "quilt," where separateness remains even as each patch becomes woven into a sustainable fabric (Guy, 2010).

The new sense of pluralism and inclusion helped many people of color, as well as many recent immigrant families, take pride in their own cultural heritage and develop their ethnic identities. It also proved confusing for many White American ethnics. Many European Americans who have been in the United States for several generations have fully assimilated into American culture to the point that their cultural connection to their European heritage has been lost (McGill & Pearce, 2005). Such persons, in particular those of Anglo heritage, find it uncomfortable and confusing to discuss ethnicity because they consider themselves "plain, regular Americans" (p. 460). This confusion over the meaning of ethnicity in the United States may be responsible for many White American ethnics' resistance to the concept of multiculturalism, as their concept of "culture" is not well defined and not personalized.

The American Dream

Another important development in the evolution of the White American ethnicity is commonly known as the American Dream. In many ways, the **American Dream** is the manifestation of White American ethnic cultural values, and it reinforces the notion of the United States as a utopia. It explains the country's political and social structure; incorporates the nation's stated ideals of liberty, equality, and the pursuit of happiness; and provides an explanation for the success of the American people, as well as a justification for other families' and even sociopolitical groups' financial stuggles (Johnson, 2015). It is a philosophical positioning of the United States as a meritocracy with the necessary social and political structures that include equality, freedom, and individual agency (McNamee & Miller, 2009).

One of the common beliefs perpetuated in the United States is that anyone can grow up to be a star, to own a business, even to be president of the country if he or she works hard enough. This is the prime example of the idea of a **meritocracy**, where individual success is based on personal skills, abilities, and work ethic, rather than on external factors. Meritocracies, therefore, rely on an egalitarian society that promises a level playing field where individual merit is the basis for advancement. At its core, the American Dream and meritocracy represent the cultural belief in the agency of the individual (Johnson, 2015). Legends of folks who have "pulled themselves up by the bootstraps" and have risen to success despite humble beginnings are commonly used to reinforce the myth of an American meritocracy. These stories are told and retold to emphasize the principles of a meritocracy, and thus it is hardly surprising that many people within the dominant culture believe the ideology is a reality.

Meritocracy, even as a myth, does provide benefits to those who believe in it. The idea that anyone can be successful provides a great deal of hope and inspiration to many people, encouraging individuals who are struggling to see beyond immediate barriers and believe that success is possible in the long run. In addition to providing a hope for success and explaining the achievement of those who are already successful, however, meritocracy also provides an explanation for how inequality exists. In fact, it justifies inequality (Johnson, 2015). Specifically, if those who obtained status in society are assumed to have earned their position through natural ability and hard work, then it follows that those without status have earned their fate as well. The implication is that those who struggle in society have brought it on themselves, which provides the middle and upper classes with both a rationale for their personal success and an excuse for withholding help from those who are less fortunate (e.g., help will be a wasted effort).

The problem, of course, is that the meritocracy, to the degree that it exists, exists for a very narrow range of the American population. For most of the population, there is not equitable access to resources, the playing field is decidedly not level, and although some are born into privilege, many others are born into oppression. This is exactly where the conflict for White American ethnics emerges. For White American ethnics to acknowledge that social factors inhibit the success of some groups is to acknowledge that the meritocracy, which is at the very core of many White Americans' ethnic identity, is an illusion. It also means that the privilege they enjoy (relatively guilt free) was not earned after all, a difficult notion for many who are privileged to accept.

The Creation of an American Heritage

One of the common factors that helps define ethnic groups is a common heritage, yet for more than a century of its existence, the United States was largely without a well-defined national heritage (Shackel, 2001). As part of a rise in nationalism in the early 1900s, the U.S. Department of Defense began funding the preservation of war monuments, which began the process of creating a collective memory and the beginning of a national heritage. The fact that the national heritage movement started with the Department of Defense may not have been coincidental and was certainly vital to the shaping of the national heritage. To further promote the dominance of the White American ethnicity within the social structure of the United States, the national heritage and collective memory must demonstrate the superiority of the dominant group. What better way to instill a sense of superiority into the collective consciousness of a nation than to highlight the military conquests led by White American ethnics?

For a national heritage to fully take hold, however, it must be institutionalized across a broad swath of educational, political, and economic practices. The U.S. educational system has provided a vital link in the promotion of national heritage and collective memory created by the dominant culture (Bankston & Caldas, 2009). Not only do American students learn a decidedly Eurocentric and White American ethnic perspective of the brief history of the United States, but the school systems serve to shape and reform students from diverse backgrounds into being acceptable participants in the idealized version of the United States put forth in the curricula. In addition to the Department of Defense, other groups have worked to promote a dominant history. (See Reflection 14.4.)

REFLECTION 14.4

In 2011, an Arizona law was used by the Tuscon public school system to rule that a Mexican-American studies program was "divisive," and therefore was eliminated. Lorenzo Lopez taught Mexican-American studies for eight years at the high school from which he had graduated before the program was eliminated. Lopez reported that it wasn't until he took a college class in Chicano Literature that he felt he had a part in American History, and that is what motivated him to teach in the Mexican-American studies program. Opponents of the program stated that in some schools, the program became less about history, and more about current politics and social power (National Public Radio, 2012). What are your thoughts on the difference in perspective between some people wanting educational systems to maintain a consistent understanding of history, and other people wanting to add new perspectives to historical understanding? What are the potential benefits and drawbacks to each perspective? Ultimately, what is the role of the educational system regarding the teaching of U.S. history?

Privilege, Oppression, and Ethnocentric Monoculturalism

> I have come to realize that most of my colleagues are well-intentioned and truly
> believe in equal access and opportunity for all but have great difficulty freeing
> themselves from their cultural conditioning. They are, in essence, trapped in a
> Euro American worldview that only allows them to see the world from one per-
> spective. To challenge that worldview as being only partially accurate, to entertain
> the notion that it represents a false illusion, and to realize that it may have resulted
> in injustice to others make seeing an alternative reality frightening and difficult.
> Although using the terms Whiteness and Whites may perpetuate the inaccurate
> notion that these terms describe a racial group, little doubt exists that skin color in
> this society exposes people to different experiences. Being a White person means
> something quite different from being a person of color. (Sue, 2004, p. 762)

An attempt to describe the history of European Americans and of the development of the
White American ethnic cannot be conducted without a discussion of privilege, oppression,
and ethnocentric monoculturalism. Although not identified as "values" of the European or
the White American ethnic, they are among the most widely recognized expressions of White
culture worldwide (Baum, 2008). The concepts of privilege and oppression are discussed in
more detail elsewhere in the text, yet it is important to cover these topics briefly here in terms
of how they contribute to the White American ethnic identity.

Because many members of the White American ethnicity do not see themselves as having
an ethnicity, they are often oblivious to their racialized identity (Baum, 2008). Embedded
within privilege is the privilege to be oblivious to culture, and many White people become
aware of their Whiteness only when they are outnumbered by persons of color.

White members of American society are given significant social and economic advantages that have nothing to do with the meritocracy that is supposed to exist in the United
States. Instead, these advantages are based on a pattern of social and political practices in the
United States to keep power in the hands of those who already have it (Baum, 2008). Just as
the advantages that privilege provides are real, so is the obliviousness of that privilege among
those who have it. This lack of awareness of advantage is not simply about White American
ethnics choosing not to see it; instead, Whites in America are taught not to see their own
privilege (McIntosh, 1989; Wise, 2008). For a true meritocracy to exist, privilege must be
denied. Therefore, the teaching of a national heritage and an American Dream based on a
meritocracy go hand in glove with the denial of privilege.

A closely related concept to privilege is **ethnocentric monoculturalism**, described by Sue
(2004) as "the invisible veil of a worldview that keeps White European-Americans from recognizing the ethno-centric basis of their beliefs, values, and assumptions" (p. 764). Sue (2013)
argues that ethnocentric monoculturalism is conditioned into individuals from birth and gains
its power from its invisibility. Ethnocentric monoculturalism instills in members of a dominant
group a belief in the superiority of the values and practices of that group, without making the
individuals aware that their beliefs are culturally based. This is an important distinction because
it allows members of the dominant culture to believe that they do not discriminate against others based on the color of the skin (a visible difference), even as they reject those who do not
hold their same values. The impact is a far more subtle and often invisible (to the majority
culture) form of racism in which members of the dominant group are conditioned and reinforced to accept their cultural values as universal truths, and thus view individuals and groups
who have differing values and practices as unprincipled. Although Sue argued that all groups

are ethnocentric by nature, the difference in the ethnocentric monoculturalism of the White American ethnic is in the ability to impose the White American reality onto other groups.

Whereas the myth of meritocracy would suggest that social stratification in the United States is primarily due to ability and effort, it is far more realistic to say that those in power have abused their power to remain so and to marginalize all others who are not. This type of systemic oppression has long been a staple of White American ethnics, but in many ways it too remains out of the awareness of many (Sue, 2013). The combination of the belief in a meritocracy, religious or virtuous rationalizations for civilizing communities deemed godless or uncivil, and common teachings that racism occurs through "individual acts of meanness" (McIntosh, 1989, p. 12) facilitates the invisibility of the systemic and systematic oppression to which European Americans and White American ethnics have subjected other groups of people.

Despite a history suggesting otherwise, being oppressive need not be synonymous with White culture. There may be certain aspects of European American culture that can contribute to oppressive dynamics—such as the ontology of absolutism, which designates a clear "right" and "wrong," and the democratic practice of "majority rule." However, many of the values that are at the core of the American ideal (e.g., liberty, equality, responsibility, the Christian "Golden Rule" of treating others the way you want to be treated) can also lay the foundations for a far more socially just society if the American people, in particular those in power, can live up to the stated values and afford *all* citizens those rights.

Just as the multiculturalism movement has asked that non-White cultures not be seen as "deficient," those of us who strive to hold a multicultural view of the world should not see White American culture as deficient. White American ethnics, and the European-based values they hold, present in their most positive form a determined and self-reliant group of individuals who value courage and adventure, who honor personal achievement and independence, and who possess a strong work ethic and an optimistic belief in the ability of the individual to conquer problems. The challenge for White American ethnics, then, becomes honoring their traditions, beliefs, customs, and values without imposing them on others or using them as a yardstick by which all other cultures and peoples are judged. The gift of pluralism comes as an opportunity for White American ethnics to explore the full complexity of their cultural identities, choose the values they wish to honor, and be intentional about living with others in accordance with the values we proclaim. (See Activity 14.2.)

ACTIVITY 14.2   WHAT DOES IT MEAN TO BE WHITE?

For students who identify themselves as White, identify some salient characteristics about what it means to you to be White, and write them down on a piece of paper. Next, identify some characteristics of being White that you think may be most salient to people of color.

For students of color, identify some characteristics of what it means to be White that are most salient to you and write them down. Next, identify characteristics that you think may be most salient to White American ethnics.

Process the activity either by having students share their thoughts, or by the instructor collecting the papers and writing some thoughts on a board or flipchart. What characteristics are salient to White American ethnics that are not as salient to people of color? What characteristics are salient to people of color but not to White American ethnics? What might be some reasons for these differences?

WHO GETS TO BE WHITE?

Previous sections have discussed the evolution of a White American ethnicity, but how did immigrants become part of this American ethnicity? Certainly some members, such as Anglo-Americans, were the forerunners to the new ethnicity, but when and how did the Irish, Italians, Polish, and other ethnicities become "White" Americans? What is the cost to the individual, family, and community?

Although members of White America now enjoy a great deal of privilege (including the privilege of not having to reflect on their privilege), every White family was, at some point, an immigrant family. The transition from European ethnic to White American ethnic is, first of all, dependent on the individual or family being identified as racially "White." Although this sounds obvious, the prerequisites for being included in this category have altered dramatically over the years. The nation has a long history of setting up a system of stratification, and access to the most exclusive levels of society have been contingent on not only physical characteristics, but also language, religious beliefs and practices, political affiliations, and economic stability, and a willingness to adopt the values and norms of the White Protestant culture (Olson & Beal, 2011; Treitler, 2013).

The idea of race as a physical reality began to emerge in the 17th century, when the Anglican settlers in the colonies used the idea that "Black" Africans were a separate race from "White" Europeans, thereby justifying their enslaving of the Africans (Baum, 2008). The White race, then, became synonymous with the dominant culture in the Western Hemisphere (and favored by their God, a remanent of the Jewish tradition underlying much of Christianity), and the idea of race influenced not only social interactions but also political decisions, scientific inquiry, and theological positions for centuries. Initially, the upper socioeconomic class in the United States was largely limited to wealthy, educated Protestants of English descent (Olson & Beal, 2011). Over time, and largely in response to new immigrants coming to the United States from areas with more visible differences to the Anglo-Americans, the parameters for defining who was White became more inclusive. Groups who were willing to adopt the values and mannerisms of the dominant culture, including assimilation efforts such as speaking English, adopting "American" names, receiving an American education, and even marrying into a White family, were all effective strategies for immigrants to assimilate into the Anglo-based White American culture (Olson & Beal, 2011). Slowly, dominant culture expanded from only English heritage to include other English-speaking or Western and Northern European ethnicities such as German, French, and Scots-Irish, although for an extensive period European descendants from the Mediterranean and Slavic areas were not as likely to be seen as White.

The world wars in Europe also had a profound effect on the development of the White American ethnicity. The atrocities of those wars, particularly World War II, and the genocide based on ethnicity prompted many Americans to take a far more accepting view of others (Winawer & Wetzel, 2005). In addition, Americans of German descent, and to a lesser extent Italian descent, would often go "underground" and hide or deny their ethnic heritage by assimilating into the White American ethnicity. In addition, a new, vast middle class was created when soldiers, from families who were largely uneducated, came home and attended college under the GI Bill (Mettler, 2012). Because the belief that the United States was a middle-class nation holding middle-class values played such a strong role in the national heritage, access to a college education and subsequent middle-class wages provided the opportunity for previously excluded groups to enter the White American ethnicity, if they so chose. As with many interrelated issues, it is often difficult to tell how much becoming middle class helped families be accepted as White, or how much being accepted as White helped families earn middle-class wages.

The Process of Becoming White

Today, we talk about acculturation as the process that non-White individuals learn about majority culture values and learn how to adapt to and work within White cultural settings. Despite the degree to which an individual of color may acculturate, however, non-European individuals are rarely able to fully "become White." Although European immigrants (and other immigrants who can trace their family histories back to Europe, such as many South Africans or Australians) can become White, there is strong debate over the process of becoming White, particularly around to what degree non-English and/or non-Christians who appear White choose to become or are coerced into becoming White (e.g., Kaye-Kantrowitz, 2007). That discussion, although a worthy one, is beyond the scope of this text. Instead, this section will focus on describing the process of becoming White and its implications on individuals and families who make that transition. We hope that you will consider, if relevant, reflecting on your own family's process of becoming White or not (see Reflection 14.5), and we have provided our stories of becoming White (see Reflection 14.6).

REFLECTION 14.5

When did your family become White? For readers who identify as White American or European American, identify your European heritage. What does that heritage mean to you? How connected do you feel to your European heritage? What cultural values and/or traditions are most salient to you? How does your heritage affect who you are today?

Think back on your family history and try to identify when you believe your family became White. Although becoming White is a process, there are often significant events we can identify that signal significant shifts. If you are not sure, ask family members about events that may have indicated steps toward becoming fully White.

REFLECTION 14.6   ETHNIC IDENTITY STATEMENTS OF THE THREE AUTHORS

H. George McMahon

My most prominent, perhaps pervasive, cultural identity comes from what I consider a culture of privilege. Having grown up a White male from a well-educated, professional family provided me with numerous opportunities and a degree of freedom that most people do not have. Part of the reason I believe this privilege plays such a prominent role in my perspective on the world is because privilege is, by its very nature, invisible to the privileged. The assumptions that I began to construct about the world and about people were perceived through glasses I was not aware I was wearing. In my professional career I have worked diligently at understanding my own culture and how my cultural perspective influences how I perceive the world. Becoming aware of my culture and my privilege has not meant that they no longer play a part in my worldview; rather, it is the awareness that I do indeed see the world through such a cultural lens that now plays a prominent role as I construct my worldview. I still see the world how I see it, for I can see it no other way; but I now understand that my view, although accurate for me, is quite a limited perspective. Although I could talk about specific cultural frameworks, such as my being White American, being male, or being from an upper-middle socioeconomic status, I believe the implications of each of these cultural views is absorbed in the overall culture of privilege, and I cannot separate them from each other.

Although the nature of privilege is that it is invisible to the privileged, it does not mean that the privileged are not aware, at least on some level, of the implications of race, ethnicity, gender, and other socioeconomic variables. I remember, for instance, a dream I had when I was a young boy, probably about third or fourth grade. I remember walking into the lobby of the office building where my father worked, a grand marble-covered lobby in a 50-storey building. I walked up to the security guard (who was African American in my dream) at the desk in front of the elevator bank and announced, "I'm Daddy's son." The guard smiled and said, "Go ahead" as he quickly waved me through. Even at such a young age, I was aware on some level that my lineage would grant me access to places and people that were off limits to so many others.

Regarding my specific ethnicity, I am, like many White American ethnics, of mixed ancestry. My ethnic background, as I understand it, is primarily British and Irish, with some French, French Canadian, and Choctaw. However, these identities mean little to me as far as my values and outlook on life. This is likely because for the most part, I was raised to be White American, not Irish American or Choctaw. One aspect of my identity that is very salient to me, however, is that I identify as a New Orleanian. This aspect of my identity means far more to me than ethnicity, and I am very aware of the influence the culture of my home city has on my outlook and my values. I believe that this is partly because the history of New Orleans is influenced by French, Spanish, Caribbean, and Indian values, which makes it quite unique among American cities. The pace of the city, therefore, is slow, with less value on a strong work ethic and achievement and more value placed on enjoying the moment and living life to its fullest. Although I usually identify myself as a White male, and I know that those aspects of my identity are very important, I believe that others must understand my New Orleans heritage in order to truly know me.

I am also aware that the New Orleanian part of my identity has become more meaningful after the tragedies surrounding Hurricanes Katrina and Rita. Although I was not directly involved in the storms or their aftermath, many friends and family members were, and my city was. Like so many other New Orleanians, the tragedy brought a stronger sense of solidarity and kinship among its citizens, a process I imagine other non-White groups have experienced throughout American history.

Pamela O. Paisley

As a European American, my ethnic heritage is somewhat mixed. Although predominately Scottish and English, I also have a bit of background from Germany and Italy. I grew up in a community that was heavily Scottish, where the Highland Games are still observed each October, and the small college located there was named for the woman, Flora MacDonald, who helped Bonnie Prince Charles escape. We were taught the Highland Fling in elementary school and were aware of an array of tartans appropriate for kilts based on a variety of family names or clans.

My own awareness of cultural difference was also influenced by context and several critical incidents. I grew up in a county in North Carolina that, in addition to European Americans, also had significant populations of African Americans and Native Americans. All three groups had their own school systems. My first year in high school was the first year of a freedom-of-choice policy in which students from any high school could optionally request to attend another school. One African-American male and two Native American (Lumbee) females opted to join our class. At the beginning of my senior year, the Black and White high schools were merged. A few more Native Americans had joined our class across the years, but the county Lumbee schools were not at that time required to merge. In May of 1969, I graduated with the first integrated class in my community. I am not sure how others in my class internalized that experience then or reflect on it now, but I have always been so grateful to have been a part of that group. It was not always easy, and we had to work through a great deal, but that experience introduced me to a set of conversations that I continue to be engaged in and committed to today.

At this point in my own development related to issues of diversity and social justice, I am committed to continuing my journey of self-discovery and staying fully engaged in the conversation—even when those discussions are very difficult. I am interested in understanding my own heritage and cultural values and am also committed to systemic social change. This journey requires awareness of my own privilege as well as challenging stereotypes, oppression, and injustice on a variety of dimensions of difference. To understand myself and the privileged society in which I have been sometimes invisibly advantaged, I have to be in honest, authentic relationships with others who are different from me. I am very fortunate to have graduate students, colleagues, and friends who challenge me daily to be a better version of myself and to question what

(Continued)

I think I know. I am trying to make peace internally with embracing my English, Scottish, German, and Italian heritage while also owning the historical and current injustices that are perpetuated by using a European American (particularly Anglo) cultural standard to the disservice of other groups. I have accepted that privilege is not something that I can "get over." Instead, commitment to social justice means a certain vigilance regarding awareness. In this process, I also try to avoid "White guilt" about these issues, as I don't find that very helpful or productive. There is not anything inherently wrong with my being White or being European American. My energy is better spent in challenging oppression and social injustice.

Bogusia Skudrzyk

I am a great-granddaughter of the people of the land, Polanie, in Polish. My ancestors come from Polish, Hungarian, Austrian, and German backgrounds. My maternal grandmother, one of my best teachers of lessons for living, used to say: "I never left my town or moved, and yet I got to live in three different countries." My ancestors lived in the same geographic location as I did until I was 14—I come from a town called Cieszyn—which means, more or less, a place of joy. Like any place on Mother Earth, it is a beautiful place where creeks rumble through the valleys, winds dance through the mountains, some fields are still filled with hay, and children and even adults still often dance, dance to the rhythm of life and yearning for love and acceptance, despite numerous systemic pressures. Singing, dancing, creating crafts together, and finding a way to honor relationships and life was deeply valued in my family, community, and society. As a child, in many ways my life was still privileged because my family was lucky to live in a home on a small piece of farmland, whereas others around us were stuck waiting for a small apartment, for over 10 years, as after World War II Poland and its life was destroyed. I was also privileged, as in my family and school systems, the word *culture* or being cultured meant knowing and understanding other cultures through literature, arts, and accomplishments.

I was and I am very proud of being Polish, and that does not mean I devalue others. I was surprised and did not know until my family moved to the United States that being Polish sometimes for those in positions of power (whether real or perceived) implies that we are the "stupid ones"—I was shocked by the jokes and lack of understanding that are even perpetuated by the textbooks from which young generations learn. I was saddened that people even in the 1980s were encouraged to change their names and to give up their identity just to be superficially accepted by the "in crowd." I was surprised to read in textbooks that Marie Curie was listed as a Frenchwoman, although her premarried name was Sklodowski—she was Polish and happened to marry a Frenchman. Copernicus is studied in Western Civilization with no mention that he was Polish, and Chopin's name was spelled in an "American" way, while it really is Szopen. I was surprised when I was encouraged by an American, a government official, to change my first name when I chose to be an American. He said there would be no fee and I told him, "Sir, I am keeping my name, which was given to me by my family. My grandmother chose it, and I am keeping it. Aren't we free in this country to be who we are?" And still today, I wonder who is free to be who they are? Although my ancestors and family members, and to a certain extent I, have encountered experiences with difficult, oppressive messages, I still have the privilege of looking "White." I recognize that the privilege of being White can be misused and at the same time is an opportunity to join the walk on a path that strives for finding ways to truly give voice to suffering that still surrounds us and to care for each other through mutuality where differences are valued, acknowledged, and not viewed as deficiencies.

As a woman I am very aware of the cultural identity construction, including cultural camouflaging, that can enter any culture and justify mistreatment of women, children, or anyone who might be viewed as the vulnerable ones, and in the process restrict opportunities for men and women to form and foster relationships based on acceptance and caring for each other without rigid roles being assigned to either gender.

I am aware that I have lived in the United States much longer than I have in Poland and that being an American is also important to me. To me that means always remembering that I am a granddaughter of the people of the land, a daughter of brave people who gave up their motherland and moved to the United States in the hopes of a better future for their children—but a better future never at the cost of hurting others. Most important to me, I believe that just like my children, and everyone's children, we are children of the universe, global visitors passing in time and place. I am lucky that others took time to care for me, and perhaps now more than ever I need to be mindful and search for ways through which caring for others can remain the rhythm of the dance of living.

When individuals become White, the privileges associated with being in the majority culture come along with it. However, the process also has clear disadvantages. Most important, individuals must give up a degree of their original cultural identity to become fully White. This process is problematic in that much of what is most meaningful about the culture of origin is lost. No doubt, this is at least partly why so many White American ethnics have difficulty understanding the concept of culture generally and their own culture specifically. At some point, cultural identity was worked out of the equation. People may know that they have Scottish, Italian, Czech, or Russian background, but those identities may not be very salient or meaningful to the individual. In addition, this process can cause conflict and tension between members of a family, or between families and the larger community. A family who is "upwardly mobile" may be discounted by their own cultural/ethnic groups for striving to be White. Similarly, members of a family may be seen as "too White," even when family members encouraged the acculturation process. Individuals might experience internal struggles, feeling pressures from the dominant culture to just be "normal" like everyone else, and in the process they might lose their source of wellness stemming from cultural practices that were repressed by those in a position of power, without ever feeling fully accepted by the dominant culture.

EUROPEAN AMERICAN HETEROGENEITY

As with other ethnic groups, European Americans have myriad intragroup differences, and understanding these differences is vital to understanding an individual. Several within-group variables can vastly affect the cultural views and the behavioral manifestations of those views, including specific European ethnic identity, socioeconomic class and educational level, geographic variables, religious views, generational differences, and nonethnic marginalized group identity (such as ability status or relationship orientation). One of the most prominent variables accounting for intragroup differences, however, among European Americans and White American ethnics is the degree to which individuals identify with their European heritage. There is great diversity among European ethnicities along several lines, including focus on achievement, individual or group focus, gender roles, conceptualizations of family, and treatment of elderly people. This is particularly true of recent European immigrants, who may be more likely to identify with the ethnic identities and values of their home culture. Even over long periods of time, some European groups have assimilated into the White American ethnicity to a greater degree, whereas others have been more intentional about holding on to their heritage.

In *Ethnicity and Family Therapy* (McGoldrick et al., 2005), the authors clearly take the position that, although there is a potential for "fusion of people and cultures" through intermarriage and intermingling of groups, "ethnicity will continue to be a distinguishing characteristic even for European Americans for a long time to come" (p. 503). They further acknowledge the complexity and elusiveness of ethnicity as a concept in part due to its basis in both conscious and unconscious processes. They note that "shared ethnic heritage hardly produces homogeneity of thought, emotions, or group loyalty" (p. 503) and in reality can be mitigated by class, gender, region, or personal circumstance. Nonetheless, certain values or characteristics are, if not culture specific, at least culture associated for a variety of groups, including those falling under the larger umbrella of European American. (For more detailed descriptions of cultural histories, values, characteristics, and contexts, see Chapters 36 to 48 in *Ethnicity and Family Therapy*.)

Page Intentionally Blank

Certainly, socioeconomic class also plays a key role in the variance among White American ethnics. The process of becoming middle class or upper class assumes, at least to some extent, the adoption of values, styles, and behaviors that are more typical of the general White American ethnicity. In addition, many of the prerequisites for becoming middle or upper class are connected to ethnic identity. For instance, the more education a student has and the more work experience a person has, particularly in white-collar or professional work, the more he or she has been indoctrinated into the White American ethnic values system. Conversely, many ethnic enclaves, which help perpetuate ethnic identity, are lower- or lower-middle-class areas.

Geography can also have a significant effect on variance within the White American ethnic. Part of this difference is historical, going back to the initial British immigrations. Anglos immigrated to the United States in four distinct waves, with each wave coming from a different area of the British Isles and bringing with them different values. These four waves also settled in different parts of the United States, setting the tone for regional differences. The Puritans, who largely settled in New England, valued an ordered world, whereas the Cavaliers, who settled largely in the southern colonies, believed that freedom meant the right to choose how to live and to conduct business without the interference of others. The Quakers, who largely settled in the Mid-Atlantic and the Midwest, valued privacy and respected the privacy of others, whereas the Appalachian and southwestern immigrants from Scotland and northern England, whose history was strongly affected by unceasing violence, valued self-preservation and protection over a formal education, which may be seen as an invasion. These initial value systems can be seen as influential in many ways today, including voting patterns, approaches to state and local governments, and even the disproportionate numbers of individuals from Appalachia and the Southwest volunteering for military service (and militias; McGill & Pearce, 2005).

Other geographic variables such as climate and terrain can certainly have an effect, from the northern midwestern United States values of hard work, planning, and saving (to manage tough winters) to the more laid-back approaches of southern California, where the gentler climate requires less effort to survive. Density of population can also affect how one approaches social life, as can the multiple options for entertainment that large cities can provide, versus the simpler approach to country living. Many larger cities develop their own cultures as well (think New York, Chicago, San Francisco, or New Orleans). These individual differences may develop for a variety of reasons, such as differing immigration patterns (New Orleans is more influenced by French, Spanish, and Caribbean immigrants than by British), or by the nature of the variety of influences (e.g., New York being the port of entry for so many European immigrants).

Other variables influence within-group heterogeneity as well. Religious affiliations, and differing views within those affiliations, can have profound effects on values. Although the original Anglo-Americans were virtually all Protestant, many Catholics, Jews, and Eastern Orthodox are often included in the White American ethnic (Olson & Beal, 2011). Even within the Protestant group, there are multiple variations, from strict fundamentalist to liberal approaches. Generational differences are also apparent, as younger generations of White American ethnics have far more exposure to people from a variety of backgrounds and may be more comfortable with and accepting of differences than previous generations.

Many White American ethnics may also be part of marginalized groups that are not based on ethnicity. People of varying levels of ability may experience discrimination, which may provide a different perspective on the role of privilege in our culture. Similarly, LGBTQI (lesbian, gay, bisexual, transgender, questioning [queer], and intersex) individuals may be White American ethnics, yet their experiences as part of a marginalized group may play a central role in their identity, contributing to a more open and liberal set of values and lifestyle common to LGBTQI culture than mainstream White America. Both ability and sexual orientation can vary in the degree to which these identities are visible, which may also affect how one identifies herself or himself. As is the case when understanding an individual from any cultural background, it should be clear that individuals must be understood and appreciated among a variety of identities rather than simply understood as a representative of their ethnic background.

RECENT EUROPEAN AMERICAN IMMIGRANTS

Although in the contemporary media and government the term *immigrants* is often used to refer to non-European immigrants, it is important to remember that the families of all White American ethnics were, at some time, immigrants. In the early part of the 21st century, 53 nationalities were identified within the larger European American umbrella, ranging in number from German American descendents (approximately 43 million) to Cypriot Americans (approximately 7,600; McGoldrick et al., 2005). European immigration continues, and in 2003 immigrants of European descent represented approximately 30% of documented immigrants. The number of European immigrants in the United States has remained steady since 2000, with current European immigrant children and families representing a very broad range of diverse and intercultural groups. According to 2014 U.S. Census data, 40% of European immigrants arrive from Eastern Europe (e.g., Poland, Russia, Ukrainia), 40% from Northern and Western Europe (e.g., United Kingdom, Germany), and 16% from Southern Europe (e.g., Italy, Portugal, Greece; Migration Policy Institute, 2014). The following section will describe the experiences of recent European immigrants. In particular, stressors related to immigration, conflicts with majority culture, and the acculturation process of recent European immigrants will be discussed.

Immigrants, Undocumented Immigrants, and Refugees

It is important to clarify and distinguish a few key terms that refer to individuals who relocate from their home countries to the United States. The term **immigrant** is often used as a general term for individuals who are living in a country other than their native country, but it is actually a specific term that refers to noncitizens of a host country who are granted legal permission to permanently reside in the new host country (Yakushko, Watson, & Thompson, 2008). Immigration to the United States from European countries continues, and in 2013 over 91,000 European immigrants were granted Legal Permanent Status (LPS) by the United States, accounting for 9% of all persons granted LPS (Office of Immigration Statistics, 2014). Of the European immigrant populations from 2013, most came from the United Kingdom (over 15,000), Russia (10,000), Germany (just under 7,000), and Poland (6,000). Voices from the Field 14.1 provides one immigrant's experiences in the United States.

Undocumented immigrants refers to noncitizens of a host country who did not go through the procedures established by the host country's policies. Undocumented immigrants are most

Voices from the Field 14.1

I began school in America in a middle school that had found a new life as a school for foreign children. None of the students spoke English, and the teachers spoke only English. This was 1958, long before ESL became part of the American educational system. Yet there was such an influx of eastern and western European immigrants during this time that the Philadelphia school system made provisions to quickly immerse these children into the culture and language of their new home. Eventually, these children would disperse to other schools where they would be assimilated into regular classrooms. . . . I loved going to school. Every morning, I would take the #5 trolley to downtown. For me, this was an exciting new experience. I was learning to become American and each day brought me closer to my goal. I also loved the freedom of moving about in the city without adult supervision. Half-way to school, there was a German section which I quickly discovered. This part of Philadelphia was my tie to the country I'd just left behind. Here, everything was familiar, and I could find magazines and books and food products from Germany. In the afternoon, on the way home, I often would leave the trolley at the Girard Avenue stop and wander from store to store. The smells and sounds were familiar and comfortable.

~ Irene Muthe of German and Russian heritage, immigrated to the United States at age 12.

commonly individuals who were in their host country on temporary status and stayed beyond the established time, or individuals who entered the host country without going through inspection (Yakushko et al., 2008). Immigration can be a stressful process for individuals and families, and those stressors can be exacerbated when combined with a fear that they will be "discovered" and detained and/or deported. Statistics are unknown regarding the number of undocumented immigrants from Europe, and although the immigration status of a client may be important information for counselors to know, it is obviously very sensitive information that many undocumented immigrants would be hesitant to share with anyone seen as an "authority."

The term **refugees** refers to people who are living outside their native country and who are granted permission to set up residence in a host country because they are either unable or unwilling to return to their native country for fear of persecution (Yakushko et al., 2008). The number of refugees coming to the United States from European countries has dropped in recent years, with under 2,500 European refugees from 2011–2013 (Office of Immigration Statistics, 2014). The majority of European refugees today come from Russia and other former Soviet Union countries (e.g., Ukraine, Moldova). In addition to struggling with issues of loss of home and acculturation to a host country, refugees may be dealing with a complex web of issues related to the circumstances leading to their being "pushed out" of their home countries (Djuraskovic & Arthur, 2009; Yakushko et al., 2008). Before the process of relocation, refugees may have witnessed traumatic events in their home countries, experienced severe oppression and persecution, and felt a strong sense of despair and loss for a home country to which returning may be impossible (Djuraskovic & Arthur, 2009).

International students are individuals living in a host country for the purpose of pursuing a degree, often an advanced degree. Although international students can apply to stay in the host country to pursue career opportunities postgraduation, most eventually return to their home countries (Crockett & Hays, 2011). The number of international students in the United States continues to rise, leading to a call for college counseling centers and career counseling centers to become more aware of this population and intentional in service delivery models (Crockett & Hays, 2011; Mitchell, Greenwood, & Guglielmi, 2007). Research shows that, of the international students seeking counseling services in the United States, approximately 11% are from European countries (Mitchell et al., 2007). Although these students have largely chosen to come to the United States to pursue their studies, they still face many of the same challenges in adapting to another culture. Moreover, international students must adapt to a new *academic* culture as well, where the policies, procedures, process, and expectations may be very different from the academic system that they are used to (and were successful in; Crockett & Hays, 2011). Furthermore, international students' high expectations regarding both their academic experience and their ability to enter into their "dream" career may lead to frustration and disillusionment.

Immigration Stressors

Like immigrants from any culture, the path of life for many European immigrants has been filled with a variety of stressors, often paired with a loss of previously used coping resources. Immigrants might experience a process similar to grieving when adjusting to living in a new country. Navigating through these complexities can be very challenging, especially when isolation and shame become part of daily life experiences. Losses associated with a sense of disconnect from one's community, family, and friends along with experiences of being devalued and silenced frequently penetrate the lives of immigrant families and children. Having to relearn or rediscover conveniences previously taken for granted, such as the layout of a new city, becoming aware of the resources available in the community, and having to find new stores, doctors, and the like can make the transition even more stressful.

For immigrants coming from non-English-speaking countries, the difficulties those immigrants may face when trying to communicate with people in their new community can also cause problems. These problems are particularly severe with first- and second-generation immigrants. Not only are the communication difficulties stressful, but the pressure to learn a new language, particularly at an advanced age, also adds additional stress, primarily because the subtle microaggressions that non-English-speakers or people learning the English language often encounter can greatly add to the level of discomfort (Sue, Capodilupo, et al., 2007).

Acculturation and Identity Deconstruction

The process of acculturation has traditionally been described as the cultural and psychological change that occurs when two cultural groups interact, often an immigrant group and a host group (Berry, 2003) In the United States, the term is often used to describe cultural groups adapting to the White American ethnic (based in Anglo Protestant) lifestyles, values, and language. The process of acculturation of several different racialized and ethnic groups has been examined, along with their ability to adapt, accept, and be accepted by the dominant group. Recent research supports the idea that acculturation does not follow a linear model; rather, it is a complex and cyclical process that is characterized by repeated experiences of interaction with host culture and the individual's interpretation of those experiences (Djuraskovic & Arthur, 2009). Moreover, research on refugees from the former Yugoslavia suggest that even European immigrants who are well grounded in the U.S. culture continue to experience conflicting thoughts and desires to both assimilate into and rebel against the host culture, suggesting that the process is ongoing.

Closely connected to the idea of acculturation is the process of ethnic identity reconstruction (Djuraskovic & Arthur, 2009). Originally viewed as a developmental model similar to other ethnic and minority identity development models, identity construction and reconstruction may be best understood as an interactional model in which inidviduals participate in a process of building ideas about one's identity through discourse with others within important social contexts (Bamberg, De Fina, & Schiffrin, 2011). These contextual negotiations can take several sociocultural factors into consideration, including culture of origin, identity attitudes, preferences and lifestyle of the immigrant population, political climate and climate of the host country, and the interaction among all these factors.

The acculturation and identity construction process for immigrants of European descent is similar to that of immigrants from other areas of the world, but with some significant differences. Although in many ways European immigrants face similar challenges as other immigrant groups, the fact that European immigrants may share physical and cultural features with the dominant culture in the United States can lead to acculturation issues and pressures that are quite unique to European immigrant populations. For instance, simply by the nature of looking "White," immigrants from European countries might not be viewed as foreigners, or might have an easier time assimilating (or being assumed to have assimilated) into the White American ethnic culture. Their physical "Whiteness" can lead to unexamined patterns of privilege and quicker opportunities for receiving the benefits of being seen as White. This often presents an opportunity, if not pressure, for immigrants to assimilate into mainstream American culture, but sometimes at the expense of their cultural heritage.

Just as non-White individuals are often assumed to be rather unacculturated to dominant culture in America, it may be that recent European immigrants, in particular those with good English language skills, may be assumed to be more acculturated than they are, thus leading to unrealistic expectations about their ability to understand and navigate dominant American culture (Parrillo, 2011). Several factors can affect the process of English-language acquisition, including whether families live in ethnic enclaves, the usage of English in the home, access to native-language media, and school support for English as a second language (ESL) programs while showing appreciation for native languages.

Moreover, because communication plays such an important role in adolescent socialization, children and adolescents are often more motivated to learn English to establish relationships with their peers. Although it is developmentally appropriate for children and adolescents to want to connect with and be like their peers, it is also important to consider that immigrant children might experience rejection and isolation within their family and community system when forming unions with individuals from diverse backgrounds. This is true not only in childhood, but also when second-generation European Americans become adults and seek intimate relationships with people outside their ethnic group.

Cultural conflicts can also come into play around family structure and gender roles with recent European immigrants. Many European immigrant families may hold onto traditional roles for the family, including father as primary authority and mother as primary nurturer and caretaker of the family. If mothers do hold jobs outside the home, it is often done without relieving any domestic duties or giving "room" to taking care of herself, as that would be viewed as selfish. Furthermore, sons are often given more freedom than daughters (who are expected to stay close to home), and the welfare of elderly family members is a high priority. This can lead to difficulties within immigrants' families in the United States, where it is more common for men and women to share responsibility for the home and family (at least to a greater degree) and for daughters have more freedom to pursue careers than in some European countries.

The difference in family structure can also lead to intrafamily stressors, particularly as children and adolescents are exposed to the majority culture within the United States. Adolescents may feel conflicted as they begin to adopt the values and lifestyle of the majority culture in school and with their friends, yet are expected to keep their European ethnic values and traditions at home. Furthermore, the focus on youth in American culture can increase feelings of isolation and even worthlessness in elderly immigrants, who were often treated with more respect in their homelands.

Oppression and Discrimination

Like most other U.S. immigrants, immigrants from Europe have faced and continue to face discrimination in a variety of ways when arriving in the United States. Many European cultural groups have been negatively stereotyped in mainstream U.S. culture by other cultural groups. Overt discrimination is more likely to exist when the immigrants have more visible or more dramatic differences from the majority culture. For instance, immigrants who do not speak English or who have strong accents, those who have ethnic names, and those who have fewer Anglo-Nordic physical attributes, such as Mediterranean or Eastern European immigrants, are more likely to face active discrimination.

In addition to more overt forms of discrimination, European immigrants may face more subtle, but just as damaging, systemic oppression. For instance, immigrants (and particularly women) who have poor English-language skills are far more likely to be unemployed or underemployed, often regardless of their skill level or education (Parrillo, 2011). This has been exacerbated by many European immigrants transitioning from a more agrarian society to an industrial setting, where jobs have been most available for recent immigrants. Similarly, because many European countries' education systems are very different from the U.S. education system, immigrants may be much better educated than they are given credit for by U.S. employers.

COUNSELING CONSIDERATIONS FOR EUROPEAN-DESCENT INDIVIDUALS

An important factor to consider when understanding mental health concerns of Americans of European descent is that mental well-being and pathology are largely Western European constructs. Like the concept of psychopathology and diagnosis, "traditional" approaches to counseling have long been considered White European male constructs (see Chapter 17). Many of the early theorists were White males of European or European American descent, and thus their approaches were developed within their cultural context. Evidence for this can be seen in the individual focus of many early therapy styles, the focus on individual responsibility, and the use of the medical model to describe diagnoses. In fact, disruption of autonomous functioning is a major consideration for diagnosis of just about any mental health issue as defined in the *Diagnostic and Statistical Manual of Mental Disorders* (APA, 2013). Thus, the "culture" of counseling and what is deemed mental health mirrors the cultural values of White American ethnicity. However, adherence to White American ethnic cultural values can create mental health concerns that should not be minimized. Risks for mental illness are even greater for newly immigrated Europeans given immigration and acculturative stress and oppression experiences.

Mental Health Issues of White American Ethnic Clients

Cultural values such as meritocracy and individualism/independence, conflicts resulting from changing values within the culture, and conflicts between personal and cultural values all may play a role in the mental health of White American ethnics. The cultural belief in a meritocracy where all individuals start from a roughly even playing field may provide some people with hope, but it can also lead to feelings of inferiority and shame ("hidden injuries") over perceived failures, particularly among working-class White men (Johnson, 2015). If poor White American ethnics believe that the United States is a true meritocracy, then they risk carrying the double burden of feeling oppressed by the upper classes as well as guilt and shame for not having been more successful. Middle-class White American ethnics are not protected from feelings of inadequacy either, as the forward- and upward-moving society puts pressure on them to constantly do better. Even wealthy individuals may suffer from a fear of inadequacy, believing that they must continue to perform or risk slipping to a lower class.

As mistakes are inevitable in life, and shame is a common side effect of the perceived "failures" of White American ethnics, many Americans develop coping strategies for dealing with such negative emotions. Scapegoating, often in the form of oppression of and discrimination against a particular ethnic, racial, or other cultural group, is a common way White American ethnics deal with their feelings of inadequacy and inferiority. These feelings of frustration and fear of inadequacy can be rechanneled into work or hobbies, or can come out as anger toward others, particularly family members (McGill & Pearce, 2005).

The Calvinist idea that good fortune is evidence of righteousness and predestined salvation leads not to only feelings of inadequacy but also to problems when tragedies strike. Without any sense of adaptive fatalism, the White American ethnic is often confused by tragedy and believes it to be "unfair" when bad things happen to "good people." This adds an additional component to tragedy, where individuals are struck with dealing with loss, also ask the existential question "Why me?" and deal with feelings of victimization by an unfair situation.

The White American ethnic value placed on independence and individualism, particularly when taken in conjunction with the notions of meritocracy and the Calvinist work ethic, can lead to difficulties as well. As most White American ethnics believe that struggles in life should be overcome by individual effort, it follows that a failure to overcome an obstacle is due to personal weakness. Furthermore, because asking for help is often seen as an admission of failure, people and families commonly build rigid boundaries and adopt a "no-help necessary" policy. These boundaries protect individuals and families from being pitied by others, but further isolate them from the help they need. As individuals and families retreat further from help, they may mask painful feelings with alcohol and other substances or may develop patterns of abusive behavior (Fall & Howard, 2011).

Many of the cultural beliefs cited have also contributed to feelings of inadequacy among many White American ethnic women. The White American culture, like many of the European cultural systems from which it has developed, has traditionally been patriarchal. Many women whose role was to manage the house and family felt inadequate or depressed because their contributions were "devalued" and earned no material benefits to demonstrate their worth. As the role of women has changed in recent years in response to the feminist movement, many women now work outside the home (albeit for unequal pay, and thus, unequal value) while maintaining many of the domestic responsibilities they held previously (McGill & Pearce, 2005).

There are also inconsistencies within the larger culture that contribute to stress and frustration for White American ethnics. Perhaps most obviously, Americans have always stated their belief in individual liberty, yet have an ongoing history of denying liberty to others. Religious and cultural values held by most White American ethnics encourage individuals to feel guilty for transgressions. But being accountable is often viewed as admitting fault, which indicates weakness and often leads to feelings of guilt. Moreover, the future orientation of the culture leads many people to prefer "moving ahead" rather than "dwelling on the past" (McGill & Pearce, 2005).

Cultural values also play a role in many family struggles within the White American ethnicity. Certainly, the focus on the individual can mean that the family good is often sacrificed for the good of the individual within the family, particularly when that individual is in a power position. Likewise, because problems are seen as individual problems, they are less likely to be discussed within the family to protect both the family member who is struggling (from shame) and the other members (from the burden of being asked to help).

The individual focus can also lead to problems during childrearing. Historically, White American ethnic children have been expected to be rather self-sufficient early, and in many communities they were expected to work as soon as they were able. Individuation from the family is widely valued, but the timing of the individuation can have profound effects on the future development of the child (McGill & Pearce, 2005). Children who are given too much responsibility too quickly are at risk for entering a "false adulthood with premature identity foreclosure" (p. 456) and may feel ignored and powerless to get their developmental needs met. Those who are protected longer than the norm are termed "enmeshed" and are often ridiculed for their dependence on their families.

Individualism can play a role in marriage problems as well. Despite the romantic notion of marriage popularly portrayed through American media, many approach marriage among the majority culture in the United States as little more than a contractual arrangement that is designed to meet each person's individual needs (McGill & Pearce, 2005). When one partner is no longer getting what he or she needs from the relationship, divorce is an acceptable alternative. Even with the high divorce rate, however, divorce can still be a very traumatic experience, at least in part because it is commonly viewed as a personal failure on the part of one or both spouses, leading once again to feelings of anger, shame, and/or guilt.

The value on youth and the characteristics commonly associated with youth (e.g., beauty, athleticism, freedom) within the White American ethnic also contributes to emotional difficulties, particularly with older White American ethnics and those who have disabilities. Whereas other cultures place a great deal of respect on elder members of society for their wisdom, White American ethnics are more likely to complain about what they "lose" as they get older than acknowledge the wisdom or respect they accumulate. As many White American ethnics reach old age and begin to lose independence, this loss of freedom is exacerbated by feelings of guilt of being a "burden" to the family members who take responsibility for caring for them (or paying for their care).

What makes all these issues even more difficult to identify is the common cultural norm that discourages expression of emotion, and in particular difficult emotions. Many European Americans and White American ethnics grew up in cultures that valued self-control and self-sufficiency, which meant that suffering was often expected to be borne in silence so that others would not be burdened with problems that were seen as the individual's responsibility. This is particularly true in the mental health field, where talking about personal problems with strangers is seen as a sign of weakness, but is also apparent in the medical fields, where studies show that Anglo males often visit the doctor only after long periods of suffering and would continue seeing a doctor only if they believed they could be healed (McGoldrick et al., 2005). Even more drastic, studies have shown that Irish males and their descendants are particularly poor at seeking help to address physical pain, to the point where they have difficulty articulating the type of pain and even identifying where pain is located in their own bodies. In fact, many European and White American ethnics, in particular males, are not likely to seek help for emotional issues (such as sadness or worry) at all; instead, they will seek help only when they see their problems as a threat to their autonomous functioning (McGill & Pearce, 2005). Although many White American ethnics are willing to suffer in isolation, the thought of being dependent on others or having something affect their ability to work or be successful is more likely to bring them to counseling.

Counseling White American Ethnic Clients

Multicultural counseling was developed largely in response to a concern that traditional counseling methods may not be appropriate or as effective for non-White or non-Western clients. The argument was never that traditional counseling methods were not effective when the counselors and clientele were European or European American. In fact, there is a solid body of research indicating that traditional counseling methods are effective (see Erford, 2014), but the assumption is that effectiveness studies were largely completed with European or European American (and often male) counselors and European or European American clientele.

Although these traditional counseling methods (e.g., think about the recurring theories that take up the first 12 or so chapters of a standard theories book) are not considered multicultural theories or approaches, a closer look reveals that culture, particularly European and White American culture, plays a big role in these approaches. Specifically, many of these approaches simultaneously use and challenge the European cultural norms to effect change in the clients. For example, person-centered and other humanist approaches rely on the therapeutic relationship as the primary (and in some cases, sole) instrument of change. The therapeutic relationship valued by humanists, based on mutual respect, unconditional positive regard, nonjudgment, free expression, and accurate empathic understanding of another, is very different from the relationship many White American ethnics are used to, and intentionally so. Although it may be uncomfortable initially for many White American ethnics, who have been socialized to be guarded, to enter into relationships where they are asked to and expected to share freely, those aspects of free empathy and non-judgment are precisely what makes the "new" relationships therapeutic. Relationships that do not conform to White American cultural norms are also used in group counseling and therapy, where the group leaders intentionally create a climate within the group that is markedly different from the world outside, where group members are free to express themselves and ask for feedback without fear of reprimand or burdening others with their troubles. In these instances, the healing of counseling comes, at least in part, from helping clients step outside the limits their cultural norms may pose regarding their self-expression and the manner in which they relate to others. Although the idea that engaging in behaviors within the counseling relationship that are not seen as culturally appropriate may contradict many of the assumptions of multicultural counseling, there is evidence that engaging in *certain* culturally restrictive behaviors can have therapeutic effects in certain circumstances, even if they are not comfortable for the clients (Nitza, 2011).

Although many humanist approaches attempt to create relationships that are not in line with cultural norms to promote therapeutic change, other traditional theories use therapeutic relationships based on culturally appropriate aspects for European Americans to build a solid working relationship. Psychodynamic, behaviorist, and some cognitive approaches place the therapist, the one who has external evidence of his status (e.g., degrees), in an expert role, directing the experience. Other approaches, such as Adlerian therapy or Reality therapy, suggest the relationship be democratic, which is different than an expert role, but no less Western. Moreover, many of these theories stress the importance of European and White American values in the healing process, such as the client's commitment to "work hard," accepting individual responsibility, valuing the client's right to privacy, and focusing on objective, measurable goals to indicate success. In addition, the processes of change these approaches use often challenge thoughts or behavior patterns that are seen as maladaptive, but may be culturally appropriate. For instance, cognitive therapies attempt to identify maladaptive thoughts and change them to healthier, more adaptive ones, yet the maladaptive thoughts (e.g., "shoulding," self-reference, blaming) can be seen as grounded in the European or Anglo culture that says each individual is responsible for his or her life and where personal achievement (and the rewards of such achievement) is highly valued.

Adlerian counseling takes this notion further by attempting to understand each client's style of life, or way of understanding the world and one's place in it. The style of life is certainly influenced by one's culture, and embedded within each person's style of life are the roots of the struggles clients encounter. The personality priorities described by Adlerians to describe the patterns in which common styles of life often manifest, including pleasing, superiority, control, and comfort, can be seen as being grounded in European cultural expectations and the values of achievement and self-reliance. At the same time, however, Adler emphasized the importance of belonging, and he valued a collectivist view where being a contributing part of the whole was healthier than holding power over others, a view that was somewhat of a departure from traditional Western European values. Furthermore, by helping clients bring their style of life into their awareness, a process that parallels the development of an understanding of one's worldview, Adlerian counselors can help their clients become more aware of the (cultural) principles that were guiding their lives, albeit without the clients' awareness, and choose whether to change their behaviors or adopt a different set of values and view of the world.

Although many traditional approaches to counseling and therapy were grounded in Western values and the evidence shows these approaches are effective with European and White American populations, the feminist and multicultural movements have provided a great gift to the process of counseling European Americans by adding the awareness of the role that culture plays both in the presentation of issues and in the helping process. With this comes the realization that all counseling can be viewed as multicultural counseling (Pedersen, Lonner, Draguns, Trimble, & Scharron-del Rio, 2016). As counselors become aware of the cultural and power dynamics in society as well as within the counseling relationship, it becomes imperative that they attend to these dynamics in all situations, including White American counselors working with White American clients.

Although many counselors and counselors-in-training have been exposed to multicultural counseling practices, there is virtually no professional literature on the effective use of multicultural counseling approaches with White American clients. Following are ideas on how to conceptualize White American clients and facilitate the helping process with White

American clients from a multicultural perspective. Implications for counselors of color working with White American clients will also be discussed.

When conceptualizing White American clients from a multicultural perspective, a primary consideration for counselors, regardless of the counselor's own cultural and ethnic identity, is to be aware of their own worldview they bring into the session, which includes not only their own cultural values but also the theoretical perspective from which they operate (Ratts, Singh, Nassar-McMillan, Butler, & McCullough, 2015). Inherent in all theories is a set of beliefs and techniques that are value based, so understanding the values underlying the techniques and beliefs is critical. Second, counselors must understand the major cultural values underlying the White American ethnicity. Although it is true that many counselors of color may understand the White American culture from their own perspective by observing it (and often having it thrust upon them), it is important that all counselors develop an understanding of the true cultural values underneath the practices and appreciate the worth those values hold to develop an accurate empathic understanding of those who are raised in the culture.

Counselors can then enter into counseling with an understanding of both their own worldview and the cultural base of the White American client. But as is true with multicultural counseling with other populations, it is not enough to know the general culture. Time must be spent in the counseling session to begin to understand the unique worldview of the White American client, which may be based in White American values but may also differ in significant ways due to a variety of social, geographic, generational, or personal factors and intersecting identities. In addition, understanding the mulitple contexts in which White American ethnics were raised and currently live, as well as the tension or incongruence between these multiple contexts, is an important step in developing a deeper cultural and ecological empathy for clients (Ratts et al., 2015). Using Bronfenbrenner's (1979) socioecological model or other ecological models of counseling (e.g., Cook, 2012; McMahon, Mason, Daluga-Guenther, & Ruiz, 2014) can help counselors to better understand a client's multiple identities and the intersection of identities, including where clients may have privilege (of which they may be unaware), and where they may experience marginalization or disconnection from majority culture and values.

It is important to remember that many White American ethnics, in particular older White American ethnics, may not be comfortable discussing their culture and in fact may be unclear about their cultural values, or even that their values are culturally based (Sue, 2013). Therefore, this discussion may begin as a more general discussion about beliefs, approaches to life, and so on. Discussing family traditions and legends, heroes and role models, and the like can also be ways to informally gather information about a client's worldview and values. It is also important to note that the term *values* is often used as an absolute rather than a relative term for some White American ethnics, and the idea of absolute values is often reinforced by the rhetoric of politicians and the media. This can be seen in the commonly used but vague term *family values,* which is often used to indicate that the speaker has the values that everyone recognizes as "family values" and that others do not hold those values. It will be important, therefore, for the counselor to help clients specifically identify what values they are talking about. This is not only a point of clarification for both counselor and client, but can also help clients start the process of understanding values as relative rather than absolute entities. Finally, as a counselor begins to develop a comprehensive conceptualization of the client's general cultural perspective and specific values and beliefs, the counselor can conceptualize the role that cultural conflicts may play in the presenting problem and/or in any underlying issues. These cultural conflicts may be understood as intracultural conflicts, where values and/or beliefs within the White American cultural framework are in conflict with one another or conflict with the reality of the situation. An example may include a client's feelings of guilt arising from his perception of himself as a failure, which may be based in a belief in the meritocracy and an absolute devotion to the principle of individual responsibility. Another example could be a mother's inner conflicting messages to nurture and protect her children without "babying" them, thereby frustrating their ability to be independent.

Conflicts can also arise between cultural beliefs and the client's personal beliefs, and in this way multicultural counseling with White American ethnics can be very similar to multicultural counseling with clients of color and other recent immigrants. The major difference is that non-White American clients may be more likely to understand the conflict as a cultural conflict (i.e., between "my culture and the dominant culture"). Because White American ethnics are less likely to be aware of "the dominant culture" in those terms, they may be more likely to personalize these differences, resulting in feelings like "I just don't fit in" or "No one understands me." Furthermore, White American ethnics whose personal beliefs are not consistent with the White American ethnic risk labeling from the majority group, ranging from rather benign (but no less marginalizing) terms such as *liberal, creative,* or *marching to the beat of a different drummer,* to more indicting terms such as *traitor, freak,* or *deviant.* Recent approaches such as Acceptance and Commitment Therapy (ACT) may be appropriate for this type of values clarification (e.g., Twohig, 2012); it can be used to initially discuss not only the values themselves, but where those values come from and the fit and potential conflict that holding those values brings into a client's life.

As with all counseling relationships, establishing a relationship with the White American client is a crucial part of the helping process. Although the counselor's chosen theoretical perspective will suggest the style of therapeutic relationship that is seen as most helpful and outline a way of being with the client, there are some important relationship variables to consider when working with White American clients. Because many White American ethnics, in particular males, are taught to withhold expression of emotion, this may be particularly difficult at first. Instead, clients will often present their problems in terms of disruption of their autonomous functioning and will want to set specific goals to work toward to combat fears of "wasting time." The White American value of hard work can actually be used to get clients to commit to the process of counseling, and even suggesting that the work will be difficult can present a challenge that many White American clients will want to rise to meet. In addition, many White American clients will appreciate the autonomy to do the work, but may also expect the counselor to provide some sense of guidance early in the counseling process and some feedback regarding progress. This style of relationship fits with different counseling approaches to varying degrees, but it is important to understand it is likely what White American clients will expect. If the counselor values a relationship that will look different, it would behoove the counselor to have an explicit discussion about his or her expectations for what the counseling relationship will look like.

Regarding the specific helping processes, there are several ways to take advantage of common counseling interventions to help White American clients from a multicultural perspective. As with most multicultural therapies, consciousness-raising will likely play an important part in the counseling process. **Consciousness-raising**, or helping clients develop insight or deepen awareness, has long been a staple of many modes of counseling and therapy (Prochaska & Norcross, 2014). In addition to whatever consciousness-raising activities a counselor's theoretical position may suggest, a multicultural counselor working with White American ethnics will also want to help build the client's cultural awareness in several different ways. First, helping clients fully understand their own culture and making the values of their culture explicit can be an important growth experience for many clients, helping to form a fuller and more accurate self-concept. In addition, counselors can help their clients better understand the power dynamics and the privilege that play out in their lives as a result of being White in America. As mentioned previously, many White American ethnics are unaware of their own culture and cultural values, and helping them become fully aware of the extent to which their Whiteness affects their lives can be a difficult process (Sue, 2013). However, this process can also be an important aspect of developing a full understanding of self and a way to help clients live more authentically.

Finally, counselors can help their clients identify the cultural values and facilitate the process of examining the congruence between White American cultural values and the values of the individual within the culture. When clients have a better understanding of themselves as cultural beings and a more accurate perception of self within a cultural context, they should be able to conceptualize their difficulties, thus being better able to get the help they need. In many ways, this process parallels the deconstruction and integration processes used in constructivist, feminist, and social justice counseling, whereby clients are able to begin to identify systemic factors, including cultural expectations, that may be contributing to the problematic experience, and then construct a new understanding of self within the larger social context (e.g., Goodman & West-Olatunji, 2010). One of the more powerful gifts that effective consciousness-raising gives to clients is the ability to choose, something commonly valued by White American culture. When clients are unaware of their difficulties or the personal and systemic factors that affect their lives, their ability to choose how to help themselves remains limited as well. However, when clients become more aware of their surroundings and of choices they never knew they had, the act of choosing can become a form of self-liberation (Prochaska & Norcross, 2014). For instance, as a White American becomes more aware of and examines the cultural values inherent in the White American ethnicity, perhaps for the first time, she can choose whether and to what degree to hold those values on a personal level. Thus, when experiencing guilt or shame due to cultural expectations placed on the individual, or struggling with isolation related to the White American culture's value of independence and self-reliance, clients can choose whether they want to accept these values or choose a new way of looking at their world and a new way of behaving. Likewise, if clients experience a conflict between a cultural value for achievement and a personal passion for spending time with the family, what may have previously felt like an impossible situation suddenly becomes a choice for the client.

Choosing can also play an important role in helping White American clients to live more according to the cultural values of freedom and equality for all people. As they become more aware of the role privilege plays in their lives, they can choose to continue accepting the privilege, choose not to accept privilege when it is not appropriate, or even work to promote a social justice agenda in which some "privileges," such as not having to worry about being ignored or maltreated in public, are extended to all people, rather than just the privileged. This form of choosing is consistent with social advocacy and social justice and can help White American ethnics live in ways that are more consistent with the values of their culture.

Although the need for multicultural counseling may be viewed in terms of White American counselors working with clients of color, it is important to remember that counselors of color need to work multiculturally as well. Regardless of the ethnicity, multicultural counselors need to have an awareness of both their own cultural values and the cultural background of their clients. Cross-cultural counseling is sometimes approached with trepidation regarding the ability to establish a therapeutic relationship, but the reality may be that cross-cultural relationships may be particularly therapeutic *because* they are cross cultural. In an instance of a counselor of color working with White American clients, the counselor's perspective of White American culture can add a new perspective to clients' explorations of their culture. Moreover, through self-disclosure of their own cultural perspective, White American clients can begin to see their own values as relative rather than absolute truths. The same process can be used to help White American clients increase their awareness of privilege, which culturally aware counselors of color should be able to identify quite readily.

It is also important for counselors of color to fully develop the therapeutic relationship with their clients and to use this relationship to further develop therapeutic insight and encourage the therapeutic process for White American clients. Although counselors of color may be nervous about how White American clients would view them, most White American ethnics prefer to assume worth and respect on individuals (if not always groups of people), in particular people with whom they establish personal relationships (McGill & Pearce, 2005). Thus, whatever biases White American clients may have about ethnicities, they are likely to treat their counselor with respect. This tendency can be used to help build relationships, but can also be used during the working stage of counseling to build awareness of and critically examine the clients' biases. Finally, it is important that counselors of color working with White American clients remember that they have a great opportunity to model an appropriate process for cross-cultural understanding and respect for different cultural values and practices. It may be strange for White American ethnics to be in a position where they are asked to explain their culture to someone else (particularly someone seen in somewhat of a power position), but this experience can be very eye opening and growth producing by itself.

Mental Health Issues of European Immigrants, Refugees, and International Students

There seems to be a greater effort in understanding the losses and challenges associated with immigration through media exposure, scholarly works, and community-based interventions, but the challenges facing immigrants remain. Any counseling with immigrant populations, including European immigrants and refugees, must be grounded in a consideration for and understanding of the various psychosocial factors that affect the immigrants' experiences with stress and coping (Bemak & Chung, 2015). Although numerous researchers have identified experiences and challenges associated with immigration and relocation (e.g., Crockett & Hays, 2011; Djuraskovic & Arthur, 2009; Yakushko et al., 2008), immigrants, refugees, and international students from European countries have been underrepresented in these studies (Crockett & Hays, 2011; Mitchell et al., 2007). Although many of these studies do provide useful information for counselors working with immigrants and international students from European countries, more research must be completed on this population, and with specific populations within the European Union, to help practitioners better understand both the transition and the acculturation experience for European immigrants so that they may better meet their clients' needs (Djuraskovic & Arthur, 2009; Phinney & Ong, 2007).

Although intragroup differences among the European immigrant population are crucial in terms of country of origin, ethnicity, and immigration status, there are also several factors that can contribute to the stress many individuals and families relocating to a new host country will experience. Yakushko et al. (2008) cited several stressors common to immigrants of all types, including "premigration stressors" (i.e., whatever challenges led to the decision to relocate) and "postmigration stressors" (e.g., relocation stress, acculturation stress, strain on relationships, oppression, loss of social supports). Understanding that difficulties encountered by the immigrant clients may have begun long before the relocation event can help the counselor better understand the clients within their multiple contexts.

In addition, many immigrants may face stress related to having high expectations for their move (Yakushko et al., 2008). Specifically, many immigrants believe that they will—and should—function just as well if not better in their new home than they did in their home country. Therefore, the dissonance many experience with the unexpected struggles in their new country and culture may create a sense of low self-efficacy, doubt, and even regret. These challenges, particularly when paired with a loss of connectedness and feelings of being misunderstood or not accepted, can lead to feelings of guilt, fear, anger, sadness, and depression in immigrant children and families. A lack of harmony and balance might become part of the fabric of living while experiences of lack of acceptance and respect further give voice to sorrow, pain, isolation, and fear.

One of the primary strains European immigrants will encounter is the cultural conflict between the dominant culture in America and the culture of their home countries. Learning a new culture and having to adapt to new expectations, particularly in the workplace and in school, is a strain in and of itself. This process is particularly difficult for older immigrants, who are likely to more closely identify with their home country culture and be more likely to resist acculturation to U.S. cultural norms. In addition, generational differences in identification with home country culture and American culture can lead to further conflict within the family.

The stress of the transition and the financial problems often associated with immigration put a severe strain on many immigrants and can lead to conflicts within marriage as well. These stressors can be exacerbated when couples feel pressure to change their spousal roles, particularly when coming from a more formal patriarchal system and moving to a community in the United States where marriages are viewed from a more egalitarian perspective. Couples who are not married, single parents, LGBTQI couples, and other non-male–female married couples may face further discrimination, depending on the community in which they settle.

European immigrant adults may initially seek counseling services due to employment and/or financial concerns as a result of their transition, often through employee assistance programs. European immigrants face a variety of the same stressors other immigrants face, including being discriminated against, being underemployed, feeling undervalued, and lacking a social support network. Loss of self-esteem at work can occur when language barriers prevent adults from working in previous careers and from being perceived as being less educated and/or skilled due to language difficulties. In addition, the loss of financial resources and increased stress that come from being unemployed or underemployed can result in family stress, particularly for males from patriarchal cultures, who may feel they cannot provide for their families.

In such cases where European immigrants are facing self-esteem and/or self-efficacy threats, one way to encourage individuals to clarify their identity, both within the context of their home culture and American culture, is to explore their source of wellness. For example, Garrett and Garrett (2002) described Native American perspectives relevant to wellness and healing, leading to centering and feeling grounded. Reflective questions such as "Where do I belong? What do I do well? What is my source of independence—what do I stand for? What can I offer others?" are examples of questions that invite reflection and tapping into one's inner wisdom. Various other models relevant to wellness are available as well, but counselors using a wellness model not based on White American values could both model multicultural respect and help their clients conceptualize wellness beyond the potentially restrictive boundaries of White American values. When the family has children, further stressors can occur over identity development. Conflicts often occur over how the different generations identify with and value the majority culture. Parents may have mixed feelings about wanting their children to acculturate in some ways (e.g., being successful in school) but may feel uncomfortable with some acculturation (e.g., American social norms, dating behavior, independence) and may not want their children to lose their original ethnic identity. This process of becoming bicultural can be difficult for children and adolescents to understand and to navigate and can lead to confusion, frustration, and guilt on both the part of the parents and the children.

European immigrant children and adolescents seeking counseling or psychological services will often be first identified within the school system and are often first identified for academic concerns. Language differences, the pace of the academic learning environment, and the individualistic structure of many classrooms may lead to students feeling overwhelmed with the new demands of the school. In addition, the relationship between teacher and student may be different from what the child is used to, and many immigrant children are unaware of whom or how to ask for help. Furthermore, the cultural foundations of many schools may be confusing to the students, leading to academic confusion or withdrawal and isolation. As classes become more difficult in middle and high schools, and students must rely more heavily on English-language skills to communicate abstract ideas, immigrant students may experience increased frustration over not being able to communicate effectively. These academic difficulties are problems in and of themselves and can also contribute to emotional issues and conflicts within the family over performance.

Children and adolescents from recent European immigrant families may also be referred for social issues, often related to the child's feeling like an outsider due to differences in dress, language, interests, and the like. Communication difficulties can also add to barriers to a child's social development. In addition, many children may feel conflicted over the peer pressure to engage in "typical" American behaviors that may be seen as inappropriate within the child's cultural norms. Many children of European immigrants may not feel comfortable going outside the family for help, which can further exacerbate the feelings of isolation and a sense of disconnectedness.

In addition to academic and social difficulties, children and adolescents may feel a sense of isolation or a lack of connectedness caused by feeling different from other children. These feelings can affect self-esteem and may lead to feelings of shame about their family or culture when in a majority culture setting such as school. These feelings of shame for one's family and/or country can lead to further feelings of guilt, initiating an emotional cycle. These feelings of social isolation may increase during adolescence, when many immigrants may become frustrated over difficulty fitting into peer groups and experience isolation and rejection at the hands of their peers. Adolescent immigrants may also have to deal with negative stereotypes other students may hold about their cultural background. In addition, many adolescent immigrants may be expected to spend nonschool hours helping out, which may leave them feeling "left out" when their American peers enjoy great freedom to socialize outside school. This may be particularly true of immigrants living in cultural enclaves, who may have difficulty spending time with friends outside the enclave or even participating in extracurricular activities such as sports teams or academic clubs.

Although many adolescents in America experience a decrease in self-esteem during adolescence, immigrant populations may be particularly prone to self-esteem issues. At a time when adolescents often want to be like their peers, immigrant adolescents may be hyperconscious of their differences. During this developmental stage, it is also common for adolescents to lose respect for and even reject their ethnicity, and many experience guilt over decisions made that reject family or cultural values to fit in with the peer group.

Counseling European Immigrants, Refugees, and International Students

Forced and "voluntary" immigrants are faced with creation of a new lifestyle in a new land and frequently must focus on survival, whereas immigrant children hope for the restoration of harmony and a semblance of normalcy in their lives. Whereas the cultural, political, economic, and geographic experiences of migrants are different, some unifying elements exist as well. These elements could be conceptualized as the search for protection from trauma, oppression, and isolation for many, and for others it might be a search for better standards of living and experiencing a new lifestyle. Yet, for most immigrants, numerous layers of stressors tend to become a typical part of life. Focusing on survival for many immigrant families might become a pattern for living generations. For many immigrant families, a sense of belonging is replaced with isolation, a sense of harmony with disruption, a sense of mastery with being devalued, and a sense of independence with dependence. Without understanding and healing, immigrants can become discouraged and might partake in the process of excluding, devaluing, and rejecting themselves and others. The experiences of shame and disconnect may lead to unhealthy patterns of behavior and/or self-medication through the use of alcohol or other substances.

In addition to helping immigrant families rediscover meaningful rituals, counselors can help immigrant individuals and families rebuild a sense of identity and self-efficacy through sharing their stories from their home countries and helping them construct new narratives of their lives in the United States that are filled with hope and meaning. The narrative approach to counseling—which focuses on allowing the client to narrate his or her life story while the counselor strives to understand, encourage, and convey empathy through mutuality leading to the generation of new possibilities and meanings—can help counselors and their clients toward this end. The narrative approach may be particularly helpful for European immigrants because of its wellness orientation that emphasizes the human potential to continually learn instead of focusing on remediation of problems, which often perpetuates feelings of shame and guilt common in European ethnicities, thus hindering growth.

NARRATIVE APPROACH IN COUNSELING   The narrative approach consists of three core phases: deconstructing the dominant culture narrative, externalizing the problem, and reauthoring the story. The deconstruction process focuses on examination of one's experiences relevant to inferiority and superiority. This can be the most challenging process, as clients feel reluctant and resistant to trusting the process of self-exploration and accepting self and others fully. Counselors may find the process of deconstructing the dominant narrative particularly helpful in working with European immigrants by enabling the clients to gain greater awareness of how their life has been influenced by experiences of inferiority or superiority and how these experiences help them in finding mutuality and authenticity in relationships.

In the second phase of the narrative approach, clients begin to externalize the problems. This may be a particularly helpful process for European American immigrants from cultures who have a tendency toward self-blame and feelings of guilt and shame. In this stage, it is important to distinguish problems as being ecological in nature, rather than pathological tendencies that exist within clients. For example, clients might be asked to identify how negative stereotyping in the majority culture affected their views of themselves, or how the feelings of isolation they felt as a result of their immigration status affected their views of themselves and their lives.

Finally, when clients are able to engage in honest reflections and attend to what may otherwise be hidden due to shame and isolation, the counselors can help clients focus on the final phase of the narrative approach: the reauthoring of the story. In this stage, clients and counselors can collaboratively reflect on being successful in life despite, or perhaps in some ways in concert with, the American culture. Counselors can prompt their European clients to reflect on personal strengths used in the past and how these strengths might be used to work through present challenges. This process can help clients as they deconstruct and reconstruct their ethnic identities.

Although storytelling and retelling seem to be conducive to healing and identifying new possibilities, the storytelling does not have to involve only verbal exchanges. Multicultural creative expressions can be used to give voice to those whose thoughts, feelings, and ideas might have been silenced, and this may be particularly effective when working across language barriers. Multicultural creative arts as therapeutic interventions focus on the importance of connectedness and provide opportunities for nonthreatening ways of communication. Various scholars and practitioners have noted the role of creative arts and interventions in counseling (Gladding, 2011; Jacobs, Masson, & Harvill, 2012). Furthermore, several classic theories and scholars emphasize the importance of supporting clients in their quest for connecting and searching for meaningful living (e.g., Adler, 1964; Frankl, 1959). Sharing of life stories, through multicultural creative expressions and practices, further supports the process of relational connectedness.

CREATIVE ARTS   Creative arts can help European immigrant clients find a means of identifying sources of disconnect and frustration, which can be particularly effective with clients who have difficulty expressing such concerns verbally due to language difficulties or cultural norms. In addition, creative techniques can yield opportunities for clients to gain awareness of the healthy source of the power of genuine care, which brings energy to living lives fully and enjoying the human experience. Frankl (2006) described several ways of finding meaning in living, such as truly and fully experiencing nature and culture, and through experiencing other human beings through genuine, caring relationships. Perhaps by helping clients gain awareness of what has given energy to their paths of life, counselors and clients might discover anew the healing power of cultural wisdom, strength, and perspectives that multicultural rituals bring to living.

One of the things that immigrant families lose in the transition to the United States is the traditions and rituals of their family and culture. These rituals and ceremonies serve several essential purposes, including maintaining and restoring wellness for individuals, families, and communities. The process of carrying out the rituals and ceremonies focuses on conveying respect, interdependence, reciprocity, emotionality, intimacy, and modesty (Jakubowska, 2003). It follows, then, that individuals and families across cultures could find healing and wellness by reconnecting with time-honored practices that derive from their culture of origin, as well as other cultural groups, as each culture has its unique rhythm for meaningful living. Counselors who can provide safe environments for immigrant clients to describe and partake in cultural traditions and practices that are meaningful and relevant to them can help the families begin to reground themselves and begin the healing process. (See Resource 14.1.)

To gain awareness of one's cultural heritage, its experiences of privilege or oppression, and its influence on identity formation through reciprocity, it is imperative to explore with clients several elements that influence cultural identity and wellness. Santiago-Rivera, Arredondo, and Gallardo-Cooper (2002) identified the following elements as being essential for exploration: primary social networks (e.g., same ethnicity,

---

Resource 14.1   Polish Wreath Exercise

In the Polish tradition, wreaths signify deep relational connections to people, nature, and life events. Wreaths are made for many reasons: to convey or express respect, honor, love, connection, new beginnings, and new endings. The sense of connectedness that the circle offers in essence is deeply embedded in the creation of the Polish wreath making. Specific flowers, herbs, and times of the year are selected for the creation of wreaths.

Wreaths can be created as part of an honoring ceremony so that the participants can reflect on their meaning making of living, and dying, while focusing on their cultural, community, and family strengths; their ability to remain generous and share their talents and skills; and reflection on how they are presently experiencing their lives. Branches, leaves, and flowers are the basic elements needed to create a wreath. Although ideally participants would be asked to go to nature and select parts for the wreaths, in modern society artificial branches, leaves, and flowers might need to suffice. When designing the wreaths, the dark leaves symbolize the fears and worries that one might encounter, while the yellow flowers represent the radiance of the sun and hope for new beginnings. Children and families might be asked to join together and form a wreath that symbolizes the events in their relationships and lives that are meaningful and essential to understand. Once the wreaths are formed, each family joins the circle and shares the meaning of the wreath. While reflecting on the process of wreath making, the facilitator might ask the following questions:

- What have been some of the toughest things that you encountered?
- How did the strengths within you and in the people in your family and community help you get through?
- How are you different now as a result of this experience?
- What kind of symbols did you come up with? What might those mean to you?
- What kind of strengths did you notice in you and your family members?
- If the flowers and branches could talk to you, what might they be saying?
- If the flowers and branches had a hearing heart, what would they hear from you?
- For you to feel safe and protected, which strengths within you will help you and those around you?

mixed, other); their cultural dimensions such as place of nativity or acculturation level (e.g., integrated, assimilated, marginalized, rejecting); native culture contacts (e.g., high, moderate, low); immigration history (e.g., premigration dynamics, precipitating events, migration experience, postmigration); and language dimensions, psychocultural dimensions, and other sources of stress (e.g., residency, oppression, gender, immigration, racism, ethnosupport, educational, vocational, prejudice, familial, language, economic, marital). In addition, exploring regional cultural differences and living experiences is essential; someone residing in Los Angeles might have totally different experiences than an immigrant living in rural Idaho.

SOCIAL JUSTICE COUNSELING   Another way counselors can work to alleviate stress associated with immigration while promoting wellness is to work from a social justice perspective. **Social justice counseling** represents an effort for counselors to promote general wellness and the common good through addressing systemic and cultural challenges to justice and equity, while helping individuals advocate for themselves within and successfully navigate systems where injustice and inequality exist. (See Chapter 3.) Furthermore, social justice counselors identify four principles that guide their work: equity, access, participation, and harmony (Crethar et al., 2008). The first principle, **equity**, pertains to involvement in a culture-centered approach. Counselors and professionals in the helping fields can be the catalysts for change by giving voice to dynamics that have been silenced and/or ignored. Counselors can become familiar with cultural practices that foster a sense of wellness for individuals representing various cultural groups. **Access**, the second principle, pertains to a counselor's choice to clarify identity construction in self and clients. How do we deconstruct deficiency models and reconstruct frameworks for counseling and educating based on differences, not deficiencies? **Participation**, the third principle, underscores the importance of mutuality and authenticity. Orr and Hulse-Killacky (2006) offered a framework through which counselors are encouraged to note whose voice is heard, and how decisions are made through construction of meaning, leading to transfer of learning that is based on mutuality. It is important for counselors to offer active support to those who are discouraged from participating and whose contributions to society are minimized, devalued, and shut down. As consultants, we need to ask whose stories are celebrated throughout the educational systems, what images are portrayed, and what kind of policies are still not questions that dominant culture members take for granted. The fourth principle, **harmony**, pertains to searching for wellness by tapping into the cultural wisdom and deconstructing the process of devaluing that immigrants may be experiencing. An important aspect of harmony will be developing relationships with clients that are based on the principles of mutuality. Through honest reflections about our ways of relating with our clients—how we connect, how we take time and make time for valuing others, and how respect and care may be withheld from clients whom we serve—we can ensure that clients experience a sense of valuing within the counseling relationship that they may not be experiencing in other aspects of their lives. Through the process of unmasking who we are and what we do, and unmasking cultural camouflage that is a fertile soil for shame and isolation, counselors can provide for their clients an atmosphere of authenticity and permission to be who they desire to be. Moreover, as clients continue the process of questioning and tap into their own sense of wisdom and authenticity, counselors working from a social justice perspective can create and take advantage of opportunities to be the voice for those who have been silenced.

Summary

The purpose of this chapter was to highlight the need for and importance of multicultural counseling with individuals and families of European descent. It is not uncommon for many White American ethnics to be viewed as being acultural (without culture), even by themselves, and not uncommon for recent immigrants from European nations to be viewed as White. Both of these misunderstandings fail to take into account important cultural values and practices that are essential to fully understanding individuals and families. A brief history of European cultures was presented, along with an overview of how European immigrants during the colonial period brought their cultural values and traditions to the colonies, forming the beginnings of a White American ethnicity. Because the English dominated much of the social and political landscape, the developing ethnic identity of the new United States was based largely on English cultural norms, including individualism, self-reliance, strong work ethic, and valuation of achievement and success. However, many other cultures added their own flavors, and in addition, factors such as the geography of the country and larger social changes affected the evolution of ethnic identity. Concepts such as meritocracy, a national heritage, and the metaphor of the United States as a melting pot were both developed from and contributed to the ongoing evolution of the White American ethicity.

A central component of the White American ethnicity was the concept of Whiteness, yet the qualifications of who is considered White are vague and have changed over time and in response to various social and cultural factors, including immigration patterns. What has remained constant, however, is that certain people, based on physical, religious, or other criteria, are allowed or expected to become White, a process by which they adopt certain privileges reserved for White American ethnics, but are also expected to give up, to varying degrees, their former ethnic cultural traditions and values.

The goal of this chapter was to help counselors better conceptualize their clients of European descent. Particular attention was given to understanding that European immigrants to the United States face many of the same stressors that other immigrants face, including grief and loss, underemployment, educational difficulties, difficulties with language, and oppression. Understanding these stressors, as well as understanding their own ethnic and cultural values and practices, is crucial to effective counseling of European immigrants from a multicultural perspective.

At the same time, it is important to remember that White American ethnics, although often not included in multicultural conversations, are indeed cultural beings whose personal, social, emotional, career, educational, or relationship problems can be understood and addressed through a cultural lens. In particular, feelings of inadequacy, incompetence, guilt, and shame within the White American ethnic population may be closely related to the cultural values of independence, success, and personal responsibility that are pervasive. Understanding these cultural values *as cultural values* can help counselors conceptualize their White American ethnic clients from a multicultural perspective and work toward ameliorating the effects of these cultural conflicts with their clients.

However, as with all multicultural counseling, it is important to respect intragroup differences. Many variables of identity, such as gender, socioeconomic status, generation, geographic location, sexual/relationship orientation, ability status, and European country of origin can have profound effects on the cultural identity of the individual, and all these intersecting identities must be explored before an individual of European descent can be understood. This understanding is a crucial component of effective multicultural counseling with both recent European immigrants and White American ethnics, as is the process of cultural self-exploration that occurs within the counseling setting.

Review Questions

1. How did European American history contribute to the development of a White American ethnic identity?

2. How do privilege, oppression, and ethnocentric monoculturalism relate to the White American ethnic experience?

3. What are some of the common European group values across European ethnicities? How did these values contribute to a White American ethnicity?

4. What are some of the issues and considerations for working with recent immigrants of European descent?

5. What are some key counseling considerations for working with individuals and families of European descent?

15 Individuals and Families of Multiracial Descent

Kelley R. Kenney and Mark E. Kenney

PREVIEW

The multiracial population is a rapidly growing segment of U.S. society, and counseling professionals may expect to encounter clients who are members of this population (Kenney & Kenney, 2010). It is the goal of this chapter to contribute to counselors developing the awareness, knowledge, and skills necessary for providing culturally competent and effective services to individuals and families of multiracial descent. The chapter begins with defining and clarifying terminology appropriate to the population. Historical perspectives of race mixing and classification in the United States are then discussed, along with the contemporary social perceptions, discrimination, and worldview experiences of the population. Readers are then introduced to the Competencies for Counseling the Multiracial Population (Kenney et al., 2015) and considerations for counseling individuals and families of the multiracial population are discussed in the framework of the Multicultural and Social Justice Counseling Competencies (Ratts, Singh, Nassar-McMillan, Butler, & McCullough, 2015). Support and other resources established and endorsed by the multiracial community are also provided and discussed.

TERMINOLOGY

Discussion of the interracial/multiracial population requires clarification of terminology and definitions used to refer to and describe who is included. An **interracial couple** is a couple including partners, married or not, who each are of different socially constructed racial backgrounds (Chito Childs, 2005; DaCosta, 2007). **Multiracial families** are families comprised of interracial couples and their multiracial offspring; single parents with biological offspring who are multiracial; and single parents with multiracial offspring as a result of a surrogate pregnancy process or artificial insemination process (Kenney, 2000). **Multiracial individuals** are individuals whose biological parents or whose lineage are of two or more different socially constructed racial backgrounds (DaCosta, 2007; Lewis, 2006).

The terminology used in discussing and describing the multiracial population has evolved over time and began with the use of terminology such as *mixed race* and *biracial* (Henriksen & Paladino, 2009; Root & Kelley, 2003). Although these terms are still used (see Chapter 2), the more commonly used, recognized, and accepted terms of the past 30 years are *interracial* and *multiracial*, with the term *multiracial* being favored for its acknowledgment of the possibility of two or more racial backgrounds (DaCosta, 2007; Henriksen & Paladino, 2009). The term *multiple heritage* has been offered recently (Henriksen & Paladino, 2009) and speaks to the multiple dimensions of identity, culture, and backgrounds of members of this population that include identities other than race. The term *multiple heritage* will be used synonymously with *interracial* and *multiracial* throughout this chapter. Before reading this chapter, complete Reflection 15.1. Then, review excerpts presented in Voices from the Field 15.1, which provides accounts related to multicultural racial identity development.

REFLECTION 15.1

Think about and describe your first experience or encounter of an interracial couple, multiracial family, or multiracial individual.

Voices from the Field 15.1

When I was asked about the development of my identity as a multiracial female, I found myself at a loss for words. Growing up and even today I had never thought in depth about the color of my skin or of others or how I have identified with it. I believe this is because I was brought up to look beyond the color of one's skin rather than to judge because of it. Thinking about the topic at hand, I have come to realize that I identify with the white half of my race rather than the black, and I believe that is how it has always been. I grew up having a better relationship with my mother who is white and went to schools that were primarily white, while I always felt as if I did not fit in with the "black crowd." The more I think about it, the more I realize that I have not identified with the black side of me as much as I believe I should have, and I hope that as time goes on I am able to identify with both shades of me.

~Felicia, Graduate Student, Age 24

My father is from Japan and my mother is from Belgium, but I grew up in the DC metro area. I have always had a very clear sense of my roots since both of my parents are expatriates and still hold their original passports. However, it wasn't until later in my adult life that I gained some perspective on being multiethnic. When I started the research that led to the creation of Loving Day, I discovered multiethnic community groups and academics. I learned terms like *multiethnic, hapa,* and *third culture kid.* I was exposed to literature, films, conferences, and other resources that helped me to put my own identity into context—and to share what I had learned with others through Loving Day.

~Ken, Founder of Loving Day Organization, Age 34

When I grew up in Queens, New York, in the early 80s, there weren't words to describe me. My family didn't talk about race or identity and when it came up it was because I asked questions. One day in the fourth grade, after a bully pulled at the corner of his eyes and yelled, "ching chong ching chong" at me, I ran home to talk to my mother about it. My brothers and I didn't grow up with a strong Asian identity because my father wanted us to be "American." I didn't understand what this bully saw in me that I barely saw in myself. In my 20s, I began to be able to say that both my Chinese and white/Jewish cultures were incorporated into my life and didn't feel compartmentalized (i.e., "I feel Chinese with this group and in this place, and Jewish with that group and in that place"). Meeting other mixed-race people and spending time processing my experiences with them helped me to get to this place. These experiences also led me to create Swirl. I never wanted another mixed child (or adult for that matter) to live without a sense of community and with a feeling that they had to choose one race/culture/ethnicity over the other.

~Jen, Founder/Executive Director of Swirl, Age 34

I'm a native New Yorker of Nigerian, Arab, and Brazilian descent. Growing up in the New York area I was always surrounded by people of varied backgrounds, but even then I noticed that the foods we ate, the clothes we wore, the languages we spoke at home, were slightly different from those around us. I often discussed these differences with my dad in particular since he was an ethnomusiciologist and anthropologist by training. As a teenager, I was fortunate to join my father on numerous field trips through west and central Africa. It was here that I added another facet to my identity, that of being a TCK (third culture kid). Returning to the United States and becoming re-immersed in my birth culture gave me a heightened awareness of my multiethnicity, and in the years since then I have also become an advocate for the multiracial, multicultural, and multiethnic communities in the U.S. and elsewhere. I wouldn't trade my life or my experiences with anyone, since I am mixed, and happy!

~Eddie, Volunteer at Loving Day Organization, Age 40

Having worked with multiple-heritage college students, I've found that honest and genuine empathy has had the strongest impact upon progress. Empathy is the path to a strong relationship as well as a safe environment for these clients to vent when discussing the uniqueness of their identity. Allowing an open space for them to explore what makes them who they are as well as how they interact with different ecological worlds allows for a deeper understanding of their multiple-heritage identity. This is an all too important issue regarding one's developmental time during their time in college. Through these lenses the client can process through any emotion associated with their identity as well as allow the opportunity to discover the strengths allied with being a multiple-heritage individual.

~Derrick, Counselor/Counselor Educator

As a counselor and counselor educator, I have been grateful for the lessons that multiracial students/clients have been willing to teach me about their lived experiences, and I think the lessons I have learned are instructive for all of us. It is so important that we see our multiracial clients as whole and complete individuals. They are not simply the sum of their multiple identities. Students have shared that they struggle when people ascribe attributes to them based on one aspect of their perceived identity. This is especially difficult when counselors do this. In an effort to show how "with it" and culturally competent we are, we presume to know what it is like to be multiracial. When we do this, we can actually make these students/clients feel invisible. As one student said, "I expect everyone else to make assumptions about who I am based on how I look, but I don't expect that from counselors."

~Peggy, Counselor/Counselor Educator

In working with multiracial teenagers as they explore their own identity development, it is important to remember that many of them will be uncovering a multiple heritage that may be new to not only them, but others in their lives as well. It is important for the clinician to work with the client on acknowledging the struggles of the multiple heritages, both in and out of session. Clinicians should assist these teenagers in establishing a strong support system as they weave their way through this path of growth in their lives. Support may take on many forms, and may come from many places; remembering it is vital that the teens have support to turn to while developing their multiple-heritage identity. Clinicians can also play an important role in the support system by remaining nonjudgmental, present, and open in sessions as these young people learn more about themselves and their place in the world.

~Ami, Counselor

HISTORICAL PERSPECTIVES

Discussion of the multiple-heritage population requires consideration of the major historical events that have informed the sociopolitical landscape of this population. Interracial couples and multiracial individuals have been part of the history of American society since the first European settlers arrived on American soil in 1607. The earliest of these documented relationships were between the indigenous female inhabitants and the early White male settlers. With the arrival of the first African slave ships and the first women of European heritage in 1619 came an increase in interracial mixing, although it is important to note that not all these encounters were voluntary (Joyner & Kao, 2005; Kaba, 2006, 2011). Notions of White racial purity and superiority and a desire to exert and maintain power and control at that time over Blacks and Native Americans gave rise to systems of racial, economic, and sociopolitical hierarchies. These structures led to the enactment of the first antimiscegenation laws in 1664. Although these initial laws were directed toward Blacks and Native Americans, subsequent laws prohibited marriages involving other groups of color that had immigrated to America (DaCosta, 2007; Kaba, 2006, 2011).

The first and most salient historical event was the landmark *Loving v. Virginia* (1967) Supreme Court decision, which struck down all U.S. laws against interracial marriage. In 1958, Mildred Jeter and Richard Loving, both of Caroline County, Virginia, decided to marry. Richard was White, and Mildred was of African and Native American heritage. Because they were aware of the laws forbidding them to marry in Virginia, they went to Washington, DC, where interracial marriages were legal. Upon returning home to Virginia to begin their married life, they were arrested on the basis of Virginia's antimiscegenation laws, which deemed their marriage unlawful. To avoid imprisonment, they agreed to leave Virginia for a period of 25 years and moved to Washington, DC (Roberts, 2014).

Encouraged by the progress being made in other arenas of the Civil Rights Movement, the Lovings sought the assistance of the U.S. Attorney General's Office and the American Civil Liberties Union. Their case was taken through several levels of the justice system before it was ultimately heard by the U.S. Supreme Court. On June 12, 1967, the U.S. Supreme Court voted unanimously in favor of the Lovings (Loving Day, 2009). According to Gold (2008), the decision made by the Supreme Court found that Virginia was in violation of both the Equal Protection and the due process clauses of the fourteenth amendment.

Thirty states had enacted antimiscegenation laws, including Virginia. States that had repealed their antimiscegenation laws prior to 1967 included Arizona, California, Colorado, Idaho, Indiana, Montana, Nebraska, Nevada, North Dakota, Oregon, South Dakota, Utah, and Wyoming. The U.S. Supreme Court's 1967 *Loving* decision made illegal the antimiscegenation laws that remained on the books of Virginia and 16 other states, including Alabama, Arkansas, Delaware, Florida, Georgia, Kentucky, Louisiana, Maryland, Mississippi, Missouri, North Carolina, Oklahoma, South Carolina, Tennessee, Texas, and West Virginia (Henriksen & Paladino, 2009; Loving Day, 2009).

The ideology of hypodescent, also known as the one-drop rule, emerged during slavery and came out of the White male colonists' need to impose and maintain control over the identities of persons of African descent, with the expressed intention of keeping them oppressed (DaCosta, 2007; Lewis, 2006). The laws of hypodescent first enacted in 1661 paralleled the laws of antimiscegenation and were initially a direct affront against unions involving White women and Black men (Chito Childs, 2005; DaCosta, 2007; Lewis, 2006). The principle of hypodescent held that the multiple-heritage individual should be assigned the racial identity of the parent of the lower social status (Kaba, 2011; Lewis, 2006). Although the historical significance of this concept has been its application to Black–White multiple-heritage individuals, it has also been applied to multiple-heritage individuals of White and other non-White backgrounds (DaCosta, 2007; Kaba, 2006; Wilt, 2011).

The prevalence, interpretation, and application of the laws of hypodescent have varied in their impact on racial classification systems, including the U.S. Census, throughout history (Henriksen & Paladino, 2009; Lewis, 2006). According to DaCosta (2007), as the various people's movements of the 1960s and 1970s (e.g., Black Power, Chicano, Asian American, and Native American) were empowering groups of color to self-determine and define, the experiences of multiple-heritage individuals relative to these groups varied, and hence the acceptance of the notion of multiracial identity by these groups also varied. With the establishment of the first multiracial organization, Interracial/Inter-cultural Pride (I-Pride), in San Francisco in 1978, came the rise of a movement that advocated for the rights of multiracial families and individuals (Douglass, 2003). The 1980s and early 1990s saw the emergence of a multiracial civil rights movement. Led by multiple-heritage individuals and families, it was a movement that saw the development of organizations around the country geared toward bringing public consciousness and positive awareness of the issues and concerns of the multiracial population to the forefront.

By the mid-1990s two of these organizations, the Association of MultiEthnic Americans (AMEA) and Project RACE (Reclassify All Children Equally), had become political forces around issues confronting the population and had begun to lobby the U.S. government for a multiracial category for the 2000 U.S. Census (Douglass, 2003). The Association of MultiEthnic Americans served as the voice for the population on this issue by serving on the 2000 U.S. Census Advisory Committee. The prospect of adding a "multiracial" category or any separate identification for multiracial individuals to the 2000 U.S. Census met with much controversy, particularly from traditional civil rights and ethnic special-interest groups, including the National Association for the Advancement of Colored People (NAACP), the Mexican American Legal Defense and Education Fund (MALDEF), and the National Coalition for the Accurate Count of Asian and Pacific Americans. In 1997 the U.S. Office of Management and Budget (OMB) decided to implement a "check one or more" format for the 2000 Census. This decision and the endorsement of it by AMEA and others within the multiracial movement was viewed as a compromise and resulted in an ideological split within the movement.

The 2000 U.S. Census's historic "check one or more" format marked the legal termination of the last vestiges of the hypodescent statutes by giving multiple-heritage individuals and their families the right to identify as they choose. However, although these laws no longer exist, they continue to influence societal thinking around the social construct of race and racial identity, including the thinking of those within the multiracial community (Lewis, 2006). There is much diversity of thought regarding the notion of embracing a collective identity within the multiracial community, and the issue of hypodescent resonates differently depending on the racial combination. This is particularly evident within the Black/White segment of the population (Kaba, 2011; Lewis, 2006).

In the 2010 U.S. Census 9 million people, including 4.2 million under the age of 18 years, identified as being of two or more races. This was an increase of 32% compared to the previous census of the number of people identifying as being of two or more races (U.S. Census Bureau, 2014d). According to the U.S. Census Bureau's American Community Survey, in 2013 9.3 million individuals or 3% of the U.S. population were identified as being multiracial (Pew Research Center, 2015a).

ACTIVITY 15.1

There is considerable demographic information provided through the Pew Research Center and the U.S. Census Bureau, and through Census Scope (multiracial individuals only). Investigate the demographics of your state and local community to determine the size of the multiracial population. Determine if and where the population is most prominent, and determine what resources are available to the population. Further, the Office of Management and Budget's (OMB) Directive 15 requires a "check all that apply" (with regard to questions of race and ethnicity) on all government forms. This coincides with the OMB mandate for the 2000 and 2010 census. How is this mandate regulated in your state and local community? How are multiracial children identified and counted in data collected by state and local school districts? Discuss in small groups how you might advocate for this population to be more accurately counted.

INTERRACIAL MARRIAGES TODAY

U.S. interracial marriages have been on the rise since the 1967 U.S. Supreme Court's *Loving* decision struck down remaining laws against interracial marriage; 6.3% of all marriages in 2013 were interracial (Wang, 2015). Results of the Pew Research Center's (2015a) analysis of census data for the same year further revealed that 12% of newly married couples were interracial.

Data on intermarriage continue to reveal that certain groups are more likely to intermarry than others. Of the 3.6 million adults who got married in 2013, 58% of Native Americans, 28% of Asians, 19% of Blacks and 7% of Whites married a person of a different racial background (Wang, 2015). In discussing intermarriage related to Hispanics, it is important to note that, since the U.S. Census Bureau identifies this population as an ethnic group, the intermarriage rates for this group are identified and reported as interethnic (Wang, 2012). According to Wang (2012) the intermarriage rates for Hispanics, including newlyweds, are also increasing. With regard to gender, while intermarriage rates have increased overall, Black men are more likely than Black women to marry someone of a different race and Asian women are more likely than Asian men to marry someone of a different race. Among Native Americans, women are only slightly more likely than men to marry outside of their race (Wang, 2015).

Regional patterns related to interracial marriage consistently reveal that the rates for these marriages tend to be highest in the western United States. Between 2008 and 2010, 22% of new marriages in the West were interracial, while 14% of those in the South, 13% of those in the Northeast and 11% of those in the Midwest were interracial (Johnson & Kreider, 2013; Wang, 2012). Research of other social trends and patterns related to interracial marriage suggest that decreases in social distance between groups in the areas of work, education, and living arrangements, as well as higher levels of assimilation and acculturation, increase the potential for intermarriage (Kaba, 2011; Passel, Wang, & Taylor, 2010). Growing public acceptance has also been cited as being related to the increasing number of intermarriages (Pew Research Center, 2014; Wang, 2015).

The discussion of public perceptions and the rising number of interracial couples would not be complete without mentioning the rise in the numbers of interracial same-sex couples. Examining data from the 2010 U.S. Census, Gates (2012) found that more than one in five (20.6%) same-sex couples were interracial or interethnic compared to 18.3% of heterosexual unmarried couples and 9.5% of heterosexual married couples. Similar to the geographic data indicating that the highest percentage of heterosexual interracial couples live in the Western region of the country, the 2010 census data on same-sex couples revealed the same, with more than half (53%) of these couples living in Hawaii (Gates, 2012). With the June 26th, 2015, Supreme Court Decision striking down all bans against same-sex marriages in the United States, there is an expected rise in the number of interracial marriages that are same-sex marriages.

Some of the professional literature has shown a slightly higher divorce rate for interracial couples (Wang, 2012; Zhang & Van Hook, 2009). For example, multiple-heritage marriages involving Blacks were found to be at greater risk for divorce, followed by those involving Hispanics. Multiple-heritage marriages involving Asians appeared to be at lower risk for ending in divorce, even when compared to same-race marriages involving Whites (Zhang & Van Hook, 2009). However, it is important to note that race/ethnicity may not be the sole risk factor or reason for divorce among these couples. Rather, other salient identities seem to better predict the success or failure of these relationships (Bratter & King, 2008). These identities include gender, level of education, and age at the time of marriage. For example, with regard to gender, interracial relationships involving White women and non-White males appear to have a greater likelihood for ending in divorce. This is especially true in the case of White women married to Black men. Findings suggest that these pairings are the most at risk for dissolving (Zhang & Van Hook, 2009).

MULTIRACIAL IDENTITY DEVELOPMENT

Working with families and individuals of multiracial descent requires counselors to have knowledge of the various models developed to explain the identity development processes of multiple-heritage individuals. Some of these models were introduced and reviewed in Chapter 2. Early models of the identity development process of multiple-heritage individuals examined this process from a stage perspective and focused solely on the racial identity development of the individual (Jacobs, 1992; Kerwin & Ponterotto, 1995; Kich, 1992; Phinney, 1993; Poston, 1990; Root, 1990). The models espoused by Poston (1990), Jacobs (1992), and Kerwin and

Ponterotto (1995) were limited in that they only examined the identity development of Black–White multiple-heritage individuals. Table 15.1 provides descriptions of these six multiracial identity development models.

Root (1998; as mentioned in Chapter 2) offered an ecological identity development model. While this model was derived from her counseling and therapeutic work with multiple-heritage individuals with Asian backgrounds, it examined the family and the individual in context to several major developmental, environmental, and other identity factors. The Root (2002) Ecological Framework for Understanding Multiracial Identity Development (see Figure 15.1) illustrates and provides a perspective of how the following influence and shape multiracial identity: various family and personal characteristics; social, psychological, and cognitive development factors; environmental factors; and visible and invisible identity factors, examined in combination with each other and through the magnifying lens of individuals' physical appearance or phenotype. One of the most valuable aspects of this model is its usefulness for understanding and working with both multiracial individuals and their families.

TABLE 15.1 Multiracial Identity Development Models

Poston (1990) Preschool–Adult	Jacobs (1992) Preschool–Age 12	Kerwin & Ponterotto (1995) Preschool–Adult	Kich (1992) Preschool–Adult	Phinney (1993) Adolescence	Root (1990) Children–Adult
Stage 1 Personal Identity Sense of self with no racial/ethnic awareness	Stage 1 (0–4½) Precolor Constancy: Play & experimentation with color	Stage 1 (Preschool–5) Awareness of differences in physical appearances	Stage 1 (3–10) Awareness and dissonance	Stage 1 Unexamined ethnic identity	Individual accepts identity assigned by society
Stage 2 Choice of Group Categorization Child is pressured to identify with one group	Stage 2 (4½–8) Postcolor Constancy: Biracial label and racial awareness	Stage 2 (Entry into school) Defines self based on physical appearance	Stage 2 (8–late adolescence) Struggle for acceptance	Stage 2 Ethnic identity search moratorium	Individual identifies with both racial groups
Stage 3 Enmeshment/Denial Individual is confused by single identity choice	Stage 3 (8–12) Biracial identity	Stage 3 (Pre-adolescence) Awareness of biracial status	Stage 3 (Adulthood) Self-acceptance and assertion of an interracial identity	Stage 3 Achieved ethnic identity	Individual identifies with a single group

(Continued)

TABLE 15.1   Multiracial Identity Development Models (Continued)

Stage 4 Appreciation Individual values multiple backgrounds, but identifies with single identity	Stage 4 (Adolescence) Pressure to identify with one racial heritage	Individual identifies with multiracial group
Stage 5 Integration Individual identifies with and has integrated multiple backgrounds	Stage 5 (College–Emerging Adult) Affiliation with one racial heritage with movement toward biracial awareness	
	Stage 6 (Adulthood) Biracial awareness and integration	

Multiracial identity development is complex (Lou, Lalonde, & Wilson, 2011) and varies depending upon numerous factors (Root, 2003). Although racial identity can provide for an individual's sense of self and sense of belonging to a group (Khanna, 2004), this sense of self may be especially complex for multiple-heritage individuals, considering their multiple racial backgrounds (Kenney et al., 2015; Mahtani, 2014) and how these are negotiated (Binning, Unzueta, Huo, & Molina, 2009; Cheng & Lee, 2009). Cheng and Lee (2009) discussed the importance of multiracial identity integration, described as the extent to which the individual perceives his or her multiple racial identities as compatible and integrated.

Assessment of multiracial identity integration involves examining levels of racial distance and racial conflict related to the ways in which multiracial individuals negotiate their varied racial group memberships. Racial distance is concerned with the perception of one's multiple racial identities as unique and separate from one another, while racial conflict is concerned with one's perception of the existence of conflict between one's multiple racial identities. Multiracial individuals with low levels of racial distance and low levels of racial conflict are deemed as having high multiracial identity integration (Cheng & Lee, 2009). According to Binning et al. (2009), who examined the psychological adjustment of multiracial individuals, those multiracial individuals who identified with multiple racial groups had significantly lower stress levels related to negotiating between their multiple racial identities and had greater levels of psychological well-being and social engagement. This supports Cheng and Lee (2009), who found that individuals with high multiracial identity integration perceived their multiple racial identities as compatible and complementary and felt good about identifying strongly with their multiple racial groups. High multiracial identity integration is associated with positive psychological adjustment.

It is important to understand race as a social construct when examining the racial identity development of multiracial individuals (Rockquemore, Brunsma, & Delgado, 2009). They found that having a multiracial identity that was validated by others was associated with higher levels of identity integration and self-concept. These findings support those of Cheng and Lee (2009) and, much like Root's (2002) framework, speak to the fact that multiracial identity is contextual and fluid. Terry and Winston (2010) further supported Root (2003) in terms of emphasizing the importance of understanding the fluctuations and adaptations of identity that occur over time with this population.

An issue salient to the identity development of multiracial individuals with White ancestry is that of privilege (Dawkins, 2012; Mahtani, 2014). The major manifestation of privilege with regard to this population is often associated with the concept of passing for White. The act of passing for White by a mixed-race individual is often in relation to the individual's response to others' perceptions of his or her racial background based upon phenotype (Mahtani, 2014). Historical and sociopolitical hierarchies of race privileges Whiteness (see Chapter 4), and the meaning given to Whiteness by the multiracial individual may be something to assess. As well, related to Cheng and Lee's (2009) multiracial identity integration, it may be important to assess the extent to which individuals embrace or renounce their White race identity and how this aspect of their identity is negotiated.

CONTEMPORARY SOCIAL PERCEPTIONS, SALIENT EXPERIENCES, AND RESILIENCE

Demographic information on multiple-heritage couples, individuals, and families makes clear their varied racial, cultural, and ethnic combinations. However, automatic thinking and images of these couples and families as only Black and White prevail, although this combination is only a small segment of the population (Kaba, 2011). The fact that multiple-heritage couples and families exist in varying racial, cultural, and ethnic combinations also means that they present counselors with multiple racial, cultural, and ethnic ideologies and beliefs. As the topic of immigration is increasingly debated in this country, feelings and responses to the issues of immigration may also need to be examined, as the multiracial population also includes individuals from other countries (DaCosta, 2007; Lee & Edmonston, 2005).

Issues and concerns salient to multiple-heritage couples, families, and individuals have always been related to the level of approval and acceptance by society, community, and family (Kenney & Kenney, 2014). This section examines the current societal perceptions, attitudes, and salient experiences of multiple-heritage individuals, couples, and families, and examines the worldview experiences that are part of their sociocultural and political landscape. The topic of resilience is also examined. Although the number of same-sex interracial couples has increased, discussion of this specific segment of the population will not be covered. Similarly, we do not include discussion on the experiences of LGBT multiple-heritage families or individuals. It is important to note, however, that all other intersecting and salient identities are important to assess for and consider in terms of the experiences of all members of the multiracial population (Kenney et al., 2015). Chapter 6 of this text addresses this population.

Individuals

Multiple-heritage individuals spend a lifetime confronting societal perceptions of them and their families borne out by myths and stereotypes that they are "confused, unhappy, and pathological" (Wardle & Cruz-Janzen, 2004, p. 189). The development of a positive racial and cultural identity and self-concept as they engage their environments is the salient issue and concern of multiple-heritage individuals (Hud-Aleem & Countryman, 2008; Laszloffy, 2005; Wilt, 2011). The achievement of a positive racial and cultural identity and self-concept depends on individuals' support systems, how concerns are managed at each age and phase of life, and the strengths, assets, and inner resources that come with developmental growth and maturity (Hud-Aleem & Countryman, 2008; Wilt, 2011).

According to Root (1994), it is important to understand that identity issues and concerns that arise for multiracial individuals across the life span emerge from six interrelated themes:

- *Uniqueness:* Multiracial individuals beginning even before birth are often treated as unique, special, or different because of their multiple heritages. Attempts to counter this image can lead to behaviors or interactions that may be misinterpreted or misunderstood.
- *Acceptance and belonging:* Multiracial individuals often find themselves straddling the lines of their multiple heritages, attempting to prove their racial loyalties and allegiances. Feeling that one does not fully belong to any one group may lead to an ongoing search for connection and fit.
- *Physical appearance:* Physical appearance affects all aspects of multiple-heritage individuals' existence and plays a major role in how they are perceived, judged, and accepted in a racial context. Physical appearance is particularly salient for multiple-heritage women because of societal pressures that place particular values on appearance.
- *Sexuality:* This theme has special significance for multiple-heritage women, as sexual myths and stereotypes prevail and fuel societal perceptions of multiracial women as sexually exotic objects to be sought and dominated.
- *Self-esteem:* This theme is concerned with individual development of a positive self-concept and internal frame of reference. Multiracial individuals' self-esteem interfaces with and is influenced by their experiences with the other five themes.
- *Identity:* Key to the multiple-heritage individual's functioning is affirmation for the development of a fluid but integrated racial identity that celebrates all aspects of one's heritages.

Root (2003) indicates that there are five identity possibilities that an individual may select over the life span. These potential identity choices are influenced by the generational cohort into which the individual is born.

1. *Assignment by hypodescent/one-drop rule.* Multiple-heritage individuals who identify in this manner have accepted the racial identity assigned to them by society. This identity is typically a monoracial minority identity based on the one-drop rule and hypodescent (Root, 2003). According to Root, this has often been the only option for older generations of multiracial individuals.
2. *Monoracial fit self-assignment.* This identity is a self-selected monoracial minority identity that is based on fit and is consistent with the experience of the individual over time. This identity option can result in challenges if it is different from how others perceive the multiracial individual based on phenotype (Root, 2003).

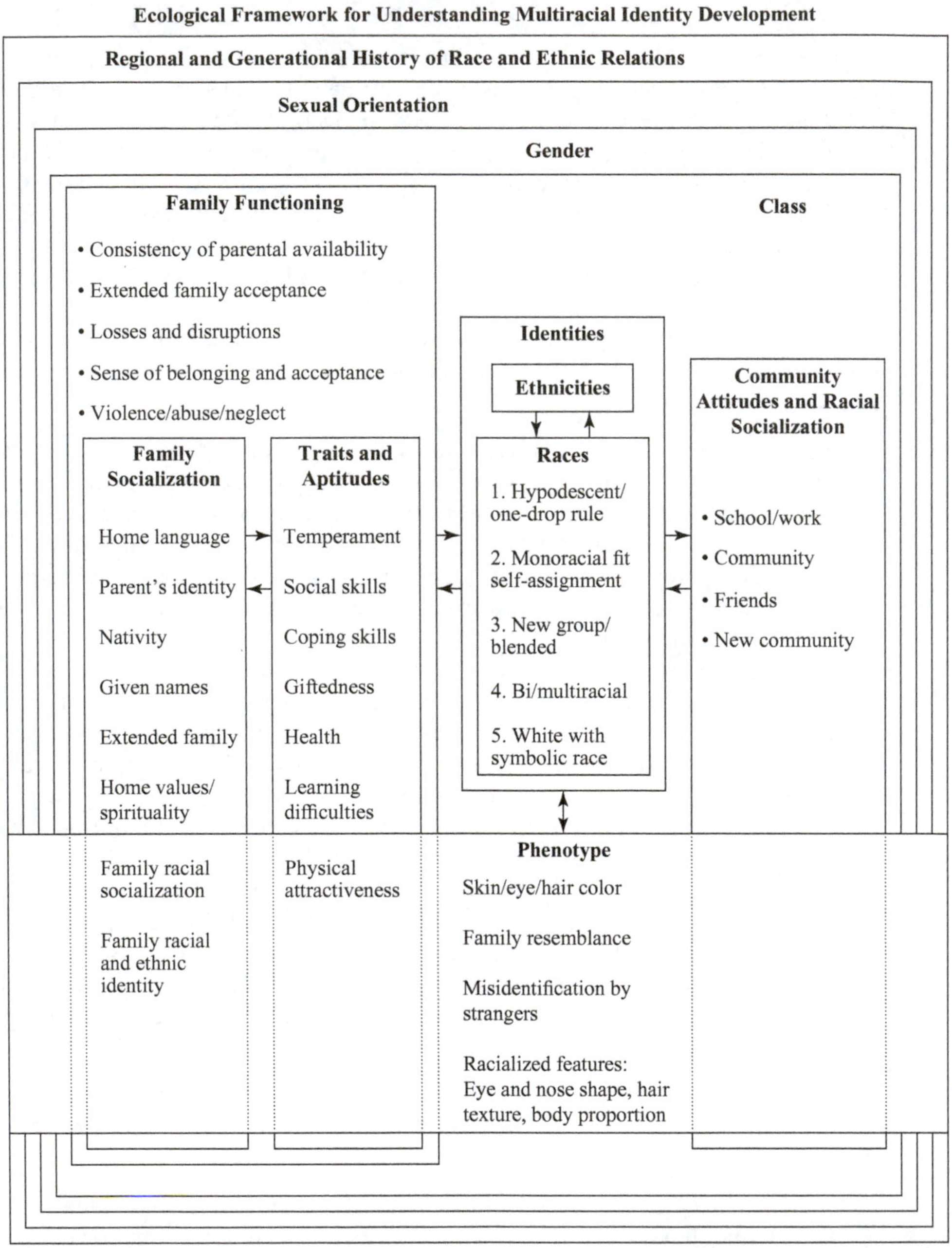

Ecological Framework for Understanding Multiracial Identity Development

FIGURE 15.1

3. *New group/blended.* According to Root (2003a), based on the situation that the individual encounters, one aspect of that individual's heritage/identity may be more salient than another, and hence the identity that surfaces or is claimed may vary and is fluid. This identity is a more recent option.

4. *Biracial/multiracial.* This identity is part of a more recent and radical phenomenon that has emerged from the experiences of younger generations of multiple-heritage individuals.

The declaration of a biracial or multiracial identity is both a refusal to break racial and ethnic identity down into categories and a celebration of all of one's racial and ethnic heritages (Root, 2003).

5. *White with symbolic identity.* According to Root (2003), this is the newest of the potential identities and is more indicative of identification with a class lifestyle and values, or a lack of exposure to and experience with an ethnic background to which one belongs. This identity can present special challenges if the individual selecting it does not have another salient identity related to a special talent or aptitude or does not have the temperament to deal with the criticism, scrutiny, or opposition that may come from others as a result of making such a selection (Root, 2003).

Jackson (2010) also discussed salient themes of experiences of multiple-heritage persons across the life span. These themes include shifting racial/ethnic expression, racial resistance, seeking community, racial ambiguity, and feeling like an outsider. **Shifting racial/ethnic expression** entails altering the expression of one's racial/ethnic identity depending upon the environmental context. This is typically an approach taken in order to accommodate and make others comfortable. **Racial resistance** is the act of defying traditional social norms and conventions of race perpetuated in U.S. society in response to inquiries about one's racial/ethnic identity. This response is often viewed as indicative of a more evolved and integrated sense of self and may also be indicative of resilience. **Seeking community** is indicative of multiracial individuals' quests to find and to connect with others with whom they share similar worldview experiences and values. It is important to note that this does not just include other multiracial persons, but others who can empathize with the experience of being different.

The final two themes espoused by Jackson substantiate and affirm the aforementioned themes from Root (1994). **Racial ambiguity** concerns the ambiguous physical features and appearance that for many multiracial individuals result in comments and questions by others regarding their racial/ethnic backgrounds and identity. **Feeling like an outsider** speaks to the essence of not fitting in, feeling marginalized and unaccepted by any of one's identity groups (Jackson, 2010). As with Root's (1994) themes, the encounters and experiences associated with these themes are unique and can vary depending upon developmental stage, other life factors, and intersecting identities. As suggested in the section on multiracial identity development, the level of understanding and support provided by family and salient others, and the manner in which the individual negotiates these themes, have implications for positive and healthy identity development, identity integration, and psychological adjustment throughout the life span (Cheng & Lee, 2009; Jackson, 2010; Rockquemore et al., 2009).

Very little has been written on the topic of resilience with regard to multiple-heritage individuals; however, when the discussion emerges it is often related to social functioning and positive psychological outcomes (Jackson, 2010; Miville, Constantine, Baysden, & So-Lloyd, 2005; Shih & Sanchez, 2005). The extent to which multiracial individuals value human differences and worldviews and have empathy for persons of different cultures is indicative of enhanced social functioning. Salahuddin and O'Brien (2011) examined enhanced social functioning and positive psychological outcomes as resilience factors that were positively related to self-esteem, social connectedness, and ethnic identity and negatively related to depression. Additional findings of their research revealed that enhanced social functioning was also related to a valuing of human and cultural differences, and positive psychological outcomes were also related to a sense of multiracial pride. Case Study 15.1 provides an opportunity to apply some of the multicultural identity frameworks presented in the chapter.

CASE STUDY 15.1

Leora is a 25-year-old single multiracial and bisexual woman who currently works and resides in a small southern U.S. city. She has ambiguous racial features and grew up and completed her education through her undergraduate degree in a Northern California metropolitan area where she lived with her African-American mother and Filipino-American father. Her family of origin talked about "race" and racism and took advantage of multicultural events and activities in the region. She feels connected to her extended family on both sides, who live in close proximity to her. Her community and school district were both very diverse.

She completed her studies in journalism with a desire to become a television reporter and eventually, a news anchor. Upon attaining her degree, she secured a position as a news reporter in a small southern U.S. city. During the past six months, she has experienced some difficulties with the transition from her diverse community of origin to a more racially segregated community. Arriving to this new community, she thought that she could readily share all of her identities, just as she had back home, but soon found herself being met with many negative and invalidating reactions. Some of these reactions were experienced in the workplace in terms of racial, gender, and sexual orientation discrimination. She also experienced a series of either challenges or rejections to her racial identity in social situations with both Whites and people of color. Not knowing how to respond to these interactions and experiences, she has become withdrawn, has begun to isolate herself, and finds that she does not enjoy her work or personal life.

- How can Root's (2002) Ecological Framework for Understanding Multiracial Identity Development be applied to understanding Leora's case?
- Which of Jackson's (2010) themes are salient for understanding the case and working with Leora?
- What are some areas to discuss with Leora in terms of these frameworks? How would you counsel Leora?

Couples

According to Wang (2012) there has been a dramatic shift in societal approval of interracial marriage in the United States, with more than 4 in 10 Americans indicating that intermarriage is good for society. Analysis of the U.S. Census Bureau's American Community Survey for 2008 to 2010 by the Pew Research Center, as well as three of the Center's own surveys on public perceptions toward intermarriage, revealed that a third of all Americans reported having a member of their immediate family or a close relative in an interracial marriage. In addition, the analysis revealed that nearly 63% of Americans responded that they would be fine if a member of their own family were to intermarry.

Despite the increase in approval rates and numbers of multiple-heritage couples, the topic continues to meet with some scrutiny and occasional opposition. However, the degree of opposition varies depending on couples' socioeconomic status, educational level, and geographical location or region of the United States (DaCosta, 2007; Wilt, 2011). Interracial couples challenge racial stratification systems and sociopolitical hierarchies that have resulted in societal perceptions that different groups of people are unequal and should not marry. This is particularly the case for Black–White couples, whose relationships often stir up unresolved tensions and other manifestations of the legacy of slavery (Chito Childs, 2005; Lewis, 2006; Yancey, 2007).

Negative perceptions of interracial couples are rooted in historical myths, stereotypes, and other forms of misinformation. Many portray persons of color as deviant and depict interracial unions, particularly those between Whites and persons of color, as problematic, wrought with difficulties, or inherently dysfunctional (Chito Childs, 2005; DaCosta, 2007; Lewis, 2006; Wilt, 2011). Common myths and stereotypes suggest that interracial coupling occurs because one or both partners are attempting to make a statement or have a desire to rebel against their family and society (Root, 2001). Other myths and stereotypes suggest that one or the other partner has ulterior motives for intermarrying, which may include presumptions of the exotic or erotic; sexual promiscuity or curiosity; desire for financial or social status; or need for control or domination (Wardle, 1999). Still other myths and stereotypes suggest that one or the other partner may be desperate, have low self-esteem, be color-blind or racially self-loathing, be seeking citizenship, or have difficulty attracting a mate of his or her own race (DaCosta, 2007; Wilt, 2011).

The relationships of multiple-heritage couples are similar to and no more problematic than same-race couples, and partners' racial and cultural differences seem to be of little or no consequence to the overall dynamics of their relationships (Joyner & Kao, 2005; Lee & Edmonston, 2005; Wilt, 2011). Although this may not be the case for some couples, generally the racial and cultural differences of partners seem to be more of a concern to those outside the relationship (Chito Childs, 2005; DaCosta, 2007). Couples report a range of experiences in dealing with parents, siblings, and extended family members, including fear and anxiety about the couple's future, lack of support and acceptance, and/or alienation and rejection. In public and social spheres, couples' experiences range from stares, racist comments, and slurs to acts of discrimination, hostility, and violence (Chito Childs, 2005; DaCosta, 2007; Kaba, 2011; Lewis, 2006; Wilt, 2011). In cases where multiple-heritage partners are at different levels of assimilation and acculturation, concerns often arise around differences in partners' cultural context and worldview experiences related to communication, language, religion, gender role expectations, parenting, traditions, and food (Crippen & Brew, 2007, 2013; Edwards, Caballero, & Puthussery, 2010).

Multiple-heritage couples, particularly those involving Whites and persons of color, may find themselves feeling vulnerable to the questions and challenges, including racism, posed by external forces. Hence, Chito Childs (2005) indicated the importance of partners understanding the role and influence that racism and privilege have in their lives and may thus play out in the relationship. Success of the relationship relies on both partners being secure within themselves and with each other. Success also relies on both partners having a strong self-concept, including a strong racial self-concept, and that the partners are clear about why they are together (Bratter & King, 2008; Chito Childs, 2005). Poulsen (2003) further emphasized that a strong and secure relational foundation is critical as couples find themselves negotiating the influences that each partner's racial and cultural traditions and identifications pose over the life span.

It is also important to discuss the issue of marital satisfaction with regard to interracial couples, as this contributes to the strength of the relationship and the success of the marriage (Wilt, 2011). A strong sense of racial identity that includes knowledge of the history of one's race and positive views about one's race on the part of both partners in the relationship is seen as a positive influence of marital satisfaction. This is especially crucial for Black partners in interracial relationships. The issue of gender role fairness with regard to household chores, child care, decision-making processes, sexual relationships, and finances has also been discussed as contributing to marital satisfaction. Perceptions of inequities and imbalance may be linked to perceptions of power and power differentials that result in one or the other partner feeling less satisfied with the marriage (Forry, Leslie, & Letiecq, 2007).

Discussions of resilience with regard to interracial couples are as limited as discussions of resilience with respect to multiracial individuals. The resilience of interracial couples may be a result of the support that they receive from friends, family, and co-workers (Nord, 2012). It may also lie within the many strengths and assets that may be afforded to them as individual partners and as couples. These strengths and assets include that they are often more socially connected, that they have gained maturity as a result of overcoming adversity, and that they have distanced "themselves from negative environments and hostility" (Wilt, 2011, p. 9). The challenges of discrimination and other negative forces experienced by interracial couples often leads to them becoming stronger and to the development of a deeper commitment to each other and to the marriage. This in and of itself speaks to their resiliency.

Families

Multiple-heritage couples must also deal with societal perceptions toward their offspring and families. Kenney and Kenney (2002) indicated that the development of a healthy family structure and a positive family identity are major issues or concerns for multiple-heritage couples as they begin to have children. Although these are issues and concerns of all couples as they begin to raise families, the realities of racism may be of more importance for those of multiple heritages. Hence, ensuring the positive identity development of their children also becomes paramount (DaCosta, 2007; Hud-Aleem & Countryman, 2008; Wilt, 2011).

Historical myths and stereotypes about multiple-heritage families suggest that the familes are either totally unsupported and rejected or only supported by communities of color (DaCosta, 2007; Yancey, 2007). Other myths and stereotypes linked to sexualized perceptions purport a specialness about multiracial couples and the children they produce, suggesting that the children are significantly more beautiful and handsome (Sue & Sue, 2013). Prevailing myths and stereotypes also portray multiple-heritage individuals as destined to have social and psychological problems (Jackman, Wagner, & Johnson, 2001); have low self-esteem; and be troubled, lost, and confused about their identity (DaCosta, 2007; Sue & Sue, 2013; Wilt, 2011). See Reflection 15.2 to consider your own views about interracial couples and their children. To consider how multiracial individuals make sense of possible challenges of multiple racial/ethnic identities, Reflection 15.3 provides an opportunity to consider how you might react to being asked to choose only one identity among the several identities that characterize you.

Issues and concerns of identity emerge for interracial couples as soon as discussions of children arise. Challenged by the question "What about the children?" and other inquiries

---

REFLECTION 15.2

What have been your perceptions of interracial couples? Where did these perceptions originate? Of what societal myths and stereotypes regarding interracial couples are you aware?

REFLECTION 15.3

Consider all the *salient* identities to which you ascribe. Now imagine being told to choose only *one* of these identities to define yourself. Describe this experience and the feelings that emerge for you. Imagine experiencing this over your life span.

---

about how their children may turn out, multiple-heritage couples are forced to think about their children and how to raise them in ways that may be different from same-race couples, including same-race couples of color (Jackson-Nakazawa, 2003). Concerns about how their multiple-heritage children will be regarded or treated because of their mixed racial backgrounds emerge for couples before their children are conceived or born (DaCosta, 2007; Laszloffy, 2005). White parents for whom race may never have been an issue often find themselves feeling completely confused and helpless to deal with their own and their children's experiences of racism (Wilt, 2011). Conversely, parents of color, including those who are multiracial but identify monoracially, may find themselves ill-equipped to understand or deal with the experiences of their children due to their own unresolved issues (Sue & Sue, 2013).

Parents and children alike frequently deal with curiosities and assumptions regarding the child's racial identity based on their physical appearance. Physical appearance or phenotype is an overarching variable that affects how the child is perceived and dealt with beginning at birth (Jackson-Nakazawa, 2003), and hence it influences his or her racial identity development (Hud-Aleem & Countryman, 2008). Physical appearance remains a salient theme over the course of the individual's life span (Root, 2003). Societal obsessions with race and racial demarcations suggest that the physical appearance of multiple-heritage individuals are not only rare and unusual, but also make it difficult to discern where they fit in terms of mainstream racial ideologies and perceptions (Jackson-Nakazawa, 2003; Wardle & Cruz-Janzen, 2004). Consideration must be given to how and when issues and matters of a racial nature will be handled and addressed (DaCosta, 2007; Laszloffy, 2005), as well as how to do so with the child in an age-appropriate manner (Wilt, 2011).

Parents of multiple-heritage children quickly discover that even the most mundane issues of child rearing can have special implications for their families. Practical concerns often take on a racial context as multiple-heritage parents make choices about where to live, work, and worship (Wilt, 2011). This may also be the case when making typical or everyday decisions regarding their children's welfare, particularly in instances where others, including extended family members, health-care providers, teachers, and other professionals, play a significant role in the children's lives (Jackson-Nakazawa, 2003; Wardle & Cruz-Janzen, 2004). Multiple-heritage parents must be cognizant and aware of matters of significance to the positive growth and development of multiracial children. This understanding is critical to helping multiracial children successfully navigate their environments, integrate all aspects of their heritages, and develop healthy and solid racial and cultural identities (Rockquemore & Laszloffy, 2005; Wilt, 2011). Again, the resiliency of the family may be a result of a healthy parent–child relationship, as well as the extent to which the family is "equipped to handle adversity, foster healthy racial identity development, and live healthy lives" (Wilt, 2011, p. 12).

CONSIDERATIONS FOR COUNSELING MULTIRACIAL INDIVIDUALS AND FAMILIES

Kenney et al. (2015) developed Competencies for Counseling the Multiracial Population. These competencies are delineated and constructed in the framework of the eight common core areas of the counseling profession: human growth and development, social and cultural diversity, helping relationships, group work, career development, assessment, research and program evaluation, and professional orientation and ethics. The competencies serve as a resource for providing competent and effective counseling services to the multiracial population in the context of each of these areas. Activity 15.2 provides readers with an opportunity to reflect on the content of the Competencies for Counseling the Multiracial Population.

ACTIVITY 15.2

Download and read the Competencies for Counseling the Multiracial Population (https://www .counseling.org/docs/default-source/competencies/competencies-for-counseling-the-multiracial-population-2-2-15-final.pdf?sfvrsn=14). Upon completion, respond to the following.

- What was the most valuable learning from each of the eight core areas in the section on Competencies for Working with Interracial Couples and Multiracial Families?
- What was the most valuable learning from each of the eight core areas in the section on Competencies for Working with Multiracial Individuals?
- The Glossary section of the document provides a variety of terms and definitions related to interracial couples, multiracial families, multiracial individuals, and transracial adoptees and families (not covered in this chapter). Of the terms that are related to interracial couples, multiracial families, and multiracial individuals, identify those that provided new knowledge for you and reflect on how you will apply this new knowledge.

In this section, we address how counseling the multiracial population should involve the domains outlined in the Multicultural and Social Justice Counseling Competencies (Ratts et al., 2015). It is important to note again that, despite the increasing numbers of same-sex interracial couples and the increasing numbers of same-sex multiple-heritage families and individuals, this segment of the multiple-heritage population is not included in this section. As indicated previously, however, counselors must assess for and consider all other intersecting and salient identities as they work with all members of the multiracial population (Kenney et al., 2015).

Counselor Self-Awareness

The counselor self-awareness domain of the Multicultural and Social Justice Counseling Competencies requires counselors to take action by engaging in ongoing self-monitoring of assumptions, values, and biases held toward multiple-heritage couples, families, and individuals. The extent to which counselors are viewed as having done such assessment and evaluation may enhance the possibility of their services being used by members of this population (Kenney et al., 2015; Wilt, 2011).

The previously mentioned myths and stereotypes about multiple-heritage couples, families, and individuals continue to pervade societal thinking and influence assumptions, values, and biases about this population. Counselors must commit to engaging in a self-reflective process where they explore their awareness of the myths and stereotypes regarding interracial unions and multiracial individuals. Counselors must also commit to assessing and evaluating the extent to which their own views and perceptions have been influenced by these myths and sterotypes about the multiple-heritage population and what it means to be multiracial (Wilt, 2011).

Multiple-heritage couples, individuals, and families do not necessarily present for counseling because of issues regarding their mixed heritages or race; other matters may be of greater significance and importance. Counselors must be self-aware of possible tendencies to assume that all issues and concerns experienced by this population are related to their mixed heritages or to race (Hud-Aleem & Countryman, 2008; Wilt, 2011).

Client Worldview

Ratts et al. (2015) indicate the importance of counselors being self-aware, knowledgeable, skilled, and action-oriented in understanding their clients' worldviews. Thus, to deliver culturally competent services to multiple-heritage couples, families, and individuals, counselors and other helping professionals must first gain knowledge of the historical and sociopolitical context of race mixing in the United States as well as knowledge of how the current landscape for the population has been shaped and influenced by past history (Pedrotti, Edwards, & Lopez, 2008; Wilt, 2011).

Counselors working with multiple-heritage couples may also need to gain knowledge of how the different worldviews and cultural backgrounds of each partner may affect the interactions and dynamics of their relationships. In cases where the racial and cultural background of one partner seems similar to that of the counselor's, it is important that the counselor not presume to know that partner's worldview experience (Wilt, 2011). Ishiyama (2006) suggested that counselors must become knowledgeable of the worldview experiences of each partner, and then use this knowledge to interpret and facilitate the partners' understanding of each other. Counselors should help partners understand the influences of culture on individual expressions of emotion and physical affection. In addition, the influences of gender roles, power distribution, family structures, views of parenting, and the meaning of love may relate to partners feeling validated. In addition, counselors should depersonalize and defuse potential problems that may exist due to partners' different cultural makeup (Crippen, 2011; Romano, 2008; Waldman & Rubalcava, 2005). Having this knowledge can also be useful when working in a multiracial family context. Again, interpreting and facilitating family members' understanding of the various cultural identities represented in the family can also help them to understand the influence of culture on the dynamics of the family (Crippen, 2011; Ishiyama, 2006; Romano, 2008; Waldman & Rubalcava, 2005; Wilt, 2011). The work of addressing worldview cultural context intensifies when working with couples and families that include individuals for whom the U.S. cultural milieu is new.

Further, as clients present for counseling, they do so having also been influenced by long-held societal myths, stereotypes, and various forms of misinformation about multiple-heritage relationships. It may therefore be necessary for counselors to assess a multiple-heritage partner's or couple's awareness and knowledge of the myths and stereotypes about these partner relationships to discern the extent to which their relationship has been influenced by stereotypical expectations or motives. Such assessment may be critical to addressing and helping the partner or couple work through issues regarding concerns presented in counseling.

This may be especially important if there are concerns around the couple being together or remaining together (Crippen, 2011; Wilt, 2011).

Counselors are also encouraged to gain knowledge of significant research on the population resulting in theories and other useful information for addressing the needs and concerns of multiracial individuals and families. For example, some theories indicate there may be particular conditions that promote interracial unions (Cottrell, 1990; Davidson, 1992). Root (2001) provided a model that examined various family "types" that may either be open to or closed to the notion of interracial coupling. Young-Ware and Ware (1998) espoused an identity development theory that examines the internal processes that both partners may progress through as their relationship evolves. A more recent model developed by Seshadri and Knudson-Martin (2013) provides insights on how interracial and intercultural couples respond to interactions with others that may be related to the partners' different racial backgrounds. All of these theories and models may be particularly useful for understanding new interracial relationships. Counselor ability to translate or interpret these theories and models can be helpful and empowering to the partner's or couple's self-understanding.

The counseling literature on couples, families, and individuals with multiple heritages has been somewhat limited. Wardle (1999) suggested acquiring knowledge of the population through training opportunities focused on the issues, needs, challenges, and strengths of the population and on working with them in a competent and effective manner. The majority of information has come from members of the population advocating for themselves. This includes the Competencies for Counseling the Multiracial Population (https://www.counseling.org/docs/default-source/competencies/competencies-for-counseling-the-multiracial-population-2-2-15-final.pdf?sfvrsn=14). Similar to the information provided by other resources from within the multiracial community, these competencies help us in our understanding of the strengths, assets, and resiliency of this population and provide for our understanding of the various factors that contribute to their lives being positive, healthy, and productive. Further, Activity 15.3 provides potential ways one could build knowledge about the multiracial population.

ACTIVITY 15.3

1. The Loving Day (www.lovingday.org) and Mixed Race Studies (www.mixedracestudies .org) Web sites offer an array of resources, including books and films related to members of the multiracial population. Select a book or film of interest to read or view. Upon completion, reflect upon the most valuable learning or take away for you as a counselor or helping professional.

2. Respectfully interview or have a discussion with a partner or partners of an interracial marriage or partnership, a multiracial family, or multiracial individual. You may center your interview or your discussion around a particular aspect of their worldview experience(s) as learned from the chapter, the Competencies, the book, or the film. Upon completion, reflect upon the most valuable learning or take away for you as a counselor or helping professional.

3. Attend a social, community, or educational gathering for members of the multiracial population or access a blog. (See Table 15.2 for examples.) Upon completion, reflect upon the most valuable learning or take away for you as a counselor or helping professional.

Counseling Relationship

The counseling relationship domain requires that counselors and helping professionals be self-aware, knowledgeable, skilled, and action-oriented in understanding the impact and influence of the counseling relationship (Ratts et al., 2015). McDowell et al. (2005) discussed the importance of emphasizing multicultural awareness within the interracial couple and family dynamic, as well as within the counseling relationship, when couples and families come in for counseling. Counselors play critical roles in conversations around race, identity, and discrimination with their clients, and as these conversations with multiple-heritage couples, individuals, and families entail close, emotional interactions, the approach taken can have a profound impact upon the counseling relationship (McDowell et al., 2005). While the therapeutic approach used in counseling is important, it is "the flexible, respectful curiosity and knowledge about cultural differences exhibited by the counselor" that positively influences the counseling experience of multiple-heritage couples (Nord, 2012, p. 6). The Competencies for Counseling the Multiracial Population detail elements that need to exist in the context of the helping relationship in order to competently and effectively work with these couples, individuals, and families (Kenney et al., 2015).

Counseling and Advocacy Interventions

This domain calls upon counselors to intervene with and on behalf of clients at the intrapersonal, interpersonal, institutional, community, public policy, and international/global levels (Ratts et al., 2015). Counselors would do well to remember that the issues, concerns, and challenges experienced by the multiple-heritages population, as well as how they negotiate these experiences, are unique, varied, and different. Hence, the counseling interventions and strategies used must be appropriate to the couple, family, or individual being served (Kenney & Kenney, 2009).

As indicated in the Client Worldview section, members of the multiple-heritages population have themselves developed models, tools, and other resources and have vetted them as appropriate, useful, and affirmative of their experiences. Dr. Maria P. P. Root has been a forerunner for the development of several tools that are useful for persons in the helping professions who may be working with the multiple-heritages population. Her model, presented earlier in the chapter, can be useful in the assessment process with multiracial families and with multiracial individuals. Two other resources provided by Root are the Bill of Rights for People of Mixed Heritage (Root, 1993; see Figure 15.2) and the Multiracial Oath of Social Responsibility (Root, 2004; see Figure 15.3). Both of these resources are useful to the advocacy aspect of counselors' work with this population, as each resource is specifically focused on affirming and empowering multiracial individuals and families and on teaching them to advocate for themselves.

Counselors working with couples, families, and individuals with multiple heritages must also familiarize themselves with the advocacy interventions and strategies that have been determined to be useful and valuable in working with this population. This includes being knowledgeable and aware of the abundance of resources available to provide support and validation for the multiple heritage population (Kenney & Kenney, 2010). Resources include social network groups and organizations and internet websites and blogs. Many of these have been organized and facilitated by interracial couples, multiracial families, and multiracial individuals. Table 15.2 provides various resources to help increase your knowledge about this population.

I HAVE THE RIGHT . . .

Not to justify my existence in this world.

Not to keep the races separate within me.

Not to justify my ethnic legitimacy.

Not to be responsible for people's discomfort with my physical or ethnic ambiguity.

I HAVE THE RIGHT . . .

To identify myself differently than strangers expect me to identify.

To identify myself differently than how my parents identify me.

To identify myself differently than my brothers and sisters.

To identify myself differently in different situations.

I HAVE THE RIGHT . . .

To create a vocabulary to communicate about being multiracial or multiethnic.

To change my identity over my lifetime—and more than once.

To have loyalties and identification with more than one group of people.

To freely choose whom I befriend and love.

FIGURE 15.2   Bill of Rights for People of Mixed Heritage.

Source: Root, M. P. P. (1993). Bill of rights for people of mixed heritage. Retrieved from http://www.drmariaroot.com/doc/BillOfRights.pdf

I want to make a difference in this world. Therefore:

I strive to improve race relations.

I know that race and ethnicity are not solely defined by one's genetic heritage;

I refuse to confine my choices in love or loyalty to a single race;

I make efforts to increase my knowledge of U.S. racial history;

I know that race and ethnicity can be used as political, economic, and social tools of oppression.

I recognize the people who have made it possible for me to affirm my multiracial identity.

They are my relatives, friends, and mentors;

They are people who have crossed color lines to fight discrimination;

They are people who identified as multiracial before this choice was recognized;

They are people who have exposed and explained the suppression of multiraciality.

I must fight all forms of oppression as the oppression of one is the oppression of all.

I recognize that oppression thrives on fear and ignorance;

I seek to recognize my prejudices and change them;

I know that it is neither helpful nor productive to argue over who is more oppressed;

I recognize that my life interconnects with all other lives.

I will make a difference!

FIGURE 15.3   Multiracial Oath of Social Responsibility.

Source: Root, M. P. P. (2004). Multiracial oath of social responsibility. Retrieved from http://www.drmariaroot.com/doc/OathOfSocialResponsibility.pdf

TABLE 15.2 Web Resources

Critical Mixed Race Studies (www.criticalmixedracestudies.org): Critical Mixed Race Studies is a biennial conference group, journal, field of study, and a scholarly/activist/artistic community. The group is in the process of forming the Critical Mixed Race Studies Association.

Loving Day (www.lovingday.org): Loving Day is a network dedicated to providing education about *Loving v. Virginia* and the history of interracial relationships. It is a project that connects the multicultural community and provides books, Web sites, multimedia, and more regarding interracial coupling and related issues.

Mixed Race Studies (www.mixedracestudies.org): Mixed Race Studies is an interdisciplinary repository of scholarly perspectives on the mixed-race experience, and provides articles, books, Web sites, multimedia, and more.

Mixed Roots Stories (www.mixedrootsstories.com): Mixed Roots Stories is a public awareness site dedicated to supporting and advocating for diverse mixed-race communities through the sharing of stories across academic and non-academic communities and across global contexts.

COUNSELING AND ADVOCACY INTERVENTIONS FOR COUNSELING MULTIRACIAL COUPLES. Although counselor training and skill level are important, the counselor's own race, culture, and gender may also have significance in the counseling process with interracial couples (McDowell et al., 2005; Wilt, 2011). Issues that arise around counselors' race, culture, and gender are often related to one or the other partner's concerns about the counselor's ability to be unbiased, sensitive, and understanding of issues being presented (Laszloffy, 2005). In addition, although a White partner may have a positive view of the potentials of the counseling process, a non-White partner may be more tentative, due either to mistrust of or lack of familiarity with the mental health field (Sue & Sue, 2013). The non-White partner may also be working from a cultural framework where personal and family concerns are not shared outside the home or family context (Crippen, 2011; Romano, 2008). The counselor should assess for all these concerns and, if necessary, address them as part of the trust- and relationship-building part of the counseling process. Of related importance is the counselor's respectful engagement and inclusion of partners and couples in deciding on and developing the goals and direction of the counseling process. This ensures that the issues, needs, values, and worldview of each individual or couple are considered and addressed (Kenney et al., 2015; McDowell et al., 2005).

There are instances where couples have become involved for reasons other than love (Kaba, 2011; Yancey, 2007). Counselors working with partners or couples where this is the case must explore the significance and impact of these other motives. If the goal of the couple is to maintain the relationship, the counselor must assist them in determining the strengths or assets that exist to help them with that goal (Wilt, 2011).

Issues and concerns related to racism experienced by partners of color at the hand of Whites often emerge and have an impact on relationships of multiple-heritage couples involving White partners and partners of color. White counselors in particular need to be comfortable assessing for and, if necessary, addressing these issues and concerns (Laszloffy, 2005; McDowell et al., 2005). The counselor will also need to examine the skills and strategies used by partners and couples in dealing with these issues and concerns within the context of the relationship. Where it appears that no skills or strategies exist, or that those used have been ineffective, the counselor will need to assist in development of effective strategies (McDowell et al., 2005).

Partners or couples who present for counseling to address race and culture-related objections to their relationship will benefit from counselors who have knowledge of the underlying racial and cultural biases associated with these objections and who can empathize with and affirm the partner's or couple's feelings (Kenney et al., 2015; Laszloffy, 2005). Partners or couples who are not familiar with the myths, stereotypes, and other historical contexts that are often the basis for these objections may internalize the objections. Counselors must assist the partner or couple in understanding and conceptualizing the objections as more a function of issues within society, than within themselves and the relationship (Killian, 2012; Seshadri & Knudson-Martin, 2013). Counselors should help the partner or couple to explore and then use their individual strengths and the strengths of the relationship to address and respond to objections and negative reactions (Crippen, 2011; Laszloffy, 2005). The counselor may also want to assess sources of support and validation available to the partner or couple for dealing with the objections and possible ramifications (Crippen, 2011; Ishiyama, 2006).

Seshadri and Knudson-Martin (2013) provide a specific set of strategies that couples may use to manage issues that arise with others around their cultural and racial differences. These strategies include creating a "we," framing differences, maintaining emotion, and positioning in relation to societal and familial context. Creating a "we" involves the partners developing a friendship with each other, finding common ground, having similar goals, working together, and establishing a commitment. Framing differences involves taking their own steps to not make racial and cultural issues central; to view differences as attractive, indicative of flexibility, and being respectful of culture; to view differences as something to learn about and celebrate. Emotional maintenance entails communicating emotions and insecurities, making adjustments related to cultural differences, and finding systems for support of the relationship. Finally, positioning entails the couple's understanding of their relationship as existing in an ecological context that may include discrimination and other forms of oppression and developing healthy ways for protecting themselves and effectively communicating with others.

Internal conflicts and stressors in interracial relationships are more likely to be related to issues of culture, gender, class, or personal and social differences, not race (Crippen, 2011; Forry et al., 2007). Tubbs and Rosenblatt (2003) indicated, however, that counselors must still be alert to the possibility that partners' or couple's racial differences are part of or linked to their presenting concerns and be comfortable assessing for this possibility. Counselors working with multiracial couples whose presenting issues are related to their different cultural worldview context must first assist the couple in examining the cultural worldview experience and context of each partner and then assist them in understanding how their different experiences and context have shaped and influenced the behaviors, dynamics, and presenting concerns (Crippen, 2011; Ishiyama, 2006; Waldman & Rubalcava, 2005). Kim, Prouty, and Roberson (2012) and Aniciete and Soloski (2011) further indicated the importance of using narrative therapy in order to help partners to explore their level of satisfaction with the relationship, the dynamics of the relationship; the effectiveness of their communication, and the level of commitment and solidarity to the relationship and to addressing and dealing with the concerns.

Ishiyama (2006) offered a self-validation model, emphasizing the need that partners in interracial marriages have to be validated by self and by their partner. Counselors can use the model's validation-gram to engage partners in a discussion that will assist them in developing empathic understanding for each other as they work together to examine and explore culturally based attitudes, behaviors, and expressions. The ultimate goal is for each to feel validated and accept that these attitudes, behaviors, and expressions are a function of who they and their partner are from a cultural standpoint. The model is similar to Ibrahim and Schroeder's (1990) psychoeducational approach and can be used to help partners better understand the cultural basis for conflicts, as well as to clarify and normalize their different cultural worldview experiences and contexts. Through discussion, partners may discover shared values and worldview experiences that can further enhance, strengthen, and solidify their relationship (Ishiyama, 2006). The most important thing to remember in helping couples to work through cultural worldview–based conflicts and differences is that both partners may need help in understanding the significant role of culture on values, attitudes, and behaviors. Failure to understand this significant role reduces the potential for partners to personalize, whereas success helps establish a climate in the relationship conducive to partners becoming allies and working more collaboratively with each other on issues and concerns (Crippen, 2011; Romano, 2008).

These suggested interventions speak to the value of personal narratives and to the utility of approaches that provide space for those narratives to be explored in counseling. A narrative counseling approach can be extremely beneficial to examining cultural context issues and to having critical conversations related to those issues (Nord, 2012). In addition, Waldman and Rubalcava (2005) suggested that a psychodynamic approach is especially useful for helping multiple-heritage couples to better understand each other and each other's cultural context as being part of a process that was internalized during childhood. This approach is useful in helping partners to empathize with each other and to thus resolve differences that may exist in their relationship.

Wong (2009) spoke to the potential benefits and usefulness of premarital work and counseling for interracial couples. Through this work couples are provided an opportunity to assess and explore issues and concerns, as well as assumptions and expectations that each partner may have, particularly related to race and culture. Watts and Henriksen's (1998) Interracial Couple Questionnaire is a tool that can be used to help couples explore and understand each partner's perceptions and experiences around the interracial relationship, taking each partner's cultural context into consideration. The questionnaire can be used to facilitate dialogue with couples regarding issues, concerns, and challenges that they have or have not already experienced, as well as to determine assets, strengths, and the potential for growth in the relationship. Counselors should be familiar with, and share with partners and couples, literature and other resources available through Internet Web sites and blogs, and through community organizations. These provide valuable options for partners and couples to gain additional information, assistance, and support (Crippen, 2011; Kenney & Kenney, 2010; Kenney & Kenney, 2014). Case Study 15.2 explores some issues that multiracial couples may experience.

CASE STUDY 15.2

Heather is of White European heritage, and David is of Japanese heritage. The two met and started dating while both were part of a year-long business externship program. They continued the relationship after the externship was over and have now been dating exclusively for over two years. Heather's friends and family have met David several times and really like him. David's family and his Japanese friends, on the other hand, wonder what he sees in Heather and wonder why he just can't date a nice Japanese girl and settle down with her.

Heather and David have been talking about next steps in their relationship, as they have developed deep feelings for each other. David invited Heather to be his date at a family wedding, where they were both made to feel very uncomfortable. David confronted his mother about his family's reaction and behavior toward Heather at the wedding. He also shared with his mother that he and Heather have begun to talk about a possible future together, at which point his mother expressed major opposition to the relationship.

- What is your reaction to Heather and David's situation?
- What are the salient issues and concerns?
- If Heather and David plan to stay together, what might they need to consider as a couple in terms of decisions or next steps related to the future of their relationship?
- How might you work with this couple?

COUNSELING AND ADVOCACY INTERVENTIONS FOR COUNSELING MULTIRACIAL FAMILIES. Wardle and Cruz-Janzen (2004) indicated that couples and families with multiple heritages may present for counseling with concerns that are very similar to those experienced by same-race couples and families. However, issues of racial identity development present special challenges and may have lasting implications. Counselors working with families on matters regarding their multiple heritages must examine how comments, questions, and concerns, particularly those expressed by children, are discussed and dealt with in the family. Multiracial couples who are parents may require education or gentle coaching in how to approach these matters, particularly when those parents are White, not comfortable with addressing these issues, or lack context for dealing with or understanding the issues. This may be especially important when dealing with experiences related to racism (Laszloffy, 2005; Rockquemore & Laszloffy, 2005; Wilt, 2011). It should be noted and may need to be explained to parents (including monoracial parents of color) that their children's experiences around race will be different due to their multiple heritages. In a similar vein, their children's experiences around issues of racism will also be different (Hud-Aleem & Countryman, 2008). In cases where a parent of color has been dealing with challenges around racism, the counselor will need to assess if and how these challenges have affected the children or the parent's interactions with the children. The counselor may need to assist both parents and children in addressing these challenges, while also helping them to address the influence on the parent–child dynamic (Hud-Aleem & Countryman, 2008; Wilt, 2011).

Henriksen and Rawlins (2003) provided suggestions for parents raising multiracial children to promote a healthy racial identity and discussed the importance of parents talking openly and age-appropriately with their children about their racial makeup, physical appearance, race, and racial identity, as well as other matters associated with these topics. This is further validated as important by McDowell et al. (2005), who emphasize the importance of these families being multiculturally aware. In addition, Henrikson and Rawlins (2003) stressed the importance of parents talking with their children in an age-appropriate manner about their own experiences and stories. Counselors may need to assess the nature and quality of the family's relationship with extended family and others, particularly others who may be significant to family. In instances where multiracial couples have experienced objections and negative reactions to their relationship that have not been resolved or dealt with, the counselor will need to assess the extent to which the children are aware. Similarly, the counselor may need to assess the extent to which they as a family have experienced objections and negative reactions, how the children have been affected, and how these objections or negative reactions were resolved. Children's experiences of objections or negative reactions outside the family context may also need to be assessed. The counselor may need to assist parents in discerning the parental dyad's and the family's strengths, skills, and sources of support for addressing, responding to, and rising above these objections and negative reactions. Counselors may also need to assist parents in helping their children to address and deal with these objections and negative reactions. Again, drawing on strengths, skills, and sources of support will be important (Laszloffy, 2005; Wilt, 2011).

Rockquemore and Laszloffy (2003) indicate that couples and families should be assisted in developing skills for resistance of the negative and harmful ramifications of racism and suggest that they be taught the strategies of "pushing back" and "pulling back." **Pushing back** involves giving expressions or acts of racism immediate acknowledgment and attention, insisting that the perpetrator be held accountable and responsible. **Pulling back** involves recognizing when it may be more advisable to take a less confrontational approach to dealing with an expression or act of racism. Although skills such as these are important for partners and couples who do not have children, they are even more important when they do, particularly as concerns arise that affect or threaten the physical and emotional safety and security of family members.

Child rearing often involves parents advocating for their children, engaging others involved in the children's life in open, honest, and frank discussions about their views of race and their children's racial and cultural identity. Counselors may need to assist and empower parents to assert themselves in this way (Wardle & Cruz-Janzen, 2004). As child-rearing practices are embedded in cultural contexts, it is very important that couples be assisted in coming to terms with and resolving differences that may exist in how they each view and approach child rearing. Kenney and Kenney (2009) indicated that whereas parenting and parental preparation classes exist for the general populace, there is limited information about the availability of these preparatory classes for parents and parents-to-be of children with multiple heritages. Counselors advocating for members of this population may be called on to develop these classes. Multiracial community organizations including MAVIN Foundation and the Mixed Race Studies Organization provide useful resources for this purpose (Kenney & Kenney, 2014). Case Study 15.3 explores some of the issues multiracial families may experience.

CASE STUDY 15.3

Maria is the 8-year-old daughter of Gina and Hector Sanchez. Gina is of Korean heritage, and Hector is of Mexican heritage. Hector's parents live nearby, as do his siblings and their families. Gina's parents and a sibling's family live two hours away. Gina and Hector have made a concerted effort to teach and expose Maria to all aspects of her heritage. She speaks Spanish and is also learning to speak Korean.

Maria has just transferred to a diverse private school that has a large Asian population. Every year the school sponsors a cultural heritage festival to celebrate the start of the school year. Children are encouraged to share their and their family's cultural foods, art, music, dress, and talents. Excited about the possibility to share some of her Korean heritage, Maria tells her classmates and teacher that she plans to bring in Asian Korean food and to display a special Korean talent. The children snicker, and Maria's teacher tells her that because she is Hispanic, she should share something from her Hispanic culture. During lunch Maria overhears some of the Asian girls laughing about Maria's offer.

The next day Maria begs not to go to school. Hector, who has typically taken Maria to school, is away on business. Gina figures she can use this opportunity to not only see what the problem is, but to meet Maria's teacher as well.

- What is your reaction to the Sanchez family and the situation with Maria?
- What are the salient issues and concerns?
- How should the situation at the school be addressed?
- How might a counselor work with the family and Maria?

COUNSELING AND ADVOCACY INTERVENTIONS FOR COUNSELING MULTIRACIAL CHILDREN. As when counseling other members of the multiracial population, counselors working with multiracial children must be cognizant of the fact that they do not always present with problems related to their multiracial status (Wardle & Cruz-Janzen, 2004). It is important to note, however, that having multiple heritages may influence an individual's life and functioning at various points in the life span, especially during childhood and adolescence. To this end, counselors must be prepared to assess the role that being of multiple heritages plays in the presenting concerns (Jackson, 2010; Jackson, Yoo, Guevarra, & Harrington, 2012). This supports Hud-Aleem and Countryman (2008), who indicated that the assessment of multiracial children's presenting concerns should give attention to whether the concerns are related to the child's developmental age or stage; the child-rearing practices of the parents, the parents' relationship, or other familial issues; or racial/ethnic issues and concerns. Because age, level of understanding, and cognitive abilities of children influence their perceptions and experiences, this information would be valuable to assess as well (Hud-Aleem & Countryman, 2008; Pedrotti et al., 2008; Wilt, 2011).

Counselors working with multiracial children must assist them in identifying and acknowledging their assets, strengths, and abilities; in developing effective coping skills; and in developing and pursuing their own unique interests (Hud-Aleem & Countryman, 2008; Pedrotti et al., 2008). According to Wardle and Cruz-Janzen (2004) and Hud-Aleem and Countryman (2008), in helping children develop a positive racial and cultural identity, it is important to encourage and assist them in learning about all aspects of their multiple heritages. This is especially important in cases in which conflict exists between parents, a parent is absent, and/or a parent's extended family is not accessible. The counselor may need to work with both the child and the significant parent/adult in this instance (Hud-Aleem & Countryman, 2008; Root, 2003).

Counselors working with multiracial children may involve siblings, parents, or significant adults in the child's life to gain understanding of the interactions and dynamics of the family. Counselors may also work with teachers and other school personnel, particularly when there appears to be a lack of understanding and/or sensitivity to issues related to the child's multiracial status (Wardle & Cruz-Janzen, 2004).

Ultimately, children need to feel that they are heard and validated. Therefore, the most important skill counselors must use in working with multiracial children is that of supportive and culturally sensitive listening (Harris, 2009). This is necessary for the development of trust, which is essential, especially if children are presenting issues and concerns that are racially or culturally oriented. Effective strategies for counseling multiracial children include bibliotherapy, role-playing, journaling, creative writing, and various art media (Wardle & Cruz-Janzen, 2004; Harris, 2009).

COUNSELING AND ADVOCACY INTERVENTIONS FOR COUNSELING MULTIRACIAL ADOLESCENTS. Maxwell and Henriksen (2009) suggested that in assessing the concerns of adolescents with multiple heritages, counselors should be cognizant of potential conflicts related to major psychosocial tasks of development in adolescence. Assessment should be conducted in the context of the adolescents' views and perceptions of their multiracial heritage. The level of support of family and others of significance to the adolescent should be established from the start of the counseling process. Perceptions and views of family members should also be assessed, along with the perceptions, views, and level of accessibility and connection with extended family members. In addition, the availability of support resources and networks in the school and community should be examined (Hud-Aleem & Countryman, 2008; Wardle & Cruz-Janzen, 2004).

Counseling multiracial adolescents requires a solid working alliance, built on trust and cultural sensitivity. The counselor must be able to validate the adolescents' feelings about their mixed-race status (Maxwell & Henriksen, 2009). The counselor must be able to assist adolescents with understanding the relationship between problem behavior and challenges they may be experiencing regarding their multiple heritages. In addition, counselors must assist them in exploring all aspects of their heritage to help individuals with multiple heritages develop a positive self-image (Hud-Aleem & Countryman, 2008; Maxwell & Henriksen, 2009).

According to Maxwell and Henriksen (2009), counseling interventions must be considerate of the adolescent's level of self-esteem and self-concept and should focus on the development of skills related to problem solving, values clarification, decision making, and goal setting. Strategies useful for assisting multiracial adolescents with exploring their racial identity and developing a positive self-concept include focused discussions, bibliotherapy, and homework assignments. Role-playing, journaling, storytelling, and behavioral goal setting may also be helpful for this age group (Maxwell & Henriksen, 2009). Counselors working in school settings can also use peer counseling and peer support groups (Wardle & Cruz-Janzen, 2004).

COUNSELING AND ADVOCACY INTERVENTIONS FOR COUNSELING MULTIRACIAL COLLEGE STUDENTS. Issues that arise for college students with multiple heritages are often related to factors of the campus environment, the students' sense of fit and belonging in the campus environment, and issues related to their identity and self-concept (Renn, 2008). Counselors working with this population must assess the extent to which these factors play a part in the students' presenting issues and concerns. According to Paladino (2004), students dealing with feelings of rejection or alienation in the campus environment may welcome that the counselor is cognizant enough to mention these factors as potential issues. Paladino indicated that several factors should be examined and attended to in working with college students with multiple heritages. These factors include positive relationships available to the student, presenting problems, opportunities the student has had to vent about feelings and concerns, student's level of self-esteem, the helping professional's level of preparation and approach, and student's level of access to family and level of family support.

Individual and group counseling that takes a psychoeducational approach can be most useful for college students with multiple heritages (Paladino, 2009). In addition, counseling that incorporates strategies of focused discussion, bibliotherapy, homework assignments, role-playing, journaling, storytelling, and behavioral goal setting are also useful for this population. Paladino (2004) discussed the benefit of establishing support groups for multiple-heritage students on campus. Members of the population suggest that campuses would do even better to establish social groups or clubs for college students with multiple heritages. Because these are focused on and derived from students' strengths and assets, social groups or clubs appear to provide more empowerment and affirmation for students as they attempt to navigate the campus environment (Ozaki & Johnston, 2008; Wong & Buckner, 2008). Counselors can advocate for students on their campuses by promoting and helping to establish these groups (Kenney & Kenney, 2010, 2014). Counselors can also take the lead and advocate for campus administrators, faculty, and staff efforts to create supportive campus environments that are conducive to improving the learning experience for these students (Renn, 2008). Case Study 15.4 explores some of the issues multiracial college students may experience.

CASE STUDY 15.4

Thomas is a college student with multiple heritages born and raised in a White suburb of a large Northeastern metropolitan area. He was raised by his African American mother and his White European father and has one younger sister. Thomas has always felt more connected to his White European family and ancestry because as a child he did not have much exposure to his mother's African American side of the family due to distance. The schools that he attended growing up were predominantly White schools.

His experiences at college are becoming increasingly difficult, as White students that he attempts to befriend on campus are not fully accepting of him as a White person and often question his racial heritage. He interacts with students of color and in fact has an African American roommate. He constantly seeks acceptance by a particular group of White students, though each time he leaves feeling more angry and frustrated. His roommate recently wondered aloud about why Thomas is so anxious to be accepted by these White students, and why he just doesn't accept his Black heritage and identity. This has caused Thomas to wonder about his entire identity.

- What is your reaction to Thomas?
- What are the salient issues and concerns of the case?
- How have family and the environment in which Thomas was raised influenced his identity and the current dilemma?
- How might Thomas's physical appearance be influencing the current dilemma?
- How might a counselor work with Thomas?

COUNSELING AND ADVOCACY INTERVENTIONS FOR COUNSELING MULTIRACIAL ADULTS. Counselors working with multiple-heritage adults may need to assess the individual's coping mechanisms and skills, as it is quite possible that the identity choice the adult has made emerged from a lack of coping skills to deal with or counter societal challenges. If this is the case, the counselor will need to assist the adult with multiple heritages in developing skills for coping that are not only effective, but that are self-validating and affirming (Miville, 2005) and foster resilience (Jackson et al., 2012).

Logan, Freeman, and McRoy's (1987) ecological approach coincides with Root's ecological framework and is useful for working with multiracial adults. The Logan et al. approach is comprised of three components (i.e., genogram, ecomap, and cultural continuum) that can be used to assist multiple-heritage adults in exploring what it means to be multiracial. The genogram can be used to help the client to examine the influences of family relationships and dynamics, roles, and significant life events. The genogram can also be used to examine the racial and ethnic backgrounds of family members, the attitudes of immediate and extended family toward the multiracial individual, and the level of functioning of family relationships. Relationships that the multiple-heritage individual and family members have had with social networks (e.g., community, neighborhood, schools, other institutions) may also be explored. Specifics pertaining to the individual and family's overall development and lifestyle may also be assessed.

The ecomap is a tool that also uses connecting lines and symbols to illustrate relationships, similar to those used in the genogram. The family of an adult with multiple heritages may be shown in a large circle, with smaller circles drawn around it to depict connections with other family and social support networks. The connecting lines are used to illustrate the individual's and family's relationships to extended family and social support. Using the ecomap, the counselor can help the adult explore his or her own and his or her family's relationship with external networks. The information that emerges regarding positive or negative experiences the individual and family have had with these networks provides information regarding where and to whom the individual can go for validation, affirmation, and support. The ecomap can also provide information regarding the potential need to reassess or reframe relationships (Logan et al., 1987).

The cultural continuum is a tool that consists of four cultural response categories: denial of cultural or racial significance, assimilation with dominant culture or race, assimilation with minority culture or race, and multiracial identification. There are advantages and disadvantages associated with each response category. Using these response categories, the counselor can help the adult to examine personal coping skills and responses to situations in which the client felt challenged about multiple heritages, while also exploring the pitfalls and outcomes of earlier and more recent choices and decisions made related to aspects of the client's heritage (Logan et al., 1987).

As indicated with regard to counseling multiple-heritage couples and families, narrative strategies that assist multiple-heritage individuals in telling their story can be extremely beneficial, especially for adult multiracial individuals. Insights gained through this approach may lead to a more comprehensive understanding of self, foster a more positive self-concept, and help build resiliency (Pedrotti et al., 2008). Psychoeducational methods, such as using Web sites, blogs, literature, or movies that present positive images of the multiracial experience, are helpful for working with adults (Paladino & Henriksen, 2009). Again, the most valuable approaches are those that empower adults with multiple heritages to assess and determine their own strengths and assets. As indicated for counselors working with individuals with multiple heritages at other developmental levels, the extent to which the adult with multiple heritages views the counselor as a sensitive, empathic, and understanding advocate enhances the possibility of the adult experiencing counseling as beneficial and effective.

Summary

The goal of this chapter was to introduce counselors and counselors-in-training to the rapidly increasing multiracial population, including interracial couples and their offspring and families. The chapter provided a historical perspective of race mixing and classification in the United States that is important for understanding contemporary social perceptions, discrimination, and worldview experiences that have shaped the sociopolitical landscape of this population. The chapter introduces readers to the Competencies for Counseling the Multiracial Population (Kenney et al., 2015) and uses the frameworks of the Multicultural and Social Justice Counseling Competencies (Ratts et al., 2015) in discussing counseling the multiracial population. Counselors, like others in society, have been influenced by myths, stereotypes, and other forms of misinformation; thus it is imperative that before working with this population counselors examine their assumptions, values, and biases, as these can dramatically influence their interactions and work with this population.

Interracial couples, multiracial individuals, and multiracial families are an extremely diverse segment of the U.S. population; hence a second imperative is that counselors intentionally increase their understanding and knowledge of the varied worldview experiences of members of this population. Finally, the multiracial population is a resilient and empowered population. This has been evidenced through the grassroots efforts of the multiracial movement that resulted in a variety of national and local advocacy and support organizations and resources. It is important that, in fulfilling their roles as advocates, counselors be aware of and knowledgeable about these organizations and resources and use them in working with and alongside multiracial clients and families.

Review Questions

1. How might knowledge of the history of race mixing and classification in the United States influence your understanding of contemporary issues and concerns affecting the multiple-heritage population?

2. How would you apply Root's Ecological Framework, Bill of Rights for People of Mixed Heritage, and Multiracial Oath of Social Responsibility when working with a multiple-heritage adult?

3. How are the issues and concerns of interracial couples similar to and different from same-race couples?

4. Discuss salient issues and concerns that may arise for multiple-heritage individuals during early childhood, childhood, middle childhood, adolescence, and emerging adulthood. What are the implications for counseling at each of these levels?

5. How might you use the various advocacy and support resources and organizations available for the multiracial population in your counseling work with the population?

16 Spiritual Diversity

Craig S. Cashwell and Amanda L. Giordano

PREVIEW

There is great religious and spiritual diversity within the United States. To the extent that a person's religious and spiritual beliefs, practices, and experiences shape his or her worldview, spirituality and religion are aspects of culture and are important in the counseling process. It is imperative that counselors understand a broad range of religious and spiritual beliefs and are able to work within these beliefs to provide culturally sensitive counseling services. Eastern and Western religions are briefly reviewed in this chapter, as well as tenets common to all major world religions. The purpose of this chapter is to discuss spiritual and religious diversity within the United States and the pitfalls of working within a culturally encapsulated framework around religious and spiritual issues in counseling.

RELIGION AND SPIRITUALITY IN AMERICA

The United States was founded on religious tolerance, diversity, and freedom, in opposition to the historical religious oppression in England. As noted by any number of the founders of the United States, freedom of religion means the right to participate in *any* religion, including no religion at all. The separation of church and state was originally intended to avoid the imposition of one set of beliefs over others, as had been the case in England (Wiggins, 2011). It is important to remember, however, that religious diversity in the United States at that time essentially meant diverse forms of Protestantism. Prior to the early settlers' arrival, though, the spirituality of American Indians already was clearly in place (Garrett, Torres-Rivera et al., 2011). In addition, over the last 250 years there has been a steady influx of immigrant populations that have brought with them diverse spiritual and religious beliefs, rituals, and traditions. As a country, the United States has maintained its emphasis on Protestantism as the cultural norm. As a result, "tensions have developed without a 'template' in which to incorporate an expanded sense of religious and cultural diversity" (Fukuyama, Siahpoush, & Sevig, 2005, p. 124).

That spirituality and religion are important cultural aspects within the United States is clear. According to the 2014 General Social Survey, the majority of American adults believe in God (Hout & Smith, 2015). Specifically, 58% believe without doubt, 17% believe even with some doubt, 4% believe sometimes, 13% believe in a Higher Power rather than a personal God, 5% do not know and do not believe there is a way to know, and only 3% do not believe in God. Thus, it is likely that counselors will encounter questions and discussion related to God or a Higher Power in their work with clients. With regard to specific faith traditions, the majority of people in the United States are Christian adherents (Pew Research Center, 2015b). There is considerable variation, however, within the Christian faith tradition. Of the 70.6% of Americans who identify as Christian, 46.6% affiliate with a Protestant denomination (e.g., Baptist, Lutheran, Methodist, Presbyterian, Pentacostal), 20.8% with Catholicism, 1.6% identify as Mormon, 0.5% identify as Orthodox, 0.8% affiliate with Jehovah's Witnesses, and 0.4% identify as other.

After Christianity, the next largest group is those who do not adhere to a religious tradition. Specifically, 22.8% of Americans claim no religions affiliation with 3.1% of those non-religious affiliates identifying as Atheist, 4.0% identifying as Agnostic, and 15.8% reporting no affiliation with a particular religious tradition (Hout & Smith, 2015). This group has been growing steadily over time. Other major world religions are less represented in the United States, comprising a combined total of 5.9% of the population. Specifically, 1.9% of Americans identify as Jewish, 0.9% Muslim, 0.7% Buddhist, 0.7% Hindu, and 0.3% other. Prevalence data from 2007 and 2014 confirm, however, that these numbers are in flux. In the seven-year span, researchers found that Christian affiliates (both Protestant and Catholic) have declined while non-Christian faith traditions and those unaffiliated with religion demonstrated an increase in affiliates (Pew Research Center, 2015b). Beyond these numbers, however, is the fact that there is tremendous within-group variance among religious traditions. That is, knowing that someone is Jewish or Hindu or Muslim or Protestant or Atheist or Buddhist affords only cursory information about the religious and spiritual beliefs, practices, experiences, rituals, and traditions of the individual.

SPIRITUALITY AND RELIGION DEFINED

The terms *spirituality* and *religion* often are misunderstood. There are two potential ways in which cultural encapsulation occurs here. In the first, people assume that others hold the same beliefs and practices that they do. Accordingly, assumptions are made regarding beliefs about the presence of a deity or deities, what occurs after death, creation stories, and spiritual practices. The second form of cultural encapsulation around spirituality and religion occurs when an individual projects his or her experiences of a religious group onto an individual. For example, a person who has experienced fundamentalism only within a specific religious group assumes that everyone who practices that form of religion is, similarly, a fundamentalist. It is important to have a working understanding of spirituality and religion and how the two may be related for individuals. Similarly, it is important for counselors to be aware of both over-identification and countertransference issues that may arise when working with clients' religion and spirituality.

Toward Defining Spirituality

Spirituality is difficult, at best, to define, largely because it is highly personal, developmental, and often beyond verbal definition. Spirituality is personal in that it is unique and idiosyncratic to each individual. Because of this, it is not possible to provide a generic definition of spirituality that is sufficiently inclusive for all people. Further, spirituality is developmental in that a person's spiritual beliefs, practices, and experiences evolve and develop over time. That is, a true spirituality is far from a static way of being. To the contrary, it is highly dynamic and evolving. Finally, when discussing the transformative aspects of religion and spirituality (which will be discussed more fully later in this chapter), transformative spiritual experiences often defy verbal explanations. As one example of this, try Activity 16.1.

ACTIVITY 16.1

The following activity is adapted from Horovitz-Darby (1994). Gather a set of art materials such as colored pencils, markers, crayons, and some art paper. Once you have gathered these materials, follow these directions:

1. Many people believe in a Divine Creator. If you hold such a belief, represent this belief visually.
2. Once this image is complete, consider that many people believe there is an opposite power of a Divine Creator. If you hold such a belief, represent this belief visually.
3. Once this image is complete, journal or discuss with someone your answers to the following questions:
   a. What are the images you have created, and what do they symbolize?
   b. How do you feel about each of the images you have created?
   c. Do you feel as though the image accurately represents your beliefs?
4. Journal or discuss how your image would have been different 5, 10, and 20 years ago, and how you expect it might evolve in the coming years.
5. Once you have completed this process, write a one- or two-sentence definition of this Divine Creator without using any of the imagery you have created in steps 1 through 4.

Note: Many people find the experience of visually representing the Divine Creator much easier than providing a verbal definition.

Source: Adapted from Horovitz-Darby, E. G. (1994). *Spiritual art therapy: An alternate path.* Springfield, IL: Charles C Thomas.

The challenges of defining spirituality notwithstanding, it seems important to provide a working definition of spirituality to serve as a starting place for discussion and to highlight the multidimensionality of the spiritual. **Spirituality**, then, is defined as a set of beliefs, practices, and experiences held by an individual that ultimately lead to a transcendence of self to be concerned with otherness (Otto, 1958). This compassion for others begins with self-compassion and involves a search for wholeness (Cashwell & Young, 2014). As such, this compassion occurs naturally as we realize that it is in giving that we receive. This framework distinguishes between compassion and codependency, where an individual helps others out of selfish reasons, albeit unconsciously, such as trying to feel worthwhile. Finally, because there needs to be a distinction between a spiritual life that is psychologically healthy and one that is not, this spiritual path allows the journeyer to mindfully and heartfully experience all emotions, even those that some religious groups might deem undesirable or a sign of weakness, and to create a collaborative relationship with a Higher Power or Higher Self. These last two points are to contrast a healthy spiritual life with a psychologically unhealthy spiritual life in which an individual is discouraged from feeling "negative" emotions, such as sadness, fear, and anger, by teachers or leaders, and a spiritual path that leads to an extreme external locus of control. It is important here to distinguish between a healthy construct, surrender, and unhealthy behaviors of abdicating personal responsibility either to a charismatic spiritual leader or a Higher Power. A co-created and collaborative relationship with a Higher Power has been found to be related to physical, emotional, and psychological health (Pargament, Falb, Ano, & Wachholtz, 2014).

Toward Defining Religion

In contrast to spirituality, religion is relatively easy to define. Where spirituality is considered to be universal, ecumenical, internal, affective, spontaneous, and private, **religion** is considered to be denominational, external, cognitive, behavioral, ritualistic, and public (Richards & Bergin, 2005); that is, religion is organized spirituality (Smith, 2006). Smith further argued that religion was the container and spirit was the essence it contained. This definition works well for those who see their spiritual and religious lives as being harmonious and mutually supportive. Others, however, argue that "the essence" is too large for most of the containers that they have experienced. Such people likely define themselves as "spiritual but not religious." A more thorough discussion of the manner in which individuals experience the relationship between religion and spirituality is warranted.

Relationships between Religion and Spirituality

The relationship between religion and spirituality differs for each individual and changes over time for each person. That is, this relationship is very personal and developmental. It is important to note that the constructs of religion and spirituality are not polar opposites, but rather interrelated. Indeed, Pargament (2011) warned against conceptualizing religion as "bad" or inferior and spirituality as "good" or superior. He posited that both constructs can have adaptive and maladaptive functions and often are integrated within one another. Furthermore, most Americans experience harmony between their religiousness and spirituality, so polarization often is unwarranted and inaccurate. Despite the integration of religion and spirituality, individuals may approach the constructs in various ways. It is possible, therefore, to delineate four major relationships that have important implications for culturally sensitive counseling processes. Reflection 16.1 proves an opportunity to consider what attitudes and skills you have for working with clients endorsing each of the four relationships. Case Study 16.1 highlights the relationship intricacies of religion and spirituality.

REFLECTION 16.1

Consider the various relationships between religion and spirituality previously chronicled and journal your responses to the following questions:

1. What type(s) would be most difficult with which to work?
2. What is it about this type that makes it a difficult match?
3. What is it about your own religious/spiritual history that makes it a difficult match?
4. Is it possible for you to be an effective counselor with a person of this type?
5. If so, what knowledge, self-awareness, and skills will be required for your work with this client to be sensitive to the client's view of religion and spirituality?

CASE STUDY 16.1

The Case of Devon

Devon is a 46-year-old White male who sought counseling as a result of issues managing his anger. Devon was encouraged to explore the option of counseling by his supervisor after Devon berated a subordinate employee for incorrectly filing paperwork. Devon appeared irritable and somewhat intimidating during the initial intake session and told his counselor he does not need counseling but, "all those morons out there do." The counselor asked Devon to tell him more about "those morons." Devon's voice grew louder as he described those individuals at his work whom he felt were inadequate and unfit for their jobs. The counselor asked Devon if he often felt that others were inadequate or lacking in some way. Devon agreed that many incompetent people held jobs that were too advanced for them, and they inevitably end up "making others' lives miserable" as a result.

In subsequent sessions. the counselor continued to explore the origins of Devon's critical view of others, as this appeared to be the source of his anger. In their fifth session, the counselor asked if Devon could reflect back to the time he first felt this anger. Devon contemplated the question for a moment and said his first experience was during his teenage years when his mother passed away. Devon described how hard it was on his father, who was tasked with raising Devon by himself. Prior to his mother's death, Devon and his parents were dedicated members of the Catholic Church, attending mass at least once per week. After his mother died, however, their priest came to visit with Devon and his father, offering his condolences. The priest also informed Devon's father that to remarry would be a sin against God, and he was forbidden to do so and remain in the Catholic Church. Devon told the counselor, "I watched my father suffer for years, without companionship and without ever trying to meet someone else because he did not want to defy what that priest said. I was so angry—surely that man was unfit to be a priest. Couldn't he see how lonely my dad was and how much he was hurting? Eventually, my dad got so depressed he stopped going to church completely and so did I. That was it for me and religion."

The counselor and Devon spent several sessions processing the anger Devon felt toward that priest and the Catholic Church. Over time, Devon revealed that underlying his anger toward the priest was a sadness that his religion had been "taken from him," as it was once an important part of his life. The counselor asked Devon if he believed his spirituality had been "taken from him" too. Devon asked if there was a difference, to which the counselor replied that some see religion as an organized expression of spirituality, whereas one's spirituality consists of personal beliefs and practices. Devon asserted that he had never stopped believing in God, and his faith remained important to him. He even prayed privately on occasion. As Devon continued to articulate and describe his spirituality to his counselor, he acknowledged that it never "left" even when he left the Catholic Church. As Devon's relationship with the spiritual dimension of his life grew, his anger began to lose its intensity, and he became less critical of others. Consider the following questions related to the case of Devon:

- Do you think the counselor took an appropriate approach to working with Devon and his anger management issues? Why or why not?
- How could the counselor ensure that he or she did not cross boundaries from counseling into spiritual direction?
- If you were working with Devon, what aspects of the counseling relationship would be most important, given his presenting demeanor and unfolding story?

HAND IN HAND For some, the relationship between religion and spirituality is either complementary or coincidental. When viewed as complementary, the religious community is an important aspect of the individual's spiritual life, but also involves disciplined spiritual practice (or multiple practices) that support spiritual growth. That is, the exoteric (i.e., public) spiritual practice (religion) complements the esoteric (i.e., private) spiritual practice, and vice versa. For others, the relationship is more coincidental. For these people, their religious life is their spiritual life. Such people have a rich spiritual life that is almost exclusively experienced and expressed within their religious community. For both complementary and coincidental individuals, the religious community is vital to the spiritual life, and the exoteric and esoteric go hand in hand.

THE JUNGIAN PATH OF PRETENDING Carl Jung (2006) once wrote that many people participate in religion to avoid having a religious experience. Essentially, this means that there are people who participate in organized religion, but more out of habit or fear of punishment than to connect to Spirit and integrate the sacred into their everyday life. For such people, religious participation is disconnected from the religious experience. In most cases, such people do not have a private spiritual practice and typically have limited spiritual experiences.

"SPIRITUAL BUT NOT RELIGIOUS" A third category of people describe themselves as spiritual but not religious. Researchers have found that this category of people is rapidly growing in the United States (Pew Forum on Religion & Public Life, 2015). Such people recognize the importance of the spiritual journey. Either because they have never participated in organized religion or because they have had negative experiences with religion, they choose not to participate in an organized religion. Such people often find a nonreligious "community" an important aspect of religion in other ways, such as through meditation or yoga groups.

There is an important distinction between two subtypes of people within this category. The first subtype, the *Accepting*, includes people who value religion and respect the place that it plays in the lives of others. That is, although they choose not to participate in organized religion themselves, they respect the importance of religion in the lives of others. The second subtype, the *Disdainful*, typically finish the phrase "I am spiritual but not religious" with a contemptuous tone. That is, they have had personal or vicarious negative experiences with organized religion. These experiences have led them not only to be nonreligious, but also to be antireligious.

Wilber (1998) provided a nice template for understanding the experiences of at least some people who describe themselves as spiritual but not religious. Within many religious communities, the focus is primarily on beliefs—that is, the translative aspect of religion is emphasized almost exclusively (i.e., the transformative potential of religion is de-emphasized). In some religious communities, the focus is even more narrowly prescribed to a communal set of beliefs in which individual variation is discouraged. Often, people in the spiritual but not religious category have previous history with organized religion, but become disenfranchised with the emphasis on the translative aspects of religion. In search of transformative experiences, their spiritual journey moves away from organized religion. If this transition is done with some resentment toward the religious community, the person typically becomes disdainful of organized religion. If the transition is more peaceful, the person becomes accepting of the importance of religion for others, although the individual does not personally participate in a religious community.

A second process that may lead to a person self-describing as spiritual but not religious occurs when religious wounding occurs. This occurs, for example, when a lesbian or gay man who has grown up within a faith community comes out to that community and is rejected by the community. In these instances, if the person is able to separate the experience in this religious community from personal spirituality, the person likely will either become disdainful of religion but maintain a private spiritual life or find another religious community that supports the LGBT community (Cashwell & Marszalek, 2007). If people are unable to separate this negative religious experience from their personal spiritual life, however, they likely operate within another category, the *Decliners*. These individuals consider themselves to be neither religious nor spiritual. Although religion is hardly universal, many argue that spirituality is innate and universal (Cashwell & Young, 2011). For a variety of reasons, though, some people develop neither their religious nor their spiritual lives.

As with the Accepting or Disdainful categories, there seem to be two subtypes of individuals in the Decliners category that are important to consider. The *Inexperienced Decliner* is a person who has never been exposed to the spiritual life or a religious community. Some may have grown up in a family that eschewed religion and spirituality or, at the very least, did not discuss such matters. When working with a client who is an Inexperienced Decliner, it is important to gently assess the openness to psychospiritual work that might be used within session (e.g., guided imagery) or between sessions (e.g., a referral to a meditation group).

The second subtype, the *Rejector*, has had some previous negative experience within a religious community that has led the individual to reject not only the religious life but also his or her own spirituality. That is, the religious and the spiritual become inseparable for the individual, and both are rejected. Any attempts to integrate spirituality into the counseling process with such a client is culturally insensitive, at best, and potentially harmful.

OVERVIEW OF MAJOR WORLD RELIGIONS

As the United States becomes increasingly diverse, it is imperative that counselors have at least a working knowledge of the major world religions. Although it is neither possible nor necessary that a counselor be an expert in all world religions, some basic working knowledge is important. In this spirit, some preliminary information about major world religions is offered. Clearly, though, it is beyond the scope of this chapter to provide an in-depth overview of the major world religions. The references contained within each section provide a nice starting place for additional reading. Further, many other sects (e.g., Aboriginal religions) are not discussed here. It is simply not possible to capture the breadth and depth of belief systems in only a few scant pages. What follows, though, provides preliminary information about the most prominent wisdom traditions of the world.

Eastern World Religions

The major Eastern religions include Buddhism, Hinduism, Sikhism, Taoism, and Confucianism. It is important to keep in mind that some Eastern religious practitioners may integrate beliefs from various traditions. For example, some consider Confucianism to be a philosophical way of living and being rather than a religion per se and, as such, may practice another religious tradition as well as Confucianism.

BUDDHISM   Buddhism defines a religion organized around the teachings of Siddhartha Gautama, who was born into a wealthy Hindu family in Nepal around 563 BC. Siddhartha began his quest for enlightenment at age 19, originally by foregoing the luxuries of his rich family and living the life of an ascetic. He later realized that the ascetic life was no more a path to enlightenment than that of luxury and began following a path he called *the middle way*, between ascetism and luxury, that remains a central tenet of contemporary Buddhism (Bien, 2011). Siddhartha developed the "divine eye" at age 35 years while meditating under a Bodhi tree and changed from a bodhisattva (i.e., enlightened person who has chosen to postpone Nirvana in order to help others become enlightened) to a Buddha (Awakened or Enlightened One). The Buddha died around 483 BC and, ostensibly in the same year, the first Buddhist Council of Rajagaha met to preserve the Buddha's teachings.

There are three major traditions of Buddhism: Theravada, Mahayana, and Vajrayana (Mitchell & Jacoby, 2013). Theravada Buddhism, also referred to as "Southern Buddhism," is practiced primarily in Sri Lanka and Southeast Asia. It is based on the Pali Canon, which is regarded as the scriptures most closely following the Buddha's own words. Theravada Buddhism is practiced more by monks than laypeople and has about 100 million followers. Mahayana (literally, "The Greater Ox-cart") Buddhism evolved as a schism from Theravada Buddhism, providing a form of Buddhism that could be practiced by the masses without requiring a monastic life. They considered enlightenment to be virtually unattainable and so created two grades of attainment below becoming a Buddha. Although the Buddha was the highest goal, one could become a pratyeka-buddha, one who has awakened to the truth but keeps it secret. Below the pratyeka-buddha is the arhant, or "worthy," who has learned the truth from others and has realized it as truth. Mahayana Buddhism establishes the arhant as the goal for all believers. Vajrayana Buddhism is an extension of Mahayana Buddhism, similar in philosophy but adding additional techniques, known as upaya or "skillful means," esoteric practices that should be learned only under the tutelage of a skilled spiritual teacher. Within the United States, 0.7% of the population identify as Buddhist (Pew Research Center, 2015b).

The most prominent teachings within Buddhism include The Four Noble Truths and The Eightfold Path (Buddha Dharma Education Association, 2018). The Four Noble Truths come from the first talk that the Buddha gave after his enlightenment. The Four Noble Truths are

1. *Dukkha:* All existence is unsatisfactory and filled with suffering. Because this is the first Noble Truth of Buddhism, some falsely think that Buddhism is a "negative" religion. This is not so at all. Rather, Buddhism, perhaps more than other religion, acknowledges the struggles and challenges of life and the path to transcend this suffering.
2. *Samudaya:* The root of suffering can be defined as a craving or clinging to the wrong things. Such a clinging is commonly referred to as an *attachment*.
3. *Dirodha:* It is possible to end suffering by abandoning our expectations of how things should be and, through this mindfulness, become more aware of how things really are.
4. *Magga:* Freedom from suffering is possible by following the Eightfold Path.

The Eightfold Path, then, is the key to practicing nonattachment and ending our suffering. Pain is inevitable, but suffering is said to occur when we resist pain. The Eightfold Path includes three major categories, Panna, Sila, and Samadhi:

Panna: Paths of discernment and wisdom
1. *Right view* occurs when we embrace the joy of life the way it is, without the maya (i.e., illusion) of hopes or fears.
2. *Right intention* occurs when we act with pure intention free of manipulation borne of our expectations, hopes, and fears.

Sila: Paths of virtue and morality

3. *Right speech* occurs when we speak from right intention in an honest, simple, and genuine way.

4. *Right discipline* occurs when we simplify life by surrendering all that complicates our life and our relationships.

5. *Right livelihood* occurs when we form a simple relationship with our job and perform it well and with attention to detail.

Samadhi: Right concentration

6. *Right effort* occurs when we surrender our tendency to struggle and see things as they are and work with them without aggression.

7. *Right mindfulness* occurs when we are precisely and clearly aware of all of our experiences, without judgment.

8. *Right concentration* occurs when we are fully aware and completely absorbed in present moment experience, free of worries for the future and regrets from the past.

HINDUISM Hinduism is the oldest known religion, with origins attributed as far back as 3200 BC, and it is the third-largest religion in the world with approximately 15% of the global population and 0.7% of Americans identifying as Hindu (Pew Research Center, 2015b). It is the predominant religion of India, where over 80% of the population is Hindu. Hinduism is unique in that it has no founder or leader whom Hindus follow (ReligionFacts, 2016). In fact, the authors of the *Four Vedas*, the holy texts of Hinduism, are unknown.

Hinduism is both a religion and a cultural way of life. It is sometimes mistakenly referred to as a polytheistic religion when, in fact, it is henotheistic, meaning that Hindus recognize a single deity, but also recognize other gods and goddesses as facets, forms, manifestations, or aspects of that supreme God.

Central to Hindu beliefs are the concepts of karma and samsara. Karma, which translates as "works" or "deeds," refers to the notion that all actions have moral consequences that one must accept as a part of life. Samsara is the idea that one's present life is only the most recent in a long chain of lives extending far into the past. Hindus believe, then, in a continuous cycle of birth, life, death, and rebirth through many lifetimes and that all past lives have some influence on the current life through karma. This cycle is represented in the Hindu trinity of Brahma (creator of the world), Vishnu (preserver of the world), and Shiva (destroyer of the world).

A final Hindu belief that may influence the counseling process is the belief that Atman (self or soul) is Brahman (God) and Brahman is Atman. Many religions separate the "self" from "God," and some mistakenly distinguish between the two when interpreting the Hindu belief system. By Atman, Hindus mean not a distinct or separate "self," as is often defined in Western traditions. Instead, by Atman Hindus are referring to that aspect of the universal consciousness that is contained within the mind, body, and soul of the individual (Klostermaier, 2007). Thus, a core belief of Hindus is that the essence of the human personality is interchangeable with God and *tat twam asi*, that one is immutable and eternal.

SIKHISM Sikhism is a fairly new religion emerging in Punjab India in the 16th century (ReligionFacts, 2016). This monotheistic religion developed in the midst of conflict between Hindus and Muslims in India. The founder, Guru Nanak Dev, preached a message of unity and equality. He declared the purpose of religion was not to create division but rather to foster unity and is quoted to say, "We are all one" (Singh, 2011). Guru Nanak Dev began acquiring followers, and the numbers continued to grow. Currently, 23 million people worldwide practice Sikhism, making it the fifth-largest religion, with 19 million Sikhs residing in India (ReligionFacts, 2016).

The religious authority of Sikhism began with Guru Nanak Dev and continued through nine Guru successors (Singh, 2011). The last Guru, Gobind Singh, claimed that Sikhs no longer needed a living Guru but that all instruction was to be found in the *Sri Guru Granth Sahib*, the sacred text of Sikhism. Today, Sikhs adhere to principles of equality, unity, and a moral code of discipline (ReligionFacts, 2016). Holy days include *gurpubs*, or anniversaries of the births and deaths of the Gurus, as well as a celebration of the Sri Guru Granth Sahib. In terms of central beliefs, reincarnation is a primary aspect of Sikhism with the cycle ending through attainment of a balanced life, a sense of community, and the avoidance of the Five Cardinal Vices. The Five Cardinal Vices include lust, anger, greed, worldly attachment, and pride. To resist and overcome these vices, the Sikhs cultivate qualities of contentment, kindness, humility, charity, and happiness (ReligionFacts, 2016). A final belief of Sikhism relates to stages of movement toward God. Rather than an afterlife of heaven or hell, Sikhs believe that the end of reincarnation is to merge with the one God (Singh, 2011). This journey to God is complete with five stages: (1) *Dharam khand* (recognition of one's spiritual duty), (2) *Gian Khand* (acquisition of divine knowledge), (3) *Sharan khand* (experience of wisdom and beauty), (4) *Karam khand* (divine grace and power), and (5) *Such khand* (truth). Thus the end of the journey is to become one with God (Singh, 2011).

TAOISM Taoism is based on ancient Chinese beliefs that over centuries have become mixed with principles from Buddhism and Confucianism (Zhao, 2010). Taoism originated with the teachings of Lao-tzu circa 604 BC, although there is some debate among scholars as to whether he really existed or whether the writings attributed to Lao-tzu were a compilation from many writers. Regardless, the *Tao Te Ching*, one of the fundamental texts of Taoism attributed to Lao-tzu, has been translated into Western languages more than any other text with the exception of the Christian Bible. There are a number of concepts central to Taoist beliefs, including:

1. *Tao:* The ultimate reality; literally, "The Way." The Tao is considered the intrinsic essence from which our existence and experience spring. The Tao is likened to water in that it is formless yet conforming, flows effortlessly yet changes, and is soft but powerful (Simpkins & Simpkins, 1999). It is through stillness and connectedness to nature that we are all connected with Tao.
2. *Te:* The life power that is the living expression of the Tao.
3. *Chi:* The life-force energy that is beyond intellectual understanding.
4. *Yin/Yang:* A symbol popularized in the West, the Yin/Yang represents opposites, most notably the masculine and feminine, that work together to bring wholeness.
5. *Wu-wei:* Literally, "actionless action," the commitment of Taoists to avoid actions that go against the natural order or Tao.

Finally, it bears mentioning that many aspects of Taoism have been integrated into Western culture, although many people do not know the origins of these aspects. Martial arts such as *Tai Chi Chuan* and *Aikido*, healing practices such as *acupuncture* and *acupressure*, and the practice of removing energetic clutter in living spaces, known as *Feng Shui*, all have roots in Taoist principles.

CONFUCIANISM **Confucianism** is a set of teachings from Confucius, whose formal name was Kong Qui (Goldin, 2011). Confucius was reportedly born into royalty but was raised in poverty.

He studied at the imperial capital of Zhou and became a renowned teacher and philosopher. He taught during a time in China considered by many to be a time of moral chaos, and his teachings were an effort to stem this moral decay—particularly among the nobility. Confucius initially attempted to teach the ruling class his doctrines, but he often was criticized and ignored, so he resigned from his formal positions and began to wander through China followed by a large group of disciples. It was during these five years of wandering through China that the majority of text that became the major sacred text of Confucianism, *The Analects*, was composed.

Although he was not accepted by the ruling class of China, Confucius gained a following of about 3,000 people, including about 70 disciples. He was not overly influential during his own generation, however, and it was not until much later that his teachings were implemented in China (Goldin, 2011). To this day, the debate goes on as to whether Confucianism is indeed a religion, with some arguing that it clearly involves that which is holy and numinous (Goldin, 2011), whereas others argue that it is more of a moral code than religion per se.

A principle belief of Confucianism is that of *ren*, or benevolence (ReligionFacts, 2016). *Ren* refers to a character of excellence comprised of altruistic behavior and human kindness (Ministry of Culture, P. R. China, 2014). *Li* is linked to *ren* and refers to the rites or rituals that result in proper conduct. This code of behavior is a guide toward benevolent acts and the outward expression of *ren*. Finally, *de*, or virtue, is the combination of *li* and *ren*. It consists of both a benevolent attitude and benevolent behaviors.

A fundamental practice among Neo-Confucianists is that of quiet-sitting, a practice that likely was inspired by Buddhist meditation (Solé-Farràs, 2013). Distinct from other forms of meditation that have the intent to empty the mind or find the Self, quiet-sitting is intended to make the mind receptive to knowledge. Quiet-sitting has been likened to brightening up a mirror so that it can more clearly reflect the original nature within oneself (Chödrön, 2013). As one becomes more fully oneself, the self can be united with God. Table 16.1 lists major observances of the religions discussed in this chapter.

TABLE 16.1 Major Religious Observances

Buddhism

Buddhist New Year: Celebrated on different days throughout the world. Theravada Buddhists celebrate the new year for 3 days from the first full moon day in April. Mahayana and Vajrayana Buddhists celebrate the new year on the first full moon day in January.

Vesak (Buddha Day): Vesak is the birthday of the Buddha and the most important festival in Buddhism. On the first full moon day in May, Buddhists celebrate the birth, enlightenment, and death of the Buddha in a single day. The name "Vesak" comes from the Indian month of that name in which it is held.

Dhamma Day: Observed on the full moon day of the eighth lunar month (July). Dhamma day commemorates the Buddha's first sermon.

Hinduism (The dates vary because the Hindu calendar is lunisolar.)

Ugadi: Hindu New Year

Holi: The festival of colors and spring (February–March)

Mashashivaratri: The sacred night for Shiva (February–March)

Rama Navami: Lord Rama's birthday (April)

Krishna Jayanti: Lord Krishna's birthday (July–August)

(Continued)

TABLE 16.1 Major Religious Observances (Continued)

Raksabandhana: Renewing the bonds of brothers and sisters (July–August)

Kmbh Mela: The pilgrimage to the four cities of India (July–August, every 12 years)

Ganesh-Chaturthi: Ganesh festival (August–September)

Dassera: The victory of Ravana (September–October)

Navaratri: The festival of Shakti (September–October)

Diwali: The festival of lights (September–October)

Sikhism

Guru Gobind Singh's Birthday: The celebration of the birth of the tenth and final Guru, who appointed the holy text as his final successor (December–January)

Hola Mohalla: A three-day festival complete with mock battles, music, poetry, and challenges for Sikhs to complete. The festival remembers the day Guru Gobind Singh designated for military exercises (March)

Vaisakhi: A day celebrating the Khalsa order, or a spiritual brotherhood of Sikhs who have evolved into total dedication to Sikhism. Many choose to be baptized into Khalsa on this day (April)

Celebration of Sri Guru Granth Sahib: The celebration of the holy text and commemoration of its completion (August–September)

Taoism

Lao Tzu's Birthday: 15th day of the 2nd lunar month

Chinese New Year: First day of the first month of the Chinese calendar

Confucianism

Teacher's Day: Honors the birth of Confucius and the teaching profession (September 28)

Christianity

Christmas: Celebrates the birth of Jesus (December 25)

Easter: Spring festival that celebrates the resurrection of Jesus

Islam

Al-Hijra: The Islam New Year. It is celebrated on the first day of Muharram, the month in which Mohammed emigrated from Mecca to Medina in AD 622.

Ramadan: Considered a holy month in which the Qur'an was sent down as a guide for Muslims. Ramadan is the ninth month of the Muslim year.

Id Al-Fitr or *Eid al-Fitr:* Festival of the breaking of the fast, a celebration on the first 3 days of the month of Shawwal to mark the end of Ramadan.

Mawlid un-Nabi: The celebration of the birthday of Mohammed. Sunni Muslims celebrate on the 12th of Rabi'-ul-Awwal. Shi'a Muslims celebrate on the 17th of Rabi'-ul-Awwal. Many Muslims do not celebrate Mawlid, as they consider it to be a *bidah,* or innovation, against Islam.

Judaism

Rosh Hashanah: Jewish New Year, occurring on the first and second days of Tishri. The Jewish New Year is a time to begin introspection, reflecting on the mistakes of the past year and planning the changes to make in the new year.

Yom Kippur: Literally "Day of Atonement," it is probably the most important holiday of the Jewish year. Yom Kippur occurs on the 10th day of Tishri.

Pesach (Passover): The primary observances of Pesach are related to the Exodus from Egypt after generations of slavery and specifically the fact that God "passed over" the houses of the Jews when he was slaying the firstborn of Egypt. Pesach begins on the 15th day of the Jewish month of Nissan.

Western World Religions

The three major Western religions are Christianity, Islam, and Judaism. Together, these three religions are professed by over 73% of the U.S. population and constitute the three largest organized religions in the United States (Pew Research Center, 2015b).

CHRISTIANITY   Christianity is overwhelmingly the largest religion in the United States, with approximately 70.6% of the U.S. population professing to be Christian (Pew Research Center, 2015b). Additionally, Christianity is the largest religious tradition worldwide with 31.4% of the global population identifying with a Christian denomination.

As with other major world religions, 2,000 years of history have resulted in a diverse religion. Within this diversity, however, there are three major divisions of Christianity: Roman Catholicism, Eastern Orthodoxy, and Protestantism. The common ground for all of these groups, however, is the historical Jesus, a man who "was born in a stable, was executed as a criminal at age 33, never traveled more than ninety miles from his birthplace, owned nothing, attended no college, marshaled no army, and instead of producing books did his only writing in the sand" (Smith, 1991, p. 317). Despite these humble roots, December 25 and the first Sunday after the first full moon of the vernal equinox in the Northern Hemisphere continue to be the holiest days of the year for Christians, who each year remember the birth and death of their "Christ" at Christmas and Easter, respectively.

A central tenet of Christianity is the Trinity, or the representation of God the parent, Jesus the Son, and the presence of the Holy Spirit. For many Christians, Jesus was sent to earth by God to fulfill messianic prophecy foretold in what is now called the Old Testament, and the life and death of Jesus created eternal life, as indicated in the Christian Bible:

> For God so loved the world that he gave his only Son, that whoever believes in Him should not perish but have eternal life. For God sent the Son into the world, not to condemn the world, but that the world might be saved through Him. (Oxford University Press, 1973, p. 1289)

Other significant principles of the religion include *baptism*, a sacrament in which individuals profess their faith in Jesus through immersion in water (ReligionFacts, 2016), as well as *communion*, the act of remembering Jesus' sacrifice by partaking of bread and wine. Finally, the term *grace* is a prominent component of Christian belief system referring to the free gift of salvation given by God to an undeserving creation.

Within each of the major divisions of Christianity (i.e., Roman Catholicism, Eastern Orthodoxy, and Protestantism), there remains great variation in the beliefs of adherents, with the most vocal divides arising between more conservative (often labeled "fundamentalist") factions and more moderate or liberal factions.

ISLAM   In the United States, 0.9% of the population identify as Muslim, adherents of Islam, and, as such, it is the third-largest religion in the country, behind only Christianity and Judaism. Of note, however, is that Islam more than doubled in the United States between 2007 (0.4% of Americans) to 2014 (0.9%; Pew Research Center, 2015b). That is, Islam is by far the most quickly growing of the Western religions in the United States. Worldwide, estimates are that there are approximately 1.5 billion Muslims, making it the second-largest religion in the world (D. W. Brown, 2009), with expected growth to 2.2 billion in the next 20 years (Pew Forum on Religion & Public Life, 2015).

The central figure to Muslims, Mohammed Ibn Abdallah, was born in AD 570 in Mecca. In 610, Mohammed had his first vision and proclaimed Allah to be the one true God and condemned idol worship. Muslims later forced the city of Mecca to submit and accept Mohammed as a prophet. Mohammed destroyed all the idols in the Kaba, or temple, in Mecca. From Mecca, Muslims waged *jihad*, or holy war, and forced surrounding cities to accept Islam and Mohammed as a prophet. Mohammed died in 632 (Lewis & Churchill, 2008).

As with other religions, it is inaccurate to consider Islam to be a monolithic group. The primary historical division is between mainstream Sunnis (the word *sunni* drawn from *sunnah*, meaning "tradition") and Shi'ites (literally, "partisans" of Ali) who believed that Ali, Mohammed's son-in-law, should have succeeded Mohammed. Ali was appointed leader of the Muslims only after being passed over three times and was assassinated soon after assuming leadership. Shi'ites comprise about 13% of all Muslims and are primarily located in Iraq and Iran. The Sunnis, comprising about 87% of all Muslims, flank the Shi'ites to both the West and the East (Smith, 1991). Recent events in the Middle East have highlighted for Westerners the divide between Sunni and Shi'ite Muslims.

There is a third subgroup of Muslims, those who are primarily interested in the mystical aspects of Islam. These practitioners are called Sufis. Focused more on the inner life than the outer, they emphasized concepts such as meaning, inner reality, and contemplation. Westerners may be most familiar with the contemplative dancers among the Sufis (known as Dervishes) and the love poetry of the Persian Sufi, Jalal ad-Din Rumi.

The most central precepts of Islam are known as The Five Pillars (Lewis & Churchill, 2008). The first pillar is Islam's creed, known as the Shahadah, that "There is no God but God, and Mohammed is His prophet." The second pillar of Islam is canonical prayer. Adherents are encouraged in the *Qur'an*, the holy text of Islam, to be constant in prayer. To this day, Muslims are required to pray five times a day, facing toward Mecca, a practice that reportedly was negotiated by Mohammed in his renowned Night Journey to Heaven (Aslan, 2011). The third pillar of Islam is charity, with a simple message. Those who have much should help lift the burden of those who have less. The fourth pillar of Islam is the observance of Ramadan, Islam's holy month, considered holy because it was the month in which Mohammed both received his first revelation and, 10 years later, made his famous migration from Mecca to Medina. Tradition dictates that able-bodied Muslims fast during Ramadan, neither eating nor drinking from dawn until dusk, and only moderately after sunset. Islam's fifth pillar is pilgrimage, dictating that each Muslim who is physically and economically able should make a pilgrimage to Mecca to heighten devotion to God.

JUDAISM   Judaism is the second largest religion in the United States with 1.9% of Americans identifying as Jewish (Pew Research Center, 2015b). Of the approximately 14 million Jews worldwide, approximately 4.7 million live in Israel. These numbers are greatly affected by one of the greatest atrocities in history, the Holocaust, in which approximately 6 million Jews were murdered.

Judaism is a religion, but much more. Judaism is a culture, and some consider it an ethnicity as well. That is, some consider themselves culturally or ethnically Jewish, but do not consider themselves to be Jewish in the religious sense. As with other religions, a variety of Jewish sects hold distinct beliefs and practices. Of those Jews affiliated with a synagogue (on which such statistics can be kept), 45% consider themselves *Reformed Jews*, 42% consider themselves *Conservative Jews*, 9% consider themselves *Orthodox*, and 4% consider themselves *Reconstructivist*. Although it oversimplifies the differences somewhat, Orthodox Jews live by the *letter* of the Torah, the five books that comprise the central Jewish holy text, whereas Reformed, Conservative, and Reconstructivist Jews live by the *spirit* of the Torah, with some variations between them.

The roots of Judaism began when God spoke to Abraham and promised a nation. This was followed some time later by a covenant between God and Moses on Mt. Sinai in which the Ten Commandments were given to Moses, land was promised, and Moses was commissioned to lead the Hebrews out of slavery. These two prophets are considered the central figures of Judaism.

Central to the Jewish tradition are rites of passage and the celebration of religious holy days. Important events in the life cycle include circumcision (and, in some instances, giving the child a Hebrew name), Bar or Bat Mitzvah, marriages, and funerals. The most important Jewish holy days often are referred to as the High Holy Days, celebrated during the first 10 days of the month of Tishri, usually in September or October. The first day is Rosh Hashanah, the Jewish New Year. For 10 days, from Rosh Hashanah until Yom Kippur, Jews think about how they have lived during the past year. They are asked to remember the wrongs they have committed and to ask forgiveness from God and those they have hurt.

Table 16.2 provides a summary comparison chart for the world's major religions, and Voices from the Field 16.1 provides anonymous perspectives on some of the major world religions discussed in this section. Activity 16.2 allows for an immersion activity into a spiritual experience in which you may be unfamiliar.

TABLE 16.2 Major Religions Comparison Chart

Religious Group	Central Figure	Key Text	Key Points	Holy Days
Buddhism	Siddhartha Gautama	Pali Canon	Four Noble Truths, Eightfold Path	Buddhist New Year, Vesak, Dhamma Day
Hinduism	No central figure or central authority	Four Vedas	Karma, Samsara, Brahman, Atman	Ugadi, Holi, Mashashivaratri, Rama Navami, Krishna Jayanti, Raksabandhana, Kmbh Mela, Ganesh-Chaturthi, Dassera, Navaratri, Diwali
Sikhism	Guru Nanak	Sri Guru Granth Sahib	Equality, Rahit Nama, Five vices, Five qualities to overcome vices, Five stages on journey to God	Birth of Guru Gobind Singh, Celebration of Sri Guru Granth Sahib, Vaisakhi, Hola Mohalla
Taoism	Lao-Tzu	Tao Te Ching	Tao, Te, Chi, Yin/Yang, Wu-wei	Lao Tzu's Birthday, Chinese New Year

(Continued)

TABLE 16.2 Major Religions Comparison Chart (Continued)

Religious Group	Central Figure	Key Text	Key Points	Holy Days
Confucianism	Confucius	The Analects	Ren, Li, De, Quiet-Sitting	Teacher's Day
Christianity	Jesus	Old and New Testaments	Trinity, Baptism, Communion, Grace	Christmas, Easter
Islam	Mohammed Ibn Abdallah	Qur'an	The Five Pillars	Al-Hijra, Ramadan, Id Al-Fitr, Mawlid un-Nabi
Judaism	Abraham and Moses	Torah	Circumcision, Bar Mitzvah, Bat Mitzvah	Rosh Hashanah, Yom Kippur, Pesach

Voices from the Field 16.1

Buddhism: "Buddhism to me is being fully present at every instant. Its practice has been valuable in helping me feel more at peace with whatever 'is' at this moment. I feel its essence as love, acceptance, compassion, and oneness."

Hinduism: "My religious and spiritual beliefs stem from one of the basic principles of Hinduism: there is no superior God, just different paths and names that individuals prescribe to based on their backgrounds and personal belief systems. My belief in religious universalism allows me to live in a space of love, acceptance, and humility."

Christianity: "The Bible is not just a book to me—it is living and active words of God. Through reading the Bible, I get to know God and strengthen my relationship with Him."

Islam: "Islam means true and infinite love to all of the creatures in the world to me. We believe that there is no God but Allah and since He created all of the creatures in this world we keep equal distance to all religions with endless tolerance and patience."

Judaism: "For me, Judaism is different than other religions in that it encourages questioning. In my synagogue, we are allowed to have opinions, feelings, and discussions from multiple views. We attempt to use these discussions to help us learn and grow into better people."

ACTIVITY 16.2

The following activity serves to provide exposure to religious experiences and spiritual practices different from your own.

1. Select one religious faith that you are least familiar/comfortable with and attend a meeting, service, or experience within that faith community (this may include attending a religious service at a Buddhist temple, an Islamic mosque, a Jewish synagogue, or a Christian church).

2. Select one spiritual practice that you are least familiar/comfortable with to experience for the duration of at least one week (this may include yoga, contemplative prayer, quiet-sitting, fasting, focusing, or a mindfulness practice). If you are unclear about the plethora of spiritual practices available, you might visit http://www.spiritualityandpractice.com /practices for ideas.

Note: When visiting a religious service it is important to express an attitude of respect for the members of the faith community. Make sure your presence is welcomed, and you are adhering to the traditions of that particular religious faith while engaging in the experience. In addition, some spiritual practices should not be attempted without guidance and instruction (such as breathwork and T'ai Chi). Be cognizant of the need for additional resources, and consult them when necessary.

ALL IS ONE: ASPECTS COMMON TO ALL RELIGIONS

"There is one river of Truth which receives tributaries from every side." ~ Clement of Alexandria

To this point, the emphasis of this chapter has been on the substantial variations of belief systems, both between and within world religions. One common precept of the spiritual life, however, is that all is connected, all is one. Within this framework, religious and spiritual diversity provides multiple paths that, at some point, converge. That is, all is connected and all is one, though the frameworks (or paths) that have evolved culturally may appear, on the surface, to be quite different. The following seven tenets are adapted from the work of Wilber (2001); these seven tenets are considered to be central to all religions.

Tenet 1: Spirit, by Whatever Name, Exists

Whether called God, Goddess, The Divine, The Absolute, Supreme Reality, Brahman, Tao, Allah, Shiva, Yahweh, Aton, Kether, Dharmakaya, or other names that have evolved from various wisdom traditions, Spirit exists. There is a certain ineffable quality to Spirit that makes the discourse around spirituality and counseling quite challenging. The proverbial hand pointing to the moon is not the moon, and the best that we can ever hope to do, given the numinous and ineffable quality of Spirit, is point toward its existence. Thousands of years of spiritual wisdom and experience across many cultural divides lead to the same conclusion. Spirit exists.

Tenet 2: Spirit Is Found "in Here," within an Open Heart and Mind

Although some individual religious groups have worked to create a disconnection between Spirit and humankind, claiming that intercessories are required, or emphasizing the "unworthiness" of humans to be connected to Spirit, the wisdom of the ages suggests quite clearly, and across many different traditions, that Spirit, or at least some collective aspect of Spirit, resides within each of us. For example, the often quoted mantra of Hinduism, previously mentioned in this chapter, that "Atman is Brahman; Brahman is Atman" is indicative of this belief, that within each of us is a Divine spark. The Buddha is quoted as saying, "We all have innate Buddha nature," and Jesus is quoted as saying, "The kingdom of heaven is within." Over time and across traditions, then, there is a recognition that we are, at the core of our being, spiritual in nature.

The second part of this tenet, "within an open heart and mind," reveals a more active process in which each of us has responsibility. Who, reading this text, could not more fully open his or her mind and heart? Increased mindfulness and heartfulness are fruits of the spiritual journey to wholeness. Opening the heart and mind is not something that is done "to us," but rather a journey co-constructed with Spirit, a journey in which each of us must accept the opportunity to discipline and tame the mind and open the heart more fully.

Tenet 3: Many/Most Don't Realize Spirit Within

There are many variations on this theme. Some have disavowed that they are spiritual beings. Such people may either be Inexperienced Decliners or Rejectors, as outlined earlier. Not acknowledging Spirit at all, they can hardly realize Spirit within. Others, though, see Spirit, using whatever name they have chosen as being an external entity, a being that (in most nomenclatures, at least) looks down on them from some ethereal realm. Such people see themselves, and label themselves, based solely on their mortal ego that hopes, at some point in the future, to be one with Spirit. Such a spirituality, which could be called a "there and then" spirituality, precludes the full experience of a "here and now" spirituality. When this contraction occurs, it is not possible to live at one with Spirit and all that exists.

Tenet 4: There Is a Path to Liberation

The path to liberation involves transcendence of the individual self or personal ego. Although the path to liberation is unique to each individual, there are common aspects of this path. Although this list is intended to be neither exhaustive nor prescriptive, some common aspects of the path to liberation include the following:

1. Study of sacred texts, either within your personal faith tradition or across faith traditions, as befits personal preference.
2. Discussion of sacred texts in some form of community.
3. A mindfulness-based practice; this might include a practice such as vipassana meditation, centering prayer, breath prayer, or Lectio Divina. Many practitioners of mindfulness, particularly those just beginning a practice, find that a teacher and/or a supportive community of practitioners deepens the practice. (See Voices from the Field 16.2.) Recommended readings on these practices include
   • Meditation—Gunaratana (2011) and LeShan (2000)
   • Centering Prayer—Keating (2006)
   • Breath Prayer—Lewis (1998)
   • Lectio Divina—Merton (1986)

Note: Although these practices are discussed in the texts from a perspective that is either nonreligious or affiliated with a particular religion, any of these practices can easily be adapted to be consistent with different belief systems.

4. Heartfulness-based practices, such as the Buddhist practice of Loving Kindness Meditation (Chödrön, 2013; Salzberg & Kabat-Zinn, 2004) and the conscious practice of forgiveness (Luskin, 2003; Tipping, 2010; Worthington & Sandage, 2015).
5. Body-centered practices, such as focusing (Cornell, 2013; Gendlin, 1982), yoga (Yee, 2015), breathwork (Grof & Grof, 2010), or T'ai Chi (Wayne, 2013).
6. Acting on increased mindfulness with acts of social justice and compassion.

Voices from the Field 16.2

"Mindfulness meditation helps me feel calm and grounded and invites the spaciousness I need to gain clarity of thought, compassion for myself and others, and a greater sense of connection to divine presence. Being mindful also allows me to feel more present and openhearted in my relationships with others"

~ Cristina, Counseling Student

"Through the practice of breathwork, my sense of spiritual connection moved from theoretical to tangible. Each breath offers the experience of connection and exchange, giving and receiving, living and dying."

~ Jamie, Professional Counselor

"Through my daily practice of Lectio Divina, I enter into relationship with my God, and become increasingly aware of my struggles in life, both those I need to actively address and those I need to surrender. This practice helps me to live out my belief in the Serenity Prayer."

Scott, Professional Counselor

Tenet 5: If This Path Is Followed, the Result Is Rebirth or Enlightenment

Through disciplined spiritual practice and study, it is possible to experience a "death" of the old self and emergence, or rebirth, of a new self, more fully authentic and self-actualized (Maslow, 1993). This transcendence may include peak experiences and epiphanies, but overall the process of rebirth or enlightenment is a gradual and lifelong process.

It is important here to distinguish between the authentic spiritual path and that which is inauthentic. One distinction that has been made is the relationship of the spiritual path to the development of ego, known as the pre/trans fallacy, discussed by Wilber (2000). Although it oversimplifies Wilber's concepts greatly, in the interest of space, consider simply the difference between a codependent and Mother Teresa. If you watch from the "outside," both will appear dedicated to a life of service to others. The difference lies, however, in intention. The codependent behaves in a manner that solidifies a nonspiritual ego, one that clings desperately to the notion that in serving others, he or she will find love and acceptance, the proverbial "good enough" irony. Such behavior is prerational in that it is not borne of, nor does it contribute to, a "rebirth" of the self. On the other hand, the selfless giving of someone like Mother Teresa has the sole intent of service to God and humankind. Such behavior is said to be transrational, in that it involves a transcending of the personal ego in lieu of compassion and service. One key distinction between the two involves self-compassion. The person functioning at a prerational level literally lives to serve others, often at personal psychological expense. On the other hand, the person functioning at a transrational level of development recognizes that compassion for others must begin with self-compassion.

Tenet 6: Rebirth or Enlightenment Results in the End of Suffering

This concept is perhaps best discussed within the Buddhist tradition, where it is commonly acknowledged that pain is inevitable but suffering is not. That is, suffering occurs when we resist the physical, emotional, and psychological pain in life (Chödrön, 2013). One of the fruits of the life of disciplined spiritual practice and study is not the eradication of pain; rather, it is the end of resistance to pain and, therefore, the end of suffering.

Tenet 7: The End of Suffering Manifests in Social Actions of Mercy and Compassion

Ultimately, rebirth or enlightenment, resulting in the end of suffering, is useful only if it manifests in acts of social justice, mercy, love, and compassion for others. Smith (2003) put this succinctly when he asserted that altered states are useful only if they lead to altered traits.

SPECIAL CONSIDERATIONS FOR COUNSELING

Having discussed diverse belief systems and a framework that provides convergence of the world's wisdom traditions, attention is now directed toward special considerations with spiritual issues in counseling. Among these are issues related to approaching spiritual issues, ethical competence, and working with spiritual bypass.

Approaching Client Spiritual Issues

Whether clients bring their spiritual issues into counseling explicitly (i.e., identifying a crisis of faith or spiritual emergency) or implicitly (i.e., presenting issues that are underlain with unspoken issues related to meaning and purpose), early responses of the counselor set the tone for the therapeutic process. Inherent in these responses from the counselor are meta-messages about the role that religious and spiritual beliefs, practices, or experiences can and should play in the counseling process.

In a seminal and frequently cited article, Zinnbauer and Pargament (2000) provided a nomenclature for the various approaches that counselors can take in working with spiritual issues that arise. In their categorization, counselors can take approaches that are rejectionist, exclusivist, constructivist, or pluralist. To this category system, we add impositional, and we will discuss this classification more fully. Reflection 16.2 offers an opportunity to consider these categories and how they might relate to your work with clients.

REFLECTION 16.2

Using the Zinnbauer and Pargament (2000) category scheme, consider what approach you will most likely or most frequently use when approaching the Sacred in counseling. Regardless of what category you place yourself in, discuss the type of religious/spiritual beliefs with which you expect you will most struggle to work. Why?

The *rejectionist* counselor denies the sacred "truths" of the client. The counseling literature is replete with examples of the rejectionist approach. Freud reduced religion and spirituality to fantasy and wish fulfillment and characterized the religious experience as "infantile regression to a primitive state of limitless narcissism" (Freud 1961, p. 19). This is far from a dated stance, however. In an interview (Master Psychotherapists, n.d.), Albert Ellis avowed that "Spirit and soul is horseshit of the worst sort" (p. 1). These are extreme examples in that they reduce the Sacred to psychological disturbance or defense (Zinnbauer & Pargament, 2000).

There are, however, many examples of more tacit and implicit rejections. For example, in any given day, how many clients across the country choose not to talk about their religious and spiritual lives, largely because the counselor does not include this as an aspect of the initial assessment? Such a bias on the part of the counselor, although clearly less malicious than the quotes of Freud and Ellis, remains no less rejectionistic in impact (Gill, Harper, & Dailey, 2011). Case Study 16.2 illustrates an example of a counselor using a rejectionist approach.

CASE STUDY 16.2

The Case of Airi

Airi was a 25-year-old graduate student of Japanese descent. She sought counseling at her college counseling center due to increasing feelings of depression, including negative thoughts, lack of energy, and difficulty concentrating. Airi had been a diligent and successful graduate student, majoring in economics and receiving honors for her academic performance. Airi's drive to succeed in school began to decline, however, and was replaced by feelings of inadequacy and hopelessness. Airi's roommate became concerned when Airi refused to get out of bed and started missing classes. Airi agreed to go to counseling and reported to her counselor that she had "lost herself" as well as her motivation to continue toward her educational goals.

In their third session, the counselor asked Airi what "finding herself" would look like. Airi considered this question for a moment and stated that she would be more "whole and balanced." When the counselor asked Airi to expand on "whole and balanced" Airi referred to the religion of her parents saying, "They seemed to have something that I don't have. Some of my earliest memories are of my parents going to Temple or meditating. I used to think it was pointless, but they were so centered and spoke of the peace that comes from being mindful. I don't think I've ever felt that way." Airi spoke at length about the influence of Buddhism she observed in the lives of her parents and her experience with religion as a youth. Once Airi entered college, she distanced herself from Buddhism and had not practiced any form of religion for several years. After this disclosure the counselor replied, "Airi, I think I may know what is going on here. It seems like this discussion of religion may be a way for you to avoid the central issue—your depression. I'd like to bring our attention back to your experience with your depressive symptoms. Depression is a medical condition with predictable symptoms that can be treated effectively with the right medication. I think we should focus on how to manage these symptoms and get you functioning again. I know how important your schooling is, and we want you back to your routine as soon as possible. Would that be alright?" Airi agreed to focus her discussion on the symptoms of her depression and from that point forward never spoke of Buddhism or her thoughts related to religion. Consider the following questions related to the case of Airi:

- How was the counselor demonstrating a rejectionist approach?
- What was the impact of this approach on Airi? On the counseling relationship?
- What are alternate responses to Airi's disclosure of the religious/spiritual aspects of her life?

The *exclusivist* counselor believes in a fundamental and exclusive reality of religious and spiritual belief and experience. As such, the exclusivist is respectful of the client's religious and spiritual views, but only to the extent that these beliefs are consistent with the exclusivist's own understanding (Zinnbauer & Pargament, 2000). To the extent that the client's religious and spiritual worldview differ from that of the counselor, the exclusivist counselor sees it as within her or his purview to "bring the client around" to what the counselor perceives as the "correct" belief system. As such, the exclusivist counselor proselytizes for a previously determined set of beliefs. Counselors using this approach have the potential to be as intolerant as a counselor working from a rejectionistic perspective. Clearly, then, both the rejectionist and exclusivist approaches to the Sacred are problematic and inconsistent with ethical standards of the counseling profession.

In contrast, the other two approaches to working with the Sacred, constructivist and pluralist approaches, are appropriate and consistent with counselors' ethical codes of conduct. Counselors working from a *constructivist* approach do not believe in an absolute reality, but that truth is constructed by humans in interactions with each other as they strive to understand their life experience. The focus, then, is on the quality of the constructions, rather than whether the counselor agrees with the constructions. When psychological symptoms appear, they are considered a manifestation of the breakdown of constructions and then, and only then, are the constructions considered problematic; at all times, the therapeutic work remains within the client's belief system and worldview (Zinnbauer & Pargament, 2000). There are, however, two substantive criticisms of the constructivist approach. First, when working with diverse religious and spiritual beliefs, it is important for the constructivist counselor to be authentic and sincere. It is possible that the impact of the constructivist counselor's work can be undermined by the client perception of insincerity on the part of the counselor. Second, in some instances, the relativistic approach to client problems and perceptions can be problematic. Zinnbauer and Pargament use the example of a parent who uses religious beliefs to justify physically abusing children as discipline. In such cases, it may be necessary for even the *constructivist* counselor to intervene on ethical and legal grounds.

The fourth approach to the Sacred, pluralism, involves an acceptance of diverse paths to Spirit as valid. Although there is agreement that Spirit exists, spiritual beliefs, practices, and experiences evolve within cultures and are expressed by different people in different ways. The **pluralistic** counselor holds personal beliefs, but at the same time prizes the different beliefs of a client. The pluralistic counselor differs from the constructivist counselor in one key way. Although the constructivist counselor works only within the religious and spiritual "template" of the client, the pluralistic counselor is willing to expose her beliefs with the client and "negotiate their social reality . . . and work to define the goals for therapy" (Zinnbauer & Pargament, 2000, p. 168). As with the constructivist approach, however, there are potential pitfalls to the pluralistic approach. Pluralistic counselors must be persistently aware of how their own beliefs and values might be affecting the therapeutic process and maintain a collaborative stance. A second problem, common to both pluralistic counselors and exclusivist counselors, occurs when the counselor and client come from a shared religious reality. In such cases, it is easy for one or both to assume that they share common beliefs and values when, in fact, there may be substantial variance between the two. In such cases, the counselor may fail to assess the client's religious worldview adequately, or the client may not sufficiently describe his problem. This occurs based on a faulty assumption that the other understands one more than he or she does.

Clearly, then, counselors who work with the Sacred need to work from either a constructivist or pluralist approach. To operate from a rejectionist or exclusivist approach risks violating the ethical and legal standards for professional conduct and, more important, has a high likelihood of, at best, minimizing the effectiveness of counseling and, at worst, causing iatrogenic harm.

With great respect toward the importance and impact of the Zinnbauer and Pargament (2000) categorization of approaches to the Sacred, with the increased attention to the important role of spirituality in the psychotherapeutic process, it may be useful to consider a fifth approach, potentially as problematic as either the rejectionist or exclusivist approach. This approach might be labeled *impositional,* in that it involves the imposition of a religious or spiritual framework with a client who is either an atheist or nonreligious. Prevalence data suggest that 15.8% of the U.S. population do not affiliate with any particular religion, 4.0% identify as Agnostic, and 3.1% identify as Atheist (Pew Research Center, 2015b). For these groups, imposing a religious or spiritual view on the presenting problems and treatment process is a disavowal of their personal beliefs and values. This is akin to the exclusivist approach in that it imposes a set of beliefs on the client. The distinction, however, is that the impositional counselor is imposing the overarching framework of spirituality onto the counseling process when this is counter to the client's desires and expectations for counseling. Within this framework, it is necessary to consider that a counselor could be both impositional and exclusivist. Such a combined stance would involve imposing a specific religious reality on a client who not only does not agree with that specific reality, but also does not want spirituality to "intrude" into the secular counseling process.

Zinnbauer and Pargament (2000) have provided an invaluable schema for considering approaches to the Sacred in counseling. It is important to realize, however, that this schema also might be applicable at more macro levels. In addition to working with individual clients, counselors must act to champion diversity and at minimum a tolerance, if not embracement, of religious diversity. Although such acts of social justice and advocacy might best be performed in a gentle and compassionate manner, such acts must also be emboldened by the knowledge that religious intolerance is detrimental to the clients we serve and society at large.

Ethical Competence

Ethical competence is at the heart of integrating spirituality and religion into the counseling process and counselors should be aware of several ethical pitfalls. First, the lack of religious/spiritual assessment, or failure to appropriately address client religious and spiritual beliefs, may undermine the counseling process. Clients' religious and spiritual beliefs often powerfully impact their worldviews. If counselors leave this realm unexamined, they likely will construct incomplete conceptualizations of clients. Indeed, the American Counseling Association *Code of Ethics* (2014) outlined several ways in which counselors should address client religion and spirituality, including the involvement of religious and spiritual leaders in counseling (A.1.d), considering religious and spiritual beliefs in assessment interpretation (E.8), avoiding discrimination based on religious and spiritual identities (C.5), respecting client diversity (including religious and spiritual identities), and refraining from the imposition of values (A.4.b.). Researchers have found, however, that although counselors deem the integration of religious/spiritual behaviors into counseling as important and appropriate, the frequency in which they implement these behaviors is significantly lower than importance ratings would suggest (Cashwell et al., 2013; Cornish, Wade, & Post, 2012). There also is evidence to suggest that counselors feel more comfortable addressing spiritual elements rather than religious elements in counseling (Cashwell & Young, 2014). The lack of attention to religious and spiritual factors of a client's identity, or the preference for spirituality over religion, reflects a lack of respect for client diversity and, potentially, an imposition of values. For example, if a counselor does not personally identify as religious or has a negative perception of religion, she may impose these values by neglecting to explore her clients' religious beliefs, underestimating the importance of religion in the lives of her clients, and refraining from using religious resources when appropriate.

Another potential ethical pitfall is to allow personal values (including religious or spiritual) to influence which clients a counselor will or will not work with in counseling. The ACA *Code of Ethics* (2014) contains a new standard explicitly stating that referrals based on a conflict in personal values are discriminatory in nature (A.11.b). Referrals are acceptable when based on a lack of competence, not diverging values (Kocet & Herlihy, 2014). If a value conflict does exist between the counselor and the client, the counselor is encouraged to seek supervision and additional training to avoid the imposition of values. To be clear, the counselor has a right to her or his own personal values, yet he or she must engage in **ethical bracketing**, or, "the intentional setting aside of the counselors' personal values in order to provide ethical and appropriate counseling to all clients" (Kocet & Herlihy, 2014, p. 182). Ethical bracketing allows the counselor to enter into the client's frame of reference and work within her or his inner world without seeking to persuade, direct, or take ownership of the client's choices.

To assist clinicians in addressing religious and spiritual issues in counseling, Barnett and Johnson (2011) provided an ethical decision-making model comprised of nine stages. When presented with client religious and spiritual issues, counselors are to 1) assess the client's belief system respectfully, 2) identify connections between the client's presenting concern and religious/spiritual beliefs, 3) infuse the attained information into the process of informed consent, 4) assess countertransference to client religion, 5) evaluate competence in addressing clients' presenting issues, 6) consult resources/experts in the field of religion and counseling, 7) if the client gives consent (and it is appropriate) consult with client's religious leaders, 8) determine whether to continue working with the client or make an appropriate referral, and 9) evaluate outcomes and adjust as needed (Barnett & Johnson, 2011). By employing this decision-making model, counselors are able to adequately attend to the religious and spiritual elements of the client's identity, work within the client's frame of reference, identify countertransference issues and bracket personal values, and provide appropriate services to uniquely meet client goals and needs. If the client is specifically seeking spiritual direction, the counselor may use the ethical decision making model to decide to make a referral, so as to avoid working outside of her or his competence. Alternatively, the counselor may decide to include a religious leader in the counseling process after seeking client consent and clearly informing the client of the distinct professional roles and responsibilities of each service provider. By relying on the ethical decision-making model, counselors can operate more objectively and effectively meet the needs of diverse clients.

Additionally, Faiver and Ingersoll (2005) provided a framework for considering ethical competence in integrating spirituality and religion into counseling by considering Wilber's (1997, 1999) concepts of translation and transformation. **Translation** refers to those aspects of the spiritual experience such as beliefs, creeds, and dogma that the individual uses as a framework with which to find meaning and purpose in life. Ethical competence related to the translational aspects of the spiritual life follows the Zinnbauer and Pargament (2000) nomenclature discussed previously; that is, the counselor works within either a constructivist or pluralist approach with the client's spiritual and religious beliefs and values.

Much more complex, however, is ethical competence related to **transformation**. According to Wilber (1997), the transformational aspect of spirituality involves progressions to higher levels of spiritual development, often accompanied by physical, emotional, cognitive, and spiritual breakthroughs. An example of a transformational experience is a near-death experience (NDE). People who have an NDE commonly become more altruistic, less materialistic, and more loving (Holden, Greyson, & James, 2009), attributes consistent with spiritual transformation.

More subtle experiences of transformation may occur, for example, for a person who has developed and sustained a disciplined contemplative practice such as vipassana meditation or centering prayer. In the case of either a spontaneous transformation, such as an NDE, or a more gradual one, the central question is whether a counselor can accept and value the spiritual experiences of the individual. At the very least, a counselor who defines herself religiously from only a translative dimension may have difficulty working effectively with someone whose current practice and experiences are more transformational in nature. The converse of this likely also is true; that is, a counselor with a bias toward the transformational function of spirituality may run the risk of imposing this on a client whose primary interest is working at the translative (i.e., beliefs and meaning-making) level.

Spiritual Bypass

Spiritual bypass is a term coined by Whitfield (2003) to refer to a phenomenon in which a person attempts to heal psychological wounds by working at the spiritual level only. In so doing, "work" in the other realms, including the cognitive, emotional, physical, and interpersonal, is relegated to "less than" status and shunned. In short, the spiritual life of the individual serves an avoidance function, as the individual avoids other aspects of his problems.

Spiritual bypass is considered a common problem among people pursuing a spiritual path (Cashwell, Myers, & Shurts, 2004). A number of common problems emerge from spiritual bypass, including compulsive goodness, repression of undesirable emotions, spiritual narcissism, extreme external locus of control, spiritual addiction, blind faith in charismatic leaders, abdication of personal responsibility, and social isolation (Cashwell, 2005; Cashwell, Bentley, & Yarborough, 2007).

From a diversity perspective, the client in spiritual bypass presents a unique challenge. Such a client often presents in counseling with an explicit interest, if not desire, to integrate the Sacred into the counseling process. To fully support the wholeness and healing of such clients, though, it likely is necessary to encourage and challenge them to work at multiple levels (i.e., cognitive, emotional, physical, and interpersonal). To do so in a respectful manner is, at times, no small accomplishment. To highlight this, consider the case of Gail presented in Case Study 16.3.

CASE STUDY 16.3

The Case of Gail

Gail was a 44-year-old White female presenting in counseling with depression that she reported battling "off and on for all of my life." She had seen three counselors previously in the past 7 years and had seen two counselors within the past 2 years, asserting that "they didn't really help me much." She specifically said that she was drawn to work with me (CC) because of my interest in spirituality.

Gail reported that she was a devout Christian who discovered in the past few years that references to reincarnation existed within early versions of the Christian Bible, and that these were deleted by the Council of Nicaea. She had begun studying reincarnation and was convinced that her problems with depression stemmed from past-life experiences. I supported her in telling the story of her lifelong battle with depression, contracted for counseling services, and requested a release to talk to her previous counselor, a local counselor I knew well.

Contacting her previous counselor proved an interesting experience. She spoke of Gail's preoccupation with past lives, and that Gail would spend a great deal of time ruminating in session about what her past lives must have been like to generate so much depression. She resisted referrals for medication evaluation because, as she said, "If I can just find the source of this depression, I believe that God and I can heal it." The client terminated after the counselor got frustrated with Gail and told her that "she shouldn't worry so much about past lives until this one wasn't so messed up," a response that the previous counselor admitted was unhelpful. Based on the initial session, I conceptualized Gail as struggling with spiritual bypass. She was, I believed, hyperfocused on karma as the cause of her depression. Although I was not in a position to say if this was true or not, I expected that her counseling process would be more complex than this. In the next session, I further assessed what Gail thought the results might be of doing past-life work. Her answers seemed to make it clear that she was not looking to lessen her depression, but was rather looking for a reason (or, perhaps, an excuse) for why she was depressed. I was prepared to refer Gail to someone who did past-life hypnotherapy as this is not part of my counseling work. Based on my conceptualization, though, I was hopeful that I might be able to work with Gail in such a way that the problem was not seen as solely spiritual or karmic while still respecting her belief system.

My treatment approach was to remind Gail that she had been depressed for, as she reported, as long as she could remember, and that it was probably important to get better slowly. I told her that I thought it was important to go back in time, but that we should not start out by going straight back to past lives; I suggested we should work to understand the early part of this life as a stepping stone back to past lives. Although I think Gail was hoping to immediately do past-life work, she agreed that this made sense and we moved forward with our work together. Using an integrated combination of early life recollections from an Adlerian framework and phenomenological experiential approaches to work with those early recollections in the here and now, Gail began to unearth and heal some early trauma, including sexual and physical abuse. She began to connect with her anger, learned to channel that energy in appropriate ways, and began to be more assertive. As she reported at the end of the ninth session, "I feel like I have found my voice." I experienced Gail as a deeply spiritual woman, and we both spoke of feeling supported in our work together by something "beyond us." As her counseling progressed, she talked less about past lives. During our termination session (session 23), Gail laughed and said, "I still feel a little down sometimes, but nothing like I did. Maybe I'll do some past-life work sometime later, just for fun, but that doesn't seem nearly as important as it once did."

Gail did some amazing work as she began to heal some very old psychological wounds. If I did anything well with Gail, it was honoring her belief systems while still working in a way that seemed psychologically grounded and sound, by using her framework of past-life work to get her to work with her early childhood trauma. In her case, the work was largely at the cognitive and emotional levels, which resulted in some clear changes in interpersonal behaviors. To have supported her in her desire to work only at the spiritual level would have, in my opinion, been a therapeutic blunder, as it would have supported her proclivity toward spiritual bypass. Consider the following questions related to the case of Gail:

- Do you think the counselor's approach to treating Gail's depression was appropriate?
- The counselor chose not to be transparent with Gail about his approach. Do you think this was appropriate?
- How would you handle a scenario where a client wanted a type of spiritual intervention that you thought might be harmful to the client?

ASERVIC Competencies

The **Association for Spiritual, Ethical, and Religious Values in Counseling (ASERVIC)** has developed competencies for integrating spirituality into the counseling process (Cashwell & Watts, 2010). Counselors may increase their levels of awareness, knowledge, and skills with respect to their own as well as their clients' spirituality by reflecting on each competency. (See Activity 16.3.) The 14 competencies are:

Culture and Worldview

1. The professional counselor can describe the similarities and differences between spirituality and religion, including the basic beliefs of various spiritual systems, major world religions, agnosticism, and atheism.
2. The professional counselor recognizes that the client's beliefs (or absence of beliefs) about spirituality and/or religion are central to his or her worldview and can influence psychosocial functioning.

Counselor Self-Awareness

3. The professional counselor actively explores his or her own attitudes, beliefs, and values about spirituality and/or religion.
4. The professional counselor continuously evaluates the influence of his or her own spiritual and/or religious beliefs and values on the client and the counseling process.
5. The professional counselor can identify the limits of his or her understanding of the client's spiritual and/or religious perspective and is acquainted with religious and spiritual resources, including leaders, who can be avenues for consultation and to whom the counselor can refer.

Human and Spiritual Development

6. The professional counselor can describe and apply various models of spiritual and/or religious development and their relationship to human development.

Communication

7. The professional counselor responds to client communications about spirituality and/or religion with acceptance and sensitivity.
8. The professional counselor uses spiritual and/or religious concepts that are consistent with the client's spiritual and/or religious perspectives and that are acceptable to the client.
9. The professional counselor can recognize spiritual and/or religious themes in client communication and is able to address these with the client when they are therapeutically relevant.

Assessment

10. During the intake and assessment processes, the professional counselor strives to understand a client's spiritual and/or religious perspective by gathering information from the client and/or other sources.

Diagnosis and Treatment

11. When making a diagnosis, the professional counselor recognizes that the client's spiritual and/or religious perspectives can a) enhance well-being; b) contribute to client problems; and/or c) exacerbate symptoms.

12. The professional counselor sets goals with the client that are consistent with the client's spiritual and/or religious perspectives.
13. The professional counselor is able to a) modify therapeutic techniques to include a client's spiritual and/or religious perspectives, and b) utilize spiritual and/or religious practices as techniques when appropriate and acceptable to a client's viewpoint.
14. The professional counselor can therapeutically apply theory and current research supporting the inclusion of a client's spiritual and/or religious perspectives and practices.

Source: Association for Spiritual, Ethical, and Religious Values in Counseling, *Competencies for Addressing Spiritual and Religious Issues in Counseling*. Copyrighted information: used by permission of ASERVIC.

The working group who developed the competencies used recent research on evidence-based practices to develop these competencies (Cashwell & Watts, 2010). Further, the sequencing of these competencies was intentional as the focus was placed first on knowledge and awareness of diverse religious and spiritual beliefs (Culture and Worldview) and then on the importance of self-knowledge and self-awareness (Counselor Self-Awareness). It is only when a counselor has addressed this knowledge of self and other that he or she is prepared to work with others within a spiritual or religious framework. That is, therapeutic communication, assessment, diagnosis, and treatment all must be grounded in a strong sense of self and a valuing of the diverse beliefs, practices, and spiritual experiences of others.

ACTIVITY 16.3

Form dyads and select three of the ASERVIC competencies. Brainstorm specific ways that you can increase your awareness, knowledge, and skills for each selected competence.

Summary

If one believes, consistent with the majority of U.S. citizens, that Spirit exists in some form and that one's religion and spirituality are aspects and expressions of culture, then counselors should be trained to address client issues related to religion and spirituality. This chapter has considered aspects of both the diversity of religious and spiritual beliefs and practices, as well as the unity that can be seen woven through the tapestry of the world religions.

Spirituality is difficult to define and has been described as a set of individual beliefs, practices, and experiences that lead to transcendence of self and connection with others. Religion may be viewed as organized spirituality. The relationship between spirituality and religion can be conceptualized in many ways: complementary or coincidental; religious practice not necessarily indicative of quality of religious or spiritual experience; or spirituality disconnected from an organized religion. Several major religions are described in this chapter, including Buddhism, Hinduism, Taoism, Confucianism, Christianity, Judaism, and Islam. Although these religions are distinct from each other, there are several common tenets across religions.

The chapter discussed several approaches counselors may take in integrating spirituality into counseling. These include (a) rejectionist (counselor dismisses or avoids discussions of spirituality); (b) exclusivist (counselor respects client's spiritual and religious beliefs to the degree they match the counselor's beliefs); (c) constructivist (counselor attends to how the spiritual or religious belief is constructed); (d) pluralist (counselor respects multiple beliefs and is willing to share his beliefs with the client); and (e) impositional (counselor imposes a spiritual or religious framework on the client who is either atheist or nonreligious).

An issue that may arise when working with clients involves spiritual bypass, in which clients attempt to solve psychological issues with spirituality alone. Finally, it is important to be ethically and culturally competent when integrating spirituality into counseling. The ASERVIC competencies are a useful framework to begin to think about ethical and cultural competence. Table 16.3 provides additional resources for facilitating multicultural counseling competence around spiritual diversity.

TABLE 16.3 Recommended Readings and Resources

Books

- Cashwell, C. S., & Young, J. S. (2011). *Integrating spirituality and religion into counseling: A guide to competent practice.* Alexandria, VA: American Counseling Association.
- Frame, M. W. (2002). *Integrating religion and spirituality into counseling: A comprehensive approach.* Brooks Cole.
- Fukuyama, M. A., & Sevig, T. D. (1999). *Integrating spirituality into multicultural counseling.* Thousand Oaks, CA: Sage.

Websites

- Ontario Consultants on Religious Tolerance (www.religioustolerance.org): The site provides information about all major religious beliefs world views, and systems of morality, ethics, and values, to promote understanding and appreciation of religious diversity.
- BN Media (www.beliefnet.com): This Web resource is the leading source of spiritual information presented without a defined editorial point-of-view.
- Harvard University-sponsored Pluralism Project (www.pluralism.org): The Pluralism Project has a mission, in part, to help Americans engage with the realities of religious diversity through research, outreach, and dissemination of information.

Within the ancient Sanskrit language, there is a word that lacks a one-word translation in English. It characterizes one way in which spirituality can be integrated within the counseling process, that of seeing the client as more than a cluster of symptoms to be reduced. It translates as "the light within me bows to the light within you."

Namaste.

The purpose of the following closing meditation is to allow people with diverse beliefs about spirituality to work with their Spirit connection.

1. Find a quiet place to sit in which you will not be interrupted during the meditation.
2. Soft, ambient background music may be used to support the meditation (e.g., *Shamanic Journey* by Anugama).
3. Begin the meditation with a few minutes of deep, full, and slow breathing in which you intentionally breathe fully both into the abdomen and then into the chest; the exhale should be used to release any remaining tension in the body.
4. After several minutes of full breathing, consider a problem or challenge that you

currently face to come into your awareness. This should be done without overthinking the problem but, rather, allowing it to emerge naturally.

5. After considering this problem, see a connection to Spirit emerging before you. This may take the form of a person, a deity, an animal, or some other form. Look at your connection to Spirit closely. Study it.

6. Ask your connection to Spirit what He/She/It has to tell you about the problem that is before you. Allow the answer(s) to emerge slowly and fully without overthinking or judging the experience. After allowing this experience to play itself out fully for you, thank the connection to Spirit for providing you with this wisdom, and allow the image before you to fade.

7. Journal your experience or, if you are doing this within a class or other community, in the coming days discuss your experience from the meditation and what it means for you.

Review Questions

1. How are religion and spirituality defined? What are various views on the relationship between the two concepts?

2. Describe the major religious groups outlined in this chapter. How do they compare with one another?

3. How might commonalities across religions be helpful when working with clients?

4. What are the four approaches counselors can take when working with clients on spiritual issues? How might these operate in counseling?

5. What is spiritual bypass? When and how might this be addressed in counseling?

SECTION 4

Multicultural Conceptualization

17 Using Counseling Theories in Multicultural Contexts

Jonathan J. Orr

PREVIEW

Theory is the foundation on which counselors build their professional identity, and it is the knowledge base that defines mental health professions. As a fundamental dimension of counselor identity, theory also forms the backbone of clinical practice and informs how a counselor works with various types of clients. Given this primacy of theory to the work of counselors, it is important to understand how theory is created and supported in a multicultural context. Throughout this chapter, the development and implementation of theory will be viewed from a perspective of intersecting identities. Embarking on this chapter, readers are encouraged to keep in mind that the development and application of theory can be as unique and varied as the clientele and clinical issues that counselors encounter in their work. This chapter cannot cover all possible ways to encounter and work with clients in counseling sessions. Readers are challenged to use this chapter as a starting point for continued exploration of how theory can inform practice in the very diverse landscape of counseling. This chapter assists readers to connect worldview to theory development, identify alternative sources for theory in multicultural contexts, trace cultural assumptions implicit in the major counseling theories, learn to use culture as a springboard for expanding the application of traditional counseling theories, and discover novel approaches to counseling that incorporate multicultural dimensions. Last, when examining the development, acquisition, and application of counseling theory in the context of culture, it is paramount to consider the cultural sources of information. This author's most current cultural identity awareness consists of the following dimensions: White, genderqueer, educated, heterosexual, spiritual, American, lower-middle SES, living in an urban area in a southern U.S. region. Although that list is in no way exhaustive, readers are invited to consider how the author's cultural lenses through which information is passed may alternatively clarify and obscure included content.

SOCIAL AND CULTURAL FOUNDATIONS OF COUNSELING THEORY

Embarking on a journey to examine the cultural dimensions and relevance of counseling theory can be a daunting task. Embarking on a journey to examine the cultural dimensions and relevance of counseling theory can be a daunting task to which some counselors have devoted entire careers. It is a challenging area of study because of the dynamic nature shared by culture and theory. Both culture and theory are founded on individuals' experiences, so as people experience more, including one another, their theoretical orientation changes. In addition to sharing similarities, culture and theory are at times at odds with one another. Theory, in its most basic sense, is reductionist and seeks to provide a consistent and all-encompassing response and explanation for various dimensions of an individual's life (Hackney & Cormier, 2012; Seligman & Reichenberg, 2013), although theory cannot be completely inclusive as a description of human behavior. However, counselors are not able to use the same type of theory to fit all people. Each person has unique perspectives and experiences that define an individual.

Theory cannot encompass all human experience; likewise, it cannot account for all the thoughts, feelings, behaviors, or contexts that contribute to individuals' identities. Counselors tend to get into trouble when they think of theory as an absolute or as all-encompassing. In other words, a theory may indicate that things should be a certain way for a client, so counselors then grow to expect that from a client (Fall, Holden, & Marquis, 2010; Murdock, 2013).

Theory is something that belongs to us as counselors. It helps us organize what a client is saying, it provides us with direction for our questioning, and it helps us make sense of our work as counselors (Fall et al., 2010; Halbur & Halbur, 2015). Our theory provides us with starting points in our work with clients. In this way, **theoretical orientation** describes both our rationale and our action. We use our theory to bring purpose to our work with clients, and theory helps us orient to our clients. Case Study 17.1 presents an example of theoretical fit and the importance it could play for clients and counselors.

CASE STUDY 17.1

Taylor visits your counseling practice and describes the challenges that are emerging in life. As you explore these presenting issues, you find that Taylor seems like a perfect fit for you and your theoretical orientation. You believe that you can truly facilitate growth in this client and make a positive life impact. Taylor endorses your belief and likewise recognizes the fit between you and potential ways to grow. In the middle of the second session, Taylor decides to ask you for the first time about your theoretical orientation. Upon hearing what it is, Taylor describes having worked before with someone who had a similar theoretical orientation and declares that there is no way that your theoretical orientation will work with the presenting issue. Taylor requests that you try a different theory.

- What are the primary issues at play in this case study?
- How do you respond to Taylor?
- How do you address Taylor's concerns and remain congruent in your own theoretical competence?

Worldview Shaping Counseling

Most people are unaware of the process underlying how they live their lives. That is, most humans do not give much thought to their philosophical or theoretical approach to life. For the most part, life proceeds for people in a more active rather than reflective manner. They are more involved and concerned with the function of their lives (i.e., what they need to get done) as opposed to the explanations, the motivations, or reasons for living their lives. At times of crisis or change, people may become more interested in the processes underlying their ways of life, and that is when they may seek assistance from helpers such as counselors or spiritual leaders. It is in these times with a professional guide that most people discover motivation for living or their personal theory for life.

Personal theories for life have been characterized in counseling literature as synonymous with worldview (Ivey, D'Andrea, & Ivey, 2012; Henderson, Spigner-Littles, & Milhouse, 2006). A person's **worldview** is comprised of personal constructs that are created within familial, cultural, and societal contexts and are typically constructed from five value orientations based on the Kluckhohn and Strodtbeck (1961) theoretical model: (a) human nature (evil, mixed, or good); (b) person/nature relations (subjugation to nature, harmony with nature, or mastery over nature); (c) social relations (lineal, collateral, or individual); (d) time sense (past, present, or future); and (e) human activity (being, being-in-becoming, or doing). The extent to which individuals combine these orientations varies based on their identification with a particular cultural group and can account for both cross-cultural and within-group differences (Ivey et al., 2012; Jun, 2010). Counselors are encouraged to consider these value orientations on a more personal level. (see Reflection 17.1.)

Assessing clients' worldviews is a dynamic process in the counseling relationship. The information gained from worldview assessments is best viewed as informative rather than

---

REFLECTION 17.1

Take a moment to answer the following questions based on the five dimensions of worldview set forth by Kluckhohn (1951, 1956). Then reflect on the value assigned to your own particular worldview:

- *Human Nature:* Do you consider humans to be essentially good, evil, or to have equal capacity for good and evil at a given moment?
- *Person/Nature Relations:* Which of the following statements would you agree with most:
- Humans are ultimately at the mercy of nature. We are not able to control how nature affects us.
- Humans are the masters of nature. We are meant to control it for our benefit.
- Humans and nature rely on one another for coexistence. One cannot continue without the other keeping it in balance.
- *Social Relations:* Which of the following statements would you agree with most:
- Ultimately, I need to take action for myself and do what is right for me in life.
- Ultimately, I need to know how my actions might reflect on my family or community and act accordingly.
- Ultimately, I need to know how my actions might reflect on my family and the legacy of those who have come before me.
- *Time Sense:* Are you more likely to be time-oriented to the past, present, or future?
- *Human Activity:* Which of the following statements would you agree with most:
- I am most satisfied being acknowledged for my activities and accomplishments.
- I am most satisfied being acknowledged for who I am and the aspirations I have for who I want to become.
- I am satisfied being acknowledged for just being me.

Consider your responses. How is your worldview supported and/or challenged by your culture? How is it challenged and/or supported by your society? How might your worldview be similar to and different from potential clients?

predictive; clients might have a tendency toward particular worldviews, and those are more indicative of a psychological, emotional, or ecological state of being rather than some inherent personality trait. Counselors interested in using assessments of clients' worldviews will find many assessments that measure a presupposed client worldview. The Belief Systems Analysis Scale (Montgomery, Fine, & James-Myers, 1990) and the Afrocentric Scale (Cokley & Williams, 2005; Grills & Longshore, 1996) are two such examples designed to measure the degree to which clients adhere to an Afrocentric worldview. Assessments to explore specific dimensions of worldview such as spirituality (Ai et al., 2014) or conditions of worldviews such as after a trauma (Pérez-Sales, Eiroa-Orosa, Olivos, Barbero-Val, Fernandez-Liria, & Vergara, 2012) also help counselors understand their clients. Assessments that characterize overall worldview can be formal, such as Worldview Analysis Scale (Obasi, Flores, & James-Myers, 2009), and informal. Refer to Reflection 17.1 for an informal assessment of worldviews and consider how you might integrate those orientations into your work.

Building on these worldview orientations, Hjelle and Ziegler (1992) identified nine basic assumptions that counselors use to create and support their approaches to counseling. The nine assumptions are freedom/determinism, rationality/irrationality, holism/elementalism, constitutionalism/environmentalism, changeability/unchangeability, subjectivity/objectivity, proactivity/reactivity, homeostasis/heterostasis, and knowability/unknowability. These assumptions may be conceptualized along a continuum. Most people find themselves between the two poles, and the combination of the assumptions dictates how persons see themselves and then view others. Counseling theorists are included among these and base the development of their approaches on these assumptions.

Transition from Worldview to Theory

From the foundation of personal worldviews, individuals begin to make sense out of their lives and account for the contexts in which they live. As people make meaning of their own life experiences, many may extend their worldview to others. Through observation, reflection, and refinement over time, those individual worldviews may soon evolve into explanations for why things happen for groups of people. Gladding (2012) pointed out that "a sound theory matches a counselor's personal philosophy of helping" (p. 4), and in this way, as worldview expands from the individual to larger groups, theory can be born. Indeed it has been suggested that most if not all of the counseling theories and techniques are derived from personal worldviews (Fall et al., 2010; Halbur & Halbur, 2015; Ivey et al., 2012).

With worldviews forming the basis for individuals' personal philosophies as well as theoretical orientations in counseling, it seems that there exists potential for both success and folly. Take, for instance, counselors whose theories are congruent with both their own worldview and their clients' worldviews. In this pairing, counselor and client could share common ground in the characterization of challenges, motivations, and goals for living. This type of congruence facilitates a stronger client–counselor alliance and counselor empathy (Kim, Ng, & Ahn, 2005). Alternatively, when clients and counselors differ on even one of the worldview dimensions, the therapeutic relationship can be affected negatively (see Activity 17.1).

From its more individualized beginnings in worldview, theory attempts to take on a more comprehensive explanation for human observations and experience. In the field of counseling, observations tend to be interpersonal in nature and deal with psychic rather than physical concerns. Furthermore, counseling theory commonly incorporates guidelines for human development and sets criteria for typical or desired functioning. It is in this area of defining

---

ACTIVITY 17.1

Discuss the following example involving competing worldviews in small groups.

A Japanese international student self-refers to a college counseling center complaining of general sadness and anxiety. During the session, the student describes to her counselor difficulty that she is having in some classes required for her major. As the counselor probes, he begins to realize that his client's sadness and anxiety seem to be directly linked to the courses with which she is struggling. However, when the counselor suggests that the student consider changing her major, she refuses, saying that her parents would never approve of that action. The counselor is confident in his assessment and believes that the change in major would greatly improve his client's disposition. He continues to focus on encouraging her to change her major and challenge her parents' expectations. He sums his suggestions to her by saying, "After all, you are here living your life, not them. You need to make decisions that will work for you." The student leaves and on returning asks for a different counselor, citing that her previous one did not understand her. How did this counselor's worldview affect his counseling? Was his worldview congruent with his client's? How might this counselor have approached his client differently?

---

typical human development and function that theory finds its limits. Human development is a social process that is influenced by individuals' culture, ethnicity, gender, and socioeconomic status, among other things. Likewise, human functioning is also socially contextualized and infinite in its scope. Within these constant processes of evolution, human development and functioning can never be fully characterized by one theory. Regardless of its reported comprehensiveness, a counseling theory will work with particular clients under particular conditions (Ivey et al., 2012). To remain multiculturally competent in their application of theory, counselors need to understand the worldview of their clients as well as the worldview supported by particular counseling theories and strive to balance the two. It may behoove counselors to consider various conceptual systems. (see Reflection 17.2.)

REFLECTION 17.2

Based on cultural differences, worldviews have been variously characterized as representative of different groups. The following worldviews adapted from Jackson and Meadows (1991, p. 75) outline three conceptual systems that are prevalent among large populations in the United States.

European Conceptual System

- Material possession and the acquisition of objects are emphasized.
- External knowledge is emphasized and is supported through measuring and/or counting.
- Logic is based on a dichotomous system (e.g., things either are or are not).
- Identity and worth are based on external criteria.

Asian Conceptual System

- Cohesiveness of the group and cosmic unity (all life and energy is connected and inseparable) are emphasized.
- A blend of internal and external knowledge is emphasized and is supported by an integration of mind, body, and spirit.

- Logic is based on unity of mind and thought with a focus on interrelations.
- Identity and worth are based on being an integration of internal and external criteria.

African Conceptual System

- Spiritual and material dimensions are emphasized and focused on the relationship between women and men.
- Self-knowledge is emphasized and is supported through symbolic imagery and rhythm.
- Logic is based on the union of opposites, with a focus on interrelationship of human and spiritual dimensions.
- Identity and worth are intrinsic.

Reflect on the following questions:

- Which of the conceptual systems is most in line with your own? Which is most different?
- How might you use this information to inform your theoretical conceptualization of particular clients?
- How might you use this information to empower your clients?
- Based on these conceptual systems, match theories that you think would be most effective with particular clients. What evidence can you use to support your matches?

Alternative Sources of Theory in Multicultural Counseling

Theories of counseling have specific definitions for mental health and parameters for typical mental functioning. Clients who are not part of the culture targeted by a particular counseling theory are set at a disadvantage. From the start, they run the risk of being considered somehow deficient because they do not fit the typical description of a client. Something that is actually a cultural difference can be misconstrued as a deficiency in the client. Take, for example, something as simple as language. If clients who do not speak English fluently as their first language were to visit an average counselor in the United States, they run the risk of misdiagnosis based on counselors misunderstanding their presentations of issues. Furthermore, when counselors and clients do not share common language, their understanding of particular meanings for concepts as well as behaviors is affected. Simply stated, without some shared understanding of what it means to be mentally healthy, no counseling theory can be effective.

The difficulties that uncommon language bases present to the counseling relationship can be minor when compared to challenges that arise when worldviews of counselors and clients differ. When counselor and client differ on worldview dimensions, the very structure and basis for mental health can be called into question. When it comes to defining and understanding what it means to be a mentally healthy and functioning person in multicultural counseling contexts, counseling theory provides only a small part of a larger picture. In many cultures, the practice of counseling is relatively unknown, and the notion of mental health is incorporated into other social systems such as religion or familial relationships. These social systems influence people's beliefs about what it means to be a "normally" functioning member of a particular group. For counselors intending to be multiculturally competent, it is important that they understand the ways in which various social systems define a person's life. The social systems of religion, government, and family are three major systems found across cultures that influence clients and shape a culture's understanding of mental health.

RELIGION AND SPIRITUALITY   Religion and spirituality have alternatively been called the greatest unifier and the greatest divider of people. Nations have been built and wars have been waged on the basis of religious and spiritual beliefs. Religious and spiritual beliefs directly influence persons' worldviews in a number of ways that in turn affect how they define mental health. In many religions, the mind and functions of mental health are closely linked to the divine. Thoughts, emotions, and even motivations for behaviors are attributed to the influence of the divine. These beliefs in the influence of the divine in all matters beyond physical action predate any notion of counseling theory and fundamentally shape how persons form their understanding of mental health.

When applying a particular theory of counseling it is important to consider how that theory interacts with clients' beliefs about the divine. Does the theory assume a humanistic perspective in that people can somehow control or influence their thoughts, behaviors, and emotions? Does the theory instead leave room for a deistic perspective in that the divine has some (if not primary) influence in people's lives? Answering these questions with each client and considering how clients conceptualize notions of the divine in their lives is an essential first step when integrating theory with religious and spiritual beliefs. A simple misunderstanding between counselor and client about the role of the divine can potentially lead to major differences in the perceptions of mental health. For example, although one may view hearing voices as an acceptable manifestation of the divine, the other may take it as a clear sign of schizophrenia.

GOVERNMENT In many ways particular forms of government are direct expressions of worldviews. Consider, for example, the American perspective of democracy. This form of democracy values equal representation in government based on certain inalienable rights that are attributed to all people. As the notions of democracy extend beyond this most basic understanding, inequities emerge, and the definition of what a democracy might represent to different individuals begins to shift. These shifts in how democracy is represented are based in large part on worldviews. Within the U.S. democratic system, two of the primary opposing worldviews are represented by political parties. The Republican and the Democrat parties share a basic conceptualization for democratic governance, but differ greatly in how to define their roles in applying and supporting that government. The political differences between Republicans and Democrats in the United States are reflected in many lifestyle choices of individuals, and often these individuals choose the political affiliation that best reflects their own principles.

Extending beyond the confines of an Amerocentric view of government, many more systems of government are in use throughout the world. Similar to democracy, each of these governments is based on worldview and lifestyle choices that are made within the context of government. Laws are created to support the structure of government and to reinforce the lifestyle choices for the governed. In this way the notions of acceptable human activity (i.e., normal functioning) are defined and shaped by government. Admittedly there is greater complexity to the intersection of government and lifestyle choices of the governed, but even in this most basic description, the effect of political or governmental views on mental health is evident. (see Activity 17.2.) Simply stated, governments set the parameters for what it means to be an accepted member of society and, by extension, how functional mental health is defined.

FAMILY Family is a social system that has the greatest potential for shaping notions of mental health. It serves as a filter through which the previously mentioned systems of religion and government are passed. Individuals learn from the members of their families how to connect with the divine and how to function socially. As such an influential social system, families play a primary role in shaping individuals' notions of mental health. Both the role of families in

ACTIVITY 17.2

In dyads, consider the following definitions of mental health:

Mental health is the foundation for the well-being and effective functioning of individuals. It is more than the absence of a mental disorder. Mental health is the ability to think and learn, and the ability to understand and live with one's emotions and the reactions of others. It is a state of balance within a person and between a person and the environment. Physical, psychological, social, cultural, spiritual and other interrelated factors participate in producing this balance (World Health Organization [WHO], 2001).

Mental health is a state of successful performance of mental function, resulting in productive activities, fulfilling relationships with other people, and the ability to adapt to change and to cope with adversity. Mental health is indispensable to personal well-being, family and interpersonal relationships, and contribution to community or society (U.S. Surgeon General, 1999).

- In what ways are these definitions similar?
- In what ways are these definitions different?
- What are some of the assumptions that support these definitions?
- How might these definitions be influenced by worldview?
- How might these definitions be influenced by systems of government or social norms?
- Using these definitions of mental health, provide examples of culturally specific behavior that could be considered unhealthy.

general within a society and the role of families in specific individuals' lives are significant factors. Specifically, how individuals relate to their particular families and how those familial relationships relate to the overall role of families are important to consider in multicultural counseling.

Families may play different roles within a particular society, and understanding these roles will provide counselors with information about mental health. For example, what constitutes a family? Is family comprised of blood relations alone, or does it include marital relations or other romantic partnerships, close friends, and/or neighbors? How are family relations connected to social status? How are families created—by choice or arrangement? Who is allowed to be considered a family and under what conditions? What are some of the taboos related to marriage? These among other questions are important to explore with clients to achieve clear meaning for how their own families are viewed in particular societal contexts. Furthermore, exploration related to the general role of families in society will provide clues to the definitions for functional and dysfunctional familial relationships.

Moving to the individual level, it is important to explore how clients interact within their own families. Typically, clients get their first definition and subsequent reinforcement of mental health from their families. These familial characterizations may or may not reflect larger societal views of mental health, but regardless, their influence on individuals is significant. Relationships between clients and their family members are important to be aware of, as are other dimensions of family. How do clients' behaviors compare to others in the family? What roles are clients expected to play in their families, and are they meeting those expectations? What is the role of ancestors in the family culture? Answers to these questions and others related to individuals' roles in family systems could illuminate the worldview that families use to shape notions of mental health.

APPLICATIONS OF COUNSELING THEORY ACROSS CULTURES

Traditional counseling theories are abundant in the counseling literature, and the degree of their relevance across cultures is gaining increased attention. In this section, traditional theoretical approaches are discussed. In addition, strategies for adapting traditional approaches and integrating Eastern approaches in counseling practice are discussed. Consider the circumstances of Clara in Case Study 17.2.

CASE STUDY 17.2

Clara is a 15-year-old client who identifies as Caucasian female and was brought to counseling because she has recently been reacting violently to social situations at home and in school. She has been involved with child protective services and foster care since the age of two and currently lives with Christa, a former partner of her biological father. Christa has been estranged from the biological father for several years and Christa's biological mother is incarcerated on charges related to drug use. Clara's father is presumed to live in another state and has occasional contact with her by phone. Clara has lit fires in the home, spray-painted walls, and made passive threats toward other children in Christa's home. These events have occurred when Clara experiences "overwhelming anger," and this has led her to counseling. Christa and Clara express a goal of learning where Clara's anger is coming from and how she can better cope with her anger.

- How would you characterize Clara's central issue that has led her to seek counseling?
- If you could provide only one targeted intervention with Clara, what would it be? How do you account for your choice of intervention?
- In what ways do you identify with Clara? In what ways do you differentiate from Clara?
- How might your answers to the previous question facilitate the counseling relationship? How might your answers impede the counseling relationship?
- Choose a counseling theory that you believe would be of greatest benefit to Clara. Account for your choice.
- Choose a counseling theory that you believe would be of least benefit to Clara. Account for your choice.

Traditional Theoretical Approaches to Counseling

Over the last 50 years, the choices for therapeutic approaches to counseling have grown to reach over 400 in number (Corsini & Wedding, 2014). Although this growth has been considerable, the foundational theories that support these approaches have grown at a more measured pace. The growth of major theoretical conceptualizations is typically characterized by the term *forces*, and authors almost universally agree that the first three **forces in counseling** theory are comprised of psychodynamic, cognitive–behavioral, and humanistic–existential (Gladding, 2012; Hackney & Cormier, 2012). The fourth force has been conceptualized as transpersonal (Moodley & West, 2005), multicultural (Ivey et al., 2012; Lee, 2007), systemic (Corey, 2013), and integrative (Seligman & Reichenberg, 2013), among others. Regardless of the specific title for this fourth force, there is clearly a shared emphasis on contextual and systemic influences among all the approaches.

Providing even a cursory overview of the major theoretical orientations in counseling is beyond the scope of this chapter. Indeed, whole texts and even series of texts have been devoted to the discussion of theories and approaches to counseling. Turning instead to some of the underlying assumptions and constructs that support development of the four forces in counseling, similarities in worldview emerge. It has become a commonly accepted assumption that most of the major theories have been developed to serve White, middle-class men of European heritage (Jones-Smith, 2014). Tracing much of counseling theory to its origins, theorists such as Freud, Adler, Perls, Ellis, and Rogers spring to mind, and it would seem that, for the most part, this assumption is supported and further reinforced by the demographic characteristics of the theorists themselves. In addition, their theories were developed to serve clients living particularly within Western European and American contexts. (see Reflection 17.3.) This means that counseling theories generally are developed in and support a particularly Westernized worldview.

The relatively limited client base targeted by the majority of counseling theories proves difficult when working with diverse client populations. Limiting theoretical and treatment options to approaches based solely on Western worldviews can prove to be both useless and potentially harmful to some clients (Jones-Smith, 2014). Are mental health and, by extension, mental distress universal concepts, or are they unique to a Westernized view of the world? Do other cultures and worldviews account for mental health through the development and

---

REFLECTION 17.3

Consider the following examples of conventional Western assumptions in counseling theories:

- The universe was created spontaneously either through physical phenomenon (e.g., Big Bang) or creation by the divine.
- Through research and study all things can be known, and reality is concrete and measurable.
- Empirical proof and intellectual knowledge and learning are highly valued.
- Consciousness is objective and only characteristic of humans.
- Personality provides unique individual identity, and context is not as important as the intrinsic characteristics of an individual.
- Living is marked by growth and progress toward an inevitable end, and the value of one's life is based on the reflection of past experiences and future goals.
- Death is an inevitable end to human life. Consciousness, personality, and existence in the physical world end with death.
- Suffering is to be avoided, and progress is marked by the alleviation of suffering.
- Emotions, learning, and consciousness are physical functions based on electrochemical systems.
- Mind, body, and spirit are divided and often at odds.
- Visual and/or auditory stimuli are more reliable than intuition (i.e., "Seeing is believing").
- Behavior, personality, and identity are individually created and modified.

Considering these assumptions, respond to the following questions:

- To what extent do your own beliefs and worldviews match these assumptions?
- Describe some of the alternative assumptions that might contradict these worldviews.
- What cultural and/or social institutions support these assumptions?
- How do mental health services create and perpetuate particular worldview assumptions?
- What are some ways in which you might become aware of other assumptions underlying counseling theory?
- How might you best use those assumptions to serve your clients rather than to alienate them?

application of theory? To fully answer these questions, it is necessary to expand the definitions of both mental health and counseling theory.

Although the traditional counseling theories that comprise the first three forces in counseling may have been developed and initially applied with specific clients in mind, they have expanded to meet the needs of a greater diversity of clients. This ability to evolve and adapt over time is one of the hallmarks of a grand theory in counseling. **Grand theories** in counseling seek to integrate all dimensions of human experience into a single overarching theoretical framework. Typically, these grand theories incorporate many different models for counseling and spawn variations on a particular theme. Psychodynamic theory provides a prime example of grand theory in counseling. From Freud's original conception of the human condition, theorists such as Jung, Adler, Erikson, Horney, and Stack-Sullivan all developed their own unique interpretation of psychodynamic theory. The grand theories in counseling coincide with the "forces" described earlier and include psychodynamic, cognitive–behavioral, and humanistic–existential theories. Voices from the Field 17.1 provides the author's perspective on applying theory to counseling practice.

Voices from the Field 17.1

There is sometimes a large gap between writing about best practices and putting them into action through practice. The greatest challenge presented in doing so lies with the ambiguity inherent in the therapeutic process. Despite thorough planning and extensive development of theory and technique, each client represents a unique opportunity to connect with cultural complexity. Here I describe how I have flexed my theoretical perspective in attempts to meet the needs of diverse clientele.

Before I share my voice, it is important for you to know a little more about how I define my voice and how I prefer to use it. I can most easily characterize my voice by sharing how I view theory functioning in the therapeutic relationship. My view of applied theory is divided into two paradigms—my theoretical orientation and the orientation of my clients. In terms of my clients, I operate from an assumption that I learned from the work of Milton Erikson that all clients represent their own unique theoretical orientation. Acting from this assumption means that I take time to learn my clients' worldview and engage their worldview on a variety of topics that are functioning in their life both successfully and unsuccessfully. For my part, I find Gestalt to be the theory that best fits my worldview. Specifically, I value the constructs of wholeness, balance, and integration and apply the following prayer coined by Fritz Perls (1969, p. 4):

> *I do my thing and you do your thing.*
> *I am not in this world to live up to your expectations*
> *And you are not in this world to live up to mine.*
> *You are you and I am I.*
> *And if by chance we find each other, it's beautiful,*
> *If not, it can't be helped.*

By integrating these perspectives of how theory operates in the therapeutic relationship, I believe I am able to achieve the seemingly contradictory goals of remaining grounded and consistent in how I conceptualize and work with clients while simultaneously being flexible to adapt to the unique identity and complexity of my diverse clientele.

So what does this look like in practice? My example involves a young man who presented with interpersonal difficulties in his career and intimate relationships that were precipitated by anxiety.

Getting to know my client over the course of several sessions, he elaborated on his internalized view that he had no worth and that the environment around him was not to be trusted at all. That sense of self was first instilled by his father and later adopted for his own sense of self. In my eagerness to help this client, I conceptualized his situation as an ideal fit for my understanding of Gestalt theory. In essence, I believed that much of his anxiety was the result of negative introjections that were first instilled by his father, and having this client adopt the Perls prayer referenced earlier appeared to be an ideal solution. This is the type of "home run" situation that I always hope for where theory and client issue seem to intersect seamlessly.

My ego would like me to say that I put my own rush of clinical excitement aside and carefully considered the effect of my evidence-based intervention in the context of client cultural identity. However, that would not make much of a story. There are many cultural nuances that I failed to consider in working with this client, but among the more dominant were his cultural identity as Southeast Asian and with that, his expressed worldview of interdependence. I confronted and challenged my client to become more self-assured, self-focused, self-aware, etc.; basically I was driving my client toward embodiment of self-defined boundaries that I understood as essential to the goals of Gestalt therapy. Simply stated, I was asking him to override his own paradigm of interdependence in favor of one that values independence.

Fortunately, I recognized early some resistance to my interventions, and I had a client who was willing to advocate for himself. Instead of pushing forward, I pulled back to examine what was happening. It was at that time that I realized my initial cultural blindness and the mistake I was making because of it. Given that information, I did not switch theories to accommodate my client; instead, I adapted my Gestalt-based intervention. He and I worked to connect him to a more supportive community that could support a more integrated self-view. I encouraged him to become more involved with his community both at work and in his residential community so that he could see the dimensionality of those with whom he interacted. The Gestalt-based goal of developing a more holistic and integrated sense of self did not change for the client, but how he achieved that goal did change. He sought to achieve the goal through relations with others rather than in the individually focused manner that I had first initiated with him. In this way, we were both able to stay true to our identities. He was able to grow within the context of his cultural identity, and I was able to flex my understanding of Gestalt theory to meet his needs.

~JJO

Culturally Responsive Use of Traditional Theories

Culturally responsive counseling is a concept that is gaining popularity, and it marks a departure from typical "one size fits all" approaches to counseling. In **culturally responsive counseling**, the counselor includes diverse perspectives in the counseling process and recognizes contextual dimensions such as culture, class, gender, race, sexual orientation, religion, and geography (Neukrug, 2015). When practicing this concept of culturally responsive counseling, counselors must also be aware of their own cultural identities and the cultural contexts for their approach to counseling. Incorporating awareness of self in the counseling process characterizes the notion of culturally responsible counseling. It is not enough for counselors to simply respond to culture in terms of their clients; counselors must also take responsibility for their own cultural contexts and the contexts of their chosen theoretical orientation.

To be culturally responsive, counselors must learn to be flexible in their theoretical approach. In this sense, counselors are expected to be chameleons, changing their theoretical approach as the therapeutic environment changes in much the same way that lizards change appearance to match their surroundings. Typically, theoretical flexibility has been characterized as eclectic or integrative practice, and in those characterizations counselors have been encouraged to use different theories based on the needs of clients. As clients present unique needs or cultural realities, an eclectic counselor might be tempted to shift from, say, a psychodynamic approach to a humanistic approach. This shift between theoretical approaches can be drastic and may bring most counselors to the brink of practicing beyond their competence. It is difficult for most counselors to fully master one theory, let alone several. The result of this type of approach can be quite harmful for clients, and instead of meeting their needs, it potentially could exacerbate their situation. After all, when a chameleon is faced with a new environment, it does not stop being a chameleon; instead, it simply changes color to adapt.

Adaptation of counseling theory is a more appropriate response to diverse clients. Through adaptation, counselors can expand their knowledge of a particular theory and deepen their competence. **Theoretical adaptation** allows counselors to remain grounded in their client conceptualization while exploring new ways to apply theory. If **eclecticism** or integration has a place in counseling it is in the techniques related to theory. Counselors are encouraged to practice technical eclecticism while maintaining a primary sense of theory across various settings and client groups.

Having introduced the concept of theoretical adaptation, it would seem natural to raise the question of how to adapt theories to fit unique client populations. Like the needs of clients, theoretical orientations are unique, and their adaptation will depend largely on the context in which they are applied. However, counselors should use some general guidelines to adapt particular theories to meet the dynamic needs of their clients.

1. *Determine Assumptions:* All theories are predicated on certain assumptions about mental health and worldview. Before using your chosen theory with any client, you need to familiarize yourself with the associated underlying assumptions.
2. *Identify Limitations:* All theories do not fit all people, so explore the limitations of your chosen theory even before you begin working with clients. Pinpoint the gaps or gray areas in your theoretical orientation and strategize ways to compensate for them.
3. *Simplify Concepts:* Theories are notorious contributors to jargon. Quite often various theories will use multiple terms to refer to similar phenomena. Consider the concept of the therapeutic alliance as first described by Freud. Subsequent theorists have used any number of terms such as *partnering, rapport building,* and so on to describe the same process. Develop a lay explanation for your chosen theory that contains easily recognizable concepts in the place of jargon.
4. *Diversify Interventions:* Many theories are accompanied by a particular set of interventions. These interventions may be primary to the theory, but they are by no means the only way to apply that theory. Consider the commonly recognized empty-chair technique that involves clients imagining and role-playing a conversation with someone whom they are in conflict with as if that person is actually present. This technique is typically attributed to Gestalt theory, but it can be adapted for use with a wide range of theoretical orientations. The empty-chair technique can be especially useful with clients who have a more collectivist worldview, regardless of counselors' primary theoretical orientation. In those situations the empty chair can be occupied by imagined family or community members, elders, or other supporters who might be needed to endorse the particular treatment.

In leaving this topic of adapting theories to address diverse populations, there are two things to keep in mind. First, theories are intended to address the questions of why: "Why is

---

REFLECTION 17.4

Identify your beliefs about human development and change and link those to a specific counseling theory. Consider the following questions in terms of adapting your chosen theory for work with diverse populations:

1. *Determine Assumptions.* Who is credited with developing the theory? What were the circumstances surrounding development of the theory (e.g., what was happening in history at that time, where was it developed)? The theory was developed to address which particular populations or issues?
2. *Identify Limitations.* For which populations or issues is the theory considered inappropriate? Which populations or issues related to the theory are missing from research, and why were they overlooked or excluded? How has professional knowledge and contextual (e.g., social, historical, political, scientific) knowledge changed since development of the theory?
3. *Simplify Concepts.* Explain the major concepts of your theory to noncounselors. Partners, friends, and family members are all good audience members for this type of explanation of your theory. Ask them which parts were easiest to understand and which were most difficult. Once you have managed to simplify the theory for those adults, try communicating the major theoretical concepts to a child younger than age 10. The process of adapting the theoretical orientation for a young child will assist in simplifying your theory for communication and application with clients who have limited language comprehension and fluency.
4. *Diversify Interventions.* Can all clients participate in the chosen interventions regardless of their physical ability? Can all clients participate in the chosen intervention regardless of their mental and comprehension abilities? What is your expected outcome for the intervention? Under what conditions would this intervention "fail" or not produce the desired result? How would you react if the intervention did not work as planned?

---

the client here?" "Why is the client having difficulty?" and so forth. Alternatively, interventions are intended to address the client's needs. The second thing to keep in mind is that human experience is finite, but interpretation and perception of experience are infinite. In other words, there is a specific range of emotions that humans are capable of expressing; however, the meaning that is assigned to those emotions is dynamic and based on the ever-evolving variables of culture and context. Now refer to Reflection 17.4 to consider how these general guidelines affect you personally.

Culturally Responsive Counseling Theories

In terms of multicultural competence, the fourth force in counseling has taken on a more global perspective in its use of worldview and offers the most opportunity when working with diverse populations. A unique characteristic of the fourth force in counseling is that it supports and encourages what Gilligan (1982) terms *alternative ways of knowing*. There is an acknowledgment that all persons are unique and, because of their uniqueness, they require flexible and adaptable approaches to counseling. That flexibility includes both the conceptualization of alternative explanations for psychic distress and the use of alternative ways to heal that distress.

Approaches to counseling that are included in this fourth force range from evolved progeny of previous counseling theories to traditional healing practices associated with a specific culture to newly developed approaches that combine the two. Besides use of an expanded worldview, cultural responsiveness is common among all these approaches. In theoretical terms, being culturally responsive means that culture and differences between cultures are primary considerations in counseling relationships. The issue of culture may have entered into previous approaches to counseling as a secondary or tertiary concern, but for approaches included in the context–systemic movement in counseling cultural identity is the starting point. As in earlier sections, a complete discussion of all approaches that are considered to be culturally responsive cannot be adequately covered in this limited space. Instead, discussion will be devoted to a grand theory that has risen to prominence as the foremost approach to multicultural counseling.

MULTICULTURAL COUNSELING AND THERAPY (MCT)   Similar to the grand theories that comprise the first three forces in counseling, **multicultural counseling and therapy (MCT)** has been presented as a metatheory that encompasses many different conceptual models and approaches to counseling (Ivey et al., 2012). Although the organizational structure and title for this metatheory are relatively new, many of the conceptual models and approaches are quite old and, in the case of many indigenous healing practices, long predate Freud's inception of psychodynamic theory. Conceptual models that are included in MCT are numerous and include feminist theory, Afrocentric theory, Naikan, and indigenous healing practices. In addition to the varied conceptualizations, MCT includes extensive numbers of interventions and approaches to counseling ranging from meditation to social consciousness raising. These various conceptual models and approaches to counseling are unified under the MCT theory by their shared recognition for the importance of cultural context in the application of counseling theory and techniques. Perhaps the most salient feature that continues to be relevant for counselors-in-training from MCT is valuing the context in which multiple layers of both counselor and client experiences take place. That is, MCT is different from what has been traditionally defined as counseling theory because it integrates the client's social and historical context (Pope-Davis, Liu, Toporek, & Brittan-Powell, 2001). The counselor is therefore the responsible party in creating a therapeutic environment where others feel comfortable sharing the development of their cultural identity over their life span.

In addition to bringing the cultural contexts to the foreground, Sue (2004) stated that MCT adheres to the following six propositions: (a) MCT is an integrative metatheory; (b) counselor and client identities are formed based on differing levels of experience and context, and the combination of these are the focus of counseling; (c) cultural identity development determines client and counselor attitudes toward self and others; (d) counseling is more effective when approaches and interventions are consistent with cultural values of the clients and no one approach to counseling will appropriately meet the needs of all clients; (e) the traditional approach to counseling is only one of many strategies for helping clients; and (f) liberation of consciousness (individual, familial, community, and organizational) is a basic goal of MCT. When reviewing some of these propositions, it is easy to see where MCT shares common ground in its approach with other metatheories such as humanistic theory. However, MCT uses cultural context as the springboard for change and provides maximum flexibility for working with diverse clientele. See Build Your Knowledge 17.1 to create a personal foundation for MCT.

Empowerment theory has roots in both feminist and multicultural theories (Hipilito-Delgado & Lee, 2007), offering counselors a way to incorporate social advocacy into their sessions when working with traditionally marginalized populations. Hipilito-Delgado and Lee described taking social action, along with developing a critical consciousness and positive identity, as the three actions for implementing this theory. Applying this approach to counseling sessions involves developing a sense of what it means to face a history of oppression and the gaps between those who identify with that oppression as part of our cultural heritage and

BUILD YOUR KNOWLEDGE 17.1

CREATING A FOUNDATION FOR MCT

As with most counseling theories, MCT does not provide specific procedural guidelines for working with clients. Instead, the MCT propositions provide a framework in which culturally responsible counselors can use a variety of therapeutic approaches and interventions. To put the MCT propositions into action, counselors must initially become aware of both themselves and their clients. This awareness is the foundation of MCT and is essential to implementing any counseling theory with any client population. To reach an initial level of self-awareness and awareness of self in relation to others, consider the following questions adapted from Hulse-Killacky, Killacky, and Donigian (2001):

Who am I?
- What do I value?
- What dimensions of my identity do I consider to be fundamental?
- What beliefs do I consider to be absolute or universally true?
- What kinds of people and institutions have contributed to and supported my development, both personally and professionally?
- What are the defining moments and experiences in my life?

Who am I with you?
- How do counselor–client similarities facilitate the counseling process? How do they inhibit it?
- How do counselor–client differences facilitate the counseling process? How do they inhibit it?
- Historically, how have relationships been characterized between individuals of similar cultural identities as the counselor and client?
- What is the dynamic of power, privilege, and oppression between counselor and client in this relationship?
- Besides counselor, what other role might I inadvertently portray in this relationship (e.g., parent, sibling, authority, subordinate)?

Who are we together?
- How will the counselor–client relationship change my life (professional development, personal development, social/contextual development)?
- How will the counselor–client relationship change my clients' lives?
- How might counseling bring greater difficulty and/or challenges for my clients?
- How will the counselor–client relationship support societal norms?
- How will the counselor–client relationship challenge societal norms?

Source: Adapted with written permission from Hulse-Killacky, Diana; Killacky, Jim; Donigian, Jeremiah, *Making Task Groups Work in Your World*, 1st Ed., © 2001. Reprinted and electronically reproduced by permission of Pearson Education, Inc., Upper Saddle River, New Jersey.

those who experience a privileged cultural identity. Positive identity formation then becomes the process of valuing one's traditionally oppressed culture as valid inside of and apart from the dominant culture. The final step of social action is the most important because it is the implementation of strategies by joining with people who face oppression to work toward liberation for self and community.

Relational-cultural theory (RCT) proposes core concepts centered on connectedness (Comstock et al., 2008). Counselors using this theory are focusing on the shift from working *for* clients to working *with* clients toward a more complete picture of traditionally underserved populations. Counseling then becomes the process of creating a therapeutic alliance between both participants, counselor and client. By focusing on the disconnections that are inherent in society at large, this therapeutic alliance is the key to providing voice to those who are trying to understand their roles and how to move beyond those roles.

COUNSELING APPROACHES BASED ON NON-WESTERN WORLDVIEWS Every culture has a means and manner for addressing the mental health needs of its residents. For example, it has been observed as a Westernized phenomenon that mind, body, and spirit are separated and compartmentalized. Furthermore, some have argued that it is due to this segregation that many find themselves in crisis (Neukrug, 2015). For many cultures, mental health is incorporated in religious or spiritual belief systems. The functions of the mind are linked to the characteristics of the soul, and in this way, problems of conscious are conceptualized as problems of conscience. Other cultures believe that the problems of an individual are linked more often to their role and participation in a larger social group or society than to intrapersonal dynamics. These different conceptualizations of mental health require unique approaches to counseling based on different worldviews. The following sections will outline three alternative approaches to counseling that have been demonstrated in counseling literature as effective. These examples are provided as snapshots of possibilities that await counselors who consider approaches to counseling that are based on non-Western worldviews. It is important to recognize that all cultures have unique approaches to healing and establishing one's mental well-being. Exploration of those varied approaches to healing can fill the life span of several careers, and integration of them into counseling practice can provide enrichment for both counselors and clients. For additional information on approaches to counseling based on a non-Western worldview, explore the resources listed in Table 17.1.

Naikan Therapy. **Naikan** is a formalized and structured method of self-reflection intended to help clients understand themselves as well as their relationships with others to gain meaning from their existence. Developed by a Jodo Shinshu Buddhist, Yoshimoto Ishin, Naikan is based on a Confucian worldview that emphasizes familial and social obligations and sustaining the harmony of social order (Ozawa-de Silva & Ozawa-de Silva, 2010). In keeping with this Confucian worldview, the practice of Naikan encourages individuals to consider their roles in and reliance on larger social systems. Inward reflection leads to a greater understanding and appreciation for the benefits of an external system.

The basic process of Naikan is fairly simple and for the most part self-guided. The meditative self-reflection is initiated by three questions: (a) What have I received from _____; (b) What have I given to _____; and (c) What troubles or difficulties have I caused _____? (Ozawa-de Silva & Ozawa-de Silva, 2010). The blanks are filled in with names of individuals with which the client has a relationship. For instance, the blanks could be filled in with names of loved ones or business associates. The blanks could also be filled in with names of institutions, such as a place of employment. Whatever relationship is chosen, the goal of reflection in Naikan is self-in-relation. In approaches that emphasize **self-in-relation**, clients are encouraged to consider how their own behaviors and attitudes contribute to or detract from a greater social system. In other words, challenges faced by an individual affect larger social systems such as family and community, and those greater systems play an integral role in healing the individual. In this way the relationship remains the primary beneficiary of reflection, and social order can be maintained. Once a subject is identified for reflection, clients

TABLE 17.1 Internet Resources for Non-Western and Alternative Approaches

- Association for Multicultural Counseling and Development (http://www. multiculturalcounseling.org/): division of American Counseling Association dedicated to "Providing global leadership, research, training and development for multicultural counseling professionals with a focus on racial and ethnic issues."
- American Psychological Association Division 52, International Psychology (www.div52.org): division of the American Psychological Association dedicated to encouraging international connections and multicultural research and practice among psychologists.
- International Association for Cross-Cultural Psychology (www.iaccp.org): association that facilitates communication and connection among individuals interested in the intersection of psychology and culture.
- Zazen meditation (https://zmm.mro.org/teachings/meditation-instructions/): basic instructions for Zazen Meditation including photos of various meditative positions. This Web site also provides information about further trainings and teachings related to practice of Zazen available from the Mountain and River Order at the Zen Mountain Monastery near Woodstock, New York.
- Kripalu Center for Yoga and Health (www.kripalu.org/): resource for practice of yoga for therapeutic purposes. The Center is located in Massachusetts and offers training in Yoga and Ayurveda.
- Thich Nhat Hahn (Buddhist psychology) (www.plumvillage.org): online community dedicated to the practice and training based on the work and life of Zen Master Thich Nhat Hanh. The focus for most of the practices and trainings is mindfulness and Buddhist concepts.
- The Chopra Center (Ayurveda; http://www.chopra.com): basic information about Ayurveda including a free quiz to identify one's Dosha (mind-body) type. Resources are also available about balancing the unique combination of mind, body, and environment characteristics.
- Indigenous Ways of Knowing (IWOK) Program at Lewis & Clark College (https://graduate. lclark.edu/programs/indigenous_ways_of_knowing/): graduate program at Lewis & Clark College that trains native and non-native teachers, counselors, and community leaders rooted in indigenous worldviews.

consider their responses to the three questions for a period of approximately 50 to 60 minutes, with the frequency of reflection varying from daily to monthly practice.

The practice of Naikan as a therapeutic intervention is effective in the treatment of a variety of issues including anxiety (Hong-Xin, Zao-Huo, & Hong-Xiang, 2006; Sengoku, Nakagome, Murata, Kawahara, & Imamura, 2010), anorexia nervosa (Morishita, 2000), and alcoholism (Suwaki, 1979, 1985). Although clients are engaged in meditative self-reflection, individualism is devalued with a goal of shifting clients' attention away from internal symptoms and blaming others to an external appreciation for interdependence and the benefits that others have brought to them (Ozawa-de Silva & Ozawa-de Silva, 2010).

Morita Therapy.   **Morita therapy** is an approach to counseling that shares some similarities with Naikan and is often used in conjunction with Naikan when working with clients. Like Naikan, Morita is based on Buddhist values but is not linked to the practice of Buddhism. It also emphasizes the importance of self-in-relation and has been used with clients dealing with anxiety in particular (Chen, 2010).

Dr. Shoma Morita created Morita therapy. He was a contemporary of Sigmund Freud and Carl Jung, practicing psychiatry in the early part of the 20th century. While serving in the

Department of Psychiatry at Jikei University School of Medicine in Tokyo, Japan, he created Morita therapy as treatment for a Japanese culturally bound anxiety disorder known as shinkeishitsu (Hofmann, 2008). Dr. Morita practiced Zen Buddhism, and the principles of that religion, especially the focus on mindfulness and an understanding of what a person can and cannot control, influenced his development of theory. The overall approach to Morita therapy can be described as purpose-centered, response-oriented, and active. Instead of attempting to reduce or alleviate symptoms, as is typical for most counseling approaches, Morita therapy stresses building clients' character to empower them to accept and respond to their life, regardless of the circumstances. Clients practicing Morita therapy can expect that their behaviors will be emphasized more than thoughts or feelings, and their decision making will be influenced by purpose rather than intuition.

Ntu Psychotherapy. Based on an African conceptual system and worldview, **Ntu** (pronounced in-too) psychotherapy incorporates ancient Eastern principles of healing and New Age conceptualizations of mind–body integration (Gregory & Harper, 2001). Beyond being simply an approach to counseling, it is a holistic philosophy and lifestyle that also provides conceptualizations for human behavior and functioning. The concept of Ntu comes from Central Africa (Bantu) and refers to universal energy or a sense of being that is shared by all things. In Ntu psychotherapy this energy is presumed to be essential to the therapeutic process and becomes the focus of the approach. As the Ntu is increased, so is the well-being of the client and vice versa. The functions of counselors in Ntu psychotherapy are those of spiritual guides as they help clients become aware of and stimulate their own self-healing processes (Gregory & Phillips, 1997).

The Ntu approach was developed by Fredrick Phillips and the staff of the Progressive Life Center. With a goal of restoring harmony, genuineness, and interconnectedness, this approach is characterized by five contextual suppositions (Phillips, 1990). As a therapeutic approach Ntu is

1. *Family-focused:* Gregory and Harper (2001) characterized this dimension of Ntu in the following way, "The family focused approach acknowledges that families are always emotionally present within each of us" (p. 306). Extending this acknowledgment, it is assumed that the entire family is with the client even if an individual presents alone for counseling. In the Ntu approach, family is typically defined based on both psychological and biological relationships, so clients are responsible for self-defining their familial group.
2. *Culturally competent:* The counselor–client relationship is collaborative and based on clients' needs. The Ntu counselor is expected to gain understanding about client populations being served and tailor interventions accordingly. Similar to any culturally competent counselor, those using the Ntu approach are expected to be self-aware and aware of any environmental circumstances (e.g., socioeconomic factors, political climate) that may affect the counseling relationship.
3. *Competence-based:* Ntu is a wellness-based approach that seeks to highlight strengths rather than deficits. In focusing on competence, an Ntu counselor can more easily avoid imposition of personal or culturally based assumptions about mental health.
4. *Holistic/systemic:* To live a full and productive life, clients must care for all dimensions of themselves (i.e., body, mind, and spirit). In addition to caring for themselves, clients must also care for the environments that support them. Ntu uses various interventions to address clients and their systems. These interventions range from traditional individual talk therapy to integrative and indigenous healing techniques such as meditation, herbology, acupuncture, and so on.

5. *Values-driven:* Unlike some typical counseling approaches that strive to suspend values in the counseling relationship and focus on unconditional regard for clients, the Ntu approach defines appropriate behavior according to particular principles. Using an Afrocentric worldview, Ntu counselors assume that contribution to family and community is essential, and clients' behaviors are assessed in terms of this contribution. In terms of specific value systems inherent to the Ntu approach, the counseling relationship focuses on the Nguzo Saba (seven principles of Kwanzaa). These seven principles are Umoja (unity), Kujichagulia (self-determination), Ujima (collective work and responsibility), Ujamaa (cooperative economy), Kuumba (creativity), Nia (purpose), and Imani (faith).

Operating from these five suppositions, Phillips (1990) described five distinct phases in Ntu psychotherapy through which the client and counselor collaborate. The first phase is *harmony*, in which rapport is built and the counselor–client relationship is established. The next phase is *awareness*, and counselor and client work together to identify and clarify the reason for counseling. *Alignment* is the third phase and core of Ntu counseling. Alignment can be alternatively characterized as congruence in that consistency among thoughts, behaviors, and feelings are sought so that family members experience one another and the presenting challenge from a common base. *Actualization* follows alignment and consists of putting into practice the changes learned during the preceding phase. The Ntu process concludes with the *synthesis* phase in which client and counselor reflect on and evaluate the overall Ntu experience. Research on the successful application of the Ntu approach is ongoing, and to date it has been used to help clients in foster care and juvenile justice systems, family counseling, school-based counseling, and in-home counseling (Gregory & Harper, 2001).

Having discussed some culturally responsive counseling approaches, it is very important to recognize that they, too, are not without their own potential pitfalls. As is the case when using theories from the psychodynamic, cognitive–behavioral, and humanistic–existential movements, counselors must be cognizant of the underlying assumptions for their chosen approaches to counseling. Most of the counseling approaches based on traditional healing practices are culture specific and require initial acceptance of particular cultural assumptions. Voices from the Field 17.2 highlights one counseling example of adapting a counseling approach to be more culturally responsive.

Voices from the Field 17.2

Culture shapes theory. One of the benefits to practicing in a major metropolitan area is that I have the opportunity to work with a wide variety of clients whose countries of origin are somewhere other than the United States. Recently, I conducted an initial intake with a client who had lived in Slovakia from birth until about age 24 and had been in the United States for about 7 years. The client presented with issues related to dissatisfaction in primary social relationships. We spent our initial session getting to know one another and building a foundation of rapport for our counseling relationship. As is typical for me in the rapport building process, I asked this client if there were any questions I could answer or if there was any information needed or wanted to help create a sense of comfort in the counseling process. We covered the anticipated questions about fee structure, scheduling, and treatment plans and then the client asked me about my theoretical orientation. Over time, I have found that most clients ask this question with the expectation that

(Continued)

I have some theoretical basis for my work; they want to hear that I have some plan and that our time together will follow some relatively predictable course. Most often, clients are not interested in the nuances of why I have chosen this theory over others nor are they invested in working with one particular type of theory related to their issue. In this particular case, when I answered the question about theory with my brief description of Gestalt and how I apply it to presenting issues similar to theirs, the client brightened and registered an expression of recognition. The client described having been to counselors in the country of origin who had also used Gestalt. The client went on to describe enjoying the use of Gestalt in session and the confidence that it would help again in this current situation. We both seemed to leave that first session encouraged—I was encouraged that my chosen theory would connect with this client and my client seemed encouraged that my theoretical framework was familiar and could be helpful.

During the next session, we continued to build rapport and I gathered more information about my client and current issues regarding relationships. I noticed during this session that the client seemed a bit impatient with some of the responses and rushed through some information sharing. The client appeared to be anticipating something and was getting more impatient as if waiting for me to get started with the work of counseling. Adhering to my Gestalt training, I confronted the client's presentation of impatience and discovered that the client was indeed waiting for me to do something, "I am waiting for you to do Gestalt with me." As we explored that statement together, my client and I realized that we had very different experiences of Gestalt counseling. Our respective cultures shaped the development of Gestalt theory; likewise, we discovered that there were linguistic differences between our two understandings of Gestalt theory. Through working with this client, I began to understand how culture and context shapes everything, including counseling theory. As a result of that experience, I spend more time in my initial sessions discussing my use of theory and exploring what resources and expectations clients bring to the implementation of that theory in practice.

~JJO

Alternative Therapies.   Interest in alternative approaches to counseling continues to rise in the field of counseling. Increasingly, counselors are focusing on the ways that mind, body, and spirit intersect to create paradigms for living, and they are implementing strategies that help clients live more fulfilled lives across all levels. Most of those alternative approaches are by no means new, and many predate the advent of talk therapy by several hundred or even thousands of years. The increased use of these alternative approaches to therapy may be a result of greater diversity among clients and among counselors entering the profession. The stereotypical portrait of a client lying on a couch engaging in talk therapy is quickly being replaced by images of clients lying on a yoga mat in asana, for example.

Multiple volumes of this text would be required to adequately explore all the alternative therapies currently being applied to healing mind, body, and spirit in the field of counseling. Many are based on holistic approaches to life that incorporate both a system of belief and a system for functioning. Contextualizing issues related to counseling in those systems often requires a complete paradigm shift of what mental health is and how it intersects individual and group identities. Pulling out discrete techniques or beliefs from the overall system can at minimum diminish therapeutic effectiveness and at most further perpetuate oppression and marginalization of nondominant approaches to healing. Recognizing these caveats, it is also important to bring recognition to how the field of counseling is evolving to apply and develop alternative therapies. The following descriptions of alternative therapies are by no means exhaustive and are included primarily to serve as introductory information from which readers are encouraged to seek more education and training. For additional information on alternative approaches to counseling, explore the resources listed in Table 17.1.

Meditation.   Meditation is a practice that has been incorporated across a wide range of interventions. Often it is coupled with progressive muscle relaxation and/or guided imagery. Taken at its simplest form, meditation can serve as a means for clients to center and ground themselves, and as such it is better characterized as a technique than as a theory. It can be applied to a wide range of belief systems but is most often associated with the practice of Zen Buddhism. Meditation has been used to address a wide range of anxiety symptoms. When meditation is used as a daily practice, it can support the efforts of clients to remain calm, focused, and mindfully aware. The focus of meditation or meditative states can range from guided to a more nondirective or Zenlike state of emptiness.

Yoga.   Yoga is one of the more popular alternative therapies being used by counselors (Adams & Puig, 2008). The practice of yoga addresses clients across the domains of mind, body, and spirit. It is equal parts physical activity and spiritual discipline that combine in a form of moving meditation. Clients engaged in yoga are encouraged to focus on breathing and the movements of their bodies as they typically assume prescribed positions referred to as asana or asanas. In therapeutic applications, yoga has been shown to be an effective treatment for a wide range of issues such as eating disorders (Carei, Fyfe-Johnson, Breuner, & Brown, 2010), substance abuse (Khalsa, Khalsa, Khalsa, & Khalsa, 2008), and stress (Forfylow, 2011). Yoga's popularity in the West has been largely centered on its physical benefits to well-being; however, the practice of yoga has traditionally been a means to achieve spiritual actualization in Hinduism. Similar to the spiritual goal of meditation, yoga is a means to transcend worldly suffering with the goal of freedom from the cycle of birth and death.

Ayurveda.   Ayurveda is an ancient and holistic system of healing that originated in India and dates back over 5,000 years. The word *Ayurveda* translates into "life knowledge" (Jayasundar, 2010). In the Ayurvedic tradition the mind, body, spirit, and senses of each individual are unique, and energetic systems or forces, known as doshas, influence them. There are three doshas: vata dosha (identified with wind), which is primarily responsible for movement in the body; pitta dosha (identified with fire), which is responsible primarily for transformation or metabolism in the body; and kapha dosha (identified with earth), which is responsible for lubrication and structure in the body. Each dosha has a balanced and imbalanced expression, and imbalances in the doshas can account for mental as well as physical disease or illness. The primary goal for Ayurveda is to balance all systems in the individual so that they work in harmony with one another and with the natural world. In order to bring balance to the overall individual, a wide variety of treatments are integrated at both the individual and environmental levels. Typical interventions include changes to diet and physical activity, use of herbs, aromatherapy, massage, and meditation.

Buddhist psychology.   Much attention in research and practice has been given to the practice of mindfulness in counseling (DeSilva, 2014). The practice of mindfulness has been shown to be effective as a treatment for mental health issues ranging from stress (Hofmann, Sawyer, Witt, & Oh, 2010) to grief (Sagula & Rice, 2004) and diagnosed chronic disease (Merkes, 2010). Mindfulness creates a doorway through which clients can learn new paradigms for viewing concepts of self and self-in-relation. Beyond the doorway of mindfulness lies a larger paradigm for living that is grounded in Buddhism, and clients who find success in living mindfully can benefit by exploring further the foundational principles that support mindful living. Summarized in its simplest form, Buddhism centers on the Four Noble Truths—suffering is an inevitable part of life, attachment is the cause for suffering, cessation of suffering is attainable, and one can follow the path to the cessation of suffering. The fourth noble truth embodies the practice of Buddhism and is subdivided into Right Understanding, Right Thought, Right Speech, Right Action, Right Livelihood, Right Effort, Right Mindfulness, and Right Concentration, collectively referred to as the Noble Eightfold Path (Nhat Hanh, 1999). Counselors who practice Buddhist psychology with their clients often use techniques grounded in the Noble Eightfold Path to shift clients' perspective of suffering and change the practice of attachment to things in their lives. Outcomes for this type of counseling relationship rely on a combination of insight and behavior change. Clients are expected to achieve relief through insight that all things are basically impermanent, and attachment to such things leads to suffering. Behavior change through disciplined practice of mindfulness can both precede and emerge from those insights.

Indigenous ways of knowing (IWOK). In addition to the approaches that have been briefly detailed previously, many more alternative approaches to counseling exist based on **indigenous ways of knowing (IWOK)**. As the term *IWOK* suggests, such approaches are predicated on a completely different paradigm for mental health (Grayshield & Mihecoby, 2010). Many of those paradigms do not support concepts for separation of mind, body, or spirit; furthermore, many IWOK reject the notion that self is separate from other or environment. When considering multicultural competence for working with indigenous populations, it is imperative to understand the perspectives of clients and to learn from them how they relate to a sense of self and self-in-relation. This creates valuable opportunities for counselors to grow and develop new approaches for working with all types of clients.

Summary

When using a counseling theory, flexibility in the approach and nimbleness of the counselor using the approach are of the highest importance. This requires adaptations in both conceptualization and intervention based on the diversity that clients bring to sessions. In any case, when working as a multiculturally competent counselor, it is critical to note that all counseling approaches ascribe to a specific worldview. These worldviews may alternatively be liberating to some and oppressive to others. Recognition of how a chosen approach to counseling influences clients is essential to ethical practice and will determine the effectiveness of therapy.

This chapter has provided a brief overview of some of the components necessary to developing and applying counseling theory in a culturally responsible manner. It started with an exploration of how theory is built from the foundation of worldview and individual concepts of how people develop within particular ecological contexts. From the exploration of worldview, this chapter turned to exploration of how to adapt various traditional theories for counseling for use with diverse populations. A strategy for adaptation of traditional theories was introduced, and you had the opportunity to apply this strategy to some of the traditional counseling theories.

We then looked at alternative sources for developing a theory of counseling that included informants such as systems of government, spiritual beliefs, and family systems. Each of these ecological factors influences to a varying degree how clients define their sense of health and wellness. Building on diverse definitions of mental health, we identified alternative sources for counseling theory and linked worldview to the development of traditional counseling theory. In terms of applying specific theory to counseling clients across cultures, multicultural counseling and therapy (MCT) theory was reviewed as a viable approach to counseling clients from many different cultures. To explore these less commonly applied conceptual models further, we examined Naikan therapy, Morita therapy, and Ntu in greater depth. Together these theories offer a more holistic approach to living that by extension results in the resolution of lapses in wellness for clients.

This chapter has largely focused on basic information about the development and application of counseling theory that responds to diverse groups of clients. It can be a common misconception among novice counselors and even those who are more advanced that the conceptualization and application of counseling theory is somehow static. Nothing could be further from the truth. A counseling theory is as alive and dynamic as the counselors who use it and the clients who benefit from it. As clients face new challenges and counselors develop a better understanding for these clients and their challenges, theory evolves.

A final area of focus in this chapter has been the use of alternative therapies and techniques within the counseling relationship. These techniques have ranged from the relatively simple (e.g., yoga) to the more complex (e.g., Aryuveda). We are reminded that theory is a tool primarily that assists counselors, and techniques are implemented for the primary benefit of our clients. It is in this spirit that exploration of some of the belief systems that support such techniques as yoga, meditation, and mindfulness was undertaken. Moving beyond the techniques, some of the basic foundations of more complex systems for healing and systems for knowing were also explored. Buddhist psychology and Ayurvedic counseling were highlighted for their comprehensive approaches to health and wellness that differ significantly from traditional Western approaches. IWOK was introduced as an opportunity for counselors to engage in a very different paradigm for relation to self, other, and the world around us.

It is on this final note of questioning paradigms that this chapter ends. The conversations that IWOK starts here in its brief appearance are ones that can carry our profession forward. Over time and with both study and practice in this field, recognize that far more people are excluded from the work that we do as counselors than are included. Considering the role that theory plays in the work we do with clients is an important part of the remedy, but we are required to do more. If something has piqued your interest or curiosity in this chapter, then take the time to read in greater depth on that topic. The challenge before us is to continue engaging the discomfort of uncertainty; we will never find a theory that works for all clients under all circumstances. As we accept that our knowledge will continue to grow and transform, we can extend that acceptance to our clients and encourage them to do the same in their lives.

Review Questions

1. What is worldview? Provide examples of Kluckhohn and Strodtbeck's (1961) five value orientations.
2. How do European, Asian, and African conceptual systems compare? How might these be used as a framework for working with multicultural populations? What might be some challenges?
3. What are some steps or guidelines mentioned in this chapter regarding adapting your theoretical orientation to work with multicultural populations?
4. What is multicultural counseling and therapy theory? How does this relate to more traditional theoretical orientations?
5. How do alternative, non-Western approaches compare with one another?

18 Multicultural Diagnosis and Conceptualization

Victoria E. Kress, Andrea L. Dixon,
and Laura R. Shannonhouse[*]

PREVIEW

Culturally diverse populations are habitually underserved by our mental health system. Evidence of health disparities reveals a gap in both physical and mental health outcomes for majority and minority populations. When counselors acknowledge attitudes and beliefs related to their enculturation and related biases, become familiar with the worldviews and values of minority populations, and acquire relevant skills and engage in clinical and advocacy interventions, they possess the multicultural counseling competence (MCC) necessary to work effectively with diverse clientele. This chapter focuses on ethnic and gender considerations that relate to mental health diagnosis, and places an emphasis on how different populations have been mischaracterized, misdiagnosed, and marginalized through diagnostic conceptualizations often normed off majority populations. These considerations are addressed by presenting the (a) challenges of ethical practice in diagnosis; (b) views of normality/abnormality; (c) culture and psychopathology; (d) feminist challenges; and (e) proposed solutions to the complex considerations presented, along with case studies, examples, and activities that can be used to apply knowledge gained. Activity 18.5 at the end of the chapter provides an opportunity for you to consider how the process of diagnosis and conceptualization can be informed from a multicultural lens.

THE CHALLENGE OF ETHICAL PRACTICE

All mental health professionals' ethical codes prohibit discrimination on the basis of such factors as age, disability, sex, race, ethnicity, religion, socioeconomic class, sexual orientation, or any other difference of the client from the mainstream. In addition, all ethical practitioners are charged with committing themselves to gaining the knowledge, personal awareness, sensitivity, and skills pertinent when working with diverse client populations. Yet how do these mandates play out in the actual diagnostic practices of counselors?

The American Counseling Association (ACA) states that "counselors [should] gain knowledge, personal awareness, sensitivity, dispositions, and skills pertinent to being a culturally competent counselor in working with a diverse client population" (p. 8). Further, cultural sensitivity is vital for counselors as "cultural experiences are considered when diagnosing

[*]The authors wish to thank Karen Eriksen and Stephanie Ford for their contributions to previous versions of this chapter.

mental disorders" (ACA, 2014, p. 11). According to LaRoche, Fuentes, and Hinton (2015), competence to work with diverse client groups when diagnosing, assessing, and providing subsequent treatment means knowing how to do an overall cultural assessment. An overall cultural assessment, from a counseling perspective, means understanding the cultural framework of the client's identity, cultural explanations of illness experiences and help-seeking behavior, cultural meanings of adaptive functioning and social context, and cultural elements in the counselor–client relationship.

Additionally, the Multicultural and Social Justice Counseling Competencies (MSJCC; Ratts, Singh, Nassar-McMillan, Butler, & McCullough, 2015), endorsed by the Association for Multicultural Counseling and Development and American Counseling Association, further provide counselors with an informed framework that can aid in the integration of multicultural and social justice competencies in counseling practice, research, and culturally appropriate assessment. The MSJCC are meant to guide counselors toward multicultural and social justice competence within the following areas: (1) counselor self-awareness, (2) client worldview, (3) counseling relationship, and (4) counseling and advocacy interventions. The MSJCC also include specific suggestions for developing this competence in counselors' attitudes and beliefs, knowledge, skills, and actions. Specifically regarding the counseling relationship, "Privileged and marginalized counselors are aware, knowledgeable, skilled, and action-oriented in understanding how client and counselor privileged and marginalized statuses influence the counseling relationship" (p. 9). As multiculturally competent and socially just counselors work with clients, they are encouraged to work to acquire and implement culturally responsive evaluation skills to conceptualize how socio-historical events and current social issues shape the worldview, cultural background, values, beliefs, biases, and experiences of clients from both privileged and marginalized backgrounds. Although it seems unlikely that a counselor could accomplish these ideals relative to several cultures, counselors should certainly work to develop these abilities for the cultures of the clients whom they predominantly serve. Counselors should also develop a referral base of counselors for clients from cultures with which they are less familiar (O'Donohue & Benuto, 2010).

Further, counselors should avoid jumping to conclusions about clients on the basis of their cultural group membership, acquire knowledge about different cultures' norms and interaction styles, and commit to ongoing awareness-building about their own values, beliefs, biases, and assumptions (American Psychiatric Association, 2013; O'Donohue & Benuto, 2010). Such practice prevents the cultural encapsulation minority clients experience when they are conceptualized through the monocultural prism of Euro-American values that pervades counseling (Shannonhouse, 2013; Sue & Sue, 2013). Culturally competent counseling extends beyond the usual attention to race and ethnicity and acknowledges differences related to religion, age, socio-economic class, gender, ethnicity, disability, and sexual orientation (Bhugra & Kalra, 2010). In the absence of this awareness of the client's context, a counselor risks engaging in the unethical practice of "imposing their values, attitudes, beliefs, and behaviors" that may be "inconsistent with the client's goals or discriminatory in nature" (ACA, 2014, p. 5).

Fully actualizing one's knowledge, skills, and awareness can be challenging. Culturally sensitive diagnosis and conceptualization, in particular, are easier to talk about than to do, especially when diagnosing clients whose cultures differ from the dominant culture, and/or the counselors' worldview. Wide variations exist among people from different cultures in their perspectives about "normal" behavior. For example, how interpersonal relationships should be conducted (e.g., parents using physical discipline with children, husbands physically abusing their wives because their wives are their property) differ among families of Western

European heritage and may be in conflict with North American laws (McGoldrick, Giordano, & Garcia-Preto, 2005). If this thinking is extended to other areas of diversity, we might ask, how can we understand gender? Sexual orientation? Religion? How can a counselor fully understand the challenges of being an immigrant if he or she is not an immigrant? Can counselors ever completely eliminate the influence of systemic oppressions—such as institutionalized racism and sexism—on themselves, the client, or relationships when diagnosing people who differ from the majority (Bhugra & Kalra, 2010)? In what forum might counselors discuss the "illness" or diagnosis of contexts or systems? How do counselors find funding for correcting "ill" systems, rather than expecting clients to correct systemic oppressions that may be contributing to or exacerbating problem issues?

Questions about counselors' cultural and gender sensitivity are not the only questions raised by those pursuing culturally sensitive diagnosis and case conceptualization. The usefulness of the various editions of the *Diagnostic and Statistical Manual of Mental Disorders* (*DSM*) published by the American Psychiatric Association has been challenged for people who differ from the dominant culture. Critics ask whether counselors can draw any definite conclusions about women, people of color, or those who are gay, lesbian, or transgender based on a diagnostic system and psychological testing system whose development was grounded in the knowledge of European American men and on evidence from research studies that did not include diverse participants (LaRoche et al., 2015).

Some may wonder whether any counseling or diagnostic system can be free of such potential bias and problems, which is a legitimate ethical query considering that counselors are called to "recognize historical and social prejudices in the misdiagnosis and pathologizing of certain individuals and groups" (ACA, 2014, p. 11). It is important to recognize that the *DSM* or any particular diagnostic, assessment, or counseling system can only be considered one assessment method among many. However, no diagnosis contains the whole or absolute "truth" about the problem issues. From this perspective, counselors might consider learning the terminology of the *DSM-5* to position themselves as advocates for their clients.

Cultural Validity in Assessment

Cultural validity is another important diagnostic concern. It is widely believed that ignoring the importance of cultural differences when diagnosing and assessing individuals from diverse backgrounds can lead to unfair and unethical testing practices and diagnoses (del Rosario Basterra, Trumbull, & Solano-Flores, 2010). For example, the wording, illustrations, layout, and contextual information embedded in diagnostic questioning reflect the language, ways of thinking, and experiences of a particular cultural group. It is likely that some diagnoses and test items might privilege individuals from one cultural group and penalize individuals from other cultural groups (Canino & Alegría, 2008). To consider fully the cultural aspects of diagnostic assessment, it is important to take a step back and consider recent fundamental changes to the *DSM* system.

The fifth edition of *DSM* (APA, 2013) has significantly affected the way counselors diagnose mental disorders by moving away from the categorical, axial system to dimensional assessments. A categorical classification approach works best when members of a diagnostic class are homogeneous and there are clear boundaries between diagnostic categories; however, this has not always been the case for certain *DSM* categorical diagnoses, with many frequently overlapping and having a high co-occurrence (i.e., comorbidity, the presence of multiple diagnoses or pathologies within the same individual). For example, depressive disorders are strongly linked with anxiety disorders (K. D. Jones, 2012), anxiety disorders are highly comorbid with one another; and depressive and anxiety disorders are often comorbid with substance-use disorders, eating disorders, and personality disorders.

The existence of excessive diagnostic comorbidity has been recognized as a significant limitation and challenges the validity of the diagnostic categories themselves (K. D. Jones, 2012). Individual presentations of problem issues are neither homogeneous nor divided by clear boundaries, which make it challenging to classify persons from varied backgrounds through discrete criteria and symptoms into specific diagnoses treated with the same evidence-based practices. As a result, clinicians have frequently used the "other" or "unspecified" categories (First, 2010) as "catch-alls" when clients experience clinically significant distress or impairment (CSDI) but fail to meet criteria for an existing diagnostic category (APA, 2013). Because of the overreliance on the other or unspecified diagnoses and the demonstrated co-occurrence of many disorders, diagnostic subtypes, specifiers, and severity ratings have been added to the *DSM-5* to "dimensionalize" assessment and make it more "continuous" (K. D. Jones, 2012).

The old binary categorical classification system where symptoms were either present or absent defined "normality" and "abnormality," which runs counter to the arguments of Kraemer (2007) and others about the purpose of diagnosis. The dimensional approach yields a greater amount of clinical information (Helzer et al., 2008) and provides "a more specific and individualized profile description of a patient's psychopathology" (Widiger & Samuel, 2005, p. 500). The new approach uses Likert-type rating scales (e.g., Level 1 and Level 2 Cross Cutting Symptom Measures) to evaluate the severity, intensity, frequency, duration, or other characteristics of *DSM* categories. This method may aid clinicians in gathering information on all of a client's symptoms and aid in developing more precise treatment plans. There is a further hope these assessments may enable clinicians to monitor treatment progress and improvements (K. D. Jones, 2012).

However, Frances (2010) expressed concern that most of the 13 *DSM-5* Work Groups created new dimensional assessments rather than selecting from hundreds of well-established rating scales that cover many aspects of psychopathology. Assessments often require years to develop, as they must be written, reviewed by experts, and pilot tested with many different populations. Subsequently, the individual items must be revised and re-tested, a process that continues until enough validity and reliability evidence is obtained to support that the scores derived from the scales measure what was intended. The *DSM-5* contains more than 67 "emerging measures" that will require score validation, including cross-cultural score validation. Further, even though these assessments are available for clinical use, it has not yet been decided how their numerical ratings will be included in the diagnostic coding system. Although the APA indicates that these assessments are intended to facilitate clinical understanding and decision making and should not be used as the only basis for ascribing a clinical diagnosis (APA, 2013), clinicians can convert scores on these emerging measures into severity specifiers that are coded in the fifth digit of a *DSM-5* diagnosis.

Finally, one emerging measure included in the *DSM-5* that was long overdue is the cultural formulation interview (CFI). The CFI was designed to aid the clinician in understanding the client's perception of the problem issue from his or her cultural context, perceptions of etiology (cause of the problem issue), context for the problem issue, perceived support, and cultural factors affecting self-coping and past/present help-seeking behavior (APA, 2013). Cultural validity in assessment requires that mental health professionals take into account specific cultural backgrounds and norms (e.g., socioeconomic status, gender, religious/spiritual beliefs, race/ethnicity, employment, individual symptoms, functional abilities, family interactions, contextual factors, environmental factors; del Rosario Basterra et al., 2010), whether through the CFI or not. While the CFI and dimensionalization are welcome changes, the limitations of any emerging measures as well as the potential harm done to clients if they are used inappropriately must be understood. Overall, assessment powerfully influences clinical decisions, particularly those related to decisions about what is "normal" or "abnormal."

NORMAL VERSUS ABNORMAL

Fundamental to any diagnostic process are questions about where the line should be drawn between normal and abnormal. Relatedly, who gets to draw the line? Who gets to decide what is abnormal? On what basis do they get to decide these things? At what point do we decide that a person is mentally ill? In answer to questions like these, some authors assert that people in power make these decisions and that agreements about those decisions change over time, depending on who is in power and the spirit of the times (Williams, 2015). Williams further argued that economics also encroach on what is normal and what is treatable, since increasing the number of reimbursable diagnoses increases the treatment domain and profits of mental health providers. Consequently, "problems in living," such as worrying, feeling blue, having obsessive thoughts, bearing grudges, lacking sexual interest, not sleeping, smoking, being alone, having trouble in school, and being hung over, may be moved into the realm of diagnosable mental illness or pathology (Wilcoxon, Magnuson, & Norem, 2008), which is particularly troubling.

For example, the recently added diagnosis of disruptive mood dysregulation disorder (DMDD), marked by severe, recurrent outbursts of temper, either verbal or behavioral, that are disproportionate in intensity and duration with situational factors and developmental level (APA, 2013), has been argued to merely demonstrate typical childhood behavior (Copeland, Angold, Costello, & Egger, 2013). Copeland et al. (2013) indicated that DMDD is uncommonly found after childhood, and it also tends to co-occur with another disorder 62% to 92% of the time. The merits of this diagnosis aside, there is an additional socio-cultural consideration regarding DMDD: affected children have been found to live in poverty and experience difficulties with social supports. If a client's context is not accurately considered, symptomatology may result in a DMDD misdiagnosis, when the behavior may actually be the result of normative adaptation to a child's environment.

As another example of normal problems in living, consider the changes made to the *DSM-5* regarding depression and bereavement. Grief reactions may, depending on cultural context, closely resemble depression. In the *DSM-5,* the bereavement exclusion for a diagnosis of major depressive disorder was removed. In other words, if a person now meets the criteria for major depression, he or she could be diagnosed with major depression even if he or she is grieving. Some argue that by changing direction in this way, the *DSM* system pathologizes the normal reaction to a universal human experience: the death of a loved one (Fox & Jones, 2013). Contrary to this belief, Kendler (2010) argued that individuals who experience other life stressors are just as likely to develop a major depressive disorder as those mourning the death of a loved one. Despite this argument, the potential to pathologize what could be a normal grief reaction is worthy of consideration by culturally sensitive clinicians.

Gender dysphoria is another new, controversial diagnosis that replaces the previously termed gender identity disorder (APA, 2013). By removing the term "disorder," the new diagnosis may reduce the stigma experienced when a client identifies with a gender other than his or her birth gender. Though this diagnosis may be argued as continued pathologizing of an ever-more-accepted variation of the human condition in the European-American cultural context, the Sexual and Gender Identity Disorders Workgroup advocated that continued inclusion of gender dysphoria in the *DSM-5* will promote access to clinical services. While the removal of the word "disorder" can be recognized as a positive symbolic shift, gender dysphoria is still a diagnosis, which requires acknowledging that an individual experiences clinically significant distress and impairment for the problem issue of his or her identity being "abnormal."

Increased pathologizing or "psychologization" locates problems at the level of the individual; the responsibility for problems and for change becomes solely the individual's, despite the availability of alternative, more systemic explanations (and potential remediation) of problems (e.g., sexism, racism, poverty). This increasing pathologization of everyday life and the expansion of the boundaries of abnormality mean that it becomes harder and harder to be assessed as "normal" and more and more likely that individuals, rather than dysfunctional social systems, will be blamed for abnormality (Wilcoxon et al., 2008).

Further, Canino and Alegría (2008) declared that many North American constructs of personality and psychopathology are culture bound and are founded in White, male, Anglo-Germanic, Protestant, and middle-class or upper-class cultural values. They indicated that *DSM* diagnostic criteria ignore much of the world's population and the most rapidly increasing segments of U.S. society. Meanwhile, nearly 20% of the U.S. population speaks a language other than English in the home (Ryan, 2013). Ethnic minorities represent roughly 38% of the population in the United States and are expected to surpass 50% in 2044 (Colby & Ortman, 2015). To illustrate, when individuals come from a culture that is more collectivistic, deferential, or passive than mainstream America, their presentation may meet the diagnostic criteria of dependent personality disorder. Such pathologizing of what is outside the cultural norm has been criticized and nearly resulted in the removal of dependent personality disorder from the *DSM* (Boeree, 2007).

Diagnostic strategies traditionally ignore the influence of cultural norms and social context on human behavior (Ho, Bluestein, & Jenkins, 2008), and fail to take cultural diversity into consideration when evaluating psychological symptoms (Wilcoxon et al., 2008). For instance, Latino clients—particularly those who have recently immigrated, are minimally acculturated into the dominant culture, or are economically disadvantaged—rarely have cultural meanings about their distress considered during the diagnostic process. Such practices result in a **category fallacy**—that is, the application of diagnostic categories to cultural groups for which they were not developed and have never been validated (Eriksen & Kress, 2005). Consider Case Study 18.1 and how culture might play into assessment and intervention.

Historically, people who have not conformed to societal conventions have been psychiatrically hospitalized, ostracized from their communities as deviants, and prevented from marrying and working (Day, Kay, Holmes, & Napier, 2011). Consider the following list of those who did or do not fit social conventions (Eriksen & Kress, 2005). Until recently, LGBTQ individuals were diagnosable as mentally ill (Jones, Brewster, & Jones, 2014). African Americans and other people of color were considered subhuman animals, so any pursuit of human "rights" was considered abnormal (Sue & Sue, 2013); African-American slaves' pursuit of freedom was given the diagnosis of drapetomania. Women of the upper classes who masturbated (and were sometimes considering divorce) were said to be treading on dangerous ground, risking idiocy, mania, and death, and therefore were "treated" with clitoridectomies. Masturbation was considered a diagnosable problem. Women pursuing higher education and/or athletics would become sterile, according to "objective" research. Women who chose not to marry, not to have children, to divorce, or to have sex outside marriage were considered abnormal and were ostracized (Day et al., 2011). Christian European Americans sought to

CASE STUDY 18.1

Sarah resides in southern California. Recently her cousin brought her to the community health center after she was attacked at a local laundromat. When her cousin first learned of the attack, it seemed that the assault resulted from a conflict over the use of a dryer; however, this was not the case. Witnesses informed him that a Mexican-American woman became frustrated with Sarah because Sarah could not speak English. The woman yelled racial slurs at Sarah and told her that she should learn English now that she was in America. Sarah has had repeated problems with communicating and interacting with members of her community who express the same sentiment as the woman in the laundromat.

- Identify multicultural counseling considerations on which you should reflect.
- How might you address these cultural considerations, particularly in assessment and diagnosis?
- What role might internalized oppression play in Sarah's interactions with some members of her community?

convert the "heathen savages" (e.g., Native Americans, Africans, Asians) who dressed differently, had different customs, and sometimes used opiates or other drugs in their spiritual activities. Few today would attribute mental illness to these groups of people, and yet, such attributions were made within the 20th century.

Some readers may assert that such past "uncivilized" and "uninformed" behavior should not be worrisome. However, research regarding transgenerational trauma (Goodman, 2013) indicates future generations are impacted as families have had to learn ways of engaging in a society in which their lived experiences are invisible to mainstream society. Research has shown that minority populations have a higher prevalence of psychological distress than Caucasians, but are half as likely to receive mental health care (U.S. Office of Minority Health, 2010). Suicide attempts and completions are significantly more frequent in minority groups, and professional counselors should be particularly concerned with the counseling attrition rate of persons of color (Worthington, Soth-McNett, & Moreno, 2007), with 50% not returning after the first session (Sue & Sue, 2013) due in part to their cultural context not being understood. A continuing lack of cultural and gender sensitivity causes harm to those who differ from Western norms or the dominant cultural group and is argued to result in overdiagnosis, underdiagnosis, misdiagnosis, and sampling bias (O'Donohue & Benuto, 2010). Use Activity 18.1 to discuss the impact of context on people's behavior and subsequent diagnosis.

Overdiagnosis, Underdiagnosis, and Misdiagnosis

Minority populations often experience psychological distress as a result of hegemony experienced in daily life. Because behavior that does not match patriarchal Western norms is sometimes labeled as pathological, gay men, lesbians, transgender, racial/ethnic minorities, women, and nontraditional men may be overdiagnosed with certain disorders or misdiagnosed entirely (Henriques-Calado et al., 2014). For instance, research indicates that African Americans have been overdiagnosed with psychosis and underdiagnosed with depression.

ACTIVITY 18.1

In small groups, discuss the relationship between a particular diagnosis and the cultural milieu. For example, in the United States during the late 20th century, anorexia nervosa was most commonly diagnosed in young European-American females. What contextual situations might contribute to this fact? The demographics of this diagnosis appear to be changing, with more variations in gender (e.g., male athletes), gender identity (e.g., transgender), and SES, and more people of color being diagnosed with an eating disorder. What contextual situations might contribute to this trend? Other examples for similar discussions might include antisocial personality disorder (overdiagnosed in those with lower SES), or dependent personality disorder in adults (overdiagnosed in females), and disruptive mood dysregulation disorder in children.

Latinos have been diagnosed with schizophrenia 1.5 times the rate of Whites, and African Americans are more likely than Whites to be diagnosed with schizophrenia, substance-use disorder, and dementia (Hernandez, Barrio, & Yamada, 2013). Women are disproportionately diagnosed with certain personality disorders (Henriques-Calado et al., 2014); antisocial personality disorder is disproportionately diagnosed in those with lower SES (Dailey, Gill, Karl, & Barrio Minton, 2014); paranoid personality disorder has been confused with reactions related to the experience of disenfranchised and oppressed groups such as minorities, immigrants, and refugees (Barlow, 2014); those who expressed personality traits outside the dominant culture have been misdiagnosed with schizoid personality disorder symptoms (Henriques-Calado et al., 2014); one's religion, family, and culture and practices such as speaking in tongues, belief in the afterlife, and practices such as voodoo can also result in misdiagnosis of schizotypal personality disorder (Peluso, 2013); LGBT clients are diagnosed 3 times and 4.7 times the rate of heterosexual clients for major depression and panic disorder, respectively (Donner & Lowry, 2013).

Evidence indicates that misdiagnosis occurs as a result of stereotyping and overlooking the perspectives of women and the poor (LaRoche et al., 2015). An additional concern related to sex and diagnosis is that if mental health professionals view certain problems as more prevalent in individuals of one sex, they may stop gathering information before they recognize its occurrence in those of the other sex (e.g., PTSD in men following rape, women's substance-abuse problems; Eriksen & Kress, 2008).

Sampling Bias

Research has ignored many who are in need of counselors' services (e.g., lower SES, women, minorities, and the unemployed; Henriques-Calado et al., 2014). Sampling has also included a disproportionate representation of the sexes and minority populations. These research omissions raise questions about how successful we have been in developing unbiased diagnostic criteria (Comas-Diaz, 2010), questions about the relevance of applying current diagnoses to marginalized groups, and questions about the appropriateness and availability of treatments that are based on such diagnoses. Reflection 18.1 can help prompt a discussion of the development of psychological difficulties.

REFLECTION 18.1

Using the example of major depression (or other disorders such as phobias, generalized anxiety disorder, or conduct disorder), explore how sociocultural factors (e.g., "isms" such as racism, sexism, classism, ageism) could legitimately lead to a diagnosis of depression in someone experiencing symptoms. Consider what characteristic such as family dynamics, geographical region, language difficulties, religion, socioeconomic status (SES), folk beliefs or cultural norms, quality of life, immigrant experiences, disabilities, discriminations, or work experiences might contribute to depression (or other disorders). Identify possible life circumstances that contribute to feelings of loneliness, isolation, sadness, and hopelessness. A discussion of these changes and contexts may help to highlight the complexities of bias in diagnosis. How might understanding cultural context alter practitioners' ways of understanding beyond the typical perception that only certain people, with certain genetic predispositions, get certain "diseases" or diagnoses?

CULTURE AND PSYCHOPATHOLOGY

One's own enculturation, or social process in which one learns one's own culture and how culture is transmitted across generations, is argued to impact one's values, beliefs, and worldview (Kottak, 2008). Culture often influences (a) what symptoms are allowed as expressions of suffering (Canino & Alegría, 2008), and (b) how individuals are allowed or encouraged to cope with distress. Culture determines how those around the individual respond to distress or problematic behaviors, in particular, deciding the intensity or severity of the problem that must be evident before intervention is deemed necessary. Culture prescribes what are considered acceptable help-seeking responses and interventions and who may intervene (Marsella & Yamada, 2010). Within a specific culture, psychological sophistication and education influence the understanding and perception of problems, as well as beliefs about what should be done about problems. Class and social position may also influence how people respond to psychological problems. Thus, Sue and Sue (2013) urged counselors to consider not only the interaction of race and ethnicity with the development of problems, but also the influence of minority status on problems or the diagnostic process.

Culture also influences counselors' perceptions of a disorder, their style of interviewing, choice of theoretical perspectives, the classification system that they use, and their purpose for making a diagnosis (Bhugra & Kalra, 2010). Cross-cultural studies reveal intricacies of culture and diagnosis, exposing behaviors that may be characteristic of particular cultures; counselors need to be aware of these intricacies to prevent misdiagnosis, underdiagnosis, or overdiagnosis, as well as cultural validity in assessment. For example:

a. Plains Indians may hear the voices of recently departed relatives calling them from the afterworld. This is considered normative for some cultural members and not evidence of psychopathology, though it would be evidence of serious mental illness for most of European ancestry.

b. Anorexia nervosa primarily exists in Western society, which regards slim female bodies as beautiful.

c. The 42 million immigrants (documented and undocumented) in the United States (Colby & Ortman, 2015) and refugees (three times as many as there were in 1980; Camorato, 2011) face tremendous challenges of which counselors may be unaware (e.g., trauma as a result of escaping persecution [Chung, Bemak, & Kudo Grabosky, 2011], such as having witnessed torture, rape, and bombings [Yakushko, Watson, & Thompson, 2008]).

PTSD is common and compounded by challenges encountered after arrival in the United States (e.g., stress of relocation and acculturation, loss of social connection, legal concerns, unemployment, language barriers, health problems, prejudice, anxiety, depression, and suicidality; Yakushko et al., 2008). Given the expanding immigrant and refugee population, counselors are charged to understand the various ways of describing psychological problems. For example, depression may be described as "congestion" in certain cultures, which could result in misdiagnosis and inappropriate treatment, and the stigma affiliated with receiving counseling services (Fulton & Shannonhouse, 2014).

d. African American and Latino adolescents in high-crime, inner-city neighborhoods may normatively demonstrate many of the *DSM* criteria for conduct disorder or antisocial personality disorder (Canino & Alegría, 2008) which is four times as high in male populations. Because violence is routine in these locales, criteria for this disorder may be considered normative or simply coping strategies that aid survival.

Thus, culture is inextricably linked with both normal and abnormal behavior. Assessing development, experience, expression of behavior, and understanding the ways in which diagnosed people are perceived and treated seems imperative. Effective diagnoses require consciousness of cultural norms, values, and typical behaviors. The *DSM* does include culture-specific psychological problems in the appendices, a selection of which are outlined in Table 18.1. Limitations of the *DSM* seem to indicate that it represents Western thought and assumptions, and thus that it currently represents a minority bias (Kress, Eriksen, Dixon Rayle, & Ford, 2005). Consider the difficulties in relating to Michael in Case Study 18.2, in determining whether a particular diagnosis or treatment might be helpful to him.

TABLE 18.1 Culture-Specific Diagnoses

Culture	Diagnosis	Description
Malaysia	Amok	"Dissociative episode characterized by a period of brooding followed by an outburst of violent, aggressive, or homicidal behavior"[1]
Laos, Philippines, Polynesia, Papua New Guinea,	Cafard or cathard	
Puerto Rico	Mal de pelea	
Navajo	Iich'aa	
Malaysia, Indonesia	Latah	Hypersensitivity to sudden fright, often with echopraxia, echolalia, command obedience, and dissociative or trancelike behavior
Siberia	Amurakh, irkunii, ikota, olan, myriachit, menkeiti	
Thailand	Bah tschi, bah-tsi, baah-ji	
Japan	Imu	
Philippines	Mali-mali, silok	
Latin	Ataques de nervios	Panic attacks, dissociation, amnesia, and out-of-control shouting, crying trembling, and aggression (usually in women whose life conditions are distressing)

(Continued)

TABLE 18.1 Culture-Specific Diagnoses (Contineud)

Culture	Diagnosis	Description
Inuit	Pibloktoq	Abrupt dissociative episode accompanied by extreme excitement (up to 20 minutes), frequently followed by seizures and coma (up to 12 hours)—sudden, erratic, irrational behavior (often in women resulting from sexual exploitation by explorers)
India	Dhat	Severe anxiety and hypochondria associated with discharge of semen, whitish discoloration of the urine, and feelings of weakness and exhaustion. Sudden, intense anxiety that the sexual organs will recede into the body and possibly cause death
Sri Lanka	Sukra prameha	
China	Shen-k'uei	
Malaysia	Koro	
South and East Asia	Shuk yang, shook yong	
China	Suo yang	
Thailand	Rok-joo	
Latin	Susto	Illness attributed to frightening event that causes the soul to leave the body and results in unhappiness and sickness. Symptoms similar to depression with somatic symptoms.
	Espanto, pasmo, tripa ida, perdida del alma, chibih	

[1]*DSM-IV TR* description

CASE STUDY 18.2

Michael, a 35-year-old African-American man with no criminal record, was brought into a community mental health clinic after a verbal confrontation with a police officer. When asked why he refused to pay a parking fee for a local event, he responded angrily, "I offered the parking attendant my credit card, and he said that they only take cash. I never carry cash! Why does everyone have to make things so difficult?"

Michael notes that he does not like to go to banks; he refuses to ever enter a bank. He handles all his finances over the phone and through writing and depositing checks at an ATM. Furthermore, he indicates that he never carries or handles cash.

"When I have to use an ATM," Michael reports, "I have a pocket knife in the passenger seat, ready to use, just in case." Michael also reported that he is leery of others and becomes suspicious when discussions involve the subject of money. He has one credit card and his driver's license in his wallet, and he carries a list of his allergies just in case he is ever wounded and unconscious. He has also posted on his refrigerator the phone number for the local police, as well as the phone number of the credit card company, in the event that his card is ever stolen.

Michael's suspicious behaviors appear bizarre, and you begin to suspect that he may be paranoid or psychotic. Address the following questions before moving on:

- What diagnoses might you be considering at this point in the interview?
- What additional questions do you need to ask Michael?

After further inquiry about past events, Michael explains that while he was in a bank approximately two years ago, he witnessed an armed robbery during which a man was shot and killed. Almost every night since then, Michael has nightmares about the event, so vivid that he can smell the money and feel the man's blood spatter onto his face. He indicates that he was afraid to tell the interviewer this because of fears that he will be found and hurt by the family of the bank robber.

- How does the context surrounding Michael's presenting problem change your evaluation of the case scenario?
- What additional traumas might a counselor ask about when assessing a client and ascribing diagnoses?
- Discuss the importance of specifically asking clients about their context versus assuming that they will tell you.
- Why might clients not tell you about their various contextual situations?
- How might Michael's ethnicity or gender affect his situation and the interpretation of that situation by authority figures or others?

FEMINIST CHALLENGES

Feminist theorists believe that women's anger, depression, and discontent have been reframed as medical or psychiatric symptoms and that, as a result, the often difficult and distressing life circumstances of women have been disregarded. They state that it is often forgotten that the roots of women's so-called psychological problems have many times been social and political, rather than individual and intrapsychic in origin (Comas-Diaz, 2010). Feminists also point out the stigmatizing effects of diagnostic labels; the classist, sexist, racist, and homophobic assumptions that they consider to be embedded in both the *International Classification of Diseases* (ICD) and the *DSM*; the resulting pathologizing of behaviors that may be normative within particular gender contexts; the underdiagnosing of problematic male behaviors; and, finally, the inability to find any use for treatment or for conceptualizing the counseling process in the *DSM* classification system. Reflection 18.2 may be helpful in stimulating readers' thinking on gender socialization; its advantages or disadvantages for men and women, boys and girls; and possible biases in diagnosis that might emerge from socialization rather than biology.

REFLECTION 18.2

Complete the following statements as they apply to your gender.

As a _____, I am a failure if I don't . . .

Real _____ do . . .

Real _____ don't . . .

How might the diagnostic process be influenced by a counselor's responses to these statements? Based on your responses, consider the following questions:

- What diagnoses might you be more likely to give to men than to women because of the beliefs inherent in your responses to these statements?

- What diagnoses might you be more likely to give to women than to men?
- What behaviors would you be likely to consider abnormal or diagnosable in men, but not in women?
- What behaviors would you be likely to consider abnormal or diagnosable in women, but not in men?

Prevalence Data of Diagnoses by Gender

Research on the prevalence of mental illness by gender yields contradictory results. Some evidence seems to confirm that more women than men are mentally ill and that women's prevalence rates are higher than those for men on many more disorders (Schwartz, Lent, & Geihsler, 2011). The reasons proposed for the conflicting results include differing definitions of mental illness (Gove, 2010), differing research strategies (Gove, 2010), and sex bias (Heo, Murphy, Fontaine, Bruce, & Alexopoulos, 2008).

However, when examining the prevalence of specific diagnoses rather than overall rates of mental illness, there do seem to be trends in gender and diagnosis. For instance, men's prevalence rates are higher for substance use and gambling disorders, whereas women's prevalence rates are higher for anxiety disorders (Schwartz et al., 2011). While prevalence for Bipolar I is equal in both men and women (APA, 2013), women have been found to experience more rapid cycling, depressive episodes, and major depression than men. Furthermore, most Cluster A (e.g., paranoid, schizoid, and schizotypal) and Cluster B (e.g., antisocial, narcissistic) personality disorders occur more frequently in men than women (APA, 2013), with the exception of borderline personality disorder (75% female) and histrionic personality disorder where research findings are equivocal (APA, 2013). In Cluster C, obsessive-compulsive personality disorder is observed twice as often in men than women (APA, 2013), while avoidant personality disorder is argued equally prevalent between the sexes, and dependent personality disorder is more common in women (Gove, 2010). Use Activity 18.2 to consider how gender biases can conceptualize two personality disorders.

ACTIVITY 18.2

Find and read the following two diagnoses from the DSM: Antisocial Personality Disorder and Dependent Personality Disorder (APA, 2013). Now, address the following:

- Imagine a man diagnosed with antisocial personality disorder and then imagine a man diagnosed with dependent personality disorder.
- Now imagine a woman diagnosed with antisocial personality disorder and then a woman diagnosed with dependent personality disorder.
- How do your perceptions of the men and women differ, even when they are diagnosed with the same disorder?
- What would be the opposite of each of the disorders? Develop the specific "opposite" criteria.
- Why are there not *DSM* diagnoses associated with these opposite criteria?
- What are some other "opposites" that are not included in the *DSM* (e.g., stoic to parallel histrionic)?
- Why do you suppose such opposites are left out?

In historic context, Landrine (1989) proposed that the personality disorder diagnoses received by men most represent role stereotypes for men of a certain age, class, and marital status, whereas personality disorder diagnoses received most by women represent female role stereotypes for females of a certain age, class, and marital status. Her research has found support for the "social role" hypothesis, a hypothesis that includes gender, age, and socioeconomic class as interacting variables. The research results indicate that stereotypes of young, lower socioeconomic class men were labeled antisocial; stereotypes of single middle-class young women were labeled histrionic/hysterical; stereotypes of married, middle-class, middle-aged women were labeled dependent; and stereotypes of the "ruling class," that is, middle-class men, were labeled prototypically normal, or corresponded with the criteria for compulsive, paranoid, and narcissistic descriptions. Borderline and schizoid descriptions were not attributed to either sex. Landrine indicated, therefore, that the gender distribution of personality disorders does not result from the misogyny of practitioners, but from the overlap between personality disorder characteristics and gender role stereotypes of both sexes.

Developmental Shifts in Prevalence Rates

Interestingly, gender prevalence studies indicate that there are few gender differences in the diagnosis of neurodevelopmental disorders (disorders that appear at the beginning of the life span and are believed to be biologically based disorders) prevalence before school age. Once children begin school, however, boys are more frequently diagnosed in the middle childhood years and girls in adolescence and beyond (Atladottir et al., 2015). Becker and Swim (2012) hypothesized that young girls with difficulties are socialized to channel them into internalized distress that is not as identifiable by teachers and parents, whereas boys are not. Therefore, it is likely that young boys' more externalized problems disrupt families and schoolrooms, potentially increasing their frequency of diagnosis and referral. Henriques-Calado et al. (2014) indicated that girls' problems are more likely to be overlooked, underdiagnosed, and untreated because of (a) the lack of ability to observe young girls' distress when it is present, and (b) the traditional notion that it is less important for girls to succeed academically. Although it may be difficult to firmly ascertain differential incidence of diagnoses during childhood by gender, beliefs about the differences seem to affect policy and funding decisions, making less money available for services for girls, who remain unreferred and undiagnosed (Atladottir et al., 2015). The very apparent needs of boys would, in contrast, result in the overpathologizing of young boys (Eriksen & Kress, 2008).

Children are, in general, often overdiagnosed or misdiagnosed. Children under age 13 are often overdiagnosed with attention-deficit/hyperactivity disorder (ADHD; Atladottir et al., 2015). Adolescents are often overdiagnosed with conduct disorders and substance-use disorders. Inappropriate diagnosis may result in labels that follow children into adulthood, thus presenting a serious ethical concern since ethical practice requires that "counselors carefully consider both the positive and negative implications of a diagnosis" (ACA, 2014, p. 11).

For those children whose problematic behavior does continue into adulthood, however, it is interesting that childhood mental disorders with male predominance, such as conduct disorder, oppositional defiant disorder, and ADHD, have only three correlates in adulthood: Antisocial Personality Disorder, ADHD, and Intermittent Explosive Disorder

(Olfson, Blanco, Liu, Moreno, & Laje 2006). However, children with disorders of female predominance experience a greater range of diagnoses as adults. From her perspective, then, the reason fewer men are considered mentally ill when they continue their problematic childhood/adolescent behavior into adulthood is that young girls' problems seem to evolve into adult problems that can receive a wide range of *DSM* diagnoses, whereas young boys' problems seem to evolve into criminality, which is not "mental illness" per se. Review Case Study 18.3 to stimulate your thinking on how male/female prevalence rates and practitioner expectations might affect assessment and treatment.

CASE STUDY 18.3

Jordan is a 41-year-old African-American male. He has a long history of receiving services within the mental health system. Jordan meets with you during a recent hospitalization for a suicide attempt. He seems uninterested during the interview, is not forthcoming with information, and states he's "been through this a million times and that you can't help" him. You are aware that you feel annoyed with Jordan.

- How would you manage your feelings of annoyance toward Jordan? What might you need from a clinical supervisor regarding countertransference?

In reviewing his charts, you see that he has historically been diagnosed with borderline personality disorder, major depression—recurrent, pathological gambling, impulsive self-mutilation, and adult antisocial behavior. Jordan has attempted suicide multiple times and is perceived by many health-care providers as "difficult" and "manipulative." Jordan often fails to follow through on recommendations made by providers and can appear "needy," "volatile," and "helpless," as documented in many of his providers' progress notes.

- What effect might Jordan's diagnoses have on his situation?
- How might the stigma of the diagnoses have made his situation worse?
- To what extent might Jordan's diagnoses help him or the treatment process?

Jordan is aware of the annoyance that many providers feel toward him. He is bitter about the multiple diagnoses and "uncaring" treatment he receives. He feels very misunderstood and has not been open about his past experiences. The reality is that his father and mother were sexually and physically abusive. His football coach also raped him in the ninth grade. He suffers many trauma reactions secondary to his childhood experiences, and many of his behaviors are his attempts to keep from committing suicide and spiralling into a deep depression.

- How might Jordan's reactions be adaptive, given his life circumstances?
- What strengths or resources might Jordan have, and how could you assess these and use them in your work together?
- How might Jordan's developmental experiences influence how he sees himself, others, and life? How might his behaviors be expected developmental reactions to abnormal situations?
- How might Jordan's gender affect his situation and his perception of his past and present situations? How might your understanding/conceptualization impact Jordan's situation?

Additional concerns about the assessment and diagnosis process emerge when considering older adult clients. Counselors may struggle with differentiating normal aging concerns from symptoms of depression or major/mild neurocognitive disorder. Disinterest and forgetfulness, for instance, may result from genetic predisposition or advancing age, emphasizing the role of the brain in one's functioning, rather than from psychological problems (Ganguli et al., 2011). Psychological symptoms may also be caused by a physical disorder or medications aimed at treating a medical problem. Approximately 66 million individuals in the United States alone are projected to struggle with neurocognitive disorders by the year 2030 (Mitchell, 2013). More than 80% of those over the age of 65 years have a chronic physical condition and may take several medications on a regular basis. As a result, psychological disorders may be overlooked among older clients and/or be inappropriately assumed when a medical problem, aging, or medication interaction is really responsible for symptoms (Heo et al., 2008). In fact, studies have demonstrated that the detection and treatment of depression with older adults have been unsatisfactory (Brown, Raue, & Halpert, 2009).

Sex Bias in Diagnosis

Recent studies demonstrate practitioners' continued sex bias in diagnosis. Researchers have found that simply knowing a client's sex may influence the diagnostic process, even among experienced practitioners (Eriksen & Kress, 2008). Female and male clients may receive different diagnoses even when they present with identical symptomatology (Gove, 2010). Angermeyer, Matschinger, Link, and Schomerus (2014) stated that women who acted in unfeminine ways received very strong negative reactions, but that men who behaved similarly did not when asking participants to respond to vignettes of men and women with alcohol dependence, major depression, or schizophrenia.

Women from traditionally marginalized groups find themselves pathologized to an even greater extent. In the United States, women of color (e.g., racial/ethnic women, immigrant women) and lesbians may experience political, legal, cultural, and personal risk factors, but may not have regular access to counseling and diagnosis that is sensitive to their particular cultural, emotional, or language needs (Caplan, 2006). Related to this issue of gender and cultural bias, sexual dysfunctions such as female orgasmic disorder varies dramatically by ethnic background (Crooks & Baur, 2013), and cultural context may be a consideration when considering symptoms such as anxiety, relationship factors, and a woman's knowledge of her own body (APA, 2013). Women from traditionally oppressed groups who claim multiple identities may find themselves "pathologized" when seen through the lenses of the upper-class-driven *DSM* characteristics, even when their behavior would be considered "normal" in ethnic/racial minority, immigrant, and/or lesbian cultures. Reflect on Case Study 18.4 as a means to assess your own tendencies toward bias in diagnosing females from nondominant cultures.

CASE STUDY 18.4

Jada is a 17-year-old girl who was brought to counseling by her parents because of the concerns and anxieties that Jada has about her English class. She indicates that it is hard for her to pay attention because her teacher is boring. She adds that she does not like her teacher because the teacher calls on her when she doesn't have her hand up. She says that the teacher tries to pick on her, knowing that it will upset her. Jada is embarrassed when this happens because she does not like to be put on the spot when she does not know the answer. She says that it is not normal for teachers to call on girls in class. She indicates that in her other classes, it is the boys who mostly talk in class.

Jada claims it is not important for her to learn English. She says she speaks English just fine and doesn't understand the point of the class. She adds that she doesn't plan on working when she graduates and has no intention of going to college. She wants to get married and support her husband in his work while she becomes a homemaker.

Jada says that she hates school because she has no friends, and people pick on her because she is different. She wishes she could drop out of school, but her parents won't let her. She says she has only one friend, but that she and her friend don't have much in common. Jada says that the only reason they are friends is because they are both "losers." Jada adds that she is used to being a "nerd," so this really doesn't bother her. The only problem, from her perspective, is her mean English teacher.

Jada indicates mounting anxiety prior to attending her English class. She says that her stomach starts to hurt about one hour before English class every day. She used to go to the school nurse instead of going to class, but the nurse told her that she couldn't come to the nurse's office anymore. Jada says that sometimes she doesn't even want to go to school because she hates English so much. When she's in English class her palms are sweaty, and she has trouble breathing. She says that her chest feels tight, and she is afraid she is going to have a heart attack.

Jada says she has trouble eating lunch because she is so nervous about going to English class. She also says that if she thinks about English class before bed, she cannot sleep and often has nightmares about going to that class. Jada wishes she could drop out of English class and take something else in order to get rid of her anxiety.

- What diagnosis might you suspect for Jada?
- Reread the case inserting "boy" and "he." How does your assessment differ?
- Now, reread the case with the assumption that Jada is of Asian descent and is from an upper-middle-class family. Her father is a doctor, and her mother is a housewife. How does that change your impressions?
- How would ascribing a *DSM* diagnosis potentially affect Jada now? In the future?
- How might your values influence your conceptualization of the situation?
- How might some of Jada's issues be related to developmental issues? Coping strategies? What strengths might she have, and why might it be important to acknowledge those or help her acknowledge those in counselling?

The battle over the inclusion in the *DSM* of Premenstrual Dysphoric Disorder (PMDD) draws particular attention to the political and gender struggles inherent in the development of *DSM* classifications. While most women experience mild physical and emotional symptoms just before menstruation (frequently referred to as PMS), 8% of women report experiencing distress that impairs their daily functioning (Pilver, Desai, Kasl, & Levy, 2011). PMDD has been linked to polymorphism of the estrogen alpha receptor gene (ESR1); women with this variant also share a polymorphism involving catechol-o-methyltransferase, which regulates mood chemistry in the prefrontal cortex (Huo et al., 2007). Correlations found between PMDD and history of sexual abuse, past or present domestic violence, and perceived sexual discrimination (Pilver et al., 2011), as well as between PMDD and past unipolar depression, anxiety, and other psychiatric disorders (Grady-Welicky, 2003), provides support for the addition of this diagnosis; however, Grady-Weliky (2003) argued although women may experience dysphoria related to their menstrual cycle, such dysphoria may result from culturally determined, negative associations with menstruation or from physiological, hormonal changes.

Socialization and Mental Health

Research and theory on the mental health implications of socialization have further clarified some of the ways that gender-specific socialization harms people or causes them distress. Historically, Gilligan's research on "voice" (Gilligan, 1993) suggested that girls silence themselves and their desires, abilities, and interests (i.e., they give up their "voice") as they move into adolescence because they believe that such silence is necessary to succeed in intimate relationships. Smolak (2002) found that voice was negatively correlated with femininity, and that the link between "lack of voice" and psychopathology was documented more clearly for women than for men. Rather than voice being related strictly to being male or female, however, higher voice ratings were related to higher ratings on masculinity and lower voice ratings to lower ratings on masculinity and higher ratings on femininity.

Hess, Ittel, and Sisler (2014) discussed individualism and relatedness, comparing these to masculinity and femininity, in their discussions of why women in North America are twice as likely as men to experience depression in their lives. Their explanations also gain support from the fact that gender differences seem to begin during adolescence, just at the time when girls' socialization becomes different from boys' (Gove, 2010). During adolescence, often boys are taught that men should be active, masterful, and autonomous, whereas girls are taught that women are to be passive, compliant, and committed to interpersonal relationships (Hess et al., 2014).

Historically, Bem (1974) indicated that suppression of the non-sex-typed part of oneself was unhealthy, and that androgyny resulted in better mental health and adjustment. Hess et al. (2014) recently confirmed Bem's findings that poor health and relationship difficulties result from a lack of balance between individualism (maleness) and relatedness (femaleness). However, being male or female turned out to be less relevant than the person's degree of masculinity and femininity. Higher femininity scores and lower masculinity scores correlated with higher depression in both sexes, and higher levels of masculinity resulted in lower levels of depression in both men and women.

What, then, are women to do about the conflict between their needs to adopt masculine characteristics to be mentally healthy and society's demands that they adopt feminine characteristics to be desirable? And how are ethnic minority females to respond to this second acculturative stress which compounds their underprivileged status and risk for diagnostic prejudice? Feminists assert that answers to these questions are unlikely to emerge from a focus on diagnosing and medically reducing the symptoms of these conflicts. At the very least, part of counselors' focus ought to be on changing the biases in society that damage both men and women. As an example of the complex interplay of gender, social adjustment, and psychological health, review the case of Tanisha in Case Study 18.5.

CASE STUDY 18.5

Tanisha earned an MBA five years ago and is working for a thriving global company. She recently became a manager in her division of the company, a role that seems to be overchallenging her. Her primary aim has been to ensure that her team meets their numbers, and she has sometimes had to discipline or terminate staff members who do not meet their weekly goals while still trying to build healthy working relationships with remaining team members.

Tanisha consults with a friend, Josh, who graduated with her from the same MBA program. She seeks his advice because he is employed with the same company, has flourished in his job, and now serves as a regional manager. The strategies he recommends to build her team seem to be punitive rather than supportive. His recommendations don't seem to mesh with her "natural" instincts to build relationships with each team member, assisting the team in becoming a cohesive unit, all while working toward company goals.

Tanisha has also been reading various books and reviewing her graduate study materials in her efforts to find help in doing her job. She further decides to use the employee assistance program at work to help her in processing her workplace struggles and questions. In her last EAP meeting, she reflected that she often hears the words of James Brown, "This is a man's world," when she feels uncomfortable or needs to make changes that threaten her team-members' job stability. She is beginning to think this might not be a good place for her to work because she feels like she has to act more like "Timothy" than "Tanisha."

- What might the counselor have to consider related to his or her perception of gender roles in the workforce?
- How is the culture of the workplace organization affecting Tanisha?
- How might Tanisha's response to the workplace culture affect her self-perception?
- How can a mental health counselor helpfully approach these questions with Tanisha as she considers her current occupational demands?
- Did you have any assumptions about Tanisha's ethnicity? How might your assumptions (and the answers to the above prompts) be different if this client was named Tabitha?

Social Conditions

Beyond the socialization questions are questions about the impact of societal conditions on women's mental health. For instance, environmental factors that may account for the high rates of depression and other disorders in women include (a) the greater restrictiveness of women's roles, which result in less financial, occupational, or social gratification; (b) the inability to measure up to standards of women who are held up as examples of those who have "made it"; (c) a lack of social networks and supports; (d) marriage, as married women are more depressed than never-married women, possibly because of isolation and not having their needs met in their roles as homemakers, or because of being employed and yet also carrying most of child-care and household responsibilities; (e) separation or divorce (because women are less likely to remarry and more likely to live longer than men); (f) single motherhood and its attendant stresses; (g) more frequent experiences of gender-based discrimination; (h) higher prevalence of living in poverty with its attendant stressors; (i) inequities related to marriage, family relationships, reproduction, child rearing, divorce, aging, education, and work; (j) work outside the home that is low status or low pay; and (k) women's roles being defined in terms of the needs of others, which serves to relegate women's own needs to secondary status, where they remain unmet (Kaiser & Spalding, 2015; Levasseur et al., 2015).

It may, therefore, be more accurate to say that disorders exist in the relationships between certain people and those with whom they relate, or between certain people and the societal norms and demands around them, rather than a disorder existing solely within an individual or her or his biology. Focusing on the individual may, in fact, lead to failures to "cure" the problem, whereas focus on correcting societal problems (e.g., providing child care, opening up employment for women, changing the definitions of proper female behavior) may actually reduce the incidence of the problems. Advocating from this systemic lens is another service that counselors provide their clients.

Women's Trauma Experiences

Some (e.g., Kaiser & Spalding, 2015) have indicated that the ongoing experiences of subordination and oppression and the previously cited negative social conditions that surround female daily existence are a type of insidious trauma. Gender differentiation in our society (Comas-Diaz, 2010) results in violence against women in the form of incest, rape, and battering; observing the abuse of other women; and sexual abuse in childhood, all of which approach normative status in girls and women. Others from nondominant groups are also repeatedly exposed to trauma and victimization. Reflect on Angela's situation in Case Study 18.6 to get a sense of how considering or not considering context affects your diagnostic impressions.

CASE STUDY 18.6

You begin counseling Angela, a 28-year-old female. Angela reports that she would like help in decreasing her anxiety. She indicates constant tension, irritableness, tiredness, worrying, and occasional panic reactions. She notes that she has a history of strained relationships and has difficulty trusting others. She also reports that she self-injures by cutting her arms and legs and has difficulty feeling at ease and "real." She states, "I don't know who I am or where I'm going. Life feels so chaotic." During your intake interview you notice that Angela is difficult to connect with and seems very distracted and agitated.

- At this point, what *DSM* diagnoses might you suspect?
- What additional information do you need before applying a formal diagnosis?

Later, you obtain a release of information to talk with Angela's mom. "Since the rape and the time she moved in with me three months ago, she begs me every day to never make her leave," says Ms. Connor about her daughter.

- How does this information change your initial diagnostic impressions?

Angela appears to be somewhat restless and guarded during your second session, but when you ask about the rape and validate her experience, she relaxes and shares her story. She reports that she was raped while walking home from work three months ago, and the rape triggered memories of early sexual abuse inflicted by her father. Now driving everywhere rather than walking, she continues to function well at work, but finds herself unable to live on her own.

When asked what prompted her to pursue counseling, Angela reluctantly pulls up the sleeves of her shirt, revealing multiple slash-type cuts and scars. In tears, Angela explains that when she feels overwhelmed by thoughts of her abuse as a child and recent rape, she distracts herself by making superficial cuts on her arms. She explains that she continually thinks about what has happened to her, especially when she's alone, and that she feels sad most of the time.

Angela reports that she was able to trust men earlier in her life. However, she has felt uncomfortable around men since her rape, and now believes that they are untrustworthy. She has recently begun working in a women's clothing store and as a result rarely has to deal with men. Angela carries pepper spray in the event that she should ever find herself alone with a man.

- Based on this additional information, what *DSM* diagnoses might you suspect?
- What additional information do you need to make a formal diagnosis?

The impact of sexual abuse and sexual assault on women's mental health and development are well documented (Comas-Diaz, 2010). For instance, women and girls who have experienced such traumas display despair, anger, and retraumatization and are given diagnoses of PTSD, depression, anxiety, eating disorders, and borderline personality disorder (Lee, Jordan, & Schuler, 2018; McLeod, Muldoon, & Jackson-Cherry, 2018; Wachter-Morris & Graves, 2018). These disorders and experiences potentially impede women from performing and enjoying activities of daily living such as work, parenting, recreation, partnerships, and friendships. Use Reflection 18.3 to stimulate your thinking about diagnosing women with histories of abuse. Then consider Case Study 18.7 and discuss the diagnostic and treatment dilemmas you might experience if you were the counselor.

REFLECTION 18.3

The trauma that women experience often negatively affects their mental health and developmental well-being. Professional counselors who work with women with histories of abuse must assess and consider their current and past social conditions. List and describe the salient variables a counselor should consider before providing a diagnosis for these women.

CASE STUDY 18.7

Lourdes is a 30-year-old immigrant from Puerto Rico who says that she is unhappy in her life because she has not made many friends in the United States. She feels very lonely and isolated. She is sad and would like to work on feeling more grateful and happy while learning how to become a better wife. She misses all her old friends in Puerto Rico and longs to see them again.

Lourdes and her husband arrived in the United States two years ago. They have no children, but do have a few other family members who came to the United States with them. Lourdes is unemployed, but her husband owns a convenience store. She works for her husband at the store when he requests her service. When she is not working for her husband, she is at home cooking and cleaning and tending to home matters. She says that "this is what women do," and she feels comfortable with this arrangement.

However, she feels lonely being in the house for days at a time. She says that in Puerto Rico when she had to stay at home all day, she could at least socialize with her neighbors and family, but she has had difficulty connecting with her neighbors here in the United States.

Lourdes says that she is having trouble sleeping and has had appetite changes, as she is often worrying about various issues. She says that she worries that she did not make the right thing for dinner or that the house will not be clean enough for her husband. She also worries that she will never make any new friends. She indicates that she often is jumpy because she is afraid she is forgetting something or will make a mistake and upset her husband. She says that, when she is not cooking or cleaning, she feels lethargic, sad, and worried.

What diagnoses might you suspect for Lourdes?
How might your values affect your conceptualization of Lourdes' situation?
How might Lourdes' gender/culture affect her perceptions of her situation?

In a later session, Lourdes wishes that her husband had more time for her, but "realizes" that she is being selfish with his time. She says that she knows that it is important for him to be at work and to tend to his social life. She indicates that her husband has several girlfriends, and although she sometimes feels jealous, she would never challenge his behaviors. She is not upset that her husband has girlfriends. Her husband gets mad at her and sometimes becomes violent if she asks him to spend more time with her. She says she also feels guilty that she has not been able to provide her husband with children, and she notes that he often castigates her for not being able to get pregnant.

The next time Lourdes comes into the office she has a black eye. The counselor also notices several bruises on her arms. When questioned about the bruises, she says that her husband hit her the night before because she was in a bad mood and asked him to stay home instead of going out with his friends. She says that she came to this appointment to tell the counselor that it would be her last appointment. Her husband does not want her to come anymore because he feels that it is disrespectful to him for her to see the counselor. He also doesn't want her participating in anything that takes away from his time with her.

- How does the domestic violence context change your diagnostic impressions?
- How do you think that long-term contexts, such as living in a domestic violence situation, affect a client's diagnostic summary?
- If Lourdes continues in counseling, how might you play a preventative role with her?
- If she ever needed to go to court to obtain a restraining order, press domestic violence charges, obtain a divorce, or the like, and the court ordered your files, what would be the implications of the different diagnoses you mentioned earlier?

TOWARD SOLUTIONS

In the literature, much of the critical discourse around professionals' use of the *DSM* has focused on what "not to do" versus "what to do," on problems rather than solutions. This section offers strategies, with activities, exercises, and cases, designed to increase counselors' incorporation into counseling the systemic, developmental, and multicultural "stories" about client problems and solutions to these problems. Begin by developing a case vignette with the prompts in Activity 18.3.

ACTIVITY 18.3

Develop a case vignette. Include the client's demographics, presenting concerns, and a brief psychosocial history. Provide a diagnosis for the client using the most current version of the *DSM*. In addition, write a couple of paragraphs about multicultural considerations that are relevant to giving the client a particular diagnosis. In small groups, discuss your vignette and your peers' vignettes. Record notes on the multicultural considerations and possible diagnoses for each client. As a class, discuss themes in multicultural diagnosis using the "clients" presented in your small group as a framework.

Comprehensive Assessment

Diagnosis should not just identify a disorder or differentiate one disorder from another. Counselors should always remain aware that *DSM* diagnosis is only one piece of a comprehensive assessment. Potential benefits of diagnosis include (a) having a framework for describing complex phenomena, (b) increasing one's understanding of symptoms, and (c) promoting self-awareness and self-acceptance within the client. Diagnosis may help clients focus on an identified external enemy and may assist family members and clinicians in developing compassion for the client. Diagnosis may help us determine whether problems are beyond the scope of our practice and assist us with the selection of intentional evidence-based interventions. Diagnosis may provide the counselor additional information regarding etiology and prognostic factors to consider in treatment planning. The dimensional approach to diagnosis (APA, 2013) may enable more accurate diagnoses contributing to meaningful research and the future development of standardized/objective inventories that are culturally appropriate. We are often required to diagnose in order to facilitate managed-care reimbursement and access to services for our clients. Further, diagnosis contributes to a common language that facilitates communication among all the individuals involved in the clients' treatment (Kress & Paylo, 2015). While the benefits of *DSM* diagnosis are important to consider, other diagnostic considerations exist.

Magnavita (2016) suggested that a comprehensive diagnosis should integrate the perspectives of the client, the counselor, and significant others, such as friends and family members. A counselor might therefore consider the *DSM* as a first step toward helping clients, while being aware of the *DSM*'s intended scope, and extending the assessment process beyond *DSM* diagnosis by including information regarding the client's developmental history, other problem areas, family relationships, medical and treatment history, and client strengths (Kress & Paylo, 2015). Diagnosis can also be specific to the case and situation, as though a wide array of potential descriptions and explanations for the presenting difficulties exist (Magnavita, 2016). With the addition of the new trait-specified personality disorder categorization, the *DSM-5* has moved in this direction. Diagnoses should continue to evolve as new information becomes available over time, rather than remain static, objective truths. The counselor is, then, not an expert *doing* diagnosis to the client, but a facilitator in forming diagnostic meanings *with* the client (Magnavita, 2016). To get a sense of how practitioners in the field ensure that their assessments are comprehensive, conduct Activity 18.4.

ACTIVITY 18.4

In your local community, select a mental health professional to interview. Ask the individual if he or she would be interested in discussing multicultural issues and diagnosis. Select two or three ideas from this chapter and develop five questions related to comprehensive assessment to ask the practitioner. Interview the practitioner. After the interview, identify the similarities or differences between the chapter information and the suggestions and practices of the mental health professional.

Universal and Culturally Specific Diagnoses

Cultural and diagnostic scholars seem to pursue two different poles or models: one suggests that there are universal diagnostic categories and descriptors that apply regardless of situational and cultural factors, and the other claims that "it is impossible to extract an individual's lifestyle from the culture that helps to mold it and through which it is expressed" (Thomas & Sillen, 1972, p. 59). Large-scale epidemiological studies that may support universal diagnostic categories have often suppressed "the voices of small groups," and have, according to Kirmayer and Minas (2000, p. 447), contributed "to the homogenization and standardization of world cultures and traditions of healing. What we gain in methodological rigor," they claim, "we lose in diversity." The relevance of culture is, as a result, undermined, and we interpret those behaviors that do not conform with a Western model as abnormal or maladaptive (Magnavita, 2016).

However, attempts to hear "the voices of small groups" by adding cultural data to the *DSM* have also generated criticism. Magnavita (2016) pointed out that separating culture-bound syndromes in the *DSM* and giving them special, restricted status makes them vulnerable to being dismissed, discounted, or not taken seriously. By separating culture-bound syndromes into a separate section, *DSM* developers assume that the European-American perspective is somehow superior or the standard or the point of reference against which all other psychiatry (including cultural psychiatry) is compared (Banzato, 2008; Baumann, 2007). If the *DSM* is not the global standard for what mental health is, then is it really applicable to those from another cultural context who move to the United States? Must they assimilate the American normative view of mental health too, just as some demand that they learn English? It is promising to note that with the fifth edition of the *DSM*, a stronger alignment has been made between *DSM* diagnostic codes and those adopted by the World Health Organization in the ICD.

The Culture and Diagnosis Group also believes that a culturally sensitive *DSM* would include (a) more extensive guidelines in the *DSM*'s introduction about how to use the *DSM* in a culturally sensitive manner; (b) a cultural axis; (c) a cultural issues section under each disease condition or chapter; (d) specific examples of culturally normative client experiences that might look like disease or of disorders that are expressed in unexpected ways for cultural reasons; (e) culture-bound syndromes; and (f) an appendix related to expectable problems in working with interpreters (Haynes, Smith, & Hunsley, 2011). Magnavita (2016) also indicated the *DSM* should (a) include information to assist the counselor to address the interactions between the client's culture and the counselor's culture; (b) assist the counselor to distinguish between pathology and culturally different (i.e., normal cultural practices that appear strange to dominant-culture practitioners); (c) clearly state that pathology should not be dismissed just because it occurs with high frequency in a particular culture; and (d) encourage counselors to avoid the temptation to assume that they cannot treat clients with culture-bound syndromes—counselors should instead assess what part of a client's psychopathology they can treat.

Magnavita (2016) outlined what more culturally sensitive assessments would look like. It is recommended that counselors begin by exploring:

- Cultural systems and structures (i.e., community structure, family, schools, interaction styles, concepts of illness, life-stage development, coping patterns, and immigration history)
- Cultural values (i.e., time, activity, relational orientation, person–nature orientation, basic nature of people)
- Gender socialization
- The effect of trauma

In the process, the counselor (and perhaps the client as well) would gain an understanding of the impact of race, class, gender, sexual orientation, and ethnicity on the presenting problem, on the client's understanding of the problem, and on the client's expression of the problem (Baumann, 2007). In practice, cultural values often overlap and intersect with other facets of our clients' identities. Voices from the Field 18.1 is an example of how one counselor worked with a Latino male with depression and guilt using a lens of religion.

Other Culturally Astute Strategies

Castillo (1997) contended that an accurate assessment of emotion or behavior is not possible without an assessment of cultural schemas. The counselor, from his perspective, needs to know:

- What types of emotions a particular cultural group experiences
- What emotions are elicited by what situations
- What particular emotions mean to indigenous observers
- What means of expression of particular emotions exist in that culture
- What emotions are considered proper or improper for a person of a particular social status
- How unexpressed emotions are handled

Castillo (1997) further urged practitioners to treat both the illness (i.e., client's subjective experience of being sick) *and* the disease (i.e., practitioner's diagnosis). He provided the following guidelines to enable mental health professionals to offer clients a culturally sensitive diagnosis:

- Assess the client's cultural identity
- Identify sources of cultural information relevant to the client

Voices from the Field 18.1

Depression and Religiosity in a Latino Male

My client requested counseling to address a "difficult to treat" depression. He was a 45-year-old Latino male who was divorced, unemployed, and a parent of two girls aged 5 and 7 years old. He had been engaged in three previous unsuccessful therapies to address his depression. During the intake he shared his story with me. Once happily married and a successful computer engineer at a nationally known candy factory, his life felt as though it came to an end after his wife asked him for a divorce. He tried to persuade her to the contrary with no success. Moreover, soon after the divorce his former wife began a new relationship and moved to a different town, preventing him from seeing his daughters. Overwhelmed by grief and unable to concentrate due to his separation from wife and daughters, he lost his job and went on a spiral of depression, crowned by his conclusion that his was a failed life.

Five years later, with significant weight loss, pervasive insomnia, deep sadness, and strong feelings of guilt, this man was sitting in my office overwhelmed, having difficulties trusting others, and feeling hopeless and lost in terms of his future. After completing the intake information and establishing a plan of action, I listened intentionally and worked collaboratively to set our goal of overcoming the depression. We built on his personal and professional strengths and competencies. Special efforts were made to capitalize on each positive action he had taken over the last years. We highlighted his efforts to find temporary jobs to make a living, his willingness to drive long miles to see his daughters, and his capacity to relate to his former wife in spite of the pain she had inflicted in his life.

We pulled on cognitive techniques, Gestalt exercises, and other interventions to address his negative cognitions and explore his emotions, but we found no success as he continually returned to his belief that he was a failure. Unable to fully capture what was at the core of his deep-seated guilt, at the end of the fifth session I suggested the use of imagery. The following session he reported an unusual dream. He was a child standing on the shadow of a tall but slender building. He was puzzled because he could not see the top of the building in spite of his efforts looking up. We processed this dream and while he was drawing the image we used his imagination to find out that at the top of the tower there was a *campanario* with church bells, topped by a big cross. Chills ran through his body and he cried profusely after the realization that as a devout Catholic he had broken a main tenet of his faith. Marrying before the eyes of God was forever and getting a divorce meant he had failed God.

The direct consequence of this deeply moving experience was to focus on his depression and guilt from a religious perspective. In his eyes, he had committed a mortal and unforgivable sin and was condemned for life. He had not set foot in a church since his divorce was finalized and he finally understood why. He could not see God approving his presence before Him. During the following three sessions we reframed God as a loving father and helped him return to his church. He decided to attend confession and the priest confirmed his view of a loving God and forgiving father, a God that asked him to treat himself with love and care . . . and he did. The client was able to find a stable job in his discipline and his adaptive functioning improved, as did his connection with his beloved daughters. A five-year follow-up revealed that he had returned to his church and was in a healthy relationship with a woman who also embraced his daughters.

~ Carlos P. Zalaquett, Counselor Educator, University Park, Pennsylvania

- Assess the cultural meaning of a client's problem and symptoms
- Consider the impacts and effects of family, work, and community on the complaint, including stigma and discrimination that may be associated with mental illness in the client's culture
- Assess personal biases
- Plan treatment collaboratively

He added the following specific suggestions for the assessment and treatment process

- Adjust the interviewing style (i.e., eye contact, personal space, rate of speech) to the norms of the client
- Do not use symptom scales without validating them in the new culture
- Remember that different symptoms mean different things in different cultures
- Consult with and work in collaboration with qualified folk healers
- Use symbols from the client's culture as part of the treatment
- Reduce the unknown by supporting the client's own understanding of the illness, as long as his or her understanding includes the possibility of treatment and eventual cure
- Increase the manageability or the client's sense of "control or competence to meet the demands of the illness" (p. 80)
- Increase understanding of the function of the illness, its purpose, and the moral or religious reason behind it
- Use symbolic, ritualistic healing in order to shift clients' cognitions about the problem, the client meanings, and thus, their emotions

Kress et al. (2005) further suggested questions that culturally sensitive counselors should ask themselves before diagnosing any client:

- Have I been able to separate what is important to me and what is important to this particular client?
- What do I know about this client's cultural heritage?
- What do I *not* know about this client's cultural heritage?
- What is this client's relationship with his or her culture from his or her perspective?
- How acculturated is the client?
- What are my stereotypes, beliefs, and biases about this culture, and how might these influence my understandings?
- What culturally appropriate strategies or techniques should be incorporated in the assessment process?
- What is my philosophy of how pathology is operationalized in individuals from this cultural group?
- Have I appropriately consulted with other mental health professionals, members from this particular culture, and/or members of this client's family or extended family?
- Has this client aided in the co-construction of my understanding of this problem? (p. 103)

Table 18.2 summarizes additional recommendations for diversity-sensitive diagnosis.

TABLE 18.2 Summary of Recommendations for Diversity-Sensitive Diagnosis: A Proactive Approach to Limiting Assessment Bias

Counselor Awareness

- Commit to assessing and overcoming personal biases and stereotypes.
- Commit to ongoing awareness about personal assumptions and cultural encapsulation, including continually questioning assumptions about what is usual or normal with respect to gender.
- Overcome own tendency to diagnose early, or to stop assessing when "usual" understandings are reached.
- Avoid jumping to conclusions about clients on the basis of their cultural group.

Counselor Knowledge

- Know and use only symptom scales validated in the client's culture.
- Acquire knowledge about different cultures' norms and interaction styles.
- Be aware of the wide variations and conflicts that may exist among people from different cultures and the conflicts that may exist between North American law and other cultures' practices.
- Avoid accepting conclusions of research if it does not include lower socioeconomic status, women, non-Whites, and the unemployed.
- Identify sources of cultural information relevant to the clients currently being seen.

Counselor Skills

- Assess the client's cultural identity.
- Assess the cultural meaning of a client's problem and symptoms.
- Understand fully what happens in the mind and body of the person who presents for care (i.e., comprehensive assessment), rather than just identifying a disorder or differentiating one disorder from another.
- Carefully describe and operationalize all relevant phenomena (e.g., individual symptoms, functional abilities, family interactions, contextual factors, and longitudinal historical information).
- Consider the effects of family, work, and community on the development and continuance of the complaint, including stigma and discrimination that may be associated with mental illness in the client's culture.
- Plan treatment collaboratively.
- Incorporate the perspective of clients and their cultures, the practitioner, and significant others, such as friends and family members.
- Work in collaboration with qualified folk healers.
- Conduct feminist clinical assessments, including questions about gender issues and experiences within the client's milieu and experiences of culture and cultural oppression.
- Attend to factors that may influence the expression of gender.
- Question the meaning to the client and to the practitioner of gendered behavior.
- Avoid the error of overdiagnosis and misdiagnosis of gay men, lesbians, African Americans, ethnic minorities, women, and nontraditional men when their behavior does not match Western norms.
- Attend to reports of somatic symptoms (e.g., headache, trouble sleeping, stomach aches), which in most societies indicate depression.

Feminist Analysis

Feminist analysis opposes traditional approaches to diagnosis and treatment that overfocus on idiosyncratic life experiences, biology (neuroscience has become more important in the *DSM-5*), or personality traits as causes of problems, and which in turn hold individuals responsible for solving these problems to too large a degree. Feminists, in contrast, begin from the position that the personal cannot be separated from the political or social, and so make no apologies for envisioning the therapy process as a political process aimed at solving social problems—which they blame for many client problems (Comas-Diaz, 2010).

By continually questioning their own assumptions about what is usual or normal with respect to gender, attending to factors that may influence the expression of gender, and questioning the meaning to both the client and to the counselor of gendered behaviors, counselors can develop an inclusive feminist identity (Baird, Szymanski, & Ruebelt, 2007). Through a feminist clinical assessment, the counselor may, for example, assess what it means to the client to be a failure or a success as a man or a woman within her or his social environment.

Counselors also need to be aware of issues, patterns, or behavior that occur with high frequency in one gender or the other, of the cultural reasons for men and women's positions in a society, and of the impact on men's and women's expressions of distress or types of problems (Eriksen & Kress, 2008). Eriksen and Kress (2008) encouraged counselors to intentionally and directly inquire into life events whose base rates are related to gender (e.g., interpersonal violence, sexual assault, covert discrimination). Use Reflection 18.4 to consider how to address some of feminists' concerns.

Function of Symptoms in Context

Counselors may experience difficulties in fully incorporating social and environmental influences on a client's problem into a *DSM* diagnosis. In fact, from a contextual perspective, we might have difficulties considering any disorder to be located within one individual. It would

---

REFLECTION 18.4

Professional counselors who adhere to a feminist perspective challenge current ways of diagnosing clients. Select one diagnostic challenge identified by the feminist perspective (as listed previously) and make recommendations to address the challenge.

---

seem that counselors who fully consider social and environmental influences will extend their assessments beyond the individual to communities, neighborhoods, and families and will define the "problem" in terms that include such entities (Kress & Paylo, 2015). Where does one find room for such conceptualizations within the medical model?

In fact, systemic counselors may also realize that what the *DSM* considers to be psychopathology is actually a very functional attempt on the client's part to adapt to or cope with a dysfunctional situation (Ivey, Ivey, Myers, & Sweeney, 2005). A compulsively overeating teenager may be offering herself nurturance when she experiences negative emotions because no one in her family is able or willing to comfort her when she needs it. A little boy may hide under his bed and refuse to see or speak to anyone as an escape from incessant parental fighting and abuse. A firefighter may dissociate following the horror of having removed bodies from the collapsed World Trade Center or following the horrors of killings in the war in Afghanistan. Including the context (e.g., rape, incest, abuse, battering) in the diagnostic discussion thus creates a very different diagnostic picture than considering symptoms without the context (e.g., PTSD vs. major depression). Central to the fifth edition of the *DSM* is a focus on the etiology of disorders. Mental health providers are tasked now with "why" a disorder exists and is causing CSDI, instead of merely categorizing "what" the specific abnormality is.

Conceptualizing symptoms as adaptations or coping strategies may also result in a different counselor–client relationship than what emerges within a medical-model relationship. That is, when viewing symptoms as coping strategies that are already being employed, a counselor might acknowledge and recognize the value of the symptom/coping strategy and how the behavior/strategy is serving/helping the client. A counselor is to appreciate all that the client is doing to manage the situation and encourage the client to use the symptom until another, less damaging or more helpful coping strategy becomes apparent. In contrast, when client problems are viewed traditionally, the counselor immediately focuses on how to reduce symptoms, viewing the client's way of handling life as inadequate or as demonstrating deficits (Baumann, 2007). Voices from the Field 18.2 provides an example of how a counselor was able to reframe a client's symptoms as a useful tool in counseling.

Voices from the Field 18.2

A Latina Woman Terrified by the Voices in Her Head

A 45-year-old female, Latina, happily married piano player with successful adult children presented for counseling extremely scared because she "heard voices in her head." Since hearing the voices, she could not sleep and eat, and she felt physically ill and emotionally terrified by the voices. She described the voices as an ongoing narrative that initially came up in her sleep, but continued during the day in an intermittent fashion. A mini-mental status examination revealed she was fully aware of time, date, and place. Drug abuse, dementia, and schizophrenia were ruled out. Furthermore, during the evaluation it was established that there was no other area of concern in her life although I noticed that this consummate piano player, with years of practice, only played for family and friends.

I asked her to maintain a diary of her voices and what they said. She recorded as much as she could and we discussed the content during our sessions. Over a brief period of time a thematic narrative describing childhood experiences became evident, as did her prolific writing abilities and her love of writing. Her voices presented her earlier experiences from the point of view of deceased relatives. "Isn't this what writers do?" I asked. She was first puzzled by the question, but responded she always wanted to do something different than playing the piano, and she had a passion for writing. Early in her life, she took piano lessons because of pressure from her family who believed that this was something an educated Latina woman should do. Writing the narrative in her head helped her to overcome her fear and created an opportunity to engage in a completely different creative venture. She took writing lessons and eventually wrote three successful novels, the first of which captured the voices she heard in her head. The voices, the fear, and the physical symptomatology she had experienced dissipated and she was able to become the artist she wanted to be: not a piano player, but a writer.

~ Carlos P. Zalaquett, Counselor Educator, University Park, Pennsylvania

ACTIVITY 18.5

With two or three of your classmates, discuss how multicultural diagnosis will influence your work as a counselor. In addition, list concerns you may have regarding multiculturalism and diagnosis. After discussing these issues for 20 to 30 minutes, share the highlights of your discussion with the class.

Summary

Diagnosis has become an essential part of a counselor's assessment toolbox, and in today's third-party payer environment, counselors may not receive payment for their services without a diagnosis. Because of the multiple ethical issues associated with diagnosis, counselors should carefully consider how they will engage in ethical diagnostic practices.

For instance, counselors need to carefully consider what to do when traditional diagnostic procedures are not well supported for nondominant client groups. They need to ask themselves how they are to justify using diagnostic codes that have not been validated for nondominant client groups and, in fact, have historically caused harm to some people from nondominant groups. They need to reflect on what to do when third-party payers only recognize certain diagnoses as reimbursable and fail to include culturally specific diagnoses. They need to find and use the diagnostic strategies that are most helpful and least harmful for all of their clients, including those from nondominant groups. Most important, they need to own their professional responsibility to change professional practices that harm those from nondominant groups.

In this chapter, we aimed to challenge readers to think about the hard questions associated with the diagnosis and assessment of those from diverse cultures. Asking these questions and searching for answers is helpful on a number of different levels. For instance, such questions require standing back from our own traditional frame of reference and thinking dialectically (Ivey et al., 2005). When we approach our craft from this developmental perspective and recognize the diverse realities of clients, the chance for successful client outcomes is enhanced (Barrio Minton & Myers, 2008). Some of the introspection that results in better counseling for those from nondominant cultures involves the following:

- Staying aware of and investing in changing societal conditions that harm people psychologically, and committing to changing these systems, rather than merely asking individuals to change.
- Becoming aware of the broader societal influences on *DSM* development, on decisions about what is normal and abnormal, on diagnostic decision making, and on treatment.
- Asking questions about who benefits from diagnosis.
- Increasing our consciousness about the broader social and economic milieus within which we operate.
- Paying constant attention to the impact of these broader milieus on our work.
- Deciding how to balance the benefits of diagnostic practices to the multiple stakeholders.

- Proactively experiencing other cultures to assist in taking our own as object.
- Increasing our cross-cultural experiences and sensitivities.
- Doing a cultural assessment with clients that includes questions about typical help seeking, what "adaptive" looks like, and how illness is explained.
- Considering traditional diagnosis to be only one story among many.

Further, with so many questions being raised about the cultural and gender limitations of diagnoses, it seems more clearly necessary for practitioners to be tentative in diagnosing those from diverse backgrounds, and, as part of a more egalitarian relationship, to co-construct an understanding of the problem *with* the client, rather than imposing a diagnosis *on* the client. The questions about diagnostic accuracy that haunt *all* research on diagnostic reliability and validity apply doubly to counselors who diagnose clients from diverse backgrounds. That is, how can counselors be accurate when assuming only an individual description of a problem, without describing strengths, support systems, and positive characteristics, and without including a broader understanding of the cultural contexts in which the person was raised and in which the person currently resides? Further, how can counselors, when diagnosing, become aware of and take into consideration the impact of culture on *themselves*, which in turn will affect the counseling relationship? Social constructionists indicate that the questions asked while diagnosing tell us more about the *diagnoser* and the culture in which diagnosis takes place, than about the *client* (Conrad & Barker, 2010). In order to maximize the benefits of diagnosis, consider the whole person, and view problems from etiological and contextual perspectives. You can start with comprehensively gathering information and using multiple sources. Consider multicultural factors, and psychosocial stressors that emerge from "isms" such as racism, sexism, classism, etc. and how those can be the cause or exacerbate problem issues. Remember that symptoms and stressors change rapidly, so consider viewing the problem issue over time, and be thoughtful/intentional when differentiating and ultimately selecting a diagnosis. Finally, make sure to include the client in the diagnostic process and resist temptations to overdiagnosis or underdiagnose (Kress & Paylo, 2015).

So, what does culturally sensitive and feminist diagnosis mean? Might it mean *not* diagnosing? Might it mean more broadly assessing the problem situation in conversation with the client, without engaging the *DSM* system? Could it mean using the *DSM* as one, perhaps minor, part of the broader scheme of diagnosis and assessment—a part currently necessary for obtaining funding for services—while considering all the parts of a typical intake interview to be the more important guides to treatment? Might *DSM* diagnosis be considered one story among many and, in the particular case of clients from groups who have historically had less power, might that story be less relevant or more harmful than other stories? Might culturally sensitive and feminist diagnosis require mental health professionals to diagnose and act to change oppressive systems, instead of confining themselves to their offices where they require clients to change? These are difficult questions, but questions that need to be asked, and asked, and asked again as mental health professionals struggle with the ethical dilemmas posed by mandates to be culturally sensitive while engaging in the diagnostic process.

Note: This chapter includes some reorganized information from K. Eriksen and V. Kress (2005), *Beyond the DSM story: Quandaries, challenges and best practices.* Pacific Grove, CA: Sage. Reprinted by permission from Sage Publications.

Review Questions

1. What are at least three things a counselor must understand about a client who is culturally different than herself or himself? What must a counselor understand about himself or herself to be culturally sensitive?
2. In what ways do overdiagnosis, underdiagnosis, misdiagnosis, and sampling bias cause harm to individuals? In what ways can they help people?
3. Consider culture and psychopathology. How are these terms used in the *DSM*? How could they be incorporated better throughout the *DSM*?

4. How do sex bias and socialization potentially cause harm to individuals?
5. What changes or inclusions can be introduced into the *DSM* diagnostic process to make it optimally culturally sensitive? What should be omitted to enhance cultural sensitivity?

APPENDIX

Multicultural and Social Justice Counseling Competencies

Developed by

The Multicultural Counseling Competencies Revisions Committee:
Dr. Manivong J. Ratts, Chair (Seattle University)
Dr. Anneliese A. Singh (University of Georgia)
Dr. Sylvia Nassar-McMillan (North Carolina State University)
Dr. S. Kent Butler (University of Central Florida)
Julian Rafferty McCullough (Georgia State University)

Commissioned by

Dr. Carlos Hipolito-Delgado
President, Association for Multicultural Counseling and Development (2014–2015)
Endorsed on June 29, 2015, by
Association for Multicultural Counseling and Development Executive Council
A Division of the American Counseling Association

MULTICULTURAL AND SOCIAL JUSTICE COUNSELING COMPETENCIES

The Multicultural and Social Justice Counseling Competencies (MSJCC), which revises the Multicultural Counseling Competencies (MCC) developed by Sue, Arredondo, and McDavis (1992) offers counselors and psychologists a framework to implement multicultural and social justice competencies into counseling theories, practices, and research. A conceptual framework (see Figure 1) of the MSJCC is provided to illustrate a visual map of the relationship between the constructs and competencies being articulated within the MSJCC. Moreover, quadrants are used to highlight the intersection of identities and the dynamics of power, privilege, and oppression that influence the counseling relationship. Developmental domains reflect the different layers that lead to multicultural and social justice competence: (1) counselor self-awareness, (2) client worldview, (3) counseling relationship, and (4) counseling and advocacy interventions. Embedded within the first three developmental domains of the MSJCC are the following aspirational competencies: attitudes and beliefs, knowledge, skills, and action (AKSA). The socioecological model is incorporated within the counseling and advocacy interventions domain to provide counselors a multilevel framework for individual counseling and social justice advocacy.

MULTICULTURAL AND SOCIAL JUSTICE COUNSELING COMPETENCIES

I. Counselor Self-Awareness

Privileged and marginalized counselors develop self-awareness, so that they may explore their attitudes and beliefs, develop knowledge, skills, and action relative to their self-awareness and worldview.

1. *Attitudes and beliefs:* Privileged and marginalized counselors are aware of their social identities, social group statuses, power, privilege, oppression, strengths, limitations, assumptions, attitudes, values, beliefs, and biases.

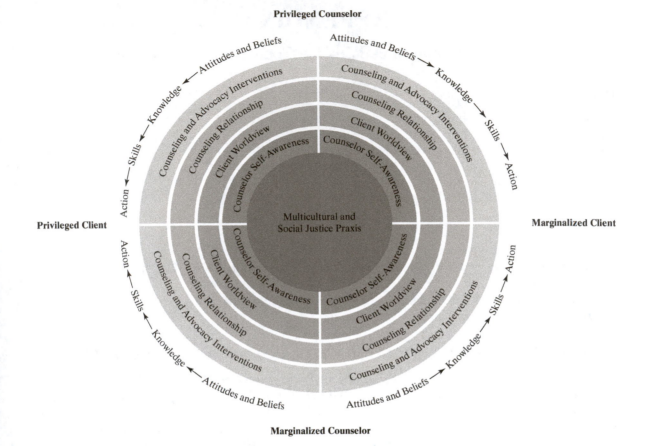

FIGURE 1   Multicultural and Social Justice Counseling Competencies Conceptual Framework.

Source: Multicultural and Social Justice Counseling Competencies Conceptual Framework. Retrieved from: www.multiculturalsocial justicecounselingcompetencies.com. © 2015 By M. J. Ratts, A. A. Singh, S. Nassar-McMillan, & J. R. McCullough. Association for Multicultural Counseling and Development Multicultural Counseling Competencies Revisions Committee.

Multicultural and social justice competent counselors:

- Acknowledge their assumptions, worldviews, values, beliefs, and biases as members of privileged and marginalized groups.
- Acknowledge their privileged and marginalized status in society.
- Acknowledge their privileged and marginalized status influences their worldview.
- Acknowledge their privileged and marginalized status provides advantages and disadvantages in society.
- Acknowledge openness to learning about their cultural background as well as their privileged and marginalized status.

2. *Knowledge:* Privileged and marginalized counselors possess an understanding of their social identities, social group statuses, power, privilege, oppression, strengths, limitations, assumptions, attitudes, values, beliefs, and biases.

Multicultural and social justice competent counselors:

- Develop knowledge of resources to become aware of their assumptions, worldviews, values, beliefs, biases, and privileged and marginalized status.
- Develop knowledge about the history and events that shape their privileged and marginalized status.
- Develop knowledge of theories that explain how their privileged and marginalized status influences their experiences and worldview.
- Develop knowledge of how their privileged and marginalized status leads to advantages and disadvantages in society.

3. *Skills:* Privileged and marginalized counselors possess skills that enrich their understanding of their social identities, social group statuses, power, privilege, oppression, limitations, assumptions, attitudes, values, beliefs, and biases.
   Multicultural and social justice competent counselors:

- Acquire reflective and critical thinking skills to gain insight into their assumptions, worldviews, values, beliefs, biases, and privileged and marginalized status.
- Acquire communication skills to explain how their privileged and marginalized status influences their worldview and experiences.
- Acquire application skills to interpret knowledge of their privileged and marginalized status in personal and professional settings.
- Acquire analytical skills to compare and contrast their privileged and marginalized status and experiences to others.
- Acquire evaluation skills to assess the degree to which their privileged and marginalized status influences their personal and professional experiences.

4. *Action:* Privileged and marginalized counselors take action to increase self-awareness of their social identities, social group statuses, power, privilege, oppression, strengths, limitations, assumptions, attitudes, values, beliefs, and biases.
   Multicultural and social justice competent counselors:

- Take action to learn about their assumptions, worldviews, values, beliefs, biases, and culture as a member of a privileged and marginalized group.
- Take action to seek out professional development opportunities to learn more about themselves as a member of a privileged or marginalized group.
- Take action to immerse themselves in their community to learn about how power, privilege, and oppression influence their privileged and marginalized experiences.
- Take action to learn about how their communication style is influenced by their privileged and marginalized status.

II. Client Worldview

Privileged and marginalized counselors are aware, knowledgeable, skilled, and action-oriented in understanding clients' worldview.

1. *Attitudes and beliefs:* Privileged and marginalized counselors are aware of clients' worldview, assumptions, attitudes, values, beliefs, biases, social identities, social group statuses, and experiences with power, privilege, and oppression.

Multicultural and social justice competent counselors:

- Acknowledge a need to possess a curiosity for privileged and marginalized clients' history, worldview, cultural background, values, beliefs, biases, and experiences.
- Acknowledge that identity development influences the worldviews and lived experiences of privileged and marginalized clients.
- Acknowledge their strengths and limitations in working with clients from privileged and marginalized groups.
- Acknowledge that learning about privileged and marginalized clients may sometimes be an uncomfortable or unfamiliar experience.
- Acknowledge that learning about clients' privileged and marginalized status is a lifelong endeavor.
- Acknowledge the importance of reflecting on the attitudes, beliefs, prejudices, and biases they hold about privileged and marginalized clients.
- Acknowledge that there are within-group differences and between-group similarities and differences among privileged and marginalized clients.
- Acknowledge clients' communication style is influenced by their privileged and marginalized status.

2. *Knowledge:* Privileged and marginalized counselors possess knowledge of clients' worldview, assumptions, attitudes, values, beliefs, biases, social identities, social group statuses, and experiences with power, privilege, and oppression.
Multicultural and social justice competent counselors:

- Develop knowledge of historical events and current issues that shape the worldview, cultural background, values, beliefs, biases, and experiences of privileged and marginalized clients.
- Develop knowledge of how stereotypes, discrimination, power, privilege, and oppression influence privileged and marginalized clients.
- Develop knowledge of multicultural and social justice theories, identity development models, and research pertaining to the worldview, culture, and life experiences of privileged and marginalized clients.
- Develop knowledge of their strengths and limitations in working with clients from privileged and marginalized groups.
- Develop knowledge of how to work through the discomfort that comes with learning about privileged and marginalized clients.
- Develop a lifelong plan to acquire knowledge of clients' privileged and marginalized status.
- Develop knowledge of the attitudes, beliefs, prejudices, and biases they hold about privileged and marginalized clients.
- Develop knowledge of the individual, group, and universal dimensions of human existence of their privileged and marginalized clients.
- Develop knowledge of the communication style of their privileged and marginalized client (e.g., high context vs. low context communication, eye contact, orientation to time and space, etc.).

3. *Skills:* Privileged and marginalized counselors possess skills that enrich their understanding of clients' worldview, assumptions, attitudes, values, beliefs, biases, social identities, social group statuses, and experiences with power, privilege, and oppression.

Multicultural and social justice competent counselors:

- Acquire culturally responsive evaluation skills to analyze how historical events and current issues shape the worldview, cultural background, values, beliefs, biases, and experiences of privileged and marginalized clients.
- Acquire culturally responsive critical thinking skills to gain insight into how stereotypes, discrimination, power, privilege, and oppression influence privileged and marginalized clients.
- Acquire culturally responsive application skills to apply knowledge of multicultural and social justice theories, identity development models, and research to one's work with privileged and marginalized clients.
- Possess culturally responsive assessment skills to identify limitations and strengths when working with privileged and marginalized clients.
- Acquire culturally responsive reflection skills needed to work through the discomfort that comes with learning about privileged and marginalized clients.
- Acquire culturally responsive conceptualization skills to explain how clients' privileged and marginalized status influence their culture, worldview, experiences, and presenting problem.
- Acquire culturally responsive analytical skills to interpret the attitudes, beliefs, prejudices, and biases they hold about privileged and marginalized clients.
- Acquire culturally responsive conceptualization skills to identify the individual, group, and universal dimensions of human existence of privileged and marginalized clients.
- Acquire culturally responsive cross-cultural communication skills to interact with privileged and marginalized clients.

4. *Action:* Privileged and marginalized counselors take action to increase self-awareness of clients' worldview, assumptions, attitudes, values, beliefs, biases, social identities, social group statuses, and experiences with power, privilege, and oppression.
Multicultural and social justice competent counselors:

- Take action by seeking out formal and informal opportunities to engage in discourse about historical events and current issues that shape the worldview, cultural background, values, beliefs, biases, and experiences of privileged and marginalized clients.
- Take action by attending professional development trainings to learn how stereotypes, discrimination, power, privilege, and oppression influence privileged and marginalized clients.
- Take action by applying multicultural and social justice theories, identity development models, and research to one's work with privileged and marginalized clients.
- Take action by assessing one's limitations and strengths when working with privileged and marginalized clients on a consistent basis.
- Take action by immersing oneself in the communities in which privileged and marginalized clients reside to work through the discomfort that comes with learning about privileged and marginalized clients.
- Take action by using language to explain how clients' privileged and marginalized status influence their culture, worldview, experiences, and presenting problem.
- Take action by pursuing culturally responsive counseling to explore the attitudes, beliefs, prejudices, and biases they hold about privileged and marginalized clients.

- Take action by collaborating with clients to identify the individual, group, and universal dimensions of human existence that shape the identities of privileged and marginalized clients.
- Take action by consistently demonstrating cross-cultural communication skills required to effectively interact with privileged and marginalized clients.

III. Counseling Relationship

Privileged and marginalized counselors are aware, knowledgeable, skilled, and action-oriented in understanding how client and counselor privileged and marginalized statuses influence the counseling relationship.

1. *Attitudes and beliefs:* Privileged and marginalized counselors are aware of how client and counselor worldviews, assumptions, attitudes, values, beliefs, biases, social identities, social group statuses, and experiences with power, privilege, and oppression influence the counseling relationship.

   Multicultural and social justice competent counselors:

   - Acknowledge that the worldviews, values, beliefs and biases held by privileged and marginalized counselors and clients will positively or negatively influence the counseling relationship.
   - Acknowledge that counselor and client identity development shapes the counseling relationship to varying degrees for privileged and marginalized clients.
   - Acknowledge that the privileged and marginalized status of counselors and clients will influence the counseling relationship to varying degrees.
   - Acknowledge that culture, stereotypes, discrimination, power, privilege, and oppression influence the counseling relationship with privileged and marginalized group clients.
   - Acknowledge that the counseling relationship may extend beyond the traditional office setting and into the community.
   - Acknowledge that cross-cultural communication is key to connecting with privileged and marginalized clients.

2. *Knowledge:* Privileged and marginalized counselors possess knowledge of how client and counselor worldviews, assumptions, attitudes, values, beliefs, biases, social identities, social group statuses, and experiences with power, privilege, and oppression influence the counseling relationship.

   Multicultural and social justice competent counselors:

   - Develop knowledge of the worldviews, values, beliefs and biases held by privileged and marginalized counselors and clients and its influence on the counseling relationship.
   - Develop knowledge of identity development theories and how they influence the counseling relationship with privileged and marginalized clients.
   - Develop knowledge of theories explaining how counselor and clients' privileged and marginalized statuses influence the counseling relationship.
   - Develop knowledge of how culture, stereotypes, discrimination, power, privilege, and oppression strengthen and hinder the counseling relationship with privileged and marginalized clients.

- Develop knowledge of when to use individual counseling and when to use systems advocacy with privileged and marginalized clients.
- Develop knowledge of cross-cultural communication theories when working with privileged and marginalized clients.

3. *Skills:* Privileged and marginalized counselors possess skills to engage in discussions with clients about how client and counselor worldviews, assumptions, attitudes, values, beliefs, biases, social identities, social group statuses, power, privilege, and oppression influence the counseling relationship.
Multicultural and social justice competent counselors:

- Acquire assessment skills to determine how the worldviews, values, beliefs and biases held by privileged and marginalized counselors and clients influence the counseling relationship.
- Acquire analytical skills to identify how the identity development of counselors and clients influence the counseling relationship.
- Acquire application skills to apply knowledge of theories explaining how counselor and clients' privileged and marginalized statuses influence the counseling relationship.
- Acquire assessment skills regarding how culture, stereotypes, prejudice, discrimination, power, privilege, and oppression influence the counseling relationship with privileged and marginalized clients.
- Acquire evaluation skills to determine when individual counseling or systems advocacy is needed with privileged and marginalized clients.
- Acquire cross-cultural communication skills to connect with privileged and marginalized clients.

4. *Action:* Privileged and marginalized counselors take action to increase their understanding of how client and counselor worldviews, assumptions, attitudes, values, beliefs, biases, social identities, social group statuses, and experiences with power, privilege, and oppression influence the counseling relationship.
Multicultural and social justice competent counselors:

- Take action by initiating conversations to determine how the worldviews, values, beliefs and biases held by privileged and marginalized counselors and clients influence the counseling relationship.
- Take action by collaborating with clients to identify the ways that privileged and marginalized counselor and client identity development influence the counseling relationship.
- Take action by exploring how counselor and clients' privileged and marginalized statuses influence the counseling relationship.
- Take action by inviting conversations about how culture, stereotypes, prejudice, discrimination, power, privilege, and oppression influence the counseling relationship with privileged and marginalized clients.
- Take action by collaborating with clients to determine whether individual counseling or systems advocacy is needed with privileged and marginalized clients.
- Take action by using cross-communication skills to connect with privileged and marginalized clients.

IV. Counseling and Advocacy Interventions

Privileged and marginalized counselors intervene with, and on behalf, of clients at the intrapersonal, interpersonal, institutional, community, public policy, and international/global levels.

A. Intrapersonal: The individual characteristics of a person such as knowledge, attitudes, behavior, self-concept, skills, and developmental history.

Intrapersonal Interventions: Privileged and marginalized counselors address the intrapersonal processes that impact privileged and marginalized clients.
Multicultural and social justice competent counselors:

- Employ empowerment-based theories to address internalized privilege experienced by privileged clients and internalized oppression experienced by marginalized clients.
- Assist privileged and marginalized clients to develop critical consciousness by understanding their situation in context of living in an oppressive society.
- Assist privileged and marginalized clients in unlearning their privilege and oppression.
- Assess the degree to which historical events, current issues, and power, privilege and oppression contribute to the presenting problems expressed by privileged and marginalized clients.
- Work in communities to better understand the attitudes, beliefs, prejudices, and biases held by privileged and marginalized clients.
- Assist privileged and marginalized clients with developing self-advocacy skills that promote multiculturalism and social justice.

Employ quantitative and qualitative research to highlight inequities present in current counseling literature and practices in order to advocate for systemic changes to the profession.

B. Interpersonal: The interpersonal processes and/or groups that provide individuals with identity and support (i.e., family, friends, and peers).

Interpersonal Interventions: Privileged and marginalized counselors address the interpersonal processes that affect privileged and marginalized clients.
Multicultural and social justice competent counselors:

- Employ advocacy to address the historical events and persons that shape and influence privileged and marginalized client's developmental history.
- Examine the relationships privileged and marginalized clients have with family, friends, and peers that may be sources of support or non-support.
- Assist privileged and marginalized clients understand that the relationships they have with others may be influenced by their privileged and marginalized status.
- Assist privileged and marginalized clients with fostering relationships with family, friends, and peers from the same privileged and marginalized group.
- Reach out to collaborate with family, friends, and peers who will be a source of support for privileged and marginalized clients.
- Assist privileged and marginalized clients in developing communication skills to discuss issues of power, privilege, and oppression with family, friends, peers, and colleagues.
- Employ evidence-based interventions that align with the cultural background and worldview of privileged and marginalized clients.

C. Institutional: Represents the social institutions in society such as schools, churches, community organizations.

Institutional Interventions: Privileged and marginalized counselors address inequities at the institutional level.
Multicultural and social justice competent counselors:

- Explore with privileged and marginalized clients the extent to which social institutions are supportive.
- Connect privileged and marginalized clients with supportive individuals within social institutions (e.g., schools, businesses, church, etc.) who are able to help alter inequities influencing marginalized clients.
- Collaborate with social institutions to address issues of power, privilege, and oppression impacting privilege and marginalized clients.
- Employ social advocacy to remove systemic barriers experienced by marginalized clients within social institutions.
- Employ social advocacy to remove systemic barriers that promote privilege that benefit privileged clients.
- Balance individual counseling with systems level social advocacy to address inequities that social institutions create that impede on human growth and development.
- Conduct multicultural and social justice based research to highlight the inequities that social institutions have on marginalized clients and that benefit privileged clients.

D. Community: The community as a whole represents the spoken and unspoken norms, value, and regulations that are embedded in society. The norms, values, and regulations of a community may either be empowering or oppressive to human growth and development.

Community Interventions: Privileged and marginalized address community norms, values, and regulations that impede on the development of individuals, groups, and communities.
Multicultural and social justice competent counselors:

- Take initiative to explore with privileged and marginalized clients regarding how community norms, values, and regulations embedded in society that hinder and contribute to their growth and development.
- Conduct qualitative and quantitative research to evaluate the degree to which community norms, values, and regulations influence privileged and marginalized clients.
- Employ social advocacy to address community norms, values, and regulations embedded in society that hinder the growth and development of privileged and marginalized clients.
- Utilize the norms, values and regulations of the marginalized client to shape the community norms, values, and regulations of the privileged client.

E. Public Policy: Public policy reflects the local, state, and federal laws and policies that regulate or influence client human growth and development.

Public Policy Interventions: Privileged and marginalized counselors address public policy issues that impede on client development with, and on behalf of, clients.
Multicultural and social justice competent counselors:

- Initiate discussions with privileged and marginalized clients on how they shape and are shaped by local, state, and federal laws and policies.

- Conduct research to examine how local, state, and federal laws and policies contribute to or hinder the growth and development of privileged and marginalized clients.
- Engage in social action to alter the local, state, and federal laws and policies that benefit privileged clients at the expense of marginalized clients.
- Employ social advocacy to ensure that local, state, and federal laws and policies are equitable toward privileged and marginalized clients.
- Employ social advocacy outside the office setting to address local, state, and federal laws and policies that hinder equitable access to employment, healthcare, and education for privileged and marginalized clients.
- Assist with creating local, state, and federal laws and policies that promote multiculturalism and social justice.
- Seek out opportunities to collaborate with privileged and marginalized clients to shape local, state, and federal laws and policies.

F. International and Global Affairs: International and global concerns reflect the events, affairs, and policies that influence psychological health and well-being.

International and Global Affairs Interventions: Privileged and marginalized counselors address international and global events, affairs and polices that impede on client development with, and on behalf of, clients.
Multicultural and social justice competent counselors:

- Stay current on international and world politics and events.
- Seek out professional development to learn about how privileged and marginalized clients influence, and are influenced by, international and global affairs.
- Acquire knowledgeable of historical and current international and global affairs that are supportive and unsupportive of privileged and marginalized clients.
- Learn about the global politics, policies, laws, and theories that influence privileged and marginalized clients.
- Utilize technology to interact and collaborate with international and global leaders on issues influencing privileged and marginalized clients.
- Take initiative to address international and global affairs to promote multicultural and social justice issues.
- Utilize research to examine how international and global affairs impact privileged and marginalized clients.

REFERENCES

Abdelhady, D. (2014). The sociopolitical history of Arabs in the United States: Assimilation, ethnicity, and global citizenship. In S. C. Nassar-McMillan, K. A. Ajrouch, & J. Hakim-Larson (Eds.), *Biopsychosocial perspectives on Arab Americans: Culture, development, and health* (pp. 7–16). New York, NY: Springer.

Abe-Kim, J., Takeuchi, D. T., Hong, S., Zane, N., Sue, S., Spencer, M. S., . . . Alegría, M. (2007). Use of mental health–related services among immigrant and US-born Asian Americans: Results from the National Latino and Asian American study. *American Journal of Public Health, 97*, 91–98. doi: 10.2105/AJPH.2006.098541

Aboul-Enein, B. H., & Aboul-Enein, F. H. (2010). The cultural gap delivering health care services to Arab American population in the United States. *Journal of Cultural Diversity, 17*, 20–23.

Acs, G. (2012). *Downward mobility from the middle class: Waking up from the American Dream.* The Pew Charitable Trusts, Economic Mobility Project. Retrieved from http://www.urban.org/research/publication/downward-mobility-middle-class-waking-american-dream

Adamczyk, A., & Cheng, Y. A. (2015). Explaining attitudes about homosexuality in Confucian and non-Confucian nations: Is there a 'cultural' influence? *Social Science Research, 51*, 276–289. doi: 10.1016/j.ssresearch.2014.10.002

Adams, C. M., & Puig, A. (2008). Incorporating yoga into college counseling. *Journal of Creativity in Mental Health, 3*, 357–372. doi: 10.1080/15401380802527456

Adams, G., & Markus, H. R. (2001). Culture as patterns: An alternative approach to the problem of reification. *Culture & Psychology, 7*, 283–296. doi: 10.1177/1354067X0173002

Adams, J. T. (1933). *The epic of America.* New Brunswick, NJ: Transaction Publishers.

Adler, A. (1964). *Individual psychology of Alfred Adler.* New York, NY: Harper Collins.

Agronick, G., O'Donnell, L., Stueve, A., Doval, A. S., Duran, R., & Vargo, S. (2004). Sexual behaviors and risks among bisexually and gay-identified young Latino men. *AIDS and Behavior, 8*, 185–197. doi: 10.1023/B:AIBE.0000030249.11679.d0

Ahmed, S., Kia-Keating, M., & Tsai, K. (2011). A structural model of racial discrimination, acculturative stress, and cultural resources among Arab American adolescents. *American Journal of Community Psychology, 48*, 181–192. doi: 10.1007/s10464-011-9424-3

Ai, A. L., Kastenmüller, A., Tice, T. N., Wink, P., Dillon, M., & Frey, D. (2014). The Connection of Soul (COS) scale: An assessment tool for afterlife perspectives in different worldviews. *Psychology of Religion and Spirituality, 6*, 316–329. doi: 10.1037/a0037455

Ainslie, R. (2011). Immigration and the psychodynamics of class. *Psychoanalytic Psychology, 28*, 560–568. doi: 10.1037/a0025262

Ajrouch, K. J., & Jamal, A. (2007). Assimilating to a White identity: The case of Arab Americans. *The International Migration Review, 41*, 860–879. doi: 10.1111/j.1747-7379.2007.00103.x

Akutsu, P. D., & Chu, J. P. (2006). Clinical problems that initiate professional help-seeking behaviors from Asian Americans. *Professional Psychology: Research and Practice, 37*, 407–415. doi: 10.1037/0735-7028.37.4.407

Albee, G. W. (2006). Historical overview of primary prevention of psychopathology: Address to the 3rd World Conference on the Promotion of Mental Health and Prevention of Mental and Behavioral Disorders, September 15–17, 2004, Auckland, New Zealand. *The Journal of Primary Prevention, 27*, 449–456. doi: 10.1007/s10935-006-0047-7

Albelda, R., Badgett, L., Gates, G. J., & Schneebaum, A. (2013). *Poverty in the lesbian, gay, and bisexual community.* Retrieved from http://williamsinstitute.law.ucla.edu/wp-content/uploads/LGB-Poverty-Update-Jun-2013.pdf

Alexander, M. (2012). *The new Jim Crow: Mass incarceration in the age of colorblindness.* New York, NY: The New Press.

Alexander-Floyd, N. (2014). Beyond superwomen: Justice for black women too. *Dissent, 61*, 42–44. doi: 10.1353/dss.2014.0018

Ali, S. (2014). Identification and approach to treatment of mental health disorders in Asian American populations. In R. Parekh (Ed). *The Massachusetts General Hospital textbook on diversity and cultural sensitivity in mental health. Current clinical psychiatry* (pp. 31–59). Totowa, NJ: Humana Press.

Al-Krenawi, A., & Jackson, S. O. (2014). Arab American marriage: Culture, tradition, religion, and the social worker. *Journal of Human Behavior in the Social Environment, 24*, 115–137. doi: 10.1080/10911359.2014.848679

Allen, J., Mohatt, G. V., Markstrom, C. A., Byers, L., & Novins, D. K. (2012). "Oh no, we are just getting to know you": The relationship in research with children and youth in indigenous communities. *Child Development Perspectives, 6*, 55–60. doi: 10.1111/j.1750-8606.2011.00199.x

Allison, M. (2014). From 'generation auclert' to 'generation ockrent': Convictions, comparisons and continuities. *Modern & Contemporary France, 22*, 143–158. doi: 10.1080/09639489.2014.886826

Altschul, I., Oyserman, D., & Bybee, D. (2006). Racial-ethnic identity in mid-adolescence: Content and change as predictors of academic achievement. *Child Development, 77*, 1155–1169. doi: 10.1111/j.1467-8624.2006.00926.x

Alvarez, A. N., & Chen, G. A. (2012). Ruth as an Asian American: A multicultural and integrative perspective. In G. Corey (Ed.), *Case approach to counseling and psychotherapy* (8th ed., pp. 304–310). Belmont, CA: Cengage.

Alvarez, A. N., & Helms, J. E. (2001). Racial identity and reflected appraisals as influences on Asian Americans' racial adjustment. *Cultural Diversity and Ethnic Minority,* 7, 217–231. doi: 10.1037/1099-9809.7.3.217

Alvarez, A. N., Juang, L., & Liang, C. (2006). Asian Americans and racism: When bad things happen to "model minorities." *Cultural Diversity and Ethnic Minority Psychology,* 12, 477–492. doi: 10.1037/1099-9809.12.3.477

Alvarez, A. N., Liang, C. T., & Neville, H. (in press). *The cost of racism for people of color: Contextualizing experiences of discrimination.* Washington, DC: American Psychological Association.

Alvarez, A. N., & Shin, J. (2013). Asian Americans and racism: Mental health and health consequences. In G. Yoo, M.-H. Le, & A. Y. Oda (Eds.), *Handbook of Asian American health* (pp. 155–172). New York, NY: Springer.

Amer, M. A. (2014). Arab American acculturation and ethnic identity across the lifespan: Sociodemographic correlates and psychological outcomes. In S. C. Nassar-McMillan, K. A. Ajrouch, & J. Hakim-Larson (Eds.), *Biopsychosocial perspectives on Arab Americans: Culture, development, and health* (pp. 89–106). New York, NY: Springer.

American Arab Anti-Discrimination Committee Education. (2012). *Home.* Retrieved from http://www.adc.org/index .php?id=203

American Arab Anti-Discrimination Committee. (2015). *Legal.* Retrieved from http://www.adc.org/legal/

American Association for Counseling and Development (AACD). (1990). *Gerontological competencies for counselors and human development specialists.* Retrieved from http://wellness-research.org/jem_info/docs/competencies .htm

American Civil Liberties Union (ACLU). (2010, June 2). New national security strategy misses the mark. *Daily Kos.* Retrieved from http://www.aclu.org/blog/national-security/new-national-security-strategy-misses-mark

American Civil Liberties Union. (2017). *ACLU.* Retrieved from https://www.aclu.org

American Counseling Association. (2014). *2014 ACA code of ethics.* Retrieved from http://www.counseling.org/docs /ethics/2014-aca-code-of-ethics.pdf?sfvrsn=4

American Immigration Council. (2015). *A guide to the immigration accountability executive action.* Retrieved from http://www.immigrationpolicy.org/special-reports /guide-immigration-accountability-executive-action

American Institute of Bisexuality. (2012). *The Klein Sexual Orientation Grid.* Retrieved from http://www. americaninstituteofbisexuality.org/thekleingrid/

American Psychiatric Association. (1973). Position statement on homosexuality and civil rights. *American Journal of Psychiatry, 131,* 497.

American Psychiatric Association. (2013). *Diagnostic and statistical manual of mental disorders* (5th ed.). Arlington, VA: Author.

American Psychological Association (APA). (2007). *Guidelines for psychological practice with girls and women. American Psychologist, 62,* 949–979. doi: 10.1037/0003-066X.62.9.949

American Psychological Association (APA). (2009). *Report of the American Psychological Association Task Force on Appropriate Therapeutic Responses to Sexual Orientation.* Retrieved from https://www.apa.org/pi/lgbt/resources /therapeutic-response.pdf

American Psychological Association (APA). (2010). *Publication manual of the American Psychological Association* (6th ed.). Washington, DC: Author.

American Psychological Association (APA). (2011). *The guidelines for psychological practice with lesbian, gay, and bisexual clients.* Retrieved from http://www.apa.org/pi /lgbt/resources/guidelines.aspx

American School Counselor Association. (2010). *Ethical standards for school counselors.* Retrieved from http:// www.schoolcounselor.org/asca/media/asca/Resource%20 Center/Legal%20and%20Ethical%20Issues/Sample%20 Documents/EthicalStandards2010.pdf

American School Counselor Association (ASCA). (2014). *The school counselor and LGBTQ youth.* Retrieved from https://www.schoolcounselor.org/asca/media/asca /PositionStatements/PS_LGBTQ.pdf

Ametrano, I. M. (2014). Teaching ethical decision making: Helping students reconcile personal and professional values. *Journal of Counseling & Development, 92,* 154–161. doi: 10.1002/j.1556-6676.2014.00143.x

Amri, S., Nassar-McMillan, S., Amen-Bryan, S., & Misenhimer, M. M. (2013). Counseling Arab Americans. In C. C. Lee (Ed.), *Counseling for diversity* (4th ed., 87–104). Alexandria, VA: American Counseling Association.

Andrade, F. C. (2009). Measuring the impact of diabetes on life expectancy and disability-free life expectancy among older adults in Mexico. *Journals of Gerontology. Series B, Psychological Sciences and Social Sciences, 64B,* S390–S401.

Andrews, M. A., & Boyle, J. S. (2011). *Transcultural concepts in nursing care* (6th ed.). Philadelphia, PA: Lippincott Williams & Wilkins.

Angermeyer, M. C., Matschinger, H., Link, B. G., & Schomerus, G. (2014). Public attitudes regarding individual and structural discrimination: Two sides of the same coin? *Structural Stigma and Population Health, Social Science & Medicine, 103,* 60–66.

Aniciete, D., & Soloski, K.L. (2011). The social construction of marriage and a narrative approach to treatment of intra-relationship diversity. *Journal of Feminist Family Therapy, 23,* 103–126. doi: 10.1080/08952833.2011.576233

Anton, B. S. (2010). Proceedings of the American Psychological Association for the legislative year 2009: Minutes of the annual meeting of the Council of Representatives and minutes of the Board of Directors. *American Psychologist, 65,* 385–475. doi: 10.1037/a0019553

Appleton, S., & Song, L. (2008). Life satisfaction in urban China: Components and determinants. *World Development, 36*(11), 2325–2340. doi: 10.1016/j.worlddev.2008.04.009

Arab American Institute. (2018). *Demographics.* Retrieved from http://www.aaiusa.org/demographics

Arbona, C., & Jimenez, C. (2014). Minority stress, ethnic identity, and depression among Latina/o college students. *Journal of Counseling Psychology, 61,* 162–168. doi: 10.1037/a0034914

Arbona, C., Olvera, N., Rodriguez, N., Hagan, J., Linares, A., & Wiesner, M. (2010). Acculturative stress among documented and undocumented Latino immigrants in the United States. *Hispanic Journal of Behavioral Sciences, 32,* 362–384. doi: 10.1177/0739986310373210

Arredondo, P., Gallardo-Cooper, M., Delgado-Romero, E. A., & Zapata, A. L. (2014). *Culturally responsive counseling with Latinas/os.* Alexandria, VA: American Counseling Association.

Ashraf, A. (2015). *Vicarious trauma and American Muslims: A mixed methods study* (Unpublished doctoral dissertation). North Carolina State University, Raleigh, North Carolina.

Asian Americans Advancing Justice. (2012). *Vincent Chin 30: Standing up then and now.* Retrieved from http://advancing-equality.org/vincent-chin-30-standing-then-and-now

Asian and Pacific Islander Institute on Domestic Violence. (2011). *Statistics on violence against API women.* Retrieved from http://www.apiidv.org/resources/violence-against-api-women.php

Aslan, R. (2011). *No god but God (updated edition): The origins, evolution, and future of Islam.* New York, NY: Random House.

Association for Lesbian, Gay, Bisexual and Transgender Issues in Counseling (ALGBTIC) Transgender Committee. (2010). American Counseling Association Competencies for Counseling with Transgender Clients. *Journal of LGBT Issues in Counseling, 4,* 135–159. doi: 10.1080/15538605.2010.524839

Atladottir, H., Gyllenberg, D., Langridge, A., Sandin, S., Hansen, S., Leonard, H., . . . Parner, E. (2015). The increasing prevalence of reported diagnoses of childhood psychiatric disorders: A descriptive multinational comparison. *European Child & Adolescent Psychiatry, 24,* 173–183. doi: 10.1007/s00787-014-0553-8

Attneave, C. L. (1987). Practical counseling with American Indian and Alaska Native clients. In P. Pedersen (Ed.), *Handbook of cross-cultural counseling and therapy* (pp. 135–140). Westport, CT: Greenwood Press.

Awosan, C. I., Sandberg, J. G., & Hall, C. A. (2011). Understanding the experience of Black clients in marriage and family therapy. *Journal of Marital and Family Therapy, 37,* 153–168. doi: 10.1111/j.1752-0606.2009.00166.x

Bae, S. W., & Kung, W. W. M. (2000). Family intervention for Asian Americans with a schizophrenic patient in the family. *American Journal of Orthopsychiatry, 70,* 532–541. doi: 10.1037/h0087789

Baillargeon, J. E. H. (2014). The help seeking behaviors of students of color: Factors influencing the utilization of mental health resources on a college campus. *Professional Psychology Doctoral Projects.* Paper 31.

Baird, M., Szymanski, D., & Ruebelt, S. (2007). Feminist identity development and practice among male therapists. *Psychology of Men and Masculinity, 8,* 67–78. doi: 10.1037/1524-9220.8.2.67

Baldridge, B. J., Hill, M. L., & Davis, J. E. (2011). New possibilities: (re)engaging Black male youth within community-based educational spaces. *Race, Ethnicity and Education, 14,* 121–136. doi: 10.1080/13613324.2011.531984

Bale, J. (2010). Arabic as a heritage language in the United States. *International Multilingual Research Journal, 4,* 125–151. doi: 10.1080/13613324.2011.531984

Bamberg, M., De Fina, A., & Schiffrin, D. (2011). Discourse and identity construction. In S. Schwartz, K. Luyckx, & V. Vignoles (Eds.) *Handbook of identity theory and research* (pp. 177–199). New York, NY: Springer.

Banks, J. A. (2008). *Teaching strategies for ethnic studies* (8th ed.). Boston, MA: Allyn & Bacon.

Banks, K. H., Murry, T., Brown, N., & Hammond, W. P. (2014). The impact of feminist attitudes on the relation between racial awareness and racial identity. *Sex Roles, 70,* 232–239. doi: 10.1007/s11199-014-0350-3

Bankston, C. L. & Caldas, S. J. (2009). *Public education: America's civil religion.* New York, NY: Columbia University Press.

Barlow, D. H. (Ed.). (2014). *The Oxford handbook of clinical psychology: Updated edition.* Oxford: Oxford University Press.

Banzato, C. E. M. (2008). Critical evaluation of current diagnostic systems. *Indian Journal of Psychiatry, 50,* 155–157. doi: 10.4103/0019-5545.43621

Barnes, D. M. & Meyer, I. H. (2012). Religious affiliation, internalized homophobia, and mental health in lesbians, gay men, and bisexuals. *American Journal of Orthopsychiatry, 82,* 505–515. doi: 10.1111/j.1939-0025.2012.01185.x

Barnes, E. F., Williams, J. M., & Barnes, F. R. (2014). Assessing and exploring racial identity development in therapy: Strategies to use with Black consumers. *Journal of Applied Rehabilitation Counseling, 45,* 11–17.

Barnett, J. E., & Johnson, W. B. (2011). Integrating spirituality and religion into psychotherapy: Persistent dilemmas, ethical issues, and a proposed decision-making process. *Ethics & Behavior, 21,* 147–164. doi: 10.1080/10508422.2011.551471

Barrett, D. C., & Pollack, L. M. (2005). Whose gay community? Social class, sexual self-expression, and gay community involvement. *The Sociological Quarterly, 46,* 437–456. doi: 10.1111/j.1533–8525.2005.00021.x

Barrio Minton, C. A., & Myers, J. E. (2008). Cognitive style and theoretical orientation: Factors affecting intervention style interest and use. *Journal of Mental Health Counseling, 30*, 330–344. doi: 10.17744/mehc.30.4.5626315033866460

Bartlett, R. (1994). *The making of Europe: Conquest, colonialism, and cultural change.* Princeton, NJ: Princeton University Press.

Baum, B. (2008). *The rise and fall of the Caucasian race: A political history of racial identity.* New York, NY: New York University Press.

Baumann, A. E. (2007). Stigmatization, social distance and exclusion because of mental illness: The individual with mental illness as a "stranger." *International Review of Psychiatry, 19*, 131–135. doi: 10.1080/09540260701278739

Baumgardner, J., & Richards, A. (2000). *Manifesta.* New York, NY: Farrar, Straus and Giroux.

Beagan, B. (2007). Experiences of social class: Learning from occupational therapy students. *Canadian Journal of Occupational Therapy, 74*, 125–133.

Beagan, B. L., & Hattie, B. (2015). Religion, spirituality, and LGBTQ identity integration. *Journal of LGBT Issues in Counseling, 9*, 92–117. doi: 10.1080/15538605.2015.1029204

Bearman, S., & Amrhein, M. (2014). Girls, women, and internalized sexism. In E. J. R. David (Ed.), *Internalized oppression: The psychology of marginalized groups* (pp. 191–226). New York, NY: Springer Publishing Company.

Becker, J. (2010). Why do women endorse hostile and benevolent sexism? The role of salient female subtypes and internalization of sexist contents. *Sex Roles, 62*(7/8), 453–467. doi: 10.1007/s11199-009-9707-4

Becker, J. C., & Swim, J. K. (2012). Reducing endorsement of benevolent and modern sexist beliefs: Differential effects of addressing harm versus pervasiveness of benevolent sexism. *Social Psychology, 43*,127–137. doi: 10.1027/1864-9335/a000091

Beemyn, B. G. (2011). Bisexuality. *GLBTQ: An encyclopedia of gay, lesbian, bisexual, transgender, & queer culture.* Retrieved from http://www.glbtq.com/social-sciences/bisex.html

Beiser, M. N., & Hou, F. (2006). Ethnic identity, resettlement stress and depressive affect among Southeast Asian refugees in Canada. *Social Science and Medicine, 63*, 137–150. doi: 10.1016/j.socscimed.2005.12.002

Beitin, B. K., & Aprahamian, M. (2014). Family values and traditions. In S. C. Nassar-McMillan, K. A. Ajrouch, & J. Hakim-Larson (Eds.), *Biopsychosocial perspectives on Arab Americans: Culture, development, and health* (pp. 67–88). New York, NY: Springer.

Bell-Tolliver, L., Burgess, R., & Brock, L. J. (2009). African American therapists working with African American families: An exploration of the strengths perspective in treatment. *Journal of Marital and Family Therapy, 35*, 293–307. doi: 10.1111/j.1752-0606.2009.00117.x

Bem, S. (1974). The measurement of psychological androgyny. *Journal of Cognitive Psychotherapy, 1*, 2–27.

Bemak, F., & Chung, R. C. (2003). Multicultural counseling with immigrant students in schools. In P. B. Pedersen & J. C. Carey (Eds.), *Multicultural counseling in schools: A practical handbook* (2nd ed., pp. 84–101). Boston, MA: Allyn & Bacon.

Bemak, F., & Chung, R. C. Y. (2008). New professional roles and advocacy strategies for school counselors: A multicultural/social justice perspective to move beyond the nice counselor syndrome. *Journal of Counseling & Development, 86*, 372–381.

Bemak, F., & Chung, R. C. Y. (2015). Counseling immigrants and refugees. In P. B. Pedersen, W. J. Lonner, J. G. Draguns, J. E. Trimble, & M. R. Scharrón-del Rio (Eds.), *Counseling across cultures* (pp. 323–346). New York, NY: Sage Publications.

Bemporad, J. R. (1997). Cultural and historical aspects of eating disorders. *International Journal of Eating Disorders, 17*, 147–152. doi: 10.1023/A:1005721808534

Bergman, J. (2005, June 22). Drugs, disease, denial. *New York Press, 18*(25). Retrieved from http://www.nypress.com

Bernasconi, R. (2012). Crossed lines in the racialization process: Race as a border concept. *Research in Phenomenology, 42*, 206–228. doi: 10.1163/156916412X651201

Berry, J. W. (2003). Conceptual approaches to acculturation. In K. Chun, P. Balls-Organista, & G. Marin (Eds.), *Acculturation: Advances in theory, measurement and applied research* (pp. 17–37). Washington, DC: APA Press.

Bethea, S., & Allen, T. (2013). Past and present societal influences on African American couples that impact love and intimacy. In K. M. Helms, & J. Carlson (Eds.), *Love, intimacy, and the African American couple* (pp. 20–59). New York, NY: Routledge/Taylor & Francis Group.

Bhugra, D., & Kalra, G. (2010). Cross cultural psychiatry: Context and issues. *Journal of Pakistan Psychiatric Society, 7*(2), 51–54.

Bidell, M. P. (2011). School counselors and social justice advocacy for lesbian, gay, bisexual, transgender, and questioning students. *Journal of School Counseling, 9*. Retrieved from http://www.eric.ed.gov/PDFS/EJ933176.pdf

Bidell, M. P. (2014). Are multicultural courses addressing disparities? Exploring multicultural and affirmative lesbian, gay, and bisexual competencies of counseling and psychology students. *Journal of Multicultural Counseling and Development, 42*, 132–146. doi: 10.1002/j.2161-1912.2014.00050.x

Bien, T. (2011). *The Buddha's way of happiness: Healing sorrow, transforming negative emotion, and finding well-being in the present moment.* Oakland, CA: New Harbinger.

BigFoot, D. S., & Funderburk, B. W. (2011). Honoring children, making relatives: The cultural translation of Parent-Child Interaction Therapy for American Indian and Alaska Native families. *Journal of Psychoactive Drugs, 43*, 309–318. doi: 10.1080/02791072.2011.628924

Binning, K. R., Unzueta, M. M., Huo, Y. J., & Molina, L. E. (2009). The interpretation of multiracial status and its relation to social engagement and psychological well-being. *Journal of Social Issues, 65*, 35–49. doi: 10.1111/j.1540-4560.2008.01586.x

Black, M. C., Basile, K. C., Breiding, M. J., Smith, S. G., Walters, M. L., Merrick, M. T., . . . Stevens, M. R. (2011). *The National Intimate Partner and Sexual Violence Survey (NISVS): 2010 summary report.* Atlanta, GA: National Center for Injury Prevention and Control, Centers for Disease Control and Prevention.

Black Lives Matter Guiding Principles. (2017). *Guiding principles.* Retrieved from http://blacklivesmatter.com /guiding-principles/

Blaise, M. (2009). What a girl wants, what a girl needs. Responding to sex, gender, and sexuality in the early childhood classroom. *Journal of Research in Childhood Education, 23*, 450–460. doi: 10.1080/02568540909594673

Bobbio, A., Canova, L., & Manganelli, A. M. (2010). Conservative ideology, economic conservatism, and causal attributions for poverty and wealth. *Current Psychology, 29*, 222–234. doi: 10.1007/s12144-010-9086-6

Boeree, G. C. (2007). *Personality disorders.* Retrieved from http://webspace.ship.edu/cgboer/persdisorders.html

Booker, C. L., & Sacker, A. (2011). Psychological well-being and reactions to multiple unemployment events: Adaption or sensitization? *Journal of Epidemiology and Community Health.* Advance online publication. doi:10.1136/jech.2010.126755

Boss, P. (2010). The trauma and complicated grief of ambiguous loss. *Pastoral Psychology, 59*, 137–145. doi: 10.1007/s 11089-009-0264-0

Bowers, R., Minichiello, V., & Plummer, D. (2010). Religious attitudes, homophobia, and professional counseling. *Journal of LGBT Issues in Counseling, 4*, 70–91. doi: 10.1080/15538605.2010.481961

Bowling Green State University. (2011, November 3). *First-time divorce rate tied to education, race.* Retrieved from http:// www.sciencedaily.com/releases/2011/11/111103161830.htm.

Boyd-Franklin, N. (2013). *Black families in therapy: Understanding the African American experience.* New York, NY: Guilford Press.

Boyd-Franklin, N., & Hafer-Bry, B. (2001). *Reaching out in family therapy: Home-based, school, and community interventions.* New York, NY: Guilford Press.

Boysen, G. A. (2010). Integrating implicit bias into counselor education. *Counselor Education & Supervision, 49*, 210–227. doi: 10.1002/j.1556-6978.2010.tb00099.x

Boysen, G. A., Fisher, M., DeJesus, M., Vogel, D. L., & Madon, S. (2011). The mental health stereotype about gay men: The relation between gay men's self-stereotype and stereotypes about heterosexual women and lesbians. *Journal of Social and Clinical Psychology, 30*, 329–360. doi: 10.1521/jscp.2011.30.4.329

Boysen, G. A., Vogel, D. L., Madon, S., & Wester, S. R. (2006). Mental health stereotypes about gay men. *Sex Roles, 54*, 69–82. doi: 10.1007/s11199-006-8870-0

Bratter, J. L., & King, R. B. (2008). "But will it last?": Marital instability among interracial and same-race

couples. *Family Relations, 57*, 160–171. doi: 10.1111/j.1741-3729.2008.00491.x

Brave Heart, M. Y. H. (2000). Wakiksuyapi: Carrying the historical trauma of the Lakota. *Tulane Studies in Social Welfare, 21–22*, 245–266.

Brave Heart, M. Y. H. (2003). The historical trauma response among Natives and its relationship with substance abuse: A Lakota illustration. *Journal of Psychoactive Drugs, 35*, 7–13.

Brave Heart, M. Y. H. (2005). *Substance abuse, co-occurring mental health disorders, and the historical trauma response among American Indians/Alaska Natives.* Research Monograph, Bureau of Indian Affairs, DASAP, Washington, DC.

Brendtro, L. K., Brokenleg, M., & Van Bockern, S. (2009). *Reclaiming youth at risk: Our hope for the future.* Bloomington, IN: National Education Service.

Brinkman, B. G., Jedinak, A., Rosen, L. A., & Zimmerman, T. S. (2011). Teaching children fairness: Decreasing gender prejudice among children. *Analyses of Social Issues & Public Policy, 11*, 61–81. doi: 10.1111/j.1530-2415.2010.01222.x

Brodkin, K. (2007). *Making democracy matter: Identity and activism in Los Angeles.* Piscataway, NJ: Rutgers University Press.

Bronfenbrenner, U. (1979). *The ecology of human development; Experiments by nature and design.* Cambridge, MA: Harvard University Press.

Brown, C. G. (2011). Sex, religion, and the single woman 1950–75: The importance of a 'short' sexual revolution to the English religious crisis of the sixties. *Twentieth Century British History, 22*, 189–215. doi: 10.1093/tcbh/hwq048

Brown, D. W. (2009). *A new introduction to Islam* (2nd ed.). New York, NY: Wiley Blackwell.

Brown, E., Raue, P., & Halpert, K. (2009). Detection of depression in older adults with dementia. *Journal of Gerontological Nursing, 35*, 11–15. doi: 10.3928/00989134-20090201-08

Brown, M. J., & Groscup, J. L. (2009). Homophobia and acceptance of stereotypes about gays and lesbians. *Individual Differences Research, 7*, 159–167.

Brubaker, M. D., Harper, A., & Singh, A. A. (2011). Implementing multicultural-social justice leadership strategies when advocating for the rights of lesbian, gay, bisexual, transgender, queer, and questioning persons. *Journal for Social Action in Counseling and Psychology, 3*, 44–58.

Bryant, W. W. (2011). Internalized racism's association with African American male youth's propensity for violence. *Journal of Black Studies, 42*, 690–707. doi: 10.1177/0021934710393243

Bryant-Davis, T., Ullan, S., Tsong, Y., Anderson, G., Counts, P., Tillman, S., . . . Gray, A. (2015). Healing pathways: Longitudinal effects of religious coping and social support on PTSD symptoms in African American sexual assault survivors. *Journal of Trauma & Dissociation, 16*, 114–128.

Buddha Dharma Education Association. (2018). *Buddhist information and education network.* Retrieved from http://www.buddhanet.net/aboutus.htm

Bullough, V. L. (2018). Homophobia. *GLBTQ: An encyclopedia of gay, lesbian, bisexual, transgender, & queer culture.* Retrieved from http://www.glbtq.com/social-sciences/homophobia.html

Burgess, D. J., Ding, Y., Hargreaves, M., Ryn, M., & Phelan, S. (2008). The association between perceived discrimination and underutilization of needed medical and mental health care in a multi-ethnic community sample. *Journal of Health Care for the Poor and Underserved, 19*, 894–911. doi: 10.1353/hpu.0.0063

Burgess, D., Lee, R., Tran, A., & van Ryn, M. (2008). Effects of perceived discrimination on mental health and mental health services utilization among gay, lesbian, bisexual and transgender persons. *Journal of LGBT Health Research, 3*(4), 1–14. doi: 10.1080/15574090802226626

Burns, J. S. (Writer), & Anderson, B. (Director). (2007). Marge the gamer [Television series episode]. In J. L. Brooks, M. Groening, & S. Simon (Producers), *The Simpsons.* Los Angeles: 20th Century Fox Television.

Burrow-Sánchez, J. J., Meyers, K., Corrales, C., & Ortiz-Jensen, C. (2015). The influence of cultural variables on treatment retention and engagement in a sample of Mexican American adolescents males with substance use disorders. *Psychology of Addictive Behaviors* [online]. doi: 10.1037/adb0000096

Burton, L. M., Bonilla-Silva, E., Ray, V., Buckelew, R., & Hordge Freeman, E. (2010). Critical race theories, colorism, and the decade's research on families of color. *Journal of Marriage and Family, 72*, 440–459. doi: 10.1111/j.1741-3737.2010.00712.x

Buse, N. A., Buker, E. J., & Bernacchio, C. (2013). Cultural variation in resilience as a response to traumatic experience. *Journal of Rehabilitation, 79*, 15–23.

Byars-Winston, A. (2010). The vocational significance of Black identity: Cultural formulation approach to career assessment and career counseling. *Journal of Career Development, 37*, 441–464. doi: 10.1177/0894845309345847

Byng, M. (2012). You can't get there from here: A social process theory of racism and race. *Critical Sociology, 39*, 705–715. doi: 10.1177/0896920512453180

Byrd, C. M., & Chavous, T. (2011). Racial identity, school racial climate, and school intrinsic motivation among African American youth: The importance of person-context congruence. *Journal of Research on Adolescence, 21*, 849–860. doi: 10.1111/j.1532-7795.2011.00743.x

Cable News Network. (2014). *Five disturbing stats on Black-White inequality.* Retrieved from http://money.cnn.com/2014/08/21/news/economy/black-white-inequality/

Cabral, R. R., & Smith, T. B. (2011). Racial/ethnic matching of clients and therapists in mental health services: A meta-analytic review of preferences, perceptions, and outcomes. *Journal of Counseling Psychology, 58*, 537–554. doi: 10.1037/a0025266

Cabrera, N. L., & Padilla, A. M. (2004). Entering and succeeding in the "culture of college": The story of two Mexican heritage students. *Hispanic Journal of Behavioral Sciences, 26*, 152–170. doi: 10.1177/0739986303262604

Cainkar, L., & Ghazal Read, J. (2014). Arab Americans and gender. In S. C. Nassar-McMillan, K. A. Ajrouch, & J. Hakim-Larson (Eds.). *Biopsychosocial perspectives on Arab Americans: Culture, development, and health* (pp. 89–106). New York, NY: Springer.

Callis, A. S. (2014). Bisexual, pansexual, queer: Non-binary identities and the sexual borderlands. *Sexualities, 17*, 63–80. doi: 10.1177/1363460713511094

Camorato, S. A. (2011). *A record-setting decade of immigration: 2000–2010.* Retrieved from http://www.cis.org/2000-2010-record-setting-decade-of-immigration

Cameron, S. C., & Wycoff, S. M. (1998). The destructive nature of the term race: Growing beyond a false paradigm. *Journal of Counseling & Development, 76*, 277–285.

Camp, S. M. H. (2015). Black is beautiful: An American history. *Journal of Southern History, 81*, 675–690.

Canino, G., & Alegría, M. (2008). Psychiatric diagnosis—is it universal or relative to culture? *The Journal of Child Psychology and Psychiatry, 49*, 237–250. doi: 10.1111/j.1469-7610.2007.01854.x

Cannon, E. P. (2008). Promoting moral reasoning and multicultural competence during internship. *Journal of Moral Education, 37*(4), 503–518. doi: 10.1080/03057240802399384

Cannon, E., Wiggins, M., Poulsen, S., & Estrada, D. (2012). Addressing heterosexist privilege during orientation: One program's experience. *Journal of LGBT Issues in Counseling, 6*, 3–17. doi: 10.1080/15538605.2011.598225

Caplan, P. J. (2006). *Psychiatric labels plague women's mental health.* Retrieved from http://womensnews.org/story/mental-health/060516/psychiatric-labels-plague-womens-mental-health

Caplan, S. (2007). Latinos, acculturation, and acculturative stress: A dimensional concept analysis. *Policy, Politics, and Nursing Practice, 8*, 93–106. doi: 10.1177/1527154407301751

Capriccioso, R. (2005). *Indian education under the microscope.* Retrieved from http://sparkaction.org/content/native-american-education-under-microscope

Carei, T. R., Fyfe-Johnson, A. L., Breuner, C. C., & Brown, M. A. (2010). Randomized controlled clinical trial of yoga in the treatment of eating disorders. *Journal of Adolescent Health, 46*, 346–351. doi: 10.1016/j.jadohealth.2009.08.007

Carlisle, S. K. (2015). Perceived discrimination and chronic health in adults from nine ethnic subgroups in the USA. *Ethnicity and Health, 20*, 309–326. doi: 10.1080/13557858.2014.921891

Carnes, T., & Yang, F. (2004). *Asian American religions: The making and remaking of borders and boundaries.* New York, NY: New York University Press.

Carroll, L. (2001). Teaching "outside the box": Incorporating queer theory in counselor education. *Journal of*

Humanistic Counseling, Education, and Development, 40, 49–57. doi: 10.1002/j.2164-490X.2001.tb00101.x

Carter, M. M., Mitchell, F. E., & Sbrocco, T. (2012). Treating ethnic minority adults with anxiety disorders: Current status and future recommendations. *Journal of Anxiety Disorders, 26,* 488–501. doi: 10.1016/j.janxdis.2012.02.002

Carter, P. L., & Weiner, K. G. (2013). *Closing the opportunity gap.* Oxford, UK: Oxford University Press.

Casas, J. M., Furlong, M. J., & Ruiz de Esparza, C. (2003). Increasing Hispanic parent participation in schools: The role of the counselor. In P. B. Pedersen & J. C. Carey (Eds.), *Multicultural counseling in the schools: A practical handbook* (pp. 105–130). Boston, MA: Allyn & Bacon.

Case, K. A., Iuzzini, J., & Hopkins, M. (2012). Systems of privilege: Intersections, awareness, and applications. *Journal of Social Issues, 68,* 1–10. doi: 10.1111/j.1540-4560.2011.01732.x

Cashwell, C. S. (2005). Spirituality and wellness. In J. E. Myers & T. J. Sweeney (Eds.), *Counseling for wellness: Theory, research, and practice* (pp. 197–206). Alexandria, VA: American Counseling Association.

Cashwell, C. S., Bentley, D. P., & Yarborough, J. P. (2007). The only way out is through: The peril of spiritual bypass. *Counseling and Values, 51,* 139–148.

Cashwell, C. S., & Marszalek, J. (2007, March). *Spiritual identity of lesbians, gay men, and bisexuals: Implications for counseling.* Paper presented at the meeting of the American Counseling Association, Detroit, MI.

Cashwell, C. S., Myers, J. E., & Shurts, M. (2004). Using the Developmental Counseling and Therapy Model to work with clients in spiritual bypass: Some preliminary considerations. *Journal of Counseling & Development, 82,* 403–409.

Cashwell, C. S., & Watts, R. E. (2010). The new ASERVIC competencies for addressing spiritual and religious issues in counseling. *Counseling and Values, 55,* 2–5.

Cashwell, C. S., & Young, J. S. (2011). *Integrating spirituality and religion into counseling: A guide to competent practice* (2nd ed.). Alexandria, VA: American Counseling Association.

Cashwell, C. S., Young, J. S., Fulton, C., Willis, B. T., Giordano, A. L., Wyatt, L. L., . . . Welch, M. (2013). Clinical behaviors for addressing religious/spiritual issues: Do we "practice what we preach?" *Counseling and Values, 58,* 45–58.

Cashwell, C. S., & Young, J. S. (2014). *Integrating spirituality and religion into counseling: A guide to competent practice.* New York, NY: John Wiley.

Cass, V. C. (1979). Homosexual identity formation: A theoretical model. *Journal of Homosexuality, 4,* 219–235. doi: 10.1300/J082v04n03_01

Cass, V. C. (1990). The implications of homosexual identity formation for the Kinsey model and scale of sexual preference. In D. P. McWhirter, S. A. Sanders, & J. M. Reinisch (Eds.), *Homosexuality/heterosexuality: Concepts of sexual orientation* (pp. 239–266). New York, NY: Oxford University Press.

Castellanos, J., Gloria, A. M., Kim, S. C., & Park, Y. S. (2014). The expression of depressive symptomatology in Korean American undergraduates: Sex and generational differences. *Journal of College Counseling, 17,* 208–221. doi: 10.1002/j.2161-1882.2014.00058.x

Castillo, R. J. (1997). *Culture and mental illness: A client centered approach.* Pacific Grove, CA: Brooks/Cole.

Cavanaugh, J. C., & Blanchard-Fields, F. (Eds.). (2014). *Adult development and aging* (7th ed.). Belmont, CA: Cengage.

Center for American Progress. (2014). *RELEASE: Teachers have lower expectations for students of color and students from low-income backgrounds.* Retrieved from https://www.americanprogress.org/press/release/2014/10/06/98317/release-teachers-have-lower-expectations-for-students-of-color-and-students-from-low-income-backgrounds/

Center on Budget and Policy Priorities. (2015). *Policy basics: An introduction to TANF.* Retrieved from http://www.cbpp.org/research/policy-basics-an-introduction-to-tanf

Centers for Disease Control and Prevention. (2013). *CDC health disparities and inequalities report—United States, 2013.* Retrieved from http://www.cdc.gov/mmwr/pdf/other/su6203.pdf.

Centers for Disease Control. (2015). *National marriage and divorce rate trends.* Retrieved from http://www.cdc.gov/nchs/nvss/marriage_divorce_tables.htm

Centers for Disease Control and Prevention (CDC). (2017). *Lesbian, gay, bisexual, and transgender health.* Retrieved from http://www.cdc.gov/lgbthealth/youth.htm

Central Intelligence Agency (CIA). (2018). *Publications: The World Factbook. country comparisons: Distribution of family income—Gini index.* Retrieved from https://www.cia.gov/library/publications/the-world-factbook/rankorder/2172rank.html

Chambers, J. R., Swan, L. K., & Heesacker, M. (2015). Perceptions of U.S. social mobility are divided (and distorted) along ideological lines. *Psychological Science, 26,* 413–423. doi: 10.1177/0956797614566657

Chandler, M. J., Lalonde, C., Sokol, B., & Hallett, D. (2003). Personal persistence, identity development, and suicide: A study of native and non-native North American adolescents. *Monographs of the Society for Research in Child Development, Serial no. 273, 68*(2).

Chaney, M. P., & Brubaker, M. (2014). The impact of substance abuse and addiction in the lives of gay men, adolescents, and boys. In M. M. Kocet (Ed.), *Counseling gay men, adolescents, and boys: A strengths-based guide for helping professionals and educators.* New York, NY: Routledge.

Chang, C. Y., Crethar, H. C., & Ratts, M. J. (2010). Social justice: A national imperative for counselor education and supervision. *Counselor Education & Supervision, 50,* 82–87. doi: 10.1002/j.1556-6978.2010.tb00110.x

Chang, C. Y., Hays, D. G., & Milliken, T. (2009). Addressing social justice issues in supervision: A call for client and professional advocacy. *The Clinical Supervisor, 28,* 20–35. doi: 10.1080/07325220902855144

Chang, D. F., Shen, B. J., & Takeuchi, D. T. (2009). Prevalence and demographic correlates of intimate partner violence in Asian Americans. *International Journal of Law and Psychiatry, 32*, 167–175. doi: 10.1016/j.ijlp.2009.02.004

Chang, J., & Smith, S. R. (2015). An exploration of how Asian Americans respond on the Personality Assessment Inventory. *Asian American Journal of Psychology, 6*, 25–30. doi: 10.1037/a0036173

Chao, R. C. (2012). Racial/ethnic identity, gender-role attitudes, and multicultural counseling competence: The role of multicultural counseling training. *Journal of Counseling & Development, 90*, 35–44. doi: 10.1111/j.1556-6676.2012.00006.x

Chao, R. C.-L., & Nath, S. R. (2011). The role of ethnic identity, gender roles, and multicultural training in college counselors' multicultural counseling competence: A mediation model. *Journal of College Counseling, 14*, 50–64. doi: 10.1002/j.2161-1882.2011.tb00063.x

Chapman, A. B. (2007). In search of love and commitment: Dealing with the challenging odds of finding romance. In H. P. McAdoo (Ed.), *Black families* (pp. 97–124). Thousand Oaks, CA: Sage Publications.

Chappell, N. L., & Cooke, H. A. (2018). Age related disabilities—Aging and quality of life. In J. H. Stone & M. Blouin (Eds.), *International encyclopedia of rehabilitation*. Retrieved from http://cirrie.buffalo.edu/encyclopedia/en/-article/189/

Chaudoir, S., & Quinn, D. (2010). Bystander sexism in the intergroup context: The impact of cat-calls on women's reactions towards men. *Sex Roles, 62*, 623–634. doi: 10.1007/s11199-009-9735-0

Chavira, D. A., Bustos, C. E., Garcia, M. S., Ng, B., & Camacho, A. (2015). Delivering CBT to rural Latino children with anxiety disorders: A qualitative study. *Community Mental Health Journal* [on-line]. doi:10.1007/s10597-015-9903-3

Cheah, C. S. L., Leung, C. Y. Y., Tahseen, M., & Schultz, D. (2009). Authoritative parenting among immigrant Chinese mothers of preschoolers. *Journal of Family Psychology, 23*, 311–320. doi: 10.1037/a0015076

Chen, C. P. (2010). Morita therapy and its counseling implications for social anxiety. *Counselling Psychology Quarterly, 23*, 67–82. doi: 10.1080/09515071003629805

Chen, S., Sullivan, N. Y., Lu, Y. E., & Shibusawa, T. (2003). Asian Americans and mental health services: A study of utilization patterns in the 1990s. *Journal of Ethnic & Cultural Diversity in Social Work, 12*, 19–42. doi: 10.1300/J051v12n02_02

Cheng, J. K. Y., Fancher, T. L., Ratanasen, M., Conner, K. R., Duberstein, P. R., Sue, S., & Takeuchi, D. (2010). Lifetime suicidal ideation and suicide attempts in Asian Americans. *Asian American Journal of Psychology 1*, 18–30. doi: 10.1037/a0018799

Cheng, C., & Lee, F. (2009). Multiracial identity integration: Perceptions of conflict and distance among multiracial individuals. *Journal of Social Issues, 65*(1), 51–68. doi: 10.1111/j.1540-4560.2008.01587.x

Cheng, C.-Y., Lee, F., & Benet-Martínez, V. (2006). Assimilation and contrast effects in cultural frame switching: Bicultural identity integration and valence of cultural cues. *Journal of Cross-Cultural Psychology, 37*, 742–760. doi: 10.1177/0022022106292081

Cheng, H., Kwan, K. K., & Sevig, T. (2013). Racial and ethnic minority college students' stigma associated with seeing psychological help: Examining psychocultural correlates. *Journal of Counseling Psychology, 60*, 98–111. doi: 10.1037/a0031169

Cheng, H., Lin, S., & Cham C. H. (2015). Perceived discrimination, intergenerational family conflicts, and depressive symptoms in foreign-born and U.S.-born Asia American emerging adults. *Asian American Journal of Psychology, 6*, 107–116. doi: 10.1037/a0038710

Cheng, P. S. (2011). Gay Asian masculinities and Christian theologies. *Cross Currents, 61*, 540–548. doi: 10.1111/j.1939-3881.2011.00202.x

Chernin, J. N., & Johnson, M. R. (2002). *Affirmative psychotherapy and counseling for lesbians and gay men*. Thousand Oaks, CA: Sage Publications.

Cheryan, S., & Monin, B. (2005). Where are you really from?: Asian Americans and identity denial. *Journal of Personality and Social Psychology, 89*, 717–730. doi: 10.1037/0022-3514.89.5.717

Cheryan, S., & Tsai, J. L. (2007). Ethnic identity. In F. T. Leong, A. G. Inman, A. Ebreo, L. H. Yang, L. Kinoshita, & M. Fu (Eds.), *Handbook of Asian American psychology* (2nd ed., pp. 125–139). Thousand Oaks, CA: Sage Publications.

Chetty, R., Hendren, N., Kline, P., & Saez, E. (2014). Where is the land of opportunity? The geography of intergenerational mobility in the United States. *Quarterly Journal of Economics, 129*, 1553–1623. doi: 10.1093/qje/qju022

Chetty, R., Hendren, N., Kline, P., Saez, E., & Turner, N. (2014). Is the United States still a land of opportunity? Recent trends in intergenerational mobility. *American Economic Review Papers and Proceedings 104*(5), 141–147.

Childstats. (2014). *America's children: Key national indicators of well-being, 2014*. Retrieved from http://www.childstats.gov/americaschildren/index3.asp

Child Welfare League of America. (2018). *Our story*. Retrieved from http://www.cwla.org/about-us/history/

Chito Childs, E. (2005). *Navigating interracial borders: Black-White couples and their social worlds*. New Brunswick, NJ: Rutgers University Press.

Chödrön, P. (2013). *How to meditate: A practical guide to making friends with your mind*. Louisville, CO: Sounds True.

Choi, K., Paul, J., Ayala, G., Boylan, R., & Gregorich, S. E. (2013). Experiences of discrimination and their impact on the mental health among African American, Asian and Pacific Islander, and Latino men who have sex with men. *American Journal of Public Health, 103*, 868–874. doi: 10.2105/AJPH.2012.301052

Choney, S. K., Berryhill-Paapke, E., & Robbins, R. (1995). The acculturation of American Indians: Developing frameworks for research and practice. In J. G. Ponterotto,

J. M. Casas, L. A. Suzuki, & C. M. Alexander (Eds.), *Handbook of multicultural counseling* (pp. 73–92). Thousand Oaks, CA: Sage Publications.

Choudhuri, D. D., Santiago-Rivera, A. L., & Garrett, M. T. (2012). *Counseling and diversity: Central concepts and themes for competent practice.* Boston, MA: Cengage/Lahaska Press.

Chu, J. A. (2011). *Rebuilding shattered lives: Treating complex PTSD and dissociative disorders.* Hoboken, NJ: John Wiley & Sons.

Chung, H., Teresi, J., Guarnaccia, P., Meyers, B., Holmes, D. Bobrowiz, T., . . . Ferran, E. (2003). Depressive symptoms and psychiatric distress in low income Asian and Latino primary care patients: Prevalence and recognition. *Community Mental Health Journal, 39,* 33–46. doi: 10.1023/A:1021221806912

Chung, R. C., & Bemak, F. (2007). Asian immigrants and refugees. In F. Leong, A. G. Inman, A. Ebreo, L. Lang, L. Kinoshita, & M. Fu (Eds.), *Handbook of Asian American psychology* (2nd ed., pp. 227–244). Thousand Oaks, CA: Sage Publications.

Chung, R. C., & Bemak, F. (2011). *Social justice counseling: The next steps beyond multiculturalism.* Thousand Oaks, CA: Sage Publications.

Chung, R. C.-Y., & Bemak, F. P. (2012). *Social justice counseling: The next steps beyond multiculturalism.* Thousand Oaks, CA: Sage Publications.

Chung, R. C.-Y., Bemak, F., & Kudo Grabosky, T. (2011). Multicultural-social justice leadership strategies: Counseling and advocacy with immigrants. *Journal of Social Action in Psychology and Counseling, 3,* 86–102.

Chung, Y. B., & Katayama, M. (1998). Ethnic and sexual identity development of Asian-American lesbian and gay adolescents. *Professional School Counseling, 1,* 21–25.

Chung, Y. B., & Singh, A. A. (2008). Lesbian, gay, bisexual, and transgender Asian Americans. In A. Alvarez & N. Tewari (Eds.), *Asian American psychology: Current perspectives* (pp. 233–246). Mahwah, NJ: Erlbaum.

Cifti, A., Jones, N., & Corrigan, P. (2013). Mental health stigma in the Muslim community. *Journal of Mental Health, 7,* 1–16.

City of Calgary. (2012). *Summary of living wage ordinance provisions in the United States.* Retrieved from http://homelesshub.ca/sites/default/files/lwp_review_living_wage_ordinance_provisions.pdf

Clance, P. C. (1985). *The impostor phenomenon: When success makes you feel like a fake.* New York, NY: Bantam Books.

Clemente, R., & Collison, B. B. (2000). The relationship among counselors, ESL teachers, and students. *Professional School Counseling, 3,* 339–349.

Coatsworth, J. D., Maldonado-Molina, M., Pantin, H., & Szapocznik, J. (2005). A person-centered and ecological investigation of acculturation strategies in Hispanic immigrant youth. *Journal of Community Psychology, 33,* 157–174. doi: 10.1002/jcop.20046

Cochran, S. D., Mays, V. M., Alegria, M., Ortega, A. N., & Takeuchi, D. (2007). Mental health and substance use disorders among Latino and Asian American lesbian, gay, and bisexual adults. *Journal of Consulting and Clinical Psychology, 75,* 785–794. doi: 10.1037/0022–006x.75.5.785

Cokley, K., & Awad, G. H. (2008). Conceptual and methodological issues related to multicultural research. In P. P. Heppner, B. E. Wampold, & D. M. Kivlighan (Eds.), *Research design in counseling* (3rd ed., pp. 366–384). Belmont, CA: Thomson Brooks/Cole.

Cokley, K., & Williams, W. (2005). A psychometric examination of the Africentric Scale: Challenges in measuring Afrocentric values. *Journal of Black Studies, 35,* 827–843. doi: 10.1177/0021934704266596

Colby, S. L., & Ortman, J. M. (2015). *Projections of the size and composition of the U.S. population: 2014 to 2060.* Retrieved from http://www.census.gov/content/dam/Census/library/publications/2015/demo/p25-1143.pdf

Coleman, E. (1981/1982). Developmental stages of the coming out process. *Journal of Homosexuality, 7,* 31–43. doi: 10.1300/J082v07n02_06

Coleman, S. (2011). Addressing the puzzle of race. *Journal of Social Work Education, 47,* 91–108. doi: 10.5175/JSWE.2011.200900086

Coleman-Jensen, A., Rabbitt, M., Gregory, C., & Singh, A. (2015). *Household food security in the United States in 2014.* Retrieved from http://www.ers.usda.gov/publications/err-economic-research-report/err194.aspx

Collier, K. L., van Beusekom, G., Bos, H. M. W., & Sandfort, T. G. M. (2013). Sexual orientation and gender identity/expression related peer victimization in adolescence: A systematic review of associated psychosocial and health outcomes. *Journal of Sex Research, 50,* 299–317. doi: 10.1080/00224499.2012.750639

Comas-Diaz, L. (2010). Healing the self, healing the world: A feminist journey. *Women & Therapy, 33,* 432–436. doi: 10.1080/02703149.2010.484679

Committee of 100. (2001). *American attitudes towards Chinese Americans and Asian Americans.* Retrieved from http://www.committee100.org/publications/survey/C100survey.pdf

Complete College America. (2018). *The completion shortfall. Access without success is an empty promise.* Retrieved from http://www.completecollege.org/completion_shortfall/

Comstock, D. L., Hammer, T. R., Strentzsch, J., Cannon, K., Parsons, J., & Salazar, G. (2008). Relational-Cultural Theory: A framework for bridging relational, multicultural, and social justice competencies. *Journal of Counseling & Development, 86,* 279–287. doi: 10.1002/j.1556-6678.2008.tb00510.x

Conger, J. J. (1975). Proceedings of the American Psychological Association, Incorporated, for the year 1974: Minutes of the annual meeting of the Council of Representatives. *American Psychologist, 30,* 620–651. doi: 10.1037/h0078455

Congress of Racial Equality. (2017). *A leader in the civil rights.* Retrieved from http://www.congressofracialequality.org

Conrad, P., & Barker, K. (2010). The social construction of illness: Key insights and policy implications. *Journal of Health and Social Behavior, 51*(S), S67–S79. doi: 10.1177/0022146510383495

Conrad, T. R. (1976). The debate about quota systems: An analysis. *American Journal of Political Science, 20*, 135–149. doi: 10.2307/2110514

Constantine, M. G., Myers, L. J., Kindaichi, M., & Moore, J. L. (2004). Exploring indigenous mental health practices: The role of healers and helpers in promoting well-being in people of color. *Counseling and Values, 48*, 110–125. doi: 10.1002/j.2161-007X.2004.tb00238.x

Cook, E. P. (2012). *Understanding people in context: The ecological perspective in counseling.* Alexandria, VA: American Counseling Association.

Copeland, V. C. (2006). Disparities in mental health service utilization among low-income African American adolescents: Closing the gap by enhancing practitioner's competency. *Child and Adolescent Social Work Journal, 23*, 407–431. doi: 10.1007/s10560-006-0061-x

Copeland, W. E., Angold, A., Costello, E. J., & Egger, H. (2013). Prevalence, comorbidity, and correlates of DSM-5 proposed disruptive mood dysregulation disorder. *American Journal of Psychiatry, 170*, 173–179. doi: 10.1176/ appi.ajp.2012.12010132

Corey, G. (2013). *Theory and practice of counseling and psychotherapy* (9th ed.). Belmont, CA: Brooks/Cole.

Cornell, A. W. (2013). *Focusing in clinical practice: The essence of change.* New York: W. W. Norton & Co.

Cornish, J. A., Schreier, B. A., Nadakarni, L. I., Metzger, L. H., & Rodolfa, E. R. (Eds.). (2010). *Handbook of multicultural counseling competencies.* Hoboken, NJ: Wiley.

Cornish, M. A., Wade, N. G., & Post, B. C. (2012). Attending to religion and spirituality in group counseling: Counselors' perceptions and practices. *Group Dynamics: Theory, Research, and Practice, 16*, 122–137. doi: 10.1037/a0026663

Corsini, R. J., & Wedding, D. (2014). *Current psychotherapies* (10th ed.). Boston, CA: Cengage.

Cottrell, A. B. (1990). Cross-national marriage: A review of the literature. *Journal of Comparative Family Studies, 21*(2), 151–169.

Courson, J., & Farris, A. (2012, January 23). *Title IX liability for anti-gay bullying.* Retrieved from http://apps.americanbar.org/litigation/committees/lgbt/articles/winter2012-title-ix-liability-anti-gay-bullying.html

Crazy Thunder, D., & Brave Heart, M. Y. H. (2005). *Cumulative trauma among tribal law enforcement officers: Search, rescue, & recovery at Ground Zero and on the reservation.* Research Monograph, Bureau of Indian Affairs, DASAP, Washington, DC.

Crippen, C., & Brew, L. (2007). Intercultural parenting and the transcultural family: A literature review. *The Family Journal, 15*, 107–115.

Crippen, C. L. (2011). *Working with intercultural couples and families: Exploring cultural dissonance to identify transformative opportunities.* Retrieved from http://www.counseling.org/docs/default-source/vistas/vistas_2011_article_21.pdf?sfvrsn=9

Crippen, C., & Brew, L. (2013). Strategies of cultural adaptation in intercultural parenting. *The Family Journal, 21*, 263–271. doi: 10.1177/1066480713476664

Crockett, S. A., & Hays, D. G. (2011). Understanding and responding to the career counseling needs of international college students on U.S. campuses. *Journal of College Counseling, 14*, 65–79. doi: 10.1002/j.2161-1882.2011.tb00064.x

Crooks, R. L., & Baur, K. (2013). *Our sexuality* (11th ed.). Belmont, CA: Cengage Learning.

Cross, W. E., Jr. (1971). The Negro-to-Black conversion experience: Toward a psychology of Black liberation. *Black World, 20*, 13–27.

Cross, W. E., Jr. (1995). The psychology of nigrescence: Revising the Cross model. In J. M. Ponterotto, J. M. Casas, L. A. Suzuki, & C. M. Alexander (Eds.), *Handbook of multicultural counseling* (pp. 93–122). Thousand Oaks, CA: Sage Publications.

Cross, W. E., Jr., & Vandiver, B. J. (2001). Nigrence theory and measurement: Introducing the Cross Racial Identity Scale (CRIS). In J. Ponterotto, J. Casas, L. Suzuki, & C. Alexander (Eds.), *Handbook of multicultural counseling* (2nd ed., pp. 371–393). Thousand Oaks, CA: Sage Publications.

Cusack, C. E., Hughes, J. L., & Nuhu, N. (2013). Connecting gender and mental health to imposter phenomenon feelings. *Psi Chi Journal of Psychological Research, 18*, 74–81.

Czopp, A. M. (2008). When is a compliment not a compliment? Evaluation expressions of positive stereotypes. *Journal of Experimental Social Psychology, 44*, 413–420. doi: 10.1016/j.jesp.2006.12.007

DaCosta, K. M. (2007). *Making multiracials: State, family, and market in the redrawing of the color line.* Stanford, CA: Stanford University Press.

Dailey, S. F., Gill, C. S., Karl, S. L., & Barrio Minton, C. A. (2014). *DSM-5 learning companion for counselors.* Alexandria, VA: American Counseling Association.

D'Andrea, M., & Daniels, J. (1999). Understanding the different psychological dispositions of White racism: A comprehensive model for counselor educators and practitioners. In M. Kiselica (Ed.), *Confronting prejudice and racism during multicultural training* (pp. 59–87). Alexandria, VA: American Counseling Association.

Daniels, J. A. (2001). Conceptualizing a case of indirect racism using the White racial identity development model. *Journal of Mental Health Counseling, 23*, 256–268.

Dasgupta, S., & Basu, J. (2011). Marital quality and gender role stereotype. *Psychological Studies, 56*, 360–367. doi: 10.1007/s12646-011-0105-y

Davidson, J. R. (1992). Theories about Black-White interracial marriage: A clinical perspective. *Journal of Multicultural Counseling and Development, 30*, 150–157. doi: 10.1002/j.2161-1912.1992.tb00573.x

Davis, F. J. (2010). *Who is black?: one nation's definition.* University Park, PA: Penn State Press.

Davis, K., Stremikis, K., Squires, D., & Schoen, C. (2014). Mirror, mirror on the wall: How the performance of the U.S. health care system compares internationally. Retrieved from http://www.commonwealthfund.org/~/media/files/publications/fund-report/2014/jun/1755_davis_mirror_mirror_2014.pdf

Dawkins, M. A. (2012). *Clearly visible: Racial passing and the color of cultural identity.* Waco, TX: Baylor University Press.

Day, M. V., Kay, A. C., Holmes, J. G., & Napier, J. L. (2011). System justification and the defense of committed relationship ideology. *Journal of Personality and Social Psychology, 101*, 291–306. doi: 10.1037/a0023197

Dearing, E., Taylor, B. A., & McCartney, K. (2004). Implications of family income dynamics for women's depressive symptoms during the first 3 years after childbirth. *American Journal of Public Health, 94*, 1372–1377.

Debnam, K., Holt, C., Clark, E., Roth, D., & Southward, P. (2012). Relationship between religious social support and general social support with health behaviors in a national sample of African Americans. *Journal of Behavioral Medicine, 35*, 179–189. doi: 10.1007/s10865-011-9338-4

deKoven, A. (2011). Engaging White college students in productive conversations about race and racism: Avoiding dominant-culture projection and condescension-judgment default. *Multicultural Perspectives, 13*, 155–159. doi: 10.1080/10509674.2011.594394

de las Fuentes, C. (2003). Latinos and mental health. In J. S. Mio & G. Y. Iwamasa (Eds.), *Culturally diverse mental health: The challenges of research and resistance* (pp. 159–172). New York, NY: Routledge.

Deloria, V., Jr. (2006). *The world we used to live in: Remembering the powers of the medicine men.* Golden, CO: Fulcrum.

del Rosario Basterra, M., Trumbull, E., & Solano-Flores, G. (2010). *Cultural validity in assessment: Addressing linguistic and cultural diversity.* New York, NY: Routledge.

DeNavas-Walt, C., & Proctor, B. D. (2014). *Income and poverty in the United States: 2013.* (Current Population Reports-P60-249). Retrieved from http://www.census.gov/content/dam/Census/library/publications/2014/demo/p60-249.pdf

Derlan, C. L., & Umaña-Taylor, A. J. (2015). Brief report: Contextual predictors of African American adolescents' ethnic-racial identity affirmation-belonging and resistance to peer pressure. *Journal of Adolescence, 41*, 1–6. doi: 10.1016/j.adolescence.2015.02.002

De Silva, P. (2005). *An introduction to Buddhist psychology* (3rd ed.). Basingstoke, United Kingdom: Palgrave Macmillan.

De Silva, P. (2014). *An introduction to Buddhist psychology and counselling: Pathways of mindfulness-based therapies* (5th ed). Basingstoke, UK: Palgrave Macmillan.

Devor, A. (2004). Witnessing and mirroring: A fourteen stage model of transsexual identity formation. *Journal of Gay and Lesbian Psychotherapy, 8*, 41–67.

de Vries, K. M. (2015). Transgender people of color at the center: Conceptualizing a new intersectional model. *Ethnicities, 15*, 3–27. doi: 10.1177/1468796814547058

Dewell, J. A., & Owen, J. (2015). Addressing mental health disparities with Asian American clients: Examining the generalizability of the common factors model. *Journal of Counseling & Development, 93*, 80–87. doi: 10.1002/j.1556-6676.2015.00183.x

Díaz, R. M., Bein, E., & Ayala, G. (2006). Homophobia, poverty, and racism: Triple oppression and mental health outcomes in Latino gay men. In A. M. Omoto & H. S. Kurtzman (Eds.)., *Sexual orientation and mental health* (pp. 207–224). Washington, DC: American Psychological Association.

Dickerson, V. (2013). Patriarchy, power, and privilege: A narrative/poststructural view of work with couples. *Family Process, 52*(1), 102–114. doi: 10.1111/famp.12018

Dik, B. J., Duffy, R. D., & Steger, M. F. (2012). Enhancing social justice by promoting prosocial values in career development. *Counseling & Values, 57*, 31–37. doi: 10.1002/j.2161-007X.2012.00005.x

Dillon, G., Hussain, R., Loxton, D., & Rahman, S. (2013). Mental and physical health and intimate partner violence against women: A review of the literature. *International Journal of Family Medicine*, 1–15. doi: 10.1155/2013/313909

Dinh, K. T., Weinstein, T. L., Nemon, M., & Rondeau, S. (2008). The effects of contact with Asians and Asian Americans on White American college students: Attitudes, awareness of racial discrimination, and psychological adjustment. *American Journal of Community Psychology, 42*(3–4), 298–308. doi: 10.1007/s10464-008-9202-z

Dinh, K. T., Weinstein, T. L., Tein, J., & Roosa, M. W. (2013). A mediation model of the relationship of cultural variables to internalizing and externalizing problem behavior among Cambodian American youth. *Asian American Journal of Psychology, 4*, 176–184. doi: 10.1037/a0030165

Dinsmore, J. A., Chapman, A., & McCollum, V. J. C. (2000, April). *Client advocacy and social justice: Strategies for developing trainee competence.* Paper presented at the annual conference of the American Counseling Association, Washington, DC.

Dion, K. K., & Dion, K. L. (2001). Gender and cultural adaptation in immigrant families. *Journal of Social Issues, 57*, 511–521. doi: 10.111/0022-4537.00226

Dispenza, F. (2015). An exploratory model of proximal minority stress and the work-life interface for men in same-sex, dual-earner relationships. *Journal of Counseling & Development, 93*, 321–332. doi: 10.1002/jcad.12030

Dixon, A. L., Tucker, C., & Clark, M. (2010). Integrating social justice advocacy with national standards of practice: Implications for school counselor education. *Counselor Education & Supervision, 50*, 103–115.

Dixon, P. (2009). Marriage among African Americans: What does the research reveal? *Journal of African American Studies, 13*, 29–46.

Djamba, Y. K., & Kimuna, S. R. (2014). Are Americans really in favor of interracial marriage? A closer look at when they are asked about Black-White marriage for their relatives. *Journal of Black Studies, 45*, 528–544. doi: 10.1177/0021934714541840

Djuraskovic, I., & Arthur, N. (2009). The acculturation of former Yugoslavian refugees. *Canadian Journal of Counselling, 43*, 18–34.

Donner, N. C., & Lowry, C. A. (2013). Sex differences in anxiety and emotional behavior. *European Journal of Physiology, 465*, 601–626. doi: 10.1007/s00424-013-1271-7

Douglass, R. E. (2003). The evolution of the multiracial movement. In M. Kelley, & M. P. P. Root (Eds.), *Multiracial child resource book: Living complex identities* (pp. 12–17). Seattle, WA: MAVIN Foundation.

Downing, N. E., & Roush, K. L. (1985). From passive-acceptance to active commitment: A model of feminist identity development for women. *The Counseling Psychologist, 13*, 695–709. doi: 10.1177/0011000085134013

Drewery, W. (2005). Why we should watch what we say: Position calls, everyday speech and the production of relational subjectivity. *Theory and Psychology, 15*(3), 305–324. doi: 10.1177/0959354305053217

Duberman, M. (1994). *Stonewall*. New York, NY: Penguin Press.

Duran, E. (2006). *Healing the soul wound: Counseling with American Indians and other native peoples*. New York, NY: Teachers College Press.

Duran, E., Firehammer, J., & Gonzalez, J. (2008). Liberation psychology as the path toward healing cultural soul wounds. *Journal of Counseling & Development, 86*, 288–295.

Durson, L. E., & Gates, G. J. (2012). *Serving our youth: Findings from a national survey of service providers working with lesbian, gay, bisexual, and transgender youth who are homeless or at risk of becoming homeless*. Los Angeles, CA: The Williams Institute with True Colors Fund and The Palette Fund.

Eap, S., Gobin, R. L., Ng, J., & Nagayama Hall, G. C. (2010). Sociocultural issues in the diagnosis and assessment of psychological disorder. In J. E. Maddux & J. P. Angney (Eds.), *Social psychological foundations of clinical psychology* (pp. 312–328). New York, NY: Guilford Press.

Edwards, R., Caballero, C., & Puthussery, S. (2010). Parenting children from mixed racial, ethnic, and faith backgrounds: Typifications of difference and belonging. *Ethnic and Racial Studies, 33*, 949–967. doi: 10.1080/01419870903318185

Eisenberg, D., Nicklett, E., Roeder, K., & Kirz, N. (2011). Eating disorder symptoms among college students: Prevalence, persistence, correlates and treatment-seeking. *Journal of American College Health, 59*, 700–707. doi: 10.1080/07448481.2010.546461

Elaasar, A. (2004). *Silent victims: The plight of Arab & Muslim Americans in post 9/11 America*. Bloomington, IN: AuthorHouse.

Erford, B. T. (Ed.). (2014). *Orientation to the counseling profession: Advocacy, ethics and essential professional foundations* (2nd ed.). Columbus, OH: Pearson Merrill.

Eriksen, K., & Kress, V. E. (2005). *Beyond the DSM story: Ethical quandaries, challenges, and best practices*. Thousand Oaks, CA: Sage Publications.

Eriksen, K., & Kress, V. E. (2008). Gender and diagnosis: Struggles and suggestions for counselors. *Journal of Counseling & Development, 86*, 152–162. doi: 10.1002/j.1556-6678.2008.tb00492.x

Estrada, F., & Arciniega, G. M. (2015). Positive masculinity among Latino men and the direct and indirect effects on well-being. *Multicultural Counseling and Development, 43*, 191–205. doi: 10.1002/jmcd.12014

Evans, G. W., & Cassells, R. C. (2014). Childhood poverty, cumulative risk exposure, and mental health in emerging adults. *Clinical Psychological Science, 2*, 287–296. doi: 10.1177/2167702613501496

Evans, G. W., & Kim, P. (2013). Childhood poverty, chronic stress, self-regulation, and coping. *Child Development Perspectives, 7*, 43–48. doi: 10.1111/cdep.12013

Evans, M. P., Zambrano, E., Cook, K., Moyer, M., & Duffey, T. (2011). Enhancing school counselor leadership in multicultural advocacy. *Journal of Professional Counseling: Practice, Theory & Research, 38*, 52–67.

Faiver, C., & Ingersoll, R. E. (2005). Knowing one's limits. In C. S. Cashwell & J. S. Young (Eds.), *Integrating spirituality and religion into counseling: A guide to competent practice* (pp. 169–183). Alexandria, VA: American Counseling Association.

Fäldt, J., & Kullberg, C. (2012). Implications of male and female same-gender dyads. *Journal of Social Service Research, 38*, 712–726. doi: 10.1080/01488376.2012.723976

Falicov, C. J. (2010). Religion and spiritual traditions in immigrant families: Significance for Latino health and mental health. In F. Walsh (Ed.), *Spiritual resources in family therapy* (pp. 157–173). New York, NY: Guilford Press.

Falicov, C. J. (2014). *Latino families in therapy* (2nd ed.). New York, NY: Guilford Press.

Fall, K. A., Holden, J. M., & Marquis, A. (2010). *Theoretical models of counseling and psychotherapy*. New York, NY: Routledge.

Fall, K. A. & Howard, S. (2011). *Alternatives to domestic violence: A homework manual for men in battering groups* (3rd ed.). New York, NY: Routledge.

Family Research Council. (2017). *Ten arguments from social science against same-sex marriage*. Retrieved from http://www.frc.org/issuebrief/ten-arguments-from-social-science-against-same-sex-marriage

Farkas, T. & Leaper, C. (2016), Chivalry's double-edged sword: How girls' and boys' paternalistic attitudes relate to their possible family and work selves. *Sex Roles, 74*, 220–230. doi: 10.1007/s11199-015-0556-z

Fassinger, R. E. (1995). From invisibility to integration: Lesbian identity in the workplace. *Career Development Quarterly, 44*, 148–167. doi: 10.1002/j.2161-0045.1995.tb00682.x

Fassinger, R. E., & Miller, B. A. (1996). Validation of an inclusive model of sexual minority identity formation on a sample of gay men. *Journal of Homosexuality, 32*, 53–78. doi: 10.1300/J082v32n02_04

Fawcett, M. L., & Evans, K. M. (2013). *Experiential approach for developing multicultural counseling competence.* Thousand Oaks, CA: Sage.

Feagin, J. R. (2014). *Racist America: Roots, current realities, and future reparations* (3rd ed.). New York, NY: Routledge.

Feagin, J., & Elias, S. (2013). Rethinking racial formation theory: a systemic racism critique. *Ethnic and Racial Studies, 36*, 931–960. doi: 10.1080/01419870.2012.669839

Federal Bureau of Investigation (FBI). (2010). *Hate Crime Statistics.* Retrieved from http://www2.fbi.gov/ucr/hc2009/victims.html

Feeding America. (2012). *Child hunger.* Retrieved from http://www.feedingamerica.org/hunger-in-america/impact-of-hunger/child-hunger/

Fennelly, K., Mulkeen, P., & Giusti, C. (1998). Coping with racism and discrimination: The experience of young Latino adolescents. In H. McCubbin, E. Thompson, A. Thompson, & J. Fromer (Eds.), *Resiliency in Native American and immigrant families* (pp. 343–366). Thousand Oaks, CA: Sage Publications.

Field, C. J., Kimuna, S. R., & Straus, M. A. (2013). Attitudes toward interracial relationships among college student's race, class, gender, and perceptions of parental views. *Journal of Black Studies, 44*, 741–776. doi: 10.1177/0021934713507580

First, M. B. (2010). Clinical utility in the revision of the *Diagnostic and Statistical Manual of Mental Disorders* (DSM). *Professional Psychology: Research and Practice, 41*, 465–473. doi: 10.1037/a0021511.

Fitzgerald, H. E., & Farrell, P. (2012). Fulfilling the promise: Creating a child development research agenda with Native communities. *Child Development Perspectives, 6*, 75–78. doi: 10.1111/j.1750-8606.2011.00216.x

Flanagan, C. A., Taehan, K., Pykett, A., Finlay, A. Gallay, E. E., & Pancer, M. (2014). Adolescents' theories about economic inequality: Why are some people poor while others are rich? *Developmental Psychology, 50*, 2512–2525. doi : 10.1037/a0037934

Flaskerud, J. H., & Hu, L. (1992). Relationship of ethnicity to psychiatric diagnosis. *Journal of Nervous and Mental Disease, 180*, 296–303.

Forfylow, A. L. (2011). Integrating yoga with psychotherapy: A complementary treatment for anxiety and depression. *Canadian Journal of Counselling and Psychotherapy, 45*, 132–150.

Forry, N. D., Leslie, L. A., & Letiecq, B. L. (2007). Marital quality in interracial relationships: The role of sex role ideology and perceived fairness. *Journal of Family Issues, 28*, 1538–1552. doi: 10.1177/0192513X07304466

Fouad, N. A., Gerstein, L. H., & Toropek, R. L. (2006). Social justice and counseling psychology in context. In R. L. Toropek, L. H. Gerstein, N. A. Fouad, G. Roysircar, & T. Israel (Eds.), *Handbook for social justice in counseling psychology* (pp. 1–16). Thousand Oaks, CA: Sage Publications.

Fowler, J. W. (1995). *Stages of faith: The psychology of human development and the quest for meaning.* San Francisco, CA: HarperOne.

Fox, J., & Jones, K. (2013). DSM-5 and bereavement: The loss of normal grief? *Journal of Counseling & Development, 91*, 113–119. doi: 10.1002/j.1556-6676.2013.00079.x

Fox, S., & Stallworth, L. E. (2005). Racial/ethnic bullying: Exploring links between bullying and racism in the U.S. workplace. *Journal of Vocational Behavior, 66*, 438–456. doi: 10.1016/j.jvb.2004.01.002

Frain, M., Bishop, M., & Bethel, M. (2010). A roadmap for rehabilitation counseling to serve military veterans with disabilities. *Journal of Rehabilitation, 76*, 13–21.

Frances, A. J. (2010). The forensic risks of DSM-V and how to avoid them. *Journal of the American Academy and Psychiatry and the Law Online, 38*, 11–14.

Francis, P. C., & Dugger, S. M. (2014). Professionalism, ethics, and value-based conflicts in counseling: An introduction to the Special Section. *Journal of Counseling & Development, 92*, 131–134. doi: 10.1002/j.1556-6676.2014.00138.x

Frankl, V. E. (1959). *From death-camp to existentialism: A psychiatrist's path to a new therapy.* Boston, MA: Beacon Press.

Frankl, V. (2006). *Man's search for meaning.* Boston, MA: Beacon Press.

Freeman, C., & Fox, M. (2005). *Status and trends in the education of American Indians and Alaska Natives (NCES 2005-108).* Washington, DC: U.S. Department of Education, National Center for Education Statistics.

Freud, S. (1924). *A general introduction to psychoanalysis.* New York, NY: Washington Square Press.

Freud, S. (1961). *Civilization and its discontents* (J. Strachey, Ed. & Trans.). New York, NY: Norton. (Original work published 1930)

Frey, L. L., & Roysircar, G. (2004). Effects of acculturation and worldview for White American, South American, South Asian, and Southeast Asian students. *International Journal for the Advancement of Counseling, 26*, 229–248. doi: 10.1023/B:ADCO.0000035527.46652.d2

Frey, L. L., & Roysircar, G. (2006). South Asian and East Asian international students' perceived prejudice, acculturation, and frequency of help resource utilization. *Journal of Multicultural Counseling and Development, 34*, 208–222.

Friedan, B. (2001). *The feminine mystique.* New York, NY: W.W. Norton.

Friedman, M. S., Marshal, M. P., Guadamuz, T. E., Wei, C., Wong, C. F., Saewyc, E. M., & Stall, R. (2011). A meta-analysis of disparities in childhood sexual abuse, parental physical abuse, and peer victimization among sexual minority and sexual nonminority individuals. *American Journal of Public Health, 101*, 1481–1494. doi: 10.2105/AJPH.2009.190009

Frye, M. (1983). *The politics of reality: Essays in feminist theory*. New York, NY: The Crossing Press.

Fukuyama, M. A., Siahpoush, F., & Sevig, T. D. (2005). Religion and spirituality in a cultural context. In C. S. Cashwell, & J. S. Young (Eds.), *Integrating spirituality and religion into counseling: A guide to competent practice* (pp. 123–142). Alexandria, VA: American Counseling Association.

Fulton, C., & Shannonhouse, L. (2014). Developing servant leadership through counselor community engagement: A case example. *Journal for Counselor Leadership and Advocacy, 1*, 98–111. doi: 10.1080/2326716X.2014.886978

Gagliardi, C., Marcellini, F., Papa, R., Giuli, C., & Mollenkopf, H. (2008). Associations of personal and mobility resources with subjective well-being among older adults in Italy and Germany. *Archives of Gerontology and Geriatrics, 50*, 42–47. doi: 10.1016/j.archger.2009.01.007

Galliher, R. V., Tsethlikai, M. M., & Stolle, D. (2012). Perspectives of Native and non-Native scholars: Opportunities for collaboration. *Child Development Perspectives, 6*, 66–74. doi: 10.1111/j.1750–8606.2011.00200.x

Gallo, L. C., Penedo, F. J., Espinosa de los Monteros, K., & Arguelles, W. (2009). Resiliency in the face of disadvantage: Do Hispanic cultural characteristics protect health outcomes. *Journal of Personality, 77*, 1707–1746. doi: 10.1111/j.1467-6494.2009.00598.x

Gamst, G., Dana, R., Der-Karabetian, A., & Kramer, T. (2001). Asian American mental health clients: Effects of ethnic match and age on global assessment and visitation. *Journal of Mental Health Counseling, 23*, 57–71.

Ganguli, M., Blacker, D., Blazer, D. G., Grant, I., Jeste, D. V., Paulsen, J. S., . . . Sachdey, P. S. (2011). Classification of neurocognitive disorders in DSM-5: A work in progress. *American Journal of Geriatric Psychiatry, 19*, 205–210. doi: 10.1097/JGP.0b013e3182051ab4

Gans, H. J. (2011). The Moynihan report and its aftermaths. *Du Bois Review: Social Science Research on Race, 8*, 315–327. doi: 10.1017/S1742058X11000385

Garrett, J. T. (1996). Reflection by the riverside: The traditional education of Native American children. *Journal of Humanistic Education and Development, 35*, 12–28.

Garrett, M. T., & Garrett, J. T. (2002). Ayeli: Centering technique based on Cherokee spiritual traditions. *Counseling and Values, 46*, 149–158.

Garrett, M. T., & Garrett, J. T. (2012). *Native American faith in America* (2nd ed.). New York, NY: Facts on File.

Garrett, M. T., Parrish, M., Williams, C., Grayshield, L., Portman, T. A. A., Torres-Rivera, E., & Maynard, E. (2014). Invited commentary: Fostering resilience among Native American youth through therapeutic intervention. *Journal of Youth and Adolescence, 43*, 470–490. doi: 10.1007/s10964-013-0020-8

Garrett, M. T., & Pichette, E. F. (2000). Red as an apple: Native American acculturation and counseling with or without reservation. *Journal of Counseling & Development, 78*, 3–13.

Garrett, M. T., Portman, T. A. A., Choudhuri, D. D., & Santiago-Rivera, A. (2011). *Counseling and diversity: Counseling Native Americans*. Boston, MA: Cengage.

Garrett, M. T., Torres-Rivera, E., Brubaker, M., Agahe Portman, T. A., Brotherton, D., West-Olatunji, C., Conwill, W., & Grayshield, L. (2011). Crying for a vision: The Native American sweat lodge ceremony as therapeutic intervention. *Journal of Counseling & Development, 89*, 318–325. doi: 10.1002/j.1556-6678.2011.tb00096.x

Garrett, M. T., Torres-Rivera, E., Dixon, A. L., & Myers, J. E. (2009). Acculturation and wellness of Native American adolescents in the United States of North America. *Perspectivas Sociales/Social Perspectives, 11*, 39–64.

Garrett, M. T., Garrett, J. T., & Melton, J. G. (2009). *Native American faith in America*. New York, NY: Infobase Publishing.

Garrett, M. T., & Portman, T. A. A. (2011). *Counseling and diversity: Counseling Native Americans*. Boston, MA: Lahaska Press.

Gates, G. J. (2011). *How many people are lesbian, gay, bisexual and transgender?* Retrieved from http://williamsinstitute.law.ucla.edu/research/census-lgbt-demographics-studies/how-many-people-are-lesbian-gay-bisexual-and-transgender/

Gates, G. J. (2012). *Same-sex couples in census 2010: Race and ethnicity*. Retrieved from http://williamsinstitute.law.ucla.edu/wp-content/uploads/Gates-CouplesRaceEthnicity-April-2012.pdf

Gates, G. J. (2013). *LGBT parenting in the United States*. The Williams Institute. UCLA School of Law. Retrieved from http://williamsinstitute.law.ucla.edu/wp-content/uploads/LGBT-Parenting.pdf

Gates, G. J. (2014a). *LGB/T Demographics: Comparisons among population-based surveys*. Williams Institute, UCLA School of Law. Retrieved from http://williamsinstitute.law.ucla.edu/wp-content/uploads/lgbt-demogs-sep-2014.pdf

Gates, G. J. (2014b). *LGBT Americans report lower well-being*. Retrieved from http://www.gallup.com/poll/175418/lgbt-americans-report-lower.aspx

Gates, G. J. (2015). *Comparing LGBT rankings by metro area: 1990–2014*. The Williams Institute. UCLA School of Law. Retrieved from http://williamsinstitute.law.ucla.edu/research/census-lgbt-demographics-studies/comparing-lgbt-rankings-by-metro-area-1990-2014/

Gay, Lesbian, and Straight Education Network. (GLSEN). (2014). *The 2013 National School Climate Survey: The experiences of lesbian, gay, bisexual, and transgender youth in our nation's schools*. Retrieved from http://www.glsen.org/sites/default/files/2013%20National%20School%20Climate%20Survey%20Full%20Report_0.pdf

Gee, G. C., Delva, J., & Takeuchi, D. T. (2006). Relationships between self-reported unfair treatment and prescription medication use, illicit drug use, and alcohol dependence among Filipino Americans. *American Journal of Public Health, 96*(8), 1–8. doi: 10.2105/AJPH.2005.075739

Gee, G. C., & Ford, C. L. (2011). Structural racism and health inequities: Old issues, new directions. *Du Bois Review, 8,* 115–132. doi: 10.1017/S1742058X11000130

Gee, G. C., & Ponce, N. (2010). Associations between racial discrimination, limited English proficiency, and health-related quality of life among 6 Asian ethnic groups in California. *American Journal of Public Health, 100,* 888–895. doi: 10.2105/AJPH.2009.178012

Gee, G. C., Ro, A., Shariff-Macro, S, & Chae, D. (2009). Racial discrimination and health among Asian Americans: Evidence, assessment, and directions for future research. *Epidemiology Reviews, 31,* 130–151. doi: 10.1093/epirev/mxp009

Gee, G. C., Spencer, M. S., Chen, J., & Takeuchi, D. (2007). A nationwide study of discrimination and chronic health conditions among Asian Americans. *American Journal of Public Health, 97,* 1275–1282. doi: 10.2105/AJPH.2006.091827

Gee, G. C., Spencer, M., Chen, J., Yip, T., & Takeuchi, D. T. (2007). The association between self-reported racial discrimination and 12-month *DSM-IV* mental disorders among Asian Americans nationwide. *Social Science & Medicine, 64,* 1984–1996. doi: 10.1016/j.socscimed.2007.02.013

Geiger, W., Harwood, J., & Hummert, M. L. (2006). College students' multiple stereotypes of lesbians: A cognitive perspective. *Journal of Homosexuality, 51,* 165–182. doi: 10.1300/J082v51n03_08

Gelman, C. R. (2003). Psychodynamic treatment of Latinos: A critical review of the theoretical literature and practice outcome research. *Psychoanalytic Social Work, 10,* 79–102. doi: 10.1300/J032v10n02_10

Gendlin, E. (1982). *Focusing.* New York, NY: Bantam.

Genia, V. (1995). *Counseling and psychotherapy of religious clients: A developmental approach.* Westport, CT: Praeger.

Gill, C. S., Harper, M. C., & Dailey, S. F. (2011). Assessing the spiritual and religious domain. In C. S. Cashwell & J. S. Young (Eds.), *Integrating spirituality and religion into counseling: A guide to competent practice* (2nd ed., pp. 141–162). Alexandria, VA: American Counseling Association.

Gilligan, C. (1982). *In a different voice: Psychological theory and women's development.* Cambridge, MA: Harvard University Press.

Gilligan, C. (1993). *In a different voice: Psychological theory and women's development* (reissue version). Cambridge, MA: Harvard University Press.

Giordono, J., McGoldrick, M., & Klages, J. G. (2005). Italian families. In M. McGoldrick, J. Giordano, & J. K. Pearce (Eds.), *Ethnicity and family therapy* (3rd ed., pp. 616–628). New York, NY: Guilford.

Gladding, S. (2011). *The counseling dictionary: Concise definitions of frequently used terms* (3rd ed.). Upper Saddle River, NJ: Pearson.

Gladding, S. T. (2012). *Counseling: A comprehensive profession* (7th ed.). Upper Saddle River, NJ: Merrill.

Glick, T. F. (2005). *Islamic and Christian Spain in the early Middle Ages* (2nd rev. ed.). Danvers, MA: BRILL.

Glosoff, H. L., & Durham, J. C. (2010). Using supervision to prepare social justice counseling advocates. *Counselor Education & Supervision, 50,* 116–129. doi: 10.1002/j.1556-6978.2010.tb00113.x

Gold, J. M. (2010). *Counseling and spirituality: Integrating spiritual and clinical orientations.* Upper Saddle River, NJ: Merrill.

Gold, S. D. (2008). *Loving v. Virginia: Lifting the ban against interracial marriage.* Tarrytown, NY: Marshall Cavendish.

Goldberg, N. G. (2009). *The impact of inequalities for same-sex partners in employer-sponsored retirement plans.* Retrieved from http://williamsinstitute.law.ucla.edu/research/-economic-impact-reports/the-impact-of-inequalities-for-same-sex-partners-in-employer-sponsored-retirement-plans/

Goldin, P. R. (2011). *Confucianism (ancient philosophies).* Berkeley CA: University of California Press.

Gomes, S. L. (2000). Factors affecting Asian Indian selection of psychotherapy: Therapist ethnicity and therapy modality. *Dissertation Abstracts International, 61*(2B), 1081.

Gone, J. P. (2009). A community-based treatment for Native American historical trauma: Prospects for evidence-based practice. *Journal of Consulting and Clinical Psychology, 77,* 751–762. doi: 10.1037/a0015390

Gonzales, J. M., Alegría, M., Prihoda, T. J., Copeland, L. A., & Zeber, J. E. (2011). How the relationship of attitudes toward mental health treatment and service use differs by age, gender, ethnicity/race, and education. *Social Psychiatry and Psychiatric Epidemiology, 46,* 45–57. doi: 10.1007/s00127-009-0168-4

Gonzales-Backen, M. (2013). An application of ecological theory to ethnic identity formation among biethnic adolescents. *Family Relations, 62,* 92–108. doi: 10.1111/j.1741-3729.2012.00749.x

Gonzalez, L. M., Borders, L. D., Hines, E., Villalba, J. A., & Henderson, A. (2013). Parental involvement in children's education: Considerations for school counselors working with Latino immigrant families. *Professional School Counseling, 16,* 185–193.

Gonzalez, L. M., Eades, M. P., & Supple, A. J. (2014). School community engaging with immigrant youth: Incorporating personal/social development and ethnic identity development. *School Community Journal, 24,* 99–117.

Gonzalez, L. M., Stein, G. L., Shannonhouse, L. R., & Prinstein, M. J. (2012). Latina/o adolescents in an emerging immigrant community: A qualitative exploration of their future goals. *Journal for Social Action in Counseling and Psychology, 4,* 83–102.

Goodman, R. D. (2013). The transgenerational trauma and resilience genogram. *Counselling Psychology Quarterly, 26,* 386–405. doi: 10.1080/09515070.2013.820172

Goodman, R., & West-Olatunji, C. A. (2010). Educational hegemony, traumatic stress, and African American and Latino American students. *Journal of Multicultural Counseling and Development, 38*, 176–186. doi: 10.1002/j.2161-1912.2010.tb00125.x

Goodrich, K. M., & Gilbride, D. D. (2010). The refinement and validation of a model of family functioning after child's disclosure as lesbian, gay, or bisexual. *Journal of LGBT Issues in Counseling, 4*, 92–121. doi: 10.1080/15538605.2010.483575

Gove, W. R. (2010). Mental illness and psychiatric treatment among women. *Psychology of Women Quarterly, 34*, 345–362. doi: 10.1111/j.1471-6402.1980.tb01109.x

Grady-Weliky, T. A. (2003). Premenstrual Dysphoric Disorder. *The New England Journal of Medicine, 348*, 433–438. doi: 10.1056/NEJMcp012067

Graham, J. R., Bradshaw, C., & Trew, J. L. (2010). Cultural considerations for social service agencies working with Muslim clients. *Social Work, 55*, 337–346. doi: 10.1093/sw/55.4.337

Graham, L. F., Aronson, R. E., Nichols, T., Stephens, C. F., & Rhodes, S. D. (2011). Factors influencing depression and anxiety among Black sexual minority men. *Depression Research and Treatment, 2011*, 1–9. doi: 10.1155/2011/587984

Grande, S. (2015). *Red pedagogy: Native American social and political thought* (10th ed.). Lanham, MD: Rowman & Littlefield.

Grant, B. F., Chou, S. P., Goldstein, R. B., Huang B., Stinson F. S., Saha T. D., . . . Ruan, W. J. (2008). Prevalence, correlates, disability, and comorbidity of *DSM-IV* borderline personality disorder: Results from the wave 2 National Epidemiologic Survey on Alcohol and Related Conditions. *Journal of Clinical Psychiatry, 69*, 533–544.

Graves, Jr., J. L. (2015). Why the nonexistence of biological races does not mean the nonexistence of racism. *American Behavioral Sciences, 59*, 1474–1495. doi: 10.1177/0002764215588810

Gray, C. (2011). President Obama's 2010 United States National Security Strategy and International Law on the Use of Force. *Chinese Journal of International Law, 10*, 35–53. doi: 10.1093/chinesejil/jmr005

Gray, G. (2018). Multicultural counseling. In B. T. Erford (Ed.), *Orientation to the counseling profession: Advocacy ethics, and essential professional foundations* (3rd ed., pp. 163–192). Columbus, OH: Pearson/Merrill.

Grayshield, L., & Mihecoby, A. (2010). Indigenous ways of knowing as a philosophical base for the promotion of peace and justice in counseling education and psychology. *Journal for Social Action in Counseling and Psychology, 2*, 1–16.

Green, K. E., & Feinstein, B. A. (2012). Substance use in lesbian, gay, and bisexual populations: An update on empirical research and implications for treatment. *Psychology of Addictive Behaviors, 26*, 265–278. doi: 10.1037/a0025424

Green, K. M., Doherty, E. E., Fothergill, K. E., & Ensminger, M. E. (2012). Marriage trajectories and health risk behaviors throughout adulthood among urban African Americans. *Journal of Family Issues, 33*, 1595–1618. doi: 10.1177/0192513X11432429

Greene, B. (2005). Psychology, diversity, and social justice: Beyond heterosexism and across the cultural divide. *Counseling Psychological Quarterly, 18*, 295–306. doi: 10.1080/09515070500385770

Greene, M. L., Way, N., & Pahl, K. (2006). Trajectories of perceived adult and peer discrimination among Black, Latino, and Asian American adolescents: Patterns and psychological correlates. *Developmental Psychology, 42*, 218–238. doi: 10.1037/0012-1649.42.2.218

Gregory, S. D. P., & Phillips, F. B. (1997). Of mind, body and spirit: Therapeutic foster care—An innovative approach to healing from an NTU perspective. *Child Welfare Journal, 76*, 127–142.

Gregory, W. H., & Harper, K. W. (2001). The NTU approach to health and healing. *Journal of Black Psychology, 27*, 304–320. doi: 10.1177/0095798401027003004

Griffin, J. M., & Friedemann-Sánchez, G. (2012). The invisible side of war: Families caring for US service members with traumatic brain injuries and polytrauma. *The Journal of Head Trauma Rehabilitation, 27*, 3. doi: 10.1097/HTR.0b013e3182274260

Grills, C., & Longshore, D. (1996). Africentrism: Psychometric analyses of a self-report measure. *Journal of Black Psychology, 22*, 86–106. doi: 10.1177/00957984960221007

Groce, N. (2005). Immigrants, disability and rehabilitation. In J. H. Stone (Ed.), *Culture and disability: Providing culturally competent services* (pp. 1–13). Thousand Oaks, CA: Sage Publications.

Grof, S., & Grof, C. (2010). *Holotropic breathwork: A new approach to self-exploration and therapy.* New York, NY: State University of New York Press.

Guardia, A. C. L., & Banner, A. T. (2012). The goal of reunification: An Adlerian approach to working for therapeutic change within the foster care system. *Family Journal, 20*, 361–368. doi: 10.1177/1066480712452390

Guindon, M. H., Green, A. G., & Hanna, F. J. (2003). Intolerance and psychopathology: Toward a general diagnosis for racism, sexism, and homophobia. *American Journal of Orthopsychiatry, 73*, 167–176. doi: 10.1037/0002-9432.73.2.167

Gullickson, A. (2010). Racial boundary formation at the dawn of Jim Crow: The determinants and effects of Black/Mulatto occupational differences in the United States, 1880. *American Journal of Sociology, 116*, 187–231. doi: 10.1086/652136

Gunaratana, B. H. (2011). *Mindfulness in plain English* (deluxe ed.). Somerville, MA: Wisdom.

Gupta, A., Leong, F., Valentine, J. C., & Canada, D. D. (2013). A meta-analytic study: The relationship between acculturation and depression among Asian Americans.

American Journal of Orthopsychiatry, 83, 372–385. doi: 10.1111/ajop.12018

Gupta, A., Szymanski, D. M., & Leong, F. T. L. (2011). The "model minority myth": Internalized racialism of positive stereotypes as correlates of psychological distress, and attitudes toward help-seeking. *Asian American Journal of Psychology, 2*, 101–114. doi: 10.1037/a0024183

Gushue, G. V., Mejia-Smith, B., Fisher, L., Cogger, A., Gonzalez-Matthews, M., Lee, Y., . . . Johnson, Y. (2013). Differentiation of self and racial identity. *Counselling Psychology Quarterly, 26*, 343–361. doi: 10.1080/09515070.2013.816839

Guy, M. E. (2010). When diversity makes a difference. *Public Integrity, 12*, 173–183. doi: 10.2753/PIN1099-9922120205

Haas, A. P., Eliason, M., Mays, V. M., Mathy, R. M., Cochran, S. D., D'Augelli, A. R., . . . Clayton, P. J. (2011). Suicide and suicide risk in lesbian, gay, bisexual, and transgender populations: Review and recommendations. *Journal of Homosexuality, 58*, 10–51. doi: 10.1080/00918369.2011.534038

Haboush, K. L., & Barakat, N. (2014). Education and employment among Arab Americans: Pathways to individual identity and community resilience. In S. C. Nassar-McMillan, J. Hakim-Larson, & K. Ajrouch (Eds.), *Biopsychosocial perspectives on Arab Americans: Culture, development, and health* (pp. 229–255). New York, NY: Springer.

Hackney, H. L., & Cormier, S. (2012). *The professional counselor: A process guide to helping* (7th ed.). Upper Saddle River, NJ: Pearson.

Haddad, Y. Y. (2004). *Not quite American? The shaping of Arab and Muslim identity in the United States.* Waco, TX: Baylor University Press.

Hakim-Larson, J., & Nassar-McMillan, S. C. (2006). *Identity development in Arab American youth: Implications for practice and research.* Paper presented at the annual American Counseling Association Conference, Montreal, Canada.

Hakim-Larson, J., Nassar-McMillan, S. C., & Patterson, A. (2012). Culturally alert counseling with Middle Eastern Americans. In G. McAuliffe (Ed.), *Culturally alert counseling: A comprehensive introduction* (2nd ed., pp. 263–292). Thousand Oaks, CA: Sage Publications.

Halbur, D. A., & Halbur, K. V. (2015). *Developing your theoretical orientation in counseling and psychotherapy* (3rd ed.). Upper Saddle River, NJ: Pearson.

Halim, M. L., Ruble, D. N., Tamis-LeMonda, C., Zosuls, K. M., Lurye, L. E., & Greulich, F. K. (2014). Pink frilly dresses and the avoidance of all things "girly": Children's appearance rigidity and cognitive theories of gender development. *Developmental Psychology, 50*, 1091–1101. doi: 10.1037/a0034906

Halkitis, P. N., & Jerome, R. C. (2008). A comparative analysis of methamphetamine use: Black gay and bisexual men in relation to men of other races. *Addictive Behaviors, 33*, 83–93. doi: 10.1016/j.addbeh.2007.07.015

Hall, G. C. N., Hong, J. J., Zane, N. W. S., & Meyer, O. L. (2011). Culturally competent treatments for Asian Americans: The relevance of mindfulness and acceptance-based psychotherapies. *Clinical Psychology: Science and Practice, 18*, 215–231. doi: 10.1111/j.1468-2850.2011.01253.x

Hall, L. J., & Donaghue, N. (2013). "Nice girls don't carry knives": Constructions of ambition in media coverage of Australia's first female prime minister. *British Journal of Social Psychology, 52*, 631–647. doi: 10.1111/j.2044-8309.2012.02114.x

Hall, M. (2004). Psychotherapy with African American women. [Review of the book *Psychotherapy with African American women: Innovations in psychodynamic perspectives in practice*]. *Smith College Studies in Social Work, 74*, 453–455.

Hall, M. L., Orzada, B. T., & Lopez-Gydosh, D. (2015). American women's wartime dress: Sociocultural ambiguity regarding women's roles during World War II. *Journal of American Culture, 38*, 232–242. doi: 10.1111/jacc.12357

Hall, P. W., & Hwang, V. M. (2001). *Anti-Asian violence in North America.* Walnut Creek, CA: Altamira Press.

Hammond, W. P. (2012). Taking it like a man: Masculine role norms as moderators of the racial discrimination-depressive symptoms association among African American men. *American Journal of Public Health, 102*, S232–S241. doi: 10.2105/AJPH.2011.300485

Han, C. S., Proctor, K., & Choi, K. H. (2014). I know a lot of gay Asian men who are actually tops: Managing and negotiating gay racial stigma. *Sexuality & Culture, 18*, 219–234. doi: 10.1007/s12119-013-9183-4

Han, H. S., West-Olatunji, C., & Thomas, M. S. (2011). Use of racial identity development theory to explore cultural competence among early childhood educators. *SRATE Journal, 20*, 1–11.

Han, M., & Lee, M. (2011). Risk and protective factors contributing to depressive symptoms in Vietnamese American college students. *Journal of College Student Development, 52*, 154–166. doi: 10.1353/csd.2011.0032

Han, M., & Pong, H. (2015). Mental health help-seeking behaviors among Asian American community college students: The effect of stigma, cultural barriers, and acculturation. *Journal of College Student Development, 56*, 1–14. doi: 10.1353/csd.2015.0001

Hanna, F. J., Talley, W. B., & Guindon, M. H. (2000). The power of perception: Toward a model of cultural oppression and liberation. *Journal of Counseling & Development, 78*, 430–441. doi: 10.1002/j.1556-6676.2000.tb01926.x

Hannon, L., & DeFina, R. (2014). Just skin deep? The impact of interviewer race on the assessment of African American respondent skin tone. *Race and Social Problems, 6*, 356–364. doi: 10.1007/s12552-014-9128-z

Hannon, M. D. (2013). *"Love him and everything else will fall into place": An analysis of narratives of African-American fathers of children with autism spectrum disorders* (Doctoral dissertation). Retrieved from ProQuest Dissertations and Theses database. (Order No. 3576535)

Harley, D., Alston, R., & Middleton, R. (2007). Infusing social justice into rehabilitation education: Making a case for curricula refinement. *Rehabilitation Education, 21*, 41–52. doi: 10.1891/088970107805059850

Harper, F. G. (2011). With all my relations: Counseling American Indians and Alaska Natives within a familial context. *The Family Journal, 19*, 434–432. doi: 10.1177/1066480711419818

Harris, A. L., & Marsh, K. (2010). Is a raceless identity an effective strategy for academic success among blacks? *Social Science Quarterly, 91*, 1242–1263. doi: 10.1111/j.1540-6237.2010.00730.x

Harris, H. (2009). Counseling multiple heritage children. In R. C. Henriksen, Jr., & D. A. Paladino (Eds.), *Counseling multiple heritage individuals, couples, and families* (pp. 45–63). Alexandria, VA: American Counseling Association.

Harris, M. S. (2014). *Racial disproportionality in child welfare.* New York, NY: Columbia University Press.

Hartung, P. J., & Blustein, D. L. (2002). Reason, intuition, and social justice: Elaborating on Parson's career decision-making model. *Journal of Counseling & Development, 80*, 41–47. doi: 10.1002/j.1556-6678.2002.tb00164.x

Hartung, P. J., Fouad, N. A., Leong, F. T. L., & Hardin, E. E. (2010). Individualism-collectivism: Links to occupational plans and work values. *Journal of Career Assessment, 18*, 34–45. doi: 10.1177/1069072709340526

Hatcher, L. S. (2012). African Americans are less likely to seek mental health treatment. *HIV Clinician, 11.*

Hatzenbuehler, M. L., Bellatorre, A., Lee, Y., Finch, B. K., Muennig, P., & Fiscella, K. (2014). Structural stigma and all-cause mortality in sexual minority populations. *Social Science and Medicine, 103*, 33–41. doi: 10.1016/j.socscimed.2013.06.005

Havighurst, R. J. (1961). The learning process. *American Journal of Public Health, 51*, 1694–1697.

Haynes, S. N., Smith, G., & Hunsley, J. (2011). *Foundations of clinical science and practice.* New York, NY: Routledge.

Hays, D. G., & Chang, C. Y. (2003). White privilege, oppression, and racial identity development: Implications for supervision. *Counselor Education & Supervision, 43*, 134–145.

Hays, D. G., Chang, C. Y., & Chaney, M. P. (2008, March). *Becoming social advocates: Counselor trainees' social justice knowledge, attitudes, and behaviors.* American Counseling Association World Conference, Honolulu, HI.

Hays, D. G., Chang, C. Y., & Dean, J. K. (2004). White counselors' conceptualization of privilege and oppression: Implications for counselor training. *Counselor Education and Supervision, 43*, 242–257.

Hays, D. G., Prosek, E., & McLeod, A. (2010). A mixed methodological analysis of the role of culture in the clinical decision-making process. *Journal of Counseling and Development, 88*, 114–121. doi: 10.1002/j.1556-6678.2010.tb00158

Heflin, C. M., Siefert, K., & Williams, D. R. (2005). Food insufficiency and women's mental health: Findings from a 3-year panel of welfare recipients. *Social Science & Medicine, 61*, 1971–1982. doi: 10.1016/j.socscimed.2005.04.014

Hehman, E., Gaertner, S. L., & Dovidio, J. F. (2011). Evaluations of presidential performance: Race, prejudice, and perceptions of Americanism. *Journal of Experimental Social Psychology, 47*, 430–435. doi: 10.1016/j.jesp.2010.11.011

Helms, J. E. (1995). An update of Helms' White and people of color racial identity. In J. G. Ponterotto, J. M. Casas, & C. M. Alexander (Eds.), *Handbook of multicultural counseling* (pp. 181–198). Thousand Oaks, CA: Sage Publications.

Helzer, J. E., Kraemer, H. C., Krueger, R. F., Wittchen, H. U., Sirovatka, P. J., & Regier, D. A. (Eds.). (2008). *Dimensional approaches in diagnostic classification.* Washington, DC: American Psychiatric Association.

Henderson, G., Spigner-Littles, D., & Milhouse, V. H. (2006). *A practitioner's guide to understanding indigenous and foreign cultures: An analysis of relationships between ethnicity, social class, and therapeutic intervention strategies.* Springfield, IL: Charles C Thomas.

Henriksen, R. C., Jr., & Paladino, D. A. (2009). *Counseling multiple heritage individuals, couples, and families.* Alexandria, VA: American Counseling Association.

Henriksen, R. C., Jr., & Rawlins, M. (2003, November). *Understanding multicultural issues: Awareness, theory and practical implications.* Paper presented at the Annual Conference of the Illinois Counseling Association.

Henriques-Calado, J., Duarte-Silva, M. E., Campos, R. C., Junqueira, D., Sacoto, C., & Keong, A. M. (2014). Personality disorders as an expression of the dimensional polarity in personality development in late adulthood women. *Bulletin of the Menninger Clinic, 78*, 283–300. doi: 10.1521/bumc.2014.78.4.283

Heo, M., Murphy, C. F., Fontaine, K. R., Bruce, M. L., & Alexopoulos, G. S. (2008). Population projection of US adults with lifetime experience of depressive disorder by age and sex from year 2005 to 2050. *International Journal of Geriatric Psychiatry, 23*, 1266–1270. doi: 10.1002/gps.2061

Herek, G. M., Norton, A. T., Allen, T. J., & Sims, C. L. (2010). Demographic, psychological, and social characteristics of self-identified lesbian, gay, and bisexual adults in a US probability sample. *Sexuality Research and Social Policy, 7*, 176–200. doi: 10.1007/s13178-010-0017-y

Herlihy, B. J., Hermann, M. A., & Greden, L. R. (2014). Legal and ethical implications of using religious beliefs as the basis for refusing to counsel certain clients. *Journal of Counseling & Development, 92*, 148–153. doi: 10.1002/j.1556-6676.2014.00142.x

Herman, J. L. (1992). Complex PTSD: A syndrome in survivors of prolonged and repeated trauma. *Journal of Traumatic Stress, 5*, 377–391. doi: 10.1002/jts.2490050305

Hernandez, M., Barrio, C., & Yamada, A. M. (2013). Hope and burden among Latino families of adults with schizophrenia. *Family Process, 52*, 697–708. doi: 10.1111/famp.12042

Hernández, M. M., Conger, R. D., Robins, R. W., Bacher, K. B., & Widaman, K. F. (2014). Cultural socialization and ethnic pride among Mexican-origin adolescents during the transition to middle school. *Child Development, 85*, 695–708. doi: 10.1111/cdev.12167

Hess, M., Ittel, A., & Sisler, A. (2014). Gender-specific macro- and micro-level processes in the transmission of gender role orientation in adolescence: The role of fathers. *European Journal of Developmental Psychology, 11*, 211–226. doi: 10.1080/17405629.2013.879055

Hewitt, N. A. (2012). Feminist frequencies: Regenerating the wave metaphor. *Feminist Studies, 38*, 658–680.

Hilton, B. A., Grewal, S., Popatia, N., Bottorff, J. L., Johnson, J. L., & Clarke, H. (2001). The desi way: Traditional health practices of South Asian women in Canada. *Health Care for Women International, 22*, 553–567. doi: 10.1080/07399330127195

Hine, R. (2011). In the margins: The impact of sexualised images on the mental health of ageing women. *Sex Roles, 65*, 632–646. doi: 10.1007/s11199-011-9978-4

Hinton, D., Field, N. P., Nickerson, A., Bryant, R. A., & Simon, N. (2013). Dreams of the dead among Cambodian refugees: Frequency, phenomenology, and relationship to complicated grief and posttraumatic stress disorder. *Death Studies, 37*, 750–767. doi: 10.1080/07481187.2012.692457

Hipilito-Delgado, C. P., & Lee, C. C. (2007). Empowerment theory for the professional school counselors: A manifesto for what really matters. *Professional School Counseling, 10*, 327–332. doi: 10.5330/prsc.10.4.fm1547261m80x744

Hirshfield, L. E., & Joseph, T. D. (2012). "We need a woman, we need a black woman": Gender, race, and identity taxation in the academy. *Gender and Education, 24*, 213–227. doi: 10.1080/09540253.2011.606208

Hjelle, L. A., & Ziegler, D. J. (1992). *Personality theories: Basic assumptions, research, and applications* (3rd ed.). New York, NY: McGraw-Hill.

Ho, C., Bluestein, D., & Jenkins, J. (2008). Cultural differences in the relationship between parenting and children's behavior. *Developmental Psychology, 44*, 507–522. doi: 10.1037/0012-1649.44.2.507

Hoeffel, E. M., Rastogi, S., Kim, M. O., & Shahid, H. (2012). *2010 Census briefs: The Asian population.* Retrieved from https://www.census.gov/prod/cen2010/briefs/c2010br-11.pdf

Hoffman, R. M. (2006). Gender self-definitions and gender self-acceptance in women: Intersections with feminist, womanist, and ethnic identities. *Journal of Counseling & Development, 84*, 358–372.

Hofmann, S. G. (2008). Acceptance and commitment therapy: New wave or Morita therapy? *Clinical Psychology: Science and Practice, 15*, 280–285.

Hofmann, S. G., Sawyer, A. T., Witt, A. A., & Oh, D. (2010). The effect of mindfulness-based therapy on anxiety and depression: A meta-analytic review. *Journal of Consulting and Clinical Psychology, 78*, 169–183. doi: 10.1037/a0018555

Holden, J. M., Greyson, B., & James, D. (2009). *The handbook of near-death experiences: Thirty years of investigation.* Santa Barbara, CA: Praeger.

Hong-Xin, W., Zao-Huo, C., & Hong-Xiang, M. (2006). Intensive Naikan therapy cure six patients with mental disorder. *Chinese Journal of Clinical Psychology, 14*, 324–325.

Hooker, S. P., Wilcox, S., Burroughs, E. L., Rheaume, C. E., & Courtenay, W. (2012). The potential influence of masculine identity on health-improving behavior in midlife and older African American men. *Journal of Men's Health, 9*, 79–88. doi: 10.1016/j.jomh.2012.02.001

hooks, b. (1981). *Ain't I a woman: Black women and feminism.* Boston, MA: South End Press.

hooks, b. (2000). *Feminist theory: From margin to center.* Boston, MA: South End Press.

Houle, J., Meunier, S., Coulombe, S., Tremblay, G., Gaboury, I., De Montigny, F., & Lavoie, B. (2015). Masculinity ideology among male workers and its relationship to self-reported health behaviors. *International Journal of Men's Health, 14*, 163–182. doi: 10.3149/jmh.1402.163

Hout, M., & Smith, T. W. (2015). *Fewer Americans affiliate with organized religions, belief and practice unchanged: Key findings from the 2014 General Social Survey.* Retrieved from www.norc.org/PDFs/GSS%20reports/GSS_REligion_2014.pdf

Howard, T. C., & Flennaugh, T. (2011). Research concerns, cautions and considerations on Black males in a "post-racial" society. *Race, Ethnicity and Education, 14*, 105–120. doi: 10.1080/13613324.2011.531983

Hsiao, A.-F., Wong, M. D., Goldstein, M. S., Becerra, L. S., Cheng, E. M., & Wenger, N. S. (2006). Complementary and alternative medicine use among Asian-American subgroups: Prevalence, predictors, and lack of relationship to acculturation and access to conventional health care. *The Journal of Alternative and Complementary Medicine, 12*, 1003–1010. doi: 10.1089/acm.2006.12.1003

Hud-Aleem, R., & Countyman, J. (2008). Biracial identity development and recommendations in therapy. *Psychiatry, 5*(11), 37–44.

Hudson, C. G. (2005). Socioeconomic status and mental illness: Tests of the social causation and selection hypothesis. *American Journal of Orthopsychiatry, 75*, 3–18. doi: 10.1037/0002-9432.75.1.3

Hulse-Killacky, D., Killacky, J., & Donigian, J. (2001). *Making task groups work in your world.* Upper Saddle River, NJ: Merrill Prentice Hall.

Human Rights Campaign Fund. (2018). *Parenting laws: Joint adoption.* Retrieved from http://www.hrc.org/state_maps

Humes, K., Jones, N. A., & Ramirez, R. A. (2011). *Overview of race and Hispanic origin. Census 2010 Briefs.* C2010BR-02. Washington, DC: U.S. Department of Commerce.

Hunt, M. O. (2004). Race/ethnicity and beliefs about wealth and poverty. *Social Science Quarterly, 85*, 827–853. doi: 10.1111/j.0038-4941.2004.00247.x

Hunter, D., & Sawyer, C. (2006). Blending Native American spirituality with individual psychology in work with children. *Journal of Individual Psychology, 62*, 234–250.

Huo, L., Straub, R. E., Roca, C., Schmidt, P. J., Shi, K., Vakkalanka, R., . . . Rubinow, D. R. (2007). Risk for premenstrual dysphoric disorder is associated with genetic variation in ESR1, the estrogen receptor alpha gene. *Biological Psychiatry, 62*, 925–933. doi: 10.1016/j.biopsych.2006.12.019

Hutchens, N., Block, J., & Young, M. (2013). Counselor educators' gatekeeping responsibilities and students' first amendment rights. *Counselor Education & Supervision, 52*, 82–95. doi: 10.1002/j.1556-6978.2013.00030.x

Ibanez, G. E., Van Oss Marin, B., Flores, S. A., Millett, G., & Diaz, R. M. (2009). General and gay-related racism experienced by Latino gay men. *Cultural Diversity and Ethnic Minority Psychology, 15*, 215–222. doi:10.1037/a0014613

Ibaraki, A. Y., Hall, G. C. N., & Sabin, J. A. (2014). Asian American Cancer disparities: The potential effects of model minority health stereotypes. *Asian American Journal of Psychology, 5*, 75–81. doi: 10.1037/a0036114

Ibrahim, F. A., & Schroeder, D. G. (1990). Cross-cultural couples counseling: A developmental, psychoeducational intervention. *Journal of Comparative Family Studies, 21*, 193–205.

Ihara, E. S., Chae, D. H., Cummings, J. R., & Lee, S. (2014). Correlates of mental health service use and type among Asian Americans. *Administration and Policy in Mental Health and Mental Health Services Research, 41*, 543–551. doi: 10.1007/s10488-013-0493-5

Ikizler, A. S., & Szymanski, D. M. (2014). A qualitative study of Middle Eastern/Arab American sexual minority identity development. *Journal of LGBT Issues in Counseling, 8*, 206–241. doi: 10.1080/15538605.2014.897295

Indian Health Service. (2014). *Trends in Indian health: 2014 edition*. Retrieved from https://www.ihs.gov/dps/index.cfm/publications/trends2014/

Ineson, E. M., Yap, H. T., & Whiting, G. (2013). Sexual discrimination and harassment in the hospitality industry. *International Journal of Hospitality Management, 35*, 1–9. doi: 10.1016/j.ijhm.2013.04.012

Inman, A. G. (2006). South Asian women: Identities and conflicts. *Cultural Diversity and Ethnic Minority Psychology, 12*, 306–319. doi: 10.1037/1099-9809.12.2.306

Inman, A. G., Constantine, M., & Ladany, N. (1999). Cultural value conflict: An examination of Asian Indian women's bicultural experience. In D. S. Sandhu (Ed.), *Asian Pacific Islander Americans: Issues and concerns for counseling psychotherapy* (pp. 31–41). Commack, NY: Nova Science.

Inman, A. G., Howard, E. E., Beaumont, L. R., & Walker, J. (2007). Cultural transmission: Influence of contextual factors in Asian Indian immigrant parents' experience. *Journal of Counseling Psychology, 54*, 93–100. doi: 10.1037/0022-0167.54.1.93

Inman, A. G., Rawls, K. N., Meza M. M., & Brown, A. L. (2002). An integrative approach to assessment and intervention with adolescents of color. In R. F. Massey & S. D. Massey (Eds.), *Comprehensive handbook of psychotherapy: Vol. 3. Interpersonal, humanistic, existential approaches* (pp. 153–178). New York, NY: Wiley.

Inman, A. G., & Tewari, N. (2003). The power of context: Counseling South Asians within a family context. In G. Roysircar, D. S. Sandhu, & V. B. Bibbins (Eds.), *A guidebook: Practices of multicultural competencies* (pp. 97–107). Alexandria, VA: American Counseling Association.

Inman, A. G., & Tummala-Narra, P. (2010). Clinical competencies working with immigrant communities. In J. Cornish, B. Schreier, L. Nadkarni, & E. Rodolfa (Eds.), *Handbook of multicultural counseling competencies* (pp. 117–152). Hoboken, NJ: John Wiley & Sons.

Inman, A. G., Tummala-Narra, P., Kaduvettoor-Davidson, A., Alvarez, A. N., & Yeh, C. (2015). Perceptions of race-based discrimination among first-generation Asian Indians in the U.S. *The Counseling Psychologist. 43*, 217–247. doi: 10.1177/0011000014566992

Inman, A. G., & Yeh, C. (2007). Stress and coping. In F. Leong, A. G. Inman, A. Ebreo, L. Lang, L. Kinoshita, & M. Fu (Eds.), *Handbook of Asian American psychology* (2nd ed., pp. 323–340). Thousand Oaks, CA: Sage Publications.

Inman, A. G., Yeh, C. J., Madan-Bahel A., & Nath, S. (2007). Bereavement and coping of South Asian families post 9/11. *Journal of Multicultural Counseling and Development, 35*, 101–115.

Institute of Medicine (IOM). (2002). *Unequal treatment: Confronting racial and ethnic disparities in health care*. Retrieved from http://www.iom.edu/Reports/2002/Unequal-Treatment-Confronting-Racial-and-Ethnic-Disparities-in-Health-Care.aspx

Intemann, K., Lee, E. S., McCartney, K., Roshanravan, S., & Schriempf, A. (2010). What lies ahead: Envisioning new futures for feminist philosophy. *Hypatia, 25*, 927–934. doi: 10.1111/j.1527-2001.2010.01136.x

Ishiyama, F. I. (2006, March). *Cultural diversity, intermarriage, and intercultural complexity in family: Self-validation model and counseling implications*. Paper presented at the Learning Institute of the Annual Conference of the American Counseling Association and the Canadian Counseling Association, Montreal, Canada.

Ivers, N. N., Ivers, J. J., & Duffey, T. (2013). Second language acquisition: Cultural, cognitive, and clinical considerations for counseling practice. *Journal of Creativity in Mental Health, 8*, 219–234. doi: 10.1080/15401383.2013.821920

Ivey, A. E., D'Andrea, M. J., & Ivey, M. B. (2012). *Theories of counseling and psychotherapy: A multicultural perspective* (7th ed.). Thousand Oaks, CA: Sage Publications.

Ivey, A., Ivey, M., Myers, J., & Sweeney, T. (2005). *Developmental counseling and therapy: Promoting wellness over the lifespan*. Boston, MA: Lahaska Press.

Ivey, A. E., Ivey, M. B., & Zalaquett, C. P. (2014). *Intentional interviewing and counseling: Facilitating client development in a multicultural society* (8th ed.). Belmont, CA: Brooks/Cole.

Iyer, D. S., & Haslam, N. (2003). Body image and eating disturbance among South Asian-American women: The role of racial teasing. *International Journal of Eating Disorders, 34*, 142–147. doi: 10.1002/eat.10170

Jackman, C. F., Wagner, W. G., & Johnson, J. T. (2001). The attitudes toward multiracial children scale. *Journal of Black Studies, 27*, 86–99. doi: 10.1177/0095798401027001005

Jackson, A. P., & Meadows, F. B. (1991). Getting to the bottom to understand the top. *Journal of Counseling & Development, 70*, 72–76.

Jackson, K. F. (2010). Living the multiracial experience: Shifting racial expressions, resisting race, and seeking community. *Qualitative Social Work, 11*, 42–60. doi: 10.1177/1473325010375646

Jackson, K. F., Yoo, H. C., Guevarra, R., Jr., & Harrington, B. A. (2012). Role of identity integration on the relationship between perceived racial discrimination and psychological adjustment of multiracial people. *Journal of Counseling Psychology, 59*, 240–250. doi: 10.1037/a0027639

Jackson, L. C., & Greene, B. (Eds.). (2000). *Psychotherapy with African American women: Innovations in psychodynamic perspectives and practice.* New York, NY: Guilford.

Jackson, L. E., Gregory, H., & Davis, M. G. (2004). NTU Psychotherapy and African American youth. In J. R. Ancis (Eds.), *Culturally responsive interventions: Innovative approaches to working with diverse populations* (pp. 49–70). New York, NY: Brunner-Routledge.

Jackson-Nakazawa, D. (2003). The identity development of 11 to 14 year old multiracial youth. In M. P. P. Root & M. Kelley (Eds.), *Multiracial child resource book: Living complex identities* (pp. 69–74). Seattle, WA: MAVIN Foundation.

Jacobs, J. H. (1992). Identity development in biracial children. In M. P. P. Root (Ed.), *Racially mixed people in America* (pp. 190–206). Newbury Park, CA: Sage Publications.

Jacobs, E. E., Masson, R. L., & Harvill, R. L. (2012). *Group counseling: Interventions and techniques.* New York, NY: Wadsworth.

Jakubowska, E. (2003). Everyday rituals in Polish and English. In K. M. Jaszolt & K. Turner (Eds.), *Meaning through language contrast* (Vol. 2). Philadelphia, PA: John Benjamins.

Jamil, H., Nassar-McMillan, S. C., Lambert, R. G., Wang, Y., Ager, J., & Arnetz, B. (2010). Pre- and post-displacement stressors and time of migration as related to self-rated health among Iraqi immigrants and refugees in southeast Michigan. *Journal of Medicine, Conflict and Survival, 26*(3), 207–222. doi: 10.1080/13623699.2010.513655

Jamil, O. B., Harper, G. W., & Fernandez, M. I. (2009). Sexual and ethnic identity development among gay-bisexual-questioning (GBQ) male ethnic minority adolescents. *Cultural Diversity and Ethnic Minority Psychology, 15*, 203–214. doi: 10.1037/a0014795

Jarvis, G. E. (2012). Changing psychiatric perception of African-Americans with affective disorders. *The Journal of Nervous and Mental Disease, 200*, 1031–1040. doi: 10.1097/NMD.0b013e318275cf43

Jaspal, R., & Cinnirella, M. (2014). Hyper-affiliation to the religious in-group among British Pakistani Muslim gay men. *Journal of Community and Applied Social Psychology, 24*, 265–277. doi: 10.1002/casp.2163

Jayasundar, R. (2010). Ayurveda: A distinctive approach to health and disease. *Current Science, 98*, 908–914.

Jennings, T. (2014). Sexual orientation curriculum in U.S. school counselor education programs. *Journal of LGBT Issues in Counseling, 8*, 43–73. doi: 10.1080/15538605.2014.853639

Johnson, A., & Jackson Williams, D. (2015). White racial identity, color-blind racial attitudes, and multicultural counseling competence. *Cultural Diversity and Ethnic Minority Psychology, 21*, 440–449. doi: 10.1037/a0037533

Johnson, H. B. (2015). *The American dream and the power of wealth: Choosing schools and inheriting inequality in the land of opportunity* (2nd ed). New York, NY: Routledge.

Johnson, S. D. (2012). Gay affirming psychotherapy with lesbian, gay, and bisexual individuals: Implications for contemporary psychotherapy research. *American Journal of Orthopsychiatry, 82*, 516–522. doi: 10.1111/j.1939-0025.2012.01180.x

Johnson, S. L., Kim, Y. M., & Church, K. (2010). Towards client-centered counseling: Development and testing of the WHO decision-making tool. *Patient Education & Counseling, 81*, 355–361. doi: 10.1016/j.pec.2010.10.011

Johnson, T. D., & Kreider, R. M. (2013). *Mapping the geographic distribution of interracial/interethnic married couples in the United States: 2010.* Paper presented at the Annual Meeting of the Population Association of America, New Orleans, LA.

Jokes, L. V. (2009). Claiming your connections: A psychosocial group intervention study of Black college women. *Social Work Research, 33*, 159–171. doi: 10.1093/swr/33.3.159

Jones, C. P. (2000). Levels of racism: A theoretic framework and a gardener's tale. *American Journal of Public Health, 90*, 1212–1215.

Jones, D. J. (2011). Coparenting in extended kinship systems: African American, Hispanic, Asian heritage, and Native American families. In K. M. Lindahl & M. Kristin (Ed.), *Coparenting: A conceptual and clinical examination of family systems* (pp. 61–79). Washington, DC: American Psychological Association.

Jones, K. D. (2012). Dimensional and cross-cutting assessment in the *DSM-5. Journal of Counseling & Development, 90*, 481–487. doi: 10.1002/j.1556-6676.2012/0059/x

Jones, K. N., Brewster, M. E., & Jones, J. A. (2014). The creation and validation of the LGBT Ally Identity Measure. *Psychology of Sexual Orientation and Gender Diversity, 1*, 181–195. doi: 10.1037/sgd0000033

Jones-Smith, E. (2014). *Theories of counseling and psychotherapy: An integrative approach*. Los Angeles, CA: Sage Publications.

Joyner, K., & Kao, G. (2005). Interracial relationship and the transition to adulthood. *American Sociological Review, 70*, 563–581. doi: 10.1177/000312240507000402

Jumper-Thurman, P., Allen, J., & Deters, P. B. (2004). The Circles of Care evaluation: Doing participatory evaluation with American Indian and Alaska Native Communities. *American Indian & Alaska Native Mental Health Research: The Journal of the National Center, 11*, 139–154.

Jun, H. (2010). *Social justice, multicultural counseling, and practice: Beyond a conventional approach*. Los Angeles, CA: Sage Publications.

Jung, C. G. (2006). *The undiscovered self*. New York, NY: Signet.

Kaba, A. J. (2006). The blood and family relations between Africans and Europeans in the United States. *African Renaissance, 3*, 105–114.

Kaba, A. J. (2011). Inter-ethnic/interracial romantic relationships in the United States: Factors responsible for the low rates of marriages between blacks and whites. *Sociology Mind, 1*(3), 121–129. doi: 10.4236/sm.2011.1

Kaiser, C. R., & Spalding, K. E. (2015). Do women who succeed in male-dominated domains help other women? The moderating role of gender identification. *European Journal of Social Psychology, 45*, 599–608. doi: 10.1002/ejsp.2113

Kandula, N. R., Kersey, M., & Lurie, N. (2004). Assuring the health of immigrants: What the leading health indicators tell us. *Annual Review of Public Health, 25*, 357–376. doi: 10.1146/annurev.publhealth.25.101802.123107

Kaplan, D. M. (2014). Ethical implications of a critical legal case for the counseling profession: Ward v. Wilbanks. *Journal of Counseling & Development, 92*, 142–146. doi: 10.1002/j.1556-6676.2014.00140.x

Kaplan, J. M., & Winther, R. G. (2013). Prisoners of abstraction? The Theory and measure of genetic variation, and the very concepts of "Race." *Biological Theory, 7*, 401–412. doi: 10.1007/s13752-012-0048-0

Karcher, M., & Sass, D. (2010). A multicultural assessment of adolescent connectedness: Testing measurement invariance across gender and ethnicity. *Journal of Counseling Psychology, 57*, 274–289. doi: 10.1037/a0019357

Kawahara, D. M., & Fu, M. (2007). The psychology and mental health of Asian American women. In F. T. Leong, A. Ebreo, L. Kinoshita, A. G. Inman, & L. H. Yang (Eds.), *Handbook of Asian American psychology* (2nd ed., pp. 181–196). Thousand Oaks, CA: Sage Publications.

Kawanga-Singer, M., & Chung, R. C. Y. (2002). A paradigm for culturally based care in ethnic minority populations. *Journal of Community Psychology, 22*, 192–208. doi: 10.1002/1520-6629(199404)22:2<192::AID-JCOP2290220213>3.0.CO;2-H

Kaye-Kantrowitz, M. (2007). *The colors of Jews: Racial politics and radical diasporism*. Bloomington: Indiana University Press.

Keeton v. Anderson-Wiley, 664 F.3d 865 (11th Cir. 2011).

Kelsey, D., & Smart, J. F. (2012). Social justice, disability, and rehabilitation education. *Rehabilitation Research, Policy, & Education, 26*, 229–239. doi: 10.1891/216866612X664970

Kendall, P. C., Hudson, J. L., Gosch, E., Flannery-Schroeder, E., & Suveg, C. (2008). Cognitive-behavioral therapy for anxiety disordered youth: A randomized clinical trial evaluating child and family modalities. *Journal of Consulting and Clinical Psychology, 76*, 282–297. doi: 10.1037/0022-006X.76.2.282

Kendler, K. (2010). *A Statement from Kenneth S. Kendler, M.D., on the proposal to eliminate the grief exclusion criterion from Major Depression*. Retrieved from http://www.dsm5.org/about/Documents/grief%20exclusion_Kendler.pdf

Kenney, K. (2000). Multiracial families. In J. Lewis & L. Bradley (Eds.), *Advocacy in counseling: Counselors, clients, community* (pp. 55–70). Greensboro, NC: ERIC/CASS.

Kenney, K. R., & Kenney, M. E. (2002). *Counseling the multiracial population: Couples, individuals, and families. Leader's Guide*. Alexandria, VA: Micro-Training Associates, Alexander Press.

Kenney, K. R., & Kenney, M. E. (2009). Counseling multiple heritage couples and families. In R. C. Henriksen, Jr. & D. A. Paladino (Eds.), *Counseling multiple heritage individuals, couples, and families* (pp. 111–124). Alexandria, VA: American Counseling Association.

Kenney, K. R., & Kenney, M. E. (2010). Advocacy with the multiracial population. In M. J. Ratts, R. L. Toporek, & J. A. Lewis (Eds.), *ACA advocacy competencies: A social justice framework for counselors* (pp. 65–74). Alexandria, VA: American Counseling Association.

Kenney, K. R., & Kenney, M. E. (2014). Counseling multiracial individuals and families. In M. J. Ratts, & P. B. Pedersen (Eds.), *Counseling for multiculturalism and social justice: Integration, theory, and application* (pp. 193–209). Alexandria, VA: American Counseling Association.

Kenney, K. R., Kenney, M. E., Alvarado, S. B., Baden, A. L., Brew, L., Chen-Hayes, S., . . . Singh, A. A. (2015). *Competencies for counseling the multiracial population*. Retrieved from http://www.counseling.org/docs/default-source/competencies/competencies-for-counseling-the-multiracial-population-2-2-15-final.pdf?sfvrsn=14

Kerwin, C., & Ponterotto, J. (1995). Biracial identity development: Theory and research. In J. Ponterotto, J. Casas, L. Suzuki, & C. Alexander (Eds.), *Handbook of multicultural counseling* (pp. 199–217). Thousand Oaks, CA: Sage Publications.

Kessler, R. C., Berglund, P., Demler, O., Jin, R., Koretz, D., Merikangas, K. R., et al. (2003). The epidemiology of Major Depressive Disorder: Results from the National Comorbidity Survey Replication (NCS-R). *Journal of the American Medical Association, 289*, 3095–3105. doi: 10.1001/jama.289.23.3095

Khalsa, S. B. S., Khalsa, G. S., Khalsa, H. K., & Khalsa, M. K. (2008). Evaluation of a residential Kundalini Yoga lifestyle pilot program for addiction in India. *Journal of Ethnicity in Substance Abuse, 7*, 67–79. doi: 10.1080/15332640802081968

Khanna, N. (2004). The role of reflected appraisals in racial identity: The case of multiracial Asians. *Social Psychology Quarterly, 67*, 115–131. doi: 10.1177/019027250406700201

Khanna, N. (2010). "If you're half Black, you're just Black": Reflected appraisals and the persistence of the one drop rule. *The Sociological Quarterly, 51*, 96–121. doi: 10.1111/j.1533-8525.2009.01162.x

Kich, G. K. (1992). The developmental process of asserting a biracial, bicultural identity. In M. P. P. Root (Ed.), *Racially mixed people in America* (pp. 304–317). Newbury Park, CA: Sage Publications.

Killian, K. D. (2012). *Interracial couples, intimacy, and therapy: Crossing racial borders.* New York, NY: Columbia University Press.

Kilpatrick, M., Ohannessian, C., & Bartholomew, J. B. (1999). Adolescent weight management and perceptions: An analysis of the National Longitudinal Study of Adolescent Health. *Journal of School Health, 69*, 148–152. doi: 10.1111/j.1746-1561.1999.tb04173.x

Kim, B. S. K., Ng, G. F., & Ahn, A. J. (2005). The Asian American Values Scale—Multidimensional: Development, reliability, and validity. *Journal of Counseling Psychology, 52*, 67–76. doi: 10.1037/1099-9809.11.3.187

Kim, C. (2015). New color lines: Racial/ethnic inequality in earnings among college-educated men. *The Sociological Quarterly, 56*, 152–184. doi: 10.1111/tsq.12078

Kim, H., Prouty, A. M., & Roberson, P. N. (2012). Narrative therapy with intercultural couples: A case study. *Journal of Family Psychotherapy, 23*, 273–286.

Kim, I., & Kim, W. (2014). Post-resettlement challenges and mental health of South East Asian refugees in the United States. *Best Practices in Mental Health: An International Journal, 10*, 63–77.

Kim, I. J., Lau, A. S., & Chang, D. F. (2007). Family violence among Asian Americans. In F. Leong, A. G. Inman, A. Ebreo, L. Lang, L. Kinoshita, & M. Fu (Eds.), *Handbook of Asian American psychology* (2nd ed., pp. 363–378). Thousand Oaks, CA: Sage.

Kim, J. L., & Ward, L. M. (2007). Silence speaks volumes: Parental sexual communication among Asian American emerging adults. *Journal of Adolescent Research, 22*, 3–31. doi: 10.1177/0743558406294916

Kim, P. Y., & Kendall, D. L. (2015). Etiology beliefs moderate the influence of emotional self-control on willingness to see a counselor through help-seeking attitudes among Asian American students. *Journal of Counseling Psychology, 62*, 148–158. doi: 10.1037/cou0000015

Kim, P. Y., & Lee, D. (2014). Internalized model minority myth, Asian values, and help-seeking attitudes among Asian American students. *Cultural Diversity, and Ethnic Minority Psychology, 20*, 98–106. doi: 10.1037/a0033351

Kim, P. Y., & Park, I. J. K. (2009). Testing a multiple mediation model of Asian American college students' willingness to see a counselor. *Cultural Diversity & Ethnic Minority Psychology, 15*, 295–302. doi: 10.1037/a0014396

Kim, S., & Cardemil, E. (2012). Effective psychotherapy with low-income clients: The importance of attending to social class. *Journal of Contemporary Psychotherapy, 42*, 27–35. doi: 10.1007/s10879-011-9194-0

Kim, S. Y., & Chao, R. K. (2009). Heritage language fluency, ethnic identity, and school effort of immigrant Chinese and Mexico adolescents. *Cultural Diversity and Ethnic Minority Psychology, 15*, 27–37. doi: 10.1037/a0013052

Kim, S. Y., Shen, Y., Huang, X., Wang, Y, & Orozco-Lapray, D. (2014). Chinese American parents' acculturation and enculturation, bicultural management difficulty, depressive symptoms, and parenting. *Asian American Journal of Psychology, 5*, 298–306. doi: 10.1037/a0035929

Kim, S. Y., Wang, Y., Chen, Q., Shen, Y., & Hou, Y. (2015). Parent-child acculturation profiles as predictors of Chinese American adolescents' academic trajectories. *Journal of Youth and Adolescence, 44*, 1263–1274. doi: 10.1007/s10964-014-01310x

Kinsey, A. C., Pomeroy, W. B., & Martin, C. E. (1948a). *Sexual behavior in the human female.* Philadelphia, PA: W. B. Saunders.

Kinsey, A. C., Pomeroy, W. B., & Martin, C. E. (1948b). *Sexual behavior in the human male.* Philadelphia, PA: W. B. Saunders.

Kira, I. A., Amer, M. A., & Wrobel, N. H. (2014). Arab refugees: Trauma, resilience, and recovery. In S. C. Nassar-McMillan, K. A. Ajrouch, & J. Hakim-Larson (Eds.). *Biopsychosocial perspectives on Arab Americans: Culture, development, and health* (pp. 89–106). New York, NY: Springer.

Kirmayer, L. J., Dandeneau, S., Marshall, S., Phillips, M. K., & Williamson, K. J. (2011). Rethinking resilience from indigenous perspectives. *The Canadian Journal of Psychiatry, 56*, 84–91.

Kirmayer, L. J., & Minas, H. (2000). The future of cultural psychiatry: An international perspective. *Canadian Journal of Psychiatry, 45*, 438–446.

Kiselica, M. S. (2004). When duty calls: The implications of social justice work for policy, education, and practice in the mental health professions. *The Counseling Psychologist, 32*, 838–854. doi: 10.1177/0011000004269272

Kiselica, M. S., & Robinson, M. (2000). Bringing advocacy counseling to life: The history, issues, and human dramas of social justice work in counseling. *Journal of Counseling & Development, 79*, 387–397.

Klar, M., & Kasser, T. (2009). Some benefits of being an activist: Measuring activism and its role in psychological well-being. *Political Psychology, 30*, 755–777. doi: 10.1111/j.1467-9221.2009.00724.x

Klostermaier, K. K. (2007). *Hinduism: A beginner's guide.* London: Oneworld.

Kluckhohn, C. (1951). Values and value orientations in the theory of action. In T. Parsons & E. A. Shields (Eds.), *Toward a general theory of action* (pp. 388–433). Cambridge, MA: Harvard University Press.

Kluckholn, C. (1956). Towards a comparison of value-emphasis in different cultures. In L. D. White (Ed.), *The state of social sciences* (pp. 116–132). Chicago, IL: University of Chicago Press.

Kluckhohn, F. R., & Strodtbeck, F. L. (1961). *Variations in value orientations.* Evanston, IL: Row, Petersen.

Knowles, E. D., & Lowery, B. S. (2012). Meritocracy, self-concerns, and Whites' denial of racial inequity. *Self and Identity, 11,* 202–222. doi: 10.1080/15298868.2010.542015

Kocet, M. M., & Herlihy, B. J. (2014). Addressing value-based conflicts within the counseling relationship: A decision making model. *Journal of Counseling & Development, 92,* 180–186. doi: 10.1002/j.1556-6676.2014.00146.x

Kosciw, J. G., Greytak, E. A., Palmer, N. A., & Boesen, M. J. (2014). *The 2013 National School Climate Survey: The experiences of lesbian, gay, bisexual and transgender youth in our nation's schools.* New York, NY: GLSEN.

Kottack, C. P. (2008). *Mirror for humanity: A concise introduction to cultural anthropology* (6th ed.). New York, NY: McGraw-Hill.

Kottak, C. (2008). *Anthropology: Exploring human diversity.* New York, NY: McGraw Hill.

Kotter, J. P. (2012). *Leading change.* Boston, MA: Harvard Business Review Press.

Kraemer, H. C. (2007). *DSM* categories and dimensions in clinical research contexts. *International Journal of Methods in Psychiatric Research, 16,* S8–S15. doi: 10.1002/mpr.211

Kress, V. E., Eriksen, K. P., Rayle, A. D., & Ford, S. J. W. (2005). The *DSM–IV–TR* and culture: Considerations for counselors. *Journal of Counseling & Development, 83,* 97–104.

Kress, V. E., & Paylo, M. (2015). *Treating those with mental disorders: A comprehensive approach to case conceptualization and treatment.* Upper Saddle River, NJ: Pearson.

Krieg, A., & Xu, Y. (2015). Ethnic differences in social anxiety between individuals of Asian heritage and European heritage: A meta-analytic review. *Asian American Journal of Psychology, 6,* 66–80. doi: 10.1037/a0036993

Krieger, N., Kosheleva, A., Waterman, P. D., Chen, J. T., & Koenen, K. (2011). Racial discrimination, psychological distress, and self-rated health among US-born and foreign-born Black Americans. *American Journal of Public Health, 101,* 1704–1713. doi: 10.2105/AJPH.2011.300168

Kwon, H. (2010). Parental pressure and expectations. In E. Wen-Chu-Chen & G. Yoo (Eds.), *Encyclopedia of Asian American issues today: Volume 1* (p. 232). Santa Barbara, CA: Greenwood Press.

LaFromboise, T. D., & Lewis, H. A. (2008). The Zuni Life Skills Development Program: A school/community-based suicide prevention intervention. *Suicide & Life-Threatening Behavior, 38,* 343–353. doi: 10.1521/suli.2008.38.3.343

Lai, E., & Arguelles, D. (2003). *The new face of Asian Pacific America: Numbers, diversity & change in the 21st century.* San Francisco, CA: Asia Week and UCLA Asian American Studies Center.

LaMantia, K., Wagner, H., & Bohecker, L. (2015). Ally development through feminist pedagogy: A systemic focus on intersectionality, *Journal of LGBT Issues in Counseling, 9,* 136–153, doi: 10.1080/15538605.2015.1029205

Lambert, S. (2005). The experience of gay male and lesbian faculty in counselor education departments: A grounded theory. *Dissertation Abstracts International, 66*(06A), 2113. (UMI No. 3177885)

Lambie, G., Davis, K., & Miller, G. (2008). Spirituality: Implications for professional school counselors' ethical practice. *Counseling and Values, 52,* 211–223.

Landrine, H. (1989). The politics of personality disorder. *Psychology of Women, 13,* 324–339. doi: 10.1111/j.1471-6402.1989.tb01005.x

Langdridge, D. (2007). Gay affirmative therapy: A theoretical framework and defense. *Journal of Gay & Lesbian Psychotherapy, 11,* 27–43. doi: 10.1300/J236v11n01_03

Lange, R., Houran, J., & Li, S. (2015). Dyadic relationship values in Chinese online daters: Love American style? *Sexuality & Culture, 19,* 190–215. doi: 10.1007/s12119-014-9255-0

Lansford, J. E., Criss, M. M., Dodge, K. A., Shaw, D. S., Pettit, G. S., & Bates, J. E. (2009). Trajectories of physical discipline: Early childhood antecedents and development outcomes. *Child Development, 80,* 1385–1402. doi: 10.1111/j.1467-8624.2009.01340.x

LaRoche, M. J., Fuentes, M. L., & Hinton, D. (2015). A cultural examination of the *DSM-5*: Research and clinical implications. *Professional Psychology: Research and Practice, 46,* 183–189. doi: 10.1037/a0039278

Laszloffy, T. A. (March–April, 2005). Multiracial families. *Family Therapy Magazine,* 38–43.

Lau, A. S., Fung, J., Wang, S., & Kang, S. M. (2009). Explaining elevated social anxiety among Asian Americans: Emotional attunement and a cultural double bind. *Cultural Diversity and Ethnic Minority Psychology, 15,* 77–85. doi: 10.1037/a0012819

Lawson, W. B., & Lawson, A. (2013). Disparities in mental health diagnosis and treatment among African Americans: Implications for the correctional systems. In B. Sanders, Y. F. Thomas, & B. Griffin Deeds (Eds.), *Crime, HIV, and health: Intersections of criminal justice and public health concerns* (pp. 81–91). Amsterdam, Netherlands: Springer.

Le, C. N. (2010). Multiracial Asian Americans: Social class, demographic, and cultural characteristics. In K. O. Korgen (Ed.), *Multiracial Americans and social class: The influence of social class on racial identity* (pp. 115–130). New York, NY: Routledge.

LeBron, A. M. W., Valerio, M. A., Kieffer, E., Sinco, B., Rosland, A., Hawkins, J., . . . Spencer, M. (2014). Everyday discrimination, diabetes-related distress, and depressive symptoms among African American and Latinos with diabetes. *Journal of Immigrant and Minority Health, 16,* 1208–1216. doi: 10.1007/s10903-013-9843-3

Lee, C. C. (Ed.). (2007). *Counseling for social justice* (2nd ed.). Alexandria, VA: American Counseling Association.

Lee, C. C. (2013). *Multicultural issues in counseling: New approaches to diversity* (4th ed.). Alexandria, VA: American Counseling Association.

Lee, C. C., & Rodgers, R. A. (2009). Counselor advocacy: Affecting systematic change in the public area. *Journal of Counseling & Development, 87,* 284–287.

Lee, C. C., & Walz, G. R. (Eds.). (1998). *Social action: A mandate for counselors.* Alexandria, VA: American Counseling Association.

Lee, C.-T., Beckert, T. E., & Goodrich, T. R. (2010). The relationship between individualistic, collectivistic, and transitional cultural value orientations and adolescents' autonomy and identity status. *Journal of Youth and Adolescence, 39,* 882–893. doi: 10.1007/s10964-009-9430-z

Lee, E. O. (2007). Religion and spirituality as predictors of well-being among Chinese American and Korean American older adults. *Journal of Religion, Spirituality, and Aging, 19,* 77–100.

Lee, E.-K. O., & Ctian, K. (2009). Religious/spiritual and other adaptive coping strategies among Chinese American older immigrants. *Journal of Gerontological Social Work, 52,* 517–533. doi: 10.1080/01634370902983203

Lee, J. (2014). Asian international students' barriers to joining group counseling. *International Journal of Group Psychotherapy, 64,* 445–464. doi: 10.1521/ijgp.2014.64.4.444

Lee, R., Jordan, J., & Schuler, E. (2018). Sexual assault. In L. R. Jackson-Cherry, & B. T. Erford (Eds.), *Crisis assessment, intervention, and prevention* (3rd ed., pp. 193–218). Columbus, OH: Pearson.

Lee, S. J., Wong, N. A., & Alvarez, A. N. (2009). The model minority and perpetual foreigner: Stereotypes of Asian Americans. In N. Tewari & A. Alvarez (Eds.), *Asian American psychology: Current perspectives* (pp. 69–84). New York, NY: Psychology Press.

Lee, S. K. (2009). *East Asian attitudes toward death— A search for the ways to help East Asian elderly dying in contemporary America.* Retrieved from http://www.ncbi.nlm.nih.gov/pmc/articles/PMC2911815/

Lee, S. M., & Edmonston, B. (2005). New marriages, new families: U.S. racial and Hispanic intermarriage. *Population Bulletin, 60,* 1–40.

Lee, S. Y., Xue, Q., Spira, A. O., & Lee, H. B. (2014). Racial and ethnic differences in depressive subtypes and access to mental health care in the United States. *Journal of Affective Disorders, 155,* 130–137. doi: 10.1016/j.jad.2013.10.037

Lemieux, A. F., & Pratto, F. (2003). Poverty and prejudice. In S. C. Carr & T. S. Sloan (Eds.), *Poverty and psychology: From global perspective to local practice* (pp. 147–162). New York, NY: Kluwer Academic/Plenum.

Leondar-Wright, B. (2012). *Class and other identities: And answers from the Class Matters book.* Retrieved from http://www.classmatters.org/bios/leondar-wright.php

Leong, F. T., Chang, D. F., & Lee, S. (2007). Counseling and psychotherapy with Asian Americans: Process and outcomes. In F. T. Leong, A. Ebreo, L. Kinoshita, A. G. Inman, & L. H. Yang (Eds.), *Handbook of Asian American psychology* (2nd ed., pp. 429–447). Thousand Oaks, CA: Sage.

Leong, F. T. L., & Kalibatseva, Z. (2011). Cross-cultural barriers to mental health services in the United States. *Cerebrum, 1–13.* Retrieved from http://dana.org/news/cerebrum/detail.aspx?id=31364

Leong, F. T. L., Kim, H. H. W., & Gupta, A. (2011). Attitudes toward professional counseling among Asian-American college students: Acculturation, conceptions of mental illness, and loss of face. *Asian American Journal of Psychology, 2,* 140–153. doi: 10.1037/a0024172

Leong, F. T. L., & Lau, A. S. L. (2001). Barriers to providing effective mental health services to Asian Americans. *Mental Health Services Research, 3,* 201–214. doi: 10.1023/A:1013177014788

Leong, F. T. L., Lee, S., & Chang, D. (2008). Counseling Asian Americans: Client and therapist variables. In P. B. Pedersen, J. G. Draguns, W. J. Lonner, & J. E. Trimble (Eds.), *Counseling across cultures* (pp. 113–129). Thousand Oaks, CA: Sage.

Lerner, G. (1986). *The creation of patriarchy.* New York, NY: Oxford University Press.

Lerner, G. (2010). Reconceptualizing differences among women. *Journal of Women's History, 1,* 106–122. doi: 10.1353/jowh.2010.0082

LeShan, L. (2000). *How to meditate: A guide to self-discovery.* New York, NY: Bantam.

Leung, A. N., Wong, S. S., Wong, I. W., & McBride-Chang, C. (2010). Filial piety and psychological adjustment in Hong Kong Chinese early adolescents. *The Journal of Early Adolescence, 30,* 651–667. doi: 10.1177/0272431609341046

Leung, P., Cheung, M., & Tsui, V. (2012). Help-seeking behaviors among Chinese Americans with depressive symptoms. *Social Work, 57,* 61–71. doi: 10.1093/sw/swr009

Lev, A. I. (2004). *Transgender emergence: Therapeutic guidelines for working with gender-variant people and their families.* Binghamton, NY: Haworth Press.

Levant, R. F., Allen, P. A., & Mei-Ching, L. (2014). Alexithymia in men: How and when do emotional processing deficiencies occur? *Psychology of Men & Masculinity, 15,* 324–334. doi: 10.1037/a0033860

Levant, R. F., Karakis, E. N., Wong, Y. J., & Welsh, M. M. (2015). Mediated moderation of the relationship between the endorsement of restrictive emotionality and alexithymia. *Psychology of Men & Masculinity, 16,* 459–467. doi: 10.1037/a0039739

Levasseur, M., Cohen, A. A., Dubois, M. F., Généreux, M., Richard, L., Therrien, F. H., & Payette, H. (2015).

Environmental factors associated with social participation of older adults living in metropolitan, urban, and rural areas: The NuAge study. *American Journal of Public Health, 105*, 718–1725. doi: 10.2105/AJPH.2014.302415

Leventhal, T., & Brooks-Gunn, J. (2003). Moving to opportunity: An experimental study of neighborhood effects on mental health. *American Journal of Public Health, 93*, 1576–1582.

Lewandowski, L. A., Chiodo, L., Peterson, B., & Kira, I. (2007). *The effects of cumulative trauma on emotional and physical health, and risky behavior of adolescents: PTSD symptomatology and parental emotional support as mediators.* Paper presented at the 18th International Nursing. Research Congress Focusing on Evidence-Based Practice, Vienna, Austria.

Lewis, B. E., & Churchill, B. E. (2008). *Islam: The religion and the people.* New York, NY: Pearson.

Lewis, E. (2006). *Fade: My journeys in multiracial America.* New York, NY: Carroll & Graf.

Lewis, J. A., Arnold, M. S., House, R., & Toporek, R. (2003). *Advocacy competencies.* Retrieved from http://counselorsforsocialjustice.com/advocacycompetencies.html

Lewis, J. A., Ratts, M. J., Paladino, D. A., & Toporek, R. L. (2011). Social justice counseling and advocacy: Developing new leadership roles and competencies. *Journal of Social Action in Counseling & Psychology, 3*, 5–16.

Lewis, K. (1998). *Prayer without ceasing: Breath prayer.* Bellevue, WA: Prescott Press.

Lewis, S. (1925). *Arrowsmith.* New York, NY: Harcourt, Brace, & World.

Lewis-McCoy, R. L. (2014). *Inequality in the promised land: Race, resources, and suburban schooling.* Redwood City, CA: Stanford University Press.

Li, M. (2014). Discrimination and psychiatric disorder among Asian American immigrants: A national analysis by subgroups. *Journal of Immigrant Minority Health, 16*, 1157–1166. doi: 10.1007/s10903-013-9920-7

Liang, C. T., Alvarez, A. N., Juang, L. J., & Liang, M. X. (2007). The role of coping in the relationship between perceived racism and racism-related stress for Asian Americans: Gender differences. *Journal of Counseling Psychology, 54*, 132–141. doi: 10.1037/0022-0167.54.2.132

Liao, M. S. (2006). Domestic violence among Asian Indian immigrant women: Risk factors, acculturation, and intervention. *Women & Therapy, 29*, 23–39. doi: 10.1300/J015v29n01_02

Lien, P. (2002). Public resistance to electing Asian Americans in Southern California. *Journal of Asian American Studies, 5*, 51–72. doi: 10.1353/jaas.2002.0005

Lind, A. (2004). Legislating the family: Heterosexist bias in social welfare policy frameworks. *Journal of Sociology and Social Welfare, 31*, 21–35.

Liu, A. (2011). Unraveling the myth of meritocracy within the contact of U.S. higher education. *Higher Education, 62*, 383–397. doi: 10.1007/s10734-010-9394-7

Liu, W. M., & Chang, T. (2007). Asian American men and masculinity. In F. Leong, A. Inman, A. Ebreo, L. Yang, L. Kinoshita, & M. Fu (Eds.), *Handbook of Asian American psychology* (2nd ed., pp. 197–212). Thousand Oaks, CA: Sage Publications.

Liu, W. M., & Iwamoto, D. K. (2006). Asian American men's gender role conflict: The role of Asian values, self-esteem, and psychological distress. *Psychology of Men & Masculinity, 7*, 153–164. doi: 10.1037/1524-9220.7.3.153

Liu, W. M., & Pope-Davis, D. B. (2004). Understanding classism to effect personal change. In T. B. Smith (Ed.), *Practicing multiculturalism: Affirming diversity in counseling and psychology* (pp. 294–310). Boston, MA: Allyn & Bacon.

Locust, C. (1988). Wounding the spirit: Discrimination and traditional American Indian belief systems. *Harvard Educational Review, 58*, 315–330. doi: 10.17763/haer.58.3.e0r224774008738p

Logan, S. L., Freeman, E. M., & McRoy, R. G. (1987). Racial identity problems of biracial clients: Implications for social work practice. *Journal of Intergroup Relations, 15*, 11–24.

Loo, C. M., Fairbank, J. A., Scurfield, R. M., Ruch, L. O., King, D. W., Adams, L. J., et al. (2001). Measuring exposure to racism: Development and validation of a Race-Related Stressor Scale (RRSS) for Asian American Vietnam veterans. *Psychological Assessment, 13*, 503–520. doi: 10.1037/1040-3590.13.4.503

Lott, B., & Bullock, H. E. (2007). *Psychology and economic injustice: Personal, professional, and political intersections.* Washington, DC: American Psychological Association.

Lou, E., Lalonde, R. N., & Wilson, C. (2011). Examining a multidimensional framework of racial identity across different biracial groups. *Asian American Journal of Psychology, 2*, 79–90. doi: 10.1037/a0023658

Love, P. (2001). Spirituality and student development: Theoretical connections. *New Directions for Student Services, 95*, 7–16. doi: 10.1002/ss.18

Loving Day Organization. (2009). *Loving v. Virginia.* Retrieved from http://lovingday.org/loving-v-virginia

Loving v. Virginia, 388 U.S. 1 (1967).

Lucier-Greer, M., O'Neal, C. W., Arnold, A. L., Mancini, J. A., & Wickrama, K. K. A. S. (2014). Adolescent mental health and academic functioning: Empirical support for contrasting models of risk and vulnerability. *Military Medicine, 179*, 1279–1287. doi: 10.7205/MILMED-D-14-00090

Lui, P. P. (2015). Intergenerational cultural conflict, mental health, and educational outcomes among Asian and Latino/a Americans: Qualitative and meta-analytic review. *Psychological Bulletin, 141*, 404–446. doi: 10.1037/a0038449

Luke, M., & Goodrich, K. (2012). LGBTQ responsive school counseling supervision. *The Clinical Supervisor, 31*, 81–102. doi: 10.1080/07325223.2012.672391

Luna, N., Evans, W. P., & Davis, B. (2015). Indigenous Mexican culture, identity and academic aspirations: Results from a community-based curriculum project for Latina/Latino students. *Race, Ethnicity and Education, 18*, 341–362. doi: 10.1080/13613324.2012.759922

Luskin, F. (2003). *Forgive for good.* San Francisco, CA: Harper.

Luu, T. D., Leung, P., & Nash, S. G. (2009). Help-seeking attitudes among Vietnamese Americans: The impact of acculturation, cultural barriers, and spiritual beliefs. *Social Work in Mental Health, 7*, 476–493. doi: 10.1080/15332980802467456

MacLeod, B. P. (2013). Social justice at the microlevel: Working with clients' prejudices. *Journal of Multicultural Counseling and Development, 41*, 169–184. doi: 10.1002/j.2161-1912.2013.00035.x

Madera, J. M., King, E. B., & Hebl, M. R. (2012). Bringing social identity to work: The influence of manifestation and suppression on perceived discrimination, job satisfaction, and turnover intentions. *Cultural Diversity and Ethnic Minority Psychology, 18*, 165–170. doi: 10.1037/a0027724

Madon, S. (1997). What do people believe about gay males? A study of stereotype content and strength. *Sex Roles, 37*, 663–685. doi: 10.1007/BF02936334

Magaldi-Dopman, D., & Park-Taylor, J. (2010). Sacred adolescence: Practical suggestions for psychologists working with adolescents' religious and spiritual identity. *Professional Psychology: Research and Practice, 41*, 382–390. doi: 10.1037/a0020941

Magnavita, J. J. (2016). *Clinical decision making in mental health practice.* Washington, DC: American Psychological Association.

Mahapatra, N. (2012). South Asian women in the U.S. and their experience of domestic violence. *Journal of Family Violence, 27*, 381–390. doi: 10.1007/s10896-012-9434-4

Mahtani, M. (2014). *Mixed race amnesia: Resisting the romanticization of multiraciality.* Vancouver, BC: UBC Press.

Maki, D. R., & Tarvydas, V. M. (2011). *The professional practice of rehabilitation counseling* (2nd ed.). New York, NY: Springer.

Malott, K. M., Paone, T. R., Schaefle, S., Cates, J., & Haizlip, B. (2015). Expanding White racial identity theory: A qualitative investigation of Whites engaged in antiracist action. *Journal of Counseling & Development, 93*, 333–343. doi: 10.1002/jcad.12031

Malott, K. M., & Schaefle, S. (2015). Addressing clients' experiences of racism: A model for clinical practice. *Journal of Counseling & Development, 93*, 361–369. doi: 10.1002/jcad.12034

Mann, C. C. (2007). *1491: New revelations of the Americas before Columbus.* New York, NY: Alfred A. Knopf.

Maparyan, L. (2012). *The womanist idea.* New York, NY: Routledge.

Markoff, L. S., Finkelstein, N., Kammerer, N., Kreiner, P., & Prost, C. A. (2005). Implementing a model of change in integrating services for women with substance abuse and mental health disorders and histories of trauma. *Journal of Behavioral Health Services and Research, 32*, 227–240.

Markovich, S. J. (Ed.). (2014). *Renewing America: Backgrounder: The income inequality debate.* Retrieved from http://www.cfr.org/united-states/income-inequality-debate/p29052

Marsella, A. J., & Kameoka, V. A. (1989). Ethno-cultural issues in the assessment of psychopathology. In S. Wetzler (Ed.), *Measuring mental illness: Psychometric assessment for clinicians* (pp. 231–256). Washington, DC: American Psychiatric Press

Marsella, A. J., & Yamada, A. M. (2010). Culture and psychopathology: Foundations, issues, directions. *Journal of Pacific Rim Psychology, 4*, 103–115. doi: 10.1375/prp.4.2.103

Marshall, G. N., Schell, T. L., Elliott, M. N., Berthold, S. M., & Chi-Ah, C. (2005). Mental health of Cambodian refugees 2 decades after resettlement in the Unites States. *The Journal of the American Medical Association, 294*, 571–579. doi: 10.1001/jama.294.5.571.

Maslow, A. (1993). *The farther reaches of human nature.* New York, NY: Penguin.

Master Psychotherapists. (2018). *Master psychotherapists discuss their lives and work: An interview with Albert Ellis, PhD.* Retrieved from http://www.psychotherapy.net/video/albert-ellis-rebt

Matsuoka, J., Breaux, C., & Ryujin, D. (1997). National utilization of mental health services by Asian Americans and Pacific Islanders. *Journal of Community Psychology, 25*, 141–145. doi: 10.1002/(SICI)1520-6629(199703)25:2<141::AID-JCOP3>3.0.CO;2-0

Matthews, C. R. (2007). Affirmative lesbian, gay, and bisexual counseling with all clients. In K. J. Bieschke, R. M. Perez, & K. A. DeBord (Eds.), *Handbook of counseling and psychotherapy with lesbian, gay, bisexual, and transgender clients* (2nd ed., pp. 201–219). Washington, DC: American Psychological Association.

Mattis, J. S., & Mattis, J. H. (2011). Religiosity and spirituality in the lives of African American children. In N. E. Hill, T. L. Mann, & H. E. Fitzgerald (Eds.), *African American children and mental health, Volumes 1 and 2: Development and context, Prevention and social policy* (pp. 125–149). Santa Barbara, CA: Praeger/ABC-CLIO.

Matus, S. R. (2010). Psychpathological speech and social control: An analysis of the relationship between regulations and exclusion. *Electronic Journal of Political Psychology, 8*, 102–114.

Maxwell, M., & Henriksen, R. C., Jr. (2009). Counseling multiple heritage adolescents. In R. C. Henriksen, Jr. & D. A. Paladino (Eds.), *Counseling multiple heritage individuals, couples, and families* (pp. 65–81). Alexandria, VA: American Counseling Association.

Maynard, C., Ehreth, J., Cox, G. B., Peterson, P. D., & McGann, M. E. (1997). Racial differences in the utilization of public mental health services in Washington state. *Administration and Policy in Mental Health, 24*, 411–424. doi: 10.1007/BF02042723

McAdoo, H. P. (Ed.). (2007). *Black families*. Thousand Oaks, CA: Sage Publications.

McAdoo, H. P., & Younge, S. N. (2009). Black families. In H. A. Neville, B. M. Tynes, & S. O. Utsey (Eds.), *Handbook of African American psychology* (pp. 103–115). Thousand Oaks, CA: Sage Publications.

McAuliffe, G., Kim, B. S. K., & Park, Y. S. (2008). Ethnicity. In G. McAuliffe & Associates (Eds.), *Culturally alert counseling: A comprehensive introduction* (pp. 84–105). Thousand Oaks, CA: Sage Publications.

McCabe, K. (2011). *African immigrants in the United States*. Washington, DC: Migration Policy Institute.

McCabe, S. E., Bostwick, W. B., Hughes, T. L., West, B. T., & Boyd, C. J. (2010). The relationship between discrimination and substance use disorders among lesbian, gay, bisexual adults in the United States. *American Journal of Public Health, 100*, 1946–1952. doi: 10.2105/AJPH.2009.163147

McCarn, S. R., & Fassinger, R. E. (1996). Re-visioning sexual minority identity formation: A new model of lesbian identity and its implications for counseling and research. *The Counseling Psychologist, 24*, 508–534. doi: 10.1177/0011000096243011

McClain, C. S. (2011). Family stories: Black/White marriage during the 1960s. *The Western Journal of Black Studies, 35*, 9–21.

McDowell, T., Ingoglia, L., Serizawa, T., Holland, C., Dashiell, J. W., Jr., & Stevens, C. (2005). Raising multiracial awareness in family therapy through critical conversations. *Journal of Marital and Family Therapy, 31*, 399–411. doi: 10.1111/j.1752-0606.2005.tb01579.x

McFadden, C. (2015). Lesbian, gay, bisexual, and transgender careers and human resource development: A systematic literature review. *Human Resources Development Review, 14*, 125–162. doi: 10.1177/1534484314549456

McFarland, L. V., Choppa, A., Betz, K., Pruden, J., & Reiber, G. E. (2010). Resources for wounded warriors with major traumatic limb loss. *Journal of Rehabilitation Research and Development, 47*(4), 1–13.

McGeorge, C., & Carlson, T. S. (2007). Deconstructing heterosexism: Becoming an LGB Affirmative heterosexual couple and family therapist. *Journal of Marital and Family Therapy, 37*, 14–26. doi: 10.1111/j.1752-0606.2009.00149.x

McGill, D. W., & Pearce, J. K. (2005). American families with English ancestors from the colonial era: Anglo Americans. In M. McGoldrick, J. Giordano, & N. Garcia-Preto (Eds.), *Ethnicity and family therapy* (3rd ed., pp. 520–533). New York, NY: Guilford Press.

McGilley, B. M., & Pryor, T. L. (1998). Assessment and treatment of Bulimia Nervosa. *American Family Physician, 57*, 2743–2750.

McGoldrick, M., Giordano, J., & Garcia-Preto, N. (2005). *Ethnicity and family therapy* (3rd ed.). New York, NY: Guilford Press.

McIntosh, P. (1988). *White privilege and male privilege: A personal account of coming to see correspondences through work in women's studies*. Working papers #189, Wellesley College Center for Research on Women, Wellesley, MA.

McIntosh, P. (1989, July/August). White privilege: Unpacking the invisible knapsack. *Peace and Freedom*, 10–12.

McLarney, E. (2011). American freedom and Islamic fascism: Ideology in the hall of mirrors. *Theory and Event, 14*(3). doi: 10.1353/tae.2011.0031

McLaughlin, D. (1994). Critical literacy for Navajo and other American Indian learners. *Journal of American Indian Education, 33*, 47–59.

McLeigh, J. D. (2010). What are the policy issues related to the mental health of Native Americans? *American Journal of Orthopsychiatry, 80*, 177–182. doi: 10.1111/j.1939-0025.2010.01021.x

McLeod, A. L., Muldoon, J., & Jackson-Cherry, L. R. (2018). Intimate partner violence. In L. R. Jackson-Cherry, & B. T. Erford (Eds.), *Crisis assessment, intervention, and prevention* (3rd ed., pp. 157–192). Columbus, OH: Pearson.

McMahon, H. G., Mason, E. C. M., Daluga-Guenther, N., & Ruiz, A. (2014). An ecological model of professional school counseling. *Journal of Counseling & Development, 92*, 459–471. doi: 10.1002/j.1556-6676.2014.00172.x

McNamee, S. J., & Miller, R. K. (2009). *The meritocracy myth*. Lanham, MD: Rowman & Littlefield.

McWhirter, E. H. (1994). *Counseling for empowerment*. Alexandria, VA: American Counseling Association.

McWhirter, E. H. (1997). Empowerment, social activism, and counseling. *Counseling and Human Development, 29*, 1–14.

Mellin, E. A., Hunt, B. & Nichols, L. M. (2011). Counselor professional identity: Findings and implications for counseling and interprofessional collaboration. *Journal of Counseling and Development, 89*, 140–147. doi: 10.1002/j.1556-6678.2011.tb00071.x

Meriam, L. (1928). *The problem of Indian administration*. Baltimore, MD: Johns Hopkins University Press.

Merriam-Webster.com. (2018). *Disability*. Retrieved from http://www.merriam-webster.com/dictionary/disability

Merkes, M. (2010). Mindfulness-based stress reduction for people with chronic diseases. *Australian Journal of Primary Health, 16*, 200–210. doi: 10.1071/PY09063

Merton, T. (1986). *Spiritual direction and meditation*. Collegeville, MN: Liturgical Press.

Mettler, S. (2012). *How the G. I. Bill built the middle class and enhanced democracy*. Retrieved from http://www.scholarsstrategynetwork.org/sites/default/files/ssn_key_findings_mettler_on_gi_bill.pdf

Meyer, I. H. (2015). Resilience in the study of minority stress and health of sexual and gender minorities. *Psychology of Sexual Orientation and Gender Diversity, 2*, 209–213. doi: 10.1037/sgd0000132

Meyer, I. H., Dietrich, J., & Schwartz, S. (2008). Lifetime prevalence of mental disorders and suicide attempts in diverse lesbian, gay, and bisexual populations. *American Journal of Public Health, 98*, 1004–1006. doi: 10.2105/AJPH.2006.096826

Meyer, I. H., Teylan, M., & Schwartz, S. (2014). The role of help-seeking in preventing suicide attempts among lesbians, gay men, and bisexuals. *Suicide and Life-threatening Behavior, 45*, 25–36. doi: 10.1111/sltb.12104

Meyer, O., Zane, N., & Cho, Y. I. (2009). Understanding the psychological processes of the racial match effect in Asian Americans. *Journal of Counseling Psychology, 58*, 335–345. doi: 10.1037/a0023605

Middleton, R. A., Ergüner-Tekinalp, B., Williams, N. F., Stadler, H. A., & Dow, J. E. (2011). Racial identity development and multicultural counseling competencies of white mental health practitioners. *International Journal of Psychology & Psychological Therapy, 11*, 201–218.

Middleton, R. A., Robinson, M. C., & Mu'min, A. S. (2010). Rehabilitation counseling: A continuing professional imperative for multiculturalism and advocacy competence. In M. J. Ratts, R. L. Toporek, & J. A. Lewis (Eds.), *ACA Advocacy Competencies: A social justice framework for counselors* (pp. 173–183). Alexandria, VA: American Counseling Association.

Migration Policy Institute. (2011). *Children of immigrants under 18 in poor and low-income families by state, 2010*. Retrieved from http://www.migrationinformation.org /DataHub/-historicaltrends.cfm#history

Migration Policy Institute (MPI). (2014). *European immigrants in the United States*. Retrieved from http://www.migration-policy.org/article/european-immigrants-united-states

Millan, J. B., & Alvarez, A. N., (2014). Asian Americans and internalized oppression: Do we deserve this? In E. J. R. David (Ed.), *Internalized oppression: The psychology of marginalized groups* (pp. 163–190). New York, NY: Springer.

Miller, M. J., Yang, M., Hui, K., Choi, N., & Lim, R. H. (2011). Acculturation, enculturation, and Asian American college students' mental health and attitudes toward seeking professional psychological help. *Journal of Counseling Psychology, 58*, 346–357. doi: 10.1037/a0023636

Miller, O. A., & Ward, K. J. (2008). Emerging strategies for reducing racial disproportionality and disparate outcomes in child welfare: The results of a national breakthrough series collaborative. *Child Welfare: Journal of Policy, Practice, and Program, 87*, 211–240.

Ministry of Culture, P. R. China. (2014). *Confucianism and its influence today*. Retrieved from http://www.chinaculture .org/focus/2014-10/10/content_567522.htm

Minow, M. (1991). *Making all the difference: Inclusion, exclusion and American law*. Ithaca, NY: Cornell University Press.

Mitchell, A. J. (2013). Redefining the syndrome of cognitive impairment in *DSM-5*. *Australian and New Zealand Journal of Psychiatry, 47*, 79–81. doi: 10.1177/0004867413495094

Mitchell, D. W., & Jacoby, S. H. (2013). *Buddhism: Introducing the Buddhist experience* (3rd ed.). New York, NY: Oxford University Press.

Mitchell, S. L., Greenwood, A. K., & Guglielmi, M. C. (2007). Utilization of counseling services: Comparing international and U.S. college students. *Journal of College Counseling, 10*, 117–130.

Mittal, S., & Thursby G. (Eds.). (2006). *Religions of South Asia: An introduction* (Vol. 69). Abingdon, UK: Routledge/Taylor & Francis Group.

Miville, M. L. (2005). Psychological functioning and identity development of biracial people: A review of current theory and research. In R. T. Carter (Ed.), *Handbook of racial-cultural psychology and counseling* (Vol. 2, pp. 295–319). New York, NY: Wiley.

Miville, M. L., Constantine, M. G., Baysden, M. F., & So-Lloyd, G. (2005). Chameleon changes: An exploration of racial identity themes of multiracial people. *Journal of Counseling Psychology, 52*, 507–516.

Monk, G., Winslade, J., & Sinclair, S. (2008). *New horizons in multicultural counseling*. Thousand Oaks, CA: Sage Publications.

Montgomery, D. E., Fine, M. A., & James-Myers, L. (1990). The development and validation of an instrument to assess an optimal Afrocentric worldview. *Journal of Black Psychology, 17*, 37–54. doi: 10.1177/00957984 900171004

Moodley, R. (2009). Multi(ple) cultural voices speaking "Outside the Sentence" of counselling and psychotherapy". *Counselling Psychology Quarterly, 22*, 297. doi: 10.1080/09515070903302364

Moodley, R., & West, W. (2005). *Integrating traditional healing practices into counseling and psychotherapy*. Thousand Oaks, CA: Sage Publications.

Moore, N., & McDowell, T. (2014). Expanding Adlerian application: The tasks, challenges, and obstacles for African American parents. *Journal of Individual Psychology, 70*, 114–127. doi: 10.1353/jip.2014.0011

Moradi, B., DeBlaere, C., & Huang, Y. (2010). Centralizing the experiences of LGB people of color in psychology. *Counseling Psychologist, 3*, 322–330. doi: 10.1177/0011000008330832

Morales, E. S. (1989). Ethnic minority families and minority gays and lesbians. *Journal of Homosexuality, 17*, 217–239. doi: 10.1300/J002v14n03_11

Morishita, S. (2000). Treatment of anorexia nervosa with Naikan therapy. *International Medical Journal, 7*, 151.

Muhammad, K. G. (2010). *The condemnation of Blackness: Race, crime, and the making of modern urban America*. Cambridge, MA: Harvard University Press.

Mui, A. C., & Kang, S.-Y. (2006). Acculturation stress and depression among Asian immigrant elders. *Social Work, 51*, 243–255.

Murdock, N. L. (2013). *Theories of counseling and psychotherapy: A case approach* (3rd ed.). Upper Saddle River, NJ: Pearson Merrill Prentice Hall.

Museus, S., & Kiang, P. N. (2009). Deconstructing the model minority myth and how it contributes to the invisible minority reality in higher education research. *New Directions for Institutional Research, 142*, 5–15. doi: 10.1002/ir.292

Museus, S. D., & Maramba, D. C. (2011). The impact of culture on Filipino American students' sense of belonging. *Review of Higher Education: Journal of the Association for the Study of Higher Education, 34*, 231–258. doi: 10.1353/rhe.2010.0022

Myers, J. E. (1992). Competencies, credentialing and standards for gerontological counselors: Implications for counselor education. *Counselor Education and Supervision, 32*, 34–42. doi: 10.1002/j.1556-6978.1992.tb00172.x

Myers, J. E., Sweeney, T. J., & White, V. E. (2002). Advocacy for counseling and counselors: A professional imperative. *Journal of Counseling & Development, 80*, 394–402.

Naber, N. (2006). Arab American femininities beyond Arab-/virgin and American(ized). *Feminist Studies, 1*, 13–21. doi: 10.1037/a0025193

Nadal, K. L. (2011). The Racial and Ethnic Microaggressions Scale (REMS): Construction, reliability, and validity. *Journal of Counseling Psychology, 58*, 470–480. doi: 10.1037/a0025193

Nadal, K. L. (2012). *Filipino American psychology: A handbook of theory, research and clinical practice.* Hoboken, NJ: Wiley.

Nadal, K. L., & Corpus, M. J. H. (2013). "Tomboys" and "baklas": Experiences of lesbian and gay Filipino Americans. *Asian American Journal of Psychology, 4*, 166–175. doi: 10.1037/a0030168

Nadal, K. L., Griffin, K. E., Wong, Y., Hamit, S., & Rasmus, M. (2014). The impact of racial microaggressions on mental health: Counseling implications for clients of color. *Journal of Counseling & Development, 92*, 57–66. doi: 10.1002/j.1556-6676.2014.00130.x

Nadal, K. L., Wong, Y., Griffin, K., Sriken, J., Vargas, V., Wideman, M., & Kolawole, A. (2011). Microaggressions and the multicultural experience. *International Journal of Humanities and Social Sciences, 1*, 36–44.

Nadal, K. L., Wong, Y., Issa, M., Meterko, V., Leon, J., & Wideman, M. (2011). Sexual orientation microaggressions: Processes and coping mechanisms for lesbian, gay, and bisexual individuals. *Journal of LGBT Issues in Counseling, 5*, 21–46. doi: 10.1080/15538605.2011.554606

Nagi, S. Z. (1965). Some conceptual issues in disability and rehabilitation. In M. B. Sussman (Ed.), *Sociology and rehabilitation* (pp. 100–113). Washington, DC: American Sociological Association.

Nagi, S. Z. (1991). Disability concepts revisited: Implications for prevention. In A. M. Pope & A. R. Tarlov (Eds.), *Disability in America: Toward a national agenda for prevention* (pp. 309–327). Washington, DC: National Academy Press.

Nandan, M. (2005). Adaptation to American culture: Voices of Asian Indian immigrants. *Journal of Gerontological Social Work, 44*, 175–203. doi: 10.1300/J083v44n03_11

Nassar-McMillan, S. C. (2003). Counseling Arab Americans: Counselors' call for advocacy and social justice. *Counseling and Human Development, 35*(5), 2–12.

Nassar-McMillan, S. C. (2007a). Applying the multicultural guidelines to Arab American populations. In D. W. Sue & M. G. Constantine (Eds.), *Multicultural competencies for working with people of color: Clinical practice implications* (pp. 85–103). New York, NY: Teachers College Press.

Nassar-McMillan, S. C. (2007b). Arab American populations. In M. G. Constantine (Ed.), *Clinical practice with people of color: A guide to becoming multiculturally competent* (pp. 85–103). New York, NY: Teachers College Press.

Nassar-McMillan, S. C. (2010). *Counseling Arab Americans.* Boston, MA: Brooks-Cole/Cengage.

Nassar-McMillan, S. C., Ajrouch, K. A., & Hakim-Larson, J. (2014). Biopsychosocial perspectives on Arab Americans: An introduction. In S. C. Nassar-McMillan, K. A. Ajrouch, & J. Hakim-Larson (Eds.), *Biopsychosocial perspectives on Arab Americans: Culture, development, and health* (pp. 7–16). New York, NY: Springer.

Nassar-McMillan, S. C., Hakim-Larson, J., & Patterson, A. (2014). From theory to practice: Clinical applications with individuals of Middle Eastern and North African descent. In D. W. Sue, M. E. Gallardo, & H. Neville (Eds.), *Case studies in multicultural counseling and therapy* (pp. 61–74). Hoboken, NJ: Wiley.

Nassar-McMillan, S. C., Lambert, R. G., & Hakim-Larson, J. (2011). Discrimination history, backlash fear, and ethnic identity among Arab Americans: Post 9-11 snapshots. *Journal of Multicultural Counseling and Development, 39*, 38–47.

Nassar-McMillan, S. C., Nour, M., & Al-Qimlass, A. M. (in press). Counseling psychology approaches for working with Arab Americans. In M. Amer & G. Awwad (Eds), *Handbook of Arab American psychology.* New York, NY: Brunner-Routledge.

Nassar-McMillan, S. C., Rezcallah, A., & Nour, M. (2014). Arab American youth: Overcoming adversity. In M. T. Garrett (Ed.), *Youth and adversity: Psychology and influences of childhood and adolescent coping strategies* (pp. 133–145). Hauppage, NY: Nova Science Publishers.

Nassar-McMillan, S. C., & Tovar, L. Z. (2012). Career counseling with Americans of Arab descent. *Career Planning and Adult Development, 28*, 72–87.

Nassar-McMillan, S. C., Tovar, L. Z., & Conley, A. H. (2014). Namadi: The case of the misunderstood Muslim. In S. G. Niles, J. Goodman, & M. Pope (Eds.), *The career counseling casebook: A resource for practitioners, students, and counselor educators* (2nd ed.). Broken Arrow, OK: NCDA.

National Alliance on Mental Illness. (2012). *NAMI establishes new multicultural action center.* Retrieved from http://www2.nami.org/Template.cfm?Section=Multicultural_Support

National Asian Pacific American Legal Consortium. (2003). *Remembering: A ten year retrospective.* Washington, DC: Author.

National Asian Women's Health Organization (NAWHO). (2002). *Silent epidemic: A survey of violence among young Asian American women.* San Francisco, CA: Author.

National Center for Health Statistics. (2011a). *Sexual behavior, sexual attraction, and sexual identity in the United States: Data from the 2006–2009 national survey of family growth.* Retrieved from http://www.cdc.gov/nchs/data/nhsr/nhsr036.pdf

National Center for Health Statistics. (2011b). *Health, United States, 2010: With special feature on death and dying.* Washington, DC: U.S. Government Printing Office.

National Coalition for Women and Girls in Education. (2008). *Title IX at 35: Beyond the headlines.* Retrieved from http://www.ncwge.org/pubs-reports.html

National Coalition of Anti-Violence Programs. (2010). *Hate violence against lesbian, gay, bisexual, transgender, queer and HIV-affected communities in the United States.* Retrieved from http://www.avp.org/storage/documents/Reports/2011_NCAVP_HV_Reports.pdf

National Commission on Asian American and Pacific Islander Research in Education. (2008). *Asian American and Pacific Islanders—Facts not fiction: Setting the record straight.* Retrieved from https://professionals.collegeboard.com/profdownload/08-0608-AAPI.pdf

National Council of La Raza. (2005). *Critical disparities in Latino mental health: Transforming research into action.* Retrieved from http://mhcaucus.napolitano.house.gov/reports/Critical_Disparities_in_Latino_Mental_Health.pdf

National Council of La Raza. (2014). *Who we are.* Retrieved from http://www.nclr.org/about-us/

National Gay and Lesbian Task Force. (2014). *State non-discrimination laws in the U.S.* Retrieved from http://www.thetaskforce.org/static_html/downloads/reports/issue_maps/non_discrimination_5_14_color_new.pdf

National Institute of Health. (2005). *PTSD, Depression epidemic among Cambodian immigrants.* Retrieved from http://www.nimh.nih.gov/news/science-news/2005/ptsd-depression-epidemic-among-cambodian-immigrants.shtml

National Public Radio. (2012). *Mexican American studies: Bad ban or bad class?* Retrieved from http://www.npr.org/2012/01/18/145397005/mexican-american-studies-bad-ban-or-bad-class

Nava, A., McFarlane, J., Gilroy, H., & Maddoux, J. (2014). Acculturation and associated effects on abused immigrant women's safety and mental functioning: Results of entry data for a 7-year prospective study. *Journal of Immigrant Minority Health, 16*, 1077–1084. doi: 10.1007/s10903-013-9816-6

Negi, N. J. (2013). Battling discrimination and social isolation: Psychological distress among Latino day laborers. *American Journal of Community Psychology, 51*, 164–174. doi: 10.1007/s10464-012-9551-5

Neukrug, E. (2015). *The SAGE encyclopedia of theory in counseling and psychotherapy.* Thousand Oaks, CA: Sage Publications.

Neuliep, J. W. (2009). *Intercultural communication: A contextual approach.* Los Angeles, CA: Sage Publications.

Neville, H. A., Awad, G. H., Brooks, J. E., Flores, M., & Bluemel, J. (2013). Color-blind racial ideology: Theory, training, and measurement implications in psychology. *American Psychologist, 68*, 455–466. doi: 10.1037/a0033282

Neville, H. A., Lilly, R. L., Duran, G., Lee, R. M., & Browne, L. (2000). Construction and initial validation of the Color-Blind Racial Attitudes Scale (CoBRAS). *Journal of Counseling Psychology, 47*, 59–70. doi: 10.1037/0022-0167.47.1.59

Neville, H. A., Spanierman, L. B., & Doan, B. (2006). Exploring the association between color-blind racial ideology and multicultural counseling competencies. *Cultural Diversity and Ethnic Minority Psychology, 12*, 272–290. doi: 10.1037/1099-9809.12.2.275

Neville, H. A., & Walters, J. M. (2004). Contextualizing Black Americans' health. In D. R. Atkinson (Ed.), *Counseling American minorities* (pp. 83–143). Boston, MA: McGraw-Hill.

Newcomb, M. E., Ryan, D. T., Greene, G. J., Garofalo, R., & Mustanski, B. (2014). Prevalence and patterns of smoking, alcohol use, and illicit drug use in young men who have sex with men. *Drug and Alcohol Dependence, 141*, 65–71. doi: 10.1016/j.drugalcdep.2014.05.005

Nguyen, D. (2011). Acculturation and perceived mental health needs among older Asian immigrants. *The Journal of Behavioral Health Services and Research, 38*, 526–533. doi: 10.1007/s11414-011-9245-z

Nguyen, P. V., & Cheung, M. (2009). Parenting styles as perceived by Vietnamese American adolescents. *Child and Adolescent Social Work Journal, 26*, 505–518. doi: 10.1007/s10560-009-0182-0

Nhât Hanh, T. (1999). *The heart of the Buddha's teaching: Transforming suffering into peace, joy & liberation: The four noble truths, the noble eightfold path, and other basic Buddhist teachings.* New York, NY: Broadway Books.

Nichols, S., Glass, G., & Berliner, B. (2006). *High-stakes testing and student achievement: Does accountability pressure increase student learning? Education Policy Analysis Archives, 14.* Retrieved from http://epaa.asu.edu/ojs/article/view/72

Nitza, A. (2011). Group processes in experiential training groups in Botswana. *Journal for Specialists in Group Work, 36*, 222–242. doi: 10.1080/01933922.2011.578116

Nolen-Hoeksema, S. (2002). Gender differences in depression. In I. H. Gotlib & C. L. Hammen (Eds.), *Handbook of depression* (pp. 492–509). New York, NY: Guilford Press.

Nord, J. (2012). *Can counseling help an interracial couple?* Retrieved from http://jeffrey-nord.com/content/view/37/33/

Nouri, R., Nadrian, H., Yari, A., Bakri, G., Ansari, B., & Ghazizadeh, A. (2012). Prevalence and determinants of intimate partner violence against women in Marivan county, Iran. *Journal of Family Violence, 27*, 391–399.

Novins, D., LeMaster, P., Jumper Thurman, P., & Plested, B. (2004). Describing community needs: Examples from the Circles of Care initiative. *American Indian & Alaska Native Mental Health Research: The Journal of the National Center, 11*, 42–58.

Nydell, M. (2012). *Understanding Arabs: A contemporary guide to Arab society.* Boston, MA: Nicholas Brealey.

Obasi, E. M., Flores, L. Y., & James-Meyers, L. (2009). Construction and initial validation of the Worldview Analysis Scale (WAS). *Journal of Black Studies, 39*, 937–961. doi: 10.1177/0021934707305411

O'Donohue, W., & Benuto, L. (2010). The many problems of cultural sensitivity. *The Scientific Review of Mental Health Practice, 7*, 34–37.

Office of Homeland Security. (2013). *Persons obtaining lawful permanent resident status by region and country of birth: FY's 2004-2013.* Retrieved from http://www.dhs.gov /publication/yearbook-immigration-statistics-2013-lawful-permanent-residents

Office of Immigration Statistics. (2014). *2013 yearbook of immigration statistics.* Retrieved from http://www.dhs .gov/sites/default/files/publications/ois_yb_2013_0.pdf

Office of Management and Budget. (OMB). (1997). *Revisions to the standards for the classification of federal data on race and ethnicity.* Retrieved from https://www.whitehouse .gov/omb/fedreg_1997standards

Oh, E., Choi, C., Neville, H. A., Anderson, C. J., & Landrum-Brown, J. (2010). Beliefs about affirmative action: A test of group self-interest and racism beliefs models. *Journal of Diversity in Higher Education, 3*, 163–176. doi: 10.1037/ a0019799

O'Hara, C. (2014). *The relationships among the experiences of racial microaggressions in supervision, traumatic experiences, and the supervisory working alliance in professional counselors and counselors-in-training [dissertation].* Retrieved from http://scholarworks.gsu.edu/cps_diss/102

Ojelade, I. I., McCray, K., Ashby, J. S., & Meyers, J. (2011). Use of Ifa as a means of addressing mental health concerns among African American clients. *Journal of Counseling & Development, 89*, 406–412.

Older Americans Act. (2012). *Older Americans Act of 1965: Programs and funding.* Retrieved from http://www.nhpf .org/library/details.cfm/2626

Olfson, M., Blanco, C., Liu, L., Moreno, C., & Laje, G. (2006). National trends in the outpatient treatment of children and adolescents with antipsychotic drugs. *Archives of General Psychiatry, 63*, 679–685. doi: 10.1001/ archpsyc.63.6.679

Olkin, R. (2009). Disability-affirmative therapy. In I. Marini & M. A. Stebnicki (Eds.), *The professional counselor's desk reference* (2nd ed.; pp. 215–223). New York, NY: Springer.

Olson, J. S., & Beal, H. O. (2011). *The ethnic dimension in American history* (4th ed.). West Sussex, UK: Wiley-Blackwell.

O'Neil, J. M. (2013). Gender role conflict research 30 years later: An evidence-based diagnostic schema to assess boys and men in counseling. *Journal of Counseling & Development, 91*, 490–498. doi: 10.1002/j.1556-6676.2013.00122.x

Organisation for Economic Co-operation and Development. (2011, May). *Growing income inequality in OECD countries: What drives it and how can policy tackle it?* Retrieved from http://www.oecd.org/els/soc/47723414.pdf

Organista, K. C. (2007). *Solving Latino psychosocial and health problems: Theory, practice, and populations.* Hoboken, NJ: John Wiley & Sons.

Orr, J. J., & Hulse-Killacky, D. (2006). Using voice, meaning, mutual construction of knowledge, and transfer of learning to apply an ecological perspective to group work training. *Journal of Specialists in Group Work, 12*, 189–200. doi: 10.1080/01933920600777824

Ortabag, T., Ozdemir, S., Bebis, H., & Ceylan, S. (2014). Perspectives of young adult men regarding violence against women: A cross-sectional study from Turkey. *Journal of Family Violence, 29*, 665–674. doi: 10.1007/ s10896-014-9617-2

Ostrove, J. M., Feldman, P., & Adler, N. E. (1999). Relations among socioeconomic status indicators and health for African Americans and Whites. *Journal of Health Psychology, 4*, 451–463. doi: 10.1177/135910539900400401

Oswalt, W. H. (2009). *This land was theirs: A study of North American Indians* (9th ed.). New York, NY: Oxford University.

Otto, R. (1958). *The idea of the holy.* New York, NY: Oxford University Press.

Owen, J., Leach, M. M., Wampold, B., & Rodolfa, E. (2011). Multicultural approaches in psychotherapy: A rejoinder. *Journal of Counseling Psychology, 58*, 22–26. doi: 10.1037/ a0022222

Oxford University Press. (1973). *The New Oxford annotated Bible: Revised standard version.* New York, NY: Author.

Ozaki, C. C., & Johnston, M. (2008). The space in between: Issues for multiracial student organizations and advising. In K. A. Renn & P. Shang (Eds.), *Biracial and multiracial students* (pp. 53–61). *New Directions for Student Services,* No. 123. San Francisco, CA: Jossey-Bass.

Ozawa-deSilva, C., & Ozawa-deSilva, B. (2010). Secularizing religious practices: A study of subjectivity and existential transformation in Naikan therapy. *Journal for the Scientific Study of Religion, 49*, 147–161. doi: 10.1111/j.1468-5906.2010.01497.x

Paceley, M. S., & Flynn, K. (2012). Media representations of bullying toward queer youth: Gender, race, and age discrepancies. *Journal of LGBT Youth, 9*, 340–356. doi: 10.1080/19361653.2012.714187

Padela, A. I., & Heisler, M. (2010). The association of perceived abuse and discrimination after Sept. 11, 2001, with psychological distress, level of happiness, and health status among Arab Americans. *Research and Practice, 100,* 284–291. doi: 10.2105/AJPH.2009.164954

Padilla, Y., & Griselda, V. (2007). Cultural responses to health among Mexican American women and their families. *Family and Community Health: The Journal of Health Promotion and Maintenance, 30*(15), S25–S33.

Pais, J. (2014). Cumulative structural disadvantage and racial health disparities: The pathways of childhood socioeconomic influence. *Demography, 51,* 1729–1753. doi: 10.1007/s13524-014-0330-9

Paladino, D. A. (2004). *The effects of cultural congruity, university alienation, and self-concept upon multiracial students' adjustment to college.* Unpublished doctoral dissertation, University of Arkansas, Fayetteville.

Paladino, D. A. (2009). Counseling multiple heritage college students. In R. C. Henriksen, Jr. & D. A. Paladino (Eds.), *Counseling multiple heritage individuals, couples, and families* (pp. 101–110). Alexandria, VA: American Counseling Association.

Paladino, D. A., & Henriksen, R. C., Jr. (2009). Counseling multiple heritage adults. In R. C. Henriksen, Jr. & D. A. Paladino (Eds.), *Counseling multiple heritage individuals, couples, and families* (pp. 101–110). Alexandria, VA: American Counseling Association.

Paniagua, F. A. (2014). *Assessing and treating culturally diverse clients: A practical guide* (4th ed.). Thousand Oaks, CA: Sage.

Paradies, Y., Ben, J., Denson, N., Elias, A., Pieterse, A., Gupta, A., Kelaher, M., & Gee, G. (2015). Racism as a determinant of health: A systematic review and meta-analysis. *PLOS One, 10,* e0138511. doi: 10.1371/journal.pone.0138511

Pargament, K. I. (2011). *Spiritually integrated psychotherapy: Understanding and addressing the sacred.* New York, NY: Guilford Press.

Pargament, K. I., Falb, M. D., Ano, G. G., & Wachholtz, A. B. (2014). The religious dimension of coping: Advances in theory, research, and practice. In R. F. Paloutzian & C. L. Park (Eds.), *Handbook of the psychology of religion and spirituality* (2nd ed.; pp. 560–579). New York, NY: Guilford.

Parham, T. A. (1989). Cycles of psychological nigrescence. *Counseling Psychologist, 17,* 187–226. doi: 10.1177/0011000089172001

Parham, T. A. (Ed.). (2002). *Counseling persons of African descent: Raising the bar of practitioner competence.* Thousand Oaks, CA: Sage.

Parham, T. A., & Helms, J. E. (1981). The influence of Black students' racial identity attitudes on preferences for counselor's race. *Journal of Counseling Psychology, 28,* 250–257. doi: 10.1037/0022-0167.28.3.250

Parrillo, V. N. (2011). *Strangers to these shores: Race and ethnic relations in the United States* (10th ed.). Boston, MA: Allyn & Bacon.

Parrillo, V. N. (2015). *Diversity in America.* New York, NY: Routledge.

Park, C. C., Endo, R., Lee, S., & Rong, X. L. (Eds.). (2007). *Asian American education: Acculturation, literacy, development, and learning.* Charlotte, NC: Information Age Publishing.

Parker, M. (2004). Memory, narrative, and myth in the construction of national identity: A rhetorical analysis of the senate debate over reparations for Japanese Americans. In G. A. Hauser & A. Grim (Eds.), *Rhetorical democracy: Discursive practices of civic engagement* (pp. 277–284). Mahwah, NJ: Lawrence Erlbaum Associates Publishers.

Parker, S. (2011). Spirituality in counseling. *Journal of Counseling & Development, 89,* 112–119. doi: 10.1002/j.1556-6678.2011.tb00067.x

Parks, S. D. (2011). *Big questions, worthy dreams: Mentoring young adults in their search for meaning, purpose, and faith.* San Francisco, CA: Jossey-Bass.

Parris, G. P., Owens, D., Johnson, T., Grbevski, S., & Holbert-Quince, J. (2010). Addressing the career development needs of high-achieving African American high school students: Implications for Counselors. *Journal for the Education of the Gifted, 33,* 417–436.

Parry, M. (2010). Betty Friedan: Feminist icon and founder of the national organization for women. *American Journal of Public Health, 100,* 1584–1585. doi: 10.2105/AJPH.2009.187534

Passel, J. S., & Cohn, D. V. (2008). *U.S. population predictions: 2005–2050.* Washington, DC: Pew Research Center.

Passel, J. S., Wang, W., & Taylor, P. (2010). *Marrying out: One-in-seven new U.S. marriages is interracial or interethnic.* Pew Research Center Publications. Retrieved from http://pewresearch.org/pubs/1616/american-marriage-interracial-interethnic

Pedersen, P. B., Lonner, W. J., Draguns, J. G., Trimble, J. E., & Scharron-del Rio, M. R. (Eds.). (2016). *Counseling across cultures* (7th ed.). Thousand Oaks, CA: Sage.

Pedrotti, J. T., Edwards, L. M., & Lopez, S. L. (2008). Working with multiracial clients in therapy: Bridging theory, research, and practice. *Professional Psychology: Research and Practice, 39,* 192–201. doi: 10.1037/0735-7028.39.2.192

Peluso, P. (2013). *DSM-5*: Personality disorders and wrap-up [Webinar]. In *DSM-5: Navigating the new terrain.* Retrieved from http://www.counseling.org/continuing-education/webinars

People for the American Way (PFAW). (2003). *Hostile climate: Report on anti-gay activity, 2003 edition.* New York, NY: Author.

Pérez-Escamilla, R. (2011). Acculturation, nutrition, and health disparities in Latinos. *American Journal of Clinical Nutrition, 93,* 1163–1167. doi: 10.3945/ajcn.110.003467

Pérez-Sales, P., Eiroa-Orosa, F. J., Olivos, P., Barbero-Val, E., Fernández-Liria, A., & Vergara, M. (2012). Vivo Questionnaire: A measure of human worldviews and identity in trauma, crisis, and loss—Validation and preliminary findings. *Journal of Loss & Trauma, 17,* 236–259. doi: 10.1080/15325024.2011.616828

Periyakoil, V. S. (2006). Working with Asian Indian American families. In G. Yeo & D. Gallagher-Thompson (Eds.), *Ethnicity and the dementias* (2nd ed., pp. 165–172). New York, NY: Routledge/Taylor & Francis Group.

Perkins-Dock, R. E. (2005). The application of Adlerian family therapy with African American families. *The Journal of Individual Psychology, 61,* 233–248.

Perls, F. S. (1969). *Gestalt therapy verbatim.* Lafayette, CA: Real People Press.

Peters, M. F. (2007). Parenting of young children in Black families. In H. P. McAdoo (Ed.), *Black families* (4th ed.; pp. 97–124). Thousand Oaks, CA: Sage.

Peters, R. M. (2004). Racism and hypertension among African Americans. *Western Journal of Nursing Research, 26,* 612–631. doi: 10.1177/0193945904265816

Pew Forum on Religion & Public Life. (2015). *Religious landscape survey.* Retrieved from http://www.pewforum.org/religious-landscape-study/

Pew Hispanic Center. (2005). *Hispanics: A people in motion.* Washington, DC: Author.

Pew Hispanic Center. (2007). *Changing faiths: Latinos and the transformation of American religion.* Washington, DC: Author.

Pew Research Center. (2013). *The rise of Asian Americans.* Retrieved from http://www.pewsocialtrends.org/2012/06/19/the-rise-of-asian-americans/

Pew Research Center. (2014). *Millennials in adulthood: Detached from institutions, networked with friends.* Retrieved from http://www.pewsocialtrends.org/2014/03/07/millennials-in-adulthood/

Pew Research Center. (2015a). *Multiracial in America: Proud, diverse, and growing in numbers.* Retrieved from http://www.pewsocialtrends.org/2015/06/11/multiracial-in-america/

Pew Research Center. (2015b). *Religious landscape study.* Retrieved from http://www.pewforum.org/religious-landscape-study/

Pew Research Center. (2015c). *A rising share of the U.S. Black population is foreign born.* Retrieved from http://www.pewsocialtrends.org/2015/04/09/a-rising-share-of-the-u-s-black-population-is-foreign-born/

Pew Research Center. (2015d). *Changing attitudes on gay marriage.* Retrieved from http://www.pewforum.org/2015/07/29/graphics-slideshow-changing-attitudes-on-gay-marriage/

Pew Hispanic Center. (2016a). *Hispanic population reaches record 55 million, but growth has cooled.* Retrieved from http://www.pewresearch.org/fact-tank/2015/06/25/u-s-hispanic-population-growth-surge-cools/

Pew Hispanic Center. (2016b). *Statistical portrait of Hispanics in the United States, 1980–2013.* Retrieved from http://www.pewhispanic.org/2015/05/12/statistical-portrait-of-hispanics-in-the-united-states-1980-2013/#current-age

Pew Hispanic Center. (2016c). *Growing public support for US ties with Cuba – And an end to the trade embargo.* Retrieved from http://www.people-press.org/2015/07/21/growing-public-support-for-u-s-ties-with-cuba-and-an-end-to-the-trade-embargo/

Pew Hispanic Center. (2016d). *Share of unauthorized immigrant workers in production, construction jobs falls since 2007.* Retrieved from http://www.pewhispanic.org/2015/03/26/share-of-unauthorized-immigrant-workers-in-production-construction-jobs-falls-since-2007/

Pew Hispanic Center. (2016e). *Broad public support for legal status for undocumented immigrants.* Retrieved from http://www.people-press.org/2015/06/04/broad-public-support-for-legal-status-for-undocumented-immigrants/

Pew Hispanic Center. (2016f). *English proficiency on the rise among Latinos.* Retrieved from http://www.pewhispanic.org/2015/05/12/english-proficiency-on-the-rise-among-latinos/

Pharr, S. (1997). *Homophobia: A weapon of sexism.* Little Rock, AR: Women's Project.

Phillips, F. B. (1990). NTU psychotherapy: An Afrocentric approach. *The Journal of Black Psychology, 17,* 55–74. doi: 10.1177/00957984900171005

Phillips, L. (2006). *The womanist reader.* New York, NY: Routledge.

Phinney, J. S. (1992). The Multigroup Ethnic Identity Measure: A new scale for use with diverse groups. *Journal of Adolescent Research, 13,* 171–184. doi: 10.1177/074355489272003

Phinney, J. S. (1993). A three-stage model of ethnic identity development in adolescence. In M. E. Bernal & G. P. Knight (Eds.), *Ethnic identity: Formation and transmission among Hispanics and other minorities* (pp. 61–79). Albany, NY: SUNY Press.

Phinney, J. S. (1996). When we talk about American ethnic groups, what do we mean? *American Psychologist, 51,* 918–927. doi: 10.1037/0003-066X.51.9.918

Phinney, J. S., Horenczyk, G., Liebkind, K., & Vedder, P. (2001). Ethnic identity, immigration, and well-being: An interactional perspective. *Journal of Social Issues, 57,* 493–510. doi: 10.1111/0022-4537.00225

Phinney, J. S. & Ong, A. D. (2007). Conceptualization and measurement of ethnic identity: Current status and future directions. *Journal of Counseling Psychology, 54,* 271–281. doi: 10.1037/0022-0167.54.3.271

Pierce, J. (2013a). Saying and doing White racism. In R. Garcia (Ed.), *Race and medicine.* Toledo, OH: University of Toledo Press.

Pierce, J. L. (2013b). White racism, social class, and the backlash against affirmative action. *Sociology Compass, 7,* 914–926. doi: 10.1111/soc4.12082

Pieterse, A. L., Todd, N. R., Neville, H. A., & Carter, R. T. (2012). Perceived racism and mental health among Black American adults: A meta-analytic review. *Journal of Counseling Psychology, 59,* 1–9. doi: 10.1037/a0026208

Pilver, C., Desai, S., Kasi, R., & Levy, B. (2011). Lifetime discrimination associated with greater likelihood of Premenstrual Dysphoric Disorder. *Journal of Women's Health, 20,* 923–931. doi: 10.1089/jwh.2010.2456

Pina, A., Silverman, W., Fuentes, R., Kurtines, W., & Weems, C. F. (2003). Exposure-based cognitive-behavioral treatment for phobic and anxiety disorders: Treatment effects and maintenance for Hispanic/Latino relative to European-American youths. *Journal of the American Academy of Child and Adolescent Psychiatry, 42*, 1179–1187. doi: 10.1097/00004583-200310000-00008

Pinyuchon, M., Gray, L. A., & House, R. M. (2003). The Pa Sook model of counseling Thai families: A culturally mindful approach. *Journal of Family Psychotherapy, 14*, 67–93. doi: 10.1300/J085v14n03_05

Pittman, C. T. (2011). Getting mad but ending up sad: The mental consequences for African Americans using anger to cope with racism. *Journal of Black Studies, 42*, 1106–1124. doi: 10.1177/0021934711401737

Pittman, C. T. (2012). Racial microaggressions: The narratives of African American faculty at a predominantly white university. *The Journal of Negro Education, 81*, 82–92.

Polivy, J., & Herman, C. P. (2002). Causes of eating disorders. *Annual Review of Psychology, 53*, 187–213. doi: 10.1146/annurev.psych.53.100901.135103

Poll, J. B., & Smith, T. B. (2003). The spiritual self: Toward a conceptualization of spiritual identity development. *Journal of Psychology and Theology, 31*, 129–142.

Pollock, E. D., Kazman, J. B., & Deuster, P. (2015). Family functioning and stress in African American families: A strength-based approach. *Journal of Black Psychology, 41*, 144–169. doi: 10.1177/0095798413520451

Ponterotto, J. G. (1988). Racial consciousness development among White counselor trainees: A stage model. *Journal of Multicultural Counseling and Development, 16*, 146–156. doi: 10.1002/j.2161-1912.1988.tb00405.x

Pope, A. M., & Tarlov, A. R. (Eds.). (1991). *Disability in America: Toward a national agenda for prevention*. Washington, DC: National Academy Press.

Pope, M., & Pangelinan, J. S. (2010). Using the ACA Advocacy Competencies in career counseling. In M. J. Ratts, R. L. Toporek, & J. A. Lewis (Eds.), *ACA Advocacy Competencies: A social justice framework for counselors* (pp. 209–223). Alexandria, VA: American Counseling Association.

Pope-Davis, D. B., Liu, W. M., Toporek, R. L., & Brittan-Powell, C. S. (2001). What's missing from multicultural competency research: Review, introspection, and recommendations. *Cultural Diversity and Ethnic Minority Psychology, 7*, 121–138. doi: 10.1037/1099-9809.7.2.121

Poston, W. S. C. (1990). The biracial identity development model: A needed addition. *Journal of Counseling & Development, 69*, 152–155.

Potoczniak, D., Crosbie-Burnett, M., & Saltzburg, N. (2009). Experiences regarding coming out to parents among African American, Hispanic, and White gay, lesbian, bisexual, transgender, and questioning adolescents. *Journal of Gay & Lesbian Social Services, 21*, 189–205. doi: 10.1080/10538720902772063

Poulsen, S. S. (2003). Therapists' perspectives on working with interracial couples. In V. Thomas, T. A. Karis, & J. L. Wetchler (Eds.), *Clinical issues with interracial couples: Theories and research* (pp. 163–177). New York, NY: Haworth.

Pramuka, M., MacAulay, J., Sporner, M., & McCue, M. (2009). Vocational rehabilitation of the combat amputee. In *Care of the combat amputee* (pp. 95–104). Falls Church, VA: Office of the Surgeon General, U.S. Army.

Pratt, R. H. (1978). The advantages of mingling Indians with Whites. In F. P. Prucha (Ed.), *Americanizing the American Indians: Writings by the "Friends of the Indian" 1880–1900* (pp. 260–271). Cambridge, MA: Harvard University Press.

President's Advisory Commission on Educational Excellence for Hispanic Americans. (2003). *From risk to opportunity: Fulfilling the educational needs of Hispanic Americans in the 21st century*. Washington, DC: Author.

Priest, N., Paradies, Y., Trenerry, B., Truong, M., Karlsen, S., & Kelly, Y. (2013). A systematic review of studies examining the relationship between reported racism and health and wellbeing for children and young people. *Social Science & Medicine, 95*, 115–127. doi: 10.1016/j.socscimed.2012.11.031

Prochaska, J. O., & Norcross, J. C. (2014). *Systems of psychotherapy: A transtheoretical analysis* (8th ed.). Belmont, CA: Thomson Brooks/Cole.

Qin, D. B. (2008). Doing well vs. feeling well: Understanding family dynamics and the psychological adjustment of Chinese immigrant adolescents. *Journal of Youth and Adolescence, 37*, 22–35. doi: 10.1007/s10964-007-9220-4

Qin, D. B. (2009). Being "good" or being "popular": Gender and ethnic identity negotiations of Chinese immigrant adolescents. *Journal of Adolescent Research, 24*, 37–66. doi: 10.1177/0743558408326912

Rasmi, S., Chuang, S. S., & Hennig, K. (2014). The acculturation gap-distress model: Extensions and application to Arab Canadian families. *Cultural Diversity and Ethnic Minority Psychology, 21*, 201–212. doi: 10.1037/cdp0000014

Ratts, M. (2011). Multiculturalism and social justice: Two sides of the same coin. *Journal of Multicultural Counseling & Development, 39*, 24–37.

Ratts, M. J., Singh, A. A., Nassar-McMillan, S., Butler, S. K., & McCullough, J. R. (2015). *Multicultural and social justice counseling competencies*. Retrieved from http://www.multiculturalcounseling.org/index.php?option=com_content&view=article&id=205:amcd-endorses-multicultural-and-social-justice-counseling-competencies&catid=1:latest&Itemid=123

Ratts, M. J., & Wood, C. (2010). The fierce urgency of now: Diffusion of innovation as a mechanism to integrate social justice in counselor education. *Counselor Education & Supervision, 50*, 207–223. doi: 10.1002/j.1556-6978.2011.tb00120.x

Raub, B., & Newcomb, J. (2012). *SOI Bulletin: Personal wealth, 2007*. Retrieved from http://www.irs.gov/pub/irs-soi/12pwwinbulwealth07.pdf

Reed, E. E. (2014). Man up: Young men's lived experiences and reflections on counseling. *Journal of Counseling & Development, 92*, 428–437. doi: 10.1002/j.1556-6676.2014.00169.x

Rees, D. (2001). *Death and bereavement: The psychological, religious, and cultural interfaces* (2nd ed.). Philadelphia, PA: Whurr.

Reeves, T. J., & Bennett, C. E. (2004). *We the people: Asians in the United States, Census 2000 special reports CENSR-17*. Washington, DC: U.S. Department of Commerce.

ReligionFacts. (2016). *Just the facts on the world's religions*. Retrieved from http://www.religionfacts.com

Renn, K. A. (2008). Research on biracial and multiracial identity development: Overview and synthesis. In K. A. Renn & P. Shang (Eds.), *Biracial and multiracial students* (pp. 13–21). *New Directions for Student Services*, No. 123. San Francisco, CA: Jossey-Bass.

Richards, P. S., & Bergin, A. E. (2005). *A spiritual strategy for counseling and psychotherapy* (2nd ed.). Washington, DC: American Psychological Association.

Richardson, M. A., Myers, H. F., Bing, E. G., & Satz, P. (1997). Substance use and psychopathology in African American men at risk for HIV infection. *Journal of Community Psychology, 25*, 353–370. doi: 10.1002/(SICI)1520-6629(199707)25:4<353::AID-JCOP4>3.0.CO;2-V

Richardson, T. Q., Bethea, A. R., Hayling, C. C., & Williamson-Taylor, C. (2010). African and Afro-Caribbean American identity development. In J. G. Ponterotto, J. M. Casas, L. A. Suzuki, & C. M. Alexander (Eds.), *Handbook of multicultural counseling* (pp. 227–239). Los Angeles, CA: Sage Publications.

Ridley, C. R. (Ed.). (2005). *Overcoming unintentional racism in counseling and therapy: A practitioner's guide to intentional intervention* (2nd ed.). Thousand Oaks, CA: Sage Publications.

Rivera, D. P., Forquer, E. E., & Rangel, R. (2010). Microaggressions and the life experience of Latina/o Americans. In D. W. Sue (Ed.), *Microaggressions and marginality: Manifestation, dynamics, and impact* (pp. 59–84). New York, NY: Wiley.

Rivers, I. (2004). Recollection of bullying at school and their long-term implications for lesbians, gay men, and bisexuals. *Crisis, 25*(4), 1–7. doi: 10.1027/0227-5910.25.4.xxx

Roberts, D. (2014). *Killing the black body: Race, reproduction, and the meaning of liberty*. New York, NY: Vintage.

Robbins, L. (2015, October 13). Syrian refugees in Jersey City are among few to start new life in U.S. *The New York Times*. Retrieved from: http://www.nytimes.com/2015/10/14/nyregion/syrian-refugees-in-jersey-city-are-among-few-to-start-new-life-in-us.html?_r=2

Robbins, M. S., Mayorga, C. C., Mitrani, V. B., Szapocznik, J., Turner, C. W., & Alexander, J. F. (2008). Adolescent and parent alliances with therapists in brief strategic family therapy with drug-using Hispanic adolescents. *Journal of Marital and Family Therapy, 34*, 316–328. doi: 10.1111/j.1752-0606.2008.00075.x

Robinson, J. (2009). American poverty cause beliefs and structured inequality legitimation. *Sociological Spectrum, 29*, 489–518. doi: 10.1080/02732170902904681

Robinson, T. N., Killen, J. D., Hammer, L. D., Wilson, D. M., Haydel, K. F., & Taylor, C. B. (1996). Ethnicity and body dissatisfaction: Are Hispanic and Asian girls at increased risk for eating disorders? *Journal of Adolescent Health, 19*, 384–393. doi: 10.1016/S1054-139X(96)00087-0

Robinson-Wood, T. L. (2013). *The convergence of race, ethnicity and gender: Multiple identities in counseling* (4th ed.). Upper Saddle River, NJ: Prentice Hall.

Rockquemore, K. A., Brunsma, D. L., & Delgado, D. J. (2009). Racing to theory or re-theorizing race? Understanding the struggle to build multiracial identity theory. *Journal of Social Issues, 65*, 13–34. doi: 10.1111/j.1540-4560.2008.01585.x

Rockquemore, K. A., & Laszloffy, T. L. (2003). Multiple realities: A relational narrative approach to therapy with Black-White mixed-race clients. *Family Relations, 52*, 119–128. doi: 10.1111/j.1741-3729.2003.00119.x

Rockquemore, K. A., & Laszloffy, T. L. (2005). *Raising biracial children: From theory to practice*. New York, NY: Altimira Press.

Roediger, D. R. (2007). *The wages of Whiteness*. New York, NY: Verso.

Rogers, B. K., Sperry, H. A., Levant, R. F. (2015). Masculinities among African American men: An intersectional perspective. *Psychology of Men & Masculinity, 16*(4), 416–425. doi: 10.1037/a0039082

Romano, D. (2008). *Intercultural marriage: Promises and pitfalls* (3rd ed.). Boston, MA: Intercultural Press.

Rong, X. L., & Fitchett, P. (2008). Socialization and identity transformation of Black immigrant youth in the United States. *Theory into Practice, 47*, 35–42. doi: 10.1080/00405840701764714

Root, M. P. P. (1990). Resolving "other" status: Identity development of biracial individuals. In L. S. Brown & M. P. P. Root (Eds.), *Diversity and complexity in feminist therapy* (pp. 185–205). New York, NY: Haworth Press.

Root, M. P. P. (1993). *Bill of rights for people of mixed heritage*. Retrieved from http://www.drmariaroot.com/doc/BillOfRights.pdf

Root, M. P. P. (1994). Mixed-race women. In L. Comas-Diaz & B. Greene (Eds.), *Women of color: Integrating ethnic and gender identities in psychotherapy* (pp. 455–478). New York, NY: Guilford Press.

Root, M. P. P. (1998). Multiracial Americans: Changing the face of Asian America. In L. C. Lee & N. W. Zane (Eds.), *Handbook of Asian American psychology* (pp. 261–287). Thousand Oaks, CA: Sage Publications.

Root, M. P. P. (2001). *Love's revolution: Interracial marriage*. Philadelphia, PA: Temple University Press.

Root, M. P. P. (2002). Methodological issues in multiracial research. In G. C. Nagayama Hall & S. Okazaki (Eds.), *Asian American psychology: The science of lives in context* (pp. 171–193). Washington, DC: American Psychological Association.

Root, M. P. P. (2003). Multiracial families and children: Implications for educational research and practice. In J. A. Banks & C. A. McGee Banks (Eds.), *Handbook of research on multicultural education* (2nd ed., pp. 110–124). San Francisco, CA: Jossey-Bass.

Root, M. P. P. (2004). *Multiracial oath of social responsibility*. Retrieved from http://www.drmariaroot.com/doc/OathOfSocialResponsibility.pdf

Root, M. P. P., & Kelley, M. (2003). *Multiracial child resource book: Living complex identities*. Seattle, WA: MAVIN Foundation.

Rose, A. M., & Hambleton, I. R. (2008). Sex and the city: Differences in disease- and disability-free life years, and active participation of elderly men and women in 7 cities in Latin America and the Caribbean. *BMC Public Health, 8*(127), 1471–2458. doi: 10.1186/1471-2458-8-127

Rosenbloom, S. R., & Way, N. (2004). Experiences of discrimination among African American, Asian American, and Latino adolescents in an urban high school. *Youth & Society, 35*, 420–451. doi: 10.1177/0044118X03261479

Rothman, E. F., Sullivan, M., Keyes, S., & Boehmer, U. (2012). Parents' supportive reactions to sexual orientation disclosure associated with better health: Results from a population-based survey of LGB adults in Massachusetts. *Journal of Homosexuality, 59*, 186–200. doi: 10.1080/00918369.2012.648878

Rowe, J. L., & Kahn, R. L. (1998). *Successful aging*. New York, NY: Pantheon.

Rudman, L. A., Dohn, M. C., & Fairchild, K. (2007). Implicit self-esteem compensation: Automatic threat defense. *Journal of Personality and Social Psychology, 93*, 798-813. doi: 10.1037/00223514.93.5.798

Ruiz, A. S. (1990). Ethnic identity: Crisis and resolution. *Journal of Multicultural Counseling and Development, 18*, 29–40. doi: 10.1002/j.2161-1912.1990.tb00434.x

Russell, G. (2004). *American Indian facts of life: A profile of today's tribes and reservations*. Phoenix, AZ: Native Data Network.

Russell, S. T., Ryan, C., Toomey, R. B., Diaz, R. M., & Sanchez, J. (2011). Lesbian, gay, bisexual, and transgender adolescent school victimization: Implications for young adult health and adjustment. *Journal of School Health, 81*(5), 223–230. doi: 10.1111/j.1746-1561.2011.00583.x

Ruzek, N. A., Nguyen, D. Q., & Herzog, D. C. (2011). Acculturation, enculturation, psychological distress and help-seeking preferences among Asian American college students. *Asian American Journal of Psychology, 2*, 181–196. doi: 10.1037/a0024302

Ryan, C. (2013). *Language use in the United States: 2011* (American Community Survey Reports-22). Retrieved from http://www.census.gov/content/dam/Census/library/publications/2013/acs/acs-22.pdf

Rybak, C. J., Eastin, C. L., & Robbins, I. (2004). Native American healing practices and counseling. *Journal of Humanistic Counseling, Education & Development, 43*, 25–32. doi: 10.1002/j.2164-490X.2004.tb00039.x

Sagardui-Villamor, J., Guallar-Castillon, P., Garcia-Ferruelo, M., Ramon Banegas, R., & Rodriguez-Artalejo, F. (2005). Trends in disability and disability-free life expectancy among elderly people in Spain: 1986–1999. *Journals of Gerontology. Series A, Biological Sciences and Medical Sciences, 62*, 408–414.

Sagula, D., & Rice, K. G. (2004). The effectiveness of mindfulness training on the grieving process and emotional well-being of chronic pain patients. *Journal of Clinical Psychology in Medical Settings, 11*, 333–342. doi: 10.1023/B:JOCS.0000045353.78755.51

Salahuddin, N. M., & O'Brien, K. M. (2011). Challenges and resilience in the lives of urban, multiracial adults: An instrument development study. *Journal of Counseling Psychology, 58*, 494–507. doi: 10.1037/a0024633

Salameh, F. (2011). Towards a new ecology of Middle Eastern identities. *Middle Eastern Studies, 47*, 237–253. doi: 10.1080/00263206.2011.544096

Salzberg, S., & Kabat-Zinn, J. (2004). *Lovingkindness: The revolutionary art of happiness*. Boulder, CO: Shambhala Publications.

Samhan, H. (2012). Intra-ethnic diversity and religion. In S. C. Nassar-McMillan, J. Hakim-Larson, & K. Ajrouch (Eds.), *Behavioral care of Arab Americans: Perspectives on culture, psychosocial development, and health*. New York, NY: Springer.

Samhan, H. H. (2014). Intra-ethnic diversity and religion. In S. C. Nassar-McMillan, K. A. Ajrouch, & J. Hakim-Larson (Eds.), *Biopsychosocial perspectives on Arab Americans: Culture, development, and health* (pp. 45–66). New York, NY: Springer.

Sanders, M. M. (2007). Family therapy: A help-seeking option among middle-class African Americans. In H. P. McAdoo (Ed.), *Black families* (pp. 97–124). Thousand Oaks, CA: Sage Publications.

Shannonhouse, L. R. (2013). *The relationships between multicultural counseling competence, cultural immersion, & cognitive/emotional developmental styles: Implications for multicultural counseling training*. Dissertation, The University of North Carolina at Greensboro.

Santiago-Rivera, A., Arredondo, P., & Gallardo-Cooper, M. (Eds.). (2002). *Counseling Latinos and la familia: A practical guide*. Thousand Oaks, CA: Sage Publications.

Santisteban, D. A., Coatsworth, J. D., Perez-Vidal, A., Kurtines, W. M., Schwartz, S. J., LaPerriere, A., et al. (2003). Efficacy of brief strategic family therapy in modifying Hispanic adolescent behavior problems and substance use. *Journal of Family Psychology, 17*, 121–133. doi: 10.1037/0893-3200.17.1.121

Sarche, M. C., & Whitesell, N. R. (2012). Child development research in North American Native communities—looking back and moving forward: Introduction. *Child Development Perspectives, 6*, 42–48. doi: 10.1111/j.1750-8606.2011.00218.x

Sawyer, P. J., Major, B., Casad, B. J., Townsend, S. S., & Mendes, W. B. (2012). Discrimination and the stress response: Psychological and physiological consequences of anticipating prejudice in interethnic interactions. *American Journal of Public Health, 102*, 1020–1026. doi: 10.2105/AJPH.2011.300620

Sayed, M. A., Collins, D. T., & Takahashi, T. (1998). West meets East: Cross-cultural issues in inpatient treatment. *Bulletin of the Menninger Clinic, 62*, 439–454. doi: 10.2105/AJPH.2011.300620

Schmitt, M. T., Branscombe, N. R., Postmes, T., & Garcia, A. (2014). The consequences of perceived discrimination for psychological well-being: A meta-analytic review. *Psychological Bulletin, 140*, 921–948. doi: 10.1037/a0035754

Schmitt, M. T., & Wirth, J. H. (2009). Evidence that gender differences in social dominance orientation result from gendered self-stereotyping and group-interested responses to patriarchy. *Psychology of Women Quarterly, 33*(4), 429–436. doi: 10.1111/j.1471-6402.2009.01520.x

Schneeberger, A. R., Dietl, M. F., Muenzenmaier, K. H., Huber, C. G., & Lang, U. E. (2014). Stressful childhood experiences and health outcomes in sexual minority populations: A systematic review. *Social Psychiatry and Psychiatric Epidemiology, 49*, 1427–1445. doi 10.1007/s00127-014-0854-8

Scholl, M. B. (2006). Native American identity development and counseling preferences: A study of Lumbee undergraduates. *Journal of College Counseling, 9*, 47–59.

Schriner, K. F., & Batavia, A. I. (1995). Disability law and social policy. In A. E. Dell Orto & R. P. Marinelli (Eds.), *Encyclopedia of disability and rehabilitation* (pp. 260–270). New York, NY: Macmillan.

Schwartz, R. C., Lent, J., & Geihsler, J. (2011). Gender and diagnosis of mental disorders: Implications for mental health counseling. *Journal of Mental Health Counseling, 33*, 347–358. doi: 10.17744/mehc.33.4.914g2n123u771316

Scott, D. A., Havice, P. A., Livingston, W. G., & Cawthon, T. W. (2012). Men's identity development: Issues and implications for residence life. *Journal of College & University Student Housing, 38/39*, 200–213.

Scott, D. A., & Robinson, T. L. (2001). White male identity development: The key model. *Journal of Counseling & Development, 79*, 415–421. doi: 10.1002/j.1556-6676.2001.tb01988.x

Scott, L. D., McCoy, H., Munson, M. R., Snowden, L. R., & McMillen, J. C. (2011). Cultural mistrust of mental health professionals among Black males transitioning from foster care. *Journal of Child & Family Studies, 20*, 605–613. doi: 10.1007/s10826-010-9434-z

Scull, N. C., Khullar, N., Al-Awadhi, N., & Erheim, R. (2014). A qualitative study of the perceptions of mental health care in Kuwait. *International Perspectives in Psychology: Research, Practice, Consultation, 3*, 284–299. doi: 10.1037/ipp0000023

Seligman, L., & Reichenberg, L. (2013). *Theories of counseling and psychotherapy: Systems, strategies, and skills* (4th ed.). Upper Saddle River, NJ: Pearson Prentice Hall.

Sellers, R. M., Smith, M. A., Shelton, J. N., Rowley, S. A. J., & Chavous, T. M. (1998). Multidimensional model of racial identity: A reconceptualization of African American racial identity. *Personality & Social Psychology, 2*, 18–39. doi: 10.1207/s15327957pspr0201_2

Sengoku, M., Nakagome, K., Murata, H., Kawahara, T., & Imamura, K. (2010). Does daily Naikan therapy maintain the efficacy of intensive Naikan therapy against depression? *Psychiatry and Clinical Neurosciences, 64*, 44–51. doi: 10.1111/j.1440-1819.2009.02049.x

Sered, S. S., & Fernandopulle, R. (2006). *Uninsured in America: Life and death in the land of opportunity*. Los Angeles, CA: University of California Press.

Seshadri, G., & Knudson-Martin, C. (2013). How couples manage interracial and intercultural differences: Implications for clinical practice. *Journal of Marital and Family Therapy, 39*(1), 43–58. doi: 10.1111/j.1752-0606.2011.00262.x

Shackel, P. A. (Ed.). (2001). *Myth, memory, and the making of the American landscape*. Gainesville, FL: University Press of Florida.

Shaheen, J. (2014). *Reel bad Arabs: How Hollywood vilifies a people* (3rd ed.). New York, NY: Olive Branch Press.

Shakir, E. (1997). *Bint Arab: Arab and Arab American women in the United States*. Westport, CT: Praeger.

Shakir, E. (2007). *Remember me to Lebanon: Stories of Lebanese women in America*. Syracuse, NY: Syracuse University Press.

Sharif, N. R. (2010). Predicting the occupational choices of foreign-born and second generation Canadians: Evidence from census data. *International Business & Economics Research Journal, 9*(6), 47–54.

Shea, M., Ma, P. W., & Yeh, C. J. (2007). Development of a culturally specific career exploration group for urban Chinese immigrant youth. *The Career Development Quarterly, 56*, 62–73. doi: 10.1002/j.2161-0045.2007.tb00020.x

Sheely-Moore, A. I., & Bratton, S. C. (2010). A strengths-based parenting intervention with low-income African American families. *Professional School Counseling, 13*, 175–183. doi: 10.5330/PSC.n.2010-13.175

Sheikh, M. F. (2009). *An exploratory study of the challenges of living in America as a Muslim adolescent attending public school* (Doctoral dissertation). Available from ProQuest dissertations and Theses database (UMI No. 3402509).

Shek, Y. L. (2006). Asian American masculinity. *Journal of Men's Studies, 14*, 379–391. doi: 10.3149/jms.1403.379

Sheu, H., & Sedlacek, E. (2004). An exploratory study of help-seeking attitudes and coping strategies among college students by race and gender. *Measurement & Evaluation in Counseling & Development, 37*, 130–143.

Shih, M., & Sanchez, D. T. (2005). Perspectives and research on the positive and negative implications of having multiple racial identities. *Psychological Bulletin, 131*, 569–591. doi: 10.1037/0033-2909.131.4.569

Shillingford, M. A., Trice-Black, S., & Butler, S. K. (2013). Wellness of minority female counselor educators. *Counselor Education & Supervision, 52*, 255–269. doi: 10.1002/j.1556-6978.2013.00041.x

Shorris, E. (2012). *Latinos: A biography of the people*. New York, NY: Norton.

Shreeve, J. (2006, March). The greatest journey. *National Geographic*, 61–69.

Simpkins, C. A., & Simpkins, A. (1999). *Simple Taoism: A guide to living in balance*. Boston, MA: Tuttle.

Singh, A. A. (2008). A social justice approach to counseling Asian American/Pacific Islanders. In C. Ellis & J. Carlson (Eds.), *Cross cultural awareness and social justice issues in counseling* (pp. 147–167). New York, NY: Routledge.

Singh, A. A., & Burnes, T. R. (2010). Introduction to the special issue: Translating the ACA Competencies for Counseling Transgender People into counseling practice, research, and advocacy. *Journal for Lesbian, Gay, Bisexual, and Transgender Issues in Counseling, 4*, 126–134.

Singh, A. A., & Crete, G. K. (2014). Counseling men with trauma histories: Moving from resilience to thriving. In M. Englar-Carlson, M. Evans, & T. Duffey (Eds.), *A counselor's guide to working with men*. Alexandria, VA: American Counseling Association.

Singh, A. A., & Hays, D. G. (2008). Feminist group counseling with South Asian women who have survived intimate partner violence. *Journal of Specialists in Group Work, 33*, 84–102. doi: 10.1080/01933920701798588

Singh, A. A., Hays, D. G., & Watson, L. S. (2011). Strength in the face of adversity: Resilience strategies of transgender individuals. *Journal of Counseling & Development, 89*, 20–27.

Singh, A. A., & McKleroy, V. (2011). "Just getting out of bed is a revolutionary act:" The resilience of transgender people of color who have survived traumatic life events. *International Journal of Traumatology, 17*, 34–44. doi: 10.1177/1534765610369261

Singh, A. A., Meng, S., & Hansen, A. (2013). It's already hard enough being a student: Developing affirming college environments for trans youth. *Journal of LGBT Youth, 10*, 208–223.

Singh, N. K. K. (2011). *Sikhism: An introduction*. London, UK: Tauris.

Singleton, G. J., Robertson, J., & Robinson, J. C. (2008). Perceived racism and coping: Joint predictors of blood pressure in Black Americans. *Negro Educational Review, 59*, 93–115.

Sink, C. (2008). Wisdom of Robert Solomon: Naturalized spirituality and counseling. *Counseling and Values, 52*, 178–180.

Sirin, S. R., Rogers-Sirin, L., Cressen, J., Gupta, T., Ahmed, S. F., & Novoa, A. D. (2015). Discrimination-related stress effects on the development of internalizing symptoms among Latino adolescents. *Child Development, 86*, 709–725. doi: 10.1111/cdev.12343

Siy, J. O., & Cheryan, S. (2013). When compliments fail to flatter: American individualism and responses to positive stereotypes. *Journal of Personality and Social Psychology, 104*, 87–102. doi: 10.1037/a0030183

Slootmaeckers, K., & Lievens, J. (2014). Cultural capital and attitudes toward homosexuals: Exploring the relation between lifestyles and homonegativity. *Journal of Homosexuality, 61*, 962–979. doi: 10.1080/00918369.2014.870848

Smart, J. F., & Smart, D. W. (2006). Models of disability: Implications for the counseling profession. *Journal of Counseling & Development, 84*, 29–40. doi: 10.1002/j.1556-6678.2006.tb00377.x

Smedley, A., & Smedley, B. D. (2011). *Race in North America: Origin and evolution of a worldview* (4th ed.). Boulder, CO: Westview Press.

Smith, H. (1991). *The world's religions: Our great wisdom traditions*. San Francisco, CA: Harper.

Smith, H. (2003). *Cleansing the doors of perception: The religious significance of entheogenic plants and chemicals*. Boulder, CO: Sentient.

Smith, H. (2006). *Why religion matters: The fate of the human spirit in an age of disbelief*. San Francisco, CA: Harper.

Smith, J. R. (2015). Mental health care services for African Americans: Parity or disparity? *Journal of Pan African Studies, 7*, 55–63.

Smith, L. (2005). Psychotherapy, classism, and the poor: Conspicuous by their absence. *American Psychologist, 60*, 687–696. doi: 10.1037/0003-066X.60.7.687

Smith, L., Foley, P. F., & Chaney, M. P. (2008). Addressing classism, ableism, and heterosexism in counselor education. *Journal of Counseling & Development, 86*, 303–309.

Smith, R. M., Parrott, D. J., Swartout, K. M., & Tharp, A. T. (2015). Deconstructing hegemonic masculinity: The roles of antifemininity, subordination to women, and sexual dominance in men's perpetration of sexual aggression. *Psychology of Men & Masculinity, 16*, 160–169. doi: 10.1037/a0035956

Smith, W. A., Hung, M., & Franklin, J. D. (2011). Racial battle fatigue and the miseducation of Black men: Racial microaggressions, societal problems, and environmental stress. *The Journal of Negro Education, 80*, 63–82.

Smolak, L. (2002). The relationship of gender and voice to depression and eating disorders. *Psychology of Women Quarterly, 26*, 234–242. doi: 10.1111/1471-6402.t01-1-00006

Snowshoe, A., Crooks, C. V., Tremblay, P. F., Craig, W. M., & Hinson, R. E. (2015). Development of a cultural connectedness scale for first nations youth. *Psychological Assessment, 27*, 249–259. doi: 10.1037/a0037867

Social Security Online. (2017). *The full retirement age is increasing*. Retrieved from https://www.ssa.gov/planners/retire/ageincrease.html

Sodowsky, G. R., Kwan, K. K., & Pannu, R. (1995). Ethnic identity of Asians in the United States. In J. G. Ponterotto, J. M. Casas, L. A. Suzuki, & C. M. Alexander (Eds.), *Handbook of multicultural counseling* (pp. 123–154). Thousand Oaks, CA: Sage Publications.

Solé-Farràs, J. (2013). *New Confucianism in twenty-first century China: The construction of a discourse.* New York, NY: Routledge.

Sondik, E. J., Huang, D. T., Klein, R. J., & Satcher, D. (2010). Progress toward the Healthy People 2010 goals and objectives. *Annual Review of Public Health, 31,* 271–281. doi: 10.1146/annurev.publhealth.012809.103613

Southern Poverty Law Center. (2012, March 01). *FBI: Dramatic spike in hate crimes targeting Muslims.* Retrieved from https://www.splcenter.org/fighting-hate/intelligence-report/2012/fbi-dramatic-spike-hate-crimes-targeting-muslims

Speight, S. L., & Vera, E. M. (2004). A social justice agenda: Ready or not? *The Counseling Psychologist, 32,* 109–118. doi: 10.1177/0011000003260005

Spero, M. H. (1992). *Religious objects as psychological structures: A critical integration of object relations theory, psychotherapy, and Judaism.* Chicago, IL: University of Chicago Press.

Spicer, P., LaFramboise, T., Markstrom, C., Niles, M., West, A., Fehringer, K., Grayson, L., & Sarche, M. (2012). Toward an applied developmental science for Native children, families, and communities. *Child Development Perspectives, 6,* 49–54. doi: 10.1111/j.1750-8606.2011.00212.x

Springer, D. W., Lynch, C., & Allen, R. (2000). Effects of a solution-focused mutual aid group for Hispanic children of incarcerated parents. *Child and Adolescent Social Work Journal, 17,* 431–442. doi: 10.1023/A:1026479727159

Statistics Canada. (2010). *Health indicators—Fact sheets: Life satisfaction.* Retrieved from http://www.statcan.gc.ca/pub/82-221-x/2009001/tblstructure/2nm/2pr/pr2lsx-eng.htm

Stevenson, D., Cohen, M., Tell, E., & Burwell, B. (2010). The complementarity of public and private long term care coverage. *Health Affairs, 29,* 35–43. doi: 10.1377/hlthaff.2009.0920

Stewart, R. E., & Chambless, D. L. (2009). Cognitive-behavioral therapy for anxiety disorders in clinical practice: A meta-analysis of effective studies. *Journal of Consulting and Clinical Psychology, 77,* 595–606. doi: 10.1037/a0016032

Stillwell, R., & Sable, J. (2013). *Public School Graduates and Dropouts from the Common Core of Data: School Year 2009–10: First Look (Provisional Data)* (NCES 2013-309). Retrieved from http://nces.ed.gov/pubsearch

Stone, C. B. (2003). Counselors as advocates for gay, lesbian, and bisexual youth: A call for equity and action. *Journal of Multicultural Counseling & Development, 31,* 143–155.

Story, M., French, S. A., Neumark-Sztainer, D., Downes, B., Resnick, M. D., & Blum, R. W. (1997). Psychosocial and behavioral correlates of dieting and purging in Native American adolescents. *Pediatrics, 99,* 1–8.

Strachan, E. D., Bennett, W. R. M., Russo, J., & Roy-Byrne, P. P. (2007). Disclosure of HIV status and sexual orientation independently predicts increased absolute CD4 cell counts over time for psychiatric patients. *Psychosomatic Medicine, 69,* 74–80. doi: 10.1097/01.psy.0000249900.34885.46

Striegel-Moore, R. (1997). Risk factors for eating disorders. *Annual New York Academy of Sciences, 817,* 98–109. doi: 10.1111/j.1749-6632.1997.tb48199.x

Striegel-Moore., R. H., & Bulik, C. M. (2007). Risk factors for eating disorders. *American Psychologist, 62,* 181–198.

Strine, T. W., Chapman, D. P., Balluz, L. S., Moriarty, D. G., & Mokdad, A. H. (2008). The associations between life satisfaction and health-related quality of life, chronic illness, and health behaviours among U.S. community-dwelling adults. *Journal of Community Health, 33,* 40–50. doi: 10.1007/s10900-007-9066-4

Substance Abuse and Mental Health Services Administration. (2014). *Results from the 2013 National Survey on Drug Use and Health: Mental health findings* (NSDUH Series H-49, HHS Publication No. (SMA) 14-4887). Retrieved from http://www.samhsa.gov/data/sites/default/files/NSDUHmhfr2013/NSDUHmhfr2013.pdf

Sue, D. W. (1994). Mental health. In N. Zane, D. T. Takeuchi, & K. Young (Eds.), *Confronting critical health issues of Asian and Pacific Islander Americans* (pp. 266–288). Newbury Park, CA: Sage Publications.

Sue, D. W. (2004). Multicultural counseling and therapy (MCT) theory. In C. A. M. Banks & J. A. Banks (Eds.), *Handbook of research on multicultural education* (2nd ed., pp. 813–827). San Francisco, CA: Jossey-Bass.

Sue, D. W. (Ed.). (2010). *Microaggressions and marginality: Manifestation, dynamics, and impact.* Hoboken, NJ: John Wiley & Sons.

Sue, D. W. (2013). Race talk: The psychology of racial dialogue. *American Psychologist, 68,* 663–672. doi: 10.1037/a0033681

Sue, D. W., Arredondo, P., & McDavis, R. J. (1992). Multicultural counseling competencies and standards: A call to the profession. *Journal of Counseling & Development, 70,* 477–486. doi: 10.1002/j.1556-6676.1992.tb01642.x

Sue, D. W., Bucceri, J., Lin, A. L., Nadal, K. L., & Torino, G. C. (2007). Racial microaggressions and the Asian American experience. *Cultural Diversity & Ethnic Minority Psychology, 13,* 72–81. doi: 10.1037/1948-1985.S.1.88

Sue, D. W., Capodilupo, C. M., & Holder, A. M. B. (2008). Racial microaggressions in the life experiences of Black Americans. *Professional Psychology: Research and Practice, 39,* 329–336. doi: 10.1037/0735-7028.39.3.329

Sue, D. W., Capodilupo, C. M., Torino, G. C., Bucceri, J. M., Holder, A. M. B., Nadal, K. L., et al. (2007). Racial microaggressions in everyday life: Implications for clinical practice. *American Psychologist, 62*, 271–286. doi: 10.1037/0003-066X.62.4.271

Sue, D. W., Nadal, K. L., Capodilupo, C. M., Lin, A. I., Torino, G. C., & Rivera, D. P. (2008). Racial microaggressions against Black Americans: Implications for counseling. *Journal of Counseling & Development, 86*, 330–338. doi: 10.1002/j.1556-6678.2008.tb00517.x

Sue, D. W., & Sue, D. (2013). *Counseling the culturally diverse: Theory and practice* (6th ed.). Hoboken, NJ: Wiley.

Sue, S. (1999). Asian American mental health: What we know and what we don't know. In W. J. Lonner, D. L. Dinnel, D. K. Forgays, & S. A. Hayes (Eds.), *Merging past, present, and future in cross-cultural psychology: Selected papers from the Fourteenth International Congress of the International Association for Cross-Cultural Psychology* (pp. 82–89). Lisse, Netherlands: Swets & Zeitlinger.

Sue, S., Cheng, J. K. Y., Saad, C. S., & Chu, J. P. (2012). Asian American mental health: A call to action. *American Psychologist, 67*, 532–544. doi: 10.1037/10028900

Sue, S., Fujino, D. C., Hu, L., Takeuchi, D. T., & Zane, N. (1991). Community mental health services for ethnic minority groups: A test of the cultural responsiveness hypothesis. *Journal of Consulting and Clinical Psychology, 59*, 533–540. doi: 10.1037/0022-006X.59.4.533

Sue, S., & Okazaki, S. (2009). Asian-American educational achievements: A phenomenon in search of an explanation. *Asian American Journal of Psychology, S*(1), 45–55. doi: 10.1037/0003-066X.45.8.913

Sue, S., Sue, D. W., Sue, L., & Takeuchi, D. T. (1995). Psychopathology among Asian Americans: A model minority? *Cultural Diversity and Mental Health, 1*, 39–51. doi: 10.1037/1099-9809.1.1.39

Sue, S., & Zane, N. (2009). The role of culture and cultural techniques in psychotherapy: A critique and reformulation. *Asian American Journal of Psychology, 1*, 3–14. doi: 10.1037/1948-1985.S.1.3

Sullivan, T. N., Scott, D. A., & Nicks, E. C. (2011). Effects of target person expression on ethnic prejudice toward Middle Easterners and Hispanics. *Journal of Multicultural Counseling & Development, 39*, 156–166. doi: 10.1002/j.2161-1912.2011.tb00148.x

Summers, F. (2014). Ethnic invisibility, identity, and the analytic process. *Psychoanalytic Psychology, 31*, 410–425. doi: 10.1037/a0037330

Suwaki, H. (1979). Naikan and Danshukai for the treatment of Japanese alcoholic patients. *British Journal of Addiction, 74*, 15–19. doi: 10.1111/j.1360-0443.1979.tb02407.x

Suwaki, H. (1985). International review series: Alcohol and alcohol problems research: II. Japan. *British Journal of Addiction, 80*, 127–132. doi: 10.1111/j.1360-0443.1985.tb03262.x

Szymanski, D. M., & Gupta, A. (2009). Examining the relationship between multiple internalized oppressions and African American Lesbian, Gay, Bisexual, and Questioning Persons' self-esteem and psychological distress. *Journal of Counseling Psychology, 56*, 110–118. doi: 10.1037/a0012981

Szymanski, D. M., & Sung, M. R. (2010). Minority stress and psychological distress among Asian American sexual minority persons. *The Counseling Psychologist, 38*, 848–872. doi: 10.1177/0011000010366167

Ta, V. M., Holck, P., & Gee, G. C. (2010). Generational status and family cohesion effects on the receipt of mental health services among Asian Americans: Findings from the national Latino and Asian American study. *American Journal of Public Health, 100*, 115–121. doi: 10.2105/AJPH.2009.160762

Tabbah, R., Miranda, A., & Wheaton, J. E. (2012). Self-concept in Arab American adolescents: Implications of social support and experiences in the schools. *Psychology in the Schools, 49*, 817–827. doi: 10.1002/pits.21640

Takaki, R. (2002). The "Indian question": From reservation to reorganization. In R. Takaki (Ed.), *Debating diversity: Clashing perspectives on race and ethnicity in America* (3rd ed., pp. 228–244). New York, NY: Oxford University Press.

Takayama, J. R. (2010). Ecological systems theory of Asian American mental health service seeking. *School of Professional Psychology. Paper 121.* Retrieved from http://commons.pacificu.edu/spp/121

Takeuchi, D. T., Hong, S., Gile, K., & Alegría, M. (2007). Developmental contexts and mental disorders among Asian Americans. *Research in Human Development, 4*, 49–69. doi: 10.1080/15427600701480998

Talleyrand, R. M. (2012). Disordered eating in women of color: Some counseling considerations. *Journal of Counseling & Development, 90*, 271–280. doi: 10.1002/j.1556-6676.2012.00035.x

Tedeschi, G. J., & Willis, F. N. (1993). Attitudes toward counseling among Asian international and native Caucasian students. *Journal of College Student Psychotherapy, 7*, 43–54. doi: 10.1300/J035v07n04_04

Terry, R. L., & Winston, C. E. (2010). Personality Characteristic Adaptations: Multiracial Adolescents' Patterns of Racial Self-Identification Change. *Journal of Research on Adolescence, 20*, 432–455.

Tewari, N., & Alvarez, A. N. (2009). *Asian American psychology: Current perspectives* (pp. 113–133). New York, NY: Routledge/Taylor & Francis Group.

Tewari, N., Inman, A. G., & Sandhu, D. S. (2003). South Asian Americans: Culture, concerns and therapeutic strategies. In J. Mio & G. Iwamasa (Eds.), *Culturally diverse mental health: The challenges of research and resistance* (pp. 191–209). New York, NY: Routledge.

Thomas, A., & Sillen, S. (1972). *Racism and psychiatry*. New York, NY: Brunner/Mazel.

Thomas, A. J., & Schwarzbaum, S. (2011). *Culture and identity: Life stories for counselors and therapists* (2nd ed.). Thousand Oaks, CA: Sage Publications.

Thomas, K. J. A. (2011). Familial influences on poverty among young children in Black immigrant, U.S.-born Black, and Nonblack immigrant families. *Demography, 48*, 437–460. doi: 10.1007/s13524-011-0018-3

Thomas, O. N., Caldwell, C. H., Faison, N., & Jackson, J. S. (2009). Promoting academic achievement: The role of racial identity in buffering perceptions of teacher discrimination on academic achievement among African American and Caribbean Black adolescents. *Journal of Educational Psychology, 101*, 420–431. doi: 10.1037/a0014578

Thompson, A. R., & Gregory, A. (2011). Examining the influence of perceived discrimination during African American adolescents' early years of high school. *Education and Urban Society, 43*, 3–25. doi: 10.1177/0013124510379827

Thornton, C., & Goldstein, L. (2006). Feminist issues in early childhood scholarship. In B. Spodek & O. Saracho (Eds.), *Handbook of research on the education of young children* (pp. 515–531). Mahwah, NJ: Erlbaum.

Tien, L., & Olson, K. (2003). Confucian past conflicted present: Working with Asian American families. In T. J. Goodrich, L. B. Silverstein, & B. Louise (Eds.), *Feminist family therapy: Empowerment in social context* (pp. 135–145). Washington, DC: American Psychological Association.

Ting, J. Y., & Hwang, W. C. (2009). Cultural influences on help-seeking attitudes in Asian American students. *American Journal of Orthopsychiatry, 79*, 125–132. doi: 10.1037/a0015394

Tipping, C. (2010). *Radical forgiveness: A revolutionary five-stage process to heal relationships, let go of anger and blame, find peace in any situation.* Northboro, MA: Quest.

Tisdell, E. J. (2007). In the new millennium: The role of spirituality and the cultural imagination in dealing with diversity and equity in the higher education classroom. *Teachers College Record, 109*, 531–560.

Tjadden, P., & Thoennes, N. (2000). *Extent, nature and consequences of intimate partner violence: Findings from the National Violence against Women Survey.* Retrieved from https://www.ncjrs.gov/pdffiles1/nij/181867.pdf

Todd, N. R., & Abrams, E. M. (2011). White dialectics: A new framework for theory, research, and practice with White students. *The Counseling Psychologist, 39*, 353–395. doi: 10.1177/0011000010377665

Toporek, R. L., & Williams, R. A. (2006). Ethics and professional issues related to the practice of social justice in counseling psychology. In R. L. Toporek, L. H. Gerstein, N. A. Fouad, G. Roysircar, & T. Israel (Eds.), *Handbook for social justice in counseling psychology* (pp. 17–34). Thousand Oaks, CA: Sage Publications.

Torche, F. (2015). Analyses of intergenerational mobility: An interdisciplinary review. *Annals of the American Academy of Political and Social Science, 657*, 37–62. doi: 10.1177/0002716214547476

Toro-Morn, M. I. (1998). The family and work experiences of Puerto Rican women migrants in Chicago. In H. McCubbin,

E. Thompson, A. Thompson, & J. Fromer (Eds.), *Resiliency in Native American and immigrant families* (pp. 277–294). Thousand Oaks, CA: Sage Publications.

Torres-Rivera, E. (2004). Psychoeducational and counseling groups with Latinos. In J. DeLucia-Waack, D. Gerrity, C. Kalodner, & M. Riva (Eds.), *Handbook of group counseling and psychotherapy* (pp. 213–223). Thousand Oaks, CA: Sage Publications.

Treitler, V. B. (2013). *The ethnic project: Transforming racial fiction into ethnic factions.* Stanford, CA: Stanford University Press.

Trinh, S. L., Ward, L. M., Day, K., Thomas, K., & Levin, D. (2014). Contributions of divergent peer and parent sexual messages to Asian American college students' sexual behaviors. *Journal of Sexuality Research, 51*, 208–220. doi: 10.1080/00224499.2012.721099.

Troiden, R. (1988). Homosexual identity development. *Journal of Adolescent Health Care, 9*, 105–113. doi: 10.1016/0197-0070(88)90056-3

Troiden, R. R. (1989). The formation of homosexual identities. *Journal of Homosexuality, 17*, 159–178. doi: 10.1300/J082v17n01_02

Tsai, J., & Kong, G. (2012). Mental health of Asian American and Pacific Islander military veterans: Brief review of an understudied group. *Military Medicine, 177*, 1438–1444. doi: 10.7205/MILMED-D-12-00214

Tuan, M. (1999). *Forever foreigners or honorary Whites? The Asian ethnic experience today.* New Brunswick, NJ: Rutgers University Press.

Tubbs, C. Y., & Rosenblatt, P. C. (2003). Assessment and intervention with Black-White multiracial couples. In V. Thomas, J. L. Wetchler, & T. A. Karis (Eds.), *Clinical issues with interracial couples: Theories and research* (pp. 115–130). New York, NY: Haworth Press.

Tuliao, A. P. (2014). Mental health help-seeking among Filipinos: A review of the literature. *Asia Pacific Journal of Counseling and Psychotherapy, 5*, 124–136. doi: 10.1080/21507686.2014.913641

Tummala-Narra, P., Inman, A. G., & Ettigi, S. P. (2011). Asian Indians' responses to discrimination: A mixed-method examination of identity, coping, and self-esteem. *Asian American Journal of Psychology, 2*, 205–218. doi: 10.1037/a0025555

Turner, R. J., & Gil, A. G. (2002). Psychiatric and substance use disorders in South Florida: Racial/ethnic and gender contrasts in a young adult cohort. *Archives of General Psychiatry, 59*, 43–50. doi: 10.1001/archpsyc.59.1.43

Turner, S. L., & Pope, M. (2009). North America's Native peoples: A social justice and trauma counseling approach. *Journal of Multicultural Counseling & Development, 37*, 194–205.

Twohig, M. P. (2012). Acceptance and commitment therapy: Introduction. *Cognitive and Behavioral Practice, 19*, 499–507.

Ukasoanya, G. (2014). Social adaptation of new immigrant students: Cultural scripts, roles, and symbolic interactionism.

International Journal for the Advancement of Counselling, 36(2), 150–161. doi: 10.1007/s10447-013-9195-7

Umemoto, K. (2000). From Vincent Chen to Joseph Ileto: Asian Pacific Americans and hate crime policy. In P. Ong (Ed.), *The state of Asian Pacific America: Transforming race relations.* Los Angeles, CA: LEAP Asian Pacific American Public Policy Institute and UCLA Asian American Studies Center.

U.S. Bureau of Indian Affairs (BIA). (2015). *Who is an American Indian or Alaska Native?* Washington, DC: Author. Retrieved from: http://www.bia.gov/FAQs/index.htm

U.S. Bureau of Labor Statistics. (2014). *Occupational outlook handbook.* Retrieved from http://www.bls.gov/ooh/a-z-index.htm

U.S. Census Bureau. (2007). *The American community—Hispanics: 2004.* Retrieved from http://www.census.gov/prod/2007pubs/acs-03.pdf

U.S. Census Bureau. (2011a). *The Black population: 2010.* Retrieved from http://www.census.gov/prod/cen2010/briefs/c2010br-06.pdf

U.S. Census Bureau. (2011b). *2010 census counts of American Indians, Eskimos, or Aleuts and American Indian and Alaska Native areas.* Washington, DC: Author.

U.S. Census Bureau. (2012a). *Poverty status of the population by sex and age, for Asian alone and White alone, not Hispanic.* Retrieved from http://www.census.gov/population/race/data/ppl-aa12.html

U.S. Census Bureau. (2012b). *Americans with disabilities: Economic household studies.* Retrieved from http://www.census.gov/prod/2012pubs/p70-131.pdf

U.S. Census Bureau. (2012c). *The Asian alone or in combination population in the United States: 2012.* Retrieved from http://www.census.gov/population/race/data/ppl-ac12.html

U.S. Census Bureau. (2014a). *Characteristics of opposite sex and same-sex couple households.* Retrieved from http://www.census.gov/hhes/samesex/

U.S. Census Bureau Population Division. (2014b). *Percentage of the projected population by Hispanic origin and race for the United States: 2015–2060* (NP2014-T11). Retrieved from http://www.census.gov/population/projections/data/national/2014/summarytables.html

U.S. Census Bureau. (2014c). *National crime victimization survey.* Retrieved from http://bjs.ojp.usdoj.gov/index.cfm?ty=dcdetail&iid=245

U.S. Census Bureau. (2014d). *Percentage distribution of the projected population by sex and selected age group for the United States: 2015–2060* (NP2014-T6). Retrieved from http://www.census.gov/population/projections/data/national/2014/summarytables.html

U.S. Census Bureau. (2015a). *Annual estimates of the resident population by sex, age, race, and Hispanic origin for the United States: April 1, 2010 to July 1, 2014.* Retrieved from http://factfinder.census.gov/faces/tableservices/jsf/pages/productview.xhtml?src=bkmk

U.S. Census Bureau. (2015b). *Historical poverty tables: Table 18.* Retrieved from http://www.census.gov/hhes/www/poverty/data/historical/people.html

U.S. Census Bureau. (2015c). *Income, poverty and health insurance coverage in the United States, 2014.* Retrieved from http://www.census.gov/content/dam/Census/library/publications/2015/demo/p60-253.pdf

U.S. Commission on Civil Rights. (2015). *Civil rights concerns in the metropolitan Washington, D.C., area in the aftermath of the September 11, 201, tragedies.* Retrieved from http://www.usccr.gov/pubs/sac/dc0603/ch2.htm

U.S. Department of Education. (2014). *Digest of educational statistics.* Retrieved from https://nces.ed.gov/programs/digest/d14/tables/dt14_326.10.asp

U.S. Department of Education. (2015). *The condition of education 2015* (National Center for Education Statistics report 2015-144). Retrieved from http://nces.ed.gov/pubs2015/2015144.pdf

U.S. Department of Health and Human Services. (2001). *Mental health: Culture, race and ethnicity—A supplement to mental health: A report of the surgeon general.* Rockville, MD: Author.

U.S. Department of Health and Human Services. (2015a). *Computations for the 2015 poverty guidelines.* Retrieved from https://aspe.hhs.gov/computations-2015-poverty-guidelines

U.S. Department of Health and Human Services, Administration on Aging. (2016). *Aging statistics.* Retrieved from http://www.aoa.acl.gov/aging_statistics/index.aspx

U.S. Department of Health and Human Services, Agency for Healthcare Research and Quality. (2012). *Conoce las Preguntas, or "Know the questions."* Retrieved from http://www.ahrq.gov/patients-consumers/patient-involvement/ask-your-doctor/index.html

U.S. Department of Health and Human Services, Centers for Disease Control and Prevention. (2015). *Health information for older adults.* Retrieved from http://www.cdc.gov/aging/info.htm#top

U.S. Department of Health and Human Services, Centers for Disease Control and Prevention, National Center for Health Statistics. (2015). *Health, United States 2014.* Retrieved from http://www.cdc.gov/nchs/data/hus/hus14.pdf

U.S. Department of Housing and Urban Development, Office of Community Planning and Development. (2014). *The 2014 annual homelessness assessment report to Congress.* Retrieved from https://www.hudexchange.info/resources/documents/2014-AHAR-Part1.pdf

U.S. Department of Justice. (2011). *Stalking victimization in the United States.* Retrieved from http://www.victimsofcrime.org/our-programs/stalking-resource-center/stalking-information/stalking-statistics

U.S. Department of Justice. (2013). *Federal Justice Statistics, 2010.* Retrieved form http://www.bjs.gov/content/pub/pdf/fjs10.pdf

U.S. Department of Justice. (2014a). *Prisoners in 2013.* Retrieved from http://www.bjs.gov/content/pub/pdf/p13.pdf

U.S. Department of Justice, Federal Bureau of Investigations. (2014b). *2013 hate crime statistics.* Retrieved from https://www.fbi.gov/about-us/cjis/ucr/hate-crime/2013/topic-pages/victims/victims_final

U.S. Department of Labor. (2017). *Wages: Minimum wage.* Retrieved from http://www.dol.gov/dol/topic/wage/minimumwage.htm

U.S. Department of Labor, Bureau of Statistics. (2015). *Highlights of women's earnings in 2000* (Report 952). Retrieved from http://www.bls.gov/cps/cpswom2000.pdf

U. S. Office of Minority Health. (2010). *Mental health data/statistics.* Retrieved from http://minorityhealth.hhs.gov/omh/browse.aspx?lvl=4&lvlid=24

U.S. Surgeon General. (1999). *Mental health: A report of the surgeon general.* Retrieved from http://www.-surgeongeneral.gov/library/mentalhealth/home.html

Uy, M. (2004). Tax and race: The impact on Asian Americans. *Asian Law Journal, 11*, 129–138.

van den Akker, H., van der Pioeg, R., & Scheepers, P. (2013). Disapproval of homosexuality: Comparative research on individual and national determinants of disapproval of homosexuality in 20 European countries. *International Journal of Public Opinion Research, 25*, 64–86. doi: 10.1093/ijpor/erd058

Velez, B. L., Moradi, B., & DeBlaere, C. (2015). Multiple oppressions and the mental health of sexual minority Latina/o individuals. *The Counseling Psychologist, 43*, 7–38. doi: 10.1177/0011000014542836

Venters, H., Adekugbe, O., Massaquoi, J., Nadeau, C., Saul, J., & Gany, F. (2011). Mental health concerns among African immigrants. *Journal of Immigrant and Minority Health, 13*, 795–797. doi: 10.1007/s10903-010-9357-1

Verbrugge, L. M., & Jette, A. M. (1994). The disablement process. *Social Science and Medicine, 38*, 1–14. doi: 10.1016/0277-9536(94)90294-1

Versola-Russo, J. (2006). Cultural and demographic factors of schizophrenia. *International Journal of Psychosocial Rehabilitation, 10*, 89–103.

Villalba, J. A. (2003). A psychoeducational group for limited-English proficient Latino/Latina children. *Journal for Specialists in Group Work, 28*, 261–276. doi: 10.1080/714860165

Villalba, J. A. (2007). Culture-specific assets to consider when counseling Latina/o children and adolescents. *Journal of Multicultural Counseling and Development, 35*, 15–25. doi: 10.1080/714860165

Villalba, J. A., Ivers, N. N., & Bartley Ohlms, A. (2010). Cuento group work in emerging rural Latino communities: Promoting personal-social development of Latina/o middle school students of Mexican heritage. *Journal for Specialists in Group Work, 35*, 23–43. doi: 10.1080/01933920903463502

Vornovitsky, M., Gottschalck, A., & Smith, A. (2015). *Distribution of household wealth in the U.S.: 2000 to 2011.* Retrieved from http://www.census.gov/people/wealth/files/Wealth%20distribution%202000%20to%202011.pdf

Wachter-Morris, C., & Graves, E. (2018). Sexual abuse. In L. R. Jackson-Cherry, & B. T. Erford (Eds.), *Crisis assessment, intervention, and prevention* (3rd ed., pp. 219–244). Columbus, OH: Pearson.

Wacquant, L. (2010). Class, race & hyperincarceration in revanchist America. *Daedalus, 139*, 74–90. doi: 10.1162/DAED_a_00024

Waite, K. R., Federman, A. D., McCarthy, D. M., Sudore, R., Curtis, L. M., Baker, D. W., . . . Paasche-Orlow, M. K. (2013). Literacy and race as risk factors for low rates of advance directives in older adults. *Journal of the American Geriatrics Society, 61*, 403–406. doi: 10.1111/jgs.12134

Wakefield, J. C. (1992). The concept of mental disorder: On the boundary between biological facts and social values. *American Psychologist, 47*, 373–388. doi: 10.1037/0003-066X.47.3.373

Waldman, K., & Rubalcava, L. (2005). Psychotherapy with intercultural couples: A contemporary psychodynamic approach. *American Journal of Psychotherapy, 59*, 227–245.

Walker, A. (1983). *In search of our mothers' gardens: Womanist prose.* San Diego, CA: Harcourt Brace Jovanovich.

Walker, J. J., & Longmire-Avital, B. (2013). The impact of religious faith and internalized homonegativity on resiliency for Black lesbian, gay, and bisexual emerging adults. *Developmental Psychology, 49*, 1723–1731. doi: 10.1037/a0031059

Wampold, B. E. (2010). *The great psychotherapy debate: Models, methods, and findings.* Mahwah, NJ: Erlbaum.

Wang, M. T., & Huguley, J. P. (2012). Parental racial socialization as a moderator of the effects of racial discrimination on educational success among African American adolescents. *Child Development, 83*, 1716–1731. doi: 10.1111/j.1467-8624.2012.01808.x

Wang, W. (2012). *The rise of intermarriage: Rates, characteristics vary by race and gender.* Retrieved from http://www.pewsocialtrends.org/2012/02/16/the-rise-of-intermarriage/

Wang, W. (2015). *Interracial marriage: Who is 'marrying out'?* Retrieved from http://www.pewresearch.org/fact-tank/2015/06/12/interracial-marriage-who-is-marrying-out/.

Ward v. Polite, 667 F.3d 727 (6th Cir. 2012).

Ward v. Wilbanks, 2010 WL 3026428 (E.D. Mich. July 26, 2010).

Ward, B. W., Dahlhamer, J. M., Galinsky, A. M,, & Joestl, S. S. (2014) Sexual orientation and health among U.S. adults: National Health Interview Survey, 2013. National health statistics reports; no 77. Hyattsville, MD: National Center for Health Statistics.

Wardle, F. (1999). *Tomorrow's children.* Denver, CO: Center for the Study of Biracial Children.

Wardle, F., & Cruz-Janzen, M. I. (2004). *Meeting the needs of multiethnic and multiracial children in schools.* Boston, MA: Pearson.

Washington, H. A. (2002). Burning love: Big tobacco takes aim at LGBT youths. *American Journal of Public Health, 92*, 1086–1095.

Watkins, M. B., Kaplan, S., Brief, A. P., Dietz, J., Mansfield, M.-T., & Cohen, R. (2006). Does it pay to be a sexist? The relationship between modern sexism and career outcomes. *Journal of Vocational Behavior, 69*, 524–537. doi: 10.1016/j.jvb.2006.07.004

Watts, R. E., & Henriksen, R. C., Jr. (1998). The Interracial Couple Questionnaire. *The Journal of Individual Psychology, 54*, 368–372.

Wayne, P. (2013). *The Harvard medical school guide to Tai Chi: 12 weeks to a healthy body, strong heart, and sharp mind.* Boulder, CO: Shambhala.

Weaver, S. (2015, March 23). Syria: Responding to an unprecedented crisis. *The Church World Services Blog.* Retrieved from: http://www.cwsglobal.org/blog/syria-unprecedented-crisis.html

Weber, G. N. (2008). Using to numb the pain: Substance use and abuse among lesbian, gay, and bisexual individuals. *Journal of Mental Health Counseling, 30*, 31–48. doi: 10.17744/mehc.30.1.2585916185422570

Weinberg, M. S., Williams, C. J., & Pryor, D. W. (1994). *Dual attraction: Understanding bisexuality.* New York, NY: Oxford University Press.

Weiner, B. A., & Zinner, L. (2015). Attitudes toward straight, gay male, and transsexual parenting. *Journal of Homosexuality, 62*, 327–339. doi: 10.1080/00918369.2014.972800

Weissman, J., Pratt, L. A., Miller, E. A., & Parker, J. D. (2015). *Serious psychological distress among adults: United States, 2009–2013.* Retrieved from https://www.researchgate.net/profile/Judith_Weissman/publication/278410177_Serious_psychological_distress_among_adults_United_States_20092013._NCHS_data_brief_no_203._Hyattsville_MD_National_Center_for_Health_Statistics._2015/links/5580757308aed40dd8cd2748.pdf

West, C. M. (2004). Black women and intimate partner violence: New directions for research. *Journal of Interpersonal Violence, 19*, 1487–1493. doi: 10.1177/0886260504269700

Westbrook, T. R., Harden, B. J., Holmes, A., Meisch, A. D., & Whittaker, J. V. (2013). Physical discipline use and child behavior problems in low-income, high-risk African American families. *Early Education and Development, 23*, 877–899. doi: 10.1080/10409289.2013.797327

Wester, S. R., & Lyubelsky, J. (2005). Supporting the thin blue line: Gender-sensitive therapy with male police officers. *Professional Psychology: Research and Practice, 36*, 51–58. doi: 10.1037/0735-7028.36.1.51

Wester, S. R., McDonough, T. A., White, M., Vogel, D. L., & Taylor, L. (2010). Using gender role conflict theory in counseling male-to-female transgender individuals. *Journal of Counseling & Development, 88*, 214–219.

Wester, S. R., Vogel, D. L., O'Neil, J. M., & Danforth, L. (2012). Development and evaluation of the Gender Role Conflict Scale Short Form (GRCS-SF). *Psychology of Men & Masculinity, 13*, 199–210. doi: 10.1037/a0025550

Whealin, J. M., Stotzer, R., Nelson, D., Li, F., Liu-Tom, H. T., & Pietzak, R. H. (2013). Evaluating PTSD prevalence and resilience factors in a predominantly Asian American and Pacific Islander sample of Iraq and Afghanistan veterans. *Journal of Affective Disorder, 150*, 1062–1068. doi: 1016/j.jad.2013.05.044

Whitfield, C. L. (2003). *My recovery: A personal plan for healing.* Deerfield Beach, FL: HCI.

Whitfield, H. W., Venable, R., & Broussard, S. (2010). Are client-counselor ethnic/racial matches associated with successful rehabilitation outcomes? *Rehabilitation Counseling Bulletin, 53*, 96–105. doi: 10.1177/0034355209338526

Wicker, L. R., & Brodie, R. E., II. (2004). The physical and mental health needs of African Americans. In D. R. Atkinson (Ed.), *Counseling American minorities* (pp. 105–124). Boston, MA: McGraw-Hill.

Widiger, T. A., & Samuel, D. B. (2005). Diagnostic categories or dimensions: A question for DSM-V. *Journal of Abnormal Psychology, 114*, 494–504. doi: 10.1037/0021-843X.114.4.494

Widner, D., & Chicoine, S. (2011). It's all in the name: Employment discrimination against Arab Americans. *Sociological Forum, 26*, 806–823. doi: 10.1111/j.1573-7861.2011.01285.x

Wiggins, M. I. (2011). Culture and worldview. In C. S. Cashwell & J. S. Young (Eds.), *Integrating spirituality and religion into counseling: A guide to competent practice* (pp. 43–70). Alexandria, VA: American Counseling Association.

Wilber, K. (1997, Fall/Winter). A spirituality that transforms. *What Is Enlightenment?, 12*, 22–32.

Wilber, K. (1998). *The essential Ken Wilber: Introductory reader.* Boston, MA: Shambhala.

Wilber, K. (1999). *The collected works of Ken Wilber* (Vol. 3). Boston, MA: Shambhala.

Wilber, K. (2000). *Sex, ecology, spirituality.* Boston, MA: Shambhala.

Wilber, K. (2001). *Grace and grit: Spirituality and healing in the life and death of Treya Killam Wilber.* Boston, MA: Shambhala.

Wilcoxon, S. A., Magnuson, S., & Norem, K. (2008). Institutional values of managed mental health care: Efficiency or oppression? *Journal of Multicultural Counseling and Development, 36*, 143–154.

Wilder, J. (2010). Revisiting "color names and color notions": A contemporary examination of the language and attitudes of skin color among young Black women. *Journal of Black Studies, 41*, 184–206. doi: 10.1177/0021934709337986

Wilder, J., & Cain, C. (2011). Teaching and learning color consciousness in Black families: Exploring family processes and women's experiences with colorism. *Journal of Family Issues, 32*, 577–604. doi: 10.1177/0192513X10390858

Wilkin, L., & Hillock, S. (2014). Enhancing MSW students' efficacy in working with trauma, violence, and oppression: An integrated feminist-trauma framework for social work education. *Feminist Teacher, 24*, 184–206.

Wilkins, C. L., Chan, J. F., & Kaiser, C. R. (2011). Racial stereotypes and interracial attraction: Phenotypic prototypicality and perceived attractiveness of Asians. *Cultural Diversity and Ethnic Minority Psychology, 17,* 427–431. doi: 10.1037/a0024733

Williams, C. B., & Wiggins, M. I. (2010). Womanist spirituality as a response to the racism-sexism double bind in African American women. *Counseling & Values, 54,* 175–186. doi: 10.1002/j.2161-007X.2010.tb00015.x

Williams, D. R., Neighbors, H. W., & Jackson, J. S. (2008). Racial/-ethnic discrimination and health: Findings from community studies. *American Journal of Public Health, 93,* 200–208.

Williams, M. T., Gooden, A. M., & Davis, D. (2012). African Americans, European Americans, and pathological stereotypes: An African-centered perspective. In G. R. Hayes, & M. H. Bryant, (Eds.), *Psychology of culture* (pp. 25–46). Hauppauge, NY: Nova Science Publishers, Inc.

Williams, R. (2015). *Eye of the storm: How mindful leaders can transform chaotic workplaces.* Vancouver, BC: Ray Williams Associates.

Williams Institute. (2011). *Occupy 2011: What Occupy Boston means to LGBTQ equality.* Retrieved from http://williamsinstitute.law.ucla.edu/press/in-the-news/occupy-2011-what-occupy-boston-means-to-lgbtq-equality/

Willie, C. V., & Reddick, R. J. (2010). *A new look at Black families* (6th ed.). Lanham, MD: Rowman & Littlefield

Wilson, B. D., Okwu, C., & Mills, S. A. (2011). Brief report: The relationship between multiple forms of oppression and subjective health among Black Lesbian and Bisexual Women. *Journal of Lesbian Studies, 15,* 15–24. doi: 10.1080/10894160.2010.508393

Wilson, W. J. (2012). *The truly disadvantaged: The inner city, the underclass, and public policy.* Chicago, IL: University of Chicago Press.

Wilt, J. (2011). Normal families facing unique challenges: The psychosocial functioning of multiracial couples, parents, and children. *The New School Psychology Bulletin, 9,* 34–41.

Winawer, H., & Wetzel, N. A. (2005). German families. In M. McGoldrick, J. Giordano, & N. Garcia-Preto (Eds.), *Ethnicity and family therapy* (3rd ed., pp. 555–572). New York, NY: Guilford Press.

Wise, T. (2008). *White like me: Reflections on race from a privileged son.* Berkeley, CA: Soft Skull Press.

Witty, M. C., & Adomaitis, R. (2014). Carl Rogers and client-centered counselling. In R. D. Parsons, & N. Zhang (Eds.), *Counseling theory: Guiding reflective practice* (pp. 171–199). Thousand Oaks, CA: Sage Publications.

Wong, E. C., Beutler, L. E., & Zane, N. W. (2007). Using mediators and moderators to test assumptions underlying culturally sensitive therapies: An exploratory example. *Cultural Diversity and Ethnic Minority Psychology, 13,* 169–177. doi: 10.1037/1099-9809.13.2.169

Wong, M. K. B. G. (2009). Strengthening connections in interracial marriages through pre-marital inventories: A critical literature review. *Contemporary Family Therapy, 31,* 251–261. doi: 10.1007/s10591-009-9099-1

Wong, M. P. A., & Buckner, J. (2008). Multiracial student services come of age: The state of multiracial student services in higher education in the United States. In K. A. Renn & P. Shang (Eds.), *Biracial and multiracial students: New Directions for Student Services,* No. 123 (pp. 43–51). San Francisco, CA: Jossey-Bass.

Wong, Y. J., Nguyen, C. P., Wang, S.-Y., Chen, W., Steinfeldt, J. A., & Kim, B. S. K. (2012). A latent profile analysis of Asian American men's and women's adherence to cultural values. *Cultural Diversity and Ethnic Minority Psychology, 18,* 258–267. doi: 10.1037/a0028423

Woo, H., Henfield, M. S., & Choi, N. (2014). Developing a unified professional identity in counselling: A review of the literature. *Journal of Counselor Leadership and Advocacy, 1,* 1–15. doi: 10.1080/2326716X.2014.895452

Woods-Giscombe, C. L., & Black, A. R. (2010). Mind-body interventions to reduce risk for health disparities related to stress and strength among African American women: The potential of mindfulness-based stress reduction, loving-kindness, and the NTU therapeutic framework. *Complementary Health Practice Review, 15,* 115–131. doi: 10.1177/1533210110386776

Worell, J., & Remer, P. (2003). *Feminist perspectives in therapy: Empowering diverse women* (2nd ed.). Hoboken, NJ: Wiley.

World Bank. (2005). *Missing in action: Teacher and medical provider absence in developing countries.* Retrieved from http://econ.worldbank.org/external/default/main?theSitePK=477916&contentMDK=20661217&pagePK=64168182&piPK=64168060

World Health Organization. (2001). *The world health report 2001-Mental health: New understanding, new hope.* Retrieved from http://www.who.int/whr/2001/en/

World Health Organization (WHO). (2007). *Breaking the vicious cycle between mental ill-health and poverty. Mental Health Core to Development Information Sheet, Sheet 1.* Retrieved from http://www.who.int/mental_health/policy/development/1_Breakingviciouscycle_Infosheet.pdf

World Health Organization. (2010). *Mental health and development: Targeting people with mental health conditions as a vulnerable group.* Geneva, Switzerland: Author.

World Health Organization (WHO). (2016). *Fact file: 10 facts on mental health.* Retrieved from http://www.who.int/-features/factfiles/mental_health/mental_health_facts/en/index.html

World Professional Association for Transgender Health's Standards of Care. (2011). *Version 7 of the World Professional Association for Transgender Health's Standards of Care.* Retrieved from http://www.wpath.org/site_page.cfm?pk_association_webpage_menu=1351&pk_association_webpage=3926

Worrell, F., Cross, W., & Vandiver, B. (2001). Nigrescence theory: Current status and challenges for the future. *Journal of Multicultural Counseling and Development, 29,* 201–213.

Worrell, F., Vandiver, B., Schaefer, B., Cross, W., & Fhagen-Smith, P. (2006). Generalizing nigrescence profiles: Cluster analyses of Cross Racial Identity Scale (CRIS) scores in three independent samples. *The Counseling Psychologist, 34*, 519–547. doi: 10.1177/0011000005278281

Worthington, E. L., Jr., & Sandage, S. J. (2015). *Forgiveness and spirituality in psychotherapy: A relational approach.* Washington, DC: American Psychological Association.

Worthington, R. L., Soth-McNett, A. M., & Moreno, M. V. (2007). Multicultural counseling competencies research: A 20-year content analysis. *Journal of Counseling Psychology, 54*, 351–361.

Wynn, R., & West-Olatunji, C. (2008). Culture-centered conceptualization using NTU psychopathology with an African American gay male client. *Journal of LGBT Issues in Counseling, 2*, 308–325.

Yakunina, E. S., & Weigold, I. K. (2011). Asian international students' intentions to seek counseling: Integrating cognitive and cultural predictors. *Asian American Journal of Psychology, 2*, 219–224. doi: 10.1037/a0024821

Yakushko, O., Watson, M., & Thompson, S. (2008). Stress and coping in the lives of recent immigrants and refugees: Considerations for counseling. *International Journal of Advanced Counseling, 30*, 167–178. doi: 10.1007/s10447-008-9054-0

Yancey, G. A. (2007). *Interracial contact and social change.* Boulder, CO: Rienner.

Yang, L. H., & WonPat-Borja, A. J. (2007). Psychopathology among Asian Americans. In F. Leong, A. G. Inman, A. Ebreo, L. Lang, L. Kinoshita, & M. Fu (Eds.), *Handbook of Asian American psychology* (2nd ed., pp. 379–405). Thousand Oaks, CA: Sage Publications.

Yarhouse, M. A., & Carrs, T. L. (2012). MTF transgender Christians' experiences: A qualitative study. *Journal of LGBT Issues in Counseling, 6*, 18–33. doi: 10.1080/15538605.2012.649405

Yee, B., DeBaryshe, B., Yuen, S., Kim, S., & McCubbin, H. (2007). Asian American and Pacific Islander families: Resiliency and life-span socialization in a cultural context. In F. Leong, A. G. Inman, A. Ebreo, L. Lang, L. Kinoshita, & M. Fu (Eds.), *Handbook of Asian American psychology* (2nd ed., pp. 69–86). Thousand Oaks, CA: Sage.

Yee, C. S. (2015). *Yoga for life: A journey to inner peace and freedom.* New York, NY: Atria.

Yeh, C. J., Inman, A., Kim, A. B., & Okubo, Y. (2006). Asian American families' collectivistic coping strategies in response to 9/11. *Cultural Diversity and Ethnic Minority Psychology, 12*, 134–148. doi: 10.1037/1099-9809.12.1.134

Yeh, C. J., & Wang, Y. W. (2000). Asian American coping attitudes, sources, and practices: Implications for indigenous counseling strategies. *Journal of College Student Development, 41*, 94–103.

Yon, A., & Scogin, F. (2008). Behavioral activation as a treatment for geriatric depression. *Clinical Gerontologist, 32*, 91–103. doi: 10.1080/07317110802478016

Yoo, H. C., Steger, M. F., & Lee, R. M. (2010). Validation of the subtle and blatant racism scale for Asian American college students (SABR-A^2). *Cultural Diversity and Ethnic Minority Psychology, 16*, 323–334. doi: 10.1037/a0018674

Yoon, E., Chang, C., Kim, S., Clawson, A., Cleary, S. E., Hansen, M., . . . Gomes, A. M. (2013). A meta-analysis of acculturation/enculturation and mental health. *Journal of Counseling Psychology, 60*, 15–30. doi: 10.1037/a0030652

Yoshikawa, H., Wilson, P. A. D., Chae, D. H., & Cheng, J. F. (2004). Do family and friendship networks protect against the influence of discrimination on mental health and HIV risk among Asian and Pacific Islander gay men? *AIDS Education and Prevention, 16*, 84–100. doi: 10.1521/aeap.16.1.84.27719

Young-Ware, D., & Ware, D. (1998). An interracial development model: A thoughtful presentation of the components of developing an interracial couple relationship and identity. *Interrace, 8*(3), 12–13.

Zane, N., Hatanaka, H., Park, S., & Akutsu, P. (1994). Ethnic-specific mental health services: Evaluation of the parallel approach for Asian American clients. *Journal of Community Psychology, 22*, 68–81. doi: 10.1002/1520-6629(199404)22:2<68::AID-JCOP2290220204>3.0.CO;2-5

Zane, N., & Ku, H. (2014). Effects of ethnic match, gender match, acculturation, cultural identity and face concern on self-disclosure in counseling for Asian Americans. *Asian American Journal of Psychology, 5*, 66–74. doi: 10.1037/a0036078

Zhang, A. Y., & Snowden, L. R. (1999). Ethnic characteristics of mental disorders in five U.S. communities. *Cultural Diversity and Ethnic Minority Psychology, 5*, 134–146. doi: 10.1037/1099-9809.5.2.134

Zhang, J., Fang, L., Wu, Y. B., & Wieczorek, W. F. (2013). Depression, anxiety, and suicidal ideation among Chinese Americans. *Journal of Nervous Mental Disorders, 201*, 17–22. doi: 10.1097/NMD.0b013e31827ab2e2

Zhang, Y., & Van Hook, J. (2009). Marital dissolution among interracial couples. *Journal of Marriage and Family, 71*, 95–107. doi: 10.1111/j.1741-3737.2008.00582.x

Zhao, Q. (2010). *Do nothing and do everything: An illustrated new Taoism.* St. Paul, MN: Paragon.

Zhou, Y., Jindal-Snape, D., Topping, K., & Todman, J. (2008). Theoretical models of culture shock and adaptation in international students in higher education. *Studies in Higher Education, 33*, 63–75. doi: 10.1080/03075070701794833

Zia, H. (2001). *Asian American dreams: The emergence of an Asian American people.* New York, NY: Farrar, Straus & Giroux.

Zinnbauer, B. J., & Pargament, K. I. (2000). Working with the sacred: Four approaches to religious and spiritual issues in counseling. *Journal of Counseling & Development, 78*, 162–171. doi: 10.1002/j.1556-6676.2000.tb02574.x

Zsembik, B. A., & Fennell, D. (2005). Ethnic variation in health and the determinants of health among Latinos. *Social Science and Medicine, 61*, 53–63. doi: 10.1016/j.socscimed.2004.11.040

INDEX